NEW

WITHDRAWN

ENCYCLOPEDIA OF
WORLD BIOGRAPHY

5

ENCYCLOPEDIA OF WORLD BIOGRAPHY

SECOND EDITION

Diderot
Forbes
5

GALE

DETROIT · NEW YORK · TORONTO · LONDON

Staff

Senior Editor: Paula K. Byers
Project Editor: Suzanne M. Bourgoin
Managing Editor: Neil E. Walker

Editorial Staff: Luann Brennan, Frank V. Castronova, Laura S. Hightower, Karen E. Lemerand, Stacy A. McConnell, Jennifer Mossman, Maria L. Munoz, Katherine H. Nemeh, Terrie M. Rooney, Geri Speace

Permissions Manager: Susan M. Tosky
Permissions Specialist: Maria L. Franklin
Permissions Associate: Michele M. Lonoconus
Image Cataloger: Mary K. Grimes

Production Director: Mary Beth Trimper
Production Manager: Evi Seoud
Production Associate: Shanna Heilveil
Product Design Manager: Cynthia Baldwin
Senior Art Director: Mary Claire Krzewinski

Research Manager: Victoria B. Cariappa
Research Specialists: Michele P. LaMeau, Andrew Guy Malonis, Barbara McNeil, Gary J. Oudersluys
Research Associates: Julia C. Daniel, Tamara C. Nott, Norma Sawaya, Cheryl L. Warnock
Research Assistant: Talitha A. Jean

Graphic Services Supervisor: Barbara Yarrow
Image Database Supervisor: Randy Bassett
Imaging Specialist: Mike Lugosz

Manager of Data Entry Services: Eleanor M. Allison
Data Entry Coordinator: Kenneth D. Benson

Manager of Technology Support Services: Theresa A. Rocklin
Programmers/Analysts: Mira Bossowska, Jeffrey Muhr, Christopher Ward

Copyright © 1998
Gale Research
835 Penobscot Bldg.
Detroit, MI 48226-4094

ISBN 0-7876-2221-4 (Set)
ISBN 0-7876-2545-0 (Volume 5)

Printed in the United States of America
10 9 8 7 6 5 4 3 2

ENCYCLOPEDIA OF WORLD BIOGRAPHY

5

D

Denis Diderot

The French philosopher, playwright, and novelist Denis Diderot (1713-1784) is best known as the editor of the *Encyclopédie*.

On Oct. 15, 1713, Denis Diderot was born in Langres, Compagne, into a family of cutlers, whose bourgeois traditions went back to the late Middle Ages. As a child, Denis was considered a brilliant student by his Jesuit teachers, and it was decided that he should enter the clergy. In 1726 he enrolled in the Jesuit college of Louis-le-Grand and probably later attended the Jansenist Collège d'Harcourt. In 1732 he earned a master of arts degree in philosophy. He then abandoned the clergy as a career and decided to study law. His legal training, however, was short-lived. In 1734 Diderot decided to seek his fortune by writing. He broke with his family and for the next 10 years lived a rather bohemian existence. He earned his living by translating English works and tutoring the children of wealthy families and spent his leisure time studying. In 1743 he further alienated his father by marrying Anne Toinette Champion.

The *Encyclopédie*

On Jan. 21, 1746, André François le Breton and his partners were granted permission to publish a 10-volume encyclopedia. On the advice of the distinguished mathematician Jean D'Alembert and with the consent of Chancellor D'Aguesseau, Diderot was named general editor of the project.

For more than 26 years Diderot devoted the bulk of his energies and his genius to the writing, editing, and publishing of the *Encyclopédie*. For Diderot, the aim of the work was "to assemble the knowledge scattered over the face of the earth; to explain its general plan to the men with whom we live . . . so that we may not die without having deserved well of the human race." Such was the plan and the purpose of the *Encyclopédie*, and it was also the credo of the Enlightenment. But the project was more than just the compilation of all available knowledge; it was also a learning experience for all those regularly connected with it. It introduced Diderot to technology, the crafts, the fine arts, and many other areas of learning. It was an outlet for his curiosity, his scholarly interests, and his creativity.

In 1751 D'Alembert's *Preliminary Discourse* and the first volume were published. In January 1752 the second volume appeared, but the opposition of the Jesuits and other orthodox critics forced a temporary suspension. Publication was soon resumed and continued at the rate of one volume a year until 1759, when the Royal Council forbade further operations. Diderot and Le Breton, however, continued to write and publish the *Encyclopédie* secretly until 1765, when official sanction was resumed. In 1772 the completed work was published in 17 volumes of text and 11 volumes of plates under the title *Encyclopédie, ou Dictionnaire raisonné des sciences, des arts, et des métiers.*

Other Writings

Throughout the period of his association with the *Encyclopédie*, Diderot continued to devote himself to other writing. In 1746 he published *Philosophical Thoughts,* which was concerned with the question of the relationship between nature and religion. He viewed life as self-sufficient and held that virtue could be sustained without religious beliefs. In *Sceptics Walk* (1747) and *Letters on the Blind* (1749) Diderot slowly turned from theism to atheism. Reli-

Diderot is one of the pre-19th-century leaders in the movement away from mathematics and physics, as a source of certain knowledge, to biological probability and historical insight. As one modern scholar has stated, Diderot's approach to nature and philosophy was that of mystical naturalism.

Later Years

Following the completion of the *Encyclopédie,* Diderot went into semiretirement; he wrote but infrequently published his works. His earnings as editor of the *Encyclopédie* guaranteed him a modest income, which he supplemented by writing literary criticism. In addition, he sold his library to Empress Catherine of Russia, who allowed him to keep it while he lived and paid him an annual salary as its librarian. On July 30, 1784, Diderot died in the home of his daughter, only 5 months after the death of his beloved mistress and intellectual companion, Sophie Voland.

The great paradox of Diderot's life is found in the tensions that existed between his basically bourgeois nature and his bohemian tendencies. This struggle was mirrored in his novel *Rameau's Nephew,* in which the staid Rameau and his bohemian nephew represent aspects of Diderot's personality. Fittingly, Diderot's last words, "The first step toward philosophy is incredulity," are an adequate measure of the man.

Further Reading

Two biographies of Diderot are outstanding: Lester G. Crocker, *Diderot: The Embattled Philosopher* (1952), an accurate and penetrating work, but with a tinge of romanticism; and Arthur M. Wilson, *Diderot: The Testing Years, 1713-1759* (1957), apparently a more scholarly work, but in reality lacking only the romanticism of Crocker. Both works show notable scholarship in the area of Diderot studies. Among the shorter works, George R. Havens, *The Age of Ideas* (1955), contains four excellent and highly original chapters on Diderot. □

gion became a central theme in his writings, and he aroused the hostility of public officials who considered him a leader of the radicals, "a clever fellow, but extremely dangerous."

In 1749 Diderot was imprisoned for 3 months because of his opinions in *Philosophical Thoughts.* Although he had stated, "If you impose silence on me about religion and government, I shall have nothing to talk about," after his release he reduced the controversial character of his published works. Therefore most of his materialistic and antireligious works and several of his novels were not published during his lifetime.

During his long literary career Diderot moved away from the mechanical approach to nature, which was characteristic of the Englishtenment's use of the discoveries of Sir Isaac Newton. Such works as *D'Alembert's Dream, Conversation between D'Alembert and Diderot, Thoughts on the Interpretation of Nature, Elements of Physiology,* and *Essay on Seneca* vividly point to the evolution of his thought and to its modernity.

In his mature writings Diderot tends to see man as an integral part of an organic and vitalistic nature, governed by laws that are incomprehensible to him. Nature, according to Diderot, is a continually unfolding process, which reveals itself, rather than being revealed by man. Forms in nature develop from earlier forms in a continually evolving process, in which all elements, animate and inanimate, are related to one another. Man can know nature only through experience; thus rationalistic speculation is useless to him in understanding nature.

Richard Diebenkorn

The American painter Richard Diebenkorn (1922-1993) was a member of the California school of abstract expressionism. His paintings move back and forth between representational and nonrepresentational imagery in his quest to translate his visual experience into painterly form.

Richard Clifford Diebenkorn, Jr. was born in Portland, Oregon, on April 22, 1922. Two years later his father, a sales executive, moved the family to San Francisco. Diebenkorn was particularly close to his grandmother, Florence Stephens, who supported his artistic interests and encouraged him to paint. She also stimulated his imagination with gifts of books illustrated by Howard Pyle and N. C. Wyeth.

In 1940 Diebenkorn enrolled at Stanford University. His father hoped that Stanford might lead his son to a more respectable career in medicine or law. Although Diebenkorn majored in art at Stanford, he also took courses in music, literature, and history. His teacher, Daniel Mendelowitz, took him to visit Sarah Stein's collection of the early European modernists Matisse, Picasso, and Cézanne. The early contact with Matisse's work, reinforced later by visits to the Phillips collection in Washington, D.C., and the Shchukin collection in Leningrad and Moscow, profoundly influenced Diebenkorn's artistic development.

From Realism to Abstraction

Diebenkorn's paintings of this early period are realistic in nature. *Palo Alto Circle* (1943) reflects his interest in Edward Hopper even as it looks forward to a more personal style. Strong shadows and the representation of a particular time and place suggest the distinctly American scene so memorialized by Hopper, while attention to flattened surface planes and a rectilinear pictorial structure reveals Diebenkorn's underlying tendency toward abstraction.

In 1943 Diebenkorn enlisted in the Marine Corps. As part of his training he attended the University of California, Berkeley, where he studied with Erle Loran, Worth Ryder, and Eugene Neuhaus. He was then assigned to the Marine base at Quantico, Virginia, near Washington, D.C. As the resident artist there he drew portraits and animated maps. Diebenkorn visited the Phillips collection several times and was particularly impressed by Matisse's *The Studio, Quai St. Michel* (1916). Like Matisse, Diebenkorn was interested in

the re-examination of pictorial vision. He wished to explore, as the French artist had done earlier, the evocative possibilities to be found in the combination of indoor and outdoor space, in the tension between spatial illusion and surface flatness, and in the relation of figures to abstract form. Other artists who held Diebenkorn's attention at this time included Cézanne, Paul Klee, and contemporary abstract expressionists Robert Motherwell and William Baziotes.

After his discharge from the Marines in 1945, Diebenkorn attended the California School of Fine Arts in San Francisco. Here he met David Park, who became his teacher and good friend; Elmer Bischoff; Clyfford Still; and Mark Rothko. Stimulated by these contacts as well as by the work of the surrealist painters Joan Miro and Archille Gorky (whose work he saw in New York City in 1946 while living briefly in Woodstock, New York), Diebenkorn began to paint more abstractly. His canvases were filled with organic, non-representational shapes that either floated in a shallow space or were covered by a thick textured brushstroke in the manner of Clyfford Still. In 1948 Diebenkorn had his first one man show at the California Palace of the Legion of Honor in San Francisco.

Moving Toward Representational Imagery

In 1950 Diebenkorn moved to Albuquerque to obtain his Master of Fine Arts degree from the University of New Mexico. During this period his paintings took on a spaciousness and a linear organization reminiscent of the sweeping desert and sharp sunlight of his surroundings. While abstract, many of these works resemble aerial landscapes with their expansive lateral flattened forms. At the same time a quirky, meandering line entered into his work, often linking forms within a shallow surface space. It has been suggested that some of the lines and forms in these paintings can be traced to the "all-purpose" symbols found in George Herriman's *Krazy Kat* comic strip, also set in New Mexico.

Diebenkorn taught one semester at the University of Illinois at Urbana in 1952, and in the fall of 1953 he moved briefly to New York where he became friends with Franz Kline. The following year he returned to Berkeley. With the aid of a Rosenberg Fellowship, Diebenkorn was then able to paint full time. His paintings took on a pink tonality and a tripartite division of form. A landscape format began to emerge, overshadowing the earlier works, which had fused images of landscape, anatomy, and still life.

With his return to the Bay Area, Diebenkorn resumed close contact with Park and Bischoff. Since 1950-1951 Park had been painting a series of genre scenes, broadly modeled with a direct and forceful brushstroke. Bischoff's paintings, characterized by their atmospheric space and strong color, were also figurative in nature. By the summer of 1955 Diebenkorn began to experiment with representational imagery. At first he painted a series of table top still lifes, simply composed of a few objects placed in a flattened space with a strong color pattern.

Diebenkorn had always worked from experience, merging the impression of his immediate environment with his own feelings into an image whose allusive space and gestured surface evoked the artist's expressive intent. He continued this direction with his representational work in still life, interior scenes, city and landscapes, and compositions with one or more figures. *Girl on a Terrace* (1956) typifies this period of Diebenkorn's work. Here a woman stands between indoors and outdoors, her body the focal point for both composition and pictorial mood. Large planes of color executed with a loose brush stroke create a structured tension that asserts the artist's underlying abstract arrangement of form. This tension is then augmented by the figure, whose presence defines and enframes space even as it enhances the contemplative mood of the work. Diebenkorn's interiors and landscapes, with their reductive simplification of form and contradictory space, assert a similar investigation of the expressive possibilities of representational imagery.

The ''Ocean Park'' Series

In 1966 Diebenkorn moved to Santa Monica, California, and soon began a series of paintings that occupied his attention for the next 20 years. Entitled ''Ocean Park'' after an amusement park near his studio, these large format reductivist paintings returned Diebenkorn to his earlier nonobjective abstraction, now combined with the lessons learned from his ten years of figurative work. In these paintings he joined broad planes of color with a superimposed linear structure. Organized on a vertical horizontal, the viewpoint is often that of looking upward or suggestive of a great distance below. Space is defined and re-defined through the relationship of line to tonal plane, a plane that is simultaneously flat and spatial due to Diebenkorn's energetic brushstroke. Warm yellows and ochres combine with azur blue to evoke the sunny atmosphere of southern California. Diebenkorn left the process of making the image visible, integrating his earlier investigations into the final painting. Through this Ocean Park series, which numbers more than 100 paintings, Diebenkorn established a dialogue between airy spatial illusion and flat surface, between spontaneity and control, between inside and outside, between rational order and evocative mood in order to represent abstractly what he called the ''tension beneath the calm.''

Throughout his career, Diebenkorn continued to explore the evocative potential of his visual experiences. Whether abstract or representational, his paintings unite formal concerns with a meditative and emotive mood.

Further Reading

An excellent summary of Diebenkorn's art can be found in an exhibition catalogue published by the Albright-Knox Art Gallery and Rizzoli press, *Richard Diebenkorn, Paintings and Drawings, 1943-1980* (1980), with essays by Maurice Tuchman, Gerald Nordland, Robert T. Buck, and Linda Cathcart. Also recommended is a catalogue published by the Marlborough Gallery: *Richard Diebenkorn—The Ocean Park Series; Recent Work,* with an introduction by John Russell (London, 1973). □

John George Diefenbaker

John George Diefenbaker (1895-1979) was prime minister of Canada and leader of the Progressive Conservative party. Though his government had some remarkable successes, he left a legacy of bitterness and disunion for his party.

John Diefenbaker was born in Neustadt, Ontario, on Sept. 18, 1895. In 1903 his family, which was of both Scottish and German descent, moved west to Fort Carlton, north of Saskatoon, to homestead. His father, William Thomas Diefenbaker, was a teacher and encouraged literacy in his family. It was from this love of books that young John learned of Canadian prime minister Sir Wilfred Laurier, and decided he would follow in his hero's footsteps.

Diefenbaker achieved a B.A. in 1915 and an M.A. in political science and economics in 1916, both from the University of Saskatchewan. After war service in England in 1916, he was invalided home, and resumed studies at Saskatchewan, graduating with an LL.B. in 1919. His law career in Wakaw, near Prince Albert, was successful from the outset, and Diefenbaker became well-known as a fierce cross-examiner. During this time, in 1929, he married Edna May Brower.

Politics was clearly his first love, though his first attempts were unsuccessful. He was defeated in five elections before he won a seat in Parliament in 1940. There he quickly established a reputation, and in 1942 and 1948 he tried but failed to win leadership of the Progressive Conservative party. Meanwhile, in 1951, Edna died, and Diefenbaker was remarried in 1953 to Olive Evangeline Freeman Palmer. In 1956, however, Diefenbaker was the overwhelming choice of a leadership convention, becoming at age 61 the leader of the Opposition Party.

In a stunning upset in the 1957 election, Diefenbaker won a minority victory and formed a remarkably successful government. New legislation flooded the statute books, helping pensioners and farmers and cutting taxes. Early in 1958 Diefenbaker dissolved Parliament and scored a devastating victory, winning 208 of 265 seats, the first non-Liberal government in 22 years. In 1958 he also sponsored a Bill of Rights for all Canadians, not just those of English or French lineage, and by this philosophy appointed James Gladstone, a Native Canadian, as senator. He also appointed Ellen Fairclough, the first woman federal Cabinet member.

The Conservative leader could only go downhill from the heights of 1958. Unemployment soon began to climb, Quebec was restive, there were difficulties with the United States over Cuba and arms, and the Liberals were recovering. The forceful image that had propelled Diefenbaker to victory was replaced with one of bumbling indecisiveness. An election in 1962 saw Diefenbaker returned to office with a minority government, and early in 1963 the administration was defeated in Parliament. The defeat was caused by the Prime Minister's inability to decide if Canada should accept nuclear warheads for the country's NORAD defense

systems. His defense minister resigned, the U.S. State Department intervened, and the Conservatives were soon in a state of collapse. It was a tribute to Diefenbaker's campaigning skills that, although his party lost the election of 1963, it survived at all.

The last four years of Diefenbaker's party leadership were stormy. Bolstered by the support of loyal westerners, he was still a force to be reckoned with, but to urbanites the "Chief" was electoral poison. An attempt to challenge him in 1964 was crushed, and although the party came together to fight the 1965 election, the final attack came in 1966, when Diefenbaker was discredited. For a year more he hung on, but at a leadership convention in 1967 he was trounced by Robert Stanfield.

Nevertheless, Diefenbaker was committed to politics, and remained active within Commons for the next twelve years. Olive died in 1976, but Diefenbaker continued on. He was re-elected in 1979, but he died that year on August 16. His body was carried by train back to Saskatoon, and he was buried beside the Right Honorable John G. Diefenbaker Centre on the campus of the University of Saskatchewan.

Further Reading

There are as yet no scholarly studies of Diefenbaker, although an official biography has been in preparation. The best sources are Peter Newman, *Renegade in Power: The Diefenbaker Years* (1964) and *The Distemper of Our Times: Canadian Politics in Transition, 1963-1968* (1968). □

Otto Paul Hermann Diels

The German organic chemist Otto Paul Hermann Diels (1876-1954) discovered a technique of atomic combination which led to the synthesis of an important group of organic compounds.

Hermann Diels was born in Hamburg on Jan. 23, 1876. After studying chemistry at the University of Berlin he was awarded a doctoral degree in 1899. In that year he joined the faculty as assistant professor and became associate professor in 1914. He became professor of chemistry at the University of Kiel in 1916 and held this position until his retirement in 1948.

In his early work at Berlin, Diels discovered carbon suboxide (1906) and investigated its properties. The compound was important because of its high degree of reactivity and because its chemical structure provided important information as to the composition of other oxides of the carbon atom. However, Diels's most important work was done at Kiel, where he was assisted by Kurt Alder. Together they were able to work out the technique of a new atomic combination.

The now famous Diels-Alder reaction involved a diene synthesis. In this reaction there appeared a new molecular structure, one which hitherto had not been recognized. It consisted of what came to be identified as a conjugated diene, that is, an organic substance containing two double-bonded carbon atoms in a ring compound. The first experiments showed that the compound butadiene would react vigorously with maleic anhydride to produce a six-membered ring compound, and further experimentation showed that the simple dienes, such as butadiene, could be changed into cyclic dienes, which, in turn, could be used as the bases for a new group of organic compounds.

One of the most remarkable aspects of the Diels-Alder reaction was the lack of a need for reagents, catalysts, or high temperatures and pressures. The process proceeded at a relatively slow pace at temperatures usually associated with animal organisms. The potentiality of the reaction was profound. Diels went on to one synthesis after another, among the most notable being that of the polymerization of the diene isoprene into synthetic rubber. Other investigators produced a whole family of plastics, alkaloids, and polymers from the technique of the Diels-Alder reaction. The synthesis of cortisone was an outcome of this technique. In addition to this work, Diels also investigated cholesterol and bile acids, and the degradation products involved in dehydrogenation brought about by the use of the metal selenium.

Although the new organic products for which Diels was so much responsible may have produced benefits for mankind, it should not be forgotten that one of the most important parts of his research was a new insight into chemical combination and molecular structure. In 1950, in recognition of his many contributions to chemical science, Diels, together with Alder, was awarded the Nobel Prize. Diels died at Kiel on March 7, 1954.

Further Reading

There is virtually nothing in English on the life of Diels. However, for discussions of his scientific achievements, the reader should consult Eduard Farber, *Nobel Prize Winners in Chemistry, 1901-1961* (1953; rev. ed. 1963); Aaron J. Ihde, *The Development of Modern Chemistry* (1964); Nobel Foundation, *Chemistry: Nobel Lectures, Including Presentation Speeches and Laureates' Biographies,* vol. 3 (1964); and James R. Partington, *A History of Chemistry,* vol. 4 (1964). □

Ngo Dinh Diem

Ngo Dinh Diem (1901-1963) was South Vietnam's first premier and president. Leader of South Vietnam after the 1954 partition, he initially provided inspiring leadership but later became dictatorial when pressed by the Vietcong assault against his government.

The son of a minister and councilor to a former Vietnamese emperor, Ngo Dinh Diem was born Jan. 3, 1901, near Hue. In the 17th century his ancestors had been converted to Catholicism by missionaries to their Buddhist homeland, subsequently suffering much persecution.

Graduating from the government's school of administration at Hue, Diem rose to be governor of Phan Thiet province at the age of 28. Four years later he was named minister of interior in Emperor Bao Dai's central administration of the protectorate of Annam at Hue. Diem soon resigned his post, however, because neither the French nor Bao Dai would support reforms he advocated. For 21 years, from 1933 to 1954, Diem played no role of importance in Vietnam. His reputation as a nationalist grew nonetheless, largely based on his abandonment of high position in protest of French colonial rule.

Twice during the wartime Japanese occupation, Diem refused invitations to serve as premier. Held captive by Ho Chi Minh's Communist Viet Minh at the war's end, he was offered the post of interior minister in Ho's government but refused. He also declined to participate in Bao Dai's pro-French government of limited "independence" in 1949.

Diem traveled to the United States in 1950, the first year of American aid to still French-ruled Vietnam. He returned after a brief stay in France and lobbied for American support of full independence for Vietnam. He left the United States a year later and took up residence in a Belgian monastery.

Following the fall of Dien Bien Phu in 1954, Diem returned to Vietnam to accept the premiership, which he assumed on July 7, two weeks before the Geneva Accords divided the country. Long opposed to Emperor Bao Dai, Diem defeated him in a noncontested election in 1955, declaring South Vietnam a republic and becoming its first president.

Diem at first displayed outstanding leadership, building new schools and roads and surprisingly quickly rehabilitating a badly shattered economy. He refused to acquiesce in the 1956 reunification elections set by the Geneva Accords, however. The Communists subsequently inaugurated a strategy of armed revolt.

Diem became more autocratic as the war years progressed. His family had always been clannish, and he became increasingly dependent on the advice of his brother, Ngo Dinh Nhu, whose attractive and assertive wife also played a major role in his government. Diem's lack of judgment was particularly evident in 1963, when government forces fired on Buddhist demonstrators in Hue, killing eight and precipitating a crisis in which several monks subsequently burned themselves to death. The Americans, who had heretofore strongly supported Diem, gave evidence of wavering, and this was all that a group of soldiers needed to depose him. Diem was overthrown and murdered on Nov. 2, 1963.

Further Reading

Probably the most accurate, although unsympathetic, portrait of Diem is in Willard A. Hanna, *Eight Nation Makers* (1964), which is a volume of portraits of major Southeast Asian leaders of the late 1950s and early 1960s. A longer and too laudatory treatment is Anthony T. Bouscaren, *The Last of the Mandarins: Diem of Vietnam* (1965). A more balanced account is in Denis Warner, *The Last Confucian* (1963; rev. ed. 1964). Robert Shaplen's excellent *The Lost Revolution: The*

U.S. in Vietnam, 1946-1966 (1965; rev. ed. 1966) contains a perceptive study of Diem. □

Rudolf Diesel

The German mechanical engineer Rudolf Diesel (1858-1913) is remembered for the compression-ignition internal combustion engine which bears his name.

Rudolf Diesel was born March 18, 1858, in Paris. His interest in mechanics was early roused by frequent visits to the Conservatoire des Arts et Métiers. Early in the Franco-Prussian War (1870) all Germans had to leave Paris, and the Diesels went to England in poverty. After a brief stay there, Rudolf went to an uncle in Augsburg, Germany, where he received a thorough scientific schooling. From 1875 he attended the Munich Polytechnikum (later the Technische Hochschule) and graduated with highest honors. He studied thermodynamics under Carl von Linde and resolved—given the opportunity—to design a heat engine with a thermodynamic cycle approximating to the ideal described by Sadi Carnot in 1824. Great fuel economy could be expected from such a machine. But the opportunity was a long time coming. Meanwhile, in 1880 he returned to Paris to assist in the construction of a refrigeration plant for Linde and then became manager of it. During this period (1881-1890) he put much effort into an abortive design for an expansion engine using ammonia as working fluid (ammonia was also the working fluid in the refrigerator). From Paris, Diesel moved to Berlin in 1890 and continued to work for Linde's refrigeration concern.

About 1890 Diesel saw that air could be used as the working fluid and worked out the elements of his engine cycle. Air, highly compressed in a cylinder, would rise in temperature; fuel injected into this hot gas would burn spontaneously. Ideally, combustion would occur at constant temperature and pressure, and expansion of the gases would drive the piston. Thus the conversion of heat to work would reach an optimum. Diesel's design was sufficiently advanced for him to patent it in 1892, and he described it in the paper "The Theory and Design of a Rational Heat Engine" (1893). With Linde's support two outstanding German concerns, Maschinenfabrik, Augsburg, and Friedrich Krupp, Essen, agreed to finance its development. From 1893 Diesel worked on the engine at Augsburg. By 1897 the engine was perfected to Diesel's satisfaction, and it was displayed in the Munich Exhibition of 1898. It used a heavier fuel oil than the then relatively explosive gasoline engines with which it was to compete. Its fuel economy was remarkable, and it ran quietly.

With success came worldwide interest, and manufactures were licensed to build the engine. In 1897 Adolphus Busch acquired the United States license for $1 million cash. In 1899 a new company was established in Augsburg to make the engine, but Diesel's illness and rife speculation in the shares made the venture a failure. However, development work forged ahead elsewhere. Illness, stemming from overwork in the development period, crippled Diesel, and thought he continued lecture tours, his direct involvement in the engine declined. He died at sea after falling from the Antwerp-Harwich steamer *Dresden* on the night of Sept. 29/30, 1913.

Further Reading

The chapter on Diesel in Eugen Diesel and others, *From Engines to Autos: Five Pioneers in Engine Development* (1960), provides valuable information. A laudatory biography of Diesel, written in a journalistic style, is Robert W. Nitske and Charles Morrow Wilson, *Rudolf Diesel: Pioneer of the Age of Power* (1965).

Additional Sources

Grosser, Morton, *Diesel, the man & the engine,* New York: Atheneum, 1978.

Moon, John Frederick, *Rudolf Diesel and the diesel engine,* London, Priory Press, 1974.

Thomas, Donald E., *Diesel: technology and society in industrial Germany,* Tuscaloosa, Ala.: University of Alabama Press, 1987. □

Kenneth Dike

Kenneth Dike (1917-1983) was an African historian noted for setting up the Nigerian National Archives

and for serving as roving ambassador for Biafra during Eastern Nigeria's bid for secession.

Kenneth Onwuka Dike was born December 17, 1917, in Awka, (East Central) Nigeria. He attended Dennis Memorial grammar school in nearby Onitsha and went on later to first Achimota College in Ghana and then to Fourah Bay College in Sierra Leone. He received his Bachelor of Science degree at the University of Durham, England. His M.A. degree was from the University of Aberdeen in Scotland, and he earned his Ph.D. in history from the University of London.

As both historian and leader of the University of Ibadan's post-graduate school in Nigeria, Dike is said to have "Nigerianized Nigerian history" (Michael Crowder). Through his work, he gave the world an understanding of the way trade was carried out along the Niger river and in the Niger Delta during the 19th century. Perhaps Dike's best known book is *Trade and Politics in the Niger Delta 1830-1890* (1956). In this work, Dike examined the "detailed process by which the existing native governments were gradually supplanted by British consular power and following it the Crown Colony administration." The work, based on his doctoral dissertation, looked at how economic change affected the political and social life of 19th century Nigeria. The 1950s proved to have been Dike's most productive scholarly years—preceding his university administrative career and later political activity in the interest of an independent Biafra.

In 1953 his *Report on the Preservation and Administration of Historical Records in Nigeria* was published. This work had to do with setting up the Nigerian National Archives which he later served as director. In this same documentation and preservation vein, Dike served for a time as well as chair of the Nigerian Antiquities Commission. Then in 1957 *A Hundred years of British Rule in Nigeria* appeared, followed in 1958 by *The Origins of the Niger Mission*.

From 1960 until late 1966 Dike was vice-chancellor at Ibadan—i.e., he was that university's chief administrative officer. Prior to assuming that post he had been director of the Institute of African Studies at Ibadan in addition to being director of the National Archives. His combined administrative/academic skills also led to his appointment as chair of the Association of Commonwealth Universities.

His resignation as Ibadan's vice-chancellor came in December 1966, at the beginning of the Nigerian civil war. As an Ibo and an Easterner, his role as a head university administrator in Western Nigeria became untenable. A long struggle to keep his position was lost to a Yoruba opponent, and Dike made the critical decision at that point to opt for "a new life in an independent Eastern state" (John de St. Jorre). Dike joined fellow Ibo people in Eastern Nigeria who were seeking secession and to form a separate nation. This new nation was to be called Biafra, named for the Bight of Biafra at the mouth of the Niger river. The name of this body of water separating the eastern and western parts of Nigeria has since been erased from maps of the reunified nation.

From Ibadan Dike, as a former vice-chancellor, went home to become Biafra's roving ambassador. He acted in this capacity from 1967 to 1970, travelling extensively and speaking out on behalf of the Biafran position in the civil conflict. In 1969 he appeared in the United States before the National Press Club in Washington, D.C. His remarks during this visit were quoted widely in a *Washington Post* article entitled "Biafra explains its case" (April 13, 1969). Dike proved to be one of Biafra's top emissaries. He was a visible and important component in negotiations at various stages throughout the conflict. His voice rang out loudly pleading for Biafran recognition. During the war years he held a new post as vice-chancellor at Nsukka University in Biafran territory. Nsukka was known for hosting a core group of "international stars of the Ibo elite" referred to as an "Nsukka secessionist group" (de St. Jorre).

By 1968 Dike's position with regard to Biafra had become unshakable. Prior to that time Eastern Nigerian attempts to achieve a loose confederation with the West had his support. These overtures, however, had been rebuffed by the West. As a result, Dike felt that "after so much sacrifice we are not prepared to go back. . . ." Biafra's eventual and necessary unconditional surrender was certainly a blow to this determined intellectual. Still, during the final days of the secession effort he served as Biafra's representative at cease-fire negotiations in Abidjan, Ivory Coast.

During the post-war years, in the 1970s, Dike went into exile and took up an academic position at Harvard University in the United States. At Harvard from 1971 to 1973 he was chair of the Committee on African Studies. Then in 1973 he was appointed the first Mellon Professor of African History at Harvard. He continued to teach there until 1978, when he found it possible to return to Nigeria.

Back in Nigeria he again went into administrative work, this time as president of Anambra State University. Anambra is located in Enugu in the Eastern part of the re-united nation northeast of his birthplace, Awka. Dike was accompanied by his wife Ona when he returned to Nigeria. Dike died in an Enugu hospital on October 26, 1983, at the age of 65. At the time of his death, one daughter, Nneka, and one son, Emeka, lived in Nigeria's capital city, Lagos, on the Western coast. Three other children (two daughters, Chinwe and Ona, and one son, Obi) remained in the United States, in Cambridge, Massachusetts.

Further Reading

There is no published biography of Kenneth Dike. His historical work is quoted and used widely in Michael Crowder's *The Story of Nigeria* (1973), published in London by Faber and Faber. The books mentioned in this biographical article, particularly his *Trade and Politics in the Niger Delta 1830-1890* (London, 1956), are available in many university libraries in the United States. Readers interested in Dike's role as a Biafran emissary may read of him in Raph Uwechue's *Reflections on the Nigerian Civil War* (1971); in N. U. Akpan's *The Struggle for Secession 1966-1970* (London, 1971); and in John de St. Jorre's book *The Nigerian Civil War* (London, 1972). □

John Dillinger

John Dillinger (1903-1934) was the most famous modern American criminal. During the Depression of the 1930s his bank robberies were generally regarded as revenge on society's financial institutions that were unfairly exploiting the economically distressed.

John Dillinger was born on June 22, 1903, in Indianapolis, Ind. His mother died when he was quite young; he was raised by an older sister and eventually, when his father remarried, by his stepmother. At 16 he quit school and began to work intermittently. A year later his father moved the family to a farm near Mooresville, Ind. Dillinger rejected rural life and spent most of his time in the surrounding cities.

In 1923 Dillinger fell in love, but the girl's father ended the romance. Embittered, Dillinger stole a car which he later abandoned. Afraid of being prosecuted, he joined the Navy but deserted a few months later. In 1924 he was arrested for assault and attempted robbery. On the advice of his father he pled guilty; not only did he receive a more severe sentence than his accomplice, who pled not guilty, but also the accomplice secured parole after 2 years, while Dillinger languished in prison.

A difficult prisoner, Dillinger served much of his time in solitary confinement. As is frequently the case, Dillinger's confinement, instead of reforming and rehabilitating him, only trained him to be a criminal. When he left prison in 1933, he carried a map, supplied by inmates, of prospective robbery sites.

Released during the worst of the Depression, as an exconvict it is unlikely that Dillinger could have secured legitimate employment. He quickly found employment robbing banks, however, and almost overnight became a kind of Robin Hood national hero. The fact that people were killed during his holdups was overlooked; instead the national press played him up as a brilliant, daring, likeable individual, beating the banks which had been inhumanely foreclosing mortgages on helpless debtors.

Dillinger became a challenge for law enforcement officials, for he often made them look like fools; conflicts between police jurisdictions made him difficult to capture. When he was captured, he was able to escape. His most famous exploit was when he broke out of heavily guarded Crown Point County Jail armed only with a wooden gun. Eventually, however, the members of his gang were killed or caught. Dillinger moved to Chicago, disguised himself, and attempted to disappear. But he was recognized by Anna Sage, a woman who lived with his girlfriend, Polly.

On July 22, 1934, Anna Sage went to a movie with Dillinger and Polly; she wore an orange skirt to identify herself, and Dillinger, to waiting Federal agents. They gunned him down. Even in death Dillinger remained a thorn in the side of the establishment. Anna Sage ("the lady in red") became a hated figure, like most informers, and the image of

law enforcement suffered through what was regarded as too little willingness to take Dillinger, then almost a national hero, alive.

Further Reading

Interesting popularized accounts of Dillinger are contained in Robert Cromie and Joseph Pinkston, *Dillinger: A Short and Violent Life* (1962), and in John Toland, *The Dillinger Days* (1963). For a perspective on Dillinger in the context of his times consult Don Congdon, ed., *The Thirties: A Time to Remember* (1962). The law enforcement viewpoint is presented in Andrew Tully, *The FBI's Most Famous Cases* (1965). See also Jay R. Nash and Ron Offen, *Dillinger: Dead or Alive* (1970).

Additional Sources

Dillinger: the untold story, Bloomington: Indiana University Press, 1994.

Nash, Jay Robert, *The Dillinger dossier,* Highland Park, Ill.: December Press; Chicago, Ill.: Distributed by Chicago Review Press, 1983.

Toland, John, *The Dillinger days,* New York: Da Capo Press, 1995. □

Wilhelm Christian Ludwig Dilthey

The German historian and philosopher Wilhelm Christian Ludwig Dilthey (1833-1911) held that psychological principles should form the basis of historical and sociological research.

Wilhelm Dilthey was born in Biebrich, a village in the Rhineland, on Nov. 19, 1833. His family was intimately connected with the dukes of Nassau, serving for generations as chaplains and councilors. His early education was at a local gymnasium, from which he graduated in 1852. Following family tradition, Dilthey entered the University of Heidelberg to study theology. After three semesters he moved to Berlin for historical studies under Friedrich Trendelenburg. To please his father, he took the examination in theology and preached his first sermon in 1856. His preferred occupation was secondary teaching, but after 2 happy years he was forced to give this up as a result of persistent ill health. The next half-dozen years were spent in historical research and philosophical study at Berlin.

In 1864, with an essay on the ethics of Friedrich Schleiermacher, Dilthey entered university teaching. In 1866 he was called to Basel; in 1882, after brief tours in Kiel and Breslau, he returned to Berlin as professor of theology, a post he held until 1905. In 1874 Dilthey married Katherine Puttmann, and the couple had one son and two daughters. He died on Oct. 3, 1911, in Seis.

Dilthey published little during his lifetime, but since his death 14 volumes of collected writings have appeared. These include profound essays in intellectual history and original work on the philosophy of the mind. He made repeated efforts to arrive at general categories for interpreting comparative *Weltanschauungen* (philosophies of life). In imitation of Immanuel Kant's opus, Dilthey aspired to write a "Critique of Historical Reason," tracing the emergence and evolution of the great systems of thought. Dilthey concluded that no overall synthesis of these varying outlooks was possible but that an awareness of a certain historical relativity was the condition for intellectual liberation and creative work.

Dilthey argued convincingly for historical interpretation in all inquiries into man and his culture. Human life and creativity cannot be understood abstractly but only as part of a historical process. The historian must sympathetically enter into the alien cultures he seeks to understand. Much of Dilthey's work was an effort to describe the characteristic differences between this approach in historical subjects and the approach of the natural scientist toward his subject matter.

Further Reading

Fragmentary biographical information on Dilthey is contained in William Kluback, *Wilhelm Dilthey's Philosophy of History* (1956). H. A. Hodges, *Wilhelm Dilthey: An Introduction*

(1944), contains a good bibliography, and his *The Philosophy of Wilhelm Dilthey* (1952) is the most comprehensive treatment.

Additional Sources

Makkreel, Rudolf A., *Dilthey: philosopher of the human studies,* Princeton, N.J.: Princeton University Press, 1992.

Rickman, H. P. (Hans Peter), *Dilthey today: a critical appraisal of the contemporary relevance of his work,* New York: Greenwood Press, 1988.

Rickman, H. P. (Hans Peter), *Wilhelm Dilthey, pioneer of the human studies,* Berkeley: University of California Press, 1979.
□

Joe DiMaggio

Named the "Greatest Living Player" in a 1969 centennial poll of sportswriters, baseball star Joe DiMaggio (born 1914) took the great American pastime to new heights during his enormously successful career and epitomizes the sports heroes of the 1940s and 1950s.

One of the most popular and fabled players to compete in Yankee Stadium, Joe DiMaggio was winner of three Most Valuable Player awards. His 1941 hitting streak of 56 games was one of the most closely watched achievements in baseball history, and he was so beloved by his fans that Japanese attempting to insult American soldiers on World War II battlefields called out insults to DiMaggio. His career batting average was .325, and he hammered 361 home runs. In 1949 he became the American League's first $100,000 player.

Before the Yankees

Son of Italian immigrant parents, Giuseppe Paolo DiMaggio Jr. grew up in the San Francisco area with his four brothers and four sisters. At seventeen DiMaggio elected to play minor league baseball with the San Francisco Seals, the team on which his brother was making his professional debut near the end of the 1932 season. With a salary of $250 a month, 6-foot-2-inch DiMaggio became a Bay Area celebrity in 1933, hitting safely in 61 consecutive games, an all-time record for professional baseball, while hitting .340 and driving in 169 runs. A year later DiMaggio hit .341 and was purchased by the New York Yankees for $25,000 and five minor league players. An impressive .398 batting average earned him a Yankee tryout in 1936, where he was billed as the next Babe Ruth. DiMaggio's debut was delayed because of an injury, yet when he appeared on the field for the first time, on 3 May 1936, 25,000 cheering, flag-waving Italian residents of New York showed up to welcome him to the team.

"Joltin Joe, the Yankee Clipper"

By 1936 "Joltin' Joe," as he was called, led the league with a career-high 46 home runs. Even with the depth of the

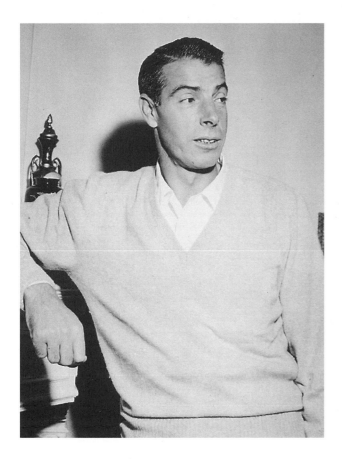

left field fence in Yankee Stadium, DiMaggio hit 361 career home runs, placing him fifth on the major league all-time home run list when he retired in 1951. In 1937 he batted an impressive .346, driving in 167 runs. The next season DiMaggio hit .324, followed in 1939 with a .381 and his first batting championship and the league Most Valuable Player award. Late in the 1939 season DiMaggio was hitting at a .412 pace, but eye trouble, and possibly the pressure, kept him from staying above the .400 mark.

The Streak

During the 1940 season DiMaggio captured his second consecutive batting title with a .352, but for the first time since he had joined the Yankees his team failed to win the pennant—setting the stage for the 1941 season that would make baseball history. DiMaggio's 56-game hitting streak during the 1941 season began on 15 May, when he singled home a run, and ended on 17 July. In between he hit .406, and fans all over the country anxiously checked each game day to see if the Yankee Clipper had kept the streak going. People jammed the ballpark; radio programs were interrupted for "DiMag" bulletins, the U.S. Congress designated a page boy to rush DiMaggio bulletins to the floor, and newspaper switchboards lit up every afternoon with the question of the day, "Did DiMaggio get his hit?" Immediately after Cleveland pitchers Al Smith and Jim Bagby held DiMaggio hitless on 17 July, with the help of two great plays at third base by Ken Keltner, he started another hitting streak that ran 17 games. At the same time, twenty-two-year-old Red Sox slugger Ted Williams was setting a modern-age

batting average of .406. During that same year, young pitcher Bob Feller won 25 games for the Cleveland Indians, and veteran pitcher Lefty Grove won his 300th game. In 1941 DiMaggio won his second Most Valuable Player award and like the rest of the nation began to feel the pressure of a nation readying itself for war. During the 1942 season DiMaggio batted .305 and was drafted into the army along with thousands of other young men. During his three years in the army DiMaggio played baseball in the Pacific and across the United States. The 1946 season was a disappointment (he batted .290), but by 1947 he was back in form, hitting .315 to win his third Most Valuable Player award and lead his team to the pennant.

Hall of Famer

Aided by the media machine of New York City and his own powerful statistics, DiMaggio became a national hero after the war—even though he played for the often-hated Yankees. He was even immortalized in a song called "Joltin' Joe DiMaggio," recorded by the Les Brown Orchestra. In 1948 DiMaggio had returned to the height of this form, winning the home run title with 39, the RBI crown with 155, and the batting title with a .320 average. DiMaggio sat out the first two months of the 1949 season with a bone spur in his heel, but as always his return was memorable. Although playing in pain, during his first games for new manager Casey Stengel, DiMaggio belted four homers in three games that broke the back of the league-leading Red Sox and helped the Yankees bring home another pennant. In 1951, with another soon-to-be Yankee superstar, young Mickey Mantle, on the scene, DiMaggio's average slipped to .263 with only 12 homers. Announcing his retirement at age thirty-seven in 1952, he turned down a fourth consecutive $100,000 contract because "when baseball is no longer fun, it's no longer a game." The Yankees, whose history is replete with heroes, retired his uniform, the world-famous pinstripe number five. In later years DiMaggio hosted pregame television shows, made television commercials, and was briefly married to the voluptuous Hollywood actress Marilyn Monroe. He was elected to the Baseball Hall of Fame in 1955, and in 1969 he was named the "Greatest Living Player" in a centennial poll of sportswriters.

Further Reading

Maury Allen, *Where Have You Gone, Joe DiMaggio? The Story of America's Last Hero* (New York: Dutton, 1975);

Jack B. Moore, *Joe DiMaggio: A Bio-Bibliography* (Westport, Conn.: Greenwood Press, 1986);

Michael Seidel, *Streak: DiMaggio and the Summer of '41* (New York: McGraw-Hill, 1988).

Durso, Joseph, *DiMaggio: the last American knight* (Boston: Little, Brown, 1995). □

Georgi Dimitrov

Georgi Dimitrov (1882-1949) was a Bulgarian and Soviet Communist leader who served as head of the Communist International (Comintern) from 1935 to

1943 and as prime minister of Bulgaria from 1944 until his death.

Georgi Dimitrov was born on June 18, 1882, in the village of Kovachevtsi, District of Pernik, near Sofia. His parents, poor peasants, came from Bulgarian Macedonia, then under Turkey, where American Protestants conducted successful missionary activities. A devout Protestant, his mother wanted him to become a clergyman, but according to his Marxist biographers, he rebelled against "the religious mysticism in which he was brought up at home" and turned to atheistic socialism. At age 12 he quit school, apprenticing as a printer and working (in 1903) in the printing shop of the American college at Samokov. He became active in the nascent labor union movement and in 1902 joined the Bulgarian Social Democratic Labor Party. As the party split in 1903 into "Narrow" (doctrinaire Marxist) Socialists, led by Dimitrov Blagoev, and "Broad" Socialists, Dimitrov took the side of Blagoev, who used him in the struggle for control of the labor unions. He was elected a member of Parliament first in 1913, serving until 1923. In 1918 he was briefly jailed for antiwar activities.

Blagoev's choice of successor to the leadership of the Narrows early fell on Vasil Kolarov, a lawyer educated in Geneva, Switzerland, and well acquainted with Georgi Plekhanov and European socialist leaders. Through the 1920s Dimitrov remained outranked and largely overshadowed by Kolarov. When the Narrows chose not to ally

with the Agrarians of Alexander Stamboliiski in 1918 a bitter enmity developed during Stamboliiski's administration (1919-1923). Together with Kolarov and other Narrows, Dimitrov led the prolonged transportation strike which threatened to turn into an armed clash with the Agrarians. After the establishment of the Communist International (Comintern) and the Narrows affiliation with it as the Bulgarian Communist Party (BCP) it was Kolarov who maintained the liaison by travelling to Soviet Russia. His standing with Lenin and other Soviet leaders became such that he was made the Comintern's general secretary in 1922. Dimitrov's first trip to Moscow was in 1921 to attend the third congress of the Comintern and take part in the establishment of the Red International of Trade Unions, or Profintern.

In the mounting crisis between the Agrarian government and its enemies on the right, ending in its overthrow in June 1923, Blagoev kept the BCP neutral and passive. To straighten out this mistaken course, the Comintern resolved that BCP should make an alliance with the overthrown Agrarians (or a "united front," in Lenin's precept) and stage an armed insurrection. Kolarov was dispatched with full powers to implement the decision. With Dimitrov and other BCP leaders who accepted the Comintern fiat, Kolarov threw the party into a futile insurrection in September 1923 which sputtered for a few days and ended in a bloodbath. He and Dimitrov escaped to neighboring Yugoslavia and thence to Vienna and Moscow where Kolarov resumed his functions at the Comintern and Dimitrov entered the ranks of its operatives.

In the ensuing ten years Dimitrov rose through various assignments involving the Balkan, Austrian, and German communist parties to the post of chief of the underground Bureau for Western Europe of the Comintern, headquartered in Berlin from 1929 to 1933. In that capacity he ran, under various aliases, a vast secret network of operations designed to keep the European communist parties in line with Soviet policies. It was in Berlin that the Gestapo arrested him on March 9, 1933, as it looked for culprits in the arson of the Reichstag (Parliament) building.

The Reichstag fire trial, held in Leipzig and Berlin, catapulted Dimitrov to world prominence. In the courtroom the prosecution tried to make a case against five defendants: Marinus van der Lubbe, a dim-witted Dutch Communist who was caught in the act; Ernst Torgler, the leader of the Communist members of the Reichstag; Dimitrov; and two other Bulgarians, Blagoi Popov and Vasil Tanev. The imperial court, still not Nazified, found only van der Lubbe guilty and sentenced him to death; Dimitrov and the others were acquitted.

After Dimitrov's arrest, the Comintern launched a camouflaged campaign, headquartered in Paris, to mobilize world public opinion against the Nazis. A so-called World Committee for the Relief of the Victims of German Fascism, made up of leftists and well-meaning liberals from various countries, set up a counter-trial in London which succeeded in embarrassing and affecting the German trial. At Leipzig, Dimitrov himself was impressive in his self-defense, especially in the confrontations with Goering and Goebbels, who appeared as witnesses for the prosecution, although he apparently knew, according to Ruth Fischer and Arthur Koestler, that he would be set free under a deal between the Gestapo and the GPU, the Soviet secret police. Indeed, soon after his acquittal he was given Soviet citizenship and taken to Moscow by special plane.

As a reward, and to capitalize on Dimitrov's new fame, Stalin put him in charge of the Comintern. In that capacity Dimitrov enunciated in 1935, at the seventh congress of the Comintern, the new line that Fascism, not the Western democracies, was the enemy and that the tactic to fight it was popular (or united) fronts—that is, coalitions of the Communists with anti-Fascist forces—in various countries. He remained in charge of the Comintern until its dissolution in 1943 and enjoyed a close relationship with Stalin during the tense period of the Great Purge and the years of World War II. From this vantage point of prestige and power he also made himself the undisputed leader of the Bulgarian exiles in the USSR and of the BCP in Bulgaria.

Dimitrov's chance to govern Bulgaria came after the Soviet Union declared war on the country in September 1944 and a coalition of BCP, Agrarians, and other anti-Fascist elements (the "Fatherland Front") took power. He returned from the Soviet Union in November 1945 amidst a mounting crisis between the BCP and the Agrarians led by Nikola Petkov and others in the coalition over BCP's drive, with Soviet support, to establish a Soviet system in Bulgaria. In November 1946 he became prime minister and presided over the destruction of all opposition and the Sovietization of Bulgaria by the harshest methods of the Stalin era. Among the victims was Petkov, who was put through a sham trial and executed; in its protest the U.S. government pointed to the contrast in Dimitrov's role in the Reichstag fire trial and the judicial murder of Petkov. In foreign policy Dimitrov toed Stalin's line and, while Stalin approved it, pursued the old Marxist vision of a Balkan federation of socialist states which was to be implemented by first federating Bulgaria and Yugoslavia. With the break between Stalin and Tito in 1948 Dimitrov abandoned the idea and took his place dutifully behind Stalin. He died on July 2, 1949, at the Borovikha Sanatorium near Moscow. His body, like Lenin's in Moscow, is on public display in a mausoleum in Sofia.

Further Reading

The main sources, *Georgi Dimitrov: biografiia*, by V. Khadzhinikolov and others (Sofia, 1982), and *Georgi Dimitrov: letopis za zhivota i revoliutsionnata mu deinost*, by E. Savova (Sofia, 1982), are not available in English; an earlier biography by the same authors, *Georgi Dimitrov, 1882-1949* (Sofia, 1972) is. Useful for context are J. D. Bell, *The Bulgarian Communist Party from Blagoev to Zhivkov* (1985); two books by N. Oren, *Bulgarian Communism* (1971) and *Revolution Administered* (1973); and F. Tobias, *The Reichstag Fire* (1964). The best bibliography is by E. Savova, *Georgi Dimitrov: bibliografiia* (Sofia, 1968), which lists materials in various languages and editions of Dimitrov's works.

Additional Sources

Mukerjee, Hirendranath, *Georgi Dimitrov, titan of our time,* New Delhi: Vision Books, 1982.

Mukherjee, G., *Georgi Dimitrov, a leader of working class,* New Delhi: Northern Book Centre, 1983.

Radenkova, Petra, *Georgi Dimitrov: a short biography,* Sofia: Sofia Press, 1982. □

Karen Dinesen Blixen-Finecke

Isak Dinesen was the pseudonym used by the Danish author Karen Dinesen Blixen-Finecke (1885-1962). Her stories place her among Denmark's greatest authors.

Isak Dinesen was born on April 17, 1885, the daughter of a wealthy landowner, adventurer, and author. In 1914 she went to Africa, married, and bought a coffee plantation. After her divorce in 1921 she managed the plantation alone until economic disaster forced her to return to Denmark in 1931, where she lived the rest of her life on the family estate, Rungstedlund, near Copenhagen.

The years in Africa were the happiest of Dinesen's life, for she felt, from the first, that she belonged there. Had she not been forced to leave, she wrote later, she would not have become an author. In the dark days just before leaving, she began to write down some of the stories she had told to her friends among the colonists and natives. She wrote in English, the language she used in Africa. Her books usually appeared simultaneously in America, England, and Denmark, written in English and then rewritten in Danish.

Dinesen's first collection, *Seven Gothic Tales,* appeared in America in 1934, where it was a literary sensation, immediately popular with both critics and public. The Danish critical reaction was cool. Danish literature was still dominated by naturalism, as it had been for the past 60 years, and her work was a reaction against this sober, realistic fiction of analysis.

Dinesen's second book, *Out of Africa* (1937), a brilliant recreation of her African years, was a critical and popular success wherever it appeared. Although it has little in common, stylistically and formally, with her stories, it describes the experiences which formed her views about life and art. The third central work in her authorship, *Winter's Tales,* appeared in 1942.

A characteristic of Dinesen's works is the sense that the reader is listening to a storyteller. She wanted to revive in her "listeners" the primitive love of mystery that she found in her African audience, which she felt was like the audiences that listened to Homer, the Old Testament stories, the *Arabian Nights,* and the sagas (elements from all of which she skillfully wove into her stories). She attempted to reawaken the sense of myth and, with myth, the sense of man's tragic grandeur, which she felt had been lost.

Fifteen years after *Winter's Tales,* Dinesen published *Last Tales* (1957), containing some of her finest stories. This volume includes "The Cardinal's First Tale," an excellent

Dingane

Dingane (ca. 1795-1840) was a Zulu king whose reign was blighted by domestic and external difficulties which culminated in fierce conflict with his white neighbors.

D ingane was a younger son of the Zulu chieftain Senzangakona. Little is known of Dingane's career until 1828, when he successfully conspired to assassinate his half brother Shaka who, after Senzangakona's death, had expanded the petty Zulu chieftainship into a powerful warrior kingdom at the expense of neighboring chiefs.

Although many welcomed Dingane's accession for the relief it offered from the fierce militarism of Shaka's reign, it is doubtful whether Dingane ever felt secure on the throne he had seized. His position was that of a usurper who owed his rise from obscurity to the achievements of the brother he had murdered. His kingdom, not yet 12 years old, was a forced creation in which national spirit had still not effectively submerged older political loyalties. And, among his subjects, assassination and social fission were established techniques for dealing with political difficulties. In 1829 the Qwabe subchief, Nqetho, led his followers south in a major secessionist movement, and defections continued during the years that followed.

Dingane lacked the qualities of the warrior leader. Indolent and inconstant, jealous and untrusting, he failed to arouse loyalty and affection in his subjects. To preserve his hold over his kingdom, he resorted to the methods of terrorism and extermination that Shaka had used; but he was unable to inject into his warriors the fierce fighting spirit that had once made them the terror of southeastern Africa, and his campaigns were either inconclusive or ended in humiliating defeat.

Probably because he valued trade and feared that injury to the interests of British subjects might bring retribution from the Cape, Dingane tolerated the small settlement of English traders and hunters that Shaka had permitted at the port of Natal, but he did so with diminishing enthusiasm. The traders possessed firearms that gave them a power disproportionate to their numbers. They defied his commands yet lacked law-enforcing authorities of their own. And their settlement became a place of refuge for thousands of deserters from Zululand.

In 1830 Dingane had sent an embassy to the Cape, but the expedition was tactlessly managed and relations with the whites deteriorated. For a while after 1835 Dingane seems to have hoped that the missionary Capt. A. F. Gardiner would serve as a "subchief" and control the Natal settlement, but again he was disappointed for Gardiner was unable to establish his authority.

Dingane's most serious difficulties began toward the end of 1837, when he was confronted by the leader of a large party of Trekkers (Afrikaner emigrants) from the Cape, seeking to establish a republic on his southern borderlands.

defense of her art and a critique of naturalism. In 1958 appeared *Anecdotes of Destiny.* Her last book, *Shadows on the Grass* (1961), is a pendant to *Out of Africa* .

Dinesen was the first Danish author to achieve world fame since Hans Christian Andersen and Søren Kierkegaard. Her influence on Danish literature was especially strong in the 1950s when, through her stories and personal contact, she was an inspiration to younger authors searching for new means of expression. She died on Sept. 6, 1962.

Further Reading

Useful studies of Dinesen in English are Eric O. Johannesson, *The World of Isak Dinesen* (1961), and Robert Langbaum, *The Gayety of Vision: A Study of Isak Dinesen's Art* (1964).

Additional Sources

Dinesen, Thomas, *My sister, Isak Dinesen,* London: Joseph, 1975.

Migel, Parmenia, *Tania: a biography and memoir of Isak Dinesen: first published as Titania,* New York: McGraw-Hill, 1987, 1967.

Pelensky, Olga Anastasia, *Isak Dinesen: the life and imagination of a seducer,* Athens: Ohio University Press, 1991.

Thurman, Judith, *Isak Dinesen: the life of a storyteller,* New York, N.Y.: St Martin's Press, 1982.

Henriksen, Aage, *Isak Dinesen/Karen Blixen: the work and the life,* New York: St. Martin's Press, 1988. □

These were rebels against British rule, injury to whose interests was unlikely to bring retaliation from the Cape. But Dingane seems to have feared that an outright refusal of their request might precipitate a conflict in which Zulu armies with a record of failure would be forced into open conflict with men whose firearms had already dispersed the great Ndebele kingdom of Mzilikazi. He therefore appeared to assent to their demands, but in February 1838 he trapped and massacred a large deputation headed by Piet Retief and then sent out his armies to fall upon the unsuspecting Trekker camps under cover of night.

This attempt to rid himself of the intruders by treachery and surprise failed in its purpose. The Trekkers rallied and in December at Blood River inflicted on the Zulu armies the heavy slaughter that Dingane seems to have anticipated from open conflict. Fission followed within the Zulu body politic. Dingane's half brother Mpande defected south with thousands of followers, entered into a client relationship with the Trekkers, and in February 1840 routed Dingane's troops at the battle of Magongo. Dingane, a refugee from his own people, sought his escape northward but was murdered in the Ubombo Mountains later in the year.

His efforts to preserve his throne and insulate his kingdom from the disturbing presence of white neighbors profoundly influenced the attitudes of the emergent Afrikaner people, amongst whom the conflict was commemorated as one between "civilization" and "barbarism."

Further Reading

Peter Becker, *Rule of Fear* (1964), is a popular account of the life and times of Dingane based on oral tradition and documentary sources. It should be read with Alfred T. Bryant, *Olden Times in Zululand and Natal* (1929); Donald R. Morris, *The Washing of the Spears* (1965); and John D. Omer-Cooper, *The Zulu Aftermath* (1966). Also helpful is Monica Wilson and Leonard Thompson, eds., *The Oxford History of South Africa* (1969). □

David Dinkins

After defeating incumbent Mayor Edward I. Koch in New York's 1989 Democratic mayoral primary, David Dinkins (born 1917) went on in November to defeat Rudolph Giuliani and become the first African American mayor of New York City.

Calm, elegant, deliberate, and dignified, David N. Dinkins overcame the suspicions of many white New Yorkers that he lacked leadership qualifications and in November of 1989 was elected the first black mayor of the United States' largest city. After announcing his candidacy in February, Dinkins became the beneficiary of a changing public attitude, one exhausted with racial strife and adjustments caused by a constricting economy. Drawing heavily on his political stronghold in Harlem, the career politician and lifelong Democrat defeated incumbent

Mayor Edward I. Koch in September. In the general election he was victorious over a political neophyte, the popular district attorney Rudolph W. Giuliani. Once in office, Dinkins faced the intimidating task of healing a city suffering from fiscal and racial hemorrhaging. The results have received mixed reviews, with supporters praising Dinkins for calming a populace that threatened to explode more than once, and detractors arguing that he has acted timidly at a time when the city was crying out for forceful leadership.

Celestine Bohlen expressed in the *New York Times:* "David Dinkins comes to the office of mayor after three decades of loyal, quiet service to the Democratic party— making him a man who is a groundbreaker and very much bound by tradition. In a race against two high-profile opponents, Mr. Dinkins was the candidate of moderation, a middle-of-the-road choice for a city that seemed eager to lower its own decibel level. His strategy was to soothe, not excite—and it worked."

Perceiving that the city he likes to call "our town" was ready for a candidate that would "take the high road," Dinkins led a campaign that was notable less for what he said than the way he said it. His English was formal and almost stilted, delivered in a calm baritone laden with "one oughts" and "pray tells." He did not raise his voice and unlike many politicians, spoke the same language at a breakfast meeting on Wall Street as he did at a street rally in Bensonhurst, a volatile area of the city. He fared well in comparison to Koch, known for his divisive politicking, and

Giuliani, who transferred his prosecutorial style to the campaign trail.

Dinkins has been called a man of deep convictions by his admirers, although few concrete programs can be linked to those convictions. Others have called him a political Bill Cosby: "Dinkins projects the kind of personality that's not threatening to whites and is acceptable to blacks," Representative Floyd H. Flake, a black Democrat from Queens, told the *New York Times.* Yet throughout his career he has received only marginal support from black political groups or voters outside his Harlem base, losing as many elections as he has won. The "rap" against him cites his inadequate support for minority issues.

Emerged as a Peacemaker

By most accounts his finest moments in the campaign involved calming the city when it seemed on the brink of racial schism. A young white woman had been raped and brutalized by black youths in Central Park, and a black teenager had been murdered in a white ethnic Brooklyn neighborhood. In the polarized atmosphere of the summer of 1989, Dinkins emerged as a peacemaker. His image as an avuncular, deliberative leader seemed a welcome balm to New Yorkers. To appear cool and unflappable in the summer heat, Dinkins had his aides carry three or four identical linen suits, allowing for quick changes.

In Bensonhurst, where black community leaders had organized a march to protest the killing of Yusef Hawkins in August, Dinkins faced an angry crowd that booed his arrival. He managed to quiet the boos and obtain his audience's respect. According to an account by Todd Purdum in the *New York Times,* he approached it this way: "Let's be clear on something. There's no need for you to agree with me. You have every right to prefer someone else. But understand this also. There will come a November 7 and then there'll be a November 8, and the people will have spoken. And after they've spoken, I'm equally confident that you're going to obey and abide by that judgment."

Such moments of eloquence were rare for Dinkins. Even his supporters joked about his wooden speaking style. On the eve of the general election, in a televised candidate's debate, he was given 60 seconds to explain why he should be mayor. To do this he needed to read aloud from a prepared text. For months on the campaign trail, reporters' eyes would glaze over when he repeated, for the umpteenth time, his vision of the city's ethnic diversity as "a gorgeous mosaic." He deviated little from his script.

Dinkins's two main campaign hurdles were civil rights leader Jesse Jackson and his own personal finances. Dinkins's association with Jackson, whose private pronouncement of New York as "Hymietown" still infuriated many, limited Dinkins's support among Jewish voters. The mayoral candidate's campaign strategists, however, were able to convince a plurality of Jewish voters that Dinkins was his own man and solidly within the Democratic party tradition.

A second obstacle was the integrity issue. Dinkins paid no income taxes from 1969 through 1972, although he later paid back taxes in full with interest. He referred to the

omission as an oversight. He also came under a cloud for his perceived unethical handling of his stock portfolio; he had transferred ownership to his son and substantially underreported its cash worth. Dinkins spent much time in the latter part of the campaign addressing those issues, often with visible reluctance and resentment.

Attended Howard University

Dinkins was born in Trenton, New Jersey, in 1927. His family had come from the South the previous year after pulling up roots in Newport News, Virginia. During Dinkins's early childhood, his parents separated, and he and his younger sister went with their mother to start a new life in Harlem. He returned to Trenton to attend high school, then went on to Howard University. His studies were interrupted by World War II, during which he served in the Marines. "Dink" was recalled by classmates as a fine student; media interviews with those classmates depict a young man with strong social skills, popular with one and all, and involved in a fraternity. It was at Howard that Dinkins met Joyce Burrows, a campus queen of a rival fraternity. The two eventually became engaged.

While strongly involved in social life at Howard—a primarily black college in Washington, D.C.—as an undergraduate, Dinkins occasionally ventured off campus to see movies in the Washington area. The capital was very much a segregated city at that time. An inveterate movie buff, Dinkins would don a turban and fake a foreign accent in order to enter movie theaters off limits to blacks. The episodes apparently did not stir any racial bitterness in the young man.

Soon after graduation Dinkins married his fiance in an Episcopalian church in Harlem, where the couple then set up housekeeping. Mrs. Dinkins had grown up in a very political family—her father was Daniel Burrows, former assemblyman and district leader—and provided strong encouragement for the young man to consider a political career. In 1953 Dinkins enrolled at Brooklyn Law School, entertaining the possibility of launching a political career. The young family soon moved to a state-subsidized, middle-class housing project in Harlem, where they raised two children.

Dinkins eventually complied with the wishes of his wife's parents. Introduced to J. Raymond Jones, the so-called "Harlem Fox," Dinkins became a cog in the powerful Harlem political machine, the Carver Club. The organization trained generations of young black business and political leaders and was well entrenched within the city's power structure. Dinkins took on the grunt work that is part of every campaign, awakening at dawn to hang posters at Harlem subway stops. He worked long and hard without complaint, and his dedication was duly noted. Within the Carver Club, racial rhetoric was rare, congeniality the byword. Dinkins mixed easily with politicos from all walks of life. Among his peers and cronies were Basil Paterson, Charles Rangel, and Percy Sutton, all of whom were to emerge as three of the city's most powerful black politicians. As Dinkins grew older and took on more responsibility, his associations came to include a number of the city's movers and shakers. He played tennis with them at the River Club, visited their estates in South Hampton, and vacationed in Europe at their expense.

None of this endeared Dinkins to black community leaders or younger, more activist voters. Yet as the momentum of his campaign grew, and it became clear he had a very real chance to become the city's first black mayor, misgivings gave way to racial pride. Blacks sporting "Dinkins" buttons on their lapels began turning up all over town. When his chauffeured car pulled into a black neighborhood, the excitement became palpable. A *Newsday* editorial writer asked Dinkins whether he feared his image was that of an Uncle Tom. He answered, "*Au contraire.* What I do is provide hope."

Elected Manhattan Borough President

In 1965 Dinkins ran for his first elective office, representing his district in the New York State Assembly, and won. At the end of his two-year term, however, his district was redrawn, and he chose not to run again. He bided his time handling local political tasks. When Mayor Abraham Beame offered him a post in his administration as deputy mayor, Dinkins accepted—then withdrew in the midst of a media hoopla over his unpaid taxes. Dinkins paid his taxes and, still very much in the party's good graces, was hastily appointed city clerk. His responsibilities mainly involved signing marriage certificates; his salary was $71,000.

In 1977 Percy Sutton resigned as Manhattan borough president and anointed Dinkins to run for the office. Dinkins did, but lost by a wide margin. Four years later he ran again, losing once more in a landslide. In 1985 he vied a third time and was elected. The post he took over included a staff of more than 100 and an annual budget of nearly $5 million. As borough president, Dinkins did little to upset the apple cart. He put together task forces on a range of urban issues, from pedestrian safety to school decentralization. Perhaps his strongest stance was in support of community-based AIDS services.

Neil Barsky wrote in the *Wall Street Journal,* "By most accounts he made little of the post, and was best known among city politicians for his problems making up his mind" on budget and land-use matters. Dinkins earned a reputation as a procrastinator, withholding his opinion or his vote until he could hold lengthy, detailed briefings with aides and consultants. To the public he was deliberate, cool-headed, and rather vague, as evidenced by an answer given to *New York Times* reporter Todd Purdum in response to a question on streamlining the city's bureaucracy: "I cannot now set forth a specific blueprint and guarantee that we can do everything in one stop. All I'm saying is there must exist the ingenuity among us if we start off with the assumption that it's a desirable goal."

Shattering of the "Gorgeous Mosaic"

Early in his tenure, Dinkins experienced firsthand the glaring difference between a candidate who can promise the sky and an office-holder who cannot, to the dismay of some constituents, deliver all things to all people. The city Dinkins inherited, in the eyes of many political pundits, was

looking more ungovernable with each passing day, presenting a string of concrete challenges to the idealism that had drawn the electorate to him during the campaign. The budget deficit was running at $1.8 billion, a national recession was robbing the city of jobs and cutting revenues, and crime continued to claim victims in cases that made the national news and further enhanced the image of New York as an archetype of urban decay.

In addition, it was by no means helpful that at a time when New Yorkers were in need of greater government services, federal aid to cities across the country had been given the budgetary ax. After being criticized for initially wavering on New York finances, Dinkins bit the bullet, avoiding deficit spending by cutting the city's work force and dramatically scaling back health, education, housing, and other social programs. These moves, while praised as fiscally prudent, had a political cost. Some claimed Dinkins hadn't done enough, particularly with the downsizing of government, and others maintained he had alienated those constituents in the labor and African American communities who had been among his most strident supporters. "I sort of get it from both sides," Dinkins was quoted as saying in *Emerge.* "You can't make political judgments about actions you take. You really need to make a judgment that's consistent with the correct thing to do and what's good for all people. When it comes to 'my constituency' so-called—I frankly see everyone as my constituency."

In addition to facing attacks on his financial handling of the city, Dinkins began to see the further shattering of his beloved "gorgeous mosaic." In 1991 violent protests erupted after a car in the entourage of a Brooklyn Jewish leader struck and killed a black youth in Queens. Dinkins appealed to both sides to follow the light of reason rather than cave in to emotion, stereotypes, and hate and was credited with having brokered a peace, albeit a fragile one.

A more rigorous test of his healing powers was delivered in 1992, when riots ravaged cities throughout the country in the wake of the not guilty verdict in the controversial Rodney King case, which involved the question of brutality inflicted by white police officers on a black citizen. Visiting neighborhoods most vulnerable to violent explosion, Dinkins again succeeded in deactivating a racial time bomb and earned, at least temporarily, a respite from his critics. "This was defining moment for him," state Democratic Chairman John A. Marino was quoted as saying in the *New York Times.* "He showed why he was elected, in a sense. I'm hearing a lot of good things about David N. Dinkins from people who a few weeks ago didn't have anything good to say about him."

Dinkins continued to have good luck in 1992, as the city prepared for the lucrative Democratic National Convention—a feather in the mayor's political cap. An unexpected budget surplus was discovered, and the Internal Revenue Service (IRS) ruled in May that the mayor had not violated federal tax rules in the 1986 stock transaction with his son. A July 2, 1992, poll indicated New Yorkers had a 41 percent favorable opinion of him, not the number of a universally loved politician, but 12 points higher than it had been in March.

Dinkins has learned, however, that luck is as fleeting in politics as it is in other fields, perhaps more so. As the 1993 election approached, Dinkins was facing a steady stream of criticism that he has hired incompetent workers to top municipal posts, that he acts reactively rather than proactively, and that, while displaying a talent for pacifying, he lacks the consistently strong leadership and stalwart vision that the city's multifaceted problems demand.

Still, Dinkins continued trumpeting the populist, idealistic themes that carried him through the 1989 election and that he hoped would serve him well in 1993, when he faced challenges from Giuliani and George Marlin, Conservative and Right to Life Parties. "I came into government hearing the voices of those in need, and I will never stop listening," the *New York Times* quoted the mayor as saying in his 1992 state-of-the-city speech. "There is more hope in this city than there are street corners." Nonetheless, Giuliani defeated him by a narrow margin and Dinkins became the first black mayor of a major American city who was not re-elected to office.

Further Reading

Black Enterprise, November 1989.
Detroit Free Press, January 5, 1992.
Economist, November 11, 1989.
Emerge, November 1991.
Jet, August 28, 1995, p. 6.
Newsday, October 28, 1989.
Newsweek, May 28, 1990.
New York, November 5, 1990; November 11, 1991; May 25, 1992.
New Yorker, July 20, 1992; November 15, 1993, pp. 52-59.
New York Times, September 13, 1989; September 14, 1989; October 20, 1989; October 26, 1989; October 28, 1989; November 2, 1989; November 8, 1989; January 2, 1990; September 13, 1990; January 9, 1991; February 4, 1991; April 7, 1991; May 11, 1991; June 24, 1991 January 3, 1992; May 6, 1992; May 11, 1992, December 23, 1995, p. 29.
Wall Street Journal, October 28, 1989. □

Robert Dinwiddie

The Scottish merchant Robert Dinwiddie (1693-1770) rose through colonial administrative ranks to the lieutenant governorship of Virginia.

Robert Dinwiddie was born of an old Scottish family. His father was a prosperous merchant, and his mother also came from a commercial family. Robert was educated at the University of Glasgow and entered his father's countinghouse. He later carried on a successful career as a merchant.

Dinwiddie's role as a colonial administrator began in 1721, when he was appointed British representative in Bermuda. After 16 years of service in Bermuda he received the important position of surveyor general, which included jurisdiction over Pennsylvania and the southern colonies of British North America. By tradition the surveyor general was

entitled to a seat on the Virginia Council, a post Dinwiddie insisted on assuming. Characteristic of Dinwiddie's service in the Colonies was his zealous attention to the offices under his authority and a tendency to maximize his position by emphasizing the royal prerogative. In recognition of these qualities, he was appointed lieutenant governor of Virginia, England's largest colony, and took office on July 4, 1751.

As lieutenant governor, Dinwiddie saw the beginnings of the conflict on Virginia's frontiers that led to the French and Indian War. He was a firm advocate of British expansion into the west. He sought the help of the Indians and the other British colonies in the struggle against the French, pressed the legislature for defense funds, and favored the use of regular armed forces in place of the less reliable militia. Dinwiddie made George Washington a lieutenant colonel in 1754.

Generally, Dinwiddie was able to work in harmony with the Virginia Legislature. He did, however, prompt a serious conflict with the House of Burgesses shortly after he took office. In hope of increasing the British king's revenues, Dinwiddie tried to levy a fee for land patents, which would also require landholders to pay quitrents to the Crown. This precipitated the famous "Pistole Fee" controversy, in which the lower house charged that the governor had imposed an unlawful tax that endangered colonial liberty—a precursor of the arguments of the American Revolution.

The pressures of office and the war badly taxed Dinwiddie's health. At his own request he was relieved of

office in 1758 and with his wife and two daughters returned to Britain. He died in London on July 27, 1770.

Further Reading

The most comprehensive study of Dinwiddie is the occasionally laudatory work by Louis Knott Koontz, *Robert Dinwiddie: His Career in American Colonial Government and Western Expansion* (1941). Also valuable are Douglas Freeman, *George Washington: A Biography* (7 vols., 1948-1957), and Richard L. Morton, *Colonial Virginia* (2 vols., 1960). The ''Pistole Fee'' controversy is best examined in Jack P. Greene, *The Quest for Power: The Lower House of Assembly in the Southern Royal Colonies, 1689-1776* (1963). □

Diocletian

Diocletian (245-ca. 313), in full Gaius Aurelius Valerius Diocletianus, was a Roman emperor. He established the characteristic form of government for the later empire, the Dominate.

Diocletian whose name before he became emperor was simply Diocles, was a Dalmatian of humble birth. He became commander of Emperor Numerian's bodyguard. When the Emperor was murdered by his praetorian prefect, the troops chose Diocletian in November 284 to succeed and avenge his master.

By early 285 Diocletian had circumvented all opposition and determined to take immediate steps to bring to an end the 50 years of military anarchy (235-284) that had seen 26 emperors gain the throne, and scores of unsuccessful pretenders. He therefore decided to appoint as his caesar (successor-designate) a man of his own age, his old fellow soldier Maximian. The wisdom of this policy was immediately demonstrated by Maximian's military successes in Gaul, Germany, and North Africa between 286 and 290. Diocletian, meanwhile, controlled the Danubian and eastern frontiers. His satisfaction with the arrangement led him in 286 to raise Maximian to the rank of augustus, or coemperor.

Consolidation of the Empire

In 293 Diocletian extended and formalized the system of joint leadership by the establishment of the so-called tetrarchy. He and Maximian adopted as their caesars and aides Galerius and Constantius (I) Chlorus, respectively, and each young man was prevailed upon to divorce his wife and become the son-in-law of his augustus. Maximian assumed the general supervision of the West (prefecture of Italy) with headquarters in Milan; Constantius had special responsibility in Gaul and Britain and Galerius in the Balkans (Illyrium). Diocletian was in general control of the East with headquarters at Nicomedia (modern Izmir, Turkey), but the others also regarded him as their superior and guide.

Diocletian's innovation proved a military success: in 296 Constantius returned Britain, which had split away nearly a decade before, to the empire; Maximian triumphed over Moorish revolts in 297; and Diocletian suppressed insurrections in Egypt in 295 and 297. Galerius held the Danubian frontier successfully, and in 297 he so thoroughly defeated Narses I of Persia that more than 50 years of peace was achieved for that area.

Roman Administration and Army

During the 3d century governors of the larger provinces of the empire had repeatedly become rival claimants for the throne. Diocletian sought to correct this danger by splitting up the provinces into far smaller units—the number rose from less than 50 to well over 100—and within these units civil and military administrations were carefully separated. The smaller units fostered more careful and personal administrative and judicial work by governors and promoted imperial stability, but resultant proliferation of bureaucratic machinery effected a severe strain on the economy.

Diocletian also began to systematize a new organization of the army, formalizing tendencies that constant 3d-century warfare had brought about. The old legions, now sedentary and in effect a militia of farmers, were stationed along the frontiers to absorb the first shock of external attack. New, mobile, and much smaller legions (1,000 to 1,500 men, as opposed to the old 6,000) were stationed in garrison cities to back up the frontier troops. Diocletian also developed the use of mounted troops and began the organization of special crack troops, the *comitatenses,* or friends of the emperor, to serve as an imperial bodyguard. All this raised the size of the army from about 400,000 to about 500,000 men. It also increased the financial burdens of the state, though the frontier troops undoubtedly largely supported themselves from the land.

Finance Reforms

Diocletian undertook an ambitious building program, which included the enormous Baths of Diocletian at Rome and his palace for retirement at Spalato (modern Split) in Dalmatia, and he also encouraged his colleagues to sponsor public works. This program, with the demands of the bureaucracy and the army, severely strained the empire's finances, and Diocletian undertook a complete reform of the tax structure to meet these needs. His new system was based on the establishment of units of approximately equal value of land or of living things: that is, the unit of land (a *jugum*) could equal 20 acres of first-class plowland, 5 acres of vineyard, or 225 olive trees; or the head unit (*caput*) could equal the labor of one man, two women, or the sale value of a given number of animals. The value of the nation's resources was to be reviewed periodically; and the emperor and his advisers, after determining the national budget, each year could then set the tax rate per *jugum* and *caput*.

A steady debasement of the coinage during the 3d century had undermined all public confidence in the monetary system. Diocletian instituted a complete currency reform, and a uniform currency for the whole empire was devised. It appears, though the details are obscure, that this reform sent prices skyrocketing, probably because much of the old coinage was still in circulation and was now suspect. In any case, the desperate plight of soldiers and bureaucrats, who were on a fixed salary, forced Diocletian in 301 to issue an edict setting maximum prices for almost every conceivable article and service throughout the empire. The penalty for nonobservance was death. The efficacy of the measure appears to have been disappointing and the need brief. The extant fragments of the edict are of immense value in calculating the standard of living in the Roman world.

The Court

Diocletian had lived and fought for many years in the East, and he had observed that the secluded Oriental potentates were victimized by their subjects far less frequently than the more democratic Romans. Therefore, though himself a man of simple tastes, he determined to surround the throne with all the trappings of Oriental monarchy. He seldom appeared in public, but when he did it was with diadem, royal purple, and robes embroidered with gold. This was supported by an appeal to religion. Diocletian was considered the special spokesman on earth for Jupiter, the king of the gods, and he assumed the epithet "Jovius"; Maximian became "Herculius" as the representative of Hercules, the industrious son and helper of Jupiter, and who, as the benefactor of mankind, was running a close race with Christ for the allegiance of the Roman masses.

Relations with Christians

For most of his reign Diocletian was tolerant of dissident religious sects, including the Christians. But some Romans, especially Galerius, felt that the Christians were subverting Diocletian's attempt to emphasize the religious basis of his government to strengthen the state. In 303 Diocletian finally was prevailed upon to issue an edict banning Christian churches, assemblies, and sacred books. This ban was soon followed by two fires of mysterious origin in the Emperor's own palace in Nicomedia, which probably suggested the need for three further and progressively more severe edicts. These edicts were observed in a very uneven fashion, however, being strictly enforced only in Galerius's domain.

Diocletian's Retirement

In 303 Diocletian visited Rome for the first time to observe his twentieth anniversary as emperor. The following year he suffered from a very severe illness, probably a stroke, which seems to have convinced him that it was high time to turn over the reins of government to the caesars. On May 1, 305, therefore, he abdicated at Nicomedia, and by prearrangement Maximian performed the same act simultaneously at Milan. Galerius and Constantius Chlorus were elevated to the rank of augusti, while Flavius Valerius Severus became caesar in the West and Maximin Daia in the East.

Diocletian retired to the palace that he had prepared for himself in Spalato. There he busied himself with his vegetable garden, refusing to return to the political scene except for one brief peacemaking conference in 308 between his squabbling successors. He died at Spalato, probably in 313.

Further Reading

The most comprehensive and thorough account of Diocletian and his government is in French. In English, there are adequate accounts in the *Cambridge Ancient History*, vol. 12 (1939), and in A. H. M. Jones, *The Later Roman Empire, 284-602* (2 vols., 1964). □

Diogenes

Diogenes (ca. 400-ca. 325 B.C.), a Greek philosopher, was the most famous exponent of Cynicism, which called for a closer imitation of nature, the repudiation of most human conventions, and complete independence of mind and spirit.

The son of Hicesias, Diogenes was born in Sinope. He arrived in Athens after he and his father had been exiled from their native city for debasing the coinage in some way. His life in Athens was one of great poverty, but it was there that he adopted Antisthenes's teachings and became the chief exponent of Cynicism.

Although late authors attribute many works to Diogenes, none survives. One persistent tradition is that he wrote tragedies, perhaps to show that the misfortunes celebrated in the works of that genre could have been averted through the way of life which he taught. Because of his great notoriety and because many people in antiquity considered him the founder of Cynicism, a body of legend soon grew up about him and obscured the true accounts of his life. One certainty is that he developed a caustic wit which he used unsparingly on his contemporaries to show them the utter disregard in which he held their conventions and beliefs. The date and place of his death are uncertain, although it is unlikely that he lived later than 325 B.C.

Diogenes was not famous for developing a strong theoretical argument for his way of life. Antisthenes, the pupil of Socrates, was his inspiration, and he put into practice his master's teachings in a way which made a striking impression upon his contemporaries. Indeed, it was Diogenes's application of Antisthenes's principles which gained for him the notoriety he enjoyed. His goals were self-sufficiency, a tough and ascetic way of life, and *anaideia,* or shamelessness.

The first was the ultimate goal at which the Cynic life aimed. It involved a search for true happiness through the realization that wealth, rank, honors, success, and other such worldly aims were as nothing compared with complete independence of mind. The second and third aims supported the first.

Diogenes held that through a rigorous denial of all but the barest necessities of life one could train the body to be free of the world and its delusions. Through *anaideia* one could show the rest of humanity the contempt in which their conventions were held.

It was perhaps this last characteristic of Diogenes and his followers which gave the sect its name, since *anaideia*

involved carrying out acts in public which most men usually do in private. Other accounts hold that the name Cynic (doglike) derives from the Gymnasium Kynosarges in Athens, where Antisthenes taught.

Crates, Diogenes's pupil, propagated the master's teachings after his death. In addition to the influence which Diogenes had on numbers of his contemporaries, he also served as a source for the development of Stoicism.

Further Reading

Excellent accounts of the life of Diogenes, as it can be pieced together from various ancient traditions, may be found in D. R. Dudley, *A History of Cynicism* (1937), and Farrand Sayre, *Diogenes of Sinope* (1938). Also good, although more for the Cynics as a group than for Diogenes, is Eduard Zeller, *Outlines of the History of Greek Philosophy* (1881; trans. 1931). ☐

Cheikh Anta Diop

Cheikh Anta Diop (1923-1986) was an African historian who, in a series of studies, dramatically and controversially maintained that the scope of Africa's contribution to world civilization was considerably larger than heretofore acknowledged.

Cheikh Anta Diop was born at the end of 1923 in Diourbel, Senegal, a city reknowned for spawning great Islamic philosophers and historians. He received his higher education at the University of Paris (France), where he earned a doctorate of letters and was active in African student politics. Upon returning to Senegal, he joined what is today the Institut Fondamentale d'Afrique Noire, where he founded and ran the only carbon-14-dating laboratory in Africa. Diop experienced the great explosion of independence which began in early 1958 in Ghana. The hope that this movement created soon turned sour, as former European colonial powers, unseen, remained in control. Diop led and founded two political parties in Senegal: the Bloc des Masses Senegalaises in 1961 and a few years later the Front Nationale Senegalaise, both of which were outlawed by the government on the grounds that they threatened destruction of the existing order.

Diop, however, left his mark in the realm of the reassessment of the role of black people in world history and culture. Combining an unusual breadth of knowledge—including linguistics, history, anthropology, chemistry, and physics—he uncovered fresh evidence about the ancient origins and common principles of classical African civilization. He believed that people who feel they possess no past of their own tend to be absorbed and assimilated into the governing system, and are made to feel inferior because of this apparent deficiency. In fact, Diop argued, African culture and history was older than any other, and influenced the course of other cultures more than usually given credit.

Diop's argumentative thesis stressed the great contributions of Egypt, in particular, to the origins of culture and science, and asserted that Egyptian civilization was of black origin, a theory that has since been corroborated with anthropological evidence. Diop also challenged the prevailing view that the flow of cultural influence was from the north, the European or "Hamitic" areas, southward to the more primitive areas. He instead believed that the beginnings of civilization arose below the Sahara.

The center of a storm of controversy, Diop nevertheless opened up new paths of exploration, gave a new generation redemptive faith in its roots, and presented, if nothing else, a poetic image of greatness. In its daring, this dream of a lofty cradle of civilization may come closer to truth than the prosaic rebuttal of its critics, and as discoveries continue to be made, it proves itself more real than any dream.

Among Diop's books is *Anteriorité des civilisations nègres: Mythe ou vérité historique* (1967; Roots of Black Civilizations: Myth or Historical Truth). In 1966 at Dakar the World Festival of Negro Arts honored Diop as "the black intellectual who has exercised the most fruitful influence in the twentieth century." In 1981, Diop's *Civilisation Ou Barbarie* ("Civilization or Barbarism") appeared. Some consider it his greatest work. Diop intended it as the intellectual summation of his previous research. Shortly before his death, he spoke of devoting the rest of his life to a master plan that would preserve Africa for Africans. He passed away on February 7, 1986.

Further Reading

The best way to understand Diop's life is through his writings. These include *Precolonial Black Africa* (trans. 1987); *The African Origins of Civilization: Myth or Reality* (1974); *The Cultural Unity of Black Africa* (trans. 1990); and his opus, *Civilization or Barbarism* (trans. 1991). Summaries of Diop's work can be found in Claude Wauthier, *The Literature and Thought of Modern Africa* (1964; trans. 1966). An important selection from Diop's *Nations, nègres, et cultures,* in which he accounts for the myths of Negro inferiority, can be found in Irving Leonard Markovitz, ed., *African Politics and Society* (1970). □

Christian Dior

Christian Dior (1905–1957) was a fashion designer who changed the look of women's clothing and gave the post-World War II French fashion industry a new feminine look.

Christian Dior, son of a wealthy Norman manufacturer of chemicals and fertilizer, wanted to be an architect, but his family insisted he enter the diplomatic service. He prepared for a diplomatic career at the Ecole des Sciences Politiques but abandoned diplomacy in 1928 and became an art dealer. Illness forced him to give up

that business in 1934, and when he returned to Paris a year later, it was as a fashion illustrator—first of hats, later of dresses.

"The New Look"

In 1946, when World War II cloth rationing was lifted, Dior opened his own salon. In the spring of 1947 the success of his first collection, called the "New Look," propelled him to the top of the French fashion industry. His idealized, ultrafeminine silhouette featured tiny waists; long, full skirts; padded busts; and rounded shoulders. Everything was made exquisitely of the best materials available. The New Look changed the shape of women's clothing and lifted the French fashion industry out of the doldrums. For this feat a grateful French government awarded him the Legion of Honor.

Subsequent Designs

His successive collections (including the "H-Line" in 1954 and the "A-Line" in 1955) continued to be popular, and throughout the 1950s the fashion world looked to Paris and Dior for inspiration and style. He expanded his company into eight firms and sixteen associate firms in twenty-four countries, reportedly grossing some $20 million a year. His Dior label went on jewelry, scarves, men's ties, furs, stockings, gloves, and ready-to-wear clothing.

After his death the House of Dior continued under other designers, including his protégé Yves St. Laurent until 1960, then Marc Bohan. □

Paul Adrien Maurice Dirac

The English physicist Paul Adrien Maurice Dirac (1902-1984) formulated a most general type of quantum mechanics and a relativistic wave equation for the electron which led to the prediction of positive electrons, the first known forms of antimatter.

Paul Adrien Maurice Dirac was born on Aug. 8, 1902, at Monk Royal in Bristol, England, the son of Charles Adrien Ladislas Dirac and Florence Hannah Holten Dirac. Paul received his secondary education at the old Merchant Venturers' College and, at the age of 16, entered Bristol University. He graduated 3 years later in electrical engineering. Unable to find employment, he studied mathematics for 2 years before moving to Cambridge as a research student and recipient of an 1851 Exhibition scholarship award. His student years (1923-1926) at Cambridge saw the emergence of the mathematical formulation of modern atomic physics in the hands of Louis de Broglie, Werner Heisenberg, Erwin Schrödinger, and Max Born. It was therefore natural that Dirac's attention should turn to a cultivation of mathematics most directly concerned with atomic physics.

Negative Kinetic Energy

Dirac's first remarkable contribution along these lines came before he earned his doctorate in 1926. In his paper

"The Fundamental Equations of Quantum Mechanics" (1925), Dirac decided to extricate the fundamental point in Heisenberg's now famous paper. Before Heisenberg, computation of energy levels of optical and x-ray spectra consisted in a somewhat empirical extension of rules provided by Niels Bohr's theory of the atom. Heisenberg succeeded in grouping terms connected with energy levels in columns forming large squares and also indicated the marvelously simple ways in which any desired energy level could be readily calculated. Dirac found that what Heisenberg really wanted to achieve consisted in a most general type of operation on a "quantum variable" x which was done by "taking the difference of its Heisenberg products with some other quantum variable."

At that time neither Heisenberg nor Dirac had realized that the "Heisenberg products" corresponded to operations in matrix calculus, a fact which was meanwhile being proved by Born and Pascual Jordan in Göttingen. They showed that the noncommutative multiplication of the "Heisenberg quantities" could be summed up in the formula $(p \times q) - (q \times p) = h/(2\pi\sqrt{-1})$, where h is Planck's constant and p and q some canonically conjugate variables. Independently of them, Dirac also obtained the same formula, but through a more fundamental approach to the problem. Dirac's crucial insight consisted in finding that a very simple operation formed the basis of the formula in question. What had to be done was to calculate the value of the classical Poisson bracket $[p, q]$ for p and q and multiply it by a modified form of Planck's constant.

That such a procedure yielded the proper values to be assigned to the difference of $p \times q$ and $q \times p$ was only one aspect of the success. The procedure also provided an outstanding justification of the principle of correspondence, tying into one logical whole the classical and modern aspects of physics. Dirac once remarked that the moment of that insight represented perhaps the most enthralling experience in his life.

But the most startling result of Dirac's equation for the electron was the recognition of the possibility of negative kinetic energy. In other words, his equations implied for the electron an entirely novel type of motion whereby energy had to be put into the electron in order to bring it to rest. The novelty was both conceptual and experimental and received a remarkably quick elucidation.

The experimental clarification came when C. D. Anderson, doing cosmic-ray research in R. A. Millikan's laboratory in Pasadena, Calif., obtained on Aug. 2, 1932, the photograph of an electron path, the curvature of which could be accounted for only if the electron had a positive charge. The positively charged electron, or positron, was, however, still unconnected with the negative energy states implied in Dirac's theory of the electron. The work needed in this respect was largely done by Dirac, though not without some promptings from others. A most lucid summary of the results was given by Dirac in the lecture which he delivered on Dec. 12, 1933, in Stockholm, when he received the Nobel Prize in physics jointly with Schrödinger.

World of Antimatter

The most startling consequences of Dirac's theory of the electron consisted in the opening up of the world of antimatter. Clearly, if negative electrons had their counterparts in positrons, it was natural to assume that protons had their counterparts as well. Here Dirac argued on the basis of the perfect symmetry that according to him had to prevail in nature. As a matter of fact, it was a lack of symmetry in Schrödinger's equation for the electron that Dirac tried to remedy by giving it a form satisfactory from the viewpoint of relativity.

All this should forcefully indicate that Dirac was a thinker of most powerful penetration who reached the most tangible conclusions from carrying to their logical extremes some utterly abstract principles and postulates. Thus by postulating the identity of all electrons, he was able to show that they had to obey one specific statistics. This fact in turn provided the long-sought clue for the particular features of the conduction of electricity in metals, a problem with which late classical physics and early quantum theory grappled in vain. This attainment of Dirac paralleled a similar, though less fundamental, work by Enrico Fermi, so that the statistics is now known as the Fermi-Dirac statistics.

This contribution of Dirac came during a marvelously creative period in his life, from 1925 to 1930. Its crowning conclusion was the publication of his *Principles of Quantum Mechanics,* a work still unsurpassed for its logical compactness and boldness. The latter quality is clearly motivated by Dirac's unlimited faith in the mathematical structuring of nature. The book is indeed a monument to his confidence that future developments will provide the exact physical counterparts that some of his mathematical symbols still lack.

A telling measure of Dirac's main achievements in physics was the recognition that greeted his work immediately. In 1932 he was elected a fellow of the Royal Society and given the most prestigious post in British science, the Lucasian chair of mathematics at Cambridge. He received the Royal Society's Royal Medal in 1939 and its Copley Medal in 1952. He was a member of many academies, held numerous honorary degrees, and was a guest lecturer in universities all over the world. He married Margaret Wigner, sister of Nobel laureate Eugene P. Wigner, in 1937.

The second half of Dirac's working life was occupied mainly with cosmology and the subject of "large numbers," or numbers with cosmic significance. In the 1972, he accepted a post as professor of physics at Florida State University, and he continued there until his death in Tallahassee on October 20, 1984.

Further Reading

Humorous details on Dirac's life can be found in George Gamow, *Biography of Physics* (1961), together with a not too technical discussion of Dirac's theory of holes. See also Niels H. de V. Heathcote, *Nobel Prize Winners in Physics, 1901-1950* (1954). For a rigorous account of Dirac's role in quantum mechanics, the standard work is Max Jammer, *The Conceptual Development of Quantum Mechanics* (1966). Background works which discuss Dirac include James Jeans, *Physics and Philosophy* (1942), and Barbara Lovett Cline, *The Questioners: Physicists and the Quantum Theory* (1965).

Additional Sources

Dirac, Paul, *The Principals of Quantum Mechanics,* Clarendon Press, 1930.

Dirac, Paul, *Spinors in Hilbert Space,* University of Miami Center for Theoretical Studies, 1974.

Dirac, Paul, *General Theory of Relativity,* Wiley, 1975.

Kursunolgu, Behram N., and Eugene P. Wigner, eds., *Reminiscences About a Great Physicist: Paul Adrien Maurice Dirac,* Cambridge University Press, 1987. □

Everett Mckinley Dirksen

Everett McKinley Dirksen (1896-1969) served as a Republican congressman and senator from Illinois for over three decades.

E verett McKinley Dirksen was born in Pekin, Illinois, on January 4, 1896, the son of Johann and Antje Dirksen who had immigrated from the Ostfriesland district of Germany in 1866. Dirksen and his twin, Thomas Reed, were named after prominent Republicans. The father died in their youth, and their mother supported her family on a small farm she purchased just inside the city limits of what was commonly referred to as "Beantown." Strong Calvinists, the family belonged to the Second Reformed Church. His mother encouraged his interest in reading, and he was the only one of her children who finished high school.

He considered becoming a teacher, actor, or lawyer and attended the University of Minnesota for three and one-half years studying liberal arts and law. He quit the university, in part because of the scorn heaped on German-Americans, to join the army to prove his Americanism during World War I. Trained at Camp Custer in Battle Creek, Michigan, Dirksen served in France and rose to the rank of second lieutenant. Forced to abandon his plans to finish his education at the university because of his mother's illness, he had several jobs but finally went into business with his brother in a wholesale bakery, which prospered. Active in local civic theater he met and married Louella Carver in 1927, and they had one daughter, Joy, who married Howard Baker.

Active in local politics, Dirksen decided he should act to combat the effects of the Depression and ran unsuccessfully against the local Republican congressman William Hull in 1930. Two years later he won the nomination and, cleverly eschewing any association with the Herbert Hoover administration, won despite the Franklin D. Roosevelt landslide.

From the outset of his career in the House of Representatives Everett Dirksen exhibited certain characteristics which would dominate his government career. He was pragmatic rather than doctrinaire, studied each piece of legislation carefully, worked hard, attended both committee and congressional sessions, and was a good speaker. For

example, he voted with much of the New Deal to bring the country out of the Depression, supporting the banking acts of 1933 and 1935, federal emergency relief, the Agricultural Adjustment Act, the National Industrial Recovery Act; social security, the Soil Conservation and Domestic Allotment Act, and the Civilian Conservation Corps. In foreign policy matters, however, he was an avowed isolationist and opposed all legislation which might lead to war until September 18, 1941, when he made a dramatic about-face and called for complete support for the Roosevelt foreign policy and unity to defeat the Nazis.

For 16 years Dirksen was easily reelected to the House of Representatives. Sought as a political speaker, he also headed the Republican National Congressional Committee from 1938 through 1946. Throughout World War II, he supported the movement towards international cooperation after the war and worked to help pass the Fulbright Resolution. He served on the Post War Advisory Council of the Republican Party which met at Mackinac Island, Michigan, in the summer of 1943. Both the resolution and the council called for participation in an international peace-keeping organization after the war. He voted for the Legislative Reorganization bill in 1946. While in Congress Dirksen finished his law degree at George Washington University in the evenings and was active in the Veterans of Foreign Wars, the American Legion, Eagles, Elks, Moose, Masons, and Shriners.

In mid-1943 he caught the presidential bug and, after 31 House members signed Illinois Congressman Leslie Arends' petition to nominate Dirksen on the GOP ticket, he

formally announced his candidacy on December 2, 1943. He failed to form a political alliance with Governor Earl Warren of California and tried to secure the vice presidential nomination with New York Governor Thomas E. Dewey. However, that nomination went to Governor John Bricker of Ohio. An early advocate of economic aid to war-torn Europe, Dirksen advocated bipartisan foreign policy and voted for most of the Harry S. Truman policies, including aid to Greece and Turkey and the Marshall Plan; but he voted against nearly all of Truman's domestic legislation.

His physician in 1948 diagnosed blurred vision as cancerous and recommended surgery, which Dirksen rejected. Instead, he announced that he would not seek reelection. Retiring briefly for rest to a Chesapeake Bay cottage where his eyesight improved, he decided to oppose his old friend Senator Scott Lucas in the 1950 general election. After a campaign in which both sides engaged in highly questionable practices and aided by a scandal in the Cook County sheriff's race, Dirksen defeated the Democratic majority leader by slightly less than 300,000 votes to become the junior senator from Illinois.

Upon entering the Senate in 1950, Dirksen became a close ally of Senator Robert Taft of Ohio, attracted by his isolationist stance in foreign affairs and his conservative opposition to the Truman Fair Deal; he also became a firm supporter of Senator Joseph McCarthy of Wisconsin.

In 1952 Dirksen made the two most memorable speeches of the GOP convention: in the first he accused Governor Thomas E. Dewey of taking "us down the path of defeat" in 1944 and 1948, and in the other he formally (but unsuccessfully) placed the name of Senator Taft in nomination. However, Dirksen the eternal pragmatist soon made peace with Dwight D. (Ike) Eisenhower, the successful nominee, and campaigned vigorously for the ticket. Although loyal to both Taft and McCarthy until their deaths, Dirksen gradually gravitated to Ike and became by 1955 one of his strongest allies in the Senate.

Vigorously endorsed by Eisenhower for reelection in 1956, Dirksen won and replaced William Knowland as Republican minority leader in 1958. Dirksen fought hard for Ike's legislative program and championed the cause of civil rights, Irish self-determination (with Sen. John F. Kennedy of Massachusetts), the state of Israel, equal rights for women, and, eventually, under Ike's persuasion, the St. Lawrence Seaway. He also voted for federal aid to education, increased social security benefits, and minimum wage levels and embraced Eisenhower's notion of modern Republicanism.

Dirksen got on particularly well with Presidents John F. Kennedy and Lyndon B. Johnson, who genuinely liked the Illinois senator, paid ample homage to his enormous ego, and needed his legislative support. His assistance was indispensable to the passage of the United Nations bond issue of 1962, the nuclear test-ban treaty, and the Civil Rights Act of 1964. As he said at the time, quoting Victor Hugo, "Stronger than all the armies is an idea whose time has come." With the advent of the Richard M. Nixon presidency in 1969, Dirksen found his status considerably diminished. Beset by multiple illnesses, he died in Washington on September 7, 1969.

Further Reading

Everett McKinley Dirksen is listed in *Political Profiles* for the Truman, Eisenhower, Kennedy, Johnson, and Nixon years and in the *Biographical Directory of Congress.* Dirksen wrote numerous plays and six novels, none of which were published. His speeches are in the *Congressional Record.* An outstanding biography of the Illinois legislator has been written by Edward L. Schapsmeier and Frederick H. Schapsmeier, entitled *Dirksen of Illinois: Senatorial Statesman* (1985). Background material is readily available in *American Epoch* (1980) by Arthur S. Link and William B. Catton; in Stephen E. Ambrose, *Eisenhower* (1983-1984), and in Lawrence S. Wittner, *Cold War America* (1974).

Additional Sources

Schapsmeier, Edward L., *Dirksen of Illinois: senatorial statesman,* Urbana: University of Illinois Press, 1985. ☐

Walter Elias Disney

An American film maker and entrepreneur, Walter Elias Disney (1901-1966) created a new kind of popular culture in feature-length animated cartoons and live-action "family" films.

Walter Elias Disney was born in Chicago, IL, on December 5, 1901, the fourth of five children born to a Canadian farmer and a mother from Ohio. He was raised on a Midwestern farm in Marceline, Missouri, and in Kansas City, where he was able to acquire some rudimentary art instruction from correspondence courses and Saturday museum classes. He would later use many of the animals and characters that he knew from that Missouri farm in his cartoons.

He dropped out of high school at 17 to serve in World War I. After serving briefly overseas as an ambulance driver, Disney returned in 1919 to Kansas City for an apprenticeship as a commercial illustrator and later made primitive animated advertising cartoons. By 1922, he had set up his own shop in association with Ub Iwerks, whose drawing ability and technical inventiveness were prime factors in Disney's eventual success.

Initial failure sent Disney to Hollywood in 1923, where in partnership with his loyal elder brother Roy, he managed to resume cartoon production. His first success came with the creation of Mickey Mouse in *Steamboat Willie. Steamboat Willie* was the first fully synchronized sound cartoon and featured Disney as the voice of a character first called "Mortimer Mouse." Disney's wife, Lillian, suggested that Mickey sounded better and Disney agreed.

Living frugally, he reinvested profits to make better pictures. His insistence on technical perfection and his unsurpassed gifts as story editor quickly pushed his firm ahead. The invention of such cartoon characters as Mickey Mouse,

Donald Duck, Minnie, and Goofy combined with the daring and innovative use of music, sound, and folk material (as in *The Three Little Pigs*) made the Disney shorts of the 1930s a phenomenon of worldwide success. This success led to the establishment of immensely profitable, Disney-controlled sidelines in advertising, publishing, and franchised goods, which helped shape popular taste for nearly 40 years.

Disney rapidly expanded his studio facilities to include a training school where a whole new generation of animators developed and made possible the production of the first feature-length cartoon, *Snow White* (1937). Other costly animated features followed, including *Pinocchio, Bambi,* and the celebrated musical experiment *Fantasia.* With *Seal Island* (1948), wildlife films became an additional source of income, and in 1950 his use of blocked funds in England to make pictures like *Treasure Island* led to what became the studio's major product, live-action films, which practically cornered the traditional "family" market. Eventually the Disney formula emphasized slick production techniques. It included, as in his biggest hit, *Mary Poppins,* occasional animation to project wholesome, exciting stories heavily laced with sentiment and, often, music.

In 1954, Disney successfully invaded television, and by the time of his death, the Disney studio's output amounted to 21 full-length animated films, 493 short subjects, 47 live-action films, seven True-Life Adventure features, 330 hours of Mickey Mouse Club television programs, 78 half-hour *Zorro* television adventures, and 280 other television shows.

On July 18, 1957, Disney opened Disneyland, a gigantic projection of his personal fantasies in Anaheim, CA, which has proved the most successful amusement park in history with 6.7 million people visiting it by 1966. The idea for the park came to him after taking his children to other amusement parks and watching them have fun on amusement rides. He decided to build a park where the entire family could have fun together. In 1971, Disney World, in Orlando, FL, opened. Since then, Disney theme parks have opened in Tokyo and Paris.

Disney had also dreamed of developing a city of the future, a dream realized in 1982 with the opening of EPCOT, which stands for Experimental Prototype Community of Tomorrow. EPCOT, which cost an initial $900 million, was conceived of as a real-life community of the future with the very latest in high technology. The two principle areas of EPCOT are Future World and World Showcase, both of which were designed to appeal to adults rather than children.

In addition to his theme parks, Disney created and endowed a new university, the California Institute of the Arts, known as Cal Arts. He thought of this as the ultimate in education for the arts, where people in many different disciplines could work together, dream and develop, and create the mixture of arts needed for the future. Disney once commented: "It's the principle thing I hope to leave when I move on to greener pastures. If I can help provide a place to develop the talent of the future, I think I will have accomplished something."

Disney's parks continue to grow with the creation of the Disney-MGM Studios, Animal Kingdom, and a extensive sports complex in Orlando. The Disney Corporation has also branched out into other types of films with the creation of Touchstone Films, into music with Hollywood Records, and even vacationing with its Disney Cruise Lines. In all, the Disney name now lends itself to a multi-billion dollar enterprise, with multiple undertakings all over the world.

In 1939, Disney received an honorary Academy Award and in 1954 he received four Academy Awards. In 1965, President Lyndon B. Johnson presented Disney with the Presidential Medal of Freedom and in the same year Disney was awarded the Freedom Foundation Award.

Happily married for 41 years, this moody, deliberately "ordinary" man was moving ahead with his plans for gigantic new outdoor recreational facilities when he died of circulatory problems on December 15, 1966, at St. Joseph's Hospital in Los Angeles, CA. At the time of his death, his enterprises had garnered him respect, admiration, and a business empire worth over $100 million-a-year, but Disney was still remembered primarily as the man who had created Mickey Mouse over two decades before.

Further Reading

The best book on Disney is Richard Schickel, *The Disney Version: The Life, Times, Art, and Commerce of Walt Disney* (1968). A useful source of technical information is Robert D. Feild, *The Art of Walt Disney* (1942). The most intimate portrait of Disney is by his daughter, Diane Disney Miller, *The Story of Walt Disney* (1957). Biographies of Disney appear in both the 1952 and 1967 issues of *Current Biography*. Disney's obituary appears in the December 16, 1966, issue of *New York Times*. □

Benjamin Disraeli

The English statesman Benjamin Disraeli, 1st Earl of Beaconsfield (1804-1881), supported imperialism while opposing free trade. The leader of the Conservative party, he served as prime minister in 1868 and from 1874 to 1880.

Benjamin Disraeli was born on Dec. 21, 1804, in London, the second child and first son of Isaac D'Israeli, a Sephardic Jew whose father, Benjamin, had come from Cento near Ferrara, Italy. (The family had originally gone to Italy from the Levant.) Disraeli's mother, whom he appears to have disliked, was a Basevi, from a Jewish family that fled Spain after 1492, settling first in Italy and at the end of the 17th century in England. Disraeli's maternal grandfather was president of the Jewish Board of Deputies in London.

Isaac D'Israeli, when elected warden of the Bevis Marks Synagogue, resigned from the congregation rather than pay the fee of £40 entailed upon refusal of office. He had his four children baptized in the Church of England in 1817. Benjamin went first to a Nonconformist, later to a Unitarian school. At 18 he left school and studied for a year at home in his father's excellent library of 25,000 books. His father was a literary man who had published *The Curiosities of Literature* (1791), a collection of anecdotes and character sketches about writers, with notes and commentary in excellent English. Though the book was published anonymously, its authorship soon became known, and Isaac achieved fame.

In November 1821 Benjamin was articled for 400 guineas by his father for 2 years to a firm of solicitors. He later held this against his father, who, he declared, had "never understood him, neither in early life, when he failed to see his utter unfitness to be a solicitor, nor in latter days when he had got into Parliament." However, Benjamin did not consider he had wasted his time, since working in the solicitor's office "gave me great facility with my pen and no inconsiderable knowledge of human nature."

In 1824, encouraged by John Murray, Disraeli wrote his first novel, the crude and jejune political satire *Aylmer Papillon*. The same year he started reading for the bar. He also speculated wildly on the stock exchange and lost heavily. He next became involved in a project sponsored by John Murray to publish a daily paper. Its failure was complete. His next novel, *Vivian Grey*, published anonymously, gave great offense to Murray, who was pilloried in it. Fifty years later this novel was still quoted against Disraeli; although he declared that it described his "active and real ambition," it was full of blunders that clearly showed he did not move in

the social circles to which he pretended. It was attacked by the powerful *Blackwood's Magazine,* and in a later novel, *Contarini Fleming* (1832), Disraeli wrote, "I was ridiculous. It was time to die." But instead of dying, he had a nervous breakdown and traveled for 3 years (1828-1831).

Political Career

On his return to England in 1832, Disraeli twice contested and lost High Wycombe in parliamentary elections. He also continued writing: *The Young Duke* (1831), *The Present Crisis Examined* (1831), and *What Is He?* (1833). He sent a copy of his *Vindication of the British Constitution* (1835) to Sir Robert Peel and received an acknowledgment. In 1835 he again ran unsuccessfully for Parliament; that year, however, he told Lord Melbourne that his ambition was to be prime minister. Disraeli at this time was a thin, dark-complexioned young man with long black ringlets; he dressed extravagantly, in black velvet suits with ruffles and black silk stockings with red clocks. His eccentric speeches were received with shouts of derision.

After failing in five elections in 5 years, Disraeli was elected to Parliament in 1837 for Maidstone in Kent, sharing a double seat with Wyndham Lewis. His maiden speech occasioned much laughter in Parliament, but he sat down shouting, "The time will come when you will hear me." In 1837 he published the novels *Venetia* and *Henrietta Temple*. In 1839 he spoke on the Chartist petition and declared "the rights of labour" to be "as sacred as the rights of property." The same year he married Mrs. Wyndham Lewis, 12 years his senior, his parliamentary colleague's widow.

He often declared jokingly that he had married for money; however, when his wife said he would do it again for love, he agreed. She made him an admirable wife. (Once, when he was on his way to make an important speech and had shut the carriage door on her hand, she never uttered a word until he got out, then she fainted.)

Disraeli was always financially incompetent. In 1840 he bought the estate of Hughenden; a year later he was £40,000 in debt, although his father had paid his debts on three occasions. In 1841 he won Shrewsbury and in 1842 wrote his wife that he found himself "without effort the leader of a party chiefly of youth." This party was called Young England and consisted basically of Disraeli and three of his friends, who openly revolted against Peel.

In 1842 more than 70 Tories voted with Disraeli against Peel, and the government was defeated by 73 votes. Peel resigned 4 days later, and Queen Victoria sent for Lord John Russell. In bringing down Peel, Disraeli nearly wrecked his party and his own career. He was in power for only 6 years out of a parliamentary life of more than 40 and spent longer in opposition than any other great British statesman.

In *Coningsby* (1844) and *Sybil* (1845), his two great political and social novels, Disraeli attacked Peel. In *Tancred* (1845), his last novel for 25 years, Disraeli wrote that the Anglican Church was one of the "few great things left in England." These three novels "have a gaiety, a sparkle, a cheerful vivacity" which carry the reader over their "improbabilities and occasional absurdities."

In 1848 Disraeli became leader of the Tories (Conservatives) in the House of Commons. In 1851, on Lord John Russell's resignation, the Queen sent for Lord Derby, who dissolved Parliament and gained 30 seats. In February 1851 Derby offered Disraeli the chancellorship of the Exchequer. Disraeli demurred, stating that the Exchequer was a "branch of which I had not knowledge"; Derby replied, "They give you the figures." Disraeli then accepted. The Cabinet was known as the "Who? Who?" from the deaf old Duke of Wellington's repeated questions to Lord Derby. Disraeli lowered the tax on tea in his 1852 budget and changed the income tax. In December 1852 the government was beaten, and Derby and his Cabinet resigned.

Disraeli commented that the Crimean War (1854-1856) was "a just but unnecessary war." During the outcry over the Indian mutiny (1857) he protested "against meeting atrocities by atrocities" and said, "You can only act upon the opinion of Eastern nations through their imaginations." In February 1858 he voted against the second reading of the Conspiracy to Murder Bill, when Lord Palmerston was defeated and resigned. Disraeli became chancellor of the Exchequer once more, and on March 26 brought in his India Bill, which "laid down the principles on which the great subcontinent was to be governed for 60 years." The following year his Reform Bill, redolent of what John Bright called "fancy franchises," was defeated. Palmerston then came in again for 6 years. In June 1865, however, Lord Derby came back as prime minister, and Disraeli once more became chancellor. When his Reform Bill passed in 1867, he went home to his wife, ate half a pie, and drank a bottle of champagne, paying his wife the compliment, "My dear, you are more like a mistress than a wife."

Prime Minister

In 1868 Lord Derby resigned, and on February 16 the Queen wrote, "Mr. Disraeli is Prime Minister. A proud thing for a man risen from the people." A minority premier, he passed the Corrupt Practices Bill, abolished public executions, and had his wife, who was dying of cancer, made a peeress. But in autumn 1868 the Liberals under William Gladstone came to power, and Disraeli became leader of the opposition. In 1870 he published *Lothair*. In 1872 his wife died.

In 1874 the Liberals and Home Rulers were defeated by the Conservatives, and "that Jew," as Mrs. Gladstone called him, became prime minister. "Power! It has come to me too late," Disraeli was heard to say. He was patient and formal with his colleagues, did not talk much, was a debater rather than an orator, but seldom relinquished his purpose. He was an intimate of the Queen and called her "the Faery." He became her favorite politician, although she began their association with reservations about his exotic appearance, dress, and style.

Although devoted to Disraeli, Victoria threatened to abdicate over the Eastern question, as she was violently pro-Turk. Constantinople was "the key to India," and Disraeli was determined not to let Russia get there. In 1875 he purchased the Egyptian khedive's interest in the Suez Canal Company and in 1876 made Victoria the empress of India. Disraeli and Salisbury represented England at the Congress of Berlin (1878), from which they returned bringing "peace with honour." (His phrase was used by Neville Chamberlain in another context in 1938.) Among the acts passed during Disraeli's premiership were the 1874 and 1878 Factory Acts and the Poor Law Amendment Act of 1878. In 1876 Disraeli became a member of the House of Lords as the 1st (and only) Earl of Beaconsfield.

In 1880 Gladstone and the Liberals returned to power. Disraeli retired to Hughenden, where he wrote *Endymion* and began another novel, *Falconet*. He died of bronchitis on April 19, 1881, and was buried next to his wife. His last recorded words were, "I had rather live but am not afraid to die."

Further Reading

The standard biography of Disraeli is William Flavelle Monypenny and George Earle Buckle, *The Life of Disraeli* (6 vols., 1911-1920; rev. ed., 2 vols., 1929). Robert Blake, *Disraeli* (1966), is also recommended. Cecil Roth, *Benjamin Disraeli, Earl of Beaconsfield* (1952), covers well the Jewish aspects of his life. B. R. Jerman, *The Young Disraeli* (1960), is a study of his career until 1837. See also C. C. Somervell, *Disraeli and Gladstone* (1925). □

Father Divine

Father Divine (c. 1877-1965) founded a cultish religious movement known as the Peace Mission. He served as its director from 1915 to 1965.

Father Divine is one of the more perplexing figures in twentieth-century African American history. The founder of a cultish religious movement whose members regarded him as God, Father Divine was also an untiring champion of equal rights for all Americans regardless of color or creed, as well as a very practical businessman whose many retail and farming establishments flourished in the midst of the Great Depression. Regarded by many members of the traditional black church as an imposter or even a lunatic, Divine was praised by other observers as a powerful agent of social change, alone among the many cult leaders in Depression-era New York in providing tangible economic benefits for thousands of his disciples.

The early biography of the man who later called himself Father Divine is little more than a patchwork of guesses: Divine was apparently unwilling to discuss his life except in its "spiritual" aspects. Believing himself to be God incarnate, he felt the details of his worldly existence were unimportant; the result is that historians are not certain even of his original name or place of birth. Most agree, however, that Father Divine was probably born ten to twenty years

after the end of the Civil War, somewhere in the Deep South, and that his given name was George Baker.

As betrayed by the accent and colloquialisms of his speaking style, Baker seemed to have grown up in the rural South, no doubt in a family of farmers struggling to survive under the twin burdens of economic exploitation and racially discriminatory Jim Crow laws. At an early age, Baker escaped the drudgery of farm work by becoming a traveling preacher, gradually working his way north to Baltimore, Maryland, in the year 1899.

"The Messenger"

In Baltimore, Baker worked as a gardener, restricting his preaching to an occasional turn at the Baptist church's Wednesday night prayer meeting, where his powerful speaking style was much encouraged by his fellow churchgoers. Though a man of stubby proportions with a high-pitched voice, Baker enthralled listeners with his fluid storytelling and highly emotional delivery, typical of the sermons given at the rural southern churches where he grew up.

But Baker was also a restless man of independent opinions, and it was not long before he felt compelled to resume the life of a traveling preacher. He returned to the South with two specific goals: to combat the spread of Jim Crow segregation and to offer an alternative to the otherworldly emphasis of most established churches. Such a crusade was not likely to meet with much success—indeed, Baker was fortunate not to be lynched—yet it reflected a concern for social issues that would remain constant throughout the long career of Father Divine.

Baker returned to Baltimore around 1906 and there fell under the influence of an eccentric preacher named Samuel Morris. Morris had been thrown out of numerous churches for proclaiming himself to be God, a belief he derived from a passage in St Paul's First Letter to the Corinthians which asks, "Know ye not that . . . the spirit of God dwelleth in you?" This teaching provided Baker with a religious foundation for his social activism: if God lived within every human being, all were therefore divine and hence equal. Baker became Morris's staunch supporter and disciple. Morris took to calling himself "Father Jehovia," while his prophet Baker adopted the appropriate title of "The Messenger." It was not long before The Messenger again felt the need to spread his gospel southward, and in 1912 Baker set off for the backwoods of Georgia.

At some point in his travels Baker apparently realized that if Samuel Morris were God, so too was he, and he henceforth referred to himself as the living incarnation of the Lord God Almighty. Such a claim was naturally alarming to the pastors of the churches where Baker stopped to preach, and in 1914 he was arrested in Valdosta, Georgia, as a public nuisance who was possibly "insane." The court recorded his name as "John Doe, alias God," but with the help of a local writer who took an interest in The Messenger's strange story, Baker was released and told to leave the state of Georgia. Instead, he was promptly rearrested in a nearby town and sent to the state insane asylum, whereupon his benefactor once again freed him after a short time.

Though Baker's theology was no doubt peculiar, he impressed most people as a man of sound mind and deep moral commitment. "I remember," his attorney later told the *New Yorker,* "that there was about the man an unmistakable quiet power that manifested itself to anyone who came in contact with him."

The Making of a Cult

Baker soon tired of his troubles in Georgia and in 1915 made his way to New York City, bringing with him a handful of disciples he had picked up along the way. With these followers, Baker set up a communal household in which income was shared and a life of chastity and abstinence was encouraged, all under the direction of "Major J. Devine," as Baker was then styling himself. Major Devine preached the doctrine of God within each individual, but there was never any doubt among his followers as to who was the actual incarnation of the deity—only Devine, or "Divine," as the name inevitably came to be spelled, could claim that honor. Divine helped his disciples find work, and they in turn entrusted him with the management of the group's finances as well as its spiritual well-being. By living simply and pooling their resources, Divine's movement was able to purchase a house in suburban Sayville, New York, in 1919, by which time Divine had also taken as his wife a disciple named Pinninnah.

In contrast to his earlier, public preaching, which had often expressed the need for racial equality and justice, Divine's spiritual work was now confined to the salvation of his followers and was based on harmony within and between individuals. To the outside world, Father Divine was a quiet, well-respected member of the Sayville community (otherwise all-white) who ran an employment agency for the many African American men and women staying at his house on Macon Street. Divine excelled at both of his professions. As his church grew by leaps and bounds, the preacher—also a shrewd businessman—not only found work for his disciples but oversaw the investment of their common earnings with the talent of a natural entrepreneur. Divine taught his followers the virtues of hard work, honesty, and service in their business dealings, exhorting them to achieve economic security in this world as preparation for salvation in the next. Under the guidance of Divine's leadership, his disciples gained a reputation as excellent employees and the operators of honest, efficient businesses.

Divine's "Peace Mission," as he called his following, remained relatively unknown until the start of the Great Depression in 1929. New York was full of such cult organizations, each boasting its own charismatic preacher and offering to the thousands of recently arrived black southern emigrants an emotional brand of religion similar to what they had known in their hometowns. With the advent of the Depression, however, desperate economic conditions made the Peace Mission's generosity all the more striking.

Each Sunday at the Sayville residence was set aside for an all-day banquet, free of charge and open to anyone who cared to attend. Father Divine would accept no payment for these feasts, nor did he take charitable contributions; he asked only that everyone who sat down to dinner behave in a Christian manner and abstain from the consumption of alcohol. Word quickly spread of Divine's "miraculous" bounty, and by the early 1930s his Sunday dinners were attracting hundreds of hungry poor people—mostly black but not exclusively so—to the house in Sayville. Disturbed by this eruption of black power in their midst, residents of Sayville had Divine arrested as a public nuisance. A thorough police investigation uncovered no signs of financial or moral improprieties at the Peace Mission, but Divine was nevertheless sentenced to one year in prison by a judge who considered him a dangerous fraud. When the judge promptly died three days later, Divine's reputation as a divine Christian being was enhanced: like Jesus, he had been wrongly accused, and now his persecutor was paid back in full. Divine was set free on bail, his conviction later overturned, and the Peace Mission attracted new followers by the thousands.

Peace Mission Flourished

Divine's success in the 1930s was indeed nothing short of "miraculous." After moving his headquarters to Harlem, the center of black artistic and cultural life in New York and the nation, his Peace Mission rapidly added scores of affiliated branches elsewhere in New York, in New Jersey, and as far away as California. About 85 percent of Peace Mission disciples were black, and at least 75 percent were female, many drawn as much by the electrifying person of Father Divine as by his social or theological message.

Since full-fledged disciples (known as "Angels") were required to donate all of their worldly possessions to the Mission, Father Divine was soon overseeing an organization of considerable financial size. By all accounts, he did so honestly and skillfully, helping his followers to find jobs, start innumerable small businesses, and after 1935 settle on farmland purchased by the Mission in upstate New York—all of this in the midst of the worst depression in the history of the United States. Divine did allow himself a few luxuries: he lived in the finest of the Mission's many Harlem properties, was chauffeured in a Rolls Royce, and was rarely seen in anything but a fashionable three-piece business suit.

Father Divine never advocated the virtues of poverty: his followers had all too much of that as it was. In his preaching, Divine combined an almost fanatical faith with strict adherence to the ethics of American life, urging his followers to rise from poverty by old-fashioned thrift, hard work, and scrupulous honesty. To work, in his eyes, was to serve God. Divine was especially wary of the dangers of borrowing money, and all of the Mission's business was conducted in cash, even real estate being paid for in cash and in advance. The flaunting of large amounts of money naturally drew the attention of the Internal Revenue Service, which never found any irregularities in the dealings of Father Divine or the Peace Mission. On the contrary, on many occasions his disciples startled former employers or tradesmen by repaying long forgotten debts; in one instance, this involved the sum of 66 cents for a train ride taken 40 years before.

Father Divine saw economic independence as a stepping stone toward his overall goal of racial equality. He was unequivocally opposed to any form of racial discrimination, or even to the recognition of racial difference. For Divine, all human beings partook of the divine essence, and all Americans were due the rights granted them by the Constitution. He therefore purposely bought many pieces of property in all-white areas, including most notably an estate on the Hudson River opposite the home of President Franklin D. Roosevelt, as well as a beachfront hotel near Atlantic City, New Jersey, and extensive tracts of farmland in upstate New York. When challenged by segregationists for such moves, Divine would often speak of the American way of life, as in an article published in *New Day,* a Mission newspaper: "My co-workers and followers are endeavoring to express our citizenry and enact the Bill of Rights in every activity and even in every community . . . to enjoy life, liberty and the reality of happiness."

Divine's Retirement

The end of the Depression also witnessed the gradual retirement of Father Divine. Already in his sixties, Divine was shaken by a lawsuit filed in 1937 by a former disciple who sought repayment of money she had given to the Peace Mission over the years. A long series of legal maneuvers eventually resulted in the incorporation of the Peace Mission and Father Divine's move to Philadelphia, beyond the reach of New York State law. Of greater fundamental importance to the Peace Mission was the advent of war in 1939, when the American economy snapped out of its long depression and jobs became plentiful. The Peace Mission's style of frugal collective living lost much of its appeal in a booming economic climate, and the organization stagnated, with Father Divine gradually retiring to a life of quiet wealth outside Philadelphia.

In 1946 Divine married his second wife, a 21-year-old white disciple named Edna Rose Ritchings—a move that required all of his rhetorical skill to explain as the act of a celibate divinity. Ritchings nevertheless went on to become de facto head of the Mission, known first by her cult name of "Sweet Angel" and later simply as Mother Divine.

Father Divine lived until 1965, little seen and not active in the few remaining Mission projects. However, he did remain a powerful symbol of hope for racial unity and a role model for later generations of people of color. Divine is probably best remembered as a man who, in his own peculiar way, acted in his own interest while skillfully advancing the cause of thousands of inner city African Americans.

Further Reading

The African-American Almanac, edited by Kenneth Estell, Gale, 1994.
Dictionary of American Negro Biography, edited by Rayford W. Logan and Michael R. Winston, Norton, 1982.
Harris, Sara, *Father Divine,* Collier Books, 1971.
Parker, Robert Allerton, *The Incredible Messiah: The Deification of Father Divine,* Little, Brown, 1937.
Weisbrot, Robert, *Father Divine and the Struggle for Racial Equality,* University of Illinois Press, 1983.
Nation, February 6, 1935.
New Day (Peace Mission publication), various issues, 1936.
New Yorker, June 13, 1936; June 20, 1936; June 27, 1936.

New York Times, September 11, 1965, p. 1.
Spoken Word (Peace Mission publication), various issues, 1934-37. □

Dorothea Lynde Dix

Dorothea Lynde Dix (1802-1887) was an American reformer whose pioneer efforts to improve treatment of mental patients stimulated broad reforms in hospitals, jails, and asylums in the United States and abroad.

On April 4, 1802, Dorothea Dix, the daughter of Joseph and Mary Dix, was born in Hampden, Maine. When Joseph failed at farming, he became an itinerant preacher and wrote, printed, and sold tracts, which his wife and daughter laboriously sewed together. Dorothea remembered her childhood in that bleak, poverty-stricken household as a time of loneliness and despair. At the age of 12 she ran away from home and made her way to Boston, where she persuaded her grandmother to take her in. Two years later Dorothea went to Worcester to live with a great aunt and opened a school, which she maintained for 3 years. She returned to Boston in 1819 to attend public school and to study with private tutors.

Teaching Career

In 1821 Dix opened an academy for wealthy young ladies in her grandmother's house. She also conducted a free school for poor children. As a teacher, she was a strict disciplinarian, a rigorous moralist, and a passionate explorer of many fields of knowledge, including the natural sciences. Her contagious joy in teaching made her schools highly successful. During convalescent periods from attacks of chronic lung disease, she wrote children's books.

In 1835 ill health forced Dix to abandon teaching; she went abroad for 2 years. When she returned to America, she was in better health but irresolute about her future. Four years of indecision ended when she volunteered to teach a Sunday school class for young women in the East Cambridge, Mass., jail. She discovered that the quarters for the insane had no heat, even in the coldest weather. When the jailer explained that insane people did not feel the cold, and ignored her pleas for heat, she boldly took the case to court and won.

Mental Institution Reforms

For 2 years Dix traveled throughout Massachusetts, visiting jails, workhouses, almshouses, and hospitals, taking notes on the deplorable conditions she observed. In 1845 Dr. Samuel Gridley Howe presented her "Memorial to the Massachusetts Legislature." The address began, "I proceed, gentlemen, briefly to call your attention to the *present* state of insane persons confined within the Commonwealth, in *cages, closets, cellars, pens; chained, naked, beaten with rods,* and *lashed* into obedience." This dramatic presentation caused a public controversy which won the support of Charles Sumner and other public figures in the resulting newspaper debate. Despite bitter opposition, the reform bill passed by a large majority.

Dix went on to other northeastern states and then throughout the country, state by state, visiting jails, almshouses, and hospitals, studying their needs, and eliciting help from philanthropists, charitable organizations, and state legislatures for building and renovating facilities and for improving treatment. During these years she founded new hospitals or additions in Massachusetts, Rhode Island, New York, New Jersey, Pennsylvania, and Canada and received approval to found state hospitals by the legislatures of Indiana, Illinois, Kentucky, Tennessee, Missouri, Maryland, Louisiana, Alabama, South Carolina, and North Carolina.

European Crusade

In 1848 Dix took her fight to Congress in an attempt to win appropriation of 12,500,000 acres of land, which would provide tax revenue for asylums. The bill finally passed both houses only to be vetoed by President Franklin Pierce. The discouraged reformer then traveled through England, Ireland, and Scotland, inspecting mental hospitals. English and Irish institutions were not bad, but Scottish facilities were appalling, and Miss Dix set about to improve them, taking her case finally to the lord advocate of Scotland.

Perhaps Dix's most significant European accomplishment was in Rome, where she discovered that "6,000 priests, 300 monks, 3,000 nuns, and a spiritual sovereignty, joined with the temporal powers, had not assured for the miserable insane a decent, much less an intelligent care." She negotiated an audience with Pius IX, who was moved by her appeal and personally verified her reports. He ordered construction of a new hospital and a thorough revision of the rules for the care of mental patients. Before her return to the United States, Dix evaluated hospitals and prisons in Turkey, Greece, Italy, France, Austria, Russia, Scandinavia, Holland, Belgium, and Germany and recommended reforms.

Civil War Nurse

In 1861 Dix volunteered her services for wartime duty in the Civil War. Appointed "superintendent of women nurses," she set up emergency training programs, established temporary hospitals, distributed supplies, and processed and deployed nurses. Despite wartime hardships she never relaxed her standards of efficient service, proper procedure, and immaculate hospital conditions. Her inspections of army hospitals did not make her popular with authorities, and her stringent ideas of duty and discipline were not shared by the relatively untrained nurses and jealous officials, who resented her autocratic manner. Although she was often discouraged by petty political opposition and the ever present problems of inadequate facilities, supplies, and staff, she carried out her duties until the end of the war.

Dix resumed her reform efforts until age forced her to retire. Until her death in 1887 she made her home in the

Trenton, N.J., hospital, which she had often referred to affectionately as her "first child."

Further Reading

The most commonly cited biographies of Dorothea Dix are early ones. Francis Tiffany, *The Life of Dorothea Lynde Dix* (1890), is a standard work which contains copious quotations from letters and reports. More recent is Helen E. Marshall, *Dorothea Dix: Forgotten Samaritan* (1937). Additional details are provided in Gladys Brooks's concise and popular *Three Wise Virgins* (1957). See also Albert Deutsch, *The Mentally Ill in America: A History of Their Care and Treatment from Colonial Times* (1937; 2d ed. 1949), and Norman Dain's brief but scholarly *Concepts of Insanity in the United States, 1789-1865* (1964). □

Otto Dix

German painter and graphic artist Otto Dix (1891-1969) became best known for his work in the 1920s as the leading exponent of Die Neue Sachlichkeit (The New Objectivity). His works of social criticism were called "degenerate" by the Nazis.

Otto Dix was born December 2, 1891, in Untermhaus (Thuringia) of working class parents with arts and crafts inclinations. While attending the Volksschule from 1899 to 1905 he showed talent enough to be apprenticed to a decorative painter in nearby Gera. Dix encountered modern art in his travels and in Dresden, where he studied at the School of Decorative Art from 1909 to 1914. Influence by the early German artists Dürer and Cranach was soon succeeded by that of the Impressionists and Post-Impressionists. By 1912 Dix had made contact with the Expressionists, experience of which provided the footing for his mature art.

It was while serving in the army from 1915 to 1918 that Dix first exhibited his famous war drawings (1916), so prophetic, both in style and in content, of his later work. Dix returned to Dresden in 1919 and worked at the Dresden Academy until 1922, during which time he became loosely associated with the Berlin Dadaists, who exhibited his work in the "scandalous" 1920 International Dada Fair. During these same years he was also a member of the politically oriented Novembergruppe and Gruppe 1919 of the Dresden Sezession. Between 1922 and 1925, years spent at the Düsseldorf Academy, Dix published his famous etching cycle, *Der Krieg*. The work was executed in a veristic style, already apparent in his work from 1920.

Even by this time Dix had become well known for his bitter socio-political criticism. The uncompromising nature of his vision and his almost forced attention to detail were part of a general reaction against abstraction following World War I. His work, along with that of others, was labeled Die Neue Sachlichkeit by Gustav Friedrich Hartlaub, director of the Mannheim Kunsthalle, on the occasion of an exhibition there. Art historian Paul Ferdinand Schmidt had coined the same name for the same tendencies at precisely the same time. His reputation grown, Dix was given his first retrospective exhibition at the Galerie Nierendorf in 1926 and served as professor at the Dresden Academy of Art from 1927 to 1933.

Although respected and shown widely during this period, he was declared "degenerate" by the Nazis in 1933 and was forbidden to teach. The following year he was also forbidden to exhibit. These were tense years, largely because Dix elected to stay in Germany. He moved frequently until settling in Hemmenhofen in 1936. The following year eight of his works were included in the Degenerate Art Exhibition in Munich, and in 1938 260 of Dix's works were confiscated and either destroyed or sold. In 1939 Dix was arrested by the Gestapo in Dresden; in 1945 he served in the Volkssturm, during which time he was taken prisoner by the Allies at Colmar.

From 1946, following his return to Hemmenhofen, Dix exhibited widely, and starting in 1948 he concentrated much of his energy on lithography. His style softened somewhat and his content became more mystical and religious in its orientation. During his late years Dix enjoyed a number of prestigious teaching posts. Suffering poor health the last few years of his life, Dix died of a stroke, at the age of 77, on July 25, 1969.

Further Reading

Although much of the Dix literature is written in German, English language studies have appeared. Linda F. McGreevy, *The Life* and Works of Otto Dix (1981) discusses the artist's entire career, while Brigid S. Barton, Otto Dix and Die Neue Sachlichkeit (1981) concentrates on the years from 1918 to 1925. Fritz Löffler, Otto Dix, Leben und Werk (1978) and Florian Karsch, Otto Dix, Das graphische Werk, 1913-1960 (1971) both remain standard works on the artist. Dix's own writing was largely confined to catalog introductions of exhibited work and introductions to his published portfolios.

Additional Sources

Otto Dix, life and work, New York: Holmes & Meier, 1982. □

Milovan Djilas

The Yugoslavian writer and political prisoner Milovan Djilas (1911-1995) was the most celebrated of the Eastern European intellectuals who supported communism in the 1930s but were disillusioned by the practices of Communist regimes after 1945.

Milovan Djilas was born on June 12, 1911, in the Kingdom of Montenegro. His family was very poor, and notoriously non-conformist: his grandfather Aleksa was an anti-Ottoman bandit leader, and was supposedly assassinated by orders from the royal family, while his father Nikola, during his time as a police commandant, resisted Montenegro's incorporation into Yugoslavia after World War I. Young Milovan's education in Podbise and Berane was rich, however, and spanned the works of Marx and Lenin to Dostoevski and Tolstoy.

When Djilas attended the University of Belgrade to study literature in 1929, he was indubitably a Communist. He joined the Yugoslavian Communist party in 1932 as a student opposed to King Alexander of Yugoslavia's dictatorial monarchy. He was jailed for eight days to scare him, but when he failed to be frightened he was tortured and sent to prison for 3 years, where he met famous Communists. Upon his release he went underground as a revolutionary, siding with Tito against Stalin, even to go so far as to recruit 1,500 Yugoslav Communists to fight in the Spanish Civil War. His progress through the ranks of the party was rapid; in 1938 he was elected by Tito to the Central Committee and in 1940 to the Politburo.

During World War II, Djilas was ranked a general among the Partisan leaders for his guerilla tactics against Axis forces. He edited the party newspapers, and was chief negotiator between Axis Powers and Soviet Allies, even to Stalin himself. In 1945, after the war, he was appointed minister for the province of Montenegro and in 1948 minister without portfolio and secretary of the Politburo. In 1953 he became vice president of the Yugoslavian Republic.

Although by this time Djilas was third in the party hierarchy and Tito's heir apparent, he had become increasingly disillusioned even with Tito's brand of "national" communism. At the beginning of 1954 he published a number of newspaper articles critical of the regime, and was promptly stripped of his various offices and given a suspended sentence. In November 1956, after the publication of similar criticisms in the American journal New Leader, he was sentenced to 3 years' hard labor.

Djilas was still in prison when his book The New Class was published in September 1957 in the United States. This acute analysis of the Communist system sought to show that communism did not lead to a "withering away" of the state, as Karl Marx had predicted, but rather to the formation of a new ruling class just as selfish as any previous oligarchy. One month after the publication of The New Class he was sentenced to a further 7-year term of imprisonment.

In January 1961 Djilas was released on condition that he abstain from all political activity, but his freedom was short-lived. He was rearrested in April 1962, charged with providing material for foreign newspaper articles critical of Yugoslavia, and was sentenced to 5 years in prison, to which was added 3 1/2 years (the unserved balance of the previous sentence). Shortly afterward his book Conversations with Stalin (1962), which developed further the arguments first expressed in The New Class, was published abroad.

Djilas was not released from prison until 1966. Two years later his confiscated manuscripts were returned, together with a passport for foreign travel. His relations with the government remained tense, however, and early in 1970 his passport was removed again. He continued to write, publishing novels set in Eastern Europe during the Cold War, some of which were published while he was still in jail. He also wrote several autobiographies, including Land Without Justice (1958), an epic about his childhood that has been said to be evocative of Serbian poetry, Memoir of a Revolutionary, chronicling his early days as a Communist, Wartime (1977), about his activities during the Yugoslav Revolution and WWII, and Rise and Fall (1983), which traces his political career. After the fall of Communism in Eastern Europe, The New Class was finally published in Yugoslavia in 1990, over 30 years since he had written it. He died in 1995, a free man.

Further Reading

The best biographies of Djilas are his own, Land Without Justice (1958), Memoir of a Revolutionary (1973), Wartime (1977) and Rise and Fall (1985). The most revealing books about him, however, could be his political writings: The New Class (1957) and Conversations with Stalin (trans. 1962). The best work on Yugoslavia is Phyllis Auty, Tito: A Biography (1970), which has a full bibliography. □

Sir William Dobell

The Australian artist Sir William Dobell (1899-1970) was one of the world's leading modern portraitists. His best portraits revealed extraordinary psychological insight.

William Dobell was born in Newcastle, New South Wales, on Sept. 24, 1899. He moved to Sydney in 1925 to study at the Julian Ashton Art School. In 1929 he went to London on a traveling scholarship to study at the Slade School, where he won prizes for draftsmanship and painting. Later he exhibited at the Royal Academy and before the New English Group.

Dobell returned to Sydney in 1939. He maintained a subjective approach to painting, and his work was very different from that of current Australian styles. In 1943 he won the Archibald Prize, Australia's principal award for portraiture, for a painting of fellow-artist Joshua Smith. The award was immediately challenged on the grounds that Dobell's entry showed a degree of distortion which made it a caricature rather than a true portrait, but the court upheld the judging panel's decision. Resultant newspaper publicity greatly expanded interest in Dobell's work, but as a result of the controversy Dobell withdrew to Wangi, a small coastal town north of Sydney, and became a shy and enigmatic figure.

Gentle by nature, Dobell was also shrewd, warm, and strong in feeling, and these characteristics shone through his work. He was intensely interested in his fellowman. He achieved some of his effects by deft underscoring of aspects that typified the subject's character, and others by sharp delineation of exciting and unusual features of the subject.

Dobell was also a notable landscapist. He painted local scenes, views of Southeast Asia, and a series of cameos capturing the strangeness of New Guinea. He belonged to no school but acknowledged inspiration from Rembrandt, William Hogarth, Pierre Auguste Renoir, and Chaim Soutine.

Dobell gained numerous significant awards and received many commissions, among them four for portraits for use as *Time* magazine cover subjects, including one of Australian prime minister Robert Menzies in 1960. Exhibitions of his work attracted exceptionally widespread attendance; and a sale in Sydney in 1962 realized record prices for an Australian artist. He was knighted in 1966 and died in Wangi on May 14, 1970.

Further Reading

A good general reference work on Dobell is *The Art of William Dobell,* edited by Sydney Ure Smith (1946). Dobell's place in Australia's art history is analyzed in several publications giving concise coverage of the work of various painters. Two of the most useful are a catalog produced by the Australian Government, Common-wealth Art Advisory Board, with commentaries by leading critics, for the 1962 Exhibition, *Australian Painting: Colonial, Impressionist, Contemporary;* and Bernard W. Smith, *Australian Painting 1788-1960* (1962). An illuminating outline of Dobell and his work is contained in James Gleeson's elaborately illustrated review, *Masterpieces of Australian Painting* (1969).

Additional Sources

Adams, Brian, *Portrait of an artist: a biography of William Dobell,* Richmond, Vic.: Hutchinson of Australia, 1983.
Gleeson, James, *William Dobell, a biographical and critical study,* London: Angus & Robertson, 1981. □

Theodosius Dobzhansky

Theodosius Dobzhansky (1900-1975) synthesized field study and laboratory experimentation in the study of natural selection, laying a foundation for Darwinian evolutionary theory.

Few biologists have made more important contributions to 20th-century evolutionary theory than Theodosius Dobzhansky. His work represents a major part of the synthesis of field study, laboratory experimentation, and classical Mendelian theory that became a powerful foundation for Darwinian theory. Dobzhansky's writings were prolific and influential, comprising over 550 papers and some dozen books. He wrote not only about the technical details of evolution in natural populations, but also about the social and philosophical sides of evolution—including the future evolution of the human species. He lived according to his own dictum, the title of a paper in 1972: "Nothing in biology makes sense except in the light of evolution."

Born on January 25, 1900, in Nemirov, Russia, a small town 200 kilometers southeast of Kiev in the Ukraine, Dobzhansky was the only child of Sophia Voinarsky and Grigory Dobzhansky (sic, the precise transliteration of the Russian name), a high school mathematics teacher. An avid butterfly collector, young Dobzhansky decided to become a biologist at about the age of 12. The family lived on the outskirts of Kiev during the tumultuous years of World War I and the Bolshevik Revolution. During this period Dobzhansky managed to complete his high school and university studies, graduating with a degree in biology from the University of Kiev in 1921.

As an instructor in zoology at the Polytechnic Institute in Kiev (1921-1924), he met Yuri Filipchenko, head of the newly-created Department of Genetics at the University of Leningrad and a strong advocate of T. H. Morgan's work at Columbia University in New York with the small fruit fly, *Drosophila melanogaster.* Dobzhansky went to work in Filipchenko's lab in 1924, where he began his first studies in genetics. In that same year he married Natalia Sivertzev, a geneticist in her own right working with the famous Russian evolutionist I. I. Schmalhausen in Kiev.

In 1927 Dobzhansky travelled to the United States under the auspices of a fellowship from the International Education Board (Rockefeller Foundation) to work in Morgan's laboratory at Columbia University. Here he began learning the techniques of cytogenetics, particularly the study of chromosome banding structures, that were to be so valuable in his later field studies of evolution in the wild *Drosophila* population. In September 1928 Dobzhansky moved to the California Institute of Technology, where Morgan had gone to organize and direct the newly-created division of biology. Dobzhansky was named assistant professor of genetics at Caltech in 1929 and professor in 1936. In 1940 he returned to New York as professor of zoology at Columbia University, where he remained for the next 22 years. In 1962 Dobzhansky was appointed professor at the

Rockefeller Institute (now Rockefeller University), and in 1971 adjunct professor in the Department of Genetics at the University of California, Davis, a position he held until his death on December 18, 1975.

Dobzhansky's contributions to evolutionary theory relate to five major issues: the amount of variation that exists in natural populations; genetic changes in wild populations due to natural selection; speciation; laboratory studies of fitness under controlled conditions; and human variation and evolution.

Genetic Variation Studies

When Dobzhansky came to the United States in 1927 the predominant view of genetic variation was that established by the work of T. H. Morgan and H. J. Muller in mutant laboratory stocks. Mutations were thought to be relatively rare and other variations in most cases deleterious. Since an organism's overall genetic make-up was the result of natural selection, with deleterious mutations weeded out, wild populations were assumed to harbor few mutations, or variations. As a result, evolution would be—as this was in line with what Darwin had predicted—a relatively slow process.

One of Dobzhansky's major contributions was to show that this view was incorrect. Applying the cytological methods of the Morgan group to the analysis of chromosome structure in wild populations of *Drosophila pseudoobscura*, Dobzhansky discovered a surprising amount of hidden variability—that is, variations not readily observed in the ap-

pearance of individual organisms. Dobzhansky suggested that preservation of extensive variation would allow populations to evolve rapidly as environmental conditions change. Dobzhansky published his findings in *Genetics and the Origin of Species* in 1937. This book was an important landmark in the evolutionary synthesis: the union of Mendelian genetics and Darwinian theory.

In Morgan's laboratory at Caltech Dobzhansky learned the cytological techniques involved in studying chromosome structure from two of Morgan's most important co-workers, A. H. Sturtevant and C. B. Bridges. In the mid- and late-1930s he had collaborated with Sturtevant on a series of papers using chromosome inversions (where a chromosome segment has been accidentally excised and reinserted in the chromosome upside down) as a way of tracing phylogenetic relationships among species and subspecies of *Drosophila*. Since inversions are inherited, two separate populations of varieties that showed similarities in chromosome inversion patterns ought to be more closely related than one having fewer similarities.

This work led to a subsequent series of papers of great importance. In the early and mid-1940s, Dobzhansky examined chromosome inversion patterns in populations of *Drosophila pseudoobscura* from Santa Barbara to central Texas. Each population, he found, had a different frequency for each of several inversion patterns. Moreover, noting that from one season to the next certain inversion patterns increased and others decreased *within the same population,* Dobzhansky correlated these changes with climatic and other environmental differences associated with changing seasons. He found that one inversion pattern predominated during warmer seasons, while another predominated during colder seasons. Bringing samples from each population back into the laboratory, Dobzhansky showed that he could vary environmental conditions so as to produce the same changes in frequency of inversion patterns that were observed with changing seasons in the field. Dobzhansky concluded that such seasonal fluctuations were the result of natural selection at work, with temperature acting as the selecting agent. These masterful studies provided concrete support for the theory of natural selection, at the same time illustrating the fruitfulness of combining field and laboratory work in the study of evolution.

Speciation and Evolution

As part of the larger question of how speciation occurs, Dobzhansky initiated a number of investigations into the basis of hybrid sterility—that is, the inability of the offspring of many hybrids (especially among animals) to be reproductively fertile. By studying the specifics of sexual, physiological, and behavioral isolating mechanisms in *Drosophila pseudoobscura* and *Drosophila paulistrorum,* Dobzhansky showed that varying degrees of reproductive isolation represented speciation in the process. Like many of his other studies, Dobzhansky's work on reproductive isolation was aimed at studying the process of evolution in action.

Although not primarily a human geneticist or paleontologist, Dobzhansky wrote frequently on human evolution, including the biology of race and the future of human evolution. His *Mankind Evolving* of 1962 was a highly influential work in directing attention to human variation and adaptation. Several subsequent works of a similar nature, such as *The Biological Basis of Human Freedom* (1956), *The Biology of Ultimate Concern* (1967), and *Genetics of the Evolutionary Process* (1970), all reflect Dobzhansky's wide-ranging and philosophical turn of mind.

Although plagued by a form of leukemia in his later years, Dobzhansky remained vigorous and active until the day before his death on December 18, 1975. During his lifetime he was the recipient of many honors and awards. He was a member of the U.S. National Academy of Sciences, the American Academy of Arts and Sciences, the American Philosophical Society, the Royal Society (Great Britain), the Academia Leopoldina (Leipzig), and the Academia Nazionale dei Lincei (Florence). He received the Daniel Giraud Elliot Medal (1946) and the Kimber Genetics Award (1958) from the National Academy of Sciences, the Darwin Medal from the Leopoldina (1959), the A. E. Verrill Award from Yale University (1966), the Gold Medal Award for Distinguished Achievement in Science from the American Museum of Natural History (1969), and the National Medal of Science (1964). In addition, Dobzhansky was awarded honorary degrees by over 20 institutions, including the Universities of São Paulo (Brazil), Münster (Germany), Sydney (Australia), Oxford (England), Padua (Italy), and Chicago, Columbia, Michigan, Syracuse, Berkeley, and Northwestern in the United States.

Further Reading

A detailed biography of Dobzhansky has been prepared by Howard Levene, Lee Ehrman, and Rollin Richmond, "Theodosius Dobzhansky up to now," in Max Hecht and William C. Steere (editors), *Essays in Evolution and Genetics in Honor of Theodosius Dobzhansky* (1970). A shorter appreciation was written by Francisco Ayala, "'Nothing in biology makes sense except in the light of evolution.' Theodosius Dobzhansky, 1900-1975," in *Journal of Heredity* (1977). Two important historical essays appear in the reprinted edition of Dobzhansky's "The Genetics of Natural Populations" Series: Richard Lewontin, "Introduction: the scientific work of Th. Dobzhansky," and William B. Provine, "Origins of the 'Genetics of Natural Population' series," in R. C. Lewontin, John A. Moore, William B. Provine, and Bruce Wallace (editors), *Dobzhansky's Genetics of Natural Populations I-XLIII* (1981). This work contains a complete bibliography. □

Grace Hoadley Dodge

Grace Hoadley Dodge (1856–1914) was one of the early feminists devoting her time and energy to improve the education and social status of women in the early 1900s.

A tireless supporter of women's issues, Grace Hoadley Dodge devoted her life to improvements in women's education, esteem, and safety at a time when women were just beginning to gain greater access to social privileges. Her vision of the possibilities for women came to fruition through her work with many associations and clubs, including the Young Women's Christian Association, the New York Travelers' Aid Society, and the Teachers College of Columbia University, which she founded. She contributed her time and talent generously to these associations, and worked actively in money-raising campaigns for them until her death in 1914.

In a letter to Mrs. Dave Hennen Morris, Dodge expounded on her efforts regarding the Teachers College: "I realized that the country needed trained teachers, and it was needed to make teaching a profession like that of law and medicine. I realized that expert professors, buildings, grounds, endowment, and so forth, were needed; in other words, money. I knew that the president, or professors could not go out and ask for money, and felt that I must. It was hard to know how to ask or whom to ask. Certain friends gave what they could, but much more was needed. I felt the spiritual force of this need. . . . I used to give months for several years to secure friends for the college. . . . God blesses the persistent effort."

Born the eldest of six children to William Earl and Sarah (Hoadley) Dodge in 1856, Grace Hoadley Dodge benefitted from the wealth and business savvy of her family. Her grandfather, William Earl Dodge, had founded the prominent New York firm of Phelps, Dodge & Co., of which her father was a partner. Her mother's father, David Hoadley, was a high ranking executive of large financial concerns. And her grandmother, Melissa Phelps Dodge, imparted the business know-how of her father, the successful Anson G. Phelps. Surrounded by such successful people, Grace Dodge developed strong business and management skills. Since she was a woman, however, she could not apply her talents as her forefathers had to ventures in copper, silk, or railroads.

Dodge's formal education came from private tutors and, starting in 1872, two years at Miss Porter's school for young ladies at Farmington, Connecticut. At Miss Porter's school, Dodge determined that her interests lay not in the program offerings, but in helping other people in need. At age eighteen, Dodge dropped out of Miss Porter's school. Unable to enter society as a desirable debutante like many of her more dainty and beautiful peers, Dodge became intrigued by the charitable activities of evangelist Dwight L. Moody.

Wishing to use her wealth and ambition to help others, Dodge began her distinguished career as a social worker and philanthropist, teaching Sunday School at Madison Square Chapel in 1874 and adding sewing classes one year later. Sympathetic to Grace's philanthropic desires, William E. Dodge put his daughter in contact with Louisa Lee Schuyler, organizer of the State Charities Aid Association; during their first interview Miss Schuyler made Grace Dodge a member of the association's Committee on the Elevation of the Poor in Their Homes. In 1876, Dodge began a five-year teaching career in the industrial school at the Children's Aid Society. Her work at the Children's Aid Society made her realize the need to instruct many working girls about fundamental aspects of household chores and health care. Dodge began holding discussion groups for silk factory girls, which developed into a fellowship program and a club with cooking and sewing classes. A resident doctor was added as well, and the club eventually grew into the Working Girls' Society. Dodge attended many Society discussion groups during this period, educating herself about the many and varied predicaments facing working-class women at this time. Armed with this information, she initiated tenement reform in 1879 from her position as chairperson of the Committee on the Elevation of the Poor.

In addition to her work at the Children's Aid Society and the State Charities Aid Association, Dodge taught "kitchen garden classes," which used kindergarten play methods to teach household arts to working-class girls. The success of the Kitchen Garden classes prompted organizers to enlist Dodge's help in forming the Kitchen Garden Association in 1880. The group was later reorganized into the Industrial Education Association in 1884, when it began to provide manual training for boys and promote the teaching of domestic and industrial classes in public schools. Dodge ran the association as its vice-president. Her efforts gained her additional recognition, and in 1886 she was given one of the first two seats given to women on New York City's board of education. During her three years of service on the board, she advocated manual training, secured evening classes for working girls, and became spokesperson for 3,500 New York women teachers.

The Industrial Education Association evolved into the Teachers College in 1889 under the guidance, vision, and dogged determination of Grace Dodge; following her suggestion, the college became a part of Columbia University in 1889. A decade after Grace Dodge's death, Mrs. Leonard Elmhurst wrote in *Founding Teachers College* of Dodge's vision and commitment to the school: "Being a trustee of Teachers College, I always feel in that institution a vivid sense of what her vision of education meant, not only to her generation but to the thousands of men and women who throng those halls today. She is still referred to in our trustee meetings and Dean Russell carries her spirit to us as if he only consulted with her yesterday."

Grace Dodge was still very active in her philanthropy until her death in 1914. She helped establish the Girls' Public School Athletic League in 1905, acted as president of the Young Women's Christian Association of the United States in 1906, and was influential in the consolidation of church groups into the New York Travelers Aid Society in 1907 and the organization of the American Social Hygiene Association in 1912. □

Samuel Kanyon Doe

Samuel Kanyon Doe (1951-1990) was the head of state of Liberia from 1980 to 1990. His seizure of

power ended 110 years of rule by the True Whig Party and changed Liberian politics and society in fundamental ways.

Samuel Kanyon Doe was born on May 6, 1951, in Turzon, Grand Gedeh County, Liberia. He belonged to the Krahn tribe, which is one of the 16 major tribal groups in Liberia. He attended primary school in Turzon and was later a student at the R. B. Richardson Baptist Junior High School in Zwedru, the capital of Grand Gedeh County. He dropped out of high school in 1967 for "economic reasons."

Doe joined the Liberian Armed Forces two years after leaving school. He had his initial military training at the John H. Tubman Military Camp in Todee, Montserrado County, and at Camp Schiefflen in the same county. In 1970 he was assigned to the Third Battalion of the Liberian Armed Forces at Barclay Training Center in Monrovia. Doe continued his high school education at Barracks Union School and at Marcus Garvey Memorial High School. He also studied at the Radio and Communications School of the Ministry of Defense, and in 1971 was awarded its advanced diploma with honors.

Military Career

Doe moved swiftly through the ranks of the military. He was appointed acting first-sergeant in command of 150 men in 1973 and two years later was promoted to corporal and shortly after to first-sergeant. While in the Liberian National Guard he gained a reputation as an agile combat fighter and an able sharpshooter. As a result, he was selected in 1979 for training by the United States Special Forces in Monrovia. On the successful completion of this training he was appointed adjutant in charge of administration in the Third Battalion at Barclay Training Center. Later in 1979 he was promoted to the rank of master sergeant.

During this period Doe was primarily concerned about his professional career in the military and was uninterested in politics. He also dismissed suggestions that his career in the armed forces would be hindered by the fact that the highest positions traditionally went to Americo-Liberians, the descendants of freed American slaves who founded the republic in 1847.

Political Upheaval

The True Whig Party had been in power since 1870, and for most of this period Liberian society was dominated by Americo-Liberians who had a privileged political, economic, and social status. Like his predecessor President Tubman (1943-1971), President Tolbert, who took office in 1971, tried to bridge the gap between Americo-Liberians and the indigenous tribal peoples who constitute the majority of the population. He stressed the importance of efficiency and initiated programs to help the poor. But the Tolbert regime was also notorious for corruption and nepotism, which led to frustration and anger within the country.

By 1979 two opposition parties had formed: the Progressive Alliance of Liberia (PAL) and the Movement for

Justice in Africa (MOJA), both of which had left-wing orientations. In 1979 the PAL organized a large demonstration against the government's decision to increase the price of rice by 50 percent. The demonstration led to widespread riots, and several PAL leaders were arrested. In an effort to diffuse the growing tension in the country, the government permitted the PAL to register as an official opposition party under the name of the Progressive People's Party (PPP) in January, 1980. However, when the PPP issued a call for a general strike two months later it was banned and its leaders were arrested.

Doe as Head of State

Early in the morning of April 12, 1980, a small group of soldiers from the First Brigade of the National Guard, led by Doe, staged a coup d'état. They stormed the executive mansion and killed President Tolbert. The coup gained immediate popular acceptance, and Doe adopted the revolutionary slogan: "In the Cause of the People, the struggle continues." A People's Redemption Council (PRC) consisting of 17 enlisted men headed by Doe was established. A cabinet of 19 members was also set up, which was made up of soldiers and civilians who were mostly from the PPP and MOJA, although there were a few from the True Whig Party as well. Shortly after the coup, the PRC imposed a price freeze on all commodities including imported foods, doubled the salaries of civil servants and military personnel, and ordered the public execution on a beach in Monrovia of 13 prominent officials of the Tolbert regime.

The early years of the Doe regime seemed promising. In 1981 he became Commander-in-Chief of the Armed Forces with the rank of general. The following year he received an honorary Ph.D. from the National University of Seoul. Doe promised the people that he would return Liberia to civilian rule and initiated reforms along those lines. A constitution drawn up by a constitutional commission was endorsed by the Liberian people in a referendum held in 1984. It provided for the dissolution of the PRC and the creation of an interim national assembly. In 1984 Doe declared his candidacy for the presidency and founded the National Democratic Party of Liberia (NDPL). He was re-elected October 15, 1985, over his chief opponent Jackson F. Doe (no relation) of the Liberian Action Party.

A Troubled Regime

However, the election was surrounded by much controversy as opponents claimed it was fraudulent. Many political leaders had been imprisoned under the infamous Decree 88A which made it a crime to criticize the head of state or his government. The Special Elections Commission (SECOM) was used to frustrate the registration of political parties. For example, some parties were unable to meet the high financial requirements for registration. This political unrest culminated in a failed coup attempt in November of 1985.

Aside from political turmoil, Doe also faced severe economic challenges. Liberia experienced a sharp decline in foreign investment and an unprecedented unemployment rate of over fifty percent. Doe tried to boost the economy by introducing a seven-cornered dollar coin as the first official Liberian currency; however, this worsened the economy. By the end of the 1980's Liberia had a foreign debt of over two billion U.S. dollars and was near bankruptcy.

Civil War

Doe's rule, which began in 1980 only lasted a decade. On December 24, 1989, a group of armed insurgents crossed the Ivory Coast border and threatened to take over the capital of Liberia, Monrovia. The rebels called themselves the National Patriotic Front of Liberia (NPFL) and were led by Charles McArthur Taylor, a former government employee. Doe tried to contain the threat with the Armed Forces of Liberia (AFL), but instead found himself amidst ethnic warfare which killed tens of thousands of Liberians and caused over 700,000 more to flee the country.

In July of 1990, a third rebel faction emerged. This was the Independent National Patriotic Front of Liberia (INPFL) led by Prince Yormie Johnson. On September 9, 1990, Johnson captured Doe and tortured and killed him. The end of the Doe regime only continued the ethnic warfare in Liberia.

Further Reading

There is no scholarly biography of Doe. A collection of his speeches, *The New Liberian Society* (1982), has been published. Pranay B. Gupte, "The Sergeant Ruling Liberia," in *New York Times* (April 24, 1980), provides a good general background. Doe is listed in *The International Year Book and Statesmen's Who's Who, 1984*. For more information, please see Jeffrey Bartholet and Jane Whitmore, "The Last Days of a Bloody Regime," *Newsweek* (June 11, 1990): 33-34; Stephen Ellis, "Liberia 1989-1994: A Study of Ethnic and Spiritual Violence," *African Affairs* 94 (1995): 165-197; Larry James, "A Seven-Cornered Solution?" *Africa Report* 31 (November-December 1986): 31-33; Reed Kramer, "Liberia: A Casualty of the Cold War's End," *Africa News Service* (1995); Tunji Lardner, Jr., "An African Tragedy," *African Affairs* 94 (1995): 165-197; Marguerite Michaels, and J.F.O. McAllister, "To the Last Man" *Time* (August 20, 1990): 51-52; Bruce W. Nelan, "The Would-Be President," *Time* (June 18, 1990): 55. □

Doi Takako

Elected the chairperson of the Japan Socialist Party in 1986, Doi Takako (born 1928) led the party to larger victories at the polls and in a financial revival of the party, but was forced to resign in 1991. She also mobilized Japanese women

Doi Takako was a unique phenomenon in Japanese political history. She was elected the tenth chairperson of the Japan Socialist Party (JSP), and the first-ever woman leader of any Japanese political party, in September 1986, in the wake of the party's devastating defeat in the House of Representatives (lower house) and House of Councillors (upper house) elections held simultaneously only a few weeks before. Not only did her arrival as the JSP's top leader overnight raise the JSP's popularity by nearly 5 percentage points, but the chronically money-starved party made nearly half a million dollars within the next 12 months by selling some 300,000 telephone cards bearing her picture and autograph, each worth 500 yen and priced at 800 yen, and some 40,000 copies of ornamental cards (*shiskishi*) with her calligraphy and autograph on them. She was, as the press immediately dubbed her, the JSP's "Great Savior" and "Jeanne d'Arc."

Doi Takako was born in Kobe on November 30, 1928, a second daughter to Niroichi, a successful 33-year-old pediatrician, and his 24-year-old wife, Kiyo. With her elder sister, two younger sisters, and two brothers, she grew up in a comfortable middle-class family in a three-storied Western-style house with a pedicab, a convenience upgraded in 1941 to a Ford coupe. She attended Suma Primary School, went to Kobe Girls' High School, and then enrolled in the Department of English Literature at Kyoto Women's College. After two years at the private women's college, she transferred in 1949 to the law school of Doshisha University as a junior and as one of two women among some 200 students in the school. Upon completion of the Bachelor of Arts degree at the well-known private Christian university two years later, she was admitted to the graduate program in the same school as a student of Professor Tabata Shinobu, a constitutional law specialist known for his commitment to pacifism and strict construction of Japan's postwar constitution, especially its famous war-renouncing clause (Article 9).

After earning the Master of Arts degree in 1956, at the age of 27, Doi taught law as a lecturer—a position roughly equivalent to an assistant professor at an American university—at Doshisha from 1957 to 1970 and, simultaneously, at Kwansei University after 1963 and Showa Women's College after 1968. During this period she also served as the secretary-general of both the Constitutional Research Institute, an academic outfit set up by Tabata, and the prefectural branch of the National Coalition to Defend the Constitution, an alliance of leftist groups formed to fight the conservatives' attempt to amend the postwar constitution. She also served on several local public bodies, such as Kobe City's Personnel Commission and Amagasaki City's Social Security Commission and Labor Council.

Doi ran for a Diet seat in the December 1969 lower house general election at the request of the JSP leadership and on her mentor Tabata's advice. She scraped in as the last of the 90 JSP winners in that election. This was the first time she officially joined the JSP. She was subsequently reelected six times before she was elected JSP chairperson in 1986. From the beginning of her parliamentary career she specialized mainly in foreign and defense policy issues, serving continuously on the lower house Foreign Affairs Committee. She quickly became a major voice of the party on a series of important, and often controversial, issues, such as Japanese relations with South Korea, aid to African famine victims, alleged involvement in widespread corruption in the Philippines under Ferdinand Marcos' rule, and above all, the revision of the Nationality Law. On the last issue, she was instrumental in the passage in 1985, after six years of intense debate both inside and outside the Diet, of the JSP-sponsored bill to amend the existing patrilineal law and make a child born of a Japanese mother and a foreign father, as well as one born of a Japanese father and a foreign mother, automatically eligible for Japanese citizenship.

In the 1983 change of the JSP's top leadership, Doi was elected one of the four vice-chairpersons. Three years later, in the wake of a "double election" of upper and lower house members in which the Liberal Democratic Party (LDP) won 300 lower house seats, or 50 more, and the JSP 85, or 27 less, than in the previous general election of 1983, she was asked by her desperate fellow JSP leaders to declare herself a candidate for the party's top position. She agreed to this after three days of agonizing indecision. In a ritual party-wide election that followed on September 8, 1986, she beat her nominal challenger, Ueda Tetsu, 58,670 to 11,748, and became the new leader of the vanquished and demoralized party.

Unlike any of her nine predecessors, Chairperson Doi had not headed a string of important party committees and bureaus, nor had she been affiliated with a major intraparty faction, nor had she been sponsored by a large and influential labor union, nor had she earned a reputation as one of the party's great theoreticians. She brought to her new job, however, several qualities that were far more important to a Japanese party leader in the late 1980s and beyond. Not beholden to any special interest groups within or without the party, she enjoyed an unsullied image as a representative of the common people. A smart and discriminating, if a little old-fashioned, dresser, she had the air of a kind and warm-hearted woman who happened, rather than deliberately chose, to stay single. At nearly 5 feet 7 inches in height, trim and athletic, she was physically not imposing but reassuring. In her childhood she played mainly with boys at boys' games, including wrestling, and usually beat them. At the girls' high school she was a great shot-putter on the school's athletic team. Above all, she was unpretentious and down-to-earth: She would sing American jazz hits and popular French *chansons* at wine bars—one of her great favorites being, not surprisingly, Ella Fitzgerald's "Mack the Knife" with its touch of feminism—and played pinball machines like a professional.

Doi's approach to politics was essentially non-ideological and pragmatic. She had, however, an unshakable belief in and commitment to defend the postwar Japanese constitution, especially its pacifism. This belief and commitment was emotionally grounded in her childhood experiences and memories of the destructive war, especially the fire bombing of Kobe on March 17, 1945, which burned down her family's lovely three-storied house before her own eyes. She and her family escaped by a hair's breadth. While enrolled at the girls' high school, she and her schoolmates were sent first to a hemp mill to help weave hemp fibers into ammunition and sand bags and then to a ball-bearing factory. Subsequently, her original emotional revulsion against war was reinforced at Doshisha University by Tabata's theory of unarmed peace and neutrality. Like her influential mentor and the JSP's contemporary leaders, Doi now came to believe that a policy of pacifism and unarmed neutrality based on Article 9 of the Japanese constitution was not only desirable but also necessary and feasible. While campaigning for the JSP chair in the summer of 1986, she pledged to stand by that very belief and commitment cultivated in her student days.

Pragmatist Doi was, however, willing to try to change the status quo gradually over a fairly long period of time rather than all at once. The JSP under her leadership continued to brand both the Self-Defense Forces and the United States-Japan Mutual Security Treaty as unconstitutional, but it now agreed that, pending amendments of relevant existing domestic laws and international agreements, both would have to be allowed to remain for the time being much as they were. On other, and more ideological, issues the party had begun substantially to soften its position even before Doi took over its leadership in 1986. In its "New Manifesto" issued in 1986, shortly before Doi's election as the new chairperson, the party had already abandoned its claim to be a "class party," renounced revolution as a means to build a socialist society, and accepted the virtues of the market economy.

The JSP's increasingly pragmatic and flexible posture that substantially accelerated under Doi's leadership earned the party handsome electoral dividends. In the 1989 Tokyo Metropolitan Assembly election, the JSP's share of the 128 seats increased from 12 to 36 and the LDP's decreased from 63 to 41; in the 1989 upper house election, the JSP's share of the 252 seats rose from 42 to 66, while the LDP's fell from 142 to 109; and in the 1990 lower house general election,

the LDP's share of the 512 seats slipped from 295 to 286, while the JSP's climbed from 83 to 140. These results were due to a number of factors, especially the newly-introduced and highly unpopular LDP's consumption (sales) tax, the equally unpopular liberalization of agricultural imports, and the Recruit stock-for-political-favor scandal. There was no doubt, however, that the "citizens," and especially women, who "moved," as they had never moved before, in response to Doi's call played a decisive role. In each of the three elections mentioned above, more women ran as candidates than ever before since the 1940s, more of them won, and most of the winners ran on the JSP ticket.

"The day has arrived for the mountain to move," Doi declared in the wake of the 1989 upper house election, reciting the opening line of the inimitable verse by her idol and one of the greatest poets of 20th-century Japan, Yosano Akiko, from the first issue (1911) of the nation's first feminist magazine, *Blue Stocking (Seito)*. For the benefit of her less literate listeners, she might have recited the rest of Yosano's simple but powerful verse: "But people don't believe what I have said/The mountain has only slept for a while/In old times, all mountains moved on the flame of fire/But one doesn't have to believe it/People, do believe only this/That all the women who were asleep have now awakened and are on the move." Doi did not start the move by herself, but she gave it a powerful push. However, following her party's severe losses in local elections Doi resigned as chairperson on June 21, 1991. However, she returned to a seat in the Lower House, as she was re-elected in 1990. In the mid 1990s she was Speaker of the Lower House.

Further Reading

For additional information on Doi and her role in Japanese politics see Hans H. Baerwald, "Japan's House of Councillors Election: A Mini-Revolution?" in *Asian Survey* (September 1989) and "Japan's 39th House of Representative Election: A Case of Mixed Signals," in *Asian Survey* (June 1990). See also Richard J. Samuels, "Japan in 1989," in *Asian Survey* (January 1990). □

Elizabeth Hanford Dole

Elizabeth Hanford Dole (born 1936), has worked as a lawyer, White House aide, cabinet officer, and president of the American Red Cross.

Elizabeth Hanford was born and grew up in Salisbury, North Carolina, the daughter of wholesale flower dealers. She was a political science major at Duke University, received a master's degree in education from Harvard in 1960, and graduated from Harvard Law School in 1965 as one of 25 female graduates in a class of 500. Dole was often described as friendly, gracious, and "brainy," attributes which led to her election as college May Queen and student body president as well as to Phi Beta Kappa, and the national honor society.

After law school Hanford went to Washington, where she earned a reputation as a consumer advocate in (what was then) the Department of Health, Education and Welfare; as executive director of the Presidential Committee for Consumer Interests; and as deputy director of the U.S. Office of Consumer Affairs. Although briefly employed in private law practice, her primary professional commitment soon became public service.

In 1973 Hanford was nominated to be one of five commissioners on the Federal Trade Commission (FTC). Once appointed she became known for her enforcement of the Equal Credit Opportunity Act of 1975 and for an FTC investigation of nursing home abuses. A colleague at the FTC remembered her priorities as " . . . the poor, the handicapped, minorities, and women. She really cared about them."

Married Republican Senator Robert Dole of Kansas

Hanford married Robert Dole, the senior senator from Kansas, in 1975 and they quickly became known as Washington's premier "Power Couple" because of their prominent roles in national politics. However glamourous that designation may seem, it referred strictly to their jobs and not their social life. According to the New York Times, the Doles often "return to their two bedroom apartment at the Watergate complex after a 12-hour day and either heat up a . . . frozen meal or go to a nearby Chinese restaurant." Their lives revolve almost totally around their work. And accord-

ing to Dole, the work experiences shared in her "dual career" marriage, often provided a source of satisfaction and enjoyment. "It's a great way of sharing even if you can't share all the information, and you don't have as much time together . . . you share a sense of pride in each other's accomplishments." Marrying late in life, she was nearly 40 and the Senator was 53, the Doles had no children and lived in Washington's famous Watergate Apartments.

Religion also played an important role in Dole's personal life. Although raised a devout Methodist she, for the most part, kept her religious views private. With little fanfare or publicity she regularly attended church and often performed charitable services for nursing home residents. A turning point came in 1987 when, in evangelical fashion, she provided her Christian "testimony" at the National Prayer Breakfast in Washington, D.C. Afterwards Dole became a favorite of Christian conservatives and began to speak regularly to religious groups around the country.

Achieved Prominence as a Republican

Previously a Democrat, Dole became a registered Independent during her early years in Washington. Following her marriage, she became a Republican and campaigned vigorously when her husband ran for vice-president on the unsuccessful Ford-Dole ticket in 1976. With her husband's own campaign for the presidency in 1979, she resigned as FTC commissioner to campaign for him full-time. Although that campaign, too, was unsuccessful, by 1980, "Liddy" Dole was becoming well-known as one of the Republican Party's most outstanding female leaders and recognized, just as much as her more famous husband, as a contender for high political office.

Served in Reagan and Bush Administrations

In 1983 President Ronald Reagan appointed Dole as Secretary of Transportation, the first woman in American history to hold that cabinet position. As "Madame Secretary" she headed an organization of 102,000 employees and administered a budget of $28 billion. Problems facing the new administrator included highways, bridges, mass transit, air traffic control, shipping, Conrail, and the Washington, D.C. public transportation system. Since the Secretary of Transportation is also the director of the U.S. Coast Guard, she was the first woman to command an armed service in the United States. At that time, Transportation was rapidly becoming an important cabinet post since it involved 20 percent of the gross national product and touched the lives of most Americans.

During her first month as Transportation Secretary, Dole "moved a mountain" and agreed to provide $70 million in existing Department of Transportation (DOT) and Amtrak funds to start making Union Station, the antiquated train station in Washington, D.C., "alive and vibrant with people . . . a center of activity for our city of Washington and for this nation."

Safety became Dole's "first issue" at the Department of Transportation. She endorsed the concept of a third brake light on cars and air bags to protect passengers in case of collision. In an effort to promote the use of airbags, DOT provided 5,000 new government cars and 500 state police cars with air bags. Her early victories at Transportation included winning government funds for new passenger railway lines and the passage of a maritime reform bill. *Washington Monthly* also credited her with adding more Federal Aviation Administration inspectors, fighting deceptive airline scheduling, and campaigning for higher drinking ages and for single-licensing of truck drivers to prevent "outlaw drivers from getting relicensed in other states.

Dole abandoned her earlier support for the Equal Rights Amendment after joining the anti-ERA Reagan administration. But she made it a point to increase the number of women at DOT as well as benefits, such as work place day care centers, designed to keep them there. Despite her identification with liberal consumer issues and former support for ERA, Dole received strong backing from the conservative Reagan administration. Critics, however, viewed her commitment to important issues as secondary to her ambition. The *Chicago Tribune* questioned the logic that transformed her from a "Democrat who had worked for President Lyndon Johnson's Great Society to a Republican who pampered big business, from a federal trade commisssioner who decried big-business mergers to a Secretary of Transportation who sanctioned almost every airline merger that came her way. The *Washington Monthly* summarized this feeling when it observed that, instead of an ideologue, Dole was "the consummate role player, her positions defined by her job description rather than deeply felt beliefs.

Dole resigned as Secretary of Transportation in 1987 to campaign for her husband's second attempt at the presidency. Although the campaign itself was unsuccessful, Dole again received high marks as a campaigner. Because of her previous cabinet-level experience under Reagan, and her immense popularity within the Republican Party, Dole was tabbed as the new Secretary of Labor by President George Bush in 1989. As Secretary of Labor, Dole negotiated a raise in the minimum wage, oversaw efforts to break "glass ceiling" restrictions that prevented movement of women and minorities into high executive positions, and was widely credited with the settlement of the United Mine Workers strike against the Pittson Coal Company.

Headed the American Red Cross

In 1990 Dole resigned as Secretary of Labor to become the president of the American Red Cross. As head of the Red Cross she oversaw a $1.8 billion annual budget, 32,000 employees, and 1.4 million volunteers. Priorities during her first tenure included issues such as improving the safety of the nation's blood supply against AIDS, responding to world emergencies caused by famine, war, and natural disasters, and improving the charitable giving by Americans to humanitarian organizations. In 1996 Dole took a one-year leave of absence to assist her husband's final campaign for the presidency.

Played Prominent Role in 1996 Campaign

According to the *New York Times*, Dole's leave of absence from the Red Cross was illustrative of her belief in and committment to her husband. It was the fourth time that she had "either quit or taken leave from powerful jobs to help along her husband's White House ambitions. Her intense loyalty was again displayed at the 1996 Republican National Convention with her talk-show style "Why I Love Bob" speech where she descended from the podium and spoke in personal terms about her husband to the nation. Saying that she would tell stories that her husband would not mention himself, Dole proceeded to deliver, in near flawless performance, a condensed biography of the Senator from his childhood days in Kansas to his current run for the White House.

So successful was Dole's speech that, after the convention, she acquired her own staff of 30, a travel budget of $1.5 million, and a leased 14-seat jet to campaign separately for her husband. Depite her efforts, though, the Senator was unable to overcome a slow campaign start and was subsequently defeated by incumbent President Bill Clinton.

Dole returned to her position as President of the American Red Cross in 1997. Her priorities for her second tenure included the reegineering of national headquarters to en sure greater responsiveness for service delivery and the strengthening of the disaster relief fund.

Dole continued her popularity as a guest speaker by delivering the 1997 commencement address to her alma mater, Duke University. Although she remained silent on future political aspirations of her own, Dole still remained a Republican Party favorite and may yet again return to high political office.

Further Reading

For more information see Elizabeth and Robert Dole, *The Doles: Unlimited Partners* (1988).

There is no book length biography of Elizabeth Hanford Dole, but she is listed in *Who's Who in America* (1984-1985, 43rd edition). Articles about Dole are in *Vogue* (October 1984) and *Working Woman* (April 1983), and a profile of her appeared in the *Washington Post* on January 8, 1983. Additional profiles appeared in *The New York Times* on July 19 and October 13, 1996. □

Robert J. Dole

Robert J. Dole (born 1923) of Kansas represented that state in the Senate from 1968 until 1996. He served as Republican National Committee chair under President Richard Nixon and was Gerald Ford's running mate in 1976. As Senate majority leader during the second administration of President Ronald Reagan and again from 1994 to 1996, Dole was an articulate spokesperson for Republican policies. Dole won the Republican presidential nomination in

1996, but lost the general election to the incumbent president, Bill Clinton.

Born in a one bedroom home in the small Kansas town of Russell on July 22, 1923, Robert J. Dole knew the hard scrabble life of Plains states' folks at first hand. Doran, his father, ran a grain elevator while his mother, Tina (Talbott), sold sewing machines. Dole and his three siblings grew up in a larger, more comfortable home than he had been born in, but his parents rented the upper floor to earn extra income.

His childhood was the commonplace one of a farmtown boy: Methodist church meetings, Boy Scouts, public schools, a strict loving home life, and a penchant for work. An honor secondary school student, Dole was extremely ambitious, at one time entertaining the dream of medical school. He had a passion for sports and won letters in running, football, and basketball. At the University of Kansas (Lawrence) he enrolled in a pre-med course and continued his athletics, becoming a star quarter-miler.

Life Threatened in War

In 1943, Dole's studies were interrupted by World War II and he began training in various military specialties at schools around the country, completing his training as an infantry second lieutenant at Fort Benning (Georgia) Officer Candidate School. Assigned as a platoon leader to the 10th Mountain Division in Italy in early 1945, he saw action

against German units in March. A month later—on April 14, 1945—he received a wound which kept him hospitalized for more than three years and left him with a permanently disabled right arm.

For a while there was no guarantee he would live, since the shell hit his shoulder and spine, paralyzing all his limbs. When the European war ended less than four weeks after he was injured, Dole's private war with deadly infection, experimental drugs, grueling therapy, and many operations had just begun. These tested his spirit and courage deeply and sharpened two qualities which characterized him later: optimism and tenacity.

In 1948, while in the hospital, he met and married Phyllis Holden, by whom he had his only child, Robin. Phyllis was a physical therapist who aided him in his return to school. He took up his education again, this time at Washburn University (Topeka) where he earned bachelor's and law degrees.

Political Career Led to Washington

Dole discarded medicine as a career in favor of politics, and even before he had earned his law degree he ran for and won a seat in the Kansas House of Representatives. After a single term as state lawmaker (1951-1953), Dole ran for Russell County prosecutor, a post he held for seven years until his successful 1960 race for the U.S. House of Representatives.

Dole served as a member of the six-person Kansas House delegation for one term, survived the 1960 reapportionment—which cost the state one seat—in his second race, and was re-elected twice more. During his eight years as a House member (1961-1969) Dole came across as a combative, rural-oriented, conservative Republican opposed on principle to much of the Great Society's program. In 1964, for example, he voted to prohibit the Supreme Court from interfering in reapportionment cases involving state legislatures, voted against the Economic Opportunity Act, and opposed the Urban Mass Transportation Act. He did support the Civil Rights Act of that year, however, and backed similar legislation throughout his career. In 1968 he took advantage of the retirement of a Republican incumbent and won the nomination as the Republican Party's candidate for the Senate. In the general election he defeated moderate Democrat William Robinson decisively, winning more than 60 percent of the popular vote.

Dole emerged in the Senate of the 91st Congress (1969-1971) as a powerful national figure. Service on the Senate Agriculture and Forestry Committee gave him the opportunity to keep fences mended at home. He also gave a good deal of time on party matters, devoting himself to the Nixon Administration's efforts to build a new national Republican coalition. Resented by some party liberals, he nevertheless became Nixon's choice for chair of the Republican National Committee and won high praise from the president for his part in the stunning victory of 1972.

Untouched by Watergate, Dole continued his growth in the Senate, winning a second term in 1974 and climbing the seniority ladder. His conservative voting record helped him win the nomination as President Gerald Ford's vice presidential candidate at the Kansas City (Missouri) Republican convention in August, 1976. The selection was viewed as a means of placating party conservatives, angry over Ford's choice of Nelson Rockefeller as his first vice president. Dole won the support of Western and Midwestern voters but was widely criticized as Ford's "hatchet man." He and Governor Jimmy Carter's vice presidential candidate, Senator Walter Mondale, participated in the explosive and precedent-setting first vice presidential debate at Houston, Texas, in October. Both Dole and Mondale emerged from the 1976 election as national figures. Dole returned to the Senate floor, Mondale mounted to the chair of president of the Senate.

Dole's life's work was also his hobby and all consuming interest: he lived politics every working hour. Meanwhile, he had experienced upheaval in his personal life. His marriage to Phyllis Holden ended in divorce in 1972, and three years later, on December 6, 1975, he married a brilliant Harvard-educated activist lawyer named Elizabeth (Liddy) Hanford. The couple became one of Washington's most powerful teams as Senator Dole won election as majority leader of the Republican-controlled Senate in January 1985; Elizabeth Dole had already been confirmed as President Reagan's Secretary of Transportation. Among numerous other posts, she also served as Secretary of Labor and director of the American Red Cross. She also assisted her husband in creating the Dole Foundation, which raised millions of dollars to assist disabled Americans.

Recurring Candidate for the Presidency

Dole made a very brief run for the presidential nomination in 1980, but he was overwhelmed by Ronald Reagan. His disappointment over his early poor showing was tempered somewhat by the fact that the Republicans gained control of the Senate as well as the Presidency. Dole became chair of the Finance Committee with an important role in ushering President Reagan's economic policies through Congress. He became majority leader of the Senate in late 1984 and helped craft a comprehensive deficit reduction bill in 1985.

In November of 1986, the Democrats regained the Senate, and Dole was demoted to leading the minority party. As the two terms of the Reagan Administration drew to a close, Dole decided once again to seek the presidency, this time with more organization, stature, and money than he had had in 1980. He battled early and often with George Bush, Reagan's vice president, who ultimately won the 1988 Republican nomination and the election.

Dole seemed to receive a new lease on life when Democratic candidate Bill Clinton was elected President in 1992. With the Presidency no longer in Republican hands, Dole became the nation's head Republican. Early in the Clinton Administration, Dole became a fixture on television news shows, positioning himself as the chief spokesperson against the president's policies. He led Senate Republicans in filibusters against Clinton's legislation, and he forced Clinton to scale back an economic stimulus bill the President tried to steer through Congress early in the Administra-

tion. Already in 1993, Dole was visiting the early presidential primary states of Iowa and New Hampshire.

In 1994, Republicans won the House for the first time in four decades, and they regained control of the Senate where Dole once again became majority leader. As the Republicans worked to fulfill the "Contract with America" with which they had won in '94, Dole planned his third attempt for presidential office.

Loses to Bill Clinton in 1996

The first primaries early in 1996 went badly. Candidate Steve Forbes made Dole the target of some $25 million in negative advertising, and Dole lost races to Forbes and Patrick Buchanan. With the Republican party establishment rallying to his defense, Dole locked up the nomination in March. He initially tried to remain majority leader while campaigning for the presidency. However, the Democrats frustrated his legislative efforts so successfully that he was forced to leave the Senate. In June of 1996, he ended his 35-year congressional career by resigning both as Senator from Kansas as well as majority leader.

Dole spent the next four months crisscrossing the country on the campaign trail. Even before the contest was over, many Republicans criticized Dole for doing a poor job of delivering the party's messages. Polls showed that the two televised presidential candidates debates in October helped Clinton and hurt Dole. In election day exit polls, seven out of ten voters said they did not believe Dole's promise to cut taxes by fifteen percent, the key theme of his campaign. It traditionally has been difficult to defeat an incumbent president during times of peace and economic prosperity. However, a *New York Times* analysis concluded that Dole's "third run for the presidency was plagued by missteps, indecision, and strategic blunders so fundamental that they bordered on amateurish."

Clinton won handily in an election marked by the lowest voter turnout in 72 years. Clinton took 49 percent of those voting and carried 31 states. Dole received 41 percent of the popular vote and won 19 states. (Reform Party candidate Ross Perot took another eight percent of the vote.) Yet the election was hardly a rout for the Republicans. The GOP maintained majority control of both the House and Senate and elected a majority of the nation's governors.

After the election, the Doles remained in Washington, D. C., where Elizabeth Dole served as president of the American Red Cross. Robert Dole joined the law firm of Verner, Liipfert, Bernhard, McPherson & Hand. A major lobbying concern, Verner Liipfert represented foreign nations as well as some of the largest business corporations in the U.S. and abroad. Dole became the senior Republican among the firm's lobbyists, whose roster included three former Democratic governors and two former Democratic senators.

Altogether—including their earnings from pensions, product endorsements, speaking fees and Elizabeth Dole's Red Cross salary—the Doles enjoyed an income well in excess of $1 million in 1997. No longer under intense public scrutiny, the former Senator traded in his 1987 Chevrolet Celebrity on a brand new Cadillac. Dole also advanced the $300,000 House Speaker Newt Gingrich owed as a penalty for violating ethics rules, giving Gingrich eight years to pay at 10 percent interest.

Further Reading

Bob Dole is referred to in the memoirs of the principal figures of his day. Former President Gerald Ford's autobiography, *A Time to Heal* (1979), for example, has insightful observations on Dole's part in the 1976 campaign. Martin Schram's *Running for President 1976* (1977) treats the same subject in less detail.

Cramer, Richard, *Bob Dole* (Random House, 1995). Dole, Bob and Elizabeth Dole, *Unlimited Partners: Our American Story* (Simon & Schuster, 1996). Dole, Bob and Jack Kemp, *Trusting the People: The Dole-Kemp Plan to Free the Economy & Create a Better America* (HarperCollins, 1996). Hilton, Stanley, *Senator for Sale* (Saint Martin's, 1996). Margolis, Jon, *The Quotable Bob Dole: Witty, Wise & Otherwise* (Avon Books, 1996). McCurry, Michael and John Buckley, "Inside Story," *New Yorker*, November 18, 1996, pages 44-60. "Masters of the Message," *Time*, November 18, 1996, pages 76-96. □

Sanford Ballard Dole

The American statesman Sanford Ballard Dole (1844-1926) was president of the Republic of Hawaii and, after its annexation to the United States in 1898, first governor of the Territory of Hawaii.

Sanford Dole was born in Honolulu, Hawaii, on April 23, 1844, the son of Protestant missionaries from New England. He grew up on the Hawaiian islands of Oahu and Kauai and went to missionary schools run by his father. He left the islands to attend Williams College in Williamstown, Mass., where he spent a year. After another year in a Boston law office, he was admitted in 1868 to the Massachusetts bar. But that same year he returned to Honolulu to practice law. He showed a good deal of interest in community affairs and often wrote for newspapers. In 1873 he married Anna P. Cate of Maine.

Dole was elected to the Hawaiian Legislature in 1884 and 1886 as a Reform party member. In 1887 he became a leader in the movement that wrested a new constitution from King David Kalakaua, reducing his power. The King, under pressure from his ministers, appointed Dole associate justice of the Supreme Court. Dole's legal decisions were marked by clarity and grace of style, and his dissents were noted for their vigor.

Dole served as a justice until 1893, when he reluctantly accepted leadership of a revolutionary movement that overthrew Queen Liliuokalani, who had succeeded her brother Kalakaua. She had tried to proclaim a new constitution that would return personal power to the throne. Dole became president of a provisional government that sought annexation to the United States. When President Grover Cleveland tried to restore the Queen (after charges that the United States had helped overthrow her), Dole wrote one of his most important state papers eloquently denying Cleveland's

right to interfere. With no prospect of quick annexation, the Republic of Hawaii was formed on July 4, 1894. The constitution named Dole president to serve until 1900.

Hawaii's support of the United States in the war with Spain in 1898 turned the balance in favor of renewed annexation efforts already under way. In 1898 President William McKinley signed a joint congressional resolution of annexation and appointed Dole a member of the commission to draft laws governing Hawaii. In 1900 McKinley appointed Dole as first governor under the Organic Act for the Territory of Hawaii. Dole served until 1903, when he resigned to become judge for the U.S. District Court for Hawaii. In 1916 he retired to private practice.

Dole is generally credited with a deep, sympathetic understanding of the native Hawaiians, although some persons might consider his attitude toward the Hawaiians slightly patronizing and paternalistic.

Further Reading

E. M. Damon, *Sanford Ballard Dole and His Hawaii* (1957), based on primary sources, is sympathetic and uncritical. The account was undertaken at Dole's express wish. Dole tells his own story of the dramatic last years of the kingdom in his *Memoirs of the Hawaiian Revolution* (1936), edited by Andrew Farrell.

Additional Sources

Allen, Helena G., *Sanford Ballard Dole: Hawaii's only president, 1844-1926*, Glendale, Calif.: A.H. Clark Co., 1988. □

Engelbert Dollfuss

The Austrian statesman Engelbert Dollfuss (1892-1934) served as chancellor of Austria from 1932 to 1934.

Engelbert Dollfuss was born on Oct. 4, 1892, near Texing, Lower Austria. Trained in law at the University of Vienna and in economics at the University of Berlin, he served as an officer in World War I. After the war he was secretary of the Peasant's Association of Lower Austria and became director of the Lower Austrian Chamber of Agriculture in 1927. In 1930 he was appointed president of the Austrian Federal Railways system because of his association with the Christian Socialist party, and in 1931 he was named minister of agriculture and forests.

On May 20, 1932, Dollfuss became chancellor of Austria, although his government possessed only a one-vote majority in the Nationalrat (lower house of Parliament) and a minority in the Bundesrat (upper house). To strengthen Austria's financial position, Dollfuss obtained a loan of £9 million sterling from the League of Nations in return for an agreement not to enter a customs union with Germany for 20 years, a stipulation which angered pan-German, Nationalist, and Socialist elements in Austria.

Subject to bitter attacks from all sides, Dollfuss suspended Parliament when its three presidents resigned on March 4, 1933, and thereafter ruled by decree. In May he founded the Vaterländische Front to mobilize support for his rule, and it was with this organization that the notorious Heimwehr merged in 1934. The latter was a defense force formed after World War I; it later espoused Italian Fascist principles, became a political party in 1930, and perpetrated acts of terror and violence against its opponents.

To bolster his foreign position and prevent Austria from uniting with Nazi Germany, Dollfuss met Mussolini at Riccione in August 1933 and received a guarantee of Austrian independence at the cost of abolishing all political parties and revising the Austrian constitution along Fascist-corporatist lines. On the prompting of Mussolini, he utilized an outbreak of rioting by leftist elements in February 1934 to destroy the Social Democratic party organization, thus removing Austria's most strongly anti-Nazi force from the scene.

Announcing his wish to order the state according to the encyclical *Quadragesimo Anno* of Pope Pius XI, Dollfuss proclaimed a new constitution on May 1, 1934, providing for state organization through professional corporations like those in Fascist Italy. The opposition of German and Austrian Nazis to his government only increased, however, as he evidenced his determination to oppose the surrender of Austrian independence. Finally, during an abortive Nazi putsch on July 25, 1934, Nazi agents entered the Chancellery in Vienna and during their brief occupation of the building assassinated Dollfuss.

While Dollfuss's dogged determination to maintain the integrity of Austria made him a martyr, the weakness of his political position coupled with that of his small state forced him to implement the very authoritarian principles antithetical to the Christian ideals articulated in his 1934 constitution and to the continued independence of Austria.

Further Reading

There is not much information on Dollfuss in English. Perhaps the most useful work is Paul R. Sweet, "Mussolini and Dollfuss: An Episode in Fascist Diplomacy," in Julius Braunthal, *The Tragedy of Austria* (1948).

Additional Sources

Brook-Shepherd, Gordon, *Dollfuss,* Westport, Conn.: Greenwood Press, 1978, 1961. □

Josef Ignaz von Döllinger

The German historian and theologian Johannes Josef Ignaz von Döllinger (1799-1890) represented the Catholic wing of the great German historical movement of the 19th century.

On Feb. 28, 1799, J. J. I. von Döllinger was born in Bamberg. His father was professor of physiology and anatomy at Bamberg and later at Würzburg and, though Catholic, markedly anticlerical. This influence was offset by the piety of Döllinger's mother, and the boy's interest turned to theology after a few semesters in Würzburg studying philosophy and philology. He entered the seminary at Bamberg and was ordained a priest in 1822. Disillusioned with academic studies, he desired only a country pastorate but, after serving as curate for barely a year, he was prevailed upon by his father to return to academic life.

Döllinger then taught canon law and Church history at the gymnasium in Aschaffenburg. His interests turned to patristic studies, and he published the first of many books on Church history, for which he achieved wide recognition. In 1827 he accepted the chair of Church history at the University of Munich, a post he held until 1872. In Munich he joined the circle of F. X. von Baader and J. von Görres. This group was monarchist in politics, strongly influenced by German romanticism, and inclined toward strengthening Church ties with Rome. Thereafter Döllinger became increasingly active in public life, always working to spread the influence of religion. He represented Lower Bavaria at the Congress of Frankfurt in 1848-1849.

In his historical studies Döllinger stressed historical continuity and organic development. Arguing that the Reformation represented a breach in this continuity, he led a counterattack against the influential school of Leopold von Ranke and other Protestant or liberal historians.

Döllinger's efforts to revive German Catholicism gradually led him to minimize dependence on Rome, and increasingly after 1850 he argued for a German national church. He also insisted on the right of scholars to be free from ecclesiastical censorship. Just prior to the opening of the Vatican Council in 1869, his book *The Pope and the Council,* which argued the supremacy of a general council, was condemned in Rome. During the proceedings he corresponded with the minority who opposed the infallibility decree. But his publication of *Roman Letters from the Council* (1870) injured the cause by its intemperate and sarcastic tone. In 1871 he was excommunicated for refusing to subscribe to the Council decrees on papal prerogatives and a year later was forced out of his professorship.

Döllinger was friendly with leaders of the schismatic group called the "Old Catholics" but refused to join their movement. In later years he worked to promote reunion among the churches. Accepting the last rites from an Old Catholic priest, he died in Munich on Jan. 10, 1890.

Further Reading

Louise von Kobell, *Conversations of Dr. Döllinger* (1891; trans. 1892), provides personal reminiscences. Lord Acton gives a lengthy estimate of Döllinger's historical work in his *History of Freedom, and Other Essays* (1907). □

Gerhard Johannes Paul Domagk

The German bacteriologist and experimental pathologist Gerhard Johannes Paul Domagk (1895-1964) was awarded the Nobel Prize in Physiology or Medicine for his discovery of the antibacterial effects of prontosil.

Gerhard Domagk was born at Lagow, Brandenburg, on Oct. 30, 1895. He began the study of medicine at the University of Kiel in 1913. After World War I, throughout which he served in the army, he graduated in medicine at Kiel in 1921. In 1924-1925 he was a lecturer in pathology in the universities of Greifswald and Münster. He became director of research in experimental pathology and bacteriology on the staff of the I.G. Farbenindustrie at Wuppertal-Elberfeld in 1927.

Beginnings of Chemotherapy

Early in the 1900s a synthetic organic arsenic compound was used to treat experimental trypanosomiasis. Paul Ehrlich confirmed this and then began to search for a similar compound for the treatment of syphilis. Successive organic compounds were synthesized and tested. In 1910 he found that his 606th compound was very effective; he called it salvarsan. During the next 20 years efficient antimalarial remedies were synthesized, but there were no such remedies against the common bacterial and streptococcal infections of temperate climates, despite many attempts to solve this problem.

Chemotherapy of Bacterial Infections

Shortly after his appointment to the I.G. Farbenindustrie, Domagk was made responsible for another massive attempt to achieve chemotherapy of the bacterial infections. His chief chemists, Fritz Mietzsch and Joseph Klarer, synthesized organic compounds, and Domagk tested the activity of these compounds against various organisms, in cultures and in laboratory animals. For a long time they were unsuccessful. But some years earlier the two chemists had synthesized a red azo dye combined with a sulfonamide radical. Intended for treating leather, it was already on the market under the name Prontosil Rubrum. Their tests had shown that it had little activity against bacteria in cultures, but in 1932 preliminary tests suggested that it might be protective against streptococcal infections in mice. In December a crucial experiment was carried out, which showed conclusively that prontosil was very effective in protecting mice against a highly virulent streptococcus. These very satisfactory laboratory results were not published for over 2 years, partly because of doubt whether prontosil would be tolerated by human subjects. But Domagk personally had no doubt, because he had as a last resort given his daughter, who was near death as a result of a streptococcal infection, a dose of prontosil. She had miraculously recovered.

When Domagk published his laboratory results in 1935 he did not mention his daughter's case, but work on prontosil was at once started in several countries. It was shown that the action of prontosil was due to its sulfona-

mide radical, which alone was active, and that sulfanilamide, a similar sulfonamide compound, was as active as prontosil and cheaper to manufacture. This was the first of the many similar drugs synthesized and tested. These sulfonamides were shown to be effective in many diseases in addition to streptococcal infections, such as puerperal fever, pneumonia, and cerebrospinal fever.

For his work in this field Domagk was awarded the Nobel Prize in Physiology or Medicine for 1939, but he was forced by the Nazis to decline the award, which he had already accepted. After the war he was presented with the medal and the diploma, but the prize money had meanwhile reverted to the Nobel Foundation.

Chemotherapy of Tuberculosis

The effective discovery of the method of concentrating penicillin, the first of the antibiotics, in 1940 stimulated a search for other antibiotics and chemotherapeutic remedies that might be effective in treating tuberculosis. Domagk's chemical coworkers supplied him with the first of the thiosemicarbazones, and in 1946 he showed their power to inhibit the growth of the tubercle bacillus in culture. But as they caused liver damage they had later to be given up. Meanwhile, in 1944, the antibiotic streptomycin had been discovered, but its undoubted effectiveness in treating tuberculosis was found to be limited by its tendency to produce resistant strains of the bacillus. A little later the effectiveness of *para*-aminosalicylic acid (PAS) was discovered and also its value in delaying the appearance of resistant strains. But the thiosemicarbazones led to the discovery in 1951, by Domagk and others, of the activity of isonicotinic acid hydrazide (isoniazid). It was found that in man isoniazid was most efficient when combined with streptomycin and PAS.

Chemotherapy of Cancer

For 30 years, beginning in 1925, Domagk wrote numerous papers on experimental tumor formation. In 1955 he turned to the chemotherapy of malignant tumors. In 1958 he published his results obtained with ethyl-eneimino quinones and their derivative Trenimon. Although then promising, these results later remained unconfirmed.

Later Life

In 1958 the University of Münster conferred on Domagk the title of professor, and on his retirement from the I.G. Farbenindustrie he worked on cancer research at that university. His many honors included honorary degrees from six universities. In 1959 he was elected a Foreign Member of the Royal Society, and he was the recipient of the Paul Ehrlich Gold Medal and of the Cameron Prize of the University of Edinburgh. He died at Burberg, Baden-Württemberg, on April 24, 1964.

Further Reading

There is a biography of Domagk in *Nobel Lectures: Physiology or Medicine,* 1922-1941 (1965), which also contains his Nobel Lecture, not delivered until 1947. For the background of Domagk's discovery see I. Galdston, *Behind the Sulfa Drugs*

(1943). For further developments see G. M. Findlay, *Recent Advances in Chemotherapy* (1930), especially the second (1939) and third (vol. 1, 1950) editions. □

Placido Domingo

Intelligence and dramatic conviction reinforced the vocal gifts of Spanish-born lyric-dramatic tenor Placido Domingo (born 1941). In addition to maintaining a large opera repertoire, he later turned to conducting; he was also an accomplished pianist.

Placido Domingo was born in the Barrio de Salamanca section of Madrid on January 21, 1941. His mother's family was Basque, and his father's half Catalan and half Aragonese. His parents, both active in music, were undoubtedly responsible for nurturing Domingo's musical abilities. His father had played the violin in opera and zarzuela orchestras and had sung baritone roles in zarzuelas. (Zarzuela is the Spanish equivalent of the Viennese operetta—a popular theatrical genre that mixes musical numbers with spoken dialogue. Its customary nationalistic plot may be serious or comic and usually involves scenes from everyday life.) What seems to have been a promising career, including a few recordings, was cut short when he damaged his voice by singing with a cold.

Domingo's mother was a professional singer who had made her debut at the Teatro Liceo in Barcelona, Spain's most important opera house. Her interest in zarzuela led to a performance in Federico Morena Torroba's *Sor Navarra,* where she had met her future husband. In 1946 Moreno Torroba formed a zarzuela company that included Domingo's parents and that eventually travelled to Mexico. Attracted to the country, Domingo's parents stayed and established their own company in Mexico City.

Domingo recalled that he was often pressed into service when the company needed a child. He began studying the piano shortly after the family moved to Mexico City, first privately and later at the National Conservatory. His interest in conducting also stemmed from these early years. At the impulsive age of 16 he met and married a fellow piano student, whom he does not name in his autobiography. A son was born within the year, and shortly thereafter the couple separated.

In Mexico and Israel

Domingo's first professional engagement was as accompanist to his mother in a concert at Mérida, Yucatan, in 1957. Immediately following this he joined his parents' zarzuela company, singing baritone roles and working with other singers as accompanist. His early career also included productions of *My Fair Lady,* in which he sang the role of the drunkard and was assistant conductor and assistant coach. The group gave 185 performances without interruption. Following this he served similarly in a production of Lehar's *The Merry Widow* as either Camille or Danilo.

Domingo auditioned for the National Opera (Mexico) in 1959 with several baritone arias, but was then asked to sight-read something in the tenor range. On the strength of the latter he received a contract as a tenor *comprimario* (singer of secondary roles) and as a coach for other singers. His first role was as Borsa in Verdi's *Rigoletto.* Other musical activities of the period included playing piano for a ballet company—no doubt to supplement his income—and running a program on Mexico's newly founded cultural television. This consisted of excerpts from zarzuelas, operettas, operas, and musical comedies, all to Domingo's piano accompaniment. A little later he played small parts on another program dedicated to the theater. Among the plays performed were those of Garcia Lorca, Pirandello, and Chekhov.

The number of his opera appearances, mostly in Monterrey (Mexico) and Mexico City, increased steadily from 1960 to 1961, and in November 1961 he made his American debut as Arturo in Donizetti's *Lucia di Lammermoor* with the Dallas Civic Orchestra, Joan Sutherland appearing in the title role. One year later, in Fort Worth, he sang Edgardo in the same opera, with Lily Pons singing the last Lucia of her career. Also in 1962 he married the former Marta Ornelas, whom he had met at the conservatory and who eventually sacrificed a promising career for his. She was voted the best Mexican singer of the year 1962.

Before their marriage they, along with baritone Franco Iglesias, formed a chamber opera company that toured Mexico, performing Wolf-Ferrari's *Il segreto di Susanna,* Menotti's *The Telephone,* and various duets and trios, with

Domingo accompanying at the piano. At the very end of 1962 the threesome signed a six month contract with the Hebrew National Opera in Tel Aviv, which proved such good experience that they extended their stay to two and one half years. Multi-lingual realizations of operas were common for the international cast gathered there. A performance of *La Traviata,* for instance, included a baritone singing in Hungarian, a soprano in German, a tenor in Italian, and the chorus in Hebrew. Domingo credits this cosmopolitan group for improving his abilities in several languages.

Move to New York City

After leaving Tel Aviv in June 1965, Domingo auditioned successfully for the New York City Opera. His New York debut was scheduled for October 21, 1965, as Don Jose in Bizet's *Carmen,* but occurred on the 17th when he was asked to fill in for an ailing tenor in Puccini's *Madame Butterfly* . In February of the following year he sang the title role in the North American premiere of Alberto Ginastera's *Don Rodrigo,* an event that also marked the opening of the City Opera's new home at Lincoln Center. *Don Rodrigo* remained the only modernist work in Domingo's repertoire. Although he had sung in open air performances by the Metropolitan Opera of Mascagni's *Cavalleria Rusticana* and Leoncavallo's *Pagliacci* in 1966, his official Met debut came on September 25, 1968, when he substituted for an indisposed Franco Corelli in Cilèa's *Adrianna Lecouveur* a week before his scheduled appearance.

Other important debuts were as follows: January 1965 at the Teatro Liceo, Barcelona, in three short operas by little-known Mexican composers; December 1969 in the title role of Verdi's *Ernani;* and December 1971 as Cavaradossi in Puccini's *Tosca,* his most frequently performed role. In 1980 Federico Moreno Torroba completed an opera, *El Poeta,* for Domingo, who sang the world premiere in June of that year. Both Domingo and the critics agreed that, although the straightforward, tonal score contained many attractive passages, the libretto was too weak to support it.

Although Domingo's repertoire concentrated mainly on the 19th century Italian and French masters, his range was considerably wider. In addition to his zarzuela roots and brief excursion into the modernism of *Don Rodrigo,* he went back as far as Rameau (Hippolyte) and Mozart (Don Giovanni) and touched on Wagner (Lohengrin, Hans Sachs). He also released two popular albums, one with American popular singer John Denver, ''Perhaps Love'' and later ''My Life for a Song.'' Domingo appeared in commercial film productions of Mascagni's *Cavalleria Rusticana,* Leoncavallo's *Pagliacci,* and Verdi's *La Traviata* (1983), all directed by Franco Zeffirelli, and Bizet's *Carmen* (1984), directed by Francesco Rosi.

Domingo actively pursued conducting opportunities during much of his career. In 1972 ''Domingo Conducts Milnes! Milnes Conducts Domingo!'' with the New Philharmonia Orchestra of London was released. Later he conducted a New York City Opera production of *La Traviata* during the 1973-1974 season and a Covent Garden production of *Die Fledermaus* at the end of 1983.

Achieved Universal Acclaim

Domingo's willingness to explore new musical territories led to *Perhaps Love,* his album of duets with the late singer John Denver in 1981. Although critics were not especially pleased, the album achieved gold status in record sales. During the nineties, Domingo achieved even greater mainstream commercial success on his Three Tenors collaborations with Jose Carreras and Luciano Pavarotti. The trio first performed together in celebration of the 1990 World Cup Championship in Rome. In 1994 their Dodger Stadium concert in Los Angeles, which was viewed on television by 1.3 billion people and sold more than 10 million CDs and videos, was billed as the most-seen and most-heard serious music event of all time. *New York* magazine called Domingo a ''phenomenon, perhaps the most compulsive overachiever the world of opera has ever known.'' The singer's immense popularity allowed him to raise millions of dollars through special benefit concerts in order to help the victims of the 1985 Mexican earthquake disaster, in which he personally lost four relatives. At the same time his Three Tenors collaborations introduced millions of new fans to the music of opera. In 1996 Domingo became the artistic director of the Washington Opera while simultaneously launching The Three Tenors World Tour which visited four continents and continued through 1997.

Further Reading

Of the many articles written on Domingo, those in *Opera News* are perhaps the most consistently revealing. An interview, ''What Makes Placido Run?'' appeared in the March 27, 1982, issue. Domingo's autobiography, *My First Forty Years,* was published in 1983. One of the better books of its kind, it is well written and insightful and probably no more self-congratulatory than his accomplishment deserves. □

St. Dominic

The Spanish churchman St. Dominic (ca. 1170-1221) founded the Dominican order, a religious community officially called the Order of Preachers.

Dominic was born to the well-to-do Guzmán family in the town of Caleruega in northern Spain. As a young man, he studied the liberal arts and theology at Palencia. After he was ordained a priest, he joined the cathedral canons of the city of Osma, who lived a community life under the rule of St. Augustine.

When he was about 30, Dominic accompanied his bishop on several diplomatic missions in northern Europe. In the course of these travels he became aware of the religious ideas of the Albigensians, a Manichaean movement in southern France. This sect believed that the soul is good and the body is evil and that man must be purified and must not indulge in any physical pleasures. The Pope had sent legates to counteract the movement, but with their sumptuous clothes, fine horses, and numerous attendants they only succeeded in reinforcing the Albigensians' beliefs.

Dominic saw that the only way to preach orthodox doctrine effectively to these people was to be as poor as they were and to be thoroughly knowledgable in Christian theology. He stayed in southern France for several years and, together with a small group of like-minded men, tried to put his ideas into practice by preaching, studying, praying, and living in poverty.

After a papal crusade crushed the heretics, in 1215 Dominic and his group of 16 were welcomed by the bishop of Toulouse and established as the official preachers of that diocese. Dominic then went to Rome, where he obtained Pope Innocent III's approval for the establishment of a religious order dedicated to preaching and based on a deep knowledge of the Scriptures and Christian truth. Until this time religious orders had been associated with monasteries, where men lived apart from the world and spent their time in prayer and physical work. But Dominic conceived of a group of men who would be dedicated primarily to preaching and thus to helping people in the mainstream of life. Living together in a city house, where they would pray and study, these men would be able to go wherever they were needed and would substitute study for the traditional manual labor of monks.

In 1217 Dominic showed his confidence in the men who shared his ideal and scattered the little group of 16 around Europe. He sent some to Paris to study theology, some to Bologna to study law, and others to Rome and Madrid. Two stayed behind in Toulouse and two more in nearby Prouille. Wherever they went, these men attracted others, and soon there were hundreds of followers of Dominic's ideal, many of them students and masters at universities.

During the next 2 years Dominic traveled over 3,000 miles on foot, visiting and encouraging his men in Toulouse, Paris, Milan, Rome and in Spain. In 1220 the first meeting or general chapter of the friars took place in Bologna, and there it was decided that the order would have a representational system of government, with the friars in each house electing their superiors for fixed terms. These representatives met again in 1221 and divided the order geographically into provinces. Shortly after this meeting Dominic died in Bologna in 1221; he was canonized in 1234.

Dominic's genius had several ingredients. He was a charismatic leader, able to evaluate a situation and act decisively. He had confidence in his own ideals and in the people who shared them. His mind was sharpened by study, but before he wrote, lectured, or preached, he turned to God in prayer. It was said of Dominic that "he loved everyone, so everyone loved him." By 1256 the group he had founded had over 13,000 members, and it continues to flourish today.

Further Reading

Marie Humbert Vicaire, *Saint Dominic and His Times* (2 vols., 1957; trans., 1 vol., 1964), is the most complete and accurate biography of St. Dominic in English. Pierre Mandonnet, *Saint Dominic and His Work* (2 vols., 1938; trans., 1 vol., 1944), contains a thorough study of the historical and religious background of Dominic's life. Bede Jarrett, *Life of Saint Dominic*

(1924; 2d ed. 1934), presents the personal warmth and genius of the saint.

Additional Sources

Monshau, Michael, *Praying with Dominic*, Winona, Minn.: Saint Mary's Press, 1993.
Bedouelle, Guy, *Saint Dominic: the grace of the word*, San Francisco: Ignatius Press, 1987. □

Domitian

The Roman emperor Domitian (51-96), in full Titus Flavius Domitianus Augustus, though reputed to be a complete tyrant, modernized Rome's fiscal administration and secured the empire's frontiers.

Born in Rome on Oct. 24, 51, the younger son of Vespasian, Domitian came to the throne when his brother Titus died young after only 2 years of rule. From the start Domitian reigned as a complete autocrat, partly perhaps because of his lack of political skills, but partly certainly because of his own nature. Domitian was personally suspicious and unlovable, and the relations between him and those around him began ill and ended worse.

Domitian's reign can be considered under two main heads: his administration, which was excellent, and his frontier policy, which was generally successful. Provincial government was so carefully supervised that the Roman biographer Suetonius admits that the empire enjoyed a period of unusually good government and security. Domitian's policy of employing members of the equestrian class rather than his own freedmen for some important posts was also a step forward. The finances, which Titus's fecklessness had plunged into confusion, were restored despite building projects and foreign wars.

Religion was a special concern of Domitian, and he vigorously strove to breathe life again into the ancient Roman faith; he built temples and established ceremonies and even tried to enforce morality by law. This zeal for religion may explain the hostility of the Christian writers, for though he was not a persecutor of Christians, he was an ardent propagator of paganism.

Frontier Policy

The northern frontiers needed Domitian's special attention. His governor Agricola pushed the conquest of Britain into Scotland, invaded the Highlands, and even proposed to add all Ireland to the empire after subduing Scotland. Tacitus, Agricola's son-in-law, writes that Agricola's recall in 84 was due to Domitian's jealousy, but more probably it reflected increasing concern with dangers on the Rhine-Danube frontier.

In Germany, Domitian himself took the field, continuing and extending his father's policy of shortening the frontier by annexing the triangle between the Rhine and

Danube. The latter part of the reign saw increasing trouble on the lower Danube from the Dacians, a tribe occupying approximately what is now Romania. Led by an able king, Decebalus, the Dacians in 85 invaded the empire. The war ended in 88 in a compromise peace which left Decebalus as king and gave him Roman "foreign aid" in return for his promise to help protect the frontier (chiefly against himself).

One of the reasons Domitian failed to crush the Dacians was a revolt in Germany by the governor Antonius Saturninus. The revolt was quickly suppressed, but henceforth Domitian's always suspicious temper grew steadily worse. It was, of course, the people nearest him who suffered, and after a reign of terror at court Domitian was murdered on Sept. 18, 96, in a plot to which even his own wife, Domitia Longina, was a party. The Senate, which had always hated him, hastened to condemn his memory and repeal his acts, and Domitian joined the ranks of the tyrants of considerable accomplishments but evil memory. He was the last of the Flavian emperors, and his murder marked the beginning of the period of the so-called Five Good Emperors.

Further Reading

Among the ancient sources, Tacitus's *Agricola* and Pliny the Younger's *Panegyric* are viciously hostile; Suetonius's *Lives of the Twelve Caesars* is scandalous but less rancorous. Among modern works, M.I. Rostovtzeff, *Social and Economic History of the Roman Empire* (1926; 2d rev. ed. 1957), and B. W. Henderson, *Five Roman Emperors* (1927), are the fullest and fairest.

Additional Sources

Jones, Brian W., *The Emperor Domitian*, London; New York: Routledge, 1992. ☐

Do Muoi

Do Muoi (born 1917) was made prime minister of the Socialist Republic of Vietnam in June 1988, capping a 35-year career in the state bureaucracy. As prime minister he became increasingly identified with the forces of conservatism at the highest level of leadership. In 1991 he became secretary general of the Vietnamese Communist Party.

In what was called the Socialist Republic of Vietnam's (SRV) biggest leadership shake-up in five years, Do Muoi was elected the Communist Party's General Secretary replacing Nguyen Van Linh, 75, in 1991. The election on June 27, 1991 replaced seven of the 12 men in the ruling Politburo and a similar personnel housecleaning took place in the party Central Committee. Like Linh, Do Muoi advocated reforming the marketplace without fundamentally altering the political system. Party officials made clear that Linh was retiring because of poor health and was not being ousted. Do Muoi told journalists at the time, "our party and our people will follow the way of socialism, of Ho Chi Minh, as the sole correct way.

Do Muoi had been the prime minister since 1988. Until then, he had maintained a somewhat low public profile, confining his activity either to technical administration of economic programs, such as increasing commercial trade, or as a trouble shooter dealing with some crisis condition. His constituency within Vietnam's Leninist political system was drawn from the state bureaucracy and from the middle cadres corps.

However, Do Moui is blamed for what was deemed one of the greatest tragedies in Vietnam; the "Destruction of Capitalism". On March 23, 1978, Do Moui sent 60,000 youth groups throughout Vietnam to close down the businesses. An estimated 35,000 businesses were closed in just one day. Thousands of business owners committed sucide and thus began the exodus out of Vietnam by boat. By US estimations, since then, over 2 million Vietnamese became 'boat-people" and about 400,000 perished at sea.

Do Muoi's earlier service had been chiefly in the economic sector. In the early years, the late 1950s, this stood him well and enhanced his reputation as a manager and problem solver. After the Vietnam War, in the last half of the 1970s, however, he became deeply involved in the unsuccessful amalgamation of the two economies, North and South. As deputy prime minister with the title Director of Socialist Transformation of Private Industry in Southern Vietnam (March 1975) he was in effect the czar who jammed together the socialist and capitalist economic systems. His detractors later asserted that he, more than any other

Vietnam's top political commissar. He was in command of the occupation of Haiphong at war's end.

Do Muoi's first post in the new Democratic Republic of Vietnam government was vice minister of commerce (1956), and there followed a series of assignments, chiefly in the domestic trade sector. He was politically inactive, out of the public eye, from February 1961 to November 1967. Western intelligence attributed this to poor health, not an entirely satisfactory explanation.

In 1969 he was assigned to the building and construction sectors. He was the Vietnamese liaison official with the USSR team that built Ho Chi Minh's mausoleum in Hanoi and with the Cuban team that built Hanoi's Thanh Loi hotel. He became vice premier in December 1969, a Central Committee member and Politburo alternate-member in March 1982, and a full Politburo member and Central Committee secretary in 1986; he was elected to the National Assembly in 1980. In the 1980s he was identified with the Council of Ministers (vice chairman in 1981), with one of his chief administrative tasks the supervision of the purge of incompetent and corrupt party cadres, part of the party's broader effort to restore its lost luster and reputation. In 1991 he was elevated to secretary-general of the Vietnamese Communist Party.

Do Muoi's public image was avuncular, as a serious, dedicated, honest government official. He carried the appearance of solid orthodoxy, one committed both to the orthodox Marxism-Leninism and to the pre-modern Vietnamese traditionalism. He seemed to regard Marxism-Leninism as a logical extension of the centuries-old Vietnamese value system. His public statements were in straightforward language unadorned by literary style or subtlety of thought. His doctrinal orations were punctuated by moral exhortation and in substance chiefly were restatements of party lines and state slogans. His economic philosophy, judged by his many speeches on economic problems, was what could be termed original Stalinism—that is, he believed in primary concentration on heavy industry, large-sized agricultural production units, highly centralized planning, use of moral exhortation more than individual incentive as chief motivating force, and a minimal role for the market in economic activity.

Although a little-known figure abroad, Do Muoi traveled extensively in Vietnam, probably was more tireless in stumping the boondocks than any other Hanoi leader. He also traveled extensively abroad, but almost entirely to socialist countries in search of economic aid.

Little is known about his personal life. At some point he was married, as it is reported that his wife died late in 1992. What her name was, when they were married, or if they had any children has not been disclosed. In July of 1996, Do Muoi's term as general secretary was extended. He declared, according to the *New York Times,* "I belong to the party and the people. The party and the people tell me what to do."

Further Reading

There is little published information on Do Muoi. See his biography in the *Yearbook on International Communist Affairs*

individual Vietnamese, was responsible for the country's postwar economic failure. His defenders argued that he simply shared the blame equally with other top leaders. Even his severest critics, however, always treated Do Muoi with respect, regarding him as an incorruptible disciplinarian who faithfully held high the banner of Communist Party idealism, one who properly was widely feared by the corrupt, the incompetent, and the slack.

Do Muoi was born in Dong My village (Thanh Tri district) on the outskirts of Hanoi on February 2, 1917, into what his official biography terms a "poor for many generations" family. He appears to have had little if any formal education—his official biography makes no reference at all to schooling—and quite probably he had less than five years in school. During World War II he was imprisoned by the French in Chi Hoa prison, Hanoi. Here he was thrown in with famed Vietnamese political prisoners, probably his chief educational experience as colonial prisons were the "university" for most Asian revolutionaries.

According to his official biography, Do Muoi became politically active at the age of 14 when he joined the antifascist Popular Front. His occupation at the time was as a house painter. He joined the Indochinese Communist Party in 1939, was sentenced to ten years in prison by the French in 1941, and escaped (or was released) in 1945.

He joined the Viet Minh in its war against the French and began service in Ha Dong province. During this war he held a succession of provincial level posts, achieving the equivalent rank of brigadier general as the People's Army of

1989, edited by Richard Staar (1990); "Hanoi Assembly Elects a New Prime Minister" in the *New York Times* (June 28, 1988); "A Premier Candidate" in *Far Eastern Economic Review* (June 23, 1988); and "Vietnam Picks a Disciplinarian as Premier" in the *Washington Post* (June 23, 1988).His recent political activities are recorded in the *LA Times]* Albright Outlines U.S. Terms for Closer Ties With Vietnam on June 28, 1997, Vietnam's Premier Becomes Party Chief; Communists: Do Muoi advocates market reform without greatly altering the political system on June 28, 1991; SOUTHEAST ASIA; New Blood, Same Policy Likely at Vietnamese Party Congress on May 17, 1991. Many of his speeches and political activities are broadcast on Radio Free Asia. □

Donatello

The Italian sculptor Donatello (1386-1466) was the greatest Florentine sculptor before Michelangelo and certainly the most influential individual artist of the 15th century in Italy. Nearly every later sculptor and numerous Florentine and Paduan painters were indebted to him.

Though Donatello was a descendant of a branch of the important Bardi family, he was brought up in a more plebeian tradition than his older contemporary Lorenzo Ghiberti. Gifted with humanistic insight and a quality of will that were highly prized in the early Renaissance, Donatello revealed the inner life of his heroic subjects, memorable images which have conditioned our very conception of 15th-century Florence. Sharing neither Ghiberti's feeling for line nor Filippo Brunelleschi's interest in proportion, Donatello worked creatively with bronze, stone, and wood, impatient with surface refinements and anxious to explore the optical qualities he observed in the world about him. His later art, saturated with the spirit of Roman antiquity, is frequently disturbing in its immediacy as it attains a level of dramatic force hitherto unknown in Italian sculpture.

Donato di Niccolò Bardi, called Donatello, was born in 1386 in Florence. Little precise biographical information has come down to us, although many anecdotes are recorded by Giorgio Vasari in his *Lives.* Donatello was apprenticed to Ghiberti, and in 1403, at the age of 17, Donatello was working for the master on the bronze reliefs of the First Doors of the Baptistery. By 1407 he had left Ghiberti for the workshops of the Cathedral.

Early Works

One of Donatello's earliest known works is the lifesized marble *David* (1408; reworked 1416; now in the Bargello, Florence). Intended to adorn a buttress of the Cathedral, in 1414 it was set up in the Palazzo Vecchio as a symbol of the Florentine republic, which was then engaged in a struggle with the king of Naples. Dramatic in posture and full of youthful energy, the *David* possesses something of the graceful late Gothic feeling of a figure by Ghiberti, though Donatello now admits us to a world of psychological tensions.

Rapidly maturing, Donatello produced a strong, original, dynamic style in two works: the large marble figure *St. Mark* in a niche on the exterior of Orsanmichele, completed between 1411 and 1413, and the seated *St. John the Evangelist* for the facade of the Cathedral (now in the Museo dell'Opera), finished in 1415. These powerful, over-life-sized figures established the sculptor's reputation. The *St. Mark* broke with tradition in its classical stance, realistically modeled drapery, and concentrated face with such optical subtleties as a detailed analysis of the eye. It became a stunning symbolic portrait of a noble Florentine hero in the embattled republic of Donatello's day.

Donatello's new style was confirmed in the famous *St. George,* carved in marble about 1416-1417 for the exterior of Orsanmichele (later replaced by a bronze copy; the original is in the Bargello). Resolute in stance, the Christian saint has the face not of an ideal hero but of a real one. Even more significant is the little marble relief *St. George and the Dragon,* that decorates the base of the niche. The marble was ordered in 1417, and the relief was completed shortly afterward. This is an important date, for the relief is the earliest example in art of the new science of perspective used to create a measurable space for the figures. Up to this time artists had conceived of a flat background in front of which, or in which, the figures were placed; now the low, pictorial forms seem to emerge from atmosphere and light. Donatello was probably influenced by the contemporary theoretical studies in perspective of the architect Brunelleschi.

Between 1415 and 1435 Donatello and his pupils completed eight life-sized marble prophets for niches in the Campanile of the Cathedral (now in the Museo dell'Opera). The most impressive of the group are the so-called *Zuccone* ("big squash" or "baldy"), perhaps representing Habakkuk, and the *Jeremiah,* in both of which there is great psychological tension and a convincing, deliberate ugliness.

Middle Period

Donatello received many commissions, which he often executed in collaboration with other artists. An unusual work is the *Marzocco,* the emblematic lion of the Florentines, carved in sandstone and imbued with a grand contrapuntal vigor; it was ordered in 1418 for the papal apartments in S. Maria Novella (now in the Museo Nazionale). Donatello's optical principles and his vigorous style in relief sculpture reached a climax in the gilded bronze *Feast of Herod,* completed in 1427 for the font in the Baptistery, Siena; Ghiberti, Jacopo della Quercia, and other sculptors also executed reliefs for the baptismal font. In Donatello's very low relief composition he approximated, but deliberately avoided the accurate construction of, one-point architectural perspective.

About 1425 Donatello entered into partnership with Michelozzo, sculptor and architect, with whom he made a trip to Rome after 1429. (Vasari states that Donatello went to Rome with Brunelleschi. This would have been much earlier, perhaps in 1409; but there is no document to confirm such a trip.) With Michelozzo he produced a series of works, including the tomb of Pope John XXIII in the Baptistery, Florence, and the tomb of Cardinal Brancacci in S. Angelo a Nilo, Naples, both of which were in progress in 1427. The first of these established a type of wall tomb that was decisive for many later Florentine examples.

Probably just after the trip to Rome, Donatello created the well-known gilded limestone *Annunciation* tabernacle in Sta Croce, Florence, enclosing a lyrical pair of Gabriel and the Virgin Mary. He was also commissioned to carve for the Cathedral a *Singing Gallery* to match the one already begun by Luca della Robbia (both now in the Museo dell'Opera). Using marble and mosaic, Donatello presented a classically inspired frieze of wildly dancing *putti.* It was begun in 1433, completed 6 years later, and installed in 1450.

Later Works

Much of Donatello's later work manifests his understanding of classical art, for example, the bronze *David* in the Bargello, a preadolescent boy clothed only in boots and a pointed hat. This enigmatic figure is in all probability the earliest existing freestanding nude since antiquity.

From 1443 to 1453 Donatello was in Padua, where he created the colossal bronze equestrian monument to the Venetian *condottiere* called Gattamelata in the Piazza del Santo. It was the first important sculptural repetition of the 2d-century equestrian statue of Marcus Aurelius in Rome. Donatello portrayed Gattamelata as the ideal man of the Renaissance. Another major commission in Padua was the high altar of S. Antonio, decorated with four large narrative reliefs representing the life of St. Anthony, smaller reliefs, and seven life-sized statues in bronze, including a seated Madonna and Child and a bronze Crucifixion. Donatello had earlier made remarkable experiments with illusionistic space in his large stucco medallions for the Old Sacristy of S. Lorenzo in Florence; now his major bronze Paduan reliefs present an explosive conception of space with sketchy figures and a very excited continuous surface. The influence of these scenes on painters in northern Italy was to prove enormous and long lasting.

Back in Florence, the aged Donatello carved a haunting, emaciated *Mary Magdalen* from poplar wood for the Baptistery (1454-1455). Romantically distorted in extreme ugliness, the figure of the penitent saint in the wilderness originally had sun-tanned skin and gilding on her monstrous hair. In 1456 Donatello made an equally disturbing group in bronze of Judith cutting off the head of Holofernes. Now in the Piazza della Signoria, Florence, it was originally commissioned, apparently as a fountain, for the courtyard of the Medici Palace.

At his death on Dec. 13, 1466, Donatello left two unfinished bronze pulpits in S. Lorenzo, Florence. On one are relief panels, showing the torture and murder of Christ by means of distorted forms and wildly emotional actions. Finished by his pupil Bertoldo di Giovanni, the pulpit scenes reveal the great master's insight into human suffering and his pioneering exploration of the dark realms of man's experience.

Further Reading

The best scholarly study of Donatello in English is H. W. Janson, *The Sculpture of Donatello* (2 vols., 1957; 1 vol., 1963). Recommended for the reproduction of wonderful photographic details of selected sculptures are Ludwig Goldscheider, *Donatello* (1941), and the small but compendious book by Luigi Grassi, *All the Sculpture of Donatello* (1958; trans., 2 vols., 1964), which includes many works of debatable authenticity. □

Donatus

Donatus (died ca. 355) was the schismatic bishop of Carthage during the first decades of the Donatist movement.

L ittle is known of Donatus before 311, when the Christian Church in North Africa was torn by schism. He is reported to have come from Casae Nigrae in Numidia, southwest of Carthage. He may also have engaged in some quasischismatic activity of an "anti-Catholic" sort before coming to Carthage.

The cause of the schism may be said to lie in the persecution of the Church in 303 by the emperor Diocletian. As in the Decian persecution and the Novatian schism that had swept Rome 50 years before, the Church was divided into two camps concerning those who had apostatized under threat of torture or death. The "laxists" sought easy and quick rehabilitation for the lapsed; the "rigorists" held that any act of compromise, even the handing over of the Scriptures to the state (those who did so were called *traditores*), deprived the lapsed Christian of the right to receive the Sacraments and, if he was a clergyman, of the right to administer the Sacraments.

In North Africa the rigorists tended to be the rural Berbers, given to a hatred of apostasy and a sometimes extreme veneration of martyrs. Donatus was a member of this faction. The more urban and urbane "Catholics" were laxist in discipline and politically and sociologically oriented more toward Rome and the empire than toward the surrounding countryside.

Some 10 years after the Diocletian persecution, the episcopal office in Carthage fell vacant upon the death of Bishop Mensurius. Amid rival factions and behind-the-scenes maneuvering, a hastily called and peremptorily administered group of Catholics met and elected Caecilian as their new bishop. Because of his severe antirigorist views, Caecilian had many enemies, not least of whom was Lucilla, a wealthy Spanish lady residing in Carthage. Caecilian, when a deacon, had alienated her by harshly criticizing her practices of martyr worship.

The opposition, consisting mostly of Lucilla and the Numidian clergy, was quick to move. They claimed that Caecilian was in fact not a bishop because one of his co-consecrators, Felix of Aptunga, had been a *traditor* during the persecution and therefore the consecration was invalid. They elected and consecrated their own bishop, Majorinus, claiming him to be the true bishop. Thus began in 312 the great schism that was to rend North Africa for the next century. "Bishop was set up against Bishop," wrote Optatus, "and altar against altar." This was the same year in which Constantine was converted to Christianity; the persecution of the Church by the state was now at an end, but the persecution of the Donatists was just beginning.

Majorinus lived only a year after his consecration as rival bishop. It was Donatus who took his place, and because of his long and powerful episcopacy, the schism was named after him. During the first year of his reign the Roman Church formally condemned Donatism at the Council of Arles in 314. But the Donatists became increasingly intransigent in their views and in their anti-Catholic activity. "Under the hot Numidian sun," one historian wrote, "nothing was forgiven or forgotten." Donatus proved an able and enthusiastic leader of his fellow schismatics; they swore by his "white hairs," wrote St. Augustine later. Finally Donatus was driven from Carthage by force in the proconsular Macarian persecution of 347. He died in exile less than 10 years later.

The schism persisted, but the Donatists were never as strong as they had been under Donatus. At the turn of the century the Donatists, with their militant activists (known as the *circumcelliones*), were to test the intellectual skills of the great Catholic bishop of Hippo, Augustine, as well as sorely to try his patience. Violence and futile attempts at reconciliation continued well into the 5th century, and not until the onslaught of Islam did the Donatists (and Catholics) of a divided and weakened Christian North Africa finally disappear.

Further Reading

Primary sources for the life of Donatus and the history of Donatism are found chiefly in the works of Optatus, Bishop of Milevis, and in the anti-Donatist writings of St. Augustine. Modern studies in English are few, but W. H. C. Frend, *The Donatist Church: A Movement of Protest in Roman North Africa* (1952), and Stanley L. Greenslade, *Schism in the Early Church* (1953; 2d ed. 1964), are important. ☐

Pham Van Dong

Pham Van Dong (born 1906) was the longtime Hanoi premier, first in the Democratic Republic of Vietnam (DRV) government and then, after reunification in 1976, of the Socialist Republic of Vietnam (SRV) government. He was considered to be one of the members of the inner "circle of five" top political power holders in Vietnam.

Pham Van Dong, a charter member of the Indochinese Communist Party in 1930, distinguished himself over the years primarily as administrator and organizer of the government bureaucracy (as opposed to the party bureaucracy). Much of his career success was traceable to the fact that he early associated with Ho Chi Minh and served him well, always seeking to emulate Ho's dedication and zeal but in a loyal and self-deprecating manner so as never to upstage Ho. To this Ho reciprocated by publicly calling Dong "my best nephew" and "my alter ego." Indeed, the two did work well as a team, in the marriage of Ho's organizational skill with Dong's managerial ability. They also shared a common philosophic outlook that put pragmatism over ideology.

In many ways Dong was a typical first generation Asian revolutionary: that is, a well-educated member of the upper class who early in life was moved to political activism by nationalist sentiment. His background was Mandarin, which means he was born into affluence and raised in a Confucian tradition of strong cultural value placed on intellectual superiority rather than social origin as the proper basis for government, education, and behavior in life in general. His radicalization was in spite of, not because of, his early years. However, there were alternate political roads that Dong could have traveled, various nationalist movements which were in fact larger and more attractive than Stalinism. Dong apparently chose Marxism-Leninism as the proper outlet for his political energies not because of the inherent appeal of Marxist thought but because of the influence of the personality of Ho Chi Minh.

Dong was born March 1, 1906, in Mo Duc village of Quang Ngai province in Central Vietnam. His father was a high ranking official in the Imperial Court in Hue and served

as court secretary to Emperor Duy Tan. The emperor was deposed by the French in 1916 for being too nationalistic, which also resulted in loss of status for Dong's father and probably began his alienation from the existing colonial arrangement.

Student Activist Turned Revolutionary

Dong received a good French *lycee* education in Hue. In 1925 he enrolled in the University of Hanoi and soon ran into trouble with the authorities by leading a student strike during the funeral of Phan Chu Trinh, a famed nationalist leader. Within a year he was expelled and left for Canton, China, where he spent a year at the Chinese Nationalist run Whampoa Military Academy, met Ho Chi Minh, and joined Ho's proto-communist revolutionary movement, the Vietnam Revolutionary Youth League (Thanh Nien).

From Revolutionary Prisoner to Guerrilla Warrior

Ho sent Dong back to Hanoi in 1927 to do revolutionary organizational work. Dong was subsequently arrested by the French and jailed at Poulo Condore, Vietnam's famed prison island. He remained there from 1929 to 1936 when a new government in France ordered general amnesty for political prisoners in French colonial jails. Dong resumed organizational work in Hanoi and Saigon for three years, then fled to China to escape the 1939 roundup of Vietnamese leftists came with the start of World War II. In 1941 he joined Ho and others at the China border for the

conference which created the Viet Minh league, the united front organization (and guerrilla force) that was to lead the struggle against French colonialism.

When the Democratic Republic of Vietnam (DRV) was formed in 1945 Dong was named its first finance minister. In the late 1950s he returned to his home province of Quang Ngai and took field command of a guerrilla force about which little is known. Also during this time he was involved in the bloody purge of non-communist nationalists from Viet Minh ranks, a dark episode for which he was never forgiven by many early Vietnamese nationalist revolutionaries. In 1951 he was named vice premier. In 1954 he became acting foreign minister and was sent to Geneva as the head of the DRV delegation to the Geneva Conference that ended the Viet Minh war. In 1955 he was named premier, a post he continued to hold until December 1986. Over the years Dong held other important governmental posts such as vice chairman of the National Defense Council, member of the National Assembly, and, within party ranks, member of the all-powerful Politburo.

International Negotiator and Party Organizer

During the Vietnam War Dong's central task was to mobilize material support for the war effort. This involved organization of the general population of North Vietnam, working through the mechanism of the National Assembly, and efforts abroad to assure the necessary flow of arms from socialist countries. He made frequent trips outside the country and is said to have been particularly effective in dealing with the former U.S.S.R.

After the end of the war in 1975 Dong concentrated his energies on the nation-building task, particularly on the vastly ambitious "district building" reorganizational effort that sought to eliminate the village in Vietnam and replace it with the giant agroville at the district level. He continued to pursue tirelessly a heavy schedule of public events. For months on end he averaged a speech or more a week, chiefly involving education or technical training activities, in between attending a variety of semisocial activities such as diplomatic receptions and tree planting ceremonies.

Dong also continued trips abroad. He was probably the most travelled member of the ruling Politburo and certainly had longer experience in diplomatic negotiations than any other Socialist Republic of Vietnam (SRV) official. In later years his external activities in the international arena tended to be goodwill visits rather than tough negotiations. He was believed by many to have remained the dominant influence on SRV foreign policy, superior to Foreign Minister Nguyen Co Thach.

Dong's personality was described by those who knew him or worked closely with him as sophisticated, self-assured, and somewhat imperious. He was said to have been highly articulate and a smooth diplomatic negotiator.

Defeated by Poor Health and Economy

Dong was known to have suffered from tuberculosis in early life. In the 1980s his health began to deteriorate. He was not seen in public as often as he once was, and his travel abroad was curtailed. Reportedly he had a heart pacemaker implanted in mid-1979 by surgeons in Moscow, and he returned there again in 1982 for extensive medical treatment of an unknown nature. In late December, 1986, at the Sixth Party Congress in Hanoi, Dong resigned as premier because of "advanced age and bad health." He was one of the last top members of the Politburo to have led the Communist defeat of the Japanese, the French, and finally the United States' soldiers in war.

In addition to his failing health, growing impatience over the country's long economic crisis was felt to have prompted his resignation along with two other top officicals, General Secretary Truong Chinh (79) and Politburo member Le Duc Tho (76). In an interview with *Time* magazine in November 1985, Dong emphasized that economic development to rebuild the country was the government's primary task. *Newsweek* also later quoted him as saying, "Waging war is simple, but running a country is very difficult." His war record was far more impressive than his success in improving economic conditions, which had reached a crisis stage when he stepped down. Vietnam could ill afford its invasion of Cambodia in 1978, and the continued engagement had adversely affected the already strained economy. Some speculated that Dong's willingness (in 1985) to discuss the long unresolved MIA dispute with the United States was prompted by the economic turmoil.

Little is known about Dong's private life. He was married late, when he was about 40, to a 20-year-old girl who, according to some reports, was later confined to an institution with mental illness, or, according to other reports, died. They are believed to have had two children, a boy and a girl. Dong was never known to have discussed his personal life with foreigners.

Further Reading

There are no full length biographies of Pham Van Dong available in English. His various writings make autobiographical references from which the facts of his life can be pieced together. A short biographical sketch was written by the French scholar Jean Lacouture in *The New York Times Sunday Magazine* (May 19, 1968). See also a short biography in the *Baltimore Sun* (September 12, 1967). The basic collection of his writings in English, published by the Foreign Languages Publishing House, Hanoi, in 1977, is titled *Pham Van Dong: Selected Writings* and contains six of his major articles written between 1954 and 1977. He also published a biography in English, *President Ho Chi Minh* (Hanoi, 1960). Dong published at least nine other books in Vietnamese between 1945 and 1985, which are mostly collections of his articles, speeches, and interviews. Periodical articles including information on Pham Van Dong are: *Newsweek* (December 29, 1986), *Time* (November 11 and 25, 1985),*Scholastic Update* (March 29, 1985), and *The New Yorker* (November 1985). □

Gaetano Donizetti

The Italian opera composer Gaetano Donizetti (1797-1848) was one of the first composers of the romantic movement in Italy.

Gaetano Donizetti was born in Bergamo on Nov. 29, 1797. He received his first instruction in music from an uncle, but the beginning of his formation as a composer came in 1806, when he was accepted as a free student in the Lezione Caritatevoli, a school supported by the church of S. Maria Maggiore for the training of musicians and choristers for its services. The director was Simon Mayr, a German who had settled in Bergamo in 1805. Although not known today, his music was held in high esteem in his lifetime. Mayr's influence seems to have been decisive. He kept young Donizetti in the school although his voice was not of the necessary quality, even writing works for student performances in which these vocal defects could be avoided.

Following this training, Donizetti went to Bologna in 1815 to study with Padre Mattei, a student of Padre Martini and a teacher of Gioacchino Rossini. Mayr gave Donizetti financial support as well as letters of introduction. Donizetti's first publication, a set of variations on a theme by Mayr, appeared in 1815.

Donizetti's first three operas date from 1816 and 1817 and were not performed during his lifetime. His first opera to

be performed was *Enrico di Borgogna,* given in Venice in 1818. From this time until 1844 he produced operas of all types at a fantastic pace. In 1827 he agreed to compose 12 operas for Venice within a 3-year period. This speed in production shows in many works that perfunctorily filled the established forms of the day. His works all allow the singer ample opportunity for display with cadenzas and brilliant coloratura writing. Many of his librettos deal with violent passions that are not always turned to best dramatic effect. However, works like *L'elisir d'amore* (1832), *Lucia di Lammermoor* (1835), *La Fille du régiment* (1840), and *Don Pasquale* (1843) have gained a place in the repertory for themselves and an important historical position for their composer.

Although now known primarily for his operas, Donizetti produced a large number of compositions in other genres. In addition to 71 operas, he composed cantatas, sacred works, symphonies, string quartets and quintets, and numerous works for piano solo, voice and piano, and piano and other instruments.

Donizetti's fame quickly spread throughout Italy; he went to Paris, where he wrote five operas, and to Vienna, where he became principal court conductor in 1842. His last years, 1844-1848, were spent in rather severe circumstances because of the progressive deterioration of his health, both physical and mental.

Further Reading

Two biographies of Donizetti are Herbert Weinstock, *Donizetti and the World of Opera* (1963), and William Ashbrook, *Donizetti* (1965), both containing numerous documents, lists of works, and librettos. Donizetti's place in early-19th-century music is discussed in Alfred Einstein, *Music in the Romantic Era* (1947), and Donald J. Grout, *A Short History of Opera* (2 vols., 1947; 2d ed. 1965). □

John Donne

John Donne (1572-1631), English metaphysical poet, Anglican divine, and pulpit orator, is ranked with Milton as one of the greatest English poets. He is also a supreme artist in sermons and devotional prose.

John Donne's masculine, ingenious style is characterized by abrupt openings, paradoxes, dislocations, argumentative structure, and "conceits"—images which yoke things seemingly unlike. These features in combination with his frequent dramatic or everyday speech rhythms, his tense syntax, and his tough eloquence were both a reaction against the smoothness of conventional Elizabethan poetry and an adaptation into English of European baroque and mannerist techniques. Since Donne's times such poetry has been unaptly called "metaphysical"—a term more appropriate for the philosophical verse of Lucretius.

Son of a prosperous ironmonger of Welsh ancestry, Donne was born between Jan. 4 and June 19, 1572, and was bred a Londoner and a Roman Catholic. His mother, a great niece of Sir (later St.) Thomas More, came from a cultured, devout family: her father, John Heywood, wrote interludes; her brother Jasper was a Jesuit; and her son Henry, John's brother, died in 1593 of a fever caught in Newgate Prison, where he was incarcerated for harboring a Roman Catholic priest. Donne's father died when John was 4, and his mother married a prominent physician.

His Poetry

After some years at Oxford (from 1584) and possibly Cambridge, Donne studied law at Lincoln's Inn (1592-1594) and became one of the first to write in English formal verse satires in the classical mode. It was also in the 1590s that he wrote many of his amatory poems. Most of them are dramatic monologues expressive of attitudes toward love, ranging from cynical fleshly realism to platonic idealism. It is sounder to see them not as autobiographical but as exposing the extremes of carnal and spiritual love and as putting in a favorable light love in which they are complementary. He also composed verse letters, elegies, epithalamia, and epigrams; they were published after his death as *Songs and Sonnets.*

Donne partook in the Earl of Essex's expeditions against the Spanish in Cadiz and the Azores in 1596-1597 and reflected this military experience in his poems "The Storm" and "The Calm." By 1597-1598, when he became secretary to Sir Thomas Egerton, the lord keeper, he had dissociated himself from Roman Catholicism. In 1601 he blasted the promise of a successful career by secretly marrying Lady

Egerton's niece, Ann More. He was dismissed from his post and temporarily imprisoned, and for about a decade he and his ever-increasing family were largely dependent on relatives and patrons.

During this middle period Donne wrote *Biathanatos,* a treatise on instances of justifiable suicide which may have been intended as a satire on casuistry; it was published by his son in 1646. His *Pseudo-Martyr* (1610) accused Roman Catholics of fostering false martyrdom for secular ends. *Ignatius His Conclave* (1611) was popular in both English and Latin versions: it brilliantly satirized the Jesuits but is interesting today because it reflects the then new astronomy of Galileo and toys with the notion of colonizing the moon.

Donne continued to write secular poems and, about 1609-1610, a powerful series of "Holy Sonnets," in which he meditated on sickness, death, sin, and the love of God. In 1611 he composed two companion poems, *The Anniversaries,* on the Idea of woman, the decay of the physical universe, the vanity of this world, and, in contrast, the permanence of God and spiritual values. These commemorated the death of little Elizabeth Drury and won him the patronage of her father, with whom Donne traveled to France and Germany. He briefly served as a member of Parliament in 1601 and again in 1614.

Church Career

About 1606 Thomas Morton offered Donne a benefice if he would take Anglican orders. But it was not until 1615, after long pious and practical hesitations, that he was ordained a priest. Appointed a royal chaplain in the same year, he also received a doctor of divinity degree from Cambridge. In 1616-1622 he was reader in divinity at Lincoln's Inn, where he preached regularly. He was desolated in 1617 by the death of his wife: she had borne him 12 children, 5 of whom died. He preached frequently at court and in 1619 was an embassy chaplain in Germany. In 1621, on James I's nomination, he became dean of St. Paul's Cathedral, attracting huge congregations with his brilliant oratory. A serious illness in 1623 gave rise to his *Devotions,* those moving meditations on sickness, death, and salvation from which Ernest Hemingway derived the title *For Whom the Bell Tolls.*

On Feb. 25, 1631, Donne left his sickbed to preach his last and most famous sermon, "Death's Duel." On March 31 he died. An effigy of him wrapped in funeral shrouds which survived the burning of St. Paul's in the Great Fire of 1666 is preserved in the present cathedral, built by Sir Christopher Wren. The effigy is that of an old, seasoned man who has thought and suffered greatly but has achieved some peace of soul. His youthful portraits show black hair, clear skin, intense eyes, an ample brow, and a pointed, bearded chin. His later pictures reveal the same intensity and alertness.

His Character

Donne's was a complex personality, an unusual blend of passion, zeal, and brilliance; God and women were his favorite themes, but his subject matter otherwise ranged over the pagan and the pious, the familiar and the esoteric, the cynical and the sincere, the wittily bright and the theologically profound.

Largely because of Izaak Walton's charming but somewhat unreliable *Life of Dr. John Donne* (1681) and because of the risqué elements in Donne's secular poetry, a myth grew up contrasting a youthful Jack Donne the rake with a pious and repentant Dr. John Donne, Dean of St. Paul's. That in his younger days he was an attractive conversationalist, socialite, and courtier is undeniable, but his works reveal that he was always a serious student and a seeker after truth; and there is no sound evidence to support the myth. Certainly after his ordination he dedicated his remarkable genius wholeheartedly to the service of God and thus became one of the most brilliant stars in that hierarchy of extraordinary Anglican priests—among them, Robert Herrick, George Herbert, and Robert Burton—whose exceptional literary genius was dedicated to the glory of God and the welfare of man.

Further Reading

Biographies of Donne written before 1960 are unreliable. Robert C. Bald's definitive *John Donne: A Life* (1970) supersedes all previous biographies. The frequently reprinted work by Izaak Walton, *Life of Dr. John Donne* (many editions) should be read as great literature, more imaginative than accurate. Edward LeComte, *Grace to a Witty Sinner: A Life of Donne* (1964), is written for the general reader.

Among the studies of Donne's work, K. W. Gransden's concise *John Donne* (1954; rev. ed. 1969) and Frank Kermode, *John Donne* (1957), are introductions for beginners. James B. Leishman, *The Monarch of Wit* (1951; 6th ed. 1962), and Clay Hunt, *Donne's Poetry* (1954), provide solid foundations for interpreting the poems. Arnold Stein, *John Donne's Lyrics* (1962), emphasizes Donne's style and wit. Varied approaches are collected in Helen Gardner, ed., *John Donne* (1962), and Leonard Unger further illuminates such approaches in *Donne's Poetry and Modern Criticism* (1950). Judah Stampfer, *John Donne and the Metaphysical Gesture* (1970), is impressionistic but stimulating. Far more reliable is Donald L. Guss, *John Donne, Petrarchist* (1966), which relates *Songs and Sonnets* to their Italian influences; N. J. C. Andreasen, *John Donne, Conservative Revolutionary* (1967), also relates the poetry to tradition. Evelyn M. Simpson, *A Study of the Prose Works* (1924; 2d ed. 1948), is fundamental. Also excellent are William R. Mueller, *John Donne, Preacher* (1962), and Joan Webber, *Contrary Music: The Prose Style of John Donne* (1963). For the scientific background, Charles M. Coffin, *John Donne and the New Philosophy* (1937), and Marjorie Hope Nicolson, *The Breaking of the Circle* (1950; rev. ed. 1960), still have value. Wilbur Sanders, *John Donne's Poetry* (1971), is a judicious survey. Among the more general works relating to Donne are George Williamson, *The Donne Tradition* (1930); Helen C. White, *The Metaphysical Poets* (1936); Joseph E. Duncan, *The Revival of Metaphysical Poetry* (1959); and, of outstanding importance, Douglas Bush, *English Literature in the Earlier Seventeenth Century* (1945; rev. ed. 1962), and Louis L. Martz, *The Poetry of Meditation* (1954; rev. ed. 1962). □

Ignatius Donnelly

Ignatius Donnelly (1831-1901) was an American politician, reformer, and author. He was an outstanding spokesperson for the political reform movements of the second half of the 19th century that culminated in the Populist revolt.

Born in Pennsylvania of Irish parents, Ignatius Donnelly attended the free public schools and read law in Philadelphia. Interested in real estate promotion, he moved to Minnesota in 1856 and established the *Emigrant Aid Journal* to promote settlement. The Panic of 1857 destroyed his projected ideal community and his fortune but not his optimism. He returned to practicing law and entered politics to help promote the organization of the Republican party.

Elected lieutenant governor of Minnesota in 1859, Donnelly was a tireless and fighting politician. He served three terms in the House of Representatives (1863-1869), where he strongly supported the Civil War and Reconstruction programs of the Republican party. In advocating the interests of the Northwest, chiefly land grants for railroad construction, he evoked the ire of economy-minded congressmen.

As the Republican party moved toward conservatism, Donnelly joined the protesters in the Liberal Republicans, the Grangers, and the Greenbackers successively. Serving in the Minnesota Senate (1874-1879), he crusaded for reforms to aid the underprivileged and published a weekly newspaper, the *Anti-Monopolist*. When his attempt to return to Congress was blocked in 1878 he abandoned politics for writing.

Capitalizing on the popular interest in science fiction, Donnelly's first book, *Atlantis: The Antediluvian World* (1882), attempted to demonstrate the existence of Plato's fabled island Atlantis. *Ragnarok: The Age of Fire and Gravel* (1883) followed. *The Great Cryptogram* (1888) tried to prove that Francis Bacon was the author of Shakespeare's plays.

After another unsuccessful bid for Congress in 1884, Donnelly became active in the Farmers' Alliance and was returned to the Minnesota Senate in 1887. In 1890 he wrote *Caesar's Column: A Story of the Twentieth Century*, painting a graphic picture of the potential horrors of life in the United States in the coming century, yet closing with a statement of what might be achieved through reform. The book was widely read. As president of the Farmers' Alliance in Minnesota, Donnelly was actively involved in the establishment of the Populist, or People's, Party. Presiding officer in caucus and conventions and author of the challenging preamble to the party's 1892 platform, he was among the Populists' foremost leaders.

Four years later Donnelly reluctantly followed the leadership of William Jennings Bryan, but he soon concluded that the fusion of the Populists with the Democrats on the free-silver issue was a betrayal of broader reforms. Donnelly ran for the vice presidency on the Populist ticket in 1900.

Late in life Donnelly married his second wife, his 21-year-old stenographer, who assisted him in publishing a newspaper, the *Representative*. He died on Jan. 1, 1901. His biographer rightly asserts that Donnelly was the hero of the Populist movement, his name synonymous with reform, a true rebel who was never without a feeling of alienation.

Further Reading

The major full-length biography of Donnelly is the excellent volume by Martin Ridge, *Ignatius Donnelly: The Portrait of a Politician* (1962). John D. Hicks published scholarly interpretations of Donnelly's life in *The Populist Revolt: A History of the Farmers' Alliance and the People's Party* (1931) and in numerous articles, the last of which is in John A. Garraty, ed., *The Unforgettable Americans* (1960). Popular interpretations of Donnelly's career are numerous and include those of Stewart H. Holbrook in *Dreamers of the American Dream* (1957) and Gerald W. Johnson in *The Lunatic Fringe* (1957).

Additional Sources

Anderson, David D., *Ignatius Donnelly*, Boston: Twayne Publishers, 1980.

Ridge, Martin, *Ignatius Donnelly: the portrait of a politician*, St. Paul: Minnesota Historical Society Press, 1991. ☐

Georg Raphael Donner

The Austrian sculptor Georg Raphael Donner (1693-1741) was the first exponent of classicism in 18th-century Austria and the greatest sculptor of the period.

Georg Raphael Donner was born in Esslingen, Lower Austria, on May 24, 1693, the son of a carpenter. After studying with Johann Kaspar Prenner, a goldsmith to the imperial court in Vienna, Donner was apprenticed at the age of 13 to the sculptor Giovanni Giuliani to assist on statuary for the Liechtenstein Palace in Vienna. Donner worked mainly in Vienna and Pressburg (modern Bratislava, Slovakia). His sculptures are largely in marble and bronze, but he early developed a fondness for lead; the soft sheen of the material was well suited to his characteristic smooth modeling, firm outlines, and gracefully elongated figures, based on his obvious study of 16th century Italian sculpture, whose manneristic qualities he blended with classical ideals in a highly individual harmony.

In 1725 Donner worked with his assistants in Salzburg on sculpture for the famous staircase in Mirabell Palace. Donner personally executed the figure *Paris* (1726). While in Salzburg he also did some work for the local mint, producing ducats with portraits and coats of arms of the prince-Bishop. In 1728 the primate of Hungary, Prince-Bishop Emre Esterhazy, called Donner to his court in Pressburg, where in the Cathedral, he carved the sculpture of the high altar of the chapel of St. Elemosynarius (1732). This chapel also contains the prelate's tomb, for which Donner carved the highly expressive kneeling figure of the primate. He also made the equestrian statue *St. Martin and the Beggar* for the high altar of the Cathedral (1735), an over-life-sized lead sculpture combining classicistic clarity with touches of realism, for the warrior saint wears an 18th-century hussar's uniform rather than classical dress. The marble statue *Emperor Charles VI* (1734) reveals the baroque qualities underlying Donner's classicism in the momentary pose of the Emperor.

Donner's most famous work is the Providentia Fountain on the Neue Markt in Vienna. Unveiled in 1739, the lead figures were replaced by bronze copies in 1873, and the originals are now in the Baroque Museum, Vienna. The figures of the four rivers on the fountain are prime examples of his debt to the late Renaissance and of his naturalistic tendencies. He also carved reliefs for the Viennese mint and cast in bronze the Andromeda Fountain in the courtyard of the Vienna city hall (now Altes Rathaus). His last important work is the moving Pietà in the Cathedral of Gurk (1741). Donner died on Feb. 15, 1741, in Vienna, where his pupils and his brother Mathias continued to work in his style until late in the century.

Further Reading

Donner's work is discussed in Nicolas Powell, *From Baroque to Rococo* (1959), and Eberhard Hempel, *Baroque Art and Ar-* chitecture in Central Europe (1965). The only monograph on Donner is in German, C. Blauensteiner, *Georg Raphael Donner* (1947); it contains excellent photographs. □

José Donoso

José Donoso (1924-1996) was one of Chile's most distinguished and widely read authors. His novels especially brought him international fame.

José Donoso was born on October 5, 1924, in Santiago, Chile, into a well-to-do family of lawyers and doctors. As a child he attended the "The Grange," an English day school where he remained for a decade and learned English well. He was a rebellious student, hating school work and compulsory sports, and, according to his own account, "this collective experience may have determined my lifelong incapacity to belong to groups of any kind—political, social or recreational."

Restless Youth Found His Passion

As a youth, he dropped out of school, traveled about to various places in Chile and abroad, and finally went back to finish his education at the University of Chile. There he won a two year scholarship to Princeton University, where he took a B.A. in 1951 and where he published his first two stories—in English—in the campus literary magazine.

After returning to Chile in 1952 Donoso held a series of teaching jobs while continuing to write stories. His first book of short stories, *Summer Vacation* (*Veraneo*), appeared in 1955 and received considerable critical notice. In 1962 he was awarded the William Faulkner Foundation Prize for Chile for his first novel, *Coronation* (*Coronación*, 1957; English translation, 1965).

Success Came Early

Donoso's fame was assured after *Coronation* appeared. This novel describes a family of Santiago's aristocratic society fallen into decay. A 90-ish grandmother rules in her imposing Victorian mansion over the remnants of her family—mainly her weakling grandson—and a bevy of servants. The book is filled with grotesque figures and situations, a constant in Donoso's work. Though the satire of upper class life seems cruel at times, Donoso also wrote of his characters with compassion and humor.

In 1960 Donoso brought out another collection of fine stories, *The Charleston* (*El Charleston*), dedicated to the young lady from Bolivia to whom he had been engaged for some time. The following year they finally married. The reader of the tales in *El Charleston* will probably be fascinated by all the frustrations and the dark world of passions portrayed in them, especially among members of the Chilean upper middle class, and also by the contrast with understatement found in the British style of Jane Austen or Henry James.

Mastered Dark Surrealism and Social Satire

During 1965-1967 Donoso taught creative writing at the Writers' Workshop at the University of Iowa, and in 1967 he moved to Spain where his only child, a daughter, was born. His second and third novels, *This Sunday* (*Este domingo*, 1966) and *Place without Limits* (*Ellugar sin límites*, 1967), were published in quick succession. *This Sunday* contains some lively, vivid characters, and the dramatic conflicts within them and between them sharpen the reader's interest. Especially noteworthy is the young narrator's grandmother Chepa, a wealthy society lady who devotes herself to charities and the poor, and Maya, a bum who is the chief recipient of her benevolence. The relationships between these two and other members of the narrator's family are complicated and filled with repressed violence which finally bursts out, bringing them to a tragic ending. As in *Coronation* and in his stories, houses and other inanimate things take on life under Donoso's powerfully descriptive pen. Symbols abound and sensations are stressed—for example, the long opening scene describes the delicious smells wafted through the house by Violeta's Sunday dinner meat pies, and these *empanadas* recur as a motif throughout the book.

"Madness" Became Reality

For a number of years Donoso and his family lived in Spain (Madrid, Mallorca, near Barcelona), and in this latter city his most ambitious novel, *The Obscene Bird of Night* (*El obsceno pájaro de la noche*), was published in 1970. While he was writing this lengthy book, which took several years to accomplish, Donoso confessed that he passed through spells of "madness"—paranoia, hallucinations, split personality, and suicide attempts. He had been prone to imaginary illness since childhood when he had pretended to have stomach aches when he didn't want to go to school and he fooled his doctor father who diagnosed appendicitis. In adult life he was plagued by psychosomatic illness, and his imagined ulcers became real.

The Obscene Bird of Night, with its catchy title—a phrase Donoso found in a letter written by Henry James, Sr. to his sons—is undoubtedly a masterpiece. This sprawling, obscure, fascinating, imaginative, 540-page novel is concerned with large problems of identity, the losing of oneself in a plurality of masks. The leading character, Humberto Peñaloza, goes through all kinds of character changes, real or imaginary. The first of these changes is motivated by the insignificance of his lowly social origins in Chilean society and his intense wish to be somebody. Later he is moved by his own feelings of inadequacy or frustration and strong desires for self-destruction. There is one long fantastic section of the novel devoted entirely to depicting a world of real physical monsters, where normal intruders become the monsters. The plot and structure, though carefully ordered, seem chaotic. *The Bird* reminds us of the distorted world of Goya's dark period and the nightmarish quality of Bosch's paintings, such as "The Seven Deadly Sins." It evokes a world filled with terror and dreams, myth and legend, at the same time that it dissects various levels of society with a sharp eye.

After *The Bird,* Donoso continued to turn out novels, including *Country House* (*Casa de campo*, 1978) and *The Garden Next Door* (*El jardín de al lado*, 1981) and shorter pieces of fiction, such as *Three Bourgeois Novelettes* (*Tres novelitas burguesas*, 1973) and the erotic novel *The Mysterious Disappearance of the Marquise of Loria* (*La misteriosa desaparición de la Marquesita de Loria*, 1980).

Returned From Exile

About 1980 Donoso returned to his homeland of Chile. Interviewed years later by Fernando Ainsa for the *UNESCO Courier* (1994), Donoso spoke of exile, his own as well as the literary theme of exile, "Wherever people go, whatever they do, they take their homeland, their home town, with them, and there is no way of going into voluntary exile from one's own self, whatever some people may think or claim to the contrary. The primary reason why I returned to Chile was homesickness, which gets worse as one gets older. . . ." Donoso reflected this philosophy in *The Garden Next Door* (1981), which conveyed a strong theme of exile, and in *Despair* (*Desesperanza*, 1986), which revolved around the theme of homecoming.

He also felt that he could make a larger contribution to society and the literary world writing from his homeland. The 1980s and 1990s, he felt, were a time when writers abandoned their desire to prescribe remedies for the world's ills, and instead focused on interpreting individual life stories. Author of numerous critically acclaimed works during this period, Donoso was awarded Chile's Premio Nacional in 1990.

Among his later novels were:*Curfew, Taratuta and Still Life with Pipe: Two Novellas* (*Taratuta. Naturaleza muerta con cachimba* (1990), *Hell Has No Limits,* and *Cuatro para Delfina* (1982). Throughout his writing the reader is aware of layer upon layer of "wrappings" around his characters' identities, so much so that some critics believe that the imposed masks or disguises become the character's identity. Donoso died of cancer in 1996 at the age of 72.

Further Reading

Donoso is listed in various guides, such as *The Oxford Companion to Spanish Literature* (1978) and D. W. Foster and V. R. Foster, editors, *Modern Latin American Literature* (1975). The journal *Review* devoted to Latin American literature and printed entirely in English focused a large part of its fall 1973 issue on Donoso and his novel *The Bird,* including a chronology of his life and works by the author himself. Briefer sketches in English appear in standard anthologies of Latin American literature, as well as articles in periodicals such as:*New York Times* (December 9, 1996), *Hispanic Review* (Summer 1994), and *UNESCO Courier* (July 1994), and *World Literature Today* (Summer 1993). □

Hilda Doolittle

The American poet, translator, and novelist Hilda Doolittle (1886-1961), generally called H. D., was an imagist whose lyric art conveys intense feelings through sharp images and "free" forms.

Hilda Doolittle was born on Sept. 10, 1886, in Bethlehem, Pa.; her father was a professor. She entered Bryn Mawr College in 1904. She had met Ezra Pound in 1901, and in 1905, while he was studying at the University of Pennsylvania, he introduced her to William Carlos Williams, then a medical school student at the university. She quit school in 1906 because of ill health. During the next 5 years she studied Greek and Latin literature, tried Latin translation, and wrote a few poems. By 1911 the apprenticeship of this tall young woman, attractive in a long-faced, large-eyed way, was nearly over.

Doolittle toured Europe and stayed on in London, where Pound took her under his wing. She and Richard Aldington found a common interest in carrying over into English the spare beauty of Greek art and literature. Pound called them *Imagistes,* thus creating a new literary movement based on common speech, the exact word, new rhythms, absolute freedom in choosing subjects, clarity, and concentration. Pound helped both poets get published, persuading Doolittle in 1913 to sign herself "H. D., Imagiste." (H. D. remained perhaps the only faithful imagist, less out of decision than because her natural way of writing simply coincided with Pound's program.)

H. D. married Aldington in 1913. In 1916 he left for World War I front lines, and she issued her first volume, *Sea Garden,* also succeeding him as literary editor of the *Egoist.* A year later she resigned because of poor health and was replaced by T. S. Eliot. The anxieties of the war, a miscarriage, and her husband's infidelity overwhelmed her. In 1919, pregnant, ill with pneumonia, and saddened by the death of her father, she separated from Aldington and later had a daughter, Perdita.

Winifred Ellerman, a wealthy novelist-to-be known as "Bryher," became H. D.'s friend and benefactor. They settled in neighboring houses in a Swiss village in 1923. Thereafter H. D. lived either in Switzerland or in London. Meanwhile she issued *Hymen* (1921) and *Heliodora* (1924). *Collected Poems* (1925) established her place in modern poetry. "Helen" and the more sustained lament "Islands" are representative selections.

H. D.'s first novel, *Palimpsest* (1926), deals with the trials of sensitive women and artists in a harsh world. Her second novel was *Hedylus* (1928). In 1927 she published a verse play, *Hippolytus Temporizes.* A new volume of poems, *Red Roses from Bronze* (1931), and *The Hedgehog* (1936), prose fiction, like her early volumes contained choruses translated from Greek plays. Her most ambitious translation was *Euripides' Ion* (1937). The following year she divorced Aldington.

H. D. was in London during World War II. *By Avon River* (1949) deals with Shakespeare and Elizabethan and Jacobean writers. *Tribute to Freud* (1956) records her gratitude for her psychoanalysis. Her novel *Bid Me to Live* (1960) is an account of a situation that approximates her marital breakup. Her most ambitious work, *Helen in Egypt* (1961), concludes that perfect love can be found only in death. She died that year in Switzerland.

In all of H. D.'s poetry, discrete colors and forms, frugal rhythms, focused emotions, and clarity of thought suggest a Greek miniaturist or, in longer works, a Japanese scroll painter.

Further Reading

There are two full-length studies of Hilda Doolittle: Thomas B. Swann, *The Classical World of H. D.* (1962), and Vincent Quinn, *H. D.* (1968). Biographical material is also available in the autobiographies of Richard Aldington, *Life for Life's Sake* (1941), and Bryher (pseudonym of Winifred Ellerman), *The Heart to Artemis: A Writer's Memoirs* (1962). Stanley K. Coffman, *Imagism: A Chapter for the History of Modern Poetry* (1951), discusses the movement of which H. D. seems the best representative. □

James Harold Doolittle

James Harold Doolittle (1896-1993) was a pilot who set two early transcontinental flying time records, pioneered advancements in aviation, led the Tokyo raid in 1942, and commanded the Eighth Air Force attack on Germany.

James Harold Doolittle was born in Alameda, California, on December 14, 1896, the only child of Frank, a carpenter, and Rosa Shephard Doolittle. Most of his youth was spent in Nome, Alaska, and Los Angeles, where he graduated from Manual Arts High School in 1914. Delicate as a child and small of stature, Doolittle nevertheless developed a love of adventure and a scrappy disposition, taking up motorbike riding and boxing as he grew older. His enthusiasm for homemade gliders developed into a lifelong commitment to aviation.

After two years at Los Angeles Junior College, Doolittle enrolled at the University of California at Berkeley to study mining engineering. He never completed his studies (several years later he was awarded a bachelor's degree, however), for in September 1917 he enrolled in the Signal Corps of the U.S. Army hoping to become a pilot. He was commissioned a second lieutenant on March 9, 1918. A few months earlier he had married Josephine "Joe" Daniels. They had two sons.

Service as an Army Pilot

Doolittle saw no overseas duty during World War I, but remained in the service after the war ended and received a first lieutenant's commission in the Regular Army in 1920. A member of Billy Mitchell's team during the controversial bomber versus battleship tests of 1921, Doolittle himself emerged as a public figure in 1922 when he flew from Pablo Beach (near Jacksonville), Florida, to San Diego in less than 22 hours flying time, the first to span the continent in less

than 24 hours. Nine years later, in the course of winning the Bendix Trophy race, he recorded the first transcontinental flying time of less than 12 hours. Doolittle, however, was much more than the daredevil aviator he was reputed to be, for at bottom he believed that one took chances in the air for a serious purpose: to further the usefulness of aviation. Selected to be one of the first participants in the army's new program in aeronautical engineering, he received a doctorate from Massachusetts Institute of Technology in 1925.

During the 1920s and early 1930s Doolittle, both as a student and as a pilot, made several important contributions to the advancement of aviation. Besides the two transcontinental speed records he established, he set additional speed records and in various ways added to the understanding of acceleration's effects. He became the first North American to fly across the Andes; and, perhaps most important, after further studies and research at the Full Flight Laboratory he made the first blind flight and landing on September 24, 1929. Doolittle's participation in the development and use of instruments such as the Sperry artificial horizon would do much to increase the safety of flying, enabling it to take place in varying weather conditions.

Given a major's rank in the reserves, Doolittle left active military service to join the Shell Oil Company in 1930. With his mother and mother-in-law in need of special medical attention he felt he needed the higher income he could earn in private industry. He did promotional and sales work for Shell and on occasion for Curtiss-Wright throughout the 1930s. Although he gave up racing in 1932, believing that after several close calls he had used up his luck, he remained active as a pilot.

World War II Hero

With the start of World War II in Europe, Doolittle asked his long-time friend, General Henry "Hap" Arnold, who was now chief of the Army Air Corps, to return him to active duty. On July 1, 1940, Doolittle re-entered uniformed service as a major assigned to straighten out aircraft production bottlenecks. After America's entry into the war he sought combat duty but instead was attached to Arnold's staff with the rank of lieutenant colonel. This new position ultimately involved him in one of the war's most daring achievements—the April 1942 bombing of Tokyo.

The idea of avenging Pearl Harbor by bombing Japan itself had originated in the highest echelons of the navy, but accomplishing it posed a dilemma. The weakened American navy could not allow an aircraft carrier to approach within 400 miles of Japan, lest it be exposed to attack by shore-based Japanese planes. Nor did any standard American carrier plane of the time have the range to fly that distance with a bomb load and continue on to landing fields in China. Implementation of the plan therefore depended on using the Army Air Corps' new two engine B-25 bomber.

Doolittle was put in charge of the intensive training required in flying such a large plane from the deck of a carrier—there was no possibility of landing on the carrier after completion of the mission—and managed to talk Arnold into letting him lead the attack itself. On April 18, 1942, the 16 planes he commanded flew from the carrier *Hornet* to bomb assorted targets in Tokyo and a few other Japanese cities and then on to landings in China. Although none of the planes landed intact in China, all but two of the crews reached safety. While some have considered the Doolittle raid, as it became known, strategically unsound in terms of the negligible damage it could inflict upon Japan, it was soon immortalized in the book and film *Thirty Seconds over Tokyo* and undeniably raised American morale while causing concern to the Japanese.

Doolittle was given a rare double promotion to brigadier general and then was awarded the Congressional Medal of Honor in a White House ceremony. He was sent to Europe to command Dwight Eisenhower's air units during the planned invasion of North Africa, after which Doolittle was promoted to major general. He had been coolly received by Eisenhower, but gradually won his commander's confidence and stayed with him throughout the remainder of World War II in Europe, in succession serving as commander of the Twelfth Air Force in North Africa (1942-1943), the Northwest African Strategic Air Forces, the Fifteenth Air Force during the Mediterranean campaigns of 1943, and, finally, from January 1944, of the Eighth Air Force based in England.

In his early commands Doolittle, who often flew missions himself, had been obliged to develop effective air forces, but the Eighth had already been built into a successful unit by its previous commander, Lieutenant General Ira Eaker. Nevertheless, Doolittle profited from the advent of more and better planes, particularly the P-51 fighter which

allowed his forces to achieve air superiority over the heart of Germany itself. A firm believer in strategic bombing, Doolittle commanded the Eighth Air Force during its greatest successes: the first American bombing of Berlin, the sustained bombing campaigns against Germany's oil industry and various manufacturing and rail facilities, and finally the virtual destruction of the Luftwaffe, the German air force.

End of the War

With the end of the war in Europe Doolittle was ordered to Okinawa to establish with new planes and personnel what would in effect be a new Eighth Air Force, but Japan surrendered before it became operational. At 49 Doolittle was the youngest lieutenant general in U.S. service and the only reservist to reach that rank (1944). Believing that he was not the right man to serve in a postwar air force due for retrenchment, Doolittle returned to reserve status in 1946 and resumed work for Shell. He remained a Shell vice president until 1958, taking occasional leave to do public service both for the Air Force and for various government bodies, among them a special board that President Truman named to report on airport safety and location.

After he left Shell, Doolittle settled in Santa Monica, California, served until 1961 as board chairman of the aerospace division of TRW, then joined Mutual of Omaha. He had given up flying in 1961. Although much of Doolittle's career was spent in civilian pursuits, he will always be remembered for his pioneering achievements in aviation in the 1920s, for his successful command of the Eighth Air Force, and particularly for his leadership of the Tokyo raid in April 1942. Doolittle, recalled Arnold, "was fearless, technically brilliant, a leader who not only could be counted upon to do a task himself if it were humanly possible, but could impart his spirit to others."

Presidential Honors

Doolittle's contributions were recognized and honored by Presidents Ronald Reagan and George Bush. In Reagan's Farewell Address to the American People (1989) he said, "We've got to teach history based on not what's in fashion, but what's important: Why the pilgrims came here, who Jimmy Doolittle was, and what those 30 seconds over Tokyo meant." Later the same year, Doolittle was awarded the Presidential Medal of Freedom by President Bush.

He died on September 27, 1993, at his son's home in Pebble Beach, California, following a stroke earlier that month.

Further Reading

The best introductions to Doolittle's fascinating life are two biographies: Carroll V. Glines, *Jimmy Doolittle, Daredevil Aviator and Scientist* (1972) and Lowell Thomas and Edward Jablonski, *Doolittle: A Biography* (1976). Some of the many changes that took place in aviation during Doolittle's years as a test pilot are related in Harry F. Guggenheim, *The Seven Skies* (1930). Doolittle's World War II exploits can be studied in many places, among them: H. H. Arnold, *Global Mission* (1949); W. F. Craven and J. L. Cate, editors, *The Army Air Forces in World War II* (1948-1958, 7 vol.); Roger Freeman, *The Mighty Eighth* (1970); Carroll V. Glines, *Doolittle's Tokyo*

Raiders (1964); Ted Lawson (Robert Considine, editor), *Thirty Seconds over Tokyo* (1943); and James M. Merrill, *Target Tokyo* (1964). A brief description of his aviation accomplishments can be found at the A&E Biography Web site on the Internet at http://www.biography.com (August 4, 1997). □

Rheta Childe Dorr

Rheta Childe Dorr (1868–1948) was a member of the National Woman Suffrage Association. Her work as a journalist was not widely accepted as proper woman's work. She fought hard for women's suffrage.

As a child in Nebraska, Rheta Childe routinely disobeyed her parents. At age twelve she sneaked out of the house to attend a women's rights rally led by Elizabeth Cady Stanton and Susan B. Anthony. Her parents found out when the newspaper printed the names of those who had joined the National Woman Suffrage Association. She began working at the age of fifteen, over the objections of her parents, so that she could become independent and prove her industry. She was conservative by nature but became a rebel upon viewing a tombstone inscribed "Also Harriet, wife of the above."

Self-Expression

In 1890 Childe went to New York City to study at the Art Students' League and decided that she would become a writer. When John Pixley Dorr, a man twenty years older than she, visited from Lincoln, they fell in love and were soon married. She was swept away by his good looks and love of books. They lived in Seattle for two years, where their son Julian was born. Rheta wrote articles for the New York newspapers, which her husband found to be an unacceptable activity. They soon parted by mutual consent, and Rhea returned to New York with their young son, determined to make a living as a journalist.

Cads and Editors

Dorr was shocked at how she was treated in New York City. Editors would not put her on the staff simply because she was a woman, and when she complained that the rates they paid for freelance articles could not support a family, they said they could find other women to work for those rates. She finally got a break by persuading Theodore Roosevelt to be photographed (something he hated) and was rewarded with an ill-paying job on the *New York Evening Post,* which she left within a year. Her first overseas assignment was to cover the coronation of a new king in Norway, and on the way back she attended the International Woman Suffrage Alliance meeting in Copenhagen, where she met prominent British suffragists.

"The Woman's Invasion"

Returning to New York almost penniless, Dorr resolved to be done with the society pages that passed for women's journalism. She proposed to the editor of *Everybody's* that she go underground as a worker and write about her experiences. She spent a year working in a laundry, a department store, on an assembly line, and as a seamstress but was often too exhausted to do more than make notes about her experiences. A cowriter named William Hard was assigned to help her, but Dorr resisted giving her notes over to him. She was shocked to see the magazine begin a series with her title, ideas, and experiences but with the byline of William Hard. She hired a lawyer and at least prevented the publication of a book by Hard exploiting her work.

International Suffrage

In 1910, with the assistance of *Hampton's Magazine,* Dorr published *What Eight Million Women Want,* an account of suffrage clubs, trade unions, and consumer leagues that had sprung up all over Europe and the United States. In 1912 she went to Sweden, Germany, and England to interview leaders in the women's movement, and she spent the winter of 1912-1913 in Paris assisting British suffragist Emmeline Pankhurst in writing Pankhurst's autobiography, *My Own Story.* When she returned to the United States, she went to work for the *New York Evening Mail* and wrote a daily column, "As a Woman Sees It." Not everyone was moved by her arguments: interviewing Woodrow Wilson in 1914, she asked him about woman's suffrage. He replied, "I think that it is not proper for me to stand here and be cross-examined by you."

The Russian Revolution

Having twice been to Russia, Dorr was anxious to observe the 1917 revolution. One night she lay in her hotel bed listening to the murder of a general in the next room. When she tried to leave the country after five months, all of her notes were confiscated by the authorities so she wrote *Inside the Russian Revolution* (1917) entirely from memory. In her opinion, Russia had become "a barbarous and half-insane land. . . . Oratory held the stupid populace spellbound while the Germans invaded the country, boosted Lenin into power and paved the way for the treaty of Brest-Litovsk. . . . Russia was done."

War Correspondence

Since her son Julian was serving in the army in France, she asked editors to send her back to Europe. When the French government refused to grant her press credentials because she was a woman, she signed on as a lecturer with the YMCA. She walked into a mess tent where her son was eating. Astonished, he cried, "Mother!" and no soldier would sit down until she found a chair. Mothers were unquestioningly better received than female war correspondents. Later Dorr covered the Women's Death Battalion in Russia and described an incident in which fellow soldiers broke into their barracks in order to rape them but were held off by the women at gunpoint. In addition to her many wartime articles, she also wrote *A Soldier's Mother in France* (1918) for women on the home front. Dorr, along with Louise Bryant, Mary Roberts Rinehart, and Bessie Beattie, pioneered the way for women to become war correspondents. After spending many more years in Europe, and writing more books, including her autobiography, *A Woman of Fifty,* Dorr died in Bucks County, Pennsylvania, in 1948 at age eighty. □

John Roderigo Dos Passos

The reputation of the American novelist John Roderigo Dos Passos (1896-1970) is based chiefly on his early work, especially the trilogy "U.S.A."

John Dos Passos was born in Chicago on Jan. 14, 1896, the illegitimate son of a noted New York lawyer, John Randolph Dos Passos, and a wealthy Virginian, Lucy Addison Sprigg. His father did not acknowledge paternity until a year before his death, when the young Dos Passos was 20. As a boy, Dos Passos lived principally on the Virginia farm of his mother's family, and he also traveled frequently with his mother to Mexico, Belgium, and England.

Dos Passos attended Choate School under the name John Roderigo Madison. He graduated from Harvard in 1916, meanwhile publishing stories, verse, and reviews in the Harvard *Monthly*.

In 1917 Dos Passos was in Spain, studying Spanish culture. During World War I he enlisted in the Norton-Harjes Ambulance Unit and served in Spain and Italy. In 1918 he became a private in the U.S. Medical Corps, serving in France. Demobilized in 1919, he remained in Europe to finish two novels: *One Man's Initiation—1917* (1920) and *Three Soldiers* (1921). During the 1920s Dos Passos worked as a newspaper correspondent and traveled extensively but, as an increasingly successful author, he lived chiefly in New York.

First Novels

One Man's Initiation—1917, based on Dos Passos' experiences as an ambulance corpsman, is poignantly antiwar. It also foreshadows a more pervasive theme of his work: contemporary technological society's crippling effects on its inhabitants.

Dos Passos' first significant novel, *Three Soldiers,* is a bitterly ironic commentary on the professed ideals for which World War I was fought and, more deeply, on the "values" by which modern, mechanized man lives. Dos Passos sees the real enemy as the army itself, which by exacerbating the ordinary weaknesses and inner conflicts of its members causes irreparable harm. His three major characters are entirely broken by army life. *Three Soldiers* is part of an anti-World War I literary tradition that includes works by Ernest Hemingway, Robert Graves, E. E. Cummings, William Faulkner, and Erich Maria Remarque.

Literary Experiment

Manhattan Transfer (1925) is Dos Passos' first major experimental novel. Set in New York, it is a panoramic view of the frustrations and defeats of contemporary urban life. Frequently shifting focus among its marginally related characters, the novel details an oppressive picture of human calamity and defeat; fires, accidents, brawls, crimes, and suicides abound, and unhappiness is pervasive. The novel is uneven; it is contrived in its plotting and confusing in its use of time but interesting and especially noteworthy for its development of formal devices that would be better employed in *U.S.A.*

Dos Passos' 1920s output also included a volume of free verse, *A Pushcart at the Curb* (1922); two impressionistic travel books, *Rosinante to the Road Again* (1922) and *Orient Express* (1927); a novel, *Streets of Night* (1923); two plays; and a tract in defense of the anarchists Sacco and Vanzetti, *Facing the Chair* (1927).

Politics and Reportage

The political implications of Dos Passos' early writings are clearly socialist, and in 1926 he helped found the *New Masses,* a Marxist political and cultural journal, to which he contributed until the early 1930s. In 1927 he was jailed in Boston for picketing on behalf of Sacco and Vanzetti. In 1928 he visited the Soviet Union. Returning to the United States in 1929, he married Katherine F. Smith.

As a political reporter for the *New Republic* and other journals during the early 1930s, Dos Passos covered labor flareups, political conventions, the Depression, and the New Deal. His fundamental distrust of organized society extended to organizations as well, and despite his sympathy with many Communist causes he was always a maverick rather than a party radical. In 1934 an overt rift developed between Dos Passos and the Communist movement, and it marked the beginning of a long shift to the right in his political sympathies.

After a one-man show of his sketches in 1937, Dos Passos went to Spain to help Hemingway and Joris Ivens make a film documentary of the Spanish Civil War, *The Spanish Earth.* Dos Passos and Hemingway, who had earlier survived an auto accident together, were good friends until Dos Passos' sympathies with the anarchist faction estranged Hemingway, who was partial to the main Loyalist forces.

In 1940 Dos Passos became active in behalf of political refugees, and during World War II did a good deal of war writing, principally for *Harper's and Life* magazines, for whom he later covered the postwar Nuremberg trials.

Major Work

U.S.A. (1937), Dos Passos' masterpiece, is a trilogy made up of *The 42nd Parallel* (1930), *Nineteen-Nineteen* (1932), and *The Big Money* (1936). To solve the time problem that flawed *Manhattan Transfer,* Dos Passos employed three unusual devices: "The Camera Eye," autobiographical episodes rendered in a Joycean stream of consciousness; "Newsreel," a Dada-like pastiche of mass culture, combining fragments of pop songs, newspaper headlines, and polit-

ical speeches; and short biographies, impressionistic sketches of some of the prominent figures of the 1900-1930 time span—Henry Ford, William Randolph Hearst, Thomas A. Edison, Charles Steinmetz, and others. These sections serve as time guides and also as markers separating the narrative chapters that constitute the bulk of the trilogy and are concerned with a cross section of American social types. Among these are Mac McCreary, a poor boy who grows to a class consciousness and revolutionary commitment so strong that he deserts his family to serve the revolution in Mexico; Eleanor Stoddard, a New York interior decorator, whose gentility and estheticism are pitiably empty responses to her sordid childhood; Evaline Hutchins, an aspiring artist with little talent whose boredom with her habit of failure leads her to suicide; J. Ward Morehouse, a self-made millionaire publicist and labor politician and a prototype of the ruthless opportunist; Richard Savage, a Harvard esthete and idealist who ultimately succumbs to the enticements of big business and becomes a Morehouse employee; Mary French, an idealistic union official who becomes disillusioned with the radical movement when her Communist fiancé marries someone of the party's choice; and Charley Anderson, a likable inventor who makes a fortune in the airplane business.

The characters' lives cross briefly and futilely. All are seen in dual perspective: publicly, as they relate to the class struggle between labor and industry; and privately, as they suffer frustration and a gnawing sense of unfulfillment. Though they are closely observed, the characters rarely get beyond social typology, so that the predominant narrative sections, ironically, are less compelling than the "device" sections. However, its scope and daring give *U.S.A.* distinction, and it had a powerful impact on the social novel in America.

Later Life and Work

In a 1947 auto accident Dos Passos lost an eye and his wife was killed. In 1950 he married Elizabeth H. Holdridge; their daughter was Dos Passos' only child. After 1949 he lived principally on his family farm in Westmoreland, Va. Dos Passos died on Sept. 28, 1970, in Baltimore.

Always prolific, after the war Dos Passos divided his writing between reportage and fiction. His later novels tend toward moodiness and romantic despair. *District of Columbia* (1952) is a trilogy consisting of *Adventures of a Young Man* (1939), *Number One* (1943), and *The Grand Design* (1949). A chronicle of the Spotswood family, it takes as its theme the destruction of individuals by a complex, mechanistic, industrial society. Critics were generally displeased with the trilogy.

Chosen Country (1951), an autobiographical novel; *Most Likely to Succeed* (1954), a novel of leftist infighting; and *The Great Days* (1958), a semiautobiographical novel, add up to little more than an anti-Communist warning to the effect that the end never justifies the means. This is also the substance and weakness of *State of the Nation* (1944), *Tour of Duty* (1946), the General Mills-commissioned *The Prospect before Us* (1950), and *The Theme Is Freedom* (1956).

Among Dos Passos' other nonfiction titles are *The Ground We Stand On* (1941), a historical survey of Anglo-American democracy; *The Head and Heart of Thomas Jefferson* (1954), a biography; *Prospects of a Golden Age* (1959), a composite biographical account of early American culture; and *The Portugal Story* (1969), a historical study.

Further Reading

Dos Passos' *The Best Times* (1966) is a fragmentary autobiography, ranging from 1896 to 1936 but focused mainly on the 1920s; it offers an especially interesting account of his literary friendships. John H. Wrenn, *John Dos Passos* (1962), is a good critical biography. Excellent critical evaluations of Dos Passos may be found in Malcolm Cowley, *Exile's Return* (1934; new ed. 1951); Joseph Warren Beach, *American Fiction, 1920-1940* (1941); Maxwell Geismar, *Writers in Crisis: The American Novel between Two Wars* (1942); Alfred Kazin, *On Native Grounds: An Interpretation of Modern American Prose Literature* (1942; abr. ed. 1956); and Jean-Paul Sartre, *Literary and Philosophical Essays* (1955).

Additional Sources

Carr, Virginia Spencer, *Dos Passos: a life,* Garden City, N.Y.: Doubleday, 1984.

Knox, George Albert, *Dos Passos and "the revolting playwrights",* Philadelphia: R. West, 1977.

Ludington, Townsend, *John Dos Passos: a twentieth century odyssey,* New York: Dutton, 1980. □

José Eduardo dos Santos

José Eduardo dos Santos (born 1942) was a leader of the Popular Movement for the Liberation of Angola (MPLA) and the second president of Angola following independence in 1975. He guided the country from a Marxist to a democratic socialist form of government.

José Eduardo dos Santos was born on August 28, 1942, in Luanda, the capital of Angola, where his father was a stonemason. Even in school he was an ardent nationalist and worked clandestinely among students for the overthrow of Portuguese colonial rule.

In 1961, at the age of 19, he joined the African nationalist organization, Popular Movement for the Liberation of Angola (MPLA), although it had been banned by the Portuguese authorities and its members persecuted by the political police. Later that same year he fled into exile in Léopoldville (now Kinshasa, Congo) where MPLA had an office. His ability was soon recognized in his appointment as deputy president of the party's youth wing. Two years later he was attached to the MPLA office in Brazzaville, capital of French Congo (now Republic of the Congo).

In 1963 dos Santos, together with several other young Angolans, received a scholarship for study in Moscow at Patrice Lumumba University. In 1969 dos Santos graduated with a degree in petroleum engineering. Mindful of the struggle to which he was returning at home, he stayed another year in the Soviet Union and took a military course in telecommunications and radar. During his student years he also married a Soviet woman.

Young Military and Political Leader

Dos Santos returned to Angola in 1970, and for the next three years he served in the liberation army of MPLA on the war front in Cabinda, a northern territory of Angola. He was appointed as second-in-command of telecommunication services. In 1974 a coup in Lisbon toppled the dictatorial regime, and the independence of Portugal's African colonies at last seemed possible. The rise of dos Santos to the top ranks of MPLA continued. In 1974 he was recognized as number five in the leadership and was appointed to the party's executive committee and to its political bureau.

At the independence of Angola in November 1975, President Agostinho Neto appointed José Eduardo dos Santos as minister of foreign affairs in his first government. For Neto, close colleagues like dos Santos were essential, for they provided a link with the old days when MPLA was chiefly a military organization. In addition, they had the education and skills to turn the party into a governing body which could direct the political and economic reconstruction of the country. In 1977, in a cabinet reshuffle, dos Santos received the important assignment of planning minister and secretary of the National Planning Commission. He also served briefly as first deputy prime minister.

Thrust into Presidency

In September 1979 Angolans were shocked by the death of Agostinho Neto after a battle with cancer. The ruling Central Committee unanimously approved the appointment of José Eduardo dos Santos as the country's second president, as head of MPLA, and as commander-in-chief of the Armed Forces. The appointment was confirmed by a party congress in May 1980. At 37 years of age, dos Santos was one of Africa's youngest presidents.

Although relatively unknown outside of his country, the appointment of dos Santos was less of a surprise in Angola itself. He had been a close adviser of Neto; he was a Kimbundu from Luanda, the ethnic group that had dominated MPLA; he had a wide range of administrative experience compared to many colleagues; his loyalty and service to MPLA over the years were unquestioned; and he was not closely identified with any of the factions within the party.

Reformer Sought Peace, Challenged by War

As president, dos Santos continued the task of economic and political reconstruction begun by his predecessor. His biggest problem was the continuing war against the National Union for the Total Integration of Angola (UNITA), a rival liberation movement during the period of Portuguese rule which never recognized MPLA as the legitimate government of Angola. Many of the human and material resources which Angola desperately needed for internal development had to be diverted to the war against UNITA led by the rebel Jonas Savimbi, who was supported by South Africa and the United States. Within his government, President dos Santos, generally considered to be a moderate, had to balance different viewpoints between those who were committed to supporting Marxist ideology and those who were more pragmatic and willing to sacrifice some ideological purity in order to achieve peace.

Despite dos Santos' efforts to negotiate an end to the war, it raged on. Angola's fate was to be positioned geographically in the midst of other turmoil that fueled continued insurgency within. In 1984 the Angolan and South African governments agreed to a cease-fire to the nearly two-decade-long war along the Angola-Namibia border. An agreement by dos Santos and Cuba's President Fidel Castro to withdraw Cuban troops from Angola quickly followed. The proposition was based on the withdrawal of South African troops from Angola, South African recognition of Namibian independence, and an end to support of Savimbi and UNITA.

New Political Philosophy Emerged

Even though Angola and South Africa maintained their cease-fire agreement, negotiations for Cuban troop withdrawal from Angola and Namibian independence dragged on for years. Meanwhile, Angola's civil war took hundreds of thousands of lives and decimated the economy. As the 1980s went by, the government gradually began to change its Marxist philosophy, established a free market economy, joined the International Monetary Fund, and announced

that Angola would adopt a multiparty system and hold elections within three years after reaching a peace settlement. These steps led the United States to join Portugal and the former Soviet Union in actively brokering negotiations between the MPLA and UNITA. Savimbi and dos Santos first agreed to stop fighting in 1989—in what became an off-and-on again cease-fire—which, after a cooling off period, led to free elections.

The long awaited elections took place September 29 and 30, 1992 under United Nations supervision. Dos Santos was the undisputed winner with almost 50 percent (49.7%) of the popular vote versus 40.1 percent received by Savimbi. Savimbi claimed the vote was rigged, and by October 30th UNITA had taken the country into civil war again. More killing and economic devastation followed, further depleting the country of its rich natural resources. The United States continued to hold peace talks to work out an acceptable power-sharing arrangement between UNITA and the dos Santos government. Savimbi refused to give up the territory won through battle, and in so doing lost the United States' support as the U.S. officially recognized the dos Santos government in the Spring of 1993.

Dos Santos addressed the United Nations on its 50th Anniversary, October 22, 1995, expressing appreciation for the understanding and assistance given Angola, particularly its humanitarian aid to refugees and economic assistance to restructure the country. He also praised UN peace keeping forces in Angola for their continued role in disarming UNITA guerillas, as well as for monitoring the long process toward reconciliation within the country.

A good-looking man who smiled easily, José Eduardo dos Santos was reported to be somewhat reserved and not given to speaking or appearing in public more than necessary. One commentator noted, however, that the apparent shyness masked an inner sureness and indefatigable spirit.

Further Reading

Recommended for general background on Angola are Lawrence W. Henderson, *Angola: Five Centuries of Conflict* (1979) and Basil Davidson, *In the Eye of the Storm* (1972). On the liberation struggle in which dos Santos participated, see John Marcum, *The Angolan Revolution*, two volumes (1969 and 1978). Also, Michael Wolfers and Jane Bergerol, *Angola in the Front Line* (1983) gives an excellent account of events since independence. Shorter articles in periodicals that offer additional details of the Angolan conflict include: *Time* (April 2, 1984 and October 17, 1988); *The Economist* (July 1, 1989, September 28, 1991, October 10, 1992, and November 7, 1992); the *US Department of State Dispatch* (September 23, 1991 and October 5, 1992); (November-December 1992); and *Presidents & Prime Ministers* (January/February, 1996). □

Marcelino dos Santos

Nationalist insurgent, statesman, and intellectual, Marcelino dos Santos (born 1929) was instrumental in coordinating the Mozambican nationalist groups into the Front for the Liberation of Mozambique

(Frelimo). The party fought a ten year war which culminated in independence in 1975.

Marcelino dos Santos was born in 1929, son of Firmindo dos Santos and Teresa Sabina dos Santos, and was raised in Lourenco Marques (now Maputo), Mozambique. When he left Mozambique in 1947 to continue his education at the Industrial Institute in Lisbon, Portugal, he already showed himself ready to carry a torch held by his father's generation. Firmindo dos Santos, a member of the African Association of Mozambique, had urged revitalization and unity among Mozambicans in their pursuit of justice and social equality. Young dos Santos, in a 1949 letter to the association from Lisbon, similarly urged members to put aside individual considerations and stand united. At the House for Students of the Empire in Lisbon, where colonial youths studying in Lisbon gathered in the late 1940s, dos Santos and others increasingly articulated their Africanist and nationalist sentiments through poetry and prose. Here dos Santos discreetly shared his ideals and aspirations with Amilcar Cabral, Agostinho Neto, and Eduardo Mondlane—men destined to become nationalist leaders in Guinea Bissau, Angola, and Mozambique, respectively. By 1950, however, the political atmosphere in Lisbon was tense. Neto was arrested, Mondlane moved to study in the United States, and dos Santos and others relocated in Paris.

Activist in Exile

In Paris dos Santos lived among leftist African writers and artists affiliated with the literary journal *Presence Africaine*. He published poetry under several pen names—Kalungano in Portuguese language publications and Lilinho Micaia in the collection of his poetry published in the Soviet Union. In the 1950s his skill as a nationalist strategist and mediator sharpened as he urged Portuguese political exiles in Paris to broaden their opposition to the Salazar regime in Portugal and embrace the nationalist cause. The Anti-colonial Movement (MAC), formed in Paris in 1957, was in part a result of dos Santos' work among this exile community. At the All-African Peoples Congress at Tunis in 1960 a broader alliance emerged incorporating the nationalist movements of Angola and Portuguese Guinea.

By 1961 nationalist groups proliferated, and all were galvanized by the outbreak of violence in Angola. Dos Santos had joined the Paris branch of the National Democratic Union of Mozambique (UDENAMO), the first nationalist party formed largely among Mozambicans living in exile, but he continued to actively pursue solidarity at the international level. At a meeting in Casablanca in April 1961 the Conference of Nationalist Organizations of the Portuguese Colonies (CONCOP) was formed. Dos Santos was elected permanent secretary charged with coordinating nationalist activity in an effort to force an immediate end to colonial rule. From CONCOP's headquarters in Rabat dos Santos assumed his role of explaining the nationalist struggle to an international audience.

Party Spokesman Waged Battle for Legitimacy

In 1962 Eduardo Mondlane assembled representatives of Mozambican nationalist groups in Dar es Salaam, Tanzania, to attempt to forge a united front to undertake the struggle for independence, and dos Santos lent his support. The result was the foundation of the Front for the Liberation of Mozambique (Frelimo). Frelimo, the party which undertook and waged the war for independence from Portugal, held its first congress in Tanzania in September 1962. While continuing with CONCOP dos Santos increasingly turned his organizational and expository skills to sculpting Frelimo's political and military goals. By 1964, with the outbreak of the hostilities in northern Mozambique, dos Santos, as Frelimo's secretary for external affairs, became one of the movement's principal spokesmen. His powerful presentations before the Organization for African Unity, the Afro-Asian Solidarity Conference, and the United Nations helped win international recognition of the legitimacy of Frelimo's petitions for political, military, and financial support.

With the tragic murder of Frelimo's president, Eduardo Mondlane, dos Santos was elected to Frelimo's temporary ruling triumvirate (dos Santos, Uria Simango, and Samora Moises Machel). In 1970 he became vice president under Samora Machel—a position he held throughout the war for independence. Working at Frelimo headquarters in Dar es Salaam and in the war zones, dos Santos focused on the key political aspects of the armed struggle. Using the bonds of friendship and the political skills he developed in the 1950s, he helped cement links of political cooperation throughout the war, during the difficult negotiations leading to the independence of Mozambique, and ultimately into the Herculean task of constituting a viable new nation.

Architect of Independence Sought Internal Stability

When the Council of Ministers of the People's Republic of Mozambique was sworn to office on July 1, 1975, dos Santos assumed the key positions of vice president of Frelimo and minister for development and economic planning. After independence he held a number of important positions within the government and remained active as a member of Frelimo's Central Committee charged with political strategy. The challenge during the late 1970s and 1980s was to rebuild the country while defending Frelimo and the government from an armed takeover by the opposition group Renamo.

From 1981 to 1983 dos Santos left government office to concentrate on strengthening the party. He returned to office in 1983 as governor of the province of Sofala in central Mozambique, and in 1989 served as president of the People's Assembly. During this time, he worked diligently to establish internal stability; some progress was finally achieved in October 1992 when a peace agreement was signed by Frelimo and Renamo.

Through the mid-1990s he continued as theoretician within Frelimo's Central Committee, working to reform the country's economic and political structures from within. The long war against Renamo had left the former Portuguese colony bankrupt, earning it the dubious distinction of the world's poorest nation. Dos Santos often led delegations representing Mozambique at important international conferences, such as the Southern Africa-Cuba Solidarity Conference in May 1995.

His essential contributions were in the area of international relations, deftly aiding Mozambique in its determined posture of non-alignment, and in the development of Frelimo policy designed to develop socialist programs to serve Mozambique's majority population.

Further Reading

There are no detailed biographies of Marcelino dos Santos, but some of his best speeches and poems are available in English. His "Address to the Sixth Pan-African Congress" in *Africa Review* (1974) and "The Voice of the Awakened Continent" in *World Marxist Review* (Prague, 1964) are exemplary. *Lotus: Afro-Asian Writings* has two articles which focus on Marcelino dos Santos as a poet and on his work in the context of nationalist poetry in Mozambique: Luis Bernardo Honwana, "The Role of Poetry in the Mozambican Revolution," volume 8 (Cairo, 1971) and "Marcelino dos Santos," volume 18 (Cairo, 1973). He is listed in *Africa South of the Sahara* (11th and 12th editions. London: Europa Publications, 1981, 1982. Biographies in " Who's Who in Africa South of the Sahara" section.) Periodicals and journals with additional information include: *Africa Report* (May-June 1989); *African Communist* (Third quarter 1995); and *Current History* (May 1993).

Three general works provide the necessary context to understand the historical contribution of Marcelino dos Santos. Allen and Barbara Isaacman's book *Mozambique: From Colonialism to Revolution, 1900-1982* considers both the role of protest poetry and Marcelino dos Santos' contribution as poet and politician (1983). Eduardo Mondlane's *The Struggle for Mozambique*, republished with an introduction by John Saul and a biographical sketch by Herbert Shore (London, 1983), is the classic work on the period. Finally, Barbara Cornwall's *The Bush Rebels: A Personal Account of Black Revolt in Africa* (1972) adds a personal glimpse of dos Santos the man. □

Fyodor Dostoevsky

The Russian novelist Fyodor Dostoevsky (1821-1881) mixed social, Gothic, and sentimental elements with psychological irrationalism and visionary religion. The form of the novel vastly increased in scope and flexibility as a result of his works.

Fyodor Dostoevsky was born in Moscow in 1821, the son of a staff doctor of a Moscow hospital. His father, a cruel man, was murdered by his serfs in 1839, when Dostoevsky was 18 and attending school in St. Petersburg. Sigmund Freud and other psychoanalysts believed that throughout his life Dostoevsky felt a secret guilt about his father's murder. Dostoevsky was trained to be a military engineer, but he disliked school and loved literature. When he finished school, he abandoned the career he was trained

for and devoted himself to writing. His earliest letters show him to be a passionate, enthusiastic, and somewhat unstable young man.

Early Works

Dostoevsky began his writing career in the tradition of the "social tale" of the early 1840s, but he transformed the fiction about poor people in abject circumstances into a powerful philosophical and psychological instrument. His entry on the literary stage was brilliant. In 1843 he finished his first novel, *Poor Folk,* a social tale about an abject civil servant. The novel was praised profusely by the reigning critic, Vissarion Belinsky. Dostoevsky's second novel, *The Double* (1846), was received less warmly; his subsequent works in the 1840s were received coldly and antagonistically by Belinsky and others, and Dostoevsky's literary star sank quickly. *The Double* has emerged, however, as his most significant early work, and in many respects it was a work far in advance of its time.

Dostoevsky was always sensitive to critical opinion, and the indifferent reception of *The Double* caused him to back off from the exciting originality of the novel. From 1846 to 1849 his life and work are characterized by some aimlessness and confusion. The short stories and novels he wrote in this period are for the most part experiments in different forms and different subject matters. He continued to write about civil servants in such tales as *Mr. Prokharchin* (1846) and *The Faint Heart* (1847). *The Landlady* (1847) is an experiment with the Gothic form; *A Jealous Husband, an Unusual Event* (1848) and *Nine Letters* (1847) are bur-

lesques; *White Nights* (1848) is a sentimental romance; and the unfinished novel *Netochka Nezvanova* (1847) is a mixture of Gothic, social, and sentimental elements. Despite the variety and lack of formal and thematic continuity, one may pick out themes and devices that reappear in the mature work of Dostoevsky.

Dostoevsky's life showed some of the same pattern of uncertain experimentation. Although he had already shown the religious and conservative traits that were to become a fixed part of his character in his mature years, he was also attracted at this time to current revolutionary thought. In 1847 he began to associate with a mildly subversive group called the "Petrashevsky Circle." In 1849, however, the members were arrested and the circle was disbanded. After 8 months of imprisonment, Dostoevsky was sentenced to death. This sentence was actually a hoax designed to impress the prisoners with the Czar's mercy, when he commuted the death penalty. At one point, however, Dostoevsky believed he had only moments to live, and he was never to forget the sensation and feelings of that experience. He was sentenced to 4 years of imprisonment and 4 years of forced service in the Siberian army.

Years of Transition (1859-1864)

Dostoevsky returned to St. Petersburg in 1859 with a consumptive wife, Maria Issaeva, a widow whom he had married in Siberia. Their marriage was not happy; Dostoevsky and his wife reinforced each other's unhealthy tendencies. To support himself, Dostoevsky edited the journal *Time* with his brother Mikhail and wrote a number of fictional works. His first published works after returning from Siberia were the comic stories *The Uncle's Dream* (1859) and *The Village Stepanchikovo* (1859). In 1861 he published *Memoirs from the House of the Dead,* a fictionalized account of his experiences in prison. That year he also published *The Insulted and the Injured,* a poorly structured novel characterized by improbable events and situations. By and large his work during this period showed no great artistic advance over his early work and gave no hint of the greatness that was to issue forth in 1864 with the publication of *Notes from the Underground.*

Dostoevsky's life during this period was characterized by poor health, poverty, and complicated emotional situations. He fell in love with the young student Polina Suslova, a girl of complicated and difficult temperament, and carried on a frustrating and torturous affair with her for several years. He went abroad in 1862 and 1863 to get away from his creditors, to repair his health, and to engage in his passion for gambling. His impressions of Europe were unfavorable; he considered European civilization to be dominated by rationalism and rampant with rapacious individualism. His views on Europe are contained in *Winter Notes and Summer Impressions* (1863).

Thus, at the point when his great talent was to become evident, Dostoevsky was pursued by creditors, his wife was dying, and he was carrying on a love affair with a young girl. His journal had been closed down by the censors, and he was fatally pursuing his self-destructive passion for gambling.

Notes from the Underground (1864) is a short novel, written partly as a philosophical monologue and partly as a narrative. In this work Dostoevsky attempts to justify the existence of individual freedom as a necessary and inevitable attribute of man. He argues against the view that man is a rational creature and that society may be so organized as to assure his happiness. He insists that man desires freedom more than happiness, but he also perceives that unqualified freedom is a destructive force since there is no guarantee that man will use his freedom constructively. Indeed, the evidence of history suggests that man seeks the destruction of others and of himself.

Crime and Punishment

Dostoevsky's first wife died in 1864, and in the following year he married Anna Grigorievna Snitkina. She was efficient, practical, and serene and therefore the very opposite of his first wife and his mistress. There is very little doubt that she was largely responsible for introducing better conditions for his work by taking over many of the practical tasks that he loathed and handled badly.

In 1866 Dostoevsky published *Crime and Punishment,* which is the most popular of his great novels, perhaps because it appeals to various levels of sophistication. It can be read as a serious and complex work of art, but it can also be enjoyed as an engrossing detective story. The novel is concerned with the murder of an old pawnbroker by a student, Raskolnikov, while he is committing robbery, ostensibly to help his family and his own career. The murder occurs at the very beginning of the novel, and the rest of the book has to do with the pursuit of Raskolnikov by the detective Porfiry and by his own conscience. In the end he gives himself up and decides to accept the punishment for his act.

Raskolnikov's intentions in committing the murder share something of the complexity and impenetrability of Hamlet's motives. One can, however, dismiss some of the aims that Raskolnikov consciously gives. The humanitarian motive of murdering a useless old woman to save the careers of many useful young men is clearly a rationalization, since Raskolnikov never makes use of, or even appears interested in, the money he has stolen. The "superman" theory divides mankind into extraordinary and ordinary people, and the extraordinary people are permitted to cross the boundaries of normal morality. This theory appears to be a more accurate representation of Raskolnikov's thoughts. But some critics consider this too a rationalization of something deeper in his nature. There is some evidence that Raskolnikov suffered from a deep sense of guilt and committed the murder to provoke punishment and thus alleviate his guilt.

The Idiot

The Dostoevskys went abroad in 1867 and remained away from Russia for more than 4 years. Their economic condition was very difficult, and Dostoevsky repeatedly lost what little they had at the gaming tables. *The Idiot* was written between 1867 and 1869, and Dostoevsky stated that in this work he intended to depict "the wholly beautiful man."

The hero·of the novel is Prince Myshkin, a kind of modern Christ. He is a good man who attempts to live in a corrupt society, and it is uncertain whether he succeeds or not, since he leaves the pages of the novel with the world about him worse than when he entered. Nastasya Fillipovna, one of Dostoevsky's great female characters, shares the stage with Prince Myshkin. When she was a young girl, her honor had been violated, and she lives to wreak vengeance on the world for the hurt she had suffered. While Prince Myshkin preaches forgiveness, Nastasya Fillipovna burns with the desire to pay others back. Nastasya Fillipovna is nevertheless attracted to Prince Myshkin, and throughout the novel she vacillates between Myshkin, the prince of light, and Rogozhin, an apostle of passion and destruction. In the end Rogozhin kills Nastasya Fillipovna, and Prince Myshkin is powerless to prevent this crime.

Some readers view *The Idiot* as Dostoevsky's finest creation, while others see it as the weakest of his great novels. It is certainly a less tidy work than *Crime and Punishment,* but it is perhaps a more challenging novel.

The Possessed

Dostoevsky began *The Possessed* (also translated as *The Devils*) in 1870 and published it in 1871-1872. The novel began as a political pamphlet and was based on a political murder that took place in Moscow on Nov. 21, 1869. A radical named Nechaev had a member of his conspiratorial group murdered because the member would not obey him unquestioningly. Nechaev escaped to Switzerland but was arrested and returned to Russia, where he died in prison. Nechaev's actual influence on revolutionary movements in Russia was small, but his bravado and his friendship with Mikhail Bakunin worked to increase his reputation. Dostoevsky saw Nechaev as the end product of pernicious tendencies in liberalism and radicalism.

In *The Possessed* Dostoevsky raises a minor contemporary event to dimensions of great political and philosophical importance. The novel is a satire of liberalism and radicalism; it is set in a small provincial town and concerns the contrasting influence of father and son. The father, Stepan Trofimovich Verkhovensky, represents the liberalism of the 1840s, and the son, Peter Verkhovensky, represents the radicalism of the 1860s. Dostoevsky believed that the earlier liberalism was responsible for the later radicalism. Nicholas Stavrogin, a mysterious and compelling figure, stands apart from the political and ideological struggle, but it is clear that Dostoevsky sees in him the ultimate principle from which the disastrous consequences stem. Stavrogin represents the totally free will, attached to nothing and responsible for nothing. In Stavrogin, Dostoevsky reconfronted the problem of free will.

Many readers see *The Possessed* not only as an accurate portrayal of certain tendencies of the politics of the time but also as a prophetic commentary on the future of politics in Russia and elsewhere.

The Brothers Karamazov

During the 1870s Dostoevsky became increasingly interested in contemporary social and political events and increasingly concerned about liberal and radical trends among the youth. Except for his brief flirtation with liberal movements in the 1840s, Dostoevsky was a staunch conservative. The novel *A Raw Youth* (1875) grew out of his interest and concern about the youth of Russia, and the theme of the novel may be described as a son in search of his father. The novel is something of a proving ground for *The Brothers Karamazov* but is not generally considered to be on the same level as the four great novels.

The Brothers Karamazov (1879-1880) is the greatest of Dostoevsky's novels and the culmination of his life-work. Sigmund Freud ranked it with *Oedipus Rex* and *Hamlet* as one of the greatest artistic achievments of all time. The novel is about four sons and and their guilt in the murder of their father, Fyodor. Each of the sons may be characterized by a dominant trait: Dmitri by passion, Ivan by reason, Alyosha by spirit, and Smerdyakov by everything that is ugly in human nature. Smerdyakov kills his father, but in varying degrees the other three brothers are guilty in thought and intention.

The greatest section of the novel is "The Legend of the Grand Inquisitor," in which Ivan narrates a meeting between Christ and the Grand Inquisitor, a devil surrogate. The Grand Inquisitor presents man as slavish, cowardly, and incapable of freedom; Christ sees him as potentially capable of true freedom. The novel, however, does not confirm the validity of either view.

Dostoevsky sent the epilogue to the *The Brothers Karamazov* to his publisher on Nov. 8, 1880, and he died soon afterward, on Jan. 28, 1881. At his death he was at the height of his career in Russia, and mourning was widespread. His reputation was beginning to penetrate into Europe, and interest in him has continued to increase.

Further Reading

Translations of Dostoevsky's works are available in many editions; those by Constance Garnett and David Magarshack are recommended.

There are many biographies of Dostoevsky. Two competent ones which differ in approach are Edward Hallett Carr, *Dostoevsky (1821-1881): A New Biography* (1931), and Henry Troyat, *Firebrand: The Life of Dostoevsky* (trans. 1946). Useful biographical data may be found in Robert Payne, *Dostoevsky: A Human Portrait* (1961), which treats Dostoevsky's life and work. An intimate view of Dostoevsky the man is presented in the reminiscences of his daughter, Aimée Dostoyevsky, *Fyodor Dostoyevsky: A Study* (1921). See also A. Steinberg, *Dostoievsky* (1966).

Ernest J. Simmons, *Dostoevski: The Making of a Novelist* (1940), is a detailed and objective account of the circumstances surrounding the production of Dostoevsky's novels, as well as a consideration of their substance. Konstantin Vasilevich Mochulski, *Dostoevsky: His Life and Work,* translated by Michael A. Minihan (1967), is the most detailed analysis of Dostoevsky's work. A critical analysis of the individual works may be found in Edward Wasiolek, *Dostoevsky: The Major Fiction* (1964). For a philosophical and theological consideration of Dostoevsky's work, Nikolai A. Berdiaev, *Dostoevsky,* translated by Donald Attwater (1957), is a classic. For a psychological approach, Sigmund Freud's widely anthologized essay "Dostoevsky and Parricide" is recommended. It may be found in William Phillips, ed., *Art and Psychoanalysis* (1957). For general historical and literary background, Prince D. S. Mirsky, *A History of Russian Literature* (2 vols., 1927), is recommended; it is also available in an abridged volume, edited by Francis J. Whitfield (1958). □

Donald Wills Douglas

The American aeronautical engineer Donald Wills Douglas (1892-1981) developed and manufactured aircraft that dominated the world market for many years.

Donald Wills Douglas was born on April 6, 1892, in Brooklyn, New York. From an early age young Donald showed an interest in the then brief history of manned flight. After high school, he attended Trinity Chapel School for college, where he was editor of the school magazine. He was appointed to the U.S. Naval Academy at Annapolis in 1909, where he became enthusiastic about the infant field of aviation. During this time he even got to see the Wright Brothers demonstrating their latest plane. In 1912 he entered the Massachusetts Institute of Technology; after two years of early wind tunnel research he became the first man to receive a bachelor of science degree in aeronautical engineering from that school.

Douglas first worked in 1915 at the Connecticut Aircraft Company on the Navy's first dirigible. That same year he joined Glenn L. Martin's aircraft firm as chief engineer. The following year he went to Washington as chief civilian aeronautical engineer for the U.S. Army Signal Corps. Within a few months he resigned over a dispute with the War Production Board and returned to the Martin Company. In 1916 he married Charlotte Marguerite Ogg, with whom he had five children.

In 1920 Douglas quit the Martin Company to set up his own firm in Los Angeles. He was president of the Douglas Company until 1957. He was the first of many manufacturers to go into production permanently in Los Angeles, where the availability of capital, skilled labor, and flying weather for most of the year made an attractive package for the aeronautical industry.

Douglas's first effort was to produce a single-engine airplane, nicknamed the "Cloudster," capable of flying nonstop across the country. The "Cloudster" never made it fully cross-country, but it was the first plane capable of lifting a payload equal to its own weight, and the design was sold as a luxury aircraft. He successfully sought a contract from the U.S. Navy for airplanes and eventually became the leading manufacturer of naval aircraft. In 1932 Douglas and other firms were asked by Transcontinental and Western airlines to design a craft capable of traveling 1,080 miles with 12 passengers at a speed of up to 185 miles per hour. Douglas accepted the challenge and produced the DC-1

(for Douglas Commercial), which was first flown on July 1, 1933, and was able to carry 12 passengers at a cruising speed of 170 mph. An all-metal, twin-engine plane, it was one of the first to establish the usefulness of wing flaps in commercial planes. This aircraft (only one was built) was a prototype for the succeeding members of the DC family.

The most famous Douglas plane, the DC-3 in 1936, carried 21 passengers at a cruising speed of 190 mph. It was so successful that within 2 years after it first appeared, it was carrying 95 percent of the nation's civil air traffic. That same year Douglas was awarded The Robert J. Collier Trophy, aviation's highest honor, for the DC-2. During the late 1930s Douglas worked on designs for a four-engine transport, eventually designated the DC-4. Both the DC-3 and the DC-4 became the workhorses of military transport during World War II. After the war, the DC-4 became the major aircraft of the new international commercial air-routes. Douglas was an expert at the art of "stretching a design." The DC-4 was elongated to become the DC-6 and later the DC-7. The DC-7 was the first airliner that permitted nonstop coast to coast scheduling. In 1955 Douglas, whose planes were flying over half the world's passenger miles, developed the jet-propelled DC-8. It was followed by the medium-range DC-9 in 1966. It was said at the time that the DC-9, in terms of popularity, was the reincarnation of the DC-3.

The merger of the firm in 1967 with McDonnell Aircraft, to make the McDonnell-Douglas Corporation, strengthened its position in the aerospace industry. The site of the original Douglas Company plant is now The Museum of Flying. Donald Douglas passed away in 1981.

Further Reading

The standard biography of Douglas is Frank Cunningham, *Sky Master: The Story of Donald Douglas* (1943). Douglas's most famous airplane, the DC-3, is covered in Charles J. Kelly, *The Sky's the Limit: The History of the Airlines* (1963). A book on the success of the DC-3 is Douglas J. Ingells *The Plane That Changed The World* (1966). The best history of the industry generally is John B. Rae, *Climb to Greatness: The American Aircraft Industry, 1920-1960* (1968). □

Gavin Douglas

The Scottish poet, prelate, and courtier Gavin Douglas (ca. 1475-1522) is best known for his vigorous translation of Virgil's *Aenied* into Scots, the English of the lowlands of Scotland. He is sometimes listed among the Scottish Chaucerians.

Gavin Douglas was the third son of Archibald "Bell-the-Cat" Douglas, 5th Earl of Angus, a man of distinguished family, very active in court affairs. Little is known about Gavin's early life, but he entered the University of St. Andrews in 1490 and earned a master of arts degree in 1494. He may have studied law at Paris under the distinguished Scottish theologian John Major (or Mair).

Douglas soon rose in ecclesiastical preferment and was appointed provost of St. Giles Church, Edinburgh, about 1501. About this time he wrote *The Place of Honor,* a poem in the form of a dream vision; in it he emphasizes the difference between worldly honor and true honor before God. He probably spent some time abroad, in England, France, and Italy, during the early years of the 16th century.

Douglas completed his translation of Virgil in July 1513. It includes not only the original 12 books of the *Aeneid* but also the thirteenth book, composed by Mapheus Vegius in 1428. Douglas wrote a prologue for each book, and these prologues contain interesting material reflecting the critical, philosophical, and moral commonplaces of the time. Rather than translating "word for word," Douglas followed the advice of St. Gregory the Great and translated "meaning for meaning." Moreover, he made Virgil's characters act and speak like his own contemporaries. There are frequent turns of phrase reminiscent of Geoffrey Chaucer. The result is an extremely lively and effective poem that has own high praise from modern critics.

After the disastrous Battle of Flodden in 1513, in which James IV and much of the Scottish nobility, including the elder brothers of Gavin Douglas, perished, Douglas ceased writing poetry and devoted himself to court affairs. The widowed Queen Margaret, who married Douglas's nephew Alexander, assisted him considerably. He was made bishop of Dunkled but was imprisoned for a time in 1515-1516 and could occupy his see only by making a show of force to dislodge another contender for the office. He died in London in 1522.

Further Reading

The Poetical Works of Gavin Douglas was eidted by John Small (4 vols., 1874). A new edition of Douglas's translation of Virgil's *Aeneid,* with a full introduction, notes, and a glossary, was prepared by David F.C. Coldwell for the Scottish Text Society (4 vols. 1957-1964). The society also issued *The Shorter Poems of Gavin Douglas,* edited by Priscilla J. Bawcutt (1967). Brief selections are available in *Gavin Douglas: A Selection from His Poetry,* edited by Sydney Goodsir Smith (1959), and in *Selections from Gavin Douglas,* edited by David F. C.Coldwell (1964). There is a stimulating discussion of Douglas in C. S.Lewis, *English Literature in the Sixteenth Century: Excluding Drama* (1954).

Additional Sources

Bawcutt, Priscilla J., *Gavin Douglas: a critical study,* Edinburgh: University Press, 1976. ☐

Sir James Douglas

The Scottish patriot Sir James Douglas (1286-1330) supported Robert Bruce, later King Robert I, in the Scottish struggle for independence from England.

James Douglas was the eldest son of a notable Scottish patriot, Sir William Douglas, called "the Hardy." Sir William had been among the early leaders of resistance to the ambitions of Edward I of England to dominate Scotland. Edward imprisoned Sir William in the Tower of London and, on the latter's death in 1297, confiscated the Douglas estates.

It is not surprising, therefore, that the young James appears to have grown up with passionate anti-English feelings. He reached manhood just as Robert Bruce laid claim to the crown of Scotland (1306) and from that time was one of Bruce's most faithful and important lieutenants.

Douglas's career may be divided into two phases. The first was the 8 years of Bruce's struggle to claim the Scottish crown. This was a period of virtual guerrilla warfare, with Douglas emerging from his hiding places for a daring raid or the capture of a strategic castle. At the decisive Scottish victory at Bannockburn in 1314, Douglas commanded one of the four divisions of the Scots and, for his skillful leadership, was knighted on the battlefield by Bruce, now firmly established on the throne.

After Bannockburn, in the second phase of his public career, Douglas served as Warden of the Marches (the disputed frontier area between England and Scotland). In 1317 he diverted an English threat to the borders by staging a raid deep into English territory. Ten years later he dispersed the danger of an English invasion by an audacious attack in which he surprised the enemy forces by night and nearly captured the young Edward III in his bed.

Bruce's reliance on, and affection for, Sir James never ceased. When the King was dying in 1329, he apparently asked Sir James to carry out the spirit of an unfulfilled crusading vow by bearing Bruce's heart to the Hold Land. During the subsequent journey Douglas joined the King of Castile in a "crusade" against the Moslems in Spain and died there in battle in 1330.

It is as a hero of Scotish romance and legend that Douglas's real fame lies. Two sobriquets, "the Good" and "the Black Douglas," indicate his differing reputations in Scotland and in England (though "black" probably referred originally to the color of his hair). His name lives on, especially through the works of Sir Walter Scott, *Castle Dangerous* and *Tales of a Grandfather.*

Further Reading

A full treatment of Douglas is in Sir Herbert E. Maxwell, *A History of the House of Douglas . . .* (2 vols., 1902). The principal near-contemporary source is John Barbour's long poem *The Bruce* (ca. 1375; trans. by W. M. Mackenzie, 1909, and by Archibald A. H. Douglas, 1964).

Additional Sources

Davis, I. M., *The Black Douglas,* London, Routledge and K. Paul, 1974. ☐

Mary Tew Douglas

Mary Tew Douglas (born 1921) was a British anthropologist and social thinker of international fame.

Mary Tew Douglas was born in San Remo, Italy, to Phyllis Twomey and Gilbert Charles Tew, and was the eldest of two daughters. She was educated as a Catholic at the Sacred Heart Convent, Roehampton, in England, and she was keenly interested in religion all her life. As an anthropologist she kept on with her faith. At Oxford (where she did a B.A. degree in 1943) she fell under the influence of the famous social anthropologist E.E. Evans-Pritchard, who was also interested in comparative religion; he died a Catholic. Douglas wrote a biography of her mentor in 1980.

She interrupted her graduate study at Oxford to be a volunteer in World War II in the British Colonial Office working on penal reform. Afterwards she earned a Bachelor of Science in 1948 in anthropology and went to Africa, to the Belgian Congo (now Zaire), to study the folkways of a tribe, the Lele of the Kasai, for her Ph.D. under Professor Evans Pritchard (1951). Also in 1951, Mary Tew married the economist James A. T. Douglas. They had one daughter and two sons. She lived in London and was associated with University College, London, from that time onwards (lecturer in anthropology, 1951-1962; reader, 1963-1970; professor, 1971 until her retirement in 1978). She was the 1994 Bernal prize recipient.

Subsequently she went to the United States. Douglas was in New York City at the Russell Sage Foundation as director of research on human culture from 1977 to 1981; in Chicago at Northwestern University in Evanston, Illinois, as Avalon Foundation professor in anthropology and religion, 1981-1985; and at Princeton University as visiting professor of religion and anthropology beginning in 1985. She maintained her residence in London.

Doctoral Dissertation

Her doctoral dissertation, published as *The Lele of the Kasai* in 1963, studied the Lele tribe "as they cooked, divided food, talked about illness, babies and proper care of the body" and examined how taboos operated within tribal society and the way in which polygamous male elders of the tribe manipulated raffia cloth debts in order to restrict the access of younger men to Lele women. This field investigation led Douglas on to other studies in what she called "social accountability" and "classification schemes" of human relations, applied equally to "primitive" societies (preindustrial, pre-modern) and to modern industrial society. She wrote books on a variety of subjects including pollution, the consumer society, and religion.

The anthropology of Douglas was derived partly from the work of the French sociologist Emile Durkheim (1858-1917). Douglas rejected his determinism, but accepted what Durkheim realized: the *social* basis for human thought. She used the Durkheimian method of drawing on "primitive" cultures to illuminate problems in modern soci-

ety. For Douglas, rituals dramatize moral order in the human universe. "Culture" is rooted in daily social relations: the most mundane and concrete things of daily life. From childhood on, the drama of life is constructed: the self concept; the linguistic code, which the individual learns as a child; the individual as a moral actor; the collective nature of human existence. Comparative studies have to be made of such things as dirt and pollution, food and meals, the biological body, speech, jokes, and material possessions. The biological body is a perfect metaphor or symbol for the social body or the tribe or nation.

Douglas' view of "culture" was of it being created afresh each day. Hers was a world of ordinary symbols, rituals, and activities, all of which dramatized the "construction of social life." Everyday life was *itself* the focus of interest. Every mundane activity carried ritual and ceremonial significance. Symbolic order reflected social order as she looked at the ritual dramatization of social patterns.

Pollution and Taboo

Douglas was perhaps noted for her writings on pollution and taboo. Dirt in "primitive" (as in modern) society is relative to location: dirty shoes are dirty on the table, not dirty on the floor; cooking utensils are dirty in the bedroom; earth is dirty on chairs. Pollution *behavior* is the reaction of our cherished classifications: dirt takes us straight to the field of symbolism, to symbols of purity. In *Purity and Danger: An Analysis of Concepts of Pollution and Taboo* (1966) she stated that modern notions express basically the same idea as "primitive" notions of pollution: "Our practices are solidly based on hygiene; theirs are symbolic; we kill germs; they ward off spirits."

It was *Purity and Danger: An Analysis of Concepts of Pollution and Taboo* and *Natural Symbols* (1970), the two early books, that had such an impact on the emerging sociology of scientific knowledge.

Four related themes were presented in that early work. First, she invited attention to culture, to knowledge of nature, and specifically to cosmological and taxonomic notions, as embedded within systems of accountability. Culture is maintained and it is modified as people use it: it is a tool in everyday social action. There is no fundamental "problem" of "the relationship between culture and social action" because culture is the means by which social action is accomplished, by which members say "good" and "bad" about each other's actions, and by which they recognize them as actions of a certain sort. Second, knowledge, including natural knowledge, is treated as constitutively social. As we bring up our children, and as we talk to each other, so we build, maintain, and modify the categories of perception, thought, and language: "The colonisation of each other's minds is the price we pay for thought." For Douglas, anything but a fully general social epistemology followed from a misunderstanding of the sort of thing knowledge was.

Third, beliefs and representations become knowledge—a collective good—by successfully making the transition from the indivudal to the communal, the private to the public. The achievement of credibility is a practical problem attached to all beliefs: no belief or representation shines by its own lights, carries its crediblity with it. "Credibility," she says, "depends so much on the consensus of a moral community that it is hardly an exaggeration to say that a given community lays on for itself the sum of the physical conditions which it experiences."

Finally in the years between Purity and Danger and Natural Symbols, she developed a set of techniques for the systematic comparative study of "cultural bias." "The Great Divide" between the "modern" and the "scientific," on the one hand, and the "primitive" and "magical," on the other, was rejected. "We " are forms of "them." There is a finite range of predicaments faced and principles available for the maintenance of order. A specific form of these predicaments and principles might be as well devised by Sepik River tribes, by the Big Men of Conservative Party Central Office, or by a community of high-energy phsycists. Cultural diversity has finite forms, and, because these forms do not map onto exisiting Great Divide theories, the comparative study of cultural bias has the capacity to join up the conversations of those who study the "primitive" and those who study the "modern": anthropologists and students of modern science.

But when Douglas attempted to write about the contemporary environmental protection movement of the 1960s and 1970s in Risk and Culture, written with Aaron Wildavsky (1982), she was less sure of the material. Half the book is an attack on the beliefs of the environmentalists. She portrayed the antinuclear and environmental movements as freakish, quasireligious cults. She did not uncover anything about the actual physical environment, or nuclear plants, or off-shore oil-drilling, or industrial pollution of rivers and lakes. Douglas was best when she was talking about the Lele and pollution and food taboos.

The World of Goods

The World of Goods: An Anthropological Theory of Consumption, written with Baron Isherwood (1979), is partly an attempt to explore the social context of modern consumer society. Goods are social markers and a means of communicating. Individuals attain and keep power in society by acts of consumption, which ritually reaffirm their status. The Douglas argument is very generalized and takes us not much further than the old (and much more informative) notion of Thorstein Veblen of "conspicuous consumption" in his book *The Theory of the Leisure Class* (1899). Modern culture is supposedly a *secular* world, in which science replaces religion and ritual. Douglas as a scholar delved into comparative religion. She disagreed with the idea that religion and science could not coexist. There would be no demise of religion in the world, whatever science discovers, because religion originates in human social relations. Modernity changes the shape of society; but there are still human social relations and religion will survive. Douglas was of the opinion that so long as there is collective life, there will be religion, ritual, myths, ceremonies, and rites.

Modernity has three allegedly negative effects on the survival of religion: Douglas dismissed all three. Science is supposed to reduce the explanatory power of religion; for Douglas, religion and science pose no tension with each other—their explanations apply to different kinds of problems. Modern life is undergoing bureaucratization, and this reduces the sense of the unknown and sacred; but Douglas thought that bureaucracy existed in the Vatican in the 15th century, and so did religion. And modern life has little direct experience of nature; but Mary Douglas felt that the discoveries of modern science itself created a new sense of awe and religion. Thus, religion does not disappear in modern society, it just reappears in new forms.

Looking back on her life as a young anthropologist in Africa in *Implicit Meanings: Essays in Anthropology* (1976), she commented: "The central task of anthropology was to explore the effects of the social dimensions on behaviour. The task was grand, but the methods were humble . . . We had to stay with a remote tribe, patiently let events unfold and let people reveal the categories of their thought." From a fundamental Durkheimian belief in the role of ritual and symbol in the construction of social life and social relations, Douglas explained the rituals of meals and food, cleaning and tidying, material possessions, speech, and numerous other concrete things of daily life—in modern as well as "primitive" society.

Further Reading

In addition to the many books mentioned in the text, Mary Douglas wrote *Natural Symbols: Explorations in Cosmology* (1970), *Rules and Meanings: The Anthropology of Everyday Knowledge* (1973), *Edward Evans-Pritchard* (1980), *In the Active Voice* (London: 1982), *Essays in the Sociology of Perception* (London: 1982), and *How Institutions Think* (1986).

Discussions of her work can be found in Adam Kuper, *Anthropologists and Anthropology: The British School, 1922-1972* (London: 1973); *The Social Science Encyclopedia,* edited by A. Kuper and J. Kuper (London: 1985); *Women Anthropologists* (1988); and Robert Wuthnow *et al.,* editors, *Cultural Analysis: The Work of Peter L. Berger, Mary Douglas, Michel Foucault, and Jurgen Habermas* (1984). □

Stephen Arnold Douglas

U.S. senator Stephen Arnold Douglas (1813-1861), the foremost leader of the Democratic party in the decade preceding the Civil War, was Lincoln's political rival for the presidency.

Stephen A. Douglas was born in Brandon, Vt., on April 23, 1813. His father's early death meant Stephen's dependence on a bachelor uncle and later, a detested apprenticeship as a cabinetmaker. When his mother remarried and went to Canandaigua, N. Y., Stephen followed. He attended the academy there, developed a formidable talent as a debater, and became an ardent follower of Andrew Jackson.

Douglas made up for his short stature (5 feet 4 inches) in aggressiveness, audacity, and consuming political ambition. When he said farewell to his mother at 20, he promised to return "on his way to Congress," a prediction he made good 10 years later. He settled in Illinois, where he became a teacher. He taught himself law with borrowed books, became active in the Democratic party, and at 27 was a member of the Illinois State Supreme Court, the youngest ever to attain that office. He was called Judge Douglas thereafter.

Career in Congress

Elected to the House of Representatives in 1843 and to the Senate in 1847, Douglas became a power in all legislation having to do with territories in the West. Known as the "Little Giant" because of his massive head, heavy brown hair, broad shoulders, and booming voice, he soon won the reputation of being the most formidable legislative pugilist in Washington. His enemies called him ruthless; his admirers strove to make him president.

In 1847 Douglas married Martha Denny Martin. The following year she inherited a Mississippi plantation with 150 slaves; by the terms of his father-in-law's will, Douglas was made manager. Though he always denied ownership of any slaves himself, he did manage the plantation up to his death, and there is little doubt that he looked upon his own marriage as symbolic of a successful bridging of North and South. When his wife, after having two sons, died in childbirth, he became depressed and turned for a time to liquor. A tour abroad rejuvenated his spirits, and in 1856 he married the beautiful Adèle Cutts, another Southern woman.

Though privately Douglas held slavery to be "a curse beyond computation," publicly he pronounced it a matter "of climate, of political economy, of self-interest, not a question of legislation." It was good for Louisiana, he said, but bad for Illinois. Essentially proslavery in his legislation, he voted against abolition petitions, favored the annexation of Texas, helped Henry Clay push through the Compromise of 1850, and encouraged the purchase of Cuba to make a new slave state.

Doctrine of "Squatter Sovereignty"

Douglas's failure to reckon with the enormity of the slavery evil, and the growing Northern resentment against it, led him to devise in 1854 what modern historian Allan Nevins called "the worst Pandora's box in our history." In planning for two new states, Kansas and Nebraska, he insisted that the slavery issue be resolved by the settlers themselves rather than by Congress, thus repudiating the 20-year-old Missouri Compromise. Southern extremists saw in this "squatter sovereignty" doctrine an opportunity to make Kansas a slave state, though a majority of the actual settlers were against slavery. Missourians crossed the border at election time to overwhelm the polls and vote in a proslavery government. The antislavery majority set up a rival government in Topeka, and soon there was a small but bloody civil was in Kansas. Douglas was denounced by the abolitionists. Charles Sumner in the Senate called him the squire of slavery, "ready to do all its humiliating offices."

When President James Buchanan recognized the proslavery government in Kansas, Douglas, angered by the misuse of his popular-sovereignty doctrine, denounced the President in 1857, thereby alienating his friends in the South and damaging his presidential chances. But his Kansas-Nebraska Bill had also alienated his antislavery followers in Illinois, who charged him with conniving with railroad speculators. In 1858 he went home to face a difficult reelection battle, with Abraham Lincoln as his opponent.

Debates with Lincoln

In his famous debates with Lincoln, Douglas opposed African American citizenship in any form and attacked as "monstrous heresy" Lincoln's insistence that "the Negro and the white man are made equal by the Declaration of Independence and by Divine Providence." Douglas held that African Americans "belong to an inferior race and must always occupy an inferior position." Lincoln denounced Douglas's popular-sovereignty idea as "a mere deceitful pretense for the benefit of slavery" and emphasized the callousness of Douglas's statement: "When the struggle is between the white man and the Negro, I am for the white man; when it is between the Negro and the crocodile, I am for the Negro."

Douglas barely won the senatorial election, but the debates won national recognition for his rival. In 1860, when Lincoln was nominated for president on the Republican ticket, Douglas said of him to Republicans, "Gentlemen, you have nominated a very able and a very honest man."

Presidential Candidate

Douglas expected to be nominated for president in the Democratic convention in Charleston, but a block of Southerners bolted the party, nominating instead John C. Breckinridge. The remaining Democrats nominated Douglas at a second convention in Baltimore. A fourth convention, organized by the Constitutional Union party, nominated John Bell. Douglas suspected that the four-candidate election would ensure Lincoln's victory but nevertheless campaigned vigorously, urging support for the Union he loved. "I wish to God," he said in New York City, "that we had an Old Hickory now alive in order that he might hang Northern and Southern traitors on the same gallows." In the South he deplored secession, which he said would make it necessary for his children to obtain a passport to visit the graves of their ancestors.

A Douglas feared, Lincoln's victory brought the immediate secession of South Carolina from the Union, and other states quickly followed. Douglas still labored for compromises to restore the Union, and he urged Lincoln to support a projected 13th Amendment which would guarantee that slavery would never be tampered with in the slave states. The firing on Ft. Sumter on Jan. 9, 1861, by Confederate forces ended his compromise efforts. He now swung behind Lincoln, urging a vigorous war effort and rallying Northern Democrats to the cause of the Union.

Douglas contracted typhoid fever and died June 3, 1861. Thus Lincoln lost his ablest rival at precisely the moment in history when he was most needed.

Further Reading

The bulk of Douglas's papers are at the University of Chicago, with additional letters in the Illinois State Historical Society Library and the Chicago Historical Society. The brief *Autobiography of Stephen A. Douglas* (1913) and a volume of his letters, *The Letters of Stephen A. Douglas,* edited by Robert W. Johannsen (1961), are good source materials. The earliest good biography is Allen Johnson, *Stephen A. Douglas: A Study in American Politics* (1908). George Fort Milton in *The Eve of Conflict: Stephen A. Douglas and the Needless War* (1934) proves to be the most sympathetic of all the biographers and contends that, had Douglas been elected president in 1860, he would have prevented the Civil War. The same thesis in echoed in Gerald M. Capers, *Stephen A. Douglas: Defender of the Union,* edited by Oscar Handlin (1959). Historians are more critical of Douglas than these laudatory biographers. □

Thomas Clement Douglas

Thomas Clement Douglas (1904-1986) was a Canadian clergyman and politician; premier of Saskatchewan (1944-1961); first federal leader, New Democratic Party (1961-1971); and member of parliament (1935-1944, 1962-1968, and 1968-1979).

"Tommy" Douglas was born in Falkirk, Scotland, October 20, 1904, the son of Thomas Douglas, an iron moulder, former soldier, and socialist, and Annie Clement Douglas, of Highland origins, who was deeply religious with a poetic gift. The Douglases emigrated to Winnipeg, Canada, in 1910. Tommy Douglas began a life-long struggle with osteomyelitis. In later fights for universal hospital and medical care insurance, he recalled his experience as a charity patient.

During World War I Douglas' father rejoined his regiment, and the family spent the war years in Glasgow. They returned to Winnipeg after the war. The young Tommy Douglas apprenticed as a printer and won the lightweight boxing championship in Manitoba in 1922 and 1923. He was persuaded to resume his education at Brandon College, graduating in 1930 as "senior stick" or head of the student body. That June he was ordained in the Baptist church at Weyburn, Saskatchewan. He also married a fellow graduate, Irma Dempsey, a farmer's daughter from Carberry.

The Depression years sharpened the thinking of a young minister already preoccupied by social and political questions. Repelled by his contact with the Communists during the bloody Estevan miners' strike of 1931, he was attracted to Saskatchewan's new Farmer-Labour Party. In 1932 it joined other western Canadian radical parties to form the Co-operative Commonwealth Federation headed by a Winnipeg mentor of the younger Douglas, James Shaver Woodsworth. In 1934 Douglas fought and lost his first election as a CCF provincial candidate in Weyburn. A year later, despite warnings from church elders, he ran

again. After a bitter campaign, he defeated a Liberal incumbent and entered Parliament as one of eight CCFers.

In Parliament Douglas emerged as a young, dynamic orator with a brilliant gift for humor. He differed from the deeply pacifist Woodsworth by supporting collective security. When war came in 1939 he helped lead the wing of the CCF that insisted on full participation. Re-elected in 1940, he joined the South Saskatchewan Regiment and narrowly missed being drafted to Hong Kong in 1941. Instead, he was chosen leader of the Saskatchewan CCF in July 1942. Two years later when a worn-out, discredited Liberal government went to the polls, the CCF won in a landslide, 47 seats to five.

Hardest hit by the Depression of any Canadian province, Saskatchewan was literally bankrupt in 1944. Wartime prosperity and improved crops only meant imminent foreclosure for debt-ridden farmers. No one could claim that "socialism" had ruined the province. Instead, Douglas and his brilliant provincial treasurer, Clarence Fines, engineered a careful economic recovery. As North America's only democratic socialist regime, Saskatchewan became a laboratory for new ideas, from a fur marketing board to the world's first government car insurance system. A large and effective grassroots organization, described by S. M. Lipset, retained a high degree of involvement and accountability. Douglas himself took special pride in Saskatchewan's pioneering role in improving rural living standards and in the creation, over intense resistance from the medical community, of hospital and health insurance programs.

As an "island of socialism in a sea of capitalism," Douglas insisted the CCF could survive in Saskatchewan only if the party grew nationally. He supported efforts to broaden the CCF and to build organic links with the Canadian Labour Congress. In 1961, when a decade of change took shape in the New Democratic Party (NDP), Douglas seemed to be the only personality strong enough to sell the idea of a labor-backed party to the prairie farmers and small business people who had backed the CCF. In August 1961 the NDP's founding convention chose him as leader by 1,391 votes to 380.

It was the beginning of ten hard years. Douglas waged four general elections in a struggle that raised the new party's share of the vote from 12 to 18 percent. Personal defeat in Regina in 1962 and in Burnaby-Coquitlam in 1968 were part of the pain; so was recurrence of his childhood struggle with osteomyelitis. For a party facing chronic poverty and with little support east of the Ottawa River, Douglas became a major asset. As a platform orator, his wit, passion, and eloquence had almost no equals. He also had a shrewd tactical skill which gave his party added influence in the minority governments of the 1960s. When Saskatchewan's pioneering medicare scheme became a nation-wide reality in 1967, Douglas deserved a full share of the credit. Many other elements of the NDP's 1961 program, from portable pensions to recognition of Peking as the legitimate government of China, were implemented though his party never held more than ten percent of the seats in the House of Commons. In 1971, when the government imposed the War

Measures Act, suspending civil liberties to crush a handful of terrorists, Douglas led his party in lonely opposition.

After a decade of national leadership, Douglas resigned his position in 1971 but continued until 1979 as the member of Parliament for the seat he had won in 1969, Nanaimo-Cowichan-the Islands. He served as the NDP's expert on energy, campaigning for greater Canadian ownership of an oil and gas industry which had fallen almost wholly into foreign hands. When he retired in 1979 he remained active in the educational work of the Cold-well-Douglas Foundation established by admirers in 1979. He and his wife lived in Ottawa. Their two daughters, Shirley and Joan, established their own careers and families. In 1984 Douglas was hit by an Ottawa bus but recovered. He died of cancer February 24, 1986.

Further Reading

Doris French Shackleton's *Tommy Douglas* (Toronto, 1975) is a sympathetic biography of someone who is clearly a hero to the author. Douglas' years as leader of North America's only democratic socialist government were described by a Regina newspaperman, Chris Higinbotham, in *Off the Record: The CCF in Saskatchewan* (Toronto, 1968). His role as leader of the New Democratic Party is described by Desmond Morton, *NDP: Social Democracy in Canada* (Toronto, 1978). Speeches always lose their impact when they are put on paper, but something of Douglas' platform skill may be found in L. D. Lovick (editor), *Tommy Douglas Speaks* (Lantzville, B.C., 1979).

Additional Sources

The making of a Socialist: the recollections of T.C. Douglas, Edmonton, Alta.: University of Alberta Press, 1982.
French, Doris Cavell Martin, *Tommy Douglas,* Toronto: McClelland and Stewart, 1975. □

William Orville Douglas

William Orville Douglas (1898-1980) was one of the most liberal and activist justices of the U.S. Supreme Court and a vigorous and controversial writer.

William Orville Douglas was born on October 16, 1898, in Maine, Minnesota, where his father, a Nova Scotian missionary, had moved as an itinerant preacher. At the age of 4 William was stricken with polio; to strengthen his spindly legs he began the hiking and later the mountain climbing that became one of his characteristic signatures. When he was 6 his father died, leaving his mother and the three children to make their way on very little, so they moved in with relatives in Yakima, Washington. There William and his two siblings worked their respective ways through school in odd chores and farming jobs. William got a scholarship to Whitman College in Walla Walla, Washington, and upon graduating spent 2 years teaching English and Latin in his hometown high school.

But Douglas's aim was the law. He arrived at Columbia University Law School in 1922 almost penniless, and had to once again work his way through school doing tutoring and research for a law textbook. He was befriended by Dean Harlan Stone and deeply influenced by Professor Underhill Moore, who had a new approach to the legal sociology of corporate business, which became Douglas' focus while at Columbia. This was also the period of the creative jurisprudence on the U.S. Supreme Court of Justice Louis D. Brandeis, and this "People's Attorney" and iconoclastic judge became one of Douglas's heroes. After graduating second highest in his class and editor of Columbia's law journal, Douglas worked for Cravath, DeGersdorff, Swaine & Wood, a huge Wall Street law firm in 1925, and practiced for a year in Yakima. He was admitted to the bar in 1926. He joined the faculty at Columbia Law School in 1927 but resigned in protest against the appointment of a new dean without faculty consultation a year later. A chance meeting with Dean Robert M. Hutchins of the Yale Law School led to Douglas's appointment to a professorship there at the age of 32, and just over a year later he was made Sterling Professor of Law.

Douglas's life was transformed by President Franklin Roosevelt's New Deal, with its sense of social urgency and unparalleled opportunity for reform. In 1934 the newly created Securities and Exchange Commission asked the young law professor for a memorandum on the abuses of corporate reorganization and how these could be remedied. Douglas's reply was an eight-volume report that led to his appointment in 1936 as a member of the Commission and

in 1937 he became its chairman. He prodded the stock exchanges into reorganizing themselves and also developed the Commission's surveillance of the prospectuses for new security issues, which did much to stabilize the exchanges.

When Justice Brandeis retired from the Commission, President Franklin Roosevelt turned to Douglas, despite his youth. Justice Douglas took his seat on April 17, 1939. There was talk of Douglas's resigning for high political office on two occasions during the intervening years. One time was in 1944, when Roosevelt sent two names to the Democratic Convention managers as his preferences for vice-presidential running mate—Douglas and Harry Truman. The choice fell to Truman, partly because political moguls mistrusted Douglas just as business moguls did. The second occasion was in 1948, when President Truman, needing a strong, liberal running mate, offered the place to Douglas, who turned it down.

As a justice, Douglas was one of the hardcore liberal "activists," in the sense that he believed that judicial neutrality was a myth and that judges could not rely on constitutional precedent or hard-and-fast constitutional texts to give them the judicial answers. Douglas believed that judicial statesmanship must keep up with social change and that a judge has the duty actively to shape the law in the desired social direction. Placed for a time in a dissenting minority with Justice Hugo Black, he later found himself part of a liberal majority, as Roosevelt's appointees gradually took over the Court. He went on the defensive again in the conservative Frederick Vinson court of the cold war period but again was part of the liberal majority of the Earl Warren court.

Douglas took a strong role in desegregation cases, in the assurance of fair governmental procedures for the accused, in the freedom of religion cases, and in the cases concerning the right of access to birth-control information. In the obscenity cases he took a firm stand for the absolute freedoms guaranteed against censorship of any sort by the 1st Amendment, which to some made him a proponent of smut and "un-American" values.

Douglas's continuous record of militant judicial liberalism was bound to awaken hostility. There were rumblings about impeaching Douglas when he granted a brief stay of execution to Julius and Ethel Rosenberg, who had been convicted of spying on American atomic bomb technology. Anti-Douglas sentiments were fed by his three divorces and by his judicial opinions in religion-in-the-schools and obscenity cases. To a growing number of people he had offended God, the home, and the purity of the printed word. His book, *Points of Revolution* (1970), compared the current American Establishment with George III's, saying that unless it accepted the pressures for nonviolent revolutionary change, it would be overthrown by violence; this also stirred ire.

The impeachment movement this time gained considerable strength in the House of Representatives, fed mainly by tensions of the era and partisan politics, and a committee looking into his affairs was formed. Gerald Ford, while still in Congress, was the leading voice against Douglas. The impeachment-mongerers had their opening in Douglas's association with the Parvin fund, whose purposes were impeccable but whose money, it turned out, came from sources tainted with gambling. He collected a small fee that, despite being negligible, he still paid income taxes on, which his attackers claimed caused a conflict of interest, despite many of the other justices and government officials having received similar compensations. The impeachment attempts were all inconclusive, but persisted until Douglas retired from the Court in 1975.

An indomitable traveler, naturalist, mountain climber, lecturer, and writer, as well as teacher, administrator, and judge, Douglas reasserted the possibility of a many-faceted Renaissance existence as against a specialized, limited life. His career covered 4 decades of stormy American experience, from the early New Deal days to the tensions of the Vietnam War and the student confrontations of the late 1960s and early 1970s. He brought to these years of turmoil legal and financial skills, a passion for individual freedom, and a plain-spoken brusqueness. He will be remembered as one of the few public figures who dared challenge convention and the Establishment during the middle of the 20th century. He died on January 19, 1980.

Further Reading

William Douglas wrote multiple books, though they are more centered around either law, political philosophy, or nature than himself. However, he did write a few autobiographies, including *Go East, Young Man: The Early Years* (1974) and *The Court Years* (1980). A biographical sketch and a selection of Douglas's judicial opinions are in Vern Countryman, ed., *Douglas of the Supreme Court: A Selection of His Opinions* (1959). Douglas and the Supreme Court are also discussed in John Paul Frank, *The Warren Court* (1964); Leo Pfeffer, *This Honorable Court: A History of the United States Supreme Court* (1965); and Henry Julian Abraham, *Freedom and the Court: Civil Rights and Liberties in the United States* (1967). See also the chapter "William O. Douglas: Diogenes on Wall Street" in Max Lerner, *Ideas Are Weapons: The History and Uses of Ideas* (1939). □

Frederick Douglass

The foremost African American abolitionist in antebellum America, Frederick Douglass (ca. 1817-1895) was the first African American leader of national stature in United States history.

Frederick Douglass was born, as can best be determined, in February 1817 (he took the 14th as his birthday) on the eastern shore of Maryland. His mother, from whom he was separated at an early age, was a slave named Harriet Bailey. She named her son Frederick Augustus Washington Bailey; he never knew or saw his father. (Frederick adopted the name Douglass much later.) Douglass's childhood, though he judged it in his autobiography as being no more cruel than that of scores of others caught in similar conditions, appears to have been extraordinarily deprived of personal warmth. The lack of familial attachments, hard work, and sights of incredible inhumanity fill the text of his early remembrances of the main plantation of Col. Edward Lloyd. In 1825 his masters decided to send him to Baltimore to live with Hugh Auld.

Mrs. Auld, Douglass's new mistress and a Northerner unacquainted with the disciplinary techniques Southern slaveholders used to preserve docility in their slaves, treated young Douglass well. She taught him the rudiments of reading and writing until her husband stopped her. With this basic background he began his self-education.

Escape to Freedom

After numerous ownership disputes and after attempting to escape from a professional slave breaker, Douglass was put to work in the Baltimore shipyards. There in 1838 he borrowed a African American sailor's protection papers and by impersonating him escaped to New York. He adopted the name Douglass and married a free African American woman from the South. They settled in New Bedford, Mass., where several of their children were born.

Douglass quickly became involved in the antislavery movement, which was gaining impetus in the North. In 1841, at an abolitionist meeting in Nantucket, Mass., he delivered a moving speech about his experiences as a slave and was immediately hired as a lecturer by the Massachusetts Antislavery Society. By all accounts he was a forceful and even eloquent speaker. His self-taught prose and manner of speaking so inspired some Harvard students that they persuaded him to write his autobiography. *The Narrative of*

the *Life of Frederick Douglass* was published in 1845. (Ten years later an enlarged autobiography, *My Bondage and My Freedom,* appeared. His third autobiography, *Life and Times of Frederick Douglass,* was published in 1881 and enlarged in 1892.) The 1845 publication, of course, meant exile for Douglass, a fugitive slave.

Fearing capture, Douglass fled to Britain, staying from 1845 to 1847 to speak on behalf of abolition and to earn enough money to purchase his freedom when he returned to America. Upon his return Douglass settled in Rochester, N.Y., and started publishing his newspaper, *North Star* (which continued to be published under various names until 1863).

In 1858, as a consequence of his fame and as unofficial spokesman for African Americans, Douglass was sought out by John Brown as a recruit for his planned attack on the Harpers Ferry arsenal. But Douglass could see no benefit from what he considered a futile plan and refused to lend his support.

Civil War and Reconstruction

The Civil War, beginning in 1861, raised several issues, not the least of which was what role the black man would play in his own liberation—since one of the main objectives of the war was emancipation of the slaves. Douglass kept this issue alive. In 1863, as a result of his continued insistence (as well as of political and military expediency), President Abraham Lincoln asked him to recruit African American soldiers for the Union Army. As the war proceeded, Douglass had two meetings with Lincoln to discuss the use and treatment of African American soldiers by the Union forces. In consequence, the role of African American soldiers was upgraded each time and their military effectiveness thereby increased.

The Reconstruction period laid serious responsibilities on Douglass. Politicians differed on the question of race and its corresponding problems, and as legislative battles were waged to establish the constitutional integrity of the slaves' emancipation, Douglass was the one African American with stature enough to make suggestions.

In 1870 Douglass and his sons began publishing the *New National Era* newspaper in Washington, D.C. In 1877 he was appointed by President Rutherford B. Hayes to the post of U.S. marshal for the District of Columbia. From this time until approximately 2 years before his death Douglass held a succession of offices, including that of recorder of deeds for the District of Columbia and minister-resident and consul-general to the Republic of Haiti, as well as chargé d'affaires to Santo Domingo. He resigned his assignments in Haiti and Santo Domingo when he discovered that American businessmen were taking advantage of his position in their dealings with the Haitian government. He died in Washington, D.C., on Feb. 20, 1895.

Further Reading

Douglass's writings can be found in *The Life and Writings of Frederick Douglass,* edited by Philip S. Foner (4 vols., 1950-1955). *Frederick Douglass,* edited by Benjamin Quarles (1968), contains excerpts from Douglass's writings, portrayals of him by his contemporaries, and appraisals by later historians.

Benjamin Quarles, *Frederick Douglass* (1948), is a well-written, scholarly biography. See also Philip S. Foner, *Frederick Douglass: A Biography* (1964), and Arna Bontemps, *Free at Last: The Life of Frederick Douglass* (1971). There is a biographical sketch of Douglass in William J. Simmons, *Men of Mark: Eminent, Progressive and Rising* (1887; repr. 1968). Works that discuss Douglass at length are John Hope Franklin, *From Slavery to Freedom: A History of American Negroes* (1947; 3d ed. 1967); Louis Filler, *The Crusade against Slavery, 1830-1860* (1960); and Martin Duberman, ed., *The Antislavery Vanguard: New Essays on the Abolitionists* (1965). □

Arthur Garfield Dove

Arthur Garfield Dove (1880-1946) was a pioneer of modern art in America. As early as 1910 he was abstracting forms in nature to suggest landscape situations.

Arthur G. Dove was born in Canandaigua, N.Y., on Aug. 2, 1880. When he graduated from Cornell University in 1903, he became a magazine illustrator, an occupation that would supply his livelihood until 1930, when, with the assistance of Duncan Phillips, he was able to devote all of his time to painting.

In 1907 Dove joined the painters Alfred Maurer and Arthur B. Carles, Jr., on a trip to Europe. Dove spent most of his time in Paris, where he saw the art of the Fauves and was particularly impressed by the work of Henri Matisse. Dove exhibited in the Salon d'Automne in 1908 and 1909.

Dove returned to America in 1910 and continued to paint in an essentially impressionistic manner, though moving more and more toward abstraction. These works closely resemble Wassily Kandinsky's first abstractions, although there is no possibility of an influence since both artists were working along the same lines at about the same time. In his paintings Dove sought to project the essence of nature by ridding forms of extraneous detail and emphasizing rhythms. He replaced bulk with pattern, heightened and modified color, and simplified contours. In 1911 Dove exhibited his Parisian works in a group show at Alfred Stieglitz's gallery in New York City. The following year Dove had his first one-man show there, exhibiting 10 of his abstract canvases.

Dove's most original and striking works are his collages, such as the *Portrait of Ralph Dusenberry* (1924). Here he assembled shingles, a page from a hymnbook, a carpenter's folding rule, and an American flag. The work is a form of pictorial biography of a man whom Dove had actually known. In his collage *Goin' Fishin'* (1925) he evoked the spirit of rural America by combining pieces of a bamboo fishing pole with a denim shirt. Dove's later painting is more and more abstract. *Fog Horns* (1929) suggests piercing but distant blasts penetrating a thick fog through fuzzy-edged, concentric forms against a solid, heavy gray sky.

Dove exhibited annually at An American Place, the new Stieglitz gallery. He was a virtual recluse for the last decade of his life, first at Geneva, N.Y., and then at Centerport, N.Y., where he died on Nov. 23, 1946.

Further Reading

A good book on Dove has not yet been written. The best available work is Frederick S. Wight, *Arthur G. Dove* (1958). It has a fine selection of plates, some in color, and includes a bibliography of Dove's catalogs and exhibitions. Background works include two works edited by Alfred H. Barr, Jr., *Fantastic Art: Dada, Surrealism* (1936; 3d ed. 1947) and *Masters of Modern Art* (1954; 3d ed. 1958); and Oliver W. Larkin, *Art and Life in America* (1949; rev. ed. 1960).

Additional Sources

Morgan, Ann Lee, *Arthur Dove: life and work, with a catalogue raisonne,* Newark: University of Delaware Press; London: Associated University Presses, 1984. □

Rita Frances Dove

Rita Frances Dove (born 1952) is a poet, writer, and educator. In 1993, she became the youngest to hold the title of poet laureate of the United States Library of Congress.

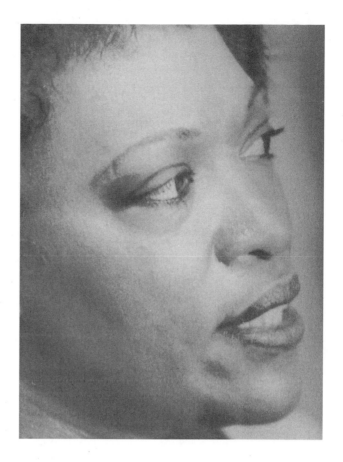

In announcing Rita Frances Dove's appointment, Librarian of Congress James H. Billington said, "I take much pleasure in announcing the selection of a younger poet of distinction and versatility. Having had a number of poet laureates who have accumulated multiple distinctions from lengthy and distinguished careers, we will be pleased to have an outstanding representative of a new and richly variegated generation of American poets. Rita Dove is an accomplished and already widely recognized poet in mid-career whose work gives special promise to explore and enrich contemporary American poetry."

Rita Frances Dove was born in Akron, Ohio, on August 28,1952. She was the second of four children born to Ray Dove and Elvira Elizabeth (Hord) Dove. Her father was one of ten children and was the first in his family to go to college, earning a master's degree in chemistry. At the time of her birth however, her father was working as an elevator operator for the Goodyear Tire and Rubber Company because he could not get hired as a research scientist. Eventually, her father broke the color barrier and became the first African American chemist to work for Goodyear.

From a young age, she wrote plays and stories which her classmates performed. In high school she wrote a comic book along with her older brother which featured characters named Jet Boy and Jet Girl who could fly and communicate telepathically. "One of the things that fascinated me when I was growing up was the way language was put together, and how words could lead you into a new place," she told Mohammed B. Taleb-Khyar in a 1991 interview for *Callaloo.* "I think one reason I became primarily a poet rather than a fiction writer is that though I am interested in stories, I am profoundly fascinated by the ways in which language can change your perceptions."

She was named a presidential scholar in 1970, when she was designated one of the hundred best high school graduates in the nation. A few months later, she enrolled at Miami University, in Oxford, Ohio, as an English major. A writers' conference she attended with one of her high school English teachers had shown her that writing could be a career. She also took many German language courses and practiced the cello consistently. She decided to become a professional poet while in college and told her parents while on a Thanksgiving break. "[My father] swallowed once," she said, recalling that day, "and said 'Well, I've never understood poetry, so don't be upset if I don't read it.'" Faculty members at Miami University were more surprised than her family with her career decision. She said that, "declaring one's intention to be a poet was analogous to putting on a dunce cap," and that many at the school treated her as if she was "throwing away [her] education."

She graduated *summa cum laude* from Miami University in 1973 and was a Fulbright fellow at the University of Tubingen, Germany from 1974 to 1975. In Germany, she studied expressionist drama and the works of twentieth-century German lyric poets Ranier Maria Rilke and Paul Celan. Her political awareness "increased dramatically" while she was in Germany because she found herself "on display in a strange environment where some people pointed with fingers at [her] and others pitied [her] as a symbol for centuries of brutality and injustice against blacks." It was also in Germany that she met her future husband, Fred Viebahn, a novelist. They married in 1979 and have a daughter, Aviva Chantal, who was born in 1983.

Early Career

After returning from Europe, she enrolled at the University of Iowa, where she was a teaching/writing fellow in the Writer's Workshop. She received her Master of Fine Arts at the University of Iowa in 1977, the year *Ten Poems,* her first chapbook of verse was published. In 1980, her second chapbook, *The Only Dark Spot in the Sky,* was published. Her first book-length poetry collection, based on her master's thesis, *The Yellow House on the Corner,* was published in 1980.

Dove's second poetry collection, *Museum,* was published in 1983 and based on her travels abroad from 1979 to 1981. In 1981, Dove joined the faculty of Arizona State University at Tempe as an assistant professor. She was the only African American out of a staff of over seventy members in the English Department. After being promoted to a full professor for the last two years of her stay at Arizona State University, she accepted a position as a professor of English at the University of Virginia at Charlottesville in 1989. In 1992, the university named her Commonwealth Professor of English.

Poet Laureate

The United States Congress created the position of poet laureate in 1985, when it upgraded the half-century-old office of poetry consultant at the Library of Congress. The official title for the position is "Library of Congress Poet Laureate Consultant in Poetry" and offers a $35,000 stipend for the one year term.

On October 1, 1993, Dove became the nation's seventh poet laureate by succeeding Mona Van Duyn. In 1993, she gave the first official poetry reading at the White House in more than a dozen years. In her role of poet laureate, she aimed to keep poetry in the public eye and to expose the mass of American society to a form of language that it might not see otherwise. She tried to be "a force" for poetry and revitalize "serious literature." She said that otherwise the country would "drown in the brutalization of a truncated, dehumanized language." Displaying her entrepreneurial energies, she said that she hoped to raise funds for readings of poetry linked with jazz; a conference among scientists, artists, and writers; and "town meetings" focused on poetry. "I'm hoping that by the end [of my tenure], people will think of a poet laureate as someone who's out there with her sleeves rolled up, not sitting in an ivory tower looking out at the Potomac." She succeeded in this aim, and James H. Billington said that she had come up with "more ideas for elevating poetry in the nation's conscienceness than there is time to carry out in one year." To this aim, he offered, and she accepted his February 1994 invitation to serve another one-year term until late-1994.

After her term finished, she went back to teaching at the University of Virginia and keeps a tireless schedule of public appearances around the country to promote poetry and literature. For the occasion of the Olympiad in Atlanta,

Georgia over the summer of 1996, Dove's works were scored for Andrew Young and read at the games.

Honors

She has held fellowships from the National Endowment for the Arts, the Guggenheim and Mellon Foundations, the National Humanities Center, and the Center for Advanced Studies at the University of Virginia. With the support of the National Endowment for the Humanities, she served as writer-in-residence at Tuskegee Institute as a Portia Pittman fellow. Robert Penn Warren, while poet laureate himself, the first to hold that designation, selected Dove for the Lavan Younger Poet Award bestowed by the Academy of American Poets. She was president of the Associated Writing Programs, made up of persons teaching creative writing in colleges and universities. She holds honorary doctorates from Miami University and Knox College and was inducted into the Ohio Women's Hall of Fame in 1991.

Dove's activities ranged widely outside the world of academia. She served on the Advisory Board for Literature of the National Endowment for the Arts, was a judge for the Walt Whitman Award, the Pulitzer Prize, the National Book Award, and the $75,000 Ruth Lilly Prize, described as "the largest poetry prize in the United States." She held the Ohio Governor's Award in the Arts and the General Electric Foundation Award. She was also an editor of *Callaloo.* She was the Phi Beta Kappa poet at a Harvard University commencement an the New York Public Library selected her as a "Literary Lion."

Dove's poems have appeared in a wide range of journals, including *Black Scholar* and the *Yale Review,* and have been reprinted in such anthologies as *Early Ripening: American Women's Poetry Now,* edited by Marge Piercy (1987). She also published five books of poetry, *The Yellow House on the Corner* (1980), *Museum* (1983), *Thomas and Beulah,* which won a Pulitzer Prize (1986), and *Grace Notes* (1989), and *Mother Love* (1995); as well as a book of short stories, *Fifth Sunday* (1985), and a novel, *Through the Ivory Gate* (1992).

Dove's sometimes intensely personal poetry displays her deeply informed grasp of literary technique. Helen Vendler, a leading critic and student of poetry, wrote in the *New York Review of Books* that "Dove has planed away unnecessary matters: pure shape, her poems exhibit the thrift that Yeats called the sign of a perfected manner."

Arnold Rampersad, director of African American Studies at Princeton University and a specialist in writing by African Americans, wrote that "Dove is perhaps the most disciplined and technically accomplished black poet to arrive since Gwendolyn Brooks began her remarkable career in the nineteen forties. . . ." He spoke also of "the absence of strain in her voice, and the almost uncanny sense of peace and grace that infuses this wide-ranging poetry. . . ."

Typical of her impressive grasp of classical prosody applied to a modern idiom is her spare free-verse sonnet "Flash Cards" from *Grace Notes,* which evokes childhood memories of studying with her father:

In math I was the whiz kid, keeper
of oranges and apples. What you don't understand,
master, my father said; the faster
I answered, the faster they came.
I could see one bud on the teacher's geranium
one clear bee sputtering at the wet pane.
The tulip trees always dragged after heavy rain
so I tucked my head as my boots slapped home.
My father put up his feet after work
and relaxed with a highball and The Life of
   Lincoln.
After supper we drilled and I climbed the dark
before sleep, before a thin voice hissed
numbers as I spun on a wheel. I had to guess.
Ten, I kept saying, I'm only ten.

"Horse and Tree," also from *Grace Notes,* catches a child's excitement about nature and carousels; "Stitches," from the same volume, tersely records the frightening tension during a moment of surgery.

Further Reading

For further biographical material on Dove, see the introductions to her books reported in the text. Articles relevant to her efforts to resuscitate poetry today are Louis Simpson's remarks in the *New York Times Book Review* (March 1, 1992), and essayist Joseph Epstein's essay "Who Killed Poetry?" in *Commentary* (August 1988).

Information on Dove's post-poet laureate career can be found in the *Atlanta Constitution* (July 22, 1996); the *Christian Science Monitor* (September 7, 1995); the *Detroit News* (April 18, 1996); and the *New York Times* (November 5, 1995). □

Neal Dow

Neal Dow (1804-1897) was an American temperance reformer. His long, successful career, together with his reputation as father of the "Maine Law," made him a national figure.

Born in Portland, Maine, on March 20, 1804, Dow was raised in a well-to-do and highly moral Quaker household. Although he read widely and had a good mind, his father was skeptical of the conduct of and influences among college students and was unwilling to send him to college. Accordingly, Dow entered his father's tannery, rose to a partnership, and expanded his business interests in several directions; these accomplishments did not, however, satisfy his need for civic participation.

Dow next entered into temperance activities. He became unusually well informed about the subject in a state which consumed large amounts of liquor, and he became an outstanding speaker against its use. Dow and others in the Maine Temperance Union developed a program aimed at total abolition of liquor sales; since a substantial number of the members were also antislavery advocates, they doubly antagonized the conservative proliquor forces.

In 1846 a measure intended to prohibit liquor sales in Maine was enacted but was so ineffective that it doubled Dow's determination to impose a better-drawn measure. In 1851 Dow became mayor of Portland and applied himself to influencing the state legislature and governor to pass the measure. Despite bitter recriminations it became law, and its passage made Dow famous. He applied the "Maine Law" firmly in Portland and accepted engagements throughout the North to express his sentiments against liquor and slavery. Opposition to the Maine Law consolidated and grew aggressive. Elected mayor again in 1855, Dow continued his fight for full enforcement. Later that year a riot was instigated by proliquor forces in which a rioter was killed and several others wounded by police defending a legally administered liquor supply. Rumor and antiprohibition propaganda accused Dow of murder, but though the Maine Law itself became subject to shifting public sentiment, Dow's good repute held firm. In 1857 he took the first of three lecture trips to England.

Despite his Quaker heritage Dow volunteered for service in the Civil War and was awarded a colonelcy of volunteers. He was active in the Gulf command, was promoted to brigadier general, and served later in Florida. Wounded in 1863, Dow was taken prisoner and spent 8 months at Libby Prison, Richmond, Va., and at Mobile, Ala., before being exchanged.

After the war Dow resumed his temperance work. Dissatisfied with the conduct of the Republican party and its chieftains, in 1880 he joined with other prohibitionists and

became their candidate for president, receiving 10,305 votes. He died in Portland on Oct. 2, 1897.

Further Reading

Dow's autobiography, published posthumously, *The Reminiscences of Neal Dow* (1898), is clearly and circumstantially presented. Dow's early temperance career receives brief but authoritative treatment in John A. Krout, *The Origins of Prohibition* (1925). □

John Dowland

The British composer and lute virtuoso John Dowland (1562-1626) was the leading English lutanist composer of his time. A sensitive, original melodist, he found his forte in pensive song-soliloquys.

John Dowland was born in December 1562 near Dublin. Nothing is known of his early training. From about 1580 until sometime before July 1584 he served as a musician to Sir Henry Cobham, the English ambassador in Paris, and his successor, Sir Edward Stafford. In 1588 Dowland received his bachelor of arts degree at Christ Church, Oxford. Unable to obtain employment in England, possibly because he had been converted to Roman Catholicism in Paris, he visited the courts of Brunswick and Hesse and then traveled to Venice and Florence.

In 1597 Dowland received a degree from Cambridge. He still could find no employment in England, so he took a position at the court of Christian IV of Denmark, whom he served from 1598 until 1607. Apparently released for unsatisfactory service, he returned to England, where it seems that his renunciation of Catholicism opened doors formerly closed to him. He entered the service of Lord Walden. At last, in 1612, he was appointed a King's Musician for the Lutes at the court of James I. He held this position until his death in 1626 and was succeeded by his son, Robert.

Dowland's reputation as a composer rests chiefly on his four books of lute songs. These works may be performed as solo ayres with lute accompaniment or as part songs for four voices. In either arrangement the chief melodic interest lies in the top voice, a feature that gives the songs considerable historical significance.

The four song collections show Dowland's mastery of a new musical idiom, with a harmonic directness that cuts through the old polyphonic complexities. His handling of the lyrics was very sensitive, and he had a remarkable gift for beautiful and expressive melody. Such songs as "Come again, sweet love" and "Lady if you so spite me" exhibit his skill in the merry vein. A diametrically opposite character is to be found in the pathetic melancholy songs for which he is better known. The most expressive of these, such as "Sorrow stay," "I saw my lady weep," and "Flow my tears," relate in literary content as in melodic substance to Dowland's instrumental collection, *Lachrimae, or Seaven Teares Figured in Seaven Passionate Pavans* (1605). The gently descending "Lachrimae" motive established its own tradition and was imitated not only by Dowland's contemporaries, but also by composers in the late 17th century.

Further Reading

Peter Warlock, *The English Ayre* (1926), discusses Dowland. Background material can be found in Paul Henry Lang, *Music in Western Civilization* (1941); Gustave Reese, *Music in the Renaissance* (1954; rev. ed. 1959); Jack A. Westrup, *An Introduction to Musical History* (1955); and Donald J. Grout, *A History of Western Music* (1960).

Additional Sources

Poulton, Diana, *John Dowland,* Berkeley, Calif.: University of California Press, 1982. □

Andrew Jackson Downing

American horticulturist and landscape architect Andrew Jackson Downing (1815-1852) was interested in all aspects of nature and how people might gain pleasure and benefit from it.

Andrew Jackson Downing was born at Newburgh, N.Y., on Oct. 31, 1815; he remained a lifelong resident there. His father was a wheelwright and later a nurseryman. He had little formal education but learned a good deal from reading, corresponding with innumerable professional horticulturists in America and abroad, and his own keen observation. When the father died in 1822, the eldest son took over the nursery business, later joined by Andrew. In 1837 Andrew bought his brother's share of the business. The following year he married Caroline E. DeWint, a grandniece of President John Quincy Adams.

For the next 14 years Downing improved his knowledge of horticulture by study and long, observant walks in the nearby hills. He published the results of his research in the horticultural magazines of Europe and the United States and in his several books. The *Treatise on the Theory and Practice of Landscape Gardening* (1841) introduced him to the American public, which gradually came to consider Downing the leading authority on the subject. He frequently received commissions for landscape projects, even from the Federal government. When his book reached England, it was highly praised.

Downing's interest in the art of landscaping led him to inquire into the relationship of the countryside to the country house and vice versa, so that several of his later books are important for their theories on architectural style. Always deeply concerned with nature, Downing thought of houses as a part of nature, and he designed them to fit their surroundings. *Cottage Residences* (1842) was the first of Downing's writings to assert that the house must fit its site.

In 1845 Downing returned to a strictly horticultural work, *The Fruits and Fruit Trees of America,* a popular book that went through many editions and contributed to his prestige as a pomologist. The next year he became editor of a newly founded magazine, *Horticulturist.* Returning to architecture again, he published *Additional Notes and Hints to Persons about Building in This Country* (1849). His most important book on architecture, *Architecture of Country Houses,* was published in 1850. In that same year Downing traveled to England, where he saw the great gardens and country landscapes he had known only from books. On his return to America he enlisted the services of Calvert Vaux as his business partner in landscape and architectural commissions. In 1851 they worked on the U.S. Capitol and the White House grounds and on estates on Long Island and in the Hudson River valley.

Downing's death on July 28, 1852, while escorting his wife and others on a boat ride down the Hudson River, is a story of heroism and tragedy. The boat caught fire from engines overheated by its negligent captain, who was attempting to outrace another boat to New York City. As people jumped overboard, Downing threw chairs to them as life preservers, and he was evidently swallowed by the river as he tried to save those unable to swim.

Further Reading

The memoir by George W. Curtis in Downing's posthumously published *Rural Essays* (1853) is a fine but typically 19th-century character sketch. George B. Tatum's introduction to a recent edition of Downing's *Architecture of Country Houses*

(1968) gives additional information. Downing's work is also discussed in Marie Luise Gothein, *A History of Garden Art,* vol. 2 (trans. 1928).

Additional Sources

Downing, A. J. (Andrew Jackson), *Pleasure grounds: Andrew Jackson Downing and Montgomery Place,* Tarrytown, N.Y.: Sleepy Hollow Press, 1988.

Schuyler, David, *Apostle of taste: Andrew Jackson Downing, 1815-1852,* Baltimore: Johns Hopkins University Press, 1996.
☐

Sir Arthur Conan Doyle

The British author Sir Arthur Conan Doyle (1859-1930) is best remembered as the creator of the famous detective Sherlock Holmes.

Arthur Conan Doyle was born in Edinburgh, Scotland, on May 22, 1859, into an Irish Roman Catholic family of noted artistic achievement. After attending Stonyhurst College, he entered Edinburgh University as a medical student in 1876. He received a doctor of medicine degree in 1885. In his spare time, however, he began to write stories, which were published anonymously in various magazines from 1878 to 1880.

After two long sea voyages as a ship's doctor, Doyle practiced medicine at Southsea, England, from 1882 to 1890. In 1885 he married Louise Hawkins and in March 1891 moved his young family to London, where he began to specialize in ophthalmology. His practice remained small, however, and since one of his anonymous stories, "Habakuk Jephson's Statement," had enjoyed considerable success when it appeared in the *Cornhill Magazine* in 1884, he began to devote himself seriously to writing. The result was his first novel, *A Study in Scarlet,* which introduced Sherlock Holmes, the detective, to the reading public in *Beeton's Christmas Annual* for 1887. This was followed by two historical novels in the tradition of Sir Walter Scott, *Micah Clarke* in 1889 and *The White Company* in 1891. The immediate and prolonged success of these works led Doyle to abandon medicine and launch his career as a man of letters.

The second Sherlock Holmes novel, *The Sign of the Four* (1890), was followed by the first Holmes short story, "A Scandal in Bohemia" (1891). The instant popularity of these tales made others like them a regular monthly feature of the *Strand Magazine,* and the famous *Adventures of Sherlock Holmes* series was begun. In subsequent stories Doyle developed Holmes into a highly individualized and eccentric character, together with his companion, Doctor Watson, the ostensible narrator of the stories, and the pair came to be readily accepted as living persons by readers in England and America. But Doyle seems to have considered these stories a distraction from his more serious writing, eventually grew tired of them, and in "The Final Problem," published in December 1893, plunged Holmes and his

archenemy, Moriarty, to their apparent deaths in the falls of Reichenbach. Nine years later, however, he published a third Sherlock Holmes novel, *The Hound of the Baskervilles,* but dated the action before Holmes's "death." Then, in October 1903, Holmes effected his mysterious resurrection in "The Empty House" and thereafter appeared intermittently until 1927, 3 years before Doyle's own death. All told, Doyle wrote 56 Sherlock Holmes stories and 4 novels (*The Valley of Fear,* 1914, was the last).

Among the other works published early in his career, which Doyle felt were more representative of his true artistry, were *Beyond the City* (1892), a short novel of contemporary urban life; *The Great Shadow* (1892), a historical novel of the Napoleonic period; *The Refugees* (1893), a historical novel about French Huguenots; and *The Stark Munro Letters* (1894), an autobiographical novel. In 1896 he issued one of his best-known historical novels, *Rodney Stone,* which was followed by another historical novel, *Uncle Bernac* (1897); a collection of poems, *Songs of Action* (1898); and two less popular novels, *The Tragedy of Korosko* (1898) and *A Duet* (1899).

After the outbreak of the Boer War, Doyle's energy and patriotic zeal led him to serve as chief surgeon of a field hospital at Bloemfontein, South Africa, in 1900. His *The Great Boer War* (1900) was widely read and praised for its fairness to both sides. In 1902 he wrote a long pamphlet, *The War in South Africa: Its Cause and Conduct,* to defend the British action in South Africa against widespread criticism by pacifist groups. In August 1902 Doyle was knighted for his service to England.

After being twice defeated, in 1900 and 1906, in a bid for a seat in Parliament, Sir Arthur published *Sir Nigel* (1906), a popular historical novel of the Middle Ages. The following year he married his second wife, Jean Leckie. The two first met in 1897 but apparently resisted the growing attraction between them successfully until after the death of his wife, in 1906, of tuberculosis. Doyle now took up a number of political and humanitarian causes. In 1909 he wrote *Divorce Law Reform,* championing equal rights for women in British law, and *The Crime of the Congo,* attacking the exploitation of that colony by Belgium. In 1911 he published a second collection of poems, *Songs of the Road,* and in 1912 began a series of science fiction stories with the novel *The Lost World,* featuring another of his famous characters, Professor Challenger.

After the outbreak of World War I, Doyle organized the Civilian National Reserve against the threat of German invasion. In 1916 he published *A Visit to Three Fronts* and in 1918 again toured the front lines. These tours, plus extensive correspondence with a number of high-ranking officers, enabled him to write his famous account *The British Campaigns in France and Flanders,* published in six volumes (1916-1919).

Doyle had been interested in spiritualism since he rejected his Roman Catholic faith in 1880. In 1915 he apparently experienced a "conversion" to "psychic religion," so that after the war he devoted the rest of his life and career to propagating his new faith in a series of works: *The New Revelation* (1918), *The Vital Message* (1919), *The Wanderings of a Spiritualist* (1921), and *History of Spiritualism* (1926). From 1917 to 1925 he lectured on spiritualism throughout Europe, Australia, the United States, and Canada. The same cause led him to South Africa in 1928 and brought him home exhausted, from Sweden, in 1929. He died on July 6, 1930, of a heart attack, at his home in Crowborough, Sussex.

Further Reading

An intimate view of Doyle emerges from his autobiography, *Memories and Adventures* (1924), and from his autobiographical novel, *The Stark Munro Letters* (1894). The best biographical and critical study of Doyle is Pierre Nordon, *Conan Doyle: A Biography,* translated by Frances Partridge (1966), although Nordon is sometimes careless about dates and bibliographical data. John Dickson Carr's "novelized" biography, *The Life of Sir Arthur Conan Doyle* (1949), is entertaining but incomplete. Two useful shorter biographies are Hesketh Pearson, *Conan Doyle: His Life and Art* (1943), and Michael and Mollie Hardwick, *The Man Who Was Sherlock Holmes* (1964). A. E. Murch, *The Development of the Detective Novel* (1958; rev. ed. 1968), gives important insight into the literary significance of the Sherlock Holmes stories. □

Luis María Drago

The Argentine international jurist and diplomat Luis María Drago (1859-1921) is known for the "Drago Doctrine," which held that international law did not

authorize European powers to use armed intervention to force American republics to pay public debts.

Luis María Drago the son of Luis María Drago and Estela Sánchez Drago, was born on May 6, 1859, in Buenos Aires. After being educated by tutors and in private schools, he began to work for newspapers and to study at the university in 1875. In 1882 he completed a doctorate of laws, served briefly in the provincial legislature, and became a judge in the Buenos Aires civil and criminal courts. Later he published a pioneer study of penal problems.

In 1902 Drago was elected to the Chamber of Deputies, but almost immediately President Julio Roca appointed him minister of foreign relations. British and German fleets at that time were blockading Venezuela's coast to force payment of debts to their nationals. Drago's instructions to Argentina's representative in Washington declared that international law did not sanction intervention to compel sovereign republics to repay public indebtedness. This "Drago Doctrine" stemmed from an 1868 pronouncement by another Argentine jurist, Carlos Calvo, who had maintained that foreign creditors must seek recourse through domestic courts of countries where they lend money.

Elected again to the Chamber of Deputies in 1906, Drago soon resigned to serve on the International Court of Justice at The Hague. The next year the Court ratified a modified version of the Drago Doctrine, which had already been adopted by the 1906 Pan-American Conference. This doctrine has been credited with developing Pan-American unity against European intervention, thereby forestalling territorial acquisitions in the Western Hemisphere like those in Asia and Africa. However, the United States' increasing strength constituted the major bulwark against European imperialism.

Drago's minor role in the Venezuelan debt crisis and his significant International Court service earned worldwide respect. In 1909 the United States and Venezuela asked him to arbitrate a claims dispute. From 1910 to 1912 Drago, at the behest of Britain and the United States, arbitrated the North Atlantic fisheries dispute, and neither side questioned his decisions. In 1912 Columbia University awarded him an honorary doctorate for contributions to international peace; and the Carnegie Endowment for International Peace acclaimed him as "the highest exponent of the intellectual culture of South America." He served again in Argentina's Chamber of Deputies from 1912 to 1916. He died in Buenos Aires on June 9, 1921.

Further Reading

The only extensive account of Drago's life is in Spanish. A brief sketch of his career appears in William Belmont Parker, ed., *Argentines of Today* (2 vols. In 1, 1920). For thorough examinations of the Drago Doctrine see Dexter Perkins, *The Monroe Doctrine, 1867-1907* (1937), and Harold F. Peterson, *Argentina and the United States, 1810-1960* (1964). □

Daniel Drake

The American physician Daniel Drake (1785-1852) was one of the founders of the medical school in Cincinnati, Ohio. He also participated in social, political, and economic movements in the Ohio Valley.

Daniel Drake was born on Oct. 20, 1785, near Plainfield, N.J. His family soon moved to Kentucky. At the age of 15 he began to study medicine with a Cincinnati doctor, later graduating from the University of Pennsylvania. Returning to the Ohio Valley in 1805, he devoted the remainder of his life to science and the development of the West.

Drake played a major role in establishing a medical school in Cincinnati. He also wrote extensively on medical subjects, his most important work being *Principal Diseases of the Interior Valley of North America*, and was cofounder in 1826 of the *Ohio Medical Repository*, a medical journal designed to improve medical standards in the West. Another project that took up his time was the establishment of adequate hospital facilities in the Ohio Valley. In his *Natural and Statistical View, or Pictures of Cincinnati*, published in 1815, Drake recorded valuable data on the geology, botany, and meteorology of this region.

Drake crusaded against the "quack" doctors who invaded the frontier. He attacked the laws which allowed such unscrupulous men to practice and the politicians who refused to pass legislation to prevent them from taking advantage of the frontier's need for doctors.

Drake also supported social reform movements. Although an active crusader against the intemperate use of alcohol, he was not for total abstinence. As a doctor, he stressed the adverse effects of alcohol on the body; as a reformer, he stressed the social implications of overindulgence. He made speeches in behalf of the temperance movement and in 1841 helped organize the Physiological Temperance Society of Louisville.

Politically, Drake advocated national unity. He violently condemned the nullification crisis of 1832-1833. On the slavery question he condemned both Northern abolitionists and Southern "fire-eaters" as disruptive forces. Firmly opposed to slavery and to its extension into the territories, he also opposed extremism. To solve the slavery problem he strongly supported a national colonization policy.

In the words of his best biographer, Drake was "a man possessing commanding talents. By some he has been called a genius. He had an unusual, almost prophetic vision, a philanthropic outlook, an abiding philosophy, as well as a scientific and inquisitive mind."

Further Reading

The most complete biography of Drake is Emmet F. Horine, *Daniel Drake, 1785-1852: Pioneer Physician of the Midwest* (1961). A description of his early life is included in Charles D.

Drake, ed., *Pioneer Letters in Kentucky: A Series of Reminiscential Letters from Daniel Drake . . . to His Children* (1870). For a contemporary view of Drake and life in the Ohio Valley see Edward D. Mansfield, *Memoirs of the Life and Services of Daniel Drake, M.D.: Physician, Professor, and Author* (1855).

Additional Sources

Mansfield, Edward Deering, *Memoirs of the life and services of Daniel Drake, M.D.,* New York: Arno Press, 1975. □

Sir Francis Drake

The English navigator Sir Francis Drake (ca. 1541-1596) was the first of his countrymen to circumnavigate the globe. His daring exploits at sea helped to establish England's naval supremacy over Spain and other European nations.

Francis Drake, the eldest son of a yeoman farmer, was born near Tavistock, Devonshire. His father later became a Calvinist lay preacher and raised his children as staunch Protestants. Young Drake received some education; he learned the rudiments of navigation and seamanship early and did some sailing near his home. The Drakes were related to the Hawkins family of Plymouth, well-to-do seamen and shipowners. The Hawkins connection got Drake a place on a 1566 slave-trading expedition to the Cape Verde Islands and the Spanish Main.

First Command

In 1567 John Hawkins made Drake an officer in a larger slave-trading expedition. Drake ultimately received command of one of Hawkins's ships, the *Judith,* and accompanied his relative to Africa, Rio de la Hacha, and Santa Marta, where Hawkins disposed of the slaves. The English were caught, however, in the harbor of San Juan de Ulúa by a Spanish fleet that opened fire without warning and destroyed most of their ships. Only Drake's *Judith* and Hawkins's small vessel escaped to England. Embittered by this, Drake resolved to devote his life to war against Spain.

Elizabeth I of England and Philip II of Spain were not at war then, but grievances were steadily mounting. The Queen declined to offend Philip and would not allow Hawkins to go to sea again immediately, but she had no objections to a voyage by the obscure Drake. In 1569 Drake had married Mary Newman of Plymouth, but finding domesticity dull, he departed in 1570 for the Spanish Main with a small crew aboard the 25-ton *Susan* . He hoped to learn how the Spaniards arranged for shipping Peruvian treasure home, and he felt that the ports of Panama City and Nombre de Dios on the Isthmus of Panama were the key. His 1570 voyage was largely one of reconnaissance during which he made friends with the Cimaroons, who were escaped slaves dwelling out of Spanish reach on the Isthmus and stood ready to help him. During a 1571 expedition he captured Nombre de Dios with Cimaroon help but lost it immediately when, wounded, he had to be carried to safety. After depre-

event, he realized that the two oceans came together and that Terra Australis would not be found there. He traveled along the coasts of Chile and Peru, capturing and destroying Spanish ships but sparing Spanish lives.

Between Callao and Panama Drake took an unarmed treasure ship, bearing gold, emeralds, and all the silver the *Golden Hind* could carry. Knowing that Spaniards would try to waylay him in the strait, Drake bypassed Panama and, near Guatalco, Nicaragua, captured charts and directions to guide him across the Pacific. Perhaps seeking the Strait of Anian, he sailed nearly 48 degrees north, and then descended to a point at or near Drake's Bay, in California, where he made friends with the Indians and overhauled the ship. He left a brass plate naming the country Nova Albion and claiming it for Elizabeth. (In 1936 a plate fitting the description was found near Drake's Bay.)

Drake then crossed the Pacific to the Moluccas and near there almost came to grief when the ship struck a reef. Skilled handling freed it, and his circumnavigation of the globe continued via the Indian Ocean and the Cape of Good Hope. Drake arrived in Plymouth in 1580, acclaimed by the public and his monarch. In April 1581 he was knighted on the deck of the *Golden Hind.*

Drake did not immediately go to sea again and in 1581 became mayor of Plymouth. After his wife died, he married a young aristocrat, Elizabeth Sydenham. Drake, now a wealthy man, made the bride a substantial settlement. He had no children by either wife.

dations off Cartagena, he intercepted a Spanish gold train near Nombre de Dios and returned to England with the bounty.

His arrival embarrassed the Queen, who still hoped for peace with Spain, and Drake evidently received a broad hint to leave the country temporarily. He is known to have served in Ireland with the Earl of Essex, who was trying to crush a rebellion in Ulster. By 1576 relations with Spain had worsened, and Drake returned to England, where a new expedition was being planned in which Elizabeth had a financial share. Drake's main instructions were to sail through the Strait of Magellan and probe for the shores of Terra Australis Incognita, the great southern continent that many thought began with Tierra del Fuego. Drake received five ships, the largest being the *Pelican* (later named the *Golden Hind*), and a crew of about 160.

Adventures on the *Golden Hind*

The fleet left Plymouth in December 1577 for the southern Atlantic, stopping at Port San Julián for the Southern Hemisphere winter. Ferdinand Magellan had once crushed a mutiny there, and Drake did the same. He tried and executed Thomas Doughty, an aristocratic member of the expedition, who had intrigued against him in an attempt to foment a rebellion.

When Drake passed through the strait and entered the Pacific, only the *Golden Hind* remained; the other ships had been lost or had parted company. Contrary winds forced him southward, and he perhaps sighted Cape Horn; in any

Expedition against Spain

By 1585 Elizabeth, after new provocations by Philip, felt ready to unleash Drake again. A large fleet was outfitted, including two of her own vessels. Drake, aboard his command ship, the *Elizabeth Bonaventure,* had instructions to release English vessels impounded by Philip, though Elizabeth certainly knew he would exceed orders.

Drake fulfilled the Queen's expectations. He sacked Vigo in Spanish Galicia and then sailed to Santo Domingo and Cartagena, capturing and holding both for ransom. He would have tried to cross the Isthmus and take Panama, a project he had cherished for years, but an epidemic so reduced his crews that he abandoned the idea. On the way to England he destroyed the Spanish settlement at St. Augustine, in Florida, and farther north, took home the last remaining settlers at Sir Walter Raleigh's unfortunate North Carolina colony.

The expedition, which reached Portsmouth in July 1586, had acquired little treasure but had inflicted great physical and moral damage on Spain, enormously raising English prestige in the bargain. Formal war was now inevitable, and Philip started plans to invade England. In February 1587 the Queen beheaded Mary of Scotland who had been connected with plots to dethrone or murder Elizabeth, to the outrage of Catholic Europe and many English Catholics. Philip began assembling his Armada in Portugal, which had been in his possession since 1580.

Spanish Armada

Elizabeth appointed Lord Charles Howard of Effingham commander of her fleet and gave Drake, Hawkins, and Martin Frobisher immediately subordinate posts. Drake advocated a strong preventive blow at Philip's unprepared Armada and received permission to strike. In April 1587 he recklessly sailed into Cadiz and destroyed or captured 37 enemy ships. He then occupied the Portuguese town of Sagres for a time and finally, in the Azores, seized a large Portuguese carrack bound homeward from Goa with a rich cargo.

The Cadiz raid damaged but did not cripple the Armada, which, under Alonso de Guzmán, Duke of Medina Sidonia, sailed in May 1588. It was alleged that Lord Howard was a figurehead and that the "sea dogs" Drake, Hawkins, and Frobisher won the victory in the July encounters. Recent evidence refutes this and shows Howard to have been in effective command. Drake took a conspicuous part in the channel fighting and captured a galleon, but he does not seem to have distinguished himself above other English commanders.

The Armada was defeated, and Drake's career thereafter proved anticlimactic. He met with his first formidable defeat in 1589, when he commanded the naval expedition sent to take Lisbon. He seemed to have lost some of his old daring, and his cautious refusal to ascend the Tagus River for a naval bombardment partly accounted for the failure. Drake did not go to sea again for 5 years. He concerned himself mainly with Plymouth matters. He sat in Parliament, but nothing of note marked his presence there.

Final Voyage

In 1595 Elizabeth thought she saw a chance of ending the war victoriously by cutting off the Spanish treasure supply from the Isthmus of Panama. For this she selected Hawkins, then 63, and Drake, in his 50s. The cautious Hawkins and the impetuous Drake could never work well together, and the Queen further complicated the situation by giving them equal authority; in effect, each commanded his own fleet. The Queen's order that they must be back in 6 months scarcely allowed time to capture Panama, and when they learned of a crippled Spanish treasure ship in San Juan, Puerto Rico, they decided to go there. Through Drake's insistence on first going to the Canary Islands, their destination was revealed, and the Spaniards sent word ahead to Puerto Rico. Hawkins died as they reached the island, leaving Drake in sole command. The Spaniards had strengthened their San Juan defenses, and Drake failed to capture the city.

Ignoring the Queen's 6-month time limit, the aging Drake, still trying to repeat his earlier successes, made for the Isthmus to capture Nombre de Dios and then Panama. He easily took the former, not knowing that it had been superseded by Puerto Bello as the Caribbean terminus of the Plate fleets. His landing party, which soon realized it was following a path long out of use, was ambushed by Spaniards and forced to retreat.

Drake knew the expedition was a failure; he cruised aimlessly to Honduras and back and then fell ill of fever and dysentery. He died off Puerto Bello on Jan. 28, 1596, and was buried at sea. Sir Thomas Baskerville, second in command, took the expedition home to England.

Further Reading

The most complete account of Drake's circumnavigation is provided by his nephew, Sir Francis Drake, in *The World Encompassed by Sir Francis Drake,* published by the Hakluyt Society (1854). Primary material can be found in John Barrow, *Life, Voyages, and Exploits of Sir Francis Drake, with Numerous Original Letters* (1844). Julian S. Corbett, *Drake and the Tudor Navy* (2 vols., 1898; rev. ed. 1899), can be supplemented with more recent studies such as James A. Williamson, *Age of Drake* (1938; 4th ed. 1960) and *Sir Francis Drake* (1966), and Kenneth R. Andrews, *Drake's Voyages: A Reassessment of Their Place in Elizabethan Maritime Expansion* (1967). For general background see J. H. Parry, *The Age of Reconnaissance* (1963). □

John William Draper

The Anglo-American scientist and historian John William Draper (1811-1882) pioneered in scientific applications of photography and popularized a "scientific" approach to social and intellectual history.

John William Draper was born near Liverpool, England, on May 5, 1811. He did premedical studies at University College, London. In 1832 Draper, his wife, mother, and sisters sailed to America.

Settling in Mecklenburg County, Va., Draper began scientific research in his own laboratory. He experimented in capillary attraction and published on a variety of scientific subjects. He completed his medical studies at the University of Pennsylvania in 1836, then returned to Virginia to become professor of chemistry and natural philosophy at Hampden-Sidney College. He contributed to British and American scholarly journals. In 1838 he was appointed professor of chemistry and botany at the University of the City of New York.

Draper's career as a research scientist flowered from 1839 to 1856. His earliest important project involved him in a race with Samuel F. B. Morse to be the first in America to apply the photographic technique of the French inventor Louis Daguerre to portraiture. In solving these problems Draper developed expansive notions about the uses of photography in scientific investigation. A brilliant experimentalist, he was especially important for outlining the scientific applications of photography. He pioneered in expanding beyond both extremes of the visible spectrum with photographic techniques and was a founder of the theory of photochemical absorption.

Draper helped establish the medical school of the University of the City of New York and became its president in

1850. His *Human Physiology* (1856) marked the end of his scientific career.

Draper's second career—in history and social analysis—grew out of his first. He believed in the possibility of progress through science and technology and wrote about history and society with the conviction that a "scientific" approach to society was desirable. His *History of the Intellectual Development of Europe* (1863) traced the history of Western thought. *Thoughts on the Future Civil Policy of America* (1865) and a three-volume *History of the American Civil War* (1867-1870), the first serious history of the war, followed. His last major work, *History of the Conflict between Religion and Science* (1874), was a condensation of his 1863 book.

Convinced that nature was the compulsive force behind history, Draper in his version of environmental determinism emphasized climate. Although his histories are seriously defective, he was a pioneer in the history of ideas. After his death on Jan. 4, 1882, Draper's reputation as a scientist diminished while his fame as a historian flourished.

Further Reading

Donald H. Fleming, *John William Draper and the Religion of Science* (1950), is an excellent biography. For background material see Nathan Reingold, ed., *Science in Nineteenth-Century America* (1964), and Howard S. Miller, *Pursuit of Science in Nineteenth Century America* (1969). □

Michael Drayton

The English poet Michael Drayton (1563-1631) attempted to create a strong national culture by turning for inspiration to English history rather than to foreign sources.

Like his contemporary William Shakespeare, Michael Drayton was the son of a prosperous Warwickshire tradesman. He received a good education as a page in the house of Sir Henry Goodere, but there is no record of his ever having studied at a university.

Drayton's first publication, *The Harmony of the Church,* a somewhat clumsy paraphrase of the Bible, appeared in 1591, when he was 28. Succeeding publications exemplify a wide variety of genres. *Idea, the Shepherd's Garland* (1593) is a collection of nine pastoral poems, celebrating ideal beauty, in imitation of Edmund Spenser. *Idea's Mirror* (1594), a sonnet sequence, also portrays the poet's beloved (probably Anne Goodere, the daughter of his patron), under the Platonic name of "Idea."

By 1593 Drayton had also written his first historical romance in verse, *Piers Gaveston.* Two heroic poems followed, drawing on incidents in English history: *Robert, Duke of Normandy* and *Mortimeriados,* both published in 1596. The latter, which portrays the evils of civil strife, was considerably revised and republished as *The Baron's Wars* (1603). The most popular of Drayton's early works, *England's Heroical Epistles,* was published in 1597. Written in imitation of Ovid's *Heroides,* it consists of a series of verse letters between lovers famous in English history.

Drayton turned to the fashionable genre of satirical verse in two rather obscure works, *The Owl* (1604) and *The Man in the Moon* (1606). Some of his most famous shorter works were published in *Poems Lyric and Pastoral* (1606), including the patriotic "Battle of Agincourt" and the "Ode to the Virginian Voyage," which celebrates English discoveries in America. Drayton's ambitious *Polyolbion* (1612-1622), a long topographical poem, describes region by region the beauties and traditions of England and attempts to provide a legendary basis for the Stuart claim to the English throne. The most important of the poems of Drayton's later years, his *Nymphidia* (1627), is a delicate mock-heroic tale of the fairy kingdom, peopled with characters like those that appear in Shakespeare's *Midsummer Night's Dream.*

Although Drayton often lacks dramatic power and intellectual depth, he has been rightly praised for his versatility, narrative skill, and insight into character. He died in London in 1631 and was buried in Westminster Abbey.

Further Reading

The Works of Michael Drayton was edited by J. William Hebel (5 vols., 1931-1941; rev. ed. 1961). An edition of Drayton's *Poems* was edited by John Buxton (2 vols., 1953). Biographical and critical studies of Drayton's life and works include Oliver Elton, *Michael Drayton* (1905); Glenn P. Haskell, *Drayton's Secondary Modes* (1936); Bernard H. Newdigate,

Michael Drayton and His Circle (1941; rev. ed. 1961); and Joseph A. Berthelot, *Michael Drayton* (1967). Recommended for general background are Lisle C. John, *The Elizabethan Sonnet Sequences* (1938); Hallett D. Smith, *Elizabethan Poetry* (1952); and Clive S. Lewis, *English Literature in the Sixteenth Century, Excluding Drama* (1954).

Additional Sources

Elton, Oliver, *An introduction to Michael Drayton,* Norwood, Pa.: Norwood Editions, 1977. □

Herman Theodore Dreiser

American novelist Herman Theodore Dreiser (1871-1945) projected a vitality and an honesty that established several of his novels as classics of world literature.

L ike other naturalistic novelists of the 1890s Theodore Dreiser believed in evolutionary and materialistic determinism and gave these ideas powerful expression. Preoccupied with sex, he demanded the freedom to write about it as he saw fit. His hard-won victories over narrow-minded censorship marked a turning point in the history of the American novel.

Dreiser was born Aug. 27, 1871, in Terre Haute, Ind., one of 12 children of a German Catholic immigrant and an

Ohio woman who gave up her Mennonite religion and her family's good opinion to marry him. Theodore was a sickly child with an almost sightless right eye; he seemed at first to have less chance of survival than the three brothers who had died before him in infancy.

Growing Up Poor

For the elder Dreiser, making a living for his large family was difficult. In 1867 he had moved them to Sullivan, Ind., where, by going deeply into debt, he bought a woolen mill that seemed promising. But in 1869 fire destroyed Dreiser's mill, leaving him even more deeply in debt. This burden was to weigh heavily upon all members of the family for years. Theodore was 7 in 1878, when his parents decided that breaking up their home was necessary for economic survival. The older children followed their father in search of jobs. The younger three, including Theodore, moved with their mother to Vincennes and then back to Sullivan. There one of the older daughters rejoined them; she was pregnant by a man who refused to marry her. When the baby was still-born in April 1878, they buried it secretly.

The family's years in Sullivan were hard for young Dreiser. He was sent home from parochial school because he had no shoes. The family was so poor that his mother took in washing (Dreiser was to remember having to deliver the bundles to affluent homes), and the boys gathered coal from the railroad tracks to keep the fire going. Dreiser's father descended upon the house-hold occasionally to rail about the children's failings in religion and morality.

The year 1881, however, brought a melodramatic reversal for the family. Paul, one of the older brothers, unexpectedly appeared, beaming with good humor and opulence. He had begun to establish his reputation as a songwriter (he would later win fame with such songs as "My Gal Sal" and "On the Banks of the Wabash"; for the latter Theodore supplied the words of the first stanza and chorus). Paul settled his mother with the younger children in a cozy home in Evansville and himself in the town's most spendid brothel, which was kept by Sallie Walker—his "Gal Sal." Food, clothing, and coal were now no problem, but Paul's flagrant life of sin troubled the religious Theodore. Paul's turbulent romance with the beautiful madam ended in 1884; he left town to seek work elsewhere. Dreiser's mother took her family to Chicago, where Theodore got a job in a dry goods store, but he was miserable and soon quit. His father rejoined the family, also out of work. Without Paul's help the Dreisers ran quickly into debt again, and soon they fled the bill collectors to Warsaw, Ind.

The nuns who had been Dreiser's teachers up to that time had made him fear school. In Warsaw he entered the public schools. A young woman teacher encouraged the shy boy to read: he fell in love with her and with the books she recommended. Again older sisters stirred town gossip: one ran off with a bar cashier who had stolen $3,500 from the bar's safe, and another had an affair with the son of a wealthy family that ended in pregnancy. These events would later provide materials for Dreiser's fiction, but at 15 he felt them only as humiliating. He left school and went to Chicago to work as a dishwasher and then a stock clerk.

In 1888 one of Dreiser's Warsaw teachers found him in Chicago and sent him to the University of Indiana the next year. College lasted only a year for him, but it was an important year. As a result of his exposure to college girls, his consciousness of the power of sex, the great theme of his fiction, became acute—and acutely painful. He returned home in 1890 to work and help care for his mother, who died that November. When a Bavarian priest refused her a funeral Mass because she had not received the last rites of the Church, Dreiser lost whatever remained of his father's religion.

Journalistic Career

Before his twenty-first birthday Dreiser had found a job on the staff of the *Chicago Globe.* Progressing rapidly in newspaper work, he moved to the *St. Louis Globe-Democrat.* In 1893 the *St. Louis Republic* sent him to the World's Columbian Exposition in Chicago as leader of a group of schoolteachers, one of whom was a pretty redhead named Sara Osborne White, called "Jug." Dreiser was then having an affair with his landlady and was romantically involved with some other women, but Jug would 6 years later become his wife. To fulfill his dream of quick success, and perhaps also to try to escape Jug, Dreiser quit his job and traveled east, taking a job on the *Pittsburgh Dispatch.* There he saw the injustices of industrial society in sharp focus, yet his editors stopped his stories about them, explaining, "The big steel men just about own the place."

If he could not write, Dreiser could read: Honoré de Balzac shaped his conception of the novel, and T.H. Huxley and Herbert Spencer gave him a new philosophy. Spencer, Dreiser reported later, "took every shred of belief away from me; showed me that I was a chemical atom in a whirl of unknown forces. . . ." In that frame of mind he moved to New York in 1894 and found work on the *World.* But the shy young man, very tall, very thin, his bad eye partially hidden by his gold-rimmed glasses, neither looked nor acted the part of the brash metropolitan reporter. If he had not quit, he would surely have been fired.

Almost destitute, Dreiser convinced his brother Paul and two other songwriters to let him edit a magazine that would give their work wider audience. Dreiser titled it *Ev'ry Month,* and filled it with popular poetry, stories, and essays, as well as the songs; he also published Stephen Crane's "A Mystery of Heroism," some other pieces of literary interest, and many of his own serious articles. He left this magazine in 1897 but found work on other magazines, for which he interviewed Thomas A. Edison, Andrew Carnegie, William Dean Howells, Marshall Field, and other celebrities, writing of their rise to success. For the first time he had money—and no further excuse for postponing marriage to the eager Jug; it took place in December 1898.

For more than a dozen years Dreiser continued his successful journalistic career in New York. He wrote features for the *Daily News;* edited dime novels; and served as editor of *Smith's Magazine, Broadway Magazine,* and three magazines published to encourage women to buy Butterick dress patterns, including the *Delineator* . He raised the *Delineator* 's circulation dramatically by anticipating the responses of its female readers. (In 1908 he secured H.L. Mencken as a contributor—the beginning of a long, important friendship.) Dreiser was one of the best-paid editors in the country in 1910, when the enraged mother of an 18-year-old girl with whom he was in love got him fired by threatening to make public the sordid history of his philandering. His marriage also suffered: his wife went home to her family in Missouri. She returned now and again, but in 1914 their separation became permanent, although neither sought a divorce.

Career as Novelist

Dreiser had begun experimenting with fiction in 1899. His first important novel, *Sister Carrie,* occupied him for about 4 months in 1899-1900. Jug helped with the grammar, and literary friends reduced the manuscript by 40,000 words after Dreiser had finished it; although Dreiser required help in polishing the surface of his work, the profundities of the novel's conceptions and characterizations prove that he was from the beginning a master of the essentials of fiction. The novel's heroine, Carrie Meeber, goes to Chicago to live with her sister and seek work but finds working conditions terrible and pay small. She becomes the mistress of a salesman but turns subsequently to Hurstwood, manager of an elegant bar. Hurstwood, whose marriage is breaking up, is tempted to steal money from the bar's safe, which he finds open. He removes the money, then decides to return it to the safe, but the safe door accidently closes and locks: chance has made him a thief. Chance operates again and again in the lives of Hurstwood and Carrie (with whom he runs away), bringing one to suicide and the other to an ungratifying success as a musical comedy star. The novel is far from explicit in its treatment of sex, but in its failure to give virtue and vice their appropriate rewards it constituted an affront to the official moral standards of the day. One publisher turned it down; but at Doubleday, Page and Company, it received a warm reception from Frank Norris, who was reader for the firm. Doubleday contracted to publish *Carrie,* but when Frank Doubleday and his wife read it, they had second thoughts. Dreiser held the firm to their contract, however, and they published the book in 1901 but did not advertise it. Norris tried hard to publicize it, but the final tally showed 456 copies sold, giving the author a royalty of $68.40. Not until 1907, when another publisher reissued it, did *Sister Carrie* attract notice and sell.

The initial failure of *Sister Carrie* drove Dreiser to a nervous and physical breakdown, but with Paul's help he recovered and turned back to his editorial work. When he lost his job at Butterick in 1910, he went to work on the other novels he had begun after *Sister Carrie.* Now he finished *Jennie Gerhardt* . Published in 1911, it received critical acclaim and sales success, in part because, without compromising his principles, Dreiser avoided affronting public morals this time: Jennie, also drawn from Dreiser's wayward sisters, does not prosper from her sins. Encouraged by the novel's success, Dreiser pressed ahead on *The Financier,* which was based on the sensational career of Charles T. Yerkes (named Frank Algernon Cowperwood in the novel), who made a fortune in Philadelphia, went to prison for embezzlement, and made another fortune after his release, while scoring almost as many romantic triumphs as business coups. *The Titan* (1914) and *The Stoic* (1947) continue with the same character.

A trip to Europe in 1911 provided material for *A Traveler at Forty* (1913), but Dreiser devoted his best efforts to fiction. *The Genius* (1915) is his most autobiographical novel. The romance with the young girl that had ended Dreiser's career at Butterick constitutes a principal incident, but the artist-hero's philosophic calm at the story's end is more wish-fulfillment fantasy than autobiography. Some critics expressed moral outrage. The New York Society for the Suppression of Vice got the book banned for over a year; yet out of the storm a critical consensus was emerging: whatever the moral or literary failings of *The Genius,* it was the work of an artist who possessed elements of genius himself.

An American Tragedy

In the following year Dreiser published several volumes of nonfiction, notably *Twelve Men* (1919). That same year he met his charming 25-year-old cousin Helen Richardson, who was fleeing an unhappy marriage. They moved to Los Angeles together, where she contributed to their household expenses by taking supporting parts in films. In nearly 3 years in California, Dreiser wrote several volumes of sketches, some bad poetry, and the first 20 chapters of his greatest novel. Based on the highly publicized 1906 murder

trial of a young New York man, *An American Tragedy* (2 vols., 1925) shows Clyde Griffiths, impoverished son of a street evangelist, working in his rich uncle's shirt factory and falling in love with a girl of beauty, wealth, and position. Only one thing blocks their marriage: Clyde has made a factory girl pregnant. Alone with the pregnant girl in a boat on a lake, he plots to murder her but loses his nerve; nevertheless, there is an accident, she drowns, and he later pays with his life. The book is genuinely tragic: Clyde is not villain but victim. If there is a villain, it is society with its conventionalism, its economic injustice, and its hypocrisy about sex. The book was a triumph: Joseph Wood Krutch spoke for most critics when he called it "the greatest American novel of our generation." The first 2 weeks' royalty check was for $11,872.02.

That splendid success was the last of Dreiser's novels to appear in his lifetime (two inferior pieces, *The Bulwark,* 1946, and *The Stoic,* 1947, appeared after his death). In 1926 he traveled with Richardson to Europe; in 1927 his trip to the Soviet Union resulted in *Dreiser Looks at Russia* (1928). In 1929 he and Richardson settled near Mount Kisco, N.Y. In 1942 Dreiser's wife died, and in 1944 he married Richardson. Travel, political activity, and a surprising turn toward mysticism occupied his late years. When he died of a heart attack in Hollywood, Calif., on Dec. 28, 1945, he was already well established in the history of world literature. Distinguished films were made in 1951 of *An American Tragedy* (under the title *A Place in the Sun*) and *Sister Carrie.*

Further Reading

Dreiser's autobiographical works include *A Hoosier Holiday* (1916), *A Book about Myself* (1922), and *Dawn* (1931). W.A. Swanberg's admirable *Dreiser* (1965) is the standard biography, but Robert H. Elias, *Theodore Dreiser: Apostle of Nature* (1949), remains valuable for its critical emphasis. Charles Shapiro, *Theodore Dreiser: Our Bitter Patriot* (1962); John J. McAleer, *Theodore Dreiser: An Introduction and Interpretation* (1968); and Ellen Moers, *Two Dreisers* (1969), are full-length discussions of the novels. Larzer Ziff, *The American 1890s: Life and Times of a Lost Generation* (1966), contains a brilliant assessment of Dreiser's accomplishments and relation to his period. □

Charles Richard Drew

African American surgeon Charles Richard Drew (1904-1950) pioneered in developing the blood bank and was an outstanding leader in the training of surgeons.

C harles R. Drew was born in Washington, D.C., on June 3, 1904, the eldest of five children. The close-knit family lived in modest circumstances and was highly respected.

Drew was educated in the Washington public schools. He earned a bachelor of arts degree from Amherst College

(1926) and his doctor of medicine and master of surgery degrees from McGill University in Canada (1933). Having decided upon a career in surgery, he went to Howard University in Washington, D.C., in 1935. After the next year as a surgical resident, he was sent by Howard for 2 years of advanced study under a General Education Board fellowship to Columbia University, which awarded him the doctor of medical science degree (1940).

At Columbia, under the direction of John Scudder, Drew completed his pioneering and definitive thesis *Banked Blood* (1940). The Blood Transfusion Betterment Association in New York funded various programs of research; one of these, on blood plasma, was conducted by Scudder and Drew. In 1940, during World War II, Scudder suggested that the association ship dried plasma to France and England. The association appointed Drew director of its "Blood for Britain" project in September 1940.

In 1941 Drew was appointed director of the first American Red Cross Bank and assistant director of blood procurement for the National Research Council, in charge of blood for use by the U.S. Army and Navy. He criticized the policy of segregating blood racially as having no scientific basis.

In October 1941 Drew returned to Howard as head of the department of surgery and was made an examiner for the American Board of Surgery. Chief of staff of Freedmen's Hospital from 1944 to 1946, he was appointed medical director of the hospital for 1946-1947. At Howard, Drew firmly established a progressive modern surgery program. He was a dynamic and inspirational teacher. While he was

still alive, eight of his residents became diplomates of the American Board of Surgery, and many more who started their training under him became board-certified and did significant work all over the world.

Drew published 19 papers, the first 13 dealing with blood therapy. The last 6 reflected broadening interests, one posthumous title being "Negro Scholars in Scientific Research."

During 6 years as chairman of the surgical section of the National Medical Association, Drew brought new vigor and standards to the group. He was in demand as a speaker, and he served on numerous boards with a wide spectrum of interests, including the 12th Street Branch of the YMCA in Washington.

Most of Drew's achievements were promptly recognized. He received the Spingarn Medal of the NAACP (1943) and honorary doctor of science degrees from Virginia State College (1945) and Amherst College (1947). In 1946 he became a fellow of the International College of Surgeons and served in 1949 as surgical consultant to the surgeon general, U.S. Army. Drew's radiant geniality and warm sense of humor endeared him to patients. He married Minnie Lenore Robbins on Sept. 23, 1939, and the couple had four children. He was killed in an automobile accident on April 1, 1950.

In 1959 the Sigma Pi Phi fraternity presented an oil portrait of Dr. Drew to the American National Red Cross. In Los Angeles the Charles R. Drew Medical Society and the Charles R. Drew Postgraduate Medical School of the Martin Luther King Jr. Hospital perpetuate his name. A health center in Brooklyn and the Harlem Hospital Center blood bank in New York City are named for him. The surgical section of the National Medical Association has an annual Charles R. Drew Forum for the presentation of original surgical research, and about 20 public schools in America have been named for him.

Further Reading

Three full-length studies of Drew are Richard Hardwick, *Charles Richard Drew: Pioneer in Blood Research* (1967); Robert Lichello, *Pioneer in Blood Plasma: Dr. Charles Richard Drew* (1968) and Roland Bertol, *Charles Drew* (1970). There are sections devoted to Drew in Ben Richardson, *Great American Negroes* (1945; rev. ed. 1956); Emma Gelders Steme, *Blood Brothers: Four Men of Science* (1959); and Louis Haber, *Black Pioneers of Science and Invention* (1970). □

Daniel Drew

Daniel Drew (1797-1879) was one of America's sensational stock manipulators, speculating particularly in Erie Railroad securities.

Born July 29, 1797, at Carmel, N.Y., Daniel Drew Grew up on the family farm. His career began as a cattle drover and horse trader: he drove cattle from the countryside into New York City. Successful, he extended activity into Ohio and Illinois, bringing livestock back to his own New York stockyard.

Drew was said to have watered his beeves heavily before bringing them to market, thus increasing their weight (hence the origin of the term "stock-watering" in connection with the issuance of fraudulent corporate securities). By 1834 he was a New York City resident, operating steamboats on the Hudson River, Lake Champlain, and long Island Sound. A bold competitor, he made money and in 1844 set up the Wall street brokerage firm of Drew, Robinson and Company.

In 1853 Drew entered the life of the Erie Railroad and in 1857 became a director. He was soon notorious as a bold manipulator of Erie securities. He sold its stock short in 1866 and made a killing.

During 1866-1868, along with Jay Gould and James Fisk (Drew was really their "front"), Drew entered into a war with Cornelius Vanderbilt for control of the Erie. Vanderbilt had put together three railroads that gave him a direct line from Buffalo to New York City; he wanted the Erie in order to monopolize entry into New York and to prevent it from becoming a serious competitor on the Lake Shore route to Chicago he was contemplating.

Meanwhile the Erie management, with Drew as treasurer, has authorized issuance of convertible bonds for improvements. In order to check Vanderbilt, Drew (with Gould and Fisk on the sidelines) sold bonds in 1868 in defiance of a court order and issued 100,000 new shares of Erie, thus creating a wild market, with Vanderbilt buying and the manipulators selling short. Drew, Gould, and Fisk fled to Jersey City to avoid court action; then Gould bribed state legislators to get conversion of the bonds into stock legalized. Vanderbilt was frustrated, but Gould settled with him and compensated him for his losses. In the end Gould owned the Erie, and Drew was forced off the board of directors.

Drew's star sank in 1870, when Gould and Fisk sold Erie stock in England to force up its price: Drew, selling short, lost $1,500,000. During the depression of 1873-1879 Drew was finished; his banking firm failed, and in 1876 he filed for bankruptcy. He died on Sept. 18, 1879, in New York, wholly dependent upon his son. In his heyday Drew played the philanthropist, building Methodist churches at Carmel and Brewster, N.Y., and spending $250,000 to set up the Drew Theological Seminary at Madison, N.J.

Further Reading

Bouck White, *The Book of Daniel Drew* (1910), is a semifictional biography. The early story of the "Erie War" is in Charles F. Adams, Jr., and Henry Adams, *Chapters of Erie and Other Essays* (1871). A more sophisticated account is in Julius Grodinsky, *Jay Gould: His Business Career, 1867-1892* (1957).

Additional Sources

Browder, Clifford, *The money game in old New York: Daniel Drew and his times,* Lexington, K.Y.: University of Kentucky, 1986. □

Katherine Drexel

Dedicating her life and her fortune to philanthropy, Katherine Drexel (1858-1955) founded a Catholic order of sisters, the Sisters of the Blessed Sacrament, to work for Native Americans and African Americans.

Katherine Drexel was born in Philadelphia on November 26, 1858, the second daughter of Francis Drexel, a highly prosperous banker, and Hannah Langstroth, a Quaker. Hannah died five weeks later; her father married Emma Bouvier in 1860. They were devout Catholics, and both gave a great deal of their time and money to philanthropic activities. The children were educated privately and were encouraged to conduct a Sunday school for children of the employees at their family's summer home. The family travelled extensively in Europe and took a 6,000 mile trip through the American West in the private railroad car lent her father by James J. Hill, head of the Great Northern Railroad.

Drexel's full social and philanthropic life was jarred by the protracted illness, and then death in 1883, of her stepmother, to whom she was very devoted; two years later, her father died. She thought seriously of entering a convent where she could be totally absorbed in contemplation and prayer, but was persuaded by her religious counsellor not to make a hasty decision. Meanwhile, the Drexel young women were begged by a stream of churchmen to use their great wealth to help, as their parents had, in meeting the many crying needs of the Church—especially for missions in the West and the South. In 1889 Drexel began a novitiate with the Sisters of Mercy in Pittsburgh, with the understanding that in two years she would found her own order, the Sisters of the Blessed Sacrament, committed to the service of Native and African Americans; she would, she vowed, "be the mother and servant of these races."

Having taken a vow of poverty, she lived the rest of her life with extreme frugality. At the same time, her income from her father's trust (which increased substantially when her older sister died in childbirth) amounted to more than a $1,000 a day; she probably was, as the newspapers regularly declared, "the richest nun in the world." Receiving innumerable requests for aid, she concentrated her gifts on works which she could inspect and where—if possible— her Sisters could serve.

In the late 19th century Americans, especially in the East, were increasingly distressed by the abuse or neglect of the American Indians. The Catholic Church, hampered by poverty and the importunate needs of Catholic immigrants in the eastern cities, had been able to do less than many religious groups; and, the Church felt, with considerable reason, that the federal government discriminated against Catholic efforts both to minister to professedly Catholic Native Americans and to proselytize among non-Christian Native Americans. In the same years, most African Americans lived in the South; the Church was weak there, and hardly needed the additional stigma that would likely attend efforts that might seem in any way to jeopardize white supremacy.

In her 60 years of service, Drexel, more than any other person, spearheaded the effort of the Church to respond more compassionately and more efficiently to the needs of Native and African Americans. She gave more than $12 million of her own money, and at her death 501 members of her order supported 49 houses in 21 states. She was in a very real sense a one-woman foundation. She reviewed personally every request, often indicating her decision with a note on the letter of inquiry. She travelled tirelessly. She gave strong priority to the creation of church buildings and schools. No believer in segregation, she recognized that in her time a segregated church or school was often the most that could be hoped for. A strong advocate of liberal education (she helped establish what came to be Xavier University in New Orleans—the first Catholic college for African Americns), she readily acquiesced in the belief that for many African Americans "vocational" education was the most pressing need. She generally confined her response to pleas for aid to inspecting, buying land, erecting buildings, and— occasionally—paying salaries. She had neither the time nor the inclination to supervise. One result of her practice was

that she almost completely avoided conflict with the priests and bishops in charge of the missions.

By the terms of her father's will, she enjoyed only the income from the trust he had established. She was urged, from time to time, to use that income to create an endowment that would sustain, after her death, the institutions she had helped create. She did not do so. Perhaps she wanted to continue to make the spending decisions herself. Probably she wanted the Catholic laity, if not the whole American people, eventually to assume the responsibility of maintaining the institutions she had help start. Certainly she wholeheartedly endorsed the traditional notion that religious institutions should ultimately put their reliance on God's grace.

She received many awards in her lifetime, including the first honorary degree given by The Catholic University to a woman. She suffered a heart attack in 1935, and though she partly recovered, she was obliged to give up her leadership of the order. She lived in retirement with the sisters until her death in 1955, in her 97th year. In 1964 the Church began the long process of determining whether Mother Katherine should be beatified.

Further Reading

Brief, informative biographies of Mother Drexel are Nancy A. Hewitt, *Notable American Women: The Modern Period* (1980) and Katherine Burton, *New Catholic Encyclopedia* (1967). Burton's *The Golden Door* (1957) is a sentimental biography of Drexel. Sister Consuela Maria Duffy, a member of the order Mother Drexel founded, has written a more balanced study, *Katherine Drexel* (1966). □

Alfred Dreyfus

The French army officer Alfred Dreyfus (1859-1935) was unjustly convicted of treason. The effort, eventually successful, to clear his name divided French society and had important political repercussions.

Alfred Dreyfus was born at Mulhouse on Oct. 9, 1859, into a Jewish textile-manufacturing family. After the Franco-Prussian War his family left Alsace in order to remain French citizens. Choosing a military career, Dreyfus entered the École Polytechnique in 1878. After further study, during which he attained the rank of captain in 1889, he was assigned as a trainee to the general staff. Dreyfus was a competent and hardworking, though not brilliant or popular, young officer. His ordeal was to prove that he was a man of great courage but limited vision: his whole life was devoted to the army, and he never lost confidence that it would recognize and remedy the wrong done him.

Arrest and Conviction

The Dreyfus case began in September 1894, when French Army Intelligence found among some papers taken from the office of the German military attaché in Paris, a list (bordereau) of secret documents given to the Germans by someone in the French army. A hasty and inadequate investigation convinced the anti-Semitic Intelligence chief, Col. Sandherr, that Dreyfus was the traitor. Apart from a certain resemblance between his handwriting and that of the bordereau, no very convincing evidence against Dreyfus could be discovered. He was arrested, however, on October 15.

Dreyfus's court-martial was held behind closed doors during December 19-21. A unanimous court found him guilty and imposed the highest legal penalty: perpetual imprisonment, loss of rank, and degradation. He was sent to the infamous Devil's Island, where he was to spend almost 5 years under the most inhumane conditions. Still protesting his innocence, Dreyfus was unaware that he had been convicted with the aid of a secret dossier prepared by Army Intelligence. Communication of the dossier to the judges without the knowledge of the defense violated due process and was the first of many actions that would bring discredit on the army and ruin the careers of the officers involved.

Convinced of his innocence, the Dreyfus family, led by his brother Mathieu, sought new evidence which would persuade the army to reopen its investigation. Aside from a few individuals such as the brilliant young writer Bernard Lazare and the respected Alsatian life-senator Scheurer-Kestner, they found few supporters, and their efforts stirred the anti-Semitic press to raise the bogey of a "Jewish syndicate" trying to corrupt the army.

Fortune came to Dreyfus's aid for the first time in July 1895, when the new Intelligence chief, Lt. Col. Marie Georges Picquart, became convinced of Dreyfus's innocence and discovered a Maj. Walsin-Esterhazy to be the real author of the bordereau. Although Picquart was unable to convince his superiors to reexamine the verdict, he remained determined to help free Dreyfus.

Still unable to persuade the government to act, the supporters of Dreyfus—the Dreyfusards—now took their case to the public, charging Esterhazy with the crime for which Dreyfus was being punished. The anti-Semitic press counterattacked, and the Dreyfus case began to turn into the Dreyfus Affair, as public passions were raised against the few who dared to challenge the verdict of the court-martial. Supported by friends within the command, Esterhazy demanded a court-martial to prove his innocence; he received a triumphant acquittal in January 1898. The evidence against Esterhazy was little better than that which had convicted Dreyfus, but his acquittal dashed the hopes of the Dreyfusards, who had expected his conviction to prove Dreyfus innocent.

Retrial and Exoneration

The controversial novelist Émile Zola, however, found a way to reopen the case: he charged in an open letter to the President of the Republic entitled *J'accuse* that the military court had acquitted Esterhazy although they knew him to be guilty. Zola hoped to bring the facts of Dreyfus's case before a civil court, where it would be more difficult for the army to conceal what had happened; he was only partially success-

ful, but increased public concern and violence in the streets forced the authorities to take further action.

The minister of war, Godefroy Cavaignac, aiming to quiet criticism, publicly revealed much of the evidence against Dreyfus. But the Dreyfusards, headed by socialist leader Jean Jaurès, charged that forgery was obvious. Cavaignac's further investigation led to the confession and suicide (Aug. 31, 1898) of an Intelligence officer, Lt. Col. Joseph Henry, who had been manufacturing evidence to strengthen the case against Dreyfus. This was the turning point of the Affair. The government brought the case before the highest appeals court, which declared (June 3, 1899) Dreyfus entitled to a new trial.

Dreyfus was brought back to France to face a new court-martial at Rennes in September 1899. It returned, by a vote of 5 to 2, the incredible verdict of guilty with extenuating circumstances and sentenced him to 10 years' imprisonment. The honor of the army had been made such an issue by the anti-Dreyfusards that no military court could ever find him innocent. No one believed in the honor of the army more than Dreyfus, and only with difficulty could he be persuaded to accept the pardon offered by President Émile Loubet.

Dreyfus continued to seek exoneration, and his record was finally cleared by the civil courts in July 1906. He was returned to service, promoted, and decorated, but he soon retired. Returning to active duty during World War I, he then spent his retirement in complete obscurity, and his death on July 11, 1935, passed almost unnoticed.

Political Consequences

Dreyfus understood little of the battle that raged in his name. The question of his innocence became a secondary matter beside the public issue of individual human rights versus the demands of state policy. Political issues also played a part in the Affair: to many conservatives the army and the Church seemed the last bulwarks of social stability; both would be undermined by the victory of the Dreyfusards. On the left many welcomed the opportunity to strike at the monarchist and clerical forces, which they saw as enemies of the Republic. Last but not least was the question of anti-Semitism. The Affair saw the first outpouring of modern political anti-Semitism, which proved a harbinger of the Nazi terror.

The immediate political consequence of the Affair was to bring the Radicals to power; they made the Church the scapegoat for the sins of the anti-Dreyfusards, taking a number of anticlerical measures culminating in the separation of Church and state in 1905. The passions exposed by the Affair were submerged in World War I but reappeared in the defeat of 1940 and under the Vichy regime.

Further Reading

There are hundreds of books dealing with the Dreyfus Affair. A well-balanced introduction is Douglas Johnson, *France and the Dreyfus Affair* (1966). The detailed study by Guy Chapman, *The Dreyfus Case: A Reassessment* (1955), upsets much of the standard Dreyfusard version but underestimates the importance of anti-Semitism. The role of crowd psychology is explored by Nicholas Halasz, *Captain Dreyfus: The Story of a Mass Hysteria* (1955). For something of the man see Dreyfus's prison memoirs, *Five Years of My Life, 1894-1899* (trans. 1901).

Additional Sources

Lewis, David L., *Prisoners of honor: the Dreyfus affair,* New York: H. Holt, 1994. □

Hans Adolf Eduard Driesch

The German biologist and philosopher Hans Adolf Eduard Driesch (1867-1941) was a leading representative of vitalism in the 20th century.

Hans Driesch was born at Bad Kreuznach on Oct. 28, 1867, into a prosperous middle-class family. After studying zoology at the University of Freiburg, he spent some semesters at Munich and then finished his degree at Jena in 1889 under the direction of Ernst Haeckel. Haeckel had apparently established mechanism as the dominant theory in biology and zoology, and Driesch's early work was a series of experimental efforts to confirm this theory. Contrary to his expectations, the experiments seemed to cast doubt on the hypothesis that living beings can be understood on purely mechanist principles.

From 1891 to 1900 Driesch worked at the Marine Biological Station in Naples, continuing his experiments and groping for a theoretical formulation of his results. At this point in his career, he began to read the classical modern philosophers, looking for an adequate philosophical theory of the organism. At the end of a long series of publications in which he explored tentative hypotheses and halfway theories, he finally presented an account of the life processes in genuinely teleological and dynamic terms in the book *The Localization of Morphogenetic Processes* (1894).

Thereafter Driesch's interests shifted from experimental work to conceptual analysis. He sought to explain the relationship between the concepts of life and the concepts of matter. In 1908 he published his Gifford Lectures, *The Science and Philosophy of the Organism,* the first full-length presentation of his ideas. At this point Driesch determined to take up a career in academic philosophy and became a lecturer at Heidelberg. Before a decade had elapsed, he had published a complete system of philosophy in three volumes, of which the most basic is his *Theory of Order* (1912).

In 1919 Driesch took a chair of systematic philosophy at Cologne and 2 years later accepted a similar post at Leipzig. In later years he was a visiting professor in China, the United States, and South America. After Hitler's assumption of power, Driesch was forced out of his position. He became interested in parapsychology and published on such phenomena as telepathy, clairvoyance, and telekinesis. Driesch was married to Margarete Relfferschneidt, and the couple had two children. He died on April 17, 1941.

Further Reading

In spite of his unusually large output of books and articles, Driesch's work has evoked little response. Ruth Moore, *The Coil of Life: The Story of the Great Discoveries in the Life Sciences* (1961), includes a biographical chapter on Driesch. His theories are discussed in Joseph Needham, *Order and Life* (1936); Rainer Schubert-Soldern, *Mechanism and Vitalism: Philosophical Aspects of Biology,* edited by Philip G. Fothergill (trans. 1962); and Jane M. Oppenheimer, *Essays in the History of Embryology and Biology* (1967). A classic critique of vitalism is Moritz Schlick, *Philosophy of Nature* (trans. 1949). □

Marcus Livius Drusus

Marcus Livius Drusus (ca. 124-91 B.C.) was a Roman statesman who attempted to unite the nobility with the equestrian order and to reconcile the cities of Italy to the rule of Rome.

Drusus was a member of a great plebeian family, the son and grandson of consuls. Drusus' mother belonged to the great patrician family of the Cornelii; his wife was Servilia, daughter of the Optimate leader Q. Servilius Caepio; and his sister Livia was married to Servilia's brother, also named Q. Servilius Caepio.

Political Career

It was inevitable that a man of Drusus' wealth and family connections should enter politics. He was elected a military tribune (ca. 105 B.C.), became one of the *decemviri stilitibus judicandis,* a court of 10 which decided cases as to whether a man was free or a slave (ca. 104), and was chosen a quaestor (ca. 102), the first step on the ladder of public office for aspiring Roman politicians. He was aedile in 94 and became a pontifex at some unknown time, an office which he held until his death.

Domestic Reforms

On Dec. 10, 92, Drusus became a plebeian tribune and used his own influence and the powers of this office to propose an extraordinary series of reforms designed to solve the major domestic problems of the day. He proposed to placate the poor citizens by suggesting the establishment of 12 colonies in Italy to which they could migrate, with a free distribution of land. To smooth relations between the Senate and the equestrian order (*equites*), Drusus wanted to restore to the senators the right, taken from them by C. Gracchus and given to the *equites,* of sitting on the juries which decided cases of alleged corruption in office. Equestrian opposition was to be overcome by doubling the size of the Senate by adding 300 *equites* to it. The restive cities of Italy Drusus wanted to conciliate by extending Roman citizenship to all Italians.

These proposals were adopted into law by the assembly of all citizens, but they violated Roman law providing that one bill of proposals could not contain several unrelated topics; force had been used as well. This gave an opportunity to Drusus' opponents to reopen the question. His brother-in-law Caepio, who had quarreled with him and had divorced his sister Livia, and the consul Marcus Philippus led the opposition. After violent agitation and threats of mass movements in support of Drusus by the Italians, Drusus' enemies persuaded a majority of the Senate to declare all of these laws invalid. The results were tragic: Drusus was murdered in his home, his supporters were subjected to prosecution in the law courts, and the Italians rose in open rebellion in the Social War (91-87).

Further Reading

There is no book-length work on Drusus. The best summary of his career is that by Hugh Last in the *Cambridge Ancient History,* vol. 9 (1932; corrected repr. 1951). For general background see Matthias Gelzer, *The Roman Nobility* (1912; trans. 1969); A. N. Sherwin-White, *The Roman Citizenship* (1939); and H. H. Scullard, *From the Gracchi to Nero* (1959). □

John Dryden

The English author John Dryden (1631-1700) is best known as a poet and critic. He also wrote almost 30 plays and was one of the great dramatists of his time.

John Dryden was born on Aug. 9, 1631, in Aldwinckle, Northamptonshire, in the parsonage of All Saints Church, where his maternal grandfather was rector. His family were supporters of Oliver Cromwell and comfortably situated. When Dryden was 15, he was sent to London to Westminster School to study under the celebrated headmaster, Dr. Richard Busby, who was known both for his rigorous discipline and for his ability to instill in his students a knowledge of Latin and Greek.

In 1649 while still at Westminster, Dryden published his first poem, "Upon the Death of Lord Hastings." The next year he was admitted to Trinity College, Cambridge. While at Trinity he published a poem in honor of a friend, John Hoddesdon, but there is no evidence that his university career was especially dedicated to poetry. In 1654, the year he earned a bachelor of arts degree, his father died, leaving him family property that yielded an income of about £40 a year. After his father's death Dryden seems to have settled in London as secretary to his cousin Sir Gilbert Pickering, but there is no record of his activities until 1659, when his third poem, "Heroic Stanzas to the Glorious Memory of Cromwell," was published.

Shortly after the death of Cromwell, Charles II was restored to the throne. Although Dryden had been brought up to support the parliamentary party, he was evidently weary of the chaos and disorder that followed upon Cromwell's death, for in 1660 he welcomed the King with his poem "Astraea redux." The following year he offered a second tribute, "To his Sacred Majesty," to celebrate Charles II's coronation. He was criticized for changing his political allegiance, but he never withdrew the loyalty proclaimed in these two poems, although it would have been advantageous for him to do so in 1688, when William III came to the throne.

Early Career

After the Restoration, Dryden settled into the business of playwriting. In the early months of 1663 his first play, *The Wild Gallant,* was produced, but it proved a failure. Late in that year he married Lady Elizabeth Howard, the sister of his friend Sir Robert Howard. The Howard family were of considerable means and had long supported the royalist cause.

Some of Dryden's most successful plays belong to a type peculiar to his own age called the heroic play. These were spectacular productions featuring exotic characters who defended their honor and proclaimed their love in rhyming couplets. Although the heroic themes of these plays were similar to those of Pierre Corneille, the sensational plots generally were derived from earlier English dramatists such as Francis Beaumont and John Fletcher. In 1665 Dryden collaborated with his brother-in-law, Sir Robert, on a heroic play, *The Indian Queen.* It was such a success that Dryden immediately wrote a sequel called *The Indian Emperor.*

In the summer of 1665 the plague hit London, and the theaters were closed. Dryden and his wife moved to the Howards' country estate at Charleton, Wiltshire. Here Dryden occupied himself with the writing of a long poem on the Dutch War and the London fire, *Annus mirabilis,* and a critical essay in prose, *An Essay of Dramatic Poesy*. He also wrote a play, *Secret Love*.

The years following the plague proved prosperous for Dryden. Both *Secret Love* and *The Indian Emperor*, whose performance had been delayed by the closing of the theaters, enjoyed great popularity. Dryden came to be regarded as the leading dramatist of the age. In 1667 he brought forth *Sir Martin Mar-All*, a new comedy adapted from Molière. He also accepted Sir William Davenant's invitation to collaborate on an operatic version of Shakespeare's *Tempest*. In 1668 the King's Company made him a shareholder in return for his promise to give them three plays a year. When Davenant died in the spring of 1668, Dryden was designated poet laureate and historiographer royal.

Heroic Plays

The years following Dryden's appointment as laureate brought his greatest heroic plays. In 1669 he produced *Tyrannic Love*, a play based on the life of St. Catherine. The next year saw the production of *The Conquest of Granada*, his most famous heroic play. Dryden continued to write dramas of this type, but it soon became apparent that he was weary of writing for the stage and tastes other than his own. He had, in fact, been eager for some time to undertake the writing of an epic poem. He had worked with epic materials in *Annus mirabilis* and the heroic plays and had even turned John Milton's *Paradise Lost* into an opera called *The State of Innocence* (1674); but the necessity of supporting himself by writing what would prove popular for the stage had deprived him of leisure to pursue his private poetical interests.

In 1676, in his dedication of his final heroic play, *Aureng-Zebe*, to the Earl of Mulgrave, Dryden expressed his discontent with the stage and begged the earl for the financial support necessary to pursue epic poetry. In 1677 he received a warrant for an additional £100 to his salary as poet laureate. This would have provided a reasonable income, but Charles's treasury was low, and Dryden was forced to abandon his epic dream because he was able to claim only about half of the £300 due him annually.

Dryden was still under contract to the King's Company. In 1677 he gave them his *All for Love*, an adaptation of Shakespeare's *Antony and Cleopatra*. Although its reception was not enthusiastic, it is generally regarded as his finest dramatic achievement. Its lack of acclaim may have been due in part to the deterioration of the King's Company, which was in financial distress. Subsequently Dryden shifted his activities to the Duke's Theatre, where his comedy *Limberham*, his adaptation of *Troilus and Cressida*, and his tragedy *Oedipus* (written in collaboration with Nathaniel Lee) were performed in 1678.

The Satires

Shortly after joining the Duke's Company, Dryden attacked the dullness of his fellow playwright Thomas Shadwell in *MacFlecknoe*. The attack seems to have been unprovoked, and the bitterness aroused by this unsolicited lampoon was heightened by political differences between the two playwrights. Dryden was a royalist; Shadwell was a Whig and a supporter of the Earl of Shaftesbury, who was

scheming among the Whigs to have Charles II's brother, the Catholic Duke of York, excluded from succession to the throne. Dryden was apparently commissioned by the King to expose the treason of the Whig sedition and the presumption of Shaftesbury, and he produced two of the finest political satires in English—*Absalom and Achitophel* (1681) and *The Medal* (1682). His next poem, *Religio laici* (1682), while nominally a defense of the authority of the English Church, was in effect also a satire on the unreason of all who dissented.

When Charles II died in 1685, Dryden was reappointed laureate by James II. At this time Dryden became a Catholic and in 1687 wrote a public apology for his new religion, *The Hind and the Panther*. Although his enemies accused him of accommodating his faith to that of his king in order to secure preferment, there is no evidence that James influenced Dryden's conversion. His adherence to his new faith after 1688 cost him the laureateship. During James's short reign Dryden was occupied primarily with poetry. He translated selections from Latin poets such as Virgil, Horace, and Lucretius. He also wrote several fine lyric odes: "Threnodia Augustalis," in memory of Charles II, "To the Memory of Anne Killigrew," and "A Song for St. Cecilia's Day."

In 1688, when William III appointed Shadwell poet laureate, Dryden was forced to return to the theater to earn a living. He produced a number of plays—*Don Sebastian* (1689), *Amphitryon* (1690), and *Cleomenes* (1690)—none of which was notably successful. He then turned to translating, which proved more profitable. His greatest translations were probably the *Satires of Juvenal and Persius* (1692), the *Works of Virgil* (1697), and the *Fables* (1700), a collection of tales from Ovid, Giovanni Boccaccio, and Geoffrey Chaucer. He was the first English author to earn his living by his writing. Dryden died on May 1, 1700.

Further Reading

The standard biography of Dryden is Charles E. Ward, *The Life of John Dryden* (1961). Sir Walter Scott's account in *The Works of John Dryden* (18 vols., 1808; revised and edited by George Saintsbury, 1882-1893) is also excellent. The best critical study of Dryden's poetry is Earl Miner, *Dryden's Poetry* (1967). Two recent studies of the heroic plays are Arthur C. Kirsch, *Dryden's Heroic Drama* (1965), and Selma Zebouni, *Dryden: A Study in Heroic Characterization* (1965).

Additional Sources

Hammond, Paul, *John Dryden: a literary life*, New York: St. Martin's Press, 1991.

Hollis, Christopher, *Dryden*, Norwood, Pa.: Norwood Editions, 1977.

Winn, James Anderson, *John Dryden and his world*, New Haven: Yale University Press, 1987. □

Sir George Russell Drysdale

The Australian painter Sir George Russell Drysdale (1912-1981) gave his countrymen a changed vision

of their continent through his landscape paintings of Australia's rural frontier.

Russell Drysdale was born on Feb. 7, 1912, at Bognor Regis, Sussex, in England. The family moved to Australia, and Russell attended Geelong Grammar School in Victoria. He intended to take up farming but developed a strong interest in art and in 1935 began studying painting in Melbourne, continuing at the Grosvenor School in London and La Grande Chaumière in Paris during 1938-1939.

Returning to Melbourne, Drysdale found a strong resistance to acceptance of the newer art forms. He decided to move to Sydney, where the art world was awakening to European influences, and he immediately found himself at home. In 1941 he traveled through the remoter sections of the hinterland; *Man Feeding His Dogs* and *Moody's Pub* capture the region's emptiness.

Painter of the Backcountry

From the early 1940s, when he began interpreting the life of Australia's rural frontier in a new and highly personalized style, Drysdale turned aside from the established Australian school. Australian impressionism had become something of a stereotype, and Sir Arthur Streeton and other landscapists had painted coastal areas and well-grassed pastoral lands accessible to the main cities. Drysdale took for his settings the wide, dry, ocher-hued heartland of the

continent, where he sensed the essence of the Australian experience. He used a warm, deeptoned palette to present somber and astringent views of desolate "heartbreak" landscapes typical of the back-country and to show how the emptiness and monotony affected those who made their lives in this environment.

Drysdale created pictorial enigmas that preserve something of the land's mystical quality and of the special response of people to it. As critic James Gleeson pointed out (1969): "Man is not shown by Drysdale as protagonist at grips with ruthless nature; rather he is drawn as a malleable creature upon whom the external forces have imposed the stamp of their authority."

Drysdale's first exhibition, in Sydney in 1942, established him as the leading exponent of a new kind of national painting. The dramatic interpretations of a rigorous and monotonous environment are compelling, evocative, and clearly Australian; yet for all their starkness the paintings reveal Drysdale's respect for the basic subtleties of classical art and his discerning awareness of the European tradition in all its richness.

Drysdale captured wartime themes in *Albury Platform* and *Home Town* (both 1942). In 1944 he did a striking series of illustrations showing soil erosion in the western region of New South Wales; published in leading newspapers, the drawings brought home the awful reality of one of the nation's severest droughts. The *Drover's Wife* (1945) and the *Cricketers* (1948) are examples of the artist's ability to place human subjects in vast settings without negating them. *Old Larsen* (1953) is an outstanding example of his character portraiture.

Prizes and Exhibitions

In 1947 Drysdale won the Wynne Prize, Australia's principal landscape award. He was selected for the Twelve Australian Artists Exhibition sponsored by the Arts Council of Great Britain (1953) and for the Venice Biennale (1954).

In 1959 Drysdale did a series of drawings to illustrate newspaper articles by A. S. Marshall on the continent's northwest frontier lands; subsequently these appeared in Marshall's *Journey among Men* (1962). Following this series, Drysdale painted aborigines of the tropical regions, showing them as symbolic figures sometimes barely distinguishable from the totems, trees, and rocks of their tribal land.

A retrospective exhibition of Drysdale's paintings was held in Sydney in 1960. He was knighted in 1969 and became a Companion of the Order of Australia in 1980. He died in 1981. After his death, three books were written about him and his work. Klepac, Lou, *The Life and Works of Russell Drysdale,* Bay Books, Sydney, 1983; Boddington, Jennie, *Drysdale Photographer*, NGV, Melbourne, 1987; and Catalano, Gary, *An Intimate Australian: The landscape and recent Australian art,* Hale & Ironmonger, Sydney, 1985.

Further Reading

A useful reference is the publication by the National Art Gallery of South Wales, Sydney, *Russell Drysdale: A Retrospective Exhibition of Paintings from 1937 to 1960;* Drysdale's views on the artist's role are included. Drysdale is discussed in relation to Australian art in Bernard Smith, *Australian Painting, 1788-1960* (1962). Drysdale's outlook and his place in the contemporary art scene are explored in James Gleeson's elaborately illustrated review *Masterpieces of Australian Art* (1969). Many of his works are featured on the Internet at The National Gallery of Victoria homepage, which can be accessed http://www.ngv.vic.gov.au/landscape/drysdale.html. ☐

William Duane

The American journalist William Duane (1760-1835) was an effective advocate of Jeffersonian democracy. He and his son William John Duane, a prominent lawyer, were embroiled in the political controversies of the time.

William Duane came from a family of Irish patriots. Born near Lake Champlain, N.Y., he was taken by his mother to Ireland when he was 5. Disinherited for marrying a Protestant, he became a printer and went to Calcutta, India. He prospered until he was deported for printing attacks against the governmental officials of the East India Company. Vain attempts to seek justice in London deepened his hatred of England. In 1796 he went to America, where bitter partisan conflict was spreading and other Irish immigrants were already bringing a special radical fervor to the experimental republican government.

Duane assisted Benjamin Franklin Bache in editing the *Aurora,* the leading journal of the Jeffersonian party. When Bache died in 1798, his widow, Margaret, continued publication; Duane, himself a widower, married her 2 years later. He also intensified the paper's vehement, often sarcastic advocacy of the Jeffersonian cause. An eloquent writer and a clever editor, he was hated by the Federalists.

John Adams's administration never succeeded in jailing or silencing Duane. But he was constantly in danger, was once attacked by armed men, and in 1799 was charged with sedition in both state and national courts. Safety came only with the election of Thomas Jefferson in 1800. To Jefferson, Duane was more than a partisan editor; he was a trusted adviser and a good printer and bookseller.

When the capital was moved from Philadelphia to Washington, Duane moved too; but he never received the patronage in printing he had expected from the Jeffersonians, and he became increasingly disillusioned with them. An unswerving Democrat, he wrote *An Epitome of Arts and Science* (1811), which attempted to make useful knowledge available to those who lacked wealth and leisure. The *Aurora* ceased publication in 1822. Duane died on Nov. 24, 1835.

Toward the end of his life Duane had joined the opposition to the National Bank. That institution, with its vast powers seemingly uncontrolled by the government, represented a new form of tyranny to many Democrats. One of Duane's five children, William John Duane (1780-1865), was a central figure in the resulting controversies. Through his state offices and through a series of publications, he became a noted opponent of banking monopolies.

President Andrew Jackson, at war with the National Bank, decided to remove the government's deposits and place them in state banks. On June 1, 1833, he appointed William J. Duane secretary of the Treasury. The Jacksonians apparently assumed that Duane, a well-known opponent of the National Bank, would carry out their wishes. He refused, and on September 23 he was dismissed. His opposition to the National Bank was actually a suspicion of all banks. He felt that Federal deposits should be where close watch was possible. More careful and astute than many other Jacksonians, Duane saw the dangers in reckless state banking that would lead to the Panic of 1837.

Further Reading

Duane's place in the development of American newspapers is noted in Frank Luther Mott, *American Journalism: A History, 1690-1960* (3d ed. 1962). He also figures prominently in James Morton Smith's authoritative study of the Alien and Sedition Laws, *Freedom's Fetters: The Alien and Sedition Laws and American Civil Liberties* (1956). See also Eugene Perry Link, *Democratic-Republican Societies, 1790-1800* (1942), for Duane and his party; Harry Tinkcom, *The Republicans and Federalists in Pennsylvania* (1950), for Duane and his home state; and Nathan Schachner, *The Founding Fathers* (1954), for Duane and national politics. For the controversies in which the younger Duane was involved see Arthur Schlesinger, Jr., *The Age of Jackson* (1945), and Bray Hammond, *Banks and Politics in America, from the Revolution to the Civil War* (1957).

Additional Sources

Phillips, Kim Tousley., *William Duane, radical journalist in the age of Jefferson,* New York: Garland Pub., 1989. ☐

José Napoleón Duarte

José Napoleón Duarte (1926-1990), a civilian reformer who was elected president of El Salvador in 1984, enjoyed the support of the United States and had a substantial popular following. But the government was badly divided between reformist and reactionary forces, leading to a continuous struggle for survival.

Duarte was born in San Salvador on November 23, 1926, to a family of comfortable means. He received an excellent education in El Salvador and the United States, graduating in civil engineering from Notre Dame University in 1948. Upon his return to El Salvador,

Duarte joined his father-in-law's construction firm and devoted his time to his profession, to part-time university teaching, and to work with service organizations. By his own account he took little interest in politics until 1960.

In 1960 a leftist-supported coup d'état overthrew the government of Col. José María Lemus (1956-1960), raising fears that El Salvador might succumb to radical contagion from Cuba where Fidel Castro had seized power the previous year. Responding to these concerns, Duarte joined other middle-class Salvadorans in founding the Christian Democratic party and was elected its first secretary general. Because of its claim to represent a "third way," one that was neither capitalist nor Communist, Christian Democracy enjoyed a brief vogue in Latin America in the 1960s. The Christian Democratic party of El Salvador grew rapidly during the decade, gaining a following especially in urban areas among professionals, teachers, organized labor, and women. Duarte, the best known and most charismatic Christian Democrat politician, won election three times (1964, 1966, and 1968) as mayor of San Salvador, the nation's capital and largest city. In 1970 he retired from the mayoralty to begin a campaign for the presidency in 1972.

First Try for the Presidency

El Salvador had not had a civilian president nor a truly free presidential election since 1931, but many progressive politicians saw 1972 as the year in which that might change. The right was alienated by what it perceived as the leftward drift of military men who controlled the government. The army had permitted greater political activity on the part of

civilian opposition parties and had even promoted reforms which made opposition electoral victories more likely. The Christian Democrats joined together with two other parties to their left to form a progressive coalition called the Unión Nacional Opositora (UNO). The UNO nominated Duarte for president and Guillermo Manuel Ungo of the democratic socialist Movimiento Nacional Revolucionario (MNR) for vice-president.

Duarte's chief rival in 1972 was Col. Arturo Armando Molina, the candidate of the army-backed Partido de Conciliación Nacional (PCN), which had dominated the government since 1961. In early returns Duarte appeared to be leading. Later, however, the government ordered a halt to broadcast coverage of the counting. The following morning the authorities announced a victory of Molina. Duarte's subsequent support of an attempted coup d'état by a group of disgruntled officers led to his arrest, torture, and expulsion from the country. He spent the balance of the 1970s in exile in Venezuela.

Following another coup d'état, on October 15, 1979, in which a group of reformist officers overthrew the corrupt and unpopular regime of Col. Carlos Humberto Romero (1977-1979), Duarte returned to El Salvador. When other progressive civilians—some of them, including Guillermo Manuel Ungo, his former political allies—resigned their positions in the new government in frustration over their inability to influence the behavior of the country's repressive armed forces and police, Duarte himself consented in March 1980 to join the ruling civilian-military junta. This action split the Christian Democratic party and led a number of its younger members to join the armed opposition on the left, but Duarte persisted in his own belief, asserted several times after his defeat and exile in 1972, that no successful program of change could come about in El Salvador without the cooperation of moderate elements in the military.

Moved to the Presidency

Duarte remained in the junta until its dissolution in December 1980, at which time he became provisional president. Once in power he pushed through a number of important measures, including an agrarian reform and the nationalization of the banking industry. These changes met violent opposition from El Salvador's right, which manifested itself in a number of assassinations, including that of San Salvador Archbishop Oscar Arnulfo Romero, widely respected as a champion of social justice for the country's exploited poor, on March 24, 1980. During succeeding months the Duarte government survived several attempts to overthrow it, thanks to the continued support of key elements in the armed forces and of the United States, which considered Duarte's "moderate" reforms the best approach to neutralizing the appeal of the leftist guerrillas and arresting the spread of radical revolution from nearby Nicaragua.

The new president's principal critic on the right was Roberto d'Aubuisson, a charismatic ex-army major whom official sources implicated in the coup attempts against Duarte. In Constituent Assembly elections held March 28, 1982, and boycotted by the left, Duarte's centrist Christian

Democrats won a plurality but lost control of the Assembly to a coalition of right-wing parties led by d'Aubuisson's Alianza Republicana Nacionalista (ARENA). The rightists ousted Duarte as provisional president and replaced him with conservative businessman Alvaro Magaña (1982-1984). The Constitutent Assembly governed the country while drafting a new constitution. Attempts by rightists within the body to dismantle the reforms initiated by Duarte led to the further polarization of Salvadoran politics.

On May 6, 1984, following a bitter and violent campaign, Duarte defeated d'Aubuisson in a runoff election to become El Salvador's first elected civilian president in 53 years. Once again the left had boycotted the vote, charging that there could be no true democracy without peace and social change. Duarte made good a campaign pledge to open a dialogue with the armed opposition, which had been waging a guerrilla war against the government for more than five years. Little came of the first talks, held at La Palma in October 1984. The ARENA-dominated Assembly's resistance to negotiations with the left as well as to further reforms compromised Duarte's effectiveness as president, although legislative elections held on March 31, 1985, strengthened his hand by giving an unexpected majority to the Christian Democrats.

Although outspokenly pro-Western and anti-Communist, Duarte occasionally criticized the United States for its support of dictatorial regimes in Latin America. For its part, Washington was sometimes reluctant to give Duarte its unqualified support. The Nixon administration failed to intervene on his behalf in 1972, perhaps because he had run that year with Communist endorsement. Following Duarte's provisional presidency (1980-1982), the United States apparently questioned his leadership ability and hoped for a victory by some other candidate in 1984. When the field narrowed to Duarte and the intransigent d'Aubuisson in the runoff, however, the Reagan administration threw its support to Duarte as the only hope for a "centrist" solution. By mid-1985 Duarte enjoyed the support of both the Assembly and the United States. Many knowledgeable observers cautioned, however, that his chances of success in the dangerous Salvadoran political climate would continue to depend upon his ability to retain the confidence of the armed forces and establish a dialogue with rebel leaders.

Throughout Duarte's administration (1984-1989), extremists from both the left and right interrupted his efforts at political, social, and economic reform. During that time, middle class Salvadorans came to associate the Christian Democratic Party with corruption, injustice, and oppression rather than its reform platform, and rebel groups became more organized and increasingly violent. The Farabundo Marti National Liberation Front (FMLN), a coalition of rebel groups, became a highly disruptive guerrilla force that craved recognition and legitimacy. Prior to the free presidential elections scheduled to take place in March 1989, the FMLN tried to pressure the government into allowing its full participation with a number of proposals that included demands for restructuring the military, as well as a six-month postponement of voting. In exchange, they offered to halt guerrilla warfare that had killed an estimated 70,000 Salvadorans in nine years, but would not promise to end their armed struggle after the election.

A Bloody Road To Democracy

Various offers were rejected by the armed forces, the Nationalist Republican Alliance (ARENA), and the ruling Christian Democrats. Yet even as late as February 26 President Duarte continued to offer options to negotiate a peace, including the postponement of elections for six weeks and the call for a cease fire until his term ended on June 1 if the rebels would do the same. Even though no single proposal satisfied every group's criteria and the election was not postponed, formal talks did begin among the Democratic Convergence (the political arm of the FMLN), the Christian Democrats, and ARENA. The government and military were not represented. Meanwhile, leftist rebels continued to attack military posts and utilities, as well as civilians.

Democratic Change Amid Extremists' Gunfire

Elections took place as planned on March 19, and Alfredo Cristiani representing the right-wing Nationalist Republican Alliance became El Salvador's new president with 54 percent of the popular vote. Ultimately, Salvadorans had become disgusted with government corruption, and voted to defeat the Christian Democrat candidate, Fidel Chavez Mena. Duarte had become increasingly frail due to his struggle against cancer. The outgoing president was proud of the peaceful transfer of power, and was quoted as saying his government had "laid the foundation for democracy in this country. I have created here a new concept of politics." He died in San Salvador on February 23, 1990, less than a year after leaving office.

In the United States, both the Reagan and Bush administrations praised Duarte for promoting democracy, while pushing to end the long civil war through a negotiated settlement. The U.S. government supported El Salvador with millions of dollars in economic and military aid, in spite of reported human rights abuse on all sides.

Further Reading

Duarte's early career is the subject of Stephen Webre, *José Napoleón Duarte and the Christian Democratic Party in Salvadoran Politics, 1960-1972* (1979). Duarte figures prominently in several general works dealing with the Salvadoran political crisis of the 1980s. Among the most important are Tommie Sue Montgomery *Revolution in El Salvador: Origins and Evolution*, 2d edition (1984); Enrique A. Baloyra, *El Salvador in Transition* (1982); and Raymond Bonner, *Weakness and Deceit: U.S. Policy and El Salvador* (1984). His autobiography, *Duarte: My Story*, was published in 1986. Additional articles can be found in the *New York Times*, March 16, 1989 and February 24, 1990; *Rolling Stone*, March 23, 1989; *Business Week*, September 12, 1988; *Newsweek*, June 13, 1988; and *National Review*, February 3, 1992. □

Alexander Dubček

The Czechoslovak politician Alexander Dubček (1921- 1992) served briefly as head of his country's Communist party. His attempts to liberalize political life led to the occupation of Czechoslovakia by the Soviet army and his dismissal from office, only to be vindicated years later when the Communist regime fell.

Alexander Dubček was born on Nov. 27, 1921, the son of a cabinetmaker who had just returned from the United States. His family lived in the U.S.S.R. from 1925 to 1938, and it was there that he received his education. During World War II he was an active member of the underground resistance to the Germans in Slovakia.

After the war Dubček made his career as a functionary of the Communist party. He was elected to the Presidium of the Slovakian and then of the Czechoslovakian Communist party in 1962, and in the following year he became first secretary of the Slovakian party's Central Committee. Yet when he succeeded Antonin Novotny in January 1968 as first secretary of the Czechoslovakian Communist party, he was not well known in his own country and was hardly known at all outside it.

Pressure for the relaxation of the rigid dogma prevailing in political life had been mounting in Czechoslovakia for a considerable time and had been strengthened by economic discontent. Dubček became the personification of this movement and promised to introduce "socialism with a human face." After coming to power, censorship was relaxed and plans were made for a new federal constitution, for new legislation to provide for a greater degree of civil liberty, and for a new electoral law to give greater freedom to non-Communist parties.

The Soviet government became increasingly alarmed by these developments and throughout the spring and summer of 1968 issued a series of warnings to Dubček and his colleagues. Dubček had attempted to steer a middle course between liberal and conservative extremes, and at a midsummer confrontation with the Soviet leaders he stood firm against their demands for a reversal of his policies.

It was thought that Dubček had won his point on this occasion, but on August 20 armies of the U.S.S.R. and the other Warsaw Pact countries occupied Czechoslovakia. Some historians believe that the immediate cause of the Soviet invasion was the Action Program, initiated by Dubcek the previous year. Mass demonstrations of support for Dubček kept him in power for the time being, but his liberal political program was abandoned.

Over the next 2 years Dubček was gradually removed from power. In April 1969 he resigned as first secretary of the party, to be replaced by the orthodox Dr. Gustav Husak. That September he was dismissed from the Presidium, and in January 1970 from the Central Committee. In December 1969 he was sent to Turkey as ambassador. The final blow came on June 27, 1970, when he was expelled from the Communist party, and shortly afterward he was dismissed from his ambassadorial post. From there he was confined for almost twenty years to a forestry camp in Bratislava, with little contact with the outside world and constant and intense supervision by the secret police.

Meanwhile, the attitudes that Dubček had set in motion continued under their own power. A small underground movement known as Charter 77, named after its inaugural declaration on January 1, 1977, grew to 2,000 members over the next twelve years. Influenced by the movement in neighboring Poland for greater openness and human rights, Charter 77 was created by a broad spectrum of leaders, including former Communists and religious activists. They were constantly hounded and persecuted by the Communist government, but did not relent. Police arrested ten of the group's leaders, including Vaclav Havel and Jiri Dienstbier, who became, respectively, President and Foreign Minister of the new Czechoslovak government in 1989. Charter 77 continued until 1995, when it became apparent it had fulfilled its function.

Dubček highly approved of Russian prime minister Mikhail Gorbachev's progressive policy of *glasnost,* and eventually its successor of *perestroika.* While he noted there were some fundamental differences, he believed it came from the same ethic he had tried to promote in the Prague Spring. After Gorbachev visited Czechoslovakia in 1987, the secret police started leaving Dubček alone.

On November 17, 1989, a student commemoration of a Nazi atrocity in 1939 was brutally assaulted by riot police with little provocation. The factionalized oppositions to the government became united to a single purpose by the event, and formed the Civic Forum, led by Havel. He obtained video of the riot, interviewed victims, and had thousands of copies distributed across the country that were surreptitiously played on available televisions. The people became inflamed, and larger and larger demonstrating crowds filled Wenceslas Square. This rapid yet peaceful movement came to be known as the Velvet Revolution. Just a week after the riot, Havel and Dubček appeared together to the throng, who in one voice demanded the latter's restoration.

At first, Havel, the playwright, insisted on standing in the shadow of Dubček; by the time of the federal elections in 1990, it had been decided that Dubček would become chairman of the federal parliament. Dubček then proposed Havel for the presidency, which was accepted unanimously.

In his last years, Dubček aligned himself with the ideas of European Social Democracy and especially with German chancellor Willy Brandt. In 1992, Dubček became leader of the Social Democratic party in Slovakia. By that time he was already sick, having worked virtually around the clock for over two years as chairman of the Czechoslovak assembly. A huge shock, one he did not get over, was the death of his wife, Anna, in September 1991. A year later, Dubček was in a car accident, and barely escaped immediate death. Physicians diagnosed him with with a broken spine, as well as other serious illnesses. He passed away on November 1, 1992. Shortly thereafter, Czechoslovakia peacefully separated into the Czech Republic and Slovakia, an event known as the Velvet Divorce.

Further Reading

The best biography of Dubček, and a successful attempt to relate his career to developments within Czechoslovakia as a whole, is William Shawcross, *Dubček* (1990). The best book on the 1968 crisis itself is Philip Windsor and Adam Roberts, *Czechoslovakia, 1968* (1969). The best way to see these events through the eyes of the man who lived them is in Dubček's autobiography, *Hope Dies Last* (1993), edited by Jiri Hochman. Valuable background is provided by Edward Taborsky, *Communism in Czechoslovakia, 1948-1960* (1961). The cultural and political climate of Eastern Europe in the late 1980's is decsribed in *Lighting the Night: Revolutions in Eastern Europe* (1990) by William Echikson. □

John Langalibalele Dube

John Langalibalele Dube (1870-1949) was a South African writer and propagandist for Zulu culture. He was one of the first writers in an African language.

John L. Dube was born on Feb. 11, 1870, at Inanda, Natal. His father was one of the first African ministers ordained by American missionaries. Dube studied at Oberlin College (1888-1890) and later at the Union Missionary Training Institute in Brooklyn.

On his return to Natal in 1901, his admiration for such leaders as Booker T. Washington drove him to found the first native-owned educational institution in South Africa, the Zulu Christian Industrial School, at Ohlange. Its purpose was to teach the Christian religion and modern skills while encouraging the development of Zulu culture. During the first decade of the 20th century, while writing articles in English for the *Missionary Review of the World,* Dube also launched the first Zulu newspaper, *Ilanga laseNatal* (The Sun of Natal), in the hope that it would provide useful training ground for future Zulu writers, as indeed it did.

In 1912, when the threat of racialist Boer supremacy in the newly formed Dominion of South Africa awoke African intellectuals to the need for unified all-black action, John Dube was elected the first president of the South African National Congress and was sent with a delegation to gain support in Great Britain. This was of no avail, and as a result of this failure, of personal quarrels among black leaders, and of financial troubles in the organization, Dube withdrew from the Congress in 1917 and dedicated himself to running his institute and his journal, to advising the Zulu royal house, and to writing *Isitha somuntu nguye uqobo lwakhe* (1922; The Black Man Is His Own Worst Enemy), in which he preached the gospel of self-help and inner change.

This was one of the first books in Zulu by a native author. But Dube's chief contribution to the growth of vernacular creative writing was *Insila kaTshaka* (1930), a semihistorical, ethnographical novel, which was later (1951) translated into English as *Jeqe, the Bodyservant of King Tshaka* and which recalls the power and the glory of the Zulu empire in the first half of the 19th century while stressing the bloodthirsty cruelty that was associated with it. Dube may be considered the founder of the Zulu novel: it was as a result of his example that the first Zulu novelist of note, R. R. R. Dhlomo (born 1901), gave up his awkward attempts at writing in English and turned to his native tongue. *Insila kaTshaka* was Dube's only venture in prose fiction: he later turned back to straight didactic writing, especially a biography of Isaiah Shembe, a Zulu prophet and founder of a dissident church, who died in 1935 after composing the earliest original hymns in the language.

But Dube had not given up politics altogether. While disappointment had caused him to renege his earlier radicalism, he had become the leader of the Natal Native Congress, which was considered eminently reliable by the South African authorities. In 1937 he was elected as Natal's delegate at the Natives' Representative Council, and he became the first African to be awarded an honorary doctorate by the University of South Africa. He died on Feb. 11, 1949.

Further Reading

George Shepperson and Thomas Price, *Independent African* (1958), a study of the Nyasaland movement of 1915, contains numerous references to Dube and his activities. For general background on the area see Donald L. Wiedner, *A History of Africa South of the Sahara* (1962), and Eric A. Walker, *A History of Southern Africa* (1964). □

Joachim du Bellay

The French poet Joachim du Bellay (ca. 1522-1560) was second only to Ronsard in his mastery of 16th-century poetic forms and showed an arresting talent for satire and simplicity.

Joachim du Bellay was born at the Château de la Turmelière in Anjou, probably in 1522. When he was about 23, he began to study law at Poitiers, but the lure of poetry was stronger and Du Bellay soon left for Paris to study along with Pierre Ronsard and Jean Antoine de Baïf under the great Jean Dorat, who taught Latin and Greek literature at the Collège de Coqueret.

In 1549 Dorat's students published the *Deffence et illustration de la langue française,* written by Du Bellay. It defended French against Latin and proposed ways by which French writers could elevate their language and literature to the perfection of the classics. The work specifically singled out the Italian sonnet, the ode, the elegy, the epic, and tragedy and comedy as practiced by the ancients as fitting genres to replace the traditional medieval forms. With the *Deffence* Du Bellay published the first major sonnet cycle in France, the *Olive.*

Du Bellay's major works, the Regrets, the *Divers jeux rustiques, Le Premier livre des antiquitez de Rome,* and the

Poemata (all published in 1558), owe a large part of their inspiration to his stay in Rome, where he went with his relative Cardinal Jean du Bellay in 1553. However, with the passage of time his enthusiasm for Rome gave way to bitter disappointment in both the city and the Church, and in August 1557 he returned to Paris.

These four works of 1558 are quite diverse. The *Poemata* contains only Latin verse. The *Jeux rustiques,* in French, is mainly a collection of light works in the tradition of Navagero and Secundus. The *Antiquitez* and the *Regrets* offer Du Bellay's most brilliant French poetry in a serious vein. The former work contrasts Rome's past glory with the decay that Du Bellay discovered. The *Regrets* can be divided into three parts. The first relates Du Bellay's unhappiness in Rome and his longing for France and includes his famous sonnet *Heureux qui comme Ulysse.* The second part is a biting satire on Rome and the Holy See, and the third treats his return to the French court.

More personal than the *Antiquitez,* the *Regrets* reveals Du Bellay as a versatile master of the sonnet form. He was derivative, like all the poets of his time, but was particularly skillful in conveying a sense of private anguish or scorn. The young poet died of a stroke on New Year's Day 1560.

Further Reading

H. W. Lawton's anthology of Joachim du Bellay's *Poems* (1961) includes a discussion of the poet's life and works. Useful for an understanding of Du Bellay's Roman poems is Gladys Dickinson, *Du Bellay in Rome* (1960). □

Membership in the Bund led to Dubinsky's arrest in 1907 during a wave of Czarist repression following the abortive 1905 Russian Revolution. After a short jail term he returned to union activity, leading a strike by bakers in Lodz, which resulted in another arrest and expulsion to Brest-Litovsk. Dubinsky, however, returned illegally to Lodz and to union affairs, only to be arrested in 1908 and this time sentenced to exile in Siberia.

He was too young to be sent to Siberia, so Dubinsky was jailed in Lodz for a year and a half, until he was old enough to be transported there. On the way to Siberia he escaped and, convinced he had no future within the Russian Empire, decided to emigrate to the New World. In 1911 Dubinsky arrived in the United States.

Within two weeks Dubinsky took out his first papers, joined the Socialist party, and enrolled in night school. He soon became a garment cutter (the most skilled craft in the garment industry) and a member of Local 10, International Ladies' Garment Workers' Union (ILGWU), the union which represented the trade's skilled-labor "aristocrats." At first Dubinsky devoted his time to Socialist party activities and to the Cooperative movement, but after his marriage to Emma Goldberg in 1914 he began to concentrate upon his craft and to take more interest in local union affairs.

Dubinsky spoke for the more recent immigrants in the union, whose increasing numbers assisted his rise to union power. In 1918 he was elected to Local 10's executive board and a year later was vice-president. Elected president in 1920, the following year Dubinsky also became general

David Dubinsky

David Dubinsky (1892-1982) was an influential American trade union official. His leadership of the International Ladies' Garment Workers' Union demonstrated his ability to combine the more mundane attributes of the labor movement with the broader social vision of a reformer.

Together with such men as John L. Lewis, Sidney Hillman, and Philip Murray, David Dubinsky built the American labor movement as it now functions. During the Great Depression and the New Deal of the 1930s, through the creation of industrial unions (as opposed to craft unions) in the mass-production industries, these leaders brought trade unionism into a position of power whereby labor influenced big business and national politics.

Dubinsky (originally Dobnievski) was born in Brest-Litovsk in Russian Poland on Feb. 22, 1892, the youngest of six children in a poor Jewish family. His father moved the family to Lodz, where he operated a bakery. At the age of 11, David went to work for his father. By 14 he was a master baker and a member of the Bakers' Union, an affiliate of the Polish Bund, a revolutionary organization of Jewish workers.

manager, a full-time, well-paid position that allowed him to leave the cutter's bench. By 1924 he added to his offices the secretary-treasurership of the local, thus becoming the most powerful figure within the New York locals that dominated the ILGWU.

A born pragmatist whose Socialist dreams had died, and eager to rise in the union hierarchy, Dubinsky joined the anti-Communist faction of the ILGWU during the 1920s in the internal war that almost tore the organization apart. With the aid of Dubinsky's powerful Local 10, the anti-Communists triumphed, but the union was wrecked and nearly bankrupt.

A member of the ILGWU's general executive board since 1923, Dubinsky was elected secretary-treasurer in 1929, allowing him to run the union since its president was desperately sick. In 1932 the president died, and Dubinsky replaced him, still retaining his secretary-treasurer's office. Until 1959 he held both positions.

Franklin Roosevelt's election to the U.S. presidency in 1932 offered Dubinsky true opportunity. Taking advantage of New Deal labor legislation, Dubinsky had increased his union's membership to over 200,000 by the end of the next year.

Elected to the American Federation of Labor (AFL) executive council in 1934, Dubinsky supported the industrial unionists' effort to organize mass-production workers. When the AFL refused its assistance, Dubinsky in 1936 resigned from the executive council. He assisted in forming the Committee on Industrial Organization (CIO). Always a firm believer in labor unity, however, when the CIO became a permanent, second national labor federation in 1938, Dubinsky took the ILGWU out. He returned his union to the AFL in 1940 and 5 years later was reelected to the AFL executive council.

During the 1930s Dubinsky broke with socialism, becoming a fervent supporter of Roosevelt's New Deal. He declared, "Trade unionism needs capitalism like a fish needs water." Because New York City's Jewish workers looked with suspicion upon the local Democratic machine, Dubinsky helped create the American Labor party to capture former Socialist voters for the New Deal. When he thought that Communists had taken over the American Labor party, he helped found the Liberal party. By the mid-1940s he was one of the nationally respected leaders of the pro-New Deal, rabidly anti-Communist wing of the American labor movement. In 1947 he helped found Americans for Democratic Action, and independent political organization.

At his retirement from union office in March 1966, Dubinsky left a thriving labor organization, though it was no longer committed to the establishment of a cooperative society. Dubinsky's heritage to the labor movement was a belief in militant economic action, a trust in reform politics, and a faith in the justice of a socially conscious capitalism.

Dubinsky died on September 17, 1982, in Manhattan after a lengthy illness. He was 90 years old. According to the *New York Times,* "Dubinsky's most notable achievement was bringingin a standard 35-hour week to the sweatshop industry that was in a constant state of chaos."

Further Reading

The World of David Dubinsky (1957) is a complete but uncritical biography by Max D. Danish, who worked for Dubinsky. Another glowing tribute to Dubinsky is the general history of the ILGWU and the needle trades by Benjamin Stolberg, *Tailor's Progress: The Story of a Famous Union and the Men Who Made It* (1944). Two books by Irving Bernstein offer the most objective account of Dubinsky's union activities in the 1920s and 1930s: *The Lean Years: A History of the American Worker, 1920-1933* (1960) and *Turbulent Years: A History of the American Worker, 1933-1941* (1969). A short but excellent general introduction to the garment industry and its unions is Joel Seidman, *The Needle Trades* (1942). Dubinsky's obituary appeared in the September 18, 1982 edition of the *New York Times.* □

Simon Dubnov

Historian, journalist, and political activist Simon Dubnov (1860-1941) was one of the founders of historical autonomism, a method of interpreting history in terms of national self-determination.

Simon Dubnov was born in Mstislav, in the district of Mohilov, in Latvia. He received a traditional Jewish education at his grandfather's home, but in his youth he turned away from Jewish tradition. He read widely and was deeply impressed by the writings of Enlightenment authors. In 1874 he started attending a Jewish state school, but soon transferred to a non-Jewish one. After graduation he attempted several times to get admitted to a teachers' seminary, but he failed in the entrance examinations.

In 1880 Dubnov moved to St. Petersburg, where he lived with his older brother. Four years later he returned to his native town, but in 1890 he moved to Odessa and began his research on eastern European Jewry. Between 1903 and 1906 he stayed in Vilnius, where he fought for the establishment of Jewish national schools. After the pogrom of Kishinev in 1903, he demanded that Jewish self-defense be organized. In 1906 he accepted the chair of Jewish history at the Institute of Natural Sciences in St. Petersburg.

Opposing the Soviet regime, in 1922 Dubnov moved to Berlin, where he resided until Hitler's accession to power in 1933. With the Nazi occupation of Riga in 1941, the entire Jewish population was expelled and exterminated. When the sick and feverish Dubnov was being loaded on a bus, a drunk Latvian policeman shot the old man in the neck and killed him. He was buried in the community grave in the old cemetery of the Riga ghetto.

His Thought

Dubnov devoted his life to Jewish historical research and to the sociological interpretation of Jewish history. He started with an evaluation of Jewish personalities in the periodicals *Razsviet, Voskhod, Pardess,* and *Hashiloakh* (1881-1901). In the years 1893-1895 he published a series of documentary studies on the history of eastern European Jewry. His central idea was that Jewish life in the Diaspora was basically the history of centers of Jewry which, with the passage of time, moved from one country to another. His sociological conception of Jewish history found its full expression in his *General History of the Jewish People.* He saw the Jewish people in the Diaspora as one that had lost some of the factors usually sustaining a nation; the Jewish people had therefore developed a unique social regime and climate which enabled it to survive as a nation in the midst of foreign communities.

Further Reading

Dubnov's *Nationalism and History: Essays on Old and New Judaism* (1958) has an excellent introductory essay on the author by Koppel S. Pinson, the editor. See also Aron Steinberg, ed., *Simon Dubnov, the Man and His Work: A Memorial Volume on the Occasion of the Centenary of His Birth, 1860-1960* (1963).

Additional Sources

The life and work of S.M. Dubnov: diaspora nationalism and Jewish history, Bloomington: Indiana University Press, 1991. ☐

William Edward Burghardt Du Bois

William Edward Burghardt Du Bois (1868-1963) was a major African American scholar, an early leader in the 20th-century African American protest movement, and an advocate of pan-Africanism.

On Feb. 23, 1868, W. E. B. Du Bois was born in Great Barrington, Mass., where he grew up. During his youth he did some newspaper reporting. In 1884 he graduated as valedictorian from high school. He got his bachelor of arts from Fisk University in Nashville, Tenn., in 1888, having spent summers teaching in African American schools in Nashville's rural areas. In 1888 he entered Harvard University as a junior, took a bachelor of arts *cum laude* in 1890, and was one of six commencement speakers. From 1892 to 1894 he pursued graduate studies in history and economics at the University of Berlin on a Slater Fund fellowship. He served for 2 years as professor of Greek and Latin at Wilberforce University in Ohio.

In 1891 Du Bois got his master of arts and in 1895 his doctorate in history from Harvard. His dissertation, *The Suppression of the African Slave Trade to the United States of America, 1638-1870,* was published as No. 1 in the Harvard Historical Series. This important work has yet to be surpassed. In 1896 he married Nina Gomer, and they had two children.

In 1896-1897 Du Bois became assistant instructor in sociology at the University of Pennsylvania. There he conducted the pioneering sociological study of an urban community, published as *The Philadelphia Negro: A Social Study* (1899). These first two works assured Du Bois's place among America's leading scholars.

Du Bois's life and work were an inseparable mixture of scholarship, protest activity, and polemics. All of his efforts were geared toward gaining equal treatment for black people in a world dominated by whites and toward marshaling and presenting evidence to refute the myths of racial inferiority.

As Racial Activist

In 1905 Du Bois was a founder and general secretary of the Niagara movement, an African American protest group of scholars and professionals. Du Bois founded and edited the *Moon* (1906) and the *Horizon* (1907-1910) as organs for the Niagara movement. In 1909 Du Bois was among the founders of the National Association for the Advancement of Colored People (NAACP) and from 1910 to 1934 served it as director of publicity and research, a member of the board of directors, and editor of the *Crisis,* its monthly magazine.

In the *Crisis,* Du Bois directed a constant stream of agitation—often bitter and sarcastic—at white Americans while serving as a source of information and pride to African Americans. The magazine always published young African American writers. Racial protest during the decade following World War I focused on securing antilynching legisla-

tion. During this period the NAACP was the leading protest organization and Du Bois its leading figure.

In 1934 Du Bois resigned from the NAACP board and from the *Crisis* because of his new advocacy of an African American nationalist strategy: African American controlled institutions, schools, and economic cooperatives. This approach opposed the NAACP's commitment to integration. However, he returned to the NAACP as director of special research from 1944 to 1948. During this period he was active in placing the grievances of African Americans before the United Nations, serving as a consultant to the UN founding convention (1945) and writing the famous "An Appeal to the World" (1947).

Du Bois was a member of the Socialist party from 1910 to 1912 and always considered himself a Socialist. In 1948 he was cochairman of the Council on African Affairs; in 1949 he attended the New York, Paris, and Moscow peace congresses; in 1950 he served as chairman of the Peace Information Center and ran for the U.S. Senate on the American Labor party ticket in New York. In 1950-1951 Du Bois was tried and acquitted as an agent of a foreign power in one of the most ludicrous actions ever taken by the American government. Du Bois traveled widely throughout Russia and China in 1958-1959 and in 1961 joined the Communist party of the United States. He also took up residence in Ghana, Africa, in 1961.

Pan-Africanism

Du Bois was also active in behalf of pan-Africanism and concerned with the conditions of people of African descent wherever they lived. In 1900 he attended the First Pan-African Conference held in London, was elected a vice president, and wrote the "Address to the Nations of the World." The Niagara movement included a "pan-African department." In 1911 Du Bois attended the First Universal Races Congress in London along with black intellectuals from Africa and the West Indies.

Du Bois organized a series of pan-African congresses around the world, in 1919, 1921, 1923, and 1927. The delegations comprised intellectuals from Africa, the West Indies, and the United States. Though resolutions condemning colonialism and calling for alleviation of the oppression of Africans were passed, little concrete action was taken. The Fifth Congress (1945, Manchester, England) elected Du Bois as chairman, but the power was clearly in the hands of younger activists, such as George Padmore and Kwame Nkrumah, who later became significant in the independence movements of their respective countries. Du Bois's final pan-African gesture was to take up citizenship in Ghana in 1961 at the request of President Kwame Nkrumah and to begin work as director of the *Encyclopedia Africana*.

As Scholar

Du Bois's most lasting contribution is his writing. As poet, playwright, novelist, essayist, sociologist, historian, and journalist, he wrote 21 books, edited 15 more, and published over 100 essays and articles. Only a few of his most significant works will be mentioned here.

From 1897 to 1910 Du Bois served as professor of economics and history at Atlanta University, where he organized conferences titled the Atlanta University Studies of the Negro Problem and edited or coedited 16 of the annual publications, on such topics as *The Negro in Business* (1899), *The Negro Artisan* (1902), *The Negro Church* (1903), *Economic Cooperation among Negro Americans* (1907), and *The Negro American Family* (1908). Other significant publications were *The Souls of Black Folk: Essays and Sketches* (1903), one of the outstanding collections of essays in American letters, and *John Brown* (1909), a sympathetic portrayal published in the American Crisis Biographies series.

Du Bois also wrote two novels, *The Quest of the Silver Fleece* (1911) and *Dark Princess: A Romance* (1928); a book of essays and poetry, *Darkwater: Voices from within the Veil* (1920); and two histories of black people, *The Negro* (1915) and *The Gift of Black Folk: Negroes in the Making of America* (1924).

From 1934 to 1944 Du Bois was chairman of the department of sociology at Atlanta University. In 1940 he founded *Phylon*, a social science quarterly. *Black Reconstruction in America, 1860-1880* (1935), perhaps his most significant historical work, details the role of African Americans in American society, specifically during the Reconstruction period. The book was criticized for its use of Marxist concepts and for its attacks on the racist character of much of American historiography. However, it remains the best single source on its subject.

Black Folk, Then and Now (1939) is an elaboration of the history of black people in Africa and the New World. *Color and Democracy: Colonies and Peace* (1945) is a brief call for the granting of independence to Africans, and *The World and Africa: An Inquiry into the Part Which Africa Has Played in World History* (1947; enlarged ed. 1965) is a major work anticipating many later scholarly conclusions regarding the significance and complexity of African history and culture. A trilogy of novels, collectively entitled *The Black Flame* (1957, 1959, 1961), and a selection of his writings, *An ABC of Color* (1963), are also worthy.

Du Bois received many honorary degrees, was a fellow and life member of the American Association for the Advancement of Science, and a member of the National Institute of Arts and Letters. He was the outstanding African American intellectual of his period in America.

Du Bois died in Ghana on Aug. 27, 1963, on the eve of the civil rights march in Washington, D.C. He was given a state funeral, at which Kwame Nkrumah remarked that he was "a phenomenon."

Further Reading

Indispensable starting points for an understanding of Du Bois's life are his autobiographical writings (the dates are of the most recent editions): *The Autobiography of W. E. B. Du Bois: A Soliloquy on Viewing My Life from the Last Decades of Its First Century* (1968); *Dusk of Dawn: An Essay toward an Autobiography of a Race Concept* (1968); *Darkwater: Voices from within the Veil* (1969); and *The Souls of Black Folk* (1969). Two critical biographies are Francis L. Broderick, *W.*

E. B. Du Bois: Negro Leader in a Time of Crisis (1959), and Elliott M. Rudwick, *W. E. B. Du Bois: A Study of Minority Group Leadership* (1960; 1968). Also of importance is the W. E. B. Du Bois memorial issue of *Freedomways* magazine (vol. 5, no. 1, 1965). This was expanded and published in book form as *Black Titan: W. E. B. Du Bois* (1970). Arna Bontemps, *100 Years of Negro Freedom* (1963), has a biographical sketch. Meyer Weinberg, Walter Wilson, Julius Lester, and Andrew G. Paschal edited Du Bois readers. Philip S. Foner edited *W. E. B. Du Bois Speaks* (1970), two volumes of speeches and addresses. □

Emil Du Bois-Reymond

The German physiologist Emil Du Bois-Reymond (1818-1896) made important discoveries about the modes of action of nerves and muscles and was the founder of modern electrophysiology.

Emil Du Bois-Reymond was born in Berlin on Nov. 7, 1818. His early education was gained partly at the French College in Berlin and later at the College of Neuchâtel. At the age of 18 he entered the faculty of philosophy at the University of Berlin. He once described himself (in 1875) as having "intellectual leanings impelling me in almost equal degree in various directions of natural knowledge." His eclectic tastes were reflected in his early years at the university when he studied philosophy, theology, mathematics, physics, and chemistry. In 1841 he became assistant to Johannes Müller, who suggested that he study some of the electrical properties of muscle and thus guided Du Bois-Reymond into a field of study which was to engross him for the next half century.

Succeeding Müller as professor of physiology in Berlin in 1858, Du Bois-Reymond agitated for a new, well-equipped department. Because of his influence with the German emperor, who much admired him, a new physiological institute was built on the Wilhelmstrasse, and it opened on Nov. 6, 1877. It served as a model for the design of physiological laboratories until the end of the 19th century. The main lecture theater contained the unusual feature of a private box for visiting royalty, which, surprisingly, was occasionally occupied by Du Bois-Reymond's imperial patron.

Du Bois-Reymond's honors and appointments were legion. In 1867 he was appointed perpetual secretary of the Berlin Academy of Sciences. Between 1859 and 1877 he was joint editor of *Müllers Archiv,* and afterward, until his death, he edited *Archiv für Physiologie.* He served as president of both the Physical and the Physiological societies of Germany and was elected a foreign fellow of the Royal Society of London.

Many physiologists during the 19th century were attracted to "vitalism." Müller himself was a protagonist of this philosophy, which held that a vital force, present in living things, could alter physical and chemical laws. It was suggested that the organism functioned as a whole and that

experimentation on its separate functions was invalid. Du Bois-Reymond rejected this indeterminate theory. He was a "materialist" and believed in the cogency of scientific analysis of the components of living processes. He was attracted to the materialistic philosophers and wrote memoirs of some of them, including Voltaire and Denis Diderot. His own philosophical views were outlined in two collections of essays, *The Limits of Natural Science* (1872) and *Seven World Riddles* (1880). His writings encompassed other nonscientific topics; among them were essays on university organization (1870) and on the relationship between natural history and natural science (1878).

Du Bois-Reymond died at Berlin on Dec. 26, 1896.

Contributions to Neurophysiology

Luigi Galvani late in the 18th century discovered that muscle has electrical properties. During the same period Alessandro Volta showed that muscles can be made to contract continuously by rapidly repeated electrical stimulation. Volta was describing tetanic contraction, though this label was introduced much later, in 1838, by Carlo Matteucci. Matteucci determined that a difference of potential exists between a nerve and its damaged muscle. Du Bois-Reymond defined the phenomenon of tetanization and first repeated Matteucci's experiments and then went on to augment them.

Du Bois-Reymond introduced the technique of stimulating nerve and muscle by means of a short-duration (faradic) current from the modified induction coil which he devised and which bears his name. He was the first to demonstrate that muscular contraction is accompanied by chemical changes in the muscle, and he also confirmed that the cut surface of a muscle exhibits a difference in electrical potential from that of its intact surface. Further, he suggested that muscles and nerves contain electromotive molecules. In 1843 he demonstrated that ions are formed within a nerve when it is stimulated by a current from a nonpolarizable electrode; this phenomenon he called electrotonus. He discovered that there is a negative change in potential from the resting state when nerves or muscles are stimulated (1843-1848). Using his induction coil, he formulated his "law of stimulation," which postulated that nerve and muscle are not excited by a constant current, no matter what its strength, but that they are very responsive to sudden changes in current intensity.

The summary of Du Bois-Reymond's hypotheses was a postulation that all the electrical phenomena accompanying neural and muscular activity depend on electromotive molecules, arranged end to end, along cylinders of tissue. He believed that electrophysiological stimulation was simply a form of electrolysis.

Du Bois-Reymond rarely published discoveries in separate papers. The bulk of his work appeared collectively in his most famous book, *Untersuchungen über Thierische Elektricitat* (Researches on Animal Electricity). The first volume appeared in 1848, the first part of the second volume in the following year. Eccentrically, the latter book ends in the middle of a sentence, which remained incomplete until the rest of the second volume was published 35 years later (1884).

Most of Du Bois-Reymond's observations were correct and have since been confirmed, but his theoretical inferences often proved to be wrong. He was, however, a pioneer in the study of neuromuscular physiology and its electrical correlates and indicated the method and the direction of future experiments. His ideas, though wrong in detail, contain in embryo form part of the modern concept of neurophysiology that nerve and muscle conduction is mediated by the passage of an electrical wave whose generation depends on a flux of ions across the tissue membrane.

Further Reading

A biography of Du Bois-Reymond and an authoritative survey of his work are given in the obituary by A. D. Waller in *Proceedings of the Royal Society*, vol. 75 (1905). A short account of his life and work is in Fielding H. Garrison, *An Introduction to the History of Medicine* (1913; 4th ed. 1929). See also Charles J. Singer, *A Short History of Medicine* (1928; 2d. ed., with E. Ashworth Underwood, 1962), and Arturo Castiglioni, *A History of Medicine* (trans. 1941; 2d ed. 1947). □

René Jules Dubos

René Jules Dubos (1901-1982), the French-born American microbiologist, pioneered in the development of antibiotics and was an important writer on humanitarian and ecological subjects.

René Dubos was born on Feb. 20, 1901, at Saint-Brice, France. After receiving a scientific education, he went to Rome in 1922, where he was on the staff of the International Institute of Agriculture. Within 2 years he left to attend Rutgers University in New Jersey, from which he received his doctorate in microbiology in 1927. Dubos immediately began his long and distinguished association with the department of pathology and bacteriology at the Rockefeller Institute for Medical Research in New York City. Except for 2 years as a professor of medicine at Harvard Medical School (1942-1944), he was continuously involved in research at the institute from 1927. In 1934 he married Marie Louise Bonnet, who died in 1942. He became a naturalized American citizen in 1938. In 1946, he married Letha Jean Porter.

Dubos was a pioneer in the development of antibiotic drugs. Shortly after joining the Rockefeller Institute, he began searching for an antibacterial substance that would destroy the microorganism causing pneumonia. In the 1930s he discovered a soil-dwelling bacterium that produced a chemical substance capable of weakening the outer capsule of pneumonia bacteria so that they would be vulnerable to the body's natural defenses. He later showed that this substance, the antibiotic tyrothricin, was composed of two chemicals—tyrocidin and gramicidin. His work paved the way for the eventual discovery of streptomycin. Upon completing his investigation of tyrothricin he turned to tuberculosis research and won new recognition in that field.

In the 1950s Dubos began writing books on scientific subjects for a more general audience. In these he touched upon the philosophical foundations and social implications of science, warned against the naive utopianism of many medical thinkers, and argued for a study of the effect of the *total* environment upon man. His wisdom, humanitarian outlook, and lucid writing made Dubos one of the most perceptive and popular contemporary science writers. He produced over 200 scientific papers and more than a dozen books, including *Louis Pasteur: Free Lance of Science* (1950), *The White Plague: Tuberculosis, Man, and Society* (1952), *The Mirage of Health* (1959), *The Dreams of Reason* (1961), *The Unseen World* (1962), *The Torch of Life* (1962), *So Human an Animal* (1968), *Man, Medicine, and Environment* (1968), *Reason Awake* (1970), and *Beast or Angel?: Choices That Make Us Human* (1974).

In his dual role as scientist and author, Dubos accumulated numerous honors, including honorary degrees from European and American universities, awards from scientific and medical organizations, membership in the National Academy of Sciences, the Arches of Sciences Award for the popularization of science, and the Pulitzer Prize in letters (1969). In 1970 he became director of environmental studies at the State University of New York at Purchase, and in that same year President Richard Nixon appointed him to the Citizens' Advisory Committee on Environmental Quality. He died in 1982.

Further Reading

Aside from the books listed, George Washington Corner's *A History of the Rockefeller Institute, 1901-1953: Origins and Growth* (1965), recounts in detail Dubos's life and work. Dubos's place in the development of microbiology can be reviewed in Hubert A. Lechevalier and Morris Solotorovsky, *Three Centuries of Microbiology* (1965). □

Jean Philippe Arthur Dubuffet

The French painter Jean Philippe Arthur Dubuffet (1901-1985) explored the possibilities of materials and surfaces in works that depict commonplace subjects. Throughout his career he reacted against conventional ideas of beauty and remained apart from artistic movements.

Jean Dubuffet was born on July 31, 1901, in Le Havre, the son of a wealthy wine merchant, whose lifestyle young Jean found *bourgeois*. He began attending art classes when he was 15 years old, and in 1918 he went to Paris to study painting at the Académie Julian. Six months later he left school to paint on his own.

Questioning his originality and the value of art and of culture, Dubuffet stopped painting in 1923, traveled to Italy and Brazil, but returned to Le Havre in 1925 to study commerce. He married Paulette Brey in 1927, with whom he had a daughter, but they divorced just a few years later, and remarried just a few years after that. In 1930 he began a wine business in Paris which he subsequently left in the hands of an associate to resume painting. He returned again to the wine business in 1937 when the associate was failing at it, but when war broke out in 1939 he closed it down. From 1942 on he devoted himself exclusively to painting, allowing a new, more capable associate run the business until it was sold in 1946.

Dubuffet had his first exhibition in 1944 in Paris. With a crudeness reminiscent of the *art brut* (raw art) he so much admired, Dubuffet portrayed such ordinary subjects as people riding the Paris subway and a girl milking a cow. He was attempting ''to bring all disparaged values into the limelight.'' These early paintings display the interest in texture, earth colors, and ironic humor that is characteristic of all Dubuffet's work. He researched the style of drawings done by children and the insane, and applied those to his works.

When Dubuffet's second major show took place in Paris in 1946, the popular response was one of outrage. Strongly influenced by graffiti, Dubuffet had broken all accepted visual conventions by his choice of subject and technique.

Spurred by his interest in naive art, Dubuffet made his first visit to North Africa in 1947. He made two subsequent visits to the Sahara between 1947 and 1949, and he responded to his experience by creating works in which landscape and texture became increasingly important.

In 1950 Dubuffet began a series of paintings of female nudes which he called *Corps de Dames.* The formless, grotesque, and often humorous figures represent the direct antithesis to classical proportion and beauty. Dubuffet wrote extensively about his rejection of esthetic conventions, which was a current running through all his work.

Because of his wife's ill health Dubuffet moved to Vence in the south of France in 1955. He was increasingly preoccupied with creating a new kind of landscape painting. With an inventiveness that is typical of his approach to his work, he tried out new methods, which included scattering sand on the painting, scratching it with a fork, and assembling pictures out of butterfly wings. From the new techniques and materials arose a rich variety of works, among them a cycle called *Texturologies.* These pictures, which celebrate the ground and contain no figures, appear to be nonrepresentational, but Dubuffet's works, however abstract they may appear, are always about something. The *Texturologies* are about matter, and by using the same thick impasto that he used to depict figures he suggests the oneness of nature and man.

When Dubuffet returned to Paris in 1961, he again took to depicting people and their environment. The bright colors and subject matter of these works recall the panoramas of city life he painted in 1943-1944. This return to an earlier style and subject matter was characteristic of Dubuffet; there was in his work a fundamental consistency in its dedication to ''disparaged values'' and in its aim of removing the boundaries between man and nature.

In 1962 Dubuffet moved to Le Touquet. At this time he began his longest series, entitled *L'Hourloupe* (a word he invented), which possess a decorative quality that is not evident in his earlier work. He also continued to paint everyday subjects, concentrating on inanimate objects such as typewriters, scissors, and clocks. In spite of their stylistic departure, these paintings are consistent with Dubuffet's entire output in their humor and naiveté.

Most of Dubuffet's later works involved large painted polyester resin sculptures, which still retain his offbeat sense of humor yet also have a grotesque and violent nature to them. Some critics consider him a predecessor to later trends in Pop Art and Neo-Dada. He died in 1985.

Further Reading

The best book on Dubuffet is by Peter Selz, *The Work of Jean Dubuffet* (1962). It is a thorough commentary on his life and work and includes translations of many of his writings. Alan Bowness's introduction in *Jean Dubuffet: Paintings* (1966), the catalog for his Tate Gallery retrospective, is very useful. An indispensable book for placing Dubuffet in the context of his century is Werner Haftmann, *Painting in the Twentieth Century* (1954; trans., 2 vols., 1961; rev. ed. 1965). □

Duccio di Buoninsegna

The Italian painter Duccio di Buoninsegna (c. 1255-c. 1318) was the first great master of the Sienese school. His art represented the culmination of the Italo-Byzantine style in Siena and created the foundation for Sienese Gothic art.

L ittle is known about the life of Duccio. It is thought that he was born in the 1250s, probably toward the end of the decade. The first documentary reference which has come down to us is dated 1278. Thereafter several documents give us some hints about the artist's personality. He was, for instance, frequently in debt, as receipts of payment indicate. He was fined several times for petty offenses such as blocking the street and once for refusing to join the militia fighting in Maremma. From these fragmentary references we might conclude that Duccio was one of the first bohemian artists. A document of 1319 indicates that he was dead.

Duccio's role in the development of early Sienese painting may be equated roughly with the roles of both Cimabue and Giotto in the development of Florentine painting. Like Cimabue, Duccio represented the culmination of the Italo-Byzantine style of the 13th century in Siena. Duccio and Cimabue, however, stamped their most Byzantine works with the marks of their personalities so that both helped to establish the character of their respective schools of painting. There was in Duccio's style an anticipation of the linear rhythmic movements and patterns that later evolved into the 14th-century Gothic style that equates him with Giotto. The some-what younger Giotto, however, actually achieved a fully developed Gothic style, whereas Duccio's art merely advanced to its threshold. After Duccio, Sienese painting became wholeheartedly Gothic in the work of Simone Martini and the Lorenzetti brothers.

The *Rucellai Madonna*

Our understanding of Duccio's style depends on two documented works: the *Madonna Enthroned,* called the *Rucellai Madonna,* and the Maestà. The *Rucellai Madonna* was commissioned on April 15, 1285, by the Confraternity of the Laudesi of S. Maria Novella in Florence. The contract was discovered in the 18th century and led to the correction of Giorgio Vasari's attribution of the *Rucellai Madonna* to Cimabue. Despite this documentary evidence and the discrepancy in style between the *Rucellai Madonna* and other authentic works by Cimabue, some scholars still cling to Vasari's attribution. Others, aware of the stylistic differences but reluctant to accept the *Rucellai Madonna* as a work by Duccio, have invented a third artist, the "Master of the Rucellai Madonna." The consensus of opinion, however, gives the painting to Duccio. There is nothing in the style of the *Rucellai Madonna* that makes its attribution to Duccio implausible. This fact plus the contract of 1285 certainly makes such an attribution acceptable.

In stylistic terms, the *Rucellai Madonna* remains within the Byzantine conventions. It shows a concern for coloristic design uncommon in the late 13th century. In the dress of the six angels flanking the throne, for instance, Duccio abandoned the strict symmetry and deep colors of the more traditional Byzantine works and substituted cool, silvery lilacs, pinks, and light blues, which give the painting a softer and more decorative appearance than was common. This decorativeness is further accentuated by the dancing gold line that traces the hem and opening of the Virgin's mantle.

The *Maestà*

The *Maestà,* Duccio's masterpiece, is fully documented. It was commissioned on Oct. 9, 1308, for the main altar of the Cathedral in Siena and was carried in triumph from Duccio's studio to the Cathedral on June 9, 1311. Between these dates there are several documents of payment and admonitions to the artist to work faster. The *Maestà* is painted on both sides. The front depicts the Madonna enthroned in majesty with saints and angels. In the predella, spandrels, and pinnacles are scenes from the life of the Virgin and portraits of the Prophets. The back is decorated with small panels depicting the life and Passion of Christ.

The *Maestà* is splendid with gold leaf and rich colors. The design of the front is conventional, with the Madonna enthroned, flanked by regular ranks of saints and angels. Duccio did, however, substitute a solid blue mantle for the gold feathered mantle of the typical Byzantine Madonna and painted a marble Cosmatesque throne in place of the Byzantine wooden throne. As in the *Rucellai Madonna,* the hem and opening of the Virgin's mantle are traced with a sinuously moving gold line. In the narrative scenes on both front and back, Duccio evolved a remarkably accurate figure-setting relationship which created convincing environments for the figures to move through.

Other Works

Other paintings generally attributed to Duccio include a half-length *Madonna and Child* for S. Cecilia in Crevole. This work, which is totally within the Byzantine style, is usually dated before the *Rucellai Madonna,* that is, before 1285, and is therefore Duccio's earliest extant work. The *Madonna and Franciscans,* dating from between the *Rucellai Madonna* and the *Maestà,* perhaps about 1300, is a charming small panel with many of the stylistic characteristics found in Duccio's larger pictures. A *Madonna Enthroned* in Bern dates from the same period as the *Madonna and Franciscans.* Other works include a half-length *Madonna* in Brussels, a half-length *Madonna* in Perugia, and a triptych in London. A polyptych with the half-length Madonna flanked by saints in Siena may be wholly or partly painted by Duccio. Duccio's pupils and followers adhered closely to his style, a fact that has created unusual difficulty for connoisseurs.

Further Reading

The best available monograph on Duccio is in Italian, Cesare Brandi, *Duccio* (1951). There is nothing comparable in English. Enzo Carli's book for the Astra Aréngarium Series, *Duccio* (1952), is available in English and includes a remarkable amount of information; the reproductions are poor. Evelyn Sandburg-Vavalà's chapters on Duccio and his school in *Sienese Studies: The Development of the School of Painting of Siena* (1953) are excellent for an understanding and appreciation of Duccio's art. ☐

Marcel Duchamp

The French painter Marcel Duchamp (1887-1968) asked questions about the importance and nature of art and the artist and challenged conventional ideas of originality. He was a major influence on 20th-century art.

Marcel Duchamp was born on July 28, 1887, the son of a notary of Rouen. One of Marcel's brothers, Gaston, known as Jacques Villon, was a painter; another brother, Raymond Duchamp-Villon, was a sculptor. Duchamp moved to Paris at the age of 17 and began to paint. By 1911 he was responding in his painting to cubism, but his subjects were unusually personal and psychologically complex compared to the typical cubist ones.

Scandal of the Armory Show

In his famous *Nude Descending a Staircase, No. 2* (1912) Duchamp used a limited cubist palette and faceting of forms but completely contradicted the cubist esthetic in his choice of an ironic title and stress on actual movement. When this painting was exhibited at the Armory Show in New York City in 1913, it created an uproar and was the focal point for derogatory criticism of the show (one critic described the work as "an explosion in a shingle factory").

In 1912-1913 a radical change took place in both Duchamp's life and art. Together with the writer Guillaume Apollinaire and the painter Francis Picabia, he began working out a highly original and mocking concept of art. Duchamp sought out methods of making art in which the artist's hand would not be stressed (using chance and mechanical methods of drawing and painting). Increasingly language and the nonvisual side of art became important to him. As he later said: "I am interested in ideas—not merely the visual products. I want to put painting once again to the service of the mind."

Inventor of Ready-Mades

In 1913 Duchamp created his first "ready-made," the *Bicycle Wheel*. This was the first of a limited number of everyday objects which Duchamp chose (sometimes making minor additions), rather than made by hand. In these he questioned conventional ideas about the artist's role in the creation of art and about original and unique artistic products, and he brought up issues as to the value of art, the market, and the art gallery. In the next few years he turned out a small number of ready-mades; the most famous was his *Fountain,* which shocked the American public in 1917

when they saw an ordinary urinal displayed in an art exhibition.

About 1915 Duchamp began work on a construction on glass, the *Bride Stripped Bare by Her Bachelors, Even,* commonly called the *Large Glass.* It was left incomplete in 1923, and the glass was cracked in 1926. Duchamp used many original and complex processes in its physical creation. The strange mechanical forms in it make up an intricate machine whose workings express his autobiographical experiences and views on sexual and emotional relations and contain many occult references, including alchemist symbolism.

In 1915 Duchamp went to America, where he immediately became part of the New York artistic scene. After World War I he divided his time between New York and Europe. He mixed briefly with the Dadaists in Paris but increasingly withdrew from actual artistic production. By 1923 he was preoccupied with chess. Occasionally he would experiment in kinetic art or create a new ready-made.

His Influence

For many years Duchamp had an underground reputation, with few exhibitions of his works. The leader of the surrealists, André Breton, and others made him into a legendary hero whose life and character were as important as his actual artistic productions. Duchamp lived an apparently contented private life, with a happy second marriage in 1954, and he maintained amicable if slightly ironic contacts with many contemporary artists. Only in the 1960s did he become internationally famous on a public level, when many American artists sought him out in New York and studied his works and ideas, because for them he was a far more important figure, with more contemporary relevance, than Pablo Picasso.

Further Reading

There are a number of brilliant earlier articles on Duchamp, but the first long study is Robert Lebel, *Marcel Duchamp* (trans. 1959). It is a moving, somewhat fragmentary, and poetic account of Duchamp, written by a longtime friend. More readable, though less thoughtful, is a succinct chapter on Duchamp in Calvin Tomkins, *The Bride and the Bachelors: The Heretical Courtship in Modern Art* (1965). Arturo Schwarz, *The Complete Works of Marcel Duchamp* (1969), is a lavishly illustrated study by Duchamp's Milanese dealer and friend. □

Raymond Duchamp-Villon

The French sculptor Raymond Duchamp-Villon (1876-1918) was one of the pioneers of the modern movement in sculpture.

Raymond Duchamp-Villon was born on Nov. 5, 1876, the second of the six children of a notary in Rouen. Christened Raymond Duchamp, he changed his name to distinguish himself from his artist brothers: Gaston, who took the name of Jacques Villon, and Marcel Duchamp. Their father encouraged them to follow careers of their own choosing. All were drawn to art, and each was given a small stipend for support.

Duchamp-Villon went to Paris to study medicine, but by 1898 he had turned to sculpture. He was essentially self-taught. His first work, which showed the influence of Auguste Rodin, was of such high quality that he was admitted to the Salon of the prestigious Société Nationale des Beaux-Arts in 1901. His sculpture then changed, away from Rodin's earthy humanitarianism toward a neoclassicism in the manner of Aristide Maillol and Charles Despiau. In 1911 Duchamp-Villon executed a head, *Baudelaire,* that owed nothing to Rodin and was far more stylized than anything by Maillol or Despiau. Forms are faceted and simplified and yet without any loss of likeness. The severity of the contours, indeed the conception as a whole, recalls ancient Egyptian portrait busts, except with the *Baudelaire* there is an intensity of expression. Equally laconic, bare, and compact is Duchamp-Villon's bust *Maggy* (1912). His *Lovers* (1913), a plaster relief with a conventional theme, reveals further trends toward abstraction.

About this time Duchamp-Villon embraced cubism as an expression of the avant-garde rather than for its post-Cézanne constructivism. His bronze *Seated Woman* (1914) indicates his concern with increasing abstraction. The bronze *Horse* (1914) shows a radical new approach. This sculpture, despite its title, resembles a turbine or some other

power-producing machine. In this respect it is closer in spirit to Italian futurism than to cubism. Duchamp-Villon knew the futurist artist Umberto Boccioni personally and was probably influenced by him. *Horse,* built on a spirallike composition, suggests involuted layers, which gather into a concentration of dynamic, aggressive energy.

Duchamp-Villon served in the army during World War I. He contracted blood poisoning and died at a military hospital in Cannes on Oct. 17, 1918.

Further Reading

An informative work on Duchamp-Villon is William C. Agee, *Raymond Duchamp-Villon, 1876-1918* (1968), the catalog for an exhibition held at Knoedler's; it contains an excellent bibliography. The Solomon R. Guggenheim Museum published *Jacques Villon, Raymond Duchamp-Villon, Marcel Duchamp* (1956), an exhibition catalog with a short text by James Johnson Sweeney. Discussions of Duchamp-Villon's work can be found in Carola Giedion-Welcker, *Contemporary Sculpture: An Evolution in Volume and Space* (1955; 2d ed. 1961); Jean Selz, *Modern Sculpture: Origins and Evolution* (trans. 1963); and Eduard Trier, *Form and Space: The Sculpture of the Twentieth Century* (trans. 1961). □

Barbara Dudley

A leading activist on behalf of global environmental protectionism, Barbara Dudley (born 1947) became executive director of Greenpeace in the United States in 1993.

Greenpeace is an organization that has garnered world attention (and new members) through its rather unorthodox approach and techniques meant to call attention to the degradation of the earth's ecosystem. Barbara Dudley served as executive director during the mid-1990s, and her exceptionally qualified background worked well within the group's emphasis upon collective efforts and its downplay of the role of individual leadership. A committed activist on issues ranging from civil and women's rights to the environment and the peace movement for 25 years, Dudley brought to Greenpeace a diverse background of activism and managerial skills precisely at a time when, at the start of the 1990s, the organization as a whole underwent restructuring and issues prioritization.

The Greenpeace movement made its first dramatic appearance in 1971. A small group of environmentalists and peace activists in Vancouver, British Columbia, calling themselves the "Don't Make a Wave Committee," sent two small boats to Amchitka in the Aleutian Islands to protest American weapons experiments in Alaska, thereby dramatizing the issue of human safety versus nuclear testing. In later years Greenpeace moved to the forefront of the struggle aimed at safeguarding the planet and its human inhabitants, animal life, vegetation, and natural resources; it came to symbolize the increasingly significant role of voluntary, nonpartisan, nongovernmental associations in international life.

Lifetime of Activism

Born in 1947, Dudley received her undergraduate degree from Stanford University and a law degree from the University of California, Berkeley. Fluent in Spanish, she worked from 1979 to 1983 for California's Agricultural Labor Relations Board in a number of positions, including senior counsel and counsel to the board. Her assignments there involved overseeing litigation as well as training staff in cases of unfair labor practice. Throughout the 1980s Dudley provided legal counsel on migrant worker issues, senior citizens' rights, and tenants' rights at the Legal Services Corporation, the California Rural Legal Assistance Program, and the National Lawyers Guild Military Law Project. From 1983 to 1987 she was president and executive director of the National Lawyers Guild in New York, overseeing some 8,000 attorneys, law students, and legal workers in the organization's 175 chapters nationwide.

Dudley also taught law and politics courses at the University of California at Berkeley. Prior to joining Greenpeace she was first a program officer and then executive director of the Veatch Program. One of the most progressive grant foundations in the United States, this program distributed some $9 million to organizations around the country to promote such causes as environmental protection and environmental justice issues, community organizing, and rural and urban development.

New Challenges

In September 1992 Dudley, then age of 46, was selected executive director of Greenpeace USA, and officially took up the post on January 1, 1993. At that point Greenpeace had branches in 30 countries, over four million registered supporters and countless enthusiasts worldwide, a staff of 400 full-time members plus part-timers and volunteers in the thousands, and a reported budget of about $150 million. Its funds came exclusively from voluntary contributions, but its finances were said to be in disarray.

Over the years Greenpeace activists served on a number of fronts, often mobilizing spontaneously, indiscriminately, and without much planning in order to stop whaling, prevent dumping of toxic and nuclear wastes, or campaign against nuclear development and weapons. In the course of doing so Greenpeace militants acquired—indeed, oftentimes consciously encouraged and sought—a confrontational image. Dudley's successful nomination as executive director of one of the main branches, Greenpeace USA, ushered in a more media-savvy approach, though she conceded in one speech before the Stanford Graduate School of Business that "we supply the media with the sound bites they need. That's what brings us the support of the public." By the late 1990s, Greenpeace press releases offered a contact person "on site"—that is, at the demonstration—who could be reached via a cellular phone number.

The "Make a Wave" Committee

Dudley's priorities involved first coordinating the efforts of nearly two million supporters across the United States; integrating activities and consulting with Stephen Sawyer, her predecessor and beginning in 1992 executive director of Greenpeace International, headquartered in Amsterdam; and finally, redefining the group's principal objectives. Accordingly, under Dudley's influence Greenpeace outlined for itself four major campaign areas: atmosphere and energy, ocean ecology and forests, toxins, and disarmament. It also recognized a need to broaden its support base, attempting to connect with minorities and the disadvantaged, while also pointing up the greater impact of environmental degradation upon the world's poor.

Equally significant, Greenpeace appeared to be shifting away from attention-grabbing stunts. Instead of being daredevils for the environment—scrambling up smokestacks in Michigan to protest sulfur dioxide emissions and acid rain, or putting themselves in inflatable boats between whales and Russian whaling vessels—Greenpeace lobbyists worked harder at strengthening legislation that protects the atmosphere, conserves dwindling natural resources, and encourages alternative energy sources. As mirrored in Dudley's own career, Greenpeace was in the process of giving up its flair for the outrageous; becoming savvy in the use of computers, the media, and a global communications network; and stimulating the world community to see "mutual security" in the larger, environmental sense by practicing the arts of lobbying and compromise. Her tenure at Greenpeace USA ended in the summer of 1997, when she resigned to pursue other interests.

Further Reading

There is little published material on Barbara Dudley. Some of her writings, speeches, and activities can be accessed on the Internet by doing a search for "Barbara Dudley" of "Greenpeace" on the World Wide Web (August 5, 1997). □

Thomas Dudley

Thomas Dudley (1576-1653), a Puritan leader of the Massachusetts Bay Colony in America, was four times elected governor of the colony.

Thomas Dudley was born in England. Little is known about his formative years except that he was an orphan and was befriended by people who saw that he was educated and placed in service to the English nobility. He rose to the post of steward to the Earl of Lincoln and took pride for having recouped the earl's diminishing fortune by raising tenant rents.

Dudley, converted to the Puritan belief by John Cotton, his pastor in England, came into contact with other emergent Puritans. By 1629 he was one of the small group who founded the Massachusetts Bay Company. Along with John Winthrop and other "persons of worth and qualitie," he became one of the eight shareholders in the company who arrived in the New World in 1630.

Dudley was second only to Winthrop among the leaders who made the crossing; once arrived, they assumed control of the new society. The former steward was now one of the "first magistrates of the Bay Company." Persecuted in the Old World, perhaps Dudley, more than the other oligarchs, became righteous and narrow in the New. "In Calvinism," historian Bernard Bailyn notes, men like Dudley "found doctrines that might be applied to every aspect of life."

For Dudley, at least, this proved all too true. He hoarded corn and lent it to his neighbors with the understanding that he would receive 10 bushels for every 7 1/2 lent; John Winthrop considered Dudley's practices usurious. Historian Edmund Morgan notes that "Dudley was a rigid, literal minded type, ready to exact his pound of flesh whenever he thought it due him." Yet, Dudley had his place in the development of the colony. He was 13 times deputy governor and was elected governor on 4 different occasions.

As might be expected, Dudley was no less rigid and fanatical in religious matters than in matters political and economic. The notorious expulsion of Roger Williams in 1635 was Dudley's most celebrated effort to thwart what he considered to be Winthrop's leniency in religious matters. Dudley also figured prominently in the persecution of Anne Hutchinson, who followed Williams into exile largely because of Dudley's allegations of her heresy. A strong believer in the political power of the oligarchy, and to his dying day (July 31, 1653) almost paranoid on the question of religious heresy, he was nevertheless a remarkable man, part of that first generation of New World Puritans who alone were able to keep the faith.

Further Reading

There is an excellent analysis of Dudley in Edmund S. Morgan, *The Puritan Dilemma: The Story of John Winthrop,* edited by Oscar Handlin (1958). James Truslow Adams, *The Founding of New England* (1921), remains useful in placing Dudley in his colonial setting. □

Guillaume Dufay

The works of the Netherlandish composer Guillaume Dufay (ca. 1400-1474) marked the beginning of the Renaissance and influenced the course of music during the 15th and 16th centuries.

Born probably in the province of Hainaut in what is now Belgium, Guillaume Dufay received his musical training at the cathedral school of Cambrai under Nicholas Malin and Richard Loqueville (1409-ca. 1419). One of Loqueville's three-voice works is preserved in a four-voice arrangement by Dufay. Cambrai was famous for its cathedral school and for its bishop, Pierre d'Ailly, one of the more influential figures in the Church at this time, who was also chancellor of the University of Paris. Dufay may have been in his retinue during the bishop's stay at the Council of Constance (1414-1418).

This gathering of churchmen from all over Europe may have been the occasion of Dufay's introduction to his first Italian patrons, the Malatesta family. He was in Rimini at the court of the Malatestas in 1419/1420; the works he wrote for members of the family date from this time until 1426.

Between 1426 and 1428 Dufay was in Cambrai. A chanson, *Adieu ces bon vins de Lannoys,* dated 1426 in a contemporary manuscript, may indicate a stay in Laon, a city in which he would hold two benefices in 1430. In 1428 he went to Italy to become a member of the papal chapel, where he remained until 1433. After 2 years in Savoy and Cambrai, Dufay returned to serve in the papal chapel until 1437. During this period his name moves from ninth to first position in the lists of singers.

In his remaining years Dufay's activities can be traced only with difficulty. He is known to have spent much of this time in Cambrai, especially after 1445. According to his will, he also spent at least 5 more years at the court of Savoy. The duchy of Savoy under Louis and his wife, Anne of Cyprus, boasted one of the best chapels in Europe. It appears that during Dufay's later stay in Savoy he received a degree in law from the University of Turin. An incomplete motet, *Juvenis qui puellam,* jokingly portrays the disputation required of a degree candidate.

Dufay became a canon at St. Waltrudis in Mons in 1446, having also received a canonicate in Cambrai in 1436. At St. Waltrudis he met the composer Gilles Binchois, who was a canon there. Dufay also had some connection with the Burgundian court in this period since he is named as a member of the chapel of the Duke of Burgundy in a document that is not, however, from that court. The title may have been an honorary one since Dufay's presence there cannot be documented.

The last 30 years of Dufay's life were centered on the Cathedral at Cambrai. Archival documents from the Cathedral contain references to the copying of his music and, on at least one occasion, to the payment to him of 60 écus for having enriched the services with his music. His fame was widespread; for example, in 1458 he was invited to Besançon to arbitrate a dispute over the mode of an antiphon, and later Piero de' Medici referred to Dufay as the ornament of his age. He died in Cambrai on Nov. 27, 1474.

Dufay's will, which is preserved, indicates that he achieved considerable material success in life. He made bequests of artworks, music books, and money to various individuals and institutions, including the bequest of four music books to Charles the Bold of Burgundy. He also requested the performance of some of his own music in his last hour and for his last rites. The motet he specified, *Ave Regina caelorum,* is preserved and has, in addition to the traditional text, a plea for "mercy on thy dying Dufay," indicating that he probably composed it for this purpose. The Requiem Mass he asked to have performed is the earliest polyphonic setting of this service; it has not been preserved.

Dufay achieved a synthesis of the different national styles of the early 15th century. His earliest works are naturally French in nature, but those written in the 1420s show the strong impression the flowing vocal lines of Italian music made on the young composer. This is especially true in his setting of Petrarch's *Vergine bella*. The works of the late 1420s and 1430s give evidence of possible contact with English music and its "sweet sound" of thirds, sixths, and full triads. This mature style is the beginning of the international style of the Renaissance, and it is the music that the theorist Johannes Tinctoris (ca. 1476) calls the "new art . . . whose fount and origin is held to be among the English, of whom Dunstable stood forth as chief. Contemporary with him in France were Dufay and Binchois, to whom directly succeeded the moderns Ockeghem, Busnois, Regis and Caron." The poet Martin le Franc in his *Le Champion des dames* (1441-1442) writes that Dufay "has taken the English countenance and follows Dunstable."

More than 200 compositions by Dufay have been preserved. These include all genres common at the time: Mass Ordinaries, both individual movements and cycles, Mass Propers, motets, and minor liturgical works, as well as French chansons and settings of Italian texts. He used the older isorhythmic technique, but only for festival motets where this older technique would carry a certain connotation suitable to the occasion. He was among the earliest Continental composers to compose cyclic Mass Ordinaries and one of the first to use a secular *cantus firmus* (in the Mass *Se la face ay pale*). He also composed a cycle of hymns for the Church year. In these works one finds the "sweet sound" of thirds, sixths, and full triads and classic examples of fauxbourdon. His chansons, datable in all periods of his creative life, show the changes in style taking place in the 15th century; changes in conception of melody, harmony, and metric flow gradually occur from the earliest to the latest of these works. His style, a fusion of features of French, Italian, and English music of the 1420s, becomes the starting point for composers whose line extends into the 16th century.

Further Reading

A good treatment of Dufay's life and work and his position in history is in Gustave Reese, *Music in the Renaissance* (1954; rev. ed. 1959).

Additional Sources

Fallows, David, *Dufay,* New York: Vintage Books, 1988, 1982. □

Alexander Duff

The Scottish Presbyterian missionary Alexander Duff (1806-1878) was a pioneer of Christian education in India and a foremost leader of the world missionary movement of his day.

Alexander Duff was born in Moulin on April 25, 1806, into a pious family. He was a brilliant student at St. Andrews University. He was ordained in 1829 and immediately volunteered for missionary service in India. The first foreign missionary of the Church of Scotland, Duff stayed in India until 1863, although his term of service was twice interrupted by long furloughs (1834-1839 and 1850-1855) necessitated by overwork and ill health. During his stays in Scotland, he organized the home base and tried to lay a firm foundation for the work overseas.

Duff was firmly convinced that education was the key to responsible missionary work and nation building. Without minimizing the vital importance of a whole network of vernacular primary schools, he focused his attention on higher education in English. When the time came to present the Gospel to the Indian people, Duff chose to work with the upper caste (Brahmin) because he planned for the creation of an Indian Christian elite who would be well versed in Eastern philosophy, Western science, and the Christian faith. Eventually a small group of high quality was expected to become the source of the evangelization of the Indian subcontinent. Duff called this the "downward filter theory." It was also intended to be one of the creative forces toward the modernization of Indian community life. Duff had the support of the best-known early Indian reformer, Raja Ram Mohun Roy, and was influential in the educational reforms of the British colonial government (1833 and 1854).

As a missionary, Duff hoped that this new style of education might "undermine" Hindu society. For him, non-Christian religion was, before anything else, a matter of ignorance. His method did not produce large numbers of converts, but the 33 who were converted during his work in India became founders of outstanding Christian families. Also as a result of his work, a number of Protestant colleges were founded in India.

After returning to Scotland, Duff continued to work out "a grand strategy of the Kingdom of God." He called for the establishment of chairs of missions in theological schools and in 1867 became the first professor of missions in a Protestant institution (New College, Edinburgh). He also planned a training institute for missionaries and a scientific journal for dealing with all aspects of the Christian world task. He died on Feb. 12, 1878, having won wide acclaim for his work.

Further Reading

The standard biography of Duff remains George Smith, *Life of Alexander Duff* (1879). For his missionary policy see Duff's *India and Indian Missions* (1839).

Additional Sources

Millar, A. A. (Andrew Alexander), *Alexander Duff of India*, Edinburgh: Canongate Press, 1992. ☐

Alan Dugan

A strictly contemporary American poet, Alan Dugan (born 1923) was noted for his intelligent, unsentimental, and humorously mocking examination of life's mundane realities.

Alan Dugan was born on February 12, 1923, in Brooklyn, New York. He attended Queens College and Olivet College, served in the Air Force during World War II, won an award from *Poetry Magazine* in 1946, and received a B.A. in English from Mexico City College in 1951. His first publication, *General Prothalamion in Populous Times,* was privately printed in 1961.

Dugan's early works are generally relegated to obscurity, but his *Poems* (1961) was greeted with enthusiasm and led to much recognition for its poet, who later held a Pulitzer Prize, National Book Award, and a Prix de Rome.

In addition to his career as a poet, Alan Dugan worked in advertising and publishing and, oddly enough, as a model maker for a medical supply house in New York. He taught at Connecticut College, Sarah Lawrence College, the University of Colorado at Boulder, and the Fine Arts Work Center in Massachusetts. In 1982 he received the Shelley Memorial Award in Literature from the American Academy and Institute of Arts and Letters.

Given some of the titles in *POEMS six,* published in 1989, it is obvious that Dugan still liked to cut through all the sentimentality and tell it like it is, for his poems are usually free of either joy or grief in their treatment of the human condition. Opting instead for self-control and fostering skepticism in his readers, Alan Dugan writes to shock his

readers into recalling memories they would rather forget because they contradict established beliefs. In his "On a Benign Bureaucratization of Death," for instance, he recounts the aftermath of his father's death. In a terse, conversational voice he recalls thinking after his father died "fighting at/my mother for life as usual,/like the yard dog with the house cat," that his mother would wither up and die "like so many old Irish ladies do." Instead, she goes to her sister's place, which is located next to a funeral home, after her husband dies, spending her days there and realizing that "mortuary talk/was all business at the dinner table,/all rational, all accountable,/and she could get a good night's sleep"—which underlines her apparent adherence to the fixed rules and a hierarchy of authority, but which really records the mourning widow's actions honestly and renders the sentiments as real and uncontrived.

In "Why There Is No Class Solidarity in America. I read it in the *Times,* Aug. 2, 1987" (*in POEMS six*), Dugan wrote about an actual crime that happened in New Jersey at the time. The witty narration tells the story of the Italian who got mad at the Jewish woman who lived downstairs in his apartment building and hired a Polish man who owned three rattlesnakes to kill her. When the snakes slipped under her door, the lady's cats raised such an uproar that the cops came and caught the culprits. One of the rattlers bit one of the cats, but the cat recovered. Dugan's moral: "All this proves/that there is no class solidarity in America,/and that cats are better than rattle-snakes/if they come from Hackensack and are Jewish cats."

The poet's point, concisely developed, brusquely stated, and full of mockery, is well taken and underpins many of his poems. Dugan was also fond of using lots of invective, vulgar slang, and scatological terms to achieve his effects. He was never dull. In, for instance, "In Memoriam: Aurelius Battaglia, and Against His Tragic Sense of Life," which appears in POEMS six. Aurelius is the "greatest loudmouth in the world." He has the reputation of having bored "everybody everywhere." When the author meets him at a bar, he can't talk: "he can only whisper, constantly" and explains that he got cancer of the larynx because "he's being punished for the sin of hubris." He claims that "he's paying out to all the people he has pissed off/by his immoral shouting domination of all conversation." The first person narrator tells Aurie not to "really believe in appropriate fates or tragedies/or just punishment for hubris" because "that's just bullshit." When your number is up, your number is up, he argues, explaining, "we live like herds of animals, impersonal personal accidents/happen regardless of personal characteristics, vices or/virtues." So it's not fate, it's not tragic, it's just death, ridiculous death; and there's no point arguing about it until after the bars close and nobody is really listening anyway.

Dugan was largely well received as a contemporary American poet. His poetry, the critics agreed, is intelligent and inventive. As Robert Boyers pointed out: "Dugan invites us to witness with him, without any redemptive qualification, the sordid spectacle of our common humiliation."

Dugan's first person persona was without self-importance or self-pity. He spoke a tough, everyday language and talks about the commonplace: jobs, money, birth, death, sex, and booze. His terrors were the grim realities that all human beings confront:

> Why
> don't I go outside and sleep
> on the ground. It is because
> I'm scared of the open night
> and stars looking down at me
> as God's eyes, full of questions

Alicia Ostriker described Dugan as an extraordinary craftsman: "He loads every rift with concrete; he makes a hard, crunching music; and his control of momentum is peerless: the poems, one after another, come barreling down the alley like big black bowling balls and down you go."

School is not out on Dugan yet. His work remained consistent throughout his career, but his predictability led some critics to accuse him of stagnation. Alan Brownjohn remarked that the "sameness of poems suggests someone who is concerned not to seek variety or development, and continue working the same weirdly attractive yet essentially limited vein." Other critics argued that his limited range was an asset since Dugan was able to focus in on his narrow range of subjects and exercise his caustic intelligence more effectively.

Dugan was different, and it's difficult to compare him to any other poet, although he created a significant number of poems. One possible explanation for this is that Dugan

had no desire to "fit in," as it were. He wrote without regard to popular approval, as some have noted. As Robert Boyers so aptly remarked, "One does not get terribly excited about his work, but one nevertheless returns to it with increasing regularity, for it successfully inhabits that middle ground of experience which our best poets today seem to loathe to admit."

Further Reading

Critical overview of Dugan's works is provided in *Contemporary Literary Criticism,* Volume 2 (1974) and Volume 6 (1976). Also worth reading are: Stephen Stepanchev, *American Poetry Since 1945* (1965); *Salmagundi* (Spring-Summer 1968); *The Hudson Review* (Autumn 1974); *Village Voice* (August 22, 1974); *Poetry* (February 1972, 1975); and *Partisan Review* (Spring 1972). □

Richard Louis Dugdale

The English-born American sociologist Richard Louis Dugdale (1841-1883), one of the first investigators to study familial feeblemindedness and criminality, is chiefly known as the author of "The Jukes."

Richard Dugdale was born in Paris of English parentage. He came to New York City with his parents in 1851, where he attended the public schools until, at the age of 14, having shown some ability in drawing, he was employed briefly as a sculptor. At the age of 17 he went with his parents to live on a farm in Indiana. Unable to perform manual labor because of heart trouble, Dugdale learned shorthand. In 1860 he obtained employment as a stenographer in New York City.

Dugdale attended night school at Cooper Union. He developed an overriding interest in sociological questions and was determined to be a social investigator. Since he lacked the academic degrees necessary for a university position, he entered business to accumulate enough money to allow him to pursue such a career.

In 1868 Dugdale became a member of the executive committee of the Prison Association of New York and 6 years later was appointed a committee of one to investigate 13 county jails. Struck by the consanguinity of many of the criminals, he used private funds to make a detailed study of one large family connection, "the Jukes," a fictitious name for a real family. The results of the research were published in 1875 as a Prison Association report, entitled *The Jukes: A Study in Crime, Pauperism, Disease, and Heredity.* The publication created a popular uproar, especially in the press. It was republished in 1877, together with his *Further Studies of Criminals.*

Dugdale believed that the results of his research indicated that heredity was of more importance than environment as a limiting factor in determining character and behavior, although at the same time he tried to give proper emphasis to environment. As evidence, he cited statistics relating to "the Jukes family." He discovered that of 709 persons (540 of "Jukes" blood and 169 of other strains connected to the family by marriage or cohabitation) 180 had been in the poorhouse or received relief for a total of 800 years, 140 had been convicted of criminal offenses, 60 had been habitual thieves, seven had been murdered, 50 had been common prostitutes, 40 women venereally diseased had infected at least 440 persons, and there had been 30 prosecutions over bastardy. All this had cost the state a minimum of $1,308,000.

Most of Dugdale's assumptions and conclusions about hereditary degeneracy are no longer accepted. What Dugdale had discerned is today known as "the poverty cycle" or "culture of poverty," and is believed to be the result of environment, not heredity. The value of his work was that it greatly stimulated discussion and controversy in areas which were much in need of investigation, and on which no unanimous agreement is yet in sight.

In 1880 Dugdale became the first secretary of the Society for Political Education. He was also a member of many sociological and civic organizations, wrote for scholarly reviews, and addressed leading scientific associations, particularly on criminology. The discovery of Dugdale's original manuscript in 1911, revealing the true names of the family, enabled Arthur H. Estabrook to make his comparative study, *The Jukes in 1915* (1916).

Further Reading

Arthur H. Estabrook, *The Jukes in 1915* (1916), contains a memoir of Dugdale and his work. See also George Haven Putnam, *Memories of a Publisher, 1865-1915* (1915; 2d ed. 1916). □

Pierre Maurice Marie Duhem

The French physicist, chemist, and historian of science Pierre Maurice Marie Duhem (1861-1916) published work in thermodynamics, physical chemistry, hydrodynamics, elasticity, electricity and magnetism, and the history and philosophy of science.

Pierre Duhem was born on June 9, 1861, in Paris. He entered the École Normale in 1882 and qualified for a teaching certificate in 1885. His first published paper on physical chemistry appeared in 1884. That year he also presented a doctoral dissertation in physics, which attacked the "maximum-work principle" of Marcelin Berthelot, a powerful figure in the French academic world. Berthelot succeeded in having the thesis rejected and is reported to have said that Duhem would never teach in Paris. The prediction came true.

Duhem stayed at the École Normale for another 2 years and in 1888 presented a doctorate in mathematics on the theory of magnetism. Meanwhile he published his first thesis and 30 articles on physics and chemistry. In 1887 he was named lecturer at Lille, but in 1893, after a fight with the dean of the faculty, he was transferred to Rennes and in 1894 to Bordeaux. There he remained for the rest of his life, deprived of the position at the Science Faculty in Paris to which his work would seem to have entitled him. He died at Cabrespine on Sept. 14, 1916.

Duhem believed that physical theories describe, condense, and classify experimental results rather than explain them. He also believed that physical theories evolve by successive changes to conform to experiment and thus gradually approach a "natural classification" that somehow reflects underlying reality. These philosophical ideas led him after 1895 to investigate the history of science, especially in the Middle Ages and Renaissance. His *Studies on Leonardo da Vinci* (3 vols., 1906-1909) revealed the works of medieval scholastics in physics and astronomy that Leonardo had used. He explored these works in *The System of the World* (10 vols., 1913-1959). Although Duhem approached his subject almost exclusively from the point of view of the ancient and medieval contribution to modern science, this history ranks him as the rediscoverer of medieval science.

As a chemist, Duhem contributed to the Gibbs-Duhem equation, which describes the relation between variations of chemical potentials. From 1884 until 1900 and after 1913 his work was predominantly concerned with thermodynamics and electromagnetism; from 1900 to 1906 he concentrated on hydrodynamics and elasticity. Trained before the discovery of radioactivity, Duhem opposed those scientists who sought a mechanical explanation of the universe through the use of atomic and molecular models. He believed that classical mechanics was a special case of a more general continuum theory and spent much of his career working on a generalized thermodynamics that would serve as a descriptive theory for all of physics and chemistry. He expressed his views most fully in his *Treatise on Energetics* (2 vols., 1911).

Further Reading

A study by Stanley L. Jaki of Duhem's life and work appears as the introductory essay to Duhem's *To Save the Phenomena: An Essay on the Idea of Physical Theory from Plato to Galileo* (trans. 1969). Armand Lowinger, *The Methodology of Pierre Duhem* (1941), is a full-length study of Duhem's work.

Additional Sources

Jaki, Stanley L., *Scientist and Catholic: an essay on Pierre Duhem*, Front Royal, VA: Christendom Press, 1991.

Jaki, Stanley L., *Uneasy genius: the life and work of Pierre Duhem*, The Hague; Boston: Nijhoff; Hingham, MA: Distributors for the U.S. and Canada, Kluwer Academic Publishers, 1984.

Martin, R. N. D. (R. Niall D.), *Pierre Duhem: philosophy and history in the work of a believing physicist*, La Salle, Ill.: Open Court, 1991. □

Michael Dukakis

Michael Dukakis (born 1933) is a former Governor of Massachusettes who lost his bid for President of the United States to George Bush in 1988.

Michael Dukakis is the type of person who would take along a book called *Swedish Land-Use Planning* as light reading on a family vacation. With Michael Dukakis the "Mike" of campaign signs is just that, a campaign device, with even his wife calling him "Michael" at home—"what you see is what you get," according to his octogenarian mother, Euterpe. What people see is a liberal Northeast ethnic governor committed to what has nearly become the archaic notion of "public service," who is also, according to *U.S. News & World Report,* "the local version of the Jack Benny joke." He rides the Green Line trolley to his Massachusetts State House office, buys his clothes at Filene's Basement discount store in downtown Boston, and frugally prepares the post-Thanksgiving turkey tetrazinni from leftovers in the Dukakis household. *Time* magazine even calls his political world-view "liberalism on the cheap" for trying to make ever rarer social service dollars stretch farther.

But Dukakis also gets high marks for intelligence and hard work. His high school yearbook calls him "Big Chief Brain in Face." If elected, he would be the nation's most conversant president, speaking Spanish and Greek easily,

and French, Italian, and Korean passably. Dukakis—the name is often shortened to "The Duke" in Massachusetts—shocked Hispanic crowds all across the country during the 1988 presidential primary season with speeches in nearly flawless Spanish. *Newsweek* may have written that Dukakis "scores high on the 'Nerdometer'" but also admitted that unlike fallen candidate Gary Hart, brought down by charges of womanizing, "nobody watches [Dukakis's] town-house door." Dukakis, the magazine wrote, has a "cable-ready glow" designed to win if not the hearts of voters, then at least their votes.

Dukakis's three-term reign as a governor in Massachusetts is broken down locally into two distinct eras. The split terms he has served are known as "Duke I" and "Duke II, The Sequel." Duke I incorporates everything through his first four-year term as governor, which ended in a disastrous defeat in 1978, an event Dukakis freely describes as the low point of his life. Duke II is everything after that, including reelection in 1982 and to a third term by record margins in 1986.

The first campaign for governor in 1974 had little humor. It ran on the official slogan "Michael Dukakis Should Be Governor." The *New York Times* observed, "It was a sign of the hubris that sometimes grows out of his self-confidence." It was also a sign of some problems to come. But in 1974, voters wanted a change after six years of Republican governor Francis Sargent, who had left the state in dire economic trouble. Dukakis won the election handily. But the honeymoon with an independent-minded state legislature was short-lived. Dukakis didn't bother to include anyone from the state House or Senate in his plans or triumphs. By the end of six months, the revolt was in the open. The biggest problem: a growing reputation for arrogance, both from Dukakis and the Harvard-trained "technocrats" who surrounded him. One Dukakis veteran of that period told *Time,* "We were brighter than anyone else and not embarrassed about showing it." But after taking office the Dukakis administration discovered a $600 million deficit in the budget they inherited from the Sargent era, which forced the new governor to cut social services and raise taxes—something he had vowed during the campaign not to do.

Dukakis's bent for "reform" of traditional backroom politics during this time made him an inflexible compromiser. Kevin Harrington, then state Senate president, told the *Chicago Tribune,*" His approach to government was: 'This is it.' It was his way or no way." Duke I, according to the *Washington Post,* was "a man of such humorless self-righteousness that he alienated most of the politicians around him; a man with visionary ideas but a distaste for traditional politics." State legislators rebelled in big ways and small. William Bulger, then House majority leader and now Senate president, told the *Post* that because they knew of Dukakis's dislike for smoking, "We'd all light up cigars [at meetings with him]. Even guys who never smoked would light up." Critics called him "Michael the Good" or "The Boy Scout." Massachusetts, on the strength of Dukakis's tax increases, became "Taxachusetts," in what the *Nation* calls "an exaggerated but effective play on words and facts." It is a sobriquet that political opponents—in the state and out—still use to bludgeon Dukakis.

By the 1978 Democratic gubernatorial primary, voters were frustrated with Dukakis. In his place, they elected conservative Edward King, who went on to win the general election. The loss, as Dukakis has frequently described it, was "the most painful thing that ever happened to me in my life." Kitty Dukakis, his wife, told the *Washington Post*, "At one point I was really worried about him." Dukakis plaintively asked, "Was I really that bad a governor?"

Shunning the public spotlight, Dukakis went into internal exile at the Kennedy School of Government at Harvard, where he was director of intergovernmental studies and led a seminar for senior managers in state and local government. He was, by appearances, just another academic. He biked to work and brown bagged his lunch—or stood in line at the school's cafeteria.

It was during this period that the transition to Duke II began. *Insight* magazine wrote that longtime friend Paul Brountas said: "I think what he learned was that he did make some mistakes. He didn't maintain the ties to the people and to the groups that got him elected [to his first term], and that was the key reason for his defeat." Dukakis explained the change to the *Washington Post* this way: "I learned how to listen, how to think a little bit longer before I do things. I learned to do better at building coalitions. I understood a lot better than I did that you've got to involve people from the beginning in what you're doing—legislators, constituency leaders—and if you involved them, you get not only greater commitment but a better product." Still, cynics wondered—and still wonder—how much of Duke II is real and how much is just an adaptation to political realities. Michael J. Widmer, Dukakis's director of communications during his first term as governor, told the *New York Times:* " He still doesn't listen easily to others. The only real change is that he's become more cautious. He may have learned how to handle politicians better, but he is also less willing to take risks because he doesn't want to lose again." And the *Chicago Tribune* reported: "Some critics complained that his new governing style lacks leadership. His aim, they say, was to avoid making enemies and ensure re-election."

After Duke II won his 1982 rematch against King, he was careful—unlike Duke I—to share credit with other elected officials in the state whenever key legislation was enacted. By 1986, *Newsweek* ranked Dukakis as the nation's most effective governor. And later that year, after winning a third term in the November general election by a landslide margin, Dukakis was already putting the machinery in place for his presidential bid two years hence.

Dukakis, born November 3, 1933, outside Boston in suburban Brookline, is, as he frequently said on the presidential campaign trail, the "son of Greek immigrants." The elder Dukakis, who died in 1979 at age 83, came to the United States in 1912 without speaking a word of English. Eight years later, he was the first Greek to enter the Harvard Medical School, where he became an obstetrician. Euterpe Dukakis went to Bates College in Maine and became a teacher. Even at 83, she campaigned for her son's presiden-

tial bid. There was no allowance and plenty of discipline in the solidly middle-class home when Dukakis was growing up. The *Chicago Tribune* wrote, "Dukakis is fond of recalling his father's admonition: 'Much has been given to you. Much is expected of you.'"

Dukakis got his start in politics early. When he was just seven, he and his older brother, Stelian, sat glued to the family radio, "listening to the Republican convention, and taking down the delegate vote state by state," he told the *Washington Post*. At Brookline High, Dukakis was president of the student council and highly regarded in athletics, including basketball, which is surprising given his adult height of just 5 feet 8 inches. As a senior, he finished 57th in the Boston Marathon, which was considered a major accomplishment for someone his age. School chum Haskell Kassler told the Washington Post:

"The marathon was something all of us watched, but none of us dreamed of running it. Michael trained, and did it." At Swarthmore College in Pennsylvania, Dukakis was again a student government leader. He also led a fight against a local barber who refused to cut the hair of black students. Dukakis set up his own barber shop, scoring a blow for civil rights and also making some money on the side. Even then, classmate Richard Burtis told *Time*, Dukakis talked of becoming governor of Massachusetts.

After Swarthmore, Dukakis entered Harvard Law School in 1957. Two years later, he tackled Brookline politics, winning a seat at the town meeting on a platform of "ousting the dominant working-class Irish politicians," whom he derided as corrupt hacks, according to the *New York Times*. That reform impulse would continue to mark his career. By 1962, now a practicing lawyer, he won a seat in the state legislature. For eight years there he was known as a maverick reformer. But Dukakis, running for lieutenant governor, lost in his first bid for statewide office when the Democratic ticket was defeated in 1970. He reentered private law practice with a big-name Boston firm and also hosted a public television talk show called "The Advocates," which gave him valuable on-camera experience. Within four years, Dukakis was back, this time running successfully for governor against Sargent.

Dukakis's decision to enter the presidential sweepstakes, like everything else he does, was made deliberately. The first seeds were planted during Walter Mondale's defeat by Ronald Reagan in 1984. John Sasso, probably Dukakis's closest aide (he was forced to resign from the Dukakis presidential campaign because of criticism over a video he secretly released to the media that attacked another Democratic contender) served as campaign manager for Mondale's running mate, Geraldine Ferraro. Dukakis himself had earlier made Mondale's list of possible running mates. The *Boston Globe* reported that a week after Mondale's humiliating loss, Sasso was back in Boston, and Dukakis asked for a postmortem on where the Democrats had gone wrong. Sasso gave his assessment, then added that Dukakis would not be likely to suffer the same fate. Dukakis was not convinced, but during the next two years Sasso marketed the "Massachusetts Miracle" across the country. By late summer in 1986, Dukakis got reassurances that enough campaign donations would roll in to fund a presidential bid. In November, he won his landslide third term and began a public exploration of a possible candidacy. Dukakis entered the presidential race on March 16, 1987. He told a Boston press conference, "I have the energy to run this marathon, the strength to run this country, the experience to manage our government and the values to lead our people."

The Dukakis strategy in the early primaries was to survive the Iowa caucus (he did, placing third against two regional candidates), win the New Hampshire primary where he was the regional candidate (he did, with nearly twice the votes of the closest competitor), and go on to a big day on Super Tuesday when 20 states voted or caucused. It worked. On Super Tuesday, Dukakis took his own state, the major delegate prizes of Texas and Florida, and several others. Overnight he became the front-runner, a distinction he would hold on to right into the Democratic convention.

How did a little-known governor pull it off? The *Boston Globe* wrote: "He was lucky. The Democratic Party's best known names—Kennedy, Bradley, Cuomo—bypassed the race. Front-runner Gary Hart dropped out just nine days after Dukakis announced his candidacy. His opponents (with the prominent exception of the Rev. Jesse Jackson) were as little known as he was, and his arsenal included a world-class fund-raising operation." The *New Yorker* observed: "Dukakis' 'Mr. Goodwrench' approach to government is selling somewhat, but it isn't the only reason he may prevail. If he does prevail, it will also be in large part because he had the best campaign plan and the money to implement it."

There were mistakes early in the campaign. The problem, according to several observers, was that Dukakis had lived virtually his whole life on the banks of the Charles River, which divides Boston from Cambridge and Harvard. That seemed to lead to cultural nearsightedness, such as the time he urged Iowa farmers to grow Belgian endive as an alternative crop—a Yuppie food few in the Bread Belt had ever heard of. The *Boston Globe* reported that at a small-town Midwest campaign stop, the candidate lectured wizened Iowa farmers "who looked as if they had never left the state" about the need to cut that "Caribbean vacation" instead of the grocery budget.

More seriously, critics—and not just in other campaigns—question how much Dukakis is responsible for the so-called "Massachusetts Miracle," which he touts at nearly every campaign stop. In *Business Week,* Dukakis said, "We took an economic basket case and turned it into an economic showcase." Opponents say key elements of the "showcase" were already in place when Dukakis won his rematch with King in 1982. Also, Massachusetts's recovery was fueled, at least in part, by the defense spending of President Reagan, something Dukakis may have to rationalize with his more liberal defense policies. Christopher Anderson of the Massachusetts High Technology Council told *Newsweek,*" We could have had a personal computer running the government and we'd still have a healthy economy." But the *New York Times* said other studies showed Dukakis indeed helped the Massachusetts boom by steering new industry into economically depressed areas outside of Boston, such as the former mill towns of Lowell and Lawrence.

Dukakis the man is more difficult to isolate than his policies. Dukakis, who comes off as cool and cerebral, "is more apt to stir the mind than the soul," according to the *Chicago Tribune.* Thomas P. O'Neill III, son of former House Speaker "Tip" O'Neill, told the paper: "Michael is not the type of person you'd have a beer with. He would consider that a waste of time." In fact, the Dukakis campaign tried to capitalize on just that stuffy image. A television commercial aired during the Illinois primary featured a bricklayers union spokesman from Boston making the same observation, but adding: "If you want somebody to drink with, call your buddy. If you care about your job, vote for Mike Dukakis." In Illinois, though, where Dukakis finished third behind the local favorites Jesse Jackson and U.S. Senator Paul Simon, this approach may have backfired. The *New Yorker* said many Illinois voters asked themselves, "What's the matter with Dukakis that he's not a shot-and-beer kind of guy?" Clearly, though, that image doesn't bother Dukakis. Close friend Boston surgeon Nicholas Zervas told the *Chicago Tribune:*" He has absolutely no material needs. He's more interested in ideas."

Lighting a cigarette, Kitty Dukakis—she has been trying to quit for years—often pleads, "Don't tell Michael." The couple has been Massachusetts' first Odd Couple since they emerged into the public eye. She is Jewish; he is Greek Orthodox. She loves spending money; he abhors it. At one point, she had to keep part of her wardrobe at her parents' home—her father is former Boston Pops associate conductor and violinist Harry Ellis Dickson—for fear of what Michael would say. They both went to Brookline High School but didn't start dating until 1961; he a Harvard Law School student, she a divorced mother working and going to school part-time. They married in 1963 and, besides Kitty's son, John, from her first marriage, have two daughters, Andrea and Kara.

One of the few bumps in Dukakis's road through the presidential primaries came when Kitty Dukakis admitted a 26-year addiction to diet pills that only ended in 1982 after treatment at a private clinic in Minnesota. She has turned the revelation to her husband's advantage, campaigning as a friend to people who have experienced chemical dependencies. But opponents of Dukakis questioned how he could not have noticed his wife's addiction over the course of more than two decades. The *New York Times* wrote, "Some wondered if he was practicing a form of self-deception." Kitty Dukakis openly despises those "silly wife questions." When she was asked how her husband's shirts always looked so wrinkle-free at the end of the day, *Time* magazine reported her answering: "I don't do his shirts. You'll have to ask him." Not surprisingly, it turns out that Dukakis does his own shirts.

Michael Dukakis chose Lloyd M. Bentsen, Jr. of Texas as his running mate in the 1988 campaign, but Dukakis's candidacy never lived up to expectations. The Massachusetts governor was buffeted by the now notorious Willie Horton television ads and repeated images of himself riding in an Army tank wearing headphones that looked like Mickey Mouse ears. Republicans George Bush and Dan Quayle easily won the White House by a margin of over 7 million popular votes. The Bush campaign also exploited the word "liberal" by claiming that Dukakis and Bentsen represented the worst that liberalism had to offer: unwarranted federal intervention and social engineering, high taxes, and the coddling of criminals. The Democrats could only rejoin after the election that it was difficult to run against the "peace and prosperity" of the Reagan years. Being a little more dispassionate,*Commentary* in a post-election analysis summed up Dukakis and his failure at national politics by quoting from *In These Times,* an "independent socialist weekly": "In three terms as governor of Massachusetts, Dukakis has been an effective liberal reformer with a strong managerial bent. Liberal groups have generally found Dukakis sympathetic to their causes and willing to devote state resources to solve social and economic problems of poor and working-class people, but often too willing to compromise on regulation and taxes for the sake of political consensus."

The voters saw Dukakis as basically a nice guy with good intentions who didn't know when to stop or say no. *Commentary* went on to claim that "Dukakis was, of course, aware from the outset of the low regard in which voters have come to hold liberalism." In his acceptance speech Dukakis told the convention's delegates that " . . . this election isn't about ideology. It's about competence." Two weeks before the election he told Ted Koppel: "Ted, I'm not a liberal." The voters weren't buying it.

In late 1989, while he was still reeling from the criticism of the media and his fellow Democrats, Dukakis's personal world began to fall apart. Reports were leaked to the press that Kitty was suffering from alcoholism and had resorted to drinking rubbing alcohol in a bout of depression on the one-year anniversary of her husband's defeat. A close friend described Kitty as giving "a cry for help." Kitty was hospitalized in Boston, and it was further revealed that she had been taking prescription antidepressants and had been attending meetings of Alcoholics Anonymous. A spokeswoman implied that Kitty's drinking rubbing alcohol may have been a suicide attempt.

Dukakis's "Massachusetts Miracle" also began falling apart during the waning years of his governorship. *Newsweek* reported in early 1990 that his unfavorable rating had climbed to an incredible 79 percent as Massachusetts faced a $825 million deficit. Upon hearing the approval rating, Howie Carr, *Boston Herald* columnist and longtime opponent of Dukakis, quipped "What's wrong with the other 21 percent of the population?" The looming flood of red ink in the state budget prompted the dismantling of many of the government programs and services the three-term governor had fought so hard to implement. Massachusetts was also facing the lowest bond rating in the country. Dukakis wisely declined to seek another term in office.

For the next two years Michael and Kitty Dukakis shunned publicity and all but disappeared from public life. Dukakis turned to the academic world and began teaching political science at the University of Australia and the Uni-

versity of Hawaii. By late 1992 the couple had returned to Massachusetts and the former governor was teaching at Northeastern University near Boston and grading papers in a cramped third-floor office. Still notorious for his personal parsimony, Dukakis was walking two miles to work and standing in the lunch line at the school's cafeteria. *People* reported in 1994 that Kitty Dukakis had enrolled in a master's program in social work at Boston University. In addition to teaching at Northeastern Michael Dukakis still feels committed to public service. "Public life *is* my life," he told one reporter. In October 1996 Dukakis, Lamar Alexander, and Richard Lamm were in Washington, D.C. to tape an episode of a television series, *Race for the Presidency,* produced by TCI News, to discuss what went wrong with their presidential campaigns.

Further Reading

Kenney, Charles, and Robert Turner, *Dukakis: An American Odyssey,* Houghton, 1988.
Boston Globe, February 14, 1988; May 8, 1988.
Business Week, March 23, 1987.
Chicago Tribune, August 7, 1987.
Insight, May 9, 1988.
Los Angeles Times, March 17, 1987.
Nation, May 16, 1987.
New Republic, October 26, 1987.
Newsweek, March 24, 1986; July 20, 1987; November 30, 1987.
New Yorker, April 4, 1988.
New York Times, April 10, 1988.
New York Times Magazine, May 8, 1988.
Time, March 30, 1987; July 27, 1987; February 22, 1988; May 2, 1988.
U.S. News & World Report, March 30, 1987; July 6, 1987.
Washington Post, June 29, 1987; August 25, 1987; October 5, 1996.
Commentary, February, 1989.
Detroit News, November 9, 1989; December 16, 1992.
Newsweek, January 8, 1990.
People, November 28, 1994.
USA Weekend, March 1-3, 1991. □

James Buchanan Duke

James Buchanan Duke (1856-1925), American industrialist and philanthropist, was the first giant of finance to emerge in the post-Civil War South.

James B. Duke was born on Dec. 23, 1856, on a small farm near Durham, N.C., the younger son of Washington Duke. Union troops during the Civil War so ravaged their farm that at war's end, when Washington Duke returned from service in the Confederate Army, the family had to begin anew with total assets of 50 cents and two blind mules. The discovery of a small load of tobacco that had somehow escaped capture by Union forces triggered their rise to wealth. This supply sold so quickly that the Dukes began production and distribution on a large scale. By 1872, at the height of the South's impoverishment, the family was selling 125,000 pounds of tobacco annually.

When, in 1881, the Dukes began to manufacture cigarettes, business boomed. Three years later, with James in control, the company moved its executive offices to New Jersey to take advantage of that state's liberal corporation laws and to exploit the virgin markets of the North and West. Thereafter, the business grew into an international combine as Duke pursued monopolistic methods. Rebates, discrimination, a nationwide secret service, bulldozer tactics against competitors, and price manipulations marked the long "Tobacco War," by which Duke gained complete ascendancy over all rivals.

By 1904 Duke's American Tobacco Company controlled 90 percent of the national market and at least 50 percent of the foreign trade in tobacco. With unlimited power and a capitalization of over $500,000,000, the Duke trust was so powerful that a 1911 Supreme Court decree ordering their monopoly be dissolved had little effect on the company's prosperity.

Duke also developed an interest in the potential of electrical power. In 1905 he organized the Southern (now Duke) Power and Light Company. Within 25 years this utility was "capable of producing more energy than all the slaves of the Old South."

Duke contributed large sums to hospitals and churches. His last notable act was the establishment of the Duke Endowment on behalf of a small Methodist school, Trinity College. He donated more than $60,000,000 toward the creation of a new campus characterized by large buildings of Gothic design. The school was renamed Duke University.

The tall, rugged, redheaded industrialist died on Oct. 10, 1925. Once asked the secret of his success, Duke replied simply, "I had confidence in myself."

Further Reading

John W. Jenkins, *James B. Duke, Master Builder* (1927), and John K. Winkler, *Tobacco Tycoon: The Story of James Buchanan Duke* (1942), give sympathetic treatments of Duke. See also Meyer Jacobstein, *The Tobacco Industry in the United States* (1907), and Nannie May Tilley, *The Bright-Tobacco Industry, 1860-1929* (1948). □

John Foster Dulles

John Foster Dulles (1888-1959), American diplomat, was secretary of state under Eisenhower. He strove to create a United States policy of "containing" communism.

John Foster Dulles was born in Washington, D.C., on Feb. 25, 1888. His grandfather, John W. Foster, had been secretary of state under Benjamin Harrison, and his uncle, Robert Lansing, had been secretary of state under Woodrow Wilson. Educated at Princeton and the law school of George Washington University, Dulles joined the international law firm of Sullivan and Cromwell in 1911,

became a partner in 1920, and was head of the firm in 1927. He was eminent in his field.

Dulles's interest in foreign affairs was of long standing; at the age of 31, he had attended the 1919 Paris Peace Conference as legal counsel to the American delegation. In 1945 he was appointed legal adviser to the United States delegation at the San Francisco conference which drew up the Charter of the United Nations.

A Republican, Dulles served in the U.S. Senate in 1949-1950. In 1951, as ambassador-at-large, he negotiated a peace treaty with Japan acquitting himself brilliantly in overcoming Soviet opposition and other difficulties.

In 1952 Dulles was an ardent partisan of Dwight D. Eisenhower for president and was rewarded the next year with the office of secretary of state, which he held until his death. In his first months in office Dulles brought about an armistice in the Korean War, probably by the threat of the resumption of the war if the negotiations did not succeed. Less successful was his effort to roll back the Iron Curtain: in the East German revolt of 1953 and the Hungarian revolt of 1956 the United States was unable to offer any support to the rebels.

Dulles was a firm supporter of the North Atlantic Treaty Organization and supported the proposal for an international defense force in Europe. This project failed, however, and it was Anthony Eden, rather than Dulles, who played the leading role in forging a new treaty that invigorated the European alliance and admitted Germany to full membership.

In 1955 came the Big Four Conference at Geneva, attended by the four heads of government—Eden of England, Edgar Faure of France, N. A. Bulganin of the U.S.S.R., and Eisenhower of the United States—with a view to bettering understanding with the Soviet Union. Dulles had a part in the proceedings, but little was accomplished. As a matter of fact, from the outset the secretary of state had regarded the project with pessimism.

In 1956 came one of the most serious crises of Dulles's career. In the summer of that year Gamal Abdel Nasser, the Egyptian dictator, seized and nationalized the Suez Canal, creating great resentment in France and Britain. Dulles labored manfully to find a peaceful solution of the problem, but in December the British and the French, using an Israeli attack on Egypt as a pretext, landed forces in the canal zone. With great courage Dulles protested this violation of the peace and brought the situation before the United Nations. As a result, the invaders were compelled to withdraw.

Dulles's activities were by no means confined to Europe. The United States played a part in the overthrow of a Communist regime in Guatemala. In the Far East, Dulles played a leading role in the formation of the Southeast Asia Treaty Organization, an alliance of the United States, Britain, France, Australia, New Zealand, the Philippines, Thailand and Pakistan. This alliance did not explicitly call for armed action, but it bound the signatories to consult whenever the integrity of any country in Southeast Asia was menaced. Importantly, it marked the extension of United States commitments in this area. Dulles also signed a defense treaty with the Chinese Nationalist government on Taiwan (Formosa) and twice thwarted hostile attacks by the (Communist) Chinese People's Republic on the Nationalists' island of Quemoy. Dulles's attempt to bring together some of the countries of the Middle East in opposition to communism resulted in an alliance that soon disintegrated.

A believer in keeping firm opposition to the Communist menace, Dulles based his diplomacy on strong ideology. He was ready to use force or the threat of force (as in the Formosa Strait) when he believed that such action would balk aggression. His diplomacy was highly personal. He was not a great administrator, but he was a dedicated public servant. In the last year of his life he suffered from cancer, which he bore with real heroism. He died on May 24, 1959.

Further Reading

Louis L. Gerson, *John Foster Dulles,* vol. 17 in Samuel F. Bemis and Robert H. Ferrell, eds., *The American Secretaries of State and Their Diplomacy* (1967), is recommended. See also John Robinson Beal, *John Foster Dulles* (1957); Roscoe Drummond and Gaston Coblentz, *Duel at the Brink: John Foster Dulles Command of American Power* (1960); and Richard Goold-Adams, *John Foster Dulles: A Reappraisal* (1962). □

Dull Knife

Although Dull Knife (1810?–1883) was active in the Cheyenne-Arapaho War in Colorado, the Sioux Wars for the Northern Plains, and also the War for the Black Hills, he is, perhaps, best remembered for attempting to lead nearly three hundred people from an assigned reservation back to their Tongue River homeland in northern Wyoming and southern Montana.

Best-known for leading his people in a courageous attempt to return from exile in Oklahoma to their Montana homeland in 1878, the Northern Cheyenne leader Morning Star was born in about 1810 on the Rosebud River. He was known mostly by his nickname of Dull Knife, given to him by his brother-in-law, who teased him about not having a sharp knife. A renowned Dog Soldier in his youth, Dull Knife became a member of the Council of 44 and in the 1870s was one of the four principal, or Old Man, Chiefs. These chiefs represented the mystical four Sacred Persons who dwelt at the cardinal points of the universe and were the guardians of creation.

Little is known of Dull Knife's early life. When he was a young man in the late 1820s, he went on a raiding party against the Pawnees. Capturing a young girl, he saved her life by asking that she replace a member of his family previously lost to the Pawnees. When he became a chief, Dull Knife made Little Woman his second wife, the union producing four daughters. Dull Knife had two other wives, Goes to Get a Drink, with whom he had two daughters, and her sister Slow Woman, by whom he had four sons and another daughter.

Dull Knife first appears in white history in 1866, when he joined Red Cloud and the Oglala Sioux in ambushing U.S. soldiers under Captain William J. Fetterman traveling along the Bozeman Trail to reach the Montana gold fields. At the end of the Bozeman Trail War, the Northern Cheyennes signed the 1868 Treaty of Fort Laramie agreeing to settle on a reservation. The U.S. government gave them the choice of joining the Crows in Montana, the Sioux in Dakota, or the Southern Cheyennes and Arapahos in Indian Territory. To force an early decision, the government withheld supplies, and the Northern Cheyennes signed an agreement on November 12, 1874, to move to Indian Territory whenever the U.S. government saw fit.

These arrangements were set aside, however, when the Black Hills Gold Rush led to war with the Sioux and their allies. The precipitating act was an ultimatum ordering the Indians to return to agencies in South Dakota by January 31, 1876. The Big Horn Expedition, intended to force the Indians back to their agencies, engaged the Sioux, Northern Cheyennes, and Northern Arapahos in several major battles, the most famous being Custer's fight on the Little Big Horn. Dull Knife was not in the Indian village that day, but his son Medicine Lodge was present and died in combat against the Seventh Cavalry.

The pivotal battle for the Northern Cheyennes occurred on the morning of November 25, 1876, when Colonel Ranald Mackenzie's force of 600 men of the 4th Cavalry and about 400 Indian scouts surprised Dull Knife's camp on the Red Forks of the Powder River. Reportedly killed in the fighting were one of Dull Knife's sons and a son-in-law. The dead numbered around 40, but destruction of the village and its contents sealed their fate. For all practical purposes, the campaign of 1876-77 ended the Indian wars on the Northern Plains.

Concern for their children caused Dull Knife and his people to surrender to the troops under Crook and Mackenzie in the spring of 1877. At Fort Robinson they learned that the government had decreed that all Northern Cheyennes would be sent to Indian Territory. Dull Knife and Little Wolf urged their tribesmen to abide by the wishes of the government. The Northern Cheyennes may have been led to believe that they could return to their tribal lands in a year if they did not like life in the south. The journey to Indian Territory began on May 28, 1877. In the group were 937 Northern Cheyennes. Seventy days later, on August 5, they arrived at the Cheyenne and Arapaho Agency, selecting a campsite about eight miles north.

Within a year, the Northern Cheyennes were ready to return to their homeland. Starved, ravaged by disease, preyed upon white gangs of horse thieves, unwilling to farm, critical of the civilized ways of their southern brethren, rankled by the fact that the Northern Arapahos had been allowed to remain in the north, and with 50 of their children dead, they had had enough. So at 10:10 p.m. on September 9 a party of 353 Cheyennes—92 men, 120 women, 69 boys, and 72 girls—quietly left the foreign place, leaving fires burning and lodge poles standing to fool distant military pickets. After discovery of their departure the next morning at three in the morning, the army's pursuit began, eventually involving 13,000 men in three military departments.

Following the route of the Texas Cattle Trail from Oklahoma through Kansas, Dull Knife and Little Wolf and their followers skirmished with army units on September 13 at Turkey Springs, September 14 at Red Hill, September 17 and 21-22 at Sand Creek, and September 27 at Punished Woman Creek, each time eluding the troops and continuing north. On the journey, Little Woman was killed by a horse that stampeded through the camp. When the fleeing Cheyennes reached northeast Kansas, warriors roamed the countryside, killing 40 male white settlers, some said in revenge for a mass killing of their kinsmen by whites in the area in 1875. In Nebraska, Dull Knife and Little Wolf separated, the former heading for Fort Robinson and Red Cloud Agency, the latter to the traditional Northern Cheyenne homeland in Montana.

On October 23, two companies of the 3rd Cavalry traveled up Chadron Creek and caught Dull Knife and his people. Taken to Fort Robinson, the Cheyennes learned on January 3 that the Washington government had decided they must be sent back to Indian Territory. When they refused, Post Commander Henry Wessells imprisoned the band in a cavalry barracks, cutting off heat, food, and water. Barricading doors and covering windows with cloth to conceal their movements, the captives tore up the floor and constructed rifle-pits to command the windows. At 10:10 at night on January 9, the Cheyennes began firing. The men moved forward through the windows with children under their arms, while the women followed, and once again Dull Knife and his band dashed for freedom. This time they were not so fortunate. Soldiers sent volley after volley into the fleeing band. Twenty-two men, eight women, and two children died in the initial exodus, including Dull Knife's daughter, Traveling Woman, who was carrying her 4-year-old sister on her back. The retreat continued for four miles in the darkness until the fugitives reached neighboring hills where pursuit was no longer possible.

Twelve days later, four companies of soldiers caught the largest number of remaining Cheyennes, pinning them down in an oblong depression about 40 miles from Fort Robinson. Twenty-three Indians were killed and nine captured, including two young girls, aged 14 and 15, discovered under the bodies of young men. The dead Indians were buried in the pit where they had hidden. In the meantime, Dull Knife, Slow Woman, and their remaining children had found a haven in the rocks, where they stayed for ten days, keeping alive by eating their moccasins. After eighteen days of wandering, they reached Pine Ridge, where they were hidden by Sioux relatives in a lodge under a little bluff on Wounded Knee Creek.

After wintering in a sheltered valley near the forks of the Niobrara River, Little Wolf and his followers headed north. On March 25, they surrendered to Lieutenant W. P. Clark on the Yellowstone and were sent to Fort Keogh. In November, Indian Bureau officials permitted the Northern Cheyenne at Pine Ridge to transfer to Montana to join the rest. At the request of General Nelson A. Miles, Dull Knife was allowed to return to the valley of the Rosebud. An Executive Order of November 26, 1884, established a permanent home for the Northern Cheyenne in south central Montana east of the Crow reservation.

Dull Knife spent his remaining years, embittered and grieving, in the hills of southern Montana. Among the dead he had left behind at Fort Robinson were two daughters and a son, bringing the total of his loved ones lost in a single year to a wife, three sons, and two daughters. Dull Knife died in 1883 at his son Bull Hump's home. In 1917 Cheyenne historian George Bird Grinnell had his remains and those of Little Wolf reinterred in the cemetery at Lame Deer, where they are today. □

Alexandre Dumas

Alexandre Dumas (1803-1870), the prolific French author of plays, popular romances, and historical novels, wrote *The Three Musketeers* and *The Count of Monte Cristo*.

Alexandre Dumas is generally called Dumas *père* to distinguish him from his illustrious son Alexandre (known as Dumas *fils*), who was also a dramatist and novelist. The son of a Creole general of the French Revolutionary armies, Dumas was brought up by his mother in straitened circumstances after his father's death. While still young, he began to write "vaudeville" plays (light musical comedies) and then historical plays in collaboration with a friend, Adolphe de Leuven. Historical themes, as well as the use of a collaborator, were to be permanent aspects of Dumas's style throughout his career.

After reading William Shakespeare, Sir Walter Scott, Friedrich von Schiller, and Lord Byron, and while employed as a secretary to the Duke of Orléans (later King Louis Philippe), Dumas wrote his first plays in 1825 and 1826. Others followed, with *Henri III et sa cour* (1829) bringing him great success and recognition. It seemed to the theatergoers of Dumas's time that here at last was serious theater which presented an alternative to effete neoclassical drama.

The Revolution of 1830 temporarily diverted Dumas from his writing, and he became an ardent supporter of the Marquis de Lafayette. His liberal activities were viewed unfavorably by the new king, his former employer, and he traveled for a time outside France. A series of amusing travel books resulted from this period of exile.

His Fiction

When Dumas returned to Paris, a new series of historical plays flowed from his pen. By 1851 he had written alone or in collaboration more than 20 plays, among the most outstanding of which are *Richard Darlington* (1831), *La Tour de Nesle* (1832), *Mademoiselle de Belle-Isle* (1839), and *La Reine Margot* (1845). He also began writing fiction at

this time, first composing short stories and then novels. In collaboration with Auguste Maquet he wrote the trilogy: *Les Trois Mousquetaires* (1844; *The Three Musketeers*), *Vingt Ans après* (1845; *Twenty Years After*), and *Le Vicomte de Bragelonne* (1850). *Le Comte de Monte-Cristo* (1846; *The Count of Monte Cristo*) was also a product of this period.

Dumas had many collaborators (Auguste Maquet, Paul Lacroix, Paul Bocage, and P.A. Fiorentino, to name only a few), but it was undoubtedly with Maquet that he produced his best novels. He had assistants who supplied him with the outlines of romances whose original form he had already drawn up; then he wrote the work himself. The scale of his "fiction factory" has often been exaggerated. Although at least a thousand works were published under his own name, most were due to his own industry and the amazing fertility of his imagination. Dumas grasped at any possible subject; he borrowed plots and material from all periods and all countries, then transformed them with ingenuity. The historian Jules Michelet once wrote admiringly to him, "You are like a force of elemental nature."

Dumas does not penetrate deeply into the psychology of his characters; he is content to identify them by characteristic tags (the lean acerbity of Athos, the spunk of D'Artagnan) and hurl them into a thicket of wild and improbable adventures where, after heroic efforts, they will at last succumb to noble and romantic deaths. His heroes and heroines, strong-willed and courageous beings with sonorous names, are carried along in the rapid movement of the dramas, in the flow of adventure and suspenseful plots. Dumas adhered to no literary theory, except to write as the spirit moved him, which it did often.

Dumas's works were received with enthusiasm by his loyal readers, and he amassed a considerable fortune. It was not sufficient, however, to meet the demands of his extravagant way of life. Among his follies was his estate of Monte-Cristo in Saint-Germain-en-Laye, a Renaissance house with a Gothic pavilion, situated in an English garden. This estate housed a horde of parasitical guests and lady admirers who lived at the author's expense.

Later Life

Dumas, who had never changed his republican opinions, greeted the Revolution of 1848 with enthusiasm and even ran as a candidate for the Assembly. In 1850 the Théâtre-Historique, which he had founded to present his plays, failed. After the coup d'état in 1851 and the seizure of power by Napoleon III, Dumas went to Brussels, where his secretary managed to restore some semblance of order to his affairs; here he continued to write prodigiously.

In 1853 Dumas returned to Paris and began the daily paper *Le Mousquetaire*. It was devoted to art and literature, and in it he first published his *Mémoires*. The paper survived until 1857, and Dumas then published the weekly paper *Monte-Cristo*. This in turn folded after 3 years.

In 1858 Dumas traveled to Russia. He then joined Giuseppe Garibaldi in Sicily, and in 1860 Garibaldi named him keeper of museums in Naples. After remaining there for 4 years, he returned to Paris, where he found himself deep in debt and at the mercy of a host of creditors. His affairs were not helped by a succession of parasitical mistresses who expected—and received—lavish gifts from Dumas.

Working compulsively to pay his debts, Dumas produced a number of rather contrived works, among them *Madame de Chamblay* (1863) and *Les Mohicans de Paris* (1864), which were not received with great enthusiasm. His last years were softened by the presence of his son, Alexandre, and his devoted daughter, Madame Petel. He died in comparative poverty and obscurity on Dec. 5, 1870.

Further Reading

A good introduction to the Dumas dynasty is André Maurois, *The Titans: A Three Generation Biography of the Dumas,* translated by Gerard Hopkins (1957). A. Craig Bell, *Alexandre Dumas: A Biography and Study* (1950), is a more serious and complete work. In a lighter vein is Herbert S. Gorman, *The Incredible Marquis: Alexandre Dumas* (1929). For a direct look at the source material, Jules E. Goodman, ed., *The Road to Monte-Cristo: A Condensation from the Memoirs of Alexandre Dumas* (1956), is recommended.

Additional Sources

Dumas, Alexandre, *My memoirs,* Westport, Conn.: Greenwood Press, 1975, 1961.

Hemmings, F. W. J. (Frederick William John), 1920-, *Alexandre Dumas, the king of romance,* New York: Scribner, 1979.

Ross, Michael, *Alexandre Dumas,* Newton Abbot, Devon; North Pomfret, Vt.: David & Charles, 1981.

Schopp, Claude, *Alexandre Dumas: genius of life,* New York: Franklin Watts, 1988. □

alteration in the basic properties of the compound. This theory was related to his belief in families of organic compounds, in which substitutions could be made with the fundamental characteristics of the family remaining unchanged. At this time Berzelius was at the height of his eminence and would accept no affront to his authority; such was the strength of his attack on Dumas that the latter did not continue the dispute. Later researches proved Dumas to have been more correct in his theories than was the Swedish master.

Dumas isolated various essences and oils from coal tar; developed a method for measuring the amount of nitrogen in organic compounds, which made quantitative organic analysis possible; and developed a new method of determining vapor densities. He also concerned himself with determining the atomic weights of such elements as carbon and oxygen and published a new list of the weights of some 30 elements in 1858-1860.

In addition to his scientific achievements, Dumas led an active public life during the reign of Napoleon III. He was minister of agriculture and commerce and then minister of education. He was also a senator, master of the French mint, and president of the municipal council of Paris. His public life ended with the downfall of the Second Empire in 1871. Dumas died in 1884 in Paris.

Further Reading

There is a chapter on Dumas by Georges Urbain, "Jean-Baptiste Dumas and Charles-Adolphe Wurtz," in Eduard Farber, ed.,

Jean Baptiste André Dumas

The French chemist Jean Baptiste André Dumas (1800-1884) worked in the field of organic chemistry and developed the "type" theory of organic structure.

On July 14, 1800, Jean Baptiste Dumas was born at Alais. In his youth he was apprenticed to an apothecary. In 1816 he moved to Geneva and studied physiological chemistry in the laboratory of A. Le Royer. In Geneva, Dumas met the famous scientist Alexander von Humboldt, who persuaded Dumas to move to Paris, where he would find greater scientific opportunities. This he did in 1823, and he was engaged as a lecture assistant in chemistry at the École Polytechnique; he became professor of chemistry in 1835. During this period Dumas began to work on his major book, *Treatise on Chemistry,* and he also participated in the founding of the Central School for Arts and Manufactures.

In 1830 Dumas challenged the so-called dualistic theory of the great Swedish chemist Jöns Jacob Berzelius. The dualistic theory stated that all compounds could be divided into positive and negative parts. Dumas presented instead a unitary theory which held that atoms of opposite charges could be substituted in compounds without causing much

Great Chemists (1961). Particularly useful is James R. Partington's monumental four-volume *History of Chemistry* (1962-1969). The life and work of Dumas are discussed in Aaron J. Ihde, *The Development of Modern Chemistry* (1964), and Isaac Asimov, *A Short History of Chemistry* (1965). □

Jean Henri Dunant

Jean Henri Dunant (1828–1910) was a Swiss merchant who, as a witness to the cruelties of the battle of Solferino, made public the inefficiency of the sanitary organizations in wartime and developed a vision for a relief society of trained volunteers that resulted in the founding of the Red Cross.

Jean Henri Dunant was born on May 8, 1828, in Geneva, Switzerland, to parents who belonged to the nobility. Combining Christian faith with a strong sense of charity, humanity, and justice, his parents taught their young son to respect and support those in need. He often accompanied his mother on her visits to the poor and sick in Geneva's suburbs, visits to dark streets that he would later recall as his first encounters with misfortune and misery. In these early years, the mother's generosity passed to the son, whose enthusiasm for improvement would accompany him throughout his life.

During his first years of adulthood, Dunant focused his efforts on the promotion of the Young Men's Christian Association (YMCA). Founded in 1844 by London merchant George Williams, the YMCA had quickly spread to the Continent and subsequently to the United States and Canada. Eight years later, Dunant was among the cofounders of the YMCA in Geneva. He promoted (and in 1855 succeeded in) the unification of the various YMCA groups that existed in Europe and overseas.

Dunant's professional career began as a merchant and banker, an occupation that led him to Algeria from 1853-59. More than 20 years earlier, in 1830, Algeria had been conquered by France, and since then many young adventurers had sought their fortunes there. Dunant had similar intentions. He opened his own business of cornmills and marble quarries, financed by influential citizens of Geneva. Though he had acquired French citizenship in 1858, he continued to be harassed by the colonial bureaucracy in Algeria. To stop these impediments, he planned to speak to French emperor Napoleon III, personally.

In his leisure hours, Dunant observed the manners and habits of the North African people, praising their hospitality, codes of honor, and chivalry—qualities that, he believed, were deficient in the European nations. Devoting some time to reading, he was deeply impressed by Harriet Beecher Stowe's *Uncle Tom's Cabin* and spoke strongly against slavery as it was practiced in the north of Africa. He especially condemned the transatlantic slave trade to the United States and remained perplexed by American members of the

YMCA who tolerated what he considered the blatant violation of the message of Christianity.

In the summer of 1859, Dunant traveled to Italy. His suitcase contained a written homage to Napoleon III who, in alliance with Sardinia, was waging a war on Austria. On June 24, the two armies met at Solferino, a few miles west of the city of Mantua. The ensuing battle—though of small strategic or political significance—was one of the most devastating battles fought in terms of casualties. Nearly 40,000 wounded men begged for help on the battlefield at the fighting's end. Dunant, known as "the man in white" because of his tropical outfit, was attempting to arrange his meeting with Napoleon, but found himself instead witnessing the shocking scene:

> Some, who had gaping wounds already beginning to show infection, were almost crazed with suffering. They begged to be put out of their misery, and writhed with faces distorted in the grip of the death-struggle. There were poor fellows who had not only been hit by bullets or knocked down by shell splinters, but whose arms and legs had been broken by artillery wheels passing over them.

Realizing that thousands of lives would be lost within the following days due to a lack of surgeons, medication, nurses, bandages, and food, Dunant headed for the French headquarters and successfully persuaded Marshal Mac-Mahon to liberate all captive Austrian surgeons so that they might be allowed to tend their wounded. Three days later, permission was officially granted by Emperor Napoleon.

Meanwhile, churches and private houses of nearby Castiglione were transformed into hospitals. But the number of convoys of wounded increased to such proportions that:

> the local authorities, the townspeople, and the troops left in Castiglione, were absolutely incapable of dealing with all the suffering. Scenes as tragic as those of the day before, though of a very different sort, began to take place. There was water and food, but even so, men died of hunger and thirst; there was plenty of lint, but there were not enough hands to dress wounds; most of the army doctors had to go on to Cavriana, there was a shortage of medical orderlies, and at this critical time no help was to be had.

With the assistance of Don Lorenzo Barzizza, priest of Castiglione, Dunant gathered several hundred women who were willing to act as nurses, cooks, and laundresses to help the wounded—regardless of their background or nationality. *Tutti fratelli* (all brothers) became the slogan that helped save hundreds of lives.

Dunant tirelessly tended the wounded, organized supplies, and wrote letters to military headquarters, as well as to personal friends in Geneva, asking them to send clothes, bandages, medication, camomile to cleanse the wounds, and tobacco (to offer a distraction to the wounded and dying). After two weeks of immense struggle, Dunant left Castiglione, exhausted. In Milano, and later in his hometown Geneva, news of his efforts spread rapidly. High-ranking families invited him to their homes and palaces. Wherever he went, he was celebrated as a great benefactor to humanity.

To improve his business in Algeria, Dunant then moved to Paris, where memories of the wounded and dying continued to haunt him. In three years' time, he wrote and published an account of these last days of June 1859. In 1862, *Un Souvenir de Solferino* (*A Memory of Solferino*) was printed in Geneva at the author's expense and distributed among his friends and the courts in Europe. *Solferino* immediately attracted a wide circle of readers; within a few years, it was translated into 12 languages. Generals and field-marshals, along with princes and dukes, expressed their willingness to support Dunant's plan to improve the care of wounded soldiers.

One of the first to compliment him on his book was the lawyer Gustave Moynier of Geneva. Dunant, Moynier, and three other friends—the "Committee of Five," as they were called—drew up a memorandum, calling for an international conference to inquire into "the means of providing for the Inadequacy of the Sanitary Service of Armies in the Field." The memorandum suggested a solution: the institutionalization of a committee designed to answer the needs of troops wounded in battle. After the International Congress of Welfare in Berlin was called off, the Committee of Five decided to bring its cause before the Congress of Statistics which was to take place in Berlin.

One of Dunant's great admirers was the surgeon-mayor Doctor Basting who had translated *Solferino* into Dutch and who, like Dunant, would be participating in the congress. When they met for the first time, Dunant and Basting immediately discovered mutual interests and became close friends. Indeed, together with Basting, Dunant rewrote the memorandum only a few days before the opening of the congress, adding aspects which would be of the utmost importance. He requested that "the Governments of Europe agree that for the future the military staff and attendants, together with the officially recognized volunteer ambulance corps, be regarded as neutrals by the belligerents."

The Congress of Statistics in Berlin proved a big success for Dunant, and delegates of various European countries were invited to an International Congress in Geneva set for October 26, 1863. But Dunant's decision to alter the memorandum without consulting the other members of the Committee of Five led to a cool reception back in Geneva. Moynier, especially, reproved Dunant for his impetuosity and sought to curb it by appointing Dunant as secretary of the congress over which Moynier was to preside.

From October 26-29, 36 delegates of 16 countries discussed the issues promoted and presented by the Committee of Five. They passed a resolution consisting of ten articles and four recommendations. In times of peace, the various National Committees would store up requisites and enlist and train a Volunteer Ambulance Corps. It was also decided:

> In times of war, the committees of the belligerent nations shall furnish the needful supplies to their respective armies. They will organize their Volunteer Ambulance Corps and arrange with the military authorities as to the places where the wounded are to receive attention. . . . The volunteer assistants will be placed under the orders of the military chiefs, and all shall wear, as a distinctive badge, a red cross on a white ground.

Among the points recommended were: the expressed protection by the government; the neutralization of the Ambulance Corps; and the adoption of a common flag for ambulances and hospitals. Thus, in October of 1863, part of Dunant's dream had come true. The Committee of the Red Cross was founded. The following year, in the Geneva Convention of 1864, the recommendations expressed were fully accepted and integrated into the resolutions. A first, important step toward a new humanitarian international law had been taken.

But as Dunant's star as the promoter of the Red Cross was rising, his career as a merchant and banker was coming to a crushing finale. Devoting himself to his humanitarian work, he had neglected his business obligations for years. The honors that were paid to him could not avert financial bankruptcy and the loss of his reputation. Expelled by his hometown Geneva, and hunted by creditors, Dunant thought it best to leave Switzerland. Even more devastating was his resignation from the Committee of the Red Cross. The other members, Gustave Moynier among them, no longer considered the bankrupt Dunant of value to their cause. Upon discovering years later that Dunant was still using the letterhead of the Red Cross for his correspondence, Moynier sharply rebuked him. Thus, one of Dunant's earliest supporters openly turned into his enemy.

Dunant then spent several years in Paris, where his work with the Red Cross had kept him in high esteem with both the royal family and the aristocracy. Acquaintances, however, became fewer as news of his financial breakdown spread. Still, in Paris, Dunant was more than welcome as an expert in organizing the French Red Cross. In the war of 1870-71, France was heavily defeated at Sedan by a superior German army. Napoleon III was taken prisoner by the Prussians. After the defeat, France proclaimed the downfall of the monarchy and the inauguration of the Third Republic. Following his release, Napoleon lived in exile in England, where he would then die in 1871.

Unexpectedly, Dunant's efforts were supported by the exiled emperor. Dunant was provided with financial aid for the *Alliance Universelle de l'ordre et de civilisation*, an institution founded to help the victims of the Siege of Paris and of the Civil War in France. Moreover, he was given a house in Paris to use as a home as well as an office. With brighter prospects in mind, in August of 1872 he went to England to win supporters for his new mission to institute a convention for prisoners of war. This enterprise proved quite successful. Among those who complimented him on the recent undertakings was Florence Nightingale, "the lady with the lamp," who had been working as a volunteer nurse during the Crimean War, 1853-56. Devastated by the poor conditions of the military hospitals and the lack of properly trained nurses, Nightingale reorganized military as well as civilian nursing in Britain.

This short period of recognition, however, could not prevent Dunant's slow drift into oblivion. In Europe, Gustave Moynier was celebrated as the founder of the Red Cross, while Dunant gradually lost what had been his hallmarks—his energy and his faith in humanity. He traveled in Europe, taking odd jobs offered to him by old friends, living on their generosity and a small annual pension of 1,200 Swiss francs provided by his family in Geneva.

In 1887, Dunant, prematurely aged and in poor health, moved to Heiden, Switzerland. There, in the hospital where he was treated for his various ailments, he lived a secluded life; few visitors ever broke the monotony and the silence of his room. Likewise, there were not many whom the former "Samaritan of Europe" wished to see. He had become pessimistic and distrustful. No longer hunted or offended, he began to recover his mental stability and was glad for the peaceful retreat in Heiden. A religious man, he spent most of his time speculating on Genesis and Salvation, considering their impact on human evolution.

One friend who remained loyal, despite Dunant's failure, was Rudolf Mueller from Stuttgart, Germany. When, in 1892, an International Congress of the Red Cross was about to take place in Rome, Italy, Mueller published an article in a German newspaper, recalling the beginnings of the Red Cross and referring to Dunant as its founder and promoter. Yet it was not until 1895 that Dunant again became a topic for the public in Europe.

Suddenly, after being presumed dead, Dunant was surrounded by previous and newly won admirers. Swiss journalist George Baumberger's article in a German magazine had revealed that Dunant was indeed alive but living a lonely life of poverty. Baumberger finished his article with an appeal to the readers that, in anyway possible, they support Dunant—a man who had done much for others and asked nothing for himself. Letters of sympathy and encouragement were sent to Dunant, often including money, to make his later years more comfortable. His biographer, Rudolf Mueller, reestablished Dunant's reputation by reminding his audiences of Dunant's situation in many speeches. Mueller and other friends vehemently fought the rumors that *Solferino* had not been written by Dunant but by a French officer. Dunant knew of these allegations, and freely admitted that in order to correctly record the military details he had consulted army officials; otherwise, *Solferino* had been completely his own doing.

In 1896, a Dunant fund was started, primarily to enable the "Father of the Red Cross" to live in dignity. In December 1901, the Nobel Committee awarded Dunant with its first Peace Prize, an honor which he shared with Frenchman Frederic Passy. From his hometown Geneva, the International Committee of the Red Cross sent the following message:

> There is no man who more deserves this honour, for it was you, forty years ago, who set on foot the international organization for the relief of the wounded on the battlefield. Without you, the Red Cross, the supreme humanitarian achievement of the nineteenth century, would probably never have been undertaken.

One honor seemed to follow another, and, in 1903, the degree of Doctor honoris causa was conferred upon Dunant by the Faculty of Medicine of the University of Heidelberg, Germany.

On October 30, 1910, 82-year-old Jean Henri Dunant died peacefully in the hospital in Heiden. According to his own wishes, he was buried in Zurich.

Further Reading

de Lisle, Arnold. *The Story of the Red Cross Movement.* London: The Banner, 1904.

Dunant, Henry. *A Memory of Solferino.* Geneva: International Committee of the Red Cross, 1986.

Heudtlass, Willy. *J. Henry Dunant, Gruender des Roten Kreuzes, Urheber der Genfer Konvention, Eine Biographie.* Stuttgart: Kohlhammer, 1977.

Huber, Max. *The Red Cross, Principles and Problems.* Geneva: A. Kundig Press, 1942.

Willemin, Georges, and Roger Heacock. "The International Committee of the Red Cross," in *International Organization and the Evolution of World Society.* Vol. 2. Martin Nijhoff, 1984. □

Paul Laurence Dunbar

Paul Laurence Dunbar (1872-1906), poet and novelist, was the first African American author to gain national recognition and a wide popular audience.

Born the son of a former slave in Dayton, Ohio, Paul Laurence Dunbar achieved a formal education through high school, graduating in 1891. He had served as editor of the school paper and as class poet. Unable to go to college, Dunbar worked as an elevator operator. He published his first book of poems, *Oak and Ivy,* in 1893 at his own expense, and his second, *Majors and Minors,* 2 years later. Seeing the second book, William Dean Howells, then one of America's most distinguished literary critics, urged the young poet to concentrate on dialect verse.

With the publication of *Lyrics of Lowly Life,* for which Howells wrote a laudatory preface, Dunbar's professional career got an auspicious start. Demand for his work was soon sufficient to enable him to earn his living as a writer. He took Howell's advice to study the "moods and traits of his own race in its own accents of our English," so that his art was best shown in those "pieces which . . . described the range between appetite and emotion . . . which is the range of the race." (This was Howells's limited view of African Americans.)

Dunbar wanted to satisfy the popular taste for the light, romantic, comic, and sentimental. His short stories, which began appearing in popular magazines in the 1890s, usually depict African American folk characters, Southern scenes, and humorous situations. His first novel, *The Uncalled* (1898), like two of the three that followed—*The Love of Landry* (1900) and *The Fanatics* (1901)—is a sentimental tale about white people. These novels are competent but undistinguished. His last long fiction, *The Sport of the Gods* (1902), is notable only for his failure to realize the potential in the story of an agrarian African American family's urbanization.

In 1898 Dunbar married Alice Moore; the marriage was unhappy, and the couple separated in 1901, when Dunbar went to Washington, D.C., as a consultant to the Library of Congress. He was unhappy with his writing too. At about this time he confided to a friend, "I see now very clearly that Mr. Howells has done me irrevocable harm in the dictum he laid down regarding my dialect verse."

Dunbar had contracted tuberculosis and tried all the "cures"; alcohol brought temporary relief, and he became addicted. He continued to turn out short stories and poems. Sick, and discouraged by the lukewarm reception of *The Heart of Happy Hollow* (1904), a collection of short stories, and of *Lyrics of Love and Sunshine* (1905), which contains some of his best verses in pure English, he returned to Dayton, where he died on Feb. 9, 1906. The *Complete Poems of Paul Laurence Dunbar* (1913; still in print) shows how well he succeeded in capturing many aspects of African American life.

Further Reading

Two full-length biographies of Dunbar are Benjamin Brawley, *Paul Laurence Dunbar: Poet of His People* (1936), and the better-balanced *Paul Laurence Dunbar and His Song* (1947) by Virginia Cunningham. Jean Gould, *That Dunbar Boy* (1958), is for children. Dunbar gets brief treatment in Sterling A. Brown, Arthur P. Davis, and Ulysses Lee, *Negro Caravan* (1941); Hugh M. Gloster, *Negro Voices in American Fiction* (1948); and James A. Emanuel and Theodore L. Gross, *Dark Symphony* (1968). □

William Dunbar

The Scottish poet and courtier William Dunbar (ca. 1460-ca. 1520) wrote satirical, occasional, and devotional works. Although he is conventionally numbered among the Scottish Chaucerians, he owed a great deal to the traditions of French poetry.

Very little is known about William Dunbar's family or early life. He received a master of arts degree from St. Andrews University in 1479. In 1500 he was granted an annual pension of £10 by James IV, most likely in recognition for his services as a court poet. Dunbar was probably in England during the winter of 1501 in connection with the negotiations for the marriage between King James and Princess Margaret.

Dunbar's most famous poem is perhaps "The Thistle and the Rose," an allegory in the Chaucerian manner, probably written in 1502 to celebrate the impending marriage between James and Margaret. The poet took holy orders in 1504 and may have written "In May as that Aurora did upspring" at about this time. This poem, which is in the form of a debate between a merle and a nightingale, celebrates love for God. The following years produced a number of occasional poems—one on the birth of Margaret's first child, petitions to the King for increased aid, and a satire on a court physician and alchemist.

In 1507 Dunbar's pension was increased to £20 and in 1510 to the substantial sum of £80. There is no record of the poet after the Battle of Flodden (1513), and he probably died a few years after that disaster for the Scottish court. During his last years he may have written his devotional poems, some of which, like the Christmas poem "Rorate celi desuper" and the aureate hymn to the Blessed Virgin "Hale, sterne superne, hale in eterne," are extremely effective.

Among Dunbar's more famous longer pieces is the satire *The Tretis of the Tua Mariit Wemen and the Wedo*. The poet overhears a nocturnal conversation among three attractive ladies whose tongues have been loosened by wine. The two married women describe the shortcomings of their husbands in very frank language, and the widow, who bears some resemblance to Chaucer's Wife of Bath, reveals her wiles. One of the more attractive moral pieces attributed to Dunbar, reminiscent of Chaucer's "Truth," is "Without glaidnes avalis no tresure," in which the poet assures his readers that if they are just and joyful, Truth will make them strong.

Further Reading

The most useful editions of Dunbar's poems are *The Poems of William Dunbar,* edited by John Small (3 vols., 1884-1893), and *The Poems of William Dunbar,* edited by W. Mackay Mackenzie (1932). A volume of selected poems was edited by

James Kinsley (1958). A careful biographical account of Dunbar based on the scanty evidence that survives is J. W. Baxter, *William Dunbar* (1952). The study by Tom Scott, *Dunbar: A Critical Exposition of the Poems* (1966), is stimulating but untrustworthy. □

William Dunbar

William Dunbar (1749-1810), Scottish-born American scientist and planter, wrote the first topographical description of the Southwest.

William Dunbar was born in Morayshire, Scotland, son of Sir Archibald Dunbar. After study at Glasgow he did advanced work in mathematics and astronomy in London until ill health forced him to seek a warmer climate. In 1771 he went to America and established a plantation in British West Florida with a partner. Plagued by misfortunes—a slave insurrection in 1775 and later plundering by Continental Army soldiers—they moved in 1792 to what is now Mississippi to start a new plantation. Applying the principles of scientific agriculture, chemical treatment of the soil, improved models of plows and harrows, and special machinery for pressing and baling cotton, Dunbar made such a success of the venture that he bought out his partner and was able to devote much of his time to scientific investigation.

Like many 18th-century gentleman amateur scientists, Dunbar's interests included astronomy, botany, zoology, ethnology, and meteorology. Appointed surveyor general of the District of Natchez in 1798, he represented the Spanish government in determining the boundaries between Spanish and United States possessions in that area. Immediately thereafter he became a United States citizen and began making the first meteorological observations in the Mississippi Valley. Dunbar attracted the attention of Thomas Jefferson, with whom he corresponded and who secured his admission to the American Philosophical Society. In 1804 President Jefferson commissioned Dunbar to explore the Ouachita River country. In 1805 Dunbar was appointed to conduct similar explorations in the Red River valley.

Among Dunbar's scientific concerns were investigations of Native American sign language, fossil mammoth bones, and plant and animal life. On his plantation he operated an observatory equipped with the latest European astronomical instruments. His particular concern was the observation of rainbows, and he was the first to study the elliptical type. One of his practical contributions was a method for finding longitude by a single observer, without knowledge of the time. His meteorological speculations included the theory that a region of calm exists within the vortex of a cyclone.

Dunbar corresponded with American and European scientists. He also served as chief justice on the Court of Quarter Sessions and as a member of the Mississippi territorial legislature. His most important writing was the first

topographical description of the little-known south-western territory. He died at his plantation in October 1810.

Further Reading

For information on Dunbar see Frank L. Riley, *Sir William Dunbar: The Pioneer Scientist of Mississippi* (1899). Additional material on his life can be found in Eron Rowland, *Life, Letters and Papers of William Dunbar* (1930).

Additional Sources

Smeaton, William Henry Oliphant, *William Dunbar,* New York: AMS Press, 1975.

Taylor, Rachel Annand, *Dunbar the poet and his period,* Folcroft, Pa.: Folcroft Library Editions, 1974. □

Isadora Duncan

The American dancer and teacher Isadora Duncan (1878-1927) is considered one of the founders of modern dance.

Isadora Duncan was born Dora Angela Duncan on May 27, 1878, in San Francisco. By the age of 6 Isadora was teaching neighborhood children to wave their arms, and by 10 she had developed a new "system" of dance with her sister Elizabeth, based on improvisation and interpretation. With her mother as accompanist and her sister as partner, Isadora taught dance and performed for the San Francisco aristocracy.

The Duncans went to Chicago and New York to advance their dancing careers. Disheartened by their reception in eastern drawing rooms, they departed for London. In Europe, Duncan won recognition. She shocked, surprised, and excited her audience and became a member of the European intellectual avantgarde, returning triumphantly to America in 1908.

Duncan attacked the system of classical ballet, which was based on movement through convention, and rejected popular theatrical dance for its superficiality. She encouraged all movement that was natural, expressive, and spontaneous. Conventional dance costumes were discarded in favor of Greek tunics and no shoes to allow the greatest possible freedom of movement.

Experimenting with body movements, she concluded that all movements were derived from running, skipping, jumping, and standing. Dance was the "movement of the human body in harmony with the movements of the earth." Inspired by Greek art, the paintings of Sandro Botticelli, Walt Whitman's poems, the instinctual movements of children and animals, and great classical music, she did not dance *to* the music as much as she danced *the* music. For her, the body expressed thoughts and feelings; each dance was unique, each movement created out of the dancer's innermost feelings. Her dances were exclusively female, celebrating the beauty and holiness of the female body and

reflecting the emergence of the "new woman" of this period.

After World War I Duncan traveled throughout Europe. Her first school (in Berlin, before the war) had collapsed for lack of funds. In 1921 she accepted the Soviet government's offer to establish a school in Moscow. But financial problems continued. Meanwhile, she married the poet Sergei Yesenin. When the couple came to America in 1924 at the height of the "Red scare," Duncan was criticized for her "Bolshevik" dances. Returning to Russia, her husband committed suicide.

By 1925 Duncan's life had been filled with tragedy. In 1913 her two illegitimate children had been accidently drowned; she had had a stillbirth; and she became disillusioned with the Soviet Union. She was famous but penniless. In 1927, while riding in an open sports car, her scarf caught in a wheel and she was strangled.

Isadora Duncan's death was mourned by many. She left no work that could be performed again, no school or teaching method, and few pupils, but with her new view of movement she had revolutionized dance.

Further Reading

There is no balanced assessment of Isadora Duncan's life. The best introduction is her own passionate and sensitive autobiography, *My Life* (1927). She has been eulogized by friends— see Mary Desti, *The Untold Story: The Life of Isadora Duncan, 1921-1927* (1929)—exposed by enemies, and sometimes appreciated by scholars. A scholarly but badly written biography is Ilya Schneider, *Isadora Duncan: The Russian Years*

(1969). Recent, more dispassionate accounts are Allan Ross Macdougall, *Isadora: A Revolutionary in Art and Love* (1960), and Walter Terry, *Isadora Duncan: Her Life, Her Art, Her Legacy* (1964). ☐

Katherine Dunham

As a dancer and choreographer, Katherine Dunham (born 1910) wowed audiences in the 1930s and 1940s when she combined classical ballet with African rhythms to create an exciting new dance style.

Dancer, choreographer, and anthropologist Katherine Dunham was born on June 22, 1910, in Glen Ellyn, Illinois, a small suburb of Chicago, to Fanny June (Guillaume) and Albert Millard Dunham. She was their second and last child together. Her brother, Albert Dunham Jr., was almost four years old when she was born. She adored him and thought of him as her protector. Their mother, who was French Canadian and Indian, was 20 years older than their African-American father.

Fanny Dunham had been married once before, to a man whose last name was Taylor. Their marriage ended in divorce and they had three children together: Louise and Fanny June (Taylor) Weir, who had families of their own by the time Dunham was born, and a son, Henry, who was mentally disabled. All of Fanny Dunham's children and grandchildren lived with her and her second husband under one roof in Glen Ellyn, making their house very crowded.

Mother Died

When Dunham was three years old, her mother died after a lengthy illness. She had owned property in Chicago, but it was sold to pay off her grown children's debts and her doctor bills. Albert Dunham, who had been working as a tailor, could no longer afford to keep his house in the mostly-white suburb of Glen Ellyn and was forced to sell it. This created a rift between him and his wife's grown children that would last for years.

Dunham and her brother, Albert Jr., went to live with their father's sister, Lulu Dunham, in a tenement slum in Chicago, while their father tried to make a better living as a traveling salesman. Lulu Dunham worked as a beautician and sometimes her relatives would baby-sit Katherine while Albert Jr. was in school.

Introduced to Theater

One of those baby-sitters, Clara Dunham, had come to Chicago with her daughter, Irene, hoping to break into show business. They and other amateur performers began rehearsing a musical/theatrical program in the basement of their apartment building, and Dunham would watch. Although the program wasn't a success, it provided Dunham with her first taste of show business.

Dunham and her brother were very fond of their Aunt Lulu. However, because she was experiencing financial difficulties, a judge granted temporary custody of the children to their half-sister Fanny June Weir, and ordered that the children be returned to their father as soon as he could prove that he could take care of them.

Home Was Dismal

When Dunham was about five years old, her father married an Iowa schoolteacher named Annette Poindexter. They moved to Chicago and were granted custody of the children, and Dunham grew to love her step-mother. Her father bought a dry cleaning business in Chicago and all four members of the family worked there, as they lived in a few rooms in back of the business.

Family problems emerged when Albert Sr. began to physically abuse his wife and children and became increasingly violent. Consequently, Dunham longed to get away from him.

In high school, Dunham excelled in athletics. She also took dancing lessons and joined an after-school club that put on dance recitals. However, her father began demanding that she spend more time working at the dry cleaners, leaving her very little time for her extra-curricular activities.

Albert Jr., who was valedictorian of his senior class, received a scholarship and went away to college, against the wishes of his father. A short time later, Annette Dunham left her abusive husband and went to live in another part of the city. Dunham, who was still in high school, went with her. However, she was forced to continue working for her father's business, in order to help support her step-mother.

Became Scholar

Dunham began attending junior college at the age of 17. During her second and final year there, her brother convinced her to take a Civil Service exam. If she passed, he said, she could become a librarian for the city. She passed the exam, graduated from junior college and began working at the Hamilton Park Branch Library, which was in a white, middle-class, suburban district of the city. The other librarians refused to eat lunch with her because she was black. However, she was not aware of the discrimination at first, because she was just glad to be free of her father.

Following in her brother's footsteps, Dunham enrolled in the University of Chicago, where she earned a master's degree and Ph.D. in anthropology. She also took dance lessons and participated in theater productions there. To help pay for her education, she opened a dance school in 1930.

Researched Dances

In 1935, Dunham received a fellowship to conduct anthropological field research. She used the grant to study African-based dances in the Caribbean. She knew that each Caribbean island had its own unique form of dance. However, all of the dances had a common denominator: They all had been influenced in some way by the African slaves who had been brought there by various colonial overseers.

Dunham wanted to discover exactly what that common denominator was and which dance moves had come from Africa. She spent 18 months in the Caribbean, documenting its various dances.

Found Answer

She found that of all the Caribbean islands, the purest forms of African dance were in Haiti. She theorized that this was because Haiti had won its independence as a nation long before any other country had freed its African slaves. "Haitians ground their hips, circled their haunches, executed mesmerizing pelvic movements, and shrugged a ritual called 'zepaules, accenting their shoulders. It was all fundamental African technique, identical to what is done in, say, Dakar, and on which variations persist in African-American communities everywhere," wrote Paula Durbin in an article about Dunham that appeared in the January/February 1996 issue of *Americas* magazine.

Dunham fell in love with Haiti and its people, and later bought a home and opened a dance school and medical clinic on the island. She chronicled her work in the Caribbean in her book, *Journey to Accompong,* and wrote about her experiences in Haiti in her book, *Island Possessed.*

Created New Style

When Dunham returned to the United States, she combined the ethnic dances she had learned in the Caribbean with classical ballet and theatrical effects. The result was an entirely new art form, called the "Dunham technique." It has also been referred to as "Afro-Caribbean dance."

In 1940, she formed The Dunham Dance Company, an all-black dance troupe, to perform her technique. The company gave its first show in New York City and performed a revue called "Tropics and le Jazz Hot." Audiences in the United States had never seen anything like it. As Durbin wrote in the *Americas* article, "Everything moved—shoulders twitched, torsos arched, hips popped—and Martha Graham proclaimed Dunham 'the high priestess of the pelvic girdle.'" Graham is considered to be the founder of modern dance.

Fought Segregation

Dunham and her company toured North and South America in the 1940s and 1950s, fighting segregation along the way. In 1952, the management of a hotel in Brazil refused to let Dunham join her husband, John Pratt, in his hotel suite because she was black and he was white. Dunham, who had been married to Pratt since 1940, filed a lawsuit against the hotel, and as a result, the Brazilian legislature quickly passed a bill outlawing discrimination in public places. In addition to touring with her company, which disbanded in 1957, Dunham operated a dance school in New York from 1944 through 1954. She also choreographed many ballets, stage shows and films, including the movies, "Stormy Weather" and "Pardon My Sarong." During this same period, she and her husband adopted their daughter, Marie Christine.

Opened Illinois School

In the 1960s, Dunham visited East St. Louis, Illinois, a very poor African-American community in the southern part of the state. She wanted to do something to help the children there and decided to open a school. In 1967 she opened the Katherine Dunham Centers for the Arts and Humanities. At the school, disadvantaged children can learn classical ballet, martial arts, the Dunham technique, foreign languages and, most importantly, self-discipline. The campus also includes the Dunham Museum, which houses costumes and other artifacts, and the Institute for Intercultural Communication.

Held Hunger Strike

In 1992 Dunham went on a 47-day hunger strike to protest the exclusionary U.S. policy toward Haitian refugees. Due to political unrest in their homeland, thousands of Haitians fled their country for the United States in the early 1990s. In 1991 and 1992, the U.S. Coast Guard intercepted some 35,000 Haitian refugees as they tried to enter the United States. Most of them were returned to Haiti.

Dunham has diabetes and arthritis and uses a wheelchair. She still lives and teaches in East St. Louis, Illinois, and has begun work on another autobiography.

Further Reading

Ben-Itzak, Paul, "Dunham Legacy Stands At Risk," in *Dance Magazine,* January 1995, pp. 42, 44.
Durbin, Paula, "The First Lady of Caribbean Cadences," in *Americas,* 1996, pp. 36-41.
Greene, Carol, *Katherine Dunham: Black Dancer,* Childrens Press, Inc., 1992. □

4th Earl of Dunmore

John Murray, 4th Earl of Dunmore (1732-1809), was the British colonial governor of Virginia during the dramatic years preceding the American Revolution.

John Murray, descended from the French line of Stuarts, succeeded to his father's title in 1765. He also held the titles of Viscount Fincastle, Baron of Blair, Baron of Moulin, and Baron of Tillymount. In 1768 he married Lady Charlotte Stewart, daughter of the Earl of Galloway. Elected in 1761 as one of the 16 Scottish peers to sit in the British Parliament, he was reelected in 1768.

Lord Dunmore was appointed governor of New York in 1770 by Lord Hillsborough, British secretary of state for the Colonies. In 1771 he was promoted to governor of Virginia. He was well liked there, as he had been in New York. His newborn daughter was adopted by the Virginia colony, and two new counties, Fincastle and Dunmore, were named for him. His popularity began to wane in 1773, when he dissolved the House of Burgesses, which had proposed a procolonial committee of correspondence; he repeated that action the following year when the legislature proposed a day of fasting and prayer because of the new Boston Port Bill.

While visiting Virginia's northwest frontier, Dunmore constructed Ft. Dunmore at the forks of the Ohio. In 1774 he led the Virginians in what is often called Dunmore's War. When the Shawnee Indians went on the warpath, the southwest Virginia militia, under Col. Andrew Lewis, advanced down the Kanawha River, while Dunmore himself led another force from Ft. Dunmore. After Lewis defeated Chief Cornstalk, Dunmore negotiated a treaty with the Native Americans at Scioto. Generally applauded at the time, the governor was later accused of inciting the Native Americans to warfare and attempting to lead the militia into a trap.

As the colonial revolutionary movement gathered momentum, Dunmore lost what remained of his popularity. To forestall rebels, he removed the powder from the Williamsburg magazine in April 1774, but this action incited so much antagonism that he paid for the powder. In June threats on his life forced him to retreat to the frigate *Fowey*. In November he declared martial law and called upon slaves to desert their masters and join his "Royal Ethiopian" Regiment in return for their freedom.

On Dec. 9, 1775, Dunmore's loyalist troops were defeated by the colonials at Great Bridge. Retiring to his ships, Dunmore bombarded and burned Norfolk. In July 1776, after a conflict on Gwynn's Island, he returned to England.

Once again Dunmore was returned to Parliament as a Scottish representative. From 1787 to 1796 he served as governor of the Bahamas. He died on March 5, 1809, at Ramsgate, England.

Further Reading

R. G. Thwaites and L. P. Kellog, *Documentary History of Dunmore's War* (1905), contains a good biographical sketch of Dunmore. Dunmore's American career is well covered in Thomas J. Wertenbaker, *Give Me Liberty: The Struggle for Self-government in Virginia* (1958), and Clifford Dowdey, *The Golden Age: A Climate for Greatness—Virginia, 1732-1775* (1970).

Additional Sources

Hagemann, James A., *Lord Dunmore: last Royal Governor of Virginia, 1771-177,* Hampton, Va., Wayfarer Enterprises 1974.
Selby, John E., *Dunmore,* Williamsburg, Va.: Virginia Independence Bicentennial Commission, 1977. □

Finley Peter Dunne

Finley Peter Dunne (1867-1936) was an American journalist. He is noted for his humorous sketches in which an Irish saloonkeeper named Mr. Dooley commented on current events.

Peter Dunne was born July 10, 1867, in Chicago, the fifth of seven children of an orthodox Catholic immigrant couple from Ireland. Peter (at 19 he added Finley to his name) graduated from high school in 1884. He covered sports and police courts for several newspapers, then became city editor of the *Chicago Times* when he was 21. Responsible positions on other papers followed. On the staff of the *Evening Post* in 1892, he met Mary Ives Abbott, a cultivated book reviewer for the *Post,* who recognized Dunne's promise and began to guide him. She introduced him to Chicago's select society.

In 1892 Dunne published his first sketch in Irish dialect in the *Post.* His protagonist, modeled upon a taciturn but witty saloonkeeper named James McGarry, was called Colonel McNerry. When the real saloonkeeper complained to Dunne's editor that McNerry sounded too much like McGarry, Dunne changed his character's name to Mr. Martin Dooley. Dunne's unsigned columns satirizing politics and society made Mr. Dooley a Chicago institution, and his fame spread to other cities. In 1898 one much-reprinted column turned Mr. Dooley into a national sensation. When Commodore George Dewey took Manila, Mr. Dooley celebrated the accomplishment of his "Cousin George"— "Dewey or Dooley, 'tis all th' same." In this piece Dunne caught the jubilant mood of victorious America, but subsequently he turned to critical satire when United States imperialism, showing its true colors, began the systematic subjugation of the Philippines. To the Filipinos, Dunne's imperialist says: "We'll treat ye th' way a father shud treat his childher if we have to break ivry bone in ye'er bodies. So come to our arms."

Publication of collections of Dooley sketches in book form began in 1898 with *Mr. Dooley in Peace and War* and continued roughly at the rate of one volume every 2 years for 2 decades.

In 1900 Dunne moved to New York. In 1902 he married Abbott's daughter Margaret; they had four children.

Dunne became associated with Lincoln Steffens and other "muckrakers" on the *American Magazine,* and he wrote for *Collier's* and several other magazines, but the articles in which he put Mr. Dooley aside and spoke in his own voice were never markedly successful. He died of cancer in New York City on April 24, 1936.

Further Reading

Elmer Ellis, *Mr. Dooley's America: A Life of Finley Peter Dunne* (1941), contains Dunne's unfinished memoirs. For Dunne's place in the history of American humor see Walter Blair, *Horse Sense in American Humor* (1942). *The Autobiography of Lincoln Steffens* (1931) contains a contemporary sketch of Dunne.

Additional Sources

Eckley, Grace, *Finley Peter Dunne,* Boston: Twayne, 1981. □

William Archibald Dunning

The American historian, author, and educator William Archibald Dunning (1857-1922) was an authority on the Civil War and Reconstruction periods and an influential teacher.

B orn in Plainfield, N.J., on May 12, 1857, William Dunning experienced as a young boy the tragic years of the Civil War, which had a profound effect on his career. For the rest of his life he devoted his energies to researching and training students in this watershed period of history.

Although he studied at Dartmouth College and the University of Berlin, Dunning received all of his degrees from Columbia University. In 1888 he married Charlotte E. Loomis of Brooklyn, who died June 13, 1917. Following completion of his doctorate in 1885, Dunning remained at Columbia, reaching the rank of full professor in 1893. In 1904 he was selected to be the first Lieber professor of history and political science.

Dunning possessed the rare talent of being both a distinguished teacher and a brilliant scholar. A perusal of his writings is impressive. After publishing his doctoral dissertation, *The Constitution of the United States in Civil War and Reconstruction, 1860-1867* (1885), he produced two other books in the same area: *Essays on the Civil War and Reconstruction and Related Topics* (1898), a scientific and scholarly investigation of the period; and *Reconstruction, Political and Economic, 1865-1877* (1907), a volume in the first "American Nation Series," which although partly refuted by revisionists, remains the best summary of the politics of the era.

Dunning was an equally competent political writer. His *A History of Political Theories: Ancient and Medieval, from Luther to Montesquieu* (1905) and *From Rousseau to Spencer* (1920) discuss the development of political theories from ancient to modern times. He also wrote *The British Empire and the United States* (1914), which analyzes the hundred years of diplomatic relations between the two powers starting with the Treaty of Ghent, and he collaborated with Frederick Bancroft on "A Sketch of Carl Schurz's Political Career" in *The Reminiscences of Carl Schurz,* vol. 3 (1908). He also wrote many articles and reviews for the *American Historical Review, Educational Review,* and the *Political Science Quarterly* and was editor of the last from 1894 to 1903.

The "Dunning school" in Civil War and Reconstruction historiography interpreted the events of the period in a manner more favorable to the South. They defended the planters of the antebellum period, blamed the abolitionists for bringing on the war, and vehemently criticized the Radical Republicans for using Lincoln's death to enhance their political ambitions and economic interests by reducing the South to colonial status.

Dunning was one of the founders of the American Historical Association, serving several years on its council and as its president in 1913. He was president of the American Political Science Association at the time of his death.

In 1914 sixteen former students published *Studies in Southern History and Politics,* and 10 years later another group published the commemorative volume *A History of Political Theories, Recent Times.* Dunning died on Aug. 15, 1922.

Further Reading

There is no single volume on the life of Dunning. For a discussion of Dunning's role in Civil War and Reconstruction historiography see Thomas J. Pressly, *Americans Interpret Their Civil War* (1954; rev. ed. 1962), and Kenneth M. Stampp, *The Era of Reconstruction, 1865-1877* (1965). ☐

John Duns Scotus

The Scottish philosopher and theologian John Duns Scotus (c. 1265-1308) contributed to the development of a metaphysical system that was compatible with Christian doctrine, an epistemology that altered the 13th-century understanding of human knowledge, and a theology that stressed both divine and human will.

The century from 1250 to 1350 can be considered the high point of the scholastic movement in philosophy and theology. During that period a number of important developments took place which influenced European thought in subsequent centuries. The first of these developments was the attempt to construct a metaphysical system that would remove or reduce apparent conflicts between natural reason and the truths of revelation, allowing each a specific domain with a certain number of truths in common. This development is often termed the "synthesis of faith and reason" and is considered one of the major achievements of medieval philosophy. A second development was the perfection of an empirical approach to knowledge and the perfection of the critical tools of logic and scientific inquiry, a movement with important long-range results for the history of modern thought. The third development was the creation of a theological system that would protect the Christian conception of the omnipotence and freedom of God while upholding a practical system in which salvation would be granted to any man who earnestly sought it. In each of these developments Duns Scotus made an important contribution.

His Life

John Duns Scotus was born into a landowning family in the southeastern corner of Scotland, an area strongly influenced by the social, political, and religious institutions of England. According to one tradition, his father was Ninian Duns, who held an estate near Maxton in Roxburghshire. After receiving his early education, possibly at Haddington, John Duns entered the Franciscan convent at Dumfries about 1277-1280 and received instruction there from his paternal uncle, Elias Duns.

Shortly before 1290 John Duns was sent to Oxford, probably to continue his study in the liberal arts. It may have been at Oxford that he received the nickname "Scotus" or "the Scot." While at Oxford he was ordained to the priesthood on March 17, 1291, by Oliver Sutton, Bishop of Northampton.

Scotus, as he eventually came to be called, seems to have completed his study in the arts before 1293, for in that year he began his study for the higher degree of theology at Paris under Gonsalvo of Balboa. Returning to Oxford in 1296, Scotus continued his study of theology and commented on the *Book of Sentences* by Peter Lombard, a standard requirement of any theological faculty in a medieval university and an activity which made the candidate a "bachelor of the *Sentences*." Having read the *Sentences* at Oxford (and possibly also at Cambridge), Scotus returned to Paris in 1302 and in that year read the *Sentences* for the second or third time.

Because of his opposition to King Philip IV's call for a general council against Pope Boniface VIII, Scotus was exiled from France in 1303 and probably returned to Oxford for a year. In 1304, however, Scotus returned to Paris and completed the requirements for the degree of master of theology in 1305. For the next 2 years he held the chair of theology at the Franciscan convent in Paris, debating with other theologians and increasing his reputation. One of his most important works, *Quaestiones quodlibetales,* contains Scotus's version of many debates in which he engaged during this period.

Scotus was transferred in 1307 to the Franciscan house of study at Cologne, Germany, where he lectured until his death on November 8, 1308. He was buried in the chapel of the convent.

Relation between Philosophy and Theology

Under the impact of the revival of Aristotle in the 13th century, several theologians attempted to argue for the "scientific" nature of theology. This movement was short-lived, and by the end of the 13th century the scientific quality of theology had been rejected on the grounds that theology did not possess the same type of evidence nor was its method demonstrative in the same sense as mathematics or Euclidean geometry.

Scotus contributed to a more exact understanding of the relation between philosophy and theology. He emphasized the practical and affective nature of theology, denying to it the rigorous demonstrative quality of the Aristotelian sciences. Scotus, however, shared with St. Thomas Aquinas the belief that truth was one and that theology and philosophy do not contradict each other but represent two different approaches to the same truth.

The relation of philosophy and theology, for Scotus, was based on the nature of their respective sources: reason and revelation. Scotus's formulation of this problem followed the pattern established by St. Thomas Aquinas, although Scotus restricted the number of theological truths that could be established by natural reason, unaided by revelation.

Metaphysical Beliefs

Scotus understood metaphysics as that aspect of philosophy that studies the nature of *being* itself rather than any particular object possessing being that exists in external reality. Being, understood in this way, was a concept common to God and man. Moreover, certain disjunctive attributes or antinomies could be applied to being, such as "infinite-finite" or "necessary-contingent." On the basis of his belief that the term "being" applied to God and man in the same sense and that one part of a disjunctive requires the other part, Scotus established a proof for God's existence based on the nature of being. The existence of finite, contingent beings requires the existence of an infinite, necessary being, namely God.

Epistemology and Empiricism

Scotus shared with St. Thomas Aquinas a strong belief in the primacy of sense experience in the process of human knowledge. Scotus, however, gave the intellect of man a more active role in cognition than was customary in the late 13th century. In opposition to the more common Aristotelian epistemology, he argued that the intellect could come into direct contact with the object to be known. Scotus therefore played a very important role in the transformation of medieval epistemology from a conception of the intellect as a passive receptacle that knows only universal concepts to a view of the intellect as an active mind that knows individual things.

Theological Beliefs

The main feature of Scotus's theology is the importance he gives to the primacy of the will in both God and man. In contrast to St. Thomas Aquinas, who tended to emphasize the intellect or reason, Scotus stressed the freedom of the divine will and the freedom of the human will within an order freely chosen by God.

The freedom of God, for Scotus, means first of all that creation was not necessary. God not only chose the *type* of world He wished to create; He chose to create. Having once chosen, however, it is the nature of God to abide by his decisions. Although He always retains the power to do otherwise, He never arbitrarily reverses His decisions.

The second area where God's freedom is evidenced is in man's salvation. God, for Scotus, predestines those He wishes to save apart from any foreseen merits. Moreover, God retains His freedom to accept or reject the Christian who fulfils the divine commandments.

This absolute power of God is limited by His own free decision to allow man freedom and to award eternal life on the basis of human merit. Man, for Scotus, is also primarily will and is united to God through love more than through reason. Man has the freedom to fulfil God's demands and thus obtain salvation.

Marian Doctor

The last important area of Scotus's thought concerns his teaching on Mary, the mother of Jesus. Duns Scotus is known as the Marian doctor because of the high status he accords to Mary. Scotus taught that Mary was born without the stain of original sin, a doctrine known as the Immaculate Conception and eventually recognized as dogma in the Roman Catholic Church. The support of Scotus's teaching by many within the Franciscan order facilitated the development and final acceptance of that doctrine.

Further Reading

The best biographical sketch of Duns Scotus can be found in Alfred B. Emden, *A Biographical Register of the University of Oxford to A.D. 1500,* vol. 1 (1957). Among the many histories of medieval philosophy that include the thought of Scotus, the clearest description can be found in Frederick Copleston, *A History of Philosophy,* vol. 2 (1950). There are several more detailed studies in English of various aspects of Scotus's thought. Two excellent studies of Scotus's metaphysics are Cyril L. Shircel, *The Univocity of the Concept of Being in the Philosophy of John Duns Scotus* (1942), and Allan Wolter, *The Transcendentals and Their Function in the Metaphysics of Duns Scotus* (1946). The best study of Scotus's epistemology is Sebastian Day, *Intuitive Cognition: A Key to the Significance of the Later Scholastics* (1947). A more general evaluation of Scotus's thought and his impact on modern philosophy is provided in J. F. Boler, *Charles Peirce and Scholastic Realism: A Study of Peirce's Relation to John Duns Scotus* (1963). □

John Dunstable

John Dunstable (ca. 1390-1453) was the most celebrated English composer of the entire 15th century.

His works were known and imitated all over western Europe.

Contemporary documentation of John Dunstable's life is sparse. From his tombstone, which was in St. Stephen Walbrook, London, until it was destroyed in the Great Fire, it is known that he died on Dec. 24, 1453, and that he was also a mathematician and astronomer. Several tracts on astronomy once in his possession are in various English libraries, and from one of these it is known that he was in the service of John, Duke of Bedford, brother of Henry V. John became regent of France in 1422 and maintained a chapel in that country until his death in 1435; thus it is likely that Dunstable was on the Continent for some years. He is mentioned by several contemporary and slightly later theorists. Other information must be deduced from his music and the manuscript sources that preserve it.

Almost all of Dunstable's known works are sacred. There are 20-odd settings of items of the Mass Ordinary (single sections, Gloria-Credo or Sanctus-Agnus pairs, and complete cyclic Masses), 12 isorhythmic motets, some 20 motets and polyphonic settings of liturgical melodies, and 2 secular pieces

Most of Dunstable's compositions are found in non-insular sources. Almost all of his motets are in a manuscript in Modena (probably copied in Ferrara); some of these motets and most of his Mass music are in sources in Trent and Aosta. Other works are in Bologna, Florence, Berlin, El Escorial, Paris, and Seville. Only a handful of English sources of his music have survived, and many of these are fragmentary. The destruction of musical manuscripts (and instruments) for religious and political reasons at a later time created a situation whereby no major sources of polyphonic music remain in England for roughly the middle years of the 15th century. It is fortunate that English music was so widely admired and copied on the Continent.

Lack of biographical information and precise datings for manuscripts makes a chronology of Dunstable's works very difficult. In a general way, the isorhythmic motets, with their rigidly structured formal frameworks and general harmonic style, look back to techniques popular in the 14th century, and such harmonizations of liturgical melodies as the *Magnificat secundi toni* and *Ave Regina celorum* are clear descendants of late-14th century English descant settings. On the other hand, the *Missa Rex seculorum* and *Missa Da gaudierum premia*, cyclic Masses with each section built over a common tenor, are innovative works, early examples of a species of composition that was to be a cornerstone of Mass composition for the next century, and some of the nonisorhythmic—and probably later—motets, such as *Quam pulchra es* and *Salve Regina mater mire*, anticipate the motet style of the generation of Josquin des Prez with their careful declamatory settings of the text, fuller harmonic style, and independence of the individual voices.

Stylistic features of English music were known to and imitated by such Continental masters as Guillaume Dufay and Gilles Binchois. This can be seen in their music, in the incorporation of a harmonic style more dependent on thirds and sixths and their taking up of such structural devices as the tenor, or *cantus firmus*, Mass. It is also attested to by writers of the time. Martin le Franc, in his lengthy poem *Le Champion des dames* (1441-1442), speaks of Dufay and Binchois as having found a new way in music, based on the English style of Dunstable. And Johannes Tinctoris in his *Proportionales musices* (ca. 1476) maintains that a fundamental change took place in music in the early 15th century, that it originated with Dunstable, and that not only Dufay and Binchois but also such men as Johannes Ockeghem, Anthoine Busnois, and their contemporaries were affected by this new style.

This statement may be exaggerated. The English influence came not only from Dunstable but also from his contemporaries, particularly Leonel Power. But a good case can be made for the suggestion that the diffusion, popularity, and influence of English music were never so great as during the first half of the 15th century, and Dunstable stands at the head of this school.

Further Reading

Stylistic and biographical commentary on Dunstable are in the following standard works: Gustave Reese, *Music in the Middle Ages* (1940); Manfred F. Bukofzer, *Studies in Medieval and Renaissance Music* (1950); Frank Llewellyn Harrison, *Music in Medieval Britain* (1958); and Donald Jay Grout, *A History of Western Music* (1960).

Additional Sources

Bent, Margaret, *Dunstable*, London; New York: Oxford University Press, 1981. □

St. Dunstan

The English monk and archbishop St. Dunstan (ca. 909-988) was a counselor of kings and a respected churchman. He made the English monasteries into centers of religion and culture.

Dunstan was born into an important family near Glastonbury in Somerset. As a young man, he lived for a time in the household of King Athelstan but incurred the displeasure of some of the officials by his love of singing and reading. Accused of black magic and pressured into leaving the court, Dunstan lived for a short time with the bishop of Winchester, who persuaded him to become a monk.

As a hermit near Glastonbury, Dunstan disciplined himself through prayer and penance. He worked as a silversmith and copied manuscripts. The next king, Edmund, called Dunstan back to court as one of his counselors and eventually made him abbot of Glastonbury. Under Edmund's successor, Edred, Dunstan practically ran the kingdom. But his luck changed when Edwy succeeded to the throne in 955. Dunstan's outspoken criticism of the king's loose conduct earned him a sentence of exile. For 2 years

Dunstan lived on the Continent, near Ghent in Flanders, with a group of monks guided by the strict rule of St. Benedict. In 957 some of King Edwy's subjects rebelled and set up a separate kingdom. Their leader, Edgar, called Dunstan back from Flanders and appointed him bishop first of Worcester and then of London. When Edwy died 2 years later, Edgar became sole king of England. He made Dunstan archbishop of Canterbury, head of the entire Church in England.

For almost 30 years, seen by some as a golden age, Dunstan and King Edgar cooperated closely, Dunstan preaching respect for the King's law and the King giving money to help build churches and monasteries. Dunstan was as strict with his clergy as he was with himself. His experiences in Flanders taught him that monks should live in an atmosphere of self-sacrifice. He enforced the law of celibacy wherever possible. He forbade the selling of Church offices (simony) and the appointing of relatives to positions of authority (nepotism). He encouraged his people to fast and preached the ideal of justice for all. Once he refused to say Mass until some counterfeiters had paid the penalty decreed by the magistrate. Their hands were chopped off.

By his forceful preaching and administrative ability, his friendship with the King, and his personal example, Dunstan succeeded in reforming the Church in England. The monasteries he influenced became sources of genuine religious spirit for the people and provided many bishops for England as well as missionaries for northern Europe. He was accepted as a saint by the English people soon after his death on May 19, 988.

Further Reading

Eleanor S. Duckett, *Saint Dunstan of Canterbury* (1955), is a clearly written historical sketch of St. Dunstan. David Knowles, *The Monastic Orders in England* (1940; 2d ed. 1963), details St. Dunstan's important contributions. For his place in the perspective of English history see G. O. Sayles, *The Medieval Foundations of England* (1948; 2d ed. 1950).

Additional Sources

Dales, Douglas, *Dunstan: saint and statesman,* Cambridge: Lutterworth Press, 1988.
St. Dunstan: his life, times, and cult, Woodbridge, Suffolk, UK; Rochester, NY: Boydell Press, 1992. □

Henry Dunster

Henry Dunster (ca. 1609-1659), an English-born American clergyman, was distinguished as the innovative and forceful first president of Harvard College.

Henry Dunster was born in Bury, Lancashire, England, the fifth child of a yeoman farmer. At 17 he entered Magdalene College at Cambridge University and, upon completion of requirements, received a bachelor of arts degree. He returned to Bury as a teacher and curate, studied Oriental languages, and in 1634 was granted a master of arts degree from Cambridge. Under spiritual stress, Dunster gravitated to Puritanism and emigrated to New England.

Although relatively unknown, Dunster was chosen president of Harvard College upon his arrival in Boston in 1640. He revived an institution that was virtually defunct, reuniting the scattered student body and establishing degree requirements. With Cambridge and Oxford as models, he was determined to put Harvard on secure foundations. The college laws were first codified in 1646, a charter obtained in 1650, and the holdings of the library increased through gifts. Dunster and Thomas Shepard, the eminent Puritan and theologian, petitioned the New England Confederation for contributions from the inhabitants, obtaining £250 in gifts of wheat by 1653. Dunster advocated 4 years residence for the bachelor of arts degree, and although protesting students refused to pay commencement fees, he successfully instituted the change. Edward Johnson in his *Wonder Working Providence* (1654) observed that "the learned reverend, and judicious Mr. Henry Dunster [was] fitted from the Lord for the work."

In 1641 Dunster married Elizabeth, the widow of Jose Glover. Marriage brought President Dunster financial security and also Glover's printing press. Operated for years in Dunster's house, this press was the first one in the Colonies and was later acquired by Harvard. His wife's death in 1643 led to conflict between her children and Dunster over the estate. In 1644 he chose a second wife, Elizabeth Atkinson, who outlived him.

While a member of the Cambridge church, Dunster refused to have an infant son baptized. Public hostility to his Baptist views led to demands for his resignation from Harvard. On Oct. 24, 1654, he resigned, later becoming a minister at Scituate in Plymouth Colony. He died there in 1659.

Further Reading

Jeremiah Chaplin, *Life of Henry Dunster: First President of Harvard College* (1872), is the standard biography. Samuel Eliot Morison, *The Founding of Harvard College* (1935), gives an excellent account of Dunster's presidency. Two informative background works are Morison's *Builders of the Bay Colony* (1930; rev. ed. 1958) and Louis B. Wright, *The Cultural Life of the American Colonies, 1607-1763* (1957). □

Marquis Dupleix

The French colonial administrator Joseph François, Marquis Dupleix (1697-1763), sought to establish a French empire in India but was frustrated by indifference at home and by growing British power.

Joseph François Dupleix was born in Landrecies on Jan. 1, 1697, into a wealthy family. After making several voyages to America and India, in 1721 he was named a member of the superior council at Pondicherry, India, of the Compagnie des Indes—the French counterpart of the English East India Company. In addition to his official duties he engaged, as was the custom, in private business ventures and gained a fortune. In 1731 he became governor or superintendent of French affairs in Chandernagor, where he administered his office with great competence and established a fruitful trade with China.

In 1742 Dupleix was appointed governor general of the company with authority over French investments in India. Ambitious to found a great French colony at a time when native governments were in a state of political dissolution and when commercial advantages were open to European nations, Dupleix found himself opposed by British designs. He was also hampered by a bitter jealousy on the part of the Comte de La Bourdonnais, governor of the isle of Bourbon, and by a lack of understanding among the company officials in France.

The War of the Austrian Succession permitted Dupleix partially to realize his aims. The capitulation of Madras to the French in 1746 fostered his purpose, but restoration of the city to British control blocked him. He sent an expedition against Fort St. David in 1747, but it was defeated by the nawab of Arcot, who was allied with the British. When the British besieged Pondicherry in 1748, Dupleix conducted a brilliant defense, but news of the peace of Aix-la-Chapelle arrived during the operations and halted further military activities.

Dupleix sought to subjugate southern India and use military forces to safeguard commercial advantages. He sent troops to aid sovereign claimants to the Carnatic and the Deccan, who were opposed by British-supported rivals. In the end, Dupleix was unable to match the British aspirations and activities directed by Robert Clive, and French influence declined as British power increased.

In 1754 the French government, wishing to avoid further conflict with the British in India, sent a special commissioner, Charles Robert Godeheu, to replace Dupleix, who returned to France that year. Although he had expended his personal fortune to support his public policy, he found that the Compagnie des Indes was unwilling to reimburse him and that the French government would do nothing to help him. Regarded at the time as an ambitious and self-serving adventurer, he died in obscurity, neglect, and poverty in Paris on Nov. 10, 1763. He was, however, one of the greatest French colonial administrators of the 18th century, but his country's lack of interest defeated him.

Further Reading

For information on Dupleix see G. B. Malleson, *Dupleix* (1895), and Henry Dodwell, *Dupleix and Clive: The Beginning of Empire* (1920). □

Éleuthère Irénée du Pont

Éleuthère Irénée du Pont (1771-1834), a French-born American manufacturer, founded the gunpowder mill which became the basis of E. I. du Pont de Nemours and Company.

Born in Paris on June 24, 1771, E. I. du Pont was the son of Pierre Samuel du Pont de Nemours, a leading economist of the physiocratic school. Irénée demonstrated little interest in school, and in 1788 he went to work for Antoine Lavoisier, the noted French chemist who was chief of the royal powder works. He became Lavoisier's first assistant in 1791.

Following the French Revolution, Irénée's father found he could not cooperate with the new government and decided the family should emigrate to the United States. The decision was undoubtedly influenced by the elder Du Pont's friend Thomas Jefferson, with whom he had become acquainted when Jefferson was serving as minister to France. Thirteen members of the family, including Irénée, his wife, and three children, sailed for the United States and arrived in Newport, R.I., on New Year's Day 1800.

On a hunting trip with Col. Louis de Toussard, an American military officer, Irénée du Pont discovered that American gunpowder was not only poor in quality but high in price. They made a study of the powder industry in America and concluded that the construction of a powder

mill might be a profitable venture. Du Pont and his brother Victor returned to France to seek the assistance of former associates. He obtained designs for machinery and the equipment he would need, plus pledges of financial support. Upon his return he purchased a farm 4 miles from Wilmington, Del., as the site for his factory. In 1803 the small mill began processing saltpeter for the government, and eventually the company produced the first powder for sale.

During the next few years the company increased its production and sales, but not without problems. Stockholders grew tired of Du Pont's continuous expansion and demanded their share of the profits. Two explosions, one in 1815 and another in 1818, resulted in 49 deaths and considerable financial loss. Orders from the U.S. government during the War of 1812, however, made Du Pont the major powder producer in America.

Du Pont had other interests besides gunpowder. In 1811, with his brother Victor and Peter Baudy, he opened a woolen mill on the Brandywine River. Du Pont helped establish a cotton mill and a tannery. In 1822 he became a director of the Bank of the United States. He died on Oct. 31, 1834, in Philadelphia.

Further Reading

Bessie Gardner du Pont edited and translated *Life of Éleuthère Irénée du Pont* (12 vols., 1923-1927), which is largely a collection of Du Pont's correspondence. His life in the United States is included in her *E. I. du Pont de Nemours & Co.: A History, 1802-1902* (1920). Max Dorian, *The Du Ponts: From Gunpowder to Nylon* (1961; trans. 1962), contains extensive references to Irénée du Pont, as does William S. Dutton, *Du Pont: One Hundred and Forty Years* (1942). □

Pierre Samuel du Pont

The American industrialist Pierre Samuel du Pont (1870-1954), as chairman of the board of E. I. du Pont de Nemours and Company, was among those responsible for its phenomenal success in the 20th century.

Pierre Samuel du Pont was born in Wilmington, Del., on Jan. 15, 1870. After receiving a bachelor of science degree from the Massachusetts Institute of Technology in 1890, he became a chemist in the family firm. He pursued a variety of business activities until 1902, when he and two cousins purchased and reorganized the family company. He became president of the firm in 1915, an office he held until he became chairman of the board in 1919. He remained in the latter post until 1940.

Du Pont guided the company through its enormous expansion during World War I and its later product diversification program outside the explosives industry. He emphasized competence rather than family membership: the company made a successful transition from a family operation to one run by professional managers. The new company structure stressed division of authority between central management and the operating departments; the former concentrated on long-run policy decision making while the latter focused on day-to-day problems. In adapting his company's organizational structure to its new marketing strategy, Du Pont was an industrial and administrative innovator.

The company first invested in the General Motors Company in 1917, with massive investment 3 years later. In 1920 William C. Durant, president of General Motors, found himself in financial difficulty. Because possible failure of General Motors might have jeopardized Du Pont's investment, a Du Pont syndicate rescued Durant, but the price was his holdings in General Motors. Reluctantly, Pierre du Pont became president of General Motors and occupied that office until 1923, when Alfred P. Sloan, Jr., replaced him.

Du Pont was also active in public affairs. He held numerous offices in the state government of Delaware, including tax commissioner. Initially a supporter of Franklin D. Roosevelt, Du Pont strongly opposed governmental intervention in business affairs and so opposed Roosevelt's reelection in 1936. He was one of the founders of the American Liberty League, which unsuccessfully appealed to voters to defeat the New Deal because it seemed to represent an infringement on individual liberties.

Du Pont died in Wilmington on April 5, 1954. As much as any other man, he can be credited with the success of the Du Pont Company in the 20th century.

Further Reading

The key source concerning Du Pont is Alfred D. Chandler and Stephen Salsbury, *Pierre S. du Pont and the Making of the Modern Corporation* (1971). Various aspects of his life and career are treated in the histories of the family and its enterprise: William S. Dutton, *Du Pont: One Hundred and Forty Years* (1942); Max Dorian, *The Du Ponts: From Gunpowder to Nylon* (1961; trans. 1962); and William H. A. Carr, *The Du Ponts of Delaware* (1964). Du Pont's years at General Motors receive extensive comment in the chapter on that firm in Alfred D. Chandler, Jr., *Strategy and Structure: Chapters in the History of the Industrial Enterprise* (1962). George Wolfskill recounts the story of the leading rightwing organization of the 1930s in *The Revolt of the Conservatives: A History of the American Liberty League, 1934-1940* (1962).

Additional Sources

Du Pont, Pierre S. (Pierre Samuel), *Life in my father's house*, Wilmington, Del.: H.R. Sharp, Jr., 1987. □

Pierre Samuel du Pont de Nemours

The French political economist, public administrator, and reformer Pierre Samuel du Pont de Nemours

(1739-1817) expounded the economic doctrines of the physiocrats.

Born in Paris on Sept. 14, 1739, Pierre Samuel du Pont was the son of Samuel du Pont, a master watchmaker, and Anne Alexandrine de Montchanin, member of a derogated noble family. After becoming a watchmaker and dabbling in medicine, he turned to letters as a means of attaining recognition. In 1763 he was introduced to François Quesnay, whose physiocratic thought greatly influenced him.

In Du Pont's early works—*Of the Exportation and Importation of Grains* (1763), *Physiocracy* (1767), and *Of the Origin and the Progress of a New Science* (1767)—he stated the core ideas of his thinking. He believed in a presocial natural order in which man had rights and duties based on the physical necessities of life. Man had propertorial rights over his life and possessions; his duties were to supply his own and others' needs and to respect others' rights and property. From these assumptions followed the belief that the natural source of wealth was land, and the labor and commerce associated with agriculture. All other forms of industry were secondary and related to luxury, which detracted from the expansion of agriculture and the accumulation of wealth. Du Pont believed that society should discourage nonproductive industries and free agriculture from all unnatural restraints. Good government, therefore, should work to eliminate custom barriers and excessive and unproductive taxation, which inhibited the growth of agri-

culture and trade. He also held that only hereditary monarchy could ensure the proper use of natural resources.

In 1774 Du Pont was appointed inspector general of commerce under his close friend A. R. J. Turgot, whom he served primarily as private secretary. With the fall of Turgot in 1775, Du Pont went into retirement at his estates near Nemours. There he finished drawing up Turgot's *Memoir on Municipalities* (1776), which in modified form served as the basis for some of the reform proposals of later ministers. Since there is no way of knowing how much of the *Memoir* was actually the work of Du Pont, there may be some justification in his claim that the bulk of later reform proposals were actually based on his ideas. It is known, however, that his role in the commercial treaties of 1783 and 1786 was considerable.

During the Assembly of the Notables (1787), Du Pont served as second secretary of the meetings—a privilege he was granted because he had been ennobled in 1783 for his services to the Crown. With the failure of the Notables, he became active in the Revolutionary movement and in 1789 was elected to represent the Third Estate from Nemours. As a member of the Constituent Assembly, he served on 11 economic committees. Du Pont was a moderate Revolutionary who believed reform should go no further than was absolutely necessary to ensure the realization of physiocratic principles. He advocated the separation of powers in government, a bicameral legislature, and a strong monarchy.

His views earned him the disfavor of most of the leaders of the Revolution, and Du Pont retired from public life in 1791. Chosen to sit in the Council of Elders in 1795, he was in constant opposition to the policies of the Directory and was proscribed in 1797, being suspected of royalism. He then resigned from the Elders and turned his thoughts to America, which he considered "the only asylum where persecuted men can find safety." He traveled to America in 1799 to introduce physiocratic ideas into the young republic.

On his return to France in 1802, Du Pont played an intermediary role in the Louisiana Purchase and was later elected to the Paris Chamber of Commerce. He did not, however, find favor with Napoleon, and his ambition of election to the Imperial Senate was never realized. In 1814 he supported the restored Bourbon monarchy, viewing the Charter of 1814 as similar to his own proposals of 1789. Napoleon's return from exile prompted Du Pont to flee to America, where he spent the last years of his life in retirement at his son's powder plant in Delaware. He died on Aug. 7, 1817, after a brief illness.

Further Reading

A full-length study is Ambrose Saricks, *Pierre Samuel du Pont de Nemours* (1965). A profile of Du Pont is the older, but useful work by Henry Higgs, *The Physiocrats: Six Lectures on the French Économistes of the 18th Century* (1896; repr. 1963). For general background see Peter Gay, *The Enlightenment* (2 vols., 1966-1969). □

Additional Sources

Du Pont de Nemours, Pierre Samuel, *The autobiography of Du Pont de Nemours,* Wilmington, Del.: Scholarly Resources, 1984. □

Asher Brown Durand

The American painter and engraver Asher Brown Durand (1796-1886) was a prominent figure in the first generation of the Hudson River school of painters.

Asher Durand was born on Aug. 21, 1796, in Jefferson Village, N.J., of a French Huguenot family. His first training was with his father, John Durand, a watchmaker. At 17 Asher was apprenticed to the engraver Peter Maverick and showed such facility that after 5 years they became partners. Durand also attended the American Academy of Fine Arts. When John Trumbull, who ran the academy, engaged Durand to engrave his painting *The Declaration of Independence,* Maverick, jealous of his former pupil, dissolved the partnership. Durand then set up his own establishment and was soon America's leading engraver. He engraved many portraits and book illustrations and executed a fine engraving of John Vanderlyn's *Ariadne.*

Although Durand had occasionally done some painting, he did not give up engraving in favor of painting until about 1834, when Luman Reed, a wealthy New York collector, commissioned him to do portraits of the early American presidents. In 1840 Durand traveled to Europe, where he admired the work of the 17th-century Dutch masters as well as Salvator Rosa and Claude Lorrain. Durand succeeded Samuel F. B. Morse as president of the National Academy of Design, New York, in 1846 and held the office until 1862, when he resigned.

Because Durand had been trained as an engraver, his earlier paintings are hard in texture and meticulous in detail, and his color is pale in tone. However, he soon developed a freer style and a richness of color. Two notable canvases, the *Morning of Life* and the *Evening of Life,* are allegories of the ages of man and depict imaginary landscapes in a rich and luxurious manner. But he was also a very factual painter. While most artists of the Hudson River school made sketches on the spot from which they worked up paintings in the studio, he was a pioneer in making actual paintings out of doors. As a result, his color is more true to nature than that used by his contemporaries. His *Monument Mountain, Berkshires* and numerous scenes done in the Catskills are remarkably fresh interpretations of the natural world.

In memory of his friend and fellow painter Thomas Cole, who died in 1848, Durand painted *Kindred Spirits,* showing Cole and the poet William Cullen Bryant standing on a cliff overlooking a Catskill stream. If overliterary in content, the painting does show the close association between writers and painters during the American romantic period.

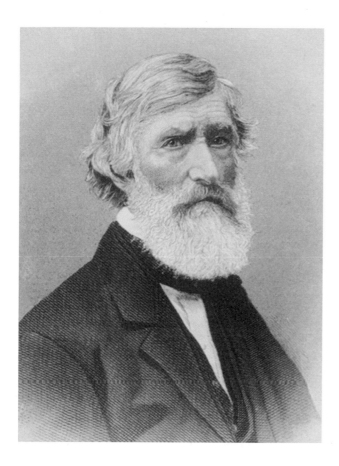

as the line's eastern terminus, although most authorities give the credit to Grenville M. Dodge. The Union Pacific ran into early financial difficulty, and Durant, vice president of the company, persuaded Congress to double the land grant and also to allow the road to issue bonds equal to those issued by the government, which was the transcontinental's major financial backer.

When the Union Pacific ran into difficulty selling its securities at par value as was required by the charter, Durant devised a scheme whereby a group of company executives formed a construction company called the Crédit Mobilier of America. This firm was awarded the construction contracts and accepted the securities as payment. To protect the firm against loss, the contracts were high enough to offset the sale of the securities below par. Regardless of the corrupt nature of the operation, money was secured and construction continued.

In 1865 Oakes and Oliver Ames, Massachusetts manufacturers, entered the Crédit Mobilier and began a battle for control with Durant. For 2 years the rival factions, known as the "Boston Crowd" and the "New York Crowd," contended for supremacy. At stake in the struggle was not only the construction company but the entire Union Pacific. Durant was forced out of the Crédit Mobilier in 1867, but efforts to sever him from the railroad failed. An agreement then followed between the two groups for construction of some 667 miles of track; the agreement proved profitable to the Crédit Mobilier, but the Union Pacific was left with a shoddily built line and heavy overcapitalization. Losing control to the Ames brothers, Durant held on just long

Further Reading

Durand is discussed in Frederick A. Sweet, *The Hudson River School and the Early American Landscape Tradition* (1945), and E. P. Richardson, *Painting in America* (1956). See also Oliver Larkin, *Art and Life in America* (1949; rev. ed. 1960).
□

Thomas Clark Durant

The American Thomas Clark Durant (1820-1885), an executive of the Union Pacific Railroad, was a major force behind the first transcontinental railroad.

Thomas C. Durant was born in Lee, Mass., on Feb. 6, 1820, the son of well-to-do parents. Although he graduated from Albany Medical College, he left medicine for his uncle's firm, which exported flour and grain. Durant later moved to New York City to open a branch office and became widely known in financial circles because of his activities in stocks.

Railroads were a popular investment in the 1850s, and Durant joined with Henry Farnam in building the Michigan Southern, the Chicago, Rock Island, and Pacific, and the Mississippi and Missouri. In 1862 the Federal government designated the Central Pacific and Union Pacific railroads to construct the first transcontinental line. Durant claimed that he influenced President Abraham Lincoln to select Omaha

enough to help Leland Stanford drive in the golden spike to complete the nation's first transcontinental railroad on May 10, 1869. On May 25 Durant was dropped from the board of directors of the Union Pacific.

Durant was married and the father of a son and daughter. His last years passed uneventfully in the Adirondacks.

Further Reading

No full-length study of Durant exists. For his role in the Union Pacific see Nelson Trottman, *History of the Union Pacific: A Financial and Economic Survey* (1923), and a popular work, Wesley S. Griswold, *A Work of Giants: Building the First Transcontinental Railroad* (1962). □

William Crapo Durant

The American industrialist William Crapo Durant (1861-1947) was the founder of General Motors, an automobile manufacturing company.

William C. Durant was born in Boston, Mass., on Dec. 8, 1861. He grew up in Flint, Mich., where he became a leading carriage manufacturer. In 1886 he organized the Durant-Dort Company and helped to make Flint the carriage capital of the nation.

Durant acquired control of the Buick Motor Car Company in 1904 and revived it; by 1908 Buick was one of the four leading automobile companies. Durant had a vision of the boundless possibilities of the automobile, particularly the moderate-priced car, and attempted to capitalize on these possibilities by establishing a large-scale enterprise based on volume production. He intended that his company would be well financed, market a variety of automobiles, and produce many of its own parts.

After an attempt to buy Ford Motor Company in 1907 failed because Henry Ford wanted to be paid in cash, Durant established the General Motors Company the next year. He began with the Buick and added Cadillac, Oldsmobile, Oakland (Pontiac), and other lesser companies. Durant overextended himself, and by 1910 General Motors needed the intervention of a bankers' syndicate to lift the burden of debt. Durant returned to the automobile business in 1911 with the Chevrolet car. In 1916, with the backing of the Du Pont family, he recovered control of General Motors.

In 1919 General Motors was one of the largest American industrial enterprises, but Durant exercised little control over its operation; General Motors was too decentralized to be effective. When the Panic of 1920 occurred, Durant was overcommitted in the stock market. He tried unsuccessfully to support the price of General Motors stock; he was forced out of the company in 1920 by the Du Ponts, who wanted to protect their sizable investment.

The remainder of Durant's life was anticlimactic. In 1921 he started Durant Motors, which failed to become a major automobile producer. Durant Motors was already shaky when the 1929 crash occurred; the Depression then

sharply reduced automobile sales and resulted in 1933 in dissolution of the firm. Durant was bankrupt by 1935. During his remaining years he engaged in a variety of business enterprises but without marked success. He died in New York City on March 18, 1947.

Durant was a pioneer in the automotive industry, and his most notable creation, General Motors, has dominated the automobile market since. Some of his chance ideas, such as the entry of General Motors into the manufacture of refrigerators, were highly successful. However, Durant never succeeded in organizing and administrative structure adequate for the giant enterprise he founded, and the task of converting General Motors into an enduring monument was left to his successors.

Further Reading

John B. Rae, *The American Automobile: A Brief History* (1965), places Durant in the context of his times and industry. Alfred D. Chandler, Jr., *Strategy and Structure: Chapters in the History of the Industrial Enterprise* (1962), has a chapter which analyzes Durant's administrative strategy. Carl Crow, *The City of Flint Grows Up: The Success Story of an American Community* (1945), includes a brief account of Durant's early years.

Additional Sources

Weisberger, Bernard A., *The dream maker: William C. Durant, founder of General Motors,* Boston: Little, Brown, 1979. □

Albrecht Dürer

The German painter and graphic artist Albrecht Dürer (1471-1528) introduced the achievements of the Italian Renaissance into northern European art. His prints diffused his new style, a fusion of the German realistic tradition with the Italian ideal of beauty.

Until the end of the 15th century late medieval realism in the north and the art of the Renaissance in Italy developed more or less independently of each other. While Italian artists invented rules of perspective and proportion to govern their representations of man in his natural environment, the German and early Netherlandish painters perfected their observation and depiction of individual natural phenomena without, however, establishing a correct perspectival space within which to contain the multiplicity of detail. Albrecht Dürer was, in effect, the first non-Italian artist to associate the humanistic disciplines with the esthetic pursuits of art.

Albrecht Dürer was born on May 21, 1471, in Nuremberg. His father, Albrecht the Elder, was a Hungarian goldsmith who went to Nuremberg in 1455, where he married Barbara Holper, daughter of a goldsmith. The young Dürer received his first training in his father's workshop as an engraver. He executed his first self-portrait, a drawing in silverpoint, at the age of 13.

His Apprenticeship

From 1486 to 1490 Dürer was apprenticed to the Nuremberg painter and woodcut illustrator Michael Wolgemut, following which he went on his bachelor's journey, the route of which is not known but which presumably led him to the Rhineland and to the Netherlands, since influences of early Netherlandish art are traceable in his works. He arrived in Colmar in 1492, soon after the death of the prominent German graphic artist Martin Schongauer in 1491, and continued on to Basel, where he stayed until late 1493 working extensively as a woodcut designer.

There is a difference of scholarly opinion in regard to Dürer's work in Basel, mostly woodcuts in books illustrated by several artists. The works generally ascribed to him show he was an extremely lively and many-faceted artist, interested in the representation of various aspects of daily life. The prints and drawings he executed at that period were influenced by Schongauer and the Housebook Master, the two major representatives of Rhenish graphic art.

In 1493 Dürer painted a self-portrait (Paris) in which he represented himself in a lyrical, romantic vein and inscribed above his head, "My affairs will go as ordained in Heaven." In May 1494 he returned to Nuremberg, and 2 months later he married Agnes Frey.

First Trip to Italy

In the fall Dürer journeyed to Venice, Padua, and Mantua. He copied works by the leading contemporary Italian masters, and it is apparent in his drawings that he soon learned how to impart to his figures perfection of anatomy, classical pathos, and harmony. It was at this time that Dürer began to be interested in the art of the ancients, although he probably had access to the classical works largely through Italian copies and interpretations. In the process of assimilating the spirit of classical art, he became aware of the necessity of art theory, to which he later devoted much of his time. Dürer's travels not only opened his eyes to the marvels of ancient art but also to the variety to be found in nature, which he captured in his excellent landscape drawings and watercolors of Alpine views.

Return to Nuremberg

In 1498 Dürer published a series of 15 woodcuts, the *Apocalypse,* which represents the highest achievement of German graphic art in that medium and which had a dramatic message to impart on the eve of the Protestant Reformation. The series is a tour de force in giving shape, in a realistic framework, to the fantastic images conjured up in the Book of Revelation. Each of the woodcuts represents a homogeneous action but at the same time contributes to create a powerful unity of the whole series. In the *Apocalypse* series as well as in the later series of prints representing the Passion of Christ (The *Great Passion,* begun before 1500 and published in 1511; the *Small Passion,* 1509-1511, repeated in copper engravings in 1507-1513; and the *Life of the Virgin,* 1500-1511), Dürer interpreted the Gospel in a new, human, and understandable language, organically fusing northern realism with the ideal beauty of Italy.

In Dürer's painting, another self-portrait (1498; Madrid) marked the turning point of his art. He represented himself as a humanist scholar and an elegant young man without the attributes of his profession. In this way he opposed the concept of art as craft current outside of Italy. "There were many talented youths in our German countries who were taught the art of painting but without fundamentals and with daily practice only. They therefore grew up unconscious as a wild uncut tree," he wrote. He wanted to be different and to change his followers: "Since geometry is the right foundation of all painting, I have decided to teach its rudiments and principles to all youngsters eager for art. . . ."

In his altarpieces Dürer revealed his interest in perspective, as in the *Paumgartner Altarpiece* (1502-1504). His portraits, such as *Oswolt Krell* (1499), were characterized by sharp psychological insight. Dürer depicted mythological and allegorical subjects in engravings on metal, for example, the *Dream of the Doctor* (after 1497) and *Sea Monster* (ca. 1498), and he also used that technique for one of his most popular prints, the *Prodigal Son* (ca. 1496). Dürer represented the hero in a novel way, the scene chosen being neither the prodigal son's sinful life nor the happy ending of his return to his father, but the moment in which the hero becomes cognizant of his sinful life and begins his repentance. In the print *Nemesis* (1501-1502) Dürer's study of human proportion is manifested, together with his taste for complicated humanistic allegory, which appears in several of his prints of that period.

Second Trip to Italy

In 1505 Dürer went to Venice again. Records of that stay abound in his letters to his humanist friend Willibald Pirckheimer. There is no mention of a visit to Rome. The assumption that Dürer visited Rome has been a subject much discussed by art historians. It was only quite recently that the inscription "Romae 1506" was discovered on his painting *Christ among the Doctors* (Lugano), which seems to argue favorably for the assumption that he did go to Rome. Until recently scholars knew only that he went as far as Balogna, but even if he really visited Rome his stay there must have been rather short as it left no visible traces in his drawings.

It was the art of Venice that profoundly influenced Dürer's work. He was on good terms there with artists, humanists, and noblemen. He wrote Pirckheimer that the painter Giovanni Bellini was his friend and wanted Dürer to paint a picture for him. It seems, however, that it was Dürer's prints rather than his paintings which established his reputation.

In 1506 Dürer painted for the church of the German merchants in Venice, S. Bartolommeo, his most Italian picture—in composition as in color: the *Feast of the Rose Garlands*. Even today, in spite of its damaged condition, "a solemn splendor of the southern town rests upon the picture," according to M. J. Friendländer. Dürer's portraits done at this time excel by nature of their soft subtlety of chiaroscuro, compositional simplicity, and lyrical mood, for example, *Portrait of a Young Girl* (1505; Vienna). The same freedom of touch, subtle and flexible, characterizes his drawings of nudes, done during and after the Italian journey.

Nuremberg Altarpieces

The large altarpieces executed when Dürer returned to Nuremberg show a mixture of colorful Italianisms with the traditional northern style. One of them is the *Heller Altarpiece* (1507-1509). The central panel was destroyed by fire in 1729 and is known only through a copy by Jobst Harrich. The wings were painted by Dürer's assistants, and four panels were executed by Mathias Grünewald.

The other two important altarpieces of that period are the *Adoration of the Trinity* (1511) and the *Martyrdom of the Ten Thousand* (1508), in which Dürer's placement of little figures in vast landscapes was a return to his early style, based on the traditions of northern painting. Dürer was also returning to his personal heritage in that he once again took up the engraver's burin as his main tool.

Melancholy and Humanism

Perhaps Dürer's most important works of the period from 1513 to 1520 were his engravings. In them his humanistic interests appear, developed through his friendships with distinguished German scholars, especially Pirckheimer. Through Pirckheimer, Dürer became acquainted with contemporary Italian thought as well as with classical philosophy and its recent revival known as Neoplatonism. The three so-called Master Engravings *Knight, Death, and the Devil* (1513), *St. Jerome in His Study* (1514), and *Melencolia I* (1514) are the climax of Dürer's graphic style and also express his thoughts on life, man, and art.

These engravings are allegories of the three kinds of virtue associated with the three spheres of human activity: in *Knight* the active sphere is depicted; in *St. Jerome,* the contemplative sphere; and in *Melencolia I,* the intellectual sphere, which Erwin Panofsky describes as an allegory of "the life of the secular genius in the rational and imaginative worlds of science and art." The three prints excel not only in transmitting their complicated allegorical messages but also in conveying a powerful expression of mood: heroic in *Kinght,* intellectually concentrated but serene in *St. Jerome,* and dramatic and gloomy in *Melencolia.* At the same time they show the greatest virtuosity in the handling of the medium; their silvery, vibrant surfaces contain both graphic and pictorial effects. It is possible that *Melencolia* was connected with a difficult moment in the development of Dürer's theoretical concepts, which he formulated at that time, although it was only later that his theoretical works were published.

Dürer was equally interested in a direct depiction of observed data. Throughout his life he drew and engraved simple motifs studied from life, as in the dramatic drawing of his old mother, emaciated and ill (1514).

Until 1519 Dürer worked for Emperor Maximilian I, taking part in the execution of various artistic projects of allegorical and decorative character, mostly in graphic media (the *Triumphal Arch* and the *Triumphal Procession of*

Maximilian I) but also in miniature (drawings in the *Maximilian I Prayer Book,* 1515).

Last Period

In July 1520 Dürer left for the Netherlands in order to receive from Charles V, Maximilian I's successor, the reconfirmation of his yearly salary of 100 florins that Maximilian had allotted him. This trip was a triumph for the artist and proved the esteem with which he was regarded. In his travel journal Dürer left a moving day-by-day record of his stay in Antwerp and of his visits to various Dutch, Belgian, and German towns. He met princes, rich merchants, and great artists. He drew portraits, landscapes, townscapes, and curiosities in his sketchbook. He met Erasmus of Rotterdam, whom he greatly admired and of whom he made a portrait drawing, which he later engraved (1526).

Dürer's last years were difficult. The Reformation was creating great religious and social changes. Dürer supported Martin Luther, whose teachings were heralded by Dürer's *Apocalypse.* In his last drawings, such as the *Oblong Passion* (10 drawings, 1520-1524), he expressed his powerful religious feelings, but held in check by a severe composition.

Dürer's last great work was the so-called *Four Apostles* (1526). The monumental, sculpturesque figures towering in their shallow space represent Saints John and Peter (left panel) and Saints Mark and Paul (right panel). The two paintings were probably intended as the wings of a triptych, the central panel of which was not executed. He gave the panels to the Town Council of Nuremberg. In the panels he included quotations from the writings of the saints represented, which contained accusations against "false prophets." Dürer's work proclaimed the unity of the new faith against the different sects arising at that time.

In 1525 Dürer published his book concerning perspective (*Instruction in Measurement*), and in 1527 his treatise on fortifications appeared. He died on April 6, 1528, a few months before his last and most important theoretical work, *The Four Books on Proportions,* was published. Excellent painter, engraver, and draftsman, Dürer was also a learned theorist. Active in art and science, he was the first true Renaissance artist outside of Italy and in his diversity a typical Renaissance man.

Dürer's Influence

Dürer's influence was greater than that of any artist of northern Europe of his time and was most widely felt through his woodcuts and engravings. He created a language of visual forms that furnished his contemporaries and followers with modern tools adapted to their needs: his art was a translation of the Italian Renaissance vocabulary into a dialect understandable north of the Alps. Dürer was beloved by the German romantic artists and writers of the 19th century, for whom he represented the quintessential German artist.

Further Reading

An English edition of Dürer's writings is William Martin Conway, *Literary Remains of Albrecht Dürer* (1889; rev. ed. 1958). A selection of his writings is included in Wolfgang Stechow, ed., *Northern Renaissance Art, 1400-1600: Sources and Documents* (1966). There are several works on Dürer in English, all overshadowed by the magisterial monograph of the foremost Dürer scholar, Erwin Panofsky, *The Life and Art of Albrecht Dürer* (2 vols., 1943; paperback ed., 1 vol., 1971). Old but good is William Martin Conway, *The Art of Albrecht Dürer* (1910). Wilhelm Waetzoldt, *Dürer and His Times* (1935; trans. 1950), written for a general audience, stresses the cultural background. For a study of Dürer's drawings see *Dürer: Drawings and Water Colours,* selected and with an introduction by Edmund Schilling (trans. 1949); and for the prints see Arthur M. Hind, *Albrecht Dürer: His Engravings and Woodcuts* (1911). The humanistic background and the symbolism of the *Melencolia I* print are discussed in Raymond Klibansky, Erwin Panofsky, and Fritz Saxl, *Saturn and Melancholy* (1964). □

1st Earl of Durham

John George Lambton, 1st Earl of Durham (1792-1840), was the tactless and energetic English statesman best known for his report on Canada, which laid the basis for the country's Dominion status.

John George Lambton was born in London on April 12, 1792. After attending Eton College, he joined the dragoons in 1809 but resigned in 1811. From 1813 to 1828 he was a member of Parliament. In 1830 he was made a privy councilor, created a baron, and appointed lord privy seal, and he also entered the House of Lords. He had a hand in preparing the First Reform Bill of 1832. In the same year he was made ambassador extraordinary in succession to St. Petersburg, Vienna, and Berlin, and he was rewarded for his service by being created viscount the following year. For the next 2 years Lord Durham led the advanced Whigs but in 1835 went once again to St. Petersburg as ambassador to Russia.

In 1837 Lord Durham returned home and in the next year was appointed high commissioner to Upper and Lower Canada and governor general of the British provinces in North America. Revolts in both Upper and Lower Canada in 1837-1838 had warned the British government that the Canadians were demanding responsible government and that the situation could not be ignored. Durham spent 6 months in Canada. He sent political prisoners to Bermuda— with which step he exceeded his orders—and it caused his fall.

But upon his return to Britain, Lord Durham published his famous *Report on the Affairs of British North America.* In it he enunciated the principle that the executive branch in Canada would have to make its peace with local interests by instituting a system of responsible government, revising the land ownership laws, fostering immigration, and providing a system of municipal government. He also urged that Upper and Lower Canada be united so as to outnumber the French Canadians. Durham died shortly after his report was completed, in Cowes, Isle of Wight, on July 28, 1840.

Energetic, vain, and high-spirited, Durham tried to keep the Canadian issue nonpartisan in British politics. It is arguable that it was not so much the tactless Durham who created responsible government as the able colonial secretaries and governors who followed him and implemented it.

Further Reading

The best biography of Durham is Leonard Cooper, *Radical Jack: The Life of John George Lambton, First Earl of Durham* (1959). The older works are Stuart J. Reid, *Life and Letters of the First Earl of Durham, 1792-1840* (2 vols., 1906), and Chester W. New, *Lord Durham: A Biography of John George Lambton, First Earl of Durham* (1929). For the place of the Durham report in the development of the British Empire see E. L. Woodward, *The Age of Reform, 1815-1870* (1938; 2d ed. 1962), and C. E. Carrington, *The British Overseas* (1950; 2d ed. 1968). □

Émile Durkheim

The French philosopher and sociologist Émile Durkheim (1858-1917) was one of the founders of 20th-century sociology.

Emile Durkheim was born at Épinal, Lorraine, on April 15, 1858. Following a long family tradition, he began as a young man to prepare himself for the rabbinate. While still in secondary school, however, he discovered his vocation for teaching and left Épinal for Paris to prepare for the École Normale, which he entered in 1879. Although Durkheim found the literary nature of instruction there a great disappointment, he was lastingly inspired by two of his teachers: the classicist Numa Denis Fustel de Coulanges and the philosopher Émile Boutroux. From Fustel he learned the importance of religion in the formation of social institutions and discovered that the sacred could be studied rationally and objectively. From Boutroux he learned that atomism, the reduction of phenomena to their smallest constituent parts, was a fallacious methodological procedure and that each science must explain phenomena in terms of its own specific principles. These ideas eventually formed the philosophical foundations of Durkheim's sociological method.

From 1882 to 1885 Durkheim taught philosophy in several provincial lycées. A leave of absence in 1885-1886 allowed him to study under the psychologist Wilhelm Wundt in Germany. In 1887 he was named lecturer in education and sociology at the University of Bordeaux, a position raised to a professorship in 1896, the first professorship of sociology in France.

On his return from Germany, Durkheim had begun to prepare review articles for the *Revue philosophique* on current work in sociology. In 1896, realizing that the task was too much for a single person to do adequately, he founded the *Année sociologique*. His purpose, he announced, was to bring the social sciences together, to promote specialization within the field of sociology, and to

make evident that sociology was a collective, not a personal, enterprise. In 1902 Durkheim was named to a professorship in sociology and education at the Sorbonne. There he remained for the rest of his career.

Achieving Consensus

The Division of Labor, Durkheim's doctoral thesis, appeared in 1893. The theme of the book was how individuals achieve the prerequisite of all social existence: consensus. Durkheim began by distinguishing two types of "solidarities," mechanical and organic. In the first, individuals differ little from each other; they harbor the same emotions, hold the same values, and believe the same religion. Society draws its coherence from this similarity. In the second, coherence is achieved by differentiation. Free individuals pursuing different functions are united by their complementary roles. For Durkheim these were both conceptual and historical distinctions. Primitive societies and European society in earlier periods were mechanical solidarities; modern European society was organic. In analyzing the nature of contractual relationships, however, Durkheim came to realize that organic solidarity could be maintained only if certain aspects of mechanical solidarity remained, only if the members of society held certain beliefs and sentiments in common. Without such collective beliefs, he argued, no contractual relationship based purely on self-interest could have any force.

Collective Beliefs

At the end of the 19th century, social theory was dominated by methodological individualism, the belief that all social phenomena should be reduced to individual psychological or biological phenomena in order to be explained. Durkheim therefore had to explain and justify his emphasis on collective beliefs, on "collective consciousness" and "collective representations." This he did theoretically in *The Rules of Sociological Method* (1895) and empirically in *Suicide* (1897). In the first, he argued that the social environment was a reality and therefore an object of study in its own right. "Sociological method," he wrote, "rests wholly on the basic principle that social facts must be studied as things; that is, as realities external to the individual." The central methodological problem was therefore the nature of these realities and their relationship to the individuals who compose society.

In *Suicide* Durkheim demonstrated his sociological method by applying it to a phenomenon that appeared quintessentially individual. How does society cause individuals to commit suicide? To answer this question, he analyzed statistical data on suicide rates, comparing them to religious beliefs, age, sex, marital status, and economic changes, and then sought to explain the systematic differences he had discovered. The suicide rate, he argued, depends upon the social context. More frequently than others, those who are ill-integrated into social groups and those whose individuality has disappeared in the social group will kill themselves. Likewise, when social values break down, when men find themselves without norms, in a state of "anomie" as Durkheim called it, suicide increases.

From what source do collective beliefs draw their force? In *The Elementary Forms of Religious Life* (1912) Durkheim argued that the binding character of the social bond, indeed the very categories of the human mind, are to be found in religion. Behind religion, however, is society itself, for religion is communal participation, and its authority is the authority of society intensified by being endowed with sacredness. It is the transcendent image of the collective consciousness.

During his lifetime Durkheim was severely criticized for claiming that social facts were irreducible, that they had a reality of their own. His ideas, however, are now accepted as the common foundations for empirical work in sociology. His concept of the collective consciousness, renamed "culture," has become part of the theoretical foundations of modern ethnography. His voice was one of the most powerful in breaking the hold of Enlightenment ideas of individualism on modern social sciences.

Durkheim died in Paris on Nov. 15, 1917.

Further Reading

Robert A. Nisbet presents a comprehensive analysis of Durkheim's ideas in *Émile Durkheim* (1965). A collection of essays on various aspects of Durkheim's work appears in Kurt Wolff, ed., *Émile Durkheim, 1858-1917: A Collection of Essays with Translations and a Bibliography* (1960). See also Charles Elmer Gehlke, *Émile Durkheim's Contribution to Sociological Theory* (1915), and Harry Alpert, *Émile Durkheim and His Sociology* (1939). A more general study is Talcott Parsons, *The Structure of Social Action: A Study in Social Theory with Special Reference to a Group of Recent European Writers* (1937; 2d ed. 1964).

Additional Sources

Giddens, Anthony, *Emile Durkheim,* New York: Penguin Books, 1979.

Lukes, Steven, *Emile Durkheim, his life and work: a historical and critical study,* Stanford, Calif.: Stanford University Press, 1985.

Mestrovic, Stjepan Gabriel, *Emile Durkheim and the reformation of sociology,* Totawa, N.J.: Rowman & Littlefield, 1988. □

Lawrence Durrell

A prolific British author, Lawrence Durrell (1912-1990) wrote several large-scale, multi-volume series of novels as well as poetry, plays, short stories, and travel books. People and places of the Mediterranean were a central theme of his work.

Lawrence Durrell was born on February 27, 1912, in Darjeeling, India, at the foothills of the Himalayas. His parents were Irish Protestants engaged in colonial service. After attending the College of St. Joseph in Darjeeling, the 11-year-old Durrell, like many Anglo-Indian children, was sent to England to complete his education. He went to St. Edmund's School, Canterbury, and, failing to gain entrance to Cambridge, took up a bohemian existence and supported himself by working as a jazz pianist in London night clubs and taking on a variety of odd jobs. He also began to work seriously on his poetry and fiction.

Oppressed by the hardship of life in a grimy quarter of London, Durrell was also stung by the stifling pressure of British society on his artistic ambitions. He wrote in a letter: "England wrung my guts out of me and tried to destroy everything singular and unique in me." In 1935, to escape "that mean, shabby little island," Durrell went with his family to the island of Corfu, off the Adriatic coast of Greece. He wanted to live the life of an expatriate writer and to recreate the life of London in his novels, much as the expatriate James Joyce had done for Dublin. At this time, Durrell read Henry Miller's *Tropic of Cancer,* a book whose plain style and sexual candor would greatly influence his own fiction. He went to Paris to meet Miller, and so began their life-long friendship.

Durrell's stay on Corfu was interrupted by the onset of World War II. His life for the next 17 years was shaped by a series of postings in government service. Durrell was in Athens and Crete from 1939 to 1941 teaching English, in Cairo and Alexandria until 1945 as an officer in the Foreign Press Service, in Rhodes until 1947 as director of public relations for the Dodecanese Islands, in Argentina in 1948 as director of the British Council Institute in Cordoba, in Belgrade through 1952 as press attaché, and in Cyprus from 1953 to 1956 as director of public relations for the island's government. The literary result was that the world of the

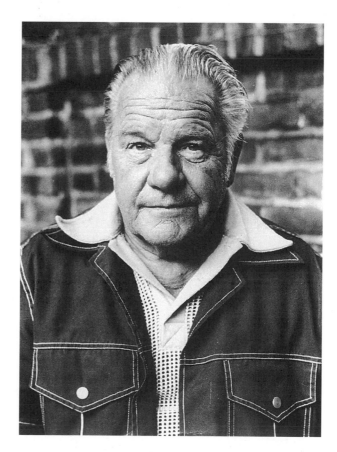

Mediterranean became Durrell's chief subject matter, in both his fiction and his many travel books. In 1957 he left government service to dedicate himself to this writing and settled in a village in the south of France, where he lived until his death in 1990.

Durrell's first important novel was *The Black Book* (1938), which, though similar in theme, represented a major stylistic break from his earlier fiction. The novel shows the influence of Miller's *Tropic of Cancer,* but *The Black Book* was no mere imitation. The novel recounts the lives and loves of struggling writers and artists in a grubby London hotel. Because of the novel's sexual frankness, Faber & Faber refused to bring out an unexpurgated edition; the book was finally published in its complete form through the efforts of Henry Miller. (*The Black Book* did not find a publisher in the United States until 1960.) With its appearance, Durrell was recognized as a major literary voice.

Durrell's subsequent fiction explores the people and places of the Mediterranean that he came to know so well. *Cefalu* (1947; later retitled *The Dark Labyrinth*) is a satirical portrait of a group of English tourists who are for a time trapped in the Cretan labyrinth, home to the legendary Minotaur.

The centerpiece of Durrell's career as novelist is *The Alexandria Quartet,* comprised of *Justine* (1957), *Balthazar* (1958), *Mountolive* (1958), and *Clea* (1960). In this ambitious and intricate series of novels, Durrell attempted to create a fictional parallel of 20th-century physics, based on theories he had expounded in his one book of literary criticism, *A Key to Modern British Poetry* (1952). In a prefatory note to *Balthazar,* Durrell wrote: "Modern literature offers us no Unities, so I have turned to science and am trying to complete a four-decker novel whose form is based on the relativity proposition. Three sides of space and one of time constitute the soup mix recipe of a continuum." The books of *The Alexandria Quartet,* which Durrell called "an investigation of modern love," are not sequential; rather, the first three books tell of the same events and characters in pre-World War II Alexandria, but from different viewpoints. The "facts" of the story of sexual liaisons and political intrigue are glimpsed only obliquely from the accounts of different narrators. There is, in a sense, no objective truth to be discovered. The fourth novel, *Clea,* is a more traditional chronological narrative which takes the characters through the war years.

In *The Alexandria Quartet,* Durrell adopted a highly ornate and sensuous narrative voice which drew much critical attention. George Steiner described the *Quartet's* style as "complex aural music" in which "light seems to play across the surface of the words in a brilliant tracery." The "baroque" style was not to everyone's taste though; Martin Green complained that "a steady diet of [Durrell's] sentences . . . makes one feel one is sickening for a bad cold."

Durrell's career as novelist continued with two other large-scale, multi-volume works. *Tunc* (1968) and *Nunquam* (1970) comprise *The Revolt of Aphrodite,* which tells a gothic story of corporate intrigue. The five-part *Avignon Quintet* is made up of *Monsieur, or the Prince of Darkness* (1974); *Livia, or Buried Alive* (1978); *Constance, or Solitary Practices* (1982); *Sebastian, or Ruling Passions* (1983); and *Quinx, or the Ripper's Tale* (1985). These later works, which are heavily weighted with allusions to gnostic mysticism and the medieval legends of the Knights Templar, are direct descendents of Durrell's *Alexandria* series. As the critic Alan Friedman points out:

> They too offer exotic settings peopled by improbable characters; multiple fictional and narrative layerings; . . . extensive mythical and metaphysical speculation on the nature of the universe and its creator, on the ego and personality, on the enterprises of being, becoming and creating; a harsh critique of western civilization and values; and an erotically charged prose style whose evocations and allusions overtly echo and invoke the *Quartet.*

In addition to his novels, Durrell is noted for a series of works generally referred to as the "island books," a hybrid genre incorporating autobiography and satiric social commentary. *Prospero's Cell* (1945) is an "island portrait" of Corfu, its geography, lore, customs, and eccentric inhabitants. Later, Durrell published *Reflections on a Marine Venus: A Companion to the Landscape of Rhodes* (1953); *Bitter Lemons* (1957), which deals with the Greek-Turkish conflict on Cyprus; *Sicilian Carousel* (1977); and *The Greek Islands* (1978).

Durrell's literary output also includes twelve volumes of poetry, three plays, several books of satiric sketches of diplomatic life, short stories, and collections of his correspondence with Henry Miller, Alfred Perles, and Richard Aldington. Durrell died of emphysema at his home in the village of Sommieres, November 7, 1990.

Further Reading

Spirit of Place (1969), edited by Alan G. Thomas, is an extensive anthology of Durrell's essays and fiction which serves as a Baedecker to Durrell's life and travels. Two important collections of criticism are Harry T. Moore's *The World of Lawrence Durrell* (1962) and Alan Warren Friedman's *Critical Essays on Lawrence Durrell* (1987). Readers interested in Durrell's friendship with Henry Miller might turn to the *Durrell-Miller Letters, 1935-1980* (1988) or to *Always Merry and Bright* (1978), Jay Martin's biography of Miller. □

Friedrich Dürrenmatt

The works of the Swiss playwright Friedrich Dürrenmatt (1921-1990) combine surface realism with an absurd and almost surreal artistic vision, expressed in an abundance of oppressive, distorted, often ironic detail.

F riedrich Dürrenmatt was born on January 5, 1921, in Konolfingen, Switzerland, near Bern. His father, Rheingold, was a pastor, while his grandfather, Ulrich, was a famous satirist and poet. At 13 he began to study theology, philosophy, German literature, and natural sciences, first at the Gymnasium in Bern and then at the University of Bern. Later he attended the University of Zurich to study art and philosophy. Inexplicably he began to write, yet he entered the field of graphic design in order to support himself. A heavy man with a penchant for cigars, in 1947 he won the heart of Lotti Geisler, a German actress, with whom he had three children. While residing in Basel, he composed *Es steht geschrieben* ("It Is Written," 1946), which caused scandal when it was produced in 1947 because of its alternative portrayal of religion, yet it earned him a prize. *Der Blinde* ("The Blind," 1948) was produced the next year.

Dürrenmatt's first success on the postwar German stage was *Romulus der Grosse* ("Romulus the Great," 1949), an "unhistorical historical comedy" about the fall of the Roman Empire. In this commentary on the absurdity of human values—with contemporary satirical implications—the last Roman emperor, more interested in breeding chickens than in politics, stoically accepts the inevitable course of history and hands his crown to the barbarian invader. The dramatist was later to write, "The world, for me, stands as something monstrous, an enigma of calamity that has to be accepted but to which there must be no surrender."

His next work and first big hit, *Die Ehe des Herrn Mississippi* ("The Marriage of Mr. Mississippi," 1950), was produced in Munich in 1952. A grotesque yet comic "dance of death" mocking ideology as a solution to man's predicament, it was briefly produced off-Broadway in 1958 as *Fools Are Passing Through* to mixed criticism. With *Ein Engel kommt nach Babylon* ("An Angel Comes to Babylon," 1953), produced in Munich, Dürrenmatt's reputation was established in Europe. It has been alternatively described as an obscure, fragmentary drama challenging "God's injustice," and as a parable of "a heavenly emissary who brings confusion instead of happiness." *Der Besuch der alten Dame* ("The Old Lady's Visit," later shortened to just "The Visit", 1955), however, extended the author's impact. Caught in a struggle between moral and material values, the dramatic protagonist of this work is an entire community which slowly succumbs to the temptation of murdering one of its members for the sake of a promised fortune. When it opened on Broadway in 1958, it was one of the most highly praised plays of the season. In 1971 Austrian composer made *The Visit* into an opera.

Dürrenmatt's nondramatic prose also explores "black comic" elements with penetrating irony. Among the radio scripts prepared during this period are *The Vega Enterprise* (1956), a science-fiction thriller which ends with the atomic bombing of the last humane sanctuary in a corrupt universe, and *Nächtliches Gespräch mit einem verachtelen Menschen* ("Nocturnal Conversation With a Scorned Man," 1957), which contains a dialogue between the secret executioner and the idealist on the futility of self-sacrifice and the art of dying. Many of his shorter efforts can be termed detective mysteries. His full-length novel *Grieche Sucht Griechin* ("Greek Man Seeks Greek Woman," 1955), however, does offer some genuine comic relief from the oppressive quality of the author's world view, but it was panned because its logic escaped its reviewers.

Three years after *The Visit* Dürrenmatt returned to the theater with *Frank V*, a poorly received musical drama. *Die Physiker* ("The Physicists," 1961), his first classically constructed work, restored the playwright to favor. Dürrenmatt preferred to term his plays "comedies," and in *Problems of the Theatre* (1955) he expressed the belief that tragedy could no longer be written because the modern age, lacking a well-ordered world—with established standards of guilt and retribution—is not suited for it. He continued writing, his plays of note including *Play Strindberg* (1969), *Die Frist* ("The Appointed Time," 1977), *Achterloo,* and *Oedipus* (1989). His last major work, *The Execution of Justice* (1989), has been described as the culmination of 400 years of European thought on the topic of justice. Dürrenmatt passed away in 1990.

Further Reading

Many of Dürrenmatt's plays can be found in print, and a good number of those in English. *The Playwrights Speak,* edited by Walter Wager (1967), includes a chapter by Dürrenmatt on his theory of theater. Murray B. Peppard, *Friedrich Dürrenmatt* (1970), contains a discussion of Dürrenmatt's writings as well as biographical details. Several critical surveys of drama devote sections to the playwright: see Hugh F. Garten, *Modern German Drama* (1959). □

François Duvalier

François Duvalier (1907-1971) was Haitian president for life. Trained as a physician and known to his people as "Papa Doc," Duvalier dominated his country and its institutions as no other Haitian chief executive.

Little is known of the origins of François Duvalier. Though some of his ancestors came from Martinique, his parents were Haitians, and he was born in Petit-Goâve in southern Haiti. An early Haitian Africanist, he was one of the founders of the Haitian intellectual Griot movement of the 1930s, and he built a reputation as a scholar, ethnologist, and folklorist.

Duvalier graduated in 1934 from the Haitian National University Medical School. He was active in the U.S. Army—directed sanitary programs initiated in Haiti during World War II. In 1944-1945 he studied at the University of Michigan. After returning to Haiti, Duvalier became minister of health and labor in President Dumarsais Estimé's government. After opposing Paul Magloire's coup d'etat in 1950, Duvalier returned to the practice of medicine, especially the anti-yaws and malaria campaigns. In 1954 he abandoned medicine and went into hiding in the Haitian backcountry, until a Magloire amnesty granted to all political opponents in 1956 enabled him to emerge from hiding. He immediately declared his candidacy for the next elections.

Accession to Power

Duvalier had a solid base of support in the countryside and, like the campaigns of the other candidates, his was based on national reconciliation and reconstruction. He made various tactical alliances with one or more of the other candidates, won the army to his cause, and finally overwhelmed Louis Déjoie, his main opponent, in what turned out to be the quietest and most accurate election in Haiti's history.

In spite of this auspicious start, Duvalier's government was dogged by problems. The defeated candidates refused to cooperate with him and, from hiding, encouraged violence and disobedience. After Fidel Castro came to power, Cuba began to harbor various Haitian refugees, who had escaped the increasingly harsh Duvalier regime. Furthermore, Gen. Rafael Trujillo, dictator of the Dominican Republic and archfoe of Castro, feared a Cuban invasion through Haiti, and this concern led to Dominican meddling in Haitian affairs.

It was during this period that Duvalier created an organization directly responsible to him, the *tontonmacoutes* (TTM), the Haitian version of a secret police. Through the late 1950s to the middle 1960s this force continued to grow and through brutality and terrorism helped to reduce elements which might oppose Duvalier.

In the 1961 Assembly elections Duvalier had his name placed on the top of the ballots. After the "election" he interpreted this impromptu act as a further mandate of 6 years. In the words of the *New York Times* of May 13, 1961, "Latin America has witnessed many fraudulent elections . . . but none will have been more outrageous than the one which has just taken place in Haiti."

After the 1961 elections the American government made it clear that the United States regarded those elections as fraudulent and that Duvalier's legal term should end in 1963. During 1962 the American AID Mission was withdrawn from Haiti, and by April 1963 an American fleet maneuvered close to Port-au-Prince. On May 15, to show its disapproval of Duvalier's continued presence, the United States suspended diplomatic relations. At the same time, with Haitian-Dominican relations at a low ebb, Duvalier's pledged ideological enemy, President Juan Bosch of the Dominican Republic, was threatening to invade Haiti. Even the Organization of the American States (OAS) became involved, sending a fact-finding mission to Haiti. However, Duvalier remained firmly in control, the Dominicans backed down, and a few days later the American ambassador was withdrawn.

President for Life

After the election of 1961 and the "continuation" of 1963, it was only a matter of time before Duvalier moved to have himself installed for life as Haitian president. "Responding" to just such a request, Duvalier consented on April 1, 1964. Duvalier's rubber-stamp Legislative Chamber rewrote the 1957 Constitution, specifically altering Article 197 so that he could be declared president for life. A "referendum" was held, and on June 22, 1964, Duvalier was formally invested.

After that time Haitian political life was relatively anticlimactic. Having dominated his country and in the process thwarted the United States, the OAS, and the Dominican Republic, Duvalier was in complete control. During the 1960s he survived several disastrous hurricanes and several *opéra-bouffe* "invasions." A small, gray-haired man, Duvalier was suffering from chronic heart disease and diabetes. In January 1971 he induced the National Assembly to change the constitution to allow his son, Jean Claude Duvalier, to succeed him. Duvalier died on April 21, 1971, and his son succeeded him without difficulty.

Further Reading

Useful works on Duvalier and his government include Leslie F. Manigat, *Haiti of the Sixties* (1964); Jean-Pierre O. Gingras, *Duvalier: Caribbean Cyclone* (1967); Al Burt and Bernard Diederich, *Papa Doc* (1969); and Robert I. Rotberg and Christopher K. Clague, *Haiti: The Politics of Squalor* (1971).
Among the several excellent background books on Haiti are Melville J. Herskovits's classic sociological study *Life in a Haitian Valley* (1937); Rayford W. Logan, *The Diplomatic Relations of the United States with Haiti, 1776-1891* (1941); Hugh B. Cave's delightful travelog, *Haiti: Highroad to Adventure* (1952); Seldon Rodman, *Haiti: The Black Republic* (1954; rev. ed. 1961); and James H. McCroklin's monographic work on the U.S. Marine occupation period, *Garde d'Haiti, 1915-1934* (1956). An excellent source of information on anything Haitian is James G. Leyburn, *The Haitian People* (1941; rev. ed. 1966). This classic scholarly work presents an interpretive overview of the history, culture, and society of Haiti and is brought up to date with a new foreword by Sidney W. Mintz. □

Jean-Claude Duvalier

Jean-Claude (Baby Doc) Duvalier (born 1951) succeeded his father, François (Papa Doc) Duvalier, as president-for-life of Haiti in 1971. He ruled with less of his father's repression but was deposed February 7, 1986. Living in exile in France, he grew increasingly destitute, having mismanaged much of the wealth he allegedly took out of Haiti.

Born in July 1951, Jean-Claude Duvalier became president of Haiti at age 19, when his father, the feared and hated Dr. François (Papa Doc) Duvalier died suddenly in April of 1971. The elder Duvalier, who rose to power in the late 1950s, had proclaimed himself president-for-life in 1964 and declared his eldest son heir apparent in 1969. "Baby Doc" Duvalier, as he came to be known, was educated entirely in Haiti. He visited Europe as a teenager, but was reportedly more interested in the continent's hedonist diversions than its other treasures. On the eve of his ascendance to the presidency, visiting journalists described him as a buffoon; his school-days nickname, "Baskethead," had followed him into adulthood.

Within a year of the younger Duvalier's accession to power Haiti experienced a marked decrease in political tension. Guided by his mother and several aides of his late father, the young president relied somewhat less than his predecessor on a reign of terror backed by Haiti's brutal secret police, the Tonton Macoutes. He also permitted limited press freedom and personal criticisms that were never tolerated by Papa Doc.

A Desperately Poor Nation

The younger Duvalier also moved closer to the United States, from whom his father had been estranged since 1961. Aid from the United States and from multilateral agencies began again. But there was no real attention, as many had hoped there would be, to the real ills of Haiti, long the poorest nation in the Western Hemisphere and the most ravaged by its rulers. The new President Duvalier—a pampered, portly playboy with a penchant for fast sports cars—had hardly been trained to succeed his enigmatic, ruthless father. Haiti had a per-capita income of $150 a year, literacy rates which hovered between five and ten percent of the population, infant mortality rates as high as 50 percent, a life expectancy of only 53 years, shrinking yields of coffee (the country's only cash crop), and a continued prevalence of tuberculosis. Moreover, Haiti's limited arable land area was shrinking dramatically every year due to deforestation, overgrazing, and violent erosion.

Nevertheless, Duvalier's first years in office offered hope. Soon more than 150 U.S. concerns were operating in Haiti, including a small chain of Holiday Inns. The sewing of baseballs, long a staple of low-wage Haiti, was expanded. New electronic assembly plants were developed. Another of the new businesses exported blood plasma, collected from the poor of Haiti's mean streets for $3 a quart, to the United States. For nearly two years, Hemo Caribbean made $5 a quart on sales of 4,000 quarts a month to hospitals and blood banks in the United States.

Political Instability

During the early years of the elder Duvalier presidency, exiled Haitians—some supported clandestinely by the United States—invaded their homeland in attempts to oust him, but all were repulsed. In late 1978 Baby Doc Duvalier's government was also threatened by an invasion in the northeast, at Cape St. Nicholas. Several dozen exiles came ashore from small boats. They proved no match for the Haitian army. A second invasion took place in 1982, when a small group of exiles led by a Miami garage owner landed on Tortuga, a small island off Haiti's northwest coast All of those who landed were imprisoned and shot.

A political crackdown on dissidents followed as a result of these two attempted coups. Senior United Nations officials complained about the all-pervasive atmosphere of family corruption. Caribbean political analysts asserted that Haiti's tobacco monopoly, among other enterprises, continued to be used as a family slush fund. The renewed authoritarianism deterred tourism and curtailed aid levels.

Island Spiraled into Crisis

When President Duvalier shortly thereafter permitted the formation of two opposition parties and publicly inaugurated a period of "liberalization," the United States and long-time opponents took cheer. The tame press was allowed to publish critical articles. By late 1979, however, the honeymoon was over. Men armed with clubs broke up Haiti's first human rights rally in Port-au-Prince. Diplomats were beaten, and hundreds were hurt. The press was again curbed. In 1980 Silvio Claude, founder of the Haitian Christian Democratic Party, was arrested and held incommunicado for two years. Gregoire Eugene, another party leader, and a number of journalists were subsequently arrested and flown out of Haiti on exit visas.

By mid-1981 Duvalier's new policies had transformed middle-class—and comparatively limited—migration of Haitians to the nearby United States into a wholesale exodus of impoverished peasants and landless laborers. In roughly made wooden sailboats, in rusty island freighters, in scows and anything that would float, 4,000 refugees a month began leaving Cap Haitien and Port de Paix secretly under the guidance of profiteering shippers for economic and political opportunity as refugees in Florida.

New Palace Power

In 1980 the president had married Michèle Bennett, the American-educated daughter of a well-to-do Haitian coffee merchant. At a cost of $3 million, the ceremony and festivities garnered infamy for its entry in the Guinness Book of World Records as the most expensive wedding ever held. The same year a son, François-Nicholas, was born. Michèle Duvalier outmaneuvered her mother-in-law in 1983 and became First Lady of Haiti. By then it had become clear that the new first lady was the power behind, next to, and perhaps in front of the throne. She began making executive decisions whenever her husband was otherwise engaged driving racing cars or cruising in his presidential yacht.

In the 1984 election to Haiti's 59-seat National Assembly, no opposition candidates were permitted to contest the election. The only plausible leaders of contrary parties were specifically excluded. Gregoire Eugene, who had earlier been exiled to New York, was prevented from returning. Silvio Claude was again arrested and tortured. Sixty of his followers were also arrested or exiled. So few Haitians voted that the government refused to reveal the turnout. The few meetings called to protest the elections were broken up by thugs. Duvalier confined his own electioneering to throwing money from the window of his speeding car.

Denied political and most other freedoms and condemned to flee their country or remain illiterate, ill-housed, ill-fed, and prone to disease, Haitians were also condemned to renewed cycles of underdevelopment. The tourist industry was destroyed by the association of AIDS with Haiti, and the farmers in 1985 were producing only 50 percent of the coffee grown in the 1960s. The roads were still rough and limited, electricity supplies haphazard, and arbitrary official taxation and corruption remained ingrained.

Kicked Out of Own Country

In the first days of February 1986 a series of riots broke out across Haiti. This time the government's usual harsh repressive measures only worsened the massive unrest. Fearing for his life, Duvalier fled to France in a U.S. cargo plane with his family and 17 associates. France granted temporary asylum, but then asked the Duvalier party to find another place of refuge; yet no other country would accept them.

After a short period of democratic rule, a junta took over the government of Haiti; elections were held in late 1990 and a former priest, Jean-Bertrand Aristide, was elected. A military coup ousted him after only a few months in office, and only an economic blockade helped see him reinstated in 1993. Meanwhile, a very small group still loyal to Duvalier continued to agitate for his return.

Duvalier has said he would be happy to return to Haiti, but it would certainly require heavy security. Scenes of the frightened Duvaliers behind the windshield of their luxury German automobile as they arrived at the airport to flee the country in 1986 became one of the lasting images of the coup. It was said that Duvalier was reportedly worth $120 million, much of it looted from Haiti's resources in one way or another. Shortly after the arrival of the Duvaliers and their entourage on the French Riviera, the U.S. government froze the former leader's American-held assets, which included a yacht in Miami, a condominium in New York's posh Trump Tower, and three other Manhattan abodes.

In the south of France Duvalier and his family lived quite comfortably, and he and Michèle Duvalier continued to spend freely—supposedly with money stored in secret Swiss accounts. On one trip to Paris, they bought nearly a half-million dollars worth of jewelry. The Duvalier fortune took a turn for the worse, however, after the couple's 1990 divorce. With his ex-wife in Paris with their two children (a daughter, Anya, arrived three years after François-Nicholas), Duvalier moved to another Cote D'Azur villa in 1990. His new rented home in Vallauris cost $9,000 a month, but legal actions taken by the current Haitian government to freeze his international assets in an attempt to recover some of the monies plundered were successful, and effectively impoverished Duvalier. By 1994 France Telecom disconnected his phone until its $14,000 balance was paid, and he was evicted from his villa for unpaid rent. He reportedly lives in a much smaller house in Vallauris, drives a humble Opel, and shares his home with his aged mother and five dogs.

Further Reading

The three books useful for the regime of the Duvaliers are Graham Greene, *The Comedians* (London, 1966), a novel which mirrored life in Haiti under the first Duvalier; Robert I. Rotberg, *Haiti: The Politics of Squalor* (1971); and David Nicholls, *From Dessalines to Duvalier* (1979). A post-coup analysis is found in Elizabeth Abbott, *The Woeful Dynasty: The Duvaliers and their Legacy* (1991). Updates on Duvalier's exile status appeared in *People* (August 22, 1994) and the *Economist* (October 22, 1994). □

Antonin Dvořák

Antonin Dvořák (1841-1904), one of the greatest Czech composers, is most noted for his attractive and apparently effortless melodic gifts and the unfailing brilliance of his orchestration.

Antonin Dvořák was a nationalistic musician, basing his style on melodic and rhythmic patterns found in the folk music of his own country. At the same time he was not excessively concerned with program music, and he worked most successfully in instrumental forms utilizing traditional classical structures, such as symphonies and chamber works. Even those compositions which contain programmatic titles tend toward a general atmosphere rather than a musical structure that follows a preconceived literary outline.

Born on Sept. 8, 1841, in a small town near Prague into a moderately poor worker's family, Dvořák showed considerable interest in music as a child. When he was 16 he moved to Prague to continue his education, studying at the Prague Organ School from 1857 to 1859. He received not only a thorough musical training that introduced him to the works of the great masters of the past, but also one that exposed him to the more "advanced" composers like Robert Schumann and Richard Wagner.

In 1861 Dvořák joined the orchestra of the National Theater in Prague as a violist, where he remained for 10 years, performing for a while under the leadership of Bedřich Smetana. During this time Dvořák wrote numerous compositions, but not until 1873, with a performance of his grand patriotic work *Hymnus* for chorus and orchestra, did he achieve some renown. His compositions attracted the attention of Johannes Brahms, who prevailed upon his publisher to print some of Dvořák's works. The two composers became close friends.

Always composing an apparently effortless output of music, including the popular *Slavonic Dances* (1878), Dvořák soon became a professor of composition at the Prague Conservatory. In 1884 he made the first of a series of trips to London to conduct his own music. There he earned a commission to compose a choral work, *The Spectre's Bride*. He received an honorary doctorate degree from Cambridge University in 1891, the same year he composed his popular *Carnival* overture.

After successful tours of Russia and Germany, Dvořák accepted an invitation in 1892 to became the director of the National Conservatory of Music in New York City. While in the United States he wrote what is probably his most famous work, the Symphony in E Minor, *From the New World* (1893). There has always been some confusion as to the extent to which Dvořák either imitated or directly borrowed melodic material from American folk music. All the music is original, however, and despite the fact that the theme of the second movement has been made into the song "Goin' Home," it is not an African American spiritual but a melodic invention by Dvořák. Perhaps the greatest problem presented by the *New World* Symphony is that it tends to blind audiences to the merits of some of his other symphonies. One in G major (1889) and another in D minor (1885) are certainly its equal in musical quality. In 1893 he also wrote his *American* String Quartet, the best-known of his 13 quartets, and a charming sonatina for violin and piano, a masterpiece in miniature.

In 1895 Dvořák returned to the Prague Conservatory, completing his cello concerto, probably the most outstanding concerto ever written for that instrument, and a perennial concert favorite. From this point on he concentrated on symphonic poems and operas. *Rusalka,* the ninth of his 10 operas, completed in 1900, was his last major work. Very popular in Czechoslovakia although rarely performed outside the country, *Rusalka* is a stunning lyric fantasy, an evocative retelling of the familiar story of the water nymph who fell in love with an all-too-human prince. In 1901 Dvořák became the director of the Prague Conservatory. He died on May 1, 1904.

Further Reading

Two major studies of Dvořák are John Clapham, *Antonin Dvořák: Musician and Craftsman* (1966), which deals mainly with the music, and Gervase Hughes, *Dvořák: His Life and Music* (1967), which treats the biographical data and the works in chronological order. An earlier but still useful work is Alec Robertson, *Dvořák* (1945). Good background studies are Gerald Abraham, *A Hundred Years of Music* (1938; 3d ed. 1964); Rosa Newmarch, *The Music of Czechoslovakia* (1942); and Alfred Einstein, *Music in the Romantic Era* (1947).

Additional Sources

Butterworth, Neil, *Dvořák,* London; New York: Omnibus Press, 1984, 1980.

Butterworth, Neil, *Dvořák: his life and times,* Speldhurst Eng.: Midas Books, 1980.

Clapham, John, *Dvořák,* New York: Norton, 1979. □

Timothy Dwight

Timothy Dwight (1752-1817), an American Congregational minister, was president of Yale College and New England's leading religious politician.

Timothy Dwight was born in Northhampton, Mass., into one of New England's most extraordinary families on May 14, 1752. His maternal grandfather was the famed theologian Jonathan Edwards. His mother, a woman of great intellect, educated him according to her own ideas. A child prodigy, Timothy was ready for college at 8, but Yale did not enroll him until he was 13. Studying 14 hours a day, he earned highest honors at graduation in 1769 but also developed an eye ailment that plagued him all his life.

Dwight assumed the headship of the Hopkins Grammar School in New Haven, Conn., for 2 years before returning to Yale as a tutor. There he joined the brilliant "Connecticut Wits," John Trumbull and Joseph Howe, who were patriotic belles-lettrists ambitious to make America "the first in letters as the first in arms." When Yale's aging president was forced to resign in 1777, Dwight, only 25, was pushed by some for the presidency. But the Yale Corporation had other opinions of the witty young man and called for his resignation instead. Before he left, Dwight married Mary Woolsey on March 3, 1777.

The following October the U.S. Congress appointed Dwight chaplain of the Connecticut Continental Brigade. A year later, on his father's death, he returned to his family in Northampton. He spent 5 vigorous years running two farms, preaching, sitting in the Massachusetts Legislature in 1781 and 1782, and founding a coeducational academy in 1779 to teach modern subjects as well as Latin and Greek. He left the school for the pulpit of Greenfield Hill, Conn., on July 20, 1783, where he established another school.

Dwight's journalistic assault against Yale started in 1783 in the *Connecticut Courant;* he used the pen name Parnassus. But when Yale's president Ezra Stiles prevented any legislative "intermeddling in college affairs," Dwight returned to the writing that had earned him prominence among the Connecticut Wits. *The Conquest of Canaan,* written earlier but published in 1785, was the first epic poem produced in America.

On June 25, 1795, Dwight accepted the presidency of Yale, a few weeks after the death of Stiles. For almost 22 years "Pope Dwight" (as the unregenerate called him) administered the college with great ability, ushering it into its modern era. No scholar himself, he had the vision to appoint men who were or would become scholars, and he allowed greater faculty participation in college government, traditionally the monopoly of the Yale Corporation and the president. Student relations were significantly improved, though Dwight held autocratic sway. Besides administering an exuberant college and giving counsel of weight in the affairs of state to visiting dignitaries, he taught the moral philosophy course to the seniors, supplied the college pulpit twice a Sabbath, and served as professor of divinity.

On Jan. 11, 1817, Dwight ceased to reign. His stormy life had personified the contradictions and strengths of New England Puritanism wedded to Federalism.

Further Reading

The definitive biography of Dwight is Charles E. Cunningham, *Timothy Dwight, 1752-1817* (1942). Kenneth Silverman, *Timothy Dwight* (1969), is a scholarly study. See also Leon Howard, *The Connecticut Wits* (1943). Ralph Henry Gabriel, *Religion and Learning at Yale: The Church of Christ in the College and University, 1757-1957* (1958), contains a chapter on Dwight and American Protestantism.

Additional Sources

Cuningham, Charles E., *Timothy Dwight, 1752-1817: a biography,* New York: AMS Press, 1976.

Wenzke, Annabelle S., *Timothy Dwight (1752-1817),* Lewiston, NY: E. Mellen Press, 1989. □

Bob Dylan

Throughout a career that has seen the better part of three decades, Bob Dylan (born 1941) has been pop music's master poet and an ever-changing performer.

I n the early 1960s Bob Dylan was heralded as the spokesman for his generation, writing and singing folk songs that were as deep and moving as those of any artist since his idol, Woody Guthrie. At the 1965 Newport Folk Festival Dylan shocked his following by going electric and venturing into rock and roll. He proved to be equally superior in that field also and by 1968 he was trying his hand at folk-rock, creating an impact that touched even the Beatles and the Rolling Stones. As the 1980s came around Dylan was undergoing a spiritual rebirth and his writing reflected a religious conviction that was truly heartfelt.

Began Exploring Folk Music

Born Robert Zimmerman in Duluth, Minnesota, Dylan was raised in the northern mining town of Hibbing from the age of six. His earliest musical influences, Hank Williams, Muddy Waters, Jimmy Reed, Howlin' Wolf and John Lee Hooker, were brought to him via the airwaves of a Shreveport, Louisiana, radio station. He played in a variety of bands during high school, including the Golden Chords, before enrolling at the University of Minnesota in 1959. It was at college that he changed his name to Dylan (probably after the poet Dylan Thomas) and began creating his own mythological background, which made him out to be everything from an Indian to a hobo to Bobby Vee. After hearing the Kingston Trio and Odetta he began to explore folk music, learning older tunes and sitting in at local coffeehouses around campus.

Just one year into college, Dylan dropped out and hitchhiked to New York to meet legendary singer Woody Guthrie, who was in an East Coast hospital suffering from Huntington's disease. "Guthrie was my last idol," Dylan said in *Rock 100* . "My future idols will be myself." Obviously in little need of self-confidence, by April 1961 he was gigging at Gerde's Folk City in New York's Greenwich Village. With the folk scene booming, Columbia executive and talent scout John Hammond had just signed Pete Seeger; Dylan followed soon after.

His debut LP, *Bob Dylan,* was released in March 1962. Recorded for a mere $402, the album featured acoustic reinterpretations of old folk songs, but also included two Dylan originals, "Song for Woody" and "Talking New York." Within a year his second LP, *The Freewheelin' Bob Dylan*—containing self-penned compositions only—was released. Protest tunes like "A Hard Rain's a-Gonna Fall," "Masters of War," and "Don't Think Twice, It's Alright" were making listeners more conscious and aware, both politically and personally. The trio of Peter, Paul & Mary recorded a version of "Blowin' in the Wind" from the LP that helped put the spotlight on Dylan. In July of that year at the Newport Folk Festival he was crowned leader of the folk movement with Joan Baez as the reigning queen. The new voice of youth, "Dylan's albums were listened to as if they were seismic readings from an impending apocalypse," reported *Rock 100.*

Unique Phrasing

The Times They Are a-Changin', with its title track and "The Lonesome Death of Hattie Carroll," broke in the new year of 1964. Imitators of his guitar/harmonica rig and odd singing (talking?) voice were sprouting up everywhere. "It's phrasing," Dylan told *Rolling Stone,* "I think I've phrased everything in a way that it's never been phrased before." In addition to his unique voice, lyrics, and meter, Dylan's physical image was just as intriguing with his wild conk of hair, stovepipe legs, and facial scowl. As much as the public and critics adored him, they also were frustrated as attempts to gain insight were met with toying word games and sometimes downright humiliation. Dylan began to question his role as guru on his fourth LP, *Another Side of Bob Dylan,* moving away from political themes and towards personal love songs. "My Back Pages" and "It Ain't Me Babe" signalled that a different Dylan had now arrived.

Bringing It All Back Home (1965) was a half-acoustic, half-electric outing that featured Dylan classics "Subterranean Homesick Blues," "Maggie's Farm," "Mr. Tambourine Man," and "It's Alright Ma (I'm Only Bleeding)." Dylan's first step into rock was also his first million-seller. Even so, his die-hard fans were not prepared for Dylan's performance at the 1965 Newport Folk Festival, when he appeared onstage backed by the electric Paul Butterfield Blues Band. Cries of "sell-out" and "gone commercial" filled the air as he was booed off the stage only to return for a final acoustic number, "It's All Over Now, Baby Blue." Anyone who doubted his commitment only needed to check out the next LP, *Highway 61 Revisited,* which was able to leap off the turntable courtesy of Michael Bloomfield's stinging guitar lines. The album featured the songs "Desolation Row," "Just Like Tom Thumb's Blues," "Queen Jane Approximately," and perhaps Dylan's most popular tune yet, "Like a Rolling Stone" (which went all the way to number two).

1966's Masterpiece *Blond on Blonde*

His masterpiece, *Blond on Blonde* (1966), is considered by some to be the finest rock album in history. A double LP recorded with Nashville session men, it is filled with an amazing display of Dylan's songwriting abilities: "Sad Eyed Lady of the Lowlands," "Absolutely Sweet Marie," "Rainy Day Women No. 12 & 35," "Memphis Blues Again," "I Want You," and others that firmly established Dylan as the most prolific stylist of all time. Just when it seemed he was in full force, Dylan was seriously injured in a motorcycle accident on July 29, 1966. He would spend the next year and a half recuperating from a broken neck in upstate New York. He recorded tracks with his backup group, the Band, but they would not be released until 1975 as *The Basement Tapes* (an LP that was bootlegged endlessly during the nine-year delay).

After flirting with death, Dylan's comeback album, *John Wesley Harding,* relied more on religious themes and a mellower country flavor. "All Along the Watchtower" became a hit shortly after for Jimi Hendrix while the entire mood of *JWH* sent an influential wave out that touched other artists of the time. Dylan carried the country style even further on *Nashville Skyline,* recording a duet with Johnny Cash, and the easy-going "Lay Lady Lay." His next release, however, was a commercial and critical disappointment. *Self-Portrait* was a double album consisting mainly of non-originals that seemed to be almost intentionally bad. *New Morning,* also from 1970, did not fare much better; Dylan's talent seemed to have peaked.

In 1973 Dylan's Columbia contract expired and he signed with Asylum just after releasing his soundtrack to the movie *Pat Garrett and Billy the Kid,* which included one of his biggest hits, "Knockin' on Heaven's Door." (Dylan also played the part of Alias in the film. Actor Sam Shepard told Rolling Stone that Dylan "knows how to play a part. He and Billy Graham are the two greatest actors in the world.") As if in retaliation for his leaving, Columbia released *Dylan,* a collection of studio outtakes and cover tunes that accomplished little more than embarrassing Dylan. His two Asylum LPs, *Planet Waves* and *Before the Flood,* were both recorded with the Band, the first being a studio album and the second featuring live recordings of the ensuing tour in early 1974.

Recordings Reflected Religious Beliefs

In 1975 Dylan re-signed with Columbia and recorded one of his best records yet, *Blood on the Tracks,* which seemed to harken back to his earlier style. "Tangled up in Blue," "Idiot Wind," "Shelter From the Storm," "Meet Me in the Morning," and "Buckets of Rain" amongst others had critics gushing with joy over yet another Dylan comeback. He then hit the road with a musically varied ensemble called the Rolling Thunder Revue: Mick Ronson, Joan Baez, T-Bone Burnett, Roger McGuinn, Ramblin' Jack Elliott, and David Mansfield, all blasting off on Dylan classics and material from his newest LP, *Desire.* That album topped both the British and U.S. charts riding a crest of popularity created by "Hurricane," Dylan's thumping plea for the release of the imprisoned boxer Ruben "Hurricane" Carter. In 1976 the live *Hard Rain* album captured the revue on vinyl. Two years later he would release another fine studio effort, *Street Legal,* featuring "Where Are You Tonight," "Baby Stop Crying," and "Changing of the Guards."

Dylan's next phase can be summed up in three albums, *Slow Train Coming, Saved,* and *Shot of Love,* and one word: Christianity. In 1979 he became "born-again," as writers coined it, studying the Bible at the Vineyard Christian Fellowship school in California. Although raised a Jew, Dylan took his new-found belief to the point of righteousness. "Dylan hadn't simply found Jesus but seemed to imply that he had His home phone number as well," wrote Kurt Loder in his *Rolling Stone* review of *Slow Train Coming.* The LP revolved around Dylan's beliefs, but it also rocked with the aid of Dire Straits guitarist Mark Knopfler. Critics and the public were split over the newest Dylan. Jann Wenner

explained his view of this period in *Rolling Stone:* "Dylan created so many images and expectations that he narrowed his room for maneuverability and finally became unsure of his own instincts."

Made MTV *Unplugged* Appearance

A rejuvenated Dylan appeared in 1983 on *Infidels,* produced by Knopfler with ex-Rolling Stone Mick Taylor on guitar. Dylan had joined an ultra-Orthodox Jewish sect, Lubavitcher Hasidim, and the songs reflected the move (although more subtly than during his Christian phase). In the mid-1980s Dylan continued to record and toured with Tom Petty and the Heartbreakers and the Grateful Dead as his backup bands. In 1988 he appeared as one of the Traveling Wilburys alongside Jeff Lynne, Tom Petty, George Harrison, and the late Roy Orbison. More changes can probably be expected from this master of the unexpected; Dylan has stayed on top by keeping ahead of the pack, knowing where his audience wants to be next, and then delivering.

Another important year for Dylan was 1995, as he reemerged as "the bard who matters most," according to the *Boston Globe.* The rock legend embarked on a U.S. tour, released an *MTV Unplugged* album, and a new CD-ROM entitled *Bob Dylan: Highway 61 Interactive,* all to favorable reviews.

Further Reading

Christgau, Robert, *Christgau's Record Guide,* Ticknor & Fields, 1981.
Dalton, David, and Lenny Kaye, *Rock 100,* Grosset & Dunlap, 1977.
Dylan, Bob, *Tarantula,* Macmillan, 1970.
Bob Dylan: The Illustrated Record, Harmony, 1978.
The Illustrated Encyclopedia of Rock, compiled by Nick Logan and Bob Woffinden, Harmony, 1977.
The Rolling Stone Illustrated History of Rock and Roll, edited by Jim Miller, Random House/Rolling Stone Press, 1976.
The Rolling Stone Record Guide, edited by Dave Marsh with John Swenson, Random House/Rolling Stone Press, 1979.
Shepard, Sam, *Rolling Thunder Logbook,* Viking Press, 1977.
Spitz, Bob, *Dylan, A Biography,* McGraw, 1989.
What's That Sound?, edited by Ben Fong-Torres, Anchor, 1976.
Boston Globe, December 8, 1995; February 9, 1995.
Detroit News, July 9, 1989.
Musician, September 1986.
New York Times, April 30, 1995.
Oakland Press, July 2, 1989.
Rolling Stone, March 11, 1976; September 21, 1978; November 16, 1978; July 12, 1979; September 20, 1979; September 18, 1980; June 21, 1984; Summer 1986; College Papers, Number 3.
USA Today, May 5, 1995.
Washington Post, May 17, 1995; February 8, 1995. □

Freeman John Dyson

The physicist Freeman Dyson (born 1923) has worked on wide-ranging projects in his field, always attracted by the latest developments. He is best known, however, for his speculations on the philo-

sophical implications of science and its political uses.

Freeman John Dyson was born in Crowthorne, Berkshire, England, on December 15, 1923. His father, Sir George Dyson, was a famed composer and musician who was from 1937 to 1952 director of London's Royal College of Music. Young Dyson's mother worried about her son's solitary pursuit of mathematics (he taught himself calculus from a textbook during one Christmas holiday), but his interests proved to be varied if not always sociable. The early science fiction of H. G. Wells and Jules Verne attracted him, and in his teens an interest in the causes of war led him to create a metaphysical faith which he called Cosmic Unity.

Wartime Service

Dyson entered Cambridge University in 1941 but was soon recruited by C. P. Snow, the future novelist, to work on statistical calculations for the Royal Air Force. The study involved the survival odds for bomber crews making runs over the European continent. There he had his first taste of technically interesting work, but he considered the bombing strategy to be a foolish endangerment of lives. He took his baccalaureate degree from Cambridge in 1945 and was made a junior fellow at Trinity College.

Two years later Dyson won a fellowship to Cornell University in the United States, where he was able to study under such internationally acclaimed scientists as Hans A. Bethe and Richard P. Feynman. It was here that he made perhaps his most significant theoretical contribution to the physics of quantum electrodynamics—the making compatible of previous work by Bethe, Feynman, and Julian Schwinger. He explained two conflicting theories on the interaction of electromagnetic waves with matter by showing them to be essentially the same.

Philosophy and Physics

Many of Dyson's new teachers had been involved with developing the atomic bomb during World War II, and the moral implications of this particular application of science was often a subject of discussion between them and their students. Dyson's continued interest in the philosophical questions concerned with physics—and particularly the practice of that science in morally and politically ambiguous contexts—led friends to introduce him to J. Robert Oppenheimer, sometimes referred to as the father of the atomic bomb. Dyson went to study with him at Princeton University's Institute for Advanced Study, which Oppenheimer then headed. During his year there, Dyson debated with, and finally convinced his mentor regarding his aforementioned synthesis of the theories of Feynman and Schwinger. In 1953, Oppenheimer was instrumental in obtaining for his protégé a faculty position in physics at the Institute.

At Princeton Dyson worked on queries into spin waves and the stability of matter. In 1956 he also began work with Edward Teller on designing an inherently "safe" nuclear reactor—that is, one which would necessarily shut itself down if it over-heated. As Dyson often had reason to complain, this technically interesting subject was cut short by more practical considerations. Although the two men came up with a design they called the High Temperature Graphite Reactor (HTGR), it was rejected by an industry that wanted lower costs for start-up. Dyson protested that "nobody any longer has any fun building reactors." Two years later he also associated himself with the Orion Project group in La Jolla, California, which was attempting to design a nuclear-powered spacecraft for manned exploration. When further work on the design was canceled by the government, Dyson complained loudly and publicly about political interference but later admitted that it was a poor way to explore space.

Grew Liberal in Beliefs

In 1959 he worked briefly with Edward Teller in developing the neutron bomb and soon became one of the leading scientific critics of the proposed nuclear test ban. At the same time, through the Federation of American Scientists (of which he became chairperson in 1962) he worked hard and effectively for the creation of the Arms Control and Disarmament Agency. Eventually he came to believe that his earlier opposition to the test ban had been "wrong technically, wrong militarily, wrong politically, and wrong morally."

Dyson went on to argue for the colonization of space, though he insisted on plans of a smaller scale and less costly than many of those which were popularly acclaimed. His own "Dyson sphere" advanced the idea of rearranging the orbit of planets to construct a ring that could support life, if it orbited an energy-producing star such as the sun. By the 1990s the Dyson sphere was so well-known among the scientific community that it was even mentioned in an episode the science-fiction television series *Star Trek: The Next Generation*.

Distinguished Author

Many of Dyson's original ideas were explored in depth in his books. Beginning with *Disturbing the Universe* (1979)—part autobiography, part treatise on morally ambiguous scientific matters such as nuclear arms and biogenetic engineering—the book won laudatory reviews for its accessibility to both learned and lay audiences. In its follow-up, *Weapons and Hope* (1984), Dyson joined a growing number of scientists who questioned the marriage of nuclear science and political strategy. During this era, many leading citizens such as Dyson became concerned about the proliferation of nuclear weapons and the growing tension between the United States and the Soviet Union, and would serve as the disarmament movement's most eloquent advocates.

Dyson, still a professor at Princeton during the 1980s, also wrote *Origins of Life* (1986) and *Infinite in All Directions* (1988). In 1991 he became president of the Space Studies Institute, an organization founded to raise more widespread awareness and support for the idea of space settlements open to the general public. Dyson advocates the idea of first sending people to colonize the Earth's moon because of its difficult environment: "Once there are people established on the Moon, if they can actually cope with that, they can cope with almost anything," he told *Ad Astra* magazine in 1994. As a leading scientist, he has also voiced criticism of the National Aeronautics and Space Administration for its misuse of resources and has called for its decentralization.

In the 1990s Dyson continued his active role in the scientific community. His 1991 book *From Eros to Gaia* is a collection of anecdotes from inside the scientific community. For instance, he relates how the rocket scientist Wernher von Braun used the strategy of the 1949 Berlin airlift in his 1952 conceptualization of a Mars colonization project. At the time, scientists actually considered the possibility of sending out four flights a day for several months. In the same lighthearted vein, Dyson includes a short piece he wrote at age ten in *From Eros to Gaia*.

New Issues for the 21st Century

Imagined Worlds (1997) was written after Dyson became professor emeritus at the Institute for Advanced Studies in 1994. Again, he examines leaps in scientific feasibility with the moral issues they raise; the colonization of space, radiotelepathy, and the use of computers to engineer human reproduction are some of the topics touched upon. Dyson's essays have also been published in *Scientific American* and the *New Yorker,* and he appeared as one of six panelists on the 15-hour PBS documentary *A Glorious Accident,* which aired in 1994.

Dyson has a son and a daughter from his first wife, Verena Haefeli-Huber, and four daughters born after his 1958 marriage to Imme Jung. He became a naturalized American citizen in 1957. His many honors include being made a member of the National Academy of Science, a fellow of the Royal Society of London, and a recipient of the German Physical Society's Max Planck Medal; in 1991 he was awarded the Oersted Medal by the American Association of Physics Teachers for his work in increasing public awareness in scientific matters.

Further Reading

Dyson's technical work can be approached undiluted through his many papers in the scientific literature. Mixed with political and philosophical thoughts, and even some autobiographical material they can be found in his books *Disturbing the Universe* (1979); *Weapons and Hope* (1984); *Values at War* (1985); *Origins of Life* (1986); *Infinite in All Directions* (1988); *From Eros to Gaia* (1991); and *Imagined Worlds* (1997). There is also a interview with Dyson in *Ad Astra* magazine (March/April, 1994). A more intimate look at Dyson can be found in Kenneth Brower's *The Starship and the Canoe* (1983), a dual biography of the visionary scientist and his back-to-nature, tree-dwelling son. □

Felix Edmundovich Dzerzhinsky

The Soviet politician Felix Edmundovich Dzerzhinsky (1877-1926) participated in the Polish and Russian revolutionary movements. He was the organizer and first administrator of the Soviet internal security apparatus.

Felix Dzerzhinsky was born in Poland of a landholding family. While still a student, he became involved in antigovernment politics, and on completion of his secondary education he embarked upon a career as a revolutionary political leader. Between 1897 and 1917 he was arrested and imprisoned or exiled five times. Although most of his actual political work was in Poland, he became more deeply involved with the Russian Social Democratic party than with the Social Democratic party of Poland and Lithuania; he was ultimately identified with the Leninist (Bolshevik) faction of the Russian revolutionary movement.

It was only after the Bolshevik seizure of power in 1917 that Dzerzhinsky's talents began to be fully exploited. In December 1917 he accepted appointment as chairman of the All Russian Extraordinary Commission, subsequently known by its Russian initials, Cheka. This organization was responsible for enforcing obedience to party and state decisions during the early days of the Revolution. The Cheka is generally regarded as the principal instrument of "Red terror" during the course of the civil war.

Although his opinions on policy frequently varied from those of Lenin, Dzerzhinsky's obedience to established policy seems to have been complete, and he held a large number and range of offices during the unsettled postrevolutionary days. In the summer of 1920 he was appointed head of the People's Commissariat for Internal Affairs (NKVD); the following spring he became commissar of the Peoples' Commissariat of Ways and Communications; and in February 1924 he was named president of the Supreme Council of National Economy (Vesenkha).

Throughout this period Dzerzhinsky supported the stated policy of the party with increasing vigor, while rejecting all alternative views. In particular he stood on the side of centralization as the Central Control Commission, originally founded to ensure that the center reflected the wishes of the party rank and file, became an agency for placing supporters of Stalin's policies in positions of power.

After the death of Lenin in 1924, the struggle for power between Stalin and his opponents sharpened, and Dzerzhinsky increasingly played the role of an apologist of both party unity and Stalin. During a particularly acute Central Committee confrontation in 1926 Dzerzhinsky, vigorously defending Stalin, suffered a fatal heart attack.

Further Reading

There is a translation of Dzerzhinsky's early work in his *Prison Diary and Letters* (1959). Although there is an extensive literature on Dzerzhinsky in periodicals, there are few full-length works. The best known of these in English are B. Jaxa-Ronikier, *The Red Executioner Dzierjinski* (trans. 1935), and Bernard Bromage, *Man of Terror: Dzherzhynski* (1956). Background material on the police apparatus can be found in Simon Wolin and Robert Slusser, eds., *The Soviet Secret Police* (1957).

Additional Sources

Felix Dzerzhinsky: a biography, Moscow: Progress Publishers, 1988. □

E

James Buchanan Eads

James Buchanan Eads (1820-1887), an American engineer and inventor, developed ironclad ships during the Civil War and designed the world's first steel-arch bridge.

James B. Eads was born in Lawrenceburg, Ind., on May 23, 1820. His father moved his family often, and James attended various public schools until the age of 13. After 5 years as a dry-goods clerk in St. Louis, he became a purser on a Mississippi River steam-boat and a self-taught expert in river navigation and hydrography.

Eads patented a diving bell in 1841 and used it on specially designed craft to salvage wrecked riverboats. After a brief, debt-ridden interval, he returned to salvaging, which proved very lucrative after 1848. He amassed a fortune and lived in semiretirement from 1857 to 1861.

In 1861 President Abraham Lincoln summoned Eads for advice on how to use western rivers for military purposes. Eads proposed a fleet of armor-plated, steam-driven gunboats and contracted to build seven 600-ton vessels. Ironclads became the mainstays of the Army's Western Flotilla and from Oct. 1, 1862, the nucleus of the Navy's Mississippi Squadron.

During the Civil War, Eads built 14 armored gunboats, 6 of them turreted; their 11-and 15-inch guns, worked by steam, could fire every 45 seconds. He converted and armed at least 11 others. These boats were indispensable in defeating the Confederacy.

In 1865 Congress authorized construction of the first bridge across the Mississippi at St. Louis, although it was

declared impractical by leading civil engineers. Eads was selected to build it. The bridge, with three arches, each over 500 feet, and a roadway 50 feet above the water, was the world's first steel-arch railroad bridge. Finished in 1874 after 6 years of building, it brought Eads international fame.

For many years the only bridge spanning the Mississippi, it was vital in opening the transcontinental railroad system.

Among engineers Eads received even greater recognition for his work on the lower Mississippi channel. Congress approved his proposal to open the river's mouth and maintain the channel at his own risk, and the job was completed in 1879. Eads's ingenious jetties redirected and accelerated the current; sediment was deposited at sea, and the channel, deepened to 30 feet, made New Orleans an ocean port.

Eads became a technical adviser on river control for many American and foreign port cities. His plan for deepening the Mississippi northward to the mouth of the Ohio later proved practicable. In 1884 he became the first American to receive England's coveted Albert Medal of the Society of Arts. Later he was the first engineer to be voted into America's Hall of Fame. He died on March 8, 1887, in Nassau, Bahamas.

Further Reading

Florence L. Dorsey, *Road to the Sea: The Story of James B. Eads and the Mississippi River* (1947), supersedes earlier biographies by Louis How (1900) and W. Sherwood Stuyvesant (1930).

Additional Sources

Baldwin, Clara, *Miracle man of the Mississippi, James B. Eads,* United States: C. Baldwin, 1985. □

Thomas Eakins

Thomas Eakins (1844-1916) was the most powerful figure painter and portrait painter of his time in America. He was a leading naturalist and one of the era's strongest painters of the current scene.

Thomas Eakins was born on July 25, 1844, in Philadelphia. After his graduation from Central High School, he studied for 5 years at the Pennsylvania Academy of the Fine Arts, where he drew chiefly from casts. To make up for his lack of study of living models, he entered Jefferson Medical College and took the regular courses in anatomy, including dissecting cadavers and observing operations.

In 1866 Eakins left for Paris, where he went through 3 years of rigorous academic training at the École des Beaux-Arts under Jean Léon Gérôme. He also traveled in Italy and Germany. In December 1869 he went to Spain, In Madrid's Prado Museum his discovery of 17th-century Spanish painting, especially the work of Diego Velázquez and Jusepe de Ribera, came as a revelation after the insipidity of the French Salons. After a winter in Seville, Eakins went back to Paris. In July 1870 he returned to Philadelphia, where he would live for the rest of his life, never going abroad again.

The Realist

Eakins now took for subjects the life of his place and period, Philadelphia of the 1870s; and with uncompromis-

ing realism he built his art out of this. His first American paintings were scenes of outdoor life in and around the city—rowing on the Schuylkill River, sailing and fishing on the Delaware River, hunting in the New Jersey marshes— and domestic genre picturing his family and friends in their homes. These works revealed utter honesty, a sure grasp of character, and an unsentimental but deep emotional attachment to his community and its people. From the first, they had the strong construction, the sense of form and of three-dimensional design, and the complete clarity of vision that were to mark Eakins's style thenceforth. The most important work of this period was the *Gross Clinic* (1875), portraying the great surgeon Samuel D. Gross operating before his students in Jefferson Medical College. The painting shocked the public and critics but established Eakins's reputation as a leader of American naturalism.

Scientific Interests

Eakins had an unusual combination of artistic and scientific gifts. Anatomy, higher mathematics, and the science of perspective were major interests to him and played an essential part in his painting. As early as 1880, he was using photography as an aid to painting, as a means of studying the body and its actions, and as an independent form of pictorial expression. In 1884 he collaborated with the pioneer photographer Eadweard Muybridge in photographing the motion of men and animals, but Eakins improved on Muybridge's method of employing a battery of cameras by using a single camera.

Another of Eakins's interests was sculpture. Sometimes he made small models for figures in his paintings, and he produced several full-scale anatomical casts. In the 1880s and early 1890s he executed eight original pieces. All of them were in relief, some in very high relief, almost in the round. Although he did not try to make sculpture his major medium, the strength and skill of his few pieces indicate that he might have achieved results as substantial as in painting.

The Teacher

A natural teacher, in 1876 Eakins began instructing at the Pennsylvania Academy and in 1879 became acting head of the school. Discarding old-fashioned methods, he subordinated drawing from casts to painting from the model, and based instruction on thorough study of the human body, including anatomy courses and dissection—innovations that were to revolutionize art education in America. But his stubborn insistence on the nude, particularly the completely nude male model in lectures on anatomy, scandalized the academy trustees and the more proper women students, and he was forced to resign in 1886. Most of his men students seceded from the academy and started the Art Students' League of Philadelphia, which continued for about 7 years, with Eakins as its unpaid head.

Until his early 40s Eakins had painted varied aspects of contemporary life, outdoors and indoors, as well as many portraits. But the academy affair and the lack of popular success for his paintings (at 36 he had sold only nine pictures for a total of a little over $2,000) probably explain why in the middle 1880s he abandoned his picturing of the broader American scene, except occasionally, and concentrated on portraiture.

His Portraiture

In this more restricted field Eakins displayed growing mastery. Those who sat for his portraits were not the wealthy and fashionable, but his friends and students and individuals who attracted him by their qualities of mind—scientists, physicians, fellow artists, musicians, the Catholic clergy. They were pictured without a trace of flattery but with a profound sense of their identity as individuals. Eakin's sure grasp of character, his thorough knowledge of the human body, and his psychological penetration gave his portraits intense vitality. His paintings of women, in contrast to the bodiless idealism of his academic contemporaries, had a flesh-and-blood reality and sense of sex. Eakin's portraiture forms the most mature pictorial record of the American people of his time, equal to John Singleton Copley's record of colonial Americans.

But none of these qualities made for worldly success. Commissions were rare. Usually Eakins asked sitters to pose, then gave them the paintings. Even so, his sitters often did not bother to take their portraits, so that he was left with a studio full of them. After the 1880s he suffered increasing neglect from the academic art world—or actual opposition, as when they refused to exhibit the masterpiece of his mature years, the *Agnew Clinic* (1889). In spite of this lack of recognition, he continued to work in the same uncompromisingly realistic style, and some of his strongest works were painted during the 1900s. Finally, in old age, he received a small shower of honors.

In 1884 Eakins had married Susan Hannah Macdowell, a former pupil and a gifted painter. They had no children but many students and friends. Fortunately he had a modest income from his father, and they lived in the family home, where he had lived since childhood. It was there that he died on June 25, 1916.

Eakins's work had a vitality, substance, and sculptural form greater than that of any other American painter of his generation. His figure compositions, particularly the relatively few based on the nude or seminude figure, achieved plastic design of a high order. The prudish limitations of his environment, combined with his own intransigent realism, thwarted full expression of his healthy sensuousness and his potentialities in design. But with all these reservations, Eakins's art was a monumental achievement. He was the first major painter of his period to accept completely the realities of contemporary American life and to create out of them a strong and profound art.

Further Reading

The first monograph on Eakins is Lloyd Goodrich, *Thomas Eakins: His Life and Work* (1933). Margaret McHenry, *Thomas Eakins Who Painted* (1946), adds personal material about the artist and his sitters and friends. Roland McKinney, *Thomas Eakins* (1942), and Fairfield Porter, *Thomas Eakins* (1959), are shorter biographical and critical accounts, with numerous illustrations. Sylvan Schendler, *Eakins* (1967), is a full-length study of Eakins and his art in relation to American society and culture of his period and includes 158 illustrations.

Additional Sources

Goodrich, Lloyd, *Thomas Eakins,* Cambridge, Mass.: Published for the National Gallery of Art by Harvard University Press, 1982.

Hendricks, Gordon, *The life and work of Thomas Eakins,* New York: Grossman Publishers, 1974.

Homer, William Innes, *Thomas Eakins: his life and art,* New York: Abbeville Press, 1992. □

Amelia Mary Earhart

The American aviator Amelia Mary Earhart Putnam (1897-1937) remains the world's best-known woman pilot long after her mysterious disappearance during a round-the-world flight in 1937.

Amelia Mary Earhart was born on July 24, 1897, the daughter of Edwin and Amy Otis Earhart. Until she was 12 she lived with her wealthy maternal grandparents, Alfred and Amelia Harres Otis, in Atcheson, Kansas, where she attended a private day school. Her summers were spent in Kansas City, Missouri, where her lawyer-father worked for the Rock Island Railroad.

In 1909 Amelia and her younger sister, Muriel, went to live with their parents in Des Moines, Iowa, where the railroad had transferred her father. Before completing high school she also attended schools in St. Paul, Minnesota, and Springfield, Illinois, while her father fought a losing battle against alcoholism. His failure and its consequent humiliation for her were the root of Amelia's lifelong dislike of alcohol and desire for financial security.

Amy Earhart left Edwin in Springfield in 1914, taking her daughters with her to live with friends in Chicago, where Amelia was graduated from Hyde Park School in 1915. The yearbook described her as "A.E.—the girl in brown (her favorite color) who walks alone."

A year later, after Amy Earhart received an inheritance from the estate of her mother, she sent Amelia to Ogontz School in Philadelphia, an exclusive high school and junior college. During Christmas vacation of her second year there Amelia went to Toronto, Canada, where Muriel was attending a private school. In Toronto Amelia saw her first amputees, returning wounded from World War I. She immediately refused to return to Ogontz and became a volunteer nurse in a hospital for veterans where she worked until after the armistice of 1918. The experience made her an ardent, life-long pacifist.

From Toronto Earhart went to live with her mother and sister in Northampton, Massachusetts, where her sister was attending Smith College. In the fall of 1919 she entered Columbia University, but left after one year to join her parents, who had reconciled and were living in Los Angeles.

In the winter of 1920 Earhart saw her first air show and took her first airplane ride. "As soon as we left the ground," she said, "I knew I had to fly." She took lessons at Bert Kinner's airfield on Long Beach Boulevard in Los Angeles from a woman—Neta Snooks—and on December 15, 1921, received her license from the National Aeronautics Association (NAA). By working part-time as a file clerk, office assistant, photographer, and truck driver, and with some help from her mother, Earhart eventually was able to buy her own plane. However, she was unable to earn enough to continue what was an expensive hobby.

In 1924, when her parents separated again, she sold her plane and bought a car in which she drove her mother to Boston where her sister was teaching school. Soon after that Earhart re-enrolled at Columbia but lacked the money to continue for more than one year. She returned to Boston where she became a social worker in a settlement house, joined the NAA, and continued to fly in her spare time.

In 1928 Earhart accepted an offer to join the crew of a flight across the Atlantic. The flight was the scheme of George Palmer Putnam, editor of WE, Charles Lindbergh's book about how he became, in 1927, the first person to fly across the Atlantic alone. The enterprising Putnam chose her for his "Lady Lindy" because of her flying experience, her education, and her lady-like appearance. Along with pilot Wilmer Stultz and mechanic Louis Gordon, she crossed the Atlantic (from Newfoundland to Wales) on June 18-19, 1928. Although she never once touched the controls (she described herself afterward as little more than a "sack of potatoes"), Earhart became world-renowned as "the first woman to fly the Atlantic."

From that time Putnam became Earhart's manager and, in 1931, her husband. He arranged all her flying engagements, many followed by often strenuous cross-country lecture tours (at one point, 29 tours in 31 days) for maximum publicity. However Earhart did initiate one flight of her own. Resenting reports that she was largely a puppet figure created by her publicist husband and something less than a competent aviator, she piloted a tiny, single-engine Lockheed Electra from Newfoundland to Ireland to become—on May 20-21, 1932, and five years after Lindbergh—the first woman to fly solo across the Atlantic.

During the scarcely more than five years remaining in her life, Earhart acted as a tireless advocate for commercial aviation and for women's rights. The numerous flying records she amassed included:

1931: Altitude record in an autogiro

First person to fly an autogiro across the United States and back

1932: Fastest non-stop transcontinental flight by a woman

1933: Breaks her own transcontinental speed record

1935: First person to fly solo across the Pacific from Hawaii to California

First person to fly solo from Los Angeles to Mexico

Breaks speed record for non-stop flight from Los Angeles to Mexico City to Newark, New Jersey

1937: Sets speed record for east-west crossing from Oakland to Honolulu

Honors and awards she received included the Distinguished Flying Cross; Cross of the Knight of the Legion of Honor, from the French Government; Gold Medal of the National Geographic Society; and the Harmon Trophy as America's outstanding airwoman in 1932, 1933, 1934, and 1935.

On July 2, 1937, 22 days before her 40th birthday and having already completed 22,000 miles of an attempt to circumnavigate the earth, Earhart and her navigator, Fred Noonan, disappeared over the Pacific somewhere between Lae, New Guinea, and Howland Island. The most extensive search ever conducted by the U.S. Navy for a single missing plane sighted neither plane nor crew. Subsequent searches since that time have been equally unsuccessful. In 1992, an expedition found certain objects (a shoe and a metal plate) on the small atoll of Nikumaroro south of Howland, which could have been left by Earhart and Noonan. In 1997 another female pilot, Linda Finch, recreated Earhart's final flight in an around the world tribute entitled "World Flight 97." The event took place on what would have been Earhart's 100th birthday. Finch successfully completed her voyage, the identical route that Earhart would have flown, around the world.

Further Reading

The first biography to tell a life story rather than a mystery tale of disappearance was Doris L. Rich, *Amelia Earhart: A Biography* (1989). Mary S. Lovell's *The Sound of Wings* (1989) is an interesting study of Putnam as well as Earhart, concluding with his death in 1950. Earhart's sister, Muriel Morrissey, in *Courage Is the Price* (1963) and Jean Backus in *Letters from Amelia* (1982) focus on family relationships. Dick Strippel's *Amelia Earhart: The Myth and the Reality* (1972) debunks the numerous theories based on Earhart's supposed capture and/ or execution by the Japanese as well as claims she was acting as a spy for the U.S. Government. Brief, accurate biographies are in the Smithsonian Institution studies *United States Women in Aviation (1919-1929)* by Kathleen Brooks-Pazmany (1983) and *United States Women in Aviation (1929-1940)* by Claudia M. Oakes (1978). See also Susan Ware, *Still Missing: Amelia Earhart and the Search for Feminism* (1994). Information on Linda Finch can be obtained from http://www.worldflight.com. (July 1997). ☐

Ralph Earl

Ralph Earl (1751-1801) was an American painter whose work recalls the archaisms of 17th-century colonial limners. He was one of America's earliest landscape artists.

Ralph Earl was born in rural Connecticut. Nothing is known of his early training. In 1775, working in New Haven, he and the engraver Amos Doolittle visited the recent battle scenes of the American Revolution at Lexington and Concord. Earl's four painted battle pictures, engraved by Doolittle, were among the earliest such scenes done in America. The forms are sharply drawn with little modeling and take on the look of flat paper cutouts.

Earl's father was a colonel in the Revolutionary Army, but Earl's own sentiments lay with the loyalists. Refusing to fight the King's troops and fearing for his safety, he fled to England in 1778, where he remained for 7 years. He left behind him Sarah Gates Earl, his wife and cousin. Later Earl married again (never having divorced his first wife) and also later left his second wife. He seems to have been a man of unstable temperament. William Dunlap's history of American art published in 1834 observed that Earl "prevented improvement and destroyed himself by habitual intemperance."

Only a handful of Earl's paintings from the period prior to his English trip still exist. The best is the portrait *Roger Sherman* (ca. 1777), in which Earl's roughhewn, laborious, but direct approach brings inner qualities of the sitter into full relief. Sherman was a slow, tenacious type who rose from humble origins through his own efforts to become lawyer, judge, and prominent civic leader. Earl painted him in browns and blacks, against a bare backdrop, seated in a plain Windsor chair, looking doggedly ahead.

When Earl returned to America, he tried to settle in New York but could not make a go of it and became an itinerant painter in Connecticut. His colors grew brighter and his figures more supple, but his paintings still had the primitive, 17th-century limner look, which was not uncommon for itinerant painters of the time. His paintings were uneven in quality. Among the best are the portrait *Daniel Boardman* (1789), in which a lovely, grassy landscape with soft mists falling over the hills stretches behind the figure; and the portrait *Mrs. William Mosley and Son Charles* (1791). His Connecticut hillscapes of the 1790s are precise and factual, yet manage to catch the personality of the place.

Earl's clumsy power was representative of the work of itinerant Connecticut painters in the late 18th and early 19th centuries.

Further Reading

Laurence B. Goodrich, *Ralph Earl: Recorder for an Era* (1967), offers a lively account of his career. William Sawitzky, *Ralph Earl, 1751-1801* (1945), is a catalog of an exhibition of Earl's works at the Whitney Museum of American Art, New York, and the Worcester Art Museum, Mass.

Additional Sources

Goodrich, Laurence B., *Ralph Earl, recorder for an era*, Albany State University of New York 1967. ☐

Sylvia A. Earle

Sylvia A. Earle (born 1935) is a leading American oceanographer and former chief scientist. Earle is a devout advocate of public education regarding the importance of the oceans as an essential environmental habitat.

Sylvia A. Earle is a former chief scientist of the National Oceanic and Atmospheric Administration (NOAA) and a leading American oceanographer. She was among the first underwater explorers to make use of modern self-contained underwater breathing apparatus (SCUBA) gear, and identified many new species of marine life. With her former husband, Graham Hawkes, Earle designed and built a submersible craft that could dive to unprecedented depths of 3,000 feet.

Sylvia Alice (Reade) Earle was born in Gibbstown, New Jersey on August 30, 1935, the daughter of Lewis Reade and Alice Freas (Richie) Earle. Both parents had an affinity for the outdoors and encouraged her love of nature after the family moved to the west coast of Florida. As Earle explained to *Scientific American,* "I wasn't shown frogs with the attitude 'yuk,' but rather my mother would show my brothers and me how beautiful they are and how fascinating it was to look at their gorgeous golden eyes." However, Earle pointed out, while her parents totally supported her interest

in biology, they also wanted her to get her teaching credentials and learn to type, "just in case."

She enrolled at Florida State University and received her Bachelor of Science degree in the spring of 1955. That fall she entered the graduate program at Duke University and obtained her master's degree in botany the following year. The Gulf of Mexico became a natural laboratory for Earle's work. Her master's dissertation, a detailed study of algae in the Gulf, is a project she still follows. She has collected more than 20,000 samples. "When I began making collections in the Gulf, it was a very different body of water than it is now—the habitats have changed. So I have a very interesting baseline," she noted in *Scientific American.*

In 1966, Earle received her Ph.D. from Duke University and immediately accepted a position as resident director of the Cape Haze Marine Laboratories in Sarasota, Florida. The following year, she moved to Massachusetts to accept dual roles as research scholar at the Radcliffe Institute and research fellow at the Farlow Herbarium, Harvard University, where she was named researcher in 1975. Earle moved to San Francisco in 1976 to become a research biologist at and curator of the California Academy of Sciences. That same year, she also was named a fellow in botany at the Natural History Museum, University of California, Berkeley.

Although her academic career could have kept her totally involved, her first love was the sea and the life within it. In 1970, Earle and four other oceanographers lived in an underwater chamber for fourteen days as part of the government-funded Tektite II Project, designed to study undersea habitats. Fortunately, technology played a major role in Earle's future. A self-contained underwater breathing apparatus had been developed in part by Jacques Cousteau as recently as 1943, and refined during the time Earle was involved in her scholarly research. SCUBA equipment was not only a boon to recreational divers, but it also dramatically changed the study of marine biology. Earle was one of the first researchers to don a mask and oxygen tank and observe the various forms of plant and animal habitats beneath the sea, identifying many new species of each. She called her discovery of undersea dunes off the Bahama Islands "a simple Lewis and Clark kind of observation." But, she said in *Scientific American,* "the presence of dunes was a significant insight into the formation of the area."

Though Earle set the unbelievable record of freely diving to a depth of 1,250 feet, there were serious depth limitations to SCUBA diving. To study deep-sea marine life would require the assistance of a submersible craft that could dive far deeper. Earle and her former husband, British-born engineer Graham Hawkes, founded Deep Ocean Technology, Inc., and Deep Ocean Engineering, Inc., in 1981, to design and build submersibles. Using a paper napkin, Earle and Hawkes rough-sketched the design for a submersible they called *Deep Rover,* which would serve as a viable tool for biologists. "In those days we were dreaming of going to thirty-five thousand feet," she told *Discover* magazine. "The idea has always been that scientists couldn't be trusted to drive a submersible by themselves because they'd get so involved in their work they'd run into things." *Deep Rover* was built and continues to operate as a mid-water machine in ocean depths ranging 3,000 feet.

In 1990, Earle was named the first woman to serve as chief scientist at the National Oceanic and Atmospheric Administration (NOAA), the agency that conducts underwater research, manages fisheries, and monitors marine spills. She left the position after eighteen months because she felt that she could accomplish more working independently of the government.

Earle, who has logged more than 6,000 hours under water, is the first to decry America's lack of research money being spent on deep-sea studies, noting that of the world's five deep-sea manned submersibles (those capable of diving to 20,000 feet or more), the U.S. has only one, the *Sea Cliff*. "That's like having one jeep for all of North America," she said in *Scientific American*. In 1993, Earle worked with a team of Japanese scientists to develop the equipment to send first a remote, then a manned submersible to 36,000 feet. "They have money from their government," she told *Scientific American*. "They do what we do not: they really make a substantial commitment to ocean technology and science." Earle also plans to lead the $10 million deep ocean engineering project, Ocean Everest, that would take her to a similar depth.

In addition to publishing numerous scientific papers on marine life, Earle is a devout advocate of public education regarding the importance of the oceans as an essential environmental habitat. She is currently the president and chief executive officer of Deep Ocean Technology and Deep Ocean Engineering in Oakland, California, as well as the coauthor of *Exploring the Deep Frontier: The Adventure of Man in the Sea* and sole author of *Sea Change: A Message of the Ocean,* published in 1995.

Further Reading

Brownlee, Shannon, "Explorers of the Dark Frontiers," in *Discover,* February, 1986, pp. 60–67.
Holloway, Marguerite, "Fire in Water," in *Scientific American,* April, 1992, pp. 37–40. □

Wyatt Barry Stepp Earp

Wyatt Barry Stepp Earp (1848-1929) was a major figure in the history and myth of the American West. Most of his fame came from his reputation as a gun-fighting marshal.

There are records of the Earps in 17th-century Fairfax County, Virginia; in the French and Indian Wars; and in the War of Independence. Earps kept moving westward, across Nebraska, Missouri, Iowa, Utah. They fought the Sioux in Wyoming. They helped develop San Bernardino, California. Wyatt Earp was born in Monmouth, Illinois, in 1848. He grew up in Iowa and is believed to have begun his western adventures as a buffalo hunter about 1869. In 1897 Earp joined the gold rush to Alaska, and

when he returned to the states in 1901 he continued to prospect for gold, now in California. While living in San Francisco he married Josephine Sarah Marcus, daughter of an early businessman there.

Differing Views of Wyatt Earp

Earp belongs in the pantheon of popular western heroes and villains, alongside names made famous in history texts, fiction, folk song, theater, musical comedy, film, and television. His contemporaries included Bat Masterson, Doc Holliday, Geronimo, Sitting Bull, Billy the Kid, Wild Bill Hickok, Annie Oakley, Kit Carson, Buffalo Bill Cody, and Matt Dillon. His name is associated with fabled places: Dodge City, Boot Hill, the O.K. Corral, and Tombstone. He achieved his particular fame, according to one biographer, Stuart Lake, as "the greatest gun-fighting marshall that the Old West knew."

Lake, who interviewed Earp in his last years, summed him up as follows: "Wyatt Earp was a man of action. He was born, reared, and lived in an environment which held words and theories of small account, in which sheer survival often, and eminence invariably, might be achieved through deeds alone. Withal, Wyatt Earp was a thinking man, whose mental processes were as quick, as direct, as unflustered by circumstance and as effective as the actions they inspired."

A less exalted image of Wyatt Earp emerges from the scrutiny of Frank Waters, a veteran observer of American Southwest landscape and history. "Wyatt," he wrote, "was an itinerant saloonkeeper, cardsharp, gunman, bigamist, church deacon, policeman, bunco artist, and a supreme confidence man. A lifelong exhibitionist ridiculed alike by members of his own family, neighbors, contemporaries, and the public press, he lived his last years in poverty, still mainly trying to find someone to publicize his life, and died two years before his fictitious biography recast him in the role of America's most famous frontier marshal."

The truth, as is common enough with historical figures about whom we know more from oral tradition than from documentation, undoubtedly lies between these extremes. The lives of those who became legend in the history of the West are perhaps even more embellished, for good or ill, as a result of sensational exaggeration by journalists and other writers. Confrontations between cowboys and Indians in the American "wild West" have long fascinated foreign audiences. British writers accompanied William F. ("Buffalo Bill") Cody on his expeditions, for example, producing "penny dreadfuls," cheap, paperbound books that sensationalized the wanton killing of Indians and of buffalo. Clint Eastwood's celebrated "anti-western," *Unforgiven*, includes a writer who takes notes throughout on the mayhem. Eastwood's earlier westerns were produced in Italy; the Japanese, in their films, found parallels between itinerant, freelance gunslingers and early samurai warriors. The raw, physical energies that supposedly characterized western pioneers fascinate French intellectuals.

Nevertheless, the mere facts about the Earp family offer an unchallenged, epical account of the turbulent, confused, sometimes noble, sometimes less than savory or honorable development and exploitation of America's western frontiers in the decades after the Civil War. To establish their hold on the variegated landscape, settlers had to contend with extravagantly hard seasons and the hostility of natives who were being callously displaced.

Gunfight at the O.K. Corral

Wyatt Earp's most well-known exploit was his killing in 1881, at the O.K. Corral in Tombstone, Arizona, of outlaws Billy Clanton and the McLowery brothers. Wyatt was aided by two of his brothers and by Doc Holliday. The event crystallized many of the mythical details about gunslinging bad guys and good guys. In 1957 Hollywood issued the critically acclaimed *Gunfight at the O.K. Corral,* the script of which was written by Leon Uris, starring Burt Lancaster, Kirk Douglas, Rhonda Fleming, and Jo Ann Fleet. It provides a reasonably authentic representation of the event.

Two years before his death, the gunfight still on his mind, Wyatt Earp wrote to Stuart Lake as follows: "For my handling of the situation at Tombstone, I have no regrets. Were it to be done over again, I would do exactly as I did at that time. If the outlaws and their friends and allies imagined that they could intimidate or exterminate the Earps by a process of assassination, and then hide behind alibis and the technicalities of the law, they simply missed their guess.

I want to call your particular attention again to one fact, which writers of Tombstone incidents and history apparently have overlooked: with the deaths of the Mc-Lowerys, the Clantons, Stillwell, Florentino Cruz, Curly Bill, and the rest, organized, politically protected crime and depredations in Cochise County ceased. Oh, yes, there were individual crimes committed thereafter, as there would be in any bailiwick, but organized outlawry ended with the deaths of Curly Bill and his gang. Let me repeat . . . Were it to be done over again, I would do exactly as I did at that time."

Many of the details of Wyatt Earp's career were gathered directly from him and those who knew him. Stuart Lake's work, *Wyatt Earp, Frontier Marshall* (1931), carries long quotations from Earp; the book is dedicated to him. *The Earp Brothers of Tombstone: The Story of Mrs. Virgil Earp* by Frank Waters (1960, 1976) disputes many conclusions in Lake's work, depending largely on examination of documents throughout the territory visited by the Earps. Its accumulation of data itself offers a fascinating narrative of Wyatt's checkered and far from inconsiderable career, which made him widely known in his time. For example, a number of ocean-going vessels were named after him.

Rich background on the complex world in which the Earps moved can be found in a range of creative efforts. Perhaps most illuminating are two theatrical works. The musical *Oklahoma!* by Richard Rodgers and Oscar Hammerstein covers the prickly relations in the settling of the West between ranchers, who needed unfenced, open land to graze their cattle, and farmers, who labored to cultivate crops on protected acreage. Arthur Kopit's *Indians* powerfully dramatizes the conflicts at the time between pioneers and Indians, giving short, sharp depictions of Buffalo Bill, about whom the play revolves, and Sitting Bull, Annie

Oakley, Chief Joseph, Geronimo, Wild Bill Hickok, and Washington politicians, among others.

Further Reading

In addition to the Lake and Waters' books discussed in the text, see *And Die in the West: The Story of the O. K. Corral Gunfight* by Paula Mitchell Marks (1989); it provides not only a full account of that event, by this time virtually akin in its complexity to the Greek siege of Troy, but also vignettes of Earp's personal life. Also relevant are Josephine Earp, ed. Glenn G. Boyer, *I Married Wyatt Earp: The Recollections of Josephine Sarah Marcus Earp* (1976), and Anne M. Butler, *Daughters of Joy, Sisters of Misery: Prostitution in the American West, 1865-90* (1987).

Additional Sources

Earp, Wyatt, *Wyatt Earp,* Sierra Vista, Ariz.: Y.V. Bissette, 1981.
Erwin, Richard E., *The truth about Wyatt Earp,* Carpinteria, CA: O.K. Press, 1992.
Lake, Stuart N., *Wyatt Earp, frontier marshal,* New York: Pocket Books, 1994.
Morton, Randall A., *Wyatt, the man called Earp,* Laguna Niguel, CA: RAMCO International, 1994. □

Edward Murray East

Edward Murray East (1879-1938), an American plant geneticist whose experiments led to the development of hybrid corn, also made distinguished contributions to genetic theory.

Edward M. East was born on Oct. 4, 1879, at Du Quoin, Ill. After high school he worked in a machine shop and in 1897 entered the Case School of Applied Science in Cleveland, Ohio. A year later he transferred to the University of Illinois, graduating with a bachelor of science degree in 1901. In 1903 he married Mary Lawrence Boggs.

East became interested in the new field of genetics. As assistant at the Illinois Agricultural Experiment Station, he analyzed the protein and fat content of Indian corn grown under an experimental breeding program. After receiving his master of science degree at Illinois in 1904, he became an agronomist at the Connecticut Agricultural Experiment Station at New Haven for 4 years. He worked mainly with corn and tobacco but continued his earlier studies with the potato, incorporating these in his doctoral thesis for the University of Illinois in 1907.

Continued experiments on the effects of inbreeding in corn, together with independent work at the nearby Carnegie Institution for Experimental Evolution, finally led East to the development of hybrid corn. This new method of seed production revolutionized corn growing throughout the world.

In 1909 East joined the faculty of the Bussey Institution of Harvard University (later reorganized as a graduate school of applied biology). He continued his corn and to-

bacco experimentation at the Connecticut Agricultural Experiment Station but also began more theoretical work. He discovered (independently of a Swedish plant breeder) the phenomenon later known as "multiple factors" which provides a Mendelian interpretation for "blending inheritance," previously thought outside of Gregor Mendel's laws. East also made distinguished studies of self-and cross-incompatibility, heterosis, cytoplasmic heredity, and hybridization.

East's work during World War I with the National Research Council and the U.S. Food Administration aroused his interest in the implications of biology for world problems and human affairs. He wrote two popular books warning of impending disaster if the exponential increase in world population was not quickly halted.

East served as president of the American Society of Naturalists (1919) and of the Genetics Society of America (1937). He was a member of the American Philosophical Society and the National Academy of Sciences. He died on Nov. 9, 1938, in Boston.

Further Reading

The only source for East's biography is the sketch by Donald F. Jones in the National Academy of Sciences, *Biographical Memoirs,* vol. 23 (1945), which contains a complete list of East's publications. ☐

Charles A. Eastman

Charles Eastman (1858–1939) was the first Native American physician to serve on the Pine Ridge Reservation and a prolific author of works about Indian life and culture.

Born near Redwood Falls, Minnesota, of mixed Santee Sioux and white parentage, Charles Eastman was much influenced in his distinguished career as a writer, physician, and Indian spokesman by two of the last bloody Indian-white conflicts on the North American prairies and plains. He published two autobiographical accounts of his youth—*Indian Boyhood* and *From the Deep Woods to Civilization*—which were widely credited with raising white awareness of Indian issues.

His parents were Jacob Eastman ["Many Lightnings"], a Wahpeton Sioux, and Mary Nancy Eastman, a mixed-blood Sioux who died when he was a baby. His maternal grandfather was artist Seth Eastman. The youngest of five children, and given the name Hakadah ["The Pitiful Last"] because of his mother's early death, Eastman fled with his family from Minnesota to British Columbia following the Sioux Indian Uprising of 1862. Ten years later, after thorough training as a hunter and warrior, he was reclaimed by his father, who had been in prison during most of that time for his part in the uprising.

At his father's insistence, Eastman enrolled in the Flandreau Indian School and thus was abruptly introduced into an alien society that he would struggle to understand for the rest of his life. Eastman went on to study at Beloit College, Knox College, Dartmouth College (where he earned a bachelor's degree in 1887), and Boston University (where he received his doctorate in 1890). In his first position as government physician at Pine Ridge Agency in South Dakota, he treated the survivors of the Wounded Knee Massacre. There he also met—and the next year married— Elaine Goodale, a poet, educator, and reformer.

A succession of positions followed with the YMCA and the Bureau of Indian Affairs, and he was much in demand in America and England throughout his life as an authority on Indian concerns. With his wife's assistance, Eastman began his career as a published author in 1893 with a series called "Recollections of the Wild Life" in *St. Nicholas* magazine. Over the next 27 years he gained increasing fame as America's distinguished Indian writer with many more articles and ten books, one of them written jointly with his wife Elaine. In addition to collaborating as writers, the couple produced six children. In 1933, Eastman was recognized by the Indian Council Fire, a national organization, with its first award for "most distinguished achievement by an American Indian."

Throughout his life, Eastman's reputation as a writer, speaker, and advocate of Indian rights rested largely on the fact that he had made the dramatic transition from the life of a traditional Sioux Indian in the wilds of Canada to the drawing rooms and lecture halls of white America. As an

articulate and accomplished physician, with a dynamic wife who spoke Lakota like a native, Eastman amazed many auditors and readers. Even some Congressmen were startled, as Rob Eshman points out in the *Dartmouth Alumni Magazine*. From 1897 to 1900 Eastman was a lobbyist for the Santee Sioux Tribe in Washington, D.C. Following one presentation before a Congressional committee, the only responses from the Congressmen were, "Where did you go to school? Why are there not more Indians like you?"

Began Literary Career with Autobiography

Eastman's literary career began in earnest in 1902 with the publication of *Indian Boyhood*. He had previously published a handful of short pieces, mostly in *Red Man* and *St. Nicholas* magazines, but this autobiography—dedicated to his son Ohiyesa the second—appealed to a wide non-Indian public with its depiction of "the freest life in the world," as Eastman called it. It consists of his earliest recollections from childhood; tributes to Uncheedah, his paternal grandmother who reared him, and to Mysterious Medicine, his uncle who taught him the lore of a life lived close to nature; and a moving conclusion that recounts the return of his father, just released from the federal penitentiary at Davenport, Iowa.

Of his grandmother, Eastman wrote, she "was a wonder to the young maidens of the tribe." Although she was 60 years old, she cared for Eastman as if he were her own child. "Every little attention that is due to a loved child she per-

formed with much skill and devotion. She made all my scanty garments and my tiny moccasins with a great deal of taste. It was said by all that I could not have had more attention had my mother been living." For his uncle, his father's brother, Eastman had the greatest admiration. He characterized the warrior as "a father to me for ten years of my life," a teacher with infinite patience who knew his subject—nature—thoroughly. Said Eastman, "Nothing irritated him more than to hear some natural fact misrepresented. I have often thought that with education he might have made a Darwin or an Agassiz." But Mysterious Medicine also realized that the things he knew and taught would soon lose their value. After telling Eastman the story of one of his most exciting hunting adventures, he concluded: "But all this life is fast disappearing, and the world is becoming different."

The world became shockingly different for Eastman when his father sought him out in Canada in 1873 and returned him to the United States, to Flandreau, Dakota Territory, where a group of Santees lived as homesteaders among the whites. "Here," wrote Eastman, "my wild life came to an end, and my school days began." It was an ironic reunion and return, for Eastman had thought his father dead, had pledged himself to take revenge upon the whites for that death, and now would be living among them with his father and adopting their ways.

Eastman would go on to publish the sequel to *Indian Boyhood* in 1916, when *From the Deep Woods to Civilization* appeared. In it, as Raymond Wilson concludes in *Ohiyesa: Charles Eastman, Santee Sioux*, Eastman presents a more realistic picture of the white world, "openly attacking the evils of white society and lamenting the sorrows Indians encountered as a result of cultural contact. . . ." In particular, his versions of the controversies in which he was embroiled at Pine Ridge and later at Crow Creek are clearly presented in a one-sided way. In addition, the pervasive tone of innocence in *Indian Boyhood* is now replaced by one of frustration, expressed in its most ironic form by his comment on his years at Dartmouth College: "It was here that I had most of my savage gentleness and native refinement knocked out of me. I do not complain, for I know that I gained more than their equivalent." Above all, Eastman was profoundly depressed by the failure of Americans to practice the Christianity that they professed, so that the meek might inherit the earth and "the peacemakers receive high honor." Instead, he wrote in *From the Deep Woods to Civilization*, "When I reduce civilization to its lowest terms, it becomes a system of life based upon trade. . . ."

All told, Eastman wrote ten books, and they established him as the leading apologist for his people and a storyteller of historic significance. Other titles include *Red Hunters and the Animal People* (1904), stories and legends for youth; *Old Indian Days* (1907), divided into stories about warriors and women; *Smoky Day's Wigwam Evenings: Indian Stories Retold* (1910), written with his wife Elaine; *The Soul of the Indian* (1911), the most fully developed statement of his religious beliefs; and *The Indian Today: The Past and Future of the First American* (1915), a review of Indian history, contributions, and problems. Eastman's last book was *Indian Heroes and Great Chieftains* (1918), a collection of short biographies of Sioux leaders written for young people.

Throughout the years that Charles and Elaine Eastman lived together, she served as his editorial assistant in all of his writing. Although on occasion Eastman resented some of Elaine's rewriting, she seems to have been essential to his publishing success, for after their separation in 1921 he published nothing more. What he had done by then was to contribute substantially to a better understanding by whites of Indians in general and the Sioux in particular. For Sioux readers, Wilson explained, Eastman's books "provide a bridge to self-respect . . . expressing their stories, beliefs, and customs in the language of White men." As a cultural bridge builder in the early twentieth century, Eastman was unequaled.

Served Sioux People in Other Capacities

Throughout his career as a writer, Eastman also served his people and the larger society in a variety of roles. His training as a physician he used on the Pine Ridge Reservation (1890-1893), in private practice in St. Paul, Minnesota (1894-1897), and at Crow Creek Reservation in South Dakota (1900-1903). While in St. Paul he began to work for the YMCA, organizing chapters around the country, and from 1897 to 1900 he lobbied for the Santee Sioux. For seven years (1903-09) Eastman was engaged, at Hamlin Garland's urging, in a BIA project to re-name the Sioux, giving them legal names in order to protect their interests. In 1910 he began a lifelong association with the Boy Scouts of America, and from 1914 to 1925 he and Elaine operated a girls' camp near Munsonville, New Hampshire. In 1923 he entered the Indian service for the last time, working until 1925 as an Indian inspector on and off the reservations. The last years of his life, until his death in 1939, Eastman devoted principally to lecturing.

In the last analysis, Charles Eastman's most important contribution to American letters is as a writer of autobiography and as a preserver of Sioux Indian legends, myths, and history. As autobiography, his *Indian Boyhood* is without equal. As William Bloodworth concludes in *Where the West Begins,* nearly all other life stories by his contemporaries consist of "coup stories, stories that explain an individual's name, and narrative elements in oratory and prophecy." Moreover, Eastman is the most prolific teller of Sioux Indian myths and legends. In her essay for *American Indian Quarterly,* Anna Lee Stensland concludes that despite our uncertainty over which stories are tribal legends and which are Eastman's own creations, and to what degree Eastman's Christianity led him to modify incompatible Indian concepts, Eastman is still the George Bird Grinnell and Stith Thompson of his people: "In the prolific writings of Charles Eastman there is probably more Sioux legend, myth, and history than is recorded any place else."

Further Reading

Copeland, Marion W., *Charles Alexander Eastman,* Boise State University Western Writers Series, 1978.

Eastman, Elaine Goodale, *Pratt, The Red Man Moses,* Norman, University of Oklahoma Press, 1935.
Graber, Kay, editor, *Sister to the Sioux: The Memoirs of Elaine Goodale Eastman, 1885-91,* Lincoln, University of Nebraska Press, 1978.
Hassrick, Royal B., *The Sioux: Life and Customs of a Warrior Society,* Norman, University of Oklahoma Press, 1964.
Meyer, Roy W., *History of the Santee Sioux: United States Indian Policy on Trial,* Lincoln, University of Nebraska Press, 1967.
Mooney, James, *The Ghost-Dance Religion and the Sioux Outbreak of 1890,* Chicago, University of Chicago Press, 1965.
Prucha, Francis Paul, editor, *Americanizing the American Indians: Writings by the "Friends of the Indian," 1880-1900,* Cambridge, Harvard University Press, 1973.
Riggs, Stephen R., *Mary and I: Forty Years with the Sioux,* Chicago, W.G. Holmes, 1880.
Utley, Robert M., *The Last Days of the Sioux Nation,* New Haven, Yale University Press, 1963.
Wilson, Raymond, *Ohiyesa: Charles Eastman, Santee Sioux,* Urbana, University of Illinois Press, 1983.
Alexander, Ruth, "Building a Cultural Bridge: Elaine and Charles Eastman," *South Dakota Leaders,* edited by Herbert T. Hoover and Larry J. Zimmerman, Vermillion, University of South Dakota Press, 1989; 355-66.
Alexander, "Finding Oneself through a Cause: Elaine Goodale Eastman and Indian Reform in the 1880s," *South Dakota History,* 22:1, Spring 1992; 1-37.
Bloodworth, William, "Neihardt, Momaday, and the Art of Indian Autobiography," *Where the West Begins,* edited by Arthur R. Huseboe and William Geyer, Sioux Falls, South Dakota, Center for Western Studies Press, 1978; 152-60.
Eastman, Charles Alexander (Ohiyesa), "A Canoe Trip among the Northern Ojibways," *The Red Man* 3, February 1911; 236-44.
Eastman, Charles, "Recollections of the Wild Life," *St. Nicholas: An Illustrated Magazine for Young Folks* 21, December 1893-May 1894.
Eastman, Charles, "Report on Sacajawea," *Annals of Wyoming* 13, July 1941; 187-94.
Eastman, Elaine Goodale, "All the Days of My Life," *South Dakota Historical Review* 2, July 1937; 171-84.
Eshman, Rob, "The Ghost Dance and Wounded Knee Massacre of 1890-91," *Nebraska History* 26, January 1945; 26-42.
Eshman, Rob, "Stranger in the Land," *Dartmouth Alumni Magazine,* January/February 1981; 20-23.
Fowler, Herbert B., "Ohiyesa, The First Sioux M.D.," *Association of American Indian Physicians Newsletter* 4, April 1976; 1, 6.
Holm, Tom, "American Indian Intellectuals and the Continuity of Tribal Ideals," *Book Forum* 5.3, 1981; 349-56.
Johnson, Stanley Edwards, "The Indian Ohiyesa," *Dartmouth Alumni Magazine,* June 1929; 521-23.
Milroy, Thomas W., "A Physician by the Name of Ohiyesa: Charles Alexander Eastman, M.D.," *Minnesota Medicine* 5, July 1971; 569-72.
Oandasan, William, "A Cross-Disciplinary Note on Charles Eastman (Santee Sioux)," *American Indian Culture and Research Journal* 7.2, 1983; 75-78.
Stensland, Anna Lee, "Charles Alexander Eastman: Sioux Storyteller and Historian," *American Indian Quarterly* 3, 1977; 199-207. □

George Eastman

By mass-producing his inventions, the American inventor and industrialist George Eastman (1854-1932) promoted photography as a popular hobby. He was also a benefactor of educational institutions.

George Eastman was born in Waterville, N.Y., on July 12, 1854, and educated in Rochester public schools. He advanced from messenger to bookkeeper in the Rochester Savings Bank by 1877. Frugal with money—his only extravagance amateur photography—he spent his savings on cameras and supplies and went to Mackinac Island. When photographic chemicals ruined his packed clothes, he became disgusted with the wet-plate process.

In the 1870s American photography was still slow, difficult, and expensive. Equipment included a huge camera, strong tripod, large plateholder, dark tent, chemicals, water container, and heavy glass plates. Eastman experimented with dry-plate techniques. He was the first American to contribute to photographic technology by coating glass plates with gelatin and silver bromide. In 1879 his coating machine was patented in England, in 1880 in America. He sold his English patent and opened a shop to manufacture photographic plates in Rochester. To eliminate glass plates, Eastman coated paper with gelatin and photographic emulsion. The developed film was stripped from the paper to make a negative. This film was rolled on spools. Eastman and William Walker devised a lightweight roll holder to fit any camera.

Amateurs could develop pictures after Eastman substituted transparent film for the paper in 1884. Flexible film was created by Hannibal Goodwin of New York and a young Eastman chemist, Henry Reichenback. The long patent dispute between Goodwin and Eastman was the most important legal controversy in photographic history. A Federal court decision on Aug. 14, 1913, favored Goodwin. Goodwin's heirs and Ansco Company, owners of his patent, received $5,000,000 from Eastman in 1914.

In 1888 Eastman designed a simple camera, the Kodak (Eastman's coined word, without meaning), which was easy to carry and eliminated focusing and lighting. With a 100-exposure roll of celluloid film, it sold for $25.00. After taking the pictures and sending the camera and $10 to the Rochester factory, the photographer received his prints and reloaded camera. Eastman's slogan, "You press the button, we do the rest," was well known.

Anticipating photography's increased popularity, in 1892 Eastman incorporated the Eastman Kodak Company. This was one of the first American firms to mass-produce standardized products and to maintain a chemical laboratory. By 1900 his factories at Rochester and at Harrow, England, employed over 3,000 people and by 1920 more than 15,000. Eastman, at first treasurer and general manager, later became president and finally board chairman.

Daylight-loading film and cameras eliminated returning them to the factory. To Eastman's old slogan was added "or you can do it yourself." A pocket Kodak was marketed in 1897, a folding Kodak in 1898, noncurling film in 1903, and color film in 1928. Eastman film was indispensable to Thomas Edison's motion pictures; Edison's incandescent bulb was used by Eastman and by photographers specializing in "portraits taken by electric light."

Eastman's staff worked on abstract problems of molecular structure and relativity, as well as on photographic improvements. During World War I his laboratory helped make America's chemical industry independent of Germany, and finally the world leader.

Concerned with employee welfare, Eastman was the first American businessman to grant workers dividends and profit sharing. He systematically gave away his huge fortune to the University of Rochester (especially the medical school and Eastman School of Music), Massachusetts Institute of Technology, Hampton Institute, Tuskegee Institute, Rochester Dental Dispensary, and European dental clinics.

After a long illness the lonely, retiring bachelor committed suicide on March 14, 1932, in Rochester. He had written to friends, "My work is done. Why wait?"

Further Reading

The best biography of Eastman is Carl W. Ackerman, *George Eastman* (1930). Robert Taft, *Photography and the American Scene: A Social History, 1839-1889* (1938), places Eastman in perspective in the evolution of photography. Mitchell Wilson, *American Science and Invention: A Pictorial History* (1954), is also helpful. □

Max Eastman

Max Eastman (1883-1969) was a poet, radical editor, translator, and author. He edited the socialist magazine *The Masses* (1912-1917) and translated Leon Trotsky into English.

Max Forrester Eastman was born on January 4, 1883, the son of two ministers. He graduated from Williams College in 1905 and studied philosophy with John Dewey at Columbia University (1907-1911), where he completed the work for a doctoral degree which he then decided not to claim. In 1909 Eastman founded the Men's League for Women's Suffrage and became a well-known and popular member of the bohemian left in New York City, where his growing reputation as a writer, lecturer, and fund-raiser led to his being invited, in 1912, to become the editor of the socialist magazine *The Masses* .

Under Eastman's leadership *The Masses* became an exuberantly anti-establishment left-wing socialist magazine featuring literary and political writing by such figures as Floyd Dell, John Reed, and Louis Untermeyer and graphic art by John Sloan, Robert Minor, and Art Young. When *The Masses* at first opposed America's entry into World War I it was banned by the government, and its editors, led by Eastman, were put on trial twice under the Espionage Act. Eastman was the star at both trials, a handsome and articulate young man whose eloquence was credited with achieving the victory of two hung juries at a time when most defendants under the Espionage Act were foredoomed to conviction.

After the death of *The Masses* Eastman founded *The Liberator* (1918-1922), then embarked enthusiastically on a sojourn to the Soviet Union, where he expected to discover the success of socialism. Eastman left the Soviet Union in 1924, disillusioned by the bitter struggle that followed Lenin's death in which Trotsky was brushed aside by Stalin. In 1925 Eastman's small book *Since Lenin Died* revealed to the world for the first time "Lenin's Testament," warning the party against allowing Stalin to succeed to power. Eastman's opposition to Stalin isolated him from American Marxists, and although he continued for some years to consider himself a radical, his views were rejected by orthodoxies of the left and the right, a position that Eastman himself, a rebellious individualist, did much to encourage.

Eastman's differences with his former comrades led him into bitterness that finally came full circle when in 1941 he published in the *Reader's Digest* (a conservative popular magazine with an enormous circulation) an article titled "Socialism Does Not Gibe with Human Nature." Eastman accepted a retainer as a roving editor for the *Reader's Digest* (which supported him until his death in 1969) and became an advocate of free enterprise and a supporter of Sen. Joseph McCarthy's attacks on alleged communists. (He did not, however, inform on his former friends, as some ex-communists and fellow travellers did).

Eastman was, according to his most sympathetic biographers, a gifted man who because of personality, conviction, and circumstance did not achieve his full possibilities. He was a prolific writer whose real text seems to have been his own contradictory life and an idiosyncratic, rebellious individualist whose journey from radical socialism to conservatism seemed to typify an American pattern. Eastman's intelligence and independence allowed him to struggle free of Marxist orthodoxies, but also prevented him from discovering a satisfying engagement with culture and politics. In his personal life, Eastman was a lifelong advocate of feminist principles who, after divorcing his first wife and through two long and apparently successful marriages, became the conscientiously self-indulgent lover of many women. Eastman's opposition to Marxist literary theory cut him off from an important part of American intellectual and artistic life during his prime; his opposition to modernist approaches to art throughout his life cut him off from much of the rest. Milton Cantor, one of Eastman's biographers, says that Eastman "we find that rare thing—the fusion of the life and the letters, the thinker and the doer, the artist and the revolutionary . . . who knew life and yet loved it, knew men and yet loved them. . . . He was, before the loss of hope, . . . [the] gnarled apple which had the sweetest taste."

Further Reading

Eastman wrote, edited, and translated many books. Among them are *Enjoyment of Poetry* (1913) and *Poems of Five Decades* (1954). His political works are better known than the poetical and include *Since Lenin Died* (1925); *The End of Socialism in*

Russia (1937); *Marxism: Is It Science?* (1940); and *Stalin's Russia and the Crisis in Socialism* (1940). Also important are two volumes of autobiography: *The Enjoyment of Living* (1948) and *Love and Revolution* (1965). For a sampling of *The Masses,* see William L. O'Neill (editor), *Echoes of Revolt: the Masses, 1911-1917.* For general biography, see William L. O'Neill, *The Last Romantic: A Life of Max Eastman* (1978) and Milton Cantor, *Max Eastman* (1970). Useful critical accounts of Eastman in the context of American radicalism may be found in Daniel Aaron, *Writers on the Left: Episodes in American Literary Communism* (1961); John P. Diggins, *Up from Communism: Conservative Odysseys in American Intellectual History* (1975); and Leslie Fishbein, *Rebels in Bohemia: The Radicals of The Masses, 1911-1917* (1982).

Additional Sources

O'Neill, William L., *The last romantic: a life of Max Eastman,* New Brunswick, U.S.A.: Transaction Publishers, 1991. □

Clint Eastwood

Clint Eastwood (born 1930) ranks among the world's best known and most successful movie stars. Most of his films have done well at the box office and he has established himself as a director of note.

A 1971 *Life* magazine cover carried his picture with the tag line "the world's favorite movie star is—no kidding—Clint Eastwood." After that he continued to win box-office and financial success—as well as increasing critical acclaim—well into the 1990s. Born Clinton Eastwood, Jr., on May 30, 1930, in San Francisco, California, he had a tough childhood because of the Great Depression, as his parents moved frequently in search of work, finally settling in Oakland. There he went to high school, graduating in 1948. Striking out on his own, he held various menial jobs before being drafted into the army. Discharged in 1953, he enrolled in Los Angeles City College as a business administration major, supporting himself with various odd jobs which included digging swimming pool foundations.

Bit Parts in "B" Movies

Army friends in the film business urged Eastwood to try his luck. He did, was screen-tested by Universal, and on the basis of his good looks was hired as a contract player in 1955. His salary was $75 a week, and his assignments included minuscule roles in forgettable movies, including *Tarantula* and *Francis in the Navy*). After Universal dropped him in 1956, the roles briefly got bigger but not better: Eastwood has described the 1958 *Ambush at Cimarron Pass,* in which he had a substantial part, as "maybe the worst film ever made."

Notwithstanding an occasional unimpressive role in television series such as "Highway Patrol," by 1958 Eastwood found himself again digging swimming pools for a living. As the result of a chance meeting, he was chosen to play Rowdy Yates, the second lead in the CBS television series "Rawhide." Characterized as "an endless cattle drive," the series lasted seven years (1959-1966), owing much of its success to Eastwood's popular "punk ramrod."

Gains Stardom with "Spaghetti Westerns"

During a hiatus from "Rawhide" in 1964, Eastwood filmed *A Fistful of Dollars* in Spain for Italian director Sergio Leone. Eastwood portrayed a hired gun, a nameless man, who successfully manipulates—and then ruthlessly kills—rival gangs of bandits. The film catapulted Eastwood from a dead-end television career to stardom in the movies. Over the next two years, Eastwood returned to Europe to film two equally popular sequels, both also featuring the "Man with No Name": *For a Few Dollars More* (1965) and *The Good, The Bad, and The Ugly* (1966).

These films defined the Eastwood screen persona which, as *New York Times* reporter John Vinocur pointed out, was "a western hero without the westerner's traditional heroic characteristics." Eastwood's character was callous, violent, cynical, tough. Facets of that character were present in his best westerns, such as *The Outlaw Josey Wales* (1976) and *Unforgiven* (1992), both stark bloody films about an outsider.

The same toughness also characterized many of Eastwood's non-western roles. His appeal lay (to use Eastwood's words) in his ability "to hack his way through" because such a person "is almost . . . a mythical character in our day and age" as everything "becomes more complicated." That capacity underlay what has been described as one of Eastwood's "enduring screen figures"—Harry Callahan, a contemporary San Francisco detective who roams the city defying a legalistic bureaucracy and practicing a vigorous populist brand of justice. Callahan was introduced in *Dirty Harry* (1971), which critic Pauline Kael found imbued with "fascist medievalism."

No matter what the critics thought, the American public flocked to see *Dirty Harry,* and the role was reprised in 1973, 1976, 1983, and 1988. All but the last did well at the box office, if not critically, because they (in the words of one writer) seized "the mood of many Americans frustrated by . . . an ineffectual law enforcement system."

His career, which by 1997 encompassed almost 40 roles, was not without weak spots. He co-starred with an orangutan in the critically attacked comedies *Every Which Way But Loose* (1978) and *Any Which Way You Can* (1980), among Warner's highest grossing films in those years. Less successful theatrically but critically well-received was *The Beguiled* (1971), a Gothic tale about a crippled Union soldier murdered by southern school girls. Critics and moviegoers both agreed the musical *Paint Your Wagon* (1969) wasted his talents. He had flops in 1989 (*The Pink Cadillac*) and 1990 (*The Rookie*).

Eastwood made a striking comeback with *Unforgiven* (1992) and *In The Line of Fire* (1993), a taut tale about a Secret Service agent and a potential presidential assassin. Both films won critical plaudits and were among their years' highest grossing films. *Unforgiven* won Eastwood numerous directing and acting awards, including Oscars for best picture and best direction and a nomination for an Oscar as best actor.

Begins Directing

Eastwood's interest in directing reached back to "Rawhide," but CBS allowed him only to direct trailers. He made an auspicious directorial debut in 1971 with *Play Misty for Me,* a thriller about a psychotic obsessed woman. It received good notices and did well at the box office, as did many of the over one dozen films he directed after it. Most starred him, but one of his finest efforts did not: *Bird* (1988) dealt movingly with the downbeat life of the jazz great Charlie Parker. Eastwood was a life-long fan of jazz, and jazz music and songs have been a frequent presence on the soundtracks of many of his films.

Eastwood's direction has been described as "a lean location sense of realism"; his technique shows economy, vitality, imagination, and a good sense of humor. In 1993 he said that "favorites among his own films" were *Play Misty for Me, The Outlaw Josey Wales, Unforgiven,* and *Bronco Billy,* a sweet 1980 movie about an ex-shoe-salesman from New Jersey (played by Eastwood) who has formed a wild West show with a group of misfits.

Finally Earns Critical Acclaim

From the early 1980s. the critical community began to reassess Eastwood's contribution to cinema. Open hostility turned to grudging acceptance and finally to admiration. More and more people began to appreciate Eastwood's contribution as producer and director, especially in his smaller, more personal films, including *Play Misty for Me* and *Honkytonk Man.* While Eastwood told the *New York Times Magazine* that he "never begged for respectability," he nonetheless flew to Paris in 1985 to accept the honor of Chevalier des Arts et Lettres, a French national award.

In 1992, with *Unforgiven,* Eastwood finally won his first Academy Awards. After the ceremony, Eastwood told reporters that the wait for the award had been worth it. "I think it means more to me now," he was quoted as saying in the *Philadelphia Inquirer.* "If you win it when you're 20 or 30 years old, you're wondering, 'Where do I go from here?' . . . You learn to take your work seriously and not yourself seriously, and that comes with time." Three years later, at the 1995 Academy Awards, the film community reaffirmed its respect for Eastwood's body of work. The Academy bestowed upon him the Irving G. Thalberg Memorial Award, which is given to producers or directors for consistently high quality of motion picture production.

Eastwood has not, however, rested on his laurels. In the summer of 1995, he directed and starred in *The Bridges of Madison County.* The film, based on the best-selling novel by Robert James Waller, follows a National Geographic photographer as he is sent on assignment to photograph covered bridges in Iowa. While there he has a passionate three-day affair with an Italian-born farm wife, played by Meryl Streep. The film enjoyed success as a classic "three-handkerchief weepie." It also received favorable notices from critics. Many praised Eastwood's even-handed and sensitive depiction of the brief affair and, especially, of the farm wife, who came across as much more realized character on screen than she did in the novel.

Absolute Power released in early 1997, was less of a triumph with the pubic and with critics. Eastwood once again directed but played a less romanic lead. His character, an aging Washington, D.C. burglar, accidently watches the president of the United States kill a woman during a sexual tryst.

Seeks Privacy in Personal Life

"Not a Hollywood type," as a 1993 profile explained, Eastwood has made his home in Carmel, California, far from filmdom's party circuit. There he lived a private life, spending time with friends who were not involved in the entertainment industry. And he is known as a loyal employer whose production crew included people who had worked for him for 15 years.

Politically conservative, Eastwood was several times approached by the Republican Party for various positions but he eschewed any public political stance except for a two-year term (1986-1988) as mayor of Carmel. Eastwood sought the position because he disapproved of zoning laws in the village. After serving one two-year term—and changing the laws—he stepped down with no regrets.

Eastwood married Maggie Johnson in 1953; they had a son Kyle (born 1968) and a daughter Alison (born 1972). They separated in the late 1970s, and the marriage ended in 1984, with Maggie Johnson reportedly receiving a settlement of $25 million.

After separating from Johnson, Eastwood spent more than a decade living with actress Sandra Locke, who appeared in many of his films. That relationship broke up acrimoniously at the end of the 1980s, resulting in a palimony suit eventually settled out of court at a cost to Eastwood of more than $7 million. He then established a relationship with Frances Fisher, an actress who appeared in *The Pink Cadillac*. The two had a baby girl in August 1993, whom they named Francesca Ruth.

In April 1993, Eastwood was interviewed by Dina Ruiz, a television news anchorwoman in Los Angeles, California. Three years later, in March 1996, Eastwood, then aged 65, married Dina Ruiz, 30, in a small private ceremony at the Las Vegas, Nevada, home of gambling casino magnate Steve Wynn.

By 1997, Eastwood had appeared in more than 40 motion pictures and directed 19 of them himself. Over the years his talents, both in front of and behind the camera, have been reevaluated. He won newfound respect for his talents as actor and director. He remained a potent force in the film industry through the 1990s, and for the public he became (to use *Newsweek*'s phrase) "An American Icon."

Further Reading

For additional reading about Eastwood see Boris Zmijewsky and Lee Pfeiffer, *The Films of Clint Eastwood* (1993), which provides an up-to-date overview of Eastwood's career; C. Frayling, *Clint Eastwood* (London, 1992), a better than average popular biography; and Paul Smith, *Clint Eastwood* (1992), a somewhat overheated attempt to deal with Eastwood's impact on American culture. There is a fascinating interview with Eastwood in *Focus on Film,* #25 (Summer-Autumn 1976), undertaken when Eastwood talked with almost no one. There are also useful and interesting articles such as Bernard Weinraub, "The Last Icon," *GQ* (March 1993); and John Vinocur, "Clint Eastwood, Seriously," *New York Times Magazine* (February 24, 1985). An intellectual approach with some good Eastwood quotes is Richard Combs, "Shadowing the Hero," in *Sight and Sound* (October 1992).

Bingham, Dennis. *Acting Male: Masculinities in the Films of James Stewart, Jack Nicholson, & Clint Eastwood* (Rutgers University Press, 1994). Clinch, Minty. *Clint Eastwood* (Hoder & Stoughthton, 1995). Gallafent, Edward. *Clint Eastwood: Filmaker and Star* (Continuum, 1994). Knapp, Laurence. *Directed by Clint Eastwood: Eighteen Films Analyzed.* (McFarland, 1996). Munn, Michael. *Clint Eastwood: Hollywood's Loner* (Parkwest, 1993). O'Brien, Daniel. *Clint Eastwood Film Maker* (Trafalgar Square, 1997). Schickel, Richard. *Clint Eastwood: A Biography* (McKay, 1996). Tanitch, Robert. *Clint Eastwood* (Studio Vista Books, 1995). Thompson, Douglas. *Clint Eastwood: Riding High* (1992). □

Dorman Bridgman Eaton

Dorman Bridgman Eaton (1823-1899), American lawyer and author, was a strong advocate of civil service reform and wrote the draft on which the Civil Service Act of 1883 was based.

Dorman Eaton was born in Hardwick, Vt., on June 27, 1823. After graduation from the University of Vermont and Harvard Law School, he practiced law in New York City. He distinguished himself as a legal scholar by editing a new edition of James Kent's *Commentaries* and other works, and as a practicing attorney, especially as counsel for the Erie Railroad. In connection with some of the bitter controversies involving the railroad, he was attacked and seriously injured by unidentified assailants.

Meanwhile, Eaton began his lifelong interest in governmental reform, assisting in the creation of a New York City municipal board of health and a professional fire department and in the reorganization of the police courts. In 1856 he married Annie Foster.

In 1870 Eaton gave up his private practice to devote full time to the cause of national civil service reform. George William Curtis, Carl Schurz, and Eaton were among the earliest advocates of ending the spoils system in national politics. Under president U.S. Grant, Eaton succeeded Curtis as chairman of the first civil service commission, serving from 1873 to 1875, when the commission became ineffectual after. Congress cut off its funds.

In the early 1870s Eaton had toured Europe to study civil service reform, and in the late 1870s, at the request of President Rutherford B. Hayes, he revisited England to make a formal report on its merit system. The result, published as *The Civil Service in Great Britain: A History of Abuses and Reforms and Their Bearing upon American Politics* (1880), was influential in the movement for reform in the United States. In the meantime, the New York Civil Service Reform Association, the nucleus of the powerful National Civil Service Reform League, had been founded in Eaton's home.

The assassination of President James Garfield in 1881 by a disappointed office seeker gave impetus to the reform movement, which culminated in the passage of the Pendleton Civil Service Act of 1883. The final bill was based on Eaton's draft. President Chester A. Arthur appointed Eaton chairman of the three-man Civil Service Commission established under the new law, a post he held until his resignation in 1886.

Renewing his interest in city government, Eaton wrote *The Government of Municipalities* (1899), one of the first such studies. He died on Dec. 23, 1899. In his will he endowed chairs at Columbia and Harvard universities to continue the study of national and municipal government.

Further Reading

The work of Eaton and his fellow reformers is covered in Frank Mann Stewart, *The National Civil Service Reform League* (1929); Paul P. Van Riper, *History of the United States Civil Service, 1789-1957* (1958); and Leonard D. White, *The Republican Era, 1869-1901: A Study in Administrative History* (1958). □

Abba Eban

The Israeli statesman, diplomat, and scholar Abba Eban (born 1915) served as Israel's United Nations representative and ambassador to the United States until 1959. He was Israel's foreign minister between 1966 and 1974.

Abba Solomon Eban was born in 1915 in Capetown, South Africa. His parents moved to Great Britain during his childhood, where Eban studied classics and oriental languages at Cambridge University. He learned seven languages, including Arabic, Hebrew, and Persian. At Cambridge he was active as a student Zionist leader, in the University Labor Society, and as president of the Student Union. During World War II he volunteered as a private in the British army, rising to the rank of major. One of his assignments between 1942 and 1944 was chief instructor at the British military's Middle East Arabic Center in Jerusalem. Because of his Zionist connections he also served as liaison officer for the British with the Jewish Agency, predecessor of the Israeli government.

Present at Israel's Founding

After the war Eban was persuaded by the Zionist leader Chaim Weizmann (later to be Israel's first president) to devote his extensive knowledge of the Middle East to service with the Jewish Agency, and in 1947 he was its liaison officer with the United Nations Special Committee on Palestine, which recommended partition of the country into

Jewish and Arab states and an international enclave including Jerusalem. Before Israel was created Eban was a principal spokesman of the Jewish Agency at the United Nations, where he spoke eloquently on behalf of establishing a Jewish state.

Eban's outstanding as skills as speech maker and diplomat led to his appointment as the United Nations representative of the new government of Israel in 1948 and as its first permanent representative from 1949 to 1959. Simultaneously he was Israel's ambassador to the United States. In this dual role Eban acquired prominence as Israel's leading spokesman abroad and as one of the most persuasive orators at the United Nations. To many Jews and other Americans Eban came to symbolize Israel and its struggle to survive during the critical first ten years. He helped Israel's first prime minister, David Ben Gurion, to explain Israel's difficult position through several international crises, including the War of Independence in 1948 and the Sinai (Suez) War with Egypt in 1956.

Lauded as Learned Politician

After more than a decade in the United States Eban returned to Israel, and in 1959 he was elected to the Knesset (parliament) as a representative of the Mapai (Labor) Party. He served in the cabinet of the Labor government, first as minister without portfolio, later as minister of education and culture between 1959 and 1963. In the latter post he attempted to introduce educational reforms including increased opportunity for the growing number of Jewish immigrants from lesser developed countries in Asia and

Africa. While active in his cabinet jobs Eban also found time to continue his activity as scholar and author of over a dozen books, including a biography of his mentor, Chaim Weizmann. He also was president of Israel's prestigious scientific research center, the Weismann Institute of Science, at Rehovot, from 1958 to 1966.

Adroit Foreign Minister

After Ben Gurion's successor, Levi Eschol, became prime minister, Eban served as deputy prime minister between 1963 and 1966. Afterwards, he served in what was perhaps his most important position, foreign minister of Israel from 1966 to 1974. During this era Israel fought two of its bloodiest wars, the June 1967 Six-Day War and the Yom Kippur War in October 1973. As foreign minister Eban had to tread a delicate balance: resisting pressures from the international community on Israel to return the territory it had seized in 1967 from Egypt, Syria, and Jordan, yet appearing willing to compromise.

After the 1973 war Eban helped to negotiate, through the United States, partial Israeli withdrawal from the Sinai territory taken from Egypt and from the Golan Heights territory taken from Syria. Within the Israeli cabinet Eban was generally perceived as the spokesman for moderation in foreign policy, preferring the use of diplomacy rather than military force to meet the many crises confronting the nation. Although his advice and recommendations were not always accepted by the government, he was the most eloquent defender of whatever policy was finally decided upon.

Although Eban left the cabinet in 1974 he remained active in the Knesset and as a leader of the Labor Party. In the Labor Party he was identified with the "doves" who called for Israel to withdraw from most of the territory occupied in the 1967 war in exchange for a genuine secure peace settlement with the Arab states. (In contrast, Israel's Likud Party took a much more conservative stance.) He feared that if Israel kept the occupied territories their large Arab populations, especially the Arabs in the West Bank of Jordan, would eventually undermine Israel's claim to be a Jewish state.

Active as Senior Statesperson

Between 1974 and 1984 Eban had more time for scholarly pursuits, publishing several new volumes on the history of the Jews and of Israel and on international affairs. These include *The New Diplomacy: International Affairs in the Modern Age* (1983) and *Heritage, Civilization, and the Jews* (1985). When the Labor Party returned to lead the government as a result of the 1984 election, Eban was appointed to be chairman of the powerful Knesset committee on foreign and security affairs. In this role he again was able to exercise a moderating influence on Israel's relations with the Arab states and in foreign policy generally.

Eban also chaired the committee that investigated the Jonathan Pollard spy scandal in 1987. Pollard was a civilian employee of the U.S. Navy who was later convicted of selling classified information from U.S. military files to Israel. The bipartisan committee itself came under fire from prominent Labor Party colleagues Shimon Peres and Yitzhak Rabin for its what they termed its pro-Likud stance.

Eban served in the Knesset until 1988. Though in his eighties, he continued to play an active role in Israeli politics, at least from the sidelines. His fifteenth book, *Personal Witness: Israel Through My Eyes,* was published in 1993 and became a five-part series hosted by Eban on American public television.

Further Reading

Eban is listed in the *Encyclopaedia Judaica* and in the *Encyclopaedia of Zionism and Israel,* also in *Who's Who 1985-1986.* A full length biography, *Eban* (1972), was written by Robert St. John. Abba Eban published his own story, *An Autobiography* (1978), along with *Personal Witness: Israel Through My Eyes* (1993). □

Hermann Ebbinghaus

The German psychologist Hermann Ebbinghaus (1850-1909) is best known for his innovative contribution to the study of memory through nonsense syllables.

Hermann Ebbinghaus was born on Jan. 24, 1850, near Bonn. In 1867 he went to the University of Bonn and somewhat later attended the universities of Berlin and Halle. After the Franco-Prussian War he continued his philosophical studies at Bonn, completing a dissertation on Eduard von Hartmann's *Philosophy of the Unconscious,* and received his doctorate in 1873.

Ebbinghaus's goal was to establish psychology on a quantitative and experimental basis. While professor at Berlin, he founded a psychological laboratory, and in 1890 he founded the journal *Zeitschrift für Psychologie und Physiologie der Sinnesorgane.* He became full professor in Breslau in 1894, where he also founded a laboratory. In 1905 he moved to Halle, where he died on Feb. 26, 1909.

In psychology Ebbinghaus found his own way. None of his instructors determined in any marked way the direction of his thinking. A major influence, however, was the combination of philosophical and scientific points of view he found in Gustav Theodor Fechner. He acknowledged his debt in the systematic treatise *Die Grundzüge der Psychologie,* which he dedicated to Fechner.

Ebbinghaus was an unusually good lecturer. His buoyancy and humor, together with the unusual clarity and ease of his presentation, assured him of large audiences. Another valuable trait was his Jamesian tolerance, which led him as editor to publish widely diverse opinions—a policy vital to a young science.

Ebbinghaus himself published relatively little. No records exist of the work he did before he published *Memory* (1885). In the introduction to this work, in the section on nonsense syllables, he says only, "I have hit upon the following method," and goes on to discuss the nature and mechanics of nonsense syllables. Memory, a fundamental central function, was thereby subjected to experimental investigation.

In 1894 William Dilthey claimed that the new psychology could never be more than descriptive and that attempts to make it explanatory and constructive were wrong in principle, leading to nothing but confusion of opinion and fact. Since this amounted to an attack on the very keystone of Ebbinghaus's faith, he undertook, despite his reluctance for controversy, to defend psychology as he understood it. In an article in the *Zeitschrift für Psychologie* for 1896, he justified the use of hypothesis and causal explanation in psychology.

When Ebbinghaus died, the *Grundzüge* that he had begun early in the 1890s was only a little more than half completed; a colleague, Ernst Dürr, finished it. The major virtues of these volumes lie in their readableness and convenient format rather than in any radical approach to psychology, but these qualities, together with their comprehensiveness and minor innovations, were sufficient to produce an enthusiastic reception. Ebbinghaus's *Abriss der Psychologie* (1908), an elementary textbook of psychology, also achieved considerable success.

Ebbinghaus's influence on psychology, great as it was, has been mostly indirect. *Memory*, undoubtedly his outstanding contribution, was the starting point for practically all of the studies that have followed in this field.

Further Reading

Ebbinghaus's *Memory: A Contribution to Experimental Psychology* was reissued with a new introduction by Ernest R. Hilgard (1964). There is no biographical work on Ebbinghaus. The most complete picture of him is in Edwin G. Boring, *A History of Experimental Psychology* (1929; 2d ed. 1950). See also Gardner Murphy, *Historical Introduction to Modern Psychology* (1929; rev ed. 1948). □

Friedrich Ebert

The German Social Democratic leader Friedrich Ebert (1871-1925) served as the first president of Germany.

Friedrich Ebert was born in Heidelberg on Feb. 4, 1871, the son of a master tailor. Trained as a saddler, he turned to socialism at the age of 18 under the influence of an uncle. Although the anti-Socialist law was repealed that same year (1889), political harassment forced the young journeyman to change jobs and residences several times until he settled in Bremen in May 1891. Elected head of the local saddlers' union shortly after his arrival, he devoted his time increasingly to politics. He left his job and joined the Social Democratic organ *Bremer Buerger-Zeitung,* becoming editor in March 1893.

A tireless agitator, popular campaigner, and able organizer, Ebert quickly rose in the Bremen Social Democratic party (SPD). In 1900 he was elected to the City Parliament and became secretary of the local consolidated union organization. From his dominant position in the Bremen labor movement he entered the national party hierarchy in 1905 as secretary of the party Executive Committee and in 1912 was elected to the Reichstag (Imperial Diet). Here his reputation as a mediator between the right and left wings of the party brought his election to the SPD Executive in 1913; in 1916 he became party floor leader in the Reichstag.

A vigorous advocate of peace and an opponent of annexations during World War I, Ebert was the man to whom the defeated monarchist leadership turned in the face of threatening revolution and chaos in 1918. Initially opposed to the proclamation of the republic, he organized a provisional People's Commission of Social Democrats and Independent Socialists on Nov. 9, 1918. This government signed the armistice with the Western Powers (Nov. 11, 1918), dealt with revolutionary threats from left and right (chiefly through an agreement with the army, the "Ebert-Groener Deal"), and made preparations for the election of a Constitutional Assembly (January 1919). On Feb. 11, 1919, the National Assembly elected Ebert provisional president of the new German Republic; he was reelected by the Reichstag in October 1922.

Ebert gave the presidential office a special dignity through his honesty, simplicity, strong convictions, and concern for the common man. Continually striving to maintain government stability, he promoted strong coalitions of the moderate forces of the Reichstag in order to combat the numerous antirepublican threats from right and left and to

strengthen a foreign policy of reconciliation. He was, however, virulently attacked by the nationalist press, and his health finally broke in a bitter struggle against a malicious accusation of high treason (December 1924) which was upheld by a reactionary court. He died in Berlin on Feb. 28, 1925.

Further Reading

There is no biography of Ebert in English. For general information see Erich Eyck, *A History of the Weimar Republic* (2 vols., 1954-1956; trans., 2 vols., 1962-1963), and Carl E. Schorske, *German Social Democracy, 1905-1917* (1955). □

Adolphe Felix Sylvestre Eboué

Adolphe Felix Sylvestre Eboué (1885-1944) was a governor of French Equatorial Africa. As a successful and apparently well-adjusted black Frenchman, he represented the epitome of French assimilationist policy.

F elix Eboué was born in Cayenne, French Guiana, on Dec. 26, 1885, the son of gold washer and of a comparatively well-educated mother. In 1901 he traveled to France on a scholarship to complete his secondary education at Bordeaux, where he also picked up an adolescent interest in the political ideas of French Socialist leader Jean Jaurès as well as a lifelong penchant for sport. Between 1904 and 1908 he pursued twin courses of study at the Paris Law School and at the École Coloniale.

Early Civil Service

Upon graduating from the École Coloniale in 1908, Eboué asked to be assigned to the French Congo (modern Republic of Congo), an area which had just acquired considerable notoriousness as a result of widespread abuses committed against the African population. He was sent to the remote and undesirable district of Ubangi-Shari (modern Central African Republic), where he labored tenaciously against administrative inertia and covert racial prejudice, making slow but steady progress on the civil service ladder and collecting anthropological material, which he later published in book form: *Les Peuples de l'Oubangui-Chari* (1931; The People of Ubangi-Shari) and *La Clef musicale des langages tambourinés et sifflés* (1935; The Musical Key to Drum and Whistle Languages).

Eboué's liberal views, his Masonic affiliations, and his friendship with West Indian novelist René Maran, whose prize-winning novel *Batouala* (1921) painted an unflattering picture of French Equatorial Africa, appear to have caused some official annoyance with Eboué during the 1920s. But Eboué was no anticolonialist and seems to have taken a dim view—at least initially—of the criticism leveled against

French rule by such men as novelist André Gide and journalist Albert Londres.

In 1932, having finally been promoted to a senior grade in the colonial civil service, Eboué was dispatched to Martinique, then served as secretary general of French Sudan (modern Mali) from 1934 to 1936. With the coming to power of the left-of-center Popular Front coalition in 1936, however, Eboué received his first gubernatorial appointment in Guadeloupe, and although political influences resulted in his recall from that West Indian island after 2 years, he was given a key post in 1938 as governor of Chad.

The appointment of a black governor by a Jewish minister (Georges Mandel) took on additional significance against the ominous backdrop provided by the rise of German and Italian fascism. Also, Chad had a considerable strategic value in view of Mussolini's expansionist policies in Africa. Eboué stepped up military preparedness by developing military roads through northern Chad, which were later used by the Free French forces in their victorious advance into Libya.

Free French Leader in Africa

When France fell in 1940, Eboué refused to follow the Vichy government's orders to break all relations with Great Britain and on Aug. 26, 1940, became the first governor in Africa to rally to De Gaulle, a move that was emulated within a few days by the governors of French Congo and Ubangi-Shari. French Equatorial Africa thus became the first bastion of the Free French government. On Nov. 12, 1940, Eboué was appointed governor general of all Equatorial Africa, and in December, Free French forces, using Chad as a base, began military operations against the Italians.

Eboué's main efforts during the next 3 years were devoted to the pursuit of the war effort, but he also found time to introduce some of the reforms he had advocated as a junior official, such as the development of secondary education and the protection of African values and institutions. At the same time, however, his opposition to any kind of nationalist movement was similar to that of any high official: during his incumbency the Amicaliste movement in the Congo was severely repressed, and its leader, André Matswa, died in jail in 1942. Eboué's last public action was his participation in the 1944 Brazzaville conference which laid down the principles of postwar French colonial policy. On May 27, 1944, while on leave from his post, he died of pneumonia in Cairo.

Further Reading

A biography of Eboué is Brian Weinstein, *Eboué* (1972). Satisfactory histories of Equatorial Africa are scarce. A survey of African history in which Eboué is mentioned is Roland Oliver and J. D. Fage, *A Short History of Africa* (1964). See also Basil Davidson and Adenekan Ademola, eds., *The New West Africa* (1953). A longer study that combines history, sociology, and anthropology is Virginia Thompson and Richard Adloff, *The Emerging States of French Equatorial Africa* (1960). □

Sir John Carew Eccles

The Australian neurophysiologist Sir John Carew Eccles (1903-1997) made a series of original contributions to the knowledge of how nerve cells communicate with each other.

John Carew Eccles was born in Melbourne, Australia, on January 27, 1903, the first of two children of two teachers. He attended high school in Warambool, Victoria, but graduated in Melbourne in 1919. He went on to Melbourne University to study medicine, and excelled at multiple athletics. He married Irene Miller in 1928, with whom he would have nine children. When he graduated from college in 1925 at the top of his class, with a bachelor of science and medicine degrees, and as a Rhodes scholar, he realized his dream to attend Oxford University. There he worked with Sir Charles Scott Sherrington, probably the greatest student of the physiology of the nervous system in the 20th century. Eccles carried on and developed further his teacher's scientific and philosophical ideas. He graduated from Magdalen College in Oxford in 1927, again with first-class honors and a scholarship to Exeter College, Oxford. Side by side with Sherrington, they investigated nerve impulses and synapses, which Sherrington had defined in 1897. In 1929 Oxford awarded Eccles a masters of arts and a doctor of philosophy degrees. Eccles continued to research the brain at Oxford until he returned to Australia in 1937.

During the early 1930s Eccles had become interested in the nature of synaptic transmission, particularly in the fundamental question of how signals are transferred from one nerve cell to another. For the next 30 years he pursued this theme in his characteristic style, which was different from that of most scientists. He generally proposed a hypothesis, made it as precise as possible, and championed it with enthusiasm and energy until eventually it was either found to be false or was greatly modified by new experimental data. While many workers feel it is a sign of failure if a pet hypothesis has to be abandoned, Eccles took pleasure in this and was stimulated into a new formulation.

In 1937 Eccles moved to Sydney, where he headed the Kanematsu Memorial Institute, a small, isolated research institute attached to a local hospital. With several younger colleagues, including Bernard Katz, who influenced him greatly, he studied the transmission of impulses from nerve to muscle until 1943. During this time, he carried out studies of synaptic transmission in the mammalian nervous system by making electrical recordings from the interior of individual nerve cells and analyzing in great detail the processes of excitation, as well as inhibition, at cell junctions. During World War II he aided in the Australian war effort by serving on committees on vision, hearing and airsickness, and by synthesizing blood serum for medical facilities.

In 1944 Eccles moved to New Zealand, and until 1951 taught physiology at the University of Otago Medical School in Dunedin. He also continued his research on

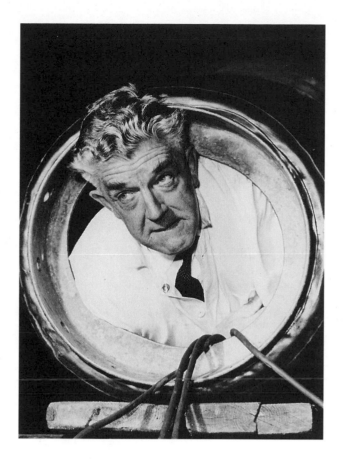

synaptic transmission, and it was in 1951 that he actually disproved his own hypothesis about the electrical nature of synaptic transmission, and henceforth championed the alternate theory of chemical neurotransmission. His own tactic of wildly espousing theories and then rigorously working to prove them wrong was reinforced when he met Dr. Karl Popper in New Zealand, who encouraged him to do just that.

These findings further crystallized when he left Otago for the John Curtin School of Medical Research of the Australian National University in Canberra, where he became professor of physiology in 1952. In league with other researcher, he discovered how to induce certain synaptic reactions on a chemical and ionic level, and how to rewire nerve endings. Due to his cumulative research, Eccles was knighted in 1958, and was jointly awarded the Nobel Prize for Medicine and Physiology with Alan Hodgkin and Andrew Huxley in 1963 for their respective studies on the production and transmission of nerve impulses.

Eccles was forced to retire from the Australian National University in 1966 upon reached their mandatory retirement age, but quickly accepted an enormous job offer from the American Medical Association to head their largest research group at their Institute for Biomedical Research in Chicago. Soon after, in 1968, he served as Distinguished Professor of Physiology and Medicine and the Dr. Henry C. and Bertha H. Buswell Research Fellow at the medical school of New York State University in Buffalo. Eccles's investigations continued to cover additional areas of the nervous system, as his aim was always an understanding of the working of the entire brain. He explored the functional interconnections in the cerebellum, summarizing his results in *The Cerebellum as a Neuronal Machine* (1967). In his personal life, he divorced his wife of almost forty years in 1968; a little over two weeks later he was remarried to Helena Taborikova, a medical researcher of some reknown.

Eccles's influence extended beyond his immediate scientific circle. In Australia he was a founder and president of the Academy of Sciences. He published in numerous scientific journals, gave many public lectures, and wrote a series of books which had wide circulation, including *Physiology of Nerve Cells* (1957) and *Physiology of Synapses* (1964). He also edited *Brain and Conscious Experience* (1966). He died on May 2, 1997, at the age of 84, in Switzerland.

Further Reading

A sketch of Eccles's life is in Theodore L. Sourkes, *Nobel Prize Winners in Medicine and Physiology, 1901-1965* (rev. ed. 1967). His work is discussed in Alan Lloyd Hodgkin, *The Conduction of the Nervous Impulse* (1964), and in much greater detail in Ragnar Granit, *Charles Scott Sherrington: An Appraisal* (1967). A brief obituary which discussed his scientific accomplishments appeared in the May 3, 1997 edition of the *Washington Post* . □

Bülent Ecevit

Turkish politician and writer Bülent Ecevit (born 1925) was alternately prime minister and leader of the opposition in the 1970s; since 1989 he has chaired the Democratic Left Party.

Bülent Ecevit was born in Istanbul on May 28, 1925 into a learned and cultured family. His father was a physician and member of Turkey's new parliament as a representative of the Republican People's Party (RPP); Ecevit's mother was a teacher and painter. He graduated from the American Robert College in Istanbul in 1944 and later studied at the universities of Ankara, London, and Harvard. Following an interlude as an official with the Press Attaché's office at the Turkish Embassy in London, he returned to Turkey in 1950 and joined *Ulus,* the daily of the RPP, as a literary critic. He would later hold positions of foreign news editor, managing editor, political director, and chief columnist at the paper over the next several years.

Entered Politics

The RPP, the party of both his father and the founder of modern Turkey, Kemal Ataturk, had governed Turkey since 1923, but in 1950 lost its parliamentary majority for ten years to the Democrat Party. Ecevit was part of a new wave of intellectuals brought in to revitalize the party, partly through his recognition by Ismet Inönü, the RPP's elder statesman. In 1957 Ecevit was elected to Turkey's National Assembly and set about modernizing RPP by establishing its research center. The following year he held the position as representative for Turkey at the Council of Europe. After a

military intervention on May 27, 1960, Ecevit was appointed to the constituent assembly which was to draft a new constitution. In 1961 he was elected to the National Assembly. Later that year, when RPP chair Inönü formed a new government, Ecevit was appointed minister of labor.

Ecevit initiated significant labor legislation during his tenure over the next few years, mainly through recognizing the importance of establishing strong ties with the country's newly emergent urban working class and courting their trade unions. Ecevit shepherded Turkey's first right-to-strike act into law, a significant labor achievement. Convinced that his party should be oriented toward socio-economic reform, he strove to steer its 1965 National Assembly election platform in a "left-of-center" direction, despite the protests of conservative circles. Inönü's support enabled Ecevit to carry through this change of orientation; however, the RPP lost the elections, perhaps because of its new stance, to another mass party, the Justice Party, which formed the new government. Nevertheless, Ecevit was appointed RPP secretary-general in 1966.

Decline, Then Comeback, of RPP

Although the RPP fared even worse in 1969 elections than in 1965, Ecevit gradually consolidated his position as the acknowledged leader of the party group advocating socio-economic reform. Soon after a second military intervention of March 12, 1971, a power struggle between Ecevit and the aging Inönü erupted. In 1972 Ecevit became the RPP's chairman, leading the party to victory in the October 1973 National Assembly elections and demonstrating his charisma in speeches before huge crowds, with whom he created successful rapport through his populist flair. However, although the RPP received a plurality, its share came to only 33.3 percent of the overall vote, which meant it had to form a coalition.

Crisis on Cyprus

On January 25, 1974, Ecevit became prime minister of a coalition government in which the RPP was the senior partner and the National Salvation Party, a newly formed political grouping with an Islamic orientation, the junior one. The government lasted only until September 11, 1974, primarily because of political rivalry and personal friction between the partners. The unavoidable give-and-take meant that few significant reforms could be achieved; the most notable success was the Turkish intervention in Cyprus in July 1974, which Ecevit had authorized. Greek forces had invaded the island and ousted its president; fearing annexation of Cyprus into Greece, Turkey sent troops to protect its citizens there. The situation threatened to launch a war between Greece and Turkey—an unprecedented danger, as both were members of the North Atlantic Treaty Organization—but instead it dissolved into a political stalemate with both countries sharing a divided island. Negotiations to resolve the dispute were still ongoing in 1997.

Though a busy politician, Ecevit also pursued his literary interests. He was the translator of part of the sacred Indian text the *Bhagwad Gita* into Turkish, and wrote poetry and numerous treatises on his country's history and politics. His list of published works include *Şiirleri* (1976), *Ortanin solu* (title means Left of the Middle'; 1966), and *Atatürk ve devrimcilik* (title means Ataturk and the Revolution'; 1970).

Beginning in November 1974 the RPP returned to parliamentary opposition, and the Justice Party formed a coalition government with smaller parties in March 1975. In the June 1977 National Assembly elections the RPP came in first again with even stronger support than in 1973, and much of its success was attributed to Ecevit's charismatic leadership. Modern Turks had come to seen the party of Ataturk as elitist and out of touch, and Ecevit helped attract fresh support by taking its platform in a new direction and somewhat distancing the party from its past. Significantly, he courted voters from among the urban working class and poor rural farmers.

New Responsibility

After a short-lived coalition government headed by the Justice Party, Ecevit succeeded in forming a government in December 1977, this time supported by two small splinter parties and several independents. This precarious majority enabled Ecevit to serve as prime minister until October 1979. The Justice Party then set up a coalition government which, in turn, was dismissed by the third military intervention on September 12, 1980. Parliament was dissolved and political parties were closed down soon afterwards, their leaders banned from political activity for ten years. When Ecevit continued to give political interviews, he was briefly jailed. Upon Turkey's return to civilian government in late 1983 neither the RPP nor Ecevit himself participated in politics, although Ecevit's wife, Rahšan, was increasingly active politically in the new Democratic Socialist Party (DSP), which he had helped organize.

In 1986 Ecevit was charged with violating the ban on political activity; he was acquitted, and the following year a national referendum voted in favor of lifting that ban altogether. He then became chair of the party. The year 1987 also brought elections, but the DSP failed to gain any seats in parliament. Ecevit resigned as a result, but was reelected its chair in 1988.

An intellectual who has also translated the works of T. S. Eliot and penned poetry himself, Ecevit showed himself to be both an ideologue and a man of action. His brief tenures in office hardly sufficed for effectively attending to Turkey's serious socio-economic problems. Ecevit, however, seemed to maintain his popular appeal throughout, advocating a brighter future based on rapid economic development and a new social order—a libertarian democracy focusing on improving living standards, yet consistent with Turkey's national interests. Ecevit considered himself a social democrat, while his political opponents saw him as a radical leftist; he aroused both unbounded admiration and intense criticism.

In the early 1990s Ecevit remained as chair of the DSP. The party won eleven percent of the vote in 1991 elections, and Ecevit returned to a seat in the National Assembly. The continued animosity between he and Inönü prevented any alliance between their respective parties, however. Ecevit also continued to pursue his scholarly interests, and this period would see the publication of several more books. These included *The Changing World and Gurhey* (1990), *Mithat Pasha and the Historical Process of the Turkish Economy* (1990), *The Impact on Turkish Politics of the Social Culture,* and *Anti-Memoirs* (1991).

Further Reading

Ecevit is listed in Marquis' *Who's Who in the World.* For his views, see Ecevit's "Labor in Turkey as a New Social and Political Force," in K. H. Karpat and Contributors, *Social Change and Politics in Turkey* (1973) and Ecevit's "Left of Center: What Is It?" in K. H. Karpat (editor), *Political and Social Thought in the Contemporary Middle East* (2nd edition, 1982).

Several books discuss recent Turkish politics and Ecevit's role therein: Geoffrey Lewis, *Modern Turkey* (1974); Jacob M. Landau, *Radical Politics in Modern Turkey* (1974); Ergun Özbudun, *Social Change and Political Participation in Turkey* (1976); Feroz Ahmad, *The Turkish Experiment in Democracy, 1950-1975* (1977); C. H. Dodd, *Democracy and Development in Turkey* (1979); Walter F. Weiker, *The Modernization of Turkey* (1981); and Frank Tachau, *Turkey: The Politics of Authority, Democracy and Development* (1984). □

José Estéban Echeverría

The Argentine author, poet, and political theorist José Estéban Echeverría (1805-1851) pioneered the romantic mood in literature in the New World and

also formulated the political ideals of a secret group combating the dictatorial regime of Rosas.

José Estéban Echeverría was born on Sept. 2, 1805, in Buenos Aires. His father died shortly thereafter, and the boy was raised by his mother and several doting aunts. For reasons unexplained and apparently beyond his control, he left school to take a job as a customshouse clerk.

Out of this reflective period came a determination to seek a fuller education than Echeverría's young country could provide. In 1826 Echeverría settled in Paris and resumed his formal studies, most significantly, political science from a sociological perspective. His reading broadened to include writers cultivating a new and exciting mode: Goethe, Schiller, and especially Byron. From these readings developed a growing sense of self-identification with romantic expression and ideas.

By 1830, Echeverría was back in Buenos Aires. His early romantic poems, including "Elvira, or the Bride of the Plate" (1832), attracted little interest. His volume of verses entitled *Consolations* (1834) had considerable public success, owing no doubt to its dominant themes of patriotism and romantic love. In *Rhymes* (1837) he included a long narrative poem called *The Captive Woman,* in which his poetic genius is wedded to national themes. In this poem, with striking descriptions of the Pampa, the Indian tribes of the area, and the romantic adventures of two young lovers, he accomplished his aim of "Americanizing" Argentine literature.

In 1838 Echeverría was instrumental in founding the Association of May, a secret society whose goal was to return Argentina to democratic rule. Its credo, composed by Echeverría and published in 1846 under the title *The Socialist Dogma,* was an idealistic work of democratic propaganda. The dictator Juan Manuel de Rosas eventually obliged many of the association members, including Echeverría, to flee to Uruguay.

During the years remaining before his death in exile on Jan. 19, 1851, Echeverría wrote some relatively unsuccessful verse—"The Guitar" (1842) and its continuation "The Fallen Angel" (1846)—which dealt with the Don Juan theme. But it was a prose sketch, "The Slaughterhouse," found among his papers and published in 1871 that secured his literary reputation. This starkly realistic anecdote, which recounts the death of a young opponent of the Rosas regime at the hands of Rosas supporters employed at the Buenos Aires slaughterhouse, is one of the most powerful and memorable prose narratives ever written in Spanish America.

Further Reading

There is no book-length study of Echeverría's work in English. For general background see Alfred Coester, *The Literary History of Spanish America* (1916); Arturo Torres-Ríoseco, *The Epic of Latin American Literature* (1942); Pedro Henriquez-Ureña, *Literary Currents in Hispanic America* (1945) and *A Concise History of Latin American Culture* (1947; trans. 1966); Enrique Anderson-Imbert, *Spanish-American Literature: A History,* vol. 1 (trans. 1963; rev. ed. 1969); and Jean Franco, *An Introduction to Spanish-American Literature* (1969). Consult also the Instituto Internacional de Literatura Iberoamericana, *An Outline History of Spanish-America,* edited by John Englekirk and others (1941; 3d ed. 1965). □

Luis Echeverría Alvarez

Luis Echeverría Alvarez (born 1922) was the president of Mexico from 1970 to 1976. Although his major interest was foreign affairs, severe economic dislocations diverted his energies to domestic policies. Forced to devalue the Mexican peso twice, he left the presidency under a cloud of despondency.

Luis Echeverría was born on January 17, 1922, in Mexico's Federal District. He received his primary and secondary education in México City schools and his law degree at the Universidad Nacional Autónoma de México in 1945. After teaching law for several years Echeverría made his decision to pursue a political career and began working his way through the ranks of Mexico's Partido Revolucionario Institucional (PRI).

Political Career

National prominence came to Echeverría in 1957 when he was named chief administrative officer of the PRI's Central Executive Committee and was chosen to give the major nominating speech for the soon to be president Adolfo López Mateos. By 1964, during the presidential administration of Gustavo Díaz Ordaz, he was a member of the cabinet and served for six years as secretary of gobernación. Controversy engulfed him for the first time as he was chosen to negotiate with Mexico City's leftist students threatening to disrupt the opening of the Summer Olympic Games in 1968. His negotiations proved unsuccessful, and political violence resulted in several hundred deaths prior to the opening ceremonies of the Olympiad. In unfounded charges Echeverría took much of the blame for the break down of negotiations. Sensitive to attacks from the left, he sought to mollify his critics by espousing Third World rhetoric for the next two years. The criticism eased off, at least for the time being.

Echeverría's nomination as the presidential candidate of the PRI in 1969 assured his election to his country's highest post the following year, but he conducted a vigorous presidential campaign anyhow. He visited some 900 municipalities, covering 35,000 miles in all 29 Mexican states and the two territories. He relished the opportunity to debate with students and used the opportunity to cultivate the Third World and to criticize the United States.

Presidential Years

As president Luis Echeverría traveled abroad more extensively than any previous Mexican president. In addition to visiting a number of Latin American countries, his travels carried him to Japan, the People's Republic of China, England, Belgium, France, and the Soviet Union. The trips

were undertaken for the express purpose of opening new avenues of trade. Under his prodding the Mexican government supported the admission of the People's Republic of China to the United Nations. He repeatedly called for Third World countries to maintain their economic independence from the United States. The success and failures of his presidential administration, however, would be measured not on his relationship with the outside world but on his domestic policies.

Luis Echeverría embarked upon a series of policies designed to repudiate the conservative stance adopted by his predecessor, Gustavo Díaz Ordaz. To the distress of the conservative Mexican business community, he argued that it was time to slow down the pace of Mexico's industrialization and to renew state initiatives in rural Mexico. In keeping with this policy he supported a new agrarian reform law which encouraged the development of the *ejidos,* Mexico's rural communal landholdings. He placed major emphasis on extending the rural road system and rural electrification. Perhaps out of conviction, but perhaps to curry favor with the left, in 1971 he released the student prisoners incarcerated during the pre-Olympic demonstrations of 1968. He nationalized the tobacco and telephone industries, and in 1972 he granted diplomatic asylum to Hortensia Allende, widow of the murdered Chilean president Salvador Allende. All of these measures alienated those on the right side of the political spectrum but did little to garner the support of the left.

From 1971 to 1974 President Echeverría learned that his country was not immune from the rural and urban

terrorism associated with other Latin American countries. A series of bank robberies were traced to the Movimiento Armado Revolucionario when self-admitted terrorists bragged that their exploits had been undertaken in behalf of a new revolution. Political kidnappings followed in rapid succession. The victims included Julio Hirschfield, director of Mexico's airports; Jaime Castrejón, rector of the University of Guerrero; Terrence Leonhardy, United States consul general in Guadalajara; and Guadalupe Zuno Hernandez, President Echeverría's father-in-law and a former governor of Jalisco. Mexico's image as a progressive and stable republic was beginning to suffer at home and abroad. As events would soon demonstrate, however, President Echeverría's most serious difficulty was not terrorism, but rather an increasingly sluggish Mexican economy.

Economic Difficulties

The Echeverría administration was marked by a huge balance of payment deficits. Tourism, a leading source of Mexico's foreign exchange earning, declined as Echeverría's Third World rhetoric dissuaded many foreign tourists from visiting the country. Spot shortages of electric power and steel prompted a decline in the rate of economic growth. Inflation and high unemployment were rampant. In the summer of 1976 rumors began to circulate that for the first time in 22 years Mexico would have to devalue the peso. President Echeverría tried to convince his fellow countrymen that no devaluation was contemplated, but his repeated assurances did not prevent the flight of hundreds of millions of pesos as wealthy Mexicans exchanged their currency for dollars and invested them in the United States.

The inevitable devaluation came in September 1976, and the peso fell from 12.50 to 20.50 to the dollar, a 60 percent decline. A month later a second devaluation of an additional 40 percent was announced. The second devaluation in a month was psychologically more painful than the first. The president's attempts to blame all of Mexico's economic woes on multi-national corporations and on the United States convinced some, but not many. To be sure, Mexico was a dependent nation and one strongly influenced by the United States, but there was no way to disguise financial mismanagement of major proportions within the Echeverría administration.

Powerful Ex-President

Many Mexicans were relieved when Luis Echeverría turned over the presidential office to his successor, José López Portillo, in 1976. Those who anticipated that relations with the United States would improve markedly and that the Mexican economy would recover would be disappointed. The trends established during Echeverría's years in office would not be easily reversed.

Echeverría did not disappear from public life after his tenure as president. He became a *cacique,* a local political boss, and retained his position as president-for-life of the Center for Economic and Social Studies of the Third World. In 1995 he publicly criticized the most recent ex-president of Mexico, Carlos Salinas de Gortari. This broke an important rule in Mexican politics whereby ex-presidents were expected to remain silent on all political matters once they left office. Echeverría's actions caused much controversy and challenged the traditional role of the ex-president.

Further Reading

The diplomacy of the Echeverría administration is examined in Yoram Shapira, *Mexican Foreign Policy Under Echeverría* (1978). His domestic policy is treated in Daniel Levy and Gabriel Székely, *Mexico: Paradoxes of Stability and Change* (1983).

Additional Sources

Divon, Sam. "Silence is No Longer Golden for Former Presidents of Mexico." *The New York Times,* 24 September 1995.
Preston, Julia. "Salinas Denies New Charges by Mexico." *The New York Times,* 5 December 1995.
Samuel Schmidt, *The Deterioration of the Mexican Presidency: The Years of Luis Echeverría.* Tucson: The University of Arizona Press, 1991. □

Johann Maier von Eck

The German theologian Johann Maier von Eck (1486-1543) was a leading Roman Catholic opponent of Luther.

Johann Eck was born at Eck in Swabia, and like Martin Luther was of peasant stock. He studied at Heidelberg and other universities before becoming a doctor of theology in 1510. Eck taught at the University of Freiburg and after 1510 at the University of Ingolstadt. His academic career was early marked by a taste for humanist scholarship and intense criticism of ecclesiastical abuses, and he soon was widely known and respected as a scholar and orthodox churchman.

In 1517, when Luther, a professor of theology at the University of Wittenberg, published his 95 theses criticizing certain religious practices, Eck responded with a set of countertheses, which he called "Obelisks" and circulated privately. Karlstadt, a supporter of Luther's, obtained a copy of Eck's work and responded publicly with a collection of 400 theses. In 1518 Eck arranged for a debate with Luther and Karlstadt at Leipzig in the following year. At the debate Eck quickly disposed of Karlstadt and then took on Luther himself, skillfully drawing the reformer into extremely heretical positions and achieving a personal triumph.

When academic recognition was slow in coming, Eck took his case to Rome and elicited a papal bull from Leo X excommunicating Luther and condemning his position. Eck then brought the bull back to Germany and urged Emperor Charles V to apply force to Luther. Following Luther's condemnation, Eck remained the defender of Catholicism against him. Since Luther, however, refused to respond to his challenges, Eck turned his attention to other reformers and in a number of works condemned various theological errors. His career as the champion of orthodoxy culminated

in his Confutation of the Protestant Augsburg Confession in 1530.

Because of his opposition to the Reformation, Eck has been criticized as a scholar and as a man, both by his contemporary opponents and by many historians since the 16th century. Although he was indeed given to excessive self-praise and could be extremely insulting to his enemies, he was a distinguished scholar, a practical administrator, and a man very much aware of and sympathetic to the various intellectual currents of his time.

Further Reading

The standard biography of Eck is in German; there is no biography of him in English. The interested reader should consult general accounts of the Reformation such as *The New Cambridge Modern History,* vol. 2: G. R. Elton, ed., *The Reformation, 1520-1599* (1958); A. G. Dickens, *Reformation and Society in Sixteenth-Century Europe* (1966); and H. G. Koenigsberger and George L. Mosse, *Europe in the Sixteenth Century* (1968). Another source of information on Eck is the scholarship on Martin Luther; for example, good short accounts are in Roland H. Bainton, *Here I Stand: A Life of Martin Luther* (1950), and Robert Herndon Fife, Jr., *The Revolt of Martin Luther* (1957). □

Johann Eckhart

The German Dominican Johann Eckhart (ca. 1260-ca. 1327), called Meister Eckhart, founded German mysticism. A theologian and preacher, he represented God as dwelling in man's soul.

Born near Gotha in Thuringia, Johann Eckhart joined the Dominican order and studied in Strassburg and Cologne. In Paris he received a master's degree in theology in 1302. He became provincial in 1303, later vicar, in Bohemia. In 1311-1313 he was again in Paris as a teacher and then was professor of theology in Strassburg until 1323. Finally, he taught and preached as regent in Cologne.

Eckhart was twice involved in ecclesiastical conflicts. He favored the Pope in the struggle between Louis IV of Bavaria and the papacy over the imperial election. He was later a victim of the displeasure of Archbishop Henry II of Cologne, who was determined to destroy the Dominican order. Cited before a hostile tribunal, Eckhart was accused of heresy on 100 counts. He appealed to Pope John XXII in Avignon and was received there but returned to Cologne because of illness. He died soon after and was posthumously condemned, or suspected, of heresy on over 20 counts.

His Thought

Eckhart's doctrine of the "little spark in man's soul" (*Seelenfünklein*) afforded direct confrontation with God. To him God is not an aloof personal deity in whose image man was created, but a shapeless, incommensurable being ever unchanged and immanent in all matter and creatures. Once man sheds the dross of personal assertiveness and selfish drives, he can merge with God, becoming one with Him, like Christ. Eckhart was deemed heretical for denying a difference between the essence of God and that of creatures and for negating the temporal nature of the world. He was not, however, a pantheist.

Eckhart ranged far in his studies. He was beholden to Aristotle, St. Albertus Magnus, and St. Thomas Aquinas, but also to the Neoplatonism of the Spanish rabbi Maimonides and the Moslem philosopher Averroës. As a preacher and prolific writer, he addressed the people in the vernacular and his fellow clerics in Latin. He coined many German philosophical terms, and scholasticism received a fresh stimulus as he preached of emotions welling from his heart and emerging from everyday life. He influenced two other mystics: Johannes Tauler of Strassburg (died 1361) and the Swiss Heinrich Seuse, or Suso (died 1366).

Further Reading

Claud H. Field translated *Meister Eckhart's Sermons* (1931). *Meister Eckhart: An Introduction to the Study of His Works, with an Anthology of His Sermons* was selected, translated, and annotated by James M. Clark (1957). An excellent background study that discusses Eckhart is Clark's *The Great German Mystics: Eckhart, Tauler, and Suso* (1949).

Additional Sources

Woods, Richard, *Eckhart's way,* Collegeville, Minn.: Liturgical Press, 1990. ☐

Sir Arthur Stanley Eddington

The English astronomer Sir Arthur Stanley Eddington (1882-1944) greatly advanced theoretical astrophysics as a consequence of his original contributions to the theory of relativity and his studies on the internal constitution of stars.

Arthur S. Eddington was born on Dec. 28, 1882, at Kendal, Westmorland. His father was the headmaster and proprietor of a school where John Dalton once taught. Arthur was a precocious child, and by his own account had mastered the 24 x 24 multiplication table before he could read. He received his bachelor's degree in 1902 from Owens College, Manchester, and immediately proceeded to Trinity College, Cambridge. At Cambridge he placed first in the mathematical tripos examination in his second year, an unprecedented achievement. In 1905 he took his bachelor's degree from Cambridge University; in 1907 he became Smith's Prize winner and was elected a fellow of Trinity College; and in 1909 he obtained his master's degree.

In 1906 Eddington was appointed chief assistant at the Royal Observatory at Greenwich. He remained there for 7 years, gaining much practical astronomical experience.

While there he initiated a program for determining latitude variation of stars which, with modifications, is still in force today, and engaged in theoretical researches on the systematic motions and distributions of the stars recorded in the Groombridge Catalog. These last studies formed the basis of his Smith's Prize essay and culminated in his book *Stellar Movements and the Structure of the Universe* (1914). One important result was that he confirmed Jacobus Kapteyn's 1904 conclusion that there are two star streams in the Milky Way.

In 1913 Eddington was appointed Plumian professor of astronomy at Cambridge; a year later he became director of the Cambridge Observatory and was elected a fellow of the Royal Society. During World War I he began studies on Albert Einstein's general theory of relativity and on stellar structure. As secretary of the Royal Astronomical Society, Eddington received for publication a copy of Einstein's paper of 1915, the only one to reach England during the war. By the end of the war Eddington had become one of the few men to master Einstein's general theory, had made original contributions to it, and had written the first account of it in English.

In 1919 Eddington led the famous solar eclipse expedition to West Africa and proved, as Einstein's theory demanded, that starlight is deflected in passing close to a massive body such as the sun. Later, Eddington generalized H. Weyl's theory of the electromagnetic field, and in 1925 W. S. Adams spectroscopically verified Eddington's 1924 prediction of a large gravitational red shift of the light emitted by Sirius's white dwarf companion. In 1930 Eddington proved that an Einstein universe is unstable, thereby lending support to the concept of an expanding universe.

In 1915 Eddington also began studying the internal constitution of stars, a subject largely of his own creation. During the ensuing years he demonstrated, for example, the importance of radiation pressure in helping thermal pressure maintain a star's stability against gravitational collapse. He, as well as Harlow Shapley, showed that variable stars change their brightness because they pulsate. He also derived his famous mass-luminosity law, which shows that the more massive a star, the brighter it is.

Eddington was a master of popular science writing, a talent which he exploited especially after 1927. He also increasingly expounded his controversial philosophical and theological convictions. Moreover, spurred on by Paul Dirac's 1928 discovery of the relativistic wave equation for the electron, Eddington during the last 16 years of his life attempted to wed relativity to quantum theory in what came to be called his fundamental theory. Undisturbed by the criticism that this elegant but speculative theory evoked, Eddington pursued it to the end. Few today accept it, but its positive elements may one day be reborn in different form.

Eddington was knighted in 1930 and received numerous honors throughout his life, including the coveted Order of Merit in 1938. He remained a bachelor and died in Cambridge on Nov. 22, 1944.

Further Reading

A full-length biography of Eddington is Allie Vibert Douglas, *The Life of Arthur Stanley Eddington* (1956). For a shorter biographical sketch see H. C. Plummer's obituary notice in the *Biographical Memoirs of the Fellows of the Royal Society,* vol. 5 (1945-1948). See also John W. Yolton, *The Philosophy of A. S. Eddington* (1960).

Additional Sources

Chandrasekhar, S. (Subrahmanyan), *Eddington, the most distinguished astrophysicist of his time,* Cambridge; New York: Cambridge University Press, 1983. □

Mary Baker Eddy

The American founder of the Christian Science Church, Mary Baker Eddy (1821-1910) showed a unique understanding of the relationship between religion and health, which resulted in one of the era's most influential religious books, "Science and Health."

Mary Baker was born July 16, 1821, at Bow, N.H. A delicate and nervous temperament led to long periods of sickness in her early years, and chronic ill health made her weak and infirm during much of her adult life. In 1843 she married George Washington Glover, but he soon died and she returned home, where she had her only child. She married Daniel Patterson, a traveling dentist, in 1853; however, his frequent trips and her invalidism led to a separation by 1866 and a divorce several years later. In 1877 she married Asa Gilbert Eddy.

In her quest for health, she had visited Dr. Phineas P. Quimby of Portland, Maine, in 1862, and found that his nonmedical principles cured her. She absorbed his system and became a disciple. In 1866 she claimed to have been completely cured of injuries suffered in a fall by what she called "Christian science." By 1870 she was teaching her new-found science in collaboration with practitioners who did the healing. Her key ideas were published in *Science and Health with Key to the Scriptures* (1875).

This book and Mary Baker Eddy's forceful personality attracted numerous followers, and on Aug. 23, 1879, the Church of Christ, Scientist, was chartered. Asa Eddy helped organize the movement. Mrs. Eddy chartered the Massachusetts Metaphysical College in 1881, where she taught her beliefs. Asa Eddy died in 1882, and the next year Mrs. Eddy began to publish the *Journal of Christian Science.*

Her fame spread, support grew, and Mrs. Eddy became wealthy. But dissensions divided the Church, and in 1889 "Mother Eddy" moved to Concord, N.H., apparently withdrawing from leadership. In seclusion, however, she restructured the Church organization: the First Church of Christ, Scientist, in Boston was established on Sept. 23, 1892, as the mother church. Mrs. Eddy was its head, and all other churches were subject to its jurisdiction. Though internal quarrels diminished, they continued to the end of her life. Partly to guarantee a trustworthy newspaper for the movement, Mrs. Eddy began publishing the *Christian Science Monitor* in 1908. That year she moved to Chestnut Hill near Boston, where she died on Dec. 3, 1910.

Further Reading

Science and Health with Key to the Scriptures (1875 and later editions) is the most important of Mrs. Eddy's writings. Sibyl Wilbur, *The Life of Mary Baker Eddy* (1908), is the laudatory official biography. A friendly but more scholarly study is Robert Peel, *Mary Baker Eddy* (2 vols., 1966-1971). Critical accounts are Edwin F. Dakin, *Mrs. Eddy: The Biography of a Virginal Mind* (1929), and Ernest S. Bates and John V. Dittemore, *Mary Baker Eddy: The Truth and the Tradition* (1932). □

Marian Wright Edelman

Marian Wright Edelman (born 1939) was a lobbyist, lawyer, civil rights activist who founded the Children's Defense Fund in 1973 to advocate children's rights.

Marian Wright Edelman was born in Bennetsville, South Carolina, on June 6, 1939 and was named for the singer Marian Anderson. She was the youngest of five children born to Arthur Jerome Wright and Maggie Leola (Bowen) Wright. She spent her early years in Bennettsville. It was, as she described it, a small-town, socially segregated childhood. She went to racially segregated public schools, but excelled academically. She took piano and voice lessons and became a drum majorette in her high school band.

Beginnings of Her Advocacy

Edelman's quest for political, economic, and social rights and justice has its beginnings in her childhood. The elder Wrights instilled in their children a strong sense of service to others by their words and deeds. Indeed, as Edelman wrote, "Service is the rent we pay to be living. It is the very purpose of life and not something you do in your spare time." She was expected to help out with chores at the nearby Wright Home For the Aged, the first such institution for African-Americans in South Carolina, which her father founded and her mother ran. "The only time my father wouldn't give me a chore was when I was reading, so I read a lot," she said of those years.

When she was 14-years-old, her father died after suffering a heart attack. "The last thing he said to me before he died was, 'Don't let anything get between you and your education,'" she said. Driven by these words, she went to Spelman College, an historic African-American institution for women in Atlanta, Georgia. While at college, she won a

Merrill scholarship to study abroad. Her search for a broad international perspective took her to classes at the Sorbonne in Paris, the University of Geneva in Switzerland, and with the help of a Lisle Fellowship, to Moscow just prior to starting her senior year.

She had planned on a career in the foreign service, but changed her plans as the events of the 1960s' civil rights movement occurred. Caught up in the African-American social consciousness of the times, she participated at sit-ins in Atlanta's City hall and was arrested. "Segregation was wrong, something to be fought against," she said. The experiences stimulated her to believe that she could contribute to social progress through the study of law. She entered Yale Law School on a scholarship after receiving her undergraduate degree in 1960. She did not love law but explained that she decided to study law "to be able to help black people, and the law seemed like a tool [I] needed."

Early Advocacy

Edelman began her career as a lawyer hired by the NAACP (National Association for the Advancement of Colored People) in New York after receiving her law degree in 1963. After one year she moved to Jackson, Mississippi, to continue her work with the association. She became the first African-American woman admitted to the Mississippi State Bar Association. Her career changed direction after she became a lawyer for the Child Development Group in Mississippi and successfully lobbied for the restoration of Federal funds for the Mississippi Head Start programs. This started her subsequent life-long effort to lobby for children's interests.

She met Peter Benjamin Edelman, a staff assistant to Democratic Senator Robert F. Kennedy, while he was conducting research in Mississippi. They were married on July 14, 1968, and have three sons: Joshua Robert, Jonah Martin, and Ezra Benjamin. They moved to Washington, D.C., where he continued to work and she began to expand her work on the problem's of Mississippi's poor to the national political arena.

Edelman started the Washington Research Project of the Southern Center for Policy Research. It was created to lobby and research programs to assist children in poverty. In 1971 the Edelmans moved to Boston, where Peter served two years as vice-president of the University of Massachusetts. She directed the Center for Law and Education at Harvard University. That year *Time* magazine named her one of the top 200 young leaders in America.

Founds CDF

Under Edelman's guidance the Children's Defense Fund (CDF) was founded in 1973. It was to become a major advocate, research, and lobbying organization designed to seek aid for children. She campaigned for a number of programs. Among these were programs to help children remain healthy, stay in school, and avoid teenage pregnancy; to prevent child abuse; and to stop drug abuse. In her words, the CDF "works with individuals and groups to change policies and practices resulting in neglect or mistreatment of millions of children."

Again the Edelmans moved as their career paths evolved. Her husband joined the faculty of Georgetown University Law Center in Washington, D.C., in 1979. She relocated with her family to join him. There she continued to be president of the Children's Defense Fund, working long hours to convince government officials of the need for her children's aid programs.

When Bill Clinton was elected U.S. president in 1992, it was expected that Edelman, a friend and intellectual soul mate to First Lady Hillary Clinton, who had served as chairman of the CDF, would command a level of attention within the new administration that had been absent during the tenures of Presidents Bush and Reagan. There were even rumors that she would join the cabinet, bet she was quick to discount such rumors. "I need to work outside government, on my own," she said.

In 1992, Edelman and the CDF began its "Leave No Child Behind" campaign. She estimated that it would cost as much as $47 billion to fulfill all the goals of a fully-funded Head Start, proper medical insurance for all children and their pregnant mothers, vaccinations for every child, and an expanded children's tax credit for children. She tirelessly lobbies for these goals because she believes that "Investing in [children] is not a national luxury or a national choice. It's a national necessity. If the foundation of your house is crumbling, you don't say you can't afford to fix it while you're building astronomically expensive fences to protect it from outside enemies. The issue is not are we going to pay—it's are we going to pay now, upfront, or are we going to pay a whole lot more later on."

On June 1, 1996, Edelman and the CDF held their "Stand For Children" in Washington, D.C. An estimated 200,000 supporters showed up to march in support of children and the CDF's goals. Many of Edelman's critics had previously criticized Edelman and her ideas as outdated. But with the large support she received during "Stand For Children," she demonstrated that she and the CDF are still a force to contend with in American politics.

In 1997, Edelman criticized President Clinton for his welfare reform package by warning it could lead to record numbers of uninsured children, increased child abuse, and rising firearms deaths. The CDF's "The State of America's Children Yearbook 1997" criticized the package and warned that "if America does not stand up now for its children, it will not stand strong in the new millennium."

Edelman has been widely recognized for her spirited activity as a lobbyist for her causes. She lectures, writes, and travels to convince others of the many needs facing young people. She is the author of the books, *Families In Peril: An Agenda For Social Change* (1987); *Portrait of Inequality: Black and White Children in America* (1990); *The Measure of Our Success: A Letter to My Children and Yours* (1992); and *Guide My Feet: Meditations and Prayers on Loving and Working for Children* (1995). She is also the author of several reports, and many articles in support of children and her causes. All the while, she stressed that she is a doer rather than a scholar. She believed that problems must be broken down and a range of strategies must be considered to achieve goals. She was less interested in forming theories

than "in feeding, clothing, housing, and educating as many American children as soon as possible." She was also able to balance her hectic, social-oriented work with the demands of a family.

Further Reading

Marian Wright Edelman has written about her spiritual, family, and community values and thoughts in *The Measure of Our Success: A Letter to My Children and Yours* (1992). She described her programs and research findings and the work of the Children's Defense Fund in *Families in Peril: An Agenda for Social Change* (1987). Her biographies appear in *Who's Who in America, Who's Who Among Black Americans, Notable Black American Women, Black Women in America,* and *African American Biographies.*

Biographical information on Edelman can be found in the May 10, 1992 issue of the *Washington Post* and the March 15, 1997 issue of *Afro-American.* □

Anthony Eden

Statesman and nobleman Anthony Eden (1897-1977) briefly succeeded Winston Churchill as prime minister of Britain during its disastrous invasion of Suez in 1956.

From a wealthy and privileged background, Robert Anthony Eden was born on June 12, 1897, at Windlestone Hall near Bishop Auckland, Durham. He was the third son of Sir William Eden, with one sister, Marjorie, older than all the brothers, of which there was a total of four. Young Eden was educated at Sandroyd Prep School in Surrey and then at Eton, where he distinguished himself in sports but little else. He interrupted his schooling to fight in the King's Royal Rifle Corps during World War I (during which his eldest and youngest brothers were killed). In the course of the war he became the youngest adjutant by 1916, won a military cross in 1917, and by the end of the war he had become a brigade major. In 1919 he attended Christ Church College, Oxford, gaining first-class honors in Oriental languages in 1922.

Despite a lack of political education, he ran for the Spenymoor division of Durham in 1922 and was trounced by 6,000 votes by his Labor opponent. The next year he ran for and won the seat he was to hold during the rest of his parliamentary career, Warwick and Leamington, on the Conservative ticket. Evidence of the peculiarities of British politics, in addition to a Liberal competitor, his Labor opponent was the Socialist Countess of Warwick, who was also his sister's mother-in-law. In 1923 he also married Beatrice Helen Beckett, the daughter of Sir Gervase Beckett; after having two sons together (the elder died in World War II), this union was dissolved in 1950.

Eden's political ascent was steady, as he moved through a series of government posts mainly dealing with foreign affairs. In 1926 he was made parliamentary private secretary to Sir Austen Chamberlain, the Foreign Secretary.

Largely on his own initiative, he followed an Israeli attack with an Anglo-French military force. But after a Soviet protest, domestic disapproval, and no support from the U.S., he withdrew them. This action led, however, to severe strains in Anglo-Arab relations, as well as between the U.S. and England, France, and Australia. Eden resigned in January 1957 on the grounds of ill health, yet he maintained his actions were justified. Queen Elizabeth II made him the Earl of Avon in 1961, though he eschewed anyone referring to him by his title.

For the next 17 years, Eden traveled the world and worked on a total of four volumes of his *Memoirs,* the last of which, *Another World,* became a success, both critically and financially. He died on January 14, 1977, with his wife and son Nicholas by his bedside.

Further Reading

There are a number of biographies on Eden available, such as Alan Campbell-Johnson's *Anthony Eden: A Biography* (1955) and Robert Rhodes James's identically titled *Anthony Eden: A Biography* (1986). Yet perhaps the most fascinating sources for Eden's career are his own *Memoirs,* which provide splendid insight into his character: *Facing the Dictators* (1962); *The Reckoning* (1965); *Full Circle* (1960), which includes his account of Suez; and *Another World: 1897-1917* (1976), his most popular and critically-acclaimed. ☐

In 1931 he became Under- Secretary of Foreign Affairs, and in 1934 he became Lord Privy Seal to the League of Nations, during the tenure of which he directly dealt with the Axis leaders to avoid war. In 1935, he became Foreign Secretary, first under the administration of Stanley Baldwin, then Neville Chamberlain in 1937. In 1938 he staunchly opposed Chamberlain's "appeasement" policy toward dictators like Hitler and Mussolini, and he resigned from the Cabinet. His book *Foreign Affairs* (1939) reflects his views in this period, and his views reflected those of a great portion of the populace. When Winston Churchill replaced Chamberlain, he immediately recalled Eden to the Cabinet, seeing him as a trustworthy ally because they shared the same view of the Nazi threat. Besides giving him the posts of secretary for dominion affairs (1939-1940), secretary for war (1940), foreign secretary (1940-1945), and leadership of the House of Commons (1942-1945), Churchill primed him to take over the leadership of the Conservative party. This succession was further cemented when Eden married Clarissa Spencer Churchill in 1952.

Deputy leader of the opposition from 1945 to 1951, Eden became deputy prime minister and foreign secretary when a Tory government was returned in 1951. When in April 1955 Winston Churchill retired as prime minister, Eden was his natural replacement. In 1956 the Suez crisis broke. Egyptian president Gamal Abdel Nasser nationalized the Suez Canal, which had been jointly owned by the British and French governments and individual shareholders. It was not an unusual nationalistic expropriation, but Eden likened the situation to that of 1938 and overreacted.

Maria Edgeworth

The British author Maria Edgeworth (1767-1849) wrote novels that are characterized by clear, vivid style, good humor, and lively dialogue.

Maria Edgeworth was born on Jan. 1, 1767, the second of the 21 children (by four wives) of Richard Edgeworth, whose family supposedly came from Edgeware, England, to Edgeworthtown, Ireland, about 1573. Richard Edgeworth was a model landlord, living on his estates and improving them. Maria's mother died when she was 6, and within a few months her father married again. Maria was happy with all her stepmothers, the last being 20 years her junior, and spent her whole life surrounded by her family, never even having a room of her own. She worked in the living room at a desk her father made for her, writing on folio sheets she sewed together in chapters.

When she was 16, Maria became her father's secretary and accountant. Edgeworth was devoted to J.J. Rousseau's ideas and brought up his children on Thomas Day's *Sandford and Merton,* a didactic educational book. Richard encouraged Maria to write, and together they produced *Practical Education,* which advised parents to deliver short sermons, to instruct gradually, and to teach mainly by conversation. Maria's own first book was *The Parents' Assistant* (1796), a delightful collection of short stories, of which the most famous is "Two Strings to His Bow." The same year appeared her *Letters from Literary Ladies.*

whom she submitted and who corrected all her writing, was thought by all to be a pompous bore. Miss Edgeworth was so modest that Lord Byron wrote, "No one would have suspected she could write her name"; he added, "Her father thought nothing except his own name worth writing." After her father's death Miss Edgeworth took two of her sisters abroad, spending more than a year in France and Switzerland. She was proposed to by the Chevalier Edencrantz, confidential secretary to the king of Sweden, but she would not leave her family, or he his monarch.

In 1823 Miss Edgeworth spent 2 weeks with Sir Walter Scott at Abbotsford, and in 1825 Scott visited her at Edgeworthtown, which had become a shrine at which all visitors to Ireland paid homage. In 1844 she was made a member of the Royal Irish Academy. At 70 she learned Spanish. During the potato famine of 1847, she worked among the starving. She died on May 22, 1849. Asked during her lifetime to furnish biographical details, she replied that "as a woman" her life had been "wholly domestic and could be of no interest to the public." Her stepmother wrote after Miss Edgeworth's death that "her whole life of eighty-three years, has been an aspiration after good."

Further Reading

Two works on Maria Edgeworth are Isabel C. Clarke, *Maria Edgeworth, Her Family and Friends* (1950), and Elizabeth Inglis-Jones, *The Great Maria* (1959). An older work is Emily Lawless, *Maria Edgeworth* (1904).

Additional Sources

Clarke, Isabel Constance, *Maria Edgeworth, her family and friends,* Philadelphia: R. West, 1976.

Inglis-Jones, Elisabeth, *The great Maria: portrait of Maria Edgeworth by Elisabeth Inglis-Jones,* Westport, Conn.: Greenwood Press, 1978 1959. □

In 1800 Miss Edgeworth published *Castle Rackrent,* of which Irish author Padraic Colum wrote, "One can read it in an hour. Then one knows why the whole force of England could not break the Irish people." She was the first to depict Irish peasants as human beings. Miss Edgeworth's *The Absentee* (1812) was written as a play, but Richard Sheridan, who wanted to produce it, found the censor would not allow public discussion of the spending of Irish rents in England. The Russian Ivan Turgenev declared he got a revelation from Maria Edgeworth's stories, and the word "absenteeism" occurs on the first page of his *Smoke.* Sir Walter Scott said that he hoped "in some distant degree to emulate the admirable Irish portraits of Miss Edgeworth" and that she had shown him his path; in fact, *Waverley* has been called a Scots *Castle Rackrent.* Jeanie Deans, in Scott's *Heart of Midlothian,* may have been modeled on Maria Edgeworth.

Later novels by Miss Edgeworth were *Belinda* (1801), *Ormond* (1817), *Frank* (1822), and *Harry and Lucy* (1825). Sir Walter Scott stated that "in natural appearance she is quite the fairy Whipity of our nursery tale . . . who came flying in through the window to work all sort of marvels. Maria writes while she reads, speaks, eats, drinks and no doubt while she sleeps." Calm, cheerful, and unselfish, she was small and slight, with bright, very blue eyes and tiny hands and feet.

In 1802 Miss Edgeworth went with her father, stepmother, and a small sister to Paris, where she met Madame de Genlis, one of whose books she had translated, and J.A. de Ségur, who had translated her *Belinda.* Her father, to

Thomas Alva Edison

The American inventor Thomas Alva Edison (1847-1931) held hundreds of patents, most for electrical devices and electric light and power. Although the phonograph and incandescent lamp are best known, perhaps his greatest invention was organized research.

Thomas Edison was born in Milan, Ohio, on Feb. 11, 1847; his father was a jack-of-all-trades, his mother a former teacher. Edison spent 3 months in school, then was taught by his mother. At the age of 12 he sold fruit, candy, and papers on the Grand Trunk Railroad. In 1862, using his small handpress in a baggage car, he wrote and printed the *Grand Trunk Herald,* which was circulated to 400 railroad employees. That year he became a telegraph operator, taught by the father of a child whose life Edison had saved. Exempt from military service because of deafness, he was a tramp telegrapher until he joined Western Union Telegraph Company in Boston in 1868.

Early Inventions

Probably Edison's first invention was an automatic telegraph repeater (1864). His first patent was for an electric vote recorder. In 1869, as a partner in a New York electrical firm, he perfected the stock ticker and sold it. This money, in addition to that from his share of the partnership, provided funds for his own factory in Newark, N.J. Edison hired technicians to collaborate on inventions; he wanted an "invention factory." As many as 80 "earnest men," including chemists, physicists, and mathematicians, were on his staff. "Invention to order" became very profitable.

From 1870 to 1875 Edison invented many telegraphic improvements: transmitters; receivers; the duplex, quadruplex, and sextuplex systems; and automatic printers and tape. He worked with Christopher Sholes, "father of the typewriter," in 1871 to improve the typing machine. Edison claimed he made 12 typewriters at Newark about 1870. The Remington Company bought his interests.

In 1876 Edison's carbon telegraph transmitter for Western Union marked a real advance toward making the Bell telephone practical. (Later, Émile Berliner's transmitter was granted patent priority by the courts.) With the money Edison received from Western Union for his transmitter, he established a factory in Menlo Park, N.J. Again he pooled scientific talent, and within 6 years he had more than 300

patents. The electric pen (1877) produced stencils to make copies. (The A. B. Dick Company licensed Edison's patent and manufactured the mimeograph machine.)

The Phonograph

Edison's most original and lucrative invention, the phonograph, was patented in 1877. From a manually operated instrument making impressions on metal foil and replaying sounds, it became a motor-driven machine playing cylindrical wax records by 1887. By 1890 he had more than 80 patents on it. The Victor Company developed from his patents. (Alexander Graham Bell impressed sound tracks on cylindrical shellac records; Berliner invented disk records. Edison's later dictating machine, the Ediphone, used disks.)

Incandescent Lamp

To research incandescence, Edison and others, including J. P. Morgan, organized the Edison Electric Light Company in 1878. (Later it became the General Electric Company.) Edison made the first practical incandescent lamp in 1879, and it was patented the following year. After months of testing metal filaments, Edison and his staff examined 6,000 organic fibers from around the world and decided that Japanese bamboo was best. Mass production soon made the lamps, although low-priced, profitable.

First Central Electric-Light Power Plant

Prior to Edison's central power station, each user of electricity needed a dynamo (generator), which was inconvenient and expensive. Edison opened the first commercial electric station in London in 1882; in September the Pearl Street Station in New York City marked the beginning of America's electrical age. Within 4 months the station was lighting more than 5,000 lamps for 230 customers, and the demand for lamps exceeded supply. By 1890 it supplied current to 20,000 lamps, mainly in office buildings, and to motors, fans, printing presses, and heating appliances. Many towns and cities installed central stations.

Increased use of electricity led to Edison-base sockets, junction boxes, safety fuses, underground conduits, meters, and the three-wire system. Jumbo dynamos, with drum-wound armatures, could maintain 110 volts with 90 percent efficiency. The three-wire system, first installed in Sunbury, Pa., in 1883, superseded the parallel circuit, used 110 volts, and necessitated high-resistance lamp filaments (metal alloys were later used).

In 1883 Edison made a significant discovery in pure science, the Edison effect—electrons flowed from incandescent filaments. With a metal-plate insert, the lamp could serve as a valve, admitting only negative electricity. Although "etheric force" had been recognized in 1875 and the Edison effect was patented in 1883, the phenomenon was little known outside the Edison laboratory. (At this time existence of electrons was not generally accepted.) This "force" underlies radio broadcasting, long-distance telephony, sound pictures, television, electric eyes, x-rays, high-frequency surgery, and electronic musical instruments. In 1885 Edison patented a method to transmit telegraphic "aerial" signals, which worked over short distances, and later sold this "wireless" patent to Guglielmo Marconi.

Creating the Modern Research Laboratory

The vast West Orange, N.J., factory, which Edison directed from 1887 to 1931, was the world's most complete research laboratory, an antecedent of modern research and development laboratories, with teams of workers systematically investigating problems. Various inventions included a method to make plate glass, a magnetic ore separator, compressing dies, composition brick, a cement process, an all-concrete house, an electric locomotive (patented 1893), a fluoroscope, a nickel-iron battery, and motion pictures. Edison refused to patent the fluoroscope, so that doctors could use it freely; but he patented the first fluorescent lamp in 1896.

The Edison battery, finally perfected in 1910, was a superior storage battery with an alkaline electrolyte. After 8000 trials Edison remarked, "Well, at least we know 8000 things that don't work." In 1902 he improved the copper oxide battery, which resembled modern dry cells.

Edison's motion picture camera, the kinetograph, could photograph action on 50-foot strips of film, 16 images per foot. A young assistant, in order to make the first Edison movies, in 1893 built a small laboratory called the "Black Maria,"—a shed, painted black inside and out, that revolved on a base to follow the sun and kept the actors illuminated. The kinetoscope projector of 1893 showed the films. The first commercial movie theater, a peepshow, opened in New York in 1884. A coin put into a slot activated the kinetoscope inside the box. Acquiring and improving the projector of Thomas Armat in 1895, Edison marketed it as the Vitascope.

Movie Production

The Edison Company produced over 1,700 movies. Synchronizing movies with the phonograph in 1904, Edison laid the basis for talking pictures. In 1908 his cinemaphone appeared, adjusting film speed to phonograph speed. In 1913 his kinetophone projected talking pictures: the phonograph, behind the screen, was synchronized by ropes and pulleys with the projector. Edison produced several "talkies."

Meanwhile, among other inventions, the universal motor, which used alternating or direct current, appeared in 1907; and the electric safety lantern, patented in 1914, greatly reduced casualties among miners. That year Edison invented the telescribe, which combined features of the telephone and dictating phonograph.

Work for the Government

During World War I Edison headed the U.S. Navy Consulting Board and contributed 45 inventions, including substitutes for previously imported chemicals (especially carbolic acid, or phenol), defensive instruments against U-boats, a ship-telephone system, an underwater searchlight, smoke screen machines, antitorpedo nets, turbine projectile

heads, collision mats, navigating equipment, and methods of aiming and firing naval guns. After the war he established the Naval Research Laboratory, the only American institution for organized weapons research until World War II.

Synthetic Rubber

With Henry Ford and the Firestone Company, Edison organized the Edison Botanic Research Company in 1927 to discover or develop a domestic source of rubber. Some 17,000 different botanical specimens were examined over 4 years—an indication of Edison's tenaciousness. By crossbreeding goldenrod, he developed a strain yielding 12 percent latex, and in 1930 he received his last patent, for this process.

The Man Himself

To raise money, Edison dramatized himself by careless dress, clowning for reporters, and playing the role of homespun sage with aphorisms like "Genius is 1 percent inspiration and 99 percent perspiration" and "Discovery is not invention." He scoffed at formal education, thought 4 hours' sleep a night enough, and often worked 40 or 50 hours straight. As a world symbol of Yankee ingenuity, he looked and acted the part. George Bernard Shaw, briefly an Edison employee in 1879, put an Edisontype hero into his novel *The Irrational Knot:* free-souled, sensitive, cheerful, and profane.

Edison had more than 10,000 books at home and masses of printed materials at the laboratory. When launching a new project, he wished to avoid others' mistakes and to know everything about a subject. Some 25,000 notebooks contained his research records, ideas, hunches, and mistakes. Supposedly, his great shortcoming was lack of interest in anything not utilitarian; yet he loved to read Shakespeare and Thomas Paine.

Edison died in West Orange, N.J., on Oct. 18, 1931. The laboratory buildings and equipment associated with his career are preserved in Greenfield Village, Detroit, Mich., thanks to Henry Ford's interest and friendship.

Further Reading

A good biography of Edison, filled with human interest, is Matthew Josephson, *Edison: A Biography* (1959). Biographies emphasizing his inventions include William Adams Simonds, *Edison: His Life, His Work, His Genius* (1934), and H. Gordon Garbedian, *Thomas Alva Edison: Builder of Civilization* (1947). There is more emphasis on industry in John Winthrop Hammond, *Men and Volts: The Story of General Electric,* edited by Arthur Pound (1941). See also Charles Singer and others, eds., *A History of Technology,* vol.5: *The Late Nineteenth Century* (1958). □

Edward I

Edward I (1239-1307), known as the "Greatest of the Plantagenets," was king of England from 1272 to 1307. His reign witnessed the growth of parliamen-

tary power, the enactment of extensive reforms, and the spread of English control over Scotland and Wales.

The eldest son of Henry III and Eleanor of Provence, Edward was born on June 17/18, 1239. In October 1254, at the age of 15, he married Eleanor of Castile, by whom he had 10 children. She died in 1290, and in September 1299 Edward married Margaret of France, by whom he had three children.

Soon after Edward's first marriage, Henry III gave him Gascony, Ireland, Bristol, and the march between the Dee and the Conway rivers. In the latter area, as the Earl of Chester, he gained experience in warfare with the Welsh. His attempt to introduce the English system of counties and hundreds provoked Llewelyn ap Gruffydd, Prince of Wales. During the Parliament of Oxford in 1258, Edward sided with his father, but in the following year he became a leader of the "Bachelorhood of England" in support of Simon de Montfort and the Provisions of Westminster. Again in support of his father, Edward attacked the Welsh who were supporting the rebellious barons, and in 1264 he attacked the barons at Northampton. Edward caused his father's defeat and his own capture at the Battle of Lewes. After his escape Edward led the victory over the barons at Evesham, and in the next years, as he received the submission of the barons, Edward became an advocate of a policy of healing.

Edward was made the steward of England in 1268 as well as warden of the city and the Tower of London. He gained popularity by abolishing the levy of customs and by urging laws against the Jewish moneylenders. He left for the Crusades in 1271 and fought bravely at Acre and Haifa. While Edward was on the way home, his father died, and he succeeded to the crown on Nov. 20, 1272.

Domestic and Foreign Policies

After his coronation on Aug. 19, 1274, Edward initiated an active legislative program to overthrow feudalism and to develop the parliamentary system of government. He earned the name of "English Justinian" as a flood of legislation was passed. The first important reform was the Statute of Westminster I, passed in 1275 to amend the evils of the earlier civil war. It was followed by the Statute of Gloucester (1278), which reformed territorial jurisdiction; the Statute of *Mortmain* (1279), which reformed ecclesiastical landholding; the Statute of *Quia Emptores* (1290), which enabled land sales; the Statute of Westminster II, which reformed legal rights; and the Statute of Winchester, which reformed the national military force.

Edward was also busily engaged in the first years of his reign in his attempts to control Wales. Prince Llewelyn at first refused to attend Parliament but submitted to the English in 1276. This submission did not last long, however, and Edward was forced to take up arms, killing Llewelyn in 1282 and bringing his brother, David, to trial in 1283. This victory over the Welsh rebels resulted in the Statute of Wales, which brought the English pattern of administration to Wales.

By 1292 Edward was also involved in Scotland, where 13 claimants sought the throne. After the Scotch asked for arbitration by the English, Edward placed John Balliol (the third son of the founder of Balliol College, Oxford) on the Scottish throne. Balliol was forced to surrender Scotland in 1296, and a second expedition was made in 1300, when the Scottish lords asked that Balliol be allowed to reign. Edward defeated the Scottish rebels under William Wallace at Linlithgow Heath in 1298 and eventually executed Wallace in London.

In addition to attempting to control Scotland and Wales, Edward was active in holding his possessions on the Continent. From 1286 to 1289 he spent much time in France and Gascony. After the loss of Gascony to Philip IV in 1294, he was able to receive support for military activities from a Parliament of all three estates in 1295, and he received financial help from the clergy in 1297. Although the barons opposed the campaign to Gascony, Edward sailed for Bruges to help the Count of Flanders against the French. The following year, at the persuasion of Boniface VIII, he deserted his ally to make a truce with France in order to recover the lost territory.

The last years of Edward's reign were spent in conflict with his barons, who were against his military activities both at home and abroad. To obtain their support, he was forced to reissue the Great Charter in 1299. While traveling north to deal with the threat of Robert Bruce, the new leader of the

Scottish rebels, he died at Burghon-Sands on July 7, 1307. His burial took place at Westminster Abbey on October 27.

Further Reading

An informative biography of Edward I is E. L. G. Stones, *Edward I* (1968). For Edward's early life see F. M. Powicke, *King Henry III and the Lord Edward* (2 vols., 1947). Various aspects of the reign are covered in John E. Morris, *The Welsh Wars of Edward I* (1901), and in two works by T. F. T. Plucknett, *Legislation of Edward I* (1949) and *Edward I and Criminal Law* (1960). General histories of the period include Sir James H. Ramsay, *The Dawn of the Constitution* (1908), and F. M. Powicke, *The Thirteenth Century, 1216-1307* (1953; 2d ed. 1962).

Additional Sources

Chancellor, John, *The life and times of Edward I,* London: Weidenfeld and Nicolson, 1981.
Edward I and Wales, Cardiff: University of Wales Press, 1988.
Prestwich, Michael., *Edward I,* Berkeley: University of California Press, 1988. □

Edward II

Edward II (1284-1327) was king of England from 1307 to 1327. His reign witnessed the decline of royal power and the rise of baronial opposition.

E dward II was born on April 25, 1284, the fourth son of Edward I and Eleanor of Castile. He acted as regent during his father's absence in Flanders in 1297-1298, signing the Confirmatio Cartarum. He was created Prince of Wales and Earl of Chester in 1301.

One of his first acts upon succeeding to the crown on July 8, 1307, was to recall his favorite, Piers Gaveston, who had been banished by Edward I, and to make him Earl of Cornwall on August 6. He also appointed Gaveston regent of Ireland and custos of the realm. In January 1308 Edward married Isabella, the daughter of Philip IV of France. These two acts aroused such baronial opposition that 21 "lords ordainers" were appointed to administer the country.

Under the pretense of attacking the Scottish rebels, Edward marched north in 1310. His real aim, however, was to avoid the ordainers and Thomas of Lancaster, the leader of the barons. Civil war broke out. The strife ended with the murder of Gaveston by the Earl of Warwick on June 19, 1312. The following year an amnesty was granted.

Hoping to win popular support, Edward resumed the war against the Scots. His sound defeat by Robert Bruce at Bannockburn in 1314 caused him to lose what little remaining influence he had. Edward's high-handed treatment of the Mortimers and other nobles alienated many of the nobility.

Edward offended his wife by his fondness for the younger Hugh le Despenser. After sending Isabella to France to negotiate a dispute between himself and her brother, he had to deal with her attempt to dethrone him when she returned in 1326 with troops and the support of Roger Mortimer. Unable to count on the support of his barons, whom he had offended by his unwillingness to consult with them, Edward fled to the west and was captured on Nov. 16, 1326, at Neath in Glamorgan. On June 20, 1327, he was forced to resign the throne. Imprisoned in Berkeley Castle, Edward was poorly treated. He was murdered on Sept. 21, 1327, and then buried at Gloucester Abbey.

Further Reading

Edward II's early life is the subject of Hilda Johnson, *Edward of Carnarvon* (1946). Harold F. Hutchison, *Edward II* (1972), emphasizes the King's political life. The basic study of his reign is T. F. Tout, *The Place of the Reign of Edward II in English History* (1913; 2d rev. ed. 1936). The constitutional history of his reign is treated in J. Conway Davies, *The Baronial Opposition to Edward II* (1918), and the relations with Scotland in W. Mackay Mackenzie's works, including *The Battle of Bannockburn* (1913). A basic general work on the period is May McKisack, *The Fourteenth Century, 1307-1399* (1959).

Additional Sources

Fryde, Natalie, *The tyranny and fall of Edward II, 1321-1326,* Cambridge Eng.; New York: Cambridge University Press, 1979. □

Edward III

Edward III (1312-1377) was king of England from 1327 to 1377. The Hundred Years War between England and France began during his reign.

The eldest son of Edward II and Isabella of France, Edward III was born on Nov. 13, 1312, at Windsor. He was created Earl of Chester 11 days after his birth; he was made Count of Ponthieu and Montreuil on Sept. 2, 1325, and Duke of Aquitaine a week later. In October 1326 Edward was named guardian of the kingdom, and he succeeded to the throne on Jan. 25, 1327.

For the first 4 years of his reign, Edward III was a figurehead for the rule of his mother and Roger Mortimer, with a regency during his minority in the hands of Henry of Lancaster. On Jan. 24, 1328, Edward married Philippa of Hainaut, with whom he had seven sons and five daughters. Later in 1328 Edward was forced to give up all claims to Scotland by the Treaty of Northampton. This treaty caused Mortimer's unpopularity to grow. In November 1330 Edward was sufficiently strong to have Mortimer executed and to confine his mother for the rest of her life at Castle Rising.

With the government in his own hands, Edward resumed the conflict with Scotland, and by 1332 he had established Edward de Balliol on the Scottish throne. Soon Balliol was ousted, and Edward again invaded Scotland,

defeating the Scots in July 1333 at Halidon Hill and conquering southern Scotland and the area north of the Forth.

Edward also concerned himself with the economic interests of the country. In 1332 he encouraged Flemish weavers to come to England and teach their skills. In 1337 he prepared for war against the French, who were hoping to cut into the Flemish wool trade with England. With the support of James van Artevelde of Ghent, Edward made an alliance with Ghent, Ypres, Bruges, and Cassel, as well as a treaty with Emperor Louis V for the hiring of troops. In July 1338 Edward went to Flanders, and the following year he laid siege to Cambrai.

Conflict with France

In order to retain Flemish support, Edward took the title of king of France in January 1340, thus reviving a claim that was to last throughout the medieval period and into the reign of George III. He returned to England for supplies, and that same year the English defeated the French in the naval battle at Sluis, the traditional beginning of the Hundred Years War. Edward returned to France in 1342, landing at Brest with the aim of securing Brittany, and laid siege to Tournai.

The following year plans were made at Sainte-Madeleine for a 3-year truce, but Edward claimed that Philip VI of France broke the truce and sent an English force to sack Harfleur, Saint-Lô, and Caen. Through a flanking movement, the English were able to destroy the French army at the Battle of Crécy near Abbeville on Aug. 6, 1346. After a year-long blockade and siege, Calais surrendered. Lacking supplies to continue the war, Edward returned to England in 1347.

Edward's activities in France had stripped England of troops, giving King David II of Scotland an opportunity to rise in revolt. Encouraged by Philip of France, Scottish troops crossed the border, raiding as far south as the Tyne, and conducted a drive to force the English out of Scotland. This attempt was foiled at the Battle of Neville's Cross in 1346. David was captured and the English recovered much of southern Scotland.

While war with France continued, with a Spanish fleet fighting for France being defeated off Winchelsea in 1350, Edward devoted his attention to internal matters. He founded the Order of the Garter, the senior British order of chivalry, probably in 1348. As a result of an out break of the plague, the Statute of Laborers was enacted in 1351 in an attempt to stabilize wages. To control the Church, the Statute of Provisors was enacted the same year and that of Praemunari 2 years later.

By the mid-1350s the war with France had been resumed, but the King now relied on his eldest son, Edward the Black Prince, who led the English to victory at the Battle of Poitiers (Sept. 19, 1356) over King John II of France. The following year, on May 8, Edward III gained vast lands and ransom at the Treaty of Bretigny in return for a promise to abandon his claim to the French throne. This promise was not carried out, and warfare continued.

In 1362 Edward reorganized Gascony and Aquitaine in an attempt to control his French holdings. The following year a plan for the union of England and Scotland was agreed upon by King David but was defeated by the Scottish Parliament. The same period saw the rise of strong English nationalism. The use of French in the law courts ended in 1362, and the payment of Peter's Pence to the papacy was discontinued in 1366. The enactment of the Statute of Kilkenny in 1367 was an attempt to check English colonists in Ireland from adopting Irish customs.

Foreign military commitments continued. In 1367 the Black Prince was sent to help Pedro of Castile regain the throne of Spain, which had been usurped by his half brother, Henry of Trastamare, with the help of the French. Major fighting broke out in France again 2 years later as a result of English "free companies"; the Black Prince seized Limoges and killed all its inhabitants. Desultory warfare occurred in Poitou and Touraine, causing the French to burn Portsmouth in 1369 in retaliation.

Later Reign

Old before his time, Edward took a mistress, Alice Perrers, after the death of his queen in 1369. He allowed the government to be administered by John of Gaunt. He remained passive in the struggles between the barons and the Church, though he attached Church lands in 1371 to raise money for the continuation of the French war. In the struggle between the reforming members of Parliament led by the Black Prince and the Lancastrians led by Henry of Lancaster, his chief minister, Edward was almost a spectator. After the death of the Black Prince in 1376, Edward appears to have been almost deserted. He died the following year on June 21.

During the early years of his reign, Edward was an enlightened king. He made a strong effort to maintain economic ties with Flanders, and his interest in building a navy caused Parliament to call him "king of the sea." However, the military exploits of his reign in the conflict with France were of no lasting benefit to the nation. His victories were due more to superior manpower and supplies rather than to any great military or tactical skill on his part. His financial management had kept the country always in debt, and by the time of his death most of the fruits of his victories had vanished, especially with the loss of Aquitaine in 1374. During the last years of his reign, Edward was unable to cope with either constitutional or social crises.

Further Reading

For the general background of the reign of Edward III see Sir James H. Ramsey, *Genesis of Lancaster, 1307-1399* (2 vols., 1913), and May McKisack, *The Fourteenth Century, 1307-1399* (1959). The conflicts with Scotland are treated in E. W. M. Balfour-Melville, *Edward III and David II* (1954), and Ronald Nicholson, *Edward III and the Scots, 1327-1335* (1965). The causes of the French conflict are treated in Henry Stephen Lucas, *The Low Countries and the Hundred Years' War, 1326-1347* (1929). For the war itself see Edouard Perroy, *The Hundred Years War* (1945; trans. 1951); Alfred H. Burne's more detailed *The Crécy War* (1955); and H. J. Hewitt, *The Black Prince's Expedition of 1355-1357* (1958).

Foreign relations are dealt with in P. E. Russell, *The English Intervention in Spain and Portugal in the Time of Edward III and Richard II* (1955); religious matters in William Abel Pantin, *The English Church in the Fourteenth Century* (1955); legal development in B. Wilkinson, *The Chancery under Edward III* (1929); and economic matters in George Unwin, ed., *Finance and Trade under Edward III* (1918). For information on the last years of Edward's life see F. George Kay's account of Edward's mistress, *Lady of the Sun: The Life and Times of Alice Perrers* (1966).

Additional Sources

Bevan, Bryan, *Edward III: monarch of chivalry,* London: Rubicon Press, 1992.

Packe, Michael St. John, *King Edward III,* London; Boston: Routledge & Kegan Paul, 1983. □

Edward IV

Edward IV (1442-1483) was the first Yorkist king of England. His reforms and innovations invigorated 15th-century English government.

Born at Rouen on April 28, 1442, Edward IV was the son of Richard, Duke of York, and Cecily Neville. He took part in the Wars of the Roses from the first battle at St. Albans (1455), and in 1460 he accompanied Richard Neville, Earl of Warwick (the "Kingmaker"), and the Calais garrison when Warwick invaded England and raised rebels in Kent and in the north demanding "good government." The success of this uprising established Richard of York as regent and heir of the ineffective Henry VI of Lancaster, but Henry's queen, Margaret of Anjou, did not accept this political disinheritance of their son, Prince Edward of Lancaster. Her Army of the North defeated and killed Richard of York at Wakefield (Dec. 30, 1460). Margaret's success in liberating Henry VI and her failure to attack London simplified Edward's position. The 6-foot teenager entered the capital and claimed the crown.

Edward's popular election by crowds at St. John's Field (March 1, 1461) and at St. Paul's, Westminster Hall, and the Abbey (March 4, 1461) was a constitutional novelty. Of at least equal importance was the march north and the 10-hour battle at Towton (March 29, 1461), which left the Lancastrians scattered fugitives. The June 28 coronation followed a Parliament that voted attainders but no funds, and it reminded the new king of his promise of better government.

Early Reign

In 1461 Edward's government was more Neville than Yorkist. The 33-year-old Warwick ruled the north, installed his brother George as chancellor, and corresponded with foreign rulers as a national spokesman. However, Edward's 1464 marriage to Elizabeth Woodville, widow of John Grey of Groby, crossed Warwick's plan for the King to marry Bona of Savoy, sister-in-law of Louis XI of France. The numerous Woodvilles advanced rapidly, and inevitably they quarreled with the Nevilles. In 1467 Edward sent

campaign, but by the time Edward had transported his army to Europe, Charles was distracted by imperial ambitions. Edward conducted his own invasion but only for a price. At Picquigny on Aug. 29, 1475, Edward agreed to give up the expedition and Margaret of Anjou. Louis agreed to pay Edward 75,000 crowns within 15 days and thereafter a secret pension totaling 50,000 crowns per year.

Financially, this settlement turned the tide for Edward. He paid his debts and amassed a comfortable fortune, thus indirectly relieving the pressure on his government's Exchequer. However, even the public form of this treaty was unpopular in England as marking an "inglorious" episode. Edward may have considered England well out of the rivalry that Louis waged against Charles until the latter's death in battle against the Swiss in 1477. Yet the French king's diplomatic net extended to Edward's family, finding a ready dupe in George of Clarence. Edward's patience with his brother's repeated betrayals was exhausted when George reportedly gossiped about the legitimacy of Edward and his children. Clarence was attainted in Parliament and executed in 1478.

Louis's 1482 publication of the secret pension seems to have alarmed Edward into searching for new diplomatic alternatives at the time of his sudden illness and death at Westminster on April 9, 1483. Edward's 12-year-old son was proclaimed Edward V, with his uncle, Richard of Gloucester, as regent.

Further Reading

Cora Scofield, *The Life and Reign of Edward the Fourth* (2 vols., 1923), is a comprehensive biography. Useful background information is supplied in E. F. Jacob, *The Fifteenth Century, 1399-1485* (1961); S. B. Chrimes, *Lancastrians, Yorkists, and Henry VII* (1964; 2d ed. 1966); and J. R. Lander, *The Wars of the Roses* (1965). On constitutional developments of the period, S. B. Chrimes, *English Constitutional Ideas in the Fifteenth Century* (1936), presents a useful commentary, while B. Wilkinson, *Constitutional History of England in the Fifteenth Century, 1399-1485* (1964), excerpts documents and chronicles on major events.

Additional Sources

Clive, Mary, Lady, *This sun of York; a biography of Edward IV,* 1st American ed., New York, Knopf, 1974.
Falkus, Gila, *The life and times of Edward IV,* London: Weidenfeld and Nicolson, 1981.
Ross, Charles Derek, *Edward IV,* London: Eyre Methuen, 1974. □

Warwick to parley with the diplomats of Burgundy, France, and Brittany. Then he struck his own bargain with Burgundy, dismissed George Neville as chancellor, and crowned the effect by marrying Warwick's wealthy 79-year-old aunt to a 19-year-old Woodville.

Warwick retaliated forcefully. With Edward's brother George of Clarence as his new candidate, the Kingmaker used the Calais garrison to capture Edward in 1469. However, this time the earl's "good government" slogans failed to win broad support, and Edward regained power. Driving Warwick and Clarence to France was a doubtful success for Edward, for with the help of Louis XI and in the cause of "Lancaster and the Old Families" they returned in 1470. Unarmed and unsupported, Edward fled to Burgundy, and Henry VI was restored.

With help and soldiers from Burgundy, Edward returned to England in 1471. Warwick was slain at Barnet (April 14), Prince Edward was killed at Tewkesbury (May 4), Margaret of Anjou was captured, and Henry VI died the night of the army's return to London (May 21). The lack of a standing army had made the English crown the prize of foreign-sponsored expeditions.

Invasion of France

Alliance with Burgundy and hostility to France was Edward's policy from 1471 to 1475, but it was difficult to coordinate a body as slow as Parliament with a man as unstable as Charles the Bold against an intriguer as seasoned as Louis XI. In 1473 Parliament voted funds for a

Edward VI

Edward VI (1537-1553) was king of England and Ireland from 1547 to 1553. His short reign witnessed the introduction of the English Prayer Book and the Forty-two Articles, and thus this period was important in the development of English Protestantism.

The son of Henry VIII and his third wife, Jane Seymour, Edward VI was born on Oct. 12, 1537. His mother died 12 days after his birth. Edward spent most of his childhood at Hampton Court, where he pursued a rigorous educational regimen. He learned Latin, Greek, and French and studied the Bible and the works of Cato, Aesop, Cicero, Aristotle, Thucydides, and the Church Fathers. Roger Ascham, the author of *The Schoolmaster,* was a sometime tutor of his penmanship, and Sir John Cheke of Cambridge instructed him in classical subjects. Philip van Wilder taught him the lute. Edward knew a little astronomy and occasionally jousted. When lost in his studies, he was cheerful.

Since Edward was only 9 years old when he became king in 1547 on the death of his father, a group of councilors stipulated in Henry VIII's will ruled the kingdom in his name. His council elected his uncle Edward Seymour, the Earl of Hertford, as lord protector, and Hertford soon was created Duke of Somerset.

Somerset's Protestantism and his interest in solving the government's financial difficulties set England on a course of religious and economic change. Thomas Cranmer, the archbishop of Canterbury, given liberty to indulge his Protestant tendencies, pushed through the repeal of Henry VIII's six Articles (1547), dissolved the chantries (1547), and through the Act of Uniformity (1549) endorsed an English Prayer Book that prescribed a new religious service. This Prayer Book was subsequently revised in 1553 (Second Act of Uniformity). All Englishmen were forced to use it and to adopt the Protestant form of worship. Reaction to the first Prayer Book stimulated an uprising, the Western Rebellion in Cornwall in 1549, which was quelled at Exeter. The Forty-two Articles of religious belief adopted by Parliament in 1551 demonstrated further movement toward Protestant doctrine and were eventually made the basis of Elizabeth's Thirty-nine Articles.

Edward had a consuming interest in religion. No study delighted him more than that of the Holy Scriptures. He daily read 12 biblical chapters, and he encouraged preachers with strong Protestant views. For example, Nicholas Ridley and Hugh Latimer, both later executed for their beliefs by Queen Mary I, were regular preachers. Even the Scottish reformer John Knox delivered a few sermons. John Calvin, the Geneva reformer, wrote to him.

Resistance to a new tax on sheep (1548) and an inquiry into enclosure led to a Norfolk rising called Ket's Rebellion (1549), which was instrumental in precipitating Somerset's fall. The rebellion fueled the antagonism of John Dudley, Earl of Warwick, who thought Somerset too lenient in dealing with the rebels. Warwick became Edward's chief minister and was created Duke of Northumberland. He had, however, little time in which to practice his authority. Edward contracted measles and smallpox in April 1552 and was never well thereafter. He was still too young for marriage. A contract made in 1543 for his marriage to Mary, Queen of Scots, had been abandoned in 1550. In 1551 a contract had been drawn for the hand of Elizabeth, the daughter of Henry II of France. But on July 6, 1553, Edward died of tuberculosis.

A priggish, austere boy, Edward had little sympathy for his uncle Somerset and almost no friends. He was short for his age and fair-complected and had weak eyes. His death at 15 left the English Protestant cause without its principal defender and caused Northumberland hastily and unlawfully to place his daughter-in-law, Lady Jane Grey, on the throne. Though Edward's reign was brief, it marks an important milestone in the development of English Protestantism.

Further Reading

The best biography of Edward VI is Hester W. Chapman's scholarly and well-written *The Last Tudor King* (1958), which underscores personal detail. See also the older, less objective study by Sir Clements R. Markham, *King Edward VI: An Appreciation* (1907). For background on the religious change consult Jasper Ridley, *Thomas Cranmer* (1962), and A. G. Dickens, *The English Reformation* (1964; rev. ed. 1967).

Additional Sources

Hayward, John, Sir, *The life and raigne of King Edward the Sixth,* Kent, Ohio: Kent State University Press, 1993 (originally published in 1630). □

Edward VII

Edward VII (1841-1910) was king of Great Britain and Ireland from 1901 to 1910. His short reign was marked by peace and prosperity.

Born on Nov. 9, 1841, at Buckingham Palace, Edward VII was the eldest son of Victoria and Albert. Bertie, as he was nicknamed, proved unresponsive to the elaborate educational scheme his parents imposed. He gained command of German and French, some skill in public speaking, and little else. Beginning in 1859, he attended Christ Church, Oxford, for four terms, interrupted by an American tour in 1860. Formal schooling ended in 1861 at Trinity College, Cambridge.

Dismayed by what Queen Victoria called "Bertie's fall," which occurred with an actress in Ireland in 1861, his parents considered travel and an early marriage the best remedy. Discussion of Princess Alexandra, whose father was heir to the Danish throne, as a suitable bride preceded the Prince Consort's death in 1861. After a trip to the Holy Land, Edward married Alexandra at Windsor on March 10, 1863.

Despite Victoria's early determination to initiate Edward into affairs of state, she withheld the key to Foreign Office boxes during his long tenure as Prince of Wales because of his indiscretion. Edward's imprudence persisted during his exclusion from apprenticeship: he had to testify in the Mordaunt divorce case (1870); he was deeply involved in the Aylesford scandal (1876); and the Tranby Croft affair (1891) brought him to court again, this time as a witness to cheating at baccarat. Understandably, the tone of the prince's set alarmed the Queen and offended nonconformist consciences. But his hearty self-indulgence had

St. Aubyn, Giles, *Edward VII, Prince and King,* New York: Atheneum, 1979. □

Edward VIII

Edward VIII (1894-1972) was King of England for only one year, 1936, abdicating the throne to marry the "woman I love," the twice-divorced Wallis Simpson. He was Duke of Windsor after his abdication.

The eldest son of George, Duke of York, and his wife, Princess Mary of Tech, Edward Albert Christian George Andrew Patrick David was born on June 23, 1894, at Richmond Park, Surrey. Upon the death of the gregarious Edward VII in May 1910, the young Prince's father became George V and Prince Edward became the heir to the throne. The new king and queen were strict, serious, and self-disciplined parents who sought to imbue their children with a strong sense of duty.

In order to prepare Prince Edward for his future responsibilities, his parents decided to have him trained for the Royal Navy. Accordingly, he was sent to Osborne in 1907 and from 1909 to 1911 attended the Royal Naval College at Dartmouth. There he was treated like the other cadets, a novel situation which he much enjoyed. In 1911 he was invested as Prince of Wales in an impressive ceremony at Caernarvon Castle, Wales. To complete his education he was sent to Oxford in 1912, where he studied—not very strenuously—until the outbreak of World War I.

During the war the prince served as an aide-de-camp to the commander in chief of the British Expeditionary Force in France, Gen. Sir John French. Although he was in a position of considerable trust, he was gravely disappointed that he was not allowed to be sent to the front. "What difference does it make if I am killed?" he asked. "The King has three other sons." His observation of the conduct of the war and the death and devastation which it caused affected him deeply, as it did many other members of his generation, making him loathe war and desire constructive social change.

Conduct as Prince

After the war the prince began his true career as prince of Wales, participating in many royal ceremonial duties and, by touring the dominions and other countries, serving as a goodwill ambassador. Prince Edward filled the role admirably: he was probably history's most popular prince of Wales up to that time—a handsome, sociable, debonair young man with considerable charm and a skilled conversationalist endowed with a natural and spontaneous, if rather superficial, sympathy. His activities were recorded enthusiastically in the press, and he was accorded a status very like that of a rock idol of the 1980s, complete with a sycophantic entourage and groupies. As the heir apparent to the world's most prestigious constitutional monarchy, he was expected

an appeal transcending classes. As a winner at the racecourse and as an arbiter of taste, the prince was genuinely popular. The European web of dynastic marriages familiarized Edward with other royalties. He relished the spectacular state visits required by British diplomacy, but he did not make foreign policy.

When he succeeded to the throne on the death of Victoria in 1901, Edward was a portly, balding, bearded figure. He created the Order of Merit and introduced automobiles as royal transport. Edward supported Lord Fisher's naval reforms and Lord Haldane's reorganization of the army, but he was not as close to any ministers as Queen Victoria had been to Lord Melbourne and Benjamin Disraeli. The great constitutional crisis of his reign—whether to promise the Liberal ministry a creation of peers sufficient to overcome the Tory majority in the House of Lords, and, if so, on what conditions—was unresolved at his death. Edward VII died of bronchitis followed by heart attacks on May 6, 1910, and he was interred at Windsor.

Further Reading

Sir Sidney Lee, *King Edward VII: A Biography* (2 vols., 1925-1927), may be supplemented by Philip Magnus, *King Edward the Seventh* (1964). For the flavor of Edward's reign see S. Nowell-Smith, ed., *Edwardian England, 1901-1914* (1964).

Additional Sources

Pearson, John, *Edward the rake: an unwholesome biography of Edward VII,* New York: Harcourt Brace Jovanovich, 1975.

to be both discreet and wise. As he was naturally neither, his activities sometimes caused friction between him and his parents. His expression of compassion for the wretched unemployed miners of Wales ("Something must be done") for example, earned his father's disapproval because of its possible political implications. His parents also strongly disapproved of the rather "fast" and trendy company he kept and of his unfortunate tendency to fall in love with married women.

In June 1931 Prince Edward met Wallis Warfield Simpson, the 33-year-old wife of a well-to-do American-born British subject, Ernest Simpson. Wallis Simpson herself was American-born and bred and grew up in a wealthy Maryland family. She was sent to private schools and made her debut in Baltimore in 1914. In 1916 she married a Navy pilot, Lt. Cmdr. Earl Spenser Junior. The marriage was not a success, and after separations and attempts at reconciliation it ended in divorce in 1927. While touring Europe with her aunt, Wallis met London resident Ernest Simpson and they were married in 1928. Wallis adjusted quickly to life as a wealthy wife in London and became a fashionable hostess. As they moved in the same social circles, it was inevitable that she and the Prince of Wales should meet, and when they did, an immediate friendship sprang up between them which rapidly became a love affair of great intensity. Although their relationship was an open secret in royal and fashionable upper class circles and was the subject of some comment in the foreign press, the British press maintained a decorous and self-imposed silence on the subject.

The Abdication Crisis

When George V died on January 20, 1936, Prince Edward became King Edward VIII. Despite his family's disapproval (because the monarch is the head of the Church of England and also is seen to serve as the exemplar of the British way of life, with an emphasis on domesticity and morality), King Edward continued his liaison with Mrs. Simpson. Their vacation together aboard a yacht in the summer of 1936 was sensationally reported in the foreign press and caused considerable anxiety in British royal and governmental circles. The crisis began in October 1936, when Wallis Simpson was granted a decree *nisi*—a divorce which would become final in six months—from Ernest Simpson. A few weeks later the king told the prime minister, the staid Conservative Stanley Baldwin, that he wanted to marry Wallis Simpson and that if he could not do so and remain king, he was "prepared to go."

The prime minister, with the support of the cabinet, the hierarchy of the Church of England, the rest of the royal family, and the bulk of public opinion at home and in the dominions, told the king he could not, as King of England, marry a woman who was twice divorced. The king, with some support from a "King's Party" consisting of Winston Churchill and press magnates Lords Beaverbrook and Rothermere, hoped he could, and desparately sought a solution. The idea of a morganatic marriage, in which the king would legally marry a woman who would not be raised to his royal rank, was suggested but ultimately rejected as being a concept alien to the English constitution. Finally, on December 10, 1936, after days of wild newspaper speculation about the constitutional crisis, the king abdicated. He could not, as he said in his famous radio speech on December 11, 1936, continue to perform his duties without the support of the "woman I love," and he left the throne to his brother, who became George VI. Throughout the crisis Edward, separated, if only temporarily, from his beloved Wallis, plagued by the controversies reported in the press, unable to find (or unwilling to listen to) wise advisers, and under great stress, acted inconsistently and unwisely. And if no other vindication for the views and actions of Baldwin and his party existed, it would be enough that the abdication of a popular king was accepted by the public so calmly and the succession of a new monarch occurred so smoothly.

Edward lived for another 35 years, but the rest of his life, though far from uneventful, served as an epilogue to the abdication crisis. He left England for Europe immediately after the abdication and, as soon as her divorce became final, married Wallis on June 3, 1937. Edward was created duke of Windsor upon his brother's succession; several months later he—but not his wife—was granted the title of "Royal Highness," a slight which hurt the duke deeply and which he continued to feel for the rest of his life.

After their marriage the duke and duchess lived in considerable style in France, where they bought a villa on the Riviera. In 1937 they made a much-publicized trip to Hitler's Germany. Although the duke's purpose—to view German labor conditions, a topic in which he had been much interested since his Prince of Wales days—was blameless, and although he was not the only prominent Englishman to visit and even to express admiration for German efficiency in the mid-1930s, he was at the time and thereafter blamed for being sympathetic to the Nazi cause.

Service in World War II

Upon the outbreak of World War II the duke hurried to England to offer his services to the government. Then, as later, the government did not quite know what to do with him. He had left the throne under something of a cloud, and he was estranged from his family. After some hesitation he was given the job of liaison officer between the British and French high commands in France. He retained this position until shortly before the fall of France, when he fled with his wife first to Spain and then to Portugal. While in the Iberian Peninsula in the summer of 1940 he was the subject of much Nazi interest. A shadowy plot was hatched through which the Nazis hoped to use the duke, whom they felt was a friend of Germany, to overthrow the British government. The details of the plot and the duke's part in it—or even his awareness of it—remain obscure, and on August 1, 1940, the duke and duchess sailed for the Bahamas, of which the duke had been appointed governor and where they remained until 1945.

After the war the Windsors returned to Europe and lived as international jet-setters. They were, by all accounts, a devoted couple. They had a home in Paris, a country house outside Paris, wintered in Biarritz, and spent several months every year in New York. The duke had much leisure to pursue his interests, which included golf and gardening, and the duchess, whose interests were mainly social, entertained and was entertained frequently. In 1951 he published *A King's Story,* his version of the abdication crisis. Her autobiography, *The Heart Has Its Reasons,* appeared in 1956.

In 1972, while dying from throat cancer, the duke was reconciled with his family at last. His niece, Queen Elizabeth II, with her husband and oldest son, came to visit the duke and duchess in Paris. He died a few days later, on May 28, 1972, and was buried at Windsor. At the funeral his wife was scrupulously accorded the respect appropriate to her rank. The duchess returned to France immediately after the funeral, where she, increasingly infirm, retired from all active life. She died April 24, 1986.

Further Reading

There is a wealth of material on the Duke of Windsor— biographies, autobiographies, and monographs—much of it poorly researched. The best place to start is with the duke's autobiography, *A King's Story* (1951), and with the duchess's *The Heart Has Its Reasons* (1956), which present their views on the abdication crisis. Many books simply and uncritically glamorize the story, such as Geoffrey Dennis' *Coronation Commentary* (1937) and Ursula Bloom's *The Duke of Windsor* (1972). Of greater interest because of his personal participation in the events of 1936, but still flattering to the duke, is Lord Beaverbrook's *The Abdication of King Edward VIII* (1966). Highly readable but superficial, *The Woman He Loved,* by Ralph G. Martin, was published in 1973. Books expressing views critical of the duke have been published since the 1930s. Among these are Hector Bolitho's *King Edward VIII: An Intimate Biography* (1937) and Brian Inglis' *Abdication* (1966). Frances Donaldson's *Edward VIII* (1974) is a learned, well-documented biography based on many primary sources and interviews which provides a portrait of a man who was stubbornly wrong-headed and almost self-destructively unwise. Two books on the duke are concerned with his relationship with the Nazis in 1940. Peter Allen's *The Crown and the Swastika: Hitler, Hess and the Duke of Windsor* (1983) takes an extreme view of the duke's activities, charging him with either treason or nearly criminal stupidity. Michael Bloch's *Operation Willi: The Plot to Kidnap the Duke of Windsor July 1940* (1984) is a detailed and interesting account of the events of July 1940 in which the duke is depicted as a loyal Briton but an unwise and indecisive man. Bloch also edited *Wallis and Edward Letters, 1931-1937: The Intimate Correspondence of the Duke and Duchess of Windsor* (1986).

Additional Sources

Birmingham, Stephen, *Duchess: the story of Wallis Warfield Windsor,* Boston: Little, Brown, 1981.

Donaldson, Frances Lonsdale, Lady, *Edward VIII,* Philadelphia: Lippincott, 1975.

Thornton, Michael, *Royal feud: the dark side of the love story of the century,* New York: Simon and Schuster, 1985.

Bryan, J. (Joseph), *The Windsor story,* New York: Morrow, 1979.

Martin, Ralph G., *The woman he loved,* New York, Simon and Schuster 1974, 1973. □

Edward the Black Prince

The English soldier-statesman Edward the Black Prince (1330-1376) was heir apparent to the English throne. Active in the military affairs of the period, particularly in the English conflict with France, he earned fame as a skillful and valorous fighter.

Born on June 15, 1330, Edward the Black Prince, also known as Edward of Woodstock (after his place of birth), as Prince of Wales, and sometimes as Edward IV, was the eldest son of Edward III and Philippa of Hainaut. On March 18, 1333, shortly before his third birthday, he was created Earl of Chester, and he was made Duke of Cornwall on March 3, 1337. During the next few years he was guardian of the kingdom while his father was absent on the Continent, and on May 12, 1343, Edward was created Prince of Wales. At the age of 15 he was knighted by his father at La Hogue, and the following year Edward took an active role in the winning of the Battle of Crécy against the French. It was at this battle that he obtained the name of "the Black Prince," possibly because he wore black armor.

In the following years Edward was active in the military expeditions of his father, taking part in the expedition to Calais in 1349. By 1355 he was the King's lieutenant in Gascony and leader of an army in Aquitaine that was invading southeastern France. In 1356 he was outflanked in battle by King John. After a failure to negotiate a peace, Edward defeated the French and captured their king at the Battle of Poitiers (September 19).

In October 1361 Edward married the 33-year-old Joan, Countess of Kent, who was the widow of Sir Thomas Holland. As an orphan, she had been brought up in the household of Edward III along with Edward. Known as the "Fair Maid of Kent," Joan had two sons by the Black Prince.

Edward continued to play an active role in the government and in military matters. On July 19, 1362, he was created prince of Aquitaine and Gascony, and during the next years he was busy in France, attempting to check the "free companies" that continued to war against the French. In 1367 he undertook an expedition into Spain to assist Don Pedro of Castile, who had been deprived of his throne by Henry of Trastamare with French aid. With an army of 30,000 men Edward crossed the Pyrenees and won a third great battle at Navarrete. Due to illness, he was forced to return to his holdings in France. When war broke out with Charles V of France in 1369, Edward laid siege to Limoges. Upon its capture all its inhabitants were put to death.

Ill health caused Edward to return to England in 1371, and in the following year he resigned his principality and began to take an active part in English internal politics. He became the champion of the constitutional policy of the Commons against the corrupt court and the party of the Lancastrians. Edward was active in the reform plans as set forth in the "Good Parliament" of 1376, but his death caused much of this work to remain undone. He died on June 8, 1376, a month before the Parliament was dissolved.

Although he is known to history as a great soldier, the Black Prince's victories were due more to superior numbers than to great skill on his part. His greater contribution was his attempt to deal with the political situation in England.

Further Reading

The primary sources on the Black Prince are Jean Froissart, *The Chronicle of Froissart,* translated by Sir John Bourchier (6 vols., 1901-1903; repr. 1967); *The Life of the Black Prince by the Herald of Sir John Chandos,* edited by Mildred K. Pope and Eleanor C. Lodge (1910); and *The Register of Edward, the Black Prince* (4 vols., 1930-1933). There is a short study of Edward by Dorothy Mills, *Edward, the Black Prince* (1963). Older works are G. P. R. James, *A History of the Life of Edward the Black Prince* (2 vols., 1836); R. P. Dunn-Pattison, *The Black Prince* (1910); and Marjorie Coryn, *The Black Prince* (1934). Edward's military activities are related in H. J. Hewitt, *The Black Prince's Expedition of 1355-57* (1958), and his burial in Sir James Mann, *The Funeral Achievements of Edward the Black Prince* (1950). For historical background on the period see May McKisack, *The Fourteenth Century, 1307-1399* (1959), and Arthur Bryant, *The Atlantic Saga,* vol. 2: *The Age of Chivalry* (1964).

Additional Sources

Barber, Richard W., *Edward, Prince of Wales and Aquitaine: a biography of the Black Prince,* New York: Scribner, 1978.
Chandos Herald, *Life of the Black Prince,* New York, AMS Press, 1974.
Cole, Hubert, *The Black Prince,* London: Hart-Davis, MacGibbon, 1976.
Emerson, Barbara, *The Black Prince,* London: Weidenfeld and Nicolson, 1976.
Harvey, John Hooper, *The Black Prince and his age,* Totowa, N.J.: Rowman and Littlefield, 1976.
The life and campaigns of the Black Prince: from contemporary letters, diaries and chronicles, including Chandos Herald's Life of the Black Prince, New York, NY: St. Martin's Press, 1986. □

Edward the Confessor

Edward the Confessor (died 1066), the last king of the house of Wessex, ruled England from 1042 to 1066. Attracted to religion and to Norman culture, he was not a vigorous leader. He gained a reputation, not fully deserved, for sanctity and was eventually canonized.

The youngest son of Ethelred the Unready and his Norman wife, Emma, Edward was born sometime after 1002. When Ethelred's authority crumbled in the face of Danish invasions and dissensions among the English nobility, Emma and her children took refuge in 1013 at the court of Richard II, Duke of Normandy. Ethelred died in 1016, and Edward's eldest brother, Edmund Ironsides, succeeded him but died later the same year. Cnut of Denmark was in possession of England, and Edward and his remaining brother Alfred were in exile in Normandy. As he grew up, Edward became thoroughly imbued with Norman manners.

After Cnut's death in 1035, England experienced several years of factional strife, during which Edward's brother Alfred returned to England and was murdered by a powerful earl, Godwin of Wessex. In 1041 Cnut's last surviving son designated Edward his successor, and the following year Edward, with widespread popular support, became king of England.

The first half of Edward's reign was full of uncertainties. Until 1047 England was threatened by a possible invasion by King Magnus of Norway, who claimed the English throne because of an agreement made with Cnut's son. Meanwhile, internal difficulties sprang from the rivalries of the great earls Godwin, Leofric, and Siward (formerly Cnut's councilors) and their ambitious descendants. Godwin, murderer of Edward's brother, was especially troublesome, but Edward, lacking the power to confront him, pacified him for several years. Edward married his daughter Edith in 1045. The match was childless, inspiring a later legend that Edward, in his saintliness, had never consummated it. Edward also met opposition from his mother, whose lands he confiscated in 1043. To counteract his lack of trusted English councilors, Edward invited to his court a number of Norman and Breton knights and clerics, whose presence angered the English magnates.

In 1051 Edward, using as an excuse Godwin's refusal to obey an order, moved against his great rival. He exiled Godwin, banished Edith from the court, designated Wil-

liam, Duke of Normandy, as heir to the throne of England, and arranged that a Norman, Robert of Jumièges, become archbishop of Canterbury. The following year the situation reversed itself. Godwin returned with a large fleet, and he and Edward were officially reconciled to prevent a civil war and resultant Norse invasion. The archbishop and most of the Norman courtiers were banished. Godwin died soon after, in 1053, but his son Harold became Earl of Wessex and Edward's most powerful adviser.

For the rest of his reign Edward, by choice or necessity, did not exercise dominant control over affairs of state, leaving to Harold, to Godwin's other son Tostig (from 1055 to 1065 Earl of Northumbria), and to other powerful nobles the prosecution of wars against the revived power of Wales and the settling of domestic policies. In 1057 Edward's nephew, since 1016 an exile in Hungary, came to visit him but died soon after his arrival in mysterious circumstances. His death made it clear that Edward's successor would be either William of Normandy or the popular Harold of Wessex.

Edward became increasingly interested in religious matters, devoting much of his attention in his later years to the founding of Westminster Abbey. He also loved hunting and was less inclined to ascetic and pious practices than his posthumous reputation, based on a miracle-laden hagiographical biography written soon after his death, suggests. Edward died on Jan. 5, 1066. Harold was quickly chosen his successor, but by the end of the year William of Normandy (known as the "Conqueror") had been crowned

at Westminster in the abbey whose construction Edward had supervised with such loving care.

Further Reading

The main historical source for Edward's life and reign is *The Anglo-Saxon Chronicle,* edited and translated by G.N. Garmonsway (1953). A full-length study is Frank Barlow, *Edward the Confessor* (1970). The hagiographical *The Life of King Edward,* edited and translated by Frank Barlow (1962), is not a historical record but testifies to the growth of the cult of Edward after his death. See also F. M. Stenton, *Anglo-Saxon England* (1943; 2d ed. 1947), and C. N. L. Brooke, *The Saxon and Norman Kings* (1963).

Additional Sources

The life of Saint Edward, king and confessor, Guildford, Surrey: St. Edward's Press, 1990.
Barlow, Frank, *Edward the Confessor,* London: Eyre Methuen, 1979, 1970.
The life of King Edward who rests at Westminster, New York: AMS Press, 1984, 1962. ☐

Edward the Elder

Son and successor of Alfred the Great, the Anglo-Saxon king Edward the Elder (died 924) continued his father's spirited defense of Anglo-Saxon domains against Danish invaders. He also greatly increased the power of the West Saxon monarchy.

Nothing of importance is known of Edward before his succession to the West Saxon Kingship in 899, on the death of his father, Alfred. At that time Wessex and its dependent kingdoms were in no immediate danger of invasion by the Danes, who had harassed England for over a century and whom Alfred had twice beaten off decisively. Nonetheless, the colonies established by the Danes in northern and eastern England were a constant threat to the Anglo-Saxons, and Edward fought occasional, inconclusive battles with the colonists during the first decade of his reign. On one occasion, shortly after his accession, his cousin Ethelwold, frustrated in his attempt to claim the rule of Wessex for himself, raised an army in Danish England and attacked Edward's lands. Edward raided East Anglia in retaliation and killed Ethelwold.

In 909 Edward sent an army to attack the Northumbrian Danes. When they retaliated the following year, the Danes were so conclusively defeated that they ceased to be a factor in the Anglo-Danish wars for some years. Edward then began a systematic campaign to subdue East Anglia and the Danish midlands with the help of his sister, Ethelfleda (Aethelflaed), Lady of the Mercians, widow of a Mercian king dependent upon Wessex. Her chain of fortresses constructed throughout northern Mercia and Edward's intelligent use of the militia system created by Alfred enabled the King to consolidate his annual gains against the Danes and to turn the chronic disunity of the colonists against themselves.

When Ethelfleda died in 918, Edward assumed closer control over Mercia. In the same year several of the princes of western Wales accepted Edward as their lord. By the end of 918 the last Danish strongholds had surrendered. Now all England south of the Humber was under Edward's authority.

In the later years of his reign Edward fought battles against new adversaries—Viking raiders stationed in Ireland who attacked the western coast of Mercia. In 920 Edward campaigned against the raiders, and at the end of the summer all the kings of Britain acknowledged his overlordship. Thereafter, Edward remodeled the administrative structure of Mercia, creating several new shires. His last battle was fought against a rebellious force of allied Mercians and Welshmen—two groups traditionally restless under West Saxon domination.

Edward died on July 17, 924, and was succeeded by his son Athelstan, who consolidated his father's considerable military and political achievements.

Further Reading

The known facts of Edward's life and reign are preserved in *The Anglo-Saxon Chronicle,* edited and translated by G. N. Garmonsway (1953). F. M. Stenton, *Anglo-Saxon England* (1943; 2d ed. 1947), provides the most lucid and thorough modern commentary. For other useful background see the chapter on Aethelflaed, Lady of the Mercians, in Peter Cleomoes, ed., *The Anglo-Saxons* (1959). □

Jonathan Edwards

Jonathan Edwards (1703-1758), colonial New England minister and missionary, was one of the greatest preachers and theologians in American history.

At the close of the 17th century, the science of Isaac Newton and the philosophy of John Locke had significantly changed man's view of his relationship to God. Man's natural ability to discover the laws of creation seemed to demonstrate that supernatural revelation was not a necessary prelude to understanding creation and the creator. God was no longer mysterious; He had endowed men with the power to comprehend His nature and with a will free to choose between good and evil.

It was Jonathan Edwards's genius that he could make full use of Locke's philosophy and Newton's discoveries to reinterpret man's relationship to God in such a way that the experience of supernatural grace became available to people living in an intellectual and cultural climate very different from that of 17th-century England. In so doing, Edwards helped transmit to later generations the richest aspect of American Puritanism: the individual heart's experience of spiritual and emotional rebirth. Further, by his leadership in the religious revivals of the early 18th century, Edwards

helped make the experience an integral part of American life for his own time and for the following century.

Jonathan Edwards was born on Oct. 5, 1703, in East Windsor, Conn., where his father was a minister. Jonathan's grandfather was pastor to the church in Northampton, Mass. Jonathan was the only boy in the family; he had 10 sisters. He graduated from Yale College in 1720, staying on there as a theology student until 1722, when, though not yet 19 years old, he was called as minister to a church in New York. Edwards served there for 8 months. In 1723, though called to a church in Connecticut, he decided to try teaching. He taught at Yale from 1724 to 1726.

Early Writings

At an early age Edwards showed a talent for science. At Yale he studied Newton's new science and read Locke with more interest "than the most greedy miser" gathering up "handfuls of silver and gold, from some newly discovered treasure." During these years he also began recording his meditations on the Bible and his observations of the natural world. Edward's central purpose was not to become a scientist but to lead a life of intense holiness.

Edwards's "Personal Narrative" (written ca. 1740) and his letters and diaries show a young man whose religious experience was of great power and beauty. As Edwards tells it, after several "seasons of awakenings," at the age of 17 he had a profound religious experience in which "there came into my mind so sweet a sense of the glorious *majesty and grace* of God, that I know not how to express. I seemed to see them both in a sweet conjunction; majesty and meekness joined together; it was a sweet, and gentle, and holy majesty; and also a majestic meekness; an awful sweetness; a high, and great, and holy gentleness." Adapting Locke's philosophy to his own purposes, Edwards interpreted the "sweet" sense of God's majesty and grace as a sixth and new sense, created supernaturally by the Holy Spirit. As he wrote later in *A Treatise of Religious Affections* (1746), the new sense is not "a new faculty of understanding, but it is a new foundation laid in the nature of the soul, for a new kind of exercises of the same faculty of understanding."

Edwards's perception of ultimate reality as supernatural is further evidenced in his statement that "the world is . . . an ideal one." He wrote in his youthful "Notes on the Mind": "The secret lies here: That, which truly is the Substance of all Bodies, is the infinitely exact, and precise, and perfectly stable Idea, in God's mind, together with his stable Will, that the same shall gradually be communicated to us, and to other minds, according to certain fixed and exact Methods and Laws."

In 1726 Edwards was called from Yale to the Northampton church to assist his grandfather; when his grandfather died in 1729, Edwards became pastor of the church. In 1727 he married the beautiful and remarkable Sarah Pierrepont of New Haven.

Early Revivals

Religious revivals had been spreading through New England for 100 years. In his youth Edwards had seen "awakenings" of his father's congregation, and his grandfather's revivals had made his Northampton church second only to Boston. In early New England Congregationalism, church membership had been open only to those who could give public profession of their experience of grace. The Halfway Covenant of 1662 modified this policy, but when Edwards's grandfather allowed all to partake of the Sacraments (including those who could not give profession of conversion), he greatly increased the number of communicants at the Lord's Supper.

Edwards's first revival took place in 1734-1735. Beginning as prayer meetings among the young in Northampton, the revivals soon spread to other towns, and Edwards's reputation as a preacher of extraordinary power grew. Standing before his congregation in his ministerial robe, he was an imposing figure, 6 feet tall, with a high forehead and intense eyes. A contemporary wrote that Edwards had "the power of presenting an important Truth before an audience, with overwhelming weight of argument, and with such intenseness of feeling, that the whole soul of the speaker is thrown into every part of the conception and delivery. . . . Mr. Edwards was the most eloquent man I ever heard speak."

Edwards endeavored to convey as directly as possible the meaning of Christ's Crucifixion and Resurrection. His words, he hoped, would lead his listeners to a conviction of their sinful state and then through the infusion of divine grace to a profound experience of joy, freedom, and beauty. Edwards's *A Faithful Narrative of the Surprising Work of God in the Conversion of Many Hundred Souls in Northampton, and the Neighboring Towns and Villages* (1737) relates the history of the 1734-1735 revival and includes careful analyses of the conversions of a 4-year old child and an adolescent girl.

Edwards's preaching and writings about the nature and process of the religious experience created powerful enemies. In western Massachusetts the opposition to Edwards was led by his relatives Israel and Solomon Williams, who maintained that a man's assurance of salvation does not lie in a direct and overpowering experience of the infusion of grace and that he may judge himself saved when he obeys the biblical injunctions to lead a virtuous life. Edwards too believed that a Christian expresses the new life within him in virtuous behavior, but he denied that a man is in a state of salvation simply because he behaves virtuously. For him, good works without the experience of grace brought neither freedom nor joy.

In 1739 Edwards preached sermons on the history of redemption. He clearly thought the biblical promises of Christ's kingdom on earth would be fulfilled soon. His interest in the history of redemption is further evidenced in the many notes he made on the prophecies he found in the Bible and in natural events.

Great Awakening

In 1740 the arrival in America of George Whitefield, the famous English revivalist, touched off the Great Awakening. Revivals now swept through the Colonies, and thousands of people experienced the infusion of grace. The emotional intensity of the revivals soon brought attacks from ministers who believed that Whitefield, Edwards, and other "evangelical" preachers were stirring up religious fanaticism. The most famous attack was made by Charles Chauncy in *Seasonable Thoughts on the State of Religion in New England* (1743).

Edwards defended the Great Awakening in several books. He acknowledged that there had been emotional excesses, but on the whole he believed the revivals were remarkable outpourings of the Holy Spirit. His works of defense include *The Distinguishing Marks of a Work of the Spirit of God* (1741), *Some Thoughts Concerning the Present Revival of Religion in New England* (1742), and *A Treatise Concerning Religious Affections* (1746), the last a classic in religious psychology. He also wrote a biography of his daughter's fiancé the Native American missionary David Brainer.

The Great Awakening intensified Edward's expectations of Christ's kingdom. With English and Scottish ministers, he began a Concert of United Prayer for the Coming of Christ's Kingdom. To engage people in the concert, he wrote *An Humble Attempt to Promote Visible Union of God's People in Extraordinary Prayer for the Revival of Religion* (1747).

Edward's Dismissal

The troubles that culminated in Edwards's dismissal from Northampton began in the 1740s. Considerable opposition to Edwards had remained from his revivals. Animosity between him and members of his congregation was increased by an embarrassing salary dispute and an incident in 1744 when Edwards discovered that some children had been secretly reading a book on midwifery. Many children of influential families were implicated; Edwards's reading of their names publicly from the pulpit was resented. But the most important factor in Edwards's dismissal was his decision, announced in 1748, that henceforth only those who publicly professed their conversion experience would be admitted to the Lord's Supper. His decision reversed his grandfather's policy, which Edwards himself had been following for 20 years.

Edwards was denied the privilege of explaining his views from the pulpit, and his written defense, *An Humble Inquiry into the Rules of the Word of God, Concerning the Qualifications Requisite to a Complete Standing and Full Communion with the Visible Christian Church* (1749), went largely unread. After a bitter struggle, the church voted 200 to 23 against Edwards, and on July 1, 1750, he preached his farewell sermon.

Late Works

In August 1751 Edwards and his large family went to Stockbridge, Mass., where he had been called as pastor to the church and missionary to the Native Americans. As a missionary, he defended the Native Americans against the greed and mismanagement of a local merchant. These struggles consumed much of his time, but he still managed to write extensively. Among the most important works are *A Careful and Strict Enquiry into the Modern Prevailing No-*

tions of That Freedom of Will . . . (1754) and *The Great Christian Doctrine of Original Sin Defended* (1758). In the first, he asserted that a man has freedom to choose but freedom of choice is not the same as freedom of will. The power which decides what a man will choose—his willing—is in the hands of God and beyond his personal control. In *Original Sin* Edwards maintained that all men live in the same unregenerate state as Adam after the fall.

Two other works show that Edwards had not become embittered by his dismissal. In *The Nature of True Virtue* (1756) he defines virtue as benevolence to "being" in general. *Concerning the End for Which God Created the World* (1756) is a prose poem, a praise to God Who is love, and Whose universe is the expression of God's desire to glorify Himself.

In January 1758 Edwards became president of the College of New Jersey (now Princeton). Two months later he died of fever resulting from a smallpox inoculation. He was buried in Princeton.

Further Reading

Two volumes of Edwards's *Works,* edited by Perry Miller, have appeared (1957). The major biography remains Samuel Hopkins, *Life of the Rev. J. Edwards* (1833), reprinted in *Jonathan Edwards: A Profile,* edited by David Levin (1969). The most important study of Edwards's thought is Perry Miller, *Jonathan Edwards* (1949). Other important studies are Ola E. Winslow, *Jonathan Edwards, 1703-1758* (1940); Douglas Elwood, *Philosophical Theology of Jonathan Edwards* (1960); and James Carse, *Jonathan Edwards and the Visibility of God* (1967). For background see Perry Miller, *The New England Mind: From Colony to Province* (1953), and Alan E. Heimert, *Religion and the American Mind* (1967). □

Melvin Edwards

Melvin Edwards (born 1937) was an American sculptor who attempted to work within accepted mainstream aesthetic standards without rejecting his African heritage. His art addressed his existence as an African-American as well as the oppression of African people in their native countries.

Melvin Edwards was born in Houston, Texas, on May 4, 1937. His early interest in art was encouraged by his parents. His father built his first easel for him when he was 14. He moved to southern California for his college education, where he attended the Los Angeles City College and the Los Angeles County Art Institute before receiving his B.F.A. degree from the University of Southern California.

After college Edwards was an educator as well as an exhibiting artist. Before leaving California he taught at the San Bernadino Valley College (1964-1965) and the Chouinard Art Institute, now the California Institute of Arts, known as Cal Arts (1965-1967). In 1967 he moved east to be nearer the New York art scene. He then taught at the

Orange County Community College, New York (1967-1969), and the University of Connecticut (1970-1972). In 1972 he went to Rutgers University's Mason Gross School of the Arts, where he was still teaching in the 1990s.

His first one-artist exhibition was mounted by the Santa Barbara Museum of Art in 1965. Later he had solo exhibitions at the Whitney Museum of American Art in New York, the Walker Art Center in Minneapolis, the Studio Museum in Harlem, and the Maison de l'UNESCO, Paris, France, to name a few. His work is in many public and corporate collections, including the Museum of Modern Art, New York; Los Angeles County Museum; New Jersey State Museum; Chase Manhattan Bank; and Peat Marwick Inc. He has outdoor sculpture in Mount Vernon Plaza, Columbus, Ohio; Lafayette Gardens, Jersey City, New Jersey; on the Winston-Salem campus of North Carolina State University; and at the U.S. Social Security Federal Plaza, Jamaica, New York. Yet he did not receive his first one-man exhibition in a New York gallery until March of 1990.

Almost from the time Edwards started making sculpture (around 1963), he began a series of small welded steel pieces he called *Lynch Fragments,* and he continued to add to this series at various times throughout his career. These wall-mounted reliefs, usually no more than a foot tall, consist of bent and welded steel frequently combined with found objects such as nails, short lengths of chain, and discarded machine parts. Like the African ceremonial masks that inspired them, the *Lynch Fragments* express emotional extremes. Edwards' use of found objects not only has its precedence in modern art, but recalls the African practice of empowering so-called "fetish" figures with nails, blades, and other materials.

Shortly after moving to New York in 1967, Edwards was commissioned to produce an outdoor sculpture for Bethune Tower, a middle-income housing project built by the New York City Housing and Development Administration. *Double Circle* (1968) consists of four eight-foot-diameter steel disks, each with an opening in the center of approximately six feet. The four rings are mounted on edge one behind the other at sidewalk level, inviting visitors to walk through and between them.

Edwards' exhibition at the Whitney Museum of American Art in 1970 featured four installations of barbed wire and chain. *Pyramid Up and Down Pyramid* consisted of strands of barbed wire of varying lengths stretched between two converging walls to create the single plane of an inverted pyramid descending from the ceiling to a point where the two walls meet the floor. *Curtain for William and Peter* was a curtain of barbed wire suspended from the ceiling and weighted at the bottom by scallops of heavy chain. These works have an affinity to the dematerialized perceptual installations of the 1960s, such as Dan Flavin's fluorescent light sculptures, but Edwards' choice of barbed wire charged his sculptures with social and political meaning.

Edwards' experiments with barbed wire formed an interim between his early *Lynch Fragments* and his *Rocker* series, begun after the Whitney exhibition. The *Rocker* series employs large semicircular steel plates on which the sculptures rock. The series was conceived when Edwards' interest in kinetic sculpture and animated film sparked childhood memories of his Grandmother Cora's oak Mission rocking chair. Like the *Lynch Fragments,* the *Rocker* series is a theme to which Edwards continued to return throughout his career. In 1978 the Studio Museum in Harlem organized a retrospective exhibition of these two aspects of his work: the *Lynch Fragments* from 1963 to 1966 and the *Rockers* of 1972 to 1978.

A third aspect of Edwards' work is his outdoor public sculpture. In 1981 the New Jersey State Museum in Trenton exhibited six monumental works around the exterior of the museum. Like his first public commission, *Double Circle,* and the *Rocker* series, his large, outdoor pieces are, for the most part, comprised of geometric shapes. *Confirmation,* a public sculpture commissioned in 1989 under the art-in-architecture program of the General Services Administration for the U.S. Social Security Federal Plaza in Jamaica, New York, is representative. It consists of a 12-foot-tall disk leaning against and welded to an arch. The surface of the entire sculpture is polished steel. The influence of African sculpture is present in the geometric compositions, albeit filtered through Western Cubism.

Edwards refused to assign specific meanings to any aspect of his art, even though it is filled with layers of symbolism and implication. Hints at the artist's intent are present in some of his titles. *Homage to Billy Holiday and the Young Ones of Soweto* stands on the campus of Morgan State University in Baltimore. *Homage to My Father and the Spirit* is at Cornell University in Ithaca, New York. *Angola,* which commemorates the independence of that country, was included in the 1976 American Bicentennial exhibition at the Museum of Modern Art, New York. Also, many of the *Lynch Fragments* have African titles, such as *Da Ten Da Mhiza.* In general terms, the *Lynch Fragments* are personal reflections on his African heritage as well as expressions of the fear and anger of the civil rights movement. The large outdoor pieces, in comparison, are open, bright, optimistic, and playful. However, the chain, a frequently recurring motif, evokes oppression, alienation, and slavery.

Edwards continued to explore his heritage, to educate others, and to accumulate awards. He traveled repeatedly to Nigeria, Ghana, Egypt, France, Mexico, and Cuba. He received a New Jersey State Arts Council grant, a Guggenheim Foundation fellowship, and two National Endowment for the Arts fellowships. In 1988 and 1989 Edwards, the great great-grandson of an African blacksmith brought to the United States as a slave, received Fulbright fellowships to travel to Zimbabwe to conduct workshops in the art of metal sculpture for artists of that country.

Further Reading

Melvin Edwards, the exhibition catalogue published by the Studio Museum in Harlem, New York, in 1978, includes an essay by Mary Schmidt Campbell and "Notes on Black Art," a statement written by Edwards at the invitation of the Whitney Museum of American Art in 1971. (The Whitney refused to publish it.) *Melvin Edwards: Sculptures 1964-84* was published by the Maison de l'UNESCO in Paris, France, in conjunction with an exhibition there in November 1984. It includes essays, in French, by April Kingsey and Mary Schmidt Campbell and a statement by the artist. "Black Art: Talking about Books," in the *Two Rivers Quarterly* (London, 1970) is an article on Edwards by Frank Bowling, a frequent contributor to *Art News* and *Arts* magazine on African-American art.

For contextual background, *Since the Harlem Renaissance: 50 Years of Afro-American Art,* the catalogue of an exhibition organized by the Center Gallery of Bucknell University, Lewisburg, Pennsylvania, in 1984, includes statements by many of the artists as well as brief essays about the history of African-American art. Also, *The Pluralist Era: American Art 1968-1981* by Corinne Robins (1984) includes a chapter on African-American art and artists. □

Edward Eggleston

Edward Eggleston (1837-1902) was an American minister and historian. He was also Indiana's leading writer of local-color fiction.

B orn in Vevay, Ind., Edward Eggleston, too frail to attend school regularly, was taught by his father to read in several languages. His religious training was intensified after his parents' conversion to Methodism and then, after his father's death in 1846, by his mother's marriage 4 years later to a Methodist minister.

Ordained as a minister himself in 1856, Eggleston served as a circuit rider, Bible agent, and minister. He was a Methodist preacher in Minnesota churches in 1858, when he married Lizzie Snyder. They had four children. Beginning in 1866 Eggleston edited and wrote for Sunday school and juvenile periodicals. By 1874 he had abandoned Methodism; in Brooklyn, N.Y., he founded the Church of Christian Endeavor, serving as its pastor until 1879. Meanwhile he had begun to publish adult fiction serially in the magazine *House and Home,* of which he was editor.

Eggleston's *The Hoosier School-Master* (1871), much admired by subscribers and later by the public, was based on the experiences of his brother George and influenced by James Russell Lowell's dialect poems and southwestern humorous works. This realistic account of life in backwoods Indiana helped launch the local-color movement that flourished in America for 3 decades. Eggleston's reputation was furthered by *The End of the World* (1872), about the Millerite religious sect in pioneer Indiana, and *The Circuit Rider* (1872), based on personal experiences. *Roxy* (1878) portrays a river town much like Vevay. Eggleton's final noteworthy novel, *The Graysons* (1888), is a historical romance in which the young Lincoln is a character.

Eggleston had long considered his fiction a kind of history. Between 1878 and 1888 he published several biographies and histories for children. In accordance with a view he expressed in 1900 as president of the American Historical Association, he planned a comprehensive account of the growth of American civilization. His belief—much more novel then than it was later—was that the best history is a record of a people's culture, not of its politics

Ilya Grigorievich Ehrenburg

The Soviet author Ilya Grigorievich Ehrenburg (1891-1967) is best known for his role as a man of letters throughout the first 50 years of Soviet history. He wrote more than 100 books and pamphlets, which range from lyric verse, to fiction, to journalism.

Ilya Ehrenburg was born on Jan. 27, 1891, in Kiev. He came from a middle-class Jewish family, and his father worked in a brewery. The rampant anti-Semitism of Kievan life at the turn of the century made a deep impression on young Ehrenburg. Throughout his life he engaged in the fight against racism. In 1896 Ehrenburg's family moved to Moscow, where Ilya entered the First Moscow Gymnasium. Although he was a poor student, he drew inspiration from Moscow life. Leo Tolstoy kept a townhouse next to the Ehrenburg home, and Maxim Gorky lived for a short while in the Ehrenburg house.

Ehrenburg's formal education ended in 1907, when he was expelled from the gymnasium for leading an anticzarist strike. He had been exposed at school to ideas of revolution and early leaned toward the Bolshevik ideology. Ehrenburg was arrested several times in 1907 and 1908 for radical writings, and he was finally exiled in 1908. His exile brought him to Paris in 1909, where he settled down in the emigre artists' colony.

The experiences of Ehrenburg in Paris from 1909 to 1917 and from 1924 to 1940 left an indelible impression on his life and art. His acquaintance with Pablo Picasso and Diego Rivera introduced him to the avant-garde in the arts. His contacts among Russian emigres led him to reflect on the problems of Russia's historical destiny in the context of European civilization. During the 1910s Ehrenburg led the life of a literary bohemian, attending lectures at the Haute École des Études Sociales, working as a tourist guide and stevedore, and testing his talent as a writer. His first literary work was poetry, and he published a book of poems entitled *Paris* at his own expense in 1910. Ehrenburg spent much of World War I working as a correspondent for various Russian newspapers.

Ehrenburg had deep reservations about the Russian Revolution. He returned to Russia in 1917 after the February Revolution, working at various literary and journalistic jobs until 1921. Ehrenburg married in 1919, and he and his family left the Soviet Union in 1921, traveling about Europe until 1924, when they settled in Paris. In 1921 in Belgium, Ehrenburg wrote his most successful novel, *The Extraordinary Adventures of Julio Jurenito and His Disciples.* This satirical novel portrays the comical adventures of a Mexican as he confronts the absurdities of capitalist and socialist life in Europe and the Soviet Union.

From 1924 until his return to Moscow in 1940, Ehrenburg lived the life of a journalist and free-lance writer throughout Europe. Although he came to accept the role of the Soviet Union in world affairs and to praise the Soviet

and wars. *The Beginners of a Nation,* subtitled "A History of the Source and Rise of the Earliest English Settlements in America with Special Reference to the Life and Character of the People," appeared in 1896, and in 1901 he published *The Transit of Civilization from England to America in the Seventeenth Century.* These were the only volumes Eggleston completed before a stroke partially disabled him in 1899; a second stroke led to his death on Sept. 2, 1902, at Lake George, N.Y. The two social histories, which Carl Van Doren called "erudite, humane, and graceful," were pioneering achievements. Eggleston was survived by his second wife, whom he had married in 1891.

Further Reading

George Cary Eggleston, Edward's brother and also a successful writer, provides an intimate memoir, *The First of the Hoosiers* (1903). William Randel wrote a superior biography, *Edward Eggleston: Author of the Hoosier School-Master* (1946). Randel is also the author of an excellent critical study, *Edward Eggleston* (1963).

Additional Sources

Randel, William Peirce, *Edward Eggleston,* New York, Twayne Publishers c1963. ☐

Union's opposition to fascism, Ehrenburg was hesitant about committing himself to life in the Soviet Union. In 1932 he became a regular correspondent for the Soviet newspaper *Izvestia*. His duties as journalist took him to Spain in the 1930s, where he wrote about the Spanish Civil War. In 1940 he was again in Paris, then occupied by German troops. His book *The Fall of Paris* (1942) presents an excellent account of the Occupation.

Ehrenburg returned to Moscow in 1940 with a world-wide reputation. He worked as a war correspondent for the Soviet newspaper *Pravda* throughout World War II. Ehrenburg's attitudes toward the unreasonable strictures placed on the Soviet writer by socialist realism were ambivalent until after the death of Stalin. In 1954, however, Ehrenburg published *The Thaw,* depicting the harm done to Soviet writing by the heavy hand of the Soviet bureaucracy. The title of this novel became the name of the liberal decade of the 1950s in Soviet literature. Ehrenburg further contributed to the thaw in Soviet literary policy with his memoirs, *People, Years, Life,* published in the late 1950s and early 1960s. Ehrenburg's memoirs are a valuable source of information for students of Soviet literature.

Ehrenburg was an urbane man, an extremely prolific writer, and a protector of the arts. He died in Moscow on Sept. 1, 1967.

Further Reading

The best source on Ehrenburg's life is his autobiography. For critical appraisals of his writings see Max Eastman, *Artists in Uniform: A Study of Literature and Bureaucratism* (1934), and Vera Alexandrova, *A History of Soviet Literature* (1963). □

pects—in which his idea of a chemical binding of heterogeneous substances to protoplasm was first expressed. Already in 1876, he had discovered the "mast" cell by its basophilic granules.

Early in his student career Ehrlich started investigations which in spite of their apparent diversity converged on a common principle: the action of drugs as a manifestation of their specific affinity for particular constituents of cells. According to Ehrlich, substances which affect bodily functions do so by virtue of combining with particular components of the animal. In chemical idiom, certain atom groups (side chains) of the drug combine with receptor atom groups of the cellular protoplasm and lead to the action. This was his famous "side-chain theory."

Ehrlich spent several years in Egypt recovering from a severe case of phthisis. On his return to Germany, Robert Koch, from whom Ehrlich had received an understanding of the modern discipline of cellular pathology and also the relation of bacteriology to disease processes, offered him a place in his new Institute for Infectious Diseases. Here Ehrlich perfected methods of preparing and standardizing diphtheria antitoxin from horses. Meanwhile he was appointed director of the State Institute for Serum Research and Serum Control at Steglitz near Berlin. Work on tumors and immunological studies occupied the forefront of his research until about 1909. In 1908 Ehrlich received the Nobel Prize in medicine for his studies on immunity.

Paul Ehrlich

The German bacteriologist Paul Ehrlich (1854-1915) advanced the science and practice of medicine by applying the fast-growing achievements of organic chemistry to the problems of disease. He is known for his discovery of Salvarsan.

Paul Ehrlich was born on March 14, 1854, at Strehlen, Upper Silesia. While still at school he took a great interest in chemical experiments and even got the local druggist to compound throat lozenges according to his original prescription.

Preparatory Work

At first Ehrlich attended Breslau University but found it dull and uninteresting because it lacked biology and organic chemistry, his favorite subjects. Accordingly, he passed on to the new University of Strasbourg, where he experimented with histological staining, but he returned to Breslau in his third term. In 1878 he graduated in medicine at Leipzig. His thesis was a contribution on the theory and practice of histological staining—the conception of the processes in their chemical, technological, and histological as-

Science of Chemotherapy

The Speyer-Ellissen family of Frankfurt offered to endow a research institute for Ehrlich's work on chemo-therapy. The institute, named George Speyer-Haus, was built, and in 1906 Ehrlich became director. The methods of chemotherapy, that is, treating infections with synthetic compounds antagonistic to pathogenic agents without seriously damaging the host, had arisen in 1891, when it was observed that methylene blue exercises a curative action on human malaria. Before the founding of the institute, Ehrlich had conducted work on an experimental scale with a small staff, and this resulted in a veritable miracle: the cure of a trypanosome infection that was invariably fatal in mice in 3—4 days. Cure followed one subcutaneous injection of a synthetic dye, trypan red, administered within 24 hours of the anticipated time of death. Other drugs were found to possess a degree of therapeutic effect, and certain organic arsenical compounds, "atoxyl" derivatives, also proved to be trypanocidal. From these the drug Salvarsan was derived, which Ehrlich found to be the most efficient curative agent for human syphilis then known, although it was sometimes liable to produce toxic effects. The science of chemotherapy was thus born.

Ehrlich's tremendous achievements were the outcome of a life of unremitting scientific preoccupation to which almost everything was sacrificed. The furor of Salvarsan made him one of the celebrities of his time, both in science and commerce. He died in Bad Homburg, Hesse, on Aug. 20, 1915.

Further Reading

For Ehrlich's own writings see F. Himmelweit, ed., *The Collected Papers of Paul Ehrlich* (1956). Accounts of Ehrlich's life and work are Herman Goodman, *Paul Ehrlich: A Man of Genius and an Inspiration to Humanitarians* (1924), and Martha Marquardt, *Paul Ehrlich* (1951). A sketch of his life is in Theodore L. Sourkes, *Nobel Prize Winners in Medicine and Physiology, 1901-1965* (1953; rev. ed. 1966). □

Adolf Eichmann

Adolf Eichmann (1906-1962) was responsible for the persecution and murder of millions of Jews in the death camps in Europe during World War II.

On May 13, 1960, Adolf Eichmann was seized by Israeli agents in Argentina and smuggled back to Jerusalem to stand trial for his role in the murder of one-third of Europe's Jewish people during World War II. The Eichmann trial of April through August 1961 gained world-wide attention as the most important trial of Nazi criminality since the Nuremberg trial of 1945-1946. For the first time a Jewish court convened in judgment upon a former persecutor. Eichmann was that SS (Schutzstaffel) officer responsible for transporting Jews and other victims to the extermination camps. What motivated him? The trial testimony showed him to be the ultimate conformist in a criminal state. As he said to an interrogator, "If they told me that my own father was a traitor and I had to kill him, I'd have done it. At that time I obeyed my orders without thinking, I just did as I was told. That's where I found my—how shall I say?—my fulfillment. It made no difference what the orders were."

(Karl) Adolf Eichmann was born into a religious middle-class Protestant family in Solingen in western Germany near the Rhine river on March 19, 1906. His father, an accountant for an electrical company, moved his family to Linz, Austria, in 1914. Eichmann's mother died when he was ten. Unlike his three brothers and one sister he was a poor student. Because of his dark looks he was apparently chided as "the little Jew." In Linz Eichmann went to the same secondary school Hitler had attended some 15 years before.

The resentment in Germany and Austria after defeat in World War I twisted an already inflamed nationalism, fed a lie that Germany had been "stabbed in the back" by the Jews. In 1919, amidst this new wave of anti-Semitism, the 13-year-old Eichmann was named in a newspaper as a member of a gang of youths who had tormented a Jewish classmate. Eichmann kept a precise record of each gang member's turn in beating up the victim (who died 20 years later in a death camp).

In the 1920s Eichmann drifted. He studied electrical engineering without success until his father decided that he should become an apprentice in an electrical appliance company, but his father wasn't satisfied with his son's progress there either. In 1928 Eichmann became a travelling salesman for an oil company through the help of Jewish relatives of his stepmother. He enjoyed his independence and his sporty car and became a joiner. As a member of the youth section of the Austro-German Veterans' Organization, he marched through the streets of Linz challenging the social democrats and cheering German nationalism. In 1932 the fanatical young Ernst Kaltenbrunner recruited Eichmann for the Austrian Nazi party and the SS. The Nazis promised that Austria would become part of a powerful German nation-state, and being a member of the SS gave Eichmann the chance to act superior after years of feeling inferior. Kaltenbrunner's father and Eichmann's father had been friends; their sons would make careers together in the SS. Kaltenbrunner became chief of the Security Service of the SS, second to Heinrich Himmler (and was hung as a war criminal in 1946).

When the Austrian government banned the Nazi Party in 1933, Eichmann, who did not have a job at the time, moved to Nazi Germany and joined the SS "Austrian Legion in exile." After a year he transferred to the Security Service where he found a niche for himself as an "expert" on Jewish affairs. He learned about Zionism and even briefly visited Palestine. When Austria was annexed by the Third Reich in 1938 Eichmann efficiently organized the expulsion of 45,000 Austrian Jews, first stripping them of their possessions. He became known in SS circles as the expert on forced emigration. When Germany invaded Poland, Hitler decided to exterminate the Polish Jews, and Eichmann's organizing ability turned towards mass murder. In the summer of 1941 he was among the first to be told of the "Final

Solution,'' and on January 20, 1942, he was one of 15 who attended the Wannsee Conference where the formal pact was drawn between the political leadership and the bureaucracy to send European Jewry to the death camps. Jews were forced to wear the yellow star of David for easy identification; they were assembled for easy transport to their doom. Eichmann's principal concern was to maintain the killing capacity of the camps by maintaining a steady flow of victims. All the principles of civilization were turned on their head. First into the gas chambers were children, mothers, and the old. About 25 percent of each train load, the strongest men and women, were spared for slave labor. Very many died of starvation, sickness, and overwork. In 1944 Eichmann reported to Himmler that some four million Jews were killed in the camps and some two million more had been shot or killed by mobile units.

Eichmann was a bureaucratic mass murderer; he avoided the extermination sites and shielded himself from his acts through a bureaucratic language that deadened his conscience. Eichmann was limited, compartmentalized in mind and spirit. ''Officialese is my only language,'' he said at his trial. Eichmann exemplified the terrifying discrepancy between the unparalleled and monstrous crime and the colorless official who carried out the evil. He viewed his victims as objects to be transported to their deaths as if they were nuts and bolts, and in 1944 he unsuccessfully sought to trade the lives of one million Jews for 10,000 trucks.

At the end of the war Eichmann was rounded up, but he managed to disguise his identity and escaped detection. ODESSA, the secret SS organization, arranged his flight to Argentina in 1952. Under the alias of Ricardo Klement, Eichmann created a new identity as the unassuming employee of the Mercedes-Benz car factory in Buenos Aires. His wife and two sons joined him.

On December 15, 1961, the Israeli court sentenced Eichmann to hang. His last words on June 1, 1962, were that he would not forget Austria, Germany, and Argentina. He was 56; his corpse was cremated, and his ashes scattered over the sea. Eichmann's inhuman acts in the name of Germany seemingly confirmed one 19th-century Austrian's fear that Europe was moving from humanity through nationality to beastiality.

Further Reading

Hannah Arendt, *Eichmann in Jerusalem: A Report on the Banality of Evil* (1963) and Jochen von Lang, editor, *Eichmann Interrogated: Transcripts from the Archives of the Israeli Police* (1984) provide additional information on Eichmann's activities and thoughts.

Additional Sources

Malkin, Peter Z., *Eichmann in my hands,* New York, NY: Warner Books, 1990. □

Alexandre Gustave Eiffel

The French engineer Alexandre Gustave Eiffel (1832-1923) is best known for the Eiffel Tower, which he built in Paris in 1889.

Born in Dijon, Gustave Eiffel studied at the École Polytechnique and the École Centrale in Paris. He designed numerous bridges, the first in 1858 in Bordeaux, viaducts, and exhibition buildings; the ultimate in exhibition architecture came in 1889, when he built his famous tower in Paris. Throughout his life he was concerned with innovative structures and especially with the effects of wind loading on plane surfaces. He built an air tunnel in his laboratory at Auteuil for experimental purposes.

Eiffel's most famous bridge, the Maria Pia over the Douro at Oporto, Portugal (1876), spans 500 feet by a single arch, 200 feet above high-water level, which with additional side pylons supports the horizontal superstructure. Also during that year Eiffel collaborated with the architect. L.A. Boileau the Younger on the Bon Marché Department Store in Paris, the first glass and cast iron department store. A glass wall along all three street facades, with circular pavilions at the corners, enclosed a store comprising open courts covered by skylights to an extent of 30,000 square feet. Slender columns supported balconies, bridges, and the glazed roof. The store still stands, although it has a masonry skin added in the 1920s.

Eiffel's Garabit viaduct over the Truyère near Ruines, France, is 1,625 feet long and 400 feet high and has a central span of 210 feet. Other works by Eiffel include a revolving cupola for the Nice Observatory, and the structure that supports F.A. Bartholdi's Statue of Liberty in New York City (1886).

An associate engineer on the Garabit viaduct, Maurice Koechlin, encouraged Eiffel in his design for the Paris exhibition tower of 1889. It was the factory-made components, fitted together on the site for the viaduct, that made the 984-foot-high Eiffel Tower possible.

Each of the 12,000 different component parts of the tower was designed to counteract wind pressures, and 2,500,000 rivets were used to create a continuous structure. Four main piers, each with a slight curve, anchored to separate foundations incorporated elevators; two acted on a combined principle of pistons and chains, and the two American Otis elevators acted on a hydraulic piston system. Other hydraulic elevator systems linked the first level to the second one and the second level to the third.

Further Reading

Jean Prévost, *Eiffel* (1929), the only monograph on Eiffel, is brief and in French. Two publications in English on the Eiffel Tower are Gaston Tissandier, *The Eiffel Tower* (1889), and Robert M. Vogel, *Elevator Systems of the Eiffel Tower, 1889* (1961). Siegfried Giedion, *Space, Time, and Architecture: The Growth of a New Tradition* (1941; 5th ed. 1967), connects

Eiffel with the development of structural techniques of the 19th century. □

Christian Eijkman

The Dutch physician and biologist Christian Eijkman (1858-1930) was a pioneer in the study of the biochemical basis of health and in the recognition and study of vitamins.

Christian Eijkman was born to a schoolteacher in Nijkerk on Aug. 11, 1858. He took his degree in medicine at Amsterdam in 1883 and then trained as medical officer for the army of the Dutch East Indies. His first official position was as assistant to the Dutch commission to study the scourge of beriberi in Batavia. The commission returned to Europe in 1887, but Eijkman remained as director from 1885 to 1896. In 1898 he was called to the chair of hygiene and forensic medicine at Utrecht. He became a member of the Royal Academy of Sciences of the Netherlands in 1907.

Eijkman arrived in Batavia at a time when there had been many severe outbreaks of beriberi. Beriberi is characterized by ascending paralysis and cardiac symptoms and edema, and it carried a frightful 80 percent mortality in some outbreaks. The epidemic nature of the disease seemed to be strong evidence that it was spread by a pathogen. As director of the civilian research laboratory, Eijkman, having been unable to isolate a causative organism, began to study the laboratory chickens which had been struck by the disease. None of the refined autopsy techniques indicated that the disease was infectious. Then fate revealed the clue to the puzzle: the chickens were being fed polished white rice, but when whole rice grain was given instead, the animals recovered. Eijkman also demonstrated that the disease could be produced at will by feeding the chickens only polished rice and that the husks removed by polishing would cure the disease if given with the polished rice.

Eijkman's work led to investigations of prisons where beriberi was rampant. It was found that men fed primarily on polished rice were stricken, while those who consumed crudely crushed whole grain rice remained healthy. Eijkman drew the conclusion that the disease was linked to the mode of rice preparation, but he incorrectly assumed that the husks contained an antidote to a toxic substance in the grain.

In 1896 ill health brought Eijkman back to Holland. Meanwhile his collaborators in Java, particularly Gerrit Grijns, continued to explore the beriberi problem and eventually demonstrated conclusively that the disease was caused by a dietary deficiency, not a poison. In 1911 the Polish chemist Casimir Funk separated a substance from grain polishings which could cure the disease. He named it Vitamine; it is now known as vitamin B_1 (thiamine). The world was a giant step closer to understanding the biochemical nature of nutrition.

Eijkman won the Nobel Prize in medicine in 1929. He died on Nov. 5, 1930.

Further Reading

Biographical sketches of Eijkman can be found in Sarah R. Riedman and Elton T. Gustofson, *Portraits of Nobel Laureates in Medicine and Physiology* (1963) and *Nobel Lectures, Physiology and Medicine: Including Presentation Speeches and Laureates' Biographies, 1922-1941* (1965). Useful general works include T. R. Parsons, *The Materials of Life: A General Presentation of Biochemistry* (1930), and F. R. Jevons, *The Biochemical Approach to Life* (1964; 2d ed. 1968). □

Albert Einstein

The German-born American physicist Albert Einstein (1879-1955) revolutionized the science of physics. He is best known for his theory of relativity.

In the history of the exact sciences, only a handful of men—men like Nicolaus Copernicus and Isaac Newton—share the honor that was Albert Einstein's: the initiation of a revolution in scientific thought. His insights into the nature of the physical world made it impossible for physicists and philosophers to view that world as they had before. When describing the achievements of other physicists, the tendency is to enumerate their major discoveries; when describing the achievements of Einstein, it is possible to say, simply, that he revolutionized physics.

Albert Einstein was born on March 14, 1879, in Ulm, but he grew up and obtained his early education in Munich. He was not a child prodigy; in fact, he was unable to speak fluently at age 9. Finding profound joy, liberation, and security in contemplating the laws of nature, already at age 5 he had experienced a deep feeling of wonder when puzzling over the invisible, yet definite, force directing the needle of a compass. Seven years later he experienced a different kind of wonder: the deep emotional stirring that accompanied his discovery of Euclidean geometry, with its lucid and certain proofs. Einstein mastered differential and integral calculus by age 16.

Education in Zurich

Einstein's formal secondary education was abruptly terminated at 16. He found life in school intolerable, and just as he was scheming to find a way to leave without impairing his chances for entering the university, his teacher expelled him for the negative effects his rebellious attitude was having on the morale of his classmates. Einstein tried to enter the Federal Institute of Technology (FIT) in Zurich, Switzerland, but his knowledge of nonmathematical disciplines was not equal to that of mathematics and he failed the entrance examination. On the advice of the principal, he thereupon first obtained his diploma at the Cantonal School in Aarau, and in 1896 he was automatically admitted into the FIT. There he came to realize that his deepest interest

and facility lay in physics, both experimental and theoretical, rather than in mathematics.

Einstein passed his diploma examination at the FIT in 1900, but due to the opposition of one of his professors he was unable to subsequently obtain the usual university assistantship. In 1902 he was engaged as a technical expert, third-class, in the patent office in Bern, Switzerland. Six months later he married Mileva Maric, a former classmate in Zurich. They had two sons. It was in Bern, too, that Einstein, at 26, completed the requirements for his doctoral degree and wrote the first of his revolutionary scientific papers.

Academic Career

These papers made Einstein famous, and universities soon began competing for his services. In 1909, after serving as a lecturer at the University of Bern, Einstein was called as an associate professor to the University of Zurich. Two years later he was appointed a full professor at the German University in Prague. Within another year and a half Einstein became a full professor at the FIT. Finally, in 1913 the well-known scientists Max Planck and Walter Nernst traveled to Zurich to persuade Einstein to accept a lucrative research professorship at the University of Berlin, as well as full membership in the Prussian Academy of Science. He accepted their offer in 1914, quipping: "The Germans are gambling on me as they would on a prize hen. I do not really know myself whether I shall ever really lay another egg." When he went to Berlin, his wife remained behind in Zurich with their two sons; after their divorce he married his cousin Elsa in 1917.

In 1920 Einstein was appointed to a lifelong honorary visiting professorship at the University of Leiden. During 1921-1922 Einstein, accompanied by Chaim Weizmann, the future president of the state of Israel, undertook extensive worldwide travels in the cause of Zionism. In Germany the attacks on Einstein began. Philipp Lenard and Johannes Stark, both Nobel Prize-winning physicists, began characterizing Einstein's theory of relativity as "Jewish physics." This callousness and brutality increased until Einstein resigned from the Prussian Academy of Science in 1933. (He was, however, expelled from the Bavarian Academy of Science.)

Career in America

On several occasions Einstein had visited the California Institute of Technology, and on his last trip to the United States Abraham Flexner offered Einstein—on Einstein's terms—a position in the newly conceived and funded Institute for Advanced Studies in Princeton. He went there in 1933.

Einstein played a key role (1939) in mobilizing the resources necessary to construct the atomic bomb by signing a famous letter to President Franklin D. Roosevelt which had been drafted by Leo Szilard and E.P. Wigner. When Einstein's famous equation $E = mc^2$ was finally demonstrated in the most awesome and terrifying way by using the bomb to destroy Hiroshima in 1945, Einstein, the pacifist and humanitarian, was deeply shocked and distressed; for a long time he could only utter "Horrible, horrible." On April 18, 1955, Einstein died in Princeton.

Theory of Brownian Motion

From numerous references in Einstein's writings it is evident that, of all areas in physics, thermodynamics made the deepest impression on him. During 1902-1904 Einstein reworked the foundations of thermodynamics and statistical mechanics; this work formed the immediate background to his revolutionary papers of 1905, one of which was on Brownian motion.

In Brownian motion (first observed in 1827 by the Scottish botanist Robert Brown), small particles suspended in a viscous liquid such as water undergo a rapid, irregular motion. Einstein, unaware of Brown's earlier observations, concluded from his theoretical studies that such a motion must exist. Guided by the thought that if the liquid in which the particles are suspended consists of atoms or molecules they should collide with the particles and set them into motion, he found that while the particle's motion is irregular, fluctuating back and forth, it will in time nevertheless experience a net forward displacement. Einstein proved that this net forward displacement of the suspended particles is directly related to the number of molecules per gram atomic weight. This point created a good deal of skepticism toward Einstein's theory at the time he developed it (1905-1906), but when it was fully confirmed many of the skeptics were converted. Brownian motion is to this day regarded as one of the most direct proofs of the existence of atoms.

Light Quanta and Wave-Particle Duality

The most common misconceptions concerning Einstein's introduction of his revolutionary light quantum (light particle) hypothesis in 1905 are that he simply applied Planck's quantum hypothesis of 1900 to radiation and that he introduced light quanta to "explain" the photoelectric effect discovered in 1887 by Heinrich Hertz and thoroughly investigated in 1902 by Philipp Lenard. Neither of these assertions is accurate. Einstein's arguments for his light quantum hypothesis—that under certain circumstances radiant energy (light) behaves as if it consists not of waves but of particles of energy proportional to their frequencies—were absolutely fundamental and, as in the case of his theory of Brownian motion, based on his own insights into the foundations of thermodynamics and statistical mechanics. Furthermore, it was only after presenting strong arguments for the necessity of his light quantum hypothesis that Einstein pursued its experimental consequences. One of several such consequences was the photoelectric effect, the experiment in which high-frequency ultraviolet light is used to eject electrons from thin metal plates. In particular, Einstein assumed that a single quantum of light transfers its entire energy to a single electron in the metal plate. The famous equation he derived was fully consistent with Lenard's observation that the energy of the ejected electrons depends only on the frequency of the ultraviolet light and not on its intensity. Einstein was not disturbed by the fact that this apparently contradicts James Clerk Maxwell's classic electromagnetic wave theory of light, because he realized that there were good reasons to doubt the universal validity of Maxwell's theory.

Although Einstein's famous equation for the photoelectric effect—for which he won the Nobel Prize of 1921—appears so natural today, it was an extremely bold prediction in 1905. Not until a decade later did R.A. Millikan finally succeed in experimentally verifying it to everyone's satisfaction. But while Einstein's equation was bold, his light quantum hypothesis was revolutionary: it amounted to reviving Newton's centuries-old idea that light consists of particles.

No one tried harder than Einstein to overcome opposition to this hypothesis. Thus, in 1907 he proved the fruitfulness of the entire quantum hypothesis by showing it could at least qualitatively account for the low-temperature behavior of the specific heats of solids. Two years later he proved that Planck's radiation law of 1900 demands the *coexistence* of particles and waves in blackbody radiation, a proof that represents the birth of the wave-particle duality. In 1917 Einstein presented a very simple and very important derivation of Planck's radiation law (the modern laser, for example, is based on the concepts Einstein introduced here), and he also proved that light quanta must carry momentum as well as energy.

Meanwhile, Einstein had become involved in another series of researches having a direct bearing on the wave-particle duality. In mid-1924 S.N. Bose produced a very insightful derivation of Planck's radiation law—the origin of Bose-Einstein statistics—which Einstein soon developed into his famous quantum theory of an ideal gas. Shortly thereafter, he became acquainted with Louis de Broglie's revolutionary new idea that ordinary material *particles,* such as electrons and gas molecules, should under certain circumstances exhibit *wave* behavior. Einstein saw immediately that De Broglie's idea was intimately related to the Bose-Einstein statistics: both indicate that material particles can at times behave like waves. Einstein told Erwin Schrödinger of De Broglie's work, and in 1926 Schrödinger made the extraordinarily important discovery of wave mechanics. Schrödinger's (as well as C. Eckart) then proved that Schrödinger's wave mechanics and Werner Heisenberg's matrix mechanics are mathematically equivalent: they are now collectively known as quantum mechanics, one of the two most fruitful physical theories of the 20th century. Since Einstein's insights formed much of the background to both Schrödinger's and Heisenberg's discoveries, the debt quantum physicists owe to Einstein can hardly be exaggerated.

Theory of Relativity

The second of the two most fruitful physical theories of the 20th century is the theory of relativity, which to scientists and laymen alike is synonymous with the name of Einstein. Once again, there is a common misconception concerning the origin of this theory, namely, that Einstein advanced it in 1905 to "explain" the famous Michelson-Morley experiment (1887), which failed to detect a relative motion of the earth with respect to the ether, the medium through which light was assumed to propagate. In fact, it is not even certain that Einstein was aware of this experiment in 1905; nor was he familiar with H.A. Lorentz's elegant 1904 paper in which Lorentz applied the transformation equations which bear his name to electrodynamic phenomena. Rather, Einstein consciously searched for a general principle of nature that would hold the key to the explanation of a paradox that had occurred to him when he was 16: if, on the one hand, one runs at, say, 4 miles per hour alongside a train moving at 4 miles per hour, the train appears to be at rest; if, on the other hand, it were possible to run alongside a ray of light, neither experiment nor theory suggests that the ray of light—an oscillating electromagnetic wave—would appear to be at rest. Einstein eventually saw that he could *postulate* that no matter what the velocity of the observer, he must always observe the same velocity c for the velocity of light: roughly 186,000 miles per second. He also saw that this postulate was consistent with a second postulate: if an observer at rest and an observer moving at constant velocity carry out the same kind of experiment, they must get the same result. These are Einstein's two postulates of his special theory of relativity. Also in 1905 Einstein proved that his theory predicted that energy E and mass m are entirely interconvertible according to his famous equation, $E = mc^2$.

For observational confirmation of his general theory of relativity, Einstein boldly predicted the gravitational red shift and the deflection of starlight (an amended value), as well as the quantitative explanation of U. J. J. Leverrier's long-unexplained observation that the perihelion of the planet Mercury precesses about the sun at the rate of 43 seconds of arc per century. In addition, Einstein in 1916 predicted the existence of gravitational waves, which have only recently been detected. Turning to cosmological problems the following year, Einstein found a solution to his field equations consistent with the picture (the Einstein universe) that the universe is static, approximately uniformly filled with a finite amount of matter, and finite but unbounded (in the same sense that the surface area of a smooth globe is finite but has no beginning or end).

The Man and His Philosophy

Fellow physicists were always struck with Einstein's uncanny ability to penetrate to the heart of a complex problem, to instantly see the physical significance of a complex mathematical result. Both in his scientific and in his personal life, he was utterly independent, a trait that manifested itself in his approach to scientific problems, in his unconventional dress, in his relationships with family and friends, and in his aloofness from university and governmental politics (in spite of his intense social consciousness). Einstein loved to discuss scientific problems with friends, but he was, fundamentally a "horse for single harness."

Einstein's belief in strict causality was closely related to his profound belief in the harmony of nature. That nature can be understood rationally, in mathematical terms, never ceased to evoke a deep—one might say, religious—feeling of admiration in him. "The most incomprehensible thing about the world," he once wrote, "is that it is comprehensible." How do we discover the basic laws and concepts of nature? Einstein argued that while we learn certain features of the world from experience, the free inventive capacity of the human mind is required to formulate physical theories. There is no logical link between the world of experience and the world of theory. Once a theory has been formulated, however, it must be "simple" (or, perhaps, "esthetically pleasing") and agree with experiment. One such esthetically pleasing and fully confirmed theory is the special theory of relativity. When Einstein was informed of D.C. Miller's experiments, which seemed to contradict the special theory by demanding the reinstatement of the ether, he expressed his belief in the spuriousness of Miller's results—and therefore in the harmoniousness of nature—with another of his famous aphorisms, "God is subtle, but he is not malicious."

This frequent use of God's name in Einstein's speeches and writings provides us with a feeling for his religious convictions. He once stated explicitly, "I believe in Spinoza's God who reveals himself in the harmony of all being, not in a God who concerns himself with the fate and actions of men." It is not difficult to see that this credo is consistent with his statement that the "less knowledge a scholar possesses, the farther he feels from God. But the greater his knowledge, the nearer is his approach to God." Since Einstein's God manifested Himself in the harmony of the universe, there could be no conflict between religion and science for Einstein.

To enumerate at this point the many honors that were bestowed upon Einstein during his lifetime would be to devote space to the kind of public acclamation that mattered so little to Einstein himself. How, indeed, can other human beings sufficiently honor one of their number who revolutionized their conception of the physical world, and who lived his life in the conviction that "the only life worth living is a life spent in the service of others"? When Einstein lay dying he could truly utter, as he did, "Here on earth I have done my job." It would be difficult to find a more suitable epitaph than the words Einstein himself used in characterizing his life: "God is inexorable in the way He has allotted His gifts. He gave me the stubbornness of a mule and nothing else; really, He also gave me a keen scent."

Further Reading

Numerous biographies of Einstein have been written. Three of the best are Philipp Frank, *Einstein: His Life and Times,* translated by George Rosen (1947); Carl Seelig, *Albert Einstein: A Documentary Biography,* translated by Mervyn Savill (1956); and Ronald W. Clark, *Einstein: The Life and Times* (1971). Einstein's illuminating "Autobiographical Notes" and bibliographies of his scientific and nonscientific writings can be found in P.A. Schilpp, ed., *Albert Einstein: Philosopher-Scientist* (1949; 2d ed. 1951). See also Max Born, *Einstein's Theory of Relativity* (trans. 1922; rev. ed. 1962); Leopold Infeld, *Albert Einstein: His Work and Its Influence on Our World* (1950); and Max Jammer, *The Conceptual Development of Quantum Mechanics* (1966). □

Eisai

The Japanese Buddhist monk Eisai (1141-1215) introduced the Zen Buddhist Rinzai sect to Japan, and under him Zen first became acknowledged as an independent school of Buddhism. He is also responsible for popularizing the cultivation of tea in Japan.

Also known by his honorific title of Zenko *kokushi* (national teacher), Eisai came from a family of Shinto priests in the district of Okayama. Like many famous priests in his period, he studied at the great Tendai center on Mt. Hiei. In 1168 he made his first trip to China, where he visited Zen centers, especially those flourishing on Mt. T'ien-t'ai. He was much impressed by what he saw and felt with growing conviction that Zen could greatly contribute to a reawakening of Buddhist faith in Japan.

In 1187 he undertook a second trip to the continent for the purpose of tracing the origins of Buddhism to India. The authorities, however, refused him permission to go beyond Chinese borders. He studied on Mt. T'ient'ai until 1191, where he was ordained in the Rinzai (Chinese, Lin-ch'i) sect and returned to Japan. He constructed the first Rinzai temple, the Shofukuji, at Hakata in Kyushu.

Eisai proclaimed the superiority of Zen mediation over other Buddhist disciplines, thus provoking the ire of the Tendai monks who sought to outlaw the new sect. However, Eisai enjoyed the protection of the shogun Minamoto Yoriie, and in 1202 he was given the direction of the Kenninji in Kyoto. Like Saicho, and particularly Nichiren, Eisai associated his type of Buddhism with national welfare and promoted Zen by publishing a tract entitled *Kozen Gokoku Ron* (The Propagation of Zen for the Protection of the Country).

But Eisai was constantly obliged to face Tendai and Shingon opposition. As a compromise, Eisai conducted the Kenninji not as a purely Zen establishment but also with places for Tendai and Shingon worship. Indeed, he continued to recite Shingon magic formulas. Shortly before his death, Eisai established by government order the third Zen monastery at Kamakura, the Jufukuji, and the close relationship of Zen with the military caste dates from this time.

Introduction of Tea

Although tea had been introduced to Japan about 800 by Buddhist monks who had gone to China, its cultivation and consumption were not widespread before Eisai's time. Eisai, returning from China in 1191, brought tea seeds with him and planted them near Kyoto. In 1214 he composed the *Kissa Yojoki* (Drink Tea to Improve Health and Prolong Life), in which he set forth the hygienic and curative value of tea. Tea was considered an important adjunct to Zen mediation, for it acted as a mild stimulant against sleepiness.

Further Reading

A discussion of Eisai and excerpts from his writings may be found in Ryusaku Tsunoda and others, eds., *Sources of the Japanese Tradition* (1958). A good book on the history of Zen is Heinrich Dumoulin, *A History of Zen Buddhism* (trans. 1963). □

Loren Corey Eiseley

Trained as an anthropologist and paleontologist, Loren Corey Eiseley (1907-1977) became one of the foremost essayists of his generation to interpret science for the layman.

Of Scots-English and German pioneering stock, Loren Corey Eiseley was born in Lincoln, Nebraska, on September 3, 1907. His father, Clyde Edwin Eiseley, had been an itinerant semi-professional actor in his youth and later worked as a hardware salesman. His mother, Daisy Corey, had artistic ambitions and was a painter of some talent. These interests undoubtedly influenced Eiseley's literary sensibilities. A far more significant aspect of his childhood, however, was his mother's deafness and her paranoid, neurotic behavior which led to marital tensions and conflicts. The strangeness of his home life and frequent moves in and around Lincoln caused young Eiseley to have, to a large extent, an isolated, lonely childhood. The fugitive-outsider imagery that is found in his work resulted, in part, from this silent, solitary youth.

Perhaps to compensate for his mother's unusual behavior, his father, although he worked long hours, was consistently kind and understanding; in addition, his uncle, William Buchanan Price, offered support and assistance. He not only introduced Eiseley to the fossil collection at the University of Nebraska Museum, thus inadvertently guiding him into his eventual career, but also helped him pay college tuition after his father died.

After attending local schools, Eiseley entered the University of Nebraska in the fall of 1925. His college career was not smooth, however, and it took him eight years to graduate. First, struck by restlessness, he dropped out to "ride the rails" and spent many months as a hobo. Next, his father's painful death from cancer caused extreme emotional and financial difficulties. He and his mother moved in with Uncle "Buck" Price, and Eiseley took a job as a night watchman in a chicken hatchery to help with expenses. About that time he developed the insomnia referred to in *The Night Country* (1971), which was to plague him for the rest of his life and, shortly thereafter, tuberculosis, which forced him to spend a year recovering in the Mojave Desert. These early years are described in detail in Eiseley's autobiography, *All the Strange Hours* (1975).

Eiseley finally returned to college and graduated in 1933 majoring in both English and sociology with emphasis on anthropology. While at the University of Nebraska he showed an interest in and talent for writing and had prose and poetry published in the *Praire Schooner,* the campus literary magazine of which he became an editor. He also developed an increasing interest in paleontology and spent five summers from 1931 on with various groups searching for fossils of early man. Anecdotal descriptions of these experiences appear in *The Night Country* and throughout many of his other writings.

Finally choosing science over literature, he enrolled in the doctoral program in anthropology at the University of Pennsylvania. From 1933 to 1937 he worked on his Ph.D. with the guidance of the department chairman, Frank Speck, whose unconventional humanistic approach to anthropology no doubt encouraged the mystical, meditative qualities that Eiseley's later work often displayed. After receiving his degree he taught at the University of Kansas for seven years. During this time he married Mabel Langdon and also continued to send money to his mother. In 1947 he was asked to return to the University of Pennsylvania to replace his ailing mentor as professor of anthropology and chairman of the department. He was later named Curator of Early Man at the university museum and was appointed to a chair as Benjamin Franklin Professor of Anthropology and the History of Science.

While still an undergraduate Eiseley published poetry. In graduate school and at the University of Kansas he published several scholarly articles, and at the same time he began writing natural history essays. His biography is important because of the kind of essays he wrote. They generally followed a common pattern as personal essays which combined biographical information or literary references with scientific fact. Watching Halley's comet with his father in "The Star Dragon," floating down the Platte in "The Flow of the River," or hunting fossils in "The Relic Men" all served as rhetorical devices to introduce the reader gradually to the scientific facts or hypotheses at the heart of the essays. In what Eiseley referred to as the "concealed essay," the personal anecdote or reminiscence established the tone and masked the purely scientific with the more engaging personal. In a similar way he drew upon his broad literary background and used allusions and quotations to clarify his themes. Citing writers ranging from Bacon to Benedict, Coleridge to Cocteau, Shakespeare to Stevenson, Eiseley enlightened his readers and strengthened the thematic ties between science and literature.

Eiseley's major theme and personal obsession was time. Time was the main concern in his first volume of essays, *The Immense Journey* (1957), and continued to be significant as even the titles of his later works indicate. *The Immense Journey*, perhaps his best known and most enduring work, focuses on the evolution of the universe and of man. The book has multiple interwoven themes—the evolutionary "journey" and possible extinction of the individual, mankind, and the universe and time past, present, and future—which run throughout his other work. *The Immense Journey* follows another of Eiseley's common practices: the essays were first published separately in diverse journals and magazines and then collected, rewritten, and organized around a unifying theme.

While still working on *The Immense Journey* Eiseley began a far more scholarly project—an intellectual history of Charles Darwin, his predecessors, and the development of the theory of evolution. *Darwin's Century: Evolution and the Men Who Discovered It* appeared in 1958 and was followed 21 years later by *Darwin and the Mysterious Mr. X: A New Light on the Evolutionists* (published posthumously). Both books reflect Eiseley's lifelong interest in evolution and his concern with time.

Another major figure admired by Eiseley and intellectually closer to him than Darwin was Sir Francis Bacon; his interest resulted in *Francis Bacon and the Modern Dilemma* (1962), which he later reworked as *The Man Who Saw Through Time* (1973). Originally presented as lectures, these essays emphasized much that Eiseley and Bacon shared—a total, visionary, and perhaps prophetic view of science with an imaginary sense of its ends rather than its more practical means.

Through *The Firmament of Time* (1960), *The Unexpected Universe* (1969), *The Invisible Pyramid* (1970), and *The Night Country* (1971), Eiseley continued his personal evolution as a thinker and a writer. He did publish four volumes of poetry, but his most lyric writing was in his prose. He was a scientist, but his most significant contributions were as a humanist.

Eiseley wrote in the tradition of the 19th-century essayists Ralph Waldo Emerson and Henry David Thoreau, observing and recording nature and stressing the contemplative rather than the factual. His work was similar to that of Jacob Bronowski, Joseph Wood Krutch, and Rachel Carson; it inspired the next generation of scientific popularizers, including Stephen Jay Gould and Carl Sagan.

Further Reading

Eiseley's autobiography, *All the Strange Hours: The Excavation of a Life* (1975), offers an impressionistic account of his life and illuminates his other writings. A variety of articles are available in scholarly publications, and three full length works

have appeared. One of the most accessible is Andrew J. Angyal's *Loren Eiseley* (1983), which contains detailed biographical information and a sound appraisal of all his work. Fred E. Carlisle's *Loren Eiseley: The Development of a Writer* (1983) is another comprehensive study, and Gerber and McFadden's *Loren Eiseley* (1983) provides additional criticism and interpretation.

Additional Sources

Christianson, Gale E., *Fox at the wood's edge: a biography of Loren Eiseley,* New York: H. Holt, 1990.
Heidtmann, Peter, *Loren Eiseley: a modern Ishmael,* Hamden, Conn.: Archon Books, 1991. □

Dwight David Eisenhower

Dwight David Eisenhower (1890-1969) was leader of the Allied forces in Europe in World War II, commander of NATO, and thirty-fourth president of the United States.

Dwight Eisenhower was born in Denison, Tex., on Oct. 14, 1890, one of seven sons. The family soon moved to Abilene, Kansas. The family was poor, and Eisenhower early learned the virtue of hard work. He graduated from West Point Military Academy in 1915. He was remarkable for his buoyant temperament and his capacity to inspire affection.

Eisenhower married Mamie Doud in 1916. One of the couple's two sons died in infancy; the other, John, followed in his father's footsteps and went to West Point, later resigning from the Army to assist in preparing his father's memoirs.

Army Career

Eisenhower's career in the Army was marked by a slow rise to distinction. He graduated first in his class in 1926 from the Army's Command and General Staff School. Following graduation from the Army War College he served in the office of the chief of staff under Gen. Douglas MacArthur. He became MacArthur's distinguished aid in the Philippines. Returning to the United States in 1939, Eisenhower became chief of staff to the 3d Army. He attracted the attention of Gen. George C. Marshall, U.S. Chief of Staff, by his brilliant conduct of war operations in Louisiana in 1941. When World War II began, Eisenhower became assistant chief of the War Plans Division of the Army General Staff. He assisted in the preparations for carrying the war to Europe and in May of 1942 was made supreme commander of European operations, arriving in London in this capacity in June.

Supreme Commander in Europe

Eisenhower's personal qualities were precisely right for the situation in the months that followed. He had to deal with British generals whose war experience exceeded his own and with a prime minister, Winston Churchill, whose strength and determination were of the first order. Eisen-

hower's post called for a combination of tact and resolution, for an ability to get along with people and yet maintain his own position as the leader of the Allied forces. In addition to his capacity to command respect and affection, Eisenhower showed high executive quality in his selection of subordinates.

In London, Eisenhower paved the way for the November 1942 invasion of North Africa. Against powerful British reluctance he prepared for the June 1944 invasion of Europe. He chose precisely the day on which massive troop landings in Normandy were feasible, and once the bridgehead was established, he swept forward triumphantly—with one short interruption—to defeat the German armies. By spring 1945, with powerful support from the Russian forces advancing from the east, the war in Europe was ended. Eisenhower became one of the best known men in the United States, and there was talk of a possible political career.

Columbia University and NATO

Eisenhower disavowed any political ambitions, however, and in 1948 he retired from military service to become president of Columbia University. It cannot be said that he filled this role with distinction. Nothing in his training suggested a special capacity to deal with university problems. Yet it was only because of a strong sense of duty that he accepted President Harry Truman's appeal to become the first commander of the newly formed North Atlantic Treaty Organization (NATO) in December 1950. Here Eisen-

hower's truly remarkable gifts in dealing with men of various views and strong will were again fully exhibited.

Eisenhower's political views had never been clearly defined. But Republican leaders in the eastern United States found him a highly acceptable candidate for the presidency, perhaps all the more so because he was not identified with any particular wing of the party. After a bitter convention fight against Robert Taft, Eisenhower emerged victorious. In the election he defeated the Democratic candidate, Adlai Stevenson, by a tremendous margin.

Eisenhower repeated this achievement in 1956. In 1955 he had suffered a serious stroke, and in 1956 he underwent an operation for ileitis. Behaving with great dignity and making it clear that he would stand for a second term only if he felt he could perform his duties to the full, he accepted renomination and won the election with 477 of the 531 electoral votes and a popular majority of over 9 million.

The President

Eisenhower's strength as a political leader rested almost entirely upon his disinterestedness and his integrity. He had little taste for political maneuvers and was never a strong partisan. His party, which attained a majority in both houses of Congress in 1952, lost control in 1954, and for 6 of 8 years in office the President was compelled to rely upon both Democrats and Republicans. His personal qualities, however, made this easier than it might have been.

Eisenhower did not conceive of the presidency as a positive executiveship, as has been the view of most of the great U.S. presidents. His personal philosophy was never very clearly defined. He was not a dynamic leader; he took a position in the center and drew his strength from that. In domestic affairs he was influenced by his strong and able secretary of the Treasury, George Humphrey. In foreign affairs he leaned heavily upon his secretary of state, John Foster Dulles. He delegated wide powers to those he trusted; in domestic affairs his personal assistant, Sherman Adams, exercised great influence. In a sense, Eisenhower's stance above the "battle" no doubt made him stronger.

Domestic Policies

To attempt to classify Eisenhower as liberal or conservative is difficult. He was undoubtedly sympathetic to business interests and had widespread support from them. He had austere views as to fiscal matters and was not generally in favor of enlarging the role of government in economic affairs. Yet he favored measures such as a far-reaching extension of social security, he signed a law fixing a minimum wage, and he recommended the formation of the Department of Health, Education and Welfare. After an initial error, he appointed to this post Marion B. Folsom, an outstanding administrator who had been a pioneer in the movement for social security in the 1930s.

Civil Rights

But the most significant development in domestic policy came through the Supreme Court. The President appointed Earl Warren to the post of chief justice. In 1954 the Warren Court handed down a unanimous decision declaring segregation in the schools unconstitutional, giving a new impetus to the civil rights movement.

Eisenhower was extremely cautious in implementing this decision. He saw that it was enforced in the District of Columbia, but in his heart he did not believe in it and thought that it was for the states rather than the Federal government to take appropriate action. Nonetheless, he was compelled to move in 1957 when Arkansas governor Orval Faubus attempted to defy the desegregation decision by using national guardsmen to bar African Americans from entering the schools of Little Rock. The President's stand was unequivocal; he made it clear that he would enforce the law. When Faubus proved obdurate, the President enjoined him and forced the removal of the national guard. When the African Americans admitted were forced by an armed mob to withdraw, the President sent Federal troops to Little Rock and federalized the national guard. A month later the Federal troops were withdrawn. But it was a long time before the situation was completely stabilized.

The President's second term saw further progress in civil rights. In 1957 he signed a measure providing further personnel for the attorney general's office for enforcing the law and barring interference with voting rights. In 1960 he signed legislation strengthening the measure and making resistance to desegregation a Federal offense.

Foreign Policies

In foreign affairs Eisenhower encouraged the strengthening of NATO, at the same time seeking an understanding with the Soviet Union. In 1955 the U.S.S.R. agreed to evacuate Austria, then under four-power occupation, but a Geneva meeting of the powers (Britain, France, the U.S.S.R., and the United States) made little progress on the problem of divided Germany. A new effort at understanding came in 1959, when the Russian leader Nikita Khrushchev visited the United States. In friendly discussions it was agreed to hold a new international conference in Paris. When that time arrived, however, the Russians had just captured an American plane engaged in spying operations over the Soviet Union (the Gary Powers incident). Khrushchev flew into a tantrum and broke up the conference. When Eisenhower's term ended, relations with the Kremlin were still unhappy.

In the Orient the President negotiated an armistice with the North Koreans to terminate the Korean War begun in 1950. It appears that Eisenhower brought the North Koreans and their Chinese Communist allies to terms by threatening to enlarge the war. He supported the Chinese Nationalists. Dulles negotiated the treaty that created SEATO (Southeast Asia Treaty Organization) and pledged the United States to consult with the other signatories and to meet any threat of peace in that region "in accordance with their constitutional practices. . . ." This treaty was of special significance with regard to Vietnam, where the French had been battling against a movement for independence. In 1954 Vietnam was divided, the North coming under Communist control, the South (anti-Communist) increasingly supported by the United States.

In the Near East, Eisenhower faced a very difficult situation. In 1956 the Egyptian dictator Gamal Abdel Nasser nationalized the Suez Canal. The government of Israel, probably encouraged by France and Great Britain, launched a preventive war, soon joined by the two great powers. The President and the secretary of state condemned this breach of the peace within the deliberations framework of the United Nations, and the three powers were obliged to sign an armistice. These events occurred at a particularly inauspicious time for the United States, since a popular revolt against the Soviet Union had broken out in Hungary. The hands of the American government were tied, though perhaps in no case could the United States have acted effectively in preventing Soviet suppression of the revolt.

In the Latin American sphere the President was confronted with events of great importance in Cuba. Cuba was ruled by an increasingly brutal and tyrannical president, Fulgencio Batista. In 1958, to mark its displeasure, the American government withdrew military support from the Batista regime. There followed a collapse of the government, and the Cuban leftist leader, Fidel Castro, installed himself in power. Almost from the beginning Castro began a flirtation with the Soviet Union, and relations between Havana and Washington were severed in January 1960.

In the meantime the United States had embarked upon a course which was to cause great embarrassment to Eisenhower's successor. It had encouraged and assisted anti-Castro Cubans to prepare to invade the island and overthrow the Castro regime. Though these plans had not crystallized when Eisenhower left office in 1961, it proved difficult to reverse them, and the result for the John F. Kennedy administration was the fiasco of the Bay of Pigs.

Assessing His Career

It will be difficult for future historians to assess Eisenhower's foreign policy objectively. Ending the Korean War was a substantial achievement. The support of NATO was most certainly in line with American opinion. In the Far East the extension of American commitments can be variously judged. It is fair to Eisenhower to say that only the first steps to the eventual deep involvement in Vietnam were taken during his presidency.

One other aspect of the Eisenhower years must be noted. The President's intention to reduce the military budget at first succeeded. But during his first term the American position with the Soviets deteriorated. Then came the Soviet launching of the Sputnik space probe in 1957—a grisly suggestion of what nuclear weapons might be like in the future. In response, United States policy was altered, and the missile gap had been closed by the time the President left office. Unhappily, the arms race was not ended but attained new intensity in the post-Eisenhower years.

Few presidents have enjoyed greater popularity than Eisenhower or left office as solidly entrenched in public opinion as when they entered it. Eisenhower was not a great orator and did not conceive of the presidency as a post of political leadership. But at the end of his administration, admiration for his integrity, modesty, and strength was undiminished among the mass of the American people.

Eisenhower played at times the role of an elder statesman in Republican politics. His death on March 26, 1969, was the occasion for national mourning and for world-wide recognition of his important role in the events of his time.

Further Reading

Works written by Eisenhower are *Crusade in Europe* (1948) and his account of the presidency, *Mandate for Change, 1953-1956: The White House Years* (1963) and *Waging Peace, 1956-1961: The White House Years* (1965). For a brief summary of Eisenhower's early career see Marquis W. Childs, *Eisenhower, Captive Hero: A Critical Study of the General and the President* (1958). For the war years see W. B. Smith, *Eisenhower's Six Great Decisions* (1950). Eisenhower's election to the presidency is covered in Arthur M. Schlesinger, Jr., ed., *History of American Presidential Elections* (4 vols., 1971). Very important is Sherman Adams, *Firsthand Report: The Story of the Eisenhower Administration* (1961). The most illuminating discussion of the President is Emmett John Hughes, *The Ordeal of Power: A Political Memoir of the Eisenhower Years* (1963). See also Robert J. Donovan, *Eisenhower: The Inside Story* (1956), and Merlo J. Pusey, *Eisenhower the President* (1956). □

Mamie Doud Eisenhower

The wife of President Dwight D. "Ike" Eisenhower, Mamie Eisenhower (1896-1979) represented what was to 1950s America the ideal American wife: exuding quiet strength, finding satisfaction in domestic duties, supporting her husband unhesitatingly.

Mamie Eisenhower was the first lady of the United States at a time when home and family were considered to be of paramount importance. As first ladies often are, she was expected to serve as a role model for the American wife. Mamie Doud and Dwight D. "Ike" Eisenhower met in 1915 in San Antonio, Texas, where Eisenhower was a young army officer and high-school football coach and Mamie was wintering with her parents. They were married the next year. For Mamie, life as a military wife was initially harsh: the Douds were a close and socially prominent family, and life with Ike was relatively lean and lonely. Over the next several decades she dutifully followed her husband when she could, and raised the family herself when she could not. Her husband, meanwhile, became increasingly prominent as a military leader.

New Pressures

At the end of World War II Eisenhower was a national hero, and for his wife this meant a measure of celebrity to which she was unaccustomed as well as the opportunity to meet important world leaders. The general became president of Columbia University in 1948; throughout Ike's tenure at Columbia Mrs. Eisenhower was a gracious hostess to scores of famous visitors. When her husband decided to enter the presidential campaign in 1952, Mamie—a self-professed homebody—found that she would have to shed her aversion to public life: "there would be nothing he would ask during the campaign that I would not do," she recalled. As a campaign wife she subjected herself to daily appearances and interviews and answered thousands of letters.

Life in the White House

After Eisenhower won the presidency, Mrs. Eisenhower was able to return to a degree of domestic stability in the White House. By this time she was used to overseeing a staff, and she saw that the executive mansion was run efficiently. She also lent her services to charitable causes, and she made the White House more historic by leading a drive to recover authentic presidential antiques. She and her husband observed a division of labor ("Ike took care of the office—I ran the house") although the president valued his wife's insights into political personalities of the time.

Public Ideal

For the eight years of the Eisenhower presidency Mamie Eisenhower represented the public ideal of the American wife: exuding quiet strength, finding satisfaction in domestic duties, supporting her husband unhesitatingly. Eisenhower observed of her: "I personally think that Mamie's biggest contribution was to make the White House livable, comfortable, and meaningful for the people who came in. She was always helpful and ready to do anything. She exuded hospitality. She saw that as one of her functions and performed it, no matter how tired she was." When Eisenhower left office in 1961, he and Mrs. Eisenhower were at last allowed something like a peaceful retirement, although Eisenhower kept busy in the role of elder statesman until his death in 1969. Mamie Eisenhower lived quietly after her husband's death until her own death in 1979.

Further Reading

Dorothy Brandon, *Mamie Doud Eisenhower* (New York: Scribners, 1954).

Steve Neal, *The Eisenhowers: Reluctant Dynasty* (Garden City, N.Y.: Doubleday, 1978). □

Milton Eisenhower

Milton Eisenhower (1899-1985) gained national recognition for his careers in government and higher education. He was best known for his advisory role to his older brother, President Dwight D. Eisenhower. He also served presidents John F. Kennedy, Lyndon B. Johnson, and Richard M. Nixon as a special consultant.

Milton Stover Eisenhower, the last of six sons of David and Ida (Stover) Eisenhower, was born on September 15, 1899, in Abilene, Kansas, a farm-oriented town of about 5,000. His paternal grandfather, Jacob, a farmer and Mennonite minister, had brought his family to the midwest from Pennsylvania after the Civil War. He prospered, but son David, despite a wedding gift of a 160-acre farm plus $2,000 in cash, did not. So Milton Eisenhower grew up in relatively poor circumstances, but he was surrounded by the support of many relatives.

Another major influence on Milton was religion. The entire family took turns reading the Bible before and after dinner. In addition, his mother held meetings of the Watchtower Society in the home. Hence, the Protestant work ethic of fairness, hard work, thrift, and community service was strongly instilled in Milton Eisenhower, and his long and illustrious career exemplified both the dream and the reality of American life in the 20th century.

Many doors were opened to the young Eisenhower. Probably the most important door proved to be that of Charles M. Harger, editor of the Abilene *Reflector* and the first of several significant mentors. Harger gave Eisenhower a job as a reporter and a year later offered to pay his way to Harvard, Harger's alma mater. By Eisenhower's account he could not accept such largesse, so Harger opened the door to Kansas State, where he was a member of the board of trustees.

College to Foreign Service to Bureaucrat

Eisenhower's initial start on his college career was not auspicious. After nearly dying of influenza in the epidemic of 1918-1919 he returned home, recuperated, and resumed his career as a journalist until returning to college in the fall of 1919. As a 20-year-old freshman, Eisenhower was a standout. He was accepted by the brothers of the Sigma Alpha Epsilon fraternity and selected as editor of the student newspaper. As the voice of the student body and protege of Harger, Eisenhower won the attention of Kansas State president William M. Jardine, who opened several more doors. So did Jardine's close friend Leroy Eakin, self-made millionaire and local businessman, whose only son, Jack, was also Eisenhower's fraternity brother. Eakin's daughter Helen was the campus belle, and Eisenhower soon won her affection.

When he graduated five years later, Eisenhower accepted a position at Kansas State teaching English and journalism. Several weeks later he was offered a job in the U.S. foreign service. Eisenhower presented his dilemma to Jardine, and with his mentor's support Eisenhower spent an enthusiastic two years in Scotland. He would have made a career in the foreign service, but he could not refuse Jardine's offer in 1926 to serve under him in his new role as secretary of agriculture. The fact that Eisenhower's fiancee, Helen Eakin, was living in Washington, D.C., with her parents was an even more compelling reason for his leaving the diplomatic corps. On Columbus Day 1926 the two were married (they subsequently had a son and daughter).

In his career as a bureaucrat Eisenhower's ability and *savoir faire* became obvious. He served successfully during the long Democratic tenure of Franklin D. Roosevelt. In fact, his skill/expertise as a go-between gained the attention of the president, who asked him to draw up a plan for an Office of War Information during World War II. Eisenhower's success with this project led to his presidential appointment as director of the board established to relocate the West Coast Japanese and Nisei (Japanese-Americans). In his own words it was "the most difficult and traumatic task of my career." When he completed the relocation Eisenhower returned to the Office of War Information, but only briefly.

President of Three Colleges

In mid-1943 he accepted the offer of the presidency of Kansas State University from his initial mentor, Charles M. Harger, then serving as chairman of the Kansas State Board of Regents. In his inaugural address Eisenhower declared, "Our concern is the education of men and women determined to be free." His ultimate goal was "to create a new American—one who had the ability and the educational background and the desire to formulate sound and creative judgments on world affairs and to take part in the world in which the United States had to be the leader." To accomplish this he borrowed heavily from the ideas of Harvard president James B. Conant. He stressed the liberal arts, and those of his own heritage, which emphasized "the old-fashioned patriotism—just that sense of loyalty and obligation to the community that is necessary to the preservation of all the privileges and rights that the community guarantees." By stumping the state with such values Eisenhower won increased legislative support for the university. He also utilized his contacts in the Department of Agriculture to obtain research funds.

By 1948 he had largely succeeded in implementing the reforms he wanted, so when he was offered the presidency of Penn State in 1950 he left his alma mater. Eisenhower replicated his Kansas State experience at Penn State, with similarly remarkable results. There were some notable controversies, however, as well as the significant additional responsibility of serving as adviser to his brother, President Dwight D. Eisenhower (1953-1961). One of the controversies involved his failure to take a strong stand for academic freedom and against the demagogic anti-Communist campaign headed by Senator Joseph R. McCarthy. Another was Eisenhower's unsuccessful campaign to change the name of State College, Pennsylvania, to Mt. Nittany after Penn State became a university. These two problems were overshadowed by the glamour that surrounded Eisenhower as presidential adviser. Not only did he make frequent trips to the White House, but he also represented his brother on official missions to Latin America, about which he wrote in *The Wine Is Bitter* (1963), and to the Soviet Union. He drew even closer to his brother in late 1955 following the death of his wife from cancer and the president's heart attack. These two factors, plus the ardent appeal of the board of trustees of Johns Hopkins University, largely accounted for Eisenhower's accepting the presidency there in mid-1956.

Philosophy of Public Service

Eisenhower was the first president of the prestigious private institution not to have an earned doctorate, but it did not deter his fundraising. He proved as successful with the heads of private foundations (notably Ford and Rockefeller) as with legislators in Kansas and Pennsylvania. Millions were received, and Johns Hopkins secured a new lease on its life as one of the leading American universities, particularly in the field of international affairs, through the establishment of the School for Advanced and International Studies (S.A.I.S.) in Washington, D.C.

In the area of desegregation Eisenhower's gradual, behind-the-scenes approach was less than stellar. Nonetheless, after the assassination of the Reverend Martin Luther King, Jr. in 1968, President Lyndon B. Johnson appointed Eisenhower (who had retired in 1967) as chairman of the National Commission on the Causes and Prevention of Violence. The report advocated gun control, reform of the criminal justice system, and improvements in law enforcement. He no sooner completed this task than he accepted the urgent call of the Johns Hopkins trustees to serve as interim president.

After his second retirement a year later, Eisenhower began to write his memoir, *The President Is Calling* (1973), in which he set forth a program of reform of the presidency. He thought that "Democracy contains the seeds of its own destruction," and hence he called for the creation of two supra-cabinet positions, both appointed by the president. One would serve as vice-president for international affairs and the other as vice-president for domestic affairs. Eisenhower also advocated empowering the president with a line-item veto and limiting presidents to a single six-year term.

His greatest concern, however, was the denegration of compromise. He rejected the prevailing notion of the time that compromise was a surrender of principle. Starting from the premise that man, individually and collectively, acted out of self-interest, he concluded that compromise was essential to human existence. Quoting Edmund Burke, Eisenhower declared, "All government—indeed every human benefit, every virtue and every prudent act—is founded on compromise and barter." This focus on public acts of agreement was in keeping with the perception that the dream of success was achieved through individual merit, yet the most notable reality of Eisenhower's career was, as he himself noted, that of "The president is calling." He died of cancer at Johns Hopkins Hospital, May 2, 1985.

Further Reading

A comprehensive account of Eisenhower's own thoughts and feelings about his public career is his memoir, "*The President Is Calling* (1973). For his account of his presidential missions to Latin America see *The Wine Is Bitter* (1963). His thinking is also imbedded in *The Rule of Law An Alternative to Violence: A Report to the National Commission on the Causes and Prevention of Crime* (1970). The most scholarly study of Eisenhower is Stephen E. Ambrose and Richard H. Immerman, *Milton S. Eisenhower: Educational Statesman* (1983). Partial accounts appear in Bela Kornitzer, *The Great American Heritage: The Story of the Five Eisenhower Brothers* (1955); Steve Neal, *The Eisenhowers: Reluctant Dynasty* (1978); and Robert P. Sharkey, *Johns Hopkins: Centennial Portrait of a University* (1975).

Additional Sources

Ambrose, Stephen E., *Milton S. Eisenhower, educational statesman,* Baltimore: Johns Hopkins University Press, 1983. □

Peter D. Eisenman

The American architect Peter D. Eisenman (born 1932) studied and made formal use of concepts from other fields—linguistics, philosophy, and mathematics—in his imaginative designs.

Peter Eisenman was born in 1932 into a middle-class setting in Newark, New Jersey. Although his grandfather had been a builder, Eisenman claimed that his decision to become an architect was not made until he discovered the world of architecture as an undergraduate at Cornell University. At Cornell (B.Arch., 1955) he studied under theorist/critic Colin Rowe, receiving the Charles G. Sands Memorial Medal awarded for exceptional merit in his senior thesis. Under the tutelage of Rowe, Eisenman was encouraged to re-examine the origins of modern architecture, particularly the early works of the French architect Le Corbusier (1887-1965), and thus was exposed to a set of ideas that were to form the core of his early practice and architectural philosophy. Following Cornell and a brief apprenticeship he matriculated first to Columbia University (M.S.Arch., 1960; William Kinne fellowship, 1960-1961) and finally to Cambridge University, England, where he received an M.A. (1962) and Ph.D. (1963) in theory of design.

Early Career

Eisenman returned to the United States in 1963 to practice from an office in New York City and to teach as an assistant professor in the School of Architecture at Princeton University. Eisenman also returned to a lively debate among young professionals concerning the future of architecture, a debate in which he played a critical role. In 1964 he was a founding member of CASE (Conference of Architects for the Study of the Environment) and in 1967 he founded and served as the director of the IAUS (Institute for Architecture and Urban Studies). The critical issues of the time were those revolving around the nature of the modern city and housing. In 1967 Eisenman, in collaboration with Michael Graves and Daniel Perry, proposed an urban megastructure for the renewal of Harlem. This project was the centerpiece of the Museum of Modern Art's exhibit *The New City: Architecture and Urban Renewal.* This was but one of innumerable exhibitions Eisenman participated in during this period, with this work seeming to clearly identify him as a third generation modernist, a perception he was soon to prove misleading.

"The New York Five"

In 1969 Eisenman, through an exhibition at the Museum of Modern Art sponsored by CASE, became associated with a group of architects who quickly gained fame and notoriety as the New York Five. This group, with Eisenman generally acknowledged as the leader, included Charles Gwathmey (born 1938), Michael Graves (born 1934), Richard Meier (born 1934), and John Hejduk (born 1929). They sought a return to the origins of 20th-century modernism, as seen in the early works of Le Corbusier, the Italian Rationalist Giuseppe Terragni (1904-1943), and the Dutch De Stijl movement architect Gerrit Rietveld (1888-1964). It was the more abstract and theoretical aspects of this architecture that drove the work of the New York Five. The resulting work was perceived, at its best, as powerful, inwardly directed, critical exercises which produced wonderful architecture for architects; at its worst it was derided for its penchant for ignoring client needs, functional requirements, and even architectural technology in its seemingly entirely self-referential pursuit of ideas. The New York Five's presence was most notable through their many exhibitions and the publicity generated by *Five Architects,* edited by Kenneth Frampton (1972). Eisenman's principal role was as intellectual provocateur with his newly proposed *cardboard architecture* at the center of the ensuing critical debate.

Cardboard Architecture

In 1967 Eisenman had begun the first of a series of residential designs, labeled cardboard architecture in reference to their thin white walls and model-like qualities, through which he explored the implications of his theories in built form. This practical application was a corollary to his intellectual investigations. These buildings embodied what Eisenman referred to as *deep structure,* through which he attempted to explore the notion of *visual syntax.* The complex nature of this work stemmed from Eisenman's interest in language and semiotics, gained through his study of noted linguist/philosopher Noam Chomsky (born 1928). His designs consisted, in essence, of a floor plan ordered by a grid of lines and a structural framework of thin round columns. These were projected in three dimensions as a cubical spatial volume on which and throughout were placed a series of layered planes. In early designs these planes were placed perpendicular to each other within the cube; in later designs some planes were dislocated by rotational shifts in the plane grid and overlaid on the original grids.

A critical component of the design process for these buildings, which are referred to by numbers rather than client name as is typical—i.e., House I (1967) through House X (1982)—was the production of a text following each design effort through which Eisenman sought to explain his work. That an observer needed to read a text to fully understand his architecture was a point of considerable debate. Eisenman's literary efforts resulted in a steady stream of articles, eventually coalescing into two books: *House X* (1982) and *Houses of Cards* (1987), the latter dealing with House I through House VI.

Post Modern Architecture

By the late 1970s Eisenman had emerged as a leader in the Post Modern movement in architecture. The terms Post Modern and Post Modernism are somewhat problematic. Having originated in reference to literary theory, they were appropriated by critic Charles Jencks (*The Language of Post Modern Architecture,* 1977) to characterize the architecture that seemed to be supplanting that of the Modernist era. Although some observers question whether current architecture constitutes a truly new era or is the logical next phase of Modernism, what is clear is Eisenman's continued presence on the cutting edge of contemporary events. His work in the early 1980s was in part an elaboration of the theories embodied in the House projects. However, now he moved beyond pure geometry to examine scalar geometry, which is used in mapping complex structures such as weather formations; he was especially interested in these ideas as discussed by scientist/mathematician Benoit Mandelbrot. From these investigations Eisenman derived what he referred to as *traces:* lines or echoes from other sources that could be perceived within any aspect of a design problem. One of the first works to demonstrate these ideas, and his first large-scale project, was the Wexner Center for the Visual Arts at Ohio State University, Columbus, Ohio (1983-1989). Two trace features are a central walkway that slices through the building, with the angle of the walkway matching that of an airport runway located miles from the site, and abstract architectural elements which recall an armory that once stood on the site. His achievements during the 1980s were recognized by the Academy of Arts and Letters, which awarded Eisenman with the Arnold W. Brunner memorial award in 1984.

Deconstruction

Eisenman's later work sprang from an even more complex set of theoretical origins. In a project for the Biology Center for J.W. Goethe University in Frankfurt, Germany, he proposed a scheme derived from the structure of a DNA molecule interpolated through fractal geometry. However, the primary impetus of his efforts in the late 1980s was the philosophical/critical movement known as Deconstruction, which was developed in large part by French philosopher Jacques Derrida (born 1930) as a response to Structuralism. In Deconstruction Eisenman was seeking a new basis for architecture. While architects have traditionally relied on *man* as the foundation which informed and governed their work, Eisenman considered this position untenable in modern society. Instead he proposed three *destabilizing* concepts to guide his architecture: discontinuity, recursibility, and self-similarity. His project for the University Museum at Long Beach, California (begun in 1986), embodies these new ideas. Here past, present, and future collide, with the 1849 Gold Rush, the 1949 founding of the university, and the 2049 *rediscovery* of the museum informing the design process. Eisenman's commitment to linking past and present were also visible in a 1994 exhibit at the Canadian Center for Architecture in Montreal called "Cities of Artificial Excavation," which featured eleven of his projects from 1978 to 1988.

What's Next?

Eisenman's work in the 1990s included a city plan for Rebstockpark in Frankfurt, Germany in which he concentrated heavily on a "fold technique." He also designed the Aronoff Center for Design and Art at the University of Cincinnati as part of that university's project to redesign the entire campus. Future projects include a San Francisco Jewish Museum and a new museum and ferry terminal for New York City's Staten Island. Eisenman's search for new architectural origins and his continued presence at the forefront of architectural criticism and debate prompt one often repeated question: What's next?

Further Reading

The two principal books by Eisenman on his work are *House X* (1982) and *Houses of Cards* (1987). Books on his architecture include *Five Architects,* edited by Kenneth Frampton (1972), *A.D. Wexner Center for the Visual Arts,* Eisenman and Trott (1990), and *Eisenman: Recent Projects 1983-1989* (1989). Charles Jencks' *The Language of Post Modern Architecture* (1977) effectively sets the stage for Eisenman's work in the 1970s and 1980s, and Geoffrey Broadbent's *Deconstruction: A Student Guide* (1991) furnishes the most accessible entry into the complex world of Eisenman's Deconstruction-based architecture.

Additional Sources

"Bunshaft, Eisenman Honored by Academy of Arts and Letters." *Architecture* (June 1984): 88, 91.

Cembarest, Robin. "The Featherman File of Noteworthy Items in the Press." *Ethnic Newswatch,* 20 December 1996. Stamford: SoftLine Information, Inc.

Dawson, Layla. "Eisenman's New Trick." *The Architectural Review* 191 (September 1992): 9.

Giovannini, Joseph. "Excavating Eisenman." *Architecture* (June 1994): 57-62.

Jacobs, Karrie. "The Ferry Godfather." *The New York Times,* 31 March 1997.

Muschamp, Herbert. "Making a Rush-Hour Battleground High Art." *The New York Times,* 6 April 1997.

———. "Eisenman's Spatial Extravaganza in Cincinnati." *The New York Times,* 21 July 1996.

———. "Repulsion is the Attraction." *The New York Times,* 24 April 1994.

Zimmerman, David. "Cincinnati: A Plan for Unity." *USA Today,* 2 April 1997. □

Sergei Mikhailovich Eisenstein

The Soviet film director and cinema theoretician Sergei Mikhailovich Eisenstein (1898-1948) achieved fame for his emotionally inflammatory political epics of the Russian Revolution.

Born in Riga, the son of a wealthy shipbuilder, Sergei Eisenstein went as a young man to St. Petersburg, where he studied architecture and engineering. During the Russian Revolution he constructed trenches and also acted in plays for the Bolshevik army. Shortly after the civil war, he managed a carnival and a small workers' theater in Moscow. Following service with the engineering corps during World War I, Eisenstein was appointed assistant director and chief dramatist for the Proletcult Theater. His most celebrated avant-garde productions included a dramatization of Jack London's story, *Mexicalia,* of A. N. Ostrovsky's *Much Simplicity in Every Wise Man,* and an experimental play, *Anti-Jesus.*

First Films

Frustrated by the stage's inability to achieve total realism, Eisenstein abandoned theater for the incipient Soviet film industry, directing his first motion picture, *Strike,* in 1924. With *Potemkin* (1925) the director was able to exploit effectively his sadistic fantasies, culminating in the apocalyptic violence of the Odessa steps scene.

Ten Days That Shook the World (1927), based on John Reed's classic account of the early days of the Russian Revolution, proved ineffective both as cinema art and as political propaganda. Critics later raised serious doubts about the historical reliability of the film and justifiable questions regarding the character of its creator. The scene in *Ten Days That Shook the World* in which a student is attacked by vicious aristocratic women and subsequently murdered, his body lying on the waterfront, his neck lacerated, his torso exposed, appeared to have more erotic than political significance for its creator. Eisenstein was not criticized so much for his homosexuality as for the frequently disconcerting emotional excesses and moral obliquities it invariably produced in his work.

Activities Abroad

Eisenstein's final revolutionary epic, *The General Line* (1929), was a leisurely and often evocative ode to the joys of agricultural collectivism. It found favor with Stalin, and that year Eisenstein was granted permission for an extended tour abroad. After a brief teaching assignment at the Sorbonne in Paris, the director went to Hollywood, intending to under-

take an American production. Under contract to Paramount studio he composed a script, *Sutter's Gold,* subsequently rejected by the studio as morally indecent. Next he began intensive work on a film adaptation of Theodore Dreiser's *An American Tragedy.* His decision to present the novel in the form of an interior monologue, in opposition to the commercial ideas of the producers, resulted in his peremptory dismissal from the project.

Eisenstein then attempted to write and direct a film on location in Mexico. He was intoxicated by the warm sensuality and primitive spontaneity of Mexican life. *Que Viva Mexico* took shape, sections of the complex scenario being composed for each day's shooting. Eisenstein was unwilling to conclude the picture after its allotted budget had been expended. The film was confiscated and turned over to a Hollywood editor who divided the footage into three separate pieces. On the basis of the hypnotic beauty and visionary power evident in several sequences from the mutilated epic (released in the United States as *Time in the Sun, Thunder over Mexico,* and *Day of Death*), it can be said that had Eisenstein been permitted to complete the production the result would have possessed considerable poetry and depth.

Later Career

Upon returning to the Soviet Union in 1932, Eisenstein was confronted with a restrictive philistinism even more oppressive than the lack of understanding he had encountered in the United States. His nearly completed film *Bezhin Meadow,* based on Ivan Turgenev's tale of peasant life, was condemned and suppressed for its religious mysticism and "formalistic excesses." Also disparaged was Eisenstein's theory of montage. Eisenstein responded by publishing an article, "The Mistakes of *Bezhin Meadow,*" in which he repudiated his former esthetic commitments, vowing to "create films of high quality, worthy of the Stalinist epoch." The result, *Alexander Nevsky,* was a simpleminded and vapid historical pageant depicting the heroic overthrow by the Russian people of their 12th-century Teutonic oppressors. Although the film was praised at first for its patriotism and its anti-German virulence, the treaty signed by the Soviet Union with Nazi Germany in 1939 necessitated its immediate withdrawal from circulation.

In 1940 Eisenstein wrote his finest study of film esthetics, *Film Form,* which contains a brilliant analysis of parallels between cinematic and novelistic techniques. The same year Eisenstein began composing the scenario for *Ivan the Terrible,* a massive historical epic with contemporary overtones; although subtler and richer in psychological nuances than his previous work, this biographical parable of Russia's first dictator-despot possesses a claustrophobic opacity that is at times physically intolerable.

While attending a party celebrating the premiere of *Ivan the Terrible* (Part I) the director collapsed from a heart attack. During his early convalescence Eisenstein was informed that the already filmed Part II of *Ivan the Terrible* would not be shown in the U.S.S.R. Ravaged by physical deterioration and the emotional torments of a lifetime, Eisenstein spent his remaining months preparing a second theoretical study, *Film Sense,* and teaching classes in cinema technique at the Soviet Cinema Institute.

Further Reading

The authorized biography is Marie Seton, *Sergei M. Eisenstein* (1952). Other valuable biographical sources are Vladimir Nizhniy, *Lessons with Eisenstein* (1962); and Ivor Montagu, *With Eisenstein* (1968). Intelligent critical analyses of his work can be found in Robert Warshow, *The Immediate Experience: Movies, Comics, Theatre and Other Aspects of Popular Culture* (1962); James Agee, *Agee on Film* (1964); Eric Rhode, *Tower of Babel: Speculations on the Cinema* (1966); and Dwight Macdonald, *Dwight Macdonald on Movies* (1969). For perceptive discussions of Eisenstein's film theory see Rudolf Arnheim, *Film as Art* (1957), and André Bazin, *What Is Cinema?,* essays selected and translated by Hugh Gray (1967).

Additional Sources

Eisenstein, Sergei, *Beyond the stars: the memoirs of Sergei Eisenstein,* Calcutta: Seagull Books, 1995.
Eisenstein, Sergei, *Immoral memories: an autobiography,* Boston: Houghton Mifflin, 1983.
Seton, Marie, *Sergei M. Eisenstein: a biography,* London: Dobson, 1978. □

Kano Eitoku

Kano Eitoku (1543-1590) was a Japanese painter of the Momoyama period. Working in the bold, colorful style typical of the decorative screen painting of the 16th century, he was the leading artist of his day and one of the most influential Japanese painters.

A member of the illustrious Kano family, Eitoku was born in Kyoto. He received his training under his father, Kano Shoei, and his grandfather, Kano Motonobu, who was the leading painter of the first half of the 16th century. Eitoku's first major work was the decoration of the Jukoin sanctuary at Daitokuji, a famous Kyoto Zen temple, a task he undertook with his father in 1566. Eitoku's fame soon spread, and he became the favorite artist of Oda Nobunaga, the military dictator of Japan, who gave him several commissions. Among those were a set of screens depicting the city of Kyoto and the decoration of Nobunaga's splendid castle at Azuchi on Lake Biwa.

After Nobunaga died in 1582, his successor, Toyotomi Hideyoshi, continued to patronize Eitoku. Among the many outstanding works he produced for Hideyoshi, the most ambitious were the paintings for the castle in Osaka and the Juraku palace in Kyoto, which Eitoku undertook in 1587. Assisted by a large team of collaborators, he produced hundreds of wall paintings, sliding screens, and folding screens, which for sheer magnificence surpassed anything seen in Japan up to that time.

None of the castles and palaces built by Nobunaga and Hideyoshi has survived, so that the works which made Eitoku famous have largely perished. However, there are several sets of screens which give a good idea of his style. Among the most remarkable are a six-fold screen representing a kind of Japanese cedar called *hinoki* (National Museum, Tokyo), a huge screen depicting lions (Imperial collection), and a pair of six-part screens showing hawks and pines (Tokyo University of Arts). All these pictures are painted in the same bold style, using powerful brushstrokes, large forms, brilliant colors, and gold leaf, and emphasizing flat decorative patterns rather than realistic representation. It is this type of painting for which Eitoku is famous and which is the most characteristic expression of the Momoyama period.

While works of this type were generally displayed in the public rooms of the palaces and castles, monochrome ink painting continued to be used for the private apartments. Good examples of Eitoku's work in this medium are the 16 sliding screen paintings, or *fusuma,* which the artist executed early in his career for the Jukoin in Kyoto. The subjects represented—such as birds and flowers in a landscape setting and the "Four Accomplishments"—are Chinese in origin, and the monochrome ink style is derived from Chinese sources through his grandfather, Kano Motonobu. Yet the way in which Eitoku handled his brush with broad, vigorous strokes, stressing pattern rather than space, is very different from the earlier painting of either the Chinese or the Japanese, showing the artist's originality.

Further Reading

Kano Eitoku's work is discussed in *Pageant of Japanese Art,* vol. 2: *Painting* (1952), edited by staff members of the Tokyo National Museum; Robert Treat Paine and Alexander Soper, *The Art and Architecture of Japan* (1955; rev. ed. 1960); and Terukazu Akiyama, *Japanese Painting* (1961).

Additional Sources

Kano, Eitoku, *Kano Eitoku,* Tokyo; New York: Kodansha International, 1977. □

Cyprian Ekwensi

Cyprian Ekwensi (born 1921) was a Nigerian writer who stressed description of the locale and whose episodic style was particularly well suited to the short story.

C yprian Odiatu Duaka Ekwensi was born at Minna in Northern Nigeria on September 26, 1921. He later lived in Onitsha in the Eastern area. He was educated at Achimota College, in Ibadan, the Gold Coast, and at the Chelsea School of Pharmacy of London University. He lectured in pharmacy at Lagos and was employed as a pharmacist by the Nigerian Medical Corporation. Ekwensi married Eunice Anyiwo, and they had five children.

After favorable reception of his early writing, he joined the Nigerian Ministry for Information and had risen to be the director of that agency by the time of the first military coup in 1966. After the continuing disturbances in the Western and Northern regions in the summer of 1966, Ekwensi gave up his position and relocated his family at Enugu. He became chair of the Bureau for External Publicity in Biafra and an adviser to the head of state, Col. Odumegwu Ojukwu.

Ekwensi began his writing career as a pamphleteer, and this perhaps explains the episodic nature of his novels. This tendency is well illustrated by *People of the City* (1954), in which Ekwensi gave a vibrant portrait of life in a West African city. It was the first major novel to be published by a Nigerian. Two novellas for children appeared in 1960; both *The Drummer Boy* and *The Passport of Mallam Ilia* were exercises in blending traditional themes with undisguised romanticism.

Ekwensi's most widely read novel, *Jagua Nana,* appeared in 1961. It was a return to the locale of *People of the City* but boasted a much more cohesive plot centered on the character of Jagua, a courtesan who had a love for the expensive. Even her name was a corruption of the expensive English auto. Her life personalized the conflict between the old traditional and modern urban Africa. Ekwensi published a sequel in 1987 titled *Jagua Nana's Daughter.*

Burning Grass (1961) is basically a collection of vignettes concerning a Fulani family. Its major contribution is the insight it presents into the life of this pastoral people. Ekwensi based the novel and the characters on a real family with whom he had previously lived. Between 1961 and 1966 Ekwensi published at least one major work every year.

The most important of these were the novels, *Beautiful Feathers* (1963) and *Iska* (1966), and two collections of short stories, *Rainmaker* (1965) and *Lokotown* (1966). Ekwensi continued to publish beyond the 1960s, and among his later works are the novel *Divided We Stand* (1980), the novella *Motherless Baby* (1980), and *The Restless City and Christmas Gold* (1975), *Behind the Convent Wall* (1987), and *Gone to Mecca* (1991).

Ekwensi also published a number works for children. Under the name C. O. D. Ekwensi, he released *Ikolo the Wrestler and Other Ibo Tales* (1947) and *The Leopard's Claw* (1950). In the 1960s, he wrote *An African Night's Entertainment* (1962), *The Great Elephant-Bird* (1965), and *Trouble in Form Six* (1966). Ekwensi's later works for children include *Coal Camp Boy* (1971), *Samankwe in the Strange Forest* (1973), *Samankwe and the Highway Robbers* (1975), *Masquerade Time!* (1992), and *King Forever!* (1992). In recognition of his skills as a writer, Ekwensi was awarded the Dag Hammarskjold International Prize for Literary Merit in 1969.

Further Reading

Among the studies in which Ekwensi's work and life are discussed are Ulli Beier, ed., *Introduction to African Literature* (1967); Ezekiel Mphahlele, ed., *African Writing Today* (1967); Oladele Taiwo, *An Introduction to West African Literature* (1967); Martin Tucker, *Africa in Modern Literature: A Survey of Contemporary Writing in English* (1967); and Margaret Laurence, *Long Drums and Cannons: Nigerian Dramatists and Novelists, 1952-1966* (1968). ☐

Joycelyn Elders

Confirmed as the 16th Surgeon General of the United States on September 7, 1993, Joycelyn Elders (born 1933) was the first African American and only the second female to head up the U.S. Public Health Service. In her brief 15-month tenure, Elders added tobacco use, national health care, and drug and alcohol abuse to her platform.

Jocelyn Elders was born Minnie Jones on August 13, 1933, in the southwestern farming community of Schaal, Arkansas. She took the name Jocelyn in college. She was the first of Haller and Curtis Jones's eight children. Living in a poor, segregated pocket of the country, she and her siblings struck a balance between laboring in the cotton fields and attending an all-black school 13 miles from home. One of her earliest childhood memories was being taught to read by her mother, Haller, who had an eighth grade education which was quite remarkable for an African American woman at that time. By the time she neared graduation from high school, Elders earned a scholarship to the all-black, liberal arts Philander Smith College in Little Rock, the state's capital. Initially, higher education looked doubtful for Elders as her father did not want to let her go. He felt that her contribution to the family was much more important. He did not see the long-term value of education. With all her pleading, Haller Jones could not get her husband to budge. Elders had resigned herself to staying home and continuing to pick cotton. She hadn't counted on her paternal grandmother, for whom she was named, to come to her aid, but whatever grandma Minnie said, she was allowed to go to college in September. Her family picked extra cotton to earn the $3.43 for her bus fare. She was the first in her family to take the road to higher education.

Found Inspiration in African American Woman Doctor

At school, Elders was particularly drawn to the study of biology and chemistry and concluded that being a lab technician was her highest calling, the professional mountaintop. But her ambitions rose a notch when she heard Edith Irby Jones (no relation), the first African American to study at the University of Arkansas School of Medicine, speak at a college sorority. Jocelyn Jones, who had not even met a doctor until she was 16 years old, imagined herself as a healer.

After graduation from college, Elders married briefly and then joined the U. S. Army's Women's Medical Specialist Corps. In 1956, she entered the Arkansas Medical School on the G.I. Bill two years after the Supreme Court, in its Brown v. Board of Education decision, ruled that separate but equal education was unconstitutional. But while segregation in some areas had been declared illegal by judicial

order, an underlying discriminatory mindset in American society could not be so easily erased. As the lone black student and only one of three students of color in her class, she was required to use a separate university dining room, where the cleaning staff ate. But she accepted this arrangement without argument, as this was the only social world to which she was accustomed. She met her second husband, Oliver Elders, when, in order to make additional money, she performed the physicals for high school students on the basketball team he managed. They were married in 1960.

After an internship in pediatrics at the University of Minnesota, Jocelyn Elders returned to Little Rock in 1961 for her residency and was quickly appointed chief pediatric resident, in charge of the all-white and all-male battery of residents and interns. Over the next 20 years, Elders combined a successful clinical practice with research in pediatric endocrinology (the study of glands), publishing well over 100 papers, most dealing with growth problems and juvenile diabetes. Her pioneering work captured the attention of the state's medical community, and physicians routinely referred to her their cases of juveniles with insulin-dependent diabetes.

It was this branch of science that led her to the study of sexual behavior and planted the seeds for her public sector advocacy. Recognizing that diabetic females face a health risk if they become pregnant at too young an age—the hazards include spontaneous abortion and possible congenital abnormalities in the infant—Elders saw the urgent need to talk about the dangers of pregnancy with her patients and to distribute contraceptives in order to limit those dangers. "If I wanted to keep those kids healthy, I decided I had no choice but to take command of their sexuality at the first sign of puberty," Elders told the *New York Times.* "I'd tell them, you're gonna have two good babies, and I'm gonna decide when you're gonna have them." The results were clear: of the 520 juvenile diabetics Elders treated, approximately half were female, and only one became pregnant.

Taking Action Against Societal Health Crises

But for every young adult in her care, there were thousands throughout the state whose sexual behavior went unmonitored and whose irresponsible, uneducated actions were contributing to America's dubious distinction of having the highest rate of teenage pregnancy in the industrialized world. Elders could not turn her back on this situation. She had done that once before, when she was a pediatric resident. A young girl with a thyroid condition, upon being told that she could go home from the hospital, had confided to Elders that she didn't want to leave the safety of her room—that her father, uncles and brothers sexually abused her every Saturday night. Elders was reluctant to believe her. This was also a time before doctors could report suspected child abuse with immunity. So Elders did nothing, and sent the child home. Inaction, she vowed, would be a sin of which she would never again be guilty.

In 1986, the year before Clinton named Elders director of the Arkansas Department of Health, 20 percent of the state's total births were to teenage mothers, compared to approximately 13 percent on a national level. The costs of the birthrate profile were, in Elder's view, enormous. Taxpayers in Arkansas dished out more than $82 million in fiscal 1987 for Arkansas adolescents and their children. Equally, if not more important, was the unquantifiable price paid by a society in which a frighteningly large number of emotionally immature young adults became parents to unwanted children. The *Boston Globe* quoted Elders as describing a poor teenager with a baby as "captive to a slavery the 13th Amendment [the Emancipation Proclamation abolishing slavery] did not anticipate." With the incidences of sexually transmitted diseases on the rise, and the specter of AIDS hanging over the heads of all sexually active people, Elders recognized the urgent need for bolder government involvement and an intense public education campaign.

Fought with Conservatives and Religious Groups

Elders glimpsed one of the approaches she would champion in office when she visited the state's first school-based health clinic in the Ozark mountain community of Lincoln, where contraceptives were given to students on request and where senior class pregnancies had subsequently fallen from 13 to one. Under Elders, 18 other school clinics opened, though only four of them were authorized by their local boards of education to distribute condoms. As Elders campaigned for the clinics and expanded sex education throughout the state, she became engaged in a heated battle with both political conservatives—who criticized her effort to increase the government's role in the lives of U.S. citizens, particularly in an area as private as sexual behavior—and members of some religious groups—who feared that the distribution of condoms would increase sexual activity, and who rejected the introduction of sex education in schools as a means of institutionally sanctioning abortion.

Elders, who is pro-choice but admits she personally opposes abortion, retaliated with both sober and emotional arguments. She said she would gladly teach abstinence if she felt that approach would work. But in the real world, she maintained, kids will continue to have sex, and it is the job of adults—and the U.S. government—to turn an irresponsible action into a responsible one. She said she considered every abortion her own personal failure, and her role, simply put, was to prevent unwanted pregnancy from ever occurring. She accused anti-abortion activists of having *a love affair with the fetus,* and pointed out in the *Washington Post* that not even abortion foes want to support "any [social] programs that will make [these unwanted children] into productive citizens."

In 1989, in great measure because of Elder's lobbying, the Arkansas State Legislature mandated a kindergarten-through-twelfth-grade course curriculum encompassing not only sex education, but instruction in hygiene, substance-abuse prevention, self-esteem, and the proposition, often overlooked, that sexual responsibility does not belong exclusively to the female. Between 1987 and 1990 though the rate of teenage pregnancy in Arkansas was up, the national rate was considerably higher.

Stood Ground during Confirmation Process

President Clinton's nomination of Elders for the post of U.S. Surgeon General made her the second African American and fifth woman tapped for a cabinet position—and galvanized on a national level the active critics who had fought her locally in Arkansas. Writing in the *National Review,* Floyd G. Brown, in a rebuttal to her favoring abortion on demand, criticized her for making what in his view is a cavalier judgment that the quality of life—that is, a loving, financially sound environment—"means more than life itself." Still others questioned her support of the abortion-inducing RU-486 pill, the medicinal use of marijuana, and her urging of television networks to lift their ban on airing condom ads. "I find it rather strange that we can advertise cigarettes and beer to the young but then get nervous when there is talk of something [condoms] that can save lives but not about some things that kill," she remarked in *Advertising Age.*

Some of the most persistent attacks against her nomination concerned her involvement with the National Bank of Arkansas. She and others serving on the bank's board of directors were sued by the bank for allegedly violating the National Banking Act by authorizing $1.5 million in bad loans. The suit was settled, but the terms were not disclosed. Elders resigned from her position as director of the Arkansas Health Department in July 1993 after questions were raised about her drawing a full-time salary there while also working two days a week as a paid consultant to U.S. Health and Human Services secretary Donna Shalala.

Although some Republicans succeeded in delaying the confirmation vote, Elders gained the backing of the American Medical Association and former U.S. Surgeon General C. Everett Koop. On September 7, 1993, the Senate gave Elders the nod 65-34. Democratic senator Edward Kennedy, citing the lashing doled out by several of his coleagues, was quoted in the *Boston Globe* as saying, "She has come through this unfair gauntlet of excessive criticism with flying colors."

Elders platform as U.S. Surgeon General was to continue with her work regarding teen pregnancy, she was also concerned with tobacco use, national health care, AIDS, and drug and alcohol abuse. In late 1993 she sparked a great debate regarding the legalization of street drugs such as heroin and cocaine which was misrepresented in the media and by her opponents. What Elders, in fact, proposed was that the issue be studied. She did not back away from this stance even after the arrest and conviction of her son, Kevin, who was appealing a ten-year sentence for selling an eighth of an ounce of cocaine to a police informant in July of 1993. Claiming entrapment, Kevin Elders, nevertheless, openly acknowledged a decade-long drug problem.

Gun control was a major issue for Elders. Every day 135,000 youngsters take guns to school, more than 100 are shot, and 30 are killed, she told the *Journal of the American Medical Association (JAMA).* She sees this issue as being intrinsic to the health of the nation.

The Surgeon General Resigns Amid Controversy

Amidst a sea of controversy over a statement made at World AIDS Day at the United Nations regarding the teaching of masturbation in schools, Dr. Jocelyn Elders was forced to resign her post as U.S. Surgeon General in December 1994. The Surgeon General had just finished a routine speech at the conference on the spread of communicable diseases when, Dr. Rob Clark a New York psychologist, asked her if she would consider promoting masturbation as a means of preventing young people from engaging in riskier forms of sexual activity. Elder, as quoted in *US News & World Report* responded, "With regard to masturbation, I think that it is something that is a part of human sexuality and a part of something that should perhaps be taught." That statement so enraged both conservatives and moderates alike, that it ended in Elder's termination. For Elders the political climate in Washington at that time was less than favorable for even the most minor misstep. The Republicans had just taken over the House of Representatives—for the first time in more than 40 years—and the Clinton administration was reeling. Elders infraction could not be overlooked.

While her departure was stongly applauded by the conservative faction, many were dismayed over the events that transpired and felt that Elders was lassoed and sacrificed to satisfy the chants of conservatives, and the desperation of Democrats to quiet them, as typified in an article by Susan Ager, *Detroit Free Press*. Elders responded not with anger but with grace. She did not buck, nor did she apologize. She stood by her comment, all of her comments, saying "Jocelyn Elders was Jocelyn Elders and I've always tried to speak what I knew to be the truth." Ager went on to say, "[Elders was a] rare public official, she said clearly and fearlessly what we didn't want to hear, but need to think about. I suspect she will be saying the same thing two years from now."

What Lies Ahead

In January 1995, Jocelyn Elders returned to the University of Arkansas as a faculty researcher, a professor of pediatric endocrinology at Arkansas Children's Hospital. Elders had both strong opponents and supporters as surgeon general. To the conservatives—her strongest opponents—she was "warped, dangerous, and a lunatic." To her supporters she was "noble, heroic, and fearless." Jocelyn Elders saw her mission as Surgeon General to create dialogue on America's health and welfare and the only way to do that, according to Elders, was to get their attention. "I think the Surgeon General's office is the office where it is very important to be able to get people listening to you, thinking about it, and talking about it . . . that is where you get change," she told Dr. Paula Wilson, assistant profession of communication studies Lynchburg College in Virginia.

Elders has no intention of fading into the background now that she is no longer U.S. Surgeon General. She made an impact on the audience she was most concerned about, the youth, and she intends to continue to be their advocate. When asked if there were any hard feelings about being asked to step down, Elders, in an interview with Steve Barnes of the *Progressive Interview,* responded candidly. "No, I don't have any hard feelings. I feel that the President, and the President alone, asked me to be Surgeon General. He gave me an opportunity to serve as Surgeon General, one that I would not have had without him. . . . I would not be the Jocelyn Elders I am today without the things the President did for me."

In February 1997, speaking to a group of 350 physicians at a conference in Long Beach, California, the former Surgeon General spoke "with the same clarity and passion . . . that won her confirmation to the post of U.S. Surgeon General in 1993, that led to her resignation in 1994," according to the *Press-Telegram*. A generation of youth is drowning in an ocean surrounded by the sharks of drugs, homicide and suicide, while many of us are sitting on the moral beach of *Just say no,* she told the opening session. Challenging her audience to become actively involved, Elders said, "There's a great big difference between being concerned and being committed. When you're concerned, its negotiable." On a more personal note she added, "When I went to Washington, I was committed. And what I was about was not negotiable."

When asked what the future holds for Dr. Jocelyn Elders, she told *Progressive* in a March 1995 interview, "I'm going to be the very best doctor I can be. I'm going to try to do some research, looking at problems that impact adolescents. And I'm going to become a real advocate. I'm going to do a lot of public speaking."

Further Reading

Detroit Free Press, December 14, 1994; October 1994; *Jet,* December 26-January 2, 1995; *Lancet,* December 24, 1994; *People,* November 4, 1996; *Playboy,* June 1995; *The Nation,* January 2, 1995; *The Progressive,* March 1995; *The Progressive Interview,* March 1995; *USA Today,* May 1997; *Washington Monthly,* January-February 1997. □

Eleanor of Aquitaine

Eleanor of Aquitaine (ca. 1122-1204) was queen of France from 1137 to 1152 and queen of England from 1154 to 1204. Her second marriage, which brought southwestern France to the English king, affected the relations of France and England for almost 300 years.

E leanor was the elder daughter of William X, Duke of Aquitaine, and Aenor (Eleanor) of Châtellerault. William died on April 9, 1137. The marriage of his heiress was of great importance because Aquitaine was one of the largest fiefs of France. Probably in accord with her father's wish, Eleanor married Louis, son of King Louis VI (July 25, 1137); they were installed as rulers of Aquitaine at Poitiers (August 8) and crowned king and queen of France at

Bourges on Christmas, Louis VI having died. The young king seems to have been fond of his beautiful wife, but Eleanor is said to have complained that she had married a monk and not a king.

In June 1147 Louis and Eleanor set out on a crusade, arriving at Antioch in March 1148. Here they quarreled, and the validity of their marriage was questioned. However, she and Louis reached home together. On March 21, 1152, their marriage was annulled on grounds of consanguinity. The King's wish for a male heir—Eleanor having borne two daughters—was probably the decisive reason.

Less than 2 months later Eleanor married Henry Plantagenet, Duke of Normandy, Count of Anjou, and soon to be king of England. They were crowned at Westminster on Dec. 19, 1154. Henry II was 11 years younger than his wife. Their marriage was a political match; he wanted her lands, and she needed a protector. Eleanor and Henry had eight children: William (1153-1156); Henry the "young king" (1155-1183); Matilda (1156-1189), who married Henry the Lion, Duke of Saxony; Richard (1157-1199); Geoffrey, Duke of Brittany (1158-1186); Eleanor (1162-1214), who married Alfonso, King of Castile; Joanna (1165-1199), who married William ll, King of Sicily, and later Raymond, Count of Toulouse; and John (1167-1216).

Richard was regarded from an early age as heir to his mother's duchy. In 1168 she brought him to live there, maintaining a court centered at Poitiers. Though Richard was given the ducal title, Eleanor had both power and responsibility. Now she also had full opportunity to give

patronage to poets and authors. This relatively happy period ended abruptly in 1173. Eleanor, goaded perhaps by Henry's unfaithfulness, allied with the king of France against him. Her young sons joined her; indeed, as the young Henry was already 18, he may have instigated the plot. King Henry crushed the rebels and forgave his sons but kept his wife in semi-imprisonment until he died.

With the accession to the English throne of her favorite son, Richard (called the "Lion-Hearted"), on Sept. 3, 1189, Eleanor resumed her royal position and regained control of her property. She arranged his coronation, and in the winter of 1190/1191 she traveled to Navarre to fetch his future wife, Berengaria, and escorted her to Sicily to join Richard before he left for Palestine. During his absence she worked with the Council of Regency in England, and she had the unpleasant task of helping to thwart the treachery of John, her youngest son. She received Richard's letters about his captivity and organized the collection of his ransom.

On Richard's sudden death (April 6, 1199), Eleanor supported John's claim to succeed to the English throne against that of her grandson Arthur of Brittany. She herself did homage to King Philip of France for Aquitaine, and she formally took control of the duchy.

In July 1202, when John and Philip were at war, Eleanor was besieged in the castle of Mirabeau by John's enemies, nominally led by her grandson Arthur. John defeated the besiegers and captured his nephew. His mother was able to spend her last months in freedom. She died on April 1, 1204, and was buried at the abbey of Fontevrault, where her effigy remains.

Further Reading

The best biography of Eleanor is Amy Ruth Kelly, *Eleanor of Aquitaine and the Four Kings* (1950). There are also Régine Pernoud's shorter and more romantic *Eleanor of Aquitaine,* translated by Peter Wiles (1967), and Curtis Howe Walker, *Eleanor of Aquitaine* (1950). These works must be used with caution because the sources do not reveal Eleanor's motives and opinions. □

Sir Edward Elgar

The works of the English composer Sir Edward Elgar (1857-1934) ushered in the modern flowering of English music. His work is characterized by brilliant orchestration and impressive craftsmanship.

Edward Elgar was born on June 2, 1857, in Worcester. His father played the organ and directed the choir in St. George's Catholic Church, was a violinist in local orchestras, and ran a music store. This musical ambience was school and conservatory for Edward, who received no formal musical education except for a few violin lessons. He served his apprenticeship as a church organist, choirmaster, and director of amateur orchestras and the band of the county mental institution. The focus of musical activity was the annual choir festival, when distinguished conductors and soloists performed oratorios by George Frederick Handel and Felix Mendelsohn, as well as newly commissioned works, with the local choir.

Elgar's earliest works were for his church choir, and in later years his most important compositions were large oratorios commissioned for choir festivals. Through these performances he became known throughout England. His first important orchestral piece was the *Enigma Variations* (1899). The "enigma" refers to the theme on which the variations are written, a countertheme to an unnamed and unplayed melody. There have been many conjectures about the mysterious theme, but its identity has never been determined. Each of the variations is labeled with the initials or nickname of friends of the composer, and each variation is a musical character sketch. The piece is beautifully orchestrated and written.

Elgar's choral masterpiece is *The Dream of Gerontius* (1900). Written to a religious poem by Cardinal Newman, it is perhaps the finest English composition of the Victorian era. It is Wagnerian in its use of leitmotivs characterizing the protagonists and situations, the rich, chromatic harmony, and the masterful orchestral writing.

Other important works by Elgar are the Violin Concerto (1910) and two overtures, *Cockaigne* (1910) and *Falstaff* (1913). His best-known piece is *Pomp and Circumstance No. 1* (1901), a concert march from which the patriotic hymn "Land of Hope and Glory" was written. Its honest,

brilliant tunes epitomize the optimism of Edwardian England.

Elgar was knighted in 1904 and named master of the king's music in 1924. By the time of his death on Feb. 23, 1934, in Worcester, the younger 20th-century composers had made his music seem old-fashioned. Later evaluations, however, have been more generous, and Elgar's place in music seems once again assured.

Further Reading

The best works on Elgar are W. H. Reed, *Elgar* (1939), which includes analyses of three major works; Diana McVeagh, *Edward Elgar: His Life and Music* (1955); Percy Marshall Young, *Elgar, O. M.: A Study of a Musician* (1955), a biography which emphasizes his music; and Michael Kennedy, *Portrait of Elgar* (1968), a study of his character. A good background study which discusses Elgar's work is Joseph Machlis, *Introduction to Contemporary Music* (1961).

Additional Sources

Anderson, Robert, *Elgar*, New York: Schirmer Books: Maxwell Macmillan International, 1993.
De-la-Noy, Michael, *Elgar, the man*, London: A. Lane, 1983.
Kennedy, Michael, *Portrait of Elgar*, Oxford; New York: Oxford University Press, 1987.
McVeagh, Diana M., *Edward Elgar, his life and music*, Westport, Conn.: Hyperion Press, 1979.
Moore, Jerrold Northrop, *Edward Elgar: a creative life*, Oxford; New York: Oxford University Press, 1990.
Mundy, Simon, *Elgar*, London; New York: Omnibus Press, 1984.
Reed, William H. (William Henry), *Elgar as I knew him*, Oxford; New York: Oxford University Press, 1989.
Young, Percy M. (Percy Marshall), *Elgar, O. M.: a study of a musician*, Westport, Conn.: Greenwood Press, 1980, 1973. □

8th Earl of Elgin

James Bruce, 8th Earl of Elgin (1811-1863), was the governor general of Canada who implemented the principle of "responsible government" in colonial administration and paved the way for the development of a Commonwealth comprising autonomous nations.

The son of the 7th Earl of Elgin, who collected the Elgin Marbles for the British Museum, James Bruce was born in London on July 20, 1811. He studied at Eton and Oxford, where he graduated in 1833. For a short time he was a Conservative member of Parliament for Southampton, but on the death of his father in 1841 he succeeded to the peerage and was thus denied a career in the House of Commons.

Elgin received a colonial appointment as governor of Jamaica in 1842 and 4 years later was given the more important post of governor general of Canada. Arriving in Canada in January 1847, he brought with him clear instructions from the Whig colonial secretary, Lord Grey, to concede "responsible government" to Canada by accepting the advice of ministers who could command the confidence of a majority in the legislature.

Acting upon these directions, Elgin called to office in March 1848 a group of reformers from Canada West and Canada East headed by Robert Baldwin and Louis-Hippolyte Lafontaine. The next year he accepted the recommendation of these ministers by signing the Rebellion Losses Bill, even though he was personally unhappy over its provision to pay compensation to the victims of the rebellion of 1837. For this act of political wisdom Elgin was subjected to personal abuse from the English Tory population of Canada East, who felt outraged by what appeared to be a payment to "traitors." Elgin's farseeing action in this crisis marked the ultimate test of "responsible government" in the senior colony of the British Empire and paved the way for the extension of the principle to other settlement colonies.

Before he left Canada in 1854, Elgin was responsible for the negotiation of a reciprocity treaty with William L. Marcy, United States Secretary of State. This provided for the free admission of natural products between the British North American colonies and the United States, and it gave a considerable spur to the economic life of the colonies before it was abrogated in 1866.

A popular governor general, who built up harmonious relationships with four ministries during his term of office, Elgin left Canada amidst general regret. He went on two diplomatic missions to China in later years and served briefly in Lord Palmerston's Cabinet in 1859-1860 as post-master general. In 1862 he was appointed to the highest post in Britain's overseas service, the position of viceroy of India, but he died suddenly in India on Nov. 20, 1863, at the beginning of his term.

Further Reading

There are a number of biographies of Elgin, mostly emphasizing his Canadian experience. One of the first was Sir John Bourinot, *Lord Elgin* (1903), in "The Makers of Canada" series. This was followed by W. P. M. Kennedy, *Lord Elgin,* in the 1926 edition of the series, which used new material. There is also a biography by J. L. Morison, *The Eighth Earl of Elgin* (1928). Elgin's correspondence on Canadian affairs with Lord Grey was published as *The Elgin-Grey Papers, 1846-1852,* edited by Sir Arthur G. Doughty (4 vols., 1837).

Additional Sources

Checkland, S. G., *The Elgins, 1766-1917: a tale of aristocrats, proconsuls and their wives,* Aberdeen: Aberdeen University Press, 1988. □

Mircea Eliade

Mircea Eliade (1907-1986) was a Rumanian-born historian of religions and a novelist whose works were known in translation the world over.

Mircea Eliade began his life in Bucharest in 1907. While still studying in the lycée he wrote numerous articles in a popular vein on entomology, the history of alchemy, Orientalism, the history of religions, impressions of his travels, stories, and literary criticism. In 1925 he entered the University of Bucharest, where he pursued the study of Renaissance philosophy. Thus began a life-long preoccupation with the great creative epochs in Western history and with the puzzle of human, especially literary, creativity itself. Eliade had seen, for example, how the Rumanian poets, writers, and historians he admired had drawn material and inspiration from folk sources, and he was fascinated to see an analogous process at work in the Italian Renaissance.

For Eliade, the rediscovery of Greek philosophy, exemplified in Marsilio Ficino's Latin translations of the *Corpus hermeticum* and the founding by Ficino of the Platonic Academies in Florence, meant "a breakthrough toward the East, toward Europe and Persia." But as he later understood, it was not a simple reacquaintance with the classical heritage that made the Renaissance such a creative period; instead, the strange "new" occult elements which Renaissance thinkers encountered in their discoveries actually represented "the fund of Neolithic culture that is the matrix of all the urban cultures of the ancient Near East and the Mediterranean world."

In 1928, while in Rome to research his degree thesis on "Italian Philosophy, from Marsilio Ficino to Giordano Bruno," Eliade wrote to Professor Surendranath Dasgupta expressing a desire to study under his direction at the University of Calcutta—which he did, thanks to a scholarship offered him by the Maharajah Manindra Chandra Mandy of Kassimbazar. Eliade's stay in India lasted three years. In 1933 he received his doctorate with a dissertation on yoga, later published in French under the title *Yoga: Essai sur les origines de las mystique indienne* (1936), and began teaching at the University of Bucharest that same year.

Shortly after his return from India, in the midst of a busy schedule that included university teaching and many commitments to write and lecture, Eliade's novel, *Maitreyi,* was released to great critical and popular acclaim. Born into a tradition which saw no incompatibility between scientific and literary occupations, Eliade, the historian of religions, continued to produce novels, stories, essays, and a travel book. Today, especially in Rumania and Germany, he is known primarily as a writer of fiction; and his popularity continues to grow as more and more of his works appear in translation.

During World War II Eliade served as cultural attaché to the Rumanian legations in London and Lisbon. After the war he elected to remain in exile in Paris where he could complete work on a number of manuscripts which had taken shape during the war years, notably *Patterns in Comparative Religion* and *The Myth of the Eternal Return,* both of which came to print in 1949. The years 1951 to 1955 saw the publication of several more volumes for which Eliade is well known: *Shamanism, Images and Symbols, Yoga, The Forge and the Crucible,* and *The Forbidden Forest.* Many regard the last title as his most important work of fiction.

Eliade travelled to the United States to deliver the 1956 Haskell Lectures at the University of Chicago, and a year later he was offered the post of professor and chairman of the History of Religions Department and professor in the Committee on Social Thought at the university. Almost 30 years later, he was professor emeritus at this same institution with the title Sewell Avery Distinguished Service Professor.

Eliade's scholarly output continued unabated. Volume I of *A History of Religious Ideas* appeared in 1974, and three of its four projected volumes had been published by 1985. *A History of Religious Ideas* marked something of a departure from his previous theoretical work. As in his sourcebook, *From Primitives to Zen,* Eliade presented the "creative moments" of the world's religious traditions in more or less chronological order, treating them in a way one might call more historical and less thematic. In addition to his scholarly writing, Eliade served as editor-in-chief of a massive encyclopedia of religion until his death in 1986.

While the differences between *homo reliosus* and nonreligious people of the modern West are clear, Eliade argued that non-religion can be likened to the biblical "fall" of man. That is, just as the original "fall" produced forgetfulness of God and a "divided" consciousness, the second "fall" of modern times marked the further descent of religion into the depths of the unconscious—an explanation for, among other things, the importance modern people attach to dreams, the role of the unconscious in artistic creativity, and the persistence of initiatory and other religious patterns in literature. Eliade's theoretical work in the history of religions can thus be said to embrace even his own literary creations, so that the two together form a single *oeuvre* consistent with his visions of a "new humanism" in modern times.

Further Reading

Perhaps the best introduction to Mircea Eliade's life and thought is *Ordeal by Labyrinth: Conversations with Claude-Heuri Rocquet,* translated from the French by Derek Coltmann (1982). Readers desirous of knowing more about Eliade's fascinating career may also wish to consult his *No Souvenirs: Journals 1957-1969* (1982) and *Autobiography: Volume I, Journey East, Journey West 1907-1937* (1981).

Additional Sources

Eliade, Mircea, *Exile's odyssey: 1937-1960,* Chicago: University of Chicago Press, 1988.

Eliade, Mircea, *Autobiography,* San Francisco: Harper & Row, 1981-1988; Chicago: University of Chicago Press, 1990.

Ricketts, Mac Linscott, *Mircea Eliade: the Romanian roots, 1907-1945,* Boulder: East European Monographs; New York: Distributed by Columbia University Press, 1988. □

Taslim Olawale Elias

Taslim Olawale Elias (1914-1991), Nigerian academic and jurist, was the president of the International Court of Justice. He also modernized and extensively revised the laws of Nigeria.

Taslim Olawale Elias was born in Lagos, the capital of Nigeria, on November 11, 1914. He received his secondary education at the Church Missionary Society Grammar School and Igbobi College in Lagos. Marriage to Ganiat Yetunde Fowosere occurred in 1932; the couple would have five children together (three sons, two daughters). After passing the Cambridge School Certificate examination in 1934 he worked as an assistant in the Government Audit Department. In 1935 he joined the Nigerian Railway and served in the Chief Accountant's Office for nine years.

While working at the Nigerian Railway Elias became an external student of London University, and later he passed the intermediate examinations for the B.A. and LL.B degrees. He left Nigeria for the United Kingdom in 1944 and was admitted to University College, London. As this was during World War II, with London the target of frequent bomb attacks, he spent some time at Cambridge's Trinity College. He graduated with a B.A. the year he entered University College and two years later received the LL.B. In 1947 he was called to the bar from the Inner Temple where he was a Yarborough Anderson Scholar, and in the same year received his LL.M degree in law. He continued his graduate education at London University and in 1949 earned a Ph.D. in law.

Entered Academia

In 1951 Elias was awarded a United Nations Economic, Social and Cultural Organization (UNESCO) Fellowship to undertake research into the legal, economic, and social problems of Africa. Later that year he had his first academic appointment, the Simon senior research fellow at Manchester University. There he was an instructor in law and social anthropology. It was also in 1951 that he published his first book, *Nigerian Land Law and Custom*.

Elias moved from Manchester to Oxford in 1954 when he became the Oppenheimer research fellow at the Institute of Commonwealth Studies, Nuffield College and Queen Elizabeth House. He continued his research into Nigerian law and published *Groundwork of Nigerian Law* in the same year. In 1956 he was visiting professor of political science at the University of Delhi. He was instrumental in organizing courses in government, law, and social anthropology and in establishing the African Studies Department. Elias also lectured at the universities of Aligarh, Allahabad, Bombay, and Calcutta. In that year he also published two books, *Makers of Nigerian Law* and *The Nature of African Customary Law*.

Turbulent Yet Promising Years

He returned to London in 1957 and was appointed a governor of the School of Oriental and African Studies, University of London. As the constitutional and legal adviser to the National Council of Nigeria and the Cameroons (which later became the National Convention of Nigerian Citizens), he participated in the 1958 Nigerian Constitutional Conference in London. He was one of the architects of Nigeria's independence constitution and in 1960 was invited to become the country's attorney-general and minister of justice. Elias served in this capacity through the whole of the first republic. Although he was dismissed after the coup d'état in January 1966, he was reinstated in November of that year.

In 1966 Elias was also appointed professor and dean of the faculty of law at Lagos University. Four years earlier he had received the LL.D. degree of the University of London for his work on Nigerian and African law and British colonial law. In 1967, Elias was appointed Nigeria's commissioner for justice and five years later, in 1972, became chief justice of the Supreme Court of Nigeria. By this point he had long been active in the international legal world. A member of the United Nations International Law Commission from 1961 to 1975, he served as general rapporteur from 1965 to 1966 and was its chairman in 1970. He was the leader of the Nigerian delegations to the conference held to consider the Draft Convention on the Settlement of Investment Disputes between States and Nationals of Other States in 1963 and to the Special Committee on the Principles of International Law concerning Friendly Relations and Co-operation among States in 1964. He was a member of the United Nations Committee of Experts which drafted the constitution of the Congo, 1961-1962. He helped to draft the charter of the Organization of African Unity (O.A.U.), and its Protocol of Mediation, Conciliation and Arbitration. Elias was also the representative of the O.A.U. and Nigeria before the International Court of Justice in the proceedings concerning the status of Namibia.

Elias held a position of great import in Nigeria as its chief justice of the Supreme Court of Nigeria, but he had to contend with a sometimes tenuous political climate and the repercussions of an oil boom that made some Nigerians rich a bit too quickly. He was ousted in 1975 by Nigeria's military regime after an investigative paper published a story accusing him of trying to influence a court case involving his brother. Those who spoke out in support of Elias noted his incorruptibility and the fact that he lived quite modestly; furthermore, unlike other esteemed Nigerians in leadership positions, Elias had never used his high position to reap financial reward.

Vindicated by High Honor

The following year Elias was appointed a judge of the International Court of Justice at The Hague. The government of Nigeria did not voice any objection to this appointment, since the elevation to the International Court carried with it a great deal of prestige, and its judges were considered to be the most exemplary (thus ethics-minded) jurists. In 1982, after the death of Sir Humphrey Waldock, Elias was elected president of the International Court of Justice, and became the first African jurist to hold that honor. Five years later Elias was also appointed to the Permanent Court of Arbitration at The Hague as well.

Esteemed Intellectual

A prolific writer, Elias published nearly 20 books and numerous articles in scholarly journals. The field of emerging legal systems in African nations was his specialty, and he wrote of it broadly and specifically in titles such as *Africa Before the World Court* (1981) and *Africa and the West: The Legacies of Empire* (1986). He was a member of several international legal associations, including the International Commission of Jurists, the World Association of Judges (he served as president in 1975) and an honorary member of the American Society of International Law. He received honorary degrees from universities all over the world.

Elias died on August 14, 1991, in Lagos, Nigeria. Sadly, he was never able to refute charges of corruption, and attempted to sue the paper that first raised them, but he passed away before the case could be decided. No doubt his 1969 treatise *Nigerian Press Law* was cited at some point in the legal documents.

Further Reading

There is no biography of Elias. Some of his many books include *British Colonial Law-A Comparative Study* (1962), *Ghana and Sierra Leone: The Development of their Laws and Constitutions* (1962), *The Nigerian Legal System* (1963), *Africa and the Development of International Law* (1972), *Africa Before the World Court* (1981), and *The International Court of Justice and Some Contemporary Problems* (1983). □

Elijah ben Solomon

The Jewish scholar Elijah ben Solomon (1720-1797) was one of the greatest authorities on classical Juda-

ism. **Known for his mental acumen and personal piety, he was given the exalted titles of Gaon (excellency) and Hasid (saint).**

E lijah ben Solomon was born and died in Vilna, Poland (Vilna is now the capital of Lithuania). He displayed a prodigious intellect as a child, and at the age of 10 he insisted that he study by himself because he refused to be influenced by any special school of thought or methodology. Complete independence of thought characterized his profound scholarship. He remained in Vilna all of his life, except for a short period of voluntary exile that many scholars imposed upon themselves as an act of penance. His pilgrimage to Palestine was aborted, and he returned to his native city, where he dedicated his life to study. The community wished to designate him as their rabbi, but he refused. Out of deference they voted him a small stipend which often proved inadequate, and he had to rely upon his wife to manage the family's financial affairs. His modesty did not prevent his fame from becoming universal, and even as a young man many queries were addressed to him from the greatest scholars and authorities.

Elijah searched for truth wherever it could be found. His intellectual horizons were very broad, and he insisted that all disciplines—mathematics, astronomy, philology, and grammar—could assist in the true understanding of the basic works of classical Judaism. He mastered these subjects and wrote treatises on them.

The number of Elijah's works is said to exceed 70. Many of them have been published, others are in manuscript, and some are lost. He wrote commentaries on a number of biblical books, on the tractates of the Mishna, and on portions of the Jerusalem Talmud. His glosses to the entire Talmud (Babylonian and Jerusalem) display great linguistic insights, and his suggested textual emendations have been confirmed by later examination of manuscripts. He wrote a commentary on Joseph Caro's *Shulhan Aruk*. He also composed a treatise on Hebrew grammar, which the traditional scholars sought to overlook. Another area in which he did pioneer work was that of the early Tannaitic Midrashim, which precede the Talmud and which provide the first stratum of Jewish legal development.

Elijah's interest in classical Talmudic studies did not deter him from study of the Cabala, or Jewish mysticism, and he wrote a commentary on the *Zohar*, the magnum opus of Cabala, which is generally considered to be the work of Moses de Leon.

While Elijah strenuously avoided involvement in communal affairs, he did emerge from his isolation by twice issuing bans of excommunication against the Hasidim (Pietists), whose deprecation of scholarly pursuits as deterrents to genuine spiritual immersion was considered by him as a serious danger to the classical Jewish tradition. Elijah Gaon has been acclaimed as the last great theologian of classical rabbinism whose writings closed one great period of Jewish history but whose personal example has been an endless inspiration to subsequent generations.

Further Reading

Detailed biographical studies of Elijah ben Solomon are in Leo Jung, ed., *The Jewish Library,* vol 6: *Jewish Leaders* (1953), and Simon Noveck, ed., *Great Jewish Personalities in Ancient and Medieval Times* (1959). See also Louis Ginzberg, *Students, Scholars and Saints* (1928).

Additional Sources

Shulman, Yaacov Dovid, *The Vilna Gaon: the story of Rabbi Eliyahu Kramer,* New York: C.I.S. Publishers, 1994. □

Gertrude B. Elion

The American biochemist Gertrude B. Elion (born 1918) won a Nobel Prize for her scientific discovery of drugs to treat leukemia and herpes and to prevent the rejection of kidney transplants.

B orn in New York City in 1918, Gertrude Elion graduated from Hunter College with a B.A. degree in chemistry in 1937. In the midst of the Great Depression it was difficult for a woman to find a job in science. Elion had decided while still in high school to become a cancer researcher but for several years worked as a lab assistant, food analyst, and high school teacher while completing her Masters degree at night. She received an M.S. in chemistry from New York University in 1941.

During World War II, women were needed in scientific laboratories and Elion was hired as a biochemist by the Wellcome Research Laboratories, then in Tuckahoe, New York. There she worked for many years with George Herbert Hitchings, co-recipient with Gertrude Elion of the Nobel Prize in Medicine in 1988. Together, they pioneered pharmaceutical research, discovering and developing drugs to treat previously incurable diseases. Elion was later promoted to senior research chemist and in 1967 became head of the Department of Experimental Therapy.

The theory behind the development of these new drugs suggested by Hitchings was that, since all cells require nucleic acids, one might be able to stop the growth of rapidly dividing cells such as bacteria and tumor cells by substituting false building blocks, or antagonists of nucleic acid bases, in the synthesis of nucleic acids. Thus the replication of the unwanted cells might be prevented. Elion set to work especially on purines, nitrogenous bases that are important constituents of DNA. She was also working part-time on her doctorate at Brooklyn Polytechnic Institute but, given the ultimatum to choose between continuing on her doctorate full-time and keeping her job, she chose the latter. She was later awarded honorary doctorate degrees from George Washington University and several other universities and colleges in recognition of her research.

The early research involved a bacterium, *Lactobacillus casei,* which could synthesize purines given the right chemical substrates. She found her research work fascinating because so little was then known about how nucleic acid

was synthesized. James Watson and Francis Crick had not yet determined the structure of DNA, the double helix. The pathways for biosynthesis of purines were not worked out until the mid-1950s by Arthur Kornberg and others.

By 1951 Elion and Hitchings succeeded in developing a number of drugs that interfered with purine utilization called purine antimetabolites. Two of these were tested at the Sloan-Kettering Institute and were found to be active against leukemia in rodents. One of these, 6-mercaptopurine (6-MP), was then tested on children with acute leukemia at ten American medical centers. At that time there were no effective drugs for these terminally ill children and not even one in three lived as long as one year. The drug 6-MP was found to produce complete, though often temporary, remission. It was approved by the Food and Drug Administration in 1953. The success of this and related purine antimetabolite drugs opened up a whole new area of research in leukemia chemotherapy. Although 6-MP is still widely used, it is now prescribed in combination with several other antileukemic drugs. Almost 80 percent of children with acute leukemia can now be cured.

In the process of studying how 6-MP worked in both animals and humans, Elion developed a closely related compound called azathioprine. It was tested first as an anticancer drug but was later found to have a quite different but important function: it blocked the immune response leading to the rejection of foreign transplants. In 1960 this drug was tried out successfully in a kidney transplant on a collie. By 1962 successful human kidney transplants from unrelated donors became a reality, using azathioprine as an

immunosuppressant drug. Cyclosporine made possible successful transplants of livers, hearts, and lungs, but azathioprine is still used in kidney transplants. It is also used to treat other serious diseases such as severe rheumatoid arthritis and systemic lupus.

Another drug that Elion and her coworkers synthesized scientifically—that is, by understanding how it works biochemically—is allopurinol. It can be used for the treatment of gout and other diseases resulting from an excess of uric acid. In gout uric acid crystals accumulate in the joints, causing extreme pain. Allopurinol inhibits the formation of the uric acid.

In 1968 Elion and her group returned to some early work she and Hitchings had done on antiviral drugs. They developed a drug found to be highly active against herpes virus. In 1970 their laboratory moved to North Carolina where they synthesized a new antiviral agent, Acyclovir. This drug is highly effective against several types of herpes virus and is not toxic to normal cells. It has been used in treating herpes since 1981, and also in treating patients with the painful disease known as shingles, caused by the varicella-zoster virus. It has even been a lifesaving drug for patients with herpes encephalitis, a frequently fatal disease. Acyclovir, approved by the Food and Drug Administration 1984, has become one of Burroughs Wellcome's most profitable drugs. Two years later, researchers trained by Elion and Hitchings developed azidothymidine, or AZT, the first drug used to treat AIDS.

Elion retired from Burroughs Wellcome in 1983 but remained there as a scientist emeritus. She served as president of the American Association for Cancer Research in 1983-1984 and on many advisory boards, including chairman of the Steering Committee on the Chemotherapy of Malaria. She also served as research professor of medicine and pharmacology at Duke University, working with advanced medical students who wish to do research on tumor biochemistry and pharmacology sharing her interest and experience.

In 1988, Elion and Hitchings shared the Nobel Prize for physiology or medicine with Sir James Black, a British biochemist. In her Nobel Prize speech, Elion noted that her 40 years of research not only resulted in many therapeutic drugs but that these life-serving agents have been tools to understand nature's mysteries. They led her into whole new areas of medical research, not only in biochemistry and pharmacology but also in immunology and virology.

Elion celebrated a momentous year in 1991 as she became the first woman to be inducted in the National Inventors Hall of Fame. She was also named to the Engineering and Science Hall of Fame and received the National Medal of Science. In 1995, she was named the Higuchi Memorial Award winner and lectured at the University of Kansas.

Elion, who resides in Chapel Hill, North Carolina, continues her work today through the World Health Organization, honorary university lectureships, and assisting students in medical research. Her hobbies include photography, travel and music. Her name appears on 45 patents

Further Reading

Gertrude Elion described her scientific work in her Nobel Prize speech, quoted in *Science* magazine (April 7, 1989); gave a personal account of her life in *Les Prix Nobel* (1988). Biographical data on Elion appears in the books *Who's Who 1997* and the St. Martin's Press' annual biographical dictionary. □

Charles William Eliot

The American educator Charles William Eliot (1834-1926) was president of Harvard from 1869 to 1909 and transformed the college into a modern university.

Born in Boston on March 20, 1834, of a distinguished New England family, Charles W. Eliot graduated from Harvard in 1853. He taught mathematics and chemistry there (1854-1863). He toured Europe (1863-1865), studying chemistry and advanced methods of instruction, and returned to become a professor at the Massachusetts Institute of Technology. In 1869, having attracted favorable attention by several articles on educational reform, he was chosen president of Harvard.

Eliot's 40-year tenure permitted him to press slowly but consistently for change. The effect of his innovations was revolutionary and thoroughly altered Harvard. He drew ideas from his European experience, and he later paid tribute to the stimulating effect of the innovations undertaken at Johns Hopkins University under Daniel Coit Gilman.

Eliot developed an organized 3-year program in the law school, using the case system of instruction based on studying actual court decisions rather than abstract principles. In the medical school he introduced laboratory work and written examinations in all subjects, and he gradually made available clinical instruction in Boston hospitals. In 1872 the university began to grant doctoral degrees, and the Graduate School of Arts and Sciences was formally organized in 1890, taught by the same faculty that served the undergraduate college.

Eliot's best-known reform was the elective system. Undergraduates could choose from a wide variety of courses in each field rather than follow a prescribed curriculum. By offering many advanced courses to undergraduates, Eliot was able to employ in the college outstanding scholars who divided their time between undergraduate and graduate schools. Harvard became a leading center for graduate study and research and by the 1890s had earned an international reputation for academic excellence.

Always interested in secondary education, Eliot was active in the National Education Association (NEA), becoming president in 1903. He strongly influenced the 1892 report of the NEA "Committee of Ten" that led to the standardization of college preparation and admissions, and he helped found the College Entrance Examination Board in 1906. In 1910 he edited *The Harvard Classics,* a "five-foot shelf" of outstanding books through which those unable to attend college might acquire a liberal education. He retired in 1909 and died at Northeast Harbor, Maine, on Aug. 22, 1926.

Further Reading

Henry James, *Charles W. Eliot: President of Harvard University, 1869-1909* (2 vols., 1930), is the best and most complete biography. Samuel Eliot Morison's two books, *The Development of Harvard University since the Inauguration of President Eliot, 1869-1929* (1930) and *Three Centuries of Harvard: 1636-1936* (1936), are invaluable on Eliot's work at Harvard. Eliot's view of his profession may be found in his *Educational Reform: Essays and Addresses* (1898) and *University Administration* (1908). *Charles W. Eliot: The Man and His Beliefs,* edited by William Allan Nielsen (2 vols., 1926), is a collection of Eliot's best essays and addresses on a variety of topics. □

George Eliot

George Eliot was the pen name used by the English novelist Mary Ann Evans (1819-1880), one of the most important writers of European fiction. Her masterpiece, *Middlemarch,* is not only a major social document but also one of the greatest novels in the history of fiction.

Mary Ann Evans was born in Warwickshire, the daughter of an estate agent or manager. Her education was a conventional one, dominated by Christian teachings and touched by the enthusiasm generated by the Evangelical movement of church reform. In her 20s she came into contact with a circle of freethinkers and underwent a radical transformation of her beliefs. Influenced by the so-called Higher Criticism—a largely German school of biblical scholarship that attempted to treat sacred writings as human and historical documents—she devoted herself to translating its findings for the English public. She published her translation of David Strauss's *Life of Jesus* in 1846 and her translation of Ludwig Andreas Feuerbach's *Essence of Christianity* in 1854.

In 1851 Evans became an editor of the *Westminster Review,* a rationalist and reformist journal. In that capacity she came into contact with the leading intellectuals of the day, among them a group known as the positivists. They were followers of the doctrines of the French philosopher Auguste Comte, who were interested in applying scientific knowledge to the problems of society. One of these men was George Henry Lewes, a brilliant philosopher, psychologist, and literary critic, with whom she formed a lasting relationship. As he was separated from his wife but unable to obtain a divorce, their relationship challenged Victorian ideas of respectability. Nevertheless, the obvious devotion and permanence of their union came to be respected.

Adam Bede

In the same period Evans turned her powerful mind from scholarly and critical writing to creative work. In 1857 she published a short story, "Amos Barton," and took the pen name "George Eliot" in order to obviate the special aura then attached to lady novelists. After collecting her short stories in *Scenes of Clerical Life* (2 vols., 1858), Eliot published her first novel, *Adam Bede* (1859). The plot was drawn from a reminiscence of Eliot's aunt, a Methodist preacher, whom she idealized as a character in the novel. The story concerns the seduction of a stupid peasant girl by a selfish young squire, and it follows the stages of the girl's pregnancy, mental disorder, conviction for child murder, and transportation to the colonies. A greater interest develops, however, in the growing love of the lady preacher and a village artisan, Adam Bede. The religious inspiration and moral elevation of their life stand in contrast to the mental limitations and selfishness that govern the personal relations of the other couple.

Eliot's next novel, *The Mill on the Floss* (1860), shows even stronger traces of her childhood and youth in small-town and rural England. It follows the development of a bright and attractive heroine, Maggie Tulliver, among the narrow-minded provincials who surround her. Through the adversities that follow her father's bankruptcy, Maggie acquires a faith in Christian humility, fostered by her reading of Thomas à Kempis. But events become more complex than her ascetic way of life can respond to, and the final pages of the novel show the heroine reaching toward a "religion of humanity," which it was Eliot's aim to instill in her readers.

Silas Marner

In 1861 Eliot published a short novel, *Silas Marner,* which through use as a school textbook is unfortunately her best-known work. It concerns the redemption from misanthropy of the lonely, long-suffering Silas Marner by a child who comes accidentally to his door and whom he adopts. The fairy-tale qualities of the plot are relieved by the realism with which Eliot invested the rural setting and by the psychological penetration with which she portrayed her somewhat grotesque characters.

In 1860 and 1861 Eliot lived abroad in Florence and studied Renaissance history and culture. She wrote a historical novel, *Romola* (published 1862-1863), set in Renaissance Florence. This work has never won a place among the author's major achievements, yet it stands as a major example of historical fiction. The story follows the broad outlines of *The Mill on the Floss*—a young woman's spiritual development amid the limitations of the world around her—but the surroundings of Florentine history are considerably more complex than those of provincial English life. Romola experiences Renaissance humanism, Machiavellian politics, and Savonarola's religious revival movement. She moves beyond them all to a "religion of humanity" expressed in social service.

Despite some lapses into doctrinaire writing, Eliot always aimed at creating conviction in her readers by her honesty in describing human beings, refraining from the tendency to make them illustrations of her ideas. In her next novel, *Felix Holt* (1866), she came as close as she ever did to setting up her fiction in order to convey her doctrines. In this work, however, it is not her ethical but her political thought that is most in evidence, as she addressed herself to the social questions that were then disturbing England. The hero of the novel is a young reformer who carries Eliot's message to the working class. This message is that their advancement beyond widespread misery could be made by the inner development of their intellectual and moral capacities and not alone through political reforms or union activities. In contrast to Holt, the conventional progressive politician is shown to be tainted by political corruption and insincere in his identification with the working class. The heroine validates this political lesson by choosing the genuine, but poor, reformer rather than the opportunist of her own class.

Middlemarch

Eliot did not publish any novel for some years after *Felix Holt,* and it might have appeared that her creative vein was exhausted. After traveling in Spain in 1867, she produced a dramatic poem, *The Spanish Gipsy,* in the following year, but neither this poem nor the other poems of the period are on a par with her prose. Then in 1871-1872 Eliot published her masterpiece, *Middlemarch,* a comprehensive vision of human life, with the breadth and profundity of Leo Tolstoy's *War and Peace.* The main strand of its complex plot is the familiar Eliot tale of a girl's awakening to the complexities of life and her formulation of a humanistic substitute for religion as a guide for her conduct. But the heroine, Dorothea Brooke, is here surrounded by other "seekers in life's ways," a man of science and a political reformer, whose struggles and discoveries command almost equal attention. Moreover, the social setting in which the heroes' challenges are presented is not merely sketched in or worked up from historical notes but rendered with a comprehensiveness and subtlety that makes *Middlemarch* a major social document as well as a work of art. The title—drawn from the name of the fictional town in which most of the action occurs—and the subtitle, *A Study of Provincial Life,* suggest that the art of fiction here develops a grasp of the life of human communities, as well as that of individuals.

Eliot's last novel was *Daniel Deronda* (1874-1876). It is perhaps her least-read work, although recent critical attention has revealed its high merits in at least one half of its plot, while raising still unanswered questions about its less successful half. The novel contrasts and interweaves two stories. One is a marriage for personal advantages by a young woman of keen intelligence who discovers that she has given herself to a scoundrel. The other story is the discovery by a young British gentleman that he is of Jewish origin and his subsequent dedication to the Jewish community by espousal of the Zionist resettlement of Palestine. The ethical relationship of these widely divergent situations and characters is one of the chief interests of the author, but although her intention is clear, her literary success is less so.

In 1880, after the death of Lewes, Eliot married a friend of long standing, John Walter Cross. She died in the same year, having reached an influence on many of her contemporaries amounting almost to the position of a prophetic teacher.

Further Reading

Gordon S. Haight edited the comprehensive edition of *The George Eliot Letters* (7 vols., 1954-1955). Haight's *George Eliot* (1968) is likely to become the standard biography of Eliot, although the "official" biography by her husband, J. W. Cross, ed., *George Eliot's Life as Related in Her Letters and Journals* (3 vols., 1885), is still useful. Two preeminent critical studies of Eliot's novels are Barbara Hardy, *The Novels of George Eliot: A Study in Form* (1959; rev. ed. 1963), and W. J. Harvey, *The Art of George Eliot* (1961). For a discussion of the intellectual currents underlying her works see Bernard J. Paris, *Experiments in Life: George Eliot's Quest for Values* (1965). □

John Eliot

John Eliot (1604-1690), English-born clergyman of the first New England generation and missionary to the Massachusetts Native Americans, translated the Bible and other books into the Algonquian tongue.

John Eliot's baptismal record, dated Aug. 5, 1604, is preserved in the church of St. John the Baptist in Widford, Hertfordshire. His father had extensive landholdings in Hertford and Essex counties. When John was a child, his parents moved to Nazeing. Just before his fourteenth birthday he matriculated at Jesus College, Cambridge, where he prepared for the ministry. He took his bachelor of arts degree in 1622. In 1629-1630 he lived with Thomas Hooker and his family in Little Baddow, Essex. After the Separatist Hooker escaped to Holland, Eliot, who as a Nonconformist minister was also unsafe, decided to emigrate to New England, as many other young ministers were doing.

To the New World

Eliot arrived in Boston on Nov. 3, 1631, when the settlement was barely a year old. While John Wilson, pastor of Boston's first church society, was absent, Eliot was asked to occupy the pulpit. On Wilson's return Eliot was invited to remain as teacher. He refused, having promised Nazeing friends who were intending to emigrate that if he was not permanently engaged when they arrived he would be their pastor. The Nazeing group settled in Roxbury, Mass., and Eliot was ordained immediately as their teacher and later as pastor.

Pastor at Roxbury

Eliot stayed at Roxbury for the remainder of his years. The pleasure of his life was increased by the arrival of two sisters and, later, two brothers. Hanna Mumford, to whom he was engaged, had also come with this group. Their

wedding, in October 1632, is the first marriage on the town record.

For his first 40 years in Roxbury, Eliot preached in the 20- by 30-foot meetinghouse with thatched roof and unplastered walls that stood on Meetinghouse Hill. The church grew with the town, and Eliot's long ministry was marked by imaginative leadership both within and without the membership circle. His share in founding the Roxbury Grammar School and his efforts to keep it independent and prosperous were only part of his contribution to the community. In addition to preaching and the care of his people, he also had the traditional share of a first-generation minister in various religious and civil affairs.

"Apostle to the Indians"

These numerous and valuable local services, however, did not give John Eliot the place he holds in American history. That place is described by his unofficial title, "Apostle to the Indians," for whose benefit he gave thought, time, and unstinted energy for over half a century. He was not sent to them as a missionary by church, town, or colony but went voluntarily in fulfillment of his duty to share in Christianizing Native Americans, which, according to the original Massachusetts charter, was expected of every settler and was "the principal end of this plantation." Long before either church or civil leaders realized that Christianization was an English wish rather than a Native American one, they had puzzled over ways of proceeding. Individual ministers had tried unsuccessfully to bring Native Americans to the meetinghouse.

Learning the Native American Language

The chief barrier between European and Native American was communication. Sign language and a jargon of pidgin English and Native American would do for barter but not for sermons. The Algonquian language, spoken by the various tribes of Massachusetts Native Americans, presented a formidable problem to those trained in classical and European languages; further, there were no written texts, dictionaries, or grammars. Eliot learned the language by taking into his home a Native American boy, a captive in the Pequot War, who had learned to speak and understand everyday English and also to read it; he could not write. The boy's pronunciation was very distinct. As Eliot listened, he made word lists which revealed inflexional endings, differentiated nouns from verbs and singulars from plurals, and gave many hints of language behavior to Eliot, who had a distinct gift for such understanding. The process of mastering this strange tongue well enough to use it for expressing his own thought was arduous, but Eliot persisted, and on Oct. 28, 1646, preached his first sermon in Algonquian to a small group of Native Americans gathered at the wigwam of a chieftain at Nonantum (now Newton). The Native Americans understood well enough to question him. They felt his friendliness and invited him to preach again.

First Native American Bible

A detailed report of the first four of these woodland meetings, taken down by another minister, was given to Edward Winslow, newly appointed agent of the colony. It was immediately printed in London under the title "The Day-Breaking, if not the Sun-Rising of the Gospell with the Indians in New England." Winslow drafted a bill which led to Parliament's chartering the Society for the Propagation of the Gospel among the Native Americans of New England. Throughout England and Wales funds were solicited. With this money Eliot bought school supplies, carpenter and farm tools, cloth, spinning wheels, and other articles needed in the work of education and civilization to which, in addition to his Roxbury parish, he devoted the remainder of his life. The first edition of his translation of the Bible into Algonquian (1661-1663) was the first Bible printed in the Colonies.

This story has many chapters. Fourteen self-governing Native American towns were founded, native teachers and preachers trained, and new skills learned and practiced. But King Philip's War (1675-1676) destroyed the Native American towns; only four were rebuilt. The "Praying Indians," exiled to Deer Island, suffered lamentably. John Eliot died in 1690, before restoration of the villages had really begun. But he had lived to see the second edition of his Native American Bible. With this book he had written the beginnings of a pioneering story in race relations for his own day. His feat of translation is still a marvel to scholars.

Further Reading

A full-length study of Eliot is Ola Elizabeth Winslow, *John Eliot, "Apostle to the Indians"* (1968). He is also discussed in Walter Eliot Thwing, *History of the First Church in Roxbury* (1908); Samuel Eliot Morison, *Builders of the Bay Colony*

(1930); and William Kellaway, *The New England Company, 1649-1776* (1961).

Additional Sources

Tinker, George E., *Missionary conquest: the Gospel and Native American cultural genocide,* Minneapolis: Fortress Press, 1993. □

Thomas Stearns Eliot

Thomas Stearns Eliot (1888-1965), American-English author, was one of the most influential poets writing in English in the 20th century, one of the most seminal critics, an interesting playwright, and an editor and publisher.

On Sept. 26, 1888, T. S. Eliot was born in St. Louis, Mo., a member of the third generation of a New England family that had come to St. Louis in 1834. Eliot's grandfather, William Greenleaf Eliot, Unitarian minister and founder of schools, a university, a learned society, and charities, was the family patriarch. While carrying on a tradition of public service, the Eliots never forgot their New England ties. T. S. Eliot claimed that he was a child of both the Southwest and New England. In Massachusetts he missed Missouri's dark river, cardinal birds, and lush vegetation. In Missouri he missed the fir trees, song sparrows, red granite shores, and blue sea of Massachusetts.

Eliot Family

Henry Ware Eliot, the father of T. S. Eliot, became chairman of the board of a brick company and served the cultural institutions his father had helped found, as well as others. He married an intellectual New Englander, Charlotte Champ. After having six children, she turned her energies to education and legal safeguards for the young. She also wrote a biography, some religious poems, and a dramatic poem (1926), with a preface by her already widely respected youngest child, Thomas.

Eliot grew up within the family's tradition of service to religion, community, and education. Years later he declared, "Missouri and the Mississippi have made a deeper impression on me than any part of the world." The Eliots also spent summers on Cape Ann, Mass. These places appear in Eliot's early poetry, but in the *Four Quartets* of his maturity his affection for them is most explicit.

Education of a Poet

In St. Louis young Eliot received a classical education privately and at Smith Academy, originally named Eliot Academy. He composed and read the valedictory poem for his graduation in 1905. After a year at Milton Academy in Massachusetts, he went to Harvard in 1906. He was shy, correct in dress, and intellectually independent. He studied under such versatile men as William James, George Santayana, Josiah Royce, and Irving Babbitt. He discovered

Dante and heard talk of reviving poetic drama. Among such student personalities as Walter Lippmann, Heywood Broun, Conrad Aiken, and E. E. Cummings, Eliot made a modest impression as a contributor and editor of the *Harvard Advocate*. He was quietly completing his bachelor of arts degree in 3 years and was hard on the track of a new poetic voice. In 1908 he discovered Arthur Symons's *The Symbolist Movement in Literature,* and through it the French poet Jules Laforgue. From the example of Laforgue, other French symbolists, and late Elizabethan dramatists, he began to develop the offhand eloquence, the pastiches and discordant juxtapositions, the rhythmic versatility, and the concern masked by evasive irony and wit that would soon dominate the American-British renascence in poetry.

Eliot's stay at Harvard to earn a master of arts in philosophy was interrupted by a year at the Sorbonne. He returned to Harvard in 1911 but in 1914 he went abroad again on a Harvard fellowship to study in Germany. When World War I broke out, he transferred to Merton College, Oxford, and studied with a disciple of F. H. Bradley, who became the subject of Eliot's dissertation. Ezra Pound, the young American poet, discovered Eliot at Oxford. Though they were quite different, they shared a devotion to learning and poetry. After Oxford, Eliot decided to stay in England and in 1915 married a vivacious Englishwoman, Vivienne Haigh Haigh-Wood. He taught at Highgate Junior School for boys near London (1915-1916) and then worked for Lloyd's Bank. While teaching, he completed his dissertation, *Knowledge and Experience in the Philosophy of F. H. Bradley.* The dissertation was accepted, but Eliot did not return to

America to defend it so as to receive his doctorate. His study of Bradley, however, contributed to his thought and prose style.

Early Poetry

When the United States entered World War I in 1917, Eliot tried to join the U.S. Navy but was rejected for physical reasons. That year his first volume of verse, *Prufrock and Other Observations,* appeared and almost immediately became the focus for discussion and controversy. Eliot's abruptly varied rhythms and his mixtures of precision and discontinuity, contemporary references and echoes of the past, and immediate experience and haunting leitmotifs spoke to the distraction and alienation that World War I had intensified in Western civilization. This quality was most effective in the ironically titled poem "The Love Song of J. Alfred Prufrock," in which the Victorian dramatic monologue is turned inward and wedded to witty disillusion and psychic privacies to present a dilettante character fearful of disturbing or being disturbed by anything in the universe. Prufrock moves through a dehumanized city of dispirited common men on an empty round of elegant but uncommunicative chitchat. The many voices within him, speaking in approximations of blank verse and in catchy couplets, contribute to what Hugh Kenner, the American critic, called an "eloquence of inadequacy."

Critic and Editor

As literary editor of the *Egoist,* a feminist magazine, from 1917 to 1919, Eliot began the editorial and critical careers that would continue until his death. The back pages of the *Egoist* were entrusted to a succession of young poet-editors, and here, with the aid of Ezra Pound, the new poetry and criticism got a hearing. Eliot was also writing anonymous reviews for the London *Times* and publishing essays that announced the appearance of a sometimes pontifical but illuminating critic. In 1919 two of his most influential pieces appeared. "Tradition and the Individual Talent" advocated the "depersonalization" of poetry and a redirection of interest away from the poet's personality to the poem, the process, and the tradition to which the poem belonged. "Hamlet and His Problems" defined "objective correlative," a term soon to achieve wide currency, as a particular object, act, sequence, or situation which the poet infuses with a particular feeling in order to be able to call it up economically by mere mention of the thing or event. In this essay Eliot demonstrated the need to cut through received opinion to the literary work itself. He declared that the "primary problem" in *Hamlet* is not the character but the play, because the character has to bear the burden of an "inexpressible" emotion "in excess of the facts as they appear."

In his early critical essays, collected as *The Sacred Wood* (1920), *Homage to John Dryden* (1924), *Selected Essays: 1917-1932* (1932), and *The Use of Poetry and the Use of Criticism* (1933), Eliot pointed to the poets, critics, and cultural figures who had been helpful to him and might assist others in adjusting 20th-century experience to literary and cultural tradition. Eliot was drawn to precision and concreteness in language, seeking "to purify the dialect of the tribe," as he later put it. He called attention to thematic or musical structure for communicating complex psychological experience, to past mergers of thought and feeling that could counteract the modern "dissociation of sensibility," and to the "mythical method" of James Joyce's novel *Ulysses* and of his own poetry—a method that contrasts the balance and sanity of masterpieces and the ages that produced them with the contemporary deracination that isolates individuals culturally and psychologically. With learned understatement he also assessed critics from Aristotle to his Harvard teacher Irving Babbitt. He found creative guides in 19th-century French symbolists; the 17th-century man of letters John Dryden and his predecessor John Donne; the Jacobean dramatists; and beyond them Dante, a bitter exile who created a serene master-piece.

A rising poet and critic, Eliot made his way into elite British circles. The Bloomsbury group led by Leonard and Virginia Woolf welcomed him; as a somewhat British American, both conservative and liberal leaders could accept him; and young writers on both sides of the Atlantic offered respect and affection. When restless Pound left London for Paris in 1920, Eliot quietly assumed the leadership of England's young intelligentsia.

In "Gerontion" (1920) Eliot offered a shorter, less fragmented perspective on Prufrock's unfocused world, resorting again to the interior monologue, this time spoken by a despairing old man who did not believe or act passionately in youth and now regrets the spiritual waste of his life.

The Waste Land

While convalescing from exhaustion in 1921, Eliot advanced his diagnosis of war-enervated, spiritually moribund Europe with a draft of *The Waste Land.* This was to become, after publication in 1922, the most influential and controversial poem of the century. Eliot corresponded with Pound about the poem, and Pound's drastic editing compressed it, no doubt unifying and sharpening it. Eliot acknowledged Pound's help by dedicating the poem to him in Dante's words as "il miglior fabbro," the better maker.

In *The Waste Land* Eliot defines alienation and also indicates a remedy. Voices such as Prufrock's and Gerontion's are still heard, but Eliot's spokesman is now a mild Jeremiah, a lonely prophet or pilgrim who seeks spiritual regeneration in person and in thought throughout a corrupt city and across a disoriented continent. Spring is no longer the joyous season of renewal: "April is the cruelest month," for it calls unwilling people to physical and spiritual regeneration, to leave off unsacramental sex and materialistic busy-ness. Eliot had intensified and extended the varied rhythms and montages of his earlier interior monologues and now organized them in a five-part structure deriving from Beethoven's late quarters. While sordid and distracted images still abound, hopeful ones have increased, and a greater tension exists between the two. Social disintegration is equated with a shattered wasteland, but the poem's central consciousness is nevertheless alert to the possibility of recreating personal and communal wholes out of the present and the past, of fertility rites, Christianity, Indian philosophy, and Western literature and art: "These fragments I have shored against my ruin."

Also in 1922 Eliot founded the *Criterion,* an influential little magazine that appeared until 1939, when he discontinued its publication. In it he stressed learning, discipline, and the constant renewal of tradition in literature. The magazine also reflected his growing religiousness and his devotion to the idea of a culture stratified by class and unified by Christianity.

As author of *The Waste Land* and editor of the *Criterion,* Eliot assumed a dominant role in literature in America and in Great Britain. He left Lloyd's Bank in 1925 and joined Faber and Faber, Ltd., a publisher, eventually rising to a directorship there.

Meanwhile Eliot was crossing a divide in his career. He ended his preoccupation with one kind of alienation in "The Hollow Men" (1925), where the will-less subjects of the poem cluster in a dead land, waiting like effigies for a galvanic revelation that does not come. They comment on their lot in a spastic chorus that includes a children's game song, a fragment of the Lord's Prayer, and a parody of "world without end" and other expressions from the Bible and the Book of Common Prayer.

"The Hollow Men," "Gerontion," and *The Waste Land* compose a triptych that delineates the estrangement of the self in a society fallen into secularism, with the central panel, *The Waste Land,* suggesting the possibility of salvaging the self by reconstituting culture out of its scattered parts.

Religious and Cultural Views

In 1927 Eliot became an Anglo-Catholic and a British citizen. With the heightened social consciousness of the worldwide economic depression, a reaction set in against his conservatism. It grew more difficult to explain away on literary grounds the anti-Semitic references in several of his poems. In *After Strange Gods* (1934) Eliot took the literary ideas of his "Tradition and the Individual Talent" and made them apply to culture. He also declared that too many freethinking Jews would be a detriment to the kind of organic Christian culture he proposed. This work, along with *The Idea of a Christian Society* (1939) and *Notes toward a Definition of Culture* (1948), indicated Eliot's stand against the pluralistic society of most Western democracies. Without a reconstruction of Christendom, the alternative, he felt, was paganism.

With *Ash Wednesday* (1930), while the literary tide was flowing Leftward, Eliot emerged as the sole orthodox Christian among important Anglo-American poets. The title of this six-part poem refers to the beginning of Lent, the most intense season of penitence and self-denial in the Christian year. The poem's central consciousness is an aging penitent closer to the convert Eliot than his spokesman in any previous major poem. Like his antecedents, the penitent is alienated—but from God, not from society or nature; and following the precedents of Dante and St. John of the Cross, the 16th-century Spanish mystic, he sets out to draw near the divine presence. The poem is his interior monologue narrating his progress and praying for guidance. The tone of

unbroken sincerity and passionate yearning, of anxiety and some joy is new for Eliot. The penitent desires to abandon ambition, his fading powers of expression, the enticements of the world, and all that may prevent his mounting the turning stairs toward salvation. Though his longing for the vision of God known in childhood is not fulfilled, he progresses toward it, and he will persist. American critic F. O. Matthiessen remarked how Eliot with "paradoxical precision in vagueness" used wonderfully concrete images to convey the mystery of a spiritual experience.

In 1934 Eliot published *After Strange Gods* and also brought his religious and dramatic interests together in *The Rock.* This pageant mingles narrative prose with poetic dialogue and choruses as part of a campaign to raise funds to restore London's churches. Eliot's speakers ask for visible gathering places, where the "Invisible Light" can do its work.

In 1935 *Murder in the Cathedral,* perhaps Eliot's best play, was produced at Canterbury Cathedral. It has to do with Archbishop Thomas Becket, who was assassinated before the altar there in 1170. Its theme is the historical competition between church and state for the allegiance of the individual. Its poetry suggests blank verse with deviations. Becket prepares, like the penitent in *Ash Wednesday,* to accept God's will, knowing that "humanity cannot bear much reality." After his death, the chorus, speaking for humanity, confesses that "in life there is not time to grieve long," even for a martyr.

Four Quartets

In 1936 Eliot concluded his *Poems 1909-1935* with "Burnt Norton," the first of what became the *Four Quartets,* an extended work that proved to be his poetic viaticum. "Burnt Norton," in which Eliot makes vivid use of his recurring rose-garden symbolism, grew out of a visit to a deserted Gloucestershire mansion. This poem engendered three others, each associated with a place. "East Coker" (1940) is set in the village of Eliot's Massachusetts ancestors. The last two quartets appeared with the publication of *Four Quartets* (1943). The third, "The Dry Salvages," named for three small islands off the Massachusetts coast where Eliot vacationed in his youth, draws on his American experiences; and the fourth, "Little Gidding," derives from a visit to the site of a religious community, now an Anglican shrine, where the British king Charles I paused before he surrendered and went to his death. Here Eliot asks forgiveness for a lifetime of mistakes, which no doubt includes his possible anti-Semitism of the years before the war. Each of the quartets is a separate whole but related to the others. All employ the thematic structure of music and the five movements of *The Waste Land.* The theme, developed differently, is the same in each: a penitential Eliot seeks the eternal in and through the temporal, the still dynamic center of the turning world. One may seek or wait in any place at any time, for God is in all places at all times. The theme and method continue those of *Ash Wednesday,* but the feeling in *Four Quartets* is less passionately personal, more compassionate and reconciled. The verse is serene, poised, and sparsely graceful.

Midway in his composition of *Four Quartets,* Eliot published *Old Possum's Book of Practical Cats* (1939). Here Eliot the fabulist appeared, and the humorist and wit resurfaced.

The Playwright

The Family Reunion, the first of Eliot's four plays for the professional stage, appeared in 1939. He later observed that its hero was a prig but its poetry the best in any of his plays. This play, like the other three, employs the familiar conventions of drawing-room comedy to encase religious matters. *The Family Reunion* and *The Cocktail Party* (1940) both involve analogs with classical Greek dramas. *The Confidential Clerk* (1954) and *The Elder Statesman* (1959) even employ potentially melodramatic situations, although they are not developed popularly, for Eliot is preoccupied with individual religiousness and the self-revelations and mutual understandings it effects within families. In fact, *The Elder Statesman,* the last and simplest of his plays, contending that true love is beyond verbal expression, is dedicated to his second wife, Valerie.

The most successful of these plays, *The Cocktail Party,* enjoyed respectable runs and revivals in London and New York. It puts the tension between the temporal and the eternal in more effective dramatic terms than do the other plays. By means of the familiar, a cocktail party, Eliot involves the audience in the unbelievable, a modern martyrdom. He contrasts lives oriented to the natural with that of a martyred missionary devoted to the supernatural. At the same time he parallels a Greek drama more subtly than he did in *The Family Reunion.*

Eliot's drawing-room plays, however, have only a limited appeal. The poetry in the last three is unobtrusively effective, carried by voices moving naturally along the hazy border between poetry and prose. They are not so much powerful plays as suggestive ones.

Honor and Old Age

Following World War II there were important changes in Eliot's life and literary activities. In 1947 his first wife died. Suffering from nervous debilities, she had been institutionalized for years, and Eliot had visited her every Sunday and kept his suffering and deprivation private. In 1948 he received the Nobel Prize and the British Order of Merit, and the list of his honors continued to grow. Publishing no important poetry after the *Four Quartets,* he devoted himself to the poetic drama, the revitalization of culture, some new criticism in *On Poetry and Poets* (1957), the readjustment of earlier critical judgments, and the editing of collections of his poetry and plays. In 1957 he married his private secretary, Valerie Fischer, and enjoyed a felicitous marriage until he died on Jan. 4, 1965, in London. In accordance with earlier arrangements his ashes were deposited in St. Michael's Church, East Coker, his ancestral village, on April 17, 1965.

Many poets and artists paid final tribute to Eliot, including Pound: "A grand poet and brotherly friend"; W. H. Auden: "A great poet and a great man"; Allen Tate: "Mr. Eliot was the greatest poet in English of the 20th century";

Robert Lowell: "He was a dear personal friend. Our American literature has had no greater poet or critic"; Robert Penn Warren: "He is the key figure of our century in America and England, the most powerful single influence." Avowedly Christian in a secular age, Eliot tried to revitalize the religious roots of Western culture. His career recalls the versatile man of letters of the 18th century.

Further Reading

An edition of Eliot's work is *The Complete Poems and Plays of T. S. Eliot* (1969). Donald C. Gallup, *T. S. Eliot: A Bibliography* (1952), lists Eliot's writings through 1951. The literature on Eliot is extensive. Herbert Howarth, *Notes on Some Figures behind T. S. Eliot* (1964), provides biographical information. Hugh Kenner, *The Invisible Poet: T. S. Eliot* (1959), is probably the standard work on Eliot. Francis O. Matthiessen, *The Achievement of T. S. Eliot* (1935; 3d ed. 1958), provides a balanced introduction. Russell H. Robbins, *The T. S. Eliot Myth* (1951), primarily because of Eliot's conservatism, offers a negative view. Other studies include Elizabeth A. Drew, *T. S. Eliot: The Design of His Poetry* (1949); Helen L. Gardner, *The Art of T. S. Eliot* (1949); and D. E. S. Maxwell, *The Poetry of T. S. Eliot* (1952). George Williamson, *A Reader's Guide to T. S. Eliot: A Poem-by-Poem Analysis* (1953; 2d ed. 1966), is a helpful reference work. Collections of critical estimates of Eliot are Balachandra Rajan, ed., *T. S. Eliot: A Study of His Writings by Several Hands* (1947); Richard March and M. J. Tambimuttu, eds., *T. S. Eliot: A Symposium* (1948); Leonard Unger, ed., *T. S. Eliot: A Selected Critique* (1948); and Neville Braybrooke, ed., *T. S. Eliot: A Symposium for His Seventieth Birthday* (1958). Studies of particular works include Raymond Preston, *"Four Quarters" Rehearsed* (1946), and Robert E. Knoll, ed., *Storm over the Waste Land* (1964). □

Elizabeth, the Queen Mother

Elizabeth Angela Marguerite Bowes-Lyon (born 1900) became queen through her marriage to George VI, king of Great Britain and Ireland from 1936 to 1952. Upon her husband's death, Elizabeth became the Queen Mother and will most likely be remembered as the most beloved royal figure in British history.

The Queen Mother was born on August 4, 1900, at St. Paul's Waldenbury, Hertfordshire. She was the youngest daughter and second youngest child in a family of ten children born to the 14th Earl of Strathmore and his wife, a cousin of the duke of Portland. Raised largely at St. Paul's Waldenbury in England and the Strathmores' other home, the large and romantically gloomy Glamis Castle in Scotland, she grew up in a warm and happy family environment surrounded by siblings, relatives, and family friends. She was privately educated, first by her mother, who taught her to read, and then by a series of governesses. Her childhood was interrupted by the outbreak of World

War I, in which one of her brothers was killed. Glamis Castle was turned into a hospital for wounded soldiers, and Lady Elizabeth helped tend the patients who were sent there.

After the war, the young woman became a much sought-after debutante, and the most persistent of her suitors was none other than the brother of her friend Princess Mary—the second son of King George V, the young Albert, duke of York. Although she twice declined his proposals, on April 26, 1923 they were married at Westminster Abbey. Afterward, she impulsively laid her bridal bouquet on the church's tomb of the Unknown Soldier, a gesture that inaugurated the British public's long love affair with their new royal.

Palace Life

The duke of York's upbringing and background were remarkably different from his wife's. His parents tended to act coldly towards their children and were strict disciplinarians. Prince Albert was a sickly child who suffered from recurrent stomach ailments and bowed legs which made it necessary for him to wear leg braces for several years. Worst of all, he stammered, which made conversation difficult, school painful, and public speaking a nightmare. Five years older than Lady Elizabeth, at the time of their marriage in 1923 he was a shy and lonely man. In his wife, however, he found constant support and encouragement. By providing him with a warm and comfortable domestic life, first at White Lodge in Windsor Park and then at 145 Piccadilly in London, she made him more confident and sociable and provided him with the greatest happiness he had known. He was aware of what he owed her and was utterly devoted to her. In a letter written 24 years after his marriage he described her as "the most marvelous person in the world in my eyes."

As duchess of York, Elizabeth became a part of the royal family. She was received readily by her parents-in-law, for whom she had great fondness if not the great awe which they inspired in their own children, and she was quickly accorded a share of royal duties. With her husband she made several goodwill trips abroad to such far corners of the Empire as East Africa and New Zealand. The years 1930 to 1936 were always viewed by the duchess as a "golden age." Living in their comfortable and attractive home at 145 Piccadilly, the Yorks raised their daughters (Elizabeth, born in 1926—called Lillibet—and Margaret Rose, born in 1930) and pursued their own interests in addition to performing their public duties.

Unexpected Duty

This pleasant interlude came to an end with the political crisis of 1936 when the Duke's older brother, Edward VIII, abdicated the throne. The Duke of York thus became King George VI in December 1936. He was strengthened by the knowledge that he could rely on the support and comfort of his wife. She provided these qualities liberally, and the king manifested his gratitude by awarding her with the Order of the Garter. Despite her sympathetic nature, she never forgave Edward VIII or the woman he gave up the

throne for, Wallis Simpson, for what she considered dereliction of duty, and she remained convinced that the burdens of the kingship shortened her husband's life.

The new king and queen sought to alleviate the damage caused by the Abdication Crisis by restoring faith in the monarchy. They did this by emphasizing their domesticity and devotion to home, becoming on the newsreels the very model of a contented English family unit, and by involving themselves and their children increasingly in public royal functions. As queen, Elizabeth's activities were many and varied. She made numerous state visits with her husband, including the first royal visit to Canada and the United States by a reigning monarch and his consort in 1939. The king and queen were given a great welcome when they returned to Britain, which demonstrated how firmly they had become established as effective and popular monarchs.

Upon the outbreak of World War II in September 1939, the queen's life and work took on added dimensions. She was very active, making patriotic and inspiring broadcasts, writing thousands of letters of thanks to Britons who had housed evacuees, making bandages and comforters for soldiers, and traveling, with or without her husband, to visit hospitals and areas devastated by bombs in order to encourage and give comfort to the people. When Buckingham Palace was bombed she said, "I'm glad we've been bombed. It makes me feel I can look the East End [the poorest section of London and that which suffered most from the German bombing] in the face." Like her husband, she was determined to offer real resistance if the Germans invaded and practiced regularly firing a revolver. When asked why she and her daughters had not gone abroad for safety, she answered, "My daughters could not go without me, I could not go with the King, and the King will never go." Recognizing the powerful symbolism of this resolute wife and mother, German dictator Adolf Hitler described her as the most dangerous woman in Europe.

Becomes Queen Mum

The post-war years, though busy, were marked by the declining health of George VI. In the summer of 1947 the king and queen and their two daughters made a trip to South Africa. Shortly after their return they announced the engagement of their daughter Elizabeth to Philip Mountbatten; the marriage took place in November 1947. Also in 1947, it was discovered that the king suffered from blood clots in his legs. This necessarily curtailed his activities, but the queen carried on gamely. The king had an operation in March 1949 which improved his condition somewhat, but he was still not fully recovered. A year later doctors found that his chronic cough was caused by lung cancer. To relieve him of some of the pressure of his duties, the queen alone received the king of Norway on his official visit in June 1951 and, with Princess Margaret, made a royal visit to Northern Ireland. Although lung surgery in 1951 helped the king to a degree, he died suddenly on February 6, 1952, at the age of 56 (and was succeeded by his elder daughter, Elizabeth).

The queen, now the Queen Mother, had been fully aware of the extent of her husband's illness. Nonetheless, his death overwhelmed her, and she spent three months in seclusion. Slowly she rejoined the world and in the more than four decades of her widowhood led a useful and ceaselessly active life. She pursued her own interests, buying and restoring the Castle of Mey in remotest northern Scotland, farming, gardening, fishing, raising Corgis, and horse-racing. She also spent time with her grandchildren, and imbued in them both a sense of royal responsibility and fondness for outdoor pursuits.

Changing Times

The Queen Mother's life of service was recognized and won for her the respect, love, and devotion of her family, as reflected in her continued—and even enhanced—popularity. Her enduring contribution to her country may well be that she was able to project, as Robert Runcie, the Archbishop of Canterbury, said at her 80th birthday commemorative service on July 15, 1980, "the human face of royalty."

Yet in the decade between her eightieth and ninetieth birthdays, it may be said that the public was offered an all-too-human visage of the British royals. This new era began in a grand way with the 1981 royal wedding of Prince Charles, heir to the throne, to Lady Diana Spencer. (Prince Charles showed his admiration for his grandmother by asking her to serve as his fiancee's guide in learning how to behave like a member of the royal family.) Their marriage produced two sons and ended in divorce. Charles's brother Prince Andrew married Lady Sarah Ferguson in 1986, but this marriage, too, was rocked by scandal and divorce during the 1990s. As the decade wore on, eager reporters chronicled every move of the younger royals in public, and even semi-private moments to a degree which had not been inflicted on the Queen Mother's generation. There emerged a new era in the relationship between the royals and the public, egged on by the press. Though still revered by their subjects, public-opinion polls evidenced that a growing number of Britons considered the Windsors frivolous in both spirit and expenses—expenditures that were covered by the public treasury.

Beloved Dowager

The Queen Mother, however, usually remains above such criticism. The occasion of her ninetieth birthday in August of 1990 launched an entire summer of celebratory festivities. Prime Minister Margaret Thatcher remarked that her affection for the nation is mirrored in the affections of the nation for her, reported the *New Statesman & Society* (August 3, 1990). Even the significance of the Queen Mother's eventual demise is somewhat of an issue. There is debate within the halls of the British Broadcasting Corporation (BBC) concerning just how long the official television curfew should last—some feel her portrait should be kept on the air, in lieu of all regular programming and accompanied by somber music, for an entire week. A grave moment it might indeed be, for the Queen Mother's appeal, wrote Rosalind Brunt in the *New Statesman & Society* article, "is also about a sprightly zest for life, a famous aura of gin-and-tonics, horse-racing and camp humour. 'Such fun!' is her favorite comment and 'Every day's an adventure' her motto

. . . But hers is also an image of 'everyone's favourite Mum,' the projected ideal of someone who is unfailingly kind, never lets you down and lives forever."

Further Reading

Much useful material about the Queen Mother can be found in biographies of her husband, George VI. Of particular value is John W. Wheeler-Bennett's *King George VI: His Life and Reign* (1958), the official biography of George VI. Though ponderous and weighty, the book is well-documented and deals at length with the Queen Mother's relationship with her husband. More analytical and more accessible to the common reader is Dennis Judd's interesting *King George VI 1895-1952* (1983).

Of more limited value are most biographies of the Queen Mother herself. Lady Cynthia Asquith's *The Duchess of York* (1927-1928) is a highly anecdotal account of the Queen Mother's early years. Equally anecdotal but more awkwardly written, as well as uncritically admiring, is *The Queen Mother: The Story of Elizabeth, the Commoner Who Became Queen* by Helen Cathcart, published in 1965. Other saccharine tributes include the surprisingly thorough but now out-of-date *Queen Elizabeth the Queen Mother* (1966) by Dorothy Laird and Geoffrey Wakeford's *Thirty Years a Queen: A Study of Her Majesty Queen Elizabeth the Queen Mother* (1968). Elizabeth Longford's *The Queen Mother* (1981) is highly recommended both for its lively style and incisive grasp of material. A later biography of the "Queen Mum" is Penelope Mortimer, *Queen Elizabeth: A Portrait of a Queen Mother* (1986). Further information can be found in Ann Morrow, *The Queen Mother* (1984) and Robert Lacey, *Queen Mother* (1987). Articles about the Queen Mother in *People* magazine (Fall 1990 Special Supplement) and *New Statesman & Society* (August 3, 1990) were written on occasion of her ninetieth birthday. □

Elizabeth I

Elizabeth I (1533-1603) was queen of England and Ireland from 1558 to 1603. She preserved stability in a nation rent by political and religious dissension and maintained the authority of the Crown against the growing pressures of Parliament.

Born at Greenwich, on Sept. 7, 1533, Elizabeth I was the daughter of Henry VIII and his second wife, Anne Boleyn. Because of her father's continuing search for a male heir, Elizabeth's early life was precarious. In May 1536 her mother was beheaded to clear the way for Henry's third marriage, and on July 1 Parliament declared that Elizabeth and her older sister, Mary, the daughter of Henry's first queen, were illegitimate and that the succession should pass to the issue of his third wife, Jane Seymour. Jane did produce a male heir, Edward, but even though Elizabeth had been declared illegitimate, she was brought up in the royal household. She received an excellent education and was reputed to be remarkably precocious, notably in languages (of which she learned Latin, French, and Italian) and music.

Edward VI and Mary

During the short reign of her brother, Edward VI, Elizabeth survived precariously, especially in 1549 when the principal persons in her household were arrested and she was to all practical purposes a prisoner at Hatfield. In this period she experienced ill health but pursued her studies under her tutor, Roger Ascham.

In 1553, following the death of Edward VI, her sister Mary I came to the throne with the intention of leading the country back to Catholicism. The young Elizabeth found herself involved in the complicated intrigue that accompanied these changes. Without her knowledge the Protestant Sir Thomas Wyatt plotted to put her on the throne by overthrowing Mary. The rebellion failed, and though Elizabeth maintained her innocence, she was sent to the Tower. After 2 months she was released against the wishes of Mary's advisers and was removed to an old royal palace at Woodstock. In 1555 she was brought to Hampton Court, still in custody, but on October 18 was allowed to take up residence at Hatfield, where she resumed her studies with Ascham.

On Nov. 17, 1558, Mary died, and Elizabeth succeeded to the throne. Elizabeth's reign was to be looked back on as a golden age, when England began to assert itself internationally through the mastery of sea power. The condition of the country seemed far different, however, when she came to the throne. A contemporary noted: "The Queen poor. The realm exhausted. The nobility poor and decayed. Want of good captains and soldiers. The people out of

order. Justice not executed." Both internationally and internally, the condition of the country was far from stable.

At the age of 25 Elizabeth was a rather tall and well-poised woman; what she lacked in feminine warmth, she made up for in the worldly wisdom she had gained from a difficult and unhappy youth. It is significant that one of her first actions as queen was to appoint Sir William Cecil (later Lord Burghley) as her chief secretary. Cecil was to remain her closest adviser; like Elizabeth, he was a political pragmatist, cautious and essentially conservative. They both appreciated England's limited position in the face of France and Spain, and both knew that the key to England's success lay in balancing the two great Continental powers off against each other, so that neither could bring its full force to bear against England.

The Succession

Since Elizabeth was unmarried, the question of the succession and the actions of other claimants to the throne bulked large. She toyed with a large number of suitors, including Philip II of Spain; Eric of Sweden; Adolphus, Duke of Holstein; and the Archduke Charles. From her first Parliament she received a petition concerning her marriage. Her answer was, in effect, her final one: "this shall be for me sufficient, that a marble stone shall declare that a Queen, having reigned such a time died a virgin." But it would be many years before the search for a suitable husband ended, and the Parliament reconciled itself to the fact that the Queen would not marry.

Elizabeth maintained what many thought were dangerously close relations with her favorite, Robert Dudley, whom she raised to the earldom of Leicester. She abandoned this flirtation when scandal arising from the mysterious death of Dudley's wife in 1560 made the connection politically disadvantageous. In the late 1570s and early 1580s she was courted in turn by the French Duke of Anjou and the Duke of Alençon. But by the mid-1580s it was clear she would not marry.

Many have praised Elizabeth for her skillful handling of the courtships. To be sure, her hand was perhaps her greatest diplomatic weapon, and any one of the proposed marriages, if carried out, would have had strong repercussions on English foreign relations. By refusing to marry, Elizabeth could further her general policy of balancing the Continental powers. Against this must be set the realization that it was a very dangerous policy. Had Elizabeth succumbed to illness, as she nearly did early in her reign, or had any one of the many assassination plots against her succeeded, the country would have been plunged into the chaos of a disputed succession. That the accession of James I on her death was peaceful was due as much to the luck of her survival as it was to the wisdom of her policy.

Religious Settlement

England had experienced both a sharp swing to Protestantism under Edward VI and a Catholic reaction under Mary. The question of the nature of the Church needed to be settled immediately, and it was hammered out in Elizabeth's first Parliament in 1559. A retention of Catholicism was not politically feasible, as the events of Mary's reign showed, but the settlement achieved in 1559 represented something more of a Puritan victory than the Queen desired. The settlement enshrined in the Acts of Supremacy and Conformity may in the long run have worked out as a compromise, but in 1559 it indicated to Elizabeth that her control of Parliament was not complete.

Though the settlement achieved in 1559 remained essentially unchanged throughout Elizabeth's reign, the conflict over religion was not stilled. The Church of England, of which Elizabeth stood as supreme governor, was attacked by both Catholics and Puritans. Estimates of Catholic strength in Elizabethan England are difficult to make, but it is clear that a number of Englishmen remained at least residual Catholics. Because of the danger of a Catholic rising against the Crown on behalf of the rival claimant, Mary, Queen of Scots, who was in custody in England from 1568 until her execution in 1587, Parliament pressed the Queen repeatedly for harsher legislation to control the recusants. It is apparent that the Queen resisted, on the whole successfully, these pressures for political repression of the English Catholics. While the legislation against the Catholics did become progressively sterner, the Queen was able to mitigate the severity of its enforcement and retain the patriotic loyalty of many Englishmen who were Catholic in sympathy.

For their part the Puritans waged a long battle in the Church, in Parliament, and in the country at large to make the religious settlement more radical. Under the influence of leaders like Thomas Cartwright and John Field, and supported in Parliament by the brothers Paul and Peter Wentworth, the Puritans subjected the Elizabethan religious settlement to great stress.

The Queen found that she could control Parliament through the agency of her privy councilors and the force of her own personality. It was, however, some time before she could control the Church and the countryside as effectively. It was only with the promotion of John Whitgift to the archbishopric of Canterbury that she found her most effective clerical weapon against the Puritans. With apparent royal support but some criticism from Burghley, Whitgift was able to use the machinery of the Church courts to curb the Puritans. By the 1590s the Puritan movement was in some considerable disarray. Many of its prominent patrons were dead, and by the publication of the bitterly satirical *Marprelate Tracts,* some Puritan leaders brought the movement into general disfavor.

Foreign Relations

At Elizabeth's accession England was not strong enough, either in men or money, to oppose vigorously either of the Continental powers, France or Spain. England was, however, at war with France. Elizabeth quickly brought this conflict to a close on more favorable terms than might have been expected.

Throughout the early years of the reign, France appeared to be the chief foreign threat to England because of the French connections of Mary, Queen of Scots. By the Treaty of Edinburgh in 1560, Elizabeth was able to close off a good part of the French threat as posed through Scotland.

The internal religious disorders of France also aided the English cause. Equally crucial was the fact that Philip II of Spain was not anxious to further the Catholic cause in England so long as its chief beneficiary would be Mary, Queen of Scots, and through her, his own French rivals.

In the 1580s Spain emerged as the chief threat to England. The years from 1570 to 1585 were ones of neither war nor peace, but Elizabeth found herself under increasing pressure from Protestant activists to take a firmer line against Catholic Spain. Increasingly she connived in privateering voyages against Spanish shipping; her decision in 1585 to intervene on behalf of the Netherlands in its revolt against Spain by sending an expeditionary force under the Earl of Leicester meant the temporary end of the Queen's policy of balance and peace.

The struggle against Spain culminated in the defeat of the Spanish Armada in 1588. The Queen showed a considerable ability to rally the people around herself. At Tilbury, where the English army massed in preparation for the threatened invasion, the Queen herself appeared to deliver one of her most stirring speeches: "I am come amongst you . . . resolved in the midst and heat of battle, to live and die amongst you all. . . . I know I have the body but of a weak and feeble woman, but I have the heart and stomach of a king and of a King of England too."

That the Armada was dispersed owed as much to luck and Spanish incapacity as it did to English skill. In some ways it marked the high point of Elizabeth's reign, for the years which followed have properly been called "the darker years." The Spanish threat did not immediately subside, and English counteroffensives proved ineffectual because of poor leadership and insufficient funds. Under the strain of war expenditure, the country suffered in the 1590s prolonged economic crisis. Moreover, the atmosphere of the court seemed to decline in the closing stages of the reign; evident corruption and sordid struggling for patronage became more common.

Difficulties in Ireland

The latter years of Elizabeth's reign were marked by increasing difficulties in Ireland. The English had never effectively controlled Ireland, and under Elizabeth the situation became acute. Given Ireland's position on England's flank and its potential use by the Spanish, it seemed essential for England to control the island. It was no easy task; four major rebellions (the rebellion of Shane O'Neill, 1559-1566; the Fitzmaurice confederacy, 1569-1572; the Desmond rebellion, 1579-1583; and Tyrone's rebellion, 1594-1603) tell the story of Ireland in this period. Fortunately, the Spaniards were slow to take advantage of Tyrone's rebellion. The 2d Earl of Essex was incapable of coping with this revolt and returned to England to lead a futile rebellion against the Queen (1601). But Lord Mountjoy, one of the few great Elizabethan land commanders, was able to break the back of the rising and bring peace in the same month in which the Queen died (March, 1603).

Internal Decline

The latter years of Elizabeth also saw tensions emerge in domestic politics. The long-term dominance of the house of Cecil, perpetuated after Burghley's death by his son, Sir Robert Cecil, was strongly contested by others, like the Earl of Essex, who sought the Queen's patronage. The Parliament of 1601 saw Elizabeth involved in a considerable fight over the granting of monopolies. Elizabeth was able to head off the conflict by promising that she herself would institute reforms. Her famous "Golden Speech" delivered to this, her last Parliament, indicated that even in old age she had the power to win her people to her side: "Though God hath raised me high, yet this I count the glory of my crown, that I have reigned with your loves. . . . It is my desire to live nor reign no longer than my life and reign shall be for your good. And though you have had, and may have, many princes more mighty and wise sitting in this seat, yet you never had, nor shall have, any that will be more careful and loving."

The words concealed the reality of the end of Elizabeth's reign. It is apparent, on retrospect, that severe tensions existed. The finances of the Crown, exhausted by war since the 1580s, were in sorry condition; the economic plight of the country was not much better. The Parliament was already sensing its power to contest issues with the monarchy, though they now held back, perhaps out of respect for their elderly queen. Religious tensions were hidden rather than removed. For all the greatness of her reign, the reign that witnessed the naval feats of Sir Francis Drake and Sir John Hawkins and the literary accomplishments of Sir Philip Sidney, Edmund Spenser, William Shakespeare, and Christopher Marlowe, it was a shaky inheritance that Elizabeth would pass on to her successor, the son of her rival claimant, Mary, Queen of Scots. On March 24, 1603, the Queen died; as one contemporary noted, she "departed this life, mildly like a lamb, easily like a ripe apple from the tree."

Further Reading

The standard biography of Elizabeth is J. E. Neale, *Queen Elizabeth* (1934), which is sometimes eulogistic. Neville Williams, *Elizabeth, Queen of England* (1967), although interesting, is not likely to replace Neale. Elizabeth Jenkins, *Elizabeth the Great* (1958), has been highly praised but contains little new information. B. W. Beckinsale, *Elizabeth I* (1963), is a useful study that indicates a cautious break from the traditional Neale view. Hilaire Belloc's well-known *Elizabeth: Creature of Circumstance* (1942) is a biased study written from the Catholic viewpoint.
Frederick Chamberlin, *The Private Character of Queen Elizabeth* (1922), is useful in some respects, such as the queen's medical history, but should be used with caution. More useful on Elizabeth's medical history is Arthur S. MacNalty, *Elizabeth Tudor: The Lonely Queen* (1954). Mandell Creighton, *Queen Elizabeth* (1899; repr. 1966), though dated, repays careful study for its assessment of the Queen. Joel Hurstfield, *Elizabeth I and the Unity of England* (1960), is a highly compressed, valuable study stressing Elizabeth's concern to achieve unity in England. Joseph M. Levine, ed., *Elizabeth I* (1969), is an able compilation of writings on Elizabeth by her contemporaries; Levine contributes an introduction, a chronology of the life of Elizabeth I, and a bibliographical note.

Important studies of aspects of Elizabeth's reign include J. E. Neale, *Elizabeth I and Her Parliaments, 1559-1581* (1952) and *Elizabeth I and Her Parliaments, 1584-1601* (1957), the best works on parliamentary politics and the role of the Queen in government; Conyers Read, *Mr. Secretary Cecil and Queen Elizabeth* (1955) and *Lord Burghley and Queen Elizabeth* (1960), which is useful on diplomacy as well as the partnership with Burghley; Mortimer Levine, *The Early Elizabethan Succession Question, 1558-1568* (1966); and Wallace MacCaffrey, *The Shaping of the Elizabethan Regime* (1968), a major new study of the early years of the reign.
Elizabeth figures prominently in many of the surviving documents of the period and in nearly all secondary accounts. Two useful bibliographies are Conyers Read, ed., *Bibliography of British History: Tudor Period, 1485-1603* (2d ed. 1959), and Mortimer Levine, *Tudor England, 1485-1603* (1968).
Recommended for general historical background are J. B. Black, *The Reign of Elizabeth, 1558-1603* (1936; 2d ed. 1959); S. T. Bindoff, *Tudor England* (1951); A. L. Rowse, *The England of Elizabeth: The Structure of Society* (1951) and *The Expansion of Elizabethan England* (1955); James A. Williamson, *The Tudor Age* (1953); and G. R. Elton, *England under the Tudors* (1955; repr. with a new bibliography, 1962). □

Elizabeth II

Elizabeth II (born 1926) became queen of Great Britain and Ireland upon the death of her father, George VI, in 1952. She was a popular queen who was also respected for her knowledge of and participation in state affairs.

Elizabeth II was born on April 21, 1926, in London, the oldest child of the Duke of York and his wife, Elizabeth. Her father became King George VI, of Great Britain and Ireland in 1936 when his older brother Edward VIII abdicated the throne. Elizabeth married Philip Mountbatten in November 1947, and they had four children—Prince Charles, Princess Anne, Prince Andrew, and Prince Edward.

Since the 1960s criticism of the monarchy and of the queen has been both positive and negative. Indeed, it may be said that is precisely *because* the monarchy has not "created a truly classless and Commonwealth court" that it has been an institution of inestimable value to the United Kingdom and the Commonwealth in the second half of the 20th century. Britain is not noticeably less a "deferential society" now than it was in Walter Bagehot's day, and there can be no doubt that considerable spiritual consolation can be derived from symbolic continuity with past glory in rapidly changing and often all too inglorious times.

There have, however, been subtle changes in the monarchy. The work of the monarch and the monarchy has increased, and the queen accordingly shared some of her duties with her children, upon whom more public attention was focussed. She pursued her functions along lines laid out by her father, George VI: diligence, duty, dignity, and compassion. Her involvement of the whole family in her duties

also reflected the influence of her father, who used to speak of his family as "The Firm."

In addition, the queen, perhaps in part influenced by her strong-willed and perceptive husband, started some new trends toward modernization and openness in the monarchy. Her efforts were not unsuccessful. The queen and her activities commanded international attention and widespread respect. The prime ministers who served under her, notably Harold Wilson and James Callaghan, were impressed by her knowledge of state affairs—gained by conscientious reading of state papers contained in the Red Boxes, dispatch cases which followed her everywhere. Her popularity at home and abroad was indisputable.

A Popular Traveller

At least part of this popularity could be attributed to her far-flung travels as the embodiment of Commonwealth unity and British nationalism. Her interested and gracious demeanor on these travels contributed to the warmth and enthusiasm of the receptions which greeted her. Between 1970 and 1985 she had a dizzyingly full schedule. She visited France in the spring of 1972, attended the Commonwealth Conference in Ottawa in 1973, took part in the U.S. bicentennial celebrations and then headed north to Montreal to open the 1976 Summer Olympics, and travelled some 56,000 miles throughout the Commonwealth as part of her Silver Jubilee celebrations. In 1979 she travelled to Kuwait, Bahrain, Saudi Arabia, Qatar, the United Arab Emirates, and Oman, where she was showered with gifts of dazzling (and dazzlingly precious) jewelry.

In April 1982 she made a less exotic but constitutionally more important visit to Ottawa, where she proclaimed the New Canadian constitution, which cut the last legal links between the United Kingdom and Canada. In March of 1984 she visited Jamaica, Grand Cayman Island, Mexico, California, and British Columbia. While in California, her first trip to the west coast of North America, she had some 20 public appearances, including a visit to a movie studio and a gala dinner in San Francisco. She also went to President Reagan's Santa Barbara ranch, to former U.S. Ambassador to Britain Walter Annenberg's luxurious estate, and, in a private capacity, to Yosemite National Park with Prince Philip. She went to North America again in 1984, visiting Canada for the 14th time and then, privately, to the United States to inspect horse-breeding farms in Kentucky and to the wild west of Sheridan County, Wyoming.

Changes in the queen's circumstances and events in her private life necessarily had a public impact. In the early 1970s there was considerable controversy over her request for an increase in her civil list funding. Although it was not unreasonable that she would require additional funds to carry out her public duties in the style to which her subjects had become accustomed and in an era of rampant inflation, some critics considered her request tactless because she was one of the world's wealthiest women. Even such supporters of the monarchy as Richard Crossman publicly resented the fact that her income was not taxable. Despite the critics, however (and perhaps also because of them: the public outcry over their disloyal attitude was loud), funding was increased.

In the early 1980s personal security around the queen was increased after two unpleasant incidents. In June of 1981, while the queen was riding to the Trooping of the Color in London's Mall, a bystander in the crowd fired six blanks in her direction. Thirteen months later an unemployed and disturbed man, Michael Fagan, managed to get into Buckingham Palace and, after wandering in the corridors, entered the queen's bedroom. With admirable aplomb she spoke soothingly to the intruder, who sat bleeding on her bed, and managed to summon help.

Happier events also had their public impact. On November 20, 1972, the queen and Prince Philip celebrated their 25th wedding anniversary with a service in Westminster Abbey. One hundred couples from all over Britain who happened to have the same anniversary were invited to share in the occasion. The queen's two older children married with great ceremony and had children of their own. On November 14, 1973, Princess Anne married commoner Mark Philips and later had two children: Peter, born in 1977, and Zara, born in 1981. Prince Charles married Lady Diana Spencer on July 29, 1981; their two sons, Prince William and Prince Henry, were born in 1982 and 1984 respectively. Another son, Prince Andrew (made Duke of York), married Sarah Ferguson, July 23, 1986; their two daughters, Princess Beatrice and Princess Eugenie were born in 1988 and 1990 respectively.

A Highly Respected Monarch

Perhaps the happiest event was the queen's Silver Jubilee in 1977, marked by an outpouring of devotion to the queen, her family, and the institution of the British monarchy in the form of innumerable sporting events, festivals, carnivals, races, concerts, commemorative stamps, and other activities in her honor. On May 4, 1977, both Houses of Parliament presented loyal addresses to her in Westminster Hall. At St. Paul's Cathedral in June the queen and her family celebrated a Thanksgiving service. The queen indicated her concern for her subjects by voicing her desire that the Silver Jubilee year be a special time "for people who find themselves the victims of human conflict," by travelling extensively to meet her subjects during the year, and by establishing the Silver Jubilee Trust Fund, headed by the Prince of Wales, which was designed "to help the young to help others." She demonstrated her interest in the jubilee through the television broadcast of two films, *Royal Heritage* and *The Queen's Garden,* the publication of a book about her private art collection, the opening of the Holbein Room at Windsor Castle to the public, and the display of some of her works of art in a special Silver Jubilee train which tracked across Australia.

Elizabeth Longford, one of the queen's biographers, has suggested that it was only after the jubilee, when she was able to see the loyalty and esteem of her subjects demonstrated, that she realized her potential as a monarch. Her inhibitions were broken down and she became more confident, more open, and more ready to reveal her keen sense of humor, strong common sense, great energy, and nearly imperturbable serenity of character.

After her accession the queen endeavored in her own way to make the British monarchy more modern, more open, and more accessible. She replaced the noxious presentation of debutantes with informal Buckingham Palace luncheons to which a variety of figures eminent in diverse fields ranging from industry to the stage to sports to Scotland Yard were invited. The guest lists at her garden parties became increasingly eclectic. She showed interest and skill in use of the broadcast media, notably in her annual Christmas television messages, in royally sanctioned documentaries such as *The Royal Palaces of Britain* (1966) and *The Royal Family* as well as the two Jubilee presentations, and in television broadcasts of Prince Charles' investiture as Prince of Wales and of the royal weddings. Perhaps the most popular of her attempts was the "walkabout," in which she left her car or entourage to meet, shake hands, and chat with ordinary people in the crowds which gathered around her. These spontaneous strolls, which she started in 1970 while on a trip to New Zealand, revealed her conviction that "I have to be seen to be believed."

Troubles Plague the House of Windsor

However, in the late 1980s, the Queen grew concerned over the state and the future of the monarchy. The British press increasingly chronicled the problems in her children's marriages. It appeared to many that Prince Charles was not interested in suceeding to the throne, preferring instead to hunt, play polo, and spend time with his longtime mistress Camilla Parker-Bowles. There were rumors that the Queen would abdicate the throne to her grandson, Prince William. Her troubles seemed to peak in 1992, and she herself called it a "annus horribilis" a horrible year.

The twenty year marriage of Princess Anne ended in divorce; Prince Charles and Prince Andrew officially separated from their wives. On the night of November 20, a good section of Windsor Castle (one of Queen Elizabeth's official residences), suffered extensive fire damage. Immediately, a public outcry arose when it was announced the castle's restoration would be paid for out of public coffers. Britons felt that the Queen, who enjoyed a tax-exempt income in the millions, should pay for the restoration. Two days later, Buckingham Palace announced that the Queen and her family would no longer be exempt from taxation. This announcement was seen as a gesture of savvy and goodwill. The year ended on a happier note, as Princess Anne remarried on December 12.

In 1995, the Queen wrote a letter to Prince Charles and Princess Diana urging them to divorce, prompted by separate television interviews where they discussed their unhappy 14-year marriage. They were divorced in 1996, as were Prince Andrew and Sarah Ferguson. Despite these very public family problems, the Queen generally remained popular.

However, her resolve was tested after the August 1997 death of her former daughter-in-law, Princess Diana. Some Britons lashed out at the Queen for "being too bound up by protocol." Surprised by the backlash, she broke tradition and addressed the nation in a live broadcast the day before the funeral, paying tribute to Diana. The significance of this gesture was seen as significant, as the Queen usually addresses the nation only on Christmas Day; this was the second exception to that rule in her 45-year reign.

In spite of turmoil and public stresses, the Queen does not appear to be slowing down. She continues to enjoy time with her family, her beloved Welsh Corgis, country life, and horses, horse-breeding, and horse-racing.

Further Reading

There is a good deal of literature about Queen Elizabeth and the state of the monarchy. Of interest to those intrigued by the private life of royalty are two books by the queen's former governess, Marion Crawford: *The Little Princesses* (1950) and *Elizabeth the Queen* (1952). A well-documented, perceptive, and flattering portrait of the queen and her family is contained in Robert Lacey's Jubilee year *Majesty: Elizabeth II and the House of Windsor* (1977). An uncritically laudatory biography is *Queen Elizabeth* (1979) by Judith Campbell, which is useful only because it has a great number of interesting photographs. Of the greatest value is Elizabeth Longford's *The Queen: The Life of Elizabeth II* (1983), which is insightful, skillfully written, and thoroughly researched. Royal biographer Anne Edwards profiled the Queen and Princess Margaret in *Royal Sisters* (1990), which provides an honest account of life as a royal. In 1996, S. Badford chronicled the Queen's life in *Elizabeth: A Biography of Her Majesty the Queen* (1996). Information on the Internet is also available. Unofficial Web sites on the Queen and royal family can be accessed through the search tool Yahoo, by searching for

"Queen Elizabeth II." (July 29, 1997). General biographical information on the Internet can be accessed through http://www.mun.ca/library/ref/qeiifaq.html#crowned. □

Elizabeth Bagaaya Nyabongo of Toro

Intelligent, eloquent, elegant, and duty-bound, Elizabeth Bagaaya Nyabongo of Toro (born c. 1940) successfully revived Uganda's tarnished international image during her tenure as roving ambassador (1971-1973), minister of foreign affairs (February-November 1974), and United Nations ambassador (1986-1988).

The daughter of the *Omukama* (King) George D. Rukiidi III of Toro (1924-1965), Bagaaya was born between the late 1930s and early 1940s in Kabalole, the capital of Toro in western Uganda. Toro became an independent state in the 18th century when it seceded from the ancient and famous empire of Bunyoro Kitara, which covered parts of present-day Burundi, Rwanda, Tanzania, Zaire, and Uganda. Toro lost its kingdom status in 1967 when Milton A. Obote's government (1962-1971) abolished monarchs in Uganda.

As her mother (Lady Kezia Byanjeru) was the king's legal wife, Bagaaya became entitled to the status of *Batebe* (head of the princesses). She, however, shared the hectic royal court life in Kabalole with the king's other children. The harmonious life in the court though, made it possible for the royal children to receive an indigenous education, including an overview of the history of the motherland empire of Bunyoro-Kitara.

Formal Education

Bagaaya received her elementary education at Kyebambe Girl's School, a Protestant missionary institution that was named after her grandfather, a champion of Christianity and Western education in Toro. She continued her education at Gayaza High School in Buganda Kingdom, the center of British colonial control of Uganda from 1894 to 1962. Though officially she was under the care of the *Kabaka* (King) of Buganda, Bagaaya resided in the school dormitory. This in essence meant she lost most of the royal privileges she had enjoyed either in the palace or in the state, since Buganda was a different kingdom from Toro. She thus participated in all school activities like any other student.

Bagaaya completed her high school education at Sherborne in England. An all-girls' school, Sherborne presented new challenges; she had to adjust not only to a new culture, but also had to learn what it means to be the only African student in a school where others were white aristocrats. There was also coping with the academic work, which proved difficult because of cultural bias.

Between 1959 and 1962 she studied law, history, and political science at the University of Cambridge, England. As Cambridge was one of the educational and political powerhouses, Bagaaya acquired a quality education and was introduced to influential people who later played key roles in her career. It was at Cambridge, for example, that in 1961 Bagaaya gave a party in honor of Jomo Kenyatta, who later became president of Kenya (1963-1978). That she identified herself with Kenyatta, an individual whom the British authorities at that time regarded with disdain because of his role in the *Mau Mau* (Kenya's violent nationalist movement, 1952-1961), was evidence that Bagaaya still remained an African.

Bagaaya continued her legal education in London, qualifying as a barrister-at-law in 1965. She became one of the few female attorneys in east, central, and southern Africa. However, 1965 was a mixed bag for Bagaaya: at the height of her academic achievement, she had to cope with the death of her father, a personal confidant, and she also faced the uncertain political future resulting from Obote's desire to abolish monarchs in Uganda.

Modeling and Acting Careers

She returned to Uganda in 1965 to attend the funeral of her father and the coronation of her brother in 1966 as *Omukama* Patrick D. Kaboyo Olimi VII. As the coronation was publicized by the international press, Bagaaya, who played a key role in the ceremony as *Batebe* (the King's first sister), was catapulted to prominence.

Desiring a career, Bagaaya went to Kampala, capital of Uganda, to work with a law firm, where she was called to the Uganda bar in 1966. Just as she was ready to start practicing law, the political landscape in Uganda changed. Partly due to Obote's republican beliefs and his personal conflicts with the *Kabaka* of Buganda, he abolished the 1962 constitution that had preserved the monarchical status of the kingdoms of Ankole, Bunyoro, Buganda, and Toro, replacing it with a republican constitution in 1967.

The political uncertainty that followed forced Bagaaya to reassess her future. In 1965 when Princess Margaret and her then husband, Lord Snowdon, had visited Uganda, they had invited Bagaaya to model in a British fashion show at Marlborough House in London in 1967. Now she accepted. After the show she opted for the modeling profession on the grounds that it would have been very difficult to make a breakthrough in the highly competitive legal business and she felt modeling would promote African culture. She thus signed up with a top agency in London and embarked on a modeling and acting career that lasted from 1967 to 1970 and was briefly resumed in 1984.

She modeled in Britain in several fashion shows that were featured in the British and American *Vogue, Harper's Bazaar,* and *Queen* magazines in 1967 and 1968. Through Lord Harlech and Jacqueline Kennedy, she embarked on a modeling career in New York between 1968 and 1970. She was featured in the American *Vogue, Look, LIFE,* and *Ebony* and became the first Black to appear on the cover of a top fashion magazine (*Harper's Bazaar*).

After taking acting classes in New York, she embarked on a new career when an American and German company requested her to play a role in a film based on Chinua Achebe's *Things Fall Apart* and *No Longer at Ease*. Set in the Igbo (Ibo) region of eastern Nigeria, the film explored the impact of Western civilization on Africa. Despite the difficulties caused by the Nigerian civil war at the time, she flew to Lagos, Nigeria, in 1970, where the film was produced.

Political changes in Uganda in 1971 interrupted her career in acting, and it was not until 1984 that she returned to the profession. The publication of her *African Princess* in 1983 prompted Columbia Pictures to invite her to participate in the making of *Sheena,* a film portraying the indigenous culture of a people known as the Zamburis and their suffering at the hands of an alien.

Serving Idi Amin's Government

Bagaaya returned to Uganda when Idi Amin overthrew Milton A. Obote's government in a coup d'état in 1971. Although Amin's military government (1971-1979) later became synonymous with massive violations of human rights, economic decline, and social disintegration, it was initially well received, particularly by southern Ugandans. Prompted by the desire to serve her country and caught up in the euphoria that followed the military takeover, Bagaaya served Amin's government between 1971 and 1974.

In her first appointment as roving ambassador (1971-1973), she acted as Amin's envoy in times of crisis, conveying messages directly from one head of state to another. By getting direct access to various presidents, she avoided the normal red tape of having to go through the various foreign ministers of each country. Bagaaya's added advantages were her having been educated at Cambridge, having lived in Britain and the United States, and having been introduced through her acting and modeling careers to influential people all over the world.

As part of the Foreign Affairs Ministry, Bagaaya participated in a campaign to dispel the prevailing international skepticism that Amin lacked the necessary sophistication to lead the country. It was not particularly easy to convince African countries, who prior to the Amin coup had agreed to hold the Organization of African Unity (OAU) meeting in Uganda with Obote as the host president. Amin's open advocation for a dialogue with South Africa's minority white government further exasperated the already delicate situation.

By 1972 it was becoming increasingly difficult to formulate a coordinated foreign policy as Amin's actions became erratic. The sudden expulsion of the Israelis, who had been his close friends, was followed later in 1972 by his declaration of the "economic war" that resulted in the expulsion of 50,000 Asian traders, many of whom held British passports. As Western influence declined, the Arabs took the upper hand, with Muamar Gaddafi of Libya becoming Amin's mentor. He also received a negative international image because of the internal political repression that forced Amin's brother-in-law and foreign minister (Wanume-Kibedi) to resign and flee Uganda in 1973. The murder in 1974 of Michael Ondoga, who replaced Kibedi

as foreign minister, was further evidence of Amin's ruthlessness.

It was during this explosive international situation that Bagaaya was appointed foreign minister in February 1974. Short as her tenure was (February to November 1974), Bagaaya revived Uganda's tarnished image abroad, tried to soothe hostilities, and encouraged heads of state to visit the country. It was partly due to her policies that Arabs generously gave aid to Uganda; Gaddafi and Siad Barre of Somalia visited Uganda in 1974; and efforts were made to compensate the expelled Asian traders.

Bagaaya's peak as foreign minister came when she gave an eloquent and inspiring speech to the United Nations late in 1974. Avoiding any perception that she was defending Amin as an individual, her speech instead was a defense of the African continent in general and Uganda as a country in particular. The distinction she subtly made between Amin's personal idiosyncrasy and the general policies of the OAU was important in that she disarmed critics of Africa who portrayed Amin as an example of failed Black leadership. Her tours to Britain, Canada, West Germany, and France after the U.N. speech further helped in dispelling many of the misconceptions these countries had developed about Uganda over the years.

Ironically, the U.N. speech was one of the causes for the downfall of Bagaaya as a foreign minister. Viewing the speech as a personal success for Bagaaya and, therefore, further boosting her international image, Amin became envious, particularly since he felt that it was he who made her in the first place. It was under this illusion that Amin unsuccessfully proposed marriage to Bagaaya on her return from overseas. It was thus envy and not Amin's ludicrous claim that she had made love to a white man in Paris in 1974 that led to Bagaaya's dismissal as foreign minister.

Serving Yoweri Museveni

After a brief arrest on her return from overseas in 1974, Bagaaya fled Uganda, taking up political asylum in Britain. Aside from suing newspapers that sensationalized Amin's claims for dismissing her as foreign minister, Bagaaya generally kept a low profile during her exile years, 1975-1979. Bagaaya won all her legal suits and cleared her name.

She returned to Uganda in 1979 when Amin's government was overthrown by a combination of Tanzanian forces and Uganda exiles. Bagaaya's stay, brief as it was (1979-1980), turned out to be important: she met Wilbur Nyabongo, whom she married in 1981. Politically, Obote's return to power in 1980 after a rigged election forced Bagaaya to leave Uganda.

The formation of Yoweri Museveni's National Resistance Movement (NRM) in 1980 with an objective of opposing Obote's second administration (1980-1985) offered Bagaaya an opportunity to register her dissatisfaction with Obote. While Museveni headed the military arm of the organization (National Resistance Army, NRA), Bagaaya and Wilbur Nyabongo worked with the External Committee (the civilian arm of the organization outside Uganda) to rally material and diplomatic support. From 1980 to 1986 Bagaaya provided the organization with valuable contacts which partially helped Museveni in his fight against Obote and in the defeat of the short-lived military government (1985-1986) that replaced Obote.

Museveni appointed Bagaaya as Uganda's ambassador to the United States between 1986 and 1988. Aside from her efforts to make the embassy in Washington function again, Bagaaya faced the difficult task of improving Uganda's negative image that had developed during the Amin and post-Amin eras. She had the difficult challenge of explaining to the United States government why President Museveni, who had assumed power in 1986, was perceived as a Marxist sympathizer and a friend of Gaddafi.

To fight back, Bagaaya used the mass media to educate the American public about Africa in general and Uganda in particular. Her appearances twice on the CBS *60 Minutes* was particularly effective in explaining the misconceptions of Uganda. She highlighted Uganda's problems and made the important point that instead of giving labels to Museveni, he should be judged by what he achieved, particularly his human rights record. Bagaaya also used her contacts from previous careers to promote Ugandan causes. It was partly due to her hard negotiations and relevant contacts that it was possible for President Yoweri Museveni to meet Vice President George Bush and President Ronald Reagan in October 1987.

Due to the untimely death of her husband (Wilbur Nyabongo) in December 1986, the pressure of work caused by her efforts to reorganize the Uganda Embassy in Washington, and her desire to continue to live temporarily in the United States, she resigned her position as Ugandan ambassador to the United States on July 21, 1988. After her retirement, Bagaaya promoted African causes through television appearances and the publication of her *Elizabeth of Toro: The Odyssey of an African Princess* (1989).

Further Reading

Princess Elizabeth Bagaaya Nyabongo's fortune may be followed in her two books, *African Princess: The Story of Elizabeth of Toro* (London: 1983) and *Elizabeth of Toro: The Odyssey of an African Princess* (1989), and in Henry Kyemba's *A State of Blood: The Inside Story of Idi Amin* (1977). □

Elizabeth of Hungary

Saint Elizabeth of Hungary (1207-1231) devoted her life and her financial resources to the improvement of the lives of the sick and poor. The daughter of the King of Hungary, she renounced her privileged life and worked to serve the less fortunate, creating such charitable institutions as a hospital for lepers and the first orphanage in Central Europe.

Elizabeth of Hungary was a thirteenth-century member of the Hungarian and German royalty who devoted her energy and fortune to the assistance of the sick

and poor in the German region of Thuringia. Her work included feeding the hungry, building a hospital, and creating the first orphanage in Central Europe. A beloved figure of selflessness and charity among her people, her death brought reports that she had worked miracles on the behalf of those who prayed for her intervention. She was canonized by the Catholic Church in 1235.

Elizabeth was born into the royal family of Hungary in 1207 in Sárospatak. Her father was King Andrew II of Hungary and her mother was Gertrud of Andechs-Meran, who was the victim of a political murder plot in 1213. Elizabeth was also connected to powerful figures in the Roman Catholic Church; her uncle Berthold was the Patriarch of Aquileia and her uncle Echbert was the Bishop of Bamberg. In 1211, a marriage was arranged for the four-year-old princess to the eldest son of Hermann I, Landgrave of the German region of Thuringia. The match provided advantages for both families—Thuringia would profit from the financial wealth Elizabeth would bring, and Hungary stood to gain political support against other German princes who threatened to invade the country. With a lavish dowry, including gold pieces and a solid silver bathtub, the young Elizabeth was sent to live at the Thuringian court at Wartburg castle near Eisenach.

Married into Thuringian Royalty

At Wartburg, an engagement celebration was held for Elizabeth and her fiancee by Hermann I and his wife, Sophia. In her new life in the Thuringian court, she was educated in subjects such as poetry, the history of royal families, art, Latin, and religion. She was surrounded by poetry and art at Wartburg, where Hermann I provided patronage for a number of writers and artists of the day. She also enjoyed the playing games, riding horses, and saying prayers in the castle's chapel. Elizabeth was an enthusiastic child with a loud laugh, but she was instructed early on by her future mother-in-law that being boisterous was not appropriate for a woman of the royal court.

After learning of the violent death of her mother in 1213, Elizabeth's disposition was changed. She took on a simple mode of dress and spent an increasing amount of time in prayer. Despite a vivid dream in which she saw the bloody body of her murdered mother, she prayed for the souls of the killers. When she was nine years old, tragedy again struck. Her fiancee died, and a year later his father was dead as well. Elizabeth's position at the court became unclear, but her status was secured when the younger son of Herman I, Louis, decided that he would marry her. The two, who had developed a close friendship, were married in 1221. The following year, the couple journeyed to visit Elizabeth's father, during which time they viewed the incredible destruction that had befallen the country with the Golden Bull revolt of the Hungarian nobles.

Built Hospital and Orphanage

Upon their return to Thuringia, Elizabeth began to focus even more heavily on the development of her spiritual life. She received religious instruction and counseling from her confessor, the Franciscan friar Father Rodinger. During this time, she also turned to public charity work, building an orphanage and founding a hospital for lepers, where she would tend the afflicted herself. Her husband was called to serve in a military campaign in 1225, leaving Elizabeth as the ruler of Thuringia. She used her increased authority to extend her work, providing food for hundreds of the poor each day. But she was a firm believer in empowering the disadvantaged to help themselves and not rely on charity; she donated tools to men who were out of work and she showed women how to spin. When natural disasters occurred, she helped people to rebuild and recover. In addition, she carried on the official duties of the court, hosting important visitors and joining in entertainments such as hunting parties.

While pregnant with her third child, Elizabeth's husband was called to war again, leaving to join in a Crusade in 1227. He never returned, falling ill and dying during his journey. Louis's brothers were concerned about Elizabeth's practice of spending large sums on the poor, and so they arranged to keep her from controlling her own money. The discord at court caused her to leave Wartburg in the fall of 1227. Unable to find refuge nearby, she placed her children in the care of others and, with two of her servants, began living in the stable of an inn and spinning to earn money. She was delivered from this situation by the abbess of Kitzingen, who provided her with a place to live in the abbey.

Turned to Life of Humble Poverty

Elizabeth received offers to return to her privileged world; her uncle, the Bishop of Bamberg, invited her to take up residence at one of his castles. He also tried to arrange a marriage between her and Emperor Frederick II. But Elizabeth declined both offers. Her only worldly interest in property and fortune was to provide for her children's future and for the poor, and with the assistance of a court official in Thuringia, she successfully fought for the control of the wealth she had inherited from her husband. With that accomplished, she turned to an austere life of material deprivation and spiritual devotion. She had come under the mentorship of a Franciscan mystic by the name of Conrad of Marburg. Under his guidance, she took religious vows rejecting earthly attachments and her own free will. She then moved to an simple earthen house in the town of Wehrda, where she worked in the leper hospital she had built and supported herself by spinning.

Conrad's methods of subjugating Elizabeth's will and forcing her to abandon all worldly things took an extreme form. As a means of teaching her denial, he limited her indulgences in charity, allowing her to donate only small amounts of money to the poor and instructing her to only give a single slice of bread to those she fed. He also forced her to endure beatings and flagellation to increase her humility. Even in her reduced physical and material state, Elizabeth used what few resources she had to aid others. She placed a boy suffering from dysentery in her own bed, where she nursed him until he died. Then she took in a leprous girl, placed her in her bed, and cared for her. But soon, the physical trials took their toll. Aware that she dying,

Elizabeth arranged for her estate to be distributed to her children and the poor, and then took to her bed.

Canonized after Reports of Miracles

For the last two weeks of her life, Elizabeth remained bed-ridden, attended only by Conrad. She died on November 17, 1231, at the age of 24. Dressed in the attire of a poor woman, her body was laid in state at the Franciscan church in Eisenach for four days. People from across Thuringia came to the coffin and prayed for the assistance of the woman who had devoted her life to spiritual matters. After she was buried, miracles were said to have occurred at her grave site. After reporting her death to Pope Gregory IX, Conrad was charged with making preparations for Elizabeth's canonization. Conrad was murdered two years later, however, and the process was continued by the Bishop of Hildsheim. As part of the evidence gathered for the canonization, the testimony of four of Elizabeth's servants were written down. Elizabeth officially was named a saint of the Catholic church on May 26, 1235. One of her brothers-in-law constructed the first church in her honor at Marburg, Germany. On May 1, 1236, her remains were brought to the church and placed on the altar in a ceremony attended by her children and in-laws as well as several bishops and archbishops. Large crowds of religious pilgrims from across Europe also came to pay tribute to the woman who had provided an inspiring example of a life of service to others.

Further Reading

See also Bihl, Michael, "Elizabeth of Hungary," *Catholic Encyclopaedia,* Volume 5, 1909, pp. 389-91; and Butler, Alban, "St. Elizabeth of Hungary," *Lives of the Saints,* Volume 4, edited by Herbert Thurston and Donald Attwater, P. J. Kennedy and Sons, 1956. □

Elizabeth Petrovna

The Russian empress Elizabeth Petrovna (1709-1761) ruled from 1741 to 1761. Her reign was marked by Russia's continuing Westernization and growth as a great power.

Born in Moscow on Dec. 18, 1709, Elizabeth was the daughter of Peter I and Catherine Alekseyevna. Her education, emphasizing French, German, and the social graces, was designed to prepare her for marriage to a member of European royalty. However, all efforts to provide a suitable husband, including her father's attempt to arrange a marriage between her and Louis XV of France, failed. The beautiful and vivacious Elizabeth was forced to accept a life of spinsterhood but not one of chastity. Over the years she had many lovers, chief among them Alexis Razumovsky.

Elizabeth spent the first 3 decades of her life in political obscurity during which time the Russian throne passed, after the death of Peter I, to a succession of her relatives: her mother, as Catherine I; a nephew, as Peter II; a cousin, as

Empress Anna; and finally her young cousin Ivan VI, whose mother, Anna Leopoldovna, served as regent.

That obscurity was lifted in 1741, when a movement began to remove the allegedly pro-German regent and her son Ivan VI and to install Elizabeth as empress. In November of that year, supported by Alexis Razumovsky, Elizabeth accepted the role of legitimate claimant to the throne. She led a detachment of guardsmen to seize the regent and her son and then dramatically proclaimed herself empress of Russia.

An intellectually limited and sensual person, Elizabeth gave little attention to the day-to-day business of government. She was shrewd enough, however, to see the importance of some political matters, particularly those that personally concerned her. To protect her position, she dealt harshly with any who might become threats, among them the family of the former regent, whom she kept imprisoned. Although Elizabeth made neither domestic nor foreign policies, she influenced both through her choice of officials and her response to their counsel.

Some notable domestic changes occurred during Elizabeth's reign. The number of Germans in the government was reduced. The privileges of the landed nobility were enhanced at the expense of the serfs. The process of Westernization was accelerated by the introduction of structural improvements in St. Petersburg; the opening of the first Russian university, in Moscow, in 1755; and the establishment of the Academy of Arts in 1757.

Elizabeth took pride in the advance of her country as a great power during her 20 years as empress. In the latter part of her reign, when Russia was at war with Prussia, she followed the battle reports closely. With victory almost in sight, Empress Elizabeth died on Dec. 25, 1761.

Further Reading

Robert Nisbet Bain, *The Daughter of Peter the Great* (1899), is both readable and useful. A more recent work is Tamara Talbot Rice, *Elizabeth, Empress of Russia* (1970). See also Herbert Harold Kaplan, *Russia and the Outbreak of the Seven Years' War* (1968).

Additional Sources

Empress Elizabeth: her reign and her Russia, 1741-1761, Gulf Breeze, FL: Academic International Press, 1995. □

Edward Kennedy Ellington

Edward Kennedy Ellington (1899-1974), certainly America's most brilliant jazz composer, was considered by many to be one of the great composers of the 20th century, irrespective of categories.

On April 29, 1899, Edward Ellington, known universally as "Duke," was born in Washington, D.C. He divided his studies between music and commercial art, and by 1918 establishing a reputation as a

bandleader and agent. In 1923 he went to New York City and soon became a successful bandleader. In 1927 he secured an important engagement at the Cotton Club in Harlem, remaining there (aside from occasional tours) until 1932.

Ellington's band made its first European trip in 1932. After World War II it toured Europe regularly, with excursions to South America, the Far East, and Australia. One peak period for the band was from 1939 to 1942, when many critics considered its performances unrivaled by any other jazz ensemble.

As a composer, Ellington was responsible for numerous works that achieved popular success, some written in collaboration with his band members and with his coarranger Billy Strayhorn. The Duke's most significant music was written specifically for his own band and soloists. Always sensitive to the nuances of tone of his soloists, Ellington wrote features for individual sidemen and used his knowledge of their characteristic sounds when composing other works. His arrangements achieved a remarkable blend of individual and ensemble contributions. However, because most of his works were written for his own band, interpretations by others have seldom been satisfactory.

With *Creole Rhapsody* (1931) and *Reminiscing in Tempo* (1935) Ellington was the first jazz composer to break the 3-minute time limitation of the 78-rpm record. After the 1940s he concentrated more on longer works, including several suites built around a central theme, frequently an aspect of African American life. Always a fine orchestral

pianist, with a style influenced by the Harlem stylists of the 1920s, Ellington remained in the background on most of his early recordings. After the 1950s he emerged as a highly imaginative piano soloist.

Ellington was nominated for the Pulitzer Prize in 1964. The City of New York gave him a prize and Yale University awarded him a doctor of music degree in 1967; Morgan State and Washington universities also gave him honorary degrees that year. On his seventieth birthday Ellington was honored by President Richard Nixon at a White House ceremony and given the Medal of Freedom. In 1970 he was elected to the National Institute of Arts and Letters.

Ellington continued to compose and perform until his death from lung cancer on May 24, 1974, in New York City. His band, headed by his son Mercer, survives him, but as Phyl Garland, writing in *Ebony* magazine, put it, the elder Ellington will always be remembered for "the daring innovations that came to mark his music—the strange modulations built upon lush melodies that ramble into unexpected places, the unorthodox construction of songs . . . ; the bold use of dissonance in advance of the time."

Further Reading

Peter Gammond, ed., *Duke Ellington: His Life and Music* (1958), contains some first-rate essays on Ellington. See also Barry Ulanov, *Duke Ellington* (1946), and George E. Lambert, *Duke Ellington* (1961). Gunther Schuller, *The History of Jazz* (1968), includes the most perspicacious and scholarly study of Ellington's recordings of the 1920s.

James Lincoln Collier, *Duke Ellington,* Oxford University Press, 1987.

Stanley Dance, *The World of Duke Ellington,* Da Capo, 1980.

Duke Ellington, *Music Is My Mistress,* Doubleday, 1973.

Mercer Ellington, and Stanley Dance, *Duke Ellington in Person,* Houghton Mifflin, 1978.

Ron Frankl, *Duke Ellington,* Chelsea House, 1988.

Derek Jewell, *Duke, A Portrait of Duke Ellington,* Norton, 1977.

Ken Rattenbury, *Duke Ellington: Jazz Composer,* Yale University Press, 1991.

Duke Ellington, *The Beginning,* Decca.

Duke Ellington, *The Best of Duke Ellington,* Capitol.

Duke Ellington, *The Ellington Era,* Columbia. □

Ralph Waldo Ellison

American author Ralph Waldo Ellison (1914-1994) wrote "Invisible Man," a classic 20th-century American novel. He was an early spokesman among African-Americans for the need for racial identity.

Ralph Ellison was born in Oklahoma City on March 1, 1914. His father, a construction worker, died when Ellison was 3, and his mother stretched a meager income as a domestic worker to support her son. He studied music at Tuskegee Institute from 1933 to 1936. He worked on the New York City Federal Writers Project, contributed stories, reviews, and essays to *New Masses,* the *Antioch*

Review, and other journals (these writings have not yet been collected); and in 1942 became editor of the *Negro Quarterly.* He met Richard Wright and Langston Hughes during these years; both had a major influence on his work, along with T.S. Eliot, Ernest Hemingway, and the Russian novelists.

After brief duty in the U.S. Merchant Marine during World War II, Ellison won a Rosenwald fellowship to work on the novel which brought him instant recognition and the National Book Award, *Invisible Man* (1952). The story of a young man's growing up, first in the South and then in Harlem, it is sensational, brutally honest, and graphic in the humiliating, often violent treatment the nameless hero suffers at the hands of the Southern white men who "educate" him and the Northern black men who "use" him. But Ellison reminds the reader that he "didn't select the surrealism, the distortion, the intensity as an experimental technique but because reality is surreal." When, at the end of the novel, the hero creeps into an empty Harlem cellar to escape from the world, it is only the last of his many bouts with "invisibility." The life of a African-American has always been relentlessly unreal, and his search for identity endless. But what Ellison's novel illuminates is the common plight of all human beings in the confrontations between dream and reality, light against darkness, idealism smothered by disillusion, injured psyche, adopted personae. In 1965, in a poll of 200 writers and critics, they voted *Invisible Man* the most distinguished novel published between 1945 and 1965 in America.

Ellison's *Shadow and Act* (1964) is a collection of 20 essays and 2 interviews. He contributed to *The Living Novel* (Granville Hicks, ed., 1957), *The Angry Black* (John A. Williams, ed., 1963), and *Soon One Morning* (Herbert Hill, ed., 1963) and to numerous literary journals. He lectured at the Salzburg Seminar in 1954; taught Russian and American literature at Bard College from 1958 to 1961; was visiting professor at the University of Chicago in 1961 and visiting professor of writing at Rutgers University from 1962 to 1964; and in 1964, became visiting fellow in American studies at Yale University.

Ellison died on April 16, 1994, in New York City, leaving his second novel unfinished. His influence on American literature has been tremendous, and the loss of this second work is a bitter pill. According to Ellison himself, it was to be a work which would "[equal] his imaginative vision of the American novel as conqueror of the frontier and [answer] the Emersonian call for a literature to release all people from the bonds of oppression."

Further Reading

Perceptive critical comment on Ellison is available in Robert Bone, *The Negro Novel in America* (1958; rev. ed. 1965); Ihab Hassan, *Radical Innocence: Studies in the Contemporary American Novel* (1961); Marcus Klein, *After Alienation: American Novels in Mid-century* (1964); Jonathan Baumbach, *The Landscape of Nightmare* (1965); and Seymour L. Gross and John Edward Hardy, eds., *Images of the Negro in American Literature* (1966).
Ralph Ellsion, *Invisible Man*, Random House, 1982.
Ralph Ellison, *Shadow and Act,* Random House, 1964.
Ralph Ellison, *Going to the Territory,* Random House, 1986.
Kimberly W. Benston, editor, *The Black American Writer,* Everett Edwards, 1969. □

Daniel Ellsberg

Daniel Ellsberg (born 1931) was a defense analyst for the Rand Corporation, a U.S. government official, and then became an anti-war activist during the Vietnam era; it was Ellsberg who leaked a top-secret Defense Department study that came to be known as the Pentagon Papers. One indirect repercussion from this act was a decline in public support for the war, and eventual discrediting of the administration of President Richard M. Nixon.

Daniel Ellsberg was born in Chicago on April 7, 1931. His father, a structural engineer, moved the family several years later to Detroit. The young Ellsberg attended Barber Elementary School in Detroit and subsequently received a scholarship to Cranbook, an exclusive preparatory school located in the Detroit suburb of Bloomfield Hills. After compiling a superb academic record there, as well as captaining the basketball team, he won a scholarship to Harvard University. Once again, Ellsberg's academic performance was outstanding; he graduated

summa cum laude in 1952 with a B.A. in economics, ranking third in a class of 1,147.

After graduation Ellsberg continued his studies for one year at Cambridge University in England as a Woodrow Wilson fellow before returning to graduate school at Harvard in 1953. He temporarily interrupted his doctoral training to enlist in the Marine Corps in April 1954. Following officers' candidate school, he received the rank of second lieutenant and served as a platoon leader at Quantico and later at Camp Lejeune. In February 1957 he was discharged from the Marine Corps as a first lieutenant. Ellsberg then returned to his graduate studies at Harvard, where he spent the next two and a half years as a member of the prestigious Society of Fellows. During this period he expanded his research interests to include political science and psychology, focusing especially on the new field of games theory, which utilized mathematical formulas to devise strategies for adversarial conflicts.

From Rand to Vietnam

In 1959 Ellsberg accepted a position with the Rand Corporation in Santa Monica, California. That firm had recently emerged as a leading center for the application of games theory to defense problems. At Rand he worked on a variety of matters, developing particular expertise in the field of nuclear strategy. During his years at Rand, Ellsberg also worked intermittently as a consultant on strategic nuclear war planning and nuclear command and control for the Office of the Secretary of Defense, the White House, and the Department of State, respectively. In 1962 he was

awarded the Ph.D. degree by Harvard; many specialists considered his doctoral dissertation, "Risk, Ambiguity, and Decision," a *tour de force.*

In August 1964 Ellsberg joined the Department of Defense as a special assistant to John McNaughton, the assistant secretary of defense for international security affairs. He devoted much of his time at the Pentagon to the growing U.S. involvement in Vietnam. In July 1965 he transferred to South Vietnam as a senior liaison officer attached to the U.S. embassy in Saigon. Ellsberg remained in Vietnam for two years. Among other duties, he worked under Major General Edward G. Lansdale, the officer in charge of the American pacification program, assessing the effectiveness of anti-guerrilla operations in the provinces.

Frustrated by U.S. Policy

By 1966 Ellsberg told friends that he was growing increasingly disillusioned with the course of the American war effort. These doubts intensified after his appointment the following year as an assistant to the deputy U.S. ambassador in South Vietnam, William Porter. In that position he prepared a report sharply critical of the U.S. pacification effort and made a special trip to Washington to present his findings to Secretary of Defense Robert S. McNamara. Shortly thereafter Ellsberg suffered a severe case of hepatitis and left Vietnam permanently.

In July 1967 he resigned his government position to return to the Rand Corporation. Ellsberg continued serving as a governmental consultant, however, until the spring of 1969. As a consultant he helped prepare a secret internal study, commissioned by Defense Secretary McNamara, that examined the history of U.S. decision-making in Vietnam. Subsequently, in his final assignment for the government, he prepared an outline of alternative Vietnam strategies for Henry A. Kissinger, President Richard M. Nixon's special assistant for national security affairs.

Ellsberg's opposition to the war in Vietnam deepened during the early years of the Nixon administration. Increasingly he spoke out publicly against American involvement, articulating an antiwar position that proved occasionally embarrassing to his employers at Rand, a major defense contractor. In the spring of 1970 he left that firm to accept a fellowship at the Center for International Studies at the Massachusetts Institute of Technology; he intended to write a book on Vietnam decision-making and to continue speaking out against a war that he now viewed as immoral. "My role in the war was as a participant," he stated at that time, "along with a lot of other people, in a conspiracy to commit a number of war crimes, including, I believe, aggressive war."

The Pentagon Papers

Acting on these new convictions, in the summer of 1971 Ellsberg leaked copies of the McNamara study to the *New York Times* and other prominent newspapers. Almost overnight the "Pentagon Papers," as the study was quickly dubbed, became a lead story in the media, and Ellsberg became a controversial national figure. As he later explained his motivations: "I felt as an American citizen, a responsible citizen, I could no longer cooperate in concealing this information from the American people. I took this action on my own initiative, and I am prepared for all the consequences." Those consequences included federal indictment on several counts under the Espionage Act for the possession and unauthorized release of classified documents.

The Pentagon Papers catapulted Ellsberg into a position of national prominence. For the antiwar movement, his conversion from ardent "hawk" to committed "dove" proved a powerful symbol. Ellsberg, for his part, warmly embraced the movement along with a series of other liberal causes. In 1972 he published a book, *Papers on the War,* that set forth his position on the Vietnam conflict.

The following year the charges against him were dropped as a result of government misconduct. In the wake of the Pentagon Papers furor, the Nixon administration had launched its secret "plumbers" operation, so named because this team of trusted presidential aides was directed to stem any further "leaks" that might embarrass the government, as the Pentagon Papers had. Nixon aides burglarized the office of Ellsberg's psychiatrist in an effort to find information that would destroy his credibility, and employed similar criminal tactics in an attempt to tap the phones at the Democratic National Headquarters at the Watergate Hotel in the summer of 1972. The ramifications from this last act forced Nixon to resign 1974.

Distinguished Protest Record

Although Ellsberg's name gradually slipped from public view in subsequent years, he continued to speak out on a series of important national issues, including the problems of nuclear power and nuclear armaments. In the 1980s he served on the strategy task force of the Nuclear Weapons Freeze Campaign, and publicly advocated nuclear disarmament; he was also an outspoken opponent of U.S. policy in Central America. Joining other prominent Americans critical of the Reagan administration policy, Ellsberg was arrested numerous times for civil disobedience, including the besieging of the CIA office in San Francisco in 1985.

Later in the decade Ellsberg was affiliated with Center for Psychological Studies in the Nuclear Age at Harvard Medical School; there he studied the impact of the Cuban missile crisis of 1962. In the early 1990s he accepted a position as director of the Manhattan Project II, a program launched by Physicians for Social Responsibility. Its goal was to dismantle the work of the first Manhattan Project— the World War II-era, top-secret government effort that developed the world's first nuclear weapon. Though no longer a board member of Physicians for Social Responsibility, Ellsberg continues to work with the activist group. He is also a popular guest lecturer. For his record of achievement he has received the Tom Paine Award and the Gandhi Peace Award.

Further Reading

Sanford Ungar's *The Papers and the Papers: An Account of the Legal and Political Battle over the Pentagon Papers* (1972) follows the First Amendment battle over Ellsberg's act. A study by Peter Schrag, *Test of Loyalty: Daniel Ellsberg and the Rituals of Secret Government* (1974), analyzes the events surrounding Ellsberg's change of position regarding the Vietnam War as well as his decision to release the *Pentagon Papers*. There are no other studies that deal directly with Ellsberg, although many of the standard works on the Vietnam conflict mention his role in passing. ☐

Lincoln Ellsworth

Lincoln Ellsworth (1880-1951), American adventurer and explorer, became the first man to cross both the Arctic and the Antarctic by air.

The son of a wealthy businessman and financier, Lincoln Ellsworth was born in Chicago on May 12, 1880. Graduating from preparatory school in 1900, he briefly attended Yale and Columbia universities, but his real interest was in outdoor life. He traveled extensively, working in Canada and Alaska as a railroad surveyor and mining engineer. He then formally studied practical astronomy and surveying in preparation for realizing his lifelong ambition—polar exploration.

A true adventurer, Ellsworth participated in the Canadian government's buffalo hunt of 1911, prospected for gold, spent 3 years with the U.S. Biological Survey on the Pacific coast, and volunteered for service in World War I, training as a pilot in France. Following the war and a protracted illness, Ellsworth in 1924 joined a geological expedition to Peru.

The following year Ellsworth joined and largely financed the expedition with Roald Amundsen, the Norwegian explorer, that initiated Arctic exploration by air. Flying from Spitsbergen for the North Pole in two planes, the party of six reached 87° 44'N before being forced down with engine trouble. One plane was badly damaged during the landing, and it took 3 weeks to get the other plane off the polar ice pack. They returned to Spitsbergen to announce that no land existed on the European side of the pole. In 1926 Amundsen and Ellsworth returned to the Arctic, this time with a semirigid airship, the *Norge*.

Ellsworth concentrated on geologic work in the American Southwest for several years, although in 1931 he represented the American Geographic Society on the Arctic flight of the *Graf Zeppelin*. He undertook the exploration of Antarctica by air in 1933. In 1935, on his third attempt, Ellsworth and his pilot crossed Antarctica, landing 16 miles short of Richard Byrd's abandoned camp at Little America, where they were rescued. On this and a subsequent flight in 1939 Ellsworth discovered and claimed for the United States 377,000 square miles of land.

Ellsworth was a bold, imaginative, superbly conditioned man. He died in New York City on May 26, 1951.

Further Reading

The only books dealing with Ellsworth's life were written by the explorer himself: *The Last Wild Buffalo Hunt* (1919); two

books written with Roald Amundsen, *Our Polar Flight* (1925) and *First Crossing of the Polar Sea* (1927); *Exploring Today* (1935); and the autobiographical *Search* (1932) and *Beyond Horizons* (1937). *Air Pioneering in the Arctic*, edited by Ellsworth (1929), is a collection of articles on his expeditions. ☐

Walter Maurice Elsasser

The American physicist Walter Maurice Elsasser (1904-1991) made original contributions to geophysics and to the discussion of the physical foundations of biology.

Walter Maurice Elsasser was born in Germany on March 20, 1904. After university studies at Heidelberg and Munich he gained a doctoral degree in physics at Göttingen in 1927. His subsequent employments were diverse, in many institutions and in three countries. He worked at the Technische Hochschule, Berlin (1928-1930) and at Frankfurt University (1930-1933). While research fellow and guest lecturer at the Sorbonne (1933-1936) in Paris, his main work was in atomic physics. He immigrated to the United States in 1936 and became a naturalized citizen in 1940. In 1937 he married Margaret Trahey, and they had a daughter and a son. After a divorce from his first wife, he married Suzanne Rosenfeld in 1964.

Elsasser's first appointments in the United States were in meteorology at the California Institute of Technology (1936-1941) and then at the Blue Hill Observatory, Harvard (1941-1942). During World War II he was employed at the Signal Corps Laboratories in New Jersey, where his researches dealt with the atmospheric transmission of radio and radar waves. Following the war, he engaged in industrial research for a short time at the New Jersey Laboratories of the Radio Corporation of America. After that he held professorial posts at several universities, including Pennsylvania (1947-1950), Utah (1950-1956), California at La Jolla (1956-1962), New Mexico at Albuquerque (1960-1961), Princeton (1962-1968), and Maryland at College Park (1968-1974). In 1985 Elsasser became adjunct professor in the department of earth and planetary science at Johns Hopkins University, and was named Homewood Professor two years later. He retired from teaching in 1989.

In 1958 Elsasser published a book, *The Physical Foundation of Biology,* an important and highly original work concerned with broad philosophical, physical, and biological matters, strikingly different from his main researches. A sequel appeared in 1966, *Atom and Organism.* Other books by Elsasser include *The Chief Abstractions of Biology* (1975), *Memoirs of a Physicist in the Atomic Age* (1978), and *Reflections on a Theory of Organisms* (1987).

Calculations of wind systems led Elsasser by 1938 to consider the possibility that convection motion might exist within the earth's metallic core and might obey certain laws of cosmic magneto-hydrodynamics. He first studied the phenomenon of "secular variation" and demonstrated that his formulation of the magneto-hydrodynamics of a spherical conductor provided quantitative results in agreement with the observed phenomenon. Elsasser also explained how eddies with the circulation of the earth's core can account for the secular variation, whose distribution is regional and whose time scale, a few centuries, differs greatly from that of surface geological changes.

Being interested in the origin of the earth's permanent geomagnetic field, Elsasser first proposed a thermoelectric origin, but this did not account for the self-sustaining nature of the permanent field, and he abandoned it in favor of a dynamo theory. According to this model, the presence of a magnetic field in the core results in motion of matter perpendicular to the field, which in turn gives rise to a field producing motion, and so on in self-sustaining action.

Elsasser was elected to the National Academy of Sciences in 1957 and awarded the Bowie Medal of the American Geophysical Union (AGU) in 1959. He received the Fleming Medal of the AGU in 1971. Elsasser was also awarded the 1987 U.S. National Medal of Science. In his late research, Elsasser concentrated his efforts on the study of the earth's upper mantle. Elsasser died October 14, 1991.

Further Reading

Elsasser's work in quantum physics is briefly discussed in William H. Cropper, *The Quantum Physicists and an Introduction to Their Physics* (1970). See also David Robert Bates, ed., *The Planet Earth* (1957; rev. ed. 1964). □

Ralph Waldo Emerson

Ralph Waldo Emerson (1803-1882) was the most thought-provoking American cultural leader of the mid-19th century. In his unorthodox ideas and actions he represented a minority of Americans, but by the end of his life he was considered a sage.

Though Ralph Waldo Emerson's origins were promising, his path to eminence was by no means easy. He was born in Boston on May 25, 1803, of a fairly well-known New England family. His father was a prominent Boston minister. However, young Emerson was only 8 when his father died and left the family to face hard times. The genteel poverty which the Emerson family endured did not prevent it from sending the promising boy to the Boston Latin School, where he received the best basic education of his day. At 14 he enrolled in Harvard College. As a scholarship boy, he studied more and relaxed less than some of his classmates. He won several minor prizes for his writing. When he was 17, he started keeping a journal and continued it for over half a century.

Unitarian Minister

Emerson was slow in finding himself. After graduation from Harvard he taught at the school of his brother William. Gradually he moved toward the ministry. He undertook studies at the Harvard Divinity School, meanwhile continuing his journal and other writing. In 1826 he began his career as a Unitarian minister. Appropriately, Unitarianism was the creed of the questioner; in particular it questioned the divine nature of the Trinity. Emerson received several offers before an unusually attractive one presented itself: the junior pastorship at Boston's noted Second Church, with the promise that it would quickly become the senior pastorship. His reputation spread swiftly. Soon he was chosen chaplain of the Massachusetts Senate, and he was elected to the Boston School Committee.

Emerson's personal life flowered even more than his professional one, for he fell in love, deeply in love, for the only time in his life. He wooed and won a charming New Hampshire girl named Ellen Tucker. Their wedding, in September 1829, marked the start of an idyllic marriage. But it was all too short, for she died a year and a half later, leaving Emerson desolate. Though he tried to find consolation in his religion, he was unsuccessful. As a result, his religious doubts developed. Even the permissive creed of Unitarianism seemed to him to be a shackle. In September 1832 he resigned his pastorate; according to his farewell sermon he could no longer believe in celebrating Holy Communion.

Emerson's decision to leave the ministry was the more difficult because it left him with no other work to do. After months of floundering and even sickness, he scraped together enough money to take a 10-month tour of Europe. He hoped that his travels would give him the perspective he

needed. They did, but only to the extent of confirming what he did not want rather than what he wanted.

Professional Lecturer

However, the times were on Emerson's side, for he found on his return to America that a new institution was emerging that held unique promise for him. This was the lyceum, a system of lecturing which started in the late 1820s, established itself in the 1830s, and rose to great popularity during the next 2 decades. The local lecture clubs that sprang up discovered that they had to pay for the best lecturers, Emerson among them. Emerson turned the lyceum into his unofficial pulpit and in the process earned at least a modest stipend. He spoke to his audiences with great, if unorthodox, effectiveness. They saw before them a tall, thin Yankee with slightly aquiline features whose words sometimes baffled but often uplifted them. After a few seasons he organized his own lecture courses as a supplement to his lyceum lectures. For example, during the winter of 1837-1838 he offered the Boston public a group of 10 lectures on "human culture" and earned more than $500. Equally to the point, his lectures grew into essays and books, and these he published from the early 1840s on.

Emerson's Creed

As a transcendentalist, Emerson spoke out against materialism, formal religion, and slavery. He could not have found targets better designed to offend the mass of Americans, most of whom considered making money a major purpose in life and church and churchgoing a mainstay and,

until they faced the hard fact of the Civil War, either supported slavery or were willing to let it alone. But Emerson spoke of slavery in the context of the Fugitive Slave Law (1850), saying, in one of his rare bursts of profanity, "I will not obey it, by God."

Emerson, however, was not merely *against* certain things; he both preached and exemplified a positive doctrine. He became America's leading transcendentalist; that is, he believed in a reality and a knowledge that transcended the everyday reality Americans were accustomed to. He believed in the integrity of the individual: "Trust thyself," he urged in one of his famous phrases. He believed in a spiritual universe governed by a mystic Over-soul with which each individual soul should try to harmonize. Touchingly enough, he believed in America. Though he ranked as his country's most searching critic, he helped as much as anyone to establish the "American identity." He not only called out for a genuinely American literature but also helped inaugurate it through his own writings. In addition, he espoused the cause of American music and American art; as a matter of fact, his grand purpose was to assist in the creation of an indigenous American national culture.

Publishing His Ideas

His first two books were brilliant. He had published a pamphlet, *Nature,* in 1836, which excited his fellow transcendentalists; but now he issued two volumes of essays for a broader public, *Essays,* First Series, in 1841 and *Essays, Second Series,* in 1844. Their overarching subjects were man, nature, and God. In such pieces as "Self-reliance," "Spiritual Laws," "Nature," "The Poet," and "The Oversoul," Emerson expounded on the innate nobility of man, the joys of nature and their spiritual significance, and the sort of deity omnipresent in the universe. The tone of the essays was optimistic, but Emerson did not neglect the gritty realities of life. In such essays as "Compensation" and "Experience," he tried to suggest how to deal with human losses and failings.

Whether he wrote prose or verse, Emerson was a poet with a poet's gift of metaphor. Both his lectures and his published works were filled from the first with telling phrases, with wisdom startlingly expressed. His next book, after the second series of essays, was a volume of his poems. They proved to be irregular in form and movingly individual in expression. After that came more than one remarkable volume of prose. In *Representative Men: Seven Lectures* (1850) Emerson pondered the uses of great men, devoting individual essays to half a dozen figures, including Plato, Shakespeare, and Goethe. *English Traits* (1856) resulted from an extended visit to Great Britain. In this volume Emerson anatomized the English people and their culture. His approach was impressionistic, but the result was the best book by an American on the subject up to that time.

Meanwhile, Emerson had been immersed—sometimes willingly, sometimes not—in things other than literature. He had found a second wife, pale and serene, in Lydia Jackson of Plymouth. He had married her in 1835 and got from her the comfort of love, if not its passion. They had four children, one of whom, Waldo, died when he was a little boy; the others outlived their eminent father. As Emerson's family life expanded, so did his friendships. After leaving his pastorate in Boston, he had moved to nearby Concord, where he stayed the rest of his life. In Concord he met a prickly young Harvard graduate who became his disciple, friend, and occasional adversary: Henry David Thoreau. Emerson added others to his circle, becoming as he did so the nexus of the transcendentalist movement. Among his close friends were Bronson Alcott, George Ripley, and Theodore Parker.

Emerson's public life also expanded. During the 1850s he was drawn deeply into the struggle against slavery. Though he found some of the abolitionists almost as distasteful as the slaveholders, he knew where his place had to be. The apolitical Emerson became a Republican, voting for Abraham Lincoln. When Lincoln signed the Emancipation Proclamation (Jan. 1, 1863), Emerson counted it a momentous day for the United States; when Lincoln was killed, Emerson considered him a martyr.

Last Years

After the Civil War, Emerson continued to lecture and write. Though he had nothing really new to say anymore, audiences continued to throng his lectures and many readers bought his books. The best of the final books were *Society and Solitude* (1870) and *Letters and Social Aims* (1876). However, he was losing his memory and needed more and more help from others, especially his daughter Ellen. He was nearly 79 when he died on April 27, 1882.

America mourned Emerson's passing, as did much of the rest of the Western world. In the general judgment, he had been both a great writer and a great man. Certainly he had been America's leading essayist for half a century. And he had been not only one of the most wise but one of the most sincere of men. He had shown his countrymen the possibilities of the human spirit, and he had done so without a trace of sanctimony or pomposity. The *Chicago Tribune,* for instance, exclaimed, "How rare he was; how original in thought; how true in character!" Some of the eulogizing was extravagant, but in general the verdict at the time of Emerson's death has been upheld.

Further Reading

Emerson's *Journals* were reedited with care by William Gilman and others (7 vols., 1960-1969). Also valuable are *The Letters of Ralph Waldo Emerson,* edited by Ralph L. Rusk (6 vols., 1939). The best biography is still Rusk's *The Life of Ralph Waldo Emerson* (1949). The best critical study of Emerson's writing is Sherman Paul, *Emerson's Angle of Vision: Man and Nature in American Experience* (1952), which concentrates on Emerson's principle of "correspondence." Stephen E. Whicher, *Freedom and Fate* (1953), is also valuable; it is called an "inner life" of Emerson and concentrates on the 1830s. The only treatment of Emerson's mind and art as they relate to the transcendentalist movement is Francis O. Matthiessen's superb *American Renaissance: Art and Expression in the Age of Emerson and Whitman* (1941). □

Mihail Eminescu

The Romanian poet Mihail Eminescu (1850-1889) inaugurated modern sensitiveness and expression in Romanian poetry through his achievements in content and craftsmanship.

Mihail Eminescu was born at Ipotesti in northern Moldavia on Jan. 15, 1850, into a family of country gentry. He spent his first years like a peasant child in the midst of nature and under the influence of folklore. His adolescence was agitated by conflicts with his family. He interrupted his studies several times, going on tours with theatrical companies. He made his literary debut at 16 in the Romanian review *Familia* (The Family), published in Budapest.

Eminescu studied philosophy in Vienna from 1869 to 1872 and in Berlin from 1872 to 1874. Returning to Romania in 1874, he held several minor jobs in Iaşi (custodian of the university library, inspector of schools, subeditor of an obscure newspaper). There, and after leaving Iaşi, he found himself under the influence of the political and esthetic literary circle Junimea ("Youth"). In 1877 Eminescu went to Bucharest to work on the staff of the newspaper *Timpul* (Time). Eminescu's steady journalistic activity filled the years from 1877 to 1883. Struck by insanity in 1883, he lived until 1889 in a dramatic alternation between lucidity and madness.

Eminescu concentrated in his work the entire evolution of Romanian national poetry. The most illustrative poems of his early years (1866-1873) are "The Dissolute Youth," "The Epigones," "Mortua Est," "Angel and Demon," and "Emperor and Proletarian." The overwhelming influences on his poetry of this period were from Shakespeare and Lord Byron.

The ever deeper influence of Romanian folklore, his close contact with German philosophy and romanticism in the years 1872 to 1874 when he was preparing for a doctor's degree in philosophy in Berlin, and the evolution of his own creative powers carried Eminescu toward a new vision of the world. His poetical universe shifted to the spheres of magical transparencies offered by folklore as ideal and possible grounds for a love that was both a dream and a transfiguration. His poetical expression became increasingly inward, simplified, and sweetened. His poetry began to show rare strength and beauty, involving a universe in which a demiurgical eye and hand seemed to have conferred a new order upon the elements and to have infused them with infinite freshness and power.

In "The Blue Flower" Eminescu offered a new interpretation of the aspiration in the fulfillment of love. The most important poem written during this period was "Câlin" ("Leaves from a Fairy Tale"), a synthesis of the epical and the lyrical, with a description of the Romanian landscape.

After 1876 the sphere of Eminescu's inner experience deepened. The poetry of his maturity reached all human dimensions, from the sensitive, emotional ones to the intellectual, spiritual ones. Until 1883 his poetry was an uninterrupted meditation on the human condition in which the artist always stood on the summits of human thinking and feeling. The most important works of his last period are "A Dacian's Prayer," "Ode in the Ancient Meter," and the "Epistles." His masterpiece is "The Evening Star" (1883), a version of the Hyperion myth. Ideas and meaning, expressed in symbols, are manifold, profoundly ambiguous, and discernible in an esthetic achievement of supreme simplicity and expressiveness. In *Barren Genius,* a posthumously published novel of romantic trend, and especially in "Poor Dyonis," a fantastic, philosophical short story, Eminescu added some demiurgical features to his romantic hero.

Further Reading

Eminescu's poems were translated by Sylvia Pankhurst and I. O. Stefanovici as *Poems of Mihail Eminescu* (1930). Eminescu is treated in E. D. Tappe, *Rumanian Prose and Verse* (1956). □

Robert Emmet

The Irish nationalist Robert Emmet (1778-1803) was executed after leading an unsuccessful revolution against British rule. His youth, passionate oratory, and courage in the face of death have made him a permanent symbol of romantic, revolutionary, Irish nationalism.

Robert Emmet was the youngest of 18 children born to a prominent Anglo-Irish Protestant family. His father, Dr. Robert Emmet, was state physician of Ireland. In 1793 Emmet enrolled at Trinity College, Dublin. He excelled in his studies and won a reputation as a fiery orator. Emmet was influenced by the liberal views of the Enlightenment and the conduct of an older brother who was a member of the Society of United Irishmen. In 1796 Emmet joined the radical group.

Inspired by the examples of the American and French revolutions, the United Irishmen demanded an Ireland free of English influence and governed by a reformed Parliament representing both Protestant and Catholic opinion, elected by a democratic franchise. Frightened by the increasing militancy of the United Irishmen, the intensity of Catholic discontent, and the threat of internal insurrection supported by French invasion, the Irish government adopted measures restricting civil liberties. The Earl of Clare, Lord Chancellor of Ireland, began to investigate student opinion at Trinity, and in 1798 Emmet was forced to leave the college.

Emmet maintained United Irishmen connections but apparently did not participate in the 1798 revolution. After the Irish and British parliaments passed the Act of Union, creating the United Kingdom of Great Britain and Ireland (1800) and completely destroying the legal existence of the Irish nation, Emmet and his friends considered revolution even more imperative. He left for the Continent to confer with Irish exiles. Napoleon and other French leaders expressed a willingness to assist an Irish revolution. In 1802 Emmet returned to Dublin to create an army of liberation, hoping for French assistance:

Emmet used his own funds to buy weapons, mostly pikes. He asked the Dublin proletariat to strike a blow for liberty. Unfortunately, he failed to establish effective communications with United Irishmen outside the metropolitan area and was unaware that the government had infiltrated his organization. When authorities discovered a cache of arms, Emmet decided to raise the standard of revolt. On July 23, 1803, he issued a proclamation establishing a provisional government for an Irish Republic; he put on a general's uniform of green and white with gold epaulets and led his band of about 80 men out to battle. No help arrived and the revolt was crushed by British soldiers. Emmet managed to escape but refused to leave for America, insisting on remaining close to his fiancée, Sarah Curran, daughter of the famous barrister, John Philpot Curran. On August 25 British soldiers captured Emmet.

On Sept. 19, 1803, the government brought Emmet to trial. Sadistic Lord Norbury was the judge, and Leonard MacNally, an informer, was defense counsel. The jury delivered a guilty verdict. Before sentencing, Emmet brilliantly defended his nationalism. He said that he was prepared to die for the future of Irish freedom, closing with the words: "Let no man write my epitaph. . . . When my country takes her place among the nations of the earth, then, and not till then, let my epitaph be written." On September 20 he was hanged.

Emmet's image among Irish nationalists far exceeds the merits of his performance as revolutionary. He was naive, impractical, flamboyant, excessively talkative, and a poor organizer. British vengeance, however, converted a pathetic effort into a triumph of martydom. Thomas Moore's poems about Emmet enhanced the image of noble and tragic martyr. Irish exiles in America were particularly loyal to Emmet's memory, learning the words of his speech and naming their children and patriotic organizations after him. Emmet's example of blood sacrifice watered Irish nationalism, motivating Fenians and the men of the Easter Rebellion of 1916 and the Anglo-Irish war.

Further Reading

Helen Landreth, *The Pursuit of Robert Emmet* (1948), claims that British government spies and informers acted as agents provoking revolt to further William Pitt the Younger's Irish policy and that Emmet was an unknowing victim of British duplicity and tyranny. Owen Dudley Edwards in ''Ireland'' in *Celtic Nationalism* (1968) recognizes Emmet's contribution to the romantic myths of revolutionary nationalism but compares his total impact unfavorably when measured against Wolfe Tone's. See also Leon O'Broin, *The Unfortunate Robert Emmet* (1958), and R. Jacobs, *The Rise of the United Irishmen* (1937). □

Empedocles

The Greek philosopher, poet, and scientist Empedocles (ca. 493-ca. 444 B.C.) propounded a pluralist cosmological scheme in which fire, air, water, and earth mingled and separated under the compulsion of love and strife.

Empedocles was born of a noble family in the Sicilian city of Acragas (modern Agrigento). He is said to have studied under Xenophanes or Parmenides. His work shows familiarity with Pythagoreanism, although stories about his banishment from the sect, like many of the legends that grew up around him, may be discounted as misinterpretations of statements in his writings. It is certain that he had a profound interest in natural science and in certain religious ideas, and although there is no hint in the surviving portion of his writings that he took an interest in political affairs, the Sicilian historian Timaeus tells of his efforts to establish a democracy in Acragas. Aristotle says that Empedocles was offered the kingship but refused it. Accounts of his death are so confused as to make it impossible to determine either the date or the place, although Aristotle noted that he did not live past the age of 60.

Of his two poems, *On Nature* and *Purifications,* which totaled some 5,000 verses, fewer than 500 lines survive. *On Nature* presents Empedocles's philosophical system. Fire, air, water, and earth, the four roots or elements of which everything is made, are eternal and move through the cosmos with a swirling motion. The problem of change is solved by positing the existence of love and strife as the two forces which affect the four basic elements. Depending on which of these two principles holds sway at a given moment, the universe is either in a state of happy unity or of warring disunity, with possible gradations between the extremes.

Purifications was an extended poem dealing with the human soul and espousing the Orphic and Pythagorean tenets of immortality and metempsychosis, which were widespread in the Greek West in the 5th century B.C. Empedocles asserted that he had been boy, girl, bush, fowl, and fish in earlier lives, and he speaks of his present life as punishment for past sins.

Empedocles is less well known as the father of Sicilian rhetoric (Aristotle called him the inventor of rhetoric) and as an important contributor to medical science.

Further Reading

Selected fragments of Empedocles's two poems, with English translation and full analysis, are found in G. S. Kirk and J. E. Raven, *The Presocratic Philosophers: A Critical History with a Selection of Texts* (1962). Useful discussions are found in John Burnet, *Early Greek Philosophy* (1892; 4th ed. 1930), and Kathleen Freeman, *The Presocratic Philosophers: A Companion to Diels, Fragmente der Vorsokratiker* (1946; 2d ed. 1959). □

Juan del Encina

Juan del Encina (1468-1529?) is called the father of Spanish drama. He was also the foremost Spanish musical composer of his time.

The original name of Juan del Encina was Fermoselle, but he adopted the name of his probable birthplace, a small village in the province of Salamanca. In all likelihood Encina studied at the University of Salamanca under Antonio de Nebrija, the foremost Spanish humanist of his time. He then entered the service of the Duke of Alba, in whose palace of Alba de Tormes he discharged the multiple functions of playwright, poet, composer, and musician for 7 years. Encina published his *Cancionero* (a collection of plays and *villancicos,* or polyphonic songs) in Salamanca in 1496; other works were added to this collection in later editions.

Encina went to Rome in 1498, where he entered the papal chapel and eventually became singer to Leo X. During this time Encina continued to write plays. While in Rome he obtained several ecclesiastical benefices in Spain, and in 1510 and 1513 he was in Málaga as archdeacon and canon. He had obtained, however, papal dispensation to collect his benefices without discharging his duties.

In 1519, aged 50, Encina took holy orders and went on a pilgrimage to the Holy Land, which he described in his poem *La Trivagia*. He celebrated his first Mass in Jerusalem. Encina returned to Spain as prior of León, where he resided from 1523 until his death.

As a poet, Encina was most successful in brief, lyrical pieces, which he set to music himself; his romances were also more lyrical than narrative. His great popularity as a composer is attested to by the fact that 61 of his *villancicos* were collected in the *Cancionero musical de Palacio* (ca. 1500). As a playwright, Encina brought to their final development the theatrical forms derived from medieval liturgical drama. He inaugurated Renaissance drama in Spain. His early dramas (such as *Egloga de las grandes lluvias*) were Nativity plays, with rustic shepherds as protagonists. His later plays (such as *Egloga de Plácida y Vitoriano*) were Italianate in spirit, much longer, and complicated in form. His shepherds were now of classical inspiration. The joy of life he sang about in his later plays was almost neopagan in its exuberance.

Further Reading

The best interpretation in English of the literary works of Encina is James R. Andrews, *Juan del Encina: Prometheus in Search of Prestige* (1959). A good appreciation of his musical works is in Gilbert Chase, *The Music of Spain* (1941), and Gustave Reese, *Music in the Renaissance* (1959). The early chapters in N. D. Shergold, *A History of the Spanish Stage: From Medieval Times until the End of the Seventeenth Century* (1967), contain valuable background information. □

Guillermo Endara

Guillermo Endara (born 1936) was a member of the Panameñista Party and an ally of Arnulfo Arias for many years prior to his installation as president of Panama by the U.S. Government in 1989.

Guillermo Endara was installed as president of Panama in the Christmas 1989 invasion (Operation Just Cause) by U.S. military forces sent to depose General Manuel Noriega. Until May 1989 Endara was virtually unknown to Americans. Then he became the presidential candidate of the Panameñista Party and the choice of Noriega's growing middle-class opposition, the Civil Democratic Opposition Alliance. Foreign dignitaries (among them former U.S. President Jimmy Carter) who monitored the May 7, 1989, election agreed that Endara won decisively. But Noriega ordered seizure of the ballot boxes and subsequently declared the election void and sent his goon squad (the Dignity Battalions) to harass the opposition, many of whom had taken to the streets in protest. Endara and vice-presidential candidate Guillermo Ford were both attacked. Endara celebrated his 53rd birthday in a hospital bed recovering from a beating with an iron bar, and his first wife, Marcela, with whom he had one daughter, died of a heart attack while he was bed-ridden. He had to await the U.S. invasion to be restored to the Panamanian executive office. He took the oath in the middle of the night of December 19-20 at a U.S. military base. On December 28, after Noriega had taken shelter within the Vatican embassy in Panama City, Endara wrote Pope John Paul II, pleading with him to have his ambassadors give Noriega over to the American invasion, since Endara could not guarantee Noriega a fair trial within Panama, which they did. Six months later Endara felt secure enough in office to marry Ann Mae Diaz Chen, a law student.

Guillermo Endara Gallimany was born on May 12, 1936, into a middle-class family. His parents were closely allied with Arnulfo Arias, founder of the nationalistic (and at one time anti-American) Panameñista movement in the late 1930s. When Arias was overthrown in a 1941 coup, the Endara family joined him in exile. During this time young Guillermo went to school in Argentina and a military school in Los Angeles, Calif. Returning to Panama, Endara attended the University of Panama Law School, graduating first in his class. He then attended New York University for further law studies until he returned to Panama in 1963, helping to found Solis, Endara, Delgado, and Guevara, now one of Panama's most successful law firms. He served two terms in the Panamanian National Assembly and taught law at the university. In 1968, when Arias returned to the presidency for the third time, Endara served as Arias' minister of planning and economic policy. When the Panamanian National Guard (which became the Panama Defense Forces in 1982) overthrew Arias in the October 1968 coup, Endara went underground, was jailed in 1971, and joined the deposed executive in exile until the ban on Arias was lifted.

In the 1980s Endara had a law practice in Panama City and continued to lecture at the University of Panama Law School. His political ties to Arias remained strong, however, and he supported Arias' continued opposition to the interference of the Panamanian military in national politics. By now the growing disenchantment of the U.S. Government (which, in the interest of national security and its efforts to wage a covert war against the government of Nicaragua, had tolerated Noriega's narcotics trafficking and arms dealing) made Arias and his cause more palatable. When Arias died in 1988, Endara took on the gargantuan task of leading the opposition to Noriega and the militarization of Panama. In the campaign of 1989 he promised to reinstitute democracy in Panamanian political life and remove Noriega from power. Seven months after the election the Christmas invasion restored the victory that Noriega's thugs denied him.

Endara and his two vice presidents—Guillermo Ford and Ricardo Arias Calderon—faced a difficult task. Six years of Noriega's rule had left much of Panama in poverty. In addition, a year after the invasion more than 2,000 people in Panama City were still homeless as a result of U.S. weaponry.

To call attention to these problems, Endara staged a public hunger strike from the steps of the Metropolitan Cathedral in Panama City. He visited then U.S. President George Bush, pressing for $1 billion in emergency relief aid and cooperative measures to curtail the Panamanian narcotics trade. The money, as it slowly came in, was applied to governmental expenditures, but where it was needed more was in a police force, since street crime and narcotics trade had skyrocketed since Noriega and his associates had been purged.

Despite this, the economy improved since Endara was able to convince foreign investors that Panamanian banks were once again safe depositories of their wealth. New construction and businesses thrived, and most businesses that existed before the invasion were once again active. Even the nearly 50 percent unemployment rate when Endara took office dropped by over 25 percent. Yet there was still criticism of the administration, since it tended to be populated by conservative, wealthy businessmen who had little connection with the poor. Endara's term as president ended in August, 1994. He was succeeded by Ernesto Pérez Balladares.

Further Reading

For more information on Guillermo Endara and Panamanian politics see Frederick Kempe, *Divorcing the Dictator: America's Bungled Affair with Noriega* (1990); and John Dinges, *Our Man in Panama: How General Noriega Used the United States—and Made Millions in Drugs and Arms* (1990); John and Mavis Biesanz, *The People of Panama* (1955); Steve C. Ropp, *Panamanian Politics: From Guarded Nation to National Guard* (1982); and William Jorden, *Panama Odyssey: From Colony to Partner* (1983). □

John Endecott

John Endecott (1588-1655) was one of the English founders of the Massachusetts Bay Colony and later its governor. He often used harsh measures against the colony's enemies.

Born in Devon, John Endecott may have seen some military service. He early became interested in colonization through the influence of John White, a Puritan clergyman. Endecott was included among the six patentees of the New England Company because he was willing to emigrate as the director of the Cape Ann settlement.

Appointed "chief-in-command" and commissioned to prepare the way for more colonists, Endecott arrived at Salem, Mass., in September 1628. Under his directorship Salem became a Puritan beachhead in New England. He sent two brothers who continued using the Anglican Prayer Book back to England as undesirable colonists, and he chopped down Thomas Morton's frivolous maypole at Merrimount. Both actions indicated his impulsiveness and partisanship. He later had the cross of St. George removed from Salem's militia flag because of its papal connotation and was reprimanded by the legislature for his political indiscretion.

In 1629 the New England Company was reorganized as the Massachusetts Bay Company, and when Governor John Winthrop arrived in 1630 Endecott relinquished his leadership, although he remained among the colony's public servants. Endecott's lack of restraint was demonstrated again in 1637, when he led an expedition against the Pequot Indians to avenge the murder of a trader. After destroying one Native American settlement, Endecott and his men went to another. Ignoring pleas for caution by Connecticut settlers, Endecott continued to destroy Native American canoes and villages until, satisfied, he returned to the safety of Boston and Salem, leaving Connecticut to suffer the reprisals of the Native Americans in the Pequot War. Later, as governor of Massachusetts during the Quaker intrusions of the 1650s, he bore much of the responsibility for the inhuman treatment of the Quakers—ranging from imprisonment and banishment to execution. King Charles II eventually rebuked Massachusetts and Governor Endecott for their cruelty.

Despite his strictness and narrowness, Endecott served the colony as best he could. His election to colonial offices attests to his honesty and willingness to serve the common good. In addition to minor posts, he served 5 yearly terms as deputy governor and 15 as governor, filling the governorship longer than anyone else. If he was overzealous in defending the truth as he saw it, he was like many others in an overzealous age.

Further Reading

The only recent biography of Endecott is Lawrence S. Mayo, *John Endecott: A Biography* (1936). Background material can be found in Herbert L. Osgood *The American Colonies in the Seventeenth Century* (3 vols., 1904-1907); James Truslow Adams, *The Founding of New England* (1921); Frances Rose-Troup, *The Massachusetts Bay Company and Its Predecessors* (1930); and Charles M. Andrews, *The Colonial Period of American History* (4 vols., 1934-1938). □

John Franklin Enders

The American virologist John Franklin Enders (1897-1985), a leader in modern virology, cultivated polio-virus in tissue cultures of human cells and developed an attenuated live vaccine for measles.

John Franklin Enders was born on Feb. 10, 1897, in West Hartford, Conn. After serving from 1917 to 1920 in the United States Naval Reserve Flying Corps, he achieved his undergraduate degree at Yale University. In 1922, he earned a master's degree in English at Harvard University. But before completing doctoral work he became attracted to the study of bacteriology under Hans Zinsser, with whom he developed methods of synthesizing anti-typhus vaccines. He was married to Sarah Bennett in 1927, with whom he had two children; she died in 1943. In 1930 he received his doctorate in microbiology. He then embarked upon a remarkable and productive career as a member of the faculty of Harvard Medical School. During World War II, he was a civilian consultant on epidemic diseases to the Secretary of War, and after 1945 was affiliated with the Civilian Commission on Virus and Rickettsial Disease until 1949. He became head of the Research Division of Infectious Diseases of Children's Hospital, Boston, in 1947. In 1951 he married again, this time to Carolyn Keane.

In the late 1930s Enders focused on virologic problems. His first major breakthrough was the development of techniques for detection of antibodies to mumps virus; he and others subsequently showed that the virus could be grown in chick embryos and tissue culture. On the basis of this work the immunology and epidemiology of mumps infection could be studied, a skin test was developed, and it was shown that the infection frequently was inapparent. Finally, the studies provided the basis for the development of preventive measures against the disease, which now include an attenuated live-virus vaccine.

While Enders and his colleagues, Dr. Frederick Robbins and Dr. Thomas Weller, were continuing the study of mumps and chicken-pox viruses, various types of human cells in culture were being used. Enders suggested that some of the cultures be inoculated with poliovirus, which at that time could be studied only with difficulty in a few species of expensive experimental animals. The poliovirus did propagate in one type of culture made up of cells which were not from the nervous system. This discovery, and the studies which it made possible, opened the way to a new era in poliovirus research, the most dramatic aspect of which was the possibility for development of poliovirus vaccines. For this work Enders, Robbins, and Weller were awarded the Nobel Prize in 1954. From the Enders-Robbins-Weller technique, Dr. Jonas Salk was able to produce the first polio vaccine in 1953.

Enders began studies with another disease, measles. In 1954 he reported success in growing the virus in tissue culture and followed this by a model series of investigations that resulted in a measles vaccine in 1962. Turning his concern to cancer-related viruses in later years, he made important contributions to this field, particularly to studies of fusion of cells from different species as a means of altering cell susceptibility to viruses.

His significant contributions to many areas of virology brought him honors from all over the world, including the Presidential Medal of Freedom in 1963, but Enders continued to devote himself to his laboratory and his students. Because of the breadth and incisiveness of his thought, many of his contributions were conceptual and definitive, representing major steps opening up whole new areas for further experimentation and extension of knowledge. Enders wrote close to 200 published papers between 1929 and 1970. In 1939 he co-authored *Immunity, Principles and Application in Medicine and Public Health*. But, while achieving wide recognition and public acclaim, Enders remained a "virologists' virologist." Towards the end of his life, he sought to apply his knowledge of immunology to the fight against AIDS, especially in trying to halt the progress of the disease during its incubation period in the human body. He died September 8, 1985, of heart failure, while at his home in Waterford, Connecticut.

Further Reading

A tribute to Enders can be found in the foreword to *Perspectives in Virology VI* (1968), which was dedicated to him. The foreword was written by Frederick C. Robbins, one of Enders's colleagues, with whom he shared the Nobel Prize. Theodore L. Sourkes, *Nobel Prize Winners in Medicine and Physiology, 1901-1965* (1953; rev. ed. 1967), includes a biography of Enders and a description of his work. A biography is also in the Nobel Foundation, *Physiology or Medicine: Nobel Lectures, Including Presentation Speeches and Laureates' Biographies* (3 vols., 1964-1967). Information on his work is in any review of the literature of medical virology and in virology textbooks. □

Friedrich Engels

The German revolutionist and social theorist Friedrich Engels (1820-1895) was the cofounder with Karl Marx of modern socialism.

riedrich Engels was born on Nov. 28, 1820, in Barmen, Rhenish Prussia, a small industrial town in the Wupper valley. He was the oldest of the six children of Friedrich and Elisabeth Franziska Mauritia Engels. The senior Engels, a textile manufacturer, was a Christian Pietist and religious fanatic. After attending elementary school at Barmen, young Friedrich entered the gymnasium in nearby Elberfeld at the age of 14, but he left it 3 years later. Although he became one of the most learned men of his time, he had no further formal schooling.

Under pressure from his tyrannical father, Friedrich became a business apprentice in Barmen and Barmen, but he soon called it a "dog's life." He left business at the age of 20, in rebellion against both his joyless home and the "penny-pinching" world of commerce. Hence-forth, Engels was a lifelong enemy of organized religion and of capitalism, although he was again forced into business for a number of years.

While doing his one-year compulsory military service (artillery) in Berlin, Engels came into contact with the radical Young Hegelians and embraced their ideas, particularly the materialist philosophy of Ludwig Feuerbach. After some free-lance journalism, part of it under the pseudonym of F. Oswald, in November 1842 Engels went to Manchester, England, to work in the office of Engels and Ermens, a spinning factory in which his father was a partner. In Manchester, the manufacturing center of the world's foremost capitalist country, Engels had the opportunity of observing capitalism's operations—and its distressing effects on the workers—at first hand. He also studied the leading economic writers, among them Adam Smith, David Ricardo, and Robert Owen in English, and Jean Baptiste Say, Charles Fourier, and Pierre Joseph Proudhon in French. He left Manchester in August 1844.

On his way back to Germany, Engels stopped in Paris, where he met Karl Marx for a second time. On this occasion a lifelong intellectual rapport was established between them. Finding they were of the same opinion about nearly everything, Marx and Engels decided to collaborate on their writing.

Engels spent the next 5 years in Germany, Belgium, and France, writing and participating in revolutionary activities. He fought in the 1849 revolutionary uprising in Baden and the Palatinate, seeing action in four military engagements. After the defeat of the revolution, he escaped to Switzerland. In October 1849, using the sea route via Genoa, he sailed to England, which became his permanent home.

In November 1850, unable to make a living as a writer in London and anxious to help support the penniless Marx, Engels reluctantly returned to his father's business in Manchester. In 1864, after his father's death, he became a partner in the firm, and by early 1869 he felt that he had enough capital to support himself and to provide Marx with a regular annuity of £350. On July 1, 1869, Engels sold his share of the business to his partner. He exulted in a letter to Marx: "Hurrah! Today I finished with sweet commerce, and I am a free man!" Marx's daughter, Eleanor, who saw Engels on that day, wrote: "I shall never forget the triumphant 'For the last time,' which he shouted as he drew on his top-boots in the morning to make his last journey to business. Some hours later, when we were standing at the door waiting for him, we saw him coming across the little field opposite his home. He was flourishing his walking stick in the air and singing, and laughing all over his face."

In September 1870 Engels moved to London, settling near the home of Marx, whom he saw daily. A generous friend and gay host, the fun-loving Engels spent the remaining 25 years of his life in London, enjoying good food, good wine, and good company. He also worked hard, doing the things he loved: writing, maintaining contact and a voluminous correspondence with radicals everywhere, and—after Marx's death in 1883—laboring over the latter's notes and manuscripts, bringing out volumes 2 and 3 of *Das Kapital* in 1885 and 1894, respectively. Engels died of cancer on Aug. 5, 1895. Following his instructions, his body was cremated and his ashes strewn over the ocean at Eastbourne, his favorite holiday resort.

Personality and Character

Engels was medium-height, slender, and athletic. His body was disciplined by swimming, fencing, and riding. He dressed and acted like an elegant English gentleman. In Manchester, where he maintained two homes—one for appearances, as befitted a member of the local stock exchange, and another for his Irish mistress—he rode to hounds with the English gentry, whom he despised as capitalists but by whose antic behavior he was sardonically amused.

Engels had a brilliant mind and was quick, sharp, and unerring in his judgments. His versatility was astonishing. A successful businessman, he also had a grasp of virtually every branch of the natural sciences, biology, chemistry, botany, and physics. He was a widely respected specialist on military affairs. He mastered numerous languages, including all the Slavic ones, on which he planned to write a comparative grammar. He also knew Gothic, Old Nordic, and Old Saxon, studied Arabic, and in 3 weeks learned Persian, which he said was "mere child's play." His English, both spoken and written, was impeccable. It was said of him that he "stutters in 20 languages."

Engels apparently never married. He loved, and lived with successively, two Irish sisters, Mary (who died in 1863) and Lydia (Lizzy) Burns (1827-1878). After he moved to London, he referred to Lizzy as "my wife." The Burns sisters, ardent Irish patriots, stirred in Engels a deep sympathy for the Irish cause. He said of Lizzy Burns: "She came of real Irish proletarian stock, and the passionate feeling for her class, which was instinctive with her, was worth more to me than all the blue-stockinged elegance of 'educated' and 'sensitive' bourgeois girls."

His Writings

Engels published hundreds of articles, a number of prefaces (mostly to Marx's works), and about half a dozen books during his lifetime. His first important book, written when he was 24 years old, was *The Condition of the Working Class in England in 1844,* based on observations made when he lived in Manchester. It was published in German in 1845 and in English in 1892. His next publication was the *Manifesto of the Communist Party (Communist Manifesto),* which he wrote in collaboration with Marx between December 1847 and January 1848, and which was published in London in German a month later. An anonymous English edition came out in London in 1850.

Engels also collaborated with Marx on *The Holy Family,* an attack on the Young Hegelian philosopher Bruno Bauer, which was published in Germany in 1845. Another collaboration with Marx, *The German Ideology,* was written in 1845-1846, but it was not published in full until 1932.

In 1870 Engels published *The Peasant War in Germany,* which consisted of a number of articles he had written in 1850; an English translation appeared in 1956. In 1878 he published perhaps his most important book, *Herr Eugen Dühring's Revolution in Science,* known in an English translation as *Anti-Dühring* (1959). This work ranks, together with Marx's *Das Kapital,* as the most comprehensive study of socialist (Marxist) theory. In it, Engels wrote, he treated "every possible subject, from the concepts of time and space to bimetallism; from the eternity of matter and motion to the perishable nature of moral ideas; from Darwin's natural selection to the education of youth in a future society."

Engels's *Development of Socialism from Utopia to Science* was published in German in 1882 and in English, under the title *Socialism, Utopian and Scientific,* in 1892. In 1884 he brought out *The Origins of the Family, Private Property and the State,* an indispensable work for understanding Marxist political theory. His last work, published in 1888, was *Ludwig Feuerbach and the End of Classical German Philosophy.* Both of these last books are available in English. Two works by Engels were published posthumously: *Germany: Revolution and Counter-Revolution* (German, 1896; English, 1933) and *Dialectics of Nature,* begun in 1895 but never completed, of which an English translation appeared in 1964.

Engels's Ideas

In his articles and books Engels elaborated and developed, both historically and logically, basic ideas that go under the name of Marxism. His work was not an imitation of Marx but constituted a consistent philosophy at which both men had arrived independently and had shared in common. Engels refined the concept of dialectical materialism, which Marx had never fully worked out, to include not only matter but also form. He stressed that the materialist conception takes into consideration the whole cultural process, including tradition, religion, and ideology, which goes through constant historical evolution. Each stage of development, containing also what Engels called "thought material," builds upon the totality of previous developments. Thus every man is a product both of his own time and of the past. Similarly, he elaborated his view of the state, which he regarded as "nothing less than a machine for the oppression of one class by another," as evolving, through class struggles, into the "dictatorship of the proletariat."

Further Reading

Although Engels's writings are available in English, there is no good biography of him in English. Some biographical information can be found in Gustav Mayer, *Friedrich Engels: A Biography* (1934; trans. 1936), a dated and incomplete work; Grace Carlton, *Friedrich Engels: The Shadow Prophet* (1965), a superficial biography not based on original sources; and Oscar J. Hammen, *The Red 48'ers: Karl Marx and Friedrich*

Engels (1969). Good general works which discuss Engels are Edmund Wilson, *To the Finland Station: A Study in the Writing and Acting of History* (1940); George Lichtheim, *Marxism: An Historical and Critical Study* (1961); and Bertram D. Wolfe, *Marxism: One Hundred Years in the Life of a Doctrine* (1965). □

John England

The Irish churchman John England (1786-1842) was a controversial figure in Ireland and America. The first Roman Catholic bishop of Charleston, S. C., he founded the first American Catholic newspaper.

Born in Cork on Sept. 23, 1786, John England was educated in a Protestant school, where he was ridiculed as the only "papist." He trained for the priesthood at the College of St. Patrick. Ordained at Cork in 1808, he served there until 1817. His labors as chaplain, educator, preacher, and writer earned favorable attention, but his political agitation displeased leaders of both Church and state. Finally, in what seemed an attempt to get him out of the way, he was appointed bishop of the new diocese of Charleston, S. C.

Arriving in America in 1820, England discovered among the disorganized flock of Catholics spread throughout the Carolinas and Georgia a strong element of "trusteeism"—that is, laymen preferred to select their own priests. He proposed to correct this by creating a democratic constitution for the diocese that would provide for conventions of priests and laity but abolish parish trustees. Though his people accepted this compromise, it was viewed unfavorably by northern bishops. In Philadelphia and New York, England attracted Irish Catholic loyalties; this was regarded by local bishops as meddling and increased England's unpopularity with the hierarchy.

During 1822 England created a seminary, where he did much of the training of priests himself. He also started publishing the *United States Catholic Miscellany* (1822-1861), the first distinctly Catholic paper in America, which sought to defend the faith against outside attacks, explain Catholic doctrine, and convey internal Church news. It stands as his greatest achievement, even though episcopal jealousies kept it from becoming a national journal.

Through the *Miscellany* and his numerous controversies, and as a preacher and speaker, England became nationally famous. In 1826, as the first Catholic to address a joint session of the U.S. Congress, he spoke for 2 hours on Catholic beliefs. Yet his anticipated appointment to a more prestigious diocese never materialized. Meanwhile, partly because of his extended absences from the diocese, his constituency failed to enlarge. A steady burden of debts and growing fatigue led to prolonged illness; he died on April 11, 1842.

Further Reading

The standard source is a critical edition of England's works, *The Works of the Right Reverend John England, First Bishop of Charleston,* edited by Sebastian G. Messmer, Archbishop of Milwaukee (7 vols., 1908). Peter Guilday, *The Life and Times of John England, First Bishop of Charleston, 1786-1842* (2 vols., 1927), remains the authoritative biography. See also Dorothy Grant, *John England* (1949). For background see Thomas T. McAvoy, *A History of the Catholic Church in the United States* (1969). □

Ennin

Ennin (794-864) was a Japanese monk who founded the Sammon branch of the Tendai sect. He studied Esoteric Buddhism in T'ang China.

The family name of Ennin was Mibu, and he was born in the Tsuga district of Shimotsuke Province (modern Tochigi Prefecture). Becoming a disciple of Saicho, the founder of the Tendai sect in Japan, Ennin led a rather colorless life as a monk and teacher at the Enryakuji (another name for this temple was Sammon). He was sent to China for study in 838. His *Nyuto Gubo Junreiki* (Record of the Pilgrimage to China in Search of the Holy Law) is full of fascinating details of his adventures, from the time he sailed from Japan until his return in 847.

At first unable to obtain the necessary Chinese authorization to visit either of China's two most important Buddhist centers on Mt. Wu-t'ai and Mt. T'ien-t'ai, Ennin later managed to secure the help of an influential general to reach Mt. Wu-t'ai and other holy sites. Ennin returned to Japan after extensive study with the masters of each of the Tendai disciplines.

Upon his return to Mt. Hiei, the Emperor conferred upon Ennin the rank of *daihosshi* (great monk). Ennin then organized study of the two Mandalas, initiated Esoteric baptism, and promoted other branches of Esoteric learning. He taught the invocation of Buddha's name (*nembutsu*), which he had heard on Mt. Wu-t'ai and which was to become in some of the popular sects an all-sufficient means of gaining salvation, though for Ennin it appeared to be of less importance than Esoteric learning.

Ennin stayed on Mt. Hiei as *zasu* (chief abbot) for more than 20 years, and during his ministry he founded the monastery called Onjoji (more usually known as Miidera) at the foot of Mt. Hiei on the shore of Lake Biwa. A measure of Ennin's success is the fact that the bestowal by the court in 866 of the posthumous title of Jikaku Daishi on him and that of Dengyo Daishi on his master Saicho marks the beginning of the custom of posthumous titles in Japan.

Further Reading

There is a brief discussion of Ennin's diary describing the hazards of his trip to T'ang China and the introduction of Esoteric cults to Japan in Edwin O. Reischauer and John K. Fairbank, *East Asia: The Great Tradition* (1960). A cogent discussion of the spread of Esoteric Buddhism in Japan is in Ryusaku Tsunoda and others, *Sources of Japanese Tradition* (1958). For a brief discussion of Ennin's role in the development of the Heian Society see George B. Sansom, *A History of Japan* (3 vols., 1958-1963). ☐

Quintus Ennius

Quintus Ennius (239-169 B.C.) was a Roman poet. Called the father of Latin poetry, he is most famous for his "Annales," a narrative poem relating the history of Rome.

Ennius was born at Rudiae in Calabria. He knew three languages or had, as he said, "three hearts": Oscan, his native tongue; Greek, in which he was educated, possibly at Tarentum; and Latin, which he learned as a centurion in the Roman army. While stationed at Sardinia during the Second Punic War, he met Cato the Elder, whom he taught Greek. Cato took him to Rome in 204 B.C.

At Rome, Ennius lived frugally on the Aventine. He supported himself at first by teaching Greek, then turned to adapting Greek tragedies and some comedies for the Roman stage, and he wrote poetry as well. He was a friend of prominent Romans of that time, especially Scipio Africanus and Marcus Fulvius Nobilior and his son Quintus, who gained for him Roman citizenship. Ennius knew the comic poet Caecilius Statius, and Pacuvius, the Roman dramatist, was his nephew.

Ennius was a very versatile poet although, according to Ovid, he possessed more genius than art. The remains of Ennius's works are fragmentary. Of the *Annales,* the most important part, some 600 lines or about one-fiftieth of the whole, remains. Some fragments are as long as 20 lines.

Naevius had written a historical epic before Ennius, but the special claim to greatness of his *Annales* is its meter, the hexameter. Henceforth, much of the greatest Latin poetry would use this meter. The poet's hexameters seem crude and clumsy beside Virgil's, often being heavily spondaic, ignoring caesuras and elisions, and carrying alliteration and assonance to extremes. Nevertheless, they can at times rise to a rugged and powerful dignity.

Euripides was a favorite model for Ennius in his adaptations of Greek tragedy. Of the 22 titles of plays known to be his, 3 are from extant tragedies of Euripides. Fragments of his tragedies number about 400 lines.

As a writer of comedy, Ennius was evidently less successful, for only two titles are known. Lesser works include *Satires* (Latin *satura,* medley), a work in varying meters on different topics, including criticism of morals and politics, and the first work of its kind; *Epigrams; Hedyphagetica,* or *The Art of Dining; Epicharmus,* a didactic poem on nature; and *Euhemerus,* a rationalization of Greek mythology.

Ennius's contribution to Roman culture was twofold. First, by adapting Greek tragedies he made Greek ideas current at Rome; and second, he had a direct influence on subsequent writers.

Ennius was of a convivial nature if Horace, who said he always composed in his cups, and Jerome, who said he died of gout, can be believed. He was writing until his death, and his version of the play *Thyestes* was produced the year he died.

Further Reading

A standard reference work on Ennius is *The Tragedies of Ennius: The Fragments,* edited by H. D. Jocelyn (1967), a comprehensive volume with a Latin text, full explanatory introduction, and extensive interpretative commentary. For more information on Ennius and his place in Latin literature see H. J. Rose, *A Handbook of Latin Literature* (1936; 3d ed. with a new bibliography, 1961), and Moses Hadas, *A History of Latin Literature* (1952). ☐

James Ensor

The Belgian painter and graphic artist James Ensor (1860-1949) populated his works with masks, skeletons, and grotesque images of humanity. A sense of existential anxiety dominates his fantastic personal visions.

was born at Ostend, on Friday, April 13, 1860, the day of Venus. At my birth Venus came toward me, smiling, and we looked into each other's eyes. She smelled pleasantly of salt water." In this imaginative recollection of his birth, James Ensor also described the duality of his art: on the one hand, the fantasies of a humanistically inclined imagination; on the other, the pleasures and terrors observed as a child living in a somber Belgian town whose existence was threatened by the same sea which was its source of life. Before beginning art studies at the Brussels Academy in 1877, Ensor painted the landscape surrounding Ostend— small houses isolated in vast light-flooded spaces. At the academy he began painting imaginative, rhetorical themes; under the influence of Dutch baroque painting and French impressionism he started using a free, divided brushstroke.

After 3 years of study Ensor returned to Ostend to the attic studio above his parents' souvenir shop; he spent the remainder of his uneventful life in Ostend. Using heavy, impasto pigments, he depicted the middle-class interiors in which his family lived. A somber, disquieting air of mystery surrounds the isolated figures as they drink tea, listen to piano music, or sit in melancholy introspection.

In 1883 Ensor became a founding member of the Belgian avant-garde artists' group Les XX, which brought works by contemporary French artists to Brussels and fought for increased artistic freedom from the dictates of official taste. From 1883 until 1887 Ensor painted little but evolved the overtly fantastic images with which his art is generally associated. The carnival masks of Ostend surrounding him in his studio made their appearance in *Scandalized Masks* (1883) and *Haunted Furniture* (1885; destroyed) and were joined by numerous skeletons bringing psychotic horror and terror into the bourgeois interiors. The life and temptations of Christ, depicted with the features of the artist, became the subject matter of numerous drawings in 1886; he developed these motifs in his first etchings that year. He created 133 prints, most of them during 1885, 1889, and 1895-1899.

In the etching *The Cathedral* (1886) Ensor first explored the theme of a mocking, destructive, roving mob. His most noted painting, the *Entry of Christ into Brussels* (1888), depicts raucous carnival crowds escorting Christ-Ensor into the city, which is decorated with Socialist banners and advertisements for mustard. The massive canvas is a caustic commentary on contemporary Belgian political, artistic, and social values. Even Les XX refused to exhibit it, and during the following years this group continued to reject his controversial work.

Probably Ensor's unique use of Christian imagery rather than his unorthodox painting technique with its impasto surfaces, slashing brushstrokes, and depersonalized images caused his works to be disclaimed by academic and "free" artists as well as by critics. By identifying himself with Christ, Ensor transformed accepted biblical imagery into personal observations on the universal conflicts of innocence and evil, as well as private attacks on his critics; opposition to his own symbolic art thereby became equated with the tortures of Christ's Passion.

Ensor's sole contact with the world around him was through the medium of his art, which reflected the imagery of his eccentric, morose broodings. Even still-life paintings and landscapes appear strangely menacing, imbued with the erotic, sadistic, and self-tormenting qualities of Ensor's narrative paintings. In the smaller and more private scale of his prints and drawings, his morbid demonology attained an even greater psychotic intensity as he condemned humanity and himself to the visual torments of his private inferno.

After 1900 Ensor's imagery became tamer, more a parody than a condemnation of society, perhaps a reflection of the esteem he finally gained in official art circles. To his achievements as a painter, he added those of a writer of essays and plays, reflecting the world of his paintings and prints. A greatly respected and honored citizen of Ostend, Ensor died on Nov. 19, 1949.

Further Reading

The most perceptive analysis of Ensor's work is Libby Tannenbaum, *James Ensor* (1951). A more subjective approach is by the poet Paul Haesaerts, *James Ensor* (1957; trans. 1959), which offers numerous color reproductions. For background information see Bernard S. Meyers, *The German Expressionists: A Generation in Revolt* (1957; concise ed. 1963), and Peter Selz, *German Expressionist Painting* (1957).

Additional Sources

Ensor, James, *Ensor,* New York: G. Braziller, 1976.
Gindertael, Roger van, *Ensor,* Boston: New York Graphic Society, 1975.
Janssens, Jacques., *James Ensor,* New York: Crown Publishers, 1978.
Lesko, Diane, *James Ensor, the creative years,* Princeton, N.J.: Princeton University Press, 1985. □

Enver Pasha

The Turkish soldier Enver Pasha (1881-1922) was the dominant member of the Young Turk triumvirate ruling the Ottoman Empire during World War I.

On Nov. 23, 1881, Enver Pasha was born of a Turkish father, a bridge keeper in the Black Sea town of Apana, and an Albanian mother. Joining the military, he was posted as a subaltern to Salonika, where he joined a secret antigovernment group. He rose rapidly in the public eye when, in the spring of 1908, he defied Sultan Abdul Hamid II and fled with fellow rebel officers into the Macedonian hills. Their demand was for restoration of the 1876 Constitution, suspended since 1877. Always action-minded, always alert to the dramatic, he enjoyed his activities as a member of the liberal Committee of Union and Progress, the "Young Turks," particularly after the 3d Army Corps threatened to march on Istanbul in July and forced Abdul Hamid to restore the constitution.

The Young Turks established a government under Mahmud Shevket but were nearly overthrown on April 14,

1909. Enver participated in both movements and then returned to Berlin, where he had been serving as military attaché. He was awed by Prussian militarism and left in 1911 to join in the Turkish defense of Benghazi against the Italians. He detailed this experience in *Tripoli* (1918).

Returning to Istanbul, Enver became chief of staff of the 10th Army Corps, which he led into the Second Balkan War in a futile landing attempt on the Gallipoli Peninsula in February 1913; in July, Enver reoccupied Edirne.

Between the wars Enver participated in the shooting of the war minister, Nazim Pasha, and the ouster of the pro-British grand vizier, Kiamil Pasha. In January 1913 the Young Turks resumed control of the government. The assassination of their premier, Mahmud Shevket, in June intensified their aggressiveness. A major purge followed, with Enver dismissing over 1,200 officers in one day alone. By Jan. 13, 1914, Enver had made himself minister of war, a strategic position from which he influenced his associates into an alliance with Germany signed secretly on August 2. Subsequently he approved the German bombardment of Odessa and Sevastopol, which precipitated the Ottoman Empire's entry into World War I.

During the winter of 1914/1915 Enver Pasha, leading a Turkish army in the Caucasus, suffered a disastrous defeat. He compounded this bloody record with acquiescence in the forced deportation and consequent death of innumerable Armenians evacuated from the frontier area.

Enver subsequently became the dominant personality in the government, but his aloofness and vanity alienated

him from other Young Turks. When the Ottoman Empire collapsed, he fled to Germany and later to Russia. Condemned to death in Istanbul, he died leading an anti-Bolshevik insurrection among the Central Asian Turks around Bukhara on Aug. 4, 1922.

Further Reading

Ernest E. Ramsaur, *The Young Turks: Prelude to the Revolution of 1908* (1957), is an excellent source on Enver Pasha. Enver Pasha's later career is recounted in detail in Ulrich Trumpener, *Germany and the Ottoman Empire, 1914-1918* (1968). Also useful is Frank G. Weber, *Eagles on the Crescent: Germany, Austria, and the Diplomacy of the Turkish Alliance, 1914-1918* (1970). □

Epaminondas

Epaminondas (ca. 425-362 B.C.) was a Theban general and statesman who overthrew Sparta and whose original battle tactics revolutionized ancient warfare.

Trained in Pythagorean philosophy, Epaminondas was said to be unselfish, devout, and generous, and he certainly had a more intellectual approach to war and politics than most Thebans. He was a friend of Pelopidas, the leader of a group of exiles, who liberated Thebes from Sparta in 379 B.C., and thereafter he played a leading part in the creation of the democratic League of Boeotian States.

As a League delegate at a peace conference in Sparta in 371, Epaminondas insisted upon full recognition of the League. Sparta refused and its army moved from Phocis to disband the League. Isolated and outnumbered, the Boeotians were thought to be helpless against the invincible Spartans, but Epaminondas used a new tactic. Advancing with an oblique line, of which the weak right was delayed and the massive left was advanced, he struck at the enemy's strongest point with a series of blows—first with cavalry, then with elite infantry, and finally with the entire massed infantry. This victory encouraged federalism in central Greece, where many states formed a coalition with Boeotian leadership in war.

From 370 to 368 Epaminondas campaigned in the Peloponnesus, ravaging Sparta's territory, liberating Messenia, and building Megalopolis as capital of the Arcadian League. Here, too, federal systems were instituted and flourished because Epaminondas tolerated existing ideologies within each League. But the Boeotians soon imposed democracy and revealed imperialist ambitions. Epaminondas lost favor and was serving in the ranks in 367, when a crisis again raised him to a position of command.

In the attempt to force Boeotian supremacy on the Grecian states, Epaminondas was entrusted with two expeditions. In 363 he sailed with 100 newly built triremes to Byzantium and back, shaking Athens's confidence in its

pictetus was born a slave in Hierapolis, Asia Minor. Early in life he was brought to Rome and, while still a slave, was sent by his master Epaphroditus (probably the famous freedman of Nero) to study under the Stoic philosopher Gaius Musonius Rufus. Some time after the death of Nero (68) Epictetus was freed. He had a physical disability from an early age, and one ancient source suggests that this was the result of brutal treatment received while he was a slave.

Perhaps as a result of criticizing the tyranny of Emperor Domitian, Epictetus along with other philosophers was expelled by the Emperor, probably in 89. He settled in the town of Nicopolis in Epirus, and soon people from all over the Roman world were coming to hear him. One of these was apparently Emperor Hadrian, another was the young Arrian, the future historian.

Epictetus seems to have lived in great simplicity and abstemiousness. Whether he ever married is in doubt; one late source says he married in old age so as to have help in bringing up a child whom its parents were about to abandon.

Philosophical Teachings

Though one source says that Epictetus wrote a good deal, nothing is extant; instead there are four books of *Discourses,* written by Arrian from lecture notes, and a synoptic version of his basic teaching, called the *Manual,* also written by Arrian.

Epictetus's philosophical and religious beliefs, drawn from Musonius Rufus, are a combination of Stoicism and Cynicism. Man can achieve complete freedom (specifically from pain, fear, and passion) if he confines his desires (positive and negative) to areas laid down by nature and by what lies within his power. Anything outside of these limits should be "indifferent" and of no concern. The world is under the control of providence, and the good man will consequently acquiesce in all events beyond his control. Within the specific realm of "what is in his power," man is free in an unqualified sense and completely responsible for his own moral progress or regress. Any harm done to his mind, or real self—the body is of negligible importance—is self-inflicted; in this sense he is the master of his fate.

invulnerability and encouraging its subjects to revolt. In 362 he invaded the Peloponnesus, moving large forces with remarkable speed and dexterity. At Mantinea he faced the combined forces of Sparta, Athens, Elis, Achaea, and Mantinea in a strong position in a plain flanked by hills. Forced into a frontal attack, Epaminondas maneuvered until noon, when the enemy thought an attack unlikely. Masked by clouds of dust raised by his cavalry, his massed infantry delivered a sudden attack against the enemy's strongest troops deployed on the right. Meanwhile, a smaller force engaged the enemy's left wing. Victory was imminent, when Epaminondas fell mortally wounded.

Further Reading

Ancient sources on Epaminondas are Xenophon and Diodorus Siculus. Modern works which discuss him include *Botsford and Robinson's Hellenic History,* revised by Donald Kagan (1922; 5th ed. 1969); J. B. Bury and R. Meiggs, *A History of Greece* (3d ed., 1952); and Nicholas G. L. Hammond, *A History of Greece to 322 B.C.* (1959; 2d ed. 1967). □

Further Reading

Percy E. Matheson edited and translated, as well as wrote the introduction for, *Epictetus: The Discourses and Manual* (trans., 2 vols., 1916). There is a short biography of Epictetus in Eduard Zeller, *Outlines of the History of Greek Philosophy* (1883; trans. 1890; 13th rev. ed. 1931). For the philosophical background see Ludwig Edelstein, *The Meaning of Stoicism* (1966). □

Epictetus

Epictetus (ca. 50-ca. 135) was a Greek philosopher who believed that man should concern himself only with what he can control and suffer what he cannot influence.

Epicurus

Epicurus (ca. 342-270 B.C.) was a Greek philosopher and the founder of Epicureanism. He was the first of

the overt therapy philosophers and an upholder of the atomic theory.

Epicurus was born either in Samos or in Athens. He spent his youth in the Athenian colony of Samos, and at the age of 18 he made his way to Athens. In the upheaval resulting from the death of Alexander the Great (323 B.C.), the Athenian colonists, including Epicurus's father, Neocles, were driven out of Samos. Epicurus rejoined his father in Colophon and spent the next several years in Colophon, Lampsacus, and Mytilene, gathering disciples to his own emerging philosophical doctrines

About 307/306 Epicurus returned to Athens, and at first, according to Diogenes Laertius, seems to have spent some time with other professional philosophers in the pursuit of philosophy. Soon, however, he founded his own school, which has since borne his name. Epicurus was subject, even in his own lifetime, to opprobrious comment; among other things he was accused of gluttony, womanizing, and unwarranted contempt for other philosophers, antecedent and contemporary. Given the strength of his own convictions, the latter accusation may have had substance; all evidence we have suggests that Epicurus spoke his mind. The other accusations appear to be groundless. He was physically infirm and lived a life of abstemiousness, if not of complete asceticism. He was characterized by his love for his parents, his generosity to his brothers, and his gentleness toward his slaves. He was also respectful to the gods, no doubt on the grounds that they were the example of that

freedom from physical pain and mental tranquility that he saw as the supreme human goal.

Written Works

Epicurus's output was very large; Diogenes Laertius, his principal biographer, lists 40 works, one of them, *On Nature,* comprising 37 books. All that has survived is what seems to be an abridged version of Epicurus's philosophy in the form of three letters, a few fragments, and a collection of his more important sayings entitled *Major Opinions.* The latter, however, is likely a compendium put together by disciples, as is undoubtedly the case with the *Senteniae Vaticanae,* discovered in the 19th century. The *Letter to Herodotus* deals with Epicurus's physics and his theory of knowledge and perception. The *Letter to Pythocles* deals with his far less confident opinions on astronomy and meteorology. And the *Letter to Menoeceus* treats his theory of conduct.

Atomic Theory

All that exists, Epicurus says, consists of matter, void, and their accidents, or properties. The universe is infinite in time and space and contains an infinite number of eternally moving indestructible elements called "atoms." The number of types of atom is, he says, "inconceivably large," and there is an infinite number of each type. The atoms are not further splittable, though they are logically divisible into "minimal parts," which serve as integral units of measurement in the distinguishing of different sizes of atoms. The atoms are like sense objects in possessing mass, size, and shape.

"Creation from nothing" and "substantial" change are meaningless terms. Any change in the universe is reducible to alteration of position. Atoms are invisible, by definition; and their motions, be it in the "free fall" of the void, or from mutual collision, or in the "vibration" within a compound body, are of equal velocity, which he equates with the "speed of thought." In this respect size, mass, and other factors are irrelevant. In the matter of speed the only difference between atoms is that, thanks to the deflections consequent upon collisions, the net distance covered by one atom will differ from that covered by another.

In the infinite universe there is an infinite number of earth systems similar to our own, constantly waxing and waning. These earth systems are of various shapes, but in each instance the "earth" is a plane, like our own. "Up" and "down" are apparently meaningful terms to Epicurus, even in an infinite universe; what is "up" for our earth system is "down" for the one immediately "above" us. The universe is an infinity of space "up" and an infinity of space "down."

The question of the first collision of atoms is not discussed in the extant works of Epicurus. The problem is an acute one, since atoms falling eternally "down" at uniform speed will never meet, and the organized world described by Epicurus becomes an impossibility. It seems clear from other ancient sources that Epicurus did in fact postulate a "swerve" of one or more atoms as the initial or eternally recurring source of the collisions that are so crucial to his physical theory.

Whether Epicurus also postulated the existence of such a swerve of one or more soul atoms, early on in life, to account for man's free will is a matter for current conjecture. What we are sure of is that, by apparent contrast with Democritus, Epicurus was an atomist who was also profoundly antideterminist.

Sensations, Feelings, and Concepts

The criteria for judging questions of truth content and moral worth are primitive sensations, primitive feelings, and "concepts" (which ultimately reduce to the first two). A life lived in accord with these will achieve the maximal human good—freedom from bodily pain and freedom from mental anxiety. In the matter of sense perception, truth is attained by direct contact with the shape and qualities of an object, either by physical contact or by apprehension of the "idols" incessantly streaming off all physical subjects and, at least for a time, retaining their form and color.

Error lies in the hasty interposition of opinion into this scheme of things, without waiting for the corroboration of further sense evidence. Concepts, being constructs of sense data and feelings, are meaningful and helpful as criteria to the degree that they stem directly from sense data and feelings, without the interposition of hasty opinion. Among such concepts are the two crucial ones of atoms and void, the existence of neither of which is amenable to empirical demonstration.

Views on the Gods, the Soul, and Death

A crucial exception to all this is constituted by the "idols" of the gods. These penetrate the mind directly to form our concepts, without previously impinging upon the sense organs or influencing our feelings. Our certitude of the gods' *existence* stems from the clarity of our mental perception of the fact; men's view of their *nature,* however, says Epicurus, is usually ridiculous—thanks again to the interposition of groundless opinion into the matter. The gods live eternal lives of contentment in the void of the universe and have no concern with men. There are no rewards or punishments after death; death is extinction. *Dying* might reasonably—though mistakenly, he feels— seem a cause for fear; to fear *death* itself, however, is absurd, since it brings nothing in its wake.

This cardinal tenet about the nature of the gods and death is bound up with Epicurus's views on the soul. In spite of his physical theory, he is still (perhaps surprisingly) a dualist in matters concerning the mind and the body. Soul or mind, however, he sees as completely material; it is composed of very small, fine, round atoms. It gives sensation to the body and in turn needs the receptacle of the body to exercise its function of sensing. The body, at the same time, is given a degree of sensation by the soul. But neither soul nor body can sense apart; hence the fact that their dissolution at death is immediate annihilation for the whole person.

Epicurus therefore suggests that the end of human life should be pleasure—defining it as freedom from physical and mental pain. The positive delights that other men call "pleasure" are merely *variations* on the true, basic, contentment man needs and can easily achieve; they in no sense *increase* his happiness. A good life is guided by practical wisdom, a sense of responsibility for our decision making, self-sufficiency, and the careful application of the hedonistic calculus. This necessarily involves freedom from all fear and knowledge of the limits of our desires. Once we see that only "necessary" and nonharmful desires need be assuaged, we have removed a major obstacle to the achieving of the plenitude of human contentment.

Epicurus advocated (and practiced) a life of withdrawal from politics. The highest human communion was for him the company of friends. The degree of happiness these gave him is eloquently attested to in a last letter to Idomeneus: "On this truly happy day of my life, as I am at the point of death, I write this to you. The disease in my bladder and stomach are pursuing their course, lacking nothing of their natural severity; but against all this is the joy in my heart at the recollection of my conversations with you."

Further Reading

For a fully annotated edition of Epicurus's extant works consult *Epicurus: The Extant Remains,* edited and translated by Cyril Bailey (1926). This book, while open to criticism on some matters of detail, is still the most reliable edition in English. Bailey's more discursive study, *The Greek Atomists and Epicurus* (1928), is also recommended. A book notable for the quality of its scholarship and the depth of its sympathy with Epicurus is A.-J. Festugière, *Epicurus and His Gods,* translated by C. W. Chilton (1955). For a sophisticated study of two basic problems in Epicurus see David J. Furley, *Two Studies in the Greek Atomists* (1967). Norman Wentworth De Witt, *Epicurus and His Philosophy* (1954), and Benjamin Farrington, *The Faith of Epicurus* (1967), should both be used with caution. See also George A. Panichas, *Epicurus* (1967). □

Abraham Epstein

Abraham Epstein (1892–1945) was an economist whose dedication and hard work for the underpriviledged led to the Social Security Act of 1935.

A pioneer of the American social-insurance movement, Abraham Epstein was born in Luban, near Pinsk, Russia, and came to the United States at the age of eighteen. He lived in New York City and worked at factory jobs for one and one-half years, until a friend got him a job teaching Hebrew in Pittsburgh, Pennsylvania. Soon after his arrival, he walked into an exclusive private boys' school, asked about enrollment, passed the entrance examination, and won a tuition scholarship to attend East Liberty Academy. Another scholarship enabled him to enter the University of Pittsburgh, where he received a B.S. in 1917. That same year he became an American citizen.

Commission on Old Age Pensions

Epstein continued to do graduate work in economics at the university and conducted a detailed survey of employment and housing conditions of Pittsburgh's black population. This study, *The Negro Migrant in Pittsburgh* (1918), won him offers of several university fellowships, but he instead took a position at the Pennsylvania Commission on Old Age Pensions. He remained there until 1927, securing the passage of a state-financed old-age-pension program in 1923, despite vigorous business opposition. The pension act was declared unconstitutional in 1924, and before the decision could be appealed, the commission had been disbanded.

Social Insurance

After leaving the commission, Epstein founded the American Association for Old Age Security in 1927, which changed its name to the American Association for Social Security in 1933. By 1927 he had published several books on aging and lectured widely for social welfare and unions. Epstein led one of the two dominant groups favoring social insurance in the 1930s: he advocated government-financed programs aimed at redistributing wealth and caring for the underprivileged. The other, more conservative group, led by John D. Andrews, favored private social-insurance programs as a means of preventing suffering and poverty. The two approaches came into conflict during the Depression: Andrews's "American plan" was adopted in Wisconsin in 1932, and Epstein's "European plan" won in the New York State legislature in 1935.

Social Security Act

A rift between Andrews and Epstein resulted in the Roosevelt administration's failure to consult Epstein on the drafting of the Social Security Act of 1935, a blow from which he never recovered. He criticized the Social Security Act for failing to provide for government contributions, for leaving unemployment compensation to the states, and for the large reserve fund it set up that reduced spending power. Many of his criticisms still plague the program today.

Further Reading

New York Times, May 3, 1942, p. 43. □

Sir Jacob Epstein

The American-born English sculptor Sir Jacob Epstein (1880-1959), known principally for his expressively modeled portrait busts, periodically returned to direct carving throughout his career, predominantly drawing on biblical themes.

Born on the East Side of New York City of Jewish immigrant parents, Jacob Epstein was a pupil of the academic sculptor George Grey Barnard at the Art Students League. Barnard's influence was a formative one, and Epstein's later slightly attenuated figurative style was reminiscent of his teacher's. While a student Epstein helped to support himself by contributing sketches to *Century Magazine;* he also illustrated Hutchins Hapgood's *The Spirit of the Ghetto* (1901). In 1902 Epstein left for Paris, where he continued his artistic education briefly at the Académie Julian and the École des Beaux-Arts. He remained in Paris until 1905, and his work of this period shows more than a passing reference to the work of Auguste Rodin, especially in the use of the fragmented figure. Several large programmatic schemes that Epstein worked on at this time, while suggestive of Rodin's ambitious *Gates of Hell,* stylistically drew upon the highly formalized Egyptian sculpture that Epstein saw in the Louvre.

Epstein moved to London in 1905 and subsequently became a British subject. His first significant work appeared in 1907, when he was commissioned to carve 18 figures for the British Medical Association Building in the Strand, London. Completed the following year, these pieces solidly established the young sculptor's reputation; thus began the many privately commissioned portraits, which continued throughout his career. However, Epstein was not content only with modeling portraits, and he simultaneously pursued his interest in direct carving, restricting his subject matter to the larger themes of mankind, a search for the primordial, archetypal image. In his carved works, especially those executed between 1910 and 1915, he addressed himself to cubist and futurist theories. About 1910 Epstein became keenly interested in African sculpture and amassed one of the finest collections of African art in Great Britain. He continued his pursuit of mastering the form language of other cultures and was drawn particularly to the sculpture of Egypt, Assyria, and pre-Columbian America. His memorial for the tomb of Oscar Wilde (1912) in the Père Lachaise cemetery, Paris, reflects that interest in stylized relief carving, which departed radically from the already established esthetic of Rodin.

On his return to London, Epstein became affiliated with two avant-garde groups of artists: the London Group and the Vorticists. From 1913 to 1915 he worked almost exclusively in a highly abstract manner, carving many of his pieces in flenite. The noted critic T. E. Hulme referred to the work of this period as the seeds of a new, constructive geometric art. Epstein's *Rock Drill* (1913) was his most ambitious statement of this prewar period. By 1915 he had returned to his modeled portraits, and it was not until a decade later that he again turned his chisel to the stone. Epstein's work from 1915 until his death in London in 1959 falls primarily into two categories: the commissioned portraits and the larger carvings. His portraits are characterized by a vigorously modeled, expressionistic surface, the most representative of which are the *Self-portrait with a Beard* (1918), *Joseph Conrad* (1924), and *Haile Selassie* (1936). Although his clientele included the famous men of his time, some of his most successful pieces in bronze are the portraits of his immediate family and the various models who sat for him. Epstein's carvings were the more controversial body of his work, more innovative and abstract than his portraits. They reflect an entirely different set of concerns, an attempt to continue the themes of the Hebraic-Christian tradition into the form language of 20th-century sculpture. His most representative works in this medium are *Rima* (1924), the W. H. Hudson memorial in the bird sanctuary in Hyde Park, London; *Day* and *Night* (1929) for St. James's Underground Station, London; and *Lazarus* (1948) for New College, Oxford. His later commissions, the *Cavendish Square Madonna and Child* (1950) at the Convent of the Holy Child, London, *Social Consciousness* (1951), the Llandaff Cathedral *Christ in Majesty* (1955), and *St. Michael and the Devil* for the new Coventry Cathedral (1958), although executed in bronze, reflect as well those continuing themes first stated in his carvings.

Further Reading

The most complete publication on Epstein's sculpture, including a *catalogue raisonné* of his work, is Richard Buckle, *Jacob Epstein, Sculptor* (1963). Statements by the artist on his work can be found in *Epstein: An Autobiography* (1955), an extended and revised edition of *Let There Be Sculpture* (1940). An excellent account of his early work appears in *The Sculptor Speaks* (1931), written by Epstein and Arnold Haskell. Bernard van Dieren, *Epstein* (1920), provides useful critical material and one of the best assessments of the sources for Epstein's style.

Additional Sources

Epstein, Jacob, Sir, *Epstein, an autobiography*, New York: Arno Press, 1975.
Gardiner, Stephen, *Epstein, artist against the establishment*, London: M. Joseph, 1992. □

Olaudah Equiano

Olaudah Equiano (1745-ca. 1801) was an African slave, freedman, and author who wrote the first outstanding autobiography in slave narrative literature.

Olaudah Equiano was born at Essaka, an Ibo village (not now known) in the Benin Province of present-day Nigeria. At age 11 he was kidnaped into domestic slavery. After short service in African households he was sold to British slavers in 1756 and sent to Barbados in the West Indies. Transshipped immediately to Virginia, Olaudah, who said his African name meant "vicissitude" or "fortune," became the personal slave of Lt. Michael Henry Pascal of the Royal Navy, who gave him his second name, Gustavus Vassa.

Thus spared the fate of plantation laborer, Equiano spent the next 30 years as servant, barber, seaman, and trader, traveling widely to such varied places as Turkey, the Arctic, Honduras, North America, and London. In the process he became a literate and articulate observer of the slave trade, slavery, and his own condition.

After service in the Seven Years War, including the siege of Louisburg on Cape Breton Island and the capture of Belle Isle, Lt. Pascal surprisingly disappointed Equiano's expectation of freedom and sent him back to the West Indies for resale in 1763. Equiano's new master, a Quaker merchant of Montserrat and Philadelphia named Robert King, gave him both recognition for his abilities and the opportunity for manumission. Employed as a clerk and captain's assistant on vessels trading in the islands and carrying slaves to the American colonies, Equiano was allowed to trade on his own account and bought his freedom in 1766 for £40, the price King had paid for him. Equiano went to London, where he qualified as a barber and musician and improved his education before taking to the sea again as a free servant in 1768.

Equiano had been baptized as a youth in 1759, but Christian religion did not deeply influence his life until during or just after participating in an Arctic expedition in search of the Northeast Passage in 1773 which nearly ended in disaster. At that time he experienced profound depression and soul-searching that resulted in his conversion to Evangelicalism in 1774. Living in London again after 1777, he petitioned the bishop of London to ordain him a missionary for service in Africa, but he failed.

Subsequently Equiano rose to prominence in London's society of free blacks, became a close friend of Ottobah Cugoano, and associated with the British humanitarians opposed to the Atlantic slave trade. In 1783, for example, he

few genuine personal recollections of the slave trade as seen by the victims themselves (Philip Curtin, 1967), Equiano's account is especially interesting in two respects: first, for its extensive recollections of the author's African childhood and his retention of an African point of view in judging experience and, second, for its rational economic argument against the slave trade. Not only did he argue the moral transgressions of the trade but also its economic insanity. On the basis of demographic projections he urged the potential of legitimate commerce for British manufactures in Africa as an economic alternative to the trade in lives. This was a view shared with Cugoano's book, and it figured prominently in the ideological preparation for abolition.

Despite his sense of mission, Equiano was destined never to return to Africa. He lectured extensively in Britain against the slave trade during the 1790s and married an English girl, Susan (or Susanne) Cullen of Ely, in April 1792. He is believed to have died in London in 1801.

Further Reading

Equiano's own *The Interesting Narrative of the Life of O. Equiano, or G. Vassa, the African* was first published in two volumes in London, 1789, with eight new editions to 1795 and several more thereafter. Recently it has appeared in an abridged edition by Paul Edwards, *Equiano's Travels: His Autobiography* (1967), and in full in Arna Bontemps, ed., *Great Slave Narratives* (1969), with a useful literary introduction by the editor.

Equiano's place in the intellectual history of the slave trade, and African European relations generally, is discussed in Philip Curtin's introduction to his collection, *Africa Remembered: Narratives by West Africans from the Era of the Slave Trade* (1967), which contains Equiano's description of his African homeland with commentary by G. I. Jones. Robert W. July, *The Origins of Modern African Thought: Its Development in Western Africa during the Nineteenth and Twentieth Centuries* (1967), also discusses Equiano's career and the importance of his book. Christopher Fyfe, *A History of Sierra Leone* (1962; rev. ed. 1963), narrates Equiano's involvement in the Sierra Leone settlement scheme, while Christopher Fyfe, ed., *Sierra Leone Inheritance* (1964), uses a letter of Equiano to Lord Hawkesbury in 1788 to exemplify the economic argument against the slave trade. □

brought the famous case of the ship *Zong* to Granville Sharp's attention. Sharp made it a cause célèbre in the parliamentary battle for abolition. One hundred thirty-two sick and shackled slaves had been thrown overboard alive and then claimed for cargo insurance. In this connection also, late in 1786 Equiano was appointed by Charles Middleton, the comptroller of the navy, to be commissary steward of Granville Sharp's subsidized expedition to repatriate London's "Poor Blacks" in Sierra Leone. However, the scheme was beset with delays and mismanagement, and in a letter which his friend Cugoano published in London before their departure, Equiano charged his superior, Joseph Irwin, with theft of stores and ill treatment of the blacks. Middleton supported Equiano, but Irwin and several colleagues, acting through London businessmen interested in the venture, engineered his dismissal by Treasury authorities.

Equiano's famous autobiography *The Interesting Narrative of the Life of O. Equiano, or G. Vassa, the African* was then written in 1787-1788 partly to vindicate his role in the Sierra Leone affair, as well as to recount his exemplary rise from slavery to freedom and to argue the case for abolition of the slave trade. Although one critic (G. I. Jones, 1967) has doubted Equiano's sole authorship because of its stylistic felicities, there is little doubt that the work was essentially his own. Unlike Ottobah Cugoano's sophisticated Bible-based discourse, Equiano's is an account of action in which the realities and iniquities of slavery and the trade emerge eloquently in the telling of his own story. Besides its importance as "the first truly notable book in the genre" of slave narratives (Arna Bontemps, 1969) and its value as one of the

Erasistratus

Erasistratus (304 BC-250 BC) is best known for his works on human cadavers and his knowledge of the human body. He is considered the father of physiology.

Erasistratus, considered the father of physiology, was born on the island of Chios in ancient Greece, to a medical family. His father and brother were doctors, and his mother was the sister of a doctor. He studied medicine in Athens and then, around 280 B.C., enrolled in the University of Cos, a center of the medical school of Praxagoras. Erasistratus then moved to Alexandria, where he taught and practiced medicine, continuing the work of

Herophilus. In his later years, he retired from medical practice and joined the Alexandrian museum, where he devoted himself to research.

Although Erasistratus wrote extensively in a number of medical fields, none of his works survive. He is best known for his observations based on his numerous dissections of human cadavers (and, it was rumored, his vivisections of criminals, a practice allowed by the Ptolemy rulers). Erasistratus accurately described the structure of the brain, including the cavities and membranes, and made a distinction between its *cerebrum* and *cerebellum* (larger and smaller parts). He viewed the brain, not the heart, as the seat of intelligence. By comparing the brains of humans and other animals, Erasistratus rightly concluded that a greater number of brain convolutions resulted in greater intelligence. He also accurately described the structure and function of the gastric (stomach) muscles, and observed the difference between motor and sensory nerves. Erasistratus promoted hygiene, diet, and exercise in medical care.

In his understanding of the heart and blood vessels, Erasistratus came very close to working out the circulation of the blood (not actually discovered until William Harvey in the seventeenth century A.D.), but he made some crucial errors. Erasistratus understood that the heart served as a pump, thereby dilating the arteries, and he found and explained the functioning of the heart valves. He theorized that the arteries and veins both spread from the heart, dividing finally into extremely fine capillaries that were invisible to the eye. However, he believed that the liver formed blood and carried it to the right side of the heart, which pumped it into the lungs and from there to the rest of the body's organs. He also believed that pneumapneuma, a vital spirit, was drawn in through the lungs to the left side of the heart, which then pumped the pneuma through the arteries to the rest of the body. The nerves, according to Erasistratus, carried another form of pneuma, animal spirit.

After Erasistratus, anatomical research through dissection ended, due to the pressure of public opinion. Egyptians believed in the need of an intact body for the afterlife—hence mummification. Real anatomical studies were not resumed until the thirteenth century. □

Desiderius Erasmus

The Dutch scholar Desiderius Erasmus (1466-1536) was the dominant figure of the early-16th-century humanist movement. The intellectual arbiter during the last years of Christian unity, he remains one of European culture's most controversial giants.

The evidence about the youth and adolescence of Erasmus is hard to evaluate. A major source of knowledge is autobiographical, a product of his middle age when international fame made him most sensitive about his illegitimate birth at Rotterdam, probably in October 1466, the second son of a priest, Roger Gerard, and a physician's daughter. School life, rather than a household environment, shaped Erasmus from his fifth year onward. He later disparaged the effort of his teachers and the guardians established after the parents' deaths about 1484; in fact, his father provided Erasmus a solid education with the Brethren of the Common Life from 1475 to 1484. From this religious community, which for a century had deflected education in the Low Countries from scholastic rigidity and had relieved its discipline of the strictest monastic severity, Erasmus obtained a firm grounding in classical Latin and an appreciation of a spirit of Christianity beyond its doctrinal basis.

From Steyn to Cambridge

His unpromising birth and his guardians' business sense gave the monastic cloister an obvious, if grim, place in Erasmus' future. He entered the Augustinian monastery at Steyn in 1487 and took monastic vows in 1488; he was ordained a priest in 1492. His reading in classical literature and Christian sources matured, but Erasmus found Steyn crude and rustic. Scholarship offered the first step out, when the bishop of Cambrai employed Erasmus as his secretary in 1493 and rewarded his work with a stipend for study at Paris in 1495.

Paris provided a diverse environment which Erasmus cultivated between recalls to the Low Countries in the late 1490s. He moved in literary circles, writing poetry and dedications and experimenting with styles of educational writing which bore fruit in the later publications *Adagia* and

Colloquia. He sought students and patrons until, in 1499, his student Lord Mountjoy took him to England.

The visit was decisive to Erasmus. English humanists were studying Scripture and the early Church fathers and advocating reform of the Church and the educational process that served it. Friendships with John Colet, Sir Thomas More, and others restored Erasmus' interest in devotional studies and turned him to the Greek language as the key for his research. *Enchiridion militis Christiani* (*Handbook of the Militant Christian,* published 1503, though begun a decade before) outlined conduct which would foster man's spiritual capacities and usher in the ethics and piety of what Erasmus' group called the "philosophy of Christ." It gave these scholars an international audience and steady patronage among educated laymen.

In 1506 Erasmus fulfilled a long-standing ambition by traveling to Italy. He watched Pope Julius II conquer Bologna that year; the sharpest edge of his wit can be discerned in a tract, *Julius exclusus* (published anonymously in 1517; he never admitted authorship), in which St. Peter bars Julius from heaven and scathingly damns his wars and treasure. Erasmus polished his Greek in Italy and formed, with Aldus Manutius's press in Venice, the first of the crucial links to publishing enterprises that secured his financial and professional independence.

Back in England by 1509, disillusioned with the Church's wars and its clergy's shortcomings, Erasmus wrote *Encomium moriae* (*The Praise of Folly*), a satiric exposition of the obstacles restricting the fulfillment of Christ's teaching. Though not formally released from monastic vows until 1517, Erasmus was now effectively freed of Steyn by his mounting reputation. He held a professorship at Cambridge (1511-1514) and settled into the vocation for which his study and travel had prepared him.

Major Publications

Erasmus' *Novum instrumentum,* a heavily annotated edition of the New Testament placing texts in Greek and revised Latin side by side, appeared in 1516 from the Basel press of Johannes Froben. As the first published Greek text and a basis for further clarification of the New Testament, it was a landmark for scholars and reformers. It attuned educated Europeans more closely to Erasmus' early works, which were now widely translated from the Latin of his originals, and paved the way for the literary and educational classics of the Christian humanist fellowship.

Erasmus had now returned to the Continent to the manuscripts and printing houses on which his massive efforts relied. Froben published his nine-volume edition of St. Jerome in 1516 and in the next 2 decades issued Erasmus' comprehensive editions of early Christian authors, including St. Cyprian (1520), St. Ambrose (1527), and St. Augustine (1529); he also circulated commentaries and treatises on divinity and revised editions of the literary works.

Another dimension to Erasmus' writing appeared in 1516, while he briefly served the future emperor Charles V as councilor. Following current humanist practice, he prepared a guide for educating princes to rule justly, *Institutio principis Christiani,* and in 1517 composed *Querela pacis* (*The Complaint of Peace*), condemning war as an instrument of tyranny and warning temporal rulers to fulfil their obligation to preserve Christian harmony. Erasmus thus demonstrated, before Luther's impact was clear, his sensitivity to Europe's impending fragmentation.

Erasmus and Reformation Europe

Erasmus' influence could not realize the vision of Christian renovation expressed in his New Testament dedication and preface, which urged Pope Leo X to make Rome the center of reform and to make Christ's words available to every plowboy in the field. Following Luther's lead, many intellectuals, impatient for action, rejected humanism's "halfway house" and used presses and pulpits to move Europe's masses as Erasmus never had. The Erasmians' style of persuasion was countered by simpler, vernacular tracts on theology, the Sacraments, and Church structure, sometimes linked with social and political issues. In 1516 Erasmus had foreseen a golden age, but by 1521, dismayed by the partisan tone and substance of the reformers' appeals, he was calling his own times the worst since Christianity began.

Erasmus' eventual response, after an important exchange with Luther in 1524-1525 about the role of human will in salvation to which he contributed *De libero arbitrio* (*On the Freedom of the Will*), was a gradual disengagement from the disputing theologians and their secular sponsors. He avoided Europe's major courts and capitals, and he left congenial intellectual homes in Catholic Louvain in 1521 and Protestant Basel in 1529, when denominational advocacy invaded their scholarship and governance. Printing presses continued to hold his audience: they were the lifelines of this complex man, rootless at birth, whose temperament, circumstances, and dislike of permanent commitments consistently separated him from friends and institutions eager to harness his talents.

He died on July 12, 1536. The embattled Catholic Church, which he never left, condemned some of Erasmus' work for its critical attitude and moderation against heretics, while much modern opinion based on Protestant, nationalist viewpoints has judged him harshly. But there is, with the ecumenical mood of current commentary, a revival of interest in, and sympathy for, Erasmus and his conviction that tolerance and rational persuasion must prevail through discordant times.

Further Reading

John P. Dolan, *The Essential Erasmus* (1964), offers an excellent selection of Erasmus' works with commentary, while Roland H. Bainton, *Erasmus of Christendom* (1969), is a fine biography which lists modern editions, translations, and critical scholarship. Important modern biographies are Margaret M. Phillips, *Erasmus and the Northern Renaissance* (1949), and Johan Huizinga, *Erasmus and the Age of Reformation* (1957). For the context of Erasmian ideas recent works include Eugene F. Rice, *The Renaissance Idea of Wisdom* (1958); Robert Pardee Adams, *The Better Part of Valor* (1962); and Heiko A. Oberman, *The Harvest of Medieval Theology* (1963). For historical background see Myron P. Gilmore, *The*

World of Humanism, 1453-1517 (1952), and Geoffrey R. Elton, *Reformation Europe, 1517-1559* (1963). □

Georges Henry Erasmus

Canadian Native American leader Georges Erasmus (born 1948) was an outspoken proponent of self-determination for the native peoples of Canada. He served as president of the Dene Nation and of the Indian Brotherhood of the Northwest Territories and later as vice-chief of the Assembly of First Nations, a national organization representing Canada's status Indians.

Georges Henry Erasmus was born August 8, 1948, at Fort Rae, Northwest Territories (NWT), Canada. His family moved to Yellowknife, NWT, when he was one year old; he was educated at the Catholic high school there. He was a member of the Dene, the Athapaskan-speaking peoples who have lived for centuries in the Mackenzie Valley and Barren Grounds of the NWT.

Erasmus has been described as "the personification of his people's demands for self-determination." As a charismatic leader with a talent for clear, impassioned oratory, Erasmus rose quickly to prominence. His political involvement began in the late 1960s with the Company of Young Canadians, where he developed organizational skills as well as a radical political stance that made his transition to the larger political scene a controversial one.

Erasmus' life and career cannot be understood without some knowledge of the history of the Dene and their relationship with the government of Canada. In the late 18th and the 19th centuries, the Dene participated in the fur trade while maintaining control over their lands. Increasing knowledge of the mineral resources of their lands, dramatized by the discovery of gold in the Yukon in 1896, brought profound changes. As prospectors poured in, the government of Canada hastily drew up Treaty No. 8, covering parts of northern British Columbia and Alberta and the NWT up to Great Slave Lake. Similarly, the discovery of extensive oil fields led in 1921 to a second treaty, No. 11, covering a large area of the NWT north of Great Slave Lake. The Dene way of life was threatened by rapidly increasing populations that brought European diseases and extensive economic and social dislocation.

The desire of the Dene to reassert their culture and to reclaim sovereignty over their lands shaped Erasmus' career. Unlike the government, which asserted for years that the treaties extinguished their title to the land, the Dene see the treaties as peace and friendship agreements. In 1970 the Indian Brotherhood of the NWT (IBNWT) was formed to address Dene concerns about Treaties 8 and 11. Erasmus was active in the IBNWT from the beginning, first as director of community development, later as president of the brotherhood and its successor organization, the Dene Nation, formed in 1978. The government of Canada introduced in 1973 a policy allowing aboriginal peoples to negotiate land claims, a belated recognition that aboriginal rights do exist. The next year the Dene started the lengthy, difficult, frustrating business of negotiating their claim to 450,000 square miles of the NWT. During these years Erasmus articulated a view of the Dene as a colonized people who had never given up their sovereignty to the dominant power. This theme of the right of self-determination, or self-government, supported by an adequate land base, is reflected in the Dene Declaration of 1975. It forms a constant theme through Erasmus' writings and public statements.

Erasmus was involved heavily in the claims process. Seeking a consensus in the traditional manner, representatives from the 25 Dene communities in the Mackenzie Valley and IBNWT leaders met a number of times to work out the wording of the claim. An on-going problem for Erasmus as IBNWT president was the issue of unity, both within the IBNWT, which tended to split along moderate/radical lines, and among the aboriginal peoples of the Mackenzie Valley. The Dene, most of whom were status Indians registered under the federal Indian Act, and the Métis, nonstatus people of mixed native and European background, presented separate claims to the federal government, which insisted that they reach consensus on a single claim. This requirement does not reflect the differences in needs and goals of the various native groups. Also, government offers involving millions of dollars and limited rights in return for the land have been turned down because they fail to include the fundamental right of self-determination.

In the mid-1970s resource development and the issue of Dene land rights entered a collision course. In 1975 the government established an inquiry, headed by Judge Thomas Berger, that held extensive hearings into the Mackenzie Valley pipeline proposal, a plan to ship natural gas from the Arctic Ocean to Alberta. Erasmus and many other witnesses gave the inquiry a clear message: no further resource development until the Dene land claim was settled. Berger recommended a ten-year moratorium on development to allow time for the settlement of the Dene claim. This time passed, and the claim was still unsettled.

When land claims negotiations ground to a halt in 1983, a tired Erasmus stepped down as president of the Dene Nation. He was not inactive for long, however. Shortly after resigning, Erasmus became northern vice-chief of the Assembly of First Nations (AFN), founded in 1980 as a national organization representing the interests of Canada's status Indians. He was elected national chief on July 30, 1985, a position he held until 1991.

The AFN takes an active role in many issues affecting Canada's native peoples, including health and welfare, education, child care, prison conditions, unemployment, economic development, and funding for native media. It lobbies both the federal government and the United Nations. As national chief, Erasmus was senior spokesperson for the AFN on many of these issues. He was also active with Indigenous Survival International, an organization set up to counter the anti-fur movement that has created serious economic difficulties for aboriginal trappers. But the achievement of self-determination is the fundamental goal for Erasmus and the AFN. In the 1980s and 1990s, this issue has led to considerable debate over the position of native peoples in Canada's Constitution. The AFN represented native peoples at a series of First Ministers' Conferences held between 1983 and 1987. Erasmus was deeply involved in this process, and its failure to place clearly in the Constitution an aboriginal right of self-government was deeply disappointing.

Erasmus was invited to participate in a special committee planning Canada's 1992 celebrations of 125 years of confederation. After years of struggle, there was little to celebrate, Erasmus told the committee, for native Canadians were still at the bottom of the economic and social order. His understandable disappointment was tempered by a stubborn optimism that eventually the rights and claims of native peoples would receive just recognition.

Erasmus has been awarded many honors, including appointment to the Order of Canada in 1987. He has received honorary degrees from Queen's University, University of Toronto, University of Winnipeg, York University, and University of British Columbia. Erasmus is also a published writer, having co-authored *Drumbeat: Anger and Renewal in Indian Country.*

Further Reading

There are no major books or articles about Georges Erasmus as yet, but a good deal has been written about the Dene and the issues they face. An extensive inquiry into the Mackenzie Valley pipeline resulted in the two-volume Berger Report, officially titled *Northern Frontier, Northern Homeland* (1977). A selection of these testimonies has been edited by Mel Watkins and published as *Dene Nation: the colony within* (Toronto: 1977). *Moratorium: Justice, Energy, the North, and the Native People* (Toronto: 1977) by High and Karmel McCullum and John Olthuis is a sympathetic analysis of the problems inherent in reconciling the conflicting claims to the resources of the north. The documentary history of Treaties 8 and 11 has been assembled by René Fumoleau in *As Long as This Land Shall Last* (Toronto: 1973). Fumoleau also contributed the photographs in the amply illustrated *Denendeh: A Dene Celebration* (1984). Those who want to know more about the traditions of the Dene can turn to *When the World Was New: Stories of the Sahtu Dene,* edited by Dene elder George Blondin (Yellowknife, Northwest Territories: 1990). Native publications such as *Windspeaker, Kahtou,* and the *Dene Nation Newsletter* contain valuable information; articles can be located through various periodical indexes.

Georges Erasmus contributed to a number of books. *Dene Nation* includes his statement "We the Dene." He wrote a lengthy introduction to *Drumbeat,* a volume published in 1990 by the Assembly of First Nations in which native leaders tell their own stories about their struggles for justice. Larry Krotz interviewed Erasmus for a chapter in Krotz' book, *Indian Country: Inside Another Canada* (Toronto: 1990). ☐

Eratosthenes of Cyrene

The Greek scholar of natural history Eratosthenes of Cyrene (ca. 284-ca. 205 B.C.) was proficient in many fields, but his most outstanding work was probably in mathematics and geography.

The *Lexicon* of Suidas (ca. 10th century A.D.) records the birth of Eratosthenes as the 126th Olympiad (276-272 B.C.), but since he was a pupil of Zeno (died 262-261) and since a number of authorities describe him as an old man of 80, it is more probable that he was born about 284 B.C. He studied grammar in Alexandria but was educated in philosophy in Athens, where he was influenced by the philosophers Arcesilaus and Ariston. About the age of 40 Eratosthenes was recalled to Alexandria by Ptolemy III to take charge eventually of the famous library of the Alexandrian Museum, succeeding Apollonius of Rhodes.

Eratosthenes wrote works of literary criticism (*On Ancient Comedy*), philosophy, history (establishing chronology as a scientific discipline), mathematics, astronomy, and geography. He also wrote a short epic dealing with the death of Hesiod, and *Erigone,* an elegy praised by Longinus. His *Geographica* comprises a history of geographical ideas, including a section on mathematical geography in which the division of the globe into zones was established and the inhabited portions were delimited. There were also some crude map-making attempts in his memoirs, and it is believed that Eratosthenes compiled a catalog of 675 stars.

Eratosthenes investigated arithmetical and geometrical problems. In his "sieve" method of distinguishing prime numbers, by which "the prime and incomposite numbers are separated by themselves as though by some instrument or sieve," there is the foundation for a logical theory of the infinite. The prime numbers were found by listing all odd numbers beginning with 3, then striking out every third number, every fifth number, and so on, with the remaining numbers being the primes. The much-attempted problem of the duplication of the cube, which dealt with the problem of finding the mean proportional between two lines, occupied Eratosthenes at an early date. To solve it, he constructed a bronze instrument called a mesolabe. He also applied geometrical methods, by ascertaining both the difference of latitude and the distance apart of two places that were supposedly located on the same meridian, to deduce the circumference of the earth. The size of the units of measure (stadia) that he employed is doubtful, but it is assumed that 10 stadia approximates 1 mile; he computed the circumference at 250,000 stadia, or 25,000 miles, very close to today's estimates.

The Alexandrian Age cultivated specialization, and Eratosthenes did not therefore win the approval of his contemporaries. He had achievements, however, which could not be denied, so he was called Beta (the second letter of the Greek alphabet), indicating that he was never "first-rate" at anything. During his last years he developed ophthalmia and became blind. The end came in Alexandria as the result of suicide by voluntary starvation.

Further Reading

A brief discussion of Eratosthenes's life appears in Carl Boyer, *A History of Mathematics* (1968). Thomas L. Heath, *A Manual of Greek Mathematics* (1931), is a full treatment of Eratosthenes's mathematical research. See also Ivor Thomas, *Greek Mathematical Works,* vol. 1 (1939). □

Alonso de Ercilla y Zúñiga

The Spanish poet, soldier, and diplomat Alonso de Ercilla y Zúñiga (1533-1594) wrote the famous historical poem "La Araucana," which was the first work of genuine poetic art about any part of America.

Alonso de Ercilla was born in Madrid on Aug. 7, 1533, the youngest child of a distinguished father high in governmental circles and a tutor of Prince Philip, later Philip II of Spain, and of an aristocratic mother of royal lineage. Ercilla practically grew up in the royal household and was a companion of Prince Philip on his early travels, including the journey to London in 1554 to wed Mary Tudor, Queen of England.

News of events in faraway Peru stirred Ercilla's spirit of adventure, and he left Europe for America, arriving in Lima on July 6, 1556. He joined the expedition to Chile headed by the Peruvian viceroy's youthful son, Garcia Hurtado de Mendoza, and participated in the warfare of the Spaniards against the natives of that remote land.

On scraps of paper in the lulls of fighting, Ercilla jotted down versified octaves about the events of the war and his own part in it. These stanzas he later gathered together and augmented in number to form his epic *La Araucana,* in three parts and 37 cantos. It was the first poem of its kind written by a participant in the course of the events narrated and the first to immortalize the beginnings of a modern country. Although his purpose was to glorify Spanish arms, the figures of Araucanian chiefs, Caupolicán, Lautaro, Tucapel, Colocolo, and Galvino, have proved the most memorable. In the minds of the Chilean people *La Araucana* is a kind of *Iliad* that exalts the heroism, pride, and contempt of pain and death of these legendary Araucanian leaders and makes them national heroes today. Ercilla thus initiated the concept of the "noble savage," destined to have wide literary currency in European literature 2 centuries later. He had, in fact, created a historical poem of the war in Chile which immediately inspired many imitations.

After Ercilla's return to Spain in 1562, he made several diplomatic journeys to Austria, where his mother was a maid of honor at the imperial court, and also to Rome. In 1570 he married the aristocratic Doña María de Bazán and, after other diplomatic missions, settled permanently in Spain in 1577. He had published the first part of *La Araucana* in 1569, and its popularity led to the composition and publication of the second part in 1578 and the third part in 1589. Ercilla's later years were saddened by the loss of his

only son, and his own death occurred in Madrid on Nov. 29, 1594.

Further Reading

There is no biography of Ercilla in English. Background information is in Bernard Moses, *Spanish Colonial Literature in South America* (1922; repr. 1961). Charles Maxwell Lancaster and Paul Thomas Manchester, *The Araucaniad* (1945), is a translation of Ercilla's epic. □

Ludwig Erhard

The German statesman Ludwig Erhard (1897–1977) is credited with the decisions that resulted in West Germany's (now part of Germany) spectacular economic recovery following World War II. He served as chancellor of the Federal Republic of Germany from 1963 to 1966.

Ludwig Erhard was born in the northern Bavarian city of Fürth on Feb. 4, 1897. After serving in World War I, during which he advanced to the rank of sergeant and was badly wounded, Erhard resumed his business training. He continued his studies in economics and sociology at the progressive University of Frankfurt. After he received a doctorate, Erhard decided to devote his career to research rather than to business. He joined the staff of the Nürnberg Business School. From 1928 to 1942 he advanced from research assistant to director of the institution. The Nazis removed him from this position, however, after he refused to join the party. Erhard spent the remaining war years as a consultant to business enterprises.

Erhard's lack of compromising political ties and his reputation as an economic expert made him a likely candidate for the administrative posts set up by the Western Allied governments that occupied Germany after 1945. First Erhard was charged with the reconstruction of the war-ravaged industries of his native Fürth-Nürnberg area. Late in 1945 he was named economics minister in the Bavarian state government. After losing this post in 1947, Erhard was named to key positions in the council set up jointly by the British and American occupation authorities to coordinate economic activities in their zones.

Pushed Social Market Economy

Erhard's economic views were summarized in his advocacy of a "social market economy," which one author has called a "free economy with a social conscience." Erhard wished to use private initiative to rebuild the shattered German economy but to check it when it tended toward monopoly, cartelization, or extreme labor union demands.

Erhard well understood the inefficiencies that come with price controls. He had authored a memorandum during the war outlining his vision for a market economy in Germany. In 1947, the Allies, who wanted Germans with

no ties to the fallen Nazi regime for the new German government, named Erhard the main economic adviser to U.S. General Lucius D. Clay, military governor of the U.S. zone. Erhard advocated a quick reform of the currency system and the decontrol of prices.

After the Soviet withdrawal from the Allied Control Authority, General Clay, along with his French and British counterparts, undertook a currency reform on Sunday, June 20, 1948. The amount of currency in circulation was dramatically reduced (by a factor of slightly more than 90 percent). Under the reform mapped by Erhard, the new legal currency, the Deutschemark, was substituted for the old Reichsmark. With the sharp contraction in the German money supply, he reasoned, there would be far fewer shortages because the controlled prices would now be stated in Deutschemarks. On the same day, over the strong objections of its Social Democratic members, Germany's Bizonal Economic Council adopted a price decontrol law that gave Erhard the authority to eliminate price controls. Between June and August of 1948, Erhard decontrolled the prices of vegetables, fruits, eggs, and almost all manufactured goods. He substantially relaxed, or simply suspended enforcement of, other price ceilings.

At the same time, the government, following Erhard's advice, cut taxes sharply. Walter Heller, a young economist with the U.S. occupation forces who was later to become chairman of President Kennedy's Council of Economic Advisers, wrote in 1949 that to "remove the repressive effect of extremely high rates, Military Government Law No. 64 cut a wide swath across the German tax system at the time of the currency reform." Individual income tax rates, in particular, fell dramatically. Previously the tax rate on any income over 6,000 Deutschemarks had been 95 percent. After tax reform, this 95 percent rate applied only to annual incomes above 250,000 Deutschemarks. For the German with an annual income of about 2,400 Deutschemarks in 1950, the marginal tax rate fell from 85 percent to 18 percent.

Economy Surged

The immediate effects of these Erhard-designed reforms on the German economy were dramatic. Another U.S. economist with occupation forces wrote that the "spirit of the country changed overnight. The gray, hungry, dead-looking figures wandering about the streets in their everlasting search for food came to life." On Monday, June 21, only a day after the announcement of currency reform, shops filled with goods as people realized that the money they sold them for would be worth much more than the old money. The reforms, wrote Heller, "quickly re-established money as the preferred medium of exchange and monetary incentives as the prime mover of economic activity."

Another phenomenon was observed in the wake of the reforms: Absenteeism, which only a month earlier was averaging more than nine hours a week, was reduced significantly. Workers who had stayed off the job to forage and barter for life's necessities found that it was no longer imperative for them to do so. By the fall of 1948, the absenteeism rate had dropped to about four hours. In the second half of 1948, Germany's industrial output rose by more than 50 percent. This growth continued to be extremely strong over the next ten years, with industrial production per capita in 1958 measuring three times its level in the six months preceding the June 1948 reforms. What looked like a miracle in reality was not. Erhard expected these results because he knew full well the damage that had been wrought by inflation, coupled with price controls and high tax rates. In turn, he also was well aware of the large productivity gains that could be unleashed by ending inflation, removing price controls, and slashing high marginal tax rates.

Named Economics Minister

Immensely popular with the German people as a result of the economic reforms, Erhard joined Konrad Adenauer's Christian Democratic Union (CDU) only shortly before the first West German parliamentary election in 1949. When the party was victorious in those elections, Erhard became economics minister in the Adenauer government, in which post he remained until he succeeded the aging and increasingly unpopular Adenauer as chancellor in 1963. Erhard led his coalition government (CDU/CSU and Free Democrats) to victory in the 1965 election, after which he actively supported a normalization of relations with the countries of the Warsaw Pact. On March 25, 1966, his government sent a peace overture to the Warsaw Pact, proposing a renunciation of force. The failure to include East Germany in this initiative resulted ultimately in its failure. Erhard and his foreign minister, Gerhard Schröder, were labeled "Atlanticists" for their support of stronger ties with the United States and the North Atlantic Treaty Organization

(NATO). This focus on West Germany's relationship with NATO and the United States weakened the country's ties with France, which Adenauer had worked so hard to build up during his years as chancellor. Erhard soon found his position untenable as recession wiped away memories of the economic miracle and those he once had considered his friends, including Adenauer, sniping at him whenever possible. He was accused of both indecision and lack of experience in foreign affairs. He resigned in 1966 and was succeeded as chancellor by Kurt-Georg Kiesinger. Erhard later confided that "soon after I took office in 1963, I had the feeling that my party friends were no friends." A year after his resignation, he was named honorary chairman of the CDU.

Erhard spent the final decade of his life as a dignified elder statesman. He displayed no bitterness at what many felt was betrayal by his fellow members of the CDU. He wrote and consulted extensively in the area of his traditional expertise—the social market economy. When he died on May 5, 1977, he was lauded by his countrymen as "the father of the economic miracle." He was 80.

Further Reading

There is no biography in English of Erhard and no major scholarly work in any language. There are informative discussions of Erhard in Arnold J. Heidenheimer, *The Governments of Germany* (1961; 2d ed. 1966). See also Michael Balfour, *West Germany* (1968), and Henry Walton, *Germany* (1969). Further information on Erhard may be found in Wayne C. Thompson et al., *Historical Dictionary of Germany* (1994); James A. Moncure, editor, *Research Guide to European Historical Biography: 1450-Present* (1992); and in the entry on Ludwig Erhard on *Britannica Online* at http://www.eb.com. □

Eric the Red

Eric the Red (active late 10th century), Viking rover and founder of the first Scandinavian settlement in Greenland, was one of the early Viking explorers of North America.

Born in Norway about 950, Eric Thorvaldsson, who is known as Eric the Red, left that country as a child when his father, Thorvald, was exiled to Iceland. The family settled in the western part of the island, where Greenland could be seen 175 miles away. He married Thorhild, daughter of Jorund Atlisson, and probably as part of her dowry received land at Eriksstadir in Haukadale. His thralls caused a landslide to overwhelm the home of Valthiof and his family, whose kinsman Eyjolf in turn slew the thralls. In retaliation Eric killed Eyjolf and as a result was banished from Haukadale.

Eric retired to an island, leaving with Thorgest his diasposts, which were Viking symbols of authority and had religious significance. On Eric's return Thorgest refused to surrender them so Eric stole them. Knowing he would be

pursued, he prepared an ambush for Thorgest in which the pursuer's sons were killed. Thorgest went to court, and the Thorness Thing in 981 outlawed Eric in Iceland and Norway for 3 years.

Having purchased a boat for such a contingency, Eric decided upon a typical Viking voyage of plunder. He had heard about the "Greater Ireland" settlements in Greenland; in the spring of 981 he steered his 100-foot-long ship westward. His was hardly a voyage based on a romantic urge to discover new lands.

Eric landed in the area of Julianehaab, but the group arrived too late to reap a full reward, for the Irish settlers had left. The first winter was spent at Eric's Island near the middle of the "eastern settlements," and the next spring he proceeded to Eriksfjord. During subsequent summers explorations were made on the western side of the island as far north as Snaefells; the Davis Strait was crossed to Baffin Island, then abundant with game. Eric returned to Iceland in 985 convinced that Greenland, more clement than now, was better adapted for stock raising than Iceland.

The next year Eric set out to found a settlement in Greenland. About 14 ships out of 25 arrived with about 350 colonists, plus livestock and gear. They settled on the eastern shore. Each sea captain claimed a fjord to which he gave his name, Eric dwelling at Brattahlid in Eriksfjord. Here he lived like a jarl (lord) with his wife and four children. The latter included sons Leif, Thorvald, and Thorstein and an illegitimate daughter, Freydis. All four explored North America.

Leif brought Christianity to Greenland in 998, but Eric remained true to his pagan gods. He became estranged from his wife, who accepted the new faith and built at Brattahlid the first church in Greenland. In 999 at odds with both wife and son Leif, Eric attempted unsuccessfully a trip to Leif's Vinland with his son Thorstein the Unlucky. They failed to reach Newfoundland, but as the doughty Eric said, "We were more cheerful when we put out of the fjord in the summer; but at least we are still alive, and it might have been worse." He is last mentioned in the sagas in 1005.

Further Reading

The best primary works in English are Sir W. A. Craigie, *The Icelandic Sagas* (1913), and Gwyn Jones, ed., *Eirik the Red and Other Icelandic Sagas* (1961). Farley Mowat, *Westviking: The Ancient Norse in Greenland and North America* (1965), contains the most readable and logical account of Eric; Gwyn Jones, *A History of the Vikings* (1968), is the most thorough. □

Arthur Charles Erickson

Arthur Charles Erickson (born 1924), Canadian architect, became the most internationally noted figure in Canadian architectural history. Sensitive to the expression of site and the response of buildings to environment, he was also recognized as a skillful landscape architect.

Arthur Erickson's early education in art was inspired by the spectacular setting of the British Columbia landscape and by the intensely art-conscious social milieu into which he was born. His parents were of the generation of "pioneers" in the city of Vancouver (which was chartered in 1886 and experienced its first large demographic and building boom in 1912) who were determined to foster the arts in their community. His mother encouraged her two sons to pursue an interest in the arts. Among Erickson's other inspirers and mentors were Canadian artists who had settled in Vancouver, such as Lauren Harris and B. C. Binding, and Victoria-born Emily Car.

Prodigy

Erickson credits these mentors with having taught him an appreciation of the dual relationship between art and nature. Twinned with his aesthetic education was a boyhood fascination with nature—he brought home countless plant samples and small animals, and was allowed to paint on his bedroom wall a giant aquatic mural. His drawing talents were so developed that by the age of fourteen Harris had arranged a show of the youth's work at the Vancouver Art Gallery.

Awareness of the larger intellectual world of architecture and design philosophies came from contacts with the Austrian-American architect Richard Neutra and especially Gordon Webber, a student and teacher at the Chicago Institute of Design who had inherited the Bauhaus ideals of George Keeps, Lasso Moholy-Nagy, and Serge Chermayeff. Erickson received his formal training in architecture at Montreal's McGill University, and graduated with honors and prizes.

Rome to Stockholm

The story of Erickson's formation as an architect is not complete without mention of his love of travel, combined with his training for keen observation and his profound respect for other cultures. After McGill, he received a one-year travel-study grant, which he stretched into two and a half years, "by frugal living and a bit of vagrancy," he recalled in *The Architecture of Arthur Erickson*. Following the path of civilization from its Middle East origins and moving west- and northward across Europe, Erickson gained an appreciation of architectural history and a building's relationship to its physical environment. Combined with later journeys taken though Asia, Africa, and South America, Erickson gained a rich repertoire of ideas and inspirations regarding spiritual and spatial forms.

In 1955, Erickson began teaching at the University of Oregon, and the following year returned to Canada after taking a position with the School of Architecture of the University of British Columbia. Though he left the school in 1964, his deep influence on the architectural philosophy of the curriculum was felt for many years after his departure.

Radical Times, Radical University

The first commission to bring him wide international recognition was the building of Simon Framer University in Burnaby, British Columbia (1965), designed in cooperation with Geoffrey Massey. They built it on the "academic village" model, and its innovative concrete shapes follow a rhythm that echoes the mountainous landscape. Erickson's creation of the Canada Pavilion (also in partnership with Massey) at the Osaka World's Fair of 1970 was described as "magical" and was cited as the best building of that fair. Others among his most acclaimed works are the Museum of Anthropology (1972) on the University of British Columbia campus and the Robin Square Civic Center (1973) in downtown Vancouver. He and Massey carried on their own joint firm from 1963 to 1972, and Erickson founded his own Vancouver-based practice in 1972.

Many of Erickson's residential designs received much attention. These include the Filbert House in Commix, British Columbia (1958); the two Smith houses (1955 and 1964), the Graham House (1962), and the Epoch house (1974), all in West Vancouver, British Columbia, and the Bagel Write house (1977) in Seattle, Washington.

All of these structures exhibit Erickson's adherence to the so-called modernist tradition of the 20th century, a philosophy which emphasizes truth in expression of materials, function, and structure in architecture. Building materials which do not require the protection of paint are left to reveal their intrinsic colors and to weather In a natural way. Interior spaces are immediately discernible or are implied on the exterior, and the transition between exterior and interior is consciously de-emphasized, resulting in an intimate interdependence of building and landscape. A typical Erickson building will exhibit a minimum variety of materials. Thus the Epoch house presents to the eye little but concrete and glass, and the Osaka pavilion appeared to be ephemerally constructed of nothing but timber and mirrors.

Interesting Optical Illusion

In the composition of his buildings and their landscapes another Erickson "signature" occurs in the repeated use of the "slipped plane." This is a formal device, refined by Mies van der Rohe, in which horizontal and often vertical planes are juxtaposed along a slightly broken line which makes them appear to be moving by one another in parallax and which induces movement through a gently shifting and meandering sequence of spaces rather than a rigidly axial one.

Erickson also received much inspiration for his forms from the cultures of Shinto Japan and the Islamic Middle East. Like Frank Lloyd Wright, Erickson was early impressed with the Japanese bittersweet, rather fatalistic acceptance of nature as an inescapable force to which human beings and human structures must submit and which they may never overpower. Many of his landscape designs, especially his own garden in Vancouver, reflect this view of accepting nature as unalterable.

Drew Upon Global Themes

Erickson was also attracted by the marriage of simple stretches of opaque walls combined with complex geometrical details characteristic of Moslem architecture. This was most obviously expressed in his Man and His World Pavilion in the Montreal Exposition of 1967, in the Sikh Temple in Vancouver (1969), and in the project for a science museum in Saudi Arabia (1982). Involvement in commissions such as these, as well as large-scale urban projects for Los Angeles, Kuala Lumpur, and countries of the Middle East, led Erickson into forms more intricate and perhaps more picturesque than was previously typical in his work.

By the late 1970s Erickson's firm had expanded with offices in Toronto, Los Angeles, and Saudi Arabia. This era of his career was noted for several other notable projects, including Toronto's Roy Thomson Hall (1982). In southern California, his most noteworthy projects include the San Diego Convention Center (1981), Fresno City Hall, and Los Angeles's largest downtown real estate development, California Plaza. His reputation was further enhanced when he was chosen to design the Canadian Chancery (Embassy) in Washington, D.C. (1989). In 1985 the American Institute of Architects awarded Erickson its prized Gold Medal.

Practice Ran Aground

Yet Erickson often encountered problems in joining his architectural visions to concrete business concerns. By the late 1980s, he began to experience difficulty in obtaining financing from lending institutions for his projects; in 1988 several prominent Canadians pooled their resources and set up a capital group for him. The following year he closed his Toronto office, citing a recession that was dampening the most ambitious of creative endeavors across North America. His Los Angeles office ran into financial troubles in time as well. He was forced to close it in 1991; there were no new commissions and he could no longer pay the $10,000-a-month rent on the space.

The recession continued to stymie Erickson. By 1992 his Vancouver office had merged into another architectural firm in the city, he filed for bankruptcy in California and declared personal bankruptcy in British Columbia. He continues to work as an architect in Vancouver.

Further Reading

Additional information on Erickson can be found in the following: *The Architecture of Arthur Erickson,* written by Erickson (Montreal, 1975), contains insights into the architect's philosophy together with excellent illustrations with plans of most of the important works completed and in progress. *Seven Stones,* by Edith Uglier (1981) presents an anecdotal biography relating the architect's life to his work. *Canadian Architecture,* by Carol Moore Dee (Toronto, 1971), includes an introduction by Erickson and photoessays on Simon Framer University, the second Gordon Smith house, and the Macmillan Blooded building; and *By Their Own Design,* edited by Abby Suckle (1980) includes a section on Erickson. There is an essay on him in *Contemporary Architects* (1993). *Time* magazine, June 4, 1979, carried a cover article on Erickson; and a profile of Erickson appeared in the *New Yorker* magazine, June 4, 1979. His later career is chornicled in *Maclean's* (July 22, 1991) and an interview with him in *Canadian Architect* (April 1992).

Articles by Erickson include "The Architecture of Japan" in *The Canadian Architect* (December 1966), "The University: The New Visual Environment," in *The Canadian Architect* (January 1968), and "Ideation as a Source of Creativity" in W. H. New's *New Political Art* (1978). □

Leif Ericson

The Norse mariner and adventurer Leif Ericson (971-ca. 1015) was the first Norseman to seek out the coast of North America. He introduced Christianity into Greenland.

Leif Ericson was born in Iceland, the son of Eric the Red. He moved with his parents to Greenland in 986. In that same year Bjarni Herjolfson, following his father to Greenland, missed that island and sailed in a southwesterly direction and sighted both the Labrador coast and Newfoundland.

Leif, 15 at the time, listened carefully to tales of Bjarni's adventures, probably from Bjarni himself, who was more interested in trade than in discovering new lands. On reaching his majority, and chafing under the patriarchal rule of his father, Leif determined to visit Bjarni's southernmost land. He undoubtedly was motivated by Bjarni's account of large timber stands sighted along the coast, for timber was scarce in Greenland. Bjarni not only furnished the idea for the voyage but also supplied Leif with the very ship that he had used on his own inadvertent exploration.

Leif's voyage was planned and had a forceful, brave, shrewd leader who was careful in all things. His discovery, then, was not an accident, as those who give too little credence to Viking navigational skills intimate. He set sail probably in 995, passed Markland (Labrador), and reached Newfoundland, where his thirsty crewmen drank dew from the grass. Here, in what probably was Leif's Vinland, the men decided to winter, noticing that the days were more equitable in length than at home.

In addition to building lodgings, the men cut timber and hunted. Their tasks were eased by the fact that there were no natives in the vicinity. On one hunting and exploratory expedition, one Tyrker, who had lived in warmer climates, returned with grapes. Consequently the men began to cut vines and harvest grapes in addition to gathering timber. Because of the new find, Leif named the area Vinland, which subsequently became known as Vinland the Good. Where in Newfoundland Leif wintered is still a matter of controversy, but most leading scholars are firmly convinced that it was on that island. Grapes grew wild in quantity in Newfoundland until as late as the middle of the 17th century, because the climate then was much more benign than it is today. On the trip home with timber and other goods of value, Leif rescued a ship of Thorer and from it obtained assorted Norwegian trade goods. Because of this highly prosperous voyage, Leif received the name "Lucky."

Blocked from further ambitions by a father who did not intend to lose political influence to his son, Leif in 997 sailed for Norway, hoping to curry favor with the king, Olaf Tryggvason. En route he visited the Hebrides and left behind a pregnant mistress, Thorgunna, who subsequently followed him with his son. He spent the winter of 997 in Norway, where, to increase his power and prestige as a

buttress to his wealth, he became one of Olaf's liege men and a Christian.

The next year Leif returned home bringing priests and the new faith with him. His mother was an early convert, but Eric clung stubbornly to the old ways. When the aged chieftain along with another son, Thorstein, decided to make a trip to Newfoundland, Leif refused him the use of his ship. At this point in the sages Leif gives place to other members of his family.

Further Reading

Farley Mowat, *Westviking: The Ancient Norse in Greenland and North America* (1965), is the most readable account; and Gwyn Jones, *A History of the Vikings* (1968), and his edition of *The Norse Atlantic Saga: Being the Norse Voyages of Discovery and Settlement to Iceland, Greenland and America* (1964) are the most detailed. Also valuable are Tryggvi J. Oleson, *Early Voyages and Northern Approaches, 1000-1632* (1963), and Pattr. Groenlendinga, *The Vinland Sagas: The Norse Discovery of America* (trans. 1966). Edward F. Gray, *Leif Ericsson: Discoverer of America A.D. 1003* (1930), provides additional material. An excellent background study is Samuel Eliot Morison, *The European Discovery of America: The Northern Voyages* (1971). □

John Ericsson

John Ericsson (1803-1889), Swedish-born American engineer and inventor, perfected the screw propeller

and constructed radically designed warships, notably the ironclad "Monitor."

John Ericsson was born in Långbanshyttan, Värmland Province, on July 31, 1803. He began as an iron miner but showed an aptitude for machinery construction, drafting, and engraving. After work as a surveyor on the Göta Ship Canal, he became an army topographic officer in 1820.

In 1826 Ericsson went to London, where he worked mainly on engines and on locomotives and screw propulsion for boats, receiving 14 patents. English railroad builders kept him profitably at work.

To devise a means of using heat more efficiently than did steam engines, Ericsson applied flame directly in a "caloric" engine. His most lucrative invention was a steam fire engine. To improve marine engines and keep propulsion apparatus underwater, he designed a screw propeller (patented 1836) which was more efficient than a paddle wheel, ensured better engine performance, and made larger ships possible. In 1836 the speed of his model vessel exceeded 10 miles per hour. His screwpropelled ships were used on English rivers, and some were taken to America; yet the British navy rejected his designs. In 1839 he migrated to America to build naval vessels.

Ericsson won a prize in 1840 for the best-designed steam fire engine. He adapted twin screw propellers to a vessel, and by 1844 there were 25 such boats on American

waters. In 1844 he completed the 1,000-ton iron frigate U.S.S. *Princeton,* the first screw-propelled warship and the first with engines and boilers underwater, out of firing range. A coal burner with a self-adjusting gunlock to compensate for roll, it was pronounced a shipbuilding marvel. But on a trial run the 12-inch wrought-iron gun (not designed by Ericsson) exploded and killed the secretaries of state and Navy and four others. This tragedy stigmatized Ericsson and delayed the building of American steam naval ships.

At the London Crystal Palace Exposition of 1851 Ericsson entered a pyrometer that measured very high temperatures, a model gas engine, an engine barometer with an alarm, a sounding instrument, a distance measurer, and a compass.

Another blow to Ericsson's career occurred in 1854, when the *Ericsson,* equipped with caloric engines, capsized in a storm. Though the engines were too heavy for ship propulsion, they were economical and thousands were used to pump water for homes.

Ericsson regained prestige with the *Monitor.* Napoleon III had rejected his model ironclad warship in 1854. A U.S. Navy board reluctantly granted him a contract to construct the craft for Union use in the Civil War: the *Monitor* was launched in January 1862. It arrived at Hampton Roads (Norfolk) on March 9 in time to drive off the Confederate ironclad, the *Merrimac.* This first, historic battle between steam-driven ironclads was a turning point in naval technology. For the rest of the war Ericsson designed and built ironclads.

After the war Ericsson built monitors for other nations and gunboats for Spain. By 1878 his torpedo boat, the *Destroyer,* was ready. It could outrun ironclads, could partially submerge, and fired a dynamite torpedo projectile underwater. During Ericsson's lifetime the U.S. Navy displayed no interest in it.

Ericsson later worked with solar energy, gravitation and tides, high-speed engines for electric lighting, a marine surface condenser, and forced-draft ventilating fans. His solar engine was never commercialized.

Ericsson died in New York City on March 8, 1889. His remains were reinterred at Filipstad, Sweden.

Further Reading

A favorable biography of Ericsson is Ruth M. White, *Yankee from Sweden: The Dream and the Reality in the Days of John Ericsson* (1960). George Iles, *Leading American Inventors* (1912), includes a short account of Ericsson. For a detailed, illustrated account of the evolution of ironclad warships and screw propellers see James Phinney Baxter III, *The Introduction of the Ironclad Warship* (1933). Ericsson's ironclads are depicted in most illustrated histories of the Civil War. □

John Scotus Erigena

The Irish philosopher and theologian John Scotus Erigena (ca. 810-ca. 877) wrote "On the Division of Nature," one of the major philosophical works of the Middle Ages.

Ireland was one of the most important cultural areas of the early Middle Ages. Irish learning, which stimulated much of the intellectual development of England and the European continent in the 7th and 8th centuries, gave to John Scotus Erigena a philosophical turn of mind as well as the linguistic ability to read the earlier sources of philosophy and Christian thought in their original languages.

Erigena, or Eriugena (meaning Irish-born), was one of several men of letters from Ireland and England to find a home on the Continent. Between 845 and 847 Erigena went to the court of Charles the Bald, king of the West Franks, who resided most frequently at the royal villa of Quierzy-sur-Oise near Laon. Erigena soon became the leading man of learning in northern France.

During the early period of Erigena's life in northern France, he took part in two controversies. One concerned the mystery of the Sacrament of the Eucharist, namely, how the bread and wine become the body and blood of Christ. The other controversy was over the doctrine of predestination, namely, the degree to which God's eternal decision is responsible for the ultimate salvation or damnation of the individual.

Erigena's contribution to the eucharistic controversy has been lost. However, his work on predestination, written in 851 in order to refute the teaching of the monk Gottschalk of Orbais, survives. Gottschalk maintained that God predestined souls to heaven or hell. Using the Neoplatonic idea that evil is only the absence of good and as such has no real being, Erigena interpreted evil actions and the concept of hell in such a way as to dissolve most of the elements of the original discussion. Hell was only metaphorical; the light of God that prevailed in the afterlife would please those whose spiritual eyes were healthy and cause pain to those whose eyes were diseased through a corrupt life. Erigena's views were condemned in 855 at the Synod of Valence and described as "Irish porridge."

In 859 Erigena, responding to a request of Charles the Bald, began the translation of several Greek works whose study became formative for the development of his thought. Having made a commentary on the writings of Martianus Capella, Erigena began to translate the works of Pseudo-Dionysius (in 859-862), Maximus the Confessor (in 862-864), and Gregory of Nyssa (in 864-865). In connection with these translations, Erigena wrote commentaries on the Gospel of John and on the works of Pseudo-Dionysius.

The Neoplatonic doctrine expressed in the Dionysian works influenced the structure and substance of Erigena's major work, which he wrote during the years 862-866, namely, *On the Division of Nature.* Divided into five books, this work outlines the creation of all things from God, concentrating initially on God (the nature that creates but is not itself created), the Divine Intelligences (natures that are created and create), man and the creatures of the world (natures that are created and do not create), and finally on the return of all creation to God, who stands thus at the end of time and creation as the nature that is uncreated and does not create.

This work expresses the Neoplatonic tendency to conceive creation in terms of an involuntary emanation or overflowing of the divine essence down through the various hierarchies of heaven and the world. Because of this doctrine of emanation and the concept of a universal return to God, Erigena's work tended toward pantheism and was read in this light in later centuries.

The events at the end of Erigena's life are not known with certainty. Some evidence suggests that he returned to England or Ireland about 870, and the date for his death is generally placed about 877.

Further Reading

Erigena's life and thought are discussed in Henry Bett, *Johannes Scotus Erigena: A Study in Mediaeval Philosophy* (1925), and John J. O'Meara, *Eriugena* (1969). A brief treatment of the contents of Erigena's most famous work is in Frederick Copleston, *A History of Philosophy,* vol. 2 (1950).

Additional Sources

O'Meara, John Joseph, *Eriugena,* Oxford England: Clarendon Press; New York: Oxford University Press, 1988. □

Erik Homburger Erikson

Erik Homburger Erikson (1902–1994) was a German-born American psychoanalyst and educator whose studies have perhaps contributed most to the understanding of the young.

On June 15, 1902, Erik Erikson was born in Frankfurt am Main, Germany, of Danish parents. His widowed mother subsequently married the pediatrician Theodore Homburger. Erikson first studied painting in Germany and Italy. Later, he joined Peter Blos and Dorothy Burlingham, Anna Freud's colleague, in the development of a small children's school in Vienna. This led to his training analysis by Anna Freud and immersion in theoretical seminars and in clinical work. Having also acquired a Montessori diploma, he graduated from the Vienna Psychoanalytic Institute in 1933.

In 1930, he had married Canadian-born Joan Mowat Serson, who was vitally interested in education, as well as the arts and crafts, and deeply shared his interest in writing. The development of their three children, Kai, Jon, and Sue, as well as Erikson's work in Anna Freud's school, may have contributed much to his eventual thinking about the "epigenetic schema" of development and the vocabulary of health, in which he described the contributions of successive psychosexual stages to ego strengths, such as trust and autonomy, initiative and industry, and identity and intimacy.

Following Hitler's accession to power, the Eriksons went to the United States, where he began private practice and a sequence of research appointments at Harvard Medical School (1934-1935), Yale School of Medicine (1936-1939), University of California at Berkeley (1939-1951), and Austen Riggs Center, Stockbridge, Mass. (1951-1960); he was visiting professor at the University of Pittsburgh School of Medicine (1951-1960). One of his later appointments was as professor of human development and lecturer in psychiatry at Harvard University. At intervals he took time off for work abroad, such as travel to India in connection with his intensive study of Gandhi.

Study of Youth

Always free from the provincialism typical of thinkers with a more static and limited background, Erikson's thinking pushed toward an understanding of the ways in which the drives dominant in successive psychoanalytically defined life stages are shaped by interaction with the persistent needs and solutions typical of a given culture. These formulations were supported by field observations made with the collaboration of anthropologists, and also by observations of children's play.

Erikson's extension of the classical Freudian psychoanalytic concept of development was published in *Childhood and Society* (1950). The book startled some orthodox Freudians, who viewed development as dominated solely by the sequential emergence of successively potent drives modified or exaggerated primarily by their intimate—depriving, indulging, or punishing—interactions with the parents. Erikson's broader concept of dynamics of inner-outer interactions provided inspiration, challenge, and insight to the spectrum of American social sciences concerned with child development.

Erikson's concern at Austen Riggs Center was focused on the troubled years of late adolescence and early adulthood. He emphasized the universal process of resolution of identity conflicts during this developmental phase in a profound study of the youthful Martin Luther, *Young Man Luther* (1958); in a monograph, *Identity and the Life Cycle* (1959); and in a volume which he edited, *Youth: Change and Challenge* (1963). His Harvard teaching and response to students' concerns with values led to two collections of essays: *Insight and Responsibility* (1964) and *Identity, Youth and Crisis* (1967). The latter is a prophetic reformulation of the relation of the concepts of ego and self, and recognition of issues of nobility and cowardice, love and hate, and greatness and pettiness, which he sees as transcending the traditional normative issues of "adjustment to society." His contribution to understanding of the problem of identity in youth at times when personal change intersects with historical change has led scores of scholars to research exploring this area. In 1969 Erikson published *Gandhi's Truth*. This book focuses on the evolution of a passionate commitment in maturity to a humane goal and on the inner dynamic precursors of Gandhi's nonviolent strategy to reach this goal.

Erikson's Personality

The sources of Erikson's fresh, subtle, and multimodal awareness are many: His artist's temperament and perceptiveness contribute both to sensory richness and to sensitivity to nuances of personality and behavior. His deeply satisfying family life and wide-ranging friendships, with people such as Lawrence K. Frank, Margaret Mead, A. L. Kroeber, and Gardner Murphy, support a sense of health as a potential for the development of human beings struggling with conflicts exacerbated by the pressures of a given life stage. His freedom from premature commitment to an academic discipline with rigid canons of concept formation released him for original formulations as well as new adaptations and implications of classical psychoanalysis. Erikson's shrewd "the Emperor has no clothes" type of realism and uninhibited daring in probing new areas of experience seem to draw on a never-suppressed child's penetrating curiosity.

His love of life in nature and in people of all ages and many different cultures underlies the predominantly warm and vital quality of his thinking and writing. This has evoked the resonance of students of many disciplines whom he has influenced more than any analyst since Freud.

Freud lived and worked at a time when the mentally ill were beginning to be understood and universal inner conflict needed to be understood more deeply. Erikson was maturing in a period when the fate of the Western world was threatened by violence and denigration of values—a time when health, "virtue," and strength and their origins needed to be asserted and understood. His later books anticipated the demands of youthful protesters who repudiated the falseness of politics and the materialism of the

economic world and who called for sincerity, peace, love, and humane values.

Erikson died in 1994; however, his words live on—even those not familiar with his work may share his passion in language. Along with his numerous theories and plethora of information, Erikson also left educators the sound advice, "Do not mistake a child for his symptom."

Further Reading

Richard I. Evans published *Dialogue with Erik Erikson* (1967). A fine recent study is Robert Coles, *Erik H. Erikson: The Growth of His Work* (1970). Henry W. Maier, *Three Theories of Child Development: The Contributions of Erik H. Erikson, Jean Piaget, and Robert R. Sears, and Their Applications* (1965; rev. ed. 1969), and Noël A. Kinsella, *Toward a Theory of Personality Development: A Study of the Works of Erik H. Erikson* (1966), contain biographical material as well as discussion of Erikson's theories. Jonas Langer, *Theories of Development* (1969), contains many references to Erikson. □

Joseph Erlanger

The American physiologist Joseph Erlanger (1874-1965) made fundamental discoveries about the way in which nerve impulses are conducted.

Joseph Erlanger, the son of Herman and Sarah Erlanger, was born on Jan. 5, 1874, in San Francisco, Calif. He studied chemistry at the University of California, where he received his bachelor's degree, and then went on to Johns Hopkins University for his medical training. After he was awarded his medical degree (1899), he spent a year as a hospital resident. Between 1900 and 1906 he worked in the department of physiology at Johns Hopkins, successively holding appointments as assistant, instructor, associate, and associate professor.

In 1906 Erlanger moved to the newly established medical school at the University of Wisconsin, where he was the first professor of physiology. Shortly afterward he married Aimee Hirstel. In 1910 he became professor at Washington University, St. Louis, Mo., where he remained until his retirement in 1946.

Erlanger's early interest was in the physiology of the circulation. He studied blood pressure using a sphygmomanometer of his own devising and investigated the effect of pulse pressure on kidney function. The "Erlanger clamp" he designed reversibly to block the conduction of the auriculoventricular nerve bundle and thus was able to define some of the functions of this bundle in carrying impulses between the chambers of the heart. He also elucidated some of the mechanisms by which the flow of blood through the arteries produces sound.

In 1921 Erlanger began his collaboration with Herbert S. Gasser, investigating the properties and functions of nerve fibers. By adapting a new technique to the study of neurophysiology, Erlanger and Gasser proved the hypothesis that thick nerve fibers conduct impulses faster than thin ones.

The potential changes in nerves, which are of the order of only a few microvolts, were amplified 100,000 times by means of a newly constructed amplifier and were recorded on a cathode-ray oscillograph, which provided a virtually inertialess recording device. Using this highly sensitive apparatus, Erlanger and Gasser found that nerve trunks contain fibers which conduct electrical impulses at different rates. They defined three groups of fibers: A fibers, those of greatest thickness, which conduct impulses at velocities between 5 and 100 meters per second (mps); B fibers of intermediate thickness, conducting at 3-14 mps; and thin, C fibers, whose conduction velocity is less than 2 mps.

In 1922 Erlanger and Gasser's preliminary observations were published, and the definitive work, ''The Compound Nature of the Action Potential of Nerve as Disclosed by the Cathode-Ray Oscillograph,'' appeared in the *American Journal of Physiology* in 1924. An augmented version, published in book form in 1937, entitled *Electrical Signs of Nervous Activity,* has become a physiological classic. For their work they were awarded the Nobel Prize in physiology in 1944.

Erlanger's later work, which continued after his retirement and after his appointment as emeritus professor, was concerned mainly with the properties of single nerve fibers and, to a lesser extent, with synaptic function.

Erlanger was a man of retiring and introspective personality. His only hobby, he said, was ''communion with nature.'' He combined a reflective mind with great manual dexterity, which made him a gifted experimentalist. He died in St. Louis on Dec. 5, 1965.

Further Reading

There is no detailed biography of Erlanger, but a short account of his life appears in *Nobel Lectures: Physiology or Medicine,* vol. 3 (1967) and in Lloyd G. Stevenson, *Nobel Prize Winners in Medicine and Physiology, 1901-1950* (1953). The best account of his work is Joseph Erlanger and Herbert S. Gasser, *Electrical Signs of Nervous Activity* (1937). See also Charles Singer and E. Ashworth Underwood, *A Short History of Medicine* (1928; 3d ed. 1962). □

Max Ernst

The German painter Max Ernst (1891-1976), a leading figure in the Dada and surrealist movements, possessed an amazing range of styles and techniques.

Max Ernst was born on April 2, 1891, in Brühl, Germany. His memories of his childhood were remarkably vivid, and they provided him with many subjects for his later paintings. He attended the University of Bonn, where he studied philosophy and abnormal psychology, which also provided material for his art. In 1912 he turned to painting seriously, but it was only in 1918, after his war service, that he began to develop his own style. He made a series of collages, using illustrations from medical and technical magazines to form bizarre juxtapositions of images.

These collages were Ernst's main production when he was active in the Dada group in Cologne from 1919 to 1922. The Dada movement with its irreverent attitude to conventional art and mores appealed to Ernst and his friends. They produced a number of publications, and their most outrageous act was the famous 1920 Cologne Dada exhibition, to enter which the public had to walk through a public urinal. Dadamax was the pseudonym Ernst used during this period.

In 1922 Ernst moved to Paris, where the surrealists were gathering around André Breton. Ernst had already started doing more illusionistic paintings, strongly influenced by Giorgio de Chirico, and Breton and his friends admired them. In 1923 Ernst finished *Les Hommes n'en sauront rein,* known as the first Surrealist painting because, as the *Phaidon Dictionary of Twentieth-Century Art* says, it possesses ''all the characteristic elements of Surealist painting: the dreamlike atmosphere, the irrational juxtaposition of images of widely different assocaitons, the digrams of celestial phenomena, the desert landscape and the central eroticism.'' In 1924 he completed one of his most famous pieces, *Two Children Are Threatened by a Nightingale.* Ernst himself was a winning figure, very charming and brilliant, and particularly fascinating to women. His romantic life was colorful, with many love affairs and several marriages; these were always accompanied by wild stories,

and the surrealists enjoyed his life-style as much as they did his art.

In 1925 Ernst introduced his new technique of *frottage;* he placed sheets of paper on floorboards, tiles, bricks, or whatever was to hand and rubbed them with graphite, producing strange obsessive shapes. This technique fitted in with the surrealist cult of automatic drawing and writing, with their reliance on chance. The texture of these *frottage* drawings was then applied by Ernst to his paintings, combined with other techniques he invented. He did a series of haunting pictures of forests, birds, and hybrid beasts executed in a rough, painterly fashion. In the 1930s he returned to a more illusionistic style, though often with the same mythology as in his early works; at the same time he began doing sculpture, at first using boulders and carving them slightly to reveal hidden poetic shapes.

At the outbreak of World War II Ernst, like many other surrealists, made his way to the United States, where he married Peggy Guggenheim, the American art collector and dealer. The marriage ended in divorce. Ernst lived in the United States until 1953, spending much of his time in Arizona, painting strange landscapes. After 1953 he returned to Europe, painting and exhibiting, and continuing his personal life in a quieter vein, with his wife, Dorothea Tanning, an American painter. In 1954 at the Venice Biennale, Ernst was awarded one of the art world's top honors for painting. Ernst died in 1976. Since his death, major retrospectives exhibitions celebrating his artistic achievements have toured both Europe and the United States.

Further Reading

Ernst wrote a short, fanciful account of his life ("to a young friend") which is in the New York Museum of Modern Art publication, *Max Ernst,* edited by William S. Lieberman (1961). Ernst also wrote poetically on his ideas on art in *Beyond Painting* (1948), which includes interesting essays by his friends. Ernst's work is remembered in Werner Spies, editor, *Max Ernst: A Retrospective,* te Neues Publishing Company, 1995; and William Camfield's *Max Ernst: Dada and the Dawn of Surrealism,* te Neues Publishing Company, 1995. A solid account of Ernst is John Russell, *Max Ernst: Life and Work* (1967). □

Hussain Mohammad Ershad

Bengali military leader and statesman Hussain Mohammad Ershad (born 1930) was chief of staff of the Bangladesh army and served as president of Bangladesh from 1983 to 1990.

A meeting of opposites, a combination of calculated indifference, humanistic compassion, and poetic fatalism that made him stand out as a modern-day Machiavellian prince of the Third World, Hussain Mohammad Ershad of Bangladesh epitomized both ability and ineptitude of leadership character and effectiveness. If he ushered in political stability and increased developmental activities, he was also perceived as installing a variety of politico-economic corruption schemes. In spite of a series of politically instigated and enforced general strikes he managed to maintain himself in power for eight years.

Born on February 1, 1930, in Rangpur, North Bengal (now Bangladesh), of an upper-class Bengali family, Ershad went to Carmichael College in his hometown. He graduated, however, from Dhaka University, the premier university of then East Bengal (eastern part of Pakistan; later to be called East Pakistan) in 1950. In 1952 he was commissioned into the Pakistani army, unusual for a budding poet with a university degree, since a military career was generally regarded by Bengali intellectuals as not worth pursuing. However, due credit goes to a few Bengali college-educated young men like Ershad who understood the importance of a career in the army, which historically has controlled the allocation of resources in most underdeveloped countries. In 1956 he married Begum Rashad, with whom he had a son and adopted a daughter.

With a commission as second lieutenant from the Pakistan Military Academy, he swiftly rose through the ranks of the military hierarchy. He was interned along with other Bengali officers stationed in West Pakistan at the outbreak of the 1971 liberation war and repatriated to Bangladesh in 1973 in accordance with the Simla Agreement between India's Indira Gandhi and Pakistan's Zulfiquar Ali Bhutto. His rise to higher command positions became meteoric after 1975 when Sheik Mujibur Rahman was assassinated by a handful of junior officers of the army. Soon he won the trust of President Ziaur ("Zia") Rahman (1978-1981), who brought a relative calm to a turbulent political situation, and ultimately catapulted Ershad to the position of lieutenant general and chief of staff of the army. Seen as a professional soldier without any political ambition due to his internment during the liberation war and with a flair for Bengali speech writing, he soon became the closest politico-military adviser of Zia.

The stages of Ershad's rise to become the country's most durable president were marked by certain political and military events. The first was the assassination (May 31, 1981) of the highly popular President Rahman at the hands of disgruntled army officers led by Major General A. Manzoor, a former comrade-in-arms who had once saved Zia from an unsuccessful yet bloody coup attempt. It was Ershad who now managed to diffuse a highly charged political atmosphere by crushing the coup and then giving his full support to the ruling Bangladesh Nationalist Party (BNP). The BNP wanted to observe the constitution, which stipulated the holding of an election for a new president within six months of the death of the incumbent. With Ershad's support the BNP nominee, Justice Abdul Sattar, Zia's vice president who had been serving as acting president since the assassination, won a landslide victory in a relatively free election. Ershad's support of constitutional government raised his popularity and built high hopes among the Bengali intellectuals about the future of democracy in Bangladesh.

The second stage of Ershad's rise to the presidency was marked by his assumption of power through a bloodless coup on March 24, 1982. His contention, which was vehemently challenged by his critics, was that President Sattar, being unable to govern himself due to ill health, willingly transferred power to the army, and as its chief of staff Ershad accepted the charge. The deposed President Sattar actually vocally agreed with this assumption. This gave him the authority to dissolve the cabinet and the parliament as well. It also empowered him to contain corruption, especially in high places, by putting a number of the former cabinet ministers, including his current vice president, behind bars.

Between 1982 and 1984 Ershad was involved in making preparations to legitimize his power. Following essentially the legitimizing process previously used by Zia and other military leaders in the developing world, Ershad scheduled and re-scheduled dates for elections at all levels. In spite of opposition from two major rival parties and their respective combines of lesser parties, Ershad managed to hold the Upazilla (sub-regional) elections as well as a referendum on himself in 1985, a presidential election in 1986, and a parliamentary election the same year. In the parliamentary election his newly floated political party—the Jatio Party—captured a comfortable majority of seats. This election also received a stamp of credibility when the main opposition party, the Awami League, not only contested the election, thus giving up its earlier boycott of the electoral process, but won about 30 percent of the seats in the parliament.

Having emerged as the elected president with an elected parliament in which the main opposition party had a voice, Ershad went about consolidating his power through a program of decentralization of civil and judicial administration, together with the constitutional incorporation of the role of the army in the political decision-making process. The legitimizing process used by Ershad assumed that the legitimization of political power for a military leader consists in striking a balance between the actual election and the participation of a major opposition party in it on the one hand and between the demand for reform and the reform attempted by the leader on the other. Ershad seemed to achieve an acceptable level of legitimacy in both presidential and parliamentary elections with his platform of reform in administrative, electoral, and economic areas.

However, in the parliamentary election of 1988, which was boycotted by the two largest opposition parties, his political legitimacy certainly dipped. The greatest challenge to Ershad's increasing political power began in August 1987. At that time parliament approved an amendment to the constitution changing the institution of electoral representation to allow for the armed forces to have variable representation at the regional level of government, depending on the size of the body. In April 1988 mass demonstrations broke out against the president-induced parliamentary bill, but Ershad managed to contain them by vetoing the bill. He then cleverly held another parliamentary election and pacified the voters by withdrawing martial law as he had done once before in 1986. Had the government attempted to introduce the electoral reform bill allowing representation from all professional and occupational groups to the regional government representative body (District Council) the tempers of the opposition parties' leadership, particularly that of the Awami League, perhaps would not have flared into the full-blown mass movement that in November 1987 put tremendous pressure on Ershad to transfer the reins of power to an interim government.

Increasing political pressure was also brought to bear on Ershad for the restoration of democratic institutions in Bangladesh by the U.S. Congress. A U.S. House of Representatives foreign affairs subcommittee hearing on Bangladesh was scheduled on April 14, 1988. With political finesse Ershad lifted martial law, lobbied the three witnesses who were about to testify, and invited the subcommittee chairman, Representative Stephen Solarz, to visit Bangladesh and see for himself Bangladesh's problems of democratization.

After the hearing Ershad again tried to improve the image of his cabinet, as he did in 1982 and 1983, by offering senior cabinet positions to reputable outsiders. Subsequently, one of the three witnesses and Chairman Solarz were invited to Bangladesh as state guests, resulting in positive American reactions to Ershad's efforts at reinforcing his image as a leader who was maintaining the political stability that could be very important for, at least, the partial restoration of democracy.

The incorporation of Islam as the state religion without making Bangladesh a theocracy, the efficient damage control of the devastating flood of 1988, the decentralization of the civilian administration, and an improvement in labor relations brought only a short-term stability to Bangladesh. Ershad called for an early election and on October 15,

1990, was re-elected for another four years. But the victory was hotly disputed. Ershad re-imposed martial law. He lifted the law November 10 after the parliament had granted the president and others freedom from prosecution for any actions taken under military rule. Now oppositions erupted and a new state of emergency failed to bring stability. Ershad resigned the presidency under pressure on December 4, 1990. He was placed under house arrest while he awaited trial on corruption and other charges. Meanwhile, Khaleda Zia, widow of the assassinated president General Ziaur Rahman, became the first woman prime minister of Bangladesh. At his trial the next year he was found guilty of corruption and illegal weapons possession, and sentenced to 20 years imprisonment.

Further Reading

Additional information on Ershad and his activities can be found in Zillur R. Khan, *From Martial Law to Martial Law: Leadership Crisis in Bangladesh* (1984), and ''Politicization of the Bangladesh Military: A Post-Independence Response to Perceived Shortcoming of Civilian Government,'' *Asian Survey* (May 1981), as well as Hussain Mohammad Ershad, *A Soldier Speaks* (no publisher, n.d.). □

Erté

Romain de Tirtoff, known as Erté (1892-1990), was a Russian fashion illustrator and stage set designer, a master of the Art Deco style.

R omain de Tirtoff was born in St. Petersburg, Russia, on November 23, 1892, of an aristocratic, musical family loyal to the tsar. His father descended from a Tartar Khan named Tirt and ranked as an admiral in the Imperial Naval School. The noble de Tirtoff family had always followed naval careers since Peter the Great. His mother was also an aristocrat of Cossack descent; one of her brothers, Nicholas, was military governor of St. Petersburg. Rimsky-Korsakov, the Russian composer, was one of the friends of the family.

Romain's idea of feminine beauty, throughout his long life, was the pale skin and dark eyes and hair of his mother. He was already designing clothes for her at the age of five, aided by the family's resident dressmaker. She took him on aristocratic summer tours abroad all over Europe while his father was on naval maneuvers.

Before World War I the Russian capital city was elegant and replete with activity—theater, music, the arts, and fashion. Three imperial theaters dominated, where young Romain could enjoy opera (he saw Rimsky-Korsakov's *Sadko* at the age of seven in the family's permanent box in the Maryinsky Theater) and the *Ballets Russes* of the famed Diaghilev. His mother took him on shopping expeditions on fashionable Nevsky Prospekt where he was enthralled by the couturier's craft. He remembered in later years that in his early teens he hated uniformed school and could hardly wait until school was out to pick up his painting and designing again.

Becomes French Even in Name

He arrived in Paris at the age of 19 (February 1912); France was to be his home thereafter. The French influence on St. Petersburg was profound, and Paris was bewitched by all things Russian in those days. In Paris Romain saw ballet-dancer Nijinsky's notorious *L'Après-Midi d'un Faune* and Stravinsky's composition *Sacre du Printemps* in 1913; Picasso and Braque had begun Cubist art-forms; Orphism, Futurism, Dadaism, and Surrealism were about to be launched. (In 1914 Romain designed costumes for a scene called ''La Musée Cubiste'' in a Paris music hall revue, *Plus Ça Change*, at the age of 22). Meanwhile, in December 1912 he landed a job as draftsman in a mediocre fashion-house and was dismissed after a month for having no aptitude for design!

In January 1913 Romain took his sketches to Paul Poiret, the paragon of Parisian couturiers, who had visited St. Petersburg some years before, and secured an 18-month contract. At least Poiret recognized his natural talent. Poiret was responsible for the name ''Erté'' (the French pronunciation of the initials of ''Romain de Tirtoff''), first used professionally by Romain in the *Gazette du Bon Ton* in May 1913. Paul Poiret revolutionized women's clothes. He abandoned the corset and fitted bodice for the *soutien-gorge* (the ''bra''); he adopted the simple, boyish, tubular ''Empire'' line, sometimes with a harem skirt (*jupe culotte*). Alternatively, the slit skirt, separated at the knee, was popular for the Argentine *tango,* a dance of the day. Poiret was the first couturier to market his own perfume, to draw on live models, and to use artists (such as Raoul Dufy) to design his fabric. Young Erté had a lot to learn from the more experienced Poiret, who was a married man in his forties. They parted with an acrimonious lawsuit, nonetheless.

Poiret's business was closed at the start of World War I, and Erté lived in Monte Carlo from 1914 to 1923. Prince Nicholas Ourousoff, a distant cousin, came to live with Erté and was his business manager. Nicholas first suggested a relationship with *Harper's Bazar* in New York; Erté's 2,500 pen-and-ink drawings and *gouache* designs in the inner pages and 240 covers lasted from January 1915 until December 1936. William Randolph Hearst (1863-1951) owned the magazine as part of his publishing empire; when he lost control of it in 1937, Erté's fate was linked with that of Hearst. The new editor made a change from fashion drawing to photography, then the rage. But with his work on *Harper's Bazar* (the spelling of *Bazaar* was changed in 1929), Erté gained an international reputation for over 20 years as the world's leading fashion illustrator. He afterwards said: "Every human being has a duty to make himself as attractive as possible. Not many of us are born beautiful; . . . . Clothes are a kind of alchemy."

A Long Career of Superb Work

Theater—the stage of the French and American music hall—was the scene of the next unfolding of Erté's talent. In the economic boom times of the 1920s, the Jazz Age, the French revue, and the Broadway show were at their summit. The ambition of Erté was to design for the stage. Through Poiret, Erté designed costumes for the Dutch exotic dancer Mata Hari (who was shot by the Germans in World War I as a spy). One of the French music hall pioneers, Madame Rasimi, invited Erté to design costumes and the stage set for her revue called *L'Orient Merveilleux* (1917), where Erté had full range of his imagination for oriental pantomime. Maurice Chevalier and Mistinguett were starring; Erté designed a series of splendid gowns with long trains and the first of the huge, plumed head-dresses, so much a specialty of Mistinguett later.

The *Folies-Bergère* was the first (1869) and most famed music hall in Paris, with its spectacle and almost-nude women. The workshops of Max Weldy at the *Folies-Bergère* were internationally known; they "exported" stage sets and costumes to theaters all over the world. Erté worked with Weldy at the *Folies* from 1919 to 1930, learning what he did not already know about theatrical dress-making and stage lighting and machinery. Erté's designs for the *Folies-Bergère* "are among his finest work," according to distinguished art historian Charles Spencer, reminiscent of *Art Nouveau* painting by Gustav Klimt and the Vienna Secessionist group he founded.

Erté's style suited Broadway. He designed sets and costumes for the *Ziegfeld Follies, George White Scandals* (with music by George Gershwin), and Irving Berlin's *Music Box Revue,* among other shows. Erté's theatrical innovations were countless, including "living curtains" (showgirls with plumes and pearls, festooned by embroidered trains—

e.g., one drawing of 1924 is in the Museum of Modern Art, New York); *costumes collectifs* (immense, single costumes shared by a group of performers, with a single theme—e.g., the collective design called "Silk" is now in the Victoria and Albert Museum, London); and *tableaux vivants* (e.g., *L'Or,* 1923, from the *Ziegfeld Follies,* which needed six and half miles of gold lamé). Erté commented: "We had no budgets in those days . . . neither White nor Ziegfeld would dream of asking the cost of anything."

Through William Randolph Hearst, Erté had a brief career in Hollywood in the 1920s, although his style did not fit too well to the film capital. He worked on *The Restless Sex* (1919) for Hearst's Cosmopolitan Films, on a sequence called "Bal des Arts"— a ballroom setting, with a "Babylonian hanging-garden," a style "between *Art Nouveau* and emergent *Art Deco* of the 1920s." But when he was again called on by Hollywood in an MGM film called *Paris* in 1925, he broke his contract and returned to Paris. Erté "found the scenario dealing with Paris life simply impossible, ghastly in fact. Neither the director, nor the scenario-writer, nor the stars, knew the least bit about life in Paris. It was a huge joke."

Dissatisfied with the Hollywood venture, apparently in 1925-1926 Erté had a "bracing change" of values toward industrial art. He began a collaboration with the French magazine *Art et Industrie.* He designed utility household objects, lamps, furniture, and domestic interiors. Erté published an article about changing women's fashions in the famous 14th edition of the *Encyclopedia Brittanica* (1929), among other projects.

During the late 1930s, World War II, and the 1940s, Erté was primarily involved in the theater in Paris, London, and elsewhere. His designs were acquired by opera, ballet, drama, and music hall companies, from the Saville Theater in London ("*It's in the Bag!,* 1937) to the surrealistic designs for Francis Poulenc's *Les Mamelles de Tirésias* in Paris (at the Opéra-Comique in 1947). On into the 1950s and 1960s he was still designing: *La Plume de Ma Tante* (Garrick Theater, London, 1955-1958 with Zizi Jéanmaire), productions at the Latin Quarter in New York (1964-1965), and numerous shows and spectacles throughout the world. But a real change in his career came in 1965 when he was 73: he met Eric and Salome Estorick, the founders of Seven Arts Ltd., of the Grosvenor Galleries, London and New York. They persuaded Erté to uncover thousands of perfectly preserved drawings from huge trunks in his cellar. They caused a mild sensation, a resurgence of *Art Deco* in the late 1960s, 1970s, and 1980s, a nostalgia craze. Also in the 1960s Erté pioneered in sheet metal sculpture with oil pigments; he called them *Formes Pictorales.* He also produced a series of lithographs and serigraphs for the Estoricks. With graphic art, he concluded, "I could reach the very large public that these Exhibitions had created."

Erté was in his seventies and eighties a slight man with a shock of luxuriant white hair, impeccably groomed, to whom his work was everything. Erté confessed: "My work has been my mother, my wife, my friend, my mistress and my children . . . ." Even though he had several distinct advantages in life—in his aristocratic background in St.

Petersburg, in his mother, in his friends (Poiret, Hearst, Weldy, White, and countless others, including Prince Nicholas)—he had the capability of utter concentration, patience in controlling the designs, and supreme talent. Erté's work has a timeless quality. *Art Deco* design is not "fine art." His art is stylized, but within its stylistic limits, his artistic designs are superb.

Aged 97, Erté fell ill in Mauritius; he was flown to Paris, his real home, where he died on April 21, 1990.

Further Reading

The major study of Erté's art by an art historian is Charles Spencer, *Erté* (London, 1970; rev. 1981). He wrote two books on his life: *Things I Remember* (1975) and *My Life/My Art: An Autobiography* (London, 1989). Studies of Erté's art include his book *Erté Fashions* (1972); Stella Blum, *Designs by Erté: Fashion Drawings in Harper's Bazaar* (1976); Salome Estorick, *Erté Graphics: 5 complete studies* (1978), *Erté's Theatrical Costumes* (1979), and *New Erté Graphics* (1984); and Marshall Lee (ed.), *Erté at 95: The Complete New Graphics* (extended edition, 1988) and *Erté Sculpture* (1986).

Additional Sources

Erté, *Things I remember: an autobiography,* New York: Quadrangle / New York Times Book Co., 1975.
Erté, *My life, my art: an autobiography,* New York: E.P. Dutton, 1989. □

Sam J. Ervin Jr.

Lawyer, judge, and U.S. senator, Sam J. Ervin, Jr. (1896-1984) became a popular figure during one of the most trying times for the United States, when he chaired the Senate Select Committee on Presidential Campaign Activities—the Watergate Committee.

Sam Ervin was born September 27, 1896, in Morganton, North Carolina. His ancestors, Scotch-Irish Presbyterians, fled from religious persecution to settle in the new land in 1732. Educated in public schools and blessed with an insatiable appetite for learning, Ervin earned his college degree from the University of North Carolina in 1917, enlisted in World War I, and was wounded in combat in France. At one point during the war Ervin resigned his commission as a lieutenant as that was the only way he could return to the front and combat. A much decorated hero for his actions, when he returned home he attended Harvard Law School, graduating in 1922. From the mid-1920s until the mid-1950s he practiced law when he was not called to higher duties: as a representative to the North Carolina General Assemblies of 1923, 1925, and 1931; as a criminal court judge (Burke County) from 1935 to 1937; as a U.S. representative for one year (1946) to finish the term of office vacated by the death of his brother; and as an associate justice of the North Carolina Supreme Court from 1948 to 1954.

Ervin was appointed to the U.S. Senate by Governor William B. Umstead when Senator Clyde R. Hoey from North Carolina died in the summer of 1954. He was elected to complete that term in November of 1954 and was re-elected by more than 60 percent of the vote in 1956, 1962, and 1968. During his 20 years in the Senate, Ervin served on several committees of note: the select committee investigating (and ultimately censuring) Senator Joseph McCarthy for activities which disgraced the Senate during McCarthy's anti-Communist smear campaign (1954); the select committee investigating labor racketeering, involving illegal activities in labor or management (1957-1960); and the Select Committee on Presidential Campaign Activities (the Watergate Committee) in 1973 and 1974, which he chaired. He also served as chairman of the Judiciary Subcommittee on Constitutional Rights and succeeded in protecting the rights of persons in the military, of the mentally ill, of the criminally accused, and of American Indians. (However, he consistently opposed a liberal interpretation of the Constitution to facilitate legislation supporting civil rights during the 1960s.) In addition to the Judiciary Committee and the select committees, Ervin's regular assignments were on the Armed Services and Government Operations committees.

Ervin's role as chairman of the Watergate Committee allowed most of the country to observe through televised hearings several characteristics for which he is remembered: a person who held the Constitution in the highest regard and found trespassers to be among the lowest of criminals; a trial judge and attorney who knew how to press witnesses and generate relevant information; and, because

of the nature of his appointment as chairman, an individual who was generally above partisan politics, even though he was usually classified as a conservative by his voting record.

Throughout his career, Ervin maintained that a strict interpretation of the Constitution was very important. He was intolerant of those who meddled with the Constitution, be they activist judges or individuals who violated the tenets of that document. While seldom outwardly critical of individuals, Ervin maintained that those individual freedoms protected by the Constitution—particularly those restrictions upon government—were the most sacred protections guaranteed by the Constitution and were necessary for the preservation of democratic government.

In retirement, Ervin practiced "a little law" in Morganton, North Carolina. He died April 23, 1984, of respiratory failure. He was survived by his wife, Margaret Bruce Bell, whom he married in 1924, and by two daughters and a son.

Further Reading

The only biography of Sam Ervin is Paul R. Clancy, *Just a Country Lawyer* (1974). Sam Ervin wrote of his experiences with the Watergate Committee in *The Whole Truth: The Watergate Conspiracy* (1980). The role of Senator Ervin during the Watergate era is documented in Samual Dash, *Chief Counsel: Inside the Ervin Committee* (1976). Ervin's views on the Constitution and the Supreme Court are presented in Sam J. Ervin, Jr. and Ramsey Clark, *Rule of the Supreme Court: Policymaker or Adjudicator?* (1970). Thad Stem and Alan Butler have presented information about Ervin's anecdotes in *Senator Sam Ervin's Best Stories* (1973), and Senator Ervin published his own account of many anecdotes in *Humor of a Country Lawyer* (1983). He summed up his long career in a 1984 book—*Preserving the Constitution: The Autobiography of Senator Sam J. Ervin, Jr.*

Additional Sources

Dabney, Dick, *A good man: the life of Sam J. Ervin,* Boston: Houghton Mifflin, 1976. ☐

Julius Winfield Erving

Julius Erving, known as Dr. J., was one of the great superstars of professional basketball during the 1970s and 1980s. He was inducted into the Basketball Hall of Fame in 1993 and went on to work for NBC as a studio analyst for their basketball coverage.

Julius Erving (Dr. J) began his career playing for the fledgling American Basketball Association, a league started to compete with the long-established National Basketball Association. He played for several years for the New York Nets, being named most valuable player for the 1973-74 and 1974-75 seasons. After the merger of the two leagues in 1976, Erving was traded to the Philadelphia Seventy-Sixers, where he continued a phenomenal career, playing in several all-star games, setting a slew of records, and altering the way the game was played forever by drawing attention away from the center-focused game. At the time of his retirement from the game, he was basketball's third-highest scorer.

Displayed Great Talent at a Young Age

Julius Erving was the middle child born to Julius and Callie Mae Erving (Lindsay). His father deserted the family when Julius was three, and his mother was left to raise three children on her own, working as a house cleaner. The family lived in a housing project in Hempstead, Long Island, among other poor families. Julius was a quiet, well behaved child, and at times his family was concerned that he was perhaps too withdrawn. In school, however, he was a bright student who liked to recite poetry. He was first attracted to basketball at about the age of nine, and began spending his free time at the public courts in Campbell Park. When he was ten, Irving joined the local Salvation Army team, leading it to a 27-3 season. The next year, his team was 31-1 and went on to win the Inter-County Basketball Association tournament.

Erving attending Roosevelt High School in Roosevelt, Long Island, a town not far from Hempstead, to which the family had moved when Julius was 13. Erving maintained his passion for basketball and was named to the All-County and All-Long Island teams. After graduation Erving was offered several basketball scholarships by some of the best

Julius Erving (no. 6)

colleges in the country. He chose the University of Massachusetts at Amherst, where his basketball mentor's friend was the coach. In his first year at U-Mass, Erving led the freshman team to an undefeated season, on the way breaking the school's freshman records for scoring and rebounding. In his next year, Erving again had a stellar season, averaging 26 points and 20 rebounds per game, leading the country in rebounds. In the summer following his sophomore year, the National Collegiate Athletic Association (NCAA) named Erving to a team of college all-stars to tour Europe and the old Soviet Union. Afterwards, Erving's teammates voted him the tour's most valuable player. In his junior year, Erving averaged 27 points and 19 rebounds per game.

Joined ABA

After completing his junior season, Erving decided to turn professional. This was a controversial decision in that the NCAA liked to see its players complete their degrees before turning pro. But there was a new basketball league forming, the ABA, to challenge the status of the NBA, and they were making Erving some lucrative offers. The year was 1971, and sports salaries were just beginning to skyrocket. Erving signed with an agent and took a four-year contract to play with the Virginia Squires for the sum of $500,000. He stayed with the Squires for two seasons. In his first, he was sixth in the ABA in scoring (27.3 points per game) and third in rebounding (15.7). The Squires went to the playoffs that year, and Erving was first in playoff scoring, with 33 points on average per game. In his next year with the Squires, Erving led the ABA with 31.9 points.

After the close of the 1972-73 season, Erving surprised many fans and hired a new agent to find a more lucrative contract for him. After considering a series of offers, Erving decided on a $1.8 million deal, with a $250,000 signing bonus, with the Atlanta Hawks of the NBA. By leaving the ABA for the NBA, however, Erving set himself up for legal troubles. The NBA, as the established professional basketball league in the country, had rules about college drafts, and because the Milwaukee Bucks had earned the right to first draft picks that year, they sued to stop the deal. Erving's old agents and his old team, the Virginia Squires also went to court. It was a complicated, highly publicized case that was finally sent to arbitration to be settled before the 1973-74 season. The arbitrators arranged a settlement that sent Erving from the Squires to the New York Nets, of the ABA, in exchange for the Nets' highest scorer and a cash payment of $750,000. The Nets also had to pay the Atlanta Hawks a settlement fee of $400,000, and then were free to sign Erving to an eight-year contract that would pay him $2.8 million.

One of the Greatest Athletes Ever

In Erving's first season with the Nets (1973-74), the young superstar won his second straight league scoring championship, averaging 27.4 points per game, and led the team to the championship against the Utah Stars. In the final series, Erving led both teams in scoring with 27.9 points per game, scoring 47 points in the last game, which brought the

Nets the championship four games to one. In the next season, the Nets floundered, playing erratically. In the first round of the play-offs that year against the St. Louis Spirits, Erving had two good games but his performance wasn't enough to keep the team afloat, and the reigning champs were defeated in the first round.

By the 1975-76 season it was pretty clear that the ABA would merge with the NBA after the season. The leaders of the ABA had attracted star talent, like Erving and others, and had many teams playing on par with the older, established league. Basketball was also becoming big business and showed signs that it would continue to grow. Although the Nets again played sporadically that year, they made it to the championship against the Denver Nuggets. It was a hard fought series coming down to an exciting final game in New York; it showcased Erving to be one of the greatest athletes of modern times, and is considered one of the best games in basketball history. At one point The Nets trailed by 20 points, but managed to come back and win the game, largely as a result of Erving's play. *Sports Illustrated* called Erving's performance "the greatest individual performance by a basketball player at any level anywhere." For the championship series, Erving averaged 37.7 points, 14.2 rebounds and six assists per game. In his ABA career, Erving scored 11,662 points in total, a per-game average of 29.

Demanded Higher Salary

As anticipated, the next year the ABA and NBA merged. Erving was offered a contract to continue playing for the Nets, but he felt the money was insufficient for a player of his caliber, so he held out for a better offer. Erving was one of the first superstar athletes outside of baseball—which had seen skyrocketing salaries and athlete hold-outs for years—to demand increasingly large sums of money. Ultimately, he signed with the Philadelphia 76ers, already a playoff team with substantial talent, including Darrel Dawkins, Caldwell Jones, Doug Collins and George McGinnis.

The 76ers led their division through most of the season, and Erving scored thirty points during the all-star game and was named MVP. In the ABA, he had been in many ways, a superstar alone and unchallenged. The Sixers, however, were loaded with big names and big egos, and consequently exhibited little team work. They made it to the championship but lost to the Portland Trailblazers after winning the first two games of the series. They had a similar season the following year with the Sixers making it into the playoffs but being eliminated early.

In the 1978-79 season, the management of the Philadelphia 76ers realized that they had a flawed strategy of hiring a team of expensive superstars and thinking that would automatically lead to championships. They traded all their big names except Erving and named him captain, deciding to build a team around their most talented, most team-oriented player. However, that first season of rebuilding did not go well, and in the next season, 1979-80, the Sixers had their best regular season record in over a decade but were eliminated in the playoffs, losing to the Los

Angeles Lakers with their soon-to-be-named rookie of the year, Magic Johnson.

Inducted into Basketball Hall of Fame

The following season, 1980-81, Erving was named MVP; the first time that award had gone to a non-center in 17 years. Erving's play had revolutionized basketball, taking offense out to the perimeter instead of just on the boards. They made it to the playoffs again, but this year they came up against their old rivals, the Boston Celtics, with their second-year superstar Larry Bird, and lost a heartbreaking series after being up three games to one. In 1981-82, the Sixers were again left without a championship. That year they made it past the Celtics, but lost to a rampaging Los Angeles Lakers in the finals.

For 1982-83, Philadelphia, by now quite tired of losing to the Celtics and Lakers, signed Moses Malone, hoping to beef up their offense to go against Jabar and Johnson on the Lakers and Bird and McHale on the Celtics. That year they played phenomenally well and made it to the championships, where, once again, they faced their perennial foes from the west, the Lakers. With Malone, however, the Sixers had an added dimension and they took the series in four games straight. It was Erving's first and last NBA championship. The Sixers' prominence steadily diminished over the next couple of years, and in 1987, Julius Erving retired from basketball, after becoming the third player, after Wilt Chamberlain and Kareem Abdul-Jabbar, to score 30,000 career points.

After retiring from basketball, Erving became a successful businessman, buying a Coca Cola bottling business. In 1993 he was inducted into the Basketball Hall of Fame and was hired by NBC as a studio analyst for their basketball coverage. In 1994 *Sports Illustrated* named him to its "40 for the Ages" list, a listing of the forty greatest athletes of all time.

Further Reading

Wilker, Josh, *Julius Erving: Basketball Great,* Chelsea House, 1995.

Porter, David L., *Biographical Dictionary of American Sports,* Greenwood Press, 1995. □

Matthias Erzberger

The German statesman Matthias Erzberger (1875-1921) is best known for his sponsorship of the German parliamentary peace resolution during World War I and for his subsequent signing of the armistice agreement.

Matthias Erzberger was born in Buttenhausen, Württemberg, on Sept. 20, 1875, the son of a Catholic tailor and postman. Trained as an elementary teacher, he gave up his teaching career in 1896 to join the Catholic (and anti-Marxist) social movement as a lecturer and pamphleteer. Later he became editor of the Catholic Center party's Stuttgart publication, *Deutsches Volksblatt.* Erzberger's energy, dedication, and polemical skill soon made his reputation. In 1903 he was elected to the Reichstag (the parliament) as a delegate of the Center party's left wing.

As a member of the parliament, Erzberger combined the qualities of a master of financial intricacies with those of a Christian crusader. Appointed to the budget committee in 1904, he immediately became the sponsor and explicator of major fiscal legislation, most significantly the Finance Reform of 1909 and the military expansion bills of 1911-1913. Meanwhile, he crusaded for the rights of Catholics and against the suppression of West Prussian Poles and abuses and injustices in the colonies.

In the early years of World War I Erzberger was a fervent annexationist and served as propaganda chief toward neutral countries. He went on several important diplomatic missions, chiefly to Italy and to the Vatican. The realities of the war, however, caused him to oppose by 1916 an escalation to unlimited submarine warfare and to advocate a negotiated peace. In July 1917 he became the main sponsor of the famous Reichstag Peace Resolution.

In the government of Prince Baden, appointed to preside over the end of the war, Erzberger became state secretary without portfolio, and he was subsequently appointed armistice commissioner. In that capacity he signed the armistice agreement for Germany at Compiène on Nov. 11, 1918, and directed all armistice negotiations with the Allies.

In 1919 he became the most prominent spokesman for the unconditional ratification of the Treaty of Versailles.

As vice-chancellor and finance minister in the first coalition government of the republic, Erzberger attempted an ambitious financial reform, which simultaneously aimed at social justice and at centralization of the financial system through radical changes in the German tax structure. This reform intensified the virulent attacks on him from the right, which climaxed in a vituperous assault by a former vice-chancellor, Karl Helfferich. The subsequent libel suit necessitated Erzberger's resignation. On Aug. 26, 1921, he was murdered by two members of an ultranationalist fraternal order.

Further Reading

Neither Erzberger's early memoirs nor his numerous books and pamphlets, with the exception of *The League of Nations: The Way to the World's Peace,* translated by Bernard Miall (1919), are available in English. The best biography is Klaus Epstein, *Matthias Erzberger and the Dilemma of German Democracy* (1959). □

Jaime Escalante

Jaime Escalante (born 1930) a high school math teacher whose dedication to his students inspired Hollywood to make a movie of how he changed the lives of his students.

Jaime Escalante, a native of La Paz, Bolivia, and the son of two elementary-school teachers, inspired a movie in the 1980s by raising the aspirations of Hispanic students in one of Los Angeles's most decaying urban high schools. Shortly after Escalante came to Garfield High, its reputation had sunk so low that its accreditation was threatened. Instead of gearing classes to poorly performing students, Escalante offered AP (advanced placement) calculus. He had already earned the criticism of an administrator who disapproved of his requiring students to answer a homework question before being allowed into the classroom. "He told me to just get them inside," Escalante reported, "but I said, there is no teaching, no learning going on." Determined to change the status quo, Escalante had to persuade the first few students who would listen to him that they could control their futures with the right education. He promised them that the jobs would be in engineering, electronics, and computers, but they would have to learn math to succeed. He told his first five calculus students in 1978 that "I'll teach you math and that's your language. With that you're going to make it. You're going to college and sit in the first row, not the back, because you're going to know more than anybody." The student body at Garfield High, more than 90 percent Mexican American, had been told by teachers for years that to be Mexican American was to be unintelligent, but many of them rose to his challenge.

Public Acclaim

Within three years of instituting the calculus class, some of Escalante's students were scoring the highest possible grade, five, on the extremely difficult AP test, which entitles a student to credit at most colleges and universities. Almost all his students were receiving at least the passing grade on the test. In 1982, however, the College Board, which supervises the AP courses and testing, challenged the scores of eighteen of the Garfield students, citing irregularities in answers. The College Board accused the students of cheating. Escalante protested and convinced the students to redeem themselves by taking another test. They all passed. This event established the academic reputation of the program, and soon thereafter the 1987 film *Stand and Deliver,* starring Edward James Olmos, introduced the nation to the dramatic story of a teacher who, through igniting a love of learning in his barrio students, changed their lives.

Program Continues

In 1980 there were thirty-two calculus students in AP courses at Garfield; by 1988, 443 students took the AP exams and 266 passed. Because of state-granted waivers and a school-sponsored corporate fund raiser, only a few of the students had to pay the seventy-one-dollar fee to take the exams. Besides calculus, Garfield added sixteen AP courses in other fields, and many of the teachers in the program feel that the intellectual ability in their school could have remained untapped had Escalante not served as a catalyst. The changes at Garfield were not only among the elite students, however; the dropout rate, which was 55 percent in 1978, dropped to only 14 percent by 1988. Fully 75 percent of Garfield's 1987 graduating seniors planned to go on to some type of postsecondary instruction. Escalante emerged from the 1980s as a national figure—praised by President Reagan on a special visit to the White House, and singled out by Vice President Bush as a personal hero during one of his presidential campaign debates. During a decade with seemingly conflicting educational goals—excellence and inclusion—Escalante served as a model of a teacher who could achieve both.

In 1991 Escalante moved on to other challenges, including teaching basic math and algebra at Hiram Johnson High School in Sacramento, California. In partnership with the Foundation for Advancements in Science and Education (FASE), he is also involved in the Production of a Peabody-Award winning PBS series, "Futures," as well as other projects based on his classroom techniques.

Further Reading

New York Times Biographical Service (January 1988): 75-78.
Technos Quarterly: For Education and Technology (Spring 1993): Vol. 2, No. 1. □

Sergei Aleksandrovich Esenin

The poetry of the Russian author Sergei Aleksandrovich Esenin (1895-1925) reflects the impact of industrialization on Russian rural life. The novelty of his works and his flamboyant personality attracted the attention of artistic circles in Russia and abroad.

Sergei Esenin was born on Oct. 3, 1895, in the Ryazan Province. His parents were of peasant stock. He was raised from the age of 2 in the home of his grandfather. Esenin's youth was rough and adventurous. He learned to ride horseback at the age of 3 and soon took part in farming and in hunting expeditions. After graduating from the local provincial school in 1909, Esenin studied for 3 years in a Russian Orthodox church school; the Russian Orthodox religion had a strong effect on his political views and on the thematics of his poetry. In 1912 Esenin went to Moscow, where he studied at the Shanyavsky People's University. While there he worked at various jobs and began to write verse. His first poems were published in 1914.

In 1914 Esenin moved to Petrograd (later Leningrad, now St. Petersburg) and immediately became a literary celebrity. He made the acquaintance of the symbolist poet Aleksandr Blok and was a frequent visitor at various literary salons. He had a completely uninhibited, raucous personality. He would often become intoxicated and proclaim his verse at the top of his voice. Army service interrupted his career in 1916, but soon after the Russian Revolution he was discharged, and he returned to Petrograd.

Shortly after the Revolution, Esenin married the dancer Isadora Duncan. She, like many Western artists of the period, was flirting with the new and promising ideas emanating from the Soviet Union after the Revolution. But Esenin had seen the devastating effect of these ideas on the traditional peasant culture which he cherished, and their marriage was stormy. In 1922 and 1923 Esenin and his wife toured abroad, stopping in Germany, France, Austria, and the United States. In 1925 Esenin found himself abandoned and alone in Leningrad, suffering from alcoholism. On the night of Dec. 27, 1925, he cut his wrists, wrote his last poem in his own blood, and hanged himself.

Esenin's poetry is inspired by a sensitivity to nature, unsullied by modern life and free of the effects of industrialization. He is a poet of the Russian village and of the Russian peasant in his rural setting. His appreciation for nature is primitive and religious, almost pantheistic. His poems after the Revolution portray the devastating effects which the encroachment of industrialization had on traditional rural life. A typical juxtaposition in his poetry is that of a colt to the iron horse of the railroad. His style and language reflect the rhythm and color of Russian peasant speech. One of the founders of the short-lived imagist movement in Russian poetry, Esenin often uses liturgical words and bright, contrasting images. He viewed human nature as fundamentally dual, and his poetry portrays the struggle between creative and destructive forces in human life.

Further Reading

An exceptionally good study of Esenin's life and personality is Frances De Graaff, *Sergei Esenin: A Biographical Sketch* (1966). Irma Duncan, *Isadora Duncan's Russian Days* (1929), is a good account of Esenin's marriage to Isadora Duncan. The best critical study of Esenin's poetry is found in Renato Poggioli, *The Poets of Russia, 1890-1930* (1960).

Additional Sources

Esenin: a biography in memoirs, letters, and documents, with previously untranslated prose works and correspondence by Esenin, Ann Arbor, Mich.: Ardis, 1982.
McVay, Gordon, *Esenin: a life,* Ann Arbor, Mich.: Ardis, 1976. □

2d Earl of Essex

The English courtier Robert Devereux, 2d Earl of Essex (1567-1601), was a favorite of Queen Elizabeth I. However, his extravagance and desire for glory compromised his delicate position in the power structure.

Robert Devereux was born on Nov. 10, 1567, at Netherwood, Herefordshire, the eldest son of Walter Devereux, 1st Earl of Essex, and his wife, Lettice Knollys. His father died when the boy was only 9, and he was placed under the guardianship of the powerful Lord Burghley, the Queen's chief counselor. Already the financial affairs of the family were much embarrassed. Essex was educated at Trinity College, Cambridge, and received a master of arts degree on July 6, 1581.

Career at Court

Although Essex first appeared at court at Christmas 1577, it was not until 1584 that his stepfather, the Earl of Leicester, induced him to enter the court seriously. It was noted that his "innate courtesy" and "goodly person" soon made him popular. In August 1585 Essex was appointed general of the horse in the expedition under Leicester to aid the Netherlands in its revolt against Spain. His gallantry in the battle of Zutphen (Sept. 21, 1586) was rewarded with the dignity of a knight banneret.

In 1587 Essex returned to court. He was now a handsome young man of 20 and very clearly had the Queen's favor. A friend remarked how the Queen and Essex were frequently together and how "he cometh not to his own lodging till birds sing in the morning." It is from this period that Essex's rivalry with Sir Walter Raleigh stemmed. It is clear that Leicester was pushing Essex forward in an attempt to reduce Raleigh's influence with the Queen.

Military Expeditions

In 1589, dissatisfied with his position at court, Essex joined a naval expedition in support of Don Antonio, a claimant to the throne of Portugal. Essex distinguished himself in this campaign, but the Queen initially showed great displeasure at his departure. On his return home he was able to effect a reconciliation, but for the moment he took little prominent part in home affairs. Essex married Sir Philip Sidney's widow in 1590.

In 1591 Essex was granted a commission to command an expedition to France in support of Henry of Navarre. Though he showed "true valor and discretion," he accomplished little and was recalled in January 1592. For the next 4 years Essex remained at home and sought to build a position of domestic power. He became a privy councilor in 1593 and was regularly in attendance in the House of Lords. Increasingly he found himself in a power struggle with Burghley's son, Robert Cecil, and he began to gather around him those opposed to the dominance of the Cecil family. He found a valuable ally in Francis Bacon, who became his political adviser. By 1595 Essex seemed to be making a rapid advance in power and position.

Cadiz Expedition

In 1596 Essex came out strongly in favor of an attack on the shipping in Spanish ports, and after some delay he was made commander of the land forces for the expedition. He played a prominent role in the capture of Cadiz and emerged as the popular hero of the expedition. The Queen, however, was suspicious of military leaders whose fame might rival her own. His rivals, especially Sir Robert Cecil, were able to exploit this fact to undermine his domestic position while he was abroad. Essex attempted a reconciliation with the Cecil faction and secured the command of

another naval expedition against Spain, this time to the Azores, but his peaceful relations with the court were short-lived. While the country increasingly sought peace, Essex was identified as a leader of the war party.

Meanwhile the situation in Ireland had grown critical. A rebellion led by the Earl of Tyrone threatened to overthrow the English dominance. After failing to secure the mastership of the wards in 1598, Essex accepted command of the army in Ireland. It was a great risk, for Ireland had been the graveyard of many a Tudor statesman's reputation. The gamble failed; the council was slow to send supplies, and Essex found himself committed to a long campaign. In defiance of the Queen he left his command in 1599 and returned to England. This action caused his situation to deteriorate even further. In June 1600 a special tribunal removed his offices.

Rebellion against Elizabeth

With the whole structure of his personal patronage collapsing, Essex took one last desperate gamble. He fostered a plot for an armed rising that would force the Queen to take on new advisers. On Feb. 8, 1601, Essex and some 200 followers attempted to ignite the rebellion in London. No one rallied to their cause, and the rebellion died stillborn. Essex was brought to trial and quickly condemned. On February 25 he was executed despite evident popular regret at his fall.

Further Reading

The best modern study of Essex is Robert Lacey, *Robert, Earl of Essex* (1971). See also G. B. Harrison, *The Life and Death of Robert Devereux, Earl of Essex* (1937). Lytton Strachey, *Elizabeth and Essex* (1928), has some interesting insights. Recommended for general historical background are John B. Black, *The Reign of Elizabeth, 1558-1603* (1936; 2d ed. 1959); Stanley T. Bindoff, *Tudor England* (1950); A. L. Rowse, *The England of Elizabeth: The Structure of Society* (1951); James A. Williamson, *The Tudor Age* (1953); Geoffrey R. Elton, *England under the Tudors* (1955); and A. L. Rowse, *The Expansion of Elizabethan England* (1955). □

Richard Estes

The American artist Richard Estes (born 1932) was one of the leading realist painters of urban genre scenes in the latter half of the 20th century.

Richard Estes was born on May 14, 1932, in Kewanee, Ill., and received art training at the School of the Art Institute of Chicago between 1952 and 1956. Much of his training was in figural and traditional subjects. Following his graduation he worked as a graphic designer in Chicago, and also in New York City from when he moved there in 1959 until 1966 when he became a full-time painter. In 1962, on his own savings, he painted in Spain for a year. His first one-man show took place at the Allan Stone Gallery in New York in 1968.

Estes' work, like that of artists who similarly produce work with a high degree of verisimilitude, has been labeled variously as super-realism, neo-realism, photo-realism, or radical realism. All these terms are useful in understanding Estes' style, but super-realism is the one used more frequently. Another term, one used as the title of an important group show in 1972, was "sharp-focus realism." This exhibition included traditional, non-abstract, illusionistic work. Most looked like large photographs.

Estes' use of photography made the sharp-focus realism show controversial because critics were not comfortable using the term "realism." Realism is the 19th-century artistic style associated with subjects of modern, everyday life, especially in the work of artists such as Courbet and Eakins. For the 20th-century artists, the use of the photograph was essential, since it was the common denominator by which most people developed norms of seeing. Estes normally used several photographs in the preparation of a single painted composition. The paintings are not reproductions of photographs, but highly organized compositions based on photographs.

Estes' paintings frequently portray anonymous streets or other urban sights, with reflective glass, metal, cars, storefronts, and other surfaces. Often scenes include elaborate signage, curved and reflective architectural shapes, and colored neon, reminiscent of Art Deco. But other details make clear that Estes was not recreating a previous era in his paintings, but rather showing structures that had endured the passage of time. The reflective surfaces concentrate

attention not only on what is inside the windows but on what is around the viewer, the context of those contents.

Most of the scenes are of Manhattan, but there are also images of Venice, Chicago, and Paris. His scenes show daylight, never night, and suggest vacant and quiet Sunday mornings. He rarely included garbage, people, slush or snow, or other details that would detract from the structures of the city. But there are numerous details in terms of signs, stickers, and window displays, often viewed backwards because reflected. An Estes painting presents more visual information than can easily be received. This wealth of familiar detail is essential to the concept of realism in painting.

Estes mostly worked in oils or acrylics, and in constructing a painting he moved from the general to the specific. He used color slides in the studio, but did not project on the canvas as did some other artists. He did, however, plan on the canvas, first sketching out entirely the general composition. His work in the studio was one of selection and organization. Thus, despite the power of the photographic illusionism, the abstract qualities are strong. The thoughtful viewer is sensitive to forms and shapes, as much as to the tactile quality of the surfaces and objects.

Estes admired the early 20th-century photographer Atget and 18th-century Venetian *vedute* (view) painters such as Canaletto and Bellotto. These artists presented detached views of their surroundings, sensitive to the particularity of places but equally concerned with strong pictorial composition. Estes' paintings are far removed from the powerful Abstract Expressionist tendency in American painting in the post-World War II period. His relationship to Pop Art was more complex. He did not share the light-hearted casual approach of those artists, but certainly relied on aspects of popular culture in his work.

Richard Estes' work emphasizes craftsmanship and traditional conventions of making a two-dimensional canvas look three-dimensional, allowing the viewer to play the impartial observer, so that the sensation of being in that scene determines a more subtle mood. He was one of the most accomplished painters in defining and presenting the urban landscape in a super-realist style.

Further Reading

An excellent monograph is L. K. Meisel, *Richard Estes: The Complete Paintings, 1966-1985* (1986). Estes and other artists working in a realist style are discussed in G. Battcock, editor, *Super Realism* (1975); F. H. Goodyear, *Contemporary American Realism Since 1960* (1981); and E. Lucie-Smith, *Super Realism* (1979). For excellent broader discussions of various art movements, including super-realism, see C. Robins, *The Pluralist Era* (1984) and H. Smagula, *Currents: Contemporary Directions in the Visual Arts* (1989). Other more general studies of this period are S. Hunter and J. Jacobus, *Modern Art* (1985) and E. Lucie-Smith, *Art in the Seventies* (1980). □

Estevanico

Estevanico (1500?-1539), often called "the Black," was a Moroccan slave who accompanied Cabeza de Vaca on his odyssey through the southwestern United States. His visit to the "Seven Cities of Cibola" preceded that of Coronado.

Estevanico (also known as Estevan and Estebanico) was born sometime around the beginning of the 16th century in the town of Azemmour on the west coast of Morocco. During that time the Arabs of Morocco were in constant warfare with their Spanish and Portuguese neighbors to the north. At some point, Estevanico was captured and sold as a slave in Spain. He was often called Estevanico the Black, and it may well be that he was African or part-African in descent, since there were many years of contact between the Arabs and Berbers of North Africa and the Blacks who lived south of the Sahara.

Estevanico (which is a Spanish diminutive for "Stephen") came into the possession of Andres Dorantes de Carranca, a nobleman of the Extremadura region of Spain. Dorantes joined the expedition to North America led by Panfilo de Narvaez that included Alvar Nuñez Cabeza de Vaca. They landed in Florida in April 1528. Disregarding the advice of his captains, Narvaez abandoned his ships and marched into the interior on May 1 in search of gold. The history of the succeeding trek comes from the report that Cabeza de Vaca made after his return to Spain. At first, there is no mention of Estevanico.

Narvaez's expedition was attacked by Native Americans near the modern city of Tallahassee. The Spaniards went to a bay on the Gulf of Mexico and constructed five boats with which to sail along the coastline to a Spanish base in Mexico. They set sail on September 22, 1528; Estevanico was in the third boat, commanded by Dorantes. In November they were hit by storms and Dorantes' boat and the one captained by Cabeza de Vaca were wrecked on Galveston Island off the coast of Texas. In the spring of 1529 only 15 men were still alive. Thirteen of them, including Estevanico, left Galveston to try to get to Mexico overland. Cabeza de Vaca was too sick to travel and was left behind.

The party commanded by Dorantes headed west and south. Several died along the way, and the rest were captured by Native Americans at San Antonio Bay. By the autumn of 1530 only Dorantes, Estevanico, and Alonzo del Castillo Maldonado were still alive. They were harshly treated by their captors. Dorantes escaped and went inland to a village of the Mariame tribe, where his life was easier. In the spring of 1532 Estevanico and Castillo also got free and made it to Dorantes' village. In the spring of 1533 they were surprised to see Cabeza de Vaca, who was working as a trader among the various tribes, turn up. The four men were forced to separate but agreed to meet the following autumn at the annual festival to celebrate the harvest of prickly pears.

They did meet in the fall of 1533 but were unable to escape. They returned with their different captors and met again in the fall of 1534 at which time they were able to escape. They came to a camp of the Avavares tribe where they were warmly welcomed as medicine men. Estevanico joined the others in healing the Indians, and was especially noted for his ability to learn to speak other languages and to use sign language. They stayed with the Avavares until the spring of 1535. Their reputation as healers preceded them, and they were welcomed wherever they went.

As the four men went farther west, they saw evidence of different cultures. They saw a metal bell and medicine gourds made by the Pueblo tribes of New Mexico. Estevanico took one of these gourds and used it in his healing act. The four Westerners reached the Rio Grande River at the end of 1535, and Castillo and Estevanico headed upstream. There they came upon the permanent towns or "pueblos" of the Jumano tribe. When the others caught up with them, they found Estevanico surrounded by Indians, who treated him like a god. Along the way, the men heard tales of a group of rich cities in the interior, which they called the Seven Cities of Cibola.

From the Rio Grande, Estevanico and the three Spaniards traveled into what is now the Mexican state of Chihuahua. As they traveled, they saw more and more evidence of contact with Europeans. They met up with a party of Spaniards in March 1536 and entered Mexico City on July 24, 1536. The four men, including Estevanico, were well received by Viceroy Antonio Mendoza, who was intrigued by their tales of wealthy cities to the north.

Cabeza de Vaca returned to Spain while Castillo and Dorantes married and settled down in Mexico. Dorantes sold or gave Estevanico to Viceroy Mendoza. Mendoza wanted to send an expedition north and eventually accepted the offer of a Spanish friar, Fray Marcos de Niza, to lead it. He appointed Estevanico to be his guide. They went north to the town of Culiacan in the autumn of 1538, where Francisco Vázquez de Coronado had recently been appointed governor. Estevanico and Fray Marcos left Culiacan on March 7, 1539. On March 21 Fray Marcos sent Estevanico ahead to scout the trail. Four days later, Native American messengers returned to Fray Marcos to report that Estevanico had heard news that he was 30 days' march from Cibola and asked Fray Marcos to join him.

Fray Marcos headed northward, but Estevanico did not wait for him. As the friar entered each new village, he found a message from Estevanico saying that he had continued on. Fray Marcos chased after him for weeks but was unable to catch up. Estevanico headed through the large desert region of the Mexican state of Sonora and southern Arizona; he was the first Westerner to enter what are now Arizona and New Mexico. Wherever he traveled, Estevanico sent his medicine gourd ahead of him to announce his arrival. In May he reached the Zuni pueblo of Hawikuh, the first of the "Seven Cities of Cibola." There he showed his magic gourd, but the chief threw it down in anger and told Estevanico to leave the town. The chief took away all his possessions and put him in a house on the edge of the town without food or water. The next morning he was attacked by a band of warriors and killed.

Several of the Native American escorts escaped and returned to tell Fray Marcos the news of Estevanico's death. In his report to Mendoza, Fray Marcos said that he continued to trael north until he could see Hawikuh, or Cibola, but did not enter the pueblo. In his report he said that it was a rich place that was even bigger than Mexico City. Since it is in fact only a small pueblo, it seems as though Fray Marcos did not make the trip he claimed. However, his report inspired Mendoza to send out the ill-fated Coronado expedition. When they reached the small village of Hawikuh they learned that Fray Marcos had been lying. They also found that the chief had appropriated Estevanico's green dinner plates, his greyhound dogs, and his metal bells.

When asked why they had killed Estevanico, the Zuni said that he had claimed that there was a huge army coming behind him with many weapons. The chiefs met in council and decided that he was a spy and that it was safer to kill him. Once dead, they cut up his body into little pieces and distributed the parts among the chiefs.

Further Reading

The original source materials that we have on Estevanico are the *Joint Report*, written by Cabeza de Vaca, Dorantes, and Castillo; Cabeza de Vaca's *Relation*; and the reports sent back to Mendoza by Fray Marcos. Fray Marcos's account is available in a new edition along with a study of his journey: Adolph F. Bandelier, *The Discovery of New Mexico by the Franciscan Monk Friar Marcos de Niza in 1539,* translated by Madeleine Turrell Rodack (Tucson: University of Arizona Press, 1981).
These original documentary sources have been used to construct a narrative of Estevanico's adventures by John Upton Terrell in *Estevanico the Black* (Los Angeles: Westernlore Press, 1968), which served as the basis for this account. Terrell includes an extensive bibliography of the original sources and selected secondary sources that discuss the role of Estevanico. □

Manuel Estrada Cabrera

Manuel Estrada Cabrera (1857-1924) is regarded as one of the worst tyrants in Guatemalan history. His presidency, which began in 1898, grew progressively more despotic until his overthrow in 1920.

Manuel Estrada Cabrera, a foundling, was born in Quezaltenango on Nov. 21, 1857. He received early schooling under Church supervision and eventually became a lawyer, practicing in both Quezaltenango and Retalhuleu. President José Maria Reyna Barrios (1891-1898) appointed him minister of government and justice, but his performance was colorless.

When Reyna Barrios was assassinated on Feb. 8, 1898, Estrada Cabrera, who had risen to vice president, became provisional president. The first Guatemalan head of state taken from civilian life in over 50 years, Estrada Cabrera

overcame resistance to his regime by August 1898 and called for September elections, which he won handily. He retained power for 22 years through controlled elections in 1904, 1910, and 1916. One Guatemalan historian has suggested that the extreme despotic characteristics of the man did not emerge until after an attempt on his life in 1907.

Estrada Cabrera's regime did bring some advances. He extended roads, the long-delayed railway from the Atlantic coast to Guatemala City was completed in 1908, and early in his reign he indicated interest in education. In 1899 he initiated feasts of Minerva, celebrating accomplishments of students and teachers. His achievements, however, were overshadowed by growing repression and blatant graft, including bribes for the president. The lot of native workers was little better than peonage, and everywhere there was a spy system to report subversive activities.

On the foreign front Estrada Cabrera was frequently concerned about plottings of Guatemalan exiles in neighboring countries. A border dispute with Mexico strained his relations with that nation, and a personal feud with Gen. Tomás Regalado led to a border clash with El Salvador when Regalado, inebriated, invaded Guatemala. Estrada Cabrera cultivated friendly relations with the United States, and he supported United States policy during the Panamanian revolution of 1903.

By 1919 strong opposition developed against the dictator, which, emboldened by rumors of United States disenchantment with Estrada Cabrera, moved in the early months of 1920 to challenge his control. Popular pressure forced

the National Assembly on April 8 to declare Estrada Cabrera insane. Fighting followed, but good offices of the diplomatic corps brought a settlement which included Estrada Cabrera's surrender and assurances of his safety. He was later tried and imprisoned but released in 1922 because of ill health. He died on Sept. 24, 1924, and was buried at Quezaltenango.

Further Reading

There are no full-length studies of Estrada Cabrera in English. Dana G. Munro, *The Five Republics of Central America* (1918) and *Intervention and Dollar Diplomacy in the Caribbean, 1900-1921* (1964), which emphasizes United States relations, contain sections on the Guatemalan leader. Chester Lloyd Jones, *Guatemala: Past and Present* (1940), also has an excellent summary of Estrada Cabrera's administration. □

Tomás Estrada Palma

The Cuban statesman Tomás Estrada Palma (1835-1908) first served as president of the provisional government during Cuba's War for Independence and then became the first president of the republic.

Tomás Estrada Palma was born near Bayamo, Oriente Province, on July 9, 1835. He attended schools in Havana and the University of Seville in Spain but failed to obtain a degree because family matters forced his return to Cuba.

As soon as Cuba's Ten-Year War (1868-1878) against Spain broke out, Estrada Palma joined the rebels. In 1876 he was selected president of the provisional government but in 1877 was captured by Spanish forces and exiled to Spain, where he remained in jail until the end of the war. After his release he traveled to Paris, New York, and Honduras. In Honduras he married Genoveva Guardiola, daughter of Honduran president Santos Guardiola, and was appointed director of the postal service. From Central America, Estrada Palma moved to Orange County, N.Y., where he opened a boys' school.

Teaching soon gave way to politics. The Cubans were resuming the war against Spain, and José Martí visited Estrada Palma to enlist his support for the revolutionary cause. When Martí was killed in Cuba in the early months of the war (May 1895), Estrada Palma was named delegate in exile and head of the Cuban junta in New York, carrying out diplomatic negotiations primarily with the United States, raising funds, and promoting the Cuban cause.

President of Cuba

In 1902 Estrada Palma became the first president of the republic, having been elected in 1901 by an overwhelming majority. The new president encouraged foreign investment and Cuba's exports. He expanded public and educational projects and in 1903 negotiated with the United States a permanent treaty which was to govern the relations be-

tween the two countries. On July 16, 1903, the United States recognized Cuba's sovereignty over the Isle of Pines, and Cuba granted the United States the right to lease and establish naval bases at Guantánamo and Bahía Honda. That same year Cuba signed a reciprocity treaty with the United States which gave Cuban products, particularly sugar, a preferential rate for import duties into the United States and gave selected American products preference in Cuban rates.

Estrada Palma was less successful in his domestic policies. A popular and well-intentioned man, he remained at first above partisan politics, conducting an honest and paternalistic government. He had little faith in the ability of his compatriots to govern themselves and scolded them for their shortcomings. Teacher turned politician, he lectured the Cubans on political virtue and good government.

As the elections of 1905 approached, political difficulties increased. Estrada Palma joined the Conservative Republican party, or Moderate party as it was then called, and sought reelection. He purged unfriendly officeholders. Corruption increased, tensions mounted, and accusing the administration of fraud, the opposition Liberal party boycotted the elections, thus allowing Estrada Palma's unopposed reelection.

The Liberals charged a corrupt election and resorted to violence. In August 1906 an uprising took place in Pinar del Río Province, which quickly spread throughout the island. Estrada Palma appealed for United States intervention. President Theodore Roosevelt sent Secretary of War William H.

Taft to mediate between government and opposition. But when Taft proposed, with Liberal backing, that all of the elections be nullified except those of the president and vice president, Estrada Palma rejected the proposal and resigned in September 1906. Taft then ordered the landing of U.S. marines. He dissuaded the Liberals from fighting and proclaimed a provisional government led first by himself as acting governor and later by Charles E. Magoon. United States intervention lasted until January 1909. Estrada Palma retired quietly to his modest holding in Bayamo, where he died on Nov. 4, 1908.

Further Reading

An account of Estrada Palma's life and presidency is in Alan Reed Millett, *The Politics of Intervention: The Military Occupation of Cuba, 1906-1909* (1968). Also useful on Estrada Palma's career are Russell Hunke Fitzgibbon, *Cuba and the United States, 1900-1935* (1964), and John E. Fagg, *Cuba, Haiti, and the Dominican Republic* (1965). ☐

Ethelred the Unready

The Anglo-Saxon king Ethelred the Unready (c. 968-1016) ruled the English from 978 to 1016. During his reign England was repeatedly attacked by Danish armies seeking to destroy the sovereignty of the Anglo-Saxons and to plunder their land.

Born into the royal house of Wessex, which was at that time the effective ruler of all the Anglo-Saxons, Ethelred was a direct descendant of Alfred the Great and the son of King Edgar, who had ruled a united and peaceful England for 16 years. At Edgar's death in 975, the realm passed to Ethelred's brother Edward, who was still a child. The nobles of the kingdom formed rival parties around Edward and Ethelred, and the latter's supporters murdered Edward on March 18, 978, making Ethelred king. Edward was soon widely honored as a martyred saint, and devotion to him gave many an excuse to withhold allegiance from his successor.

From the time of Ethelred's accession at the age of 9 or 10, his reign was tragically marred by the treason and revolt of his leading thegns (noblemen). The ensuing disorder was nourished by his own indecisive character and by the renewal of Danish raids on England in 980 after a pause of 25 years. Increasing Danish aggressiveness complemented the increasing English disunity and military ineffectiveness. In 991 Ethelred instituted a policy of buying off Danish raiders with lavish payments of silver. Given the inadequacy of English defenses, it was a strategically sound but psychologically demoralizing decision that mocked the heroic traditions of the Anglo-Saxons.

In 1009 an enormous army, sent by King Swein of Denmark, arrived in England to depose Ethelred. Although the English bought the invaders off in 1012, the following year Swein led another invasion. Much of the demoralized

English nation submitted to his rule. Ethelred resisted from London for some months, then finally fled to Normandy. After Swein died suddenly in February 1014, Ethelred was reinstated as king. His rule was challenged by Cnut, Swein's younger son, and apparently by his own son Edmund Ironsides.

Cnut's first campaign misfired, and he retreated to Denmark, only to return to England with a new army in 1015. Ethelred and Edmund joined forces against the invader early in 1016 at London. But on April 23, 1016, Ethelred died. Edmund succeeded him and struggled on for a few months. However, by the end of the year Edmund too was dead, and Cnut became the ruler of England.

Further Reading

The primary source for Ethelred's reign is *The Anglo-Saxon Chronicle,* edited and translated by G. N. Garmonsway (1953; 2d ed. 1955); its account of these troubled years is unusually thorough and impassioned. The best analysis of Ethelred's policies and shortcomings is in F. M. Stenton, *Anglo-Saxon England* (1943; 2d ed. 1947). See also Christopher N. L. Brooke, *The Saxon and Norman Kings* (1963). ☐

Euclid

The Greek mathematician Euclid (active 300 B.C.) wrote the *Elements,* a collection of geometrical theorems. The oldest extant major mathematical work in the Western world, it set a standard for logical exposition for over 2,000 years.

Virtually nothing is known of Euclid personally. It is not even known for certain whether he was a creative mathematician himself or was simply good at compiling the work of others. Most of the information about Euclid comes from Proclus, a 5th-century-A.D. Greek scholar. Since Archimedes refers to Euclid and Archimedes lived immediately after the time of Ptolemy I, King of Egypt (ca. 306-283 B.C.), Proclus concludes they were contemporaries. Euclid's mathematical education may well have been obtained from Plato's pupils in Athens, since it was there that most of the earlier mathematicians upon whose work the *Elements* is based had studied and taught.

No earlier writings comparable to the *Elements* of Euclid have survived. One reason is that Euclid's *Elements* superseded all previous writings of this type, making it unnecessary to preserve them. This makes it difficult for the historian to investigate those earlier mathematicians whose works were probably more important in the development of Greek mathematics than Euclid's. About 600 B.C. the Greek mathematician Thales is said to have discovered a number of theorems that appear in the *Elements*. It might be noted too that Eudoxus is also given credit for the discovery of the method of exhaustion, whereby the area of a circle and volume of a sphere and other figures can be calculated. Book XII of the *Elements* makes use of this method. Although mathematics may have been initiated by concrete

problems, such as determining areas and volumes, by the time of Euclid mathematics had developed into an abstract construction, an intellectual occupation for philosophers rather than scientists.

The *Elements*

The *Elements* consists of 13 books. Within each book is a sequence of propositions or theorems, varying from about 10 to 100, preceded by definitions. In Book I, 23 definitions are followed by five postulates. After the postulates, five common notions or axioms are listed. The first is, "Things which are equal to the same thing are also equal to each other." Next are 48 propositions which relate some of the objects that were defined and which lead up to Pythagoras's theorem: in right-angled triangles the square on the side subtending the right angle is equal to the sum of the squares on the sides containing the right angle. The usual elementary course in Euclidean geometry is based on Book I.

The remaining books, although not so well known, are more advanced mathematically. Book II is a continuation of Book I, proving geometrically what today would be called algebraic identities, such as $(a + b)^2 = a^2 + b^2 + 2ab$, and generalizing some propositions of Book I. Book III is on circles, intersections of circles, and properties of tangents to circles. Book IV continues with circles, emphasizing inscribed and circumscribed rectilinear figures.

Book V of the *Elements* is one of the finest works in Greek mathematics. The theory of proportions discovered by Eudoxus is here expounded masterfully by Euclid. The theory of proportions is concerned with the ratios of magnitudes (rational or irrational numbers) and their integral multiples. Book VI applies the propositions of Book V to the figures of plane geometry. A basic proposition in this book is that a line parallel to one side of a triangle will divide the other two sides in the same ratio.

As in Book V, Books VII, VIII, and IX are concerned with properties of (positive integral) numbers. In Book VII a prime number is defined as that which is measured by a unit alone (a prime number is divisible only by itself and 1). In Book IX proposition 20 asserts that there are infinitely many prime numbers, and Euclid's proof is essentially the one usually given in modern algebra textbooks. Book X is an impressively well-finished treatment of irrational numbers or, more precisely, straight lines whose lengths cannot be measured exactly by a given line assumed as rational.

Books XI-XIII are principally concerned with three-dimensional figures. In Book XII the method of exhaustion is used extensively. The final book shows how to construct and circumscribe by a sphere the five Platonic, or regular, solids: the regular pyramid or tetrahedron, octahedron, cube, icosahedron, and dodecahedron.

Manuscript translations of the *Elements* were made in Latin and Arabic, but it was not until the first printed edition, published in Venice in 1482, that geometry, which meant in effect the *Elements,* became important in European education. The first complete English translation was printed in 1570. It was during the most active mathematical period in England, about 1700, that Greek mathematics was studied most intensively. Euclid was admired, mastered, and utilized by all major mathematicians, including Isaac Newton.

The growing predominance of the sciences and mathematics in the 18th and 19th centuries helped to keep Euclid in a prominent place in the curriculum of schools and universities throughout the Western world. But also the *Elements* was considered educational as a primer in logic.

Euclid's Other Works

Some of Euclid's other works are known only through references by other writers. The *Data* is on plane geometry. The word "data" means "things given." The treatise contains 94 propositions concerned with the kind of problem where certain data are given about a figure and from which other data can be deduced, for example: if a triangle has one angle given, the rectangle contained by the sides including the angle has to the area of the triangle a given ratio.

On Division (of figures), also on plane geometry, is known only in the Arabic, from which English translations were made. Proclus refers to it when speaking of dividing a figure into other figures different in kind, for example, dividing a triangle into a triangle and a quadrilateral. *On Division* is concerned with more general problems of division. As an example, one problem is to draw in a given circle two parallel chords cutting off between them a given fraction of the area of the circle.

The *Conics* appears to have been lost by the time of the Greek astronomer Pappus (late 3d century A.D.). It is frequently referred to by Archimedes. As the name suggests, it dealt with the conic sections: the ellipse, parabola, and hyperbola, to use the names given them later by Apollonius of Perga.

A work which has survived is *Phaenomena*. This is what today would be called applied mathematics; it is about the geometry of spheres applicable to astronomy. Another applied work which has survived is the *Optics*. It was maintained by some that the sun and other heavenly bodies are actually the size they appear to be to the eye. This work refuted such a view by analyzing the relationship between what the eye sees of an object and what the object actually is. For example, the eye always sees less than half of a sphere, and as the observer moves closer to the sphere the part of it seen is decreased although it appears larger.

Another lost work is the *Porisms*, known only through Pappus. A porism is intermediate between a theorem and a problem; that is, rather than something to be proved or something to be constructed, a porism is concerned with bringing out another aspect of something that is already there. To find the center of a circle or to find the greatest common divisor of two numbers are examples of porisms. This work appears to have been more advanced than the *Elements* and perhaps if known would give Euclid a higher place in the history of mathematics.

Further Reading

The standard English translation of the *Elements* is Thomas L. Heath, *The Thirteen Books of Euclid's Elements* (3 vols., 1908; 2d ed. 1926); the introduction and commentary contain much information on Euclid. A full-length study of Euclid is Thomas Smith, *Euclid: His Life and System* (1902). General studies with good discussions of Euclid include Thomas L. Heath, *A Manual of Greek Mathematics* (1931); Carl B. Boyer, *The History of the Calculus and Its Conceptual Development* (1939; rev. ed. 1949); Bartel L. van der Waerden, *Science Awakening* (1950; trans. 1954); Morris Kline, *Mathematics in Western Culture* (1953); Joseph Frederick Scott, *A History of Mathematics: From Antiquity to the Beginning of the Nineteenth Century* (1958); and Howard Eves, *Fundamentals of Geometry* (1969). □

Eudoxus of Cnidus

The astronomer, mathematician, and physician Eudoxus of Cnidus (ca. 408-ca. 355 B.C.) was the first Greek astronomer to properly apply mathematics to astronomy.

Eudoxus was born in Cnidus, a Greek colony in Asia Minor, into a family of physicians; he studied at the medical school there. At the age of 23 he went to Athens as an assistant to a doctor. He attended lectures at the Academy, recently founded by Plato. On returning to Cnidus, Eudoxus completed his studies.

A few years later Eudoxus went to Egypt with another doctor. He studied the heavens from an observatory at Heliopolis on the Nile. His astronomical observations appear in his *Phaenomena*, but apparently this book did not contain theories such as those he was later to expound. The book locates the constellations relative to each other and to imaginary lines on the celestial sphere. Much space is given to a compilation of lists of stars which rise above or fall below the horizon at the beginning of each month.

During Eudoxus' 14 months in Egypt, one of his objectives was to produce a satisfactory calendar. His skill at making the detailed observations required for a good calendar is probably a result of his medical training, for although the teaching of medicine in Eudoxus' time may not have been very strong in the area of cures, it did emphasize the detailed description of symptoms.

Astronomical Theory

On returning to Asia Minor, Eudoxus established his own school in Cyzicus. While here he wrote *On Speeds*, his most important astronomical work, in which he expounded his theory of the motions of the stars, sun, moon, and planets. The recent discovery of the spherical shape of the earth may have inspired Eudoxus' hypothesis of homocentric planetary spheres. According to this theory, the motion of a planet can be explained by imagining that the planet is attached to the equator of a sphere; this sphere, with the center of the earth as its center, rotates uniformly about its polar axis. The poles are implanted in a second sphere that is concentric with the first; the second sphere also rotates uniformly about its polar axis, which is at a fixed angle to the axis of the first sphere. This relationship continues successively to other spheres.

If the sun, for example, is imagined as fixed on the equator of one sphere, then rotations of the spheres, with appropriate speed and direction, will give the path of the sun. The fixed stars are imagined to be on the largest concentric sphere, which rotates about the polar axis of the earth. Altogether 27 spheres are required to picture the motions of all the important bodies. Although this theory did not explain all the observable planetary motions, it was accurate enough to cause many of Eudoxus' successors to assume that only minor modifications would be needed to make it more accurate.

Contribution to Mathematics

It is fairly certain that Eudoxus' principal contributions to mathematics were his theory of proportions and his method of exhaustion. Both of these appear in Euclid's collection of geometrical theorems, the *Elements*, and are fundamental in the work of later mathematicians.

Eudoxus' theory of proportions is concerned with the ratio of magnitudes. One problem in describing the theory is that many of the theorems appear to be very obvious formulas. A typical example is the following (using modern terminology): given the positive numbers a, b, and c, if a is greater than b then a/c is greater than b/c. Only a person who has investigated the not so obvious way in which such simple properties are proved would begin to appreciate the significance of Eudoxus' work. Another source of possible difficulty for the modern reader of Eudoxus' theory of proportions is that, although it was valid for irrational numbers, to the Greeks "numbers" meant the natural numbers. Thus Eudoxus used more general "magnitudes," which were represented by lengths of line segments.

Eudoxus' method of exhaustion was a rigorous way of calculating areas and volumes; it puts him closer to modern mathematics than any of his other works. Archimedes quotes two theorems which were considered to be true before Eudoxus' time but which were first proved by Eudoxus: the volume of a pyramid is one-third the volume of a prism with the same base and height; and the volume of a cone is one-third the volume of a cylinder with the same base and height.

Later Life

Eudoxus moved next to Athens, but his stay there was short. The rulers of Cnidus had been overthrown and a democracy established. The people sent a request to Eudoxus to write a constitution for a new government. He returned to Cnidus and composed the legislation. He made his home there for the rest of his life, continuing his teaching and establishing an astronomical observatory. He revised some of his earlier writings and composed a description of his travels in seven books entitled *Circuit of the Earth*.

Eudoxus also had a reputation as a philosopher. According to Aristotle, Eudoxus held pleasure to be the chief good, for all creatures sought it and all attempted to escape its opposite, pain. Also, according to Eudoxus, pleasure was an end in itself and not a relative good. But Eudoxus was not an immoderate hedonist, for Aristotle, who may have known Eudoxus personally, gives a picture of him that is quite the contrary: "His arguments about pleasure carried conviction more on account of the perfection of his character than through their contents. Eudoxus passed indeed for a man of remarkable moderation. Again he did not seem to embrace these arguments as being a friend of pleasure, but because he regarded them as conforming to the truth."

Further Reading

Brief accounts of Eudoxus' life and work are given in Thomas L. Heath, *A Manual of Greek Mathematics* (1931), and in Bartel L. van der Waerden, *Science Awakening* (1950; trans. 1954). A number of interesting theories involving Eudoxus are discussed in François Lasserre, *The Birth of Mathematics in the Age of Plato* (1964). An authoritative description of Eudoxus' astronomical theory is given by Otto Neugebauer in *The Exact Sciences in Antiquity* (1952; 2d ed. 1957). For the place of Eudoxus' mathematical contribution in the development of the modern calculus see Carl B. Boyer, *The History of the Calculus and Its Conceptual Development* (1939; rev. ed. 1949). □

Eugene of Savoy

The French-born Austrian general Eugene of Savoy (1663-1736) led the military campaigns that laid the foundation of Hapsburg power in central Europe. He was widely admired as a model soldier, diplomat, and patron of the arts.

Prince Eugene of Savoy was born in Paris on Oct. 18, 1663, the fifth son of Count Eugene Maurice of Soissons and Olympia Mancini. His father died in 1673, and Eugene was brought up haphazardly at the French court, where he acquired a longing for military glory and a dislike for the ecclesiastical career intended for him. When Louis XIV denied him permission to join the battle against the Turks besieging Vienna in 1683, Eugene left Paris secretly and went to Austria, casting his lot thenceforth with the house of Hapsburg.

Fighting in Hungary against the retreating Turks, Prince Eugene rose from colonel to major general in 1685 and to lieutenant general in 1687. Wounded at Belgrade in 1688 and again at Mainz the following year, he was sent on a diplomatic mission to Savoy in 1691, where he showed a political understanding equal to his military talents. In 1693 he was named field marshal, the highest rank in the imperial service. In 1697 he was given the supreme command of imperial forces in Hungary, and on September 11 he destroyed the much larger Turkish army at Zenta. Leopold I gratefully rewarded Eugene with honors and estates, which, together with his share of the enormous booty won at Zenta, made him one of the richest men in Europe.

When Leopold I challenged France for the Spanish succession in 1701, Eugene opened hostilities in northern Italy, establishing a firm position there in spite of weak support from his government. A series of financial and political crises in Vienna led in 1703 to his appointment as president of the imperial war council. He began at once to reorganize the army. In 1704 he joined forces with the Duke

of Marlborough in southern Germany, and together they destroyed the French and Bavarian armies on August 13 at Blenheim.

With Austria now safe from invasion, Eugene returned to Italy. By Sept. 6, 1706, he had driven the French from Turin, and in 1707 he invaded southern France, only to withdraw after besieging Toulon. Leaving Italy secure, he resumed his collaboration with Marlborough. Together they defeated the French at Oudenaarde on July 10, 1708, and the next month laid siege to Lille. It was the high tide of allied victory against France. Their victory at Malplaquet in 1709 left the allies demoralized by their tremendous losses. The unexpected death of Joseph I, Leopold's successor, changed the political balance of Europe. A new ministry in England dismissed Marlborough and negotiated a separate peace with France. Eugene carried on the hopeless war briefly, then in 1714 negotiated the Treaty of Rastadt between Louis XIV and the new emperor Charles VI.

In 1716 Eugene undertook another campaign in Hungary, where the Turkish menace arose once again. His victories at Peterwardein and Belgrade in August led to the triumphant Peace of Passarowitz in 1718 and to the end of the Turkish threat to Europe.

During the years of peace that followed, Eugene's political influence waned. Though he was still involved in the pressing military and political affairs of Austria, his relationship with Charles VI was cool. Eugene turned more and more to his books and gardens, his menagerie of exotic animals, his paintings, and his buildings. In 1734 he again led Austria in war against France over the Polish succession. His powers had gone, and the war ended ingloriously. On his return to Vienna in October 1735, he laid down his official duties. He died in the night of April 20/21, 1736.

Further Reading

The best biography of Eugene in English in Nicholas Henderson, *Prince Eugene of Savoy* (1965), which unfortunately was written before the appearance of the definitive treatment of Eugene's career in German by Max Braubach. Readers should be warned that the so-called *Memoirs of Prince Eugene of Savoy, Written by Himself,* a book found in many libraries, is a fabrication written by Prince Charles Joseph of Ligne (trans. 1811).

Additional Sources

McKay, Derek, *Prince Eugene of Savoy,* London: Thames and Hudson, 1977. □

Leonard Euler

The Swiss mathematician Leonhard Euler (1707-1783) made important original contributions to every branch of mathematics studied in his day.

The son of a clergyman, Leonhard Euler, was born in Basel on April 15, 1707. He graduated from the University of Basel in 1724. In 1727 Catherine I invited him to join the Academy of Sciences in St. Petersburg, Russia; he became professor of physics in 1730 and professor of mathematics in 1733. In 1741 Frederick the Great called him to Berlin. Euler was director of mathematics at the Academy of Sciences there until 1766, when he returned to St. Petersburg, as director of the academy. Soon after his return to St. Petersburg, Euler became blind but continued to dictate books and papers. In 1776, having lost his first wife, he married his sister-in-law. Euler died in St. Petersburg on Sept. 7, 1783.

Analysis and the Calculus

Euler's textbooks presented all that was known of mathematics in a clear and orderly manner, setting fashions in notation and method which have been influential to the present day. At various times he used the notations $f(x)$, e, π, i, Σ, though he was not in every case the first to do so. Angles of a triangle he represented by A, B, C and the corresponding sides by a, b, c, thus simplifying trigonometric formulas. Moreover, he defined the trigonometric values as ratios and introduced the modern notation.

Euler's first great textbook was *Introductio in analysin infinitorum* (1748). The first volume is devoted to the theory of functions, and in particular the exponential, logarithmic, and trigonometric functions. These functions are developed as infinite series. At this time no clear notion of convergence existed; it is not surprising, therefore, that although Euler

warned against the use of divergent series, he himself did not always succeed in avoiding such series. He also resolved the subtle problem of the logarithms of negative and imaginary numbers, and he proved that e is irrational.

The second volume of the *Introductio* contains an analytical study of curves and surfaces. First Euler considered the general equation of the second degree in two dimensions, showing that it represents the various conic sections; the discussion included a treatment of asymptotes, centers of curvature, and curves of higher degree. Turning to the case of three dimensions, Euler gave the first complete classification of surfaces represented by the general equation of the second degree. This part of the *Introductio* really constituted the first treatise on analytical geometry.

Euler wrote two great textbooks on the calculus: *Institutiones calculi differentialis* (1755) and *Institutiones calculi integralis* (3 vols., 1768-1770). His outstanding achievement in this field was the invention of the calculus of variations, described in *The Art of Finding Curves Which Possess Some Property of Maximum or Minimum* (in Latin; 1744). This subject grew out of the isoperimetric problems which had created great interest among the mathematicians of the time. Such problems, involving the determination of the form of a curve having a certain maximum or minimum property, were quite different from the ordinary maximum and minimum problems of the differential calculus. Although particular problems had been solved by others, it was Euler who developed a general method. His method was essentially geometrical, and this made the solution of the simpler problems very clear.

Theory of Numbers

Another of Euler's outstanding textbooks was *Vollständige Anleitung zur Algebra* (1770). The first volume takes algebra up to cubic and biquadratic equations, while the second is devoted to the theory of numbers.

Euler proved many of the results that had been stated by Pierre Fermat. Fermat's most famous proposition, the general proof of which has defeated the efforts of the ablest mathematicians to the present day, states that the equation $x^n + y^n = z^n$ has no solution in integers for n greater than 2. Euler made the first attack on the problem, demonstrating the theorem for $n = 3$ and $n = 4$.

Fermat also stated that the Diophantine equation $x^2 - ay^2 = 1$ always has an infinity of solutions. Although Euler failed to prove this assertion, he used successive solutions of the equation to compute approximations to $\sqrt{a}$ and, reversing the procedure, found solutions of the equation by developing $\sqrt{a}$ as a continued fraction.

Mechanics and Hydrodynamics

Euler's *Mechanica* (1736) was the first textbook in which Newtonian particle dynamics was developed using analytical methods. Another of Euler's works, *Theoria motus corpus solidorum seu rigidorum* (1765), treated the mechanics of solid bodies in the same way; by resolving the motion of a solid body into a motion of the center of mass and a rotation about this point, Euler arrived at the general equations of motion. The term "moment of inertia" was

here introduced for the first time. A memoir presented by Euler to the Paris Academy of Sciences in 1755 contained an even greater achievement, namely, the general equations of hydrodynamics, consisting of the equation of continuity, expressing the constancy of mass of a fluid element and the effects of pressure on it as it moves along, and the equations of motion, relating the forces to the acceleration of the fluid element.

Euler also devoted much attention to the problems of astronomy. He studied the attraction of ellipsoids and recognized that the tides are effectively generated by the horizontal components of the disturbing forces. Euler also contributed to the three-body problem, which was important in the theory of the moon's motion.

Euler's general knowledge was extensive. Like his contemporary Jean d'Alembert, he wrote a book on the theory of music. His interests also extended to mathematical puzzles, optics, the theory of heat, and acoustics. Finally, Euler attempted a popularization of philosophy and natural science in *Lettres à une princesse d'allemagne,* a work in three volumes which comprises his full range of scientific endeavors.

Further Reading

Euler's contributions to mechanics and hydrodynamics are presented in historical perspective in René Dugas, *A History of Mechanics* (trans. 1955). General background works which discuss Euler include Eric Temple Bell, *Men of Mathematics* (1937); Dirk J. Struick, *A Concise History of Mathematics* (1948; 3d ed. 1967); and James R. Newman, ed., *The World of Mathematics* (4 vols., 1956). □

Euripides

Euripides (480-406 B.C.) was a Greek playwright whom Aristotle called the most tragic of the Greek poets. He is certainly the most revolutionary Greek tragedian known in modern times.

Euripides was the son of Mnesarchus. The family owned property on the island of Salamis, and Euripides was twice married (Melito and Choirile) and had three sons (Mnesarchides, Mnesilochus, and Euripides). Euripides was raised in an atmosphere of culture, was witness to the rebuilding of the Athenian walls after the Persian Wars, but above all belonged to the period of the Peloponnesian War. Influenced by Aeschylus, Euripides has been described as the most intellectual poet of his time and was a product of the Sophistic movement. He has been called the philosopher of the stage. In addition to his literary talents, he is said to have been an excellent athlete and painter.

The first play by Euripides, *Daughters of Pelias* (455 B.C.; lost), was concerned with the Medea story. His first victory in a literary competition was in 442. Euripides's *Cyclops* is the only satyr play to have survived in its entirety.

The *Rhesus,* sometimes assigned to Euripides, may or may not be genuine. The remainder of his plays constitute a partial commentary on Athens's war with Sparta.

Euripides was well ahead of his times, and though popular later (more papyri of Euripides survive than of any other Greek poet except Homer), he irritated people in his own day by his sharp criticism and won only five dramatic prizes during the course of his career. He is reputed to have owned a library and to have spent a great deal of his time in his cave by the sea in Salamis.

We know nothing of Euripides's military or political career, and he may have served as a local priest of Zeus at Phyla and traveled on one occasion to Syracuse. Toward the end of his life he stayed briefly in Thessaly (at Magnesia) and at the court of King Archelaus in Macedonia, where he wrote his masterpiece, the *Bacchae.* He died in Macedonia and was buried at Arethusa. The Athenians built him a cenotaph in Athens.

Euripides's Style

Euripides was a most remarkable tragedian who had a way of baffling and startling his audiences. He radically humanized and popularized Greek tragedy and was responsible for bringing tragedy closer to the experience of the ordinary citizen. Though he used the traditional form of the drama, he had some very unconventional things to say, and he said them in a language that was much easier to comprehend than that of Aeschylus or even Sophocles. Euripides rejected rare and archaic words. He popularized diction

and utilized many everyday expressions. But he was also the Ibsen of his day because he was the first to introduce heroes in rags and crutches and in tears. He treated slaves, women, and children as human beings and insisted that nobility was not necessarily an attribute of social status.

Euripides's plays generally are comparatively loose in structure and use the prologue and *deus ex machina* to simplify plot structure. The prologue has the effect of relieving the author from working into his play the background and information necessary for its understanding. The use of the *deus ex machina,* or the appearance of a god at the end of the play, indicates that the playwright was unable to bring his play to a close in the proper dramaturgical manner. In Euripides's case this often indicates that he was much more interested in the ideas he was exploring than in the form of the play.

A critic of society, Euripides was a serious questioner of the values of his day. As a realist, he often placed modern ideas and opinions in the mouths of traditional characters. Up to the time of Euripides, the aristocracy were the only ones depicted on stage as worthy of serious consideration. Euripides felt for all classes of people and was particularly sensitive to the humanity of women and slaves. He studied female psychology with an acute eye and with unbelievably powerful perception. Euripides also could and did probe religious ecstasy, dreadful revenge, and all-consuming love. As a rationalist, Euripides was relentlessly attacked by conservative Aristophanes and accused of being an atheist. Euripides treated myths rationally and expected men to use their rational powers.

Influenced by the rhetoric of the Sophists, Euripides engaged in considerable rhetorical argument (*agon*), hairsplitting, and well-put platitudes. His plots are replete with sensationalism, surprise, and suspense, and Euripides tried to achieve the maximum of tragic effect.

All of Euripides's extant plays are concerned with three basic themes: war, women, and religion. He repudiated and despised aggressive wars. He advocated women's equal rights, and he severely questioned anthropomorphic divinity and its fallible human institutions. Euripides knew both the rational and the irrational aspects of human life and probed deeply into the social, political, religious, and philosophical issues of his day. Despite the verbal flagellation of his fellow Athenians, he truly loved Athens and sympathized genuinely with suffering humanity.

His Plays

Euripides's extant plays (excepting the *Cyclops*) can be divided into three basic categories. The true tragedies include *Medea* (431 B.C.), *Andromache* (early in the Pel ponnesian War, 431 B.C.-404 B.C.), *Heraclidae* (ca. 430 B.C.), *Hippolytus* (428 B.C.), *Hecuba* (ca. 425 B.C.), *Suppliants* (ca. 420 B.C.-419 B.C.), *Heracles* (ca. 420 B.C.-418 B.C.), *Trojan Women* (415 B.C.), and *Bacchae* (ca. 407 B.C.). The tragicomedies comprise *Alcestis* (438 B.C.), *Ion* (ca. 418 B.C.-413 B.C.), *Iphigenia at Tauris* (414 B.C.-412 B.C.), and *Helen* (412 B.C.). And the melodramas are *Electra* (ca. 415 B.C.), *Phoenician Women* (ca. 409 B.C.), *Orestes* (408 B.C.), and *Iphigenia at Aulis* (ca. 407 B.C.).

The *Alcestis* is the earliest of the Euripidean plays that is preserved and was presented in 438 in place of the satyr play. A tragicomedy, it has a happy ending and has fascinated critics for countless years. Alcestis is willing to die instead of her husband, Admetus. Heracles visits Admetus and, when he learns that Alcestis has died, struggles with Death, recovers Alcestis, and restores her to her husband.

Medea, though it won only third prize, is perhaps Euripides's most famous and most influential play. Medea, a princess, who has left family and country to marry Jason (whom she helped procure the Golden Fleece), lives peacefully in Corinth. However, when Jason suddenly sees the opportunity to gain the Corinthian throne by marrying the daughter of the king of Corinth, he ruthlessly abandons wife and children. Medea, who is also a sorceress, vows revenge and, just before she is about to be banished, sends poisoned gifts to the new bride and slays her own children to vent her hate for Jason.

In *Medea,* Euripides demonstrates that "hell hath no fury like a woman scorned," and he berates his fellow men for mistreating women and particularly for treating foreign women as inferiors. But perhaps even more brilliantly, Euripides shows that man is both rational and irrational, that the irrational can bring disaster when it gets out of control, and that a woman is particularly susceptible to passions.

Hippolytus shows clearly Euripides's concern about the claims of religion on the one hand and sexuality on the other. Hippolytus is a chaste young man dedicated to Artemis, goddess of the hunt and of purity. Phaedra, wife of King Theseus, falls in love with her stepson, Hippolytus, and reveals her overpowering "incestuous" love to her nurse. The nurse takes pity on Phaedra and informs Hippolytus of the cause of his stepmother's distress. In a rage Hippolytus denounces her and all women. Phaedra commits suicide, implicating Hippolytus, and Theseus banishes him. As Hippolytus leaves Troezen, he is mortally wounded but survives long enough for Artemis to reveal the truth to his father Theseus, who then becomes remorseful and forgiving.

The *Trojan Women* is typical of Euripides's war plays. Written during the Peloponnesian War after the brutal subjugation of the island of Melos by the Athenians, this play is perhaps the weakest of all Euripidean plays because of its episodic nature. However, it is a powerful condemnation of war and exhibits universal compassion for suffering mankind by portraying the devastating effect of war on the innocent, particularly women and children.

Euripides's *Electra* beautifully illustrates Euripidean realism and rationalism. In this play Electra is married off to a peasant who does not consummate the marriage but who is noble in heart and respectful of his princess wife. Clytemnestra, the adulterous wife of Agamemnon who is fighting in the Trojan War, is lured to the mean hut of her daughter Electra on the pretense that Electra is having a baby. Aegisthus, Clytemnestra's lover, is killed first, and Electra prepares for her mother's arrival with his corpse in the hut. Though Clytemnestra is moved to remorse over her past treatment of Electra, it does not save her from being killed by Electra and the brother, Orestes, who are over-whelmed by their actions and are bewildered. A *deus ex machina* in the form of the Dioscuri (Castor and Pollux) is needed to bridge the dilemma between an excusable murder and a mandatory punishment. Electra is to be punished by exile; Orestes will be pursued by the Furies until his trial in Athens, when he will be acquitted.

Euripides radically changes Electra from a ruthless seeker of vengeance to a tortured human being who suffers intensely as a result of her actions. Matricide is strongly condemned and the gods are vigorously castigated.

The *Bacchae,* Euripides's masterpiece, is tightly structured and closely follows the pattern of the Dionysiac ritual itself. Pantheus, a young king of Thebes, refuses to acknowledge the divinity of the newly introduced Asiatic god Dionysus, and even though grandfather Cadmus and prophet Tiresias accept him, Pentheus defiantly but unsuccessfully tries to incarcerate him. Pentheus, attracted by descriptions of the orgiastic rites, attempts to participate in one and is caught and decapitated by his own triumphant mother, Agave. She gradually recovers her senses and realizes the terrible deed she has done. The whole family of Pentheus is to be punished, asserts Dionysus, who appears as a *deus ex machina.*

The *Bacchae* is a very powerful play, Euripides's swan song. He is again showing how the irrational, when not acknowledged and properly moderated, can get out of control and destroy all those around it. Dionysus is not a god that can be worshiped in the ordinary sense. He symbolizes the bestiality in nature and in man, and the Bacchic rites provide a release, as the Greeks see it.

In his day Euripides managed to call the attention of his countrymen to many flagrant abuses and wrongs in his own society. He subjected all to a merciless rational examination, but he was fundamentally tolerant and understanding and fully sympathized with the troubles and suffering of humanity.

Further Reading

Purely biographical material on Euripides is scant. Gilbert Murray, *Euripides and His Age* (1913; 2d ed. 1946; with rev. bibl. 1965), contains a chapter on Euripides's life; the rest of the book deals with the background of the plays and the plays themselves. Some editions of Euripides's plays with the texts in Greek and long introductions and analyses in English by the editors are *Euripides' Medea,* by Denys L. Page (1938); *Euripides' Iphigenia in Tauris,* by Maurice Platnauer (1938); *Euripides' Electra,* by John D. Denniston (1939); *Euripides' Ion,* by Arthur S. Owen (1939); *Euripides' Bacchae,* by E. R. Dodds (1944); and *Euripides' Alcestis,* by Amy M. Dale (1954).
Other analyses of specific plays include Reginald P. Winninton-Ingram, *Euripides and Dionysus: An Interpretation of the Bacchae* (1948), and John R. Wilson, ed., *Twentieth Century Interpretations of Euripides' Alcestis* (1968). Paul Decharme, *Euripides and the Spirit of His Dramas* (1893; trans. 1906), is an older study. Georges M. A. Grube, *The Drama of Euripides* (1941), focuses on the structure and dramatic technique of the plays. Two works which treat all the extant plays of Euripides are D. J. Conacher, *Euripidean Drama: Myth, Themes and Structure* (1967), and Thomas Bertram Lonsdale Webster, *The Tragedies of Euripides* (1967). □

Eutyches

The Byzantine monk Eutyches (ca. 380-455) preached the doctrine of Monophysitism, the belief that Christ had only a divine nature. His teachings were condemned as heresy by the Council of Chalcedon in 451.

Few facts are known concerning the life of Eutyches. By 450 he was in charge of a large monastery in Constantinople. He was respected for his holiness after long years of prayer and penance, and he had great influence at court through his godson, who was an important official of the emperor. The Church had not fully recovered from the recent theological controversy of Nestorianism, concerning the true personality of Christ. In 431 Bishop Nestorius of Constantinople had been condemned and exiled for teaching that Jesus had, in effect, two personalities, one human, the other divine. Despite Nestorius's condemnation, his followers were not convinced he was wrong. Theodoret of Cyrrhus, a learned and able frontier bishop, had drawn up a formula of reconciliation that described Christ as having a "union of two natures."

In 448 Eutyches protested loudly against Theodoret of Cyrrhus, calling his attempt heretical. Eutyches said he himself professed "the ancient faith." He believed that Jesus was the Son of God, Jesus was God Himself. Jesus, said Eutyches, had only one nature, the divine, which absorbed his humanity. The current bishop of Constantinople, Flavian, condemned Eutyches for misrepresenting Christ, and the controversy—which had simmered for 15 years—boiled over again. Many of the churchmen and political figures who had opposed Nestorius earlier now supported Eutyches, whom they saw as the voice of orthodoxy. Those who had supported Nestorius rallied around Theodoret. Emperor Theodosius II appointed Dioscoros, Bishop of Alexandria and a friend of Eutyches, to preside at a church council called to settle the matter in Ephesus in 449. Pope Leo I sent his legates to the council with clear instructions to denounce Eutyches, whom the pope called "an ignorant, imprudent old man." Dioscoros succeeded in railroading through the council a series of resolutions that completely supported Eutyches. On the emperor's authority he imprisoned all who disagreed. The pope's legates barely escaped to return to Rome and report what had happened.

Pope Leo was furious. The emperor refused to call another council, but within months he died from an accidental fall from his horse. His successor, pressed by the pope, called the general council that met at Chalcedon in 451. This time the tables were reversed. Eutyches was condemned, and his supporter, Bishop Dioscoros of Alexandria, was exiled. The officials of the council described Christ in a way that agreed with neither Nestorius nor Eutyches. Christ, they said, was one person with two separate and distinct natures, united but unmixed. The decisions of this council have been respected since then by all orthodox Christian faiths.

Further Reading

For information about Eutyches the best work is Robert V. Sellers, *The Council of Chalcedon* (1953), which describes in detail the political and ecclesiastical controversies of his time. □

Sir Arthur John Evans

The English archeologist Sir Arthur John Evans (1851-1941) discovered and excavated the most important sites of Minoan civilization in Crete and thus made the greatest single contribution to the knowledge of European and Mediterranean prehistory.

Arthur Evans, the eldest son of archeologist Sir John Evans, was born on July 8, 1851, at Nash Mills, Hertfordshire. He received his education at Harrow and at the universities of Oxford and Göttingen and was appointed a fellow of Brasenose College, Oxford. In 1884 he became curator of the Ashmolean Museum, Oxford, a post he held until 1908, when he was appointed extraordinary professor of prehistoric archeology at the university.

Evans was made a fellow of the Royal Society in 1901, was knighted in 1911, and served as president of the Society of Antiquities (1914-1919) and president of the British Association (1916-1919). His important publications date from his early years of excavations in Crete. He died near Oxford on July 11, 1941.

Evans was originally led to take an interest in prehistoric Crete following a visit to Athens, where he examined some engraved gems and ascertained that they were of Cretan origin. He visited Crete in 1894, and 5 years later he purchased the Kephala site near Knossos. He worked at Knossos until 1935. His excavations in Crete were carried out simultaneously with Italian, American, and other British excavations, but his were by far the most productive.

Evans uncovered a hitherto unknown civilization of the Bronze Age which he named Minoan after the legendary Cretan king Minos. He divided the materials that he excavated into three main epochs, Early, Middle, and Late, stretching in time from 3000 B.C. to 1200 B.C. Within each epoch he distinguished successive phases of pottery art which he established as indexes of technical and artistic development. His dating, as well as some of his important historical conclusions, was challenged by some scholars as late as 1960.

Evans's findings, supplemented by the work of other archeologists, showed that Minoan culture was to a certain degree a formative cause in the Mycenaean culture of mainland Greece. He also found indications of contacts between the Minoan civilization and that of Europe and Egypt. He unearthed many samples of two pictographic scripts named Linear A and Linear B, which he was unable to decipher. (In 1953 Michael Ventris and John Chadwick proposed a decipherment of Linear B, and they concluded that it was written in archaic Greek. Linear A is still undeciphered.) Evans's work on Crete supplied vital chronological indexes for the Mediterranean culture of the 3d and 2d millennia B.C.

Further Reading

Biographical studies are John Linton Myres, *Sir Arthur Evans, 1851-1941,* in British Academy Proceedings, vol. 27 (1941), and Joan Evans, *Time and Change* (1943). □

Edith Evans

Edith Evans (1888-1976) was a distinguished English actress most known for her portrayals of comic character roles.

E dith Evans was born in London in 1888. After finishing her schooling at the age of 15 she worked as a milliner for a number of years. Eventually, and rather haphazardly, she began to attend evening classes in acting. In 1912 she appeared in an amateur program of Shakespeare scenes. William Poel, a director particularly noted for his innovative staging of Shakespeare plays, happened to be in the audience that evening. He immediately recognized Evans' talent and cast her in a minor role in his next production at Cambridge. By the end of that same year Evans had made her London debut—as Cressida in Poel's production of *Troilus and Cressida.*

Evans then turned professional, acting mainly in contemporary plays at various theaters, although in 1917 and 1918 she toured in Shakespeare scenes with the celebrated senior actress Ellen Terry. In 1921 she created the role of Lady Utterwood in the premiere of George Bernard Shaw's *Heartbreak House.* Two years later she acted in the English premiere of Shaw's *Back to Methusaleh,* playing the Serpent, the Oracle, and the She-Ancient.

However, it was a 1924 revival of Congreve's Restoration comedy, *The Way of the World,* that ultimately solidified Evans' reputation as one of the outstanding actresses of her generation. Under Nigel Playfair's direction at the Lyric, Hammersmith, she played the role of Millamant to rave reviews that singled out her intelligence, her polish, and her comic flair. Throughout her career Evans continued to create memorable characterizations in revivals of classic comedies. Some of her most important roles in this genre were Mrs. Sullen in Farquhar's *The Beaux Stratagem* (1927), Mrs. Fidget in Wycherly's *The Country Wife* (1936), and Mrs. Malaprop in Sheridan's *The Rivals* (1945).

A year after her triumph as Millamant Evans, determined to tackle Shakespeare's challenging repertoire, joined the Old Vic company for the 1925-1926 season. Cast in no less than 13 roles, she played some of Shakespeare's finest heroines that season, including Katharina in *The Taming of the Shrew,* Beatrice in *Much Ado About Nothing,* Cleopatra in *Antony and Cleopatra,* and Portia in both *The Merchant of Venice* and *Julius Caesar.* Her portrayal of Rosalind in *As You Like It* was her most applauded performance of that season.

During the early 1930s Evans enjoyed success with a number of modern plays, beginning with the role of Florence Nightingale in Reginald Berkeley's *The Lady With the Lamp* (1929), in which she made her New York debut two years later. Two other important roles of this period were the temperamental prima donna Irela in *Evensong* by Edward Knoblock and Beverley Nichols (1932) and the Welsh maid Gwenny in *The Late Christopher Bean,* adapted by Emelyn Williams (1933).

Evans also continued to act in the classical repertoire, performing Emilia in *Othello* and Viola in *Twelfth Night* at the Old Vic in 1932. That same year she returned to a character role which she had first played during her busy 1925-1926 Shakespeare season and which was to grow into a definitive Evans characterization—the nurse in *Romeo and Juliet.* In the 1932 production John Gielgud directed and Peggy Ashcroft played Juliet. Katherine Cornell as Juliet played opposite Evans' nurse in New York in 1934. The following year she took part in the historic New Theatre production in which John Gielgud and Laurence Olivier alternated the roles of Romeo and Mercutio and Peggy Ashcroft once again played Juliet. Evans appeared as the nurse for the last time in 1961 under Peter Hall's direction for the Royal Shakespeare Company. Rosalind from *As You Like It* was another character from Evans' initial Old Vic season to which she successfully returned ten years later, playing opposite Michael Redgrave's Orlando in 1936.

Evans first played what is often considered her most famous role, Lady Bracknell in Wilde's *The Importance of Being Earnest,* in 1939. Evans' beautifully modulated voice was always one of her strongest assets as an actress, and as Bracknell she used her distinctive voice and delivery to extraordinary comic effect. During World War II she appeared in several revues and toured as far as India to entertain troops as Gwenny in *The Late Christopher Bean* and as Hesione Hushabye in *Heartbreak House*. In 1948 Evans again appeared in the play that had first brought her serious recognition almost a quarter of a century previously—*The Way of the World*. Once more Congreve's comedy brought her acting accolades, this time for her performance of the "old peeled wall," Lady Wishfort.

Upon reaching 60, Evans began to appear in a series of new plays that provided her with some of her best roles—the brandy-swigging Lady Pitts in James Bridie's *Daphne Laureola* (1949), Helen Lancaster in N. C. Hunter's comedy *Water of the Moon* (1951), and the eccentric Mrs. St. Maugham in Enid Bagnold's *The Chalk Garden* (1956).

Early in her career Evans acted in two silent films, but she did not return to the screen until 1948. She committed two of her most remarkable stage performances to film, appearing as Lady Bracknell in *Earnest* in 1952 and as Mrs. St. Maugham in *The Chalk Garden* in 1964. Other memorable character parts in films were Ma Tanner in *Look Back in Anger* (1959), the intrepid aunt in *Tom Jones* (1963), and the Spirit of Christmas Past in *Scrooge* (1970). For her performance as Mrs. Ross in *Whisperers* (1966) she received a number of international film awards. Evans was awarded the D.B.E. (Dame of the British Empire) in 1946. She gave her last performance in *Edith Evans . . . and Friends* in 1974. She died two years later.

Further Reading

An affectionate portrait of Evans by her former secretary and friend is Jean Batters, *Edith Evans: A Personal Memoir* (1977). The authorized biography of Evans is Bryan Forbes, *Ned's Girl* (1977).

Additional Sources

Batters, Jean, *Edith Evans: a personal memoir,* London: Hart-Davis MacGibbon, 1977.

Forbes, Bryan, *Ned's girl: the authorised biography of Dame Edith Evans,* San Francisco: Mercury House, 1991. □

George Henry Evans

George Henry Evans (1805-1856), American social radical, was a leader in the first stirrings of labor unrest and an advocate of the free distribution of western lands to homesteaders.

George Evans was born in Herefordshire, England, on March 25, 1805. At the age of 15 he, his father, and brother emigrated to the United States, settling in New York State. George was apprenticed to a printer. His wide reading, especially in the works of Thomas Paine, made him a confirmed atheist and a social radical

who believed that every man had an inalienable right to the "materials of Nature," including land and water.

Evans soon founded *The Man,* the first of his many radical publications. He immersed himself in the labor movement in New York City, helped found the Workingmen's party, and became editor of its magazine, the *Advocate.* He believed that all individuals should have equal education and equal property, though he soon retreated to advocating simply an equal amount of land for every person. The Workingmen's party achieved small successes in New York elections, and the movement spread to other states. But the party (as with most radical movements) soon dissolved into feuding factions, and by 1835 reform efforts were concentrated on building labor unions. When the Panic of 1837 struck the nation, the union movement collapsed.

Evans waited out the depression years on a farm in New Jersey. He published *History of the Origin and Progress of the Workingmen's Party* (1840) to explain the party's failure and to lay philosophical foundations for further reform. He argued that public lands should be free, that each American had an inalienable right to his part of them, and that if the lands were opened to the public most of America's problems would disappear. The panacea of homesteads was intended to make the West serve as a "safety valve" for the laboring men of the East. He theorized that, if surplus workers went west to farm, a balance in the supply of and the demand for urban labor would be effected, thus forcing higher wages and improved conditions for the workers.

Evans helped organize the National Reformers to implement his agrarian principles. In the late 1840s he and his associates urged politicians to back the movement for free western lands. He published many pamphlets and continued in the reform movement until his death. He did not live to see the passage of the Homestead Law or to witness its failure to solve the nation's problems.

Further Reading

An account of Evans's life and work is included in John R. Commons and others, eds., *A Documentary History of American Industrial Society,* vol. 7 (11 vols., 1910-1911). Information is also available in John R. Commons and others, *History of Labour in the United States,* vol. 1 (4 vols., 1918-1935); Stewart H. Holbrook, *Dreamers of the American Dream* (1957); and most histories of United States labor movements. □

Oliver Evans

Oliver Evans (1755-1819) was one of America's first and most important inventors. He made major contributions to the technology of flour milling and steam engines.

Oliver Evans was born near Newport, Del. He was apprenticed to a wagon maker. About the age of 21 he began work on his first important invention: a machine to make the cards with which wool was brushed preparatory to spinning. In 1780 he married and joined his brothers in a flour milling business near Wilmington, Del., the center of that industry. Within 5 years he had made spectacular improvements in the ancient design of flour mills; these remained standard for a century.

Previously flour mills had required an enormous amount of difficult hand labor, and the flour was often dirty as a result. By harnessing the energy of the water-wheel to move the grain and flour both horizontally and vertically through the mill, Evans reduced the hand labor and improved the product's cleanliness. Although he patented his improvements, he had great difficulty in enforcing his legal rights to the invention. Soon after making these improvements, he moved to Philadelphia and established a manufactory of mill equipment.

Evans then turned to a problem which had long interested him: the production and harnessing of steam power. James Watt's low-pressure engine had been introduced into America by 1802, when Evans began to operate his first high-pressure engine. In the Watt engine, steam was condensed in the cylinder, creating a vacuum so that atmospheric pressure pushed the piston down. In Evans's new engine (which was independently invented in England at the same time) the steam was introduced into the cylinder under high pressure and used to push the piston down directly. In 1804 Evans built a steam-powered amphibious vehicle, but his hopes to introduce steam vehicles on common roads were not realized. However, his high-pressure engines soon became standard for American mills, railroads, and steamboats.

By the time Evans died in 1819, his large iron foundries in Philadelphia and Pittsburgh were turning out quantities of steam engines, mill equipment, and other types of ironwork. His two books, *The Young Mill-Wright and Miller's Guide* (1795) and *The Abortion of the Young Steam Engineer's Guide* (1805), were America's earliest handbooks on those subjects.

Further Reading

The only full-length biography of Evans is Greville and Dorothy Bathe, *Oliver Evans: A Chronicle of Early American Engineering* (1935). The story of steam engineering in America during Evans's time is told by Carroll W. Pursell, Jr., *Early Stationary Steam Engines in America: A Study in the Migration of a Technology* (1969). An old but still useful book on flour milling is Charles Byron Kuhlmann, *The Development of the Flour-Milling Industry in the United States* (1929).

Additional Sources

Ferguson, Eugene S., *Oliver Evans, inventive genius of the American Industrial Revolution,* Greenville, Del.: Hagley Museum, 1980. □

Walker Evans

An American photographer, Walker Evans (1903-1975) was best known for his photographs of American life between the world wars. Everyday objects and people—the urban and rural poor, abandoned buildings, storefronts, street signs, and the like—are encapsulated in his laconic images of the 1930s and 1940s.

Walker Evans was born in St. Louis, Missouri, on November 3, 1903. His family moved to Toledo, Ohio, shortly after his birth but eventually settled in Kenilworth, Illinois, a well-to-do suburb of Chicago, where his father worked as a successful member of an advertising firm. Walker attended several private schools, graduating in 1922 from Phillips Academy, Andover, Massachusetts, with the ambition to become a writer. He attended Williams College but dropped out after his freshman year.

With an allowance from his father, Evans in 1926 moved to Paris, along with other hopeful American expatriot writers bent on absorbing the artistic and intellectual climate of avant-garde postwar Europe. Yet, in Evans' own words, "I wanted so much to write that I couldn't write a word."

Back in the United States in 1928 he turned to photography and instantly felt at home in that medium. Entering the active field of American photography at the end of the 1920s, Evans was confronted with the two dominant modes of the moment, the "artistic" posture of Alfred Stieglitz and what Evans considered the blatantly "commercial" approach of Edward Steichen, both positions rejected by Evans in favor of, in his own words, "the elevated expression, the literate, authoritative, and transcendant statement which a photograph allows." In other words, he looked for something more than the esthetic or the commercial aspects of photography. He aimed for visual statements alluding to stories and values beyond the literal or the artistic.

During the early years of his career he supported himself with an assortment of jobs in New York City, where he became friends with several men who were themselves to become distinguished writers. For example, Hart Crane, a friend, published Evans' first work in *The Bridge* (1930). In 1931 the photographer worked with the critic Lincoln Kirstein, who published some of Evans' work in *Hound and Horn,* an avant garde magazine covering modernist thought and art around 1930.

The first exhibition of the photographer's production was at the Julien Levy Gallery in New York in 1932, and during the following year many of his pictures were used to illustrate *The Crime of Cuba,* Carleton Beal's study of social conditions in Cuba. From 1935 to 1937 Evans worked with a group of sociologists and photographers in a study of poverty in the United States during the Great Depression sponsored by the Farm Security Administration (FSA). This mid-to-late 1930s period was the most productive and photographically successful time of his life.

The quality of Evans' work gained wide recognition in 1938 with an exhibition in New York City's Museum of Modern Art and publication of *American Photographs,* an important book on the history of photography. In an introductory essay, Lincoln Kirstein characterized American photography in general and Walker Evans' work in particular when he wrote in this 1938 publication that "the use of the visual arts to show us our own moral and economic situation has almost completely fallen into the hands of the photographer . . . and [Walker Evans'] pictures with all their clear, hideous and beautiful detail, their open insanity and pitiful grandeur, [is a] vision of a continent as it is, not as it might be or as it was."

On leave from FSA in 1936 Evans collaborated with James Agee on assignment from *Fortune* magazine in a study of the life of Southern sharecroppers. *Let Us Now Praise Famous Men* (1941) was seen in the later decades as one of the best of the crop of social commentaries of the period.

From 1945 until 1965 Evans was an associate editor of *Fortune,* and from 1965 until his death in 1975 he taught a course at Yale University, which he called "Seeing."

Walker Evans' work is impossible to categorize neatly; it has little of the meticulous composition of the formalist, none of the literary quality of the photographic storyteller, and exhibits no signs of the noisy punch of the photojournalist. His subjects, seen generally from eye level, have the uncontaminated, clear vision of an observant youngster, a Huck Finn perception of America in the 1930s. His work implies the complex of values, judgments, hopes, and fantasies that brought the particular subject into existence.

Further Reading

Walker Evans: American Photographs, with an introductory essay by Lincoln Kirstein and published by the Museum of Modern Art in 1938, remains a central work for the understanding of the photographer's view of his subject. *Walker Evans,* with an introduction by John Szarkowski and also published by the Museum of Modern Art (1971), provides an excellent contemporary view of his work. Leslie Katz's "Interview with Walker Evans" (1971), included in Vicki Goldberg, *Photography in Print* (1981), provides a great deal of insight into Evans as a person. *Walker Evans at Work* (1982) is a useful collection of letters, interviews, and photographs.

Additional Sources

Mora, Gilles, *Walker Evans: the hungry eye,* New York: H.N. Abrams, 1993.
Rathbone, Belinda, *Walker Evans: a biography,* Boston: Houghton Mifflin, 1995. □

Sir Edward Evan Evans-Pritchard

The English social anthropologist Sir Edward Evan Evans-Pritchard (1902–1973) did pioneer research in the social structure, history, and religion of African and Arab peoples.

Edward Evans-Pritchard was one of the foremost anthropologists of the mid-twentieth century. The son of an Anglican clergyman, Evans-Pritchard read history at Exeter College, Oxford, and received a doctorate in anthropology at the London School of Economics. His first research was from 1926 to 1932 with the Azande of the southern Sudan and the Congo. He did further fieldwork in 1935-1936 and in 1938, mainly with the Nuer and other Nilotic peoples of the southern Sudan.

Acclaimed Scholar

Before World War II Evans-Pritchard served on the faculties of the London School of Economics, the Egyptian University in Cairo, and Cambridge University. During this period he produced his two most famous works: *Witchcraft: Oracles and Magic among the Azande* (1937) and *The Nuer* (1940). The first is a brilliant exposition of the internal logic of a preliterate philosophy, indicating how such ideas may reasonably persist in the face of what, to an outsider, may appear to be damning discrepancies and disproofs. The second volume examines the mode of political organization of the Nuer, a society lacking any formal government. It served as a model for much of the subsequent anthropological research in the social organization of African societies. In its analysis of the blood feud, conflict, and limits set by environment on a seminomadic society, it owes much to the earlier work of William Robertson Smith.

During World War II Evans-Pritchard served as an officer in military intelligence in East Africa, Ethiopia, Libya, and the Middle East, and he was able to do some anthropological fieldwork in these areas. He converted to Roman Catholicism in 1944, which may have influenced his subsequent attempts to reconcile the purported differences between social science and religious faith. In 1946 he was appointed to the chair of social anthropology at All Souls College at Oxford, which he held until his retirement in 1970. Twice he journeyed to the United States for scholarly pursuits: in 1950 he was a visiting professor at the University of Chicago, and seven years later he spent a year at Stanford University's Center for Advanced Study in the Behavioral Sciences.

Set a Standard for Anthropology Writing

An extraordinarily prolific writer, Evans-Pritchard produced works that touch upon nearly every facet of social anthropology. In general his writings exhibit a blend of rich ethnographic detail with subtle and suggestive theoretical insights. Among his better-known books are *The Sanusi of Cyrenaica* (1949), *Kinship and Marriage among the Nuer* (1951), *Social Anthropology* (1951), *Nuer Religion* (1956), and *Theories of Primitive Religion* (1965).

A year following his retirement, Evans-Pritchard was knighted for his contributions to science. He was father to five children with Ioma Nicholls, whom he married in 1939. Even after he retired from Oxford, he continued to teach and to produce influential publications in his field, including *Man and Woman Among the Azande* (1971). He was one of the strongest proponents of the value of historical perspective in anthropology and of recording African oral literature. Evans-Pritchard died in Oxford on September 11, 1973.

Further Reading

Evans-Pritchard and his importance in anthropology are discussed in Max Gluckman, *Custom and Conflict in Africa* (1955); Thomas Bieldelman, ed., *The Translation of Culture* (1971), and Mary Douglas, *Edward Evans-Pritchard* (1980). □

William Maxwell Evarts

The American lawyer and statesman William Maxwell Evarts (1818-1901) was secretary of state under President Rutherford B. Hayes.

Born in Boston, William M. Evarts was educated at Boston Latin School and Yale College, from which he graduated in 1837. He attended the Dane Law School at Harvard and entered practice in New York City in 1841. In 1843 he married Helen Minerva Wardner. Evarts achieved early eminence at the New York bar, and in 1859 he formed what became one of the nation's most successful corporate law firms.

As a Whig, Evarts defended the Compromise of 1850 and played no part in the antislavery movement except to win the Lemmon slave case (1860). The decision upheld the right of the state of New York not to return to slavery any African Americans brought by sea from a slave state and sequestered in a free state for subsequent shipment back into slavery in a third state.

In 1860 Evarts, now a Republican, preferred William Seward to Abraham Lincoln as the Republican presidential candidate. During the Civil War, Evarts played only a minor diplomatic role; he was sent to England to help prevent the equipping of the Confederate Navy. As a conservative Republican, he found favor with Lincoln's successor, Andrew Johnson, by successfully leading the defense of the President in the 1868 impeachment proceedings. Evarts was named attorney general, serving until the end of Johnson's term in 1869.

Although never a favorite of President U.S. Grant, Evarts was named, with Caleb Cushing and Morrison R. Waite, as counsel before the Geneva arbitration tribunal in the Alabama Claims case. The three lawyers won a settlement for Civil War damages from England and established a precedent for the arbitration of international disputes.

In 1877 Evarts was counsel for the Republican party before the electoral commission appointed to settle the disputed presidential election between Rutherford B. Hayes and Samuel Tilden. As Evarts urged, the commission counted the disputed votes for Hayes.

During the Hayes administration (1877-1881) Evarts served as secretary of state. He worked for the expansion of American trade around the world. Like many New Yorkers of his class, Evarts was friendly to England, despite the commercial competition of the two countries. However, he did protest the English intrusion into Guatemala and negotiated with Colombia to frustrate the French attempt to build a canal across the Isthmus of Panama. The French failed for other reasons, but Evarts had foreseen that the United States could powerfully enhance its world trade position by having such a canal under its domination. Evarts's most significant achievement was in Far Eastern affairs. He pursued an aggressive policy, increasing American trade with Japan; and after aiding Hayes in writing the veto for a flagrantly anti-Chinese bill favored in California, he negotiated a treaty with China limiting the importation of coolie laborers into the United States and relaxing the barriers against American exporters trading in China. He also arranged for the establishment of an American base in Samoa.

From the days of the Lincoln administration onward, Evarts's name was mentioned whenever a vacancy occurred on the Supreme Court, but that goal always eluded him. In 1885 the New York Legislature sent him to the U.S. Senate for one term.

Second in fame only to his defense of President Johnson was Evarts's winning of acquittal for Henry Ward Beecher in the sensational trial involving alleged sexual improprieties. Still, it was in the realm of corporate law that Evarts made his great reputation as a lawyer. He won innumerable cases important in the advancement of business enterprise and was long regarded as a leader of the New York bar. He died in his New York home in 1901.

Further Reading

Chester L. Barrows, *William M. Evarts: Lawyer, Diplomat, Statesman* (1941), is an excellent biography. □

Herbert Vere Evatt

Herbert Vere Evatt (1894-1965) was an Australian statesman, judge, and author. He laid the foundations of Australia's foreign policy and played an important part in establishing the United Nations.

Herbert Vere Evatt was a noted internationalist. He championed the role of the small and middle powers in the maintenance of world order and sought to advance international protection of human rights and the ideal of full employment in all countries. Believing as he did in the value of regional arrangements, Evatt was the decisive influence in the creation in 1947 of the South Pacific Commission, which has done so much to advance economic and human welfare in the South Pacific region.

Evatt was born on April 30, 1894, at East Maitland, New South Wales. His father died in 1901, and the family thereupon moved to Sydney, where Evatt was educated at Fort Street High School and Sydney University. At this university he achieved a remarkable academic record, consisting of arts and law degrees with multiple first-class honors, a doctorate of laws, and a doctorate of literature. He was admitted to the Sydney bar in 1918 and in 1920 married Mary Alice Sheffer.

Evatt was a man of medium height and solid physique, conveying an impression of rugged strength. He was intensely energetic and was tenacious in pursuing any cause to which he became attached. His public image of dedicated earnestness and seriousness was offset by ability to relax in private, as reflected in an excellent sense of humor and a genuine interest in art, literature, and sport. He had a wide range of friends throughout the world, including U.S. Supreme Court justices Benjamin Cardozo and Felix Frankfurter. It was Frankfurter who caused Evatt to be introduced to President Franklin Roosevelt in 1938 and thus to form a personal friendship with Roosevelt which was to facilitate Australian-American cooperation in World War II.

Career as Lawyer and Judge

Evatt had a spectacularly successful career at the Sydney bar, being appointed king's counsel at the early age of 35 and enjoying a large practice in appellate work. In 1930,

at the age of 36, he was appointed a justice of the High Court of Australia, becoming the youngest justice ever to sit on that Court. He remained in office until 1940, when he resigned to enter politics in order to assist in Australia's war effort. While on the bench, he brought to his position not only depth of learning but a judicial approach which demanded that judges should not regard legal rules as ultimate ends in themselves but should relate legal and constitutional issues to the demands of society.

In the field of constitutional law, Evatt sought to maintain a balance between the Australian states and federation, while insisting that all federal legislation must be sufficiently related to the subject matter of power relied upon, yet interpreting federal powers expansively for the purpose of compliance with Australia's international obligations.

He returned to judicial office in 1960 as chief justice of the Supreme Court of New South Wales but resigned in 1962 owing to ill health.

Political Career

Evatt, a member of the Australian Labour party, had his first political experience as member of the Legislative Assembly of New South Wales (1925-1930). In the federal sphere, he was a member of the House of Representatives from 1940 until his return to judicial office in 1960. When a Labour government came to power in 1941 under John Curtin, Evatt became attorney general and minister for external affairs, holding both offices until his government was defeated in 1949. He was appointed to the Privy Council in 1942 and was deputy prime minister from 1946 to 1949 under Prime Minister Joseph Benedict Chifley.

As attorney general, Evatt was responsible for the amendment to the Constitution enabling the Parliament to legislate in the field of social services. As minister for external affairs, Evatt not only laid the foundations of Australia's foreign policy but completely reorganized its foreign service. In 1942 and 1943 he undertook missions to the United States and Britain and was successful in obtaining essential war supplies, including Spitfire aircraft; and in 1942 he achieved the creation of the Pacific War Council in Washington. In January 1944 he was instrumental in securing the signature of an Australia-New Zealand agreement for political and economic collaboration.

Evatt was a prominent delegate at the San Francisco Conference of 1945, which drew up the United Nations Charter. As spokesman for the lesser powers, he pleaded unsuccessfully for the modification of the veto provisions. Nevertheless, many important clauses in the Charter were due to him, for example, those giving wider powers than first proposed to the General Assembly and the Economic and Social Council. At the Paris Peace Conference in 1946, Evatt unsuccessfully advocated the creation of a European Court of Human Rights; his foresight was later vindicated with the establishment of the Court in 1959. As chairman of the United Nations ad hoc committee on Palestine in 1948, he influenced the adoption of the Palestine partition plan, which led to the creation of Israel as a new state, and Israel's admission to the United Nations in 1949. In 1948 he was elected president of the General Assembly for its third session, during which the Universal Declaration of Human Rights was adopted, and Evatt took the initiative of seeking to bring about a peaceful solution of the Berlin blockade situation of 1948 by calling on the Soviet Union and the Western powers to enter into direct conversations.

In respect to Pacific affairs, Evatt sought without success to obtain an early peace settlement with Japan and a Pacific regional security pact. His efforts nevertheless provided the groundwork for the signature in 1951 of the ANZUS Security Treaty, between Australia, New Zealand, and the United States.

Evatt was leader of the Opposition for the Labour party during 1951-1960. In that capacity he unsuccessfully contested several elections against the Liberal party led by Robert Gordon Menzies. A split developed in the Labour party in 1954/1955, and Evatt's leadership came under attack, partly because of his alleged failure to take a stronger anti-Communist line and partly because of his criticism of certain aspects of the Petrov case, which concerned the defection in Canberra of a Soviet diplomat.

The strain of these stormy years and a series of cerebral hemorrhages eventually told on Evatt, and he died in retirement at Canberra on Nov. 2, 1965.

Evatt's Writings

Evatt's books are major works of historical and legal scholarship, reflecting a passionate interest in the upholding of civil liberties. His first book, *Liberalism in Australia* (1918), is a short historical treatment, from one special angle, of Australian politics down to the year 1915. *The King and His Dominion Governors* (1936) is an exposition of the royal prerogative powers in the political sphere, with a plea that, for the purpose of clarification, the body of practices and precedents in this domain should be reduced to a set of systematic guidelines. In *Injustice within the Law* (1937) Evatt examines the case of the six "Tolpuddle martyrs," who were transported from Britain to Australia in 1834 for the offense of forming a trade union, then deemed to be a conspiracy in restraint of trade. Evatt's most popular book is *The Rum Rebellion* (1938), an account of the rebellion in New South Wales in 1808 against Governor Bligh, better known as Capt. Bligh of the affair of the mutiny on the *Bounty. Australian Labor Leader* (1940) is a biography of W.A. Holman, a noted Sydney political and legal figure. *The United Nations* (1947) and *The Task of Nations* (1949) are useful treatments of the formation and functions of the United Nations. Apart from these books, Evatt was a prolific writer of articles, a number of which, together with certain speeches of 1941-1946, were collected as *The Foreign Policy of Australia* (1945) and *Australia in World Affairs* (1946).

Further Reading

A full-length biography of Evatt is Kylie Tennant, *Evatt: Politics and Justice* (1970). A general picture of Evatt and his career is given in Allan Dalziel, *Evatt the Enigma* (1967). Certain aspects of his foreign policy and his part in the formation and development of the United Nations are treated in Norman Harper and David Sissons, *Australia and the United Nations* (1959); Richard N. Rosecrance, *Australian Diplomacy and Japan, 1945-1951* (1962); Joseph G. Starke, *The ANZUS Treaty Alliance* (1965); Fred Alexander, *Australia since Federation: A Narrative and Critical Analysis* (1967); and Alan S. Watt, *The Evolution of Australian Foreign Policy, 1938-1965* (1967). Recommended for general background are Paul Hasluck, *The Government and the People, 1939-1941* (1952); Lionel Wigmore, *The Japanese Thrust* (1957); and Dudley McCarthy, *South-west Pacific Area: First Year* (1959).
□

John Evelyn

The English author John Evelyn (1620-1706) is remembered today for his diary. He was known to his contemporaries as the author of a number of treatises on gardening, engraving, pollution, coins, conservation of forests, and navigation.

John Evelyn was born on Oct. 31, 1620, at Wotton in Surrey. He was brought up by his maternal grandmother and attended the Southborough free school. In 1637 he entered the Middle Temple and later, Balliol College, Oxford, where he remained 3 years. He then returned to the Middle Temple, but he seems never to have studied law.

Evelyn spent most of the years after he left Oxford traveling in France and Italy, learning the languages of those countries, and studying art and architecture. Although he was a devout Anglican, during the English civil war he did not join the King's forces for fear that the family estates, which were in parliamentary territory, would be forfeited. In 1647 he married Mary Browne, daughter of the English ambassador at Paris. In 1652 the Evelyns returned to England and acquired the Browne estate at Sayes Court, Deptford.

In the years preceding the Restoration, Evelyn became acquainted with many of the men who eventually constituted the Royal Society. In 1656 he published a verse translation of Lucretius's *De rerum natura*. When the Royal Society was formally constituted in 1660, Evelyn was elected a member.

Most of Evelyn's writing in the next few years was scientific. In 1661 he published *Fumifugium*, a tract offering suggestions for freeing London of smog. The following year he brought out *Sculptura*, an essay on mezzotint engraving. In 1664 the first edition of *Sylva*, his most widely read work, on the conservation of trees, appeared.

Evelyn was also occupied with public service and was appointed by Charles II to a number of commissions. In 1685, shortly after James's accession, Evelyn was appointed one of the commissioners of the privy seal. In 1694 he accepted King William's invitation to serve as treasurer of Greenwich Hospital. In 1699 Evelyn inherited the family estate at Wotton. He spent his last days there, dying on Feb. 3, 1706.

Evelyn's diary was published in 1818, although the first complete and accurate edition did not appear until 1955. It

is not a record of daily life but a transcription of notes made of various historical events from the time Evelyn was 11.

Further Reading

The most accurate information about Evelyn is in volume 1 of his *Diary,* edited by E. S. de Beer (6 vols., 1955). Two excellent full-length biographies are Arthur Ponsonby, *John Evelyn* (1933), and Clara Marburg Kirk, *Mr. Pepys and Mr. Evelyn* (1935). W. G. Hiscock presents less favorable views of Evelyn in *John Evelyn and Mrs. Godolphin* (1951) and *John Evelyn and His Family Circle* (1955).

Additional Sources

Bowle, John, *John Evelyn and his world: a biography,* London; Boston: Routledge & Kegan Paul, 1981.

Kirk, Clara Marburg, *Mr. Pepys and Mr. Evelyn,* Folcroft, Pa.: Folcroft Library Editions, 1974. □

Edward Everett

Edward Everett (1794-1865), American statesman and orator, was renowned for his elegant speeches, the most famous of which was his address at Gettysburg, overshadowed by President Lincoln's remarks from the same platform.

On Apr. 11, 1794, Edward Everett was born in Dorchester, Mass. He obtained a bachelor of arts degree with highest honors from Harvard in 1811 and a master of arts in divinity in 1814. Appointed to the newly created chair in Greek at Harvard, he prepared for the post by obtaining a doctor's degree from the University of Göttingen in 1817. His marriage to Charlotte Gray Brooks in 1822 allied him to Boston's social elite.

More interested in politics than in an academic career, Everett entered the U.S. House of Representatives in 1824, serving until 1835. A spokesman of the conservative Whig party, he was closely associated with Daniel Webster, the Whig senator from Massachusetts. Everett labored to preserve the Bank of the United States and adopted pro-Southern views on issues relating to slavery. In 1835 he was elected governor of Massachusetts by a coalition of Whigs and Anti-Masons; he served until 1839. During this time he aided in creating a state board of education and in establishing the first normal schools.

Appointed minister to Great Britain by President William Henry Harrison, Everett did much to improve diplomatic relations between the two countries. The British admired this elegant, cultured, and charming ambassador. Recalled by President James Polk in 1845, Everett became president of Harvard the next year, but he disliked the post and resigned in 1849. During the last 4 months of President Millard Fillmore's administration, Everett was secretary of state and gained momentary fame for his sharp note rejecting a proposal that France and the United States jointly guarantee Spain's possession of Cuba. In 1853 he entered the Senate but resigned 15 months later in the face of public

protest over his failure (he was ill at the time) to vote against the Kansas-Nebraska Bill. This ended his political career, for many New Englanders doubted his integrity.

Everett began to lecture widely, raising $70,000 for the Mount Vernon Ladies Association, which sought to preserve George Washington's home. In 1860 he was vice-presidential candidate on the Constitutional Union ticket. During the Civil War he spoke extensively in support of the Union cause. His most famous wartime address, delivered at the dedication of the Gettysburg Cemetery on Nov. 19, 1863, was much admired but has been overshadowed by Lincoln's simpler and more moving phrases. Worn out by his activities in behalf of the Union, Everett died on Jan. 15, 1865.

Further Reading

A full-length biography of Everett is Paul Revere Frothingham, *Edward Everett: Orator and Statesman* (1925). See also Claude Moore Fuess, *Daniel Webster* (2 vols., 1930).

Additional Sources

Reid, Ronald F. (Ronald Forrest), *Edward Everett: Unionist orator,* New York: Greenwood Press, 1990.

Varg, Paul A., *Edward Everett: the intellectual in the turmoil of politics,* Selinsgrove Pa.: Susquehanna University Press; London; Cranbury, NJ: Associated University Press, 1992. □

Philip Evergood

The paintings of American artist Philip Evergood (1901-1973), especially those executed during the 1930s, reveal his concern for social causes; although realistic, they are also marked by elements of fantasy.

Philip Evergood, whose real name was Philip Blashki, was born in New York City on October 26, 1901. He was the son of an unsuccessful Polish painter who had come to America from Australia. After attending boarding schools in England, Blashki graduated from Eton in 1919. He changed his name to Evergood because British Prime Minister Winston Churchill had written that Anglo-Saxons were full of prejudice. When Evergood discovered that he wanted to be an artist, he left Cambridge University to study drawing under Henry Tonks, head of the Slade School of Fine Art, London.

In 1923 Evergood returned to America, where he studied with George Luks at the Art Students League in New York City, and then went to Paris, where he attended the Académie Julian. He went back to New York in 1926. In 1927 he held his first one-man show in New York and exhibited frequently thereafter. In 1929 Evergood returned to France. In 1931, traveling through Spain, he was impressed by the work of El Greco. That year he also married the dancer Julia Cross.

In America during the 1930s Evergood painted huge murals under the auspices of the Federal Arts Project, such as the *Story of Richmond Hill* (1936-1937). In 1936 he moved to Woodstock, NY, and that year he took part in the "219" strike protesting layoffs from the Federal Arts Project. In 1952 he moved to Southbury, CT. He died in Bridgewater, CT on March 11, 1973.

Evergood has been classified as an expressionist, a social realist, and a surrealist. To some degree, all the labels are appropriate. His work, turning on social causes especially during the 1930s, is marked throughout by strong elements of fantasy and the bizarre. He acknowledged the influence of painters Mathias Grünewald, Pieter Bruegel, Hieronymus Bosch, and El Greco and the graphic work of Francisco Goya, Honoré Daumier, and Henri de Toulouse-Lautrec. But his art is also closely tied to reality and often deals with actual events, as in the *Burial of the Queen of Sheba* (1933), which shows Evergood and his wife illegally burying their cat in a backyard. In *My Forebears Were Pioneers* (1940), Evergood pictures a staunch old woman sitting placidly in her rocking chair before huge, uprooted trees and her picturesque 19th century house. The scene was based on a woman he had encountered while driving in the countryside. In *Enigma of the Collective American Soul* (1959), Evergood combines the grotesque with social commentary by juxtaposing portraits of U.S. President Dwight Eisenhower and Churchill with an insipid beauty contest winner, while in a corner of the painting two small boys steal a smoke.

Further Reading

John I. H. Baur, *Philip Evergood* (1960), is the only monograph on Evergood. It contains much biographical information and 91 illustrations.

Additional Sources

The Dictionary of Art Grove's Dictionaires Inc., 1996.
Evergood, Philip, *Philip Evergood,* New York: H. N. Abrams, 1975.
Taylor, Kendall, *Philip Evergood: Never Separate From the Heart,* Lewisburg, PA: Bucknell University Press, 1987. □

Medgar Evers

Medgar Evers (1925-1963), field secretary for the National Association for the Advancement of Colored People (NAACP), was one of the first martyrs of the civil-rights movement. His death prompted President John Kennedy to ask Congress for a comprehensive civil-rights bill, which President Lyndon Johnson signed into law the following year.

The Mississippi in which Medgar Evers lived was a place of blatant discrimination where blacks dared not even speak of civil rights, much less actively campaign for them. Evers, a thoughtful and committed member of the National Association for the Advancement of Colored People (NAACP), wanted to change his native state. He paid for his convictions with his life, becoming the first major civil rights leader to be assassinated in the 1960s. He was shot in the back on June 12, 1963, after returning late from a meeting. He was 37 years old.

Evers was featured on a nine-man death list in the deep South as early as 1955. He and his family endured numerous threats and other violent acts, making them well aware of the danger surrounding Evers because of his activism. Still he persisted in his efforts to integrate public facilities, schools, and restaurants. He organized voter registration drives and demonstrations. He spoke eloquently about the plight of his people and pleaded with the all-white government of Mississippi for some sort of progress in race relations. To those people who opposed such things, he was thought to be a very dangerous man. "We both knew he was going to die," Myrlie Evers said of her husband in *Esquire*. "Medgar didn't want to be a martyr. But if he had to die to get us that far, he was willing to do it."

In some ways, the death of Medgar Evers was a milestone in the hard-fought integration war that rocked America in the 1950s and 1960s. While the assassination of such a prominent black figure foreshadowed the violence to come, it also spurred other civil rights leaders—themselves targets of white supremacists—to new fervor. They, in turn, were able to infuse their followers—both black and white—with a new and expanded sense of purpose, one that replaced apprehension with anger. *Esquire* contributor

Maryanne Vollers wrote: "People who lived through those days will tell you that something shifted in their hearts after Medgar Evers died, something that put them beyond fear. . . . At that point a new motto was born: After Medgar, no more fear."

A Course in Racism

Evers was born in 1925 in Decatur, Mississippi. He was the third of four children of a small farm owner who also worked at a nearby sawmill. Young Medgar grew up fast in Mississippi. His social standing was impressed upon him every day. In *The Martyrs: Sixteen Who Gave Their Lives for Racial Justice,* Jack Mendelsohn quoted Evers at length about his childhood. "I was born in Decatur here in Mississippi, and when we were walking to school in the first grade white kids in their schoolbuses would throw things at us and yell filthy things," the civil rights leader recollected. "This was a mild start. If you're a kid in Mississippi this is the elementary course.

"I graduated pretty quickly. When I was eleven or twelve a close friend of the family got lynched. I guess he was about forty years old, married, and we used to play with his kids. I remember the Saturday night a bunch of white men beat him to death at the Decatur fairgrounds because he sassed back a white woman. They just left him dead on the ground. Everyone in town knew it but never [said] a word in public. I went down and saw his bloody clothes. They left those clothes on a fence for about a year. Every Negro in town was supposed to get the message from those clothes and I can see those clothes now in my mind's eye. . . . But nothing was said in public. No sermons in church. No news. No protest. It was as though this man just dissolved except for the bloody clothes. . . . Just before I went into the Army I began wondering how long I could stand it. I used to watch the Saturday night sport of white men trying to run down a Negro with their car, or white gangs coming through town to beat up a Negro."

Evers was determined not to cave in under such pressure. He walked twelve miles *each way* to earn his high school diploma, and then he joined the Army during the Second World War. Perhaps it was during the years of fighting in both France and Germany for his and other countries' freedom that convinced Evers to fight on his own shores for the freedom of blacks. After serving honorably in the war he was discharged in 1946.

Evers returned to Decatur where he was reunited with his brother Charlie, who had also fought in the war. The young men decided they wanted to vote in the next election. They registered to vote without incident, but as the election drew near, whites in the area began to warn and threaten Evers's father. When election day came, the Evers brothers found their polling place blocked by an armed crowd of white Mississippians, estimated by Evers to be 200 strong. "All we wanted to be was ordinary citizens," he declared in *Martyrs*. "We fought during the war for America and Mississippi was included. Now after the Germans and the Japanese hadn't killed us, it looked as though the white Mississippians would." Evers and his brother did not vote that day.

What they did instead was join the NAACP and become active in its ranks. Evers was already busy with NAACP projects when he was a student at Alcorn A & M College in Lorman, Mississippi. He entered college in 1948, majored in business administration, and graduated in 1952. During his senior year he married a fellow student, Myrlie Beasley. After graduation the young couple moved near Evers's hometown and were able to live comfortably on his earnings as an insurance salesman.

Mandated Change for Mississippi

Still the scars of racism kept accumulating. Evers was astounded by the living conditions of the rural blacks he visited on behalf of his insurance company. Then in 1954 he witnessed yet another attempted lynching. "[My father] was on his deathbed in the hospital in Union [Mississippi]," Evers related in *Martyrs*. "The Negro ward was in the basement and it was terribly stuffy. My Daddy was dying slowly, in the basement of a hospital and at one point I just had to walk outside so I wouldn't burst. On that very night a Negro had fought with a white man in Union and a white mob had shot the Negro in the leg. The police brought the Negro to the hospital but the mob was outside the hospital, armed with pistols and rifles, yelling for the Negro. I walked out into the middle of it. I just stood there and everything was too much for me. . . . It seemed that this would never change. It was that way for my Daddy, it was that way for me, and it looked as though it would be that way for my children. I was so mad I just stood there trembling and tears rolled down my cheeks."

Evers quit the insurance business and went to work for the NAACP full-time as a chapter organizer. He applied to the University of Mississippi law school but was denied admission and did not press his case. Within two years he was named state field secretary of the NAACP. Still in his early thirties, he was one of the most vocal and recognizable NAACP members in his state. In his dealings with whites and blacks alike, Evers spoke constantly of the need to overcome hatred, to promote understanding and equality between the races. It was not a message that everyone in Mississippi wanted to hear.

The Evers family—Medgar, Myrlie and their children—moved to the state capital of Jackson, where Evers worked closely with black church leaders and other civil rights activists. Telephone threats were a constant source of anxiety in the home, and at one point Evers taught his children to fall on the floor whenever they heard a strange noise outside. "We lived with death as a constant companion 24 hours a day," Myrlie Evers remembered in *Ebony* magazine. "Medgar knew what he was doing, and he knew what the risks were. He just decided that he had to do what he had to do. But I knew at some point in time that he would be taken from me."

Evers must have also had a sense that his life would be cut short when what had begun as threats turned increasingly to violence. A few weeks prior to his death, someone threw a firebomb at his home. Afraid that snipers were waiting for her outside, Mrs. Evers put the fire out with the garden hose. The incident did not deter Evers from his rounds of voter registration nor from his strident plea for a biracial committee to address social concerns in Jackson. His days were filled with meetings, economic boycotts, marches, prayer vigils, and picket lines—and with bailing out demonstrators arrested by the all-white police force. It was not uncommon for Evers to work twenty hours a day.

Some weeks before his death, Evers delivered a radio address about the NAACP and its aims in Mississippi. "The NAACP believes that Jackson *can* change if it *wills* to do so," he stated, as quoted in *Martyrs*. "If there should be resistance, how much better to have turbulence to effect improvement, rather than turbulence to maintain a stand-pat policy. We believe that there are white Mississippians who want to go forward on the race question. Their religion tells them there is something wrong with the old system. Their sense of justice and fair play sends them the same message. But whether Jackson and the State choose to change or not, the years of change are upon us. In the racial picture, things will never be as they once were."

Two Fallen Leaders—One Theme

On June 12, 1963, U.S. president John F. Kennedy—who would be assassinated only a few short months later—echoed this sentiment in an address to the nation. Kennedy called the white resistance to civil rights for blacks "a moral crisis" and pledged his support to federal action on integration.

That same night, Evers returned home just after midnight from a series of NAACP functions. As he left his car with a handful of t-shirts that read "Jim Crow Must Go," he was shot in the back. His wife and children, who had been waiting up for him, found him bleeding to death on the doorstep. "I opened the door, and there was Medgar at the steps, face down in blood," Myrlie Evers remembered in *People* magazine. "The children ran out and were shouting, 'Daddy, get up!'"

Evers died fifty minutes later at the hospital. On the day of his funeral in Jackson, even the use of beatings and other strong-arm police tactics could not quell the anger among the thousands of black mourners. The NAACP posthumously awarded its 1963 Spingarn medal to Medgar Evers. It was a fitting tribute to a man who had given so much to the organization and had given his life for its cause.

Rewards were offered by the governor of Mississippi and several all-white newspapers for information about Evers's murderer, but few came forward with information. However, an FBI investigation uncovered a suspect, Byron de la Beckwith, an outspoken opponent of integration and a founding member of Mississippi's White Citizens Council. A gun found 150 feet from the site of the shooting had Beckwith's fingerprint on it. Several witnesses placed Beckwith in Evers's neighborhood that night. On the other hand, Beckwith denied shooting Evers and claimed that his gun had been stolen days before the incident. He too produced witnesses—one of them a policeman—who swore before the court that Beckwith was some 60 miles from Evers's home on the night he was killed.

Beckwith was tried twice in Mississippi for Evers's murder, once in 1964 and again the following year. Both trials ended in hung juries. Sam Baily, an Evers associate, commented in *Esquire* that during those years "a white man got more time for killing a rabbit out of season than for killing a Negro in Mississippi."

After the second trial, Myrlie Evers took her children and moved to California, where she earned a degree from Pomona College and was eventually named to the Los Angeles Commission of Public Works. However, her conviction that justice was never served in her husband's case kept Mrs. Evers involved in the search for new evidence. As recently as 1991, Byron de la Beckwith was arrested a third time on charges of murdering Medgar Evers. Beckwith was extradited to Mississippi to await trial again, still maintaining his innocence and still committed to the platform of white supremacy.

The Evers Legacy

Perhaps the most encouraging aspect of Medgar Evers's story lies in the attitudes of his two sons and one daughter. Though they experienced firsthand the destructive ways of bigotry and hatred, Evers's children appear to be very well-adjusted individuals. "My children turned out to be wonderfully strong and loving adults," Myrlie Evers concluded *Ebony*. "It has taken time to heal the wounds [from their father's assassination] and I'm not really sure all the wounds are healed. We still hurt, but we can talk about it now and cry about it openly with each other, and the bitterness and anger have gone."

At the same time, Mrs. Evers asserted in *People* that she hopes for Beckwith's conviction on the murder charges. (He was, indeed, convicted after the third trial.) "People have said, 'Let it go, it's been a long time. Why bring up all the pain and anger again?'" she explained. "But I *can't* let it go. It's not finished for me, my children or . . . grandchildren. I walked side by side with Medgar in everything he did. This [new] trial is going the last mile of the way."

Further Reading

Altman, Susan, *Extraordinary Black Americans from Colonial to Contemporary Times,* Children's Press, 1989.
Branch, Taylor, *Parting the Waters: America in the King Years, 1954-63,* Simon and Schuster, 1988.
Mendelsohn, Jack, *The Martyrs: Sixteen Who Gave Their Lives for Racial Justice,* Harper, 1966.
Ebony, June 1988.
Esquire, July 1991.
Essence, February 1986.
Newsweek, July 23, 1990.
People, February 11, 1991. □

Myrlie Evers-Williams

Myrlie Evers-Williams's name may forever evoke the legacy of her first husband, slain civil rights leader Medgar Evers, but Myrlie Evers-Williams (born 1933) has never rested quietly on his laurels. Instead, the first woman elected Board of Directors Chair of

the National Association for the Advancement of Colored People (NAACP) has spent a lifetime carving out a formidable civil rights legacy of her own.

Myrlie Evers-Williams was born in the Mississippi city of Vicksburg in 1933 in her maternal grandmother's frame house to a 16-year-old mother and a 28-year-old father, Evers-Williams was the only child born to the couple, who separated before her first birthday. Because of her mother's age, the family decided that it would be best if Evers-Williams was left in the care of her paternal grandmother, Annie McCain Beasley, a retired school teacher whom she called "Mama."

Though her mother left Vicksburg shortly after her marriage to James Van Dyke Beasley dissolved, Evers-Williams was surrounded by family while growing up. Besides her father and grandmother, with whom she lived, Evers-Williams regularly saw her maternal grandmother, and took piano lessons from her aunt, teacher Myrlie Beasley Polk. It is not surprising, then, that Evers-Williams remembered "only warmth and love and protectiveness from all of the people around me" in *For Us, the Living,* a 1967 memoir she wrote (with William Peters) about her life, and that of Medgar Evers.

Nor is it surprising, in this environment filled with educators, that Evers-Williams would develop a taste and an appetite for learning. A gifted pianist, she hoped to study music in college. However, Evers-Williams was denied the

Mississippi state financial aid that would have enabled her to attend the respected school of music at Fisk University in Nashville and was forced because of segregation to choose a school from Mississippi's two state colleges for African Americans, neither of which offered a major in music. She settled on Alcorn A&M College, where she planned to major in education and minor in music.

It was at Alcorn, during her first day on campus, that Evers-Williams met Medgar Evers, a business student who had started his studies there in the fall term of 1948. Her family initially disapproved of her romance with the older Evers—a World War II veteran roughly eight years her senior—but they continued to see each other steadily. They married on December 24, 1951, in a church in the bride's hometown of Vicksburg.

After roughly two years of study (around the time that Evers graduated from Alcorn), Evers-Williams left college, and the pair eventually settled in Jackson, Mississippi, where Evers (after a stint as an insurance agent) became the state's first NAACP field secretary. Evers-Williams worked alongside him, joining her husband's staff as his secretary. Like her husband, she was incensed by the appalling living conditions endured by sharecroppers.

Evers's efforts in the Mississippi civil rights movement, including attempts to desegregate schools and public buildings and secure voting rights for all citizens, are what led to his murder. He was shot in front of the family house in Jackson on June 12, 1963, as his wife and three children watched helplessly. His killer, white supremacist Byron De La Beckwith, was quickly arrested and charged in the shooting, but all-white juries deadlocked in two trials in 1964, freeing Beckwith. Evers-Williams, who had become active in the NAACP during her marriage, spent the next 30 years trying to bring Beckwith to justice.

Evers-Williams's dogged pursuit of the man who killed Medgar Evers paid off. When the Jackson, Mississippi *Clarion-Ledger* uncovered new information around 1989 suggesting jury tampering and official intervention in the case, Evers-Williams used the fresh evidence to convince reluctant Mississippi officials to conduct a new trial. As she told *People* magazine in 1991, shortly after Beckwith was arrested again, "People have said, 'Let it go, it's been a long time. Why bring up all the pain and anger again?' But I *can't* let it go. It's not finished for me, my children or four grandchildren." On February 5, 1994, a racially diverse Hinds County, Mississippi, jury found Beckwith guilty of the slaying. The victory was especially important for Evers-Williams. "When (the trial) was over, every pore was wide open and the demons left," she told Claudia Dreifus of the *New York Times Magazine* in 1994. "I was reborn when that jury said, 'Guilty!'"

After the murder and the failure of the initial trials to bring a conviction, Evers-Williams moved to the middle class college town of Claremont, California, with her three children. There, she completed work on a bachelor's degree in sociology in 1968 at Pomona College, one of the five Claremont colleges. While in school, Evers-Williams accepted speaking engagements for the NAACP and worked on *For Us, the Living*. In 1983, the book was adapted for a television movie starring Irene Cara and Howard Rollins. The Claremont Colleges hired Evers-Williams after her graduation as a development director in 1968. Two years later, at the behest of local residents, she made her first foray into the political arena with a run for U.S. Congress as a Democrat in the primarily Republican 24th District. Her bid for office was unsuccessful, but she did capture over 30 percent of the vote in the area.

By the early 1970s, Evers-Williams had moved with her children to New York, where she was a vice president at the advertising firm of Seligman and Latz. In 1975, she joined Atlantic Richfield, a petroleum, chemical, and natural resource firm based in Los Angeles, where she eventually rose to director of community affairs. During this period, she also became a columnist for *Ladies' Home Journal.*

Evers-Williams met the man who would become her second husband at the Claremont Colleges. In 1976 she married longshoreman and civil rights and union activist Walter Williams at Little Bridges Chapel at Claremont College. She did not take Williams's surname at that time out of respect for Medgar Evers. Williams—referred to by Evers-Williams in an article in the July 1991 issue of *Esquire* as "my best friend, my Rock of Gibraltar"—reportedly understood this, and stood by her decision.

Following an unsuccessful run for city council in Los Angeles in 1987, Evers-Williams was appointed one of the five commissioners on the Board of Public Works by Los Angeles Mayor Tom Bradley, where she was in charge of some 5,000 to 6,000 employees and a multi-million dollar budget for basic city services and improvements such as road maintenance. Evers-Williams continued her work with the NAACP along with her other commitments. As vice-chair of the board of the NAACP in 1994, she knew that the group had fallen on difficult times, as it faced mounting debt and scandal. As she acknowledged in the *New York Times Magazine* in 1994, "We need strong leadership, which I hope will include more women at the helm. We need more leaders who guard the monies of the association very carefully—and who do not abuse the privileges that come with leadership."

After considerable deliberation, especially in light of the failing health of her second husband, Evers-Williams announced her decision to run for the position of chair of the NAACP in mid-February of 1995. In a close race for control of the organization's 64-member board of directors later that month, Evers-Williams defeated incumbent William Gibson, a South Carolina dentist who had led the NAACP board since 1985, by 30-to-29.

Following her win, Jack W. White in *Time* magazine quoted Evers-Williams as having told participants at an NAACP meeting in New York, "Duty beckons me. I am strong. Test me and you will see." As White observed, Evers-Williams will need that strength to bolster the organization. As Evers-Williams begins her tenure, she must address the internal troubles and tensions that have shaken the NAACP in recent years. Former executive director Benjamin Chavis was ousted in 1994 after 15 months on the job for sexual harassment and financial mismanagement. Gibson reportedly misspent organization funds as well. The

NAACP was about $4 million in debt when Evers-Williams entered office, and charges of gender discrimination, beyond those levied at Chavis, abounded in the ranks.

Those who know Evers-Williams believed that she was up to the task. Arthur Johnson, president of the Detroit chapter of the NAACP from 1986 to 1993, told the *Detroit Free Press* in February of 1995 that he felt that "Myrlie Evers will raise the sights of NAACP members around the country and will generate a stronger and better feeling of common cause among the members." A February 21, 1995 editorial in the *New York Times* expressed similar confidence in Evers-Williams, arguing that she "seems well suited to the task of reasserting the NAACP's trademark blend of militance and inclusivity," and that she "has given the NAACP a new chance at what looked like the last minute." A writer for the *Nation* was likewise upbeat about her prospects, saying that she brings "a long history of struggle, a large slice of NAACP tradition and great integrity to her new task." Paul Ruffins in the *Nation,* similarly, noted that Evers-Williams offers "a model of life and leadership in the post-civil rights era" as well as significant management experience.

For her part, Evers-Williams has said that she will reach out to younger members of the African American community, that she will work to restore the organization's image and financial state, and that she will focus on present threats to past civil rights achievements, such as affirmative action and fair housing and lending rules. Even this triumph for Evers-Williams was tempered by tragedy, though. Williams, who had urged his wife to seek the top post of the NAACP, lost a lengthy battle with cancer on February 22, 1995, at the couple's Oregon home. Evers-Williams, who had been elected to the post just days earlier, was at his side when he died. "I kept telling him, 'I need to be with you,' and he kept saying, 'This is something you've got to do,'" Evers-Williams related in *Jet.*

Evers-Williams was sworn in as chairperson of the NAACP on Mother's Day, May 14, 1995, at the Metropolitan AME Church in Washington, before over 1,000 supporters. There, according to a report in the *Detroit Free Press,* she renewed her pledge to restore the NAACP in name and deed, telling the assembly, "I will give my all to the NAACP to see that it becomes stronger, to see that we regain our rightful place as the premier civil rights organization in this country." After Evers-Williams' inauguration, Ruffins asserted that the NAACP had "regained its moral center of gravity." Although she faced opposition by some board members, Evers-Williams' involvement seemed to bring a renewal of support for the organization. *Harper's Bazaar* reported a flood of dues from the group's 2200 branches, and noted that much-needed corporate and celebrity donations were coming in again. As Evers-Williams pointed out in *Harper's Bazaar,* the NAACP still has a long way to go. "The perception that we don't have a financial crisis jsut because I was elected is totally erroneous," she noted. However, it appeared that if anyone could get the NAACP back into shape, Evers-Williams could. During her first year of chairmanship, Ever-Williams generated much praise for reducing the organization's deficit, healing wounded souls

on the divided board, and hiring Kweisi Mfume as president to guide the NAACP into the next century.

Further Reading

Black Enterprise, May 1995, p. 20.
Chicago Tribune, January 14, 1996, Sec. 13, p. 8.
Detroit Free Press, February 22, 1995, p. 5A; May 15, 1995, p. 5A.
Ebony, June 1988, p. 108.
Esquire, July 1991, p. 58.
Harper's Bazaar, July 1995, pp. 58-59.
Jet, March 6, 1995, p. 32; March 13, 1995, p. 53.
Nation, March 13, 1995, p. 332; October 30, 1995, pp. 494-500.
New York Times, February 20, 1995, p. A1; February 20, 1995, p. C8; February 21, 1995, p. A14; February 26, 1995, p. A20; February 26, 1995, p. E2.
New York Times Magazine, November 27, 1994, p. 68.
People, February 11, 1991, p. 45.
Time, February 27, 1995, p. 23.
U.S. News & World Report, March 6, 1995, p. 32. □

William Maurice Ewing

The American oceanographer William Maurice Ewing (1906-1974) was a leader in modern earth science research, especially in the applications of geophysics to oceanography.

Maurice Ewing was born in Lockney, Texas, on May 12, 1906. He was the fourth of 10 children of Floyd Ford Ewing, a farmer and hardware merchant, and Hope Hamilton Ewing. His older siblings died at very young ages, so he grew up as the eldest of seven. He preferred to be known as Maurice, rather than William. His parents stressed the importance of education, and Ewing studied diligently and received a scholarship to college. Working at night to support himself, he received his bachelor's (1926), master's (1927), and doctoral (1931) degrees from Rice Institute in Houston. He first majored in electrical engineering and later switched to mathematics and physics, which he found more interesting. One physicist, H. A. Wilson, had a major influence on Ewing. Wilson held a weekly series at Rice attended by many prestigious scientists who made a big impression on Ewing.

Won Geological Grant

Ewing was instructor in physics at the University of Pittsburgh from 1929 to 1930. He moved to Lehigh University as instructor of physics in 1930, becoming assistant professor in 1936 and associate professor of geology in 1940. Probably the most important event of his professional life occurred in 1935, when a committee of distinguished geologists asked if he would undertake the task of applying the techniques of geophysics to the ocean areas. He jumped at the chance and with their support obtained a grant from the Geological Society of America for a classic refraction study of the structure of the Continental Shelf off the East Coast of the United States. This was quickly followed by a successful gravity-measuring cruise on the *Barracuda*, using the newly developed gravity pendulum apparatus introduced by F.A. Vening Meinesz.

With the aid of some of his students, Ewing built ocean-bottom cameras and automatic apparatus for making seismic refraction measurements at the bottom of the deep-ocean basins. Several seismic measurements had been successfully made by the time World War II broke out. In September 1940 the National Defense Research Committee (NDRC) was being discussed by leaders of the scientific community as an important adjunct to the military in the event of U.S. involvement in the war. Early recognizing the importance and probable results of the war, Ewing obtained a leave of absence from Lehigh University and moved to the Woods Hole Oceanographic Institution (WHOI) to commence defense research. Without recompense, until the NDRC was officially formed in January 1941, he and his former students wrote *Sound Transmission in Sea Water*, the standard manual throughout the war and long after for understanding and predicting the results of sound-echo ranging. They also redesigned the bathythermograph from a bulky, tedious, and unreliable instrument to one capable of obtaining temperature-depth information to depths of 900 feet from ships underway at speeds up to 20 knots. It was adopted by the Navy and was the standard instrument with only minor changes for over 20 years.

During the war Ewing was the leading physicist at WHOI in the development and application of underwater photography and underwater sound for use by the Navy. It was in this period that he introduced the long-range sound transmission studies, resulting in the SOFAR system and providing the basic ideas behind the Navy's long-range surveillance and detection systems.

Lamont-Doherty Geological Observatory

In 1946 Ewing initiated an extensive program of geophysical training for graduate students at Columbia University. He was promoted to professor in 1947 and was made Higgins Professor of Geology in 1949. That year Columbia made available the former Thomas W. Lamont estate for the use of the geophysics group to undertake studies in earthquake seismology. The Lamont Geological Observatory was formed as a part of the department of geology with Ewing named director. In 1961 the observatory was changed to a research institute within the university to promote research with other university departments; in 1969 the name was changed to the Lamont-Doherty Geological Observatory.

From 1947 to his retirement Ewing continued his work at Columbia and WHOI. During his career, he carried out an extensive research career authoring or coauthoring 280 papers and three books. He received 10 honorary degrees from universities in four countries and 26 medals and awards from institutions and scientific societies of eight nations. He died at the age of 67 in 1974. His wife, Harriet, collected many of his private papers and donated them to the University of Texas. They are housed at the Harry Ransom Humanities Research Center in Austin.

Further Reading

Ewing's contributions to oceanography are discussed in Robert C. Cowen, *Frontiers of the Sea: The Story of Oceanographic Exploration* (1963); and Warren E. Yasso, *Oceanography: A Study of Inner Space* (1965). Additional material on Ewing is in David Robert Bates, ed., *The Planet Earth* (1957; rev. ed. 1964); William S. von Arx, *An Introduction to Physical Oceanography* (1962); and Günter Dietrich, *General Oceanography: An Introduction* (trans. 1963). Further information on Ewing can be found in Frederic L. Holmes, ed., *Dictionary of Scientific Biography*, vol. 17 (1970; rev. ed. 1990), and Roy Porter, ed., *The Biographical Dictionary of Scientists* (1994). □

Benedict Chuka Ewonwu

Benedict Chuka Ewonwu (born 1921) was the first Nigerian artist to win international acclaim. His sculpture and painting reflect his conviction that art must be a personal statement and not a stereotyped conformity to any particular style.

The talent of Benedict Ewonwu for woodcarving was recognized early. In 1944 the Nigerian government sponsored his further study in England, and he won his diploma in fine arts at the University of London. His first major exhibition, at the Apollinaire Gallery in London in September 1950, was a popular success, and his work was applauded by art critics. In the period after Nigerian independence Ewonwu held the post of federal art adviser.

During the early period in his career Ewonwu's favorite medium was woodcarving. Although his reputation rests on his bronze and terra-cotta work, his skill at exploiting the natural grain of wood to express the desired motion of the figure remains his greatest strength. In wood he seems more introspective and not as torn by the conflicting demands of the public. This public is either European, which demands of him some expression of the traditional in his work, or African, which until recently considered European naturalism to be superior to African motifs. He maintained with considerable justification that he could change from one style to another just as he was able to create in stone, wood, or bronze.

Whatever the reason, Ewonwu produced prolifically in all styles, utilizing various materials. His terra-cotta sculptures are usually naturalistic renderings of African subjects. Among the best of these are the *Head of Kofi* and the *Head of Koyi*. The statue of Queen Elizabeth II in front of the old Federal House of Representatives in Lagos is probably his best-known public monumental statue.

A key to understanding Ewonwu's blend of the traditional and the natural and the conflict between these two is the bronze statue entitled *The Awakening*, outside the Nigerian Museum in Lagos. It is a female figure with an abstract body which rises in an elongated shaft from a thin base. To this Ewonwu affixed a face and hands rendered in a realistic fashion.

Ewonwu was also a painter of considerable merit. His landscapes executed in bold colors have had a wide appeal among middle-class Nigerians. By contrast, he also created a series of paintings called *Africa Dances,* in which he attempted to recapture the mysterious rhythm of old Africa by abandoning naturalism. He was also commissioned to do large-scale murals. The best examples of this type are those he created for the Nigerian Corporation Building in Lagos.

Further Reading

A short biography of Ewonwu and a discussion of contemporary Nigerian art are in Evelyn S. Brown, *Africa's Contemporary Art and Artist* (1966). See also Ulli Beier's two works, *Art in Nigeria* (1960); and *Contemporary Art in Africa* (1968); and Tibor Bodrogi, *Art in Africa* (1968). □

Hubert and Jan van Eyck

The Flemish painters Hubert (died 1426) and Jan (ca. 1390-1441) van Eyck were the founders of the early Netherlandish school of painting.

I n the third decade of the 15th century an elaborate technique of painting in oil glazes on wooden panels emerged and was perfected in the Low Countries. Although ultimately the brothers Van Eyck cannot be credited with its discovery, they were the acknowledged leaders of this new practice. The brilliant coloration, luminous surfaces, and detailed precision of their paintings remain to this day one of the greatest achievements of Western art.

The birth dates of Hubert and Jan van Eyck are unknown, but it is generally held that Hubert was the elder and Jan was born about 1390. According to a 16th-century tradition, their place of birth was Maaseyck near Maastricht in the province of Limburg.

Jan is first heard of between 1422 and 1425 at The Hague, where he held the title of *peintre et varlet de chambre* to John, Count of Bavaria-Holland. The general background and early training of the two artists, however, can only be surmised, as Jan already had apprentices when he arrived at The Hague. After the count's death Jan moved to Bruges, where on May 19, 1425, he assumed the title of *peintre et varlet de chambre* to Philip the Good, Duke of Burgundy. Jan retained this title until his death. He also served the duke as a kind of roving ambassador, traveling to Spain in 1427 in search of a bride for his employer and to Portugal in 1428. On the latter occasion Jan was successful in obtaining the hand of Isabella, the Infanta of Portugal, for Philip. Their marriage took place at Bruges on Jan. 7, 1430.

In 1432 Jan is recorded as owning a house in Bruges, and about this time he married Margaret, who bore him 10 children. Jan's great reputation during his lifetime is evidenced by numerous accounts and documents as well as a large gift that the Duke of Burgundy gave Margaret van Eyck on Jan's death.

Jan Van Eyck

Hubert van Eyck

While Jan van Eyck is the best-documented Flemish artist of the 15th century, there are so few records relating to Hubert that some art historians have strongly doubted his very existence. Moreover, not a single painting survives that can be attributed without question to Hubert. Indeed, but for the evidence of a quatrain painted on the frame of the famous *Ghent Altarpiece,* it is unlikely that his identity would have survived his own time. In translation the verse reads: "The painter Hubert van Eyck, greater than whom none was to be found, began this work and Jan, his brother—second in art—having carried through the task at the expense of Judocus Vyd, invites you by this verse to look at what has been done, 1432."

Although the question has not been laid completely to rest, most authorities today accept the authenticity of the inscription. In the opinion of Erwin Panofsky and others, the hand of Hubert is discernible on parts of the interior wings of the altarpiece. According to this view, Hubert's style, as seen, for example, in the high-horizoned landscape of the central panel, is far less progressive than Jan's.

Despite several attempts to attribute paintings to Hubert, none has met with any substantial measure of acceptance. The work scholars most generally agree upon, however, is an *Annunciation* in New York that is sufficiently archaic in its conception and treatment to merit a date in the first quarter of the 15th century.

Jan van Eyck

Among the surviving works of Jan van Eyck, the earliest is probably the diminutive *Virgin in a Church* in Berlin (ca. 1425). Although the treatment of the figures of the Virgin and Child is relatively conservative, the conception of architectural space, filled with a softly diffused and atmospheric light, is totally new. A similar handling of a warmly lighted interior space can be seen in the *Annunciation* in Washington (ca. 1428), but in addition there is a new feeling for weight and volume in the figures of the Virgin and the angel Gabriel. Also present is a strong sense of the tangible reality of objects, each of which is invested with sacred and supernatural meaning. This type of "disguised symbolism" partially derives from the somewhat earlier works of Robert Campin (the Master of Flémalle), but Jan raised it to a new level of consistency and meaning.

The *Ince Hall Madonna* (1433) is the first independent panel among a dozen surviving signed and dated works. It also contains the inscription of Jan's personal motto, *Als ick kan* ("As best I can"), an indication of the painter's great self-esteem as well as his somewhat princely aspirations. Like almost all of Jan's paintings, this work is a landmark of Western art for the numerous innovations in style and technique.

From approximately the same period is the unsigned *Madonna with Chancellor Nicholas Rolin*. A work of extraordinary clarity and precision, it shows the shrewd and

Obijt Gaudauit an 1426. ibidem in cathedrali æde sepultus

Hubert Van Eyck

powerful chancellor of Burgundy kneeling at prayer before the Virgin and Child. Every detail of the landscape and architectural setting is rendered with such exactitude that these sacred events have become profoundly real. The painter's use of bright primary hues overlaid with numerous transparent glazes enlivens the entire surface of the painting, which glows with the intensity of a precious jewel.

The famous double portrait *Giovanni Arnolfini and His Wife* is signed and dated 1434. This brilliant panel, as Panofsky has shown, functioned both as a portrait and a legal document to commemorate the sacrament of marriage between an Italian banker and his wife. The strong piety and intense spirituality of this painting are characteristic of the mature phase of Jan's art. At the same time the painter's feeling for space, lighting, and plastic form reaches new heights of actualization. A further tendency toward monumentality and static immobility can also be witnessed in this panel.

These stylistic qualities attained their finest expression in the *Madonna of Canon George van der Paele with Saints Donatien and George*. Of all Jan's surviving works, this brilliant panel (1434-1436) most fully realizes the painter's twin goals of pictorial richness and spiritual grandeur.

Only a few paintings are known from Jan's last years. The *Lucca Madonna* can probably be dated after 1436; the strangely archaic *Virgin at the Fountain* is signed and dated 1439. With only minor variations both works retain the formal beauty and compositional balance of Jan's mature style.

As a portraitist, Jan van Eyck has few rivals among northern painters. His keen and objective vision, in combination with an intuitive reserve, endows his subjects with both individuality and dignity. The portrait *Tymotheos*, which is thought to represent Philip the Good's court musician Gilles Binchois, is signed and dated Oct. 10, 1432. With characteristic Eyckian precision, the sitter is depicted in a dense spatial ambient from which he emerges through a boldly directed use of lighting.

In the *Man in a Red Turban* (1433), which is probably a self-portrait, the penetrating glance of the eyes involves the spectator more directly with the sitter. Through this remarkable innovation Jan was able to achieve the result, so aptly described by one writer, that "it is the viewer that is the observed, not the observer."

With the single exception of Rogier van der Weyden, Jan van Eyck was the most influential Flemish painter of the 15th century. The technical brilliance and formal balance of his style served as a model to generations of painters (including Rogier) both north and south of the Alps.

Further Reading

Since the rediscovery of the Van Eycks in the 19th century, many studies of them have appeared. The most complete work in English is Ludwig von Baldass, *Jan van Eyck* (1952); it contains a thorough catalog of the works as well as a full bibliography up to 1952. For the most authoritative survey of the Van Eyck problem as well as a brilliant appreciation of their art see the relevant chapters in Erwin Panofsky, *Early Netherlandish*

Painting (1953). C.D. Cuttler, *Northern Painting from Pucelle to Bruegel* (1968), is a recent excellent summary. □

Edward John Eyre

Edward John Eyre (1815-1901) was an English explorer of Australia and an administrator in New Zealand and the West Indies. He was tried for murder in the ruthless suppression of a Jamaican uprising and was acquitted.

Contrary to general belief, Edward John Eyre was born not at Hornsea, Yorkshire, but at Whipsnade in Bedfordshire on Aug. 5, 1815. His father was the Reverend Anthony Eyre, Vicar of Hornsea and Long Riston. Edward lived and was educated in Yorkshire. He completed his schooling at Sedbergh Grammar School and soon after decided to seek his fortune in the colony of New South Wales, where considerable opportunities were opened up by the expansion of the pastoral industry. Arriving at Sydney on March 20, 1833, he moved to the rich Hunter River district. In 1834 he acquired a property near Queanbeyan in New South Wales, but his stock were struck by disease. In January 1837 he returned to Sydney to start a fresh life driving sheep overland, first to Port Phillip and then even farther afield to Adelaide. There he established a home in 1838.

A young man of adventurous disposition who had become accustomed to the hardships of the bush, Eyre turned his attention to exploring. He undertook two expeditions to the north of Adelaide in 1839, and in 1840, at the invitation of a committee of Adelaide interests, prepared for an exploration of the Australian interior. Nothing was known of the central part of Australia, but there were rumors of an inland sea and of the existence of rich pastoral land, for which there was a strong demand. On June 18, 1840, Eyre set out with a small party of two aborigines and three white men, including his foreman and companion on previous trips, John Baxter, to clear up some of these mysteries. For over a month they journeyed in a northerly direction through hot, dry land, eventually turning back in despair at a point which Eyre sadly named Mount Hopeless.

To amend his failure, which weighed heavily on his mind, Eyre resolved to do what no one had previously accomplished, namely, to follow the coast westward around the Great Australian Bight and examine its practicability as a stock route. Despite initial setbacks and the attempts of friends and the governor of South Australia to dissuade him from this hazardous undertaking, he set out from Fowler's Bay on Feb. 25, 1841. Water was short, the terrain difficult, and the temperature extreme. Baxter was murdered by the natives, and only Eyre and a boy named Wylie completed the trip to Albany, a chance meeting with a French whaling ship at Rossiter Bay having provided much-needed assistance.

As an explorer, Eyre was noted more for his courage and perseverance than for finding anything of great value. He had failed to penetrate into the interior, and he discovered little that was not already suspected about the coastal country.

Career as Bureaucrat

After returning to Adelaide, Eyre was made a magistrate and protector of the aborigines at Moorundie. In December 1844 he sailed for England and in 1846 was appointed lieutenant governor of New Zealand, where he served under and clashed with the governor, Sir George Grey. In 1853 Eyre returned to England and a year later sailed for the West Indies, where he served as lieutenant governor of St. Vincent, acting governor of the Leeward Islands, and governor of Jamaica. He suppressed a serious mutiny in October 1865 but he was recalled following the court-martial and hanging of a member of the local legislature who had been implicated in the uprising.

In England there was a public outcry in which leading figures like John Stuart Mill, Julian Huxley, and Herbert Spencer attacked Eyre, while others such as Thomas Carlyle, Alfred Lord Tennyson, and John Ruskin sprang to his support. Eyre was twice tried and acquitted, but it was not until 1874 that he was allowed to retire on a governor's pension. He died on Nov. 30, 1901, in Devonshire.

Further Reading

For Eyre's own account of his work in Australia see his *Journals of Expeditions of Discovery into Central Australia, and Overland from Adelaide to King George's Sound, in the Years 1840-1841* (1845). Recent biographies are M. J. L. Uren, *Edward John Eyre* (1964), and Geoffrey Dutton, *The Hero as Murderer* (1967). Eyre's conduct as governor of Jamaica is treated in William Law Mathieson, *The Sugar Colonies and Governor Eyre, 1849-1866* (1936), while the resultant controversy in England is discussed in Bernard Semmel, *The Governor Eyre Controversy* (1962).

Additional Sources

Dutton, Geoffrey, *In search of Edward John Eyre,* South Melbourne; New York: Macmillan, 1982. □

Ezana

Ezana (active early to middle 4th century) was an Ethiopian king during the Axumite period. His reign marked a turning point in Ethiopian history because Christianity became the state religion when he became the first Christian king.

Very little indeed is known about Ethiopia before the 12th century, but the reign of Ezana in the early to middle 4th century stands out because of the relatively abundant inscriptions which he left. Axum was the predecessor kingdom of modern Ethiopia and was located in the northern part of the country. Ezana succeeded his father, Ella Amida, to the kingship while still a child, and Ezana's mother, Sofya, acted as his regent until he grew up. The young Ezana was tutored by one of his father's counselors, Frumentius, who was a Christian from Syria. Frumentius later converted Ezana to Christianity and became the head of the new Ethiopian Church.

The first known inscription left by Ezana was written on a stone stele in three languages, Geez (Old Ethiopic), Sabean, and Greek. By this time Ezana was ruling the kingdom himself, and he records the extent of his domains and some details of military expeditions to the north. He sent his brothers, Shaiazana and Hadefan, to subdue the Beja people, who had been raiding trading caravans in the north. Ezana showed his diplomatic skill by his wise treatment of these people after they were conquered. Instead of suppressing or enslaving them, he lavished wealth upon them and had them resettled in a fertile area within Axum where they were able to live in prosperity and peace. Several other, later inscriptions have been found that mention expeditions to places which can no longer be identified, and the general confusion of terminology makes it difficult to determine the precise extent of Axum at that time. It is not, for example, clear whether Ezana himself either ruled or invaded southern Arabia.

Through such men as Frumentius, Axum maintained close contacts with the Christian nations of the eastern Mediterranean. It was the rise of Islam several centuries later which isolated Christian Ethiopia from the rest of the world. There is no official and explicit record of Ezana's conversion to Christianity, but the fact of this event is shown by the changes in the symbols used in Axumite coins. Ezana's fifth and last known inscription pays tribute to the Christian god for the first time, and it goes on to describe his very important conquest of the ancient city of Meroë in northern Sudan. This conquest completed the downfall of the kingdom of Kush, which had once ruled Lower Egypt.

Traditions, which were written centuries later, say that Ezana adopted the Christian name of Abreha; however, this identification is controversial, and some modern historians believe that Abreha was another individual who ruled centuries later. Ezana is also remembered as having been a great builder, and he may have been responsible for the erection of the great obelisks still visible in the town of Axum.

Further Reading

An English translation of Ezana's last inscription is in Basil Davidson, ed., *The African Past* (1964). Very little is known about Ezana, and there is no biography of him. A useful account of early Ethiopia by G. W. B. Huntingford, "The Kingdom of Axum," is in Roland Oliver, ed., *The Dawn of African History* (1961; 2d ed. 1968). E. Sylvia Pankhurst, *Ethiopia: A Cultural History* (1955), contains more material on Ezana than most general histories. Edward Ullendorff, *The Ethiopians* (1960; 2d ed. 1965), is a good general source. □

Ezekiel

Ezekiel (active 6th century B.C.) was a Hebrew priest and prophet. He held that each man is responsible for his own acts.

Little is known about Ezekiel's personal life. The son of Buzi, he was apparently a descendant of the priestly family of Zadok. While in Jerusalem, he had been influenced by his older contemporary Jeremiah. Ezekiel was exiled to Babylonia with King Jehoiachin in 597 B.C. or shortly thereafter. Five years later he lived in the Babylonian Jewish settlement of Tel Aviv (Tel Abubu, the hill of the storm god) by the Chebar River. It was there that he received his call to prophecy in a mystical vision (Ezekiel 8:1 ff). Josephus speaks of Ezekiel as having been young at the time of his exile, but that is probably not correct. Ezekiel demonstrated the kind of precise knowledge of the Temple and its ritual that could be acquired only from personal and active participation as a priest in the Temple worship.

For 22 years Ezekiel continued his ministry. In his early period as a prophet, he denounced his people for their sins and corruption. After the destruction of Jerusalem in 586, however, Ezekiel became the consoler and comforter of the exiles, holding out to them the promise of return to the homeland and the restoration of the Temple and of the throne of David. Ezekiel's loftiest vision, that of the Valley of Dry Bones (37:1-14), has rarely been matched in its grandeur. It is the prophet's response to the despair of the exiles, and it has become a powerful symbol of hope, resurrection, and regeneration.

In the early days of his ministry, Ezekiel found it difficult to impress his doctrines upon his people. Later, particularly after the destruction of Jerusalem, they recognized him as their spiritual leader, and they turned to him for counsel in their religious dilemmas and perplexities. The community elders evidently assembled in his home for instruction and guidance (8:1 ff, 14:1 ff), and it is possible that the institution of the synagogue grew out of these gatherings. One of the primary religious issues raised in these meetings was the problem of God's justice. The exiles thought they were sinless and should not have to suffer for the sins of their ancestors. In his reply Ezekiel laid down a vital principle in Judaism. Before Ezekiel, Jeremiah had asserted that children are not answerable for their parents' sins. Ezekiel proclaimed a new doctrine, which represents an ethical advance. The individual alone, he said, bears responsibility for his deeds. The belief "If the fathers have eaten sour grapes, the children's teeth should be set on edge" (18:2) is no longer tenable. The truth is that "the soul that sinneth, it shall die" (18:4). In other words, one is not liable for another's actions, and the innocent cannot be held liable for the guilty; each one, moreover, must atone for his own sins. This idea was a powerful motivation for ethical living.

Ezekiel speaks of an attack of "Gog of the land of Magog, the chief prince of Meshech and Tubal" (38:2), who is to lead an armed horde of nations from the north against Israel before the inauguration of God's sovereignty. This idiom is obscure and has never been adequately explained. Gog is often mentioned in the apocalyptic works; it is to be found also in the Dead Sea Scrolls. In rabbinic works the wars of Gog and Magog are to precede the coming of the Messiah.

Ezekiel was the only Hebrew prophet who ministered to his people outside the Holy Land. He is unique in his frequent use of the term "son of man" as the manner of the divine address. Unlike other Hebrew prophets, who placed the ethical above the ritual, Ezekiel fused the two elements, thereby reflecting his dual role as a pious priest and inspired prophet.

Further Reading

H. H. Rowley, *Book of Ezekiel in Modern Study* (1953), and H. L. Ellison, *Ezekiel: The Man and His Message* (1956), are recommended. □

Ezra

Ezra (active 5th century B.C.) was a Hebrew priest, scribe, religious leader, and reformer who vitally influenced Judaism.

The son of Seraiah, Ezra was a descendant of the ancient priestly house of Zadok. In 458 B.C., the seventh year of the reign of King Artaxerxes of Persia, Ezra obtained the King's permission to visit Judea, bearing with him the latter's gifts for the Holy Temple. The primary purpose of his mission, however, was to inquire into the deteriorating religious conditions of the Jewish community in Judea.

Ezra came at the head of a caravan of about 1,800 men, not including their women and children. They made the 4-month journey from Babylon without the benefit of military escort, thereby demonstrating their trust and reliance upon God.

Soon after his arrival in Jerusalem, Ezra proceeded to reorganize the Temple services. In response to his vigorous program to persuade the people to observe the Mosaic Law, they entered into a covenant to keep the Sabbath and the Sabbatical year, as well as other precepts of the Torah. But the problem that perplexed Ezra most was that many of the Judean settlers had taken heathen wives from among the neighboring peoples. Mixed marriages had become so prevalent as to threaten the very survival of the Jewish community. Ezra induced his people to divorce their pagan wives and to separate from the community those who refused to do so.

Ezra's action was an extreme measure, but he felt that the critical situation warranted it. It aroused the ire of the Samaritans and other peoples, who resented the affront to their women. In retaliation the Samaritans denounced Ezra to the Persian king for attempting to rebuild the walls of Jerusalem, which he evidently was not authorized to do. The King stopped the work, and the rebuilt part was razed.

Ezra convened an assembly of the people in Jerusalem (ca. 445) in order to bring about a religious revival. Standing on a wooden pulpit, he read aloud a portion of the Law of Moses, which the Levites expounded. At that time, too, Ezra reinstituted the celebration of the Feast of Tabernacles. It is probable that he died shortly after this episode. The traditional tomb of Ezra is located in Basra, Iraq, though Josephus stated that he was buried in Jerusalem.

The Talmud ascribes a far more important role to Ezra than that recorded in the scriptural book bearing his name. The Talmud asserts that Ezra would have been worthy of having the Torah given through him to Israel had not Moses preceded him. It also attributes to him many ancient laws, perhaps to give them prestige and authority. It states that he introduced the use of the square Hebrew script. Ezra also is said to have determined the precise text of the Pentateuch. Tradition regards him, moreover, as the founder of the Kenesset Hagdolah, the Great Assembly, which exercised supreme religious authority until the end of the 4th century B.C.

Scholars believe it was Ezra who replaced the altars and shrines in the villages with synagogues. Other prominent Jewish religious customs are associated with Ezra, who is generally credited with having removed the Torah from the monopoly of the priesthood and democratized it by teaching it to the people. Finally, Ezra is regarded as the savior of the national and religious life of Judaism at a most critical period.

Further Reading

R. Travers Herford discusses the period of Ezra in *The Pharisees* (1924). For background see John Bright, *A History of Israel* (1959), and G. A. Buttrick and others, eds., *Interpreter's Dictionary of the Bible,* vol. 2 (1962). □

F

Laurent Fabius

Laurent Fabius (born 1946) was the Socialist wunderkind of French politics in the 1980s. He was not yet forty when President François Mitterrand named him prime minister in 1984 and gave him primary responsibility for producing an economic recovery.

Laurent Fabius was born on August 20, 1946, in Paris. Like many French politicians of the left as well as the right, he was a product of an elite, rigorous schooling. He was a graduate of institutions that are training grounds for academics (École Normale Supérieure), bureaucrats (École National de l'Administration) and future leaders (Institut d'Etudes Politiques). Like most of the leading lights of French politics at that time, he began his career as a civil servant with Council of State. In fact, as prime minister he was still technically on leave from the council, to which he could conceivably return when he left office.

Rising Star

While still in the early stages of his bureaucratic career, Fabius developed close connections with Socialist Party secretary François Mitterrand and his entourage. By 1974 Fabius had officially joined the party, which was then achieving greater success in elections under Mitterrand's helm. During the late 1970s he became one of Mitterrand's closest personal advisers, often serving as the spokesperson for the senior Socialist politician and the party as a whole. Fabius served on the party's steering committee beginning in 1977 and was one of the coordinators of the 1981 presidential and legislative elections that brought the Left into power on its own for the first time since the Popular Front of 1936; Mitterrand became the Fifth Republic's first Socialist president.

Fabius had been establishing his own electoral career during this time as well. From 1977 to 1981 he served as deputy mayor on the municipal council of Grand-Queville, a town of about 30,000 in Normandy. In 1978 he ran for and was elected to the National Assembly from Grand-Queville's district in the Seine-Maritime department. He was reelected in 1981, but in compliance with the French constitution had to resign his seat in parliament when he was named to Prime Minister Pierre Mauroy's first cabinet. By 1981 Fabius had developed a reputation as one of France's brightest young politicians, especially for his firm grasp on economic problems. Despite his youth, he was someone the Socialist elders in general, and Mitterrand in particular, were turning to for difficult and even delicate assignments.

In Mauroy's first cabinets Fabius served as minister for the budget (1981-1983). Later he took on the even more challenging ministry of industry and research (1983-1984). In those jobs Fabius was given the primary responsibility for reviving the lagging industrial economy and overseeing a strategized shift from a "smokestack" to a "high technology" base for the economy as a whole. The task was a difficult one indeed and a plan certainly regarded with suspicion by the electorate: the country's industries were instructed to become more competitive in world markets, while the government attempted to deal with increasingly dissatisfied labor unions.

Heir Apparent

Upon taking office, the Socialists had nationalized France's banks and instituted other measures in an effort to

account the government's procedures for testing blood products, and why certain precautions were not followed. Over 1,200 hemophiliacs in France became HIV-positive as a result, and 300 had died. Fabius and his then secretary of state for health, Edmond Hervé, and minister for social affairs Georgina Dufoix, came under fire. It was in part due to the public statements made by the Hervé and Dufoix that public outcry became vehement enough for the Court of Justice for the Republic to place all three under examination for manslaughter.

In Fabius's case, he faced charges as the leader of government at the time. Though it was understood he was not directly to blame, his statements also aroused furor and may have stalled his political career and presidential ambitions indefinitely in the public eye. He remains a strong force within his party, however: he continued as president of Haute Normandie's regional council, was again reelected to the National Assembly in 1993, and in 1995 was named leader of the Socialists in the National Assembly. He is the author of several books, including *La France inégale* (1975), *Le Coeur de Futur* (1985), and *Les Blessures de la Vérité* (1995).

Further Reading

Little is available in English specifically regarding Fabius. None of his books have been translated into English. For a good overview of the Socialist Party and the generation of activists of which Laurent Fabius was a part, see D. S. Bell and Byron Criddle, *The French Socialist Party: Resurgence and Victory* (1984); and Denis Mac-Shane, *François Mitterrand* (1982). □

reverse a long economic decline, but this led to difficulties and an austerity program went into effect in 1983. As the decade continued, the economic slump and problems with the unions continued. But President Mitterrand increasingly came to the conclusion that Fabius was the only person with the economic and political skills to reverse the decline under the Socialist government. He therefore replaced Mauroy with Fabius on July 17, 1984.

Fabius served as prime minister for two years. One of his most controversial decisions was the 1985 agreement negotiated with the Walt Disney corporate empire to build a theme park in France; there was great public outcry against it. But Fabius would be charged with a far more serious transgression some years later when he was replaced following the 1986 elections. During the interim time, he served as President of the French National Assembly from 1988 to 1992 (he had consistently won re-election from his Seine-Maritime district), and in 1992 was tapped to serve as secretary of the Socialist Party (Mitterrand's one-time post). However, by now the party was severely fractionalized, and it was hoped that under Fabius's guidance it might re-emerge as a united front, and that he would then run for President. It was known that Mitterrand himself favored him as his successor.

Charged with Manslaughter

But in the early 1990s a scandal grew of monstrous notoriety. It became known that in 1985, the blood distributed to hemophiliacs by the French ministry of health was contaminated with the HIV virus. The scandal called into

Emil Ludwig Fackenheim

Liberal Jewish theologian Emil Fackenheim (born 1916) explored new horizons relating the Holocaust to Jewish theology and examining the relationships among modern philosophical issues.

Emil Ludwig Fackenheim represents the odyssey of contemporary liberal Jewish theologians both in his thought and in his life. He was born in Halle, Germany, on June 22, 1916. Liberal Jews at this time looked to Germany's cultured, middle-class Jewish population as the beacon of enlightenment and progress. Fackenheim shared these views and studied for the Reform Jewish rabbinate in the Hochschule für die Wissenschaft des Judentums, where he was ordained in 1939. He maintained a keen interest in non-Jewish philosophy as well by studying at the University of Halle. Shortly after his ordination he was interned for three months in a concentration camp—a profoundly traumatic experience, but one with a fortunate outcome, as he was one of the few lucky ones to be released. After leaving Germany he studied briefly at the University of Aberdeen and was then called as rabbi to Congregation Anshe Sholom in Hamilton, Ontario, Canada, where he served from 1943 to 1948.

In North America, Fackenheim came to represent a growing number of Reform rabbis in both the United States and Canada who explored new theological horizons. He embraced a "neo-Orthodoxy" inspired in part by the German Protestant thinker Karl Barth. His philosophical training led him beyond existentialism to investigate Hegel, who seemed to point towards new avenues in religious thinking. He received a Guggenheim fellowship for 1957-1958 which enabled him to develop his ideas more fully. These ideas reached full expression in his book *The Religious Dimension in Hegel's Thought* (1968).

Fackenheim's thinking challenged the youth of his congregation to take Judaism seriously as an intellectual system. He took up this challenge himself while studying at the University of Toronto's Department of Philosophy, from which he received a Ph.D. in 1945. In 1948 he joined the faculty of that department, an appointment he continued for over three decades. He was an intellectual leader whose struggles with liberal thought and neo-Orthodox beliefs were well represented in his anthology of essays *Quest for Past and Future: Essays in Jewish Theology* (1968).

Holocaust and the State of Israel

The introduction to the *Quest* book represented a change in Fackenheim's approach. In March 1967 he was asked to speak at a symposium concerning the Nazi Holocaust and Jewish theology. The symposium occurred on a Sunday which celebrated both the Christian Easter and the Jewish holiday of Purim. Fackenheim noted that for Christians redemption occurs because of divine suffering, while Purim suggests that Jews must struggle in history for their own redemption. He recalled the psychic pain of confronting his own memories at a time when Christians seemed to be demanding that Jews play out their drama of suffering and abandon the lessons of Purim. These were the weeks leading up to Israel's Six-Day War, a time in which the Jewish state was threatened by the Arab world's military stronghold of Egypt. Fackenheim took the opportunity to enunciate what he called the "614th commandment," which forbids Jews to hand Hitler yet another, posthumous victory.' Thus, he asserted, Jews are compelled to learn from and remember constantly the lessons of the past—in essence, to survive.

In the following years Fackenheim developed the ideas expressed in that symposium. He explored their meaning in the Charles F. Deems Lectures given at New York University in 1968 and later published as *God's Presence in History: Jewish Affirmations and Philosophical Reflections* (1970). He explained the relevance of this new position for his continuing study of non-Jewish philosophy in *Encounters Between Judaism and Philosophy: A Preface to Future Jewish Thought* (1973).

During the 1970s Fackenheim's thought matured as he devoted five summers to study in Israel supported by research grants of the Canada Council. In 1971 he affirmed the relevance of Holocaust theology not only for Jews but for all humanity in the B. G. Rudolf Lecture in Judaica Studies at Syracuse University. In 1976 he presented a new methodological approach—that of taking *midrash* (medi-eval commentaries on Hebrew scripture) as the point of departure for Jewish theology. In a conference devoted to Elie Wiesel, the Jewish writer and Holocaust survivor, Fackenheim described this new approach to Jewish thinking: stories, images, and mystical concepts rather than philosophy could supply the keys to the meaning of Judaism. His new view of Jewish ethnicity, the relevance of the Holocaust for all humanity, and midrashic method of theologizing were expressed in *The Jewish Return into History: Reflections in the Age of Auschwitz and a New Jerusalem* (1978) and *To Mend the World: Foundations of Future Jewish Thought* (1982).

Confronting Kant and Hegel

Fackenheim's most important contribution to contemporary religious thinking was his clear account of how modern theology must confront philosophical issues. While he traced the history of modern philosophical thought in general, his analyses of Kant and Hegel are of special importance. No contemporary Jewish thinking can fail to encounter Kant's ethical challenge. Kant contended that only a self-willed, autonomous ethic is morally good. A religious ethic which is based on mere obedience to the divine will is morally suspect. Fackenheim examined this claim in a number of essays and sought to show that in Judaism the problem of God's unconditional demand is related to martyrdom and a sense of divine purpose.

From Hegel, Fackenheim learned the necessity of taking historical processes seriously—in other words, the patterns of the past do indeed shape destiny. In both cases the Nazi experience is crucial. The Holocaust brought the question of purpose into direct light; God's unconditional command is ethical because it serves a purpose even if human beings cannot comprehend that purpose. Fackenheim asserted that Kant was wrong because he does not allow for the surprise that comes when human beings recognize a purpose that they cannot comprehend. The Holocaust also revealed God's presence in history, not as an inevitable hand but as a commanding voice. Listening to that voice enabled Jews to transform the reality of human history and thus move beyond Hegel.

The Eclipse of God

Fackenheim and his family emigrated to Israel in 1974, where he continued to write books and articles on theological matters. Moving beyond Hegel and Kant into the twentieth century, Fackenheim also explored the idea put forth by modern Jewish philosopher Martin Buber, who argued that the occurrence of the Holocaust is sufficient evidence that God must have abandoned humanity for a time. Yet Fackenheim disagreed, arguing that the surviving Jews and the resistance to Nazi Germany pointed to evidence that many indeed heard the voice of God, and in essence was indeed true to that 614th commandment. Fackenheim's other titles include *To Mend the World* (1980), *What Is Judaism? An Interpretation for the Present Age* (1987), *The Jewish Bible After the Holocaust: A Re-Reading* (1990), and *Jewish Philosophers and Jewish Philosophy* (1996).

Further Reading

There is no easy way to be introduced to Emil L. Fackenheim the thinker and person. His essays and books are the best introduction since they contain both autobiographical material and his maturing thought. A critical but fair study of his work is found in Steven T. Katz, *Post-Holocaust Dialogues: Critical Studies in Modern Jewish Thought* (1983). Other scholarly studies include David Ellenson, "Emil Fackenheim and the Revealed Morality of Judaism," in *Judaism* (1976); Sandra Lubarsky, "Ethics and Theodicy: Tensions in Emil Fackenheim's Thought," in *Encounter* (1983); and Norbert Samuelson, "Revealed Morality and Modern Thought," in *Journal of the Central Conference of American Rabbis* (1969). Each of these essays is difficult but rewarding reading.

Additional Sources

Michael W. Morgan, ed., *The Jewish Thought of Emil Fackenheim* (1987).

Robert M. Seltzer, "Judaism According to Emil Fackenheim," in *Commentary* (September 1988).

Harvey Shulman, "The Theo-Political Thought of Emil Fackenheim," in *Judaism* (Spring 1990). □

Muhammad Fādil al-Jamālī

Muhammad Fādil al-Jamālī (born 1903) was an Iraqi educator, writer, diplomat, and politician who served at various times as foreign minister and premier of Iraq.

Muhammad Fādil al-Jamālī was born in 1903 in Kazimayn (hence he is called al Kāzimīyah), site of an important Shiite religious shrine immediately to the north of Baghdad. His father, Shaykh (Sheik) ʿAbbās al-Jamālī, was a local religious leader of the Shiite sect to which the family belonged. He first entered the mosque school in Kazimayn at age seven to study the Koran but continued his studies in a modern school in Kazimayn and in several different institutions in Baghdad.

Won Coveted Scholarship

Fādil al-Jamālī graduated first in his class from the Elementary Teachers' Training College in Baghdad in 1920 and taught for four years. He was then chosen as one of the first six persons to receive scholarships from the Iraqi government to attend the American University of Beirut, from which he graduated with the B.A. degree in education in 1927. In Beirut he was active in the society known as al-Urwah al-Wuthqah (based on the ideas of Jamāl al-Dīn al-Afghānī and Muhammad ʿAbduh). This society wanted to achieve a modern and progressive interpretation of Islam. He also took part in the activities of an interfaith society, demonstrating his interest in religious matters.

Upon returning to Iraq, Fādil al-Jamālī was appointed to the Higher Teachers' Training College in Baghdad, where he distinguished himself by advocating education for females—at the time a rather radical concept in the Arab world. In 1929 he was awarded a Macy grant from the International Institute of Teachers' College, Columbia University, for higher studies in education. He achieved the M.A. degree of Columbia University in 1930 and the Ph.D. in 1934. The latter was awarded for a thesis on the *New Iraq; Its Problems of Bedouin Education*. During his American sojourn, in a summer school at the University of Chicago, he met his future wife, Sarah Hayden Powell, a Canadian; the couple would have three children together.

From Education to Politics

Back in Iraq in 1932 Fādil al-Jamālī served in his country's educational establishment. He first worked as the Iraqi attaché to the Commission of Educational Inquiry sent to Iraq by the League of Nations (known as the Monroe Commission), but soon joined the Department of Education where he became successively supervisor general, director general, inspector general, and director general of education and public instruction. During all of this time he continued lecturing and working in the Higher Teachers' Training College. Most of his writings on educational subjects date from this period of his life; they include studies (in Arabic) on education in the Arab world, in Turkey, and in England, France, and Germany. He wrote also on the philosophy of education in the Koran.

In 1942 Fādil al-Jamālī joined the Iraqi foreign ministry, in which he served out the balance of his public career. He was made director general of the foreign ministry with rank of minister in 1944. In 1945, as an Iraqi delegate, he attended the conferences in San Francisco at which the United Nations was founded. When the Iraqi foreign minister, Arshād al-ʾUmarī, refused to sign the United Nations charter because of dissatisfaction over the trusteeship issue, Fādil al Jamālī was authorized to sign for Iraq.

Key Player in Arab League

Fādil al-Jamālī was an ardent exponent of Arab causes. He was among the founders of the Arab League in 1945 and afterwards served as its president. He played a particularly important role as Arab spokesperson in the debates that led up to the partition of Palestine and the establishment of the state of Israel in 1948. His position as a delegate to the first General Assembly of the United Nations in 1946, his attendance at the London Conference on Palestine in the same year, as well as his position as president of the Arab League gave him ample opportunity for the expression of his views. In 1946, he warned the representative of President Truman of the danger of revolution among all the Arabs if the rights of the Palestinians were violated.

At this time, the Arab League favored the immediate termination of the British mandate over Palestine and an independent Arab state in the country, and Fādil al-Jamālī was a principal upholder of these views. In 1947 he became foreign minister of Iraq and also co-chair of the Iraqi delegation to the UN Assembly of that year. He strove to protect Arab interests in the debates that led to the UN decision to partition Palestine, and he was among the Arab leaders who walked out of the United Nations in protest when the partition decision was finally reached.

Became Premier of Iraq

Fādil al-Jamālī gave up the post of foreign minister in 1948 and served for a time as ambassador to Egypt before taking up the foreign ministry portfolio once more in 1949. He acted as Iraq's permanent delegate to the United Nations in both 1949 and 1950, when he was made president of the Iraqi Chamber of Deputies in December. In August of 1952 he once more became foreign minister under Premier Mustafā al-'Umarī and again acted as Iraq's chief delegate to the United Nations. In the United Nations he continued his efforts on behalf of the Palestinian Arabs, initiated moves to amend the UN charter in order to abolish the veto of the Security Council, acted to block face-to-face negotiations of Israel and the Arabs with regard to Palestine, and sought to bring about negotiations between France and the Sultan of Morocco to resolve their disputes. He resigned from the foreign ministry and the conjoint post of minister of the interior in 1953, but in September of that year was asked to form a cabinet as premier of Iraq. He served as prime minister until April of the following year.

Fādil al-Jamālī resigned under the impact of severe criticism in the press, and on the part of nationalist and leftist elements, for his handling of relief to the victims of the great floods of that year. Nūrī al-Sa'īd, who succeeded to power in August, wished to have Fādil al-Jamālī as a member of his new government, but in a show of independence Fādil al-Jamālī refused. He was, nonetheless, greatly indebted to Nūrī al-Sa'īd, who had launched him on his public career. Nūrī later appointed him as head of the Iraqi delegation to the Bandung Conference in April 1955. Fādil al-Jamālī also acted as Nūrī's personal representative at the Cairo Conferences in which the Turkish-Iraqi alliance and the Baghdad Pact were discussed. In this connection, acting as Nūrī's envoy, he played an important role in trying to gain Lebanese and Syrian support for the proposed Turkish-Iraqi alliance but was unsuccessful in this mission.

In the United Nations Fādil al-Jamālī on several occasions returned to the theme of the necessity for member nations to observe and uphold the resolutions of the international body. He believed that the organization could not be effective and there could be no international peace if UN resolutions were flaunted by member states. In the early 1950s such criticisms were directed especially at the Israelis, but in 1956 he spoke out strongly against the Hungarian and Soviet governments for their suppression of the Hungarian uprising. Fādil al-Jamālī's tenure as delegate to the United Nations may, in general, be said to correspond with a period during which Iraq's foreign policy was pro-Western.

Tried, Convicted, and Imprisoned

Following the military coup of July 14, 1958 (led by Abd al-Karīm Qāsim), which overthrew the Iraqi monarch, Fādil al-Jamālī was one of 106 former officials who were arrested and brought to trial; at the time of the coup he was foreign minister under Nūrī al-Sa'īd. The trials were conducted by a special military court, later called the People's Court, in a circus-like atmosphere which mocked all judi-cial procedure and propriety. Their purpose was plainly to discredit and ridicule the defendants.

Fādil al-Jamālī, whose trial began on September 20, was accused of plotting against Iraqi national security, of corruption, of fixing elections, of plotting against Syria, of aiding imperialism, of attempting to unify Syria and Iraq, of attacking Egypt's Gamal Abdel Nasser ('Abd al-Nāsir) at the last session of the Security Council, and of criticizing Nasser for his intervention in Lebanon. On November 10 he was condemned to death, but in his case the sentence was not carried out. He was, instead, remanded to prison, where he remained until July 14, 1961. During this incarceration he wrote *Letters on Islam, Written by a Father in Prison to his Son,* published in London in 1965.

Some time after his release from prison, Fādil al-Jamālī left Iraq and public life to take up residence elsewhere. He established himself for a time at Caux in France but ultimately settled in Tunis where he taught in the university. He occasionally contributed articles on Arab affairs to the press in France, Britain, and Tunisia. He is the recipient of numerous honors and has been a member of several civic organizations. These include an honorary degree from the University of Southern California and decorations from the governments of Jordan, Iran, Spain, and China as well as Iraq. He was also a Free Mason.

Further Reading

Harry J. Almond wrote a biography of Fādil al-Jamālī, *Iraqi Statesman: A Portrait of Mohammed Fadhel Jamali* (1993). Further details of his diplomatic and political involvements may be followed by pursuing the references given in the indexes of the *New York Times* and *The Times* of London. Information concerning his arrest and trial is available in George M. Haddad, *Revolutions and Military Rule in the Middle East: the Arab States,* volume II (1971). □

Sayyid Muhammad Husayn Fadlallah

The Shi'i Muslim cleric Sayyid Muhammad Husayn Fadlallah (born 1935) was a leading political leader in Lebanon beginning in the 1980s.

Sayyid Muhammad Husayn (Hussein) Fadlallah was born in Najaf, Iraq, in November, 1935, but his roots were in Lebanon. He was the son of the late 'Abd al-Ra'uf Fadlallah, a major Shi'i Muslim cleric from the town of Ainata in southern Lebanon. In the 1980s Fadlallah emerged as one of the leading political figures in Lebanon, where he attracted a wide following in the large Shi'i community, particularly within the ranks of Hizballah (or Hezbollah), the "Party of God." From the pulpit of the Imam Rida mosque in Bir al-'Abd, a suburb of Beirut, Fadlallah's sermons gave shape to the political currents among the Shi'is, especially during the latter half of the 1980s.

As a young man Fadlallah trained in the Shi'i seminaries of Najaf, where he mastered the arcane intricacies of religious law and was certified as a *mujtahid* (a Shi'i cleric competent to independently interpret religious law). In 1966 he moved to Beirut, where he witnessed the eruption of the Lebanese civil war in 1975 and the progressive disintegration of the Lebanese state. During his first decade in Beirut he devoted much of his time to scholarship and authored several books in Arabic, including the influential *Islam and the Logic of Force.*

The Rise of the Shi'is

The 1950s and 1960s were times of ferment and concern among the learned men of Shi'ism. In Iraq, as in Lebanon, young Shi'is were becoming increasingly active in politics, but they were more attracted by the revolutionary rhetoric of the left than they were by the seemingly anachronistic language of Islam. In both countries the Shi'is found themselves at the bottom of the socioeconomic ladder and Communist ideology, with its emphasis on class exploitation, rang true. In reaction to the successes of the left, some of the leading religious scholars of Najaf created the Hizb al-Da'wa (or the party of the call), and it is entirely possible that Fadlallah was an influential voice within the party. Notwithstanding the creation of al-Da'wa, it was not until the so-called "Islamic revolution" in Iran toppled the Shah in 1979 that the potential for Shi'ism as a language of revolution was understood.

For many years Fadlallah lived in the shadow of Sayyid Musa al-Sadr, the Iranian cleric of Lebanese descent who began to organize the Lebanese Shi'is in the early 1960s. But al-Sadr disappeared in 1978 during a visit to Libya, and his still-unexplained disappearance left a gaping hole which aspiring Shi'i leaders have been competing to fill ever since. Clearly, Fadlallah saw himself as the successor to Musa al-Sadr, but he faced an impressive range of competitors, including Muhammad Mahdi Shams al-Din, the vice-chair of the Supreme Shi'i Islamic Council (al-Sadr was still considered the chair in 1991); 'Abd al-Amr Qabalan, the senior jurisprudent for Shi'i religious law; Nabih Berri, the lawyer who led the important Amal movement; and Husayn al-Husayn, who as speaker of the Parliament held the highest position available to a Shi'i under the Lebanese constitution. Although the competitors often used the highly evocative religious symbolism of Shi'ism to rally supporters and undermine adversaries, it should be borne in mind that the dynamics of Shi'i politics in Lebanon largely reflect an intense struggle for political position.

The Israeli invasion of Lebanon in 1982 was a watershed event for the Lebanese Shi'is and for the public career of Fadlallah. Although many Shi'is, particularly in South Lebanon, greeted the invasion with enthusiasm, by 1983 the mood had shifted from joy to anger. The invading army became an army of occupation, which bore down heavily upon the Shi'is, and a war of resistance began against the Israelis. Eventually, in January 1985, reeling from heavy losses, the Israeli government decided to cut its losses and reduce its occupation to a "security zone" in the south that covered a little less than 10 percent of Lebanese territory.

Although a wide assortment of Lebanese factions participated in the anti-occupation campaign, it was the self-styled Islamic Resistance that captured the imagination of observers all over the world. Fadlallah was an influential proponent of conducting a defensive *jihad al-difa'* (or defensive holy war) against the Israelis, but he was by no means the only Shi'i cleric to do so. Moreover, Fadlallah seemed to have no direct operational role in the attacks.

After the destruction of the U.S. Marine barracks (237 killed) in October of 1983, Fadlallah was said to have played a direct role in encouraging the attack, but subsequent evidence casts doubt on the claim. Indeed, it now seems that the Iranian ambassador to Syria at the time, 'Ali Akbar Mohteshemi, played the major role in organizing the attack, probably with assistance from Syria. This is not to say that Fadlallah opposed the attack. In fact, he applauded it. The Marines were members of the Multinational Force (MNF) that had been dispatched to Lebanon in 1982 following the awful massacres in the Sabra and Chatila refugee camps (the killings were the work of Christian Maronite militiamen allied to Israel). Initially, the international force was warmly received, but its fulsome support for the unpopular government under President Amin Gemayel progressively eroded support for the MNF. In addition, in the ideology promulgated by Tehran, the West—and particularly the United States—was an evil and insidious influence in Lebanon and only through its expulsion would the Lebanese win their freedom from colonialist designs and intrigues. (Incidentally, it was precisely this ideology of hatred that helped to inspire the plague of hostage-taking in the 1980s.)

Dealing with Iran and the Amal

The Iranian role in the attack on the Marines points up the expanding role of Tehran in Lebanese Shi'i politics. By 1982 Iran had dispatched a contingent of *Pasdaran* (revolutionary guards) to Lebanon. The Pasdaran served as a cadre, training Lebanese Shi'is to serve under the banner of the Islamic Revolution. Iran also dispensed relatively large sums of money, much of it flowing into the coffers of Hizballah, to pay military expenses, as well as to fund a relatively broad range of social welfare programs designed to benefit Lebanese Shi'is. Fadlallah, of course, was a vocal supporter of Ayatollah Khomeini and the Iranian revolution, but he believed that Iran was misjudging Lebanon. In particular, he argued that Iran was insensitive to the social complexity of Lebanon, where there are 17 recognized sects, including three Muslim sects and a rich variety of Christians. In contrast, almost 95 percent of the Iranian population follows Shi'i Islam. During a 1985 visit to Iran, Fadlallah found himself in some heated exchanges with Iranian counterparts who exaggerated the ease with which an Islamic state might be created in Lebanon. For his part, Fadlallah stressed a more gradual strategy, one which took fuller account of the realities of Lebanon. Fadlallah also held an independent stance on the matter of hostage-taking, which he generally criticized on moral grounds, but he had little direct influence in such matters.

The latter half of the 1980s was marked by fierce internecine fighting among the two major Shi'i groupings, Amal and Hizballah. The outcome of the fighting left Amal more or less in control of the Shi'i heartland in southern Lebanon, but the more radical Hizballah emerged victorious in the crowded Shi'i suburbs of Beirut. Fadlallah denied any organizational role in Hizballah, but he was popularly associated with the ideals of Hizballah, if not with its organizational infrastructure, so he clearly was a beneficiary of the victory. In fact, many members of the growing Shi'i professional class shifted their political loyalties from Amal to Hizballah.

But Fadlallah maintained his own political identity distinct from Hizballah. His personal ambitions were hardly modest, and by eschewing political labels Fadlallah stood a better chance of broadly appealing to the Shi'is, many of whom avoid any formal political affiliations. Nonetheless, Fadlallah rejected the reformism of the Amal movement and generally opposed efforts to renovate the Lebanese government. Not surprisingly, he refused to support the 1989 Ta'if Accord mediated by the Arab League, which took little account of the fact that the Shi'is are now Lebanon's largest community, representing as much as 40 percent of the total population. But by late 1990 the accord was being implemented under Syrian tutelage as provided in the agreement. Fadlallah certainly had the capacity to eclipse militia leaders made obsolete by a return to civility in Lebanon. But even in an environment of continuing chaos he can be expected to continue to be a formidable presence on the Lebanese scene.

Further Reading

Although none of his major writings are available in English translation, by the late 1980s Fadlallah was regularly interviewed by leading Western newspapers and magazines.
Additional information on religious and political developments in Lebanon and the Middle East can be found in Fouad Ajami, *The Vanished Imam* (1986); John Esposito and James Piscatori, editors, *The Iranian Revolution* (1990); Fuad I. Khuri, *Imams and Emirs* (1990); Moojan Momen, *An Introduction to Shi'i Islam;* Augustus Richard Norton, *Amal and the Shi'a: Struggle for the Soul of Lebanon* (1987); and Robin Wright, *Sacred Rage* (1985). □

Fahd ibn Abdul Aziz Al-Saud

King Fahd ibn Abdul Aziz Al-Saud (born 1920)—the son of the founder of modern Saudi Arabia— succeeded his brothers Saud, Faisal, and Khalid in guiding a traditional Islamic society through the astonishing economic and social development made possible by his country's vast petroleum resources.

Born in 1920, Fahd ibn Abdul Aziz Al-Saud, son of King Ibn Saud, was educated in Islamic history and religion, traditional politics, Arabic language, and desert lore at his father's court in Riyadh. His mother belonged to the Sudeiri clan, a prominent family, and Fahd was one of the couple's seven sons. King Saud had founded Saudi Arabia in 1932 after a thirty-year effort to unite the vast Arabian peninsula. Oil was discovered a few years later and the treasure beneath Saudi sand made both the ruling family and the new nation extremely wealthy within the space of a few short years.

The Fast Lane

As a young man, the king's son acquired a reputation as somewhat of a rake on the international social circuit. He was known to drink alcohol—in violation of his conservative Wahhabi Muslim upbringing—and reportedly gambled freely with his generous allowance in the casinos of Monte Carlo. In an attempt to ready his sons for future political roles, King Saud sent both Fahd and his brother, Faisal ibn Abdul Aziz, to San Francisco in 1945 for the founding convention of the United Nations, and the visit marked a turning point for Fahd. He was captivated by America, and later, as king, would conduct relations with both the U.S. political and business establishments that were surprisingly cordial—to the dismay of some of the other Arab heads of state.

Back in Saudi Arabia, Fahd honed his competence in political matters as regional governor of Jauf and of Um Laj. In his early thirties by then, Fahd was reportedly warned by his brother Faisal, then Crown Prince, to curb his hedonistic streak, or the family would consider him to be an unsuitable candidate for the throne. When his father died in 1953, Faisal ascended to the throne, and a decidedly subdued Fahd was appointed Saudi Arabia's first minister of education. The country's educational system was virtually nonexistent at the time, but revenues from Saudi Arabia's rich oil reserves helped fund the construction and staffing of hundreds of secondary schools and numerous universities under Fahd's direction.

Gained Increasing Authority

Fahd became Saudi Arabia's minister of the interior in 1962. Five years later he was also made second deputy prime minister, enabling him to preside over cabinet meetings. As a member of the Council of Ministers during Faisal's reign, Fahd served as chairman of ministerial councils and committees for national security, educational policy, universities, petroleum and minerals, youth welfare, and pilgrimage affairs. These duties gave him broad exposure to vital issues in the development of Saudi society.

In 1975 King Faisal was assassinated and another brother, Khalid, came to the throne. Fahd then became first deputy prime minister and next in the line of succession . The new Crown Prince took an active role in the kingdom's second five-year development plan (1975-1980), and with it the Saudi government's effort to achieve orderly economic progress and careful financial planning for its oil revenue during an extraordinary period of booming development. With the king, Fahd actively worked for the formation of the Gulf Cooperation Council (GCC), a regional organization founded in 1981 to help coordinate and unify Saudi economic, industrial, and defense policies with those of Bahrain, Kuwait, Oman, Qatar, and the United Arab Emirates. Yet it was also known during this era that Khalid suffered from heart trouble and delegated much of his job to Fahd.

Over a period of years, Fahd developed his experience as a spokesperson abroad by leading Saudi delegations to Arab League meetings in Casablanca (1959) and Lebanon (1960) and to Arab summit conferences in Cairo (1965). He represented Saudi Arabia on official trips to France (1967), Britain (1970), Egypt (1974), Spain (1977), and the United States (1974, 1977, and 1985). He headed the Saudi delegation to the OPEC (Organization of Petroleum Exporting Countries) summit conference in Algiers in 1975 and to the North-South Conference at Cancun, Mexico, in 1981. He was especially active in developing the foreign policy objectives of Saudi Arabia, often working behind the scenes in a mediating role. In 1976 Fahd was instrumental in devising an Arab League peacekeeping force to assist in Lebanon while avoiding direct intervention in the civil war there.

Arab Peacemaker

After the Camp David Accords of 1978, which isolated Egypt from the rest of the Arab world, Fahd worked toward an alternative framework that would permit broader participation by Arab nations. His Eight Point Peace Plan of August 1981 was adopted by the Arab summit conference in Fez, Morocco, as the basis for the "Fez Declaration." This plan summarized a consensus of Arab views and proposals concerning political tensions in the Middle East based on a belief that recognition of the rights of the Palestinian people was an essential factor in working toward a comprehensive peace in the area. The Eight Point Peace Plan suggested that mainstream Palestinian representatives participate in negotiations and called for the eventual creation of a Palestinian state.

Another of Fahd's achievements was his savvy financial management of the state treasury—he had always insisted that when a new public-works project was approved (the country constructed much of the housing its citizens enjoy for a negligible amount, for instance), he insisted that the funds be set aside, rather than allowed to earn interest. At one point during the 1970s, the country's revenues topped $100 billion annually, but a drop in crude oil prices lessened that to $20 billion in the space of a few years; yet there were relatively few financial repercussions for the Saudi economy.

Crowned King

On June 13, 1982 Fahd acceded to the throne. He took over a nation of sixteen million—roughly 25 percent of that foreign workers, who must also abide by the strict Wahhabi Islamic tenets that are the law of the land. Part of Fahd's new official title was "Custodian of the Two Holy Mosques," referring to the venerable mosques in the cities of Medina and Mecca that are the Islamic world's most important sites of worship. As king, Fahd also assumed the presidency of

Saudi Aramco, a state-owned firm that controls the country's oil reserves—estimated to be one-quarter of the planet's stores. The new ruler was also one of the world's richest citizens: prior to 1980, Fahd had received a percentage of every barrel of oil drawn in Saudi Arabia. A decade later, his fortune was estimated at $18 billion.

The Gulf War

Fahd continued his active role in Arab politics during the 1980s. He attempted to mediate a devastating war between Iran and Iraq that dragged on through the decade, and thorough his involvement in the Tripartite Committee on Lebanon, formed by the League of Arab States, helped bring about an end to that country's civil war. Fahd also continued to conduct friendly relations with a succession of American presidential administrations, and each of his sons were educated at American colleges. That cordiality proceeded in a new direction in 1990, when Iraq invaded neighboring Kuwait. Iraqi leader Saddam Hussein refused to obey United Nations Security Council directives to withdraw his forces. In response, Fahd allowed U.S. troops to gather on Saudi soil, and after negotiations failed in January of 1991 the Persian Gulf War began from the northern sector of Saudi Arabia.

Fahd's lifetime witnessed the transformation of Saudi Arabia from a collection of Bedouin desert tribes to a modern, high-tech world economic leader that offered its citizens low-cost housing, free health care, and fully subsidized university degrees. Yet the country, and its autocratic ruling family, were sometimes criticized for interference in delicate Middle East politics and human-rights violations at home. In an attempt to deflect criticism, Fahd decreed a new constitution in 1992, and the following year the nation's first national council was seated; its appointed members reviewed, but could not veto, government directives. Fahd also tried to demonstrate goodwill through massive humanitarian aid to certain causes; he founded the Supreme Commission for the Collection of Donations for Bosnian Muslims in 1992 to provide aid to Muslim victims of the war in the former Yugoslavia.

Declining Health

By the early 1990s there were reports that the aging Fahd was in poor health. Overweight for many years, the king was also diabetic and suffered from back and knee problems. Affairs of state had not kept him from enjoying his vast personal wealth: he had counted among his residences 12 palaces and a villa in Marbella, Spain. One of his yachts was accompanied by a warship that could launch anti-aircraft missiles. In late 1995 Fahd suffered a stroke, which plunged the royal family into a succession crisis—albeit one that went on behind closed doors in Riyadh. At the same time, some of the minor personal freedoms that had been allowed in the years following the Gulf War were rescinded, and the kingdom's economic picture was said to be heavily debt-ridden.

Political analysts hinted at an intense struggle within the Saud family regarding who might succeed Fahd, and the crackdown on shops that remained open during prayer times was symptomatic of the ascendance of a more conservative leadership. After his stroke, the 75-year-old Fahd issued a statement announcing that his brother Abdullah, 73, was assuming temporary duties as head of state; six weeks later he announced himself back in power, but it was reported that he was bedridden and in a state of failing mental deterioration. There was speculation that his family would force him into retirement at his villa in Marbella.

Further Reading

Additional information on King Fahd can be found in David Holden and Richard Johns, *The House of Saud: the Rise of the Most Powerful Dynasty in the Arab World* (1981); Alexander Bligh, *From Prince to King, Royal Succession in the House of Saud in the Twentieth Century* (1984); Rashid Nasser Ibrahim and Shaheen Esber Ibrahim, *King Fahd and Saudi Arabia's Great Evolution* (1987); and David E. Long's *The Kingdom of Saudi Arabia* (1997). Further information can be found in articles in *Time* (September 24, 1990; June 3, 1996); and *U.S. News and World Report* (June 24, 1996). □

Gabriel Daniel Fahrenheit

The German instrument maker Gabriel Daniel Fahrenheit (1686-1736) made the first reliable thermometers. The temperature scale he originated is named after him.

Born in Danzig on May 14, 1686, Gabriel Fahrenheit was the son of a well-to-do merchant. He lost both parents on the same day, Aug. 14, 1701, and was thereafter apprenticed to a shopkeeper in Amsterdam. After completing a term of 4 years there, he turned to physics and became an instrument maker and glassblower. Although he lived in Amsterdam most of his life, he traveled widely and spent considerable time in England, where he became a member of the Royal Society.

Fahrenheit completed his first two thermometers by 1714. They contained alcohol and agreed exactly in readings. The scale which was to bear Fahrenheit's name had not yet been calibrated, and many different scales were tried before he settled on one. He soon decided to replace the alcohol with mercury and completed a series of investigations based on the work of G. Amontons, in which he determined the boiling point of water and other liquids and studied the expansion properties of mercury. These experiments led to the discovery that the boiling point of water varied with changes in atmospheric pressure. Fahrenheit also discovered the phenomenon of supercooling of water, that is, cooling water to below its normal freezing point without converting it to ice.

Taking all of these factors into consideration, Fahrenheit was led to doubt the reliability of the freezing and boiling points of water and finally settled on a temperature scale ranging from 0 to 212. In 1724, announcing his method of making thermometers in the *Philosophical Transactions* of the Royal Society, he wrote concerning his scale,

" . . . degree 48, which in my thermometers holds the middle place between the limit of the most intense cold obtainable artificially in a mixture of water, of ice, and of sal ammoniac or even of sea salt, and the limit of heat which is found in the blood of a healthy man." (It has been suggested that the 96-degree range was chosen simply for the convenience of that number when laying off the scale by halving spaces on the thermometer stem.) Thus, finding the temperatures of the human body and of his freezing mixture to be reliable parameters, he set 0 as the temperature of the mixture; 32 as the temperature of water and ice; and 212, a point selected by chance, as about the boiling point of water.

Fahrenheit's thermometers were highly esteemed. He used mercury successfully because of his technique for cleaning it, and he introduced the use of cylindrical bulbs instead of spherical ones. However, his detailed technique for making thermometers was not disclosed for some 18 years, since it was a trade secret. Among the other instruments which he devised were a constant-weight hydrometer of excellent design and a "thermobarometer" for estimating barometric pressure by determining the boiling point of water.

On Sept. 16, 1736, Fahrenheit died, unmarried, in the Netherlands, presumably in The Hague, where he was buried.

Further Reading

Henry Lipson, *The Great Experiments in Physics* (1968), includes a chapter on heat with reference to Fahrenheit. For background and additional material on Fahrenheit see Florian Cajori, *A History of Physics* (1899; rev. ed. 1929); Max von Laue, *History of Physics* (1947; trans. 1950); and Allen L. King, *Thermophysics* (1962). □

Louis Léon César Faidherbe

Louis Léon César Faidherbe (1818-1889) was a French colonial governor. One of France's great military conquerors, he carved out the boundaries of contemporary Senegal.

Louis Faidherbe, the son of a poor enlisted man, was born in Lille on June 3, 1818. An engineering graduate of the famed École Polytechnique, he had a lengthy colonial experience in Algeria and Guadeloupe, where he participated in the emancipation of the slaves in 1848, before he was stationed in Senegal in 1852. For 2 years he completed many engineering surveys, gaining a detailed knowledge of the region before the administration named him governor of the area at the age of 36.

During Faidherbe's tenure as governor from 1854 to 1865 his major accomplishment was to create a vast colony dominated by Europeans. From 1854 to 1858 he subdued a number of tribes in the western African hinterland through a combination of military victories and negotiated treaties.

His greatest opponent, al-Hajj Omar, was the leader of an Islamic holy war. Al-Hajj Omar was born into a noble and well-educated family, made the pilgrimage to Mecca, and sought to create a religious empire in West Africa.

To defeat al-Hajj Omar and secure the colony, Faidherbe recruited the first batallion of Senegalese troops, the origin of all the African soldiers that fought the wars of France. He also developed a system of administration that relied on indigenous personnel, a system designed to enable trade to prosper. An educational system, geared to accomplish the French goals of assimilation, included a school for the sons of chiefs. The encouragement of trade involving Africans as businessmen was a pillar of his policy, and for this purpose he developed Dakar into a great maritime city.

Faidherbe later served in the Franco-Prussian War (1870-1871) in command of the Army of the North after the fall of Sedan. He won victories at Pont-Noyelles and Bapaune and suffered a defeat at Saint-Quentin. In 1872 he led a French government expedition to study monuments in Upper Egypt and as a result wrote a book on Numidian inscriptions. Other books treated of the campaign of the Army of the North (1871), of Senegalese languages (1887), and of Senegal (1889). He died in Paris on Sept. 29, 1889.

Faidherbe left a mark on Dakar and Senegal that has lasted to this day. The development of France's entire empire in West Africa was based largely on the foundations that he constructed.

Further Reading

The best assessment of Faidherbe's role in the development of the French Empire is in French. A good brief account in English is in J. D. Fage, *An Introduction to the History of West Africa* (1955; 3d ed. 1962). □

Ellen Louks Fairclough

Ellen Louks Fairclough (born 1905) was Canada's first female Cabinet minister. Preferring example to preaching in advancing women's rights, she was her country's outstanding example of a woman successful as wife, mother, businesswoman, and public servant.

Born in Hamilton, Ontario, on Jan. 28, 1905, Ellen Louks was the daughter of Norman Ellsworth Cook and Nellie Bell Louks. She was educated in Hamilton public and secondary schools, graduating at the age of 16. After a brief stint as a stenographer, she became an accountant. In 1931 she married D. H. Gordon Fairclough, owner and operator of a printing company.

Attracted by Politics

Fairclough's interest in politics dated from the time she and her husband helped organize the Young Conservative Association of Hamilton. In 1935 she started her own accounting firm and continued to operate it until becoming a member of the government in 1957. After World War II she decided to seek municipal office. She was defeated in her first attempt for the office of alderman of Hamilton. However, when the sitting alderman resigned within a few months, she was elected to fill the vacant post, in which she served from 1946 to 1949. In 1950 she served as municipal controller and deputy mayor.

In 1949 in the general election Fairclough won the nomination as the Progressive Conservative candidate for a seat in the House of Commons from the constituency of Hamilton West, but she failed to unseat the incumbent. When he resigned, she won his seat in a by-election in 1950.

As the new member of the opposition party, Fairclough soon made her mark as an informed and constructive critic of the government. Representing a riding, or electoral district, in a large urban industrial city, she had a compelling interest in labor matters. In the fall of 1950, she served as a member of Canada's delegation to the United Nations. In 1951 she was named chairman of the Labour Committee of the Opposition caucus and chief spokesperson of her party on labor matters.

Sought Equality for Women

Fairclough's efforts in the House of Commons, however, were not confined to one area. She had fought from her earliest political days for equal pay for equal work for

women and was delighted when the St. Laurent administration enshrined the principle in federal legislation. She was never a strident feminist but deplored the waste of womanly talents in business and public affairs. She knew that the traditionally conservative attitude of men, and particularly of women themselves, militated against full participation.

In 1953 and in 1957 she was reelected to Parliament. The latter was the election that brought John Diefenbaker to office as prime minister. He had promised, if elected, to name a woman to his Cabinet, and Fairclough was named Canada's first female Cabinet minister as secretary of state. In the landslide government victory of 1958 she was reelected and was named to a new post as minister of citizenship and immigration, in which position she also had responsibility for Indian affairs. In the general election of 1962 she held her seat, and shortly after, she became postmaster general of the new Diefenbaker government.

Away from Politics

In 1963 Fairclough met defeat in the election that turned out the Progressive Conservative administration. After leaving politics, she returned to Hamilton and private business. She first occupied a senior executive position with a trust company, moving from that job to the chairmanship of Hamilton Hydro. Before her retirement, she served as treasurer of the Zonta International women's group.

She has been the recipient of a number of honors during her political career and also during her retirement years in Hamilton. The Canadian Blackfoot Tribe and the

Six Nations Indian Band Council have recognized her efforts on the behalf of native Canadian peoples. The Canadian Council of Christians and Jews awarded her its Human Relations Award. The former Cabinet member received the Coronation Award in 1963, the Centennial Award in 1967, and the Jubilee Medal in 1977. In 1985, Fairclough was invested Dame of Grace in the Order of St. John of Jerusalem, Knights Hospitaler. Among her honors, perhaps the most gratifying was her investment in 1992 with the title "The Right Honorable" in the presence of Queen Elizabeth II. In the fall of 1996, she received the Order of Ontario, the highest honor awarded by the province of her birth.

Further Reading

For material on Canadian politics and Fairclough's role see Peter Charles Newman, *Renegade in Power: The Diefenbaker Years* (1964); Blair Fraser, *The Search for Identity: Canada, 1945-1967* (1967); and Patrick Nicholson, *Vision and Indecision* (1968). For further information on Fairclough, see *The Canadian Encyclopedia,* Second Edition, Vol. II (1988) and "The Right Honourable Ellen Louks Fairclough, PC" at http://www.cmhf.on.ca/fairclou.htm. □

Fairuz

Probably the greatest Arabic singer of modern times, Fairuz (neé Nuhad Haddad; born 1933), also known as Fayrouz, led the creation of a new musical language in the Middle East.

Fairuz was born Nuhad Haddad in 1933 in Beirut, Lebanon. She was raised in humble surroundings in the old neighborhood of Zukak el Blat in Beirut, where her father, Wadi Haddad, was a simple typesetter in a small print shop. Nuhad attended the Saint Joseph School for Girls in Beirut until the hardships of World War II forced her father to move her to a public school.

In 1947, at age 14, she was discovered by Mohammad Fleifel, one of the founders of the National Conservatory of Music in Beirut, who was in search of talent for a newly formed choral group. Fleifel was instrumental in Fairuz's admission to the National Conservatory, where she spent five years training. But perhaps his greatest contribution to her development as a singer was the instruction he gave her in the classical tradition of the *tajwid,* or classical chanting of Koranic verse.

Fairuz began her musical career as a member of the chorus at the Lebanese Radio Station. There Halim Al-Rumi, a composer and musical director at the radio, recognized her unique talent and made her lead soloist. He composed songs especially for her and gave her the stage name of Fairuz (turquoise) because her voice reminded him of a precious stone.

The young Fairuz met with unprecedented enthusiasm from listeners everywhere in Lebanon. This led to a meeting between her and the Rahbani brothers, Assi and Mansour, themselves rising talents as composer and lyricist, respectively. The collaboration between them at first took the form of adaptation by the Rahbanis of modern Western dance tunes into Arabic songs. This gave the team of three a certain amount of public exposure. However, the song that catapulted them into the limelight on the popular scale was not a Western dance tune but a melancholy love song entitled "Itab" (Blame) that they had recorded on November 2, 1952, at the Damascus Radio Station. What followed was a period of experimentation in a variety of musical forms. In all instances Fairuz's songs expressed artistic qualities that extended their appeal to listeners from a wide variety of social and national backgrounds.

In July 1954 Fairuz married Assi Al-Rahbani in a church wedding attended by a large crowd of adoring fans. They set up house in a villa in Antelias, a suburb of Beirut. The beautiful setting of their new home was to serve often as inspiration for many of their future songs.

Becoming an International Star

In 1955 Fairuz and Assi traveled to Egypt for the first time. Cairo, which was then the center of the Arab theater, cinema, and song, was conquered by the young Lebanese singer. Fairuz's triumph in Egypt led to many offers by celebrated Egyptian composers and filmmakers, but by then she was expecting her first child. She returned to Lebanon and gave birth to her son Ziad on January 1, 1957. She was later to have four more children, three girls and one boy. But it was Ziad who remained closest to her of all her children and who in later years wrote and composed the music for many of her songs.

In the summer of 1957 Fairuz appeared for the first time before a live audience. Until then she had been restricted to the recording studios. She sang in a musical review ("Ayam el Hissad," or "Harvest Days") before a large spellbound audience seated in the Roman ruins of the Temple of Jupiter in Baalback. This was her first appearance at the Baalback International Festival, and she was awarded the highest medal for artistic achievement there, the Cavalier, by the president of Lebanon, Camille Chamoun. Fourteen years later a stamp was issued by the government to commemorate her name.

Fairuz became one of the main attractions at the annual International Festival of Baalback, where she sang in musical plays or *massrahiyaat* that were written especially for her by the Rahbanis. In 1975 the 15-year civil was in Lebanon began, putting an end to the Baalback Festival, and some time later Fairuz's separation from her husband Assi ended her artistic collaboration with the Rahbani brothers.

With a reputation that had grown to include all the Arab world and the expatriate communities in Europe and the Americas, poets and composers everywhere rushed to write for Fairuz. The result was a repertoire of more than 800 songs, three feature films, and 400 LP recordings during a period of three decades. She was invited to appear in the major Arab capitals. She gave concerts in New York, San Francisco, Montreal, London, and Paris. She was awarded the Medal of Honor in 1963 and the Gold Medal in 1975 by King Hussein of Jordan. Fairuz had become a legend in her own time.

The Fairuz Legacy

The Fairuz-Rahbani artistic legacy was in tune with the social and cultural developments in Lebanon and the Middle East. The post-World War II years had begun to see the expansion of urban communities and the growing importance of Western influences on the daily lives of the people in that region. Furthermore, the growing role of the media (radio and television) and public entertainment (concert halls and theaters) led to the rise of an urban audience with new demands for entertainment. The new public was further impassioned by a nationalistic sentiment that had followed Lebanon's independence in 1943. The conviction was growing that the cultural heritage was in need of a more developed national expression suitable to the new image of the country. The music of the Rahbanis came to reinforce and project this image by combining the discoveries of contemporary Western techniques of composition with the forms, patterns, and sounds of Middle Eastern traditional music, thereby creating a modern musical language hitherto unheard in Lebanon. The context was unmistakably urban but the inspiration was folk and rural.

Fairuz's songs were a superb manifestation of this new musical expression. Her repertoire as a whole, both in text and music, was marked by innovation. It testified to her own broad musical background. She sang of love and the simple life, of love of country, and of the longing for a lost Jerusalem; she sang old bedouin chants and obscure shepherd's songs; she brought back the *muashahat,* a musical form first heard in the gardens of Andalusia; she interpreted the *quasida* and the *nashid,* two highly structured lyrical verse forms and, with equal success, the improvisational vocal expressions known as the *mawal* and *meyjana.* It was this special combination of lyrics, music, and vocal quality that earned Fairuz the name of "ambassador to the stars." Fairuz became a major influence on contemporary Arab music and culture.

In March 1994, at the age of 60, Fairuz performed a concert at the Olympia in London, drawing over 6000 fans. Western critics compare her to Billie Holiday and call her the "Callas of Arabia."

Further Reading

A list of Fairuz's musical plays, records, and songs in Arabic and English, along with a biography and photographs, may be found in a publication entitled "Fayrouz Legend and Legacy" published by the Forum for International Art and Culture (Washington, D.C.: 1981). The following cassettes and albums by Fairuz may also be obtained from the above forum: "A Christmas Album," "Fairuz sings Gibran," "Fairuz in Concert," and the "United Nations Concert Album." A brief article on Fairuz and her March 1994 London concert can be found in *New Statesman & Society* March 18, 1994.

A copy of a 37-mm. color documentary entitled "Fayrouz in America and Canada" (1971), filmed by Parker and Associates, may be obtained from the United States Information Agency. The main source of information about Fairuz remains the annual programs and catalogues of the Baalback International Festival, 1957-1974, Beirut, Lebanon. □

Faisal I

Faisal I (1883-1933) was an Arab nationalist and political leader during and following World War I. He led Arab troops in the revolt against Turkish rule and became king of newly created Iraq.

On May 20, 1883, Faisal was born in Taif near the Islamic holy city of Mecca in western Arabia, the third son of Husein ibn Ali and a member of one of Mecca's leading families, which claimed descent from the prophet Mohammed. In 1891 Faisal moved to Constantinople (Istanbul) with his father and brothers because the suspicious Sultan wished to keep Husein under political surveillance. Faisal was raised and educated in the imperial capital. A year after the Young Turk Revolution of 1908, Husein was appointed by the new Ottoman government sharif of Mecca, or protector of the holy places, a position his family had often held before. Faisal returned to Mecca and became a member of the Ottoman Parliament for western Arabia in 1913.

Faisal began working toward an accommodation with the Turks for Arab home rule. While his father was negotiating with the British in Egypt in 1915-1916 through the Husein-McMahon correspondence, Faisal had unsuccessfully sought to reach an agreement in Istanbul. En route back to Arabia in 1915, he met with Arab nationalist leaders in Syria, joined their organization, and participated in drafting the secret Damascus Protocol. This supported his father's negotiations for an Arab revolt against the Ottoman Empire in return for British aid for a postwar independent Arab state for Arabia and the Fertile Crescent.

Arab Revolt

After Husein's proclamation of the Arab Revolt in Mecca in June 1916, Faisal and his older brother Abdullah led Arab troops against the Ottomans, assisted the British invasion of Palestine from Egypt, harassed Ottoman supply lines, and occupied the Syrian interior, reaching Damascus in October 1918.

Following the war the British, who had promised territorial and political gains to the French, the Zionists, and the Arabs, found themselves unable to harmonize their conflicting wartime agreements. They encouraged Faisal to come to terms with the French over Syria, which both claimed, but France rejected him as a tool of the British who sought to deny France its just colonial rewards.

Faisal did conclude an agreement in 1919 with Chaim Weizmann, head of the World Zionist Organization, in which he accepted large-scale Jewish immigration into Palestine, provided that the rights of Arab farmers were protected and that the promised Arab state in the Fertile Crescent was actually established. In March 1920 an Arab National Congress in Damascus proclaimed Faisal king of Syria.

The British hope to establish Faisal as ruler of an interior Arab kingdom collapsed when France determined to maintain control of all of northern Syria. Despite the British commitment to Husein and Faisal, Britain took no action in July 1920, when France ousted Faisal from his newly proclaimed Syrian kingdom. Following a costly revolt in British-occupied Mesopotamia, Britain secured Faisal's selection as king of newly created Iraq in 1921.

King of Iraq

The British reasoned that Faisal had lost one kingdom and would take care about any actions that might threaten the loss of another. Faisal was a popular choice in the new state of Iraq because of his nationalist and military reputation, his personal charm and integrity, and his noble birth in the Prophet's Hashemite clan. The several hundred officers of Iraqi origin who had served with Faisal during the war strongly supported his selection. They backed Faisal with the experience and strength to rule capably and responsibly as he shrewdly balanced among the British authorities, tribal sheiks, and nationalist politicians. Iraq became the first Arab state in south-west Asia to eliminate the mandatory status and to join the League of Nations in 1932, but Faisal's death on Sept. 8, 1933, introduced a decade of confusion and instability in Iraq under his inexperienced young son, Ghazi.

Further Reading

There is an old biography of Faisal by Beatrice Erskine, *King Faisal of Iraq* (1933), and a more recent and popular treatment of Husein and his sons in James Morris, *The Hashemite Kings* (1959). World War I and its aftermath are well covered in Jukka Nevakivi, *Britain, France, and the Arab Middle East,*

1914-1920 (1969), and in Zeine N. Zeine, *The Struggle for Arab Independence: Western Diplomacy and the Rise and Fall of Feisal's Kingdom in Syria* (1960). See Henry A. Foster, *The Making of Modern Iraq* (1935), and Stephen H. Longrigg, *Iraq 1900 to 1950* (1953), for a discussion of Iraq under Faisal's rule. Elizabeth Monroe provides good background in *Britain's Moment in the Middle East, 1914-1956* (1963).

Additional Sources

Sheean, Vincent, *Faisal: the king and his kingdom,* Tavistock, Eng.: University Press of Arabia, 1975. □

Faisal ibn Abd al Aziz ibn Saud

King Faisal ibn Abd al Aziz ibn Saud of Saudi Arabia (1904-1975) was the most prominent Arab leader in the early 1970s. He participated for more than a half century in the creation of modern Saudi Arabia and, as king, was known for his conservative Islamic policies and his staunch anti-Communism.

Faisal was born in Riyadh in 1904, the son of Abd al-Aziz ibn Saud, founder of Saudi Arabia. His mother, Tarfa, a member of the leading religious family of the Al al-Shaikh, died when he was quite young, and he was raised by his maternal grandfather, who taught him the Koran and the principles of the Islamic religion, an education which left an impact on him for the remainder of his life.

Faisal gradually assumed state responsibilities, starting at the age of 13 as a soldier in his father's army. At the age of 18 he became commander of the Saudi army in Asir (southwest Arabia), successfully leading the Saudi military campaigns which brought the Hijaz into the kingdom (1925). His father selected him as early as the age of 15 for diplomatic missions abroad, and later he became the first Saudi foreign minister in 1930. In 1935 King ibn Saud gave his two most promising sons permanent positions in the state. Prince Saud, who was two years older than Faisal, was made viceroy of Najd, in the center of the kingdom, and Faisal, viceroy of the Hijaz on the Red Sea.

Rivalry between Faisal and Saud, 1953-1964

In 1953 King ibn Saud designated his older son, Saud, as crown prince. After the death of the king in November 1953 and the accession of Saud, the contrast in character and personality between the two brothers became evident. While Saud was flamboyant and extravagant in his spending, Faisal was frugal, reserved, and efficient. Faisal expressed his displeasure at Saud's ineffective administration by repeated withdrawals from politics.

By 1958 Saud's weaknesses as a king were evident. He had brought discord to the government by his profligacy, his inability to develop an effective bureaucracy, his continued reliance on personal advisers, and his failure to mobilize and direct for national development the massive wealth accruing to the country from oil resources.

Interference by senior members of the royal family led to a palace coup in April 1958 in which Faisal was named prime minister with all executive powers. Between 1958 and 1964 King Saud twice tried to regain his lost powers, but failed. Finally, on November 2, 1964, King Saud was forced to abdicate in favor of Faisal, who became king.

Faisal as King

When Faisal assumed office as king, Saudi Arabia was facing major internal and external challenges. Externally, a hostile relationship with Egypt under Gamal Abdul Nasser and a civil war in neighboring Yemen had forced Saudi Arabia to turn away from its traditional isolation. In 1962 a military coup had removed the monarch in Northern Yemen, which proclaimed itself a republic. Saudi Arabia supported the monarch; Egypt supported the republicans.

Internally, King Faisal continued a policy of economic and social reform, which he had already begun as prime minister. He introduced sound fiscal administration and a policy of austerity to counter the extravagance and corruption which had characterized his brother's rule. His social reforms were equally significant. In 1962 he abolished slavery, and his wife, Iffat, made a substantial contribution to women's education. He encouraged public education through the press, radio, and television, which, however, remained under strict government control. He introduced important development projects in agriculture and industry and improved the country's infrastructure.

It was on the international scene that Faisal gained much of his reputation as a leader, especially through his rivalry with Egyptian president Nasser. Faisal opposed Nasser's involvement in the war in Yemen and his hostile relations with the United States. As a countermeasure Faisal attempted to construct an anti-Communist "Islamic Front" to contain the spread of Nasser's Arab nationalism and socialism.

It was not until the Khartoum conference of August 1967, in the wake of the Arab-Israeli (Six Day) War, that Faisal and Nasser met and came to an agreement which led to the withdrawal of Egyptian troops from Yemen. The Egyptian (and Arab) defeat in 1967, the death of Nasser in 1970, and the tilt of President Anwar Sadat of Egypt toward the West all weakened Egypt's influence in Arab affairs. Gradually Faisal replaced Nasser as the most prominent leader in the Arab world and the moderator of Arab disputes.

King Faisal established strong ties with the West, making his country the strongest Arab ally of the United States. He refused any political ties with the Soviet Union and other Communist bloc countries, professing to see a complete incompatibility between Communism and Islam.

However, Faisal faced some internal opposition. Plots against the regime involving Saudi military officers and civilians, and some Yemenis, surfaced in 1966, 1969, and

1974. Terms of imprisonment and death sentences were pronounced against the perpetrators.

Faisal was criticized for his pro-American foreign policy, his conservative Islamic ideology, and the slowness of his reforms. He was finally the victim of a successful assassination attempt. On March 25, 1975, he was murdered by one of his nephews. There was no public trial and hence the real motives of the assassin remain obscure. However, they are believed to lie in a long-standing family feud and the young prince's dislike of policies he considered too conservative.

Further Reading

Additional information on Faisal can be found in David Holden and Richard Johns, *The House of Saud: the Rise of the Most Powerful Dynasty in the Arab World* (1981); Gerald de Gaury, *Faisal, King of Saudi Arabia* (1966); Alexander Bligh, *From Prince to King, Royal Succession in the House of Saud in the Twentieth Century* (1984); and Willard A. Beling, *King Faisal and the Modernization of Saudi Arabia* (London, 1980). □

Étienne Maurice Falconet

Étienne Maurice Falconet (1716-1791), a versatile and facile French sculptor, incorporated late baroque, rococo, and neoclassic elements in his work and reflected the changes in artistic taste that occurred during his era.

Born in Paris on Dec. 1, 1716, Étienne Maurice Falconet studied with the sculptor Jean Baptiste Lemoyne. In 1754 Falconet was admitted to membership in the Royal Academy of Painting and Sculpture. In 1757 he became director of sculpture at the Sevrès porcelain factory and was responsible for designing statuettes and decorative objects. The Sevrès factory was owned by the Crown, had great prestige, and produced some of the finest porcelain of the 18th century. One of Falconet's most important patrons was Louis XV's mistress, Madame de Pompadour, a leader of taste and fashion who had a particular interest in the Sevrès factory.

Falconet was strongly influenced by Gian Lorenzo Bernini, the great Italian baroque sculptor of the 17th century, and by Pierre Puget, the most important sculptor in 17th-century France to reflect the dynamic, emotional style created by Bernini. These influences are seen in some of Falconet's early productions, such as his marble *Milo of Croton and the Lion* (1754), notable for its energetic drama, rich texture, and explosive composition.

During the 1750s, however, Falconet was also creating decorative, intimate sculptures very different from the *Milo*. These small pieces, some commissioned by Madame de Pompadour, were originally executed in marble, terra-cotta, or plaster; they became extremely popular and were much reproduced in a variety of media, including bisque pottery. Examples of this aspect of Falconet's talent are the marble

Allegory of Music, the terra-cotta *Allegory of Hunting,* and the marble *Cupid's Warning.* In these works Falconet displays great virtuosity in combining a rococo taste for intimacy, refined elegance, and delicate textures with simplicity of composition, sleek modeling, and smooth lines—characteristics of style that reflect advancing neoclassicism and adapt it to the still vibrant rococo.

Falconet's most important commission was executed for Empress Catherine the Great of Russia: the large bronze *Equestrian Monument to Peter the Great* in Leningrad (1766-1782). In this imperial monument, which depicts the Emperor calmly astride an excited, plunging horse, Falconet reverts to the grandiose splendor of the baroque and echoes Bernini's dramatic equestrian statue of Louis XIV. The work makes references to antiquity and to neoclassicism, however, in the clarity of the composition, smooth modeling of the horse, majestic figure of the Emperor, and restrained treatment of his draperies.

Falconet produced a relatively small number of sculptures, but his work is remarkable in its variety and skill. He died in Paris on Jan. 24, 1791.

Further Reading

The most important works on Falconet are in French. His life and works are discussed in Lady Emilia Francis Dilke, *French Architects and Sculptors of the 18th Century* (1900). There are references to Falconet and photographs of three of his works in Arno Schönberger and Halldor Soehner, *The Rococo Age* (1960). □

Manuel de Falla

The Spanish composer Manuel de Falla (1876-1946) infused his compositions with the distinctive idioms of native folk song and dance to create music on nationalistic lines.

Manuel de Falla was born on Nov. 23, 1876, in Cadiz into a family that had a lively interest in music. His mother gave him piano lessons, and from local musicians he had instruction in harmony, counterpoint, and solfeggio. At the age of 20 he enrolled in the Madrid Conservatory and earned the school's highest awards in piano. More important to him, though, since he did not want to be a concert pianist, was his composition study with Felipe Pedrell. Working with that ardent nationalist for 3 years, Falla entered deeply into the study of his country's folk music and made his goal the development of an expressive mode of composition rooted in Spanish culture.

In *Siete canciones populares españoles* (1914) Falla took folk songs whole and put them in simple but imaginative settings; generally, however, he freely used only certain aspects of folk originals to give a Spanish quality to his compositions. Examples occur in his first important work, the two-act opera *La vida breve* (1905), which calls up memories of Giacomo Puccini and Richard Wagner but makes its best effects from the employment of two varieties of folk music native to Andalusia: lively flamenco dance rhythms and melodic patterns of the passionate, sometimes melancholic, type of song known as the *cante hondo*. These two elements also served Falla in his work through 1919, which includes music written in France as well as at home.

Living in Paris from 1907 to 1914, Falla came under the influence of Claude Debussy, whose impressionistic techniques are plainly audible in *Quatres pièces espagnoles* (1908) for piano and *Noches en los jardines de España* (1916) for piano and orchestra. The image of Spain shines through, though, in their thematic material and in Falla's evocation of guitar qualities in his treatment of both piano and orchestra. The same may be said of the music that closed what is commonly called his Andalusian period: *El amor brujo* (1915), a ballet containing the well-known "Ritual Fire Dance;" *El sombrero de tres picos* (1919), another ballet; and his single large piece for solo piano, *Fantasía bética* (1919).

The balance of Falla's production is less locally centered, less picturesque, but no less Spanish in impulse. Its high spots are a delightful puppet opera, *El retablo de Maese Pedro* (1923), based on a scene from Cervantes' *Don Quixote,* and a rather severe-sounding concerto in neoclassic vein for harpsichord and chamber orchestra (1926). His last work, an enormous cantata entitled *La Atlántida,* which occupied him from 1928 until his death, was left unfinished.

Falla died on Nov. 14, 1946, in Argentina, where he had moved in 1939 after deciding that he could no longer adapt himself to the Franco regime. Long before then he had been accepted as the foremost creative musician of his time in Spain. Present-day criticism is less favorable, viewing his music as expressively strong but limited in range and technical originality.

Further Reading

Falla's life and place in the panorama of Spanish music are most fully discussed in J. B. Trend, *Manuel de Falla and Spanish Music* (1929), and Gilbert Chase, *The Music of Spain* (1941; 2d ed. 1959). Joseph Machlis, *Introduction to Contemporary Music* (1961), gives a generally sympathetic view of Falla in the light of 20th-century musical composition.

Additional Sources

Demarquez, Suzanne, *Manuel de Falla,* New York: Da Capo Press, 1983, 1968.

Pahissa, Jaime, *Manuel de Falla, his life and works,* Westport, Conn.: Hyperion Press, 1979. □

JoAnn Falletta

The American conductor JoAnn Falletta (born 1954) served as music director of three orchestras simultaneously while still a young woman. She chose to perform pieces from the non-standard repertoire, **trying to select pieces suited to the particular audience.**

JoAnn Falletta was an American conductor whose perseverance and talent helped to place her simultaneously at the helm of three orchestras at a young age. Her success was due to the fresh and electric performances she conducted. This freshness and excitement came from performing pieces that were not in the standard repertoire, but were rather either little-known works by well-known composers or works by unfamiliar composers of the past and present. Falletta aimed to introduce these composers to the regular audiences for classical music and to young listeners who were looking for "something that will put them more in touch with themselves" and who can listen with an open ear and mind to music that is energetic and crisply presented.

The ability to communicate her ideas about particular pieces to orchestra members and to convince and enable them to carry out her conceptions did not come easily or quickly to Falletta, but the desire to do so developed in her as a child. She was born in New York City on February 27, 1954. Raised in the borough of Queens in an Italian-American household, her home was filled with music. As there was no room in the apartment for a piano, JoAnn's father bought her a guitar, which she loved as "it was the perfect instrument, quiet and personal, because I was painfully shy as a child." Her ability to play the guitar earned her entry into the guitar department at Mannes College of Music, and later she was called by the Metropolitan Opera and the New York Philharmonic whenever music for guitar, mandolin, or lute was required.

Uncertainty About a Woman Conductor

Her love of the guitar did not diminish her love of conducting. She led the student orchestra at Mannes when she was 18 and requested that she be accepted into the conducting studies program at the college. At first the administration was resistant because of the long period of study necessary combined with the unlikely prospect that a woman would be chosen as musical director of an orchestra. Mannes permitted her transfer, however, and she went on for further study to Queens College (M.A. in orchestral conducting) and the Juilliard School of Music (M.M., D.M.A. in orchestral conducting). Juilliard was no more encouraging to Falletta than Mannes had been, but she persisted and her obvious technical abilities overcame the school's uncertainty about her viability as a conductor.

None of the discouragements she received showed in her attitude toward her training, perhaps because the climate had changed in the years she was studying and, though she was still breaking ground, the concept of a female conductor was no longer considered unthinkable. Jorge Mester helped her to establish a more assertive manner on the podium while still remaining true to her own personality. This meant that she had to discard some of her self-effacing ways of dealing with orchestra players and resulted in a quiet control based on her extraordinary command of the literature. Her talent for communicating a single vision of a work through her baton technique and her explanations of musical phrasing to the players produced exciting concerts from coast to coast.

Her career began with the Jamaica (New York) Symphony, which she founded in 1978. It was, in her own words, "absolutely horrible, terrible and an embarrassment to think of now." It consisted of 15 players who rehearsed Monday nights. Gradually the original members were replaced by friends from Juilliard who wanted more orchestral experience and the number of players rose to 80. The name of the orchestra was changed to Queens Symphony and Falletta had her first taste of success in building up an orchestra. At the time she was founding the Queens Symphony, she was also studying at Juilliard and beginning to receive conducting fellowships. She won the Leopold Stokowski Conducting Competition in 1985, the same year she was appointed associate conductor of the Milwaukee Symphony Orchestra where she worked from 1985 to 1988.

Earlier, in 1983, the Denver Chamber Orchestra had appointed her as music director and the growth of that orchestra in popularity and quality matched the transformation of the Queens Symphony. It was just this talent of Falletta's to tap the interest of the community that caused the Bay Area Women's Philharmonic in 1986 and the Long Beach Symphony Orchestra in 1989 to appoint her to be their musical director, bringing the total of orchestras of which she was musical director to three. Each group required a different repertoire, which provided a challenge to JoAnn Falletta. As she admitted, before she accepted the position with the Bay Area Women's Philharmonic, "I didn't know who (the composers) Amy Beach or Louise Farrenc were. It was a whole new world for me." No novice to creative programming, she presented in the spring of 1988 works by Marianne Martines, a student of Haydn's, and a work by Germaine Tailleferre, a 20th-century French composer. In addition, works by Pulitzer prize winner Ellen Taafe Zwilich and Joan Tower expanded her repertoire to include prominent living women composers. She left the Bay Area Women's Philharmonic after 10 years, but remained its artistic director.

Her approach to her audiences was to educate them about and interest them in what was being performed. Frequently she gave talks before performances about the music to be performed. She also presented youth concerts, hoping to create an appreciative audience for classical music in the future, and sought out pieces that reflected the ethnic mix of her constituency. In the case of the Long Beach Symphony, she sought contemporary Asian works to reflect the large Asian population in the area. In 1986, 1987, 1988, and 1989 ASCAP awarded Falletta first and third prizes for creative programming. It was a fitting public recognition of her efforts not to recreate the standard repertoire. To offer this unusual mix of pieces she had learned an extraodinary number of pieces.

Critical Kudos

Critical acclaim was extremely favorable. *Newsday* referred to her as "one of the finest conductors of her genera-

tion. Her baton technique is so utterly communicative that one might as well plug one's ears and simply watch the music take shape through her sensitive, graceful gestures." The *Los Angeles Times* wrote of a performance of Prokofiev's "Symphony No. 5" by the Long Beach Symphony, "Her deliberate tempo in the first movement gave the music an extra-weighty flow, culminating spectacularly in a broad, muscular and percussive climax. This overall measured pace was ever-flexible on a local level, however, pointing up details in the massive architectural design." It was her total command of her score and the clarity of her own conception of it that was transmitted by her baton to the members of the orchestra. The communication from conductor to players to audience depends on strong, forceful leadership, which Falletta was able to provide. *USA Today* wrote: "A cool, precise presence, Falletta is the master of eventful legato. When many conductors try to establish rounded, smooth phrasing, the results are often bland, but Falletta can be suave while maintaining a rich sense of incident. As shown by the famous Nimrod variation, as well as the more introspective moments of Barber's Symphony No. 1, she was best when precipitating an ecstatic moment, inspiring an emotional candidness from the players but never slipping into the sort of self-indulgence that would tax the piece's overall architecture. Her performance of the Barber symphony had a Mahlerian grandeur." The Denver *Rocky Mountain News* wrote that "Falletta is surely destined for classical music stardom."

Stardom in the form of an appointment to a major national orchestra may not come for a time to Falletta, however, although she retained her place with the Long Beach Symphony and had also joined the Virginia Beach Symphony by 1997. Since she maintained a busy schedule of guest conducting around the country and abroad beginning in 1982, she may find herself sought by a major orchestra rather sooner than that. Even while waiting for greater exposure nationally, her ideas about the presentation of music to new audiences will provide guidelines for the future of classical music performance in this country. Falletta favored small, intimate spaces for listening to music, avoiding large, impersonal concert halls. In addition, an exciting repertoire related to the audience's background plus an effort to educate them about music was the formula for her continued success as an orchestral conductor. At the heart of her achievements, however, was the stunning control, the expertise, and the well-thought-out conceptions of the music she conducted.

Further Reading

Articles about JoAnn Falletta have appeared in newspapers and magazines on both coasts as well as in national magazines. An extensive article appeared in the *San Francisco Magazine* (November 1987) in which her early training and subsequent success are described. On September 9, 1990, the *Los Angeles Times Calendar* published an article by Greta Beigel on Falletta which went into some detail about her development as a conductor. *Musical America* ran a cover story about her (September 1990) and reviewed a concert by the Bay Area Women's Philharmonic (November 1989). The *Los Angeles Times* (September 30, 1990) wrote an article that discussed her musical directorship of the Long Beach Symphony which contained comments by those whom she conducted about her style of leadership. □

Jerry Falwell

Jerry Falwell (born 1933) is a fundamentalist religious leader who combined his religious activities, which included a nationwide television program, with promotion of a variety of right-wing political causes. He is perhaps best known as the founder of Moral Majority, Inc.

Jerry Falwell was born on August 11, 1933, in Lynchburg, Virginia. He attended public schools, excelled at sports, and earned a 98.6 percent average in high school before entering Lynchburg College in 1950. Midway through his sophomore year, on January 20, 1952, he underwent a religious conversion. Declining an offer to play baseball with the St. Louis Cardinals, Falwell transferred to the Baptist Bible College in Springfield, Missouri. On April 12, 1958, he married Macel Pate, a church pianist.

Ministry's Humble Origins

Ordained to the ministry in 1956, Falwell founded the Thomas Road Baptist Church in his home town of Lynchburg with an initial congregation of 35 adults and their families, using an abandoned building owned by the Donald Duck Bottling Company. Their first project was to scrub cola off the old brick walls. From this modest start the Thomas Road Church grew to a membership of 22,000, and eventually included a day school, a live-in rehabilitation center for alcoholics (Falwell's father drank excessively, and died when his son was just 15), a summer camp for children, a transportation service, and missionary and relief work in Guatemala, Haiti, South Korea, and elsewhere. A half-hour daily radio broadcast, "The Old-Time Gospel Hour," launched when the church was only a week old, grew into a television show which went national in 1971 and soon reached an audience estimated in the millions.

Mixing Church and State

The religion preached from Falwell's pulpit was what used to be called "fundamentalist." "The entire Bible, from Genesis to Revelation," Falwell said, "is the inerrant Word of God, and totally accurate in all respects." At times he sounded an apocalyptic trumpet: "This is the terminal generation before Jesus comes." Unlike the folkish "oldtime religion" formerly practiced in some rural areas, Falwell's gospel employed modern urban methods of persuasion. A symposium in June 1972 on "how to build a superaggressive local church" drew 5,000 Baptist church workers from all over the United States to hear one of Falwell's close associates declare: "God is impressed with a growing church. We believe Jesus must be sold as effectively as Coca-Cola."

By the late 1970s the conservative Christian movement had grown substantially, and Falwell's television ministry was just one of several thriving media pulpits. He had taken on a series of political causes: for voluntary prayer in schools, free enterprise, balanced budgets, military strength, and aid to Israel and against the Equal Rights Amendment, pornography, abortion, homosexuality, parimutuel betting, and rock and roll music.

Recognizing the political potential of his flock and others like it, Falwell founded the Moral Majority in 1979. The lobbying group's aim was to "reverse the politicization of immorality in our society," and it aimed to impel America's political leadership to demonstrate whether or not they were indeed religiously and morally committed, according to Falwell. The news magazine *Time* (October 1, 1979) described him at one rally holding up a Bible and saying, "If a man stands by this book, vote for him. If he doesn't, don't." He was also quoted as saying, "The liberal churches are not only the enemy of God but the enemy of the nation." This citizen action group soon operated with an annual budget of some $7 million.

The Reagan Years

It is difficult to assess the extent of Jerry Falwell's contribution to the wave of political conservatism that crested in the election of Ronald Reagan in 1980 and the first Republican-controlled Senate in 26 years, but it was surely substantial. Certainly he (and ministers like him), using his slogan "Get them saved, baptized, and registered," compelled many Americans to register as voters—citizens who, in some cases, had never participated in politics at any level before. During the Eighties, Republican politicians seemed to heed Falwell's warnings, and toeing the conservative line on a number of controversial issues (such as opposition to reproductive rights) became virtually obligatory in campaign strategies against Democrats.

To broaden his advocacy of purely political issues Falwell founded the Liberty Federation in 1986. Other victories directly and indirectly attributed to the influence of the Moral Majority included the election of President George Bush in 1988 and a number of conservative Supreme Court decisions beginning in the late 1980s. The Moral Majority's success was repeated in a number of offshoot groups, including the powerful Christian Coalition.

Projects Faltered

However, by the late 1980s Christian televangelism was suffering from serious blows to its credibility. While Falwell himself remained untainted by scandal, the names of other prominent ministers—most notably Jim Bakker and Jimmy Swaggart—appeared in newspaper headlines that included the words "prostitute," "adultery," and "payoff." Bakker's Praise the Lord (PTL) ministry, which included its own cable television network, was accused of financial mismanagement, and Falwell took over the organization in 1987, ostensibly in an effort to rescue it. This was ideologically akin to a Protestant becoming Pope; some within the organization later asserted that Falwell had deliberately mismanaged PTL, his ministry's main competition, to steer it into bankruptcy.

Falwell also made headlines when he sued a pornographic magazine and its publisher for a vicious parody that appeared in it. He was awarded $200,000 in emotional damages, but the case was appealed all the way to the Supreme Court, who struck down the previous verdict. The incident was woven into the plot of a 1996 feature film, *The People vs. Larry Flynt.*

In 1989 Falwell announced the dissolution of the Moral Majority, asserting its political aims had succeeded to such an extent that the organization was no longer necessary. He planned to concentrate on his other projects, most notably his Thomas Road Baptist Church, where he remained senior pastor, and Liberty University, a full-fledged educational institution he had founded in 1971. But Falwell, as chancellor, had pushed for an expansion of the university during the 1980s, and built facilities on borrowed money. The school also issued bonds and sold them on "The Old-Time Gospel Hour," later defaulting on interest payments to bondholders, many of whom were elderly and poor. Scholarships to Liberty were given away freely, and by 1990 the school was $110 million in debt. Repeated requests on "The Old-Time Gospel Hour" for donations to shore up the faltering ministry sent Falwell's trio of organizations into a downward spiral. Contributions dropped, and his financial troubles multiplied. His long-running show even went off the air for a time.

A New Direction

By the mid-1990s Falwell had ventured into political issues once again, selling a video that accused President Bill Clinton of a number of crimes; elsewhere, the minister described Clinton in one sermon as an "ungodly liar," (*Christianity Today,* December 9, 1996, p, 63). Falwell appeared on an infomercial for a videocassette bible-study course sold by his ministry, in which he asserted that it was possible that human beings and dinosaurs once coexisted. Marking his return to the political arena, Falwell delivered the benediction at the Republican National Convention in 1996, and launched his God Save America tour later that year.

Falwell also began to ally with powerful Southern Baptist leadership, who would exhibit a more conservative and outspoken outlook by their 1997 national convention. Now in his sixties, Falwell still preaches Sunday services at the Thomas Road church, and there are hints that the youngest of his three children, Jonathan, may someday assume its pastorship. The younger Falwell was appointed administrator of the church in 1995; his brother Jerry Jr. serves as in-house counsel for his father's projects, and Falwell's only daughter is a surgeon in Richmond, Virginia.

Further Reading

Falwell and his Moral Majority were the subjects of a shrewd and pertinent essay by Frances Fitzgerald, "A Disciplined, Charging Army," in the *New Yorker* (May 18, 1981). There is an admiring and uncritical biography by Jerry Strober and Ruth Tomczak, *Jerry Falwell: Aflame for God* (1979). Journalist Dinesh D'Souza is the author of *Falwell: Before the Millennium* (1984). Falwell was frank and self-revelatory in his books, such as *How You Can Clean Up America* (1978), *America Can Be Saved* (1979), and especially *Listen, America* (1980). He has also written *The Fundamentalist Phenomenon* (1981), *Strength for the Journey* (1987), and *The New American Family* (1992). *Falwell: An Autobiography* , was published in 1996. Contemporary appraisals are in *Newsweek* (July 24, 1972), and September 15, 1980), *Time* (October 1, 1979), and *Christianity Today,* December 9, 1996. □

Fan Chung-yen

The Chinese statesman Fan Chung-yen (989-1052) initiated the first important Sung reform program. He was famous for defining the ideal Confucian scholar as "one who is first in worrying about the world's troubles and last in enjoying its pleasures."

Fan Chung-yen was born into an old scholar-official family of modest importance which had settled in Soochow in the 9th century. When Fan's father died in 990, his mother remarried and took her infant son along to her new home in Shantung, where he was given the new family surname, Chu. At the age of 21 he was shocked to learn of his true father's identity and left the Chu family. In 1017 he received official permission to resume his original surname. Intense family feeling remained a strong motive force throughout Fan's life, as exemplified by the well-known charitable estate he later established for the Fan clan.

After study in Ying-t'ien, Honan Province, Fan obtained the highest academic degree (*chin-shih*) in 1015 and was assigned to a succession of provincial posts. In 1026 he resigned from his last post to perform the obligatory mourning for his mother. Called to the Sung capital for the first time in 1028, he was forced to return to the provinces the following year after incurring the displeasure of the empress dowager Chang-hsien, mother of the emperor Jen-tsung. Fan served in the capital again in 1033 and in 1035-1036 but was sent back each time after defeat by his arch political opponent, Lü I-chien.

Fan was serving in disgrace in the southeast when he was transferred to the northwest to participate in a war against the Tangut state of Hsi-Hsia. Although he had no military experience, he distinguished himself in the training and deployment of troops, the restoration of destroyed fortifications, the establishment of military colonies, and negotiations with Ch'iang tribesmen. He and his associate Han Ch'i were opposed to the Peace of 1043, but Fan's military success led to his first appointment as a high-ranking official and gave him an opportunity to initiate reforms.

The main thrust of Fan's efforts was in the reform of the bureaucracy. He replaced officials (especially in local government), limited the privilege of the well-connected to enter the bureaucracy without examination, changed the content and the procedure of the examinations, and raised the caliber of local officials through increased rigor in promotions and supervision. He reformed office land-holdings to improve the economic situation of officials, and his wider economic interests were revealed in proposals for land reclamation, irrigation, and other projects to increase agricultural productivity. As a provincial official, too, Fan was concerned with economic matters and even implemented work relief projects.

Although Fan's reforms were modest, the opposition was strong. Fan was dismissed in 1044, and most of his reforms were rescinded the following year. Fan again served in various provincial posts and did not return to power. His reforms became the precursors of the more ambitious program of Wang An-shih.

Further Reading

For Fan's reforms see James T. C. Liu's "An Early Sung Reformer: Fan Chung-yen" in John K. Fairbank, ed., *Chinese Thought and Institutions* (1957) as well as Liu's *Ou-yang Hsiu: An Eleventh-Century Neo-Confucianist* (1967). An important study of a different aspect of Fan's activities is Denis Twitchett's "The Fan Clan's Charitable Estate, 1050-1760" in David S. Nivison and Arthur F. Wright, eds., *Confucianism in Action* (1959). Recommended for general background is James T. C. Liu and Peter Golas, eds., *Change in Sung China: Innovation or Renovation?* (1969). □

Peter Faneuil

Peter Faneuil (1700-1743) was a wealthy American colonial merchant and philanthropist who donated Faneuil Hall to Boston.

Eldest child of one of three Huguenot brothers who fled France after the revocation of the Edict of Nantes, Peter Faneuil was born on June 20, 1700, in New Rochelle, N. Y. Having emigrated to America about 10 years earlier, Peter's father, Benjamin, and his uncle, Andrew, had been early settlers of New Rochelle. Shortly afterward Andrew made Boston his permanent residence. Benjamin married Anne Bureau in 1699, and they had at least two sons and three daughters who lived to maturity.

Little is known of Peter's boyhood. His father, prominent and fairly well-to-do, died when Peter was 18, and soon Peter and his brother, Benjamin, Jr., moved to Boston. Their widowed, childless uncle Andrew had become one of New England's wealthiest men through shrewd trading and Boston real estate investments. Andrew may have formally adopted his two nephews.

Peter Faneuil entered Boston's commission and shipping business and soon proved a competent trader. He handled merchandise from Europe and the West Indies, exported rum, fish, and produce, and engaged in ship-building. When he ventured both ship and cargo in transatlantic or coastal commerce, he customarily shared the risk with others. Charging 5 percent for handling consignments, he used advanced business methods and kept careful records. Fishing-grounds agents kept him informed of market prices and furthered his commercial connections. When Benjamin, Jr., married against his uncle's wishes, Andrew made Peter heir to most of his fortune. Peter, swarthy, stocky, and lame since childhood, remained a bachelor all his life.

During his uncle's final illness Peter managed Andrew's business as well as his own. Prominent in the "triangular trade," Peter shipped slaves to the West Indies and brought molasses and sugar to the Colonies. When his uncle died in 1738 Peter became—despite handsome bequests to his sisters—one of America's wealthiest men, living sumptuously in a Beacon Street mansion.

Among Faneuil's lavish gifts to his community were an endowment for the families of Trinity Church's deceased clergymen and a public market for Boston. This structure was completed in 1742, shortly before Faneuil died of dropsy on March 3, 1743. The room above the market stalls became a civic center where so many prerevolutionary meetings were held that Faneuil Hall became known as America's "Cradle of Liberty."

Further Reading

Data on Faneuil are scattered and sometimes contradictory. The best descriptions of his way of life and business practices are in Samuel Adams Drake, *Old Landmarks and Historic Personages of Boston* (1873; rev. ed. 1900), and Abram E. Brown, *Faneuil Hall and Faneuil Hall Market* (1900). □

Amintore Fanfani

The Italian statesman Amintore Fanfani (born 1908) was a major leader of influence on the post-World War II Christian Democratic Party and held many important political offices, including that of prime minister.

Amintore Fanfani was born in Pieve Santo Stefano (Arezzo Province) February 6, 1908, the son of an attorney and supporter of the Partito Popolare, the forerunner of the postwar Christian Democrats. His mother was very religious. At the Catholic University of the Sacred Heart in Milan he excelled in mathematics and physics, but later chose to study political economy and earned his doctorate in 1932.

Professor and Politician

Fanfani pursued a dual career of university professor and politician. As a student of economic history he was the author of a number of important works dealing with religion and the development of capitalism in Renaissance and Reformation Europe. His thesis was published in Italian and then in English as *Catholicism, Capitalism and Protestantism* in 1935. Fanfani accepted a chair at the Catholic University of Milan in 1936. During this period he joined a group known as the "little professors" who lived ascetically in monastery cells and walked barefoot. These men formed the nucleus of Democratic Initiative, the liberal wing of the postwar Christian Democratic Party. From 1938 to 1943 he taught at the University of Venice. Called up for military service in 1943, Fanfani took refuge in Switzerland where during the remainder of the war he taught interned Italians at the universities of Geneva and Lausanne. After 1955 he served on the faculty at the University of Rome.

His political career began with his participation in Catholic youth groups during the Fascist period, especially the Federazione Universitaria Cattolica Italiana (FUCI) (University Federation of Italian Catholics) and the Laureati (Catholic university graduates.) With the end of the war, Fanfani emerged as one of the youngest leaders of the Christian Democrats and a protege of Alcide De Gasperi, the party's leader.

Balancing Capitalism and Christianity

An able administrator and organizer, Fanfani represented the socially more progressive left-wing of the Christian Democratic Party. In his politics, as in his academic interests, Fanfani always struggled to resolve the tensions between capitalism and Christianity. In line with his devoutly Christian beliefs, his goal was to mitigate the less charitable aspects of free enterprise and to infuse capitalism with a more socially conscious spirit.

In June 1946 Fanfani was elected to represent the Arezzo-Siena-Grosseto area in the constituent assembly which drafted a new constitution effective January 1, 1948. The very first article of the constitution reflects Fanfani's

work and philosophy. Staunchly anti-Communist, but socially progressive, Fanfani proposed an article which read: "Italy is a democratic republic founded on work." His proposal, which was eventually accepted, countered the Communist version: "Italy is a democratic republic of workers." By a seemingly harmless change in the wording he avoided the class implication inherent in the Communist formula.

In 1948 he was elected to the Chamber of Deputies. He joined Alcide De Gasperi's fourth, fifth, and sixth cabinets and served from 1947 to 1950 as minister of labor and social welfare. During this period he put into operation a seven year plan to build workers' houses financed jointly by workers, the government, and employers. Fanfani also played a significant role in the creation of non-Communist labor unions which broke the monopoly of the Communist-controlled General Federation of Labor. In 1951 he held cabinet rank as minister of agriculture and forestry and expedited land reforms. In 1953 he was appointed minister of the interior under Giuseppe Pella, and subsequently he became secretary-general of the Christian Democrats in 1954-1959 and in 1973-1975.

Political Apex

From 1954 to the mid-1960s Fanfani's influence both in the party and in national politics was at its height. Fanfani served as premier in a series of governments, some of them short-lived. His first government in 1954 lasted only 21 days. Later he headed governments from July 1958 to January 1959, from July 1960 to February 1962, from February

1962 to May 1963. From 1965 to 1966 Fanfani served as president of the United National General Assembly. In 1972 he was elected as Life Senator of the Italian Senate. He was chosen as the president of the Senate from 1968-1973, 1976-1982, and 1985-1987.

Together with Aldo Moro, in the early 1960s Fanfani became the architect of the Center-Left Coalition. De Gasperi's coalition governments during the immediate postwar period had been staunchly anti-Communist and based on collaboration with the Right—Social Democrats, Liberals, and Republicans. However, during the 1950s clerical influence on the Christian Democrats diminished; a liberal Pope, John XXIII, was elected in 1958; and the Socialists loosened their ties with the Communists. Coalitions on the Left now became possible, and Fanfani led his party in this direction. At the Christian Democratic congress of January 1962 in Naples an overwhelming majority voted for the "opening to the left." The Center-Left Coalition program called for increased participation by the masses in the exercise of political power, the nationalization of the electrical industry, the democratization of the educational system, the expansion of regional governments, and improvements in agriculture. In foreign affairs, the program reaffirmed Italy's alignment with the West, but pledged to work for an easing of East-West tensions.

In 1986 when the Italian government was in crisis, President Francesco Cossiga turned to Fanfani for help. He first served as a mediator between the Socialist and Christian Democratic parties. However, when these efforts failed, President Cossiga asked Fanfani to form a new Parliament in 1987. Fanfani was once again Prime Mnister of Italy, but this position lasted only ten days as his government lost a vote of confidence on April 28, 1987.

Further Reading

Sources on Fanfani in English are scarce. See "Fanfani" in Frank J. Coppa, ed., *Dictionary of Modern Italian History* (1985). Italian sources are Piero Ottone, *Fanfani* (Milan, 1966); and Giorgio Galli, *Fanfani* (Milan, 1975).
"Amintore Fanfani." *The International Who's Who,* 57th Edition. England: Europa Publications Limited, 1993.
"Fanfani Forms Cabinet in Italy; June Vote Seen." *New York Times,* 17 April 1987.
"Italy Turns to Fanfani to Form Government." *New York Times,* 16 April 1987.
Suro, Roberto. "Mediator Named to Untangle Italy's Cabinet Crisis." *New York Times,* 5 July 1986.
——"Italy's Government Falls and a June Election is Called." *New York Times,* 29 April 1987.
Tagliabul, John. "Fanfani is Sworn in as Head of Italy's 46th Postwar Cabinet." *New York Times,* 19 April 1987. □

Frantz Fanon

The Algerian political theorist Frantz Fanon (1925-1961) analyzed the nature of racism and colonialism and developed a theory of violent anticolonialist struggle.

Frantz Fanon was born in the French colony of Martinique. He volunteered for the French army during World War II, and then, after being released from military service, he went to France, where he studied medicine and psychiatry from 1945 to 1950. In 1953 he was appointed head of the psychiatric department of a government hospital in Algeria, then a French territory. As a black man searching for his own identity in a white colonial culture, he experienced racism; as a psychiatrist, he studied the dynamics of racism and its effects on the individual.

In his first book, *Black Skin, White Masks* (1952), Fanon examined the social and psychological processes by which the white colonizers alienated the black natives from any indigenous black culture; he showed that blacks were made to feel inferior because of their color and thus strove to emulate white culture and society. Fanon hoped that the old myths of superiority would be abandoned so that a real equality and integration could be achieved.

Alienated from the dominant French culture, except for that represented by such radicals as the philosopher Jean Paul Sartre, Fanon deeply identified with Algeria's revolutionary struggle for independence. He had secretly aided the rebels from 1954 to 1956, when he resigned from the hospital post to openly work for the Algerian revolutionaries' National Liberation Front (FLN) in Tunis. He worked on the revolutionaries' newspaper, becoming one of the leading ideologists of the revolution, and developed a theory of anticolonial struggle in the "third world."

Using Marxist, psychoanalytic, and sociological analysis, Fanon summed up his views in *The Wretched of the Earth* (1961), arguing that only a thorough, truly socialist revolution carried out by the oppressed peasantry (the wretched of the earth) could bring justice to the colonized. He believed that the revolution could only be carried out by violent armed conflict; only revolutionary violence could completely break the psychological and physical shackles of a racist colonialism. Violence would regenerate and unite the population by a "collective catharsis;" out of this violence a new, humane man would arise and create a new culture. Through all this Fanon stressed the need to reject Europe and its culture and accomplish the revolution alone.

Fanon, the antiracist and revolutionary prophet, never saw the end result of the process he described: full independence of his adopted Algeria. In 1960 he served as ambassador to Ghana for the Algerian provisional government, but it was soon discovered that he had leukemia. After treatment in the Soviet Union, he went to the United States to seek further treatment but died there in 1961.

Further Reading

Peter Geismar, *Fanon* (1971), is a useful biography. David Caute, *Fanon* (1970), is not a full biography but a study of Fanon's ideas. Fanon's *The Wretched of the Earth* (1961; trans. 1965) has an interesting introduction by Jean Paul Sartre. For a concise background of Algeria see Richard M. Brace, *Morocco, Algeria, Tunisia* (1964).

Additional Sources

Bulhan, Hussein Abdilahi., *Frantz Fanon and the psychology of oppression,* New York: Plenum Press, 1985.
Gendzier, Irene L., *Frantz Fano,* London: Panaf Books, 1975. □

Michael Faraday

The English physicist and chemist Michael Faraday (1791-1867) discovered benzene and the principles of current induction.

One of a blacksmith's 10 children, Michael Faraday was born on Sept. 22, 1791, in Newington, Surrey. The family soon moved to London, where young Michael picked up the rudiments of reading, writing, and arithmetic. At the age of 14 he was apprenticed to a bookbinder and bookseller. He read ravenously and attended public lectures, including some by Sir Humphry Davy.

Faraday's career began when Davy, temporarily blinded in a laboratory accident, appointed Faraday as his assistant at the Royal Institution. With Davy as a teacher in analytical chemistry, Faraday advanced in his scientific apprenticeship and began independent chemical studies. By 1825 he discovered benzene and had become the first to describe compounds of chlorine and carbon. He adopted the atomic theory to explain that chemical qualities were the result of attraction and repulsion between united atoms. This proved to be the theoretical foundation for much of his future work.

Faraday had already done some work in magnetism and electricity, and it was in this field that he made his most outstanding contributions. His first triumph came when he found a solution to the problem of producing continuous rotation by use of electric current, thus making electric motors possible. Hans Oersted had discovered the magnetic effect of a current, but Faraday grasped the fact that a conductor at rest and a steady magnetic field do not interact and that to get an induced current either the conductor or the field has to move. On Aug. 29, 1831, he discovered electromagnetic induction.

During the next 10 years Faraday explored and expanded the field of electricity. In 1834 he announced his famous two laws of electrolysis. Briefly, they state that for any given amount of electrical force in an electrochemical cell, chemical substances are released at the electrodes in the ratio of their chemical equivalents. He also invented the voltameter, a device for measuring electrical charges, which was the first step toward the later standardization of electrical quantities.

Faraday continued to work in his laboratory, but his health began to deteriorate and he had to stop work entirely in 1841. Almost miraculously, however, his health improved and he resumed work in 1844. He began a search for an interaction between magnetism and light and in 1845 turned his attention from electrostatics to electromagnetism.

He discovered that an intense magnetic field can rotate the plane of polarized light, a phenomenon known today as the Faraday effect. In conjunction with these experiments he showed that the magnetic line of force is conducted by all matter. Those which were good conductors he called paramagnetics, while those which conducted the force poorly he named diamagnetics. Thus, the energy of a magnet is in the space around it, not in the magnet itself. This is the fundamental idea of the field theory.

Faraday was a brilliant lecturer, and through his public lectures he did a great deal to popularize science. Shortly after he became head of the Royal Institution in 1825, he inaugurated the custom of giving a series of lectures for young people during the Christmas season. This tradition has been maintained, and over the years the series have frequently been the basis for fascinating, simply written, and informative books.

On Aug. 25, 1867, Faraday died in London.

The admiration of physicists for Faraday has been demonstrated by naming the unit of capacitance the farad and a unit of charge, the faraday. No other man has been doubly honored in this way. His name also appears frequently in connection with effects, laws, and apparatus. These honors are proper tribute to the man who was possibly the greatest experimentalist who ever lived.

Further Reading

Much has been written about Faraday, but the student should first read the account by his successor at the Royal Institution, John Tyndall, *Faraday as a Discoverer* (1961). The sketch of Faraday in James Gerald Crowther, *Men of Science* (1936), is also recommended. Leslie Pearce Williams, *Michael Faraday: A Biography* (1965), appraises Faraday's work in relation to modern science and contains many previously unpublished manuscripts. □

William George Fargo

William George Fargo (1818-1881), American entrepreneur, was a founder of Wells, Fargo and Company and the American Express Company.

William Fargo was born on May 20, 1818, in Pompey, N.Y., the eldest of 12 children. His formal education ended at 13, when he began carrying mail over a 30-mile circuit for a local contractor. He subsequently worked in the grocery business, as a baker, and in a village inn. In 1840 he married Anna H. Williams; they had three children.

In 1842 Fargo became a messenger for an express firm operating between Albany and Buffalo. Soon he was appointed agent of Pomeroy and Company in Buffalo. Through his association with Wells and Company (which operated the first express company west of Buffalo), Fargo became one of the founders of the American Express Company, which quickly became the largest express concern in the United States.

In 1852 Fargo and some associates formed Wells, Fargo and Company to bring the services of an express company to the gold fields of California. American Express and Wells, Fargo combined facilities to provide rapid transportation of goods and communications between California, the Atlantic coast, Europe, and points in between.

After an 1855 financial panic drove its most formidable rival into bankruptcy, Wells, Fargo was the dominant express company in the West, with hundreds of employees, thousands of head of stock, and hundreds of thousands of dollars in capital invested. For the vast population then moving into the territory west of the Rocky Mountains, it provided unrivaled banking, express, and mail services. In 1857 Fargo and some of his associates from American Express established the Overland Mail, the first transcontinental stage line. It served the West until the coming of the railroad in 1869.

After the Civil War, the exemplary success of Wells, Fargo brought other concerns into the field, and in 1869 Wells, Fargo merged with the Pacific Express Company, which had contracted for the express business on the new transcontinental railroad. American Express was involved in similar mergers in the East.

Fargo had served as mayor of the city of Buffalo for two terms during the Civil War. A lifelong Democrat, he had stood against secession and supported the Union during the war by paying a part of their salary to those of his employees

who were drafted. He became a director of the New York Central and the Northern Pacific railroads. He was also involved in a number of manufacturing enterprises and was for a time the majority stockholder of the *Buffalo Courier.* He died on Aug. 3, 1881, having amassed a tremendous fortune.

Further Reading

Among the studies in which Fargo figures prominently are A. L. Stimson, *History of the Express Business, Including the Origin of the Railway System in America* (1881); LeRoy R. Hafen, *The Overland Mail, 1849-1869: Promoter of Settlement, Precursor of Railroads* (1926); Edward Hungerford, *Wells Fargo: Advancing the American Frontier* (1949); and Noel M. Loomis, *Wells Fargo* (1968). □

James A. Farley

James A. Farley (1888-1976) served President Franklin D. Roosevelt as the New Deal's patronage-dispensing postmaster general and official political prophet.

When President Franklin D. Roosevelt ran for reelection in 1936, Democratic National Committee Chairman Jim Farley wrote him a note saying, "I am still definitely of the opinion that you will carry every state but two, Maine and Vermont." F.D.R., master politician though he was, had predicted a loss of 171 electoral votes for himself. Farley's estimate of a mere eight vote loss, and his ability to pick the very states, confirmed him as one of America's most brilliant politicians.

Born on May 30, 1888, in upstate (Rockland County) Grassy Point, New York, James Aloysius Farley was the son of brick maker James and his wife Ellen (Goldrick), both children of Irish immigrants. He resembled F.D.R., six years his senior and his Dutchess County neighbor, in being born a Democrat in a heavily Republican county. There the resemblance ended, however. Where Roosevelt was well-born, rich, and Harvard educated, Jim Farley lost his father as boy of nine, spent much of his spare time as a brickyard worker or helping his mother in a family-owned combination grocery-bar, and after graduation from local schools attended Packard Commercial School in New York City.

His early interest in politics confirmed his attachment to the Democratic Party, and despite the Republican voter preponderance he served several terms as the elected (unsalaried) town clerk. An affable manner, dedication to extra service (he refused his share of license fees and saved prospective brides the embarrassment of an office visit by bringing the marriage license to their homes), and a phenomenal memory for names and faces made him one of Rockland County's best-liked citizens. These traits never left him, and when coupled with an uncanny capacity for political predictions would earn him his reputation as a political seer.

A Power Behind the Scenes

During his lifetime Farley won several positions in general elections, the highest being one term to the New York State Assembly. But despite his ability to win elections, Farley's forte became that of king maker. He recalled in later life how as an unknown Rockland County Democratic chairman he brashly urged Alfred E. Smith to run for governor in 1918, making light of the doubts of Smith and his advisers. Farley voted for him at the state convention and campaigned actively for the Smith ticket. Smith's victory changed his fortunes, bringing him appointment as a New York City port warden, a post he later frankly described as a sinecure and from which he was eliminated by Republican legislative cut-backs.

At the beginning of the 1920s Farley became a power in Rockland County; by the end of the decade he was a power in the state. His political career brought him little financial security and in this respect was only an avocation. To support himself, Elizabeth A. Finnegan (whom he married in 1920), and their three children, he was first a salesman in the building materials field and later a partner in a firm called General Builders Supply Corporation.

Farley was a strong supporter of Governor Smith's reelection bids, but he also felt a great admiration for Franklin D. Roosevelt, whom he first met in 1920. At the illstarred Democratic convention of 1924, Franklin Roosevelt, then a private citizen recovering from polio, nominated Smith for the presidency, proclaiming him "the Happy Warrior." Smith did not get the nomination in 1924 but was renominated by Roosevelt in 1928, at which time F.D.R. also ran for the governorship of New York.

Farley, by this time secretary to the state Democratic committee, worked tirelessly for both Smith and Roosevelt, but only the latter won, and he by a mere 25,000 votes. During the next two years Farley became chairman of the state Democratic committee, rebuilt the Democratic Party in New York State, and was gratified by Roosevelt's landslide reelection plurality of over 700,000 votes. At that point, in November 1930, Farley and Louis Howe, another Roosevelt supporter, predicted in public that the governor would be the Democratic nominee for president in 1932.

Building Up a Candidate

Farley, Howe, and a few other faithful workers created over the next two years what for the time was an astonishing organizational effort based on personal meetings, letter writing, and telephoning. Building up county by county in the state, the organization was expanded into other states with a whirlwind national trip taken by Farley in mid-1931 covering 18 states in 19 days.

At the Chicago convention of 1932 Roosevelt was one of nine candidates, but under Farley's management his organization overwhelmed his opponents. The selection of Texas favorite John Nance Garner as running-mate added the last touch. Forty-four year old Jim Farley went to the Chicago convention a well-known New York politician. He left it a national figure whose guiding motive was to elect Democrats, not alienate them. Every characteristic he had possessed throughout life—his memory, personable qualities, party loyalty, organizational ability, and tireless energy—was taxed in the extreme in the 1932 campaign, but the result was victory. Farley predicted Roosevelt would defeat Hoover by 7.5 million votes, and came within a few hundred thousand of his estimate.

Farley's reward for this service was an invitation to join F.D.R.'s New Deal as postmaster general, an appointment which made him the first Catholic cabinet member in this century. As postmaster general Farley exercised the traditional patronage dispensing function with masterful skill, rewarding loyalty; cementing regional, ethnic, and occupational alliances; and providing the president with bargaining chips for congressional dealings.

The high point of Farley's career came with management of F.D.R.'s 1936 reelection campaign, which wrote Roosevelt and himself into history as record setters. Thereafter, disenchanted with some New Deal policies and angered by the third term bid, Farley lost Roosevelt's confidence and therefore his effectiveness.

A Break with F.D.R.

During 1940 he privately made no bones about his antipathy to a Roosevelt third term. Unable to avert it, he allowed a few stalwart friends to nominate him as presidential candidate in Chicago, gaining 72 votes to Roosevelt's 946. While this gave him great personal satisfaction, it further alienated him from the president, and he resigned his cabinet post and national party chairmanship a few weeks later.

In private life, he became chairman of a Coca-Cola division but remained active in public life, particularly in New York state.

His autobiographies, *Behind the Ballots* (1938) and *Jim Farley's Story* (1948), are valuable and candid insider accounts of vital days in the nation's history. A modest man, he knew what he was—a "political drummer," as he once put it—and never apologized for it. As Roosevelt's political spoilsman, he dispensed thousands of patronage jobs unabashedly to deserving Democrats but made no financial gain himself out of politics. He always had private business interests, and these he kept scrupulously separate from his government work. As a young man he refused to accept fees due him for his services as unsalaried town clerk, later observing "I never accepted the ten-cent fee from hunters and fishermen . . . and as a result they remembered me on election day." To Farley, good neighborliness and good manners were good politics.

After many years spent as a businessman and elder statesman Jim Farley died on June 9, 1976.

Further Reading

James A. Farley's two autobiographies, *Jim Farley's Story* (1938) and *Behind the Ballots* (1948), remain the most complete accounts of his life and provide illuminating insights into American politics between the world wars. Also helpful is *American Catholics and the Roosevelt Presidency* (1968) by George Q. Flynn.

Additional Sources

Farley, James Aloysius, *Jim Farley's story: the Roosevelt years*, Westport, Conn.: Greenwood Press, 1984. □

Fannie Merritt Farmer

Fannie Merritt Farmer (1857-1915) was an American authority in the art of cookery and the author of six books about food preparation.

Fannie Farmer was born in Boston, Mass., on March 23, 1857. Her parents had hopes of sending her to college. But after high school graduation she suffered a paralytic stroke, and her doctor discouraged all thoughts of further schooling.

While at home as an invalid, Fannie Farmer became interested in cooking. When her physical condition had markedly improved, her parents advised her to seek schooling which would develop and refine her knowledge and abilities in cookery. She liked the idea and enrolled in the Boston Cooking School, where her performance was outstanding. Because of the excellence of her work, upon graduation in 1889 she was invited to serve as assistant director of the school under Carrie M. Dearborn. Farmer's inquiring mind led her into studies, including a summer course at the Harvard Medical School.

After Dearborn's death in 1891, Farmer was appointed director of the school. While there she published her monumental work, *Boston Cooking School Cookbook* (1896), of which 21 editions were printed before her death. It has remained a standard work. She served as director of the school for 11 years. After her resignation in 1902, she established her own school and named it Miss Farmer's School of Cookery. It was decidedly innovative, emphasizing the practice of cooking instead of theory. Its program was designed to educate housewives rather than to prepare teachers. The school also developed cookery for the sick and the invalid. Farmer became an undisputed authority in her field, and she was invited to deliver lectures to nurses, women's clubs, and even the Harvard Medical School.

One of Farmer's major contributions was teaching cooks to follow recipes carefully. She pioneered the use of standard level measurement in cooking. Farmer, her school, and her cook-books were extremely popular. She received favorable newspaper coverage in many American cities, and her influence was widespread. The well-attended weekly lectures at the school were tributes to the value of the work she and her assistants were doing. She also wrote a popular cookery column, which ran for nearly 10 years in the *Woman's Home Companion*, a national magazine.

Farmer was a woman of unusual motivation, intelligence, and courage. Though she suffered another paralytic stroke, she continued lecturing. In fact, 10 days before her death in 1915, she delivered a lecture from a wheelchair.

Further Reading

For general background on cooking and a brief discussion of Fanny Farmer see Kathleen Ann Smallzried, *The Everlasting Pleasure: Influences on America's Kitchens, Cooks, and Cookery from 1565 to the Year 2000* (1956). □

James Farmer

A Black civil rights activist, James Farmer (born 1920) helped organize the 1960s "freedom rides" which led to the desegregation of interstate buses and bus terminals. He also played a major role in the activities of the Congress of Racial Equality (CORE).

James Farmer along with a group of University of Chicago students founded the Congress of Racial Equality (CORE) in Chicago in 1942. The purpose of this interracial group was to work for an end to racial segregation using non-violent tactics similar to those developed by Mahatma Gandhi. Farmer was the first leader of CORE but became inactive after several years. In the 1960s when the civil rights movement was gaining momentum Farmer was reelected as the director of CORE. He also was one of the group of civil rights leaders who planned the March on Washington in 1963.

Farmer was born in Marshall, Texas, in 1920. His father held a doctorate in theology from Boston University and his mother a teaching certificate from Bethune-Cookman Institute. Farmer entered Wiley College in Texas at 14 years of age with the idea of becoming a doctor. However, after he received a Bachelor of Science degree in chemistry he decided that he would enter the ministry. When his father joined the faculty at Howard University in Washington, D.C., Farmer entered the School of Religion there. He graduated in 1941 but refused to work in a segregated church. He accepted a job with a pacifist group based in New York called the Fellowship of Reconciliation (FOR) and was assigned to work in Chicago. From his Chicago base he visited other areas in the midwest speaking about pacifism and racial equality.

As a consequence of this work and his study and observation of the Gandhi movement he addressed several proposals to FOR leaders suggesting the formation of a committee dedicated to racial equality. It was first called the Committee of Racial Equality and, finally, the Congress of Racial Equality. Farmer served as national chairman of CORE from 1942 to 1944 and again in 1950. He was elected national director in 1961 and served in that position until 1966. Even during the years that Farmer was not leading CORE he remained interested in the organization's work. During the period from about 1945 to 1959 Farmer worked as a labor union organizer. For the next two years, 1960-1961, he worked as a program director for the National Association for the Advancement of Colored People (NAACP).

Farmer was working for the NAACP when he was called back to CORE to lead the 1961 "freedom ride."

Several Supreme Court rulings led to CORE's decision to sponsor freedom rides. In 1946 the Supreme Court had ruled that racially segregated seating on interstate buses was unconstitutional, and in 1960 it declared that segregation in terminals used by interstate passengers was also unconstitutional. Yet the southern states continued to force blacks to sit in the back of the bus and to use segregated facilities. The 13 CORE freedom riders decided to travel by bus from Washington, D.C., to New Orleans with white members sitting in the back and black riders in the front. All of the riders were instructed to refuse to move when they were asked. They also decided that at the bus terminals the white riders would use the "for colored" facilities and the black the "for white."

The riders left from Washington, D.C., and made their historic trip without violence until they arrived in Alabama. In that state the freedom riders were attacked and beaten. Finally, the bus was burned by hostile whites. Youths who were members of the Student Non-Violent Coordinating Committee (SNCC) volunteered to act as replacements or reinforcements for the original 13 CORE riders. Although hundreds of riders spent weeks in Alabama prisons, new recruits continued to come forward. The conditions in the jails were almost primitive and the guards usually hostile. Although many riders continued to be attacked in other southern states, the idea of freedom rides caught on. CORE received nationwide attention, and James Farmer became well-known as a civil rights leader. The freedom ride, along with sit-ins at lunch counters and the Montgomery bus boycott led by Martin Luther King, Jr., captured the imagination of the nation and exposed to the world through photographs, newspaper accounts, and motion pictures the brutal retaliation of many southern whites against the actions of the demonstrators. Concerned whites and blacks decided that it was time for racial discrimination and segregation to come to an end.

Farmer began to meet regularly with a group of black leaders that came to be known as the "big six" of civil rights. The group included Farmer; King, leader of the Southern Christian Leadership Conference; Dorothy Height of the National Council of Negro Women; John Lewis (or sometimes James Forman) from SNCC; Roy Wilkins of the NAACP; and Whitney Young of the National Urban League. This group of leaders met regularly and sometimes invited other civil rights leaders to attend. When A. Philip Randolph, a labor leader, asked to make a presentation before the group, he proposed that the group revise his idea of a massive march on Washington, D.C., a plan that he originally had formulated in 1941. The purpose of the march was to dramatize the need for jobs, freedom, and civil rights legislation. The group agreed to support the march. When it took place in Washington, D.C., on August 28, 1963, over 250,000 blacks and whites participated. However, Farmer was in jail and could not attend.

Farmer continued to lead CORE, which grew quickly during the early 1960s. Numerous sit-ins and boycotts occurred and thousands of people, many of them students, were involved. When Farmer resigned as the leader of CORE in 1966 he continued to be active in a number of areas. He taught at several universities and in 1968 he ran unsuccessfully against Shirley Chisholm for the New York 12th district seat in the House of Representatives. In 1969 President Nixon appointed him assistant secretary for administration of the Department of Health, Education and Welfare. In that position, he initiated affirmative action and hiring practices at the HEW. Unhappy with the Nixon administration, Farmer resigned the following year to resume teaching.

Over the years Farmer taught and lectured at numerous institutions, and in the mid 1980s began teaching at Mary Washington College in Fredericksburg, Virginia, eventually joining their staff as a history professor. In 1996 he had over 250 students on his roster, more than any other history teacher at the liberal arts college. He remains a vital and active presence, despite a battle with diabetes that has left him blind in one eye, and without the use of his left leg.

Further Reading

Farmer wrote numerous articles, as well as two books entitled *Freedom, When?* (1965) and *Lay Bare the Heart; An Autobiography of the Civil Rights Movement* (1985). August Meier wrote *CORE; A Study in the Civil Rights Movement, 1942-1968* (1973), which includes important information about Farmer's role in the organization. □

Moses Gerrish Farmer

Moses Gerrish Farmer (1820-1893), an American inventor and manufacturer, pioneered in the practical applications of electricity.

Moses Farmer was born in Boscawen, N.H., where his father was a farmer and prosperous merchant. After his father died in 1837, Moses attended preparatory school and then Dartmouth College. He gave piano lessons to earn money for school, but the combination of work and study made him ill and brought his schooling to an end. He taught for several years in Maine and New Hampshire.

While teaching, Farmer pursued his interest in mechanical problems. He built a machine to manufacture printed-paper window shades, which proved a modest success. In 1845 he turned his attention to the problems of electricity. One of his first projects was an electric railroad, powered by batteries, which he built and operated at home in 1847. This invention was typical of much of his subsequent work in the field-ingenious and forward-looking but not profitable.

Farmer gave up teaching and in 1847 became a wire examiner for a telegraph line between Boston and Worcester. While on this job he studied telegraphy and the following year was made an operator at Salem, Mass. About this time he began the work that led to his invention of an electric fire alarm system. In 1851, with William F. Channing, he installed his system in Boston, the first such system in the United States. Farmer became its superintendent. He resigned this post in 1853 and for many years held a succession of jobs, not all of which were connected with electricity.

Farmer continued to invent, however, and developed such devices as an electric clock, a method of electroplating aluminum, and a self-exciting dynamo. His most dramatic success was lighting a house in Cambridge, Mass., in 1868, with 40 of his incandescent lamps. In 1872 his proposals for detonating naval torpedoes by an electric charge led to his appointment as electrician at the U.S. Torpedo Station in Newport, R.I. He resigned because of ill health in 1881. He died while on a visit to the 1893 World's Columbian Exposition in Chicago, where he was exhibiting some of his inventions.

Farmer's success as an inventor in the developing field of electricity and yet his failure to benefit financially from his efforts led one sympathetic electrician to comment at his death that he had "invented not wisely, but too well."

Further Reading

There is no satisfactory biography of Farmer. Information on his career must be pieced together from such general sources as Malcolm MacLaren, *The Rise of the Electrical Industry during the Nineteenth Century* (1943); Robert L. Thompson, *Wiring a Continent: The History of the Telegraph Industry in the United States, 1832-1866* (1947); and Harold C. Passer, *The Electrical Manufacturers, 1875-1900* (1953). □

Philo T. Farnsworth

Philo T. Farnsworth (1906–1971) is known as the father of television by proving, as a young man, that pictures could be televised electronically.

On the statue erected in his honor in the U. S. Capitol Statuary Hall, Philo T. Farnsworth is called the Father of Television. He was the first person to propose that pictures could be televised electronically, which he did when he was 14 years old. By the time he was 21, Farnsworth had proved his ideas by televising the world's first electronically-produced image. From the day he sketched out for his high school chemistry teacher his ideas for harnessing electricity to transmit images, until his death in 1971, Farnsworth amassed a portfolio of over 100 television-related patents, some of which are still in use today.

Farnsworth was born in Indian Creek, Utah, on August 19, 1906. The first of five children born to Serena Bastian and Lewis Edwin Farnsworth, he was named after his grandfather, Philo Taylor Farnsworth I, the leader of the Mormon pioneers who settled that area of southwestern Utah. Although there was no electricity where he lived, Farnsworth learned as much as he could about it from his father and from technical and radio magazines. Lewis Farnsworth was a farmer and regaled his son with technical discussions about the telephone, gramophone, locomotives, and anything else the younger Farnsworth was curious about. When the family moved to a farm in Idaho with its own power plant, he poked and probed and mastered the lighting system and was soon put in charge of maintaining it. It had never run so smoothly. Farnsworth was adept at inventing gadgets even before he went to high school, and he won a national invention contest when he was 13 years old.

Dreaming of Television

In 1920, he read that some inventors were attempting to transmit visual images by mechanical means. For the next two years, he worked on an electronic alternative that he was convinced would be faster and better; he came up with the basic design for an apparatus in 1922. Farnsworth discussed his ideas and showed sketches of the apparatus to his high school chemistry teacher Justin Tolman. Little did they know that this discussion would later be critical in settling a patent dispute between Farnsworth and his competitor at the Radio Corporation of America (RCA), Vladimir Zworykin.

Farnsworth took physics courses by correspondence from the University of Utah and later enrolled at Brigham Young University. He was largely self-taught but so impressed two of his chemistry professors at BYU with his ideas about television that they gave him the run of the chemistry and glass labs to start work on his theories.

In 1924, Farnsworth's father died and he was left with the responsibility of supporting the family. After a short time in the navy, he moved to Salt Lake City to work as a canvasser for the Community Chest. There Farnsworth made friends with George Everson, the businessman who was organizing the fund-raising effort, and his associate Leslie Gorrell. Farnsworth told Everson and Gorrell about his ideas for a television, and they invested $6,000 in his venture. With additional backing from a group of bankers in San Francisco, Farnsworth was given a research lab and a year to prove his concepts.

Building the First Television System

Farnsworth was married to his college sweetheart Elma Pem Gardner on May 27, 1926, and the next day they left for California, where Farnsworth would set up his lab in San Francisco. With assistance from his wife, Elma, better known as Pem, and her brother Cliff, Farnsworth designed and built all the components—from the vacuum transmitter tubes to the image scanner and the receiver—that made up his first television system. The key invention was his Image Dissector camera, which scanned relatively slowly in one direction and relatively quickly in the opposite direction, making possible much greater scanning speeds than had been achieved earlier. All television receivers use this basic system of scanning.

On September 7, 1927, three weeks before the deadline, Farnsworth gathered his friends and engineering colleagues in a room adjoining the lab and amazed them with the first two-dimensional image ever transmitted by television—the image of his wife and assistant, Pem. His backers continued their support for a year and in September 1928, the first television system was unveiled to the world. In 1929, some of the bankers who invested in the research formed a company called Television Laboratories Inc., of which Farnsworth was named vice president and director of research.

The Challenge of the Marketplace

At the same time, RCA began aggressively competing with Farnsworth for control of the emerging television market and challenged the patent on his invention. With the testimony of Farnsworth's high school teacher, Justin Tolman, it was determined that Farnsworth had indeed documented his ideas one year before RCA's Vladimir Zworykin. This was but the first of many challenges from RCA, but in the end the corporate giant was forced to work out a cross-licensing arrangement with Farnsworth.

The victor in dozens of legal challenges by RCA, Farnsworth eventually licensed his television patents to the growing industry and let others refine and develop his basic inventions. His patents were first licensed in Germany and Great Britain, and only later did the Federal Communications Commission allocate broadcast channels in the United States. During his early years in San Francisco, Farnsworth did other important work as well. He made the first cold cathode-ray tube, the first simple electron microscope, and a means for using radio waves to sense direction—an innovation now known as radar. He received more than 300 patents worldwide during his career.

Farnsworth eventually set up his own company, which boomed during World War II with government contracts to develop electronic surveillance and other equipment. The Farnsworth Radio and Television Corp. took a downturn after the war and was sold to the International Telephone and Telegraph Company (ITT) in 1949. Farnsworth remained with the company for some time as a research consultant. Late in his life he turned his attention to the field of atomic energy. Farnsworth died of emphysema on March 11, 1971, in Holladay, a suburb of Salt Lake City.

For his pioneering work, Farnsworth received the First Gold Medal awarded by the National Television Broadcasters Association in 1944. During his lifetime he also was presented with honorary doctorates in science from Indiana Technical College (1951) and Brigham Young University (1968). Posthumously, the inventor was remembered with a twenty-cent stamp with his likeness, issued in 1983, and his induction into the National Inventors Hall of Fame in 1984. The Philo T. Farnsworth Memorial Museum was dedicated in his honor in Rigby, Idaho, in 1988.

Further Reading

Dedication of the Statue of Philo T. Farnsworth, Proceedings in the U.S. Capital Rotunda, U.S. Government Printing Office, 1990.
The Story of Television: The Life of Philo T. Farnsworth by George Everson. Norton, 1949.
Distant Vision: Romance and Discovery on an Invisible Frontier by Elma Farnsworth. Pemberly-Kent, 1990.
BYU Today, "Philo T. Farnsworth: The Father of Television" by Dennis May (May 1989), pp. 33–36. □

Farouk I

Farouk I (1920-1965) was the second king of modern Egypt. Though he was dynamic and a nationalist, the realization of being powerless under British sovereignty turned his interests from statecraft to the gratification of his desires.

Farouk, the only son of Fuad I, was born in Cairo on Feb. 11, 1920. Educated first in Cairo and later at the Royal Military Academy at Woolwich, he was recalled to ascend the Egyptian throne in 1936 and crowned in 1937. Though he was most promising in his early days and was thought to be dedicated to the interests of Egypt, Farouk soon resumed the old struggle between the populist forces of the Wafd and the palace, and drifted toward intrigue, absolutism, and debauchery that ultimately caused the collapse of the monarchy in Egypt.

Seeds of Discontent

In 1936 more favorable terms had been reached between Britain and Egypt, but nevertheless the relationship was characterized and perceived as one permitting Britain to dominate Egypt. Farouk's rule was further complicated by new domestic developments in Egypt, particularly in political and economic matters.

The rise of the Society of Moslem Brothers, first started in 1928 and eventually catapulted into position of dominance in Egyptian politics, was one of the more critical political forces to affect the political stability of Egypt during Farouk's reign. The Moslem Brothers championed a program of Islamic reform, advocated struggle against all foreign influence, and challenged the legitimacy of the parliamentary system. The increasing literacy of Egypt and thus the increasing social and economic awareness of large segments of the Egyptian masses gave rise to various other protest movements seeking an alteration in the social, economic, and political systems. Farouk's tendency toward authoritarianism and his insistence on active intervention in politics made it impossible for any legitimately elected government to meet the expectations of the newer elements in society and complicated infinitely the task of governing the country.

World War II

The approaching storm of World War II made British interference in internal Egyptian affairs inevitable, for Britain was primarily concerned with the security of the British Empire, and Egyptian national needs, as perceived by Egyptians, had to be subordinated to Britain's security needs. Egypt's desire to steer a neutral course during World War II and its alleged flirtation with Italy prompted Britain to make strong representation to Farouk. On Feb. 4, 1942, the British ambassador, escorted by British tanks, surrounded Abdin Palace and forced King Farouk to dismiss an allegedly pro-Italian Cabinet and to replace it with the popular Wafd Cabinet. The King surrendered to British demands, and the Wafd ruled till 1944.

This overt intervention by the British in the internal affairs of Egypt and their dictation of a specific prime minister led to the discredit of both King and party. Farouk, recognizing his impotence on the world scene, reacted unusually, indulging himself in the frivolities of life. The personal corruption of Farouk, though he might have shown a tendency in that direction earlier, can be traced directly to his recognition of the futility of his position within his own country. The Wafd was similarly discredited for serving as a result of a military intervention by Britain, the power that it had tried to dislodge from the scene.

Crisis and Exile

The old liberal constitutionalism that had characterized Egyptian politics was discredited, and it was only a question of time when the whole system would collapse. In 1952 the Egyptian army led by Col. Gamal Abdel Nasser seized power and forced Farouk to abdicate on July 26 and go into exile in Italy.

Despite the negative nature of Farouk's reign, his personal corruption, and his lust for power and for women, his reign had some very positive qualities as well. He was very active in inter-Arab politics, helped in increasing the Arab orientation of Egypt, assisted in developing the League of Arab States whose headquarters became Cairo, and took an interest in the aspirations of the Palestinians. Under his rule Egypt developed economically, industrialization assumed more concrete form, and Egyptians took greater roles in the economy. Many of the measures later adopted by Nasser designed to increase the economic viability of Egypt were in fact initiated during Farouk's reign. Farouk founded many institutions of higher learning, such as Farouk I University (renamed Alexandria) and Ain Shams University.

Farouk had three daughters by his first marriage and one son, Fuad II, by his second marriage, to Narriman. Upon Farouk's abdication and exile, his son was declared king and a regency council was established, but eventually Egypt was declared a republic and the Alawid dynasty, which had ruled Egypt since Mohammed Ali assumed power in 1805, came to an end. Farouk died in exile in Rome on March 18, 1965, of a heart attack and was brought back to Egypt for burial.

Further Reading

Studies of recent Egyptian history include Austin L. Moore, *Fare-well Farouk* (1954); Hisham B. Sharabi, *Governments and Politics of the Middle East in the Twentieth Century* (1962); Tom Little, *Modern Egypt* (1967); and Harry Hopkins, *Egypt the Crucible* (1969). □

David Glasgow Farragut

The American naval officer David Glasgow Farragut (1801-1870) was the hero of two of the most important Union naval victories in the Civil War. He became the first admiral in the U.S. Navy.

James (later David) G. Farragut was born on July 5, 1801, near Knoxville, Tenn., the son of George Farragut, a U.S. Army and Navy officer. After his mother's death in 1808, James was informally adopted by Commander David Porter, who had the boy appointed a midshipman 2 years later. Farragut changed his first name from James to David while sailing with Porter on the *Essex* during the War of 1812. Farragut brought a prize ship into Valparaiso, Chile, in 1813. The following year the British captured the *Essex*.

Farragut served in the Mediterranean (1815-1820) and temporarily commanded the brig *Spark*. After passing the midshipman's exam in 1821, he hunted pirates in the Caribbean (1822-1824) with Porter and for a short time commanded the schooner *Ferret*. On Sept. 2, 1824, he married Susan C. Marchant and in 1825 became a lieutenant.

From the 1820s to 1861 Farragut frequently served ashore at the Norfolk, Va., naval yard. In 1833 his ship was stationed off Charleston, S.C., during the Nullification Crisis. Promoted to commander in 1841, Farragut commanded the sloop *Decatur* on the Brazil station the next year. His first wife had died in 1840, and 3 years later he married Virginia D. Loyall, with whom he had one son. Farragut commanded the sloop *Saratoga* on blockade duty during the Mexican War. From 1854 to 1858 he supervised the construction of the naval yard at Mare Island, Calif. When Virginia seceded from the Union in 1861, he switched his

permanent residence from Virginia to New York and offered his services to the North, but he remained under suspicion for months.

In January 1862 the Department of the Navy, convinced of his loyalty, made Farragut commander of the West Gulf Blockading Squadron. On April 24, after a 6-day bombardment, he ran past the forts below New Orleans with 17 ships and captured the South's largest port the next day. He continued up the Mississippi past the Vicksburg batteries on June 28 but could not capture the town. He passed the batteries again on July 14 in an unsuccessful effort to sink the *Arkansas*. Two days later he became the first rear admiral in the U.S. Navy.

In March 1863 Farragut led two ships past the batteries at Port Hudson on the Mississippi, but the fort surrendered in July only after a siege—several days after the Vicksburg victory. His next objective was the port of Mobile. On Aug. 5, 1864, under heavy fire, he sailed 18 ships between the Confederate forts at the heavily mined mouth of Mobile Bay. He captured the ironclad *Tennessee* following a fierce struggle inside the harbor and then received the surrender of the forts, thus sealing off the second-largest Confederate port on the Gulf of Mexico. That fall Farragut was relieved of command because of ill health. In December he received the new rank of vice-admiral. He became the first admiral of the U.S. Navy in 1866.

Farragut commanded the European squadron on a goodwill tour in 1867-1868. He died while visiting the Portsmouth, N.H., naval yard on Aug. 14, 1870.

date Jesse Jackson. Farrakhan, who had earlier counseled his devoted followers to avoid political involvements, had thrown his movement behind Jackson, providing, in addition to rhetorical support before African American audiences, bodyguards for the candidate. Farrakhan had registered to vote for the first time and urged his followers to do the same. Jackson had returned the favor by appearing as the featured speaker at the Muslim Savior's Day rally in February 1984.

In March, however, Farrakhan condemned Milton Coleman, an African American reporter for *Washington Post*, as a traitor after Coleman disclosed that Jackson had, in a conversation with campaign aides, referred to Jews as "Hymies" and to New York City as "Hymietown." In a speech, Farrakhan said of Coleman, "One day soon we will punish you with death," although he later denied that he was threatening Coleman's life. In the ensuing controversy it became known that Farrakhan had acclaimed Hitler as "a very great man" and had pronounced Judaism a "gutter religion." He also described the creation of Israel as an "outlaw act." Jackson never repudiated Farrakhan's support, but the Muslim's profile was lowered throughout the rest of the campaign.

Controversy about Farrakhan deepened when it became known that during the 1980s he had visited Libya and received a $5-million interest-free loan from dictator Muammar Gaddafi to help build Muslim institutions and businesses. Farrakhan explained that he sought to raise hundreds of millions of dollars for African American self-improvement programs from all of the groups, including Arabs, that had been involved in the slave trade and the destruction of African culture.

After his time of greatest publicity during the presidential campaign of 1984, Farrakhan continued his extensive public speaking schedule and continued to wield influence among African Americans far beyond the membership of his own movement. He and his wife, Betsy, had nine children and lived in a mainly white upscale neighborhood on the far South Side of Chicago.

In 1993, on his 60th birthday, Farrakhan performed a violin concert on Chicago's South Side in an attempt to better his image. The "concert" was held at a Temple, in hopes that tensions between Farrakhan and the Jewish community could be mended. Besides the "Clean n Fresh" product line, Farrakhan opened a $5 million restaurant in March 1995. The Salaam Restaurant and Bakery was built with funds collected from followers and the sale of the *Final Call*, an Islamic newspaper.

Farrakhan has always had a loyal following. This fact was most evident on October 16, 1995 in Washington D.C. Farrakhan had called upon at least one million African American men to converge on the nation's capital to reinvigorate their community. The "Million Man March" was to create a solidarity amongst the African American community. Many feel that the march was also designed to help bridge a gap between white and African America. Farrakhan had support from the likes of Maya Angelou, Jesse Jackson, Stevie Wonder and a host of other notable personalities. The march surprised many, not only because of the sheer force

of attendance, but because Farrakhan was able to not only promote, but deliver a non-violent protest in Washington D.C.

Further Reading

Farrakhan has given few interviews and has not been the subject of a major biographical study. One helpful article is Clarence Page's "Deciphering Farrakhan," in *Chicago* magazine (August 1984). The Nation of Islam's newspaper, *The Final Call*, provides a general exposition of Farrakhan's outlook. Other articles pertaining to Farrakhan include "No Innocent Abroad" by Jack E. White, *Time* (February 26, 1996) and "Million Man March" by Eric Pooley, *Time* (October 16, 1995). □

James Thomas Farrell

James Thomas Farrell (1904-1979), novelist and social and literary critic, was one of the most unrelenting naturalists in American literature.

B orn in Chicago, James Thomas Farrell attended Catholic parochial school. He worked at various jobs before attending the University of Chicago for three years. Here he composed a story called "Studs," which, at his professor's suggestion, he expanded into *Young Lonigan* (1932), a semi-autobiographical novel about a troubled 15-year-old Chicago youth. A sequel, *The Young Manhood of Studs Lonigan* (1934), deals with the protagonist's moral dissolution as a result of his involvement with the Chicago underworld. *Judgment Day* (1935) closes the trilogy with an affecting account of Stud's death at the age of 29, a helpless victim of biological and environmental conditions. Despite its stylistic dreariness and turgidity, *Studs Lonigan* is a work of power and a classic of naturalism.

After completing this widely acclaimed but controversial trilogy, Farrell began the Danny O'Neill tetralogy, consisting of *A World I Never Made* (1936), *No Star Is Lost* (1938), *Father and Son* (1940), *My Days of Anger* (1943), and *The Face of Time* (1953). The sensitive, spectacled Danny is a close fictional version of the author. Although Danny is able to escape the constricting familial, religious, and environmental forces of his formative years in Chicago by pursuing a writing career in New York, his inability to reconcile himself with his past endows this series with a philosophical despair more overriding than the sociological pessimism of *Studs Lonigan*.

Farrell's graphic studies of lower-middle-class Irish Catholic life in the slums of Chicago, although written with the seeming objectivity of a social scientist, possess a heated moral indignation over the crass materialism and spiritual barrenness of urban life in a capitalist society. An ardent admirer of the realistic novels of Honoré de Balzac, Charles Dickens, and Leo Tolstoy, Farrell used a fictional style and tone closer to the work of fellow Chicagoan Theodore Dreiser. Less penetrating and less impressive in overall ef-

Further Reading

The most complete biography of Farragut is Charles Lee Lewis, *David Glasgow Farragut* (2 vols., 1941-1943). Briefer volumes are Alfred Thayer Mahan, *Admiral Farragut* (1892), and John Randolph Spears, *David G. Farragut* (1905). His son, Loyall Farragut, collected source material in *The Life of David Glasgow Farragut* (1879).

Additional Sources

Lewis, Charles Lee, *David Glasgow Farragut,* New York: Arno Press, 1941-43, 1980. □

Louis Farrakhan

Louis Farrakhan (born Louis Eugene Walcott, 1933) is a leader of one branch of the Nation of Islam, more popularly known as the Black Muslims. Beginning in the mid-1970s he emerged as a popular and militant spokesman for Black Nationalism.

Louis Eugene Walcott was born on May 11, 1933, and grew up in the Roxbury neighborhood of Boston. After joining the Nation of Islam in the 1950s, he took the name Louis X (a standard Nation of Islam practice indicating that one's identity and culture were stolen during slavery) and later Louis Farrakhan. In high school he was an honor student, a good track athlete, and an active Episcopalian. After two years of college he embarked on a career as a professional violinist and singer who used such stage names as "Calypso Gene" and "The Charmer."

At the age of 21, in 1955, Farrakhan was taken by a friend to hear Elijah Muhammad, the leader of the Nation of Islam. Muhammad was the second head of the movement, having attained his position following the mysterious disappearance of founder W.D. Fard in 1934, and had overseen its growth to tens or hundreds of thousands of members with an extensive network of farms, restaurants, stores, schools, and other businesses and institutions. Muhammad's message excoriated "white devils" and promised that the day would soon arrive when God would restore African Americans, who were regarded as the original humans, to their rightful position as leaders of the world. Muhammad also imposed strict standards of behavior on his followers, who were forbidden from smoking, drinking, fighting, eating pork, and other behaviors regarded as destructive and were commanded to say prayers, attend religious services regularly, improve their education, and provide extensive service to the movement. Farrakhan joined the movement soon after hearing its leader speak.

The newcomer's ability and dedication were quickly appreciated by Muhammad, who appointed him minister of the Boston mosque. After the death of Malcolm X in 1965 he was appointed leader of the important Harlem Temple No. 7 and official spokesperson for Elijah Muhammad. He was also given the symbolically important task of introducing

Muhammad at rallies on Savior's Day, a major Islam holiday celebrating Fard's birthday.

Elijah Muhammad died in 1975 and was succ his son Wallace Muhammad, who proved much qu more moderate than his father. At Wallace Muh invitation Farrakhan moved to Chicago to wo movement's headquarters. Soon Wallace Muhan gan to pursue a program of moderation for the m abandoning its antiwhite rhetoric (and even whites to membership) and building bridges to world from the Islamic community. That progran in a movement that today functions as a relativel tional expression of Islam.

Farrakhan became a major voice of the "puris composed of members who rejected the move tow eration. He resigned from the movement in 1978 nized a new Nation of Islam that closely resembl Muhammad's original movement, with dress and codes and Muslim institutions and businesses. T theology and bitterly antiwhite rhetoric of Elijah mad once again became standard. The reconstitut ment grew quietly but steadily as Farrakhan mosques in American cities and reached out to t African American community through publicatio radio show.

Farrakhan's movement, which in 1983 was e to have between five and ten thousand members, r relatively obscure until March 1984, when controv denly erupted over his association with presidenti

In the 1950s Farrell served as chairman of the Committee for Cultural Freedom and in the 1960s he supported Hubert Humphrey and was a harsh critic of the New Left. By the 1970s his views on affirmative action and Israel were similar to that of many conservatives.

Although he had come to be known for his activism, the publication of his 50th book, *The Dunne Family,* in 1976 created a renewed interest in Farrell's works and he was honored for this literary milestone with a "Salute To James T. Farrell" at the St. Regis Hotel in New York City. In 1979, the National Broadcasting Company presented Studs Lonigan as a television miniseries and shortly afterwards he was presented with the Emerson-Thoreau Award from the American Academy of Arts and Sciences.

Farrell completed his last novel, *Sam Holman,* just five weeks before his death on August 22, 1979 and it was published posthumously in 1983. *Sam Holman* was a candid look at the world of a left-wing Jewish intellectual in New York City in the 1930s and has been seen by many as vaguely biographical of the New York radicalism of that time.

Farrell's literary career suffered somewhat of a stagnation in the 1940s, 50s, and 60s after reaching its peak in the late 30s. Never distressed, Farrell stuck to his individuality, always doing things the way he wanted to. At possibly the lowest point of his literary career in 1961, he said "I began writing in my own way and I shall go on doing it. This is my first and last word on the subject."

Further Reading

The strongest argument for Farrell's endurance as a fiction writer is in Joseph Warren Beach, *American Fiction, 1920-1940* (1941). Other assessments include sections in Alfred Kazin, *On Native Grounds: An Interpretation of Modern American Prose Literature* (1942; abr. 1956); W. M. Frohock, *The Novel of Violence in America, 1920-1950* (1950); and Chester E. Eisinger, *Fiction of the Forties* (1963). Farrell's life, politics, and works are discussed in Alan M. Wald *The New York Intellectuals* (1987); Edgar Marquess Branch *James T. Farrell* (1971); and by Farrell himself in a *New Leader* essay, "Reflections at Fifty" (1954). Farrell is also listed with a brief biography in the A&E Television Networks online biography at www.biography.com (1997). □

fect than Dreiser, Farrell is like Dreiser in his honesty, moral earnestness, and intuitive grasp of social realities.

In his later years Farrell continued to write novels and short stories, but few had the impact of his early work. Nevertheless, Farrell maintained his importance as a man of letters with valuable works of literary and social criticism. *A Note on Literary Criticism* (1936) is an unusual example of enlightened Marxist critical theory, and *The League of Frightened Philistines* (1945) presents a reasonable argument for literary naturalism. Farrell wrote of the founding of Israel in *It Has Come To Pass* (1955).

Farrell maintained his radical beliefs throughout his entire life and took his disdain of materialism and his belief in Communism outside literature. He was an ally of the Socialist Workers Party (SWP), a group advocating Marxism and Trotskyism, throughout the 1940s. From 1941 to 1945 he served as chairman of the Civil Rights Defense Committee which had been formed by the SWP to defend trade unionists and SWP members being prosecuted in Minneapolis, Minnesota under the Smith Act. This act made it unlawful to advocate the overthrow of the U.S. government or to belong to any group advocating such an overthrow.

Stalinism and its defense by many SWP members forced Farrell to break with the group and in 1948 he became an advocate of the Marshall Plan which was rebuilding post-war Europe to the surprise of many of his associates. Farrell became an staunch anti-Stalinists and felt democratic capitalism was the only means to fight it.

Suzanne Farrell

Suzanne Farrell (neé Roberta Sue Ficker; born 1945) was a versatile classical ballerina who performed with Balanchine and the Ballet of the Twentieth Century. During her almost 30-year career she performed 75 roles in 70 ballets.

Roberta Sue Ficker, who later selected the name Suzanne Farrell from a phone book, was born on August 16, 1945. She was the third of three daughters of a lower-middle-class family who lived in Mt. Healthy, a quiet town outside Cincinnati, Ohio. Her parents divorced when Farrell was nine. Her main concern was her mother's happiness, and she claims this experience taught her to be adaptable at an early age.

Farrell always dreamed of being a clown but began to dance when she was eight to overcome being an imaginative and spunky tomboy. She and her sisters frequently invited neighbors to attend carnivals held in their garage or back yard. It was not unusual for Suzanne to have choreographed a dance in which her partners were kitchen chairs. By age 10, she had organized the New York City Ballet Juniors, a group of girls from her dance classes. Her first stage experience, at age 12, was with the Cincinnati Summer Opera where she performed in various ballets.

Succeeding in the Arts

Farrell's mother recognized her daughter's talents and was determined that she succeed in the arts. She studied ballet at the Cincinnati Conservatory of Music after her school day at Ursuline Academy. Her mother supported her interest in performing and in attending concerts. She once wrote an excuse for her to miss school so she could see the New York City Ballet dance in Bloomington, Indiana. After seeing "Symphony in C," Farrell decided she wanted to dance with that company, where she felt she would fit in. The company seemed more alive and energetic than other companies.

One day Diana Adams, a scout from the School of American Ballet in New York, observed Farrell and invited her to audition for entrance to the school. In 1960, at age

15, Farrell was one of 12 students to be awarded a full Ford Foundation scholarship into their preparatory program for professional dancers. Without money or housing, her family moved to New York, a strange city to them, and lived in a one-room apartment. Farrell's mother worked 20-hour shifts as a night nurse to support them.

As a "small fish in a big pond," Farrell realized that only she was in charge of her life. The program's major goal was to develop the technical strength and the unique creativity of each student. George Balanchine, head of the school, stressed that what they did with the technique was important. Having it was not enough. Within a year, Farrell joined the company while attending high school at Rhodes. She made her corps de ballet debut in Todd Bolender's "Creation of the World" and George Balanchine's "Stars and Stripes." At 19, she was the youngest principal dancer to dance a solo while in the corps. She was the Dark Angel in "Serenade." Two years later she performed in the world premiere of "Jewels," a signature work.

Balanchine

One cannot talk about Suzanne Farrell without discussing her relationship with Balanchine. Very early, he began to give her opportunities to learn ballets and parts, sometimes superseding more veteran dancers. He collaborated with her on choreography by pushing her to take risks and allowing her to express herself through the choreography. Until she left four years after becoming a star, she was central to him and he to her. Often referred to as his "muse," she attributed this to her strong belief in him and what he was doing. He trained and perhaps molded her as he wanted. Farrell embodied his ideal and this became the norm for the company. Long-legged, gorgeous, and extraordinarily musical, she became known for her backbends, high extensions, and versatility.

Balanchine had not separated his art from life in the past and Farrell, who was immature, was very focused on her dancing. Pleasing him on stage was all she thought about, and in fact she said later that it was like the child for whom time and distance do not shake the ties he has with his parents. She described him as a feminist celebrating the independence of women while he had them on a pedestal. Some say some of his choreography, such as "Don Quixote" and "Meditation," were autobiographical, reflecting the blending of their private and professional lives. Farrell was referred to as the "5th Mrs. B" since Balanchine had previously married four of his ballerinas. They never married but other company members resented their relationship and some resigned from the company. Farrell became isolated. Despite this friction, she danced with and appreciated the uniqueness of each of her many outstanding partners, claiming that each brought out something different in her dancing. They included Balanchine, Jacques d'Amboise, Peter Martins, Edward Villela, and Jean-Pierre Bonnefeux. She performed in numerous premiers, including "Tzigane," "Caconne," "Union Jack," and "Vienna Waltzes," as well as in "Meditation," "Mozartiana," "Don Quixote," "Four Temperaments," and "Apollo," to mention only a few which are considered to be some of the most dazzling ballets of this century.

Self-imposed Exile

In 1969 her marriage to Paul Mejia, a young company dancer from Peru, created some confusion for her and affected his career. (They divorced in the mid-1990s.) He felt Balanchine was not casting him appropriately and finally, in mid-season in May of that year, they left the company with their three cats, Top, Bottom, and Middle. Maurice Bejart had seen Farrell perform the first full length "Swan Lake" with the National Ballet of Canada and sent her a telegram inviting her to join his company. They joined his Brussels-based Ballet of the Twentieth Century the following year. They both enjoyed touring and the experience of working with a style and approach which in its theatrically and reputation for being avant-garde was a dramatic departure from Balanchine's classicism. Even though Farrell performed in over 30 ballets which were composed or revived for her, she referred to this time as "exile."

A series of knee and hip injuries which had begun 20 years before developed into severe and increasingly limiting arthritis. By the 1970s doctors predicted that Farrell would never again dance. After a hip replacement and the emotional, psychological, and physical struggle involved in a prolonged hospitalization and rigorous program of physical therapy, she did in fact return to perform on pointe.

Reconciliation and Return to New York

After seeing the New York City Ballet perform again in 1974, she asked to return and did so in 1975. She also reconciled with Balanchine, and from it came the late masterworks created for Farrell: "Chaconne," "Davidsbundlertanze" and "Mozartiana." Farrell demonstrated her versatility by dancing leads in ballets choreographed by Jerome Robbins, Jacques d'Amboise, and Stanley Williams and to choreographically innovative ballets with a variety of scores, such as serial music of Stravinsky and "chance" music of Xanakis.

Balanchine died in 1983 and Farrel gave her last performance six years later, at the age of 44, on November 26, 1989, in a performance of "Vienna Waltzes" and "Sophisticated Lady." Farrell made her last bow to "Mr. B" in the presence of Lincoln Kirstein and Peter Martin. She commented that it was easy to get there but difficult to stay there or to hold on to the air. She now restages Balanchine ballets all over the world. Their famously unconsummated relationship lives on in an Oscar-nominated *Suzanne Farrell: Elusive Muse*—a relationship so consuming, that she says she considered suicide.

According to Arlene Croce, she was thought of as "the supreme classicist of our time." She had a reputation for versatility, having performed 75 roles in 70 ballets, starred in three feature-length ballet films, and performed in the Dance in America series and nationally telecast concert at the Kennedy Center in honor of Balanchine. In 1965 she was the recipient of the Merit Award of *Mademoiselle* magazine and the Award of Merit in Creative and Performing Arts at the University of Cincinnati. In 1979 Farrell received New York City's Award of Honor for Arts and Culture for a record of distinguished achievement in the world of dance, and in 1980 Brandeis University's Creative Arts Award.

Further Reading

Holding On To The Air (1954) by Suzanne Farrell with Toni Bentley is the only book about her. Objectivity is a problem, particularly where Balanchine is involved. A sense of overwhelming debt to him pervades the book and may cloud her account. □

Brian Faulkner

Brian Faulkner (1921-1977) was the last prime minister (1971-1972) of Northern Ireland under Great Britain's experiment in devolution that began in 1921.

Arthur Brian Deane Faulkner was unusual in being from a strictly business rather than a landed background. Born on February 18, 1921, and educated at St. Columba's College, Dublin, he entered the family firm, The Belfast Collar Company, at the age of 18 and simultaneously began farming 120 acres of land for wartime food production. In 1949, at age 28, he entered the Northern Ireland parliament for the East Down constituency, retaining the seat until the end of that parliament's life. Government chief whip from 1956 to 1959, he became minister for home affairs in 1959 and served as minister of commerce from 1963 to 1969, when he resigned from Terence O'Neill's government.

Faulkner returned to office under Chichester-Clark as minister of development, 1969-1971, before becoming prime minister (with home affairs), 1971-1972. Subsequently he served as chief executive of the short-lived coalition experiment in power-sharing from January to May 1974 and was leader of the Unionist Party of Northern Ireland from 1974 to 1976. In 1977 he was raised to the peerage as Lord Faulkner of Downpatrick, taking his seat on February 22. He was killed in a hunting accident shortly afterwards on March 3, 1977.

The Road to Prime Minister

A Presbyterian, teetotaller, country-lover, and hunting enthusiast, Faulkner was also a family man (he married Lucy Forsythe in 1951 and they had three children) and a determined politician who never lost touch with his business background. Ambitious from the start of his political career (he had already joined the Orange Order in 1946), he was prepared to take an uncompromising traditional line in defense of the Union and to play a prominent role in asserting the rights of the Protestant settler community as he saw them. He thus early carried a hardline reputation, but he also showed a concern for modern economic issues and saw himself apart from the usual landed figures of the Unionist leadership. By careful attention to detail and hard

work he rose to prominence, severing his connection with the family firm and becoming a full time politician on his appointment to ministerial office in 1959. Conservative and cautious, he upheld tough law and order policies at Home Affairs, favoring capital punishment and resisting franchise reform.

As minister of commerce under O'Neill, 1963-1969, he did much to extend the positive side of his image, bringing badly needed jobs to the province, building up a modern industrial base, and developing economic planning. He had not easily accepted O'Neill's premiership, however, and at successive crises in these years was accused of giving O'Neill less than wholehearted support. The tension between the two men, compounded by contrasts in style and background and political instinct, eventually brought Faulkner's resignation on January 24, 1969. When O'Neill resigned in April 1969, Faulkner contested the succession. He lost by one vote to James Chichester-Clark but then supported him loyally until Chichester-Clark in turn resigned in March 1971. This time Faulkner easily won the premiership by 26 votes to four. It can be argued, however, that his opportunity had come too late in the history of the troubled province.

A Troubled Government

Faulkner—hardman of the Union, Orangeman, and bigot to some; fair and flexible political pragmatist to others—continued to show both sides of his character as prime minister. His first moves showed more imagination and his first months more action and experimentation than

had been witnessed in the previous 50 years. In March he set out his intention to serve all the people of Northern Ireland and to open participation in decision-making to the elected representatives of the Catholic minority: he also appointed Labour politician David Bleakley to a new Ministry of Community Relations (later in the year he added G. B. Newe, a Roman Catholic, to his cabinet, another startling break with tradition). In June, Faulkner outlined many practical and radical steps to bring confidence and cooperation to the divided province, including the offer of parliamentary committee chairmanships to the Opposition. He had already legislated against discrimination in employment, and he now admitted past mistakes and looked to the future harnessing of Protestant and Catholic alike to the cause of the Union.

Alas, street violence and community suspicions soured feelings, led the opposition to withdraw from Parliament, and in the end led Faulkner himself to gamble on the introduction, in August 1971, of internment of suspected subversives without trial. This one move, accompanied though it was by an account of all the positive political reforms and an outline of a brave new economic program, outraged his opponents. Its unfair application undid much of his positive achievement, drove the communities apart once more, and opened a Pandora's box of civil disobedience. The atmosphere was worsened further on January 30, 1972, by the shooting by the army of 13 people in Derry in the confused circumstances of an illegal demonstration. On March 22 Edward Heath, prime minister of the United Kingdom, insisted on taking over control of all security matters in Northern Ireland. Brian Faulkner and his cabinet refused to carry on under such conditions, and the Westminster government then assumed direct responsibility once more for Northern Ireland. Fifty-one years of local, devolved autonomy came to a close on March 30, 1972.

This did not bring to an end Brian Faulkner's political career nor to his attempts to find a form of provincial authority acceptable to all moderate shades of opinion. William Craig and the Reverend Ian Paisley from the Unionist right jockeyed to oust him, while the IRA (Irish Republican Army) sought by physical force to impose republican Irish unity from the nationalist left. Only the partnership of moderate men seemed capable of winning respite and permitting economic, political, and social progress. At a conference in Darlington in September 1972 and throughout 1973 Brian Faulkner worked to this end. Through an elected assembly which met in July 1973 agreement was reached in November between Unionists, the Social Democratic and Labour Party, and the Alliance Party to form a power-sharing executive. This came into being under Faulkner's leadership in January 1974, but only after a preparatory conference at Sunningdale in December 1973 had worked out details, including the creation of a Council of Ireland to give a role to the Dublin government. This alarmed Unionist grass-root opinion. Unfortunately for this hopeful experiment, the British government called a snap general election in February, which allowed early electoral expression of this alarm, and subsequent weak handling of an anti-power-sharing strike by loyalists brought down the executive in May. Faulkner's promising final bid had not had sufficient time to win credibility. Direct rule from London was resumed.

There seems little doubt that Brian Faulkner was the most pragmatic and imaginative of the holders of the office of prime minister of Northern Ireland. Perhaps ambitious for office and traditional in outlook early on, he learned from experience that the Union could best be served by harnessing all interests to it and ending the exclusive domination of one section only. His plans, the reforms he helped to introduce, and the institutions he suggested did give an opportunity for equality of opportunity and benefit for all. Traditional animosities and community hatreds exacerbated by para-military violence and by sectarian extremism could not easily be overcome. Thus, like his two immediate predecessors, Faulkner proved unable to survive long enough to see reason prevail over emotion. Described as "the Prime Minister who came too late," Faulkner gave a frank statement to his autobiography which perhaps fairly sums up his philosophy: "You can do three things in Irish politics, the right thing, the wrong thing, or nothing at all. I have always thought it better to do the wrong thing than to do nothing at all."

Further Reading

Brian Faulkner, *Memoirs of a Statesman* (1978), largely completed at the time of his death and published posthumously, gives the most valuable insights. *Faulkner: Conflict and Consent in Irish Politics* (1974), by David Bleakley (a Labour opponent who served in his cabinet), gives a largely favorable view of a man whose career was always controversial, while *Brian Faulkner and the Crisis of Ulster Unionism* by Andrew Boyd (1972) is unremittingly harsh and critical. There is much background information as well as a short profile in W. D. Flackes' *Northern Ireland: A Political Directory, 1968-83* (1983). □

William Faulkner

William Faulkner (1897-1962), a major American 20th-century novelist, chronicled the decline and decay of the aristocratic South with an imaginative power and psychological depth that transcend mere regionalism.

William Faulkner was born on Sept. 25, 1897, in New Albany, Miss. He grew up in Oxford, Miss., which appears in his fiction as "Jefferson" in "Yoknapatawpha County." William was the oldest of four brothers. Both parents came from wealthy families reduced to genteel poverty by the Civil War. A great-grandfather, Col. William Falkner (as the family spelled its name), had authored *The White Rose of Memphis,* a popular success of the 1880s. William's father owned a hardware store and livery stable in Oxford and later became business manager of the state university. William attended public school only fitfully after the fifth grade; he never graduated from high school.

In 1918, after the U.S. Army rejected him for being underweight and too short (5 feet 5 inches), Faulkner enlisted in the Canadian Air Force. During his brief service in World War I, he suffered a leg injury in a plane accident. In 1918 he was demobilized and made an honorary second lieutenant.

In 1919 Faulkner enrolled at the University of Mississippi as a special student but left the next year for New York City. After several odd jobs in New York and Mississippi, he became postmaster at the Mississippi University Station; he was fired in 1924. In 1925 he and a friend made a walking tour of Europe, returning home in 1926.

During the years 1926-1930 Faulkner published a series of distinguished novels, none commercially successful. But in 1931 the success of *Sanctuary,* written expressly to make money, freed him of financial worries. He went to Hollywood for a year as a scenarist and an adviser.

It was not until after World War II that Faulkner received critical acclaim. French critics recognized his power first; André Malraux wrote an appreciative preface to *Sanctuary,* and Jean Paul Sartre wrote a long critical essay on Faulkner. The turning point for Faulkner's reputation came in 1946, when Malcolm Cowley published the influential *The Portable Faulkner* (at this time all of Faulkner's books were out of print!).

The groundswell of praise for Faulkner's work culminated in a 1950 Nobel Prize for literature. His 1955 lecture tour of Japan is recorded in *Faulkner at Nagano* (1956). In 1957-1958 he was writer-in-residence at the University of

Virginia; his dialogues with students make up *Faulkner in the University* (1959). *William Faulkner: Essays, Speeches and Public Letters* (1965) and *The Faulkner-Cowley File* (1966) offer further insights into the man.

Faulkner had married Estelle Oldham in 1929, and they lived together in Oxford until his death on July 6, 1962. He was a quiet, dapper, courteous man, mustachioed and sharp-eyed. He steadfastly refused the role of celebrity: he permitted no prying into his private life and rarely granted interviews.

Poetry and Short Stories

During the early 1920s Faulkner wrote poetry and fiction. In the volume of verse *The Marble Faun* (1922), a printer's error allegedly introduced the "u" into the author's name, which he decided to retain. The money for another book of poems, *The Green Bough* (1933), was supplied by a lawyer friend, Philip Stone, on whom the lawyer in Faulkner's later fiction is modeled. Faulkner's poetry shows the poet's taste for language but lacks stylistic discipline.

Faulkner is considered a fine practitioner of the short-story form, and some of his stories, such as "A Rose for Emily," are widely anthologized. His collections—*These Thirteen* (1931), *Doctor Martino and Other Stories* (1934), *Go Down, Moses and Other Stories* (1942), and *Knight's Gambit* (1949)—deal with themes similar to those in his novels and include many of the same characters.

Early Novels

Soldiers' Pay (1926) and *Mosquitoes* (1927) precede *Sartoris* (1927), Faulkner's first important work, in which he begins his Yoknapatawpha saga. This saga, Faulkner's imaginative recreation of the tragedy of the American South, is a Balzacian provincial cycle in which each novel interrelates, clarifies, and redefines the characters. The central figure is Bayard Sartoris, returned from the war, who drives and drinks violently to compensate for his sense of alienation. He seems determined to find some extraordinary form of self-destruction. He becomes an experimental aviator and dies in a crash, leaving his pregnant wife to sustain the family name. The novel introduces families that reappear in many of Faulkner's novels and stories: the Sartoris and Compson families, representing the agrarian, aristocratic Old South; and the Snopes clan, representing the ruthless, mercantile New South.

"The Sound and the Fury"

The book generally regarded as Faulkner's masterpiece, *The Sound and the Fury* (1929), is a radical departure from conventional novelistic form. It uses a stream-of-consciousness method, rendering a different type of mentality in each of its four sections. The title, taken from Macbeth's utterance of cosmic despair in Shakespeare's play, is a clue to the profound pessimism of the novel, which records the decay and degeneracy of the Compson family and, by implication, of the aristocratic South. It is difficult to read, and Faulkner's "Appendix," written much later at the publisher's request, hardly clarifies it.

Each section takes place in a single day; three sections are set in 1928 and one in 1910. The difficulties begin with the fact that the 1910 section is placed second in the book, and the other three are not sequential in their 1928 three-day span. Further, the opening section is rendered in the stream of consciousness of an idiot, who cannot distinguish past from present.

Unquestionably the most difficult for Faulkner to write, the Benjy section (of April 7, 1928) is also the most difficult to read. It has been likened to a prose poem, with the succeeding three sections being simply variations on its theme of futility. Because the mentally impaired Benjy lives in a state of timelessness, his report is purely sensuous, and the reader must figure out his own chronology. Faulkner gives two aids: the device of signaling time shifts by alternating the typeface between bold and italic, and the variance of the African American attending Benjy (Roskus and Dilsey ca. 1898; Versh, T.P., and Frony ca. 1910; Luster ca. 1928).

Out of Benjy's garbled report come a number of facts and motifs. He is 33 years old, in the constant care of an African American youth named Luster. Benjy is tormented by the absence of his sister, Candace, though she has been out of the household for 18 years; each time he hears golfers on the neighboring course call "Caddy!" (coincidentally her nickname), he is painfully reminded of her. The golf course, formerly part of the Compson estate, was sold so that Benjy's older brother, Quentin, could attend Harvard, where he committed suicide in 1910. Mrs. Compson is a self-pitying woman; Mr. Compson was a drunkard; Uncle Maury was a womanizer; Candace was sexually promiscuous and, in turn, her daughter, confusingly called Quentin (after her dead uncle), is also promiscuous. Benjy has been castrated at his brother Jason's order.

Ironically, the most sensitive and intelligent Compson, Quentin (whose day in the novel is June 1, 1910), shares Benjy's obsession about their sister. Candace and the past dominate Quentin's section, which is set in Boston on the day he commits suicide. His musings add more facts in the novel's mosaic. The head of the family, Mr. Compson, is wise but cynical and despairing. Quentin has falsely confessed incest with Candace to his father; the father has not believed him. Quentin had fought one of Candace's lovers over her "honor." He is oppressed by knowing that the pregnant Candace is to be married off to a northern banker; the impending marriage is symbolic to Quentin of his irremediable and intolerable severance from Candace and is the reason for his suicidal state. Quentin's ludicrously methodical preparations for his suicide culminate when the last thing he does before leaving to kill himself is brush his teeth.

Jason (his day in the novel is April 6, 1928) is one of the great comic villains of literature. He has an irrational, jealous loathing of Candace. Now head of the family, he complains bitterly of his responsibilities as guardian of Candace's daughter, Quentin, while systematically stealing the money Candace sends for her care. Jason is cast in the Snopes mold—materialistic, greedy, and cunning. What makes him humorous is his self-pity. He sees himself as victim—of Candace, who he feels has cost him a desired job; of his niece, whose promiscuity seems a personal affront; of Benjy, whose condition causes embarrassment; of Mrs. Compson, whom he constantly bullies and whose inefficiency has burdened him; of the Jews, whom he blames for his stock market losses; of the servants, whose employment necessitates his own work at a menial job. Jason's lack of soul is evident in all his habits. He leaves no mark on anything and lives totally in the present—the perfect Philistine of the New South.

The novel's final section, the only one told in the third person, gives the point of view of the sensible old black servant, Dilsey (her day is April 8, 1928). As with other Faulkner African Americans, her presence is chiefly functional: her good sense and solidity point up the decadence of the whites. In this section Jason meets with an ironic, overwhelming defeat. The novel's chief social implication is that the South is doomed.

Novels of the 1930s

As I Lay Dying (1930) is a farcical burlesque epic, again using the multiple stream-of-consciousness method to tell the grotesque, humorous story of a family of poor whites intent on fulfilling the mother's deathbed request for burial. *Sanctuary* (1931), taken seriously by most critics, was discounted by Faulkner as a "potboiler." It is the lurid tale of Popeye, a sexually mutilated bootlegger, who has degenerate sexual acts performed for his gratification. One of his victims is a college girl whose lie in Popeye's behalf at the trial of another bootlegger results in the latter's conviction of Popeye's crime. In an ironic ending, Popeye is hanged for a crime of which he is innocent.

The story in *Light in August* (1932) takes place in a single day. It is overly complicated by a subplot. Beginning with a pregnant girl searching for her lover, this plot is subordinated to the story of Joe Christmas (same initials as Jesus Christ), whose uncertain racial identity perplexes him. Though structurally unsound, *Light in August* generates enormous power and probably ranks second among Faulkner's books.

Late Novels

Faulkner's creativity ebbed after 1935. Though occasionally interesting and fitfully brilliant, his work tended to be increasingly repetitive, perverse, and mannered to the point of self-parody.

Pylon (1935), one of Faulkner's weakest novels, is the story of a flying circus team. *Absalom, Absalom!* (1936) is an extremely complex novel; the title comes from the biblical cry of David ("My son, my son!"). This novel tells of a poor white from the Virginia hills who marries an aristocractic Mississippi woman, inadvertently launching a three-generation family cycle of violence, degeneracy, and mental retardation.

Two minor novels, *The Unvanquished* (1938) and *The Wild Palms* (1939), were followed by an uneven but intriguing satire of the Snopes clan, *The Hamlet* (1940). Of this novel's four parts, the first and the last manifest Faulkner's greatest faults: they are talky and oblique and seem out of

focus. The middle sections, however, are Faulkner at his best.

Intruder in the Dust (1948) takes a liberal view of southern race relations. Lucas Beauchamp, an eccentric old African American, is saved from a false murder charge through the efforts of fair-minded whites. *A Fable* (1954) is a very poor parable of Christ and Judas. *The Town* (1957), *The Mansion* (1959), and *The Reivers* (1962), a trilogy that is part of the Yoknapatawpha saga, are generally regarded as minor works.

Further Reading

Faulkner's thoughts on literature and many other subjects can be found in James B. Meriwether and Michael Millgate, eds., *Lion in the Garden: Interviews with William Faulkner, 1926-1962* (1968). Faulkner is discussed in several memoirs: John Faulkner, *My Brother Bill: An Affectionate Reminiscence* (1963), and Murry C. Falkner, *The Falkners of Mississippi: A Memoir* (1967). A biography of Faulkner is in the introduction of Edmond L. Volpe, *A Reader's Guide to William Faulkner* (1964).

Some of the best critical work on Faulkner is in Frederick J. Hoffman and Olga W. Vickery, eds., *William Faulkner: Three Decades of Criticism* (1960). Although Joseph Blotner's biography, in progress, should be the definitive work, useful studies of Faulkner's life and work include Irving Malin, *William Faulkner: An Interpretation* (1957); William Van O'Connor, *William Faulkner* (1959); Hyatt Howe Waggoner, *William Faulkner: From Jefferson to the World* (1959); Michael Millgate, *The Achievement of William Faulkner* (1966); and H. Edward Richardson, *William Faulkner: Journey to Self-Discovery* (1969). See also Robert Penn Warren, ed., *Faulkner: A Collection of Critical Essays* (1966), and Richard P. Adams, *Faulkner: Myth and Motion* (1968). □

Gabriel Urbain Fauré

The French composer Gabriel Urbain Fauré (1845-1924) is best known for his songs and his typically French exquisiteness of taste.

Gabriel Fauré was born on May 12, 1845, in the provincial town of Pamiers, where his father was superintendent of schools. When Gabriel was 9, he was sent to Paris to attend the École Niedermeyer, a school for the education of church musicians, where he had won a scholarship. Fauré received a thorough grounding in organ playing and theory and became acquainted with Gregorian chant, whose modal melodies influenced his later compositions. Camille Saint-Saëns, a teacher at the school, exerted a strong influence on the young provincial.

When Fauré graduated in 1865, he accepted a position as organist in Rennes, but within a year he returned to Paris. He served as assistant organist at St-Sulpice and later at the Madeleine, Paris's most fashionable church, eventually becoming principal organist. He was professor of composition at the Paris Conservatory from 1896 until 1905 and director until 1920, when his growing deafness forced him to resign.

Fauré was not a prolific composer, and with few exceptions he avoided the larger dramatic forms of opera and symphony. His compositions fall into three periods stylistically. Most of his songs were written during the first period, which ended in 1886. Their beautiful melodies and flowing accompaniments make the songs small masterpieces of the genre. Many of the piano pieces belong to this period. These nocturnes, barcarolles, and impromptus do not show off the performer's technique, but their subtle melodies, arpeggio accompaniments, and surprising harmonic progressions give them a special charm. Other early works are the Sonata No. 1 for violin and piano (1876) and the two Piano Quartets (1879 and 1886), which have an immediate charm and soaring lyricism.

Important works of Fauré's second period, which lasted until 1908, are the song cycle *La Bonne chanson* (1892), settings of Paul Verlaine's poems, and the *Requiem* (1887). In contrast with the dramatic Requiems of most of his predecessors and contemporaries, Fauré's is calm and resigned, a profound and moving meditation.

Works of the third period include two song cycles, *La Chanson d'Eve* (1910) and *Le Jardin clos* (1917); an austere opera, *Penelope* (1913); Sonata No. 2 for violin and piano (1917); Piano Quintet No. 2 (1921); and a Piano Trio (1924). These compositions, the works of a man in his 70s, are remarkable for their original harmonic progressions, serenity, and clarity. Fauré died in Paris on Nov. 4, 1924.

Further Reading

Norman Suckling, *Fauré* (1946; rev. ed. 1951), is the best study of the composer's life and works. Martin Cooper, *French Music from the Death of Berlioz to the Death of Fauré* (1951), discusses distinguishing stylistic characteristics of major French composers of that period. See also Rey M. Longyear, *Nineteenth-Century Romanticism in Music* (1969).

Additional Sources

Fauré, Gabriel, *Gabriel Fauré: a life in letters,* London: Batsford, 1989.
Gabriel Faurâe, 1845-1924, New York: AMS Press, 1976.
Orledge, Robert, *Gabriel Fauré,* London: Eulenburg Books, 1979.
Suckling, Norman, *Fauré,* Westport, Conn.: Hyperion Press, 1979.
Vuillermoz, Émile, *Gabriel Fauré,* New York: Da Capo Press, 1983. □

Millicent Garrett Fawcett

Millicent Garrett Fawcett (1847–1929) was a British feminist, who led the nonviolent campaign for votes for women.

At the turn of the century, Millicent Garrett Fawcett was Britain's most important leader in the fight for women's suffrage. Although people today often identify the militant Emmeline Pankhurst and her daughters with the struggle, Fawcett contributed more than anyone

else to British women obtaining the right to vote in parliamentary elections. Valuing rational thought and her own privacy, she rejected the cult of personality that surrounded more dramatic and emotional leaders.

Changing times make Fawcett appear old-fashioned, an unchanging adherent of the ideology of individual rights popular in the mid-19th century who was surprisingly conventional in many of her opinions. She seems frozen in the late 1860s, opposing free schools as undermining a healthy spirit of independence, defending the severe sexual code that prevailed among the middle classes during her youth, and glorying in an unthinking patriotism. The modern feminist Ann Oakley described Fawcett's life as "marked by monotony and by great tranquility of spirit, and by no detectable change or development in her moral philosophy or political attitudes." Significantly, nobody has bothered to write a full-length biography of this unrevolutionary suffragist since 1931 when a friend did the rather bland, official life. As a result, Fawcett is a half-forgotten giant of British reform.

Millicent Garrett was born at Aldeburgh, Suffolk, in England, on June 11, 1847, one of the younger children in a large, middle-class family. She had a close relationship with her admiring and independent-minded father, but she rejected her mother's rigidly evangelical religion. Although Milly, as she was known to family and friends, obtained very little formal schooling, she benefited from a supportive family that expected much of her. Her older sister Elizabeth (Garrett Anderson) set an example by becoming Britain's second woman physician.

In 1867, the 19-year-old Millicent Garrett married Henry Fawcett (who had previously proposed to her sister Elizabeth and to the prominent feminist, Bessie Rayner Parkes). Already committed before her marriage to liberal principles in politics and economics, Millicent Garrett Fawcett fully shared the interests and convictions of her husband and served for several years as his secretary. A Liberal Party member of the House of Commons, he had been blinded in a shooting accident ten years earlier. As she read what he had to read and wrote what he had to write, she acquired a political education, along with one in economics, the subject which he taught at Cambridge University. She also learned from her husband's friends, including John Stuart Mill, the most influential liberal thinker in mid-Victorian Britain.

As a young woman, Fawcett pursued many interests. Along with a novel, she wrote two books on economics, one in collaboration with her husband; worked to promote higher education for women, particularly Newnham College at Cambridge where her daughter eventually studied; and, most important, enlisted in the campaign to provide women with the vote, in her opinion the key to equality between the sexes. She also joined the first organization advocating votes for women, the London Women's Suffrage Committee.

After her husband's sudden death in 1884, leaving her a widow at age 37, she made the cause of women's suffrage her life's work. Following the death of the longtime suffrage leader Lydia Becker in 1890, Fawcett emerged as the most influential figure in Britain's small band of suffragists. When the organizations united in 1897 as the National Union of Women's Suffrage Societies, she became the first president (and served until her retirement in 1919).

Although most suffragist women supported the Liberal Party, Fawcett broke with the Liberals in 1886 out of opposition to Irish Home Rule, a proposal that Ireland enjoy political autonomy but not independence. She was active in the new breakaway Liberal Unionist Party that cooperated closely with the Conservative Party, but she never put political party over her principles. For instance, in the mid-1890s, she offended many important men in the Conservative-Liberal Unionist alliance when she tried to hound out of politics a Conservative who had seduced a young woman and then failed to marry her. In 1901, her prominence in Liberal Unionist affairs earned her an appointment to head an investigation of conditions at interment camps for Boer civilians during the South African war. Some old friends accused her of collaborating with brutal imperialism. In 1903, she broke with the Liberal Unionist party because she could not support its leader Joseph Chamberlain in his new policy of tariff reform. Fawcett remained loyal to the mid-19th-century principles of free trade and laissez-faire.

The problems confronting the suffragists were complex. Although some women could vote in local government elections (and hold office), none could vote for members of the national legislature. Influential newspapers scoffed at the notion of women voting in parliamentary elections (which might deal with questions leading to war) and feared the political role of women (i.e., making possible moral reform legislation to restrict the sale of alcoholic drink). A majority of the House of Commons, particularly Liberal Party members, probably sympathized with women's suffrage in principle, but this did not mean voting for a bill that would enfranchise women. Part of the problem was the personal opposition of turn-of-the-century Liberal leaders William Gladstone and Herbert Asquith. Another part of the problem was the absence of universal male suffrage. If the vote went only to those women who met the existing requirements for men, the change would likely benefit the Conservative Party by enfranchising prosperous widows but not married women. Moreover, some politicians tried to entangle the enfranchisement of any women with the more controversial reform of universal male suffrage. Finally, women's suffrage never became the central question for ordinary voters and politicians in the way that, for instance, Irish Home Rule did.

Fawcett struggled to keep her cause alive when prospects for success seemed remote. Known for her sense of humor, she never allowed herself to be discouraged: she was an inexhaustible worker who without the aid of a secretary answered all her correspondence on the day it was received. Though she detested speechmaking, she became an effective public speaker whose unemotional speeches were distinguished by the clarity of her logic. Self-reliant, she ordinarily traveled on foot to her interviews with politicians even when that meant walking for miles and, a bit old-fashioned, she refused to have a telephone in her home.

But in the early 20th century, women's suffrage could not be ignored. Beginning in 1905, the organization headed by Emmeline Pankhurst and her daughters Christabel and Sylvia adopted militant tactics: they disrupted political meetings, destroyed private and public property and, when arrested, resisted with hunger strikes. Although Fawcett and her much larger National Union rejected such tactics, the constitutional suffragists benefited from the attention that the militants provoked.

Probably some form of women's suffrage would have been enacted, sooner or later, even without the First World War, but the war of 1914-18 promoted women's suffrage in many ways. The contribution of women to the war effort converted some former antisuffragists and allowed others a pretext for a change of position that political expediency had forced. The desire to enfranchise voteless soldiers forced politicians to deal with a general enlargement of the suffrage. Prime Minister Asquith, an old enemy of women's suffrage, was replaced by the more sympathetic David Lloyd George. On the other hand, the war presented a brief but severe challenge to Fawcett's leadership of the National Union in 1915. She wanted to use the suffragist organization to work for military victory. In contrast, pacifist-minded officers wanted to negotiate a peace without insisting on the defeat of Germany.

Fawcett supported the compromise in 1918 that enfranchised women age 30 and older and men age 21 and older. Having succeeded in obtaining women's suffrage, she retired as president of the National Union at the beginning of 1919. Remaining active in the promotion of the status of women, she was gratified by the legislation in 1928 that gave women voting rights equal to those of men. Ironically, by this time she had resigned her membership in the National Union to protest her successor's advocacy of family allowances, subsidies paid to mothers for the upbringing of children. Fawcett also continued writing books, including one about Palestine where she had traveled with a sister. Although her religious principles remained essentially agnostic, she often attended Church of England services in her last years. In 1924, she was honored with the Grand Cross of the Order of the British Empire and became Dame Millicent Fawcett, a woman's title equivalent to a man's knighthood. Two years later, activists in the women's movement established the Fawcett Library, a collection of the materials for women's history that acquired most of her papers. (It is now located at the City of London Polytechnic.) She died at her London home on August 5, 1929.

Her only child, Philippa Garrett Fawcett (1868-1948), was a brilliant mathematics student at Newnham College, Cambridge. In 1890, refuting the notion of women's intellectual inferiority at a time when Cambridge University let women take the exams but would not award them degrees, she earned higher grades in the mathematics examination than the ablest male student. She served as principal assistant to the director of education, London County Council, from 1904 until her retirement in 1934.

Further Reading

Banks, Oliver. *The Biographical Dictionary of British Feminists, 1880-1930.* Vol 1. New York University Press, 1985.

Fawcett, Millicent Garrett. *What I Remember.* T. Fisher Unwin, 1924.

Oakley, Ann. "Millicent Garrett Fawcett: Duty and Determination (1847-1929)," in Dale Spender, ed., *Feminist Theorists*, Pantheon Books, 1983.

Strachey, Ray (Rachel). *Millicent Garrett Fawcett.* John Murray, 1931.

Caine, Barbara. *Victorian Feminists.* Oxford University Press, 1992.

Dodd, Kathryn. "Cultural Politics and Women's Historical Writings: The Case of Ray Strachey's *The Cause,*" in *Women's Studies International Forum.* Vol. 13 (1990): 127-137.

Harrison, Brian. *Separate Spheres: the Opposition to Woman Suffrage in Britain.* Croom Helm, 1978.

Hume, Leslie Parker. *The National Union of Women's Suffrage Societies, 1897-1914.* Garland, 1982.

Kent, Susan Kingsley. *Sex and Suffrage in Britain, 1860-1914.* Princeton University Press, 1987.

Liddington, Jill, and Jill Norris. *One Hand Tied Behind Us: The Rise of the Women's Suffrage Movement.* Virago, 1978.

Mantin, Jo. *Elizabeth Garrett Anderson.* Dutton, 1965.

Pugh, Martin. *Women's Suffrage in Britain, 1867-1928.* Historical Association, 1980.

Rubinstein, David. "Victorian Feminists: Henry and Millicent Garrett Fawcett," in Lawrence Goldman, ed., *The Blind Victorian: Henry Fawcett and British Liberalism.* Cambridge University Press, 1989.

Strachey, Ray (Rachel). *The Cause: A Short History of the Women's Movement in Great Britain.* G. Bell, 1928. □

Safi Faye

Safi Faye (born 1943), the Senegalese filmmaker and ethnologist who made her home in Paris, was the best-known woman filmmaker in sub-Saharan Africa.

Safi Faye was born in 1943 in Fad Jal, Senegal, a village south of Dakar, where she made the ethnographic films that brought her international acclaim. She was educated in Senegal, where she obtained her teacher's certificate at Rufisque normal school. Faye was teaching in Dakar in 1966 when she met Jean Rouch, the foremost French ethnographic filmmaker and father of *cinema verité*, at FESTAC, the World Black and African Festival of Arts and Cultures. Subsequently she played a role in Rouch's *Petit à Petit* (1969), and with Rouch's encouragement she studied ethnology at the University of Paris, first earning a diploma in 1977 and then a doctorate in 1979 based on research on the religion of the Serer, her own ethnic group. While in Paris she attended the Louis Lumière Film School and in 1979-1980 she studied video production in Berlin.

Ethnographic Filmmaking

Faye's documentary films on Senegal were related to her training as an ethnologist. She was interested in showing the real problems of people's daily lives from their perspective, an advantage she had as a member of the society she filmed. Although she included some fictional events in her documentary films, such as the love story in *Kaddu Beykat,* she did not find this contradictory since the fiction was grounded in reality and was typical of the society.

Faye made her first films in France. *Revanche* (*Revenge;* 1973), made collectively with other students in Paris, is about a madman who wants to climb the Pont Neuf, a bridge in Paris. She acted in her second film, *La Passant* (*The Passerby;* 1972-1975), about an African woman in France, which reflects in part the solitude she felt in Paris at that time. This film has a soundtrack of music and poetry, but no dialogue.

Kaddu Beykat (*Peasant Letter;* 1975), the first ethnographic film Faye made in Senegal, brought her international attention through film awards at FIFEF (Festival International du Film d'Expression Française), FESPACO (Festival Panafricain du Cinéma d'Ouagadougou), and the Berlin Film Festival and through receipt of the Georges Sadoul Prize in France. It remained her most widely reviewed and analyzed film. *Kaddu Beykat,* a feature-length film made in black and white, is about Fad Jal, her natal village in Senegal. It follows the slow pace of Serer life, providing an overview of such topics as agriculture, family structure, domestic life, children's games, social gatherings, the migration of young people, and comparisons between the abundance of the past and the scarcity of the present. To investigate economic problems Faye suggested topics for discussion to which the villagers responded, thus providing a discourse between Faye and the villagers reflecting both their views. A fictional love story provides the "organization" for the ethnographic information.

Fad Jal (1979), a feature-length film, and Goob Na Nu (The Harvest Is In; 1979), both in color, also are about Faye's natal village. While Goob Na Nu focuses on agricultural issues, Fad Jal is about life-cycle rituals, especially those of birth and death, which are part of the village's history. It includes reenactments of the past and shows what has been lost due to labor migration and other changes in post-independence Senegal. Faye's three Senegalese documentaries were made in the Serer language.

Other Films

After 1980 Faye's documentary and feature films were on diverse topics and had diverse sponsorship. For example, the United Nations produced Les ames au soleil (Souls Under the Sun; 1980) about the difficult lives of women and children in rural Senegal, with a focus on health and education, while UNICEF sponsored Selbe et tant d'autres (One and So Many Others; 1982) about the daily life of a Senegalese village woman whose husband has gone to work in town. In contrast, Ambassades nourriciers (Cultural Embassies; 1984), made for French television, is about Chinese, Indian, Hungarian, and other ethnic restaurants in Paris and includes interviews with their owners. Man Sa Yay (I Your Mother; 1980), made for German television, combines fiction and documentary in depicting an African student's adjustment to studying at a polytechnic university in West Berlin. The student expresses many of his feelings in letters to his mother. Faye's later fiction film, Mossane (1991), about a beautiful girl betrothed at birth who is in love with a student her own age, was coproduced by television stations in France, Germany, and Great Britain.

Safi Faye was acknowledged as one of the most accomplished women filmmakers in sub-Saharan Africa. However, because she lived and worked in Europe, far more Europeans have seen her films than have Senegalese and other Africans.

Further Reading

Safi Faye has not yet been the subject of a book. Most interviews with Faye and reviews and analyses of her work have been written in French. The most comprehensive discussion in English of her training and analysis of her work is by Françoise Pfaff in Twenty-five Black African Filmmakers (1988). Brief biographical information and a list of her films appear in Keith Shiri's Directory of African Film-Makers and Films (1992).
Martin, Michael T. Cinemas of the Black Diaspora Detroit: Wayne State University Press, 1995. □

Gustav Theodor Fechner

The German experimental psychologist Gustav Theodor Fechner (1801-1887) founded psychophysics and formulated Fechner's law, a landmark in the emergence of psychology as an experimental science.

Gustav Theodor Fechner was born on April 19, 1801, at Gross-Särchen, Lower Lusatia. He earned his degree in biological science in 1822 at the University of Leipzig and taught there until his death on Nov. 18, 1887. Having developed an interest in mathematics and physics, he was appointed professor of physics in 1834.

About 1839 Fechner had a breakdown, having injured his eyes while experimenting on afterimages by gazing at the sun. His response was to isolate himself from the world for 3 years. During this period there was an increase in his interest in philosophy. Fechner believed that everything is endowed with a soul; nothing is without a material basis; mind and matter are the same essence, but seen from different sides. Moreover, he believed that, by means of psychophysical experiments in psychology, the foregoing assertions were demonstrated and proved. He authored many books and monographs on such diverse subjects as medicine, esthetics, and experimental psychology, affixing the pseudonym Dr. Mises to some of them.

The ultimate philosophic problem which concerned Fechner, and to which his psychophysics was a solution, was the perennial mind-body problem. His solution has been called the identity hypothesis: mind and body are not regarded as a real dualism, but are different sides of one reality. They are separated in the form of sensation and stimulus; that is, what appears from a subjective viewpoint as the mind, appears from an external or objective viewpoint as the body. In the expression of the equation of Fechner's law (sensation intensity = C log stimulus inten-

sity), it becomes evident that the dualism is not real. While this law has been criticized as illogical, and for not having universal applicability, it has been useful in research on hearing and vision.

Fechner's most significant contribution was made in his *Elemente der Psychophysik* (1860), a text of the "exact science of the functional relations, or relations of dependency, between body and mind," and in his *Revision der Hauptpunkte der Psychophysik* (1882). Upon these works mainly rests Fechner's fame as a psychologist, for in them he conceived, developed, and established new methods of mental measurement, and hence the beginning of quantitative experimental psychology. The three methods of measurement were the method of just-noticeable differences, the method of constant stimuli, and the method of average error. According to the authorities, the method of constant stimuli, called also the method of right and wrong cases, has become the most important of the three methods. It was further developed by G. E. Müller and F. M. Urban.

William James, who did not care for quantitative analysis or the statistical approach in psychology, dismisses the psychophysic law as an "idol of the den," the psychological outcome of which is nothing. However, the verdict of other appraisers is kinder, for they honor Fechner as the founder of experimental psychology.

Further Reading

The major biographies of Fechner are in German. An account of him in English, with the original German bibliography, is in G. Stanley Hall, *Founders of Modern Psychology* (1912). For a treatment of Fechner's works and thought see T. Ribot, *German Psychology of Today: The Empirical School* (trans. 1886). For his philosophy see O. Klemm, *History of Psychology* (1911; trans. 1914), and George Sidney Brett, *History of Psychology,* vol. 3 (1921). □

John Gregg Fee

John Gregg Fee (1816-1901) was an unusual American abolitionist, for he carried out his agitation in a border state, where slavery was legal and antiabolitionist feelings ran strong.

John Fee was born in Bracken County, Ky., on Sept. 9, 1816. His father was a land and slave owner of enough means to support Fee's studies at Miami and Augusta colleges. Religiously inclined, Fee entered Lane Theological Seminary in 1842. Like a great many Protestant schools of the time, Lane was full of antislavery feeling, and the moralistic appeal of abolitionism made Fee an ardent enemy of slavery. Kentucky was not dominated by the extreme anti-Northern feeling that characterized the cotton states, and Fee found some local followers. But this was still the South: for his antislavery stand Fee was disinherited by his family, and the two churches to which he ministered were ostra-

cized by other clergymen. Even Northern abolitionists were abused by rowdy crowds during the 1840s, but Fee found himself "shot at, clubbed, stoned."

By 1853 Fee felt obligated to move to Berea, Ky., where he became pastor of Berea Union Church and in 1855 founded the abolitionist school that became Berea College. He drew generous financial support from wealthy Northern sympathizers like Lewis Tappan, and he continued to sponsor abolitionist meetings, but local hostility hardly abated. In 1859, in the wake of John Brown's uprising at Harpers Ferry, Va., it was rumored that Fee had received a box of rifles and intended to launch a slave rebellion in Kentucky. He fled Berea for the North.

Fee was back in Kentucky by 1863, acting as chaplain to a detachment of African American Union soldiers at Camp Nelson. But his exile from Berea ended only after the war, when he resumed his positions as pastor and trustee of Berea College. Fee retired to a relatively quiet life; he died on Jan. 11, 1901.

Not so well known as William Lloyd Garrison or Wendell Phillips, Fee was an indefatigable and indispensable part of the abolitionist movement, which eventually resulted in the emancipation of 3 million slaves. A fanatic by one standard, other ages would have seen him as a steadfast, righteous man of principle who would sacrifice all to his beliefs.

Further Reading

Fee's *Autobiography* (1891), which is difficult to secure and just as difficult to read, is the most comprehensive source for his life. Elisabeth Peck, *Berea's First Century, 1855-1955* (1955), includes some interesting material on Fee's activities. Louis Filler, *The Crusade against Slavery, 1830-1860* (1960), has little on Fee specifically but helps to place him in context.

Additional Sources

Howard, Victor B., *The Evangelical war against slavery and caste: the life and times of John G. Fee,* Selinsgrove, Pa.: Susquehanna University Press, 1996. □

Jules Ralph Feiffer

American artist and writer Jules Ralph Feiffer (born 1929) was best known for his satirical cartoons, but his artistic creations and acclaim also extended to plays, screenplays, and novels.

Jules Feiffer, who was born on January 26, 1929, in Bronx, New York, to David and Rhoda (nee Davis) Feiffer, always had an interest in drawing. By age five he had won a gold medal in a contest sponsored by John Wanamaker's department store in New York for his picture of Tom Mix arresting outlaws. After graduating from high school, Feiffer studied at the Art Students League and Pratt Institute. From 1946 to 1951 he worked as an assistant to legendary cartoonist Will Eisner, creator of the popular comic book "The Spirit." Feiffer so impressed Eisner with his writing ability that he was given responsibility for scripting "The Spirit." During this period Feiffer also created a comic strip of his own called "Clifford," a Sunday cartoon-page feature about the adventures of a little boy and his dog. His budding career was interrupted in 1951 when he was drafted into the Army. Although military service was repugnant to Feiffer, the two-year hitch actually changed the course of his work.

The Satirist

Before the service, Feiffer said his ambition "was no more and no less than to do a daily comic strip and a Sunday page in whatever style I found." His anger at being in the Army and his rage against authority, however, led him to satire and the desire to make pointed social and political comments through his art. Feiffer's first effort in that direction was the creation of "Munro," the story of a four-year-old boy mistakenly drafted into the Army.

After leaving the military, though, Feiffer had difficulty getting started as a satirist. Unable to interest a publisher in his book of cartoons about "Munro," he drifted from one art job to another between periods of unemployment. Then, in 1956, Feiffer took some of his cartoons to the *Village Voice,* the weekly newspaper in New York's Greenwich Village that was just getting started. Although it could not pay, the *Voice* provided Feiffer with a platform and complete freedom to express his thoughts. Feiffer's simple drawings, which combined the commentary of editorial cartoons with the multi-panel structure of comic strips, were an instant success. After two years Feiffer's cartoons from the Voice were compiled into a best-selling book called *Sick, Sick, Sick.* Then *Playboy* magazine put him on a $500-a-week retainer and his career was firmly launched.

Feiffer's cartoons attracted attention and a devoted following because they differed so markedly from the norm. His work looked like comic strips, but instead of gags and preposterous situations, Feiffer offered biting vignettes of contemporary life in an attempt to expose society's ills and do something about them. Feiffer spoke of "writing" his cartoons because he believed in the supremacy of wording over illustration. Indeed, while drawing the cartoons came easily, he sometimes rewrote his captions fifteen times.

Characters and Themes

The characters in Feiffer's sharp pen drawings, which included introspective adults, precocious children, nonconformists, politicians, and army generals, experienced and explained emotional anxiety and political upheaval. Feiffer was once described as being "at war with complacency, with the cliche mongers who provide society with meaningless slogans to live by, with the pomposity of officialdom, and with the carefully cultivated dullness of our carefully protected daily lives." Summarizing his own work, Feiffer said that it dealt "with going up against authority and conventional wisdom, and how people use language *not* to communicate, and the use of power in relationships." Feiffer used his signature character, the dancer in the black leotard, to offer a ray of optimism. He said of her: "Whatever the problems and disasters, and however often hope is dashed, she rises up and dances again. She'll never be defeated by the realities."

Beginning in the 1960s, Feiffer, an outspoken liberal, increasingly concentrated on political themes such as race relations, Vietnam, and the presidency. Of the latter he said, "I really go after the presidents and seem to have a good time slapping them around." Explaining why Reagan was a special target, he said, "I rage at his smugness, ignorance and ideological blindness." Feiffer's rage at presidents and the problems he saw in America, even after nearly four decades of cartooning, never moderated. "When I see something that makes me angry, drawing a cartoon about it provides a temporary 'fix'," he said. "When the system is not corrected overnight—or even in twenty-five years—my temper tends to rise again."

Awards and Publications

In addition to appearing in the *Village Voice* and *Playboy,* Feiffer's cartoons were syndicated to more than a hundred newspapers in the United States and abroad and were compiled into numerous books. His work earned him a Pulitzer Prize for editorial cartooning in 1986, a special George Polk Memorial Award, a Newspaper Guild Page One Award, an Overseas Press Club Award, and a Capital Press Club Award. In 1995 he was elected into the American Academy of Arts and Letters. Besides these honors, Feiffer influenced a generation of cartoonists, including "Doonesbury" creator Garry Trudeau, who always credited Feiffer as his guru.

Although cartooning was his anchor, Feiffer's artistic creations and acclaim were wide-ranging. He also wrote plays, screenplays, novels, and teleplays as well as doing illustrations for several books. He won an Academy Award for his 1961 animated feature, "Munro," and wrote the screenplays for "Carnal Knowledge," "Little Murders," "Popeye," and "I Want To Go Home," which was made and released in France. His plays, which included "Little Murders," "The White House Murder Case," and "Elliott Loves," won him two Outer Circle Critics Awards, an Obie, and the London Theatre Critics Award. Feiffer was also named most promising playwright of the 1966-1967 season by New York drama critics. His novels include *Harry, the Rat with Women* and *Ackroyd.* Recently he has focued on writing children's books. In 1993 he published *The Man in the Ceiling* and *A Barrel of Laughs, A Vale of Tears* was published in 1995. In 1996 Feiffer donated his papers and drawings to the Library of Congress.

Feiffer always tried to be innovative in whatever artistic endeavor he attempted. He once said that as both writer and cartoonist, he enjoyed "understanding, acknowledging, respecting, and then ignoring the limitations of the different mediums I'm working in."

Further Reading

There are numerous books of Feiffer's cartoons, including: *Ronald Reagan in Movie America: A Jules Feiffer Production;*

Feiffer's Children; Marriage Is an Invasion of Privacy and Other Dangerous Views. □

Mitchell Jay Feigenbaum

The American physicist Mitchell Jay Feigenbaum (born 1944) laid the foundations for studying the world of complicated events in nature by recognizing patterns underlying the application of mathematical equations.

Mitchell Jay Feigenbaum was born in Philadelphia, Pennsylvania, on December 19, 1944. His father was a chemist working for the government and subsequently for industry, while his mother taught in the public schools. Feigenbaum proceeded from Samuel J. Tilden High School to the City College of New York, whereby he received a Bachelor's degree in electrical engineering in 1964. Although that field had been his first love, he found his tastes moving in the direction of physics and went to the Massachusetts Institute of Technology for his graduate work. He earned his doctorate in elementary particle physics there in 1970 and took a position at Cornell the same year.

There was little to distinguish Feigenbaum's career at Cornell and later at Virginia Polytechnic Institute. Although he felt a strong attachment to the study of hard problems (phenomena governed by equations more complicated than traditional linear equations), he had not been able to publish much on the subject. It was not clear how to approach the problems in which he was interested since the classical methods of physics were not applicable to nonlinear equations.

Almost simultaneously with his move to the National Laboratory in Los Alamos, New Mexico, however, Feigenbaum was inspired with a method of approach to nonlinear phenomena. The computers that were in use around him could perform complicated tasks by a sequence of simple steps. The question that Feigenbaum asked himself dealt with how the computer would handle the same computation if it were repeated a large number of times. Without necessarily being able to predict what would happen, he felt that the results might illustrate the behavior of nonlinear systems.

What he discovered was that if two numbers very close together were plugged into the same formula, it did not require a large number of repetitions of the formula for the values to be quite far removed from one another. This kind of behavior had been known to occur experimentally in nonlinear phenomena but Feigenbaum's results were the closest to a theoretical model that anyone had come. So far at least, however, there was not much by way of explanation of why nonlinear equations should behave this way.

In 1975 Feigenbaum heard a talk by the mathematician Stephen Smale, who had already contributed to both pure and applied mathematics. Putting Smale's theoretical work together with his own observations led Feigenbaum to an intense period of work in the spring of 1976, during which he studied with care the behavior of large numbers of values when treated with repeated applications of the same simple but nonlinear equations. The pictures that emerged from studying the behavior of the values convinced Feigenbaum that they reflected how nonlinear systems behaved.

Although he had always been interested in numbers and calculations, the work that Feigenbaum was doing and the discoveries that he was making were not readily accepted as mathematics by the mathematical community. At the same time, because he seemed to be studying computations themselves and not their physical significance, it was not always clear to physicists that he was doing physics. A new branch of science emerged, situated somewhere on the border of mathematics and physics with a heavy dose of computer science. The name attached to the new domain was "chaos theory," referring to the apparently disordered behavior of nearby points. The moral of the new subject, however, was that the chaos was only apparent and gave rise to patterns of regularity when studied more generally.

The pictures that Feigenbaum generated turned out to have the feature of looking the same at different scales. Mathematical curves with this property had been given the name "fractals" and had received some attention earlier in the 20th century. As a result, Feigenbaum was able to use some of the work done earlier to describe the patterns that he had discovered. At the same time his work gave a great impetus to the mathematical study of fractals, and mathematicians followed in Feigenbaum's footsteps. Feigenbaum's reluctance to spend time looking for proofs of his results left mathematicians with plenty to do, and Oscar Lanford III supplied some of the fundamental proofs for chaos theory in 1979.

Feigenbaum returned to Cornell University in 1982. He retained his ties to Los Alamos into the 1990s, but also took a position as professor of mathematics and physics at Rockefeller University in 1986. His accomplishments led to his spending time as a visiting researcher at the Institute for Advanced Study in Princeton and the French IHES. He and Benoit Mandelbrot of IBM share much of the credit for the study and popularization of chaos theory and fractals, although there is disagreement about exactly how the credit should be assigned. Further recognition came in the form of awards. He received a MacArthur foundation award in 1984 and a Wolf Foundation prize in physics in 1986.

Nonlinear phenomena (that is, events whose behavior seems to be governed by nonlinear equations) occur throughout nature. Among the best known applications is that of weather prediction, a proverbially inexact science. Chaos theory has not been able to bring about improvements in the ability to predict the weather, but it supplies a theoretical basis for the difficulties. Insofar as physics is about the quest for understanding, Feigenbaum's work is in the grand tradition of physics and has a universality that cuts across disciplines. His observations are at the heart of theoretical limitations to the predictive power of science.

Further Reading

Much of the work by Feigenbaum remains either unpublished or in the form of journal articles, but there is an excellent chapter in James Gleick's book *Chaos* (1988) on Feigenbaum. It talks about both Feigenbaum's contributions to chaos theory and the way his personality is interwoven with the way he does science. □

Diogo Antônio Feijó

Diogo Antônio Feijó (1784-1843) was a Brazilian liberal priest and minister of justice. He did much to establish order during the first regency but was plagued with insurmountable difficulties as the first single regent.

Diogo Antônio Feijó was born in São Paulo on Aug. 17, 1784, the natural son of a priest and the daughter of a powerful landowning family. He was instructed by private tutors and admitted to minor religious orders in 1804. Four years later he was ordained, and he spent the next 10 years of his life as a planter, priest, and teacher in São Carlos, a small village north of São Paulo. In 1818 he renounced this life and entered the ascetic community of the Fathers of Protection at Itú, the Brazilian center of religious liberalism.

In 1820 Feijó was elected deputy to the Cortes of Lisbon, and in his only speech before the Cortes, on April 25, 1822, he demanded Brazilian autonomy. He later refused to sign the constitution drafted by that body and fled to Brazil. He was chosen as a substitute delegate to the short-lived Brazilian Constitutional Assembly of 1823 and from 1826 to 1829 was a member of the Chamber of Deputies as representative from São Paulo. Among the liberal reforms he advocated was the abolition of the rule of clerical celibacy.

After the abdication of Pedro I in April 1831, Feijó aligned with the moderates and became minister of justice in the first permanent tripartite regency. His vigorous measures did much to bring the near anarchy of the period under control. When his success in putting down rebellion was not followed by success in his reform program, he resigned in 1832. After a brief retirement in São Paulo, he was elected senator by Rio moderates and campaigned in the Senate for the social, juridical, and military reforms he failed to achieve as minister.

In 1835 the moderates elected Feijó as the first permanent single regent, as provided for in the Additional Act of 1834, an amendment to the constitution. But the vigor and leadership Feijó had demonstrated as minister of justice failed him as regent. One month before he assumed leadership of the government on Oct. 12, 1835, the 10-year War of the Farropos broke out. A week before taking office, he suffered the first in a number of recurring paralytic strokes.

Feijó's 2-year regency was marred by a series of civil uprisings and political disputes. His demands for liberal reforms met the unyielding opposition of an increasingly

Lyonel Feininger

The American painter and illustrator Lyonel Feininger (1871-1956) was one of the leading artists of the German Bauhaus.

L yonel Feininger was born on July 17, 1871, in New York, the son of German musicians who had emigrated to the United States. In 1887 he went to Germany to study music, but he decided on the visual arts and attended the Hamburg School of Arts and Crafts and the Berlin Academy of Arts until 1891. He then went to Paris and studied at the Académie Colarossi until 1893.

Feininger showed an outspoken talent for caricature and became a contributor to the German humorous periodicals *Ulk* and *Fliegende Blätter* in Berlin, where he lived from 1894 to 1906. He then returned to Paris and produced drawings for the *Chicago Sunday Tribune* and the Parisian paper *Le Témoin*. His caricatures, which were capricious and fantastic, had much in common with Paul Klee's early drawings.

In 1908 Feininger returned to Berlin. On a visit to Paris in 1911 he met Robert Delaunay and became acquainted with cubist painting. It was the constructive-ordering principle dominating cubism that attracted Feininger most and appealed to his personal taste. Cubism and the Section d'Or group had a decisive influence on the formation of his painting. His first cubist paintings date from 1912. His own style was representational and two-dimensional, rendered in a prismatic protocubist manner. Light played a predominant role in his work; the rays of light were used in both the structure and the coloring of the composition.

In 1913 the artists of the Blaue Reiter group invited Feininger to exhibit with them in Berlin's First German Autumn Salon. His friendships with Wassily Kandinsky, Klee, and Alexei von Jawlensky began at this time, and later, in 1924, the four artists founded the Blaue Vier group.

Feininger's personal style was established about 1915. Abstract elements, however, had appeared in his earlier compositions. In 1919 the architect Walter Gropius, the founder of the Bauhaus in Weimar, asked Feininger to teach painting there. Architecture, which was one of Feininger's main themes, came even more into the foreground during his Bauhaus period. The other main theme in the artist's oeuvre (both oils and watercolors) was seascapes with high skies and sailing boats. When the Bauhaus moved to Dessau in 1925, Feininger left as a teacher but remained in contact with this institution until it closed in 1933. He exhibited with the Blaue Vier group from 1933 to 1936.

In 1937 Feininger returned to New York, where he died on Jan. 11, 1956. His late pictures have a pristine classical character. His art, with its emphasis on proportion, transparency, and serenity, is well balanced and harmonious.

Further Reading

The most comprehensive book on Feininger is Hans Hess, *Lyonel Feininger* (1961), which contains a works list and a good

conservative Congress. His refusal to organize a government on the principle of ministerial responsibility to the legislature further alienated that body. He failed to end the African slave trade and came into conflict with Pope Gregory XVI over the appointment of a liberal bishop of Rio de Janeiro. The latter incident was complicated by Brazilian proposals to allow civil marriage and Feijó's own advocacy of the abolition of clerical celibacy. The intransigent Congress refused to approve the measures necessary to deal effectively with the war in Rio Grande do Sul. Finally, when the Conservative victory in the congressional elections of 1836 intensified opposition of the legislature, Feijó resigned on Sept. 19, 1837.

On his return to the Senate in 1839, Feijó continued to press for reform. Frustrated again by Conservative opposition, he returned to São Paulo and joined an uprising of *paulista* liberals in May 1842. The Duque de Caxias quickly subdued the rebelling province and personally took Feijó prisoner in August. Following a 6-month banishment to Espírito Santo, Feijó resumed his seat in the Senate. He presented his own defense and retired to São Paulo to await the Senate's judgment. He died on Nov. 10, 1843.

Further Reading

The best treatment of Feijó in English is the brief sketch in Harold E. Davis, *Latin American Leaders* (1949). C. H. Haring, *Empire in Brazil: A New World Experiment with Monarchy* (1958), is recommended for general background. □

bibliography. Ernst Scheyer, *Lyonel Feininger: Caricature and Fantasy* (1964), is a detailed study of Feininger as a cartoonist. The Museum of Modern Art's *Lyonel Feininger,* edited by Dorothy C. Miller (1944), includes essays on Feininger and excerpts from his letters.

Additional Sources

Feininger, Lyonel, *Lyonel Feininge,* New York, Praeger 1974. ☐

Dianne Feinstein

Politician and public official, Dianne Feinstein (born 1933) was elected San Francisco's first female mayor in 1979 and became one of the nation's most visible and publicly recognized leaders. In 1992 she was elected to the Senate, becoming along with Barbara Boxer the first female senator from California.

Born in San Francisco on June 22, 1933, to a Jewish physician father (Leon Goldman) and a Catholic Russian-American mother (Betty Rosenburg Goldman), Dianne laid claim to having been brought up in both religious traditions. She attended a Roman Catholic school and a Jewish temple during her youth, which cultivated in her a deep respect for religious diversity. After having graduated from San Francisco's Sacred Heart High School she enrolled at Stanford where she studied history and political science and was active in student government. She was awarded a B.S. degree in 1955.

Combining marriage and family with a career, Feinstein was employed by a public affairs foundation interested in criminal justice. She worked as an administrative assistant for California's Industrial Welfare Commission and was appointed in 1962 to a four-year term on the state's Women's Board of Paroles. When her first marriage broke up, Feinstein withdrew temporarily from public life but emerged again on a county advisory committee on adult detention and on San Francisco's Mayor's Commission on Crime. During that period she also became the mother of one daughter, divorced her first husband, and organized her household tasks with a professional housekeeper in order to be free to concentrate on her public career. A second husband died in 1978, and she later married Richard Blum, an investment banker.

Early Public Career

Introduced to politics by a kindly uncle who began taking her to San Francisco Board of Supervisors (city council) meetings when she was 16, Feinstein recalled later that this was a catalyst that would turn her toward a career in public service. She won election to San Francisco's Board of Supervisors in 1969 and served on the board through the 1970s. Politically ambitious, Feinstein ran twice for the mayoralty, being defeated by Joseph Alioto in 1971 and finishing a poor third in George Moscone's 1975 election. In 1975 she was an early and firm supporter of presidential candidate Jimmy Carter, and when he won the White House, she lobbied actively for a cabinet post in Washington. Turned down in her quest for higher office, discouraged by the deaths of her father and her second husband, and afflicted by illness while abroad, Feinstein told writer Jerome Brondfield: "I decided I would not again be a candidate—for anything."

Concluding that her series of political and personal reversals had exhausted her future political prospects, Supervisor Feinstein scheduled a press conference to announce the same on what would become one of the most fateful days of her career, November 27, 1978. A half an hour before the anticipated announcement, a disgruntled former supervisor, Dan White, fatally shot Mayor George Moscone and Supervisor Harvey Milk, a homosexual political activist. This grisly assault propelled board president Feinstein into the position of acting mayor, and a month later the board selected her to serve out the balance of Moscone's term. As mayor, Feinstein sought to calm the political turbulence and violence, balance the demands of conflicting pressure groups (she appointed another gay to replace Milk), and sought what she called an "emotional reconstruction" of the city's agitated polity.

Mayor in Her Own Right

Feinstein was elected to a full four-year term as mayor beginning in 1979. During her early tenure she followed an even-handed course which incorporated some off-beat cultural politics as well as conventional politics to appeal to the varied constituencies in the community. She also focused her attention on the problem of crime, took a keen interest in police staffing and policies, and succeeded in reducing the crime rates. The biggest challenge that she first faced was fiscal—the problem of balancing the budget exacerbated by cutbacks in state and federal spending for cities. A proponent of "management by objectives" and utilizing a high-powered group of business and labor leaders in the Mayor's Fiscal Advisory Committee, Feinstein brought the city budget under control, inaugurated enlightened management and personnel policies, and supported downtown development and economic expansion.

Her occasional indulgence in whimsy delighted and amused the citizenry. She once appeared at a ribbon cutting ceremony for a reclamation project in a black wool, knee-length, old fashioned bathing suit, prompted by a wager with the contractor. At a testimonial dinner at which she was guest of honor she applied the Heimlich maneuver to save a guest from choking on a piece of meat. Yet the city's colorful and dynamic mayor occasionally stumbled, as she apparently did in pushing through an ordinance banning handguns, which led to an attempt at recall. Arrayed against her was an anti-ban group that attracted other dissidents, including the homosexual interest group. This part of the community was angered by Feinstein's veto of a measure extending medical and welfare benefits to gays and live-in companions of unmarried city employees. Although the recall movement gathered sufficient signatures, the threat quickly dissipated when Mayor Feinstein easily survived the challenge by polling an 83 percent favorable vote in April and handily winning her second and last full term in the November 1983 election (mayors were limited to two terms by the city charter).

Although beginning her career as a liberal, Mayor Feinstein was considered a moderate on matters of lifestyle tolerance and a conservative on fiscal issues. In 1984 her city hosted the Democratic National Convention, which many of the mayor's backers hoped might lead to the nomination for the vice presidency, but it did not.

In 1990 Feinstein ran for governor of California against Republican candidate Pete Wilson. Although she ran a tough campaign, and one that was well-financed by her investment banker husband, she lost to Wilson by a narrow margin. Feinstein immediately re-focused and in early 1991 announced her intention to run for Pete Wilson's former Senate seat in the 1992 election. Along with fellow Democrat Barbara Boxer, Feinstein was elected to the Senate in 1992; the two became the first women Senators ever elected in California. Their election was part of a new women's revolution, since prior to January 1993 only 15 women had ever served in the Senate, and certainly there had never been more than two serving at any given time. After her re-election in 1996, Feinstein shared the floor with 8 fellow women Senators, representing a spectrum of political viewpoints. Of the change, Senator Tom Harkin said, "Just by being on the Senate floor, they've changed the male mindset."

As Senator, Feinstein took a firm stand on a range of issues: she was outspoken against President Clinton's certification of Mexico as being an ally in the drug war, she argued that China should be granted Most Favored Nation status, and argued against the leasing of a former Navy base to China's state-owned shipping company.

Further Reading

For her political career, see Jerome Brondfield, "She Gives Her Heart to San Francisco," in *Readers Digest* (July 1984); M. Holli and P. Jones, *Biographical Dictionary of American Mayors* (1981); and biographical materials from the Office of the Mayor. For the assassination and its aftermath, see *New York Times* and *Chicago Tribune,* November 28, 1978, and *United States News and World Report,* June 6, 1979. For the recall election, see *Chicago Tribune,* April 27, 1983.

For further reading on her race against Pete Wilson for Governor, see Celia Morris's book *Storming the Statehouse: Running for Governor with Ann Richards and Dianne Feinstein* (1992). For a discussion of her role as Senator, see *Year of the Woman,* by Linda Witt, Karen Paget, and Glenna Matthews. □

Federico Fellini

The Italian film director Federico Fellini (1920-1993) began as an exponent of poetic neorealism and later became the cinema's undisputed master of psychological expressionism and surrealist fantasy.

Federico Fellini was born of middle-class family on the rocky Adriatic coast of Rimini. At the age of 12 he ran away from home to join a traveling circus and in following years supported himself as a minor stage actor, newspaper cartoonist, and radio scriptwriter. Shortly after his marriage to actress Giulietta Masina, who would later play important roles in several of his major films, Fellini was asked by the noted actor and director Aldo Fabrizi to collaborate with him on several motion picture scenarios.

In 1945 Fabrizi introduced Fellini to the celebrated cinema director Roberto Rosselini, who offered him the opportunity to work on the script and serve as assistant director of *Open City,* a powerfully realistic work which depicted the Italian underground resistance to Nazi occupation. The pair continued their collaboration on the successful wartime drama *Paisan* (1946), and the controversial religious parable *The Miracle* (1948), the story of an innocent peasant woman who mistakes a crude tramp for St. Joseph. Although *The Miracle* was in style and execution essentially a Rosselini production, its thematic ambiguity and elusive poetry distinguished it from the director's more literal neorealist efforts. Two years later, under the technical supervision of Alberto Lattuada, Fellini made his directorial debut with *Variety Lights,* an intensely personal study of theatrical life, strikingly anticipatory in its images of the desolation and ennui of the bleak emotional landscapes of his later masterpieces. He then examined the tawdry, shallow world of movie stardom in a pathetic comedy, *The White Sheik.*

With *I Vitelloni* (1953) Fellini's social microcosm expanded to include the frustrated, maladjusted lives of the provincial middle class, in a penetrating analysis of youthful malaise. But more than any of his previous work, *La Strada* (1954) established Fellini as one of the great cinematic minds of the postwar years. Painfully touching and allegorically suggestive, it told of a bizarre and tortured relationship involving a kindhearted but simpleminded girl, a brutal itinerant strongman, and a poetic, self-sacrificing clown. Less ambitious philosophically though equally brilliant in execution, *Il bidone* (1955) presented with sympathy and wit the lives of a group of small-time swindlers. Finally, with *Nights of Cabiria* (1957), the moving tale of a prostitute, Fellini reached the artistic culmination of his career as a romantic realist.

The director's fondness for jesuitical symbolism, sexual degradation, grotesquerie, and psychological Grand Guignol, visible in even his more naturalistic works, achieved overt expression in *La Dolce Vita* (1960), a monumental morality-play fresco. Although extravagantly praised at the time (it received the Academy Award for best foreign film of 1963, as had *La Strada* in 1955) and still his most popular production, the film, despite several memorable sequences, seems in retrospect curiously contrived and unconvincing.

Fellini's brief segment in *Boccaccio 70* (1962), depicting the prurient fantasies of a middle-aged bachelor, is of little interest except as an indicator of the director's future work as evidenced in *8 1/2* (1963, Fellini's 3rd Oscar winner), an expressionistic, stream-of-consciousness, auto-

biographical disclosure. Fellini's attempt to probe the psyche of his wife in *Juliet of the Spirits* (1964), while evocative, was far less successful, and his version of *The Satyricon* (1969) carried his expressionistic phase into a formless, psychedelic fantasy that lacked his usual humanity and visual grace.

An autobiographical film, *Amarcord,* came out in 1970, and again critics universally praised Fellini's talents, and the film earned Fellini another Oscar. *Amarcord* was the last film to gain great praise; in fact, most of Fellini's later work earned poor reviews. The lack of critical acclaim didn't diminish Fellini in the eyes of his fans, and he is generally regarded as the greatest Italian filmmaker. In 1993 Fellini earned his fifth and final Oscar, a lifetime achievement award. Later that year he suffered either a massive heart attack or a stroke, which left him unconscious and soon after, on October 31, he died of heart and lung failure.

Although widely praised for their visual boldness and exuberant spontaneity, Fellini's works, at their best, possess an emotional authenticity and intuitive intelligence commensurate with the dazzling brilliance of their surfaces. Fellini's greatest work was appreciated most during the 1950s through early 1970s, and he was considered a major innovator in cinematic production. Since then, his work has been dismissed as both self-indulgent and sexist.

Further Reading

Constanzo Constantini, *Conversations with Fellini,* translated by Sohrab Sorooshian, Harcourt Brace & Co., 1997; and Peter E. Bondanell, editor, *Critical Essays on Federico Fellini,* G.K. Hall & Co., 1993, are useful studies of Fellini's life and work, as is Peter Bondanella, *The Cinema of Federico Fellini,* Princeton University Press, 1992. Deena Boyer, *The Two Hundred Days of 8 1/2* (1964), is a fascinating diary about the creation of the movie. Perceptive analyses of Fellini's art are in the relevant sections of John Simon, *Acid Test* (1963); Stanley Kauffmann, *A World on Film* (1966); Pauline Kael, *Kiss Kiss Bang Bang* (1968); Dwight Macdonald, *Dwight Macdonald on Movies* (1969); and Robert Richardson, *Literature and Film* (1969). □

Vittorino da Feltre

The Italian humanist and teacher Vittorino da Feltre (1378-1446) was one of the greatest educational theorists and schoolmasters of the Italian Renaissance.

Vittorino da Feltre was born Vittorino Ramboldini at Feltre in the north of Italy. He was the son of Bruto di Ramboldini, a notary whose family, once of some social importance, had fallen on hard times. When he was 18 years old, Vittorino left Feltre for the University of Padua, where he supported himself for a time by teaching grammar to boys. After receiving his degree of doctor of arts in Latin composition and logic, he began the study of mathematics. He remained in Padua until 1415, teaching both grammar and mathematics. In 1415-1416 he studied with Guarino da Verona in Venice. Vittorino then rejoined the university in Padua. As was then the custom, he took a number of students to live in his house and closely supervised their studies.

Upon his promotion to the chair of rhetoric at Padua in 1422, Vittorino was one of the most popular masters at the university. Small but wiry and graceful, he was a dedicated teacher whose sympathy with the revolutionary scholarly methods of humanism did not in the least move him from his profound Christian convictions. In 1422, however, conditions at Padua forced him to move briefly to Venice and then, at the invitation of Gianfrancesco Gonzaga, Marquis of Mantua, to the city of Mantua, where he opened a school to tutor the marquis's children. Mantua then became Vittorino's home for the rest of his life.

Vittorino's school was created with the ideal of educating the Christian boy by using the newly discovered disciplines of classical, particularly Roman, antiquity in moral philosophy and literature. Vittorino was one of the greatest classical scholars of his day. In his school, a palace provided by the marquis, he trained not only the Gonzaga children but also children from the town and from other cities. He supervised the physical as well as the moral and intellectual development of his students.

The chief direction of Vittorino's school was training in the classics, and Latin was the language of teaching as well as of conversation. Students learned to write Greek, often by the age of 12. Vittorino collected an exceptionally fine library in Mantua, and he retained the devotion of his patrons and students throughout his life. Vittorino's name was known throughout Italy as one of the greatest humanist scholars of his day. He died in Mantua.

Further Reading

The best biography of Vittorino is in William Harrison Woodward, *Vittorino da Feltre and Other Humanist Educators* (1897), and the movements with which he was associated are further discussed in Woodward's *Studies in Education during the Age of the Renaissance, 1400-1600* (1906). □

François de Salignac de la Mothe Fénelon

The French prelate, theologian, and preacher François de Salignac de la Mothe Fénelon (1651-1715) is best known for his advocacy of quietism.

Born on Aug. 6, 1651, François Fénelon was educated by the Jesuits. He became a priest at the famous Seminary of St-Sulpice and spent 3 years preaching to Protestants. He became an ardent disciple and friend of Jacques Bossuet. Fénelon produced his *Treatise on the Existence of God* as well as his *Treatise on the Education of Young Girls* at this time. Both were highly successful.

In 1688 Fénelon met Madame Guyon, who claimed to have mystical experiences and to have the secret of loving God. She had been imprisoned by the archbishop of Paris in a convent because he feared that she was in error. Fénelon believed in her stoutly; he visited her infrequently but corresponded with her voluminously. He was suffering at this time from an intense aridity of mind in regard to God. Intellectually he could prove God's existence, but emotionally he felt little or nothing toward God. Guyon seemed to him to have discovered or received the secret of such "feeling" in her childlike surrender to God and the simplicity of her approach to divine things.

About this time there was a controversy in the French Church about a heresy called quietism, a teaching according to which progress in virtue and in the love of God was achieved by submitting to God's action and grace. Its opponents maintained that quietists made no positive effort at being virtuous, that they depended passively on God's grace, and even neglected basic rules of Christian virtue and behavior. Fénelon was involved in this unpleasant controversy through his association with Guyon. She used to visit, on Fénelon's suggestion, a school for girls run by Madame de Maintenon. The latter disliked Guyon and reported her to the authorities. Guyon also submitted her doctrine for approval to Bossuet on Fénelon's suggestion. Bossuet, although fundamentally ignorant of theology, attacked both Guyon and Fénelon in 1697.

Hate now replaced friendship for Fénelon in Bossuet's mind. He saw him as a rival in public speaking and as the nation's foremost theologian and religious counselor. He sought to have Fénelon discredited. The teaching of Fénelon and Guyon was condemned by Pope Innocent XII on the

insistence of Louis XIV under Bossuet's constant prodding. Fénelon submitted and then set out to outline his teaching on Catholic mysticism on a scale never before attempted.

In February 1695 Fénelon was made archbishop of Cambrai and from then until his death he spent his time in writing, teaching, and preaching. He was appointed tutor to Louis XIV's eldest grandson, the Duc de Bourgogne. For the duke he composed his *Dialogues* and *Telemachus,* together with other minor works. His ideas on politics were based on the universal brotherhood of man, an unpopular idea in the 18th century. He proved himself a first-rate literary judge in his *Letter* to the French Academy in 1714. He spent his last years writing against Jansenism. In his writings he explained the love of God and the simplicity of heart required in man in order to be able to practice that love. Fénelon died on Jan. 7, 1715.

Further Reading

Katherine Day Little's biography, *François de Fénelon: A Study of a Personality* (1951), is recommended. A popularly written account, sympathetic to Fénelon, is Michael de la Bedoyere, *The Archbishop and the Lady: The Story of Fénelon and Madame Guyon* (1956). Thomas Merton wrote a useful introduction to Fénelon's *Letters of Love and Counsel,* edited by John McEwen (1964). Fénelon's works are discussed in W. D. Howarth, *Life and Letters in France: The Seventeenth Century* (1965), and Philip John Yarrow, *The Seventeenth Century, 1600-1715* (1967). □

Feng Kuei-fen

Feng Kuei-fen (1809-1874) was a Chinese scholar, teacher, and official and one of the leading theorists of reform during the second half of the 19th century.

In the 1860s the Ch'ing dynasty (1644-1912), which had appeared to be toppling in the preceding decade, took on new life. The Taiping Rebellion (1850-1864) was finally crushed, and the Arrow War (1856-1860) with Britain and France was concluded. Of the new leaders who rallied in support of the dynasty, Feng Kuei-fen was one of the less well known but most influential.

Feng Kuei-fen was a native of Soochow. He passed the provincial examinations in 1832, obtained the *chin-shih* degree (the highest academic degree) with honors in 1840, and was made a compiler of the Hanlin Academy (the most prestigious academic body in China). His 7-year service in this organization gave him an intimate knowledge of the internal workings of the government, and his essays on waterways, the salt tax, and military organization showed a grasp of current affairs and economics which resulted in his being "recommended" to the Emperor in 1850 as an able official. Feng's promising official career was interrupted in the same year, when he returned home to Soochow for the required 3 years of mourning for his father.

After the Taiping rebels had occupied Nanking in 1853, Feng organized a local volunteer force to defend Soochow against the rebels. His military service was rewarded by raising him to the fifth rank (there were 10 official ranks). In 1856 he returned to government service but resigned in 1859 and spent the remainder of his life as a director of academies in Shanghai and Soochow.

Reform Ideas

In 1860, when the Taiping rebels attacked Soochow, Feng took refuge in Shanghai. It was while in Shanghai, where he had a chance to see at firsthand the military strength of the West, that Feng began to think in terms of what he called *tzu-ch'iang* (self-strengthening)—a term that was to typify Chinese efforts at reform up to 1895. He was probably the first to use this term in reference to borrowing the superior military techniques of the West, while retaining Chinese traditional culture, in order to build up China so that it could resist the West.

The essence of Feng's ideas can be found in a collection of about 50 of his essays which were compiled in 1861 under the title *Chiao-pin-lu k'ang-i* (Personal Protests from the Study of Chiao-pin).

These essays are unique in that they show a genuine realistic concern for true learning in an age when most Chinese were willfully and abysmally ignorant of the West. Feng advocated the establishment of a school for translators who could provide Chinese, through translations of Western books, with an accurate picture of the West, and a change in the sacrosanct examination requirements to include Western science and mathematics. He believed that the power of the West was based on mathematics and science. In foreign affairs he stressed the need to deal honestly and fairly with the foreigners instead of treating them with distrust and suspicion.

Even though Feng admitted that China had much to learn from the foreigners, he felt that it could be done within a Chinese context and that Chinese civilization was innately superior to that of the West. He was an accomplished Confucian scholar and thoroughly believed in the efficacy of Chinese culture. He was austere and exacting in his behavior and shunned even the most simple enjoyments. Yet, he had a rare independence of mind and a desire for truth that made it possible for him to recognize worth wherever he found it. In his attempt to blend what he considered to be the best of both worlds, Feng, nevertheless, inadvertently contributed to the further undermining of Chinese civilization. The ships and guns of the West were a product of its essence, and if China was to effectively utilize the one, it would have to accept the other.

Political Influence

Feng's influence upon the leaders of China began in 1861, when he wrote a letter to Tseng Kuo-fan on behalf of the Soochow refugees in Shanghai, explaining the strategic importance of the Soochow area. This letter resulted in the creation of Li Hung-chang's Huai army, which was sent to Shanghai. In 1862 Li Hung-chang, a leader of the "self-strengthening" movement, had Feng attached to his staff, and from then until 1865 he served Li as an independent adviser, leaving an indelible imprint on Li's future thinking.

It was at Feng's suggestion that Li undertook the rehabilitation of the Soochow area in 1865 and that Li established a school for the translation of foreign mathematical and scientific texts in 1863. Many of Li's proposals for reform were actually written, or at least influenced, by Feng Kuei-fen. In 1870 Li Hung-chang acknowledged his great debt to Feng in a memorial to the throne, which resulted in Feng's being raised to the honorary position of the third rank in 1871. In 1898, 24 years after Feng's death, the Kuang-hsü emperor ordered 1,000 copies of Feng's collected essays printed to be read and discussed in all government offices.

Further Reading

The only complete biography of Feng in English appears in Arthur W. Hummel, ed., *Eminent Chinese of the Ch'ing Period, 1644-1912* (2 vols., 1943-1944). Ssuyü Teng and John K. Fairbank, *China's Response to the West: A Documentary Survey, 1839-1923* (1954), devotes several pages to Feng, as does William Theodore de Bary, ed., *Sources of Chinese Tradition* (1964). Mary C. Wright, *The Last Stand of Chinese Conservatism: The T'ung-chih Restoration, 1862-1874* (1957; new ed. 1966), discusses many of Feng's ideas and proposals. □

Feng Yü-hsiang

Feng Yü-hsiang (1882-1948) was a Chinese warlord. Commanding the Kuominchün, or National People's Army, Feng controlled major parts of North China during the 1920s. He was known as the "Christian general."

Son of a low-ranking army officer, Feng Yü-hsiang was born in Hsingchi-chen, Chihli (Hopei). He grew up in military surroundings and received little formal schooling. He nonetheless taught himself to read works in the vernacular. From 1896 to 1911 Feng advanced through the ranks of the army of Li Hung-chang and his successor, Yüan Shih-k'ai. As a company commander in the northeast, Feng helped to organize an anti-Manchu military association, but he was exposed and imprisoned following the Wuchang uprising of October 1911. Released and readmitted to the army through the efforts of his protector, Lu Chien-chang, Feng gained increasing military power and independence.

Feng was one of the most colorful figures during the "warlord era," from 1916 to 1928. A man of imposing stature, he liked to dress in the clothes of the common soldier to demonstrate his identity with the masses. He became a Methodist in 1914 and eventually became known as the "Christian general." He was said to have baptized his troops with a fire hose. However, Feng was one of the more serious social reformers among the warlords. His troops were well trained, tightly disciplined, and indoctrinated with a Spartan ethic stressing duty and responsibility. The eclectic ideological basis for this included principles drawn from Confucius and Christ and shifted with Feng's attach-

ments to a succession of allies, including the Soviet Union and the Chinese nationalist Sun Yat-sen.

Lacking a stable territorial base, Feng found it difficult to apply his ideals to society. Exigencies of war and politics also made him an unsteady friend, and he climbed to power over a series of betrayed allies, most notably Wu P'ei-fu. By late 1924 Feng had become one of the select group of powerful generals who fought and schemed for control of North China and access to the organs of the central government in Peking (now Beijing). However, he was soon forced to retreat into northwest China. He formed an uneasy relationship with the Kuomintang and its Soviet associates in April 1925, and from May to July 1926 he toured the Soviet Union.

During the Kuomintang's Northern Expedition, Feng moved into central China after declaring himself a Kuomintang member. When the Nationalists split into two camps, the Wuhan wing allied with the Chinese Communists and the Nanking faction under Chiang Kai-shek, Feng threw his support to Chiang, enabling him to eliminate his left-wing rivals. Feng also played a significant role in the second stage of the Northern Expedition that culminated in the capture of Peking in June 1928.

Feng was one of the military leaders who split with Chiang over the issue of troop disbandment. In February 1930 Feng formed a coalition with Yen Hsi-shan. The collapse of this venture cost Feng control of his troops, and he was thereafter reduced to the role of a minor political figure. Feng moved into the spotlight only briefly—as a supporter of the anti-Japanese movement during the mid-1930s and as an émigré critic of Chiang Kai-shek after the war. On Sept. 1, 1948, Feng died in an apparently accidental fire on board the Soviet ship *Pobeda* near Odessa.

Further Reading

A first-rate biography is James E. Sheridan, *Chinese Warlord: The Career of Feng Yü-hsiang* (1966). For a detailed narrative of the warlord era see Li Chien-nung, *The Political History of China, 1840-1928* (1956). Oliver Edmund Clubb, *20th Century China* (1964), is another useful survey. □

Edna Ferber

American author Edna Ferber (1887-1968) wrote popular fiction and collaborated on several successful Broadway plays.

Born in Kalamazoo, Mich., Edna Ferber at an early age moved with her family to Appleton, Wis., where she spent most of her childhood. When her father lost his vision, she was forced to forsake her acting ambitions and, at the age of 17, began full-time work as a reporter for the *Appleton Daily Crescent*. Shortly afterward she joined the staff of the *Milwaukee Journal* and later the *Chicago Tribune*. During this period she wrote several short stories, some of which were published in *Everybody's Magazine*. She discarded a novel which her mother salvaged and had published in 1911 as *Dawn O'Hara*. Two short-story collections followed, *Buttered Side Down* (1912) and *Roast Beef Medium* (1913), and the novels *Fanny Herself* (1917), *The Girls* (1921), and *Gigolo* (1922).

Ferber won her first popular success with the novel *So Big*, the story of a young widow on a truck farm in Illinois who sacrifices everything for her son's happiness. She was awarded the Pulitzer Prize for it in 1924. *Show Boat* (1926), perhaps her best novel, tells the story of a showboat performer's love for an unscrupulous gambler. The novel was adapted as a successful Broadway musical the following year. *Cimarron,* another best seller, dealt with the spectacular Oklahoma land rush of 1889. In the early 1920s Ferber began a fruitful collaboration with playwright George S. Kaufman, producing such plays as *Minick* (1924), *The Royal Family* (1927), *Dinner at Eight* (1932), and *Stage Door* (1936).

In her later novels Ferber continued to explore various geographical and historical settings. *American Beauty* (1931) describes Polish immigrants in Connecticut; *Come and Get It* (1935) is about Wisconsin lumbermen; and *Great Son* (1945) depicts four generations of a Seattle family.

Many of Ferber's novels have been made into movies, including *Saratoga Trunk* (1941), which is set in New Orleans and Saratoga Springs, N.Y., and deals with the founding of railroad dynasties; *Giant* (1950), a story of oil fortunes in contemporary Texas; and *Ice Palace* (1958), about Alaska, from exploration to the fight for statehood.

Ferber published her first autobiography, *A Peculiar Treasure,* in 1939 and her second, *A Kind of Magic,* in 1963. Her often energetic and pleasantly nostalgic work was immensely popular with both the reading public and movie- and playgoers, making her one of America's best-known authors. She died on April 16, 1968, in New York City.

Further Reading

Miss Ferber's fiction is reviewed in Robert Van Gelder, *Writers and Writing* (1946), and W. Tasker Witham, *Panorama of American Literature* (1947).

Additional Sources

Gilbert, Julie Goldsmith., *Ferber, a biography,* Garden City, N.Y.: Doubleday, 1978. □

Ferdinand

Ferdinand (1865-1927) was king of Romania from 1914 to 1927. He presided over the expansion of Romania and the implementation of important reforms.

The second son of Prince Leopold von Hohenzollern-Sigmaringen and Princess Antonia of Portugal, Ferdinand von Hohenzollern-Sigmaringen was born on Aug. 24, 1865, at Sigmaringen, Prussia. Adopted as heir to the Romanian throne by his childless uncle, Carol I, in March 1889, Ferdinand married Princess Marie, the strong-willed granddaughter of both Queen Victoria and Czar Alexander II, on Jan. 15, 1893. The marriage produced six children, of whom the eldest, Prince Carol (1893-1953), assumed the throne in 1930.

As crown prince, Ferdinand reorganized Romania's armed forces, which he commanded in the Second Balkan War against Bulgaria in 1913. Upon the death of King Carol I, Ferdinand became king of Romania on Oct. 14, 1914. Although a Hohenzollern, Ferdinand declared war on Germany and Austria-Hungary in August 1916 to gain the Hapsburg Romanian-inhabited territories and to join all Romanians to their national state. The Austro-German forces, under Gen. August von Mackensen, occupied Bucharest in December 1916, forcing the royal family to flee to Iasi, in Moldavia. The Romanian forces were defeated, an armistice was signed on Dec. 6, 1917, and the Peace of Bucharest was concluded on May 7, 1918. After the Allied victory of 1918, however, the dream of "Greater Romania" was realized by Romania's acquisition of Bessarabia, Bucovina, a portion of the Banat of Temesvar, and Transylvania. Ferdinand was crowned king of Greater Romania at Alba Iulia on Oct. 15, 1922.

The most important reform measure enacted during Ferdinand's reign was the land reform promised his peasant soldiers during the war to reward them for their sacrifices and to prevent a peasant revolt such as had occurred under Carol I in 1907. Ferdinand himself set a notable example by being the first great landholder to give over his estates for distribution among the peasants.

The land reform measure and the decree of universal suffrage strengthened the National peasant party, strong in Romania's Transylvanian areas, but because of the party's demands for further radical land redistribution, the King refused its members entry into the government. Ferdinand also busied himself with extending full civil and military rights to all Romanian-born Jews and with reorganizing the army.

During Ferdinand's reign, Romania adhered to the Little Entente (including Czechoslovakia and Yugoslavia), concluded to oppose Hungarian revisionism; backed by France, entered a treaty with Poland to defend against Soviet attack; and followed a pro-French foreign policy. Ferdinand died in the royal palace near Bucharest on July 20, 1927. Because his heir, Carol, had renounced the succession in 1925 to live abroad with his mistress, Magda Lupescu, Ferdinand was succeeded by his young grandson, Michael, under a regency lasting until Carol's return to Romania in 1930.

Further Reading

Perhaps the most useful discussions of Ferdinand's career and his influence are contained in Robert William Seton-Watson, *A History of the Roumanians* (1934), and Henry Lithgow Roberts, *Rumania: Political Problems of an Agrarian State* (1951). Princess Marthe L. Bibesco, *Royal Portraits* (1928), includes a chapter on Ferdinand. □

Ferdinand I

Ferdinand I (1503-1564) was Holy Roman emperor from 1555 to 1564. Before his accession and during his reign he pursued conciliatory policies toward the Protestants and the powerful German princes.

Born at Alcalá de Henares, Spain, on March 10, 1503, Ferdinand was the second son of Philip the Fair, Duke of Burgundy, and Joanna the Mad of Aragon and Castile. He lived for a long time in the shadow of his older brother, Charles, who was heir to the Hapsburg holdings in Germany and the Netherlands as well as to Spain and its Italian and South American possessions. In 1517 Charles went to Spain to take over the government, and the brothers met for the first time. Ferdinand was sent to the Netherlands to complete his education; there contact with Erasmian ideas had a lasting effect upon his attitude toward the Reformation.

On the death of their grandfather Emperor Maximilian I in 1519, Ferdinand's brother became Emperor Charles V, but Ferdinand received only the Hapsburg possessions of Upper and Lower Austria, Carinthia, Carniola, and, until 1534, Württemburg. In 1526, on the death of his brother-in-law Louis, Ferdinand became king of Bohemia and Hungary. His political position became rather ambiguous, for he had to combine the roles of German representative of imperial policy, German territorial prince, and independent king of Hungary, constantly harassed by the Turks. The necessity of finding support against the Turkish threat dictated much of his conciliatory attitude toward the Protestants.

The dangerous opposition of the Lutheran princes forced Charles V to secure Ferdinand's support. In 1531 Charles had Ferdinand elected king of the Romans, that is, designated successor to the imperial dignity. Later (1548-1551) Charles tried to dissuade Ferdinand from the imperial succession in order to preserve the empire for his own son Philip II. In 1551 a compromise was reached securing Philip's succession after Ferdinand's death. The agreement was not executed, however, and the imperial office remained in the hands of Ferdinand's direct descendants.

In German politics, which were closely connected to the religious issue, Ferdinand acted as a mediator between his brother and the Protestant princes. Although he remained a Catholic, Ferdinand supported efforts to reunite the confessions and to refer the disputed points to a general council. After Charles suffered a humiliating defeat by the Protestant princes in 1552, Ferdinand arranged the Treaty of Passau (1552), the first step toward the granting of religious freedom for the Lutheran princes (Treaty of Augsburg, 1555). Charles, however, refused to accept the decisions of the Augsburg Diet and abdicated. As emperor, Ferdinand continued his efforts toward reunion of the confessions with important concessions to the Protestants. He died in Vienna on July 25, 1564.

Further Reading

The life of Ferdinand I is recounted in Johannes Janssen, *History of the German People at the Close of the Middle Ages* (8 vols., 1883-1894; trans., 16 vols., 1896-1925). For additional information see Karl Brandi, *The Emperor Charles V* (1937; trans. 1939), and Friedrich Heer, *The Holy Roman Empire* (1967; trans. 1968). □

Ferdinand II

Ferdinand II (1578-1637) was Holy Roman emperor from 1619 to 1637. He attempted to revive imperial authority in Germany and to restore Catholicism in his domain.

Born in Graz in Styria on July 9, 1578, Ferdinand of Hapsburg was the son of Archduke Charles of inner Austria and Maria of Bavaria. His father, a devout Catholic, ruled a province which had been strongly influenced by the Protestant Reformation. To protect his heir from Lutheran influences, Charles in 1590 sent Ferdinand to school at Ingolstadt in Catholic Bavaria. Archduke Charles died shortly thereafter, and Ferdinand ruled Styria under a regency until he was declared of age in 1596.

His Jesuit teachers, militant missionaries of the Catholic restoration, were enormously influential in forming Ferdinand's conception of his duties as a Christian prince, and from the beginning he dedicated himself to restoring the Roman faith in his lands. In 1602 he expelled Protestant teachers and preachers from Styria, closed or destroyed their churches, and gave his nonnoble Protestant subjects the choice of conversion or exile.

When his cousins the emperors Rudolf II and Matthias died childless, Ferdinand fell heir to the Hapsburg dominions in Austria, Bohemia, and Hungary. In 1617 he was elected king of Bohemia and in 1618 king of Hungary, intimidating the noble assemblies in both instances. In 1619 he succeeded Matthias as Holy Roman emperor. His Protestant subjects, fearing an attack on their right to worship, refused the oath of homage, and in May 1618 the Bohemian nobility rose in revolt. With the support of Maximilian of Bavaria and the forces of the Catholic League under Count Tilly, he bloodily suppressed the Protestant rebels in Austria and Bohemia in 1620.

His efforts to restore Catholicism precipitated the Thirty Years War, a European conflict in which the religious issue ultimately became submerged in a conflict for domination of the Continent. In 1629 and again in 1635 Ferdinand II was in a position to dictate a favorable peace in Germany. But both times he refused to make reasonable compromises with the Protestant princes and their powerful foreign protectors, France and Sweden.

Ferdinand II has been judged harshly for his religious fanaticism and his lack of political realism. In an age of brutal power politics he persisted in subordinating his political goals to his religious convictions. He was easily outwitted in a bargain and naive about issues that went beyond the uplifting religious tracts that made up his only reading. By dynastic accident he reunited the main Hapsburg domains in central Europe, but in pursuing the chimera of Catholic restoration he widened the rift between imperial authority and the German princes. He died in Vienna on Feb. 15, 1637.

Further Reading

The only major source for the reign of Ferdinand II is in German. In English the best references are in general works on the period. The most important are C. V. Wedgwood, *The Thirty Years War* (1939); S. H. Steinberg, *The "Thirty Years War" and the Conflict for European Hegemony, 1600-1660* (1966); and H. G. Koenigsberger, *The Habsburgs and Europe, 1516-1660* (1971). □

Ferdinand II

Ferdinand II (1810-1859) was king of the Two Sicilies from 1830 to 1859. He stoutly resisted Italian liberalism and independence movements. His bombardment of Sicilian cities earned him the nickname of King Bomba.

Born in Palermo on Jan. 12, 1810, Ferdinand II was the son of the future Francis I and the grandson of the violently anti-revolutionary Ferdinand I, both of the Bourbon line of Naples. His mother was the Spanish Infanta Maria Isabel. When Ferdinand ascended the throne of the Southern Kingdom in 1830, it was hoped that he might head up an attack on reaction from within Italy and the domination of Austria from without Italy. His first marriage was to Christina of Savoy, daughter of Victor Emmanuel I of Piedmont, the only other Italian monarch capable of resisting Austrian pressure. His reign began with an amnesty of political prisoners. He refused to sign a treaty of alliance with Austria, and he worked out a foreign-policy orientation toward France. However, Christina died in 1836 (having given birth to the last of the Bourbon line, Francis II), and with his marriage to the Austrian archduchess Theresa, Ferdinand instituted a new policy of repression at home and of friendship with the Hapsburgs.

Ferdinand put down insurrections in Sicily and Calabria in 1844; but with the revolutionary movement of 1848 the former province declared its independence. In Naples, Ferdinand instituted a constitutional monarchy, patterned on that of the 1830 July Monarchy in France. According to the constitution of January 29, there was to be a bicameral legislature and civil liberties. The constitutional movement spread to the rest of Italy and, spearheaded by Piedmont, the Italians launched their First War of Independence against Austria.

Ferdinand had contributed troops to the war effort. They were recalled after further radical activity at Naples, which resulted in the revocation of the new constitution. On May 15 the new Parliament convened, only to be immediately dispersed. (The constitution was formally discontinued on March 13, 1849.) Sicily was reconquered, and Ferdinand contributed troops to the crushing of the last Roman Republic. The savage repression which followed the defeat of the liberals had by 1850 earned Ferdinand the condemnation of the British liberal statesman William Gladstone, who described Ferdinand's regime as "the negation of God erected into a system of government."

The restoration of the old regime in the south by no means put an end to conspiracies and uprisings against Ferdinand, and there was an assassination attempt on the King's life in 1856. However, by the time Ferdinand died at Caserta on May 22, 1859, the Risorgimento (Italian unification movement) was well under way.

Further Reading

Background on Ferdinand II is in Harold Acton, *The Last Bourbons of Naples, 1825-1861* (1961), and Denis Mack Smith, *A History of Sicily: Modern Sicily after 1713* (1968). □

Ferdinand III

Ferdinand III (1608-1657) reigned as Holy Roman emperor from 1637 to 1657. He unwillingly presided over the triumph of Protestantism in Germany.

Ferdinand of Hapsburg was born in Graz in Styria on July 13, 1608, son of the later emperor Ferdinand II and Maria Anna of Bavaria. Family tradition dictated his Jesuit upbringing. As heir to the newly reunited Hapsburg patrimony in central Europe, he was elected king of Hungary in 1626 and king of Bohemia in 1627. From 1626 onward his father brought him into the councils of state. Ferdinand was intrigued by military affairs and coveted a field command. Frustrated by his father's dependence on Albrecht von Wallenstein, he became an ardent opponent of the Bohemian mercenary. After Wallenstein's murder, Ferdinand commanded nominally at the battle of Nördlingen in 1634 and won reflected glory. In December 1636 he was elected king of Rome and succeeded as Holy Roman emperor when his father died on Feb. 15, 1637.

Ferdinand III shared his father's deep piety relying constantly on the advice of his Jesuit confessors. He firmly upheld the Catholic restoration in Bohemia and Austria but showed more willingness to negotiate with the established Protestant states of Germany. Twice during the protracted peace negotiations, in 1645 and in 1647, he took personal command of his armies in an effort to win on the battlefield what he could not gain at the bargaining table. Both times he blundered disastrously, and thereafter he remained in Vienna at the center of the administration.

The Westphalian treaties of 1648 were a great disappointment to him, and Ferdinand had to be forced by his supporters to accede to them. Although he never lost sight of the goal of restoring Catholicism, he turned his attention thenceforth more to the dynastic interests of his family. In

1653 he engineered the election of his oldest son, Ferdinand Maria, as king of Rome, only to have his hopes dashed with his heir's sudden death in 1654. The last years of his reign were largely taken up by his ultimately successful efforts to secure the imperial throne for his second son, the Archduke Leopold.

Aside from his passion for the hunt, Ferdinand III had a love of learning and a special fondness for music which became a family tradition. Unlike his father, he was a gifted linguist and spoke the languages of all his subjects: German, Hungarian, Czech, Italian, Spanish, and French as well as Latin. Frugal, stolid, and rather shy, he grew mistrustful and ill-tempered in his later years. He died in Vienna on April 2, 1657.

Further Reading

Ferdinand III has never attracted a good biographer. The main source is in German. For general works on the period see C. V. Wedgwood, *The Thirty Years War* (1939); S. H. Steinberg, *The "Thirty Years War" and the Conflict for European Hegemony, 1600-1660* (1966); Friedrich Heer, *The Holy Roman Empire* (1967; trans. 1968); and H. G. Koenigsberger, *The Habsburgs and Europe, 1516-1660* (1971). ☐

Ferdinand V

Ferdinand V (1452-1516), or Ferdinand the Catholic, and his wife, Isabella I, were joint sovereigns of Castile. As Ferdinand II, he was king of Aragon. He laid the foundations of Spanish unity and imperial power.

Born on March 10, 1452, at Sos, in Aragon, Ferdinand was the son of John II of Aragon and Juana Enriquez of Castile. In 1469 he married Isabella, heiress apparent to the Castilian crown. They became joint monarchs of Castile on the death of her brother Henry IV in 1474. In 1479 John II died, and Ferdinand became king of Aragon as well as of Castile (in whose government, however, he officially occupied second place).

Domestic Policy

In the union of crowns thus achieved, Castile's growing wealth and larger population gave it predominance. At the same time the lands of the two crowns retained their separate constitutional identities; and while the Catholic Monarchs might achieve a measure of centralization in Castile, they were prevented from doing so in the Aragonese realms by a jealous defense of local *fueros* (liberties).

In only one important respect did Ferdinand intervene in Aragonese politics—over all local protests he revived the moribund medieval Inquisition which, like the new Inquisition in Castile (after 1478), was placed under royal control. In both Castile and Aragon the Inquisition attacked the political and economic positions that had been won by middle-class *conversos* (Jews who had previously been forced to accept baptism). *Conversos* emigrated in large numbers; their place in commerce and finance tended to be taken by foreigners. In Castile, the Genoese, Flemings, and Germans grew fat on the wealth of the new Atlantic trades.

Ferdinand and Isabella exerted unrelenting pressure on the papacy in order to gain control of the wealth and power of the Spanish Church. In 1486 they were handed full patronage rights over bishoprics to be established in the newly conquered Moorish lands in Granada. Papal bulls of 1493, 1501, and 1508 also made the Crown master of ecclesiastical appointments and revenues in the New World. Ferdinand and Isabella also gradually assumed control of major ecclesiastical offices in their realm, thus gaining an important new source of patronage and revenue.

The sphere of government also saw a dramatic extension of royal power. At the Castilian Cortes (Parliament) of 1476 and 1480 the Catholic Monarchs won assent to a number of important measures. They revived and centralized a medieval urban police force, the *hermandad*. Nobles were deprived of a significant share of the revenues that they had alienated from the Crown. The Royal Council was reorganized, and the financial administration was purged and pruned. Henceforth government was conducted through an interlocking system of royal councils, while newly powerful royal secretaries tied the whole apparatus to the will of the sovereign.

The Cortes also accepted a vigorous extension of royal control over municipal government. Finally, the higher court system was augmented and reorganized, restoring final determination of appeals to the Royal Council and the monarchs themselves.

Foreign Policy

All of these changes were tied together and legitimized by the last great crusade of medieval Spain. This was the war of conquest launched against Moorish Granada in 1481 and successfully concluded in 1492. While Christendom was in retreat before the Turks to the east, Ferdinand achieved through force and diplomacy a signal triumph for the Faith to the south. The year 1492 was decisive for Spain in other ways. That year Isabella gave Christopher Columbus her support, thus launching a vast new crusade to the west. And the end of medieval Spanish religious pluralism was confirmed by the expulsion of all Jews refusing baptism.

But while continued crusading appealed to religious zealots like Cardinal Jiménez de Cisneros, whom Ferdinand allowed to campaign against the Moors in North Africa (1505-1510), the King pursued traditional Aragonese interests in Spain and Italy. Charles VIII of France invaded Italy in 1494 but was defeated the following year by an Italian coalition in part engineered and aided by Ferdinand. And when another French king, Louis XII, desired to follow up his conquest of Milan (1500) by a renewed attempt on Naples, he too was caught in Ferdinand's net.

Gulled into a Spanish alliance for the division of the Neapolitan kingdom between the two monarchs, Louis found himself driven out, and in 1504 he was forced to recognize Ferdinand's exclusive right to Naples. Louis declared himself twice deceived by Ferdinand, and the latter replied: "He lies! I have deceived him ten!" Ferdinand thus firmly established Spanish preponderance in the western Mediterranean. He also involved the kingdom in a series of Italian wars which were to continue through the middle of the 16th century.

Last Years

Isabella's death in 1504 made Ferdinand's position in Castile precarious. Pursuing their policies of isolating France diplomatically and of dynastic aggrandizement, the Catholic Monarchs had linked their five children with the royal houses of Portugal, England, and the empire. But only one of these unions bore fruit—that of their daughter Joanna the Mad and Philip of Burgundy. Adhering strictly to the lawful succession, Isabella willed Castile to Joanna (and Philip).

Forced to retreat from Castile, in 1505 Ferdinand married Germaine de Foix, niece of Louis XII. But after the death of Philip of Burgundy in 1506, Ferdinand resumed his administration of Castile as regent for the insane Joanna. Using his wife's connection with the royal family of Navarre to bolster his claims, Ferdinand conquered the larger, Iberian part of that kingdom in 1512 and annexed it to Castile in 1515.

Ferdinand died on Jan. 23, 1516, at Madrigalejo, Estremadura. Niccolò Machiavelli had already written: "We have in our day Ferdinand . . . who may . . . be called a new prince, since he has been transformed from a small and weak king into the greatest monarch in Christendom."

Further Reading

Townsend Miller, *The Castles and the Crown: Spain, 1451-1555* (1963), is a stimulating biography of the Catholic Monarchs. The various aspects of their reigns can be best studied in J. H. Elliott, *Imperial Spain, 1469-1716* (1963), and J. M. Batista in Roca's chapter, "The Hispanic Kingdoms and the Catholic Kings," in *The New Cambridge Modern History,* vol. 1: G. R. Potter, ed., *The Renaissance, 1493-1520* (1957). The significance of the period in the framework of Spanish history is assessed in Jaime Vicens Vives, *Approaches to the History of Spain* (1952; 2d ed. 1960; translated and edited by Joan Connelly Ullman, 1967). For Ferdinand's successful Italian diplomacy see Garrett Mattingly, *Renaissance Diplomacy* (1955); for the crusade to the west see J. H. Parry, *The Spanish Seaborne Empire* (1966). □

Ferdinand VII

The reign of Ferdinand VII (1784-1833) was one of the most complex and important in the history of Spain. It was characterized by a popular war against French occupation and by the struggle of liberal groups to establish a constitutional monarchy.

On Oct. 14, 1784, Ferdinand was born in San Lorenzo del Escorial to the timid Charles, heir to the throne of Spain, and the domineering Maria Luisa of Parma. Two years later his mother became infatuated with Manuel de Godoy, a handsome officer of the Royal Guards. When Charles became king of Spain in early 1789, Godoy began his meteoric rise to power. By the end of 1792, at the age of 25, Godoy was virtual dictator of Spain. In 1796 he worked out an alliance with France against England, and from then till 1808 Spain and England were to be almost constantly at war.

During these years the weak and sickly Ferdinand was educated by Juan Escoiquiz, an ambitious man who inculcated in him a deep-seated hatred for Godoy. Beyond this, Ferdinand's education was one of the worst received by a Spanish monarch. The young prince hated studying, spoke little, rarely smiled, and, it was said, found sardonic satisfaction in all kinds of petty acts of cruelty.

In October 1802 Ferdinand married his cousin Maria Antonieta of Naples. An unattractive 18-year-old, he was described at this time by his mother-in-law as "an absolute blockhead, and not even a husband in the flesh. He is a fool who neither hunts nor fishes, who hangs all day about the room of his unfortunate wife, who busies himself with nothing, and is not even her husband from an animal point of view."

Plots against Godoy

Maria Antonieta soon joined Escoiquiz in his desire to overthrow Godoy, who was becoming more and more unpopular because of the inflation brought on by the war against England. Furthermore, Godoy's confiscation of clerical property had alienated the Church, and the high nobil-

ity resented being governed by a man of humble background. Escoiquiz was able to raise a conspiracy against him and organize it around the figure of Ferdinand. When Maria Antonieta died in May 1806, Godoy was accused by rumor of having poisoned her.

In 1807 Godoy told Charles that his son was plotting against him, and Ferdinand was placed under house arrest. Fearing for his life, he wrote his father: "I have done wrong; I have sinned against you both as King and as Father; but I have repented, and I now offer Your Majesty the most humble obedience." Ferdinand was freed and Escoiquiz was exiled to Toledo, but the plotting against Godoy continued.

By this time Napoleon had decided to unseat the Spanish Bourbons, and early in 1808 French troops began to occupy the main cities of Spain. Godoy and the royal family went to Aranjuez, planning to escape from Napoleon's clutches by going to the New World. Ferdinand, however, believed that the French troops were in Spain to support him, and on March 17 he overthrew Godoy at Aranjuez with the help of the aristocracy and a well-organized riot. Godoy was imprisoned, and the frightened Charles abdicated in favor of his son.

Abdication and Captivity

On March 24 Ferdinand made his triumphal entry into Madrid, which had been occupied on the previous day by a large French force commanded by Gen. Murat. A few days later he received an invitation from Napoleon to meet with him at Bayonne. Already the French emperor had offered the throne of Spain to his brother Joseph, and Joseph had accepted it.

Ferdinand still believed that Napoleon was his friend, and in spite of the warnings of Escoiquiz and others he traveled to Bayonne, where he was shocked by Napoleon's demand that he abdicate. When he refused, the French brought Charles, Maria Luisa, and Godoy to Bayonne in order to increase the pressure on him. Finally, on May 2, when the people of Madrid rose against the French army of occupation, Napoleon became furious and threatened Ferdinand with death. The frightened King quickly abdicated in favor of Charles, who then abdicated in favor of Napoleon. A few months later Napoleon's younger brother entered Spain as Joseph I.

But the Spanish people refused to accept Joseph as their king and were joined in their resistance against the French by the armies of the Duke of Wellington. By 1813 the French position in Spain had become untenable, and Napoleon decided to withdraw his troops. Hoping that Ferdinand would honor his promise to keep Spain neutral, Napoleon allowed him to return to Spain in March 1814.

Ferdinand and the Liberals

During the war against the French a group of liberal Spaniards had written the Constitution of 1812, which placed severe limitations on the power of the monarchy. Ferdinand had no intention of accepting this document, and after making sure that the army would support him, he issued a decree on May 4 restoring royal absolutism and suspending the Constitution of 1812. A week later he entered Madrid.

Ferdinand now launched a systematic persecution of those who had collaborated with the French and of those who had dreamed of a constitutional monarchy. He also began to organize an army to send against the rebellious American colonies that had taken advantage of the French occupation of Spain to launch their struggle for independence.

The persecuted liberals began to establish contacts within the army, where service in America was very unpopular. In early 1820 Col. Rafael Riego declared himself for the Constitution of 1812. All over Spain army garrisons either joined the revolt or remained neutral. The frightened Ferdinand gave in and in March took the oath to the constitution.

The liberals, however, proved unable to set up a viable government. In 1822 a royalist revolt broke out in favor of the "imprisoned" Ferdinand, and in the spring of 1823 a royalist army from France was sent to restore Ferdinand to the throne. Everywhere the French were received with enthusiasm. The liberals fled to Seville and then to Cadiz, taking Ferdinand with them. In August they gave up and freed Ferdinand, who had promised a general amnesty.

Ferdinand did not keep his promise, and as in 1814, many liberals found themselves either in prison or in exile. As the years passed, however, Ferdinand's rule became less harsh, and gradually the more moderate liberals were allowed back into the country. This angered the more conservative groups in Spain, who now turned to Ferdinand's brother, the pious and reactionary Don Carlos, for inspiration and leadership.

After the death of his first wife in 1806, Ferdinand had married twice. His third wife died in May 1829, and Ferdinand still had not produced an heir. On Dec. 12, 1829, he married his fourth wife, the beautiful and capable Maria Cristina of Naples, who in October 1830 bore him an heir, the future Isabella II.

In 1713 Philip V had introduced into Spain the so-called Salic Law, which prevented females from succeeding to the throne of Spain. Don Carlos claimed that he would be the legitimate king of Spain if his brother Ferdinand died without a male heir. In 1830 Ferdinand annulled the Salic Law, but Don Carlos still refused to give up his claims. Between 1830 and 1833, therefore, Ferdinand turned more and more to the liberals who, afraid of the reactionary Don Carlos, were solidly behind the princess Isabella. By early 1833 the government of Spain was in the hands of the liberals, the men who had been so harshly persecuted by Ferdinand in the past.

After the summer of 1832 Ferdinand's health began to fail, and he died on Sept. 29, 1833. The Queen would not allow his body to be touched for 48 hours. It lay in state in the throne room of the Palacio Real, where it was seen by that conscientious traveler Richard Ford, who claimed that the face, hideous enough in life, was "now purple, like a ripe fig." Five days after his death, the King was buried among the other kings of Spain in the vault of the Escorial. Ferdinand VII has been praised by conservative Spanish historians as a capable and popular king who struggled to preserve the traditional Spanish way of life. But he has also been attacked by liberal historians as a coward and bloody ogre who tried to sweep back the tide of progress.

Further Reading

There is no biography of Ferdinand VII available in English. Sir Charles Petrie, *The Spanish Royal House* (1958), is useful. For a scholarly account of the politics and economics of Spain during Ferdinand's reign see Raymond Carr, *Spain, 1808-1939* (1966). □

Adam Ferguson

The Scottish philosopher, moralist, and historian Adam Ferguson (1723-1816) produced a number of notable works concerning the nature of society. He is regarded as one of the founders of modern sociology.

Adam Ferguson was born in Logierat, Perthshire. In 1739 he went to the University of St. Andrews, where he received his master of arts degree in 1742. Determined on a clerical career, he began to study divinity at St. Andrews, continuing these studies in Edinburgh. In 1745 he became first deputy chaplain and later

chaplain of the Black Watch Regiment, but in 1754 he left the regiment and abandoned the ministry.

In 1757 Ferguson replaced David Hume as librarian to the Advocates Library in Edinburgh. In 1759 he became professor of natural philosophy at the University of Edinburgh and in 1764 was appointed to the coveted chair of "pneumatics [mental philosophy] and moral philosophy." Ferguson held this post until 1785 and retired from university life soon after. For the rest of his remarkably long life, however, he remained active as a writer, traveler, and speaker, amassing a considerable contemporary reputation for his *Essay on the History of Civil Society* (1767) and *Principles of Moral and Political Science* (1792). In 1793, on a trip to Germany, he was elected an honorary member of the Berlin Academy of Sciences.

Ferguson's importance as a thinker rests on his recognition of the important role played by society in shaping human values. He particularly rejected any notion of a "state of nature" in which men lived as individuals before society was established. Being a social animal, man was conditioned by necessity, habit, language, and familial or societal guidance. Societies as a whole, Ferguson asserted, are dynamic, following a pattern of change from "savagery" to "barbarism" to "civilization." Like individuals, they learn from and build upon the past. Different societies may, however, reflect particular characteristics based on factors such as geography or climate.

As any society becomes civilized, Ferguson suggested, it becomes more prone to conflict. Commerce breeds eco-

nomic competition, and the state system breeds war. Although some benefits do result from conflict—industrial growth, scientific and esthetic advances—Ferguson stressed that, when the division of labor results in economic class stratification and when warfare becomes the province of the professional military, a society faces decay and despotism and conflict is then no longer present. It should be noted that Ferguson was one of the first thinkers to point to conflict as a positive factor in human development and to argue that such conflict is more pronounced in civilized societies than in primitive ones.

Further Reading

Ferguson's *An Essay on the History of Civil Society* was recently edited with an introduction by Duncan Forbes (1966). Two useful studies of Ferguson are William C. Lehman, *Adam Ferguson and the Beginnings of Modern Sociology* (1930), and David Kettler, *The Social and Political Thought of Adam Ferguson* (1965). □

Pierre de Fermat

The French mathematician Pierre de Fermat (1601-1665) played an important part in the foundation and development of analytic geometry, the calculus of probabilities, and especially the theory of numbers.

Pierre de Fermat was born on Aug. 17, 1601, at Beaumont-de-Lamagne near Montaubon. There is some doubt as to the precise date of his birth. He is said to have been baptized on Aug. 20, 1601, but his tombstone puts his birth as 1608, and others have stated 1595. He was the son of Dominique Fermat, a leather merchant, and Claire de Long.

It was decided that Fermat should be trained as a magistrate, and he was sent to Toulouse. The general lines on which he was educated can only be guessed, and so far as his career as jurist is concerned, there is a record of his installation at Toulouse on May 14, 1631. In 1648 he was promoted to king's counselor in the Parliament of Toulouse, a post which he held until his death on Jan. 12, 1665. In 1631 he married his mother's cousin, Louise de Long; they had three sons and two daughters.

Theory of Numbers

It was perhaps C. G. Bachet's translation (1621) of Diophantus of Alexandria that stimulated Fermat's interest in the theory of numbers. That same edition was republished in 1670, with the addition of Fermat's notes edited by his son, who tells of the immense difficulties of collecting his father's writings, because they were only known from letters and notes in which Fermat usually stated theorems without proof. Much of Fermat's notes on Diophantus's problems were taken from the margin of his copy of Bachet's work.

As a specimen of Fermat's genius, there is his theorem that every number is either a square or the sum of two, three, or four squares. He arrived at his proof after long attempts to break down the solution into a multitude of minor solutions. In so doing, he also found many lesser but still important results. His final technique made use of his method of infinite descent, which may be faintly appreciated from a quotation. After saying that the theorem alluded to was beyond the power of René Descartes, by his own admission, Fermat goes on: "I have at last brought this under my method, and I prove that, if a given number were not of this nature, there would exist a number smaller than it which would not be so either, and again a third number smaller than the second, etc. *ad infinitum;* whence we infer that all numbers are of the nature indicated." Later, to prove an even more general proposition, he had to prove first five lesser theorems, and there again he made use of the same technique. The first of these theorems is worth singling out for comment. It is the theorem that every prime number of the form $4n + 1$ is the sum of two squares (thus $4 \times 1 + 1 = 1^2 + 2^2; 4 \times 2 + 1 = 0^2 + 3^2; 4 \times 3 + 1 = 2^2 + 3^2$; and so on). The great mathematician Leonhard Euler was the first to supply and publish a proof of this (1770).

There is one theorem, however, which has never been proved, and this has become something of a legend as Fermat's "Last Theorem," which states that there is no solution in integers of the equation $x^n + y^n = z^n$ $(xyz \neq 0, n > 2)$. There is a method in Diophantus for dividing a given square into two squares. Against this proposition in the margin of Bachet's edition Fermat wrote the following note:

"On the other hand, it is impossible to separate a cube into two cubes, a fourth power into two fourth powers, or, generally, any power except a square into two powers with the same exponent (i.e., of the same degree). I have discovered a truly marvelous proof of this, which however, the margin is not large enough to contain." Did Fermat have a proof of what, for 3 centuries, others have failed to prove? Euler proved it when the exponent (n) was equal to 3 or 4. Others have extended enormously the range of related theorems which are provable, but none has found a "truly marvelous proof" such as Fermat claimed to have found.

Analytical Geometry

Some of Fermat's first original mathematics appears to have been inspired by a famous problem of Apollonius. The crucial problem was this: if from a point in a plane four fixed lines are drawn, and four other lines through a point P cross the first four, all at the given angle; and if, furthermore, the distance along the four variable lines from P to where they cross the others is known as a, b, c, and d; then if $a \cdot c$ is in constant ratio to $b \cdot d$, the point P moves on a conic section (an ellipse, parabola, hyperbola, circle, or pair of straight lines). This theorem, which is not easy to write more concisely in simple language, may be called the "four-line theorem." If two of the fixed lines coincide, then the path of P is still a conic, but the problem, the "three-line problem," is easier.

Fermat provided his own proof of the three-line theorem, and in doing so he made use of analytical methods, determining points in a plane by two coordinates, showing that if the coordinates are related by equations like $2x + 3y = 5$, then the point lies on a straight line, and so on. He also worked out the equations of the curves known as conic sections, and he was quite familiar with coordinate methods in three dimensions.

Other work of a similar character by Fermat relates to the problem of constructing a tangent to a curve using infinitesimals. He found a method of calculating the length of a curve (involving the method of tangents) by first solving a problem of areas. Almost as important was his method of maxima and minima. This was first published in 1638 and was used for finding centers of gravity.

Principle of Light Transmission

It was shown by Hero of Alexandria that light traveling between two points, and undergoing a reflection in the process, follows the shortest path. For example, to follow the shortest path, light passing through a bowl of water would travel in a straight line; but observation shows that this is not true. Fermat demonstrated that such refracted (bent) light must be measured by optical distance, and this is always a minimum. The optical distance is the sum of the products of the distances and the corresponding refractive indexes. Fermat's conception involved the (correct) belief that light travels more slowly in more optically dense media. As subsequently developed, it was of great importance to the derivation of geometrical optics and also influenced J. Bernoulli in founding the calculus of variations.

Fermat did important work in the foundation of a theory of probability, which grew out of his early researches into the theory of numbers. In this theory he was without equal in his century and perhaps in any century. By any standards he was a great mathematician, but his name is less often encountered than it would have been had his personal life been better known.

Further Reading

L. J. Mordell, *Three Lectures on Fermat's Last Theorem* (1921), gives a short résumé of Fermat's life. Eric Temple Bell, *Men of Mathematics* (1937), contains a chapter on Fermat. See also James R. Newman, ed., *The World of Mathematics* (4 vols., 1956), and Joseph Frederick Scott, *A History of Mathematics: From Antiquity to the Beginning of the Nineteenth Century* (1958). ☐

Enrico Fermi

The Italian-American physicist Enrico Fermi (1901-1954) discovered "Fermi statistics," described beta decay, established the properties of slow neutrons, and constructed the first atomic pile.

In Enrico Fermi, the theorist and experimentalist were combined in a supremely intimate, complementary, and creative way. He possessed an almost uncanny physical intuition which, together with his personal simplicity, made him universally admired and respected.

Fermi was born on Sept. 29, 1901, in Rome, the third child of an official in the Ministry of Railroads. At about the age of 10 his interest in mathematics and physics awakened. A perceptive colleague of his father's, the engineer A. Amidei, recognized Fermi's truly exceptional intellectual qualities and guided his mathematical and physical studies between ages 13 and 17.

By the time Fermi received his doctorate from the University of Pisa in 1922, he had written several papers on relativistic electrodynamics, using the methods of Albert Einstein's general theory. Fermi received a fellowship to study at the University of Göttingen. In spite of the fact that he attacked problems of interest to the Göttingen physicists, his 8 months there were not very satisfactory. In 1924, on George E. Uhlenbeck's urging, Fermi went to study at the University of Leiden with Uhlenbeck's teacher, Paul Ehrenfest. Several years later, when Uhlenbeck was at the University of Michigan, he arranged for Fermi to spend the summers of 1930, 1933, and 1935 at Michigan's Summer School for Theoretical Physics.

Fermi Statistics

Late in 1924, after leaving Leiden, Fermi went to the University of Florence, where he taught mathematical physics and theoretical mechanics. In 1926 he published his first major discovery, namely, the quantum statistics now uni-

structure; and in quantum electrodynamics. His most celebrated theoretical work of this period was his 1933 theory of nuclear beta decay, a theory that nicely supplemented the theory of nuclear alpha decay of George Gamow, R. W. Gurney, and Edward U. Condon.

In beta decay a negatively charged particle (beta particle), known to be identical to an electron, is emitted from the nucleus of an atom, thereby increasing the atomic number of the nucleus by one unit. Fermi worked out in a short time an elegant theory of beta decay based on the idea that a neutron in the nucleus is transformed (decays) into three particles: a proton, an electron (beta particle), and a neutrino. Actually, the neutrino—an elusive, massless, chargeless particle—was not detected experimentally until the 1950s.

Slow Neutrons

In the late 1920s Fermi decided to attack experimental problems in nuclear physics rather than continue his ongoing spectroscopic researches. By mixing beryllium powder with some radon gas, he had a source of neutrons with which to experiment and determine whether neutrons could induce radioactivity. He constructed a crude Geiger-counter detector and, methodically, he started bombarding hydrogen, then went on to elements of higher atomic number. All results were negative until he bombarded fluorium and detected a weak radioactivity. This key date in neutron physics was March 21, 1934.

With high excitement Fermi and his coworkers continued. By summer 1934 they had bombarded many substances, discovering, for example, that neutrons can liberate protons as well as alpha particles. In addition, they had detected a slight radioactivity when bombarding uranium, and they attempted, without success, to understand why aluminum, when bombarded with neutrons, could not decide, in effect, which of two different nuclear reactions to undergo.

Their next discovery was a milestone. They found that the level of radioactivity induced in a substance was increased if a paraffin filter was placed in the beam of neutrons irradiating the substance. Fermi's hypothesis for this miracle, which he immediately confirmed, was that in passing through the paraffin, a compound containing a large amount of hydrogen, the neutrons had their velocity much reduced by collisions with the hydrogen nuclei; and these very slow neutrons—contrary to all expectations—induced a much higher radioactivity in substances than did fast neutrons. Furthermore, the old aluminum mystery had been solved: slow neutrons produce one kind of reaction, fast neutrons another. The discovery of the remarkable properties of slow neutrons was the key discovery in neutron physics.

By 1937 Fermi's wife and their children became directly affected by the racial laws in Fascist Italy. In December 1938 the Fermi family went to Stockholm for the presentation of the Nobel Prize in physics to Fermi. He and his family then left for the United States, arriving in New York on Jan. 2, 1939, where Fermi accepted a position at Columbia University.

versally known as Fermi-Dirac statistics. The particles obeying these statistics are now known as fermions.

Fermi's discovery did not stem basically from the concurrently emerging quantum theory, as might be expected, but rather from his own studies in statistical mechanics. These studies began as early as 1923 but were frustrated because a key concept, Wolfgang Pauli's exclusion principle, was still missing. Fermi saw immediately that all particles (fermions) obeying Pauli's exclusion principle would behave in a definite way, quantum-mechanically and statistically speaking. Fermi's discovery led to an understanding of certain important features of gas theory, of how electrons in metals conduct electricity, of why electrons do not contribute to the specific heats of substances, and of many other phenomena. It also undergirded Fermi's widely used 1927 statistical model of the atom, an approximate model in which the atom is envisioned as a statistical assemblage of electrons.

Theory of Beta Decay

The years between 1926 and 1938 constituted Fermi's "golden age." He accepted the chair of theoretical physics at the University of Rome in 1926 and only 3 years later became one of the first 30 members (and sole physicist) to be elected to the Royal Academy of Italy. In 1928 he married Laura Capon; they had a son and a daughter.

Fermi made significant contributions to a wide variety of problems in atomic, molecular, and nuclear spectroscopy; in particle scattering theory; in atomic and nuclear

Atomic Age

With the assistance of Herbert L. Anderson, Fermi produced a beam of neutrons with the Columbia cyclotron, thus verifying the fission of uranium. Then he quantitatively explored the conditions governing its production. He and his coworkers also proved, using a minute sample, that the fissionable isotope of uranium is U^{235}. By mid-1939 there was clear evidence that a self-sustaining chain reaction might be realizable. Furthermore, the stupendous military importance of nuclear fission had become clear. By July 1941 Arthur H. Compton, chairman of a special committee of the National Academy of Sciences, could report the possibility not only of a uranium bomb but also of a plutonium bomb.

Fermi was asked to assume the huge responsibility of directing the construction of the first atomic pile. He, and other key physicists, moved to the University of Chicago in the spring of 1942; by early October their researches had progressed to the point where Fermi was confident he knew how to construct the pile, and the project (the "Manhattan Project") was under way. Construction of the pile began in mid-November 1942, and on December 2 Fermi directed the operation of the first self-sustaining chain reaction created by man. The actual length of time it was operated on that historic day was 40 minutes; its maximum power was 1/2 watt, enough to activate a penlight. It was the opening of a new age, the Atomic Age.

Fermi's experiment was far more than an experiment in pure research. Huge national laboratories were constructed, one of which, Los Alamos, had immediate responsibility for the construction of the nuclear bomb. Its director was J. Robert Oppenheimer. In September 1944 he brought Fermi from Chicago primarily to have him on hand during the last, critical stages in the construction of the bomb. By early 1945 the project had proceeded to the point where the greatest amount of new information could be obtained only by actually exploding the fearsome weapon. The test, which bore the code name "Project Trinity," was successfully carried out on July 16, 1945, in the desert near Alamogordo in southern New Mexico.

Last Years

On Dec. 31, 1945, Fermi became Charles H. Swift distinguished service professor of physics and a member of the newly established Institute (now the Enrico Fermi Institute) for Nuclear Studies at the University of Chicago. This was the beginning of a period during which his reading and range of interests—always confined largely to physics—contracted considerably. For a few years he continued working in the fields of nuclear and neutron physics. In 1949 he demonstrated theoretically that the extremely high cosmic-ray energies can be accounted for by the accelerations imparted to them by vast interstellar magnetic fields. At about the same time his interest shifted away from nuclear physics to high-energy (particle) physics. In a number of his researches he used the Chicago synchrocyclotron to explore pi-meson interactions in an effort to discover the means by which the nucleus is held together in a stable configuration.

Fermi died in Chicago on Nov. 29, 1954.

Further Reading

The best existing guides to Fermi's scientific work are Emilio Segrè's *Enrico Fermi, Physicist* and his "Biographical Introduction" and various physicists' "Notes" in *The Collected Papers of Enrico Fermi,* edited by Segrè and others (2 vols., 1962-1965). Personal aspects of Fermi's life are recounted in the delightful work by his wife, Laura Fermi, *Atoms in the Family: My Life with Enrico Fermi* (1954) and *Illustrious Immigrants: The Intellectual Migration from Europe, 1930-41* (1968). See also Niels H. de V. Heathcote, *Nobel Prize Winners in Physics, 1901-1950* (1954); the obituary notices of Fermi by E. Bretscher and John D. Cockcroft in the Royal Society of London, *Biographical Memoirs of Fellows of the Royal Society,* vol. 1 (1955), and by Samuel K. Allison in the National Academy of Sciences of the United States, *Biographical Memoirs,* vol. 30 (1957); Pierre de Latil, *Enrico Fermi: The Man and His Theories* (trans. 1965); and Nobel Foundation, *Nobel Lectures, Including Presentation Speeches and Laureates' Biographies, 1922-1941* (1965). □

José Joaquin Fernández de Lizardi

José Joaquin Fernández de Lizardi (1776-1827) was a Mexican Journalist and novelist, commonly known by his pen name, "El Pensador Mexicano," or "The Mexican Thinker." He is regarded as the father of Mexican journalism.

José Fernández de Lizardi was born in the city of Mexico to a lower-middle-class family. Nevertheless, Fernández's parents managed to send their son to the University of Mexico, where he matriculated in the College of San Ildefonso in 1793. Five years later he withdrew without receiving his bachelor's degree, possibly because the death of his father deprived him of financial support.

Beginnings as a Journalist

Without inheritance or profession Fernández de Lizardi was forced to live by his wits, which, as it transpired, meant political journalism. It was a natural occupation for him: he had an agile and restless mind which could not help but be stimulated by the political revolutions in Spain and Mexico. It was also an occupation which involved considerable risks since political revolution fired political passions.

Lizardi's hazards were enhanced by his incapacity to identify for any length of time with any particular party or movement. He was a representative of the Enlightenment who believed that man is basically good and that society corrupts him. He was for the ideals of liberty, justice, and humanity and against slavery, oppression, intolerance, venality, and hypocrisy. Since neither contending royalists nor insurgents nor the factions that succeeded them met his standards, he found himself in perpetual opposition and the victim of almost constant suspicion and persecution.

Publisher of Political Satire

Although Lizardi had published earlier a substantial quantity of prose and verse satirizing Mexican society, his fame as a journalist began in 1812, when a decree of the liberal Spanish government establishing freedom of the press encouraged him to found his first periodical, *El pensador mexicano* (The Mexican Thinker). In it he attacked the vices of colonial government so vigorously that the viceroy suspended the decree and Lizardi was jailed for some 7 months. He continued to publish his paper until absolutism and rigorous censorship were restored in 1814, but his experience in prison and the surveillance of the Inquisition, which he had offended, induced him to turn to fiction as a less risky medium for his opinions.

Between 1816 and 1820 Lizardi wrote several novels, of which *The Itching Parrot* (*El perequillo sarniento*) became the most famous. Appearing serially, it ran into trouble with the censors, and although Lizardi managed to finish it, it was not published in full until 1830, 3 years after his death.

In 1820 the restoration of constitutional government and freedom of the press in Spain prompted Lizardi to establish a new periodical, *El conductor eléctrica* (The Lightning Conductor), in which he attacked the enemies of the constitutional system; but conservative forces were still powerful in Mexico, and after 24 numbers he could no longer find a printer. The following year insurgent and royalist forces under the leadership of Col. Agustín de Iturbide proclaimed independence, and Lizardi was summoned to operate their press. After the victory of the liberating army, however, his criticisms of Iturbide and the Church led to his excommunication and temporary imprisonment.

Lizardi had one more chance at respectability and security. In 1825, after the overthrow of Iturbide's short-lived empire, Mexico's republican government made him editor of its official gazette, but his incorrigible propensity for criticism soon caused him to fall into disfavor with its leaders. Two years later he died in poverty and obscurity.

The Itching Parrot

Lizardi is remembered as the father of Mexican journalism, but his most lasting claim to fame rests on *The Itching Parrot,* a novel of the Spanish picaresque genre. Its antihero, Perequillo, is a rogue, a scoundrel, and something of a buffoon whose life consists of an unrelieved series of escapades and misfortunes in the teeming streets, tenements, taverns, jails, and hospitals of Mexico City. Perequillo never learns from his misadventures and invariably emerges unrepentant.

The novel also has a pervasive didactic quality conveyed by digressive moral preachments and reflections on the vices of rich and poor. Its appeal to readers of successive generations, however, lies not in its narrative style or in its social and moral content but in the clarity and faithfulness with which it evokes the sights and sounds and smells of the popular culture of Mexico City at the end of the viceregal period.

Further Reading

The fullest English version of Fernández de Lizardi's most famous work, *The Itching Parrot,* translated with an introduction by Katherine Anne Porter (1942), omits the sermons which constitute over half of the work. The most complete study of Lizardi in English is Jefferson Rea Spell, *The Life and Works of José Fernández de Lizardi* (1931). For general background see Carlos Gonzalez-Pena, *History of Mexican Literature* (1940; trans. and rev. ed. 1943). ☐

Jean François Fernel

The French physician Jean François Fernel (ca. 1497-1558) reformed, systematized, and reorganized Renaissance medicine, popularizing the terms "physiology" and "pathology."

Born at Montdidier near Amiens, son of an innkeeper, Jean François Fernel was educated at the Collège de Ste-Barbe in Paris and received an arts degree from the University of Paris in 1519. Caught up in the rising tide of the new humanism led by Erasmus and Guillaume Budé, after graduating he recast his entire program to perfect himself in the classics, with special emphasis on mathematics. However, serious illness and loss of parental support compelled him to seek a living in medicine. He earned his way through medical school by lecturing and writing on astronomy, astrology, and mathematics, quickly achieving recognition not only as a learned physician and teacher but as a most modest and humane man. A highly successful medical practice created a reputation for him which spread throughout Europe, and he was called to the court by the Dauphin, later Henry II, to whom he became medical consultant and personal physician. Soon after the fall of Calais on April 26, 1558, Fernel fell ill and died at Fontainebleau.

Fernel is a classic example of the Renaissance physician. Characteristically, he approached medicine through humanistic studies, attempting to codify and clarify the accumulated knowledge of the past. He dealt with the customary topics of the day such as the elements and the humors and their functions in both health and disease. Unfortunately, he continued the medieval association of astronomy and astrology in medicine. His writings in this field were very influential on his successors. Nonetheless, his improvements on the astrolabe and his accurate estimate of the length of a degree were considerable scientific contributions.

Fernel greatly influenced medicine through his written works, of which there are no less than 100 editions. Great powers of systematization are evident in his most important publications, *Dialogues* and *Medicina,* on the basic sciences. In the first part of his *Medicina,* published in 1542 and entitled *Physiology,* he presented human physiology as an integral subject. The second part dealt with pathology and, unlike the usual approach of outlining case histories, attempted to treat the individual organs systematically. It may be said that Fernel popularized the terms "physiology" and "pathology." But his contribution was to draw together into a comprehensive treatise of ordered relationships what had been diffusely expressed by earlier writers. In his pathology, by relating theory to practice, he began to approach the conception of a clinical entity.

The distinctive features of Fernel's thought are his rationalism, analytical powers, insistence on observation. In formulating the new medicine, he carried forward the best of the old winnowed from its accumulated dross. This systematization and clarification formed an important platform from which medicine could evolve.

Further Reading

The only complete biography of Fernel in English is Sir Charles Sherrington, *The Endeavour of Jean Fernel* (1946). It contains a translation of Guillaume Plancy's *Life of Fernel* (1607). Although it is an important work, brilliantly presented, caution must be exercised in accepting many of its claims of Fernel's originality. A good corrective is Lynn Thorndike, *History of Magic and Experimental Science,* vols. 5 and 6 (1941). □

Geraldine Ferraro

Sixty-four years after American women won the right to vote Geraldine Ferraro (born 1935) became the first woman candidate for the vice presidency of a major political party. She had previously served three consecutive terms in the U.S. House of Representatives.

Geraldine Ferraro was born on August 26, 1935. She was the third child of Dominick and Antonetta Ferraro. The Ferraro's had only one surviving son, Carl, at the time of Geraldine's birth—the other, Gerard, had been killed in a family automobile accident two years earlier. Dominick Ferraro, an Italian immigrant, operated a night club in Newburgh, a small city north of New York City reputed to be wide-open to organized crime.

In 1944, when Ferraro was eight years old, her father was arrested and charged with operating a numbers racket. He died of a heart attack the day he was to appear for trial. The Ferraro family was forced to move, first to the Bronx, and then to a working-class neighborhood in Queens. Here Antonetta Ferraro worked in the garment industry, crocheting beads on wedding dresses and evening gowns in order to support herself and her children.

As a young girl Ferraro attended Marymount School in Tarrytown, New York. She consistently excelled at school, skipping from the sixth to the eighth grade and graduating from high school at 16. She won a full scholarship to Marymount Manhattan College, where she was the editor of the school newspaper. While still at Marymount Ferraro also took education courses at Hunter College. In this way she prepared herself to teach English in the New York City Public School system after she graduated college. While teaching, Ferraro attended Fordham University's evening law classes. She received her law degree in 1960. The week she passed the bar exam she married John Zaccaro, an old sweetheart, but kept her maiden name in honor of her mother.

Attorney and Congresswoman

From 1961 to 1974 Ferraro practiced law, had her three children—Donna, John Jr., and Laura—and worked in her husband's real estate business. In 1974, with her youngest child in the second grade, Ferraro agreed to serve as an assistant district attorney in Queens County. As an assistant DA, she created two special units, the Special Victims Bureau and the Confidential Unit. As chief of these units, Ferraro specialized in trying cases involving sex crimes, crimes against the elderly, family violence, and child abuse. From 1974 to 1978 she also served on the Advisory Council for the Housing Court of the City of New York and as president of the Queens County Women's Bar Association.

In 1978 Ferraro decided to run for Congress. In the primary campaign, in an intensely ethnic area of Queens, she faced Thomas Manton, an Irish city councilman, and Patrick Deignan, an Irish district leader. Outspending both opponents, Geraldine Ferraro won the nomination. Against a conservative Republican in the general election Ferraro chose to wage a campaign stressing law and order. Her slogan, "Finally, a Tough Democrat," appealed to voters, and she was elected with 54 percent of the vote.

In Congress Ferraro balanced the conservative demands of her constituency with her own feminist and liberal politics. She voted, for example, against school busing and supported tax credits for private and parochial school parents. Yet she was also a prime mover in opposing economic discrimination against housewives and working women. Ferraro easily won her re-election in 1980 and 1982 and was elected secretary of the Democratic Caucus in her second term. As secretary, she sat on the Democratic Steering and Policy Committee.

In 1982 she received an appointment to the powerful House Budget Committee, which sets national spending priorities. In the House she also served as a member of the House Committee on Public Works and Transportation. Coming from a district with two major airports close by, Ferraro was a strong advocate of air safety and noise control. As a member of the Select Committee on Aging she worked to combat crimes against the elderly and to expand health care and provide senior citizen centers. As a member of the Congressional Caucus for Women's Issues Ferraro helped lead the successful battle for passage of the Economic Equity Act and the unsuccessful campaign for the Equal Rights Amendment. She was the author of those sections of the Equity Act dealing with private pension reform and expanding retirement savings options for the elderly.

A Leader in the Democratic Party

Ferraro continued her active role within the Democratic Party. She served as a delegate to the Democratic Party's 1982 mid-term convention and was a key member of the Hunt Commission, which developed delegate selection rules for the 1984 convention. Then, in January of 1984, Ferraro was named chair of the Democratic Party Platform Committee for the 1984 national convention.

During the years between the mid-term convention and the national convention Ferraro worked hard to achieve national recognition and to correct any impression that she lacked real foreign policy experience and expertise. In 1983 she travelled to Central America and to the Middle East, and, as nomination time approached, she talked frequently about these trips and about her other international experience, including her membership in congressional groups on United States-Soviet relations.

After a grueling series of interviews—climaxing perhaps the most thorough vice-presidential search in history—Geraldine Ferraro was chosen by Democratic presidential nominee Walter F. Mondale as his running-mate. Thus, 64 years to the day that American women won the right to vote, the first woman candidate for the vice presidency was named by a major party.

The 1984 Campaign

Politically, Ferraro was seen to have several assets as a candidate. Democrats hoped that she would help to exploit the gender gap—that is, the clear difference in voting patterns between men and women that seemed to have emerged in the 1970s and 1980s, with women voting in greater numbers than men and voting for Democratic candidates and peace issues more consistently than men. A na-

tional poll taken in July of 1984 had reported that men favored Reagan 58 percent to 36 percent, but that women favored Mondale 49 percent to 41 percent. Widespread efforts on the part of organized feminists to register large numbers of new women voters also promised to widen the gender gap and increase the value of a woman candidate. Ferraro was also politically appealing as a candidate from a strong working-class and ethnic background and district. Democratic strategists felt it was essential for Mondale to win among such voters.

President Reagan's popularity with the voters, however, resulted in a solid re-election victory. Reagan-Bush received 59 percent of the popular vote and 525 of the 538 electoral votes; Mondale-Ferraro received only 41 percent of the popular vote and 13 electoral votes (Minnesota and the District of Columbia). Mondale was hurt most by his perceived ties to "special interests," his plan to raise taxes, and his lack of a clearly defined economic program. Ferraro's chief problem as a candidate was the investigation of her husband John Zaccaro's real estate business and tax records, begun during the campaign months.

The gender gap had not made the difference that the Democrats had hoped. Although women voted for the Democratic ticket in slightly larger numbers than men, the difference had fallen to 4.5 percentage points in 1984, from 8.5 percentage points in 1980. Instead, in one of the most polarized elections in the history of the United States, the vote split first along racial lines, with Blacks voting 91 to 9 percent for the Mondale-Ferraro ticket and whites voting 66 to 34 percent for Reagan-Bush, and secondly, along economic lines, with those making under $12,500 voting for Mondale-Ferraro 53 to 46 percent, and those in the over $35,000 range voting for Reagan-Bush 67 to 31.5 percent.

Keeping the Liberal Faith

After Ferraro's term as a congresswoman expired in January of 1985, she wrote a book about the vice-presidential campaign. For a time, she chose to to keep a low political profile. In 1986, she passed up the opportunity to challenge Alphonse D'Amato, the incumbent Republican senator from New York. Still under public scrutiny her husband pleaded guilty to overstating his net worth in getting a loan and was sentenced to community service. Also, police affidavits surfaced detailing a 1985 meeting between Zacarro and Robert DiBernardo, a captain and porno kingpin for mob boss John Gambino. Later, Ferraro's son John, a college student, was arrested for possessing cocaine.

In 1990 Ferraro campaigned aggressively on behalf of female Democratic candidates in New York. She launched her own political comeback in 1992, when she entered the New York Democratic primary as a candidate for the United States Senate. Competing against three other candidates in the primary, including New York state comptroller and former congressional representative Elizabeth Holtzman, Ferraro faced a tough battle. Typically optimistic to the end, Ferraro finished second, fewer than 10,000 votes behind Holtzman, who ultimately was defeated in the general election.

Undaunted, Ferraro tested support for possible campaigns for mayor of New York City in 1997 or for Senator or governor of New York in 1998. Meanwhile, she remains true to her Liberal faith and continues to speak out for Liberal policies. In 1993, she published a book demanding more power for women. Beginning in 1996, she appeared every other week on "Crossfire," a half-hour political talk show on Cable News Network—the same show that made Pat Buchanan nationally famous. Occupying the liberal chair opposite John Sununu, President Bush's Chief of Staff, Geraldine Ferraro continued to press for increased government spending and more federal programs on behalf of those she considers "underprivileged."

Further Reading

Most of the written work on Ferraro is in the popular press. Articles appeared in *US News and World Report* on July 16 and 23, 1984; *Time* on June 4, 1984; *MS* for July 1984; *New York Magazine* on July 16,1984; *Working Woman* for October 1984; and *McCall's* for October 1984. In 1985 she wrote, with Linda Bird Francke, *Ferraro: My Story* (Bantam Books), which was favorably reviewed.

Geraldine, Ferraro *Changing History: Women, Power, and Politics* (Moyer Bell, 1993). Lee Michael Katz, *My name is Geraldine Ferraro: An Unauthorized biography.* (New American Library, 1984). Eugene Larson, "Geraldine Ferraro," *Great Lives from History,* Frank N. Magill ed. Vol. 2. (Salem Press, 1995). Jan Russell, "Geraldine Ferraro" *Working Woman ,* November 1996, pages 28-31. Linda Witt, Karen M. Paget, and Glenna Matthews. *Running as a Woman; Gender and Power in American Politics* (Free Press, 1993). ☐

Gabriel Miró Ferrer

The Spanish author Gabriel Miró Ferrer (1879-1930) was one of the outstanding prose stylists of the 20th century. His preferred form was the impressionistic vignette, which appealed to the senses rather than to the intellect.

Gabriel Miró Ferrer was born on July 28, 1879, in Alicante in the bright and sunny southeastern Mediterranean region of Spain. He attended the Jesuit school in Orihuela as a boarding student during the years 1886-1891, and he graduated from secondary school in 1896. Miró began studying law in Valencia in 1896, graduating in 1900.

In 1901 Miró married Clemencia Maignon, daughter of the French consul in Alicante, and later two daughters, Olympia and Clemencia, were born to them. His first important book was *Del vivir* (1904). In it he introduced the character Sigüenza (Miró himself) and also began to develop the sensuous and impressionistic descriptions for which he is remembered. His first important novels were published in 1908: *La novela de mi amigo* and *Nómada.*

Perhaps Miró's most remembered writing (in literary circles) is *Libro de Sigüenza,* a continuing series of impressionistic vignettes beginning in 1907. In the style of this book Miró shows his affiliation with the *Modernista* movement of Rubén Dario. Sigüenza is a Franciscan monk; he is meditative, withdrawn, a lover of helpless animals. Above all, he is interested in colors and sights and sounds. He lives an intense life of the senses, though in a limited way; he lacks moral and intellectual fervor and thus the capacity for action.

In 1914 Miró moved to Barcelona to work in various journalistic ventures. One of the projects was the development of a religious encyclopedia, and his studies during this undertaking led him to write one of his distinctive books, *Figuras de la pasión del Señor* (1916). In this work, Miró focused upon various scenes in the life of Jesus, with concentration upon plastic effects and impressionistic description.

In 1921 Miró published *Nuestro Padre San Daniel,* followed by *El obispo leproso* (1926). These two novels, generally considered his finest, treat in his usual impressionistic manner his formative years in the Jesuit schools. What the novels lack in structure they make up for in sensitive presentation of the boy's emotional formation. Although Miró was not, like Miguel de Unamuno, an overt critic of the Roman Catholic Church, his criticism of its religious teaching is subtle but nevertheless effective.

After 1920 Miró lived in Madrid and worked in the Ministry of Education. He continued to write and publish until almost the time of his death on May 27, 1930.

Further Reading

There is no biography of Miró in English. Some background is in Salvador de Madariaga, *The Genius of Spain* (1923); Aubrey F.G. Bell, *Contemporary Spanish Literature* (1925; rev. ed. 1933); Richard Chandler and Kessel Schwartz, *A New History of Spanish Literature* (1961); and James R. Stamm, *A Short History of Spanish Literature* (1967). ☐

José Figuéres Ferrer

The Costa Rican political leader José Figuéres Ferrer (born 1906) was president of Costa Rica and one of its most influential figures.

José Figuéres was born in San Ramon on Sept. 25, 1906, soon after his parents' arrival from Spain. He received most of his education in Costa Rica but also studied in the United States, as an unmatriculated student at the Massachusetts Institute of Technology.

Upon his return home Figuéres took over a small plantation in the mountains and during the 1930s devoted most of his attention to converting it into a modern enterprise. He gained some local fame for the progressive manner in which he treated his employees.

Figuéres gained sudden national fame when he bought radio time to denounce a riot on July 4, 1942, and the government of President Rafael Calderon Guardia as encouraging violence by Communists to divert attention from its own failures. In the middle of his talk he was arrested and was subsequently deported to Mexico.

Upon his return in 1944 Figuéres helped to organize the campaign of Leon Cortes, opposition candidate in the 1944 presidential election. The opposition claimed that government nominee Teodoro Picado won by fraud and insisted on special guarantees for the presidential poll of 1948. Figuéres and his colleagues, organized in the Social Democratic party, supported Otilio Ulate Blanco against former president Calderon Guardia, the government's nominee.

First Presidency

When Congress negated Ulate's victory, Figuéres started a successful revolt and became president of the provisional government. The Junta Fundidora de la Segunda República (Founding Junta of the Second Republic), the government headed by Figuéres, enacted a number of reforms. It nationalized all banks and set up a government electric power company and a housing institute. In November 1949 it turned the government over to Otilio Ulate, victor in the 1948 election.

During the conservative Ulate regime, Figuéres organized the Partido Liberación Nacional (PLN; National Liberation Party). He was the PLN candidate in the 1953 presidential election and was overwhelmingly elected. The principal innovation of the second Figuéres government was a new agreement with the United Fruit Company, the major exporter of the country's bananas, providing for a much larger return to the government from the company's profits. The administration also carried out ambitious public housing and electrification programs.

Figuéres's party did not win the next election because of a split in its ranks. However, in 1962 Liberación Nacional returned to power under President Francisco Orlich, a boyhood friend of Figuéres. PLN lost again at the end of Orlich's administration in 1966.

During these years Figuéres devoted most of his attention to private business affairs, although he remained a major figure in the PLN. He also traveled widely in Latin America, the United States, Europe, and Israel, and was again nominated for president by the PLN for the election of March 1970, which he won.

Figuéres had an importance which transcended his small country. He was a major spokesman for a broad range of Latin American public opinion and in many speeches and articles laid particular stress on the importance of the highly industrialized countries paying "just" prices for the foodstuffs and raw materials purchased from the underdeveloped nations as a possible substitute for economic aid.

Further Reading

There is no general study in English on Figuéres's career. However, a summary version is in Robert J. Alexander, *Prophets of the Revolution: Profiles of Latin American Leaders* (1962). Additional information can be found in John Martz, *Central America: The Crisis and the Challenge* (1959); Franklin D. Parker, *The Central American Republics* (1964); and Mario Rodriguez, *Central America* (1965). □

Guglielmo Ferrero

The Italian journalist, novelist, and historian Guglielmo Ferrero (1871-1942) devoted his life and his writings to the cause of liberalism.

Guglielmo Ferrero was born in Portica, Piedmont, on July 21, 1871. While a law student at Pisa, Bologna, and Turin, his interest was in contemporary problems, an orientation confirmed by his first meeting in 1889 with the Italian sociologist and historian Cesare Lombroso. In 1893 the two collaborated on a study of female criminality, The *Female Offender,* and soon afterward Lombroso's daughter Gina became Ferrero's wife.

From 1891 to 1894 Ferrero traveled extensively in Europe, working in the libraries of London, Berlin, and Paris on a projected history of justice. The principal result of his travels was *Young Europe* (1897). He was already active in the Italian Socialist movement and engaged in polemics in the press with the leading nationalist writers of the country. Also concerned with the problems of recognizing whether a civilization is in its ascendance or becoming decadent, he soon turned to the history of Rome.

Ferrero's *Greatness and Decline of Rome* (6 vols., 1903-1908) was soon translated into all the major European languages. A popular success, it was met with scorn by professional classicists, who looked unkindly on his constant contemporary references, on his passion for brilliant narrative, and on his attempts at sociological analysis of Roman politics. Above all, they took exception to his portrayal of such figures as Julius Caesar. For 19th-century classical historians Caesar had been an antique Napoleon, bringing order out of chaos. Ferrero portrayed him as the cause of the ruin of the Roman Republic.

Ferrero next turned to political essays and novels: *Between Two Worlds* (1913), *Speeches to the Deaf* (1925), and *The Two Truths* (2 vols., 1933-1939); and to articles for journals in Europe, Latin America, and the United States. In these he analyzed the European crisis of values and sought to recover what he called "the geniuses of the city," which governed collective life and had been forgotten by humanity.

By 1924 Ferrero's opposition to fascism was well known. When the reign of Black Shirt terror forced liberal intellectuals to leave Italy in 1925, he refused and was placed under house arrest. In 1929, after officials of the League of Nations and King Albert of Belgium intervened, he was allowed to accept a professorship at Geneva.

Ferrero's last works were devoted to the French Revolution, Napoleon, and the restoration. The Revolution, as he saw it, had tried to create a liberal order but had ended by establishing the first modern dictatorship. The books— *Adventure* (1936), *The Reconstruction of Europe* (1940), *Power* (1942), and *The Two French Revolutions* (1951)— were filled with the political preoccupations of the interwar years. Ferrero died at Mont-Pelerin-sur-Vevey on Aug. 3, 1942.

Further Reading

Ferrero is briefly noted in Matthew A. Fitzsimons and others, eds., *The Development of Historiography* (1954). ☐

Jules François Camille Ferry

The French statesman Jules François Camille Ferry (1832-1893) was a major political leader during the first 2 decades of the Third Republic. He played a key role in expanding public education and in developing France's colonial empire.

Jules Ferry was born at Saint-Dié, Vosges Department, on April 5, 1832. On receiving his law degree in 1851, he was admitted to the Paris bar, but he first made his name in journalism as one of the most vigorous critics of the Second Empire. His successes led him into more active politics, and in 1869 he was elected to the legislature from Paris.

Entering the Government of National Defense after the fall of the Empire, Ferry became the top civil administrator for Paris and had to struggle with the difficult problems caused by the siege. His stringent but necessary measures earned him an unpopularity in the capital that lasted throughout his career.

Ferry became minister of public instruction in 1879 and initiated a number of reforms, the most controversial being those aimed at reducing the influence of the Church on education. The state recovered its monopoly in the awarding of degrees, but his proposal to prohibit teaching by members of religious orders (the famous Article 7) was defeated in the Senate. In 1880 he took administrative measures to dissolve unauthorized religious orders. More important was his introduction of legislation to make elementary education compulsory, free, and laic. In September 1880 he became premier and was able to further his program by decrees, but lack of funds and personnel prevented his ambitious plans from being implemented at once.

An ardent colonial expansionist when most republican politicians saw foreign questions only in terms of Alsace-Lorraine and the German menace, Ferry was charged with diverting attention—and troops—away from the Continent. His first ministry ended in November 1881 as a result of criticism of the Tunisian expedition which led to the French protectorate.

Ferry returned to the Ministry of Public Instruction in January 1882. In February 1883 he was again premier and carried out a purge of antirepublican elements in the judiciary. Although his power and prestige seemed as great as ever, this time the opposition to his foreign policy proved fatal to Ferry's career. He supported French involvement in Indochina, but news of a minor defeat there, much exaggerated in the first report, compelled his resignation on March 30, 1885. He was an unsuccessful candidate for the presi-

dency in 1887 and never again played a leading role in government. Shot by an Alsatian fanatic on Dec. 10, 1892, Ferry died in Paris on March 17, 1893.

Further Reading

For an important aspect of Ferry's career see Thomas F. Power, Jr., *Jules Ferry and the Renaissance of French Imperialism* (1944).

Additional Sources

Guilhaume, Philippe, *Jules Ferry,* Paris: Encre, 1980. ☐

Lion Feuchtwanger

Lion Feuchtwanger (1884-1958), a distinguished member of the post-World War I German literary scene, lived and wrote in political exile for the last quarter-century of his life. His masterwork, *Success,* is one of the great novels of the 20th century.

Lion Feuchtwanger was born on July 7, 1884, in Munich, Germany, the son of a wealthy Jewish industrialist. At Berlin and Munich universities he studied philosophy, literature, and ancient and modern languages and also developed a working interest in theater; in fact, while still a student he composed three short Old Testament plays—*Joel, King Saul,* and *Uriah's Wife* (1905-1906). After graduation he became a drama critic for *Die Schaubühne* (*The Stage*) from 1908 to 1911. In 1912 he married Martha Loffler.

Feuchtwanger was an inveterate traveller, and in 1914, shortly after the outbreak of World War I, he was in Tunisia (which was then French) and was arrested as an enemy alien and imprisoned. He escaped after a short internment, returned to Germany, and served in the army. After his discharge he wrote several anti-war plays (one, entitled *Peace,* was modeled on an Aristophanes anti-war play), but wartime patriotic fervor led to their suppression. Back in Berlin he began graduate work in literature and received a Ph.D. in 1918; his thesis subject was the great 19th-century German-Jewish poet Heinrich Heine.

Feuchtwanger's own early poetry reflected his socialist and pacifist views, and in 1918 he founded a literary newspaper, *Der Spiegel* (*The Mirror*), to promote "revolutionary artistic tendencies." His editorship led to the discovery of the experimental radical playwright Bertolt Brecht, whose work Feuchtwanger enthusiastically promoted; they later collaborated on several plays, including *Das Leben Eduard des zweiten von England* (1928), an adaptation of Christopher Marlowe's *Edward II.*

Feuchtwanger was an energetic man and a prolific writer: he translated literary classics from the Spanish, the English, and the ancient Greek and worked as an editor and a reviewer, yet still found time for his own plays, novels, and poems. He finished his first novel, *Jew Süss* (*Power*), in 1921 but was unable to find a publisher for it until 1925, when it became an international best-seller. Set in the 18th century, it deals with an identity crisis: in order to gain social power, the novel's protagonist renounces his Jewish heritage and becomes assimilated into the mainstream of German culture. In 1928, although he had not yet visited the United States, Feuchtwanger, under the pseudonym J. L. Wetcheek (a literal translation of "Feuchtwanger"), wrote *Pep,* a book of satirical poems about America.

The Novel Success

Feuchtwanger's reputation was initially as a playwright and later as a historical novelist, but his masterpiece, *Erfolg* (1930; *Success*), was a contemporary *roman à clef,* a novel of a gloriously liberal but doomed Weimar Republic moving inexorably toward fascism. Published just three years before Hitler's rise to power, the novel is not only prophetic of Germany's totalitarianism, but uncanny in its multi-level depiction of the corruptive process.

The narrative scheme of *Success* was almost certainly influenced by movie techniques. As in John Dos Passos' *USA* trilogy and Aldous Huxley's *Point Counter Point,* the main plot line, where it exists at all, is subordinated to multiple parallel sub-plots, so that there is, as in film, frequent "cross-cutting." Dozens of characters are successfully manipulated, and so skillfully that when a character reappears after an absence of 40 or 50 pages he is almost immediately recalled by the reader.

The widely diffuse central story line concerns the futile efforts of a young woman, Johanna Krain, to free her lover,

Krüger, from prison. As an art museum curator he has grievously offended the conservative Bavarian folk by exhibiting two unconventional paintings: one is an unusual treatment of "Joseph and His Brothers," and the other is a female nude. With the first painting Feuchtwanger hit upon a sly symbol; the Munich populace is too unimaginative to see the connection between themselves and Joseph's business-like, short-memoried brothers, but they are nevertheless troubled by the painting. Much less subtle is the second painting, which leads to Krüger's trial for adultery with the painting's nude subject (of which he is actually innocent) and breach of public morality; unfortunately for Krüger, too many marginal matters obtrude, and he is found guilty and languishes in prison for several dispiriting years before dying there. Krüger is, even before Hitler's advent, a victim of Hitlerism, of provincial mentality and rigged justice.

Hitler is represented in the novel as a character named Rupert Kutzner, leader of a lunatic-fringe right-wing group whose power grows and moves centerward as ministers and industrialists find the group useful. Other important replications are Kaspar Pröckl (Bertolt Brecht), Jacques Tüverlin (Feuchtwanger himself), and Hessreiter (either Krupp or I. G. Farben). Quite probably all of the characters have real-life models, just as the depicted events mirror actual developments in the decline of German democracy. But it's not the historical literalness that accounts for the novel's greatness; rather, it's the wealth and depth of Feuchtwanger's moral imagination. Dotting the book's landscapes are startling ironies and haunting tableaux: the testimony that sinks the decent, civilized Krüger comes from an arrant perjurer, the hooligan chauffeur Ratzenberger, who is not so incidentally a member of Kutzner's party; the liberal defense attorney, Geyer, is mugged by his own cadging, nihilistic son, Erich; the folksy Chaplinesque comic, Balthasar Hierl, secretly fears and detests his adoring public; the once-liberal minister Klenk, swept to the right by the political winds, finds himself strangely and deeply moved by the left-revolutionary film "Orlov" (actually Eisenstein's masterpiece, "Potemkin"); the great painter Landholzer has slyly found "asylum" in a mental institution, which he finds more congenial than the outside world.

Success's approximately 800 pages constitute a conspectus of Germany in the 1920s, brilliantly dissecting the private and public tensions that were building to a national crisis and, ultimately, to a European calamity. Few novels have been as ambitious and fewer still as fulfilling. English language readers are the beneficiaries of an exemplary translation by Willa and Edwin Muir (1930).

Exile in the United States

In 1932 and 1933 Feuchtwanger travelled in America and began writing a trilogy that reached back into Roman antiquity, focusing on the complex figure of Josephus, the Roman-Jewish soldier-historian. Upon his return to Germany Feuchtwanger's Berlin house and his fortune were confiscated by the Nazi government. He fled to France, where he lived and wrote until French capitulation in 1940 led to his confinement in a concentration camp; that incarceration and his escape in female disguise are described in

Der Teufel in Frankreich (1941; *The Devil in France*). Still under a German death sentence for his writings and his avowed politics, Feuchtwanger fled with his wife to Spain, then to Portugal, and in late 1940 reached the United States, which became his permanent home.

Feuchtwanger's political militancy and creative powers were not at all blunted by exile. In addition to his Josephus trilogy, he wrote *Die Geschwister Oppenheim* (1933; *The Oppermanns*, 1934), a powerful novel of a wealthy Jewish family cheated of their department store through the connivance of a competitor and the government; an allegorical novel followed, *Der Falsche Nero* (1936; *The Pretender*), in which a lowly potter (read "Hitler") is elevated by a capitalist to a position of pseudo emperor, but is finally overthrown and crucified along with his supporters.

After World War II's end, Feuchtwanger reverted to his first fictional love, the historical novel: *Die Füchse Im Weinberg* (1947; *Proud Destiny*) documents Benjamin Franklin's role in forging an alliance between France and the American insurrectionists during the revolutionary struggle against England. *Goya* (1951; *This Is the Hour*) portrays the tempestuous personality of the great Spanish painter against the background of his times. *Spanische Ballade* (1955; *Raquel*) is an intriguing romance of medieval Spain, exploring the interactions of its three central types—the businessman, the adventurer, and the historian.

Feuchtwanger died in Los Angeles, California, on December 21, 1958.

Further Reading

Two English-language studies of Feuchtwanger are Lothar Kahn's *Insight and Action* (1975) and John M. Spalek's *Lion Feuchtwanger: the man, his ideas, his work* (1972). Two important works in German are Günther Horst Gottschalk's *Die "Verkleidungstrachnik" Lion Feuchtwanger in Waffen für Amerika* (1965) and a full-length critical study of *Success* Egon Bruckener's *Lion Feuchtwanger's Roman "Erfolg"* (1978). □

Ludwig Andreas Feuerbach

The German philosopher Ludwig Andreas Feuerbach (1804-1872) is noted for his criticism of orthodox religion. It may be said that he humanized God while deifying man.

Ludwig Feuerbach was born on July 28, 1804, in Landshut, Bavaria. He studied at the University of Heidelberg and then switched from theology to philosophy and moved to the University of Berlin, where he became a diligent student of G. W. F. Hegel. In 1828 he received his doctorate at the University of Erlangen.

Feuerbach's first publication was an essay entitled *Thoughts about Death and Immortality* (1830). Because it was so controversial at that time to deny the immortality of the soul, he published his work anonymously. In the following years he tried unsuccessfully to obtain a professorship. Even his scholarly books were of no help: *From Bacon to Spinoza* (1833), *Leibniz* (1836), and *Pierre Bayle* (1838). In 1839 his criticism of Hegel became evident. Later he vigorously began his criticism of religion.

Feuerbach's primary work is *The Essence of Christianity* (1841), one of the first attempts at understanding religion from a strictly human point of view. He holds that the sources of religion are human wishes, imagination, feelings, emotions, and, above all, man's desire to elucidate his own essence. Accordingly, Feuerbach sees in God the purified essence of man himself and the unlimited ideal of man's capabilities. He insists that religion is necessary for man's search for himself and that it separates man from the animals. Furthermore, he concedes that among all religions Christianity has a special mandate, seen in the doctrine that God became man. However, for him it was not God who became man; in fact, it is man who intends to conceive his own real essence in Jesus Christ. Consequently, Feuerbach suggests that theology and Christology should be transmuted into anthropology, into a theory about the divine nature of man.

Besides shaking the foundation of theology, Feuerbach outlined the principles of new ways of philosophizing: *Preparatory Theses on the Reform of Philosophy* (1842) and *Principles of the Philosophy of the Future* (1843). In these he explained that the basis of philosophy is not reason and abstraction but human sensuality, sexuality, and emotions. He was one of the first in modern times to emphasize the problem of communication; hence, he understood the human ego as a relation to another human being, to a "thou."

In 1844 Feuerbach revised *The Essence of Christianity*. Further writings clarified his position, among them *The Essence of Faith according to Luther* (1844) and *The Essence of Religion* (1846). Because of his strong criticism of religion he was never given opportunity to join any faculty in Germany. He lived in an idyllic retreat at Bruckberg and in 1857 published his Theogony. He died at Rechenberg on Sept. 13, 1872.

Further Reading

Feuerbach's life and thought are examined in Friedrich Engels, *Ludwig Feuerbach and the Outcome of Classical German Philosophy* (1895; trans. 1934); William B. Chamberlain, *Heaven Wasn't His Destination* (1941); and Martin Buber, *Between Man and Man* (1947). Recommended introductions to various aspects of Feuerbach's writings are Karl Barth's introductory essay to Feuerbach's *The Essence of Christianity* (1957) and Manfred H. Vogel, *Principles of the Philosophy of the Future* (1965). □

Richard Phillips Feynman

The theoretical work of the American physicist Richard Phillips Feynman (1918-1988) opened up the doors to research in quantum electrodynamics. He shared the 1965 Nobel Prize in Physics.

Richard Feynman was born on May 11, 1918, in Far Rockaway, a suburb of New York City. He lived there until 1935, when he left to attend the Massachusetts Institute of Technology. After receiving a bachelor's degree in physics in 1939, he went to Princeton University, where he received a Ph.D. in 1942. While at Princeton, Feynman worked on the Manhattan Project, which eventually led him to Los Alamos, New Mexico, in 1943 to work on the atomic bomb. In 1946 he went to Cornell University, where he remained as an associate professor of theoretical physics until 1951. He spent half of that year in Brazil lecturing at the University of Rio and then became a Tolman professor of physics at the California Institute of Technology, where he stayed for more than 30 years. He had three wives and two children, Carl and Michelle.

Solves Problems in the Theory of Quantum Electrodynamics

Feynman's primary contribution to physics was in the field of quantum electrodynamics, which is the study of the interactions of electromagnetic radiation with atoms and with fundamental particles, such as electrons. Because the equations that compose it are applicable to atomic physics, chemistry, and electromagnetism, quantum electrodynamics is one of the most useful tools in understanding physical phenomena.

The field initially grew out of work done by P. Dirac, W. Heisenberg, W. Pauli, and E. Fermi in the late 1920s.

The original theory was constructed by integrating quantum mechanics into classical electrodynamics. It provided a reasonable explanation of the dual wave-particle nature of light by explaining how it was possible for light to behave like a wave under certain conditions and like a particle (a "photon") on other occasions. Dirac in particular introduced a theory that described the behavior of an electron in accordance with both relativity and quantum mechanics. His theory brought together almost everything that was known about particle physics in the 1920s. However, when the principles behind electromagnetic interactions were brought into Dirac's equation, numerous mathematical problems arose: meaningless or infinite answers were obtained when the theory was applied to certain experimental data.

Feynman found a way to bypass, though not solve, these problems. Be redefining the existing value of the charge and the mass of the electron (a process known as "renormalization"), he managed to make the "divergent integrals" irrelevant—these were the terms in the theory which had previously led to meaningless answers. Thus, while some divergent terms still exist in quantum electrodynamics, they no longer enter the calculations of measurable quantities from theory.

The significance of Feynman's contribution is enormous. He gave the theory of quantum electrodynamics a true physical meaning as well as an experimental use. The renormalized values for the electron's charge and mass provide finite, accurate means of measuring electron properties such as magnetic moment. This theory has also made a detailed description of the fine structure of the hydrogen atom possible. It also presents a precise picture of the collisions of electrons, positrons (anti-electrons), and photons in matter.

Feynman was awarded the Nobel Prize for his work in quantum electrodynamics in 1965, together with fellow American Julian Schwinger and Shinichiro Tomonaga of Japan, both of whom had separately developed similar theories, but using different mathematical methods. Feynman's theory was especially distinct from the other two in its use of graphic models to describe the intermediate states that a changing electrodynamic system passes through. These models are known as "Feynman diagrams" and are widely used in the analysis of problems involving pair production, Compton scattering, and many other quantum-electrodynamic problems.

Feynman was fond of using visual techniques to solve problems. In addition to his Feynman diagrams, he developed a method of analyzing MASER (microwave amplification by stimulated emission of radiation) devices that relies heavily on creating accurate pictorial representations of the interactions involved. A MASER device is one that uses the natural oscillations of molecules to generate or amplify signals in the microwave region of the electromagnetic spectrum; they are used in radios and amplifiers, among other things. Feynman's method for analyzing these devices greatly simplified and shortened the solutions, as well as brought out the important features of the device much more rapidly.

Feynman also worked on the theory of liquid helium, supporting the work of the Russian physicist L. D. Landau. Landau had shown that below a certain temperature the properties of liquid helium were similar to those of a mixture of two fluids; this is known as the two-fluid model. Feynman showed that a roton, which is a quantity of rotational motion that can be found in liquid helium, is the quantum mechanical equivalent of a rapidly spinning ring whose diameter is almost equal to the distance between the helium atoms in the liquid. This discovery gave Landau's theory a foundation in atomic theory.

Contributes to Knowledge of Quarks

Richard Feynman did work in many other areas of physics, including important work on the theory of Beta-decay, a process whereby the nucleus of a radioactive atom emits an electron, thereby transforming into a different atom with a different atomic number. His interest in the weak nuclear force—which is the force that makes the process of radioactive decay possible—led Feynman and American physicist Murray Gell-Mann to the supposition that the emission of beta-particles from radioactive nuclei acts as the chief agitator in the decay process. As James Gleick explained in *Genius,* Feynman also contributed to a "theory of partons, hypothetical hard particles inside the atom's nucleus, that helped produce the modern understanding of quarks." Quarks are the most elementary subatomic particles.

Feynman wrote many theoretical physics books which are in use in universities around the country, as well as a series entitled Feynman's Lectures in Physics, which he put together based on several terms of physics lectures he gave at the California Institute of Technology in 1965. The lectures presented a completely revolutionary approach to teaching university physics, providing a valuable resource to all physics majors. He also dabbled in many areas outside of physics, including drumming and drawing.

Feynman received the Albert Einstein Award in 1954, and he was warded the Niels Bohr International Gold Medal in 1973. He was a member of the National Academy of Science and a foreign member of the Royal Society in London.

Explains Why the Shuttle Exploded

In January 1986, the space shuttle *Challenger* exploded above Cape Kennedy, Florida. Feynman was named to the 12-member special (Rogers) commission that investigated the accident. When public hearings began in February, the discussion quickly turned toward the effect of cold temperatures on O-rings. These rubber rings seal the joints of the solid rocket boosters on either side of the large external tank that holds the liquid oxygen and hydrogen fuel for the shuttle. Using a glass of ice water, Feynman demonstrated how slowly the O-ring regained its original shape when it was cold. Because of the O-ring's slow reaction time, hot gases had escaped, eroded the ring, and burned a hole in the side of the right solid rocket booster, ultimately causing the explosion of the space craft.

In October 1979, Feynman was diagnosed with Myxoid liposarcoma, a rare cancer that affects the soft tissues of the body. The tumor from the cancer weighed six pounds and was located in the back of his abdomen, where it destroyed his left kidney. Feynman was diagnosed with another cancerous abdominal tumor in October 1987 and died of complications on February 19, 1988.

Further Reading

Feynman wrote two volumes of autobiographical sketches. *Surely You're Joking, Mr. Feynman"* (1985) is a collection of anecdotes that gives the reader an excellent sense of Feynman's personality. This was followed by *What Do You Care What Other People Think? Further Adventures of a Curious Character* (1988). A short biography of him and a slightly more detailed description of the work that led him to the Nobel Prize can be found in *Nobel Prizes 1965,* published by the Nobel Foundation. The physicist Freeman Dyson's autobiography, *Disturbing the Universe* (1979), tells about Feynman's method of work. An explanation of elementary particle and quantum physics, including Feynman diagrams, can be found in Douglas C. Gianocoli's *Physics* (1980). In *Genius: The Life and Science of Richard Feynman,* James Gleick describes both the nature of the problems with which Feynman dealt and also the ways in which Feynman's solutions differed form those of other physicists. David L. and Judith R. Goodstein describe one of his solutions in *Feynman's Lost Lecture: The Motion of Planets Around the Sun* (1996).

Additional Sources

Gribbin, John and Mary Gribbin, *Richard Feynman: A Life in Science* (1997).
Jagdish Mehra, *The Beat of a Different Drum: The Life and Science of Richard Feynman.* Oxford University Press, 1994. □

Leonardo Fibonacci

The Italian mathematician and merchant Leonardo Fibonacci (ca. 1180-ca. 1250), also known as Leonardo of Pisa, was the most original and capable mathematician of the medieval Christian world.

L eonardo Fibonacci was born in Pisa and was brought up in Bougie, Algeria, where his father was a warehouse official. Fibonacci traveled extensively for business and pleasure throughout Europe and in Egypt, Syria, and Greece. During his travels he observed and analyzed the arithmetical systems employed in commerce and learned the Hindu-Arabic numerals. He helped to introduce them into European mathematics.

In the *Liber abaci* (1202; revised version 1228), a thorough treatise on algebraic methods and problems, Fibonacci strongly advocates the use of the new Indian numerals, that is, the nine numerals, plus the *zephirum,* or symbol for zero. This work can be regarded as symptomatic of the mathematical renaissance of the West. In it, Fibonacci deals with the fundamental operations on integers, with fractions, with the extraction of roots, and with mathematical applications to commercial transactions. The *Liber abaci* also contains the famous "Fibonacci sequence," where each term after the first two is the sum of the two terms immediately preceding it, a sequence that has been found to have many significant and interesting properties. The *Liber abaci* remained a standard work for about 2 centuries.

In another work, entitled *Flos* (1225), Fibonacci considers indeterminate problems that are reminiscent of the work of Diophantus and analyzes determinate problems with methods similar to those employed by Euclid, the Chinese, and the Arabs. Another mathematical treatise by Fibonacci, the *Liber quadratorum* (1225), is an original and brilliant work on indeterminate analysis. Some of the problems dealt with in this book derived from the mathematical contests sponsored by the court of Frederick II, to which Fibonacci had been invited.

Though he was primarily an arithmetician and an algebraist, Fibonacci also wrote a book on geometry entitled *Practica geometriae* (1220), which seems to be based on Euclid's lost work *On the Division of Figures*. In his work Fibonacci uses algebraic methods to solve a large number of arithmetical and geometrical problems.

Further Reading

Despite Fibonacci's importance, none of his work has been translated into English. Some appreciation of his significance in Florian Cajori, *A History of Mathematical Notations* (2 vols., 1928-1929), and N. N. Vorobev, *Fibonacci Numbers*, edited by Ian N. Sneddon (trans. 1961). See also Cajori's *A History of Elementary Mathematics* (1896; 2d ed. 1917); David Eugene Smith, *History of Mathematics* (2 vols., 1923-1925); W. W. Rouse Ball, *A Short Account of the History of Mathematics* (1924); George Sarton, *Introduction to the History of Science*, vol. 2 (1931); and H. A. Freebury, *A History of Mathematics* (1958). ☐

Johann Gottlieb Fichte

The German philosopher of ethical idealism Johann Gottlieb Fichte (1762-1814) posited the spiritual activity of an "infinite ego" as the ground of self and world. He believed that human life must be guided by the practical maxims of philosophy.

Johann Gottlieb Fichte was born Rammenau on May 19, 1762, the son of a Saxon peasant. As a child, he impressed a visiting nobleman, Baron Miltitz, who adopted him and had him schooled at Pforta. In 1780 he became a student of theology at the University of Jena and later studied at Wittenberg and Leipzig. He soon assimilated three major ideas that became the foundations of his own philosophy: Spinoza's pantheism, Lessing's concept of striving, and Kant's concept of duty.

Zurich Years

Fichte's patron died in 1788, leaving him destitute and jobless, but Fichte was able to obtain a position as tutor in Zurich, where he met Johanna Rahn, whom he would marry in 1794. Having unsuccessfully tried to make his mark in the world of letters, he finally succeeded in 1792, when he wrote his *Versuch einer Kritik aller Offenbarung* (*Critique of All Revelation*), an application of Kant's ethical principle of duty to religion. Since this work was published anonymously, it was believed to be Kant's; but Kant publicly praised Fichte as the author, earning him the attention of Goethe and the other great minds at the court of Weimar.

Teaching at Jena

In 1794, through the influence of Goethe, Fichte was offered a professorship at Jena, where he proved an impassioned, dynamic teacher. He was a short, strongly built man with sharp, commanding features. His language had a cryptic ring; to Madame de Staël he once remarked, "Grasp my metaphysics, Madame; you will then understand my ethics."

Fichte displayed a strong moral concern for the lives of his students; he criticized the fraternities and gave public lectures on university life, which were published as *Einige Vorlesungen über die Bestimmung des Gelehrten* (1794; *The Vocation of the Scholar*). Despite all this extracurricular activity, Fichte developed his basic system, the *Wissenschaftslehre*, the doctrine of knowledge and metaphysics, in two works, *Über de Begriff der Wissenschaftslehre*

and *Grundlage der gesamten Wissenschaftslehre* (both 1794). Since he was obsessively concerned with the clarity of his writings, these works were later revised and published in several different versions in his lifetime (the English translation was entitled *The Science of Knowledge*).

Metaphysics and Ethics

Fichte's metaphysics is called subjective idealism because it bases the reality of the self and the empirical world on the spiritual activity of an infinite ego. From the principle of the infinite ego, Fichte deduced the finite ego, or subject, and the non-ego, or object. This split, or "oppositing," between subject and object cannot be overcome through knowledge. Only through moral striving and the creation of a moral order can the self be reunited with the infinite ego. The *System der Sittenlehre nach den Principien der Wissenschaftslehre* (1798; *The Science of Ethics as Based on the Science of Knowledge*) expresses the necessity of moral striving in the formula, "If I ought I can." Even God is identified with the moral order in the essay "On the Ground of Our Belief in a Divine World Order" (1798). Fichte was wont to claim that in his own life "he created God every day."

Charges of Atheism

Because of his radical political ideas and his intense moral earnestness, Fichte attracted the hostility of several groups: fraternity students, monarchists, and the clergy. The last group charged Fichte with atheism, since he had stated that "there can be no doubt that the notion of God as a separate substance is impossible and contradictory." He refused to compromise with his critics, even publicly attacking their idolatry of a personal God, and was forced to leave Jena in 1799.

Berlin and Later Writings

These years of professional insecurity did not diminish Fichte's philosophical activity. He produced a popular account of his philosophy in *Die Bestimmung des Menschen* (1800; *The Vocation of Man*). In *Der geschlossene Handelsstaat* (1800; *The Closed Commercial State*) he argued for state socialism, and in *Grundzüge der Gegenwärtigun Zeitalters* (1806; *Characteristics of the Present Age*) he presented his philosophy of history. Fichte's metaphysics became more theologically oriented in *Die Anweisung zum seligen Leben, order Religionslehre* (1806; *The Way towards the Blessed Life*). But his most memorable accomplishment during the time of the siege of Napoleon was his *Reden au die deutsche Nation* (*Addresses to the German Nation*), given in the winter of 1807-1808. These speeches rallied the German people on the cultural and educational "leadership of humanity."

In 1810, after teaching two terms at the universities of Erlangen and Königsberg, Fichte was appointed dean of the philosophy faculty and later rector of the University of Berlin. But Napoleon's siege of Berlin was to cut short his new teaching career. Johanna, his wife, nursing the wounded, fell ill with typhus and recovered; Fichte, however, succumbed to the disease and died on Jan. 27, 1814.

His philosophy was quickly superseded by the philosophies of Schelling and Hegel.

Further Reading

William Smith provided an extensive memoir of Fichte's life in his translation of *The Popular Works of Johann Gottlieb Fichte* (2 vols., 1848-1849; 4th ed. 1889). A study of an important aspect of Fichte's work is H. C. Engelbrecht, *Johann Gottlieb Fichte: A Study of His Political Writings with Special Reference to His Nationalism* (1933). For general accounts of Fichte's philosophy, the best sources in English are Robert Adamson, *Fichte* (1881; repr. 1969); Ellen Bliss Talbot, *The Fundamental Principle of Fichte's Philosophy* (1906); and Frederick Copleston, *A History of Philosophy,* vol. 7 (1946; new ed. 1963). Recommended for the historical background of idealism are Josiah Royce, *The Spirit of Modern Philosophy* (1892; repr. 1967), and John Herman Randall, *The Career of Philosophy,* vol. 2 (1965). □

Marsilio Ficino

The Italian philosopher and humanist Marsilio Ficino (1433-1499) influenced Renaissance thought through his translation and explication of the works of Plato.

Marsilio Ficino was born at Figline near Florence on Oct. 19, 1433, the son of a prominent physician. He received a traditional education in humane letters at the universities of Florence and Pisa and studied medicine briefly at Bologna. Although his teacher of philosophy at Florence was the celebrated Aristotelian Nicolo di Tignosi da Foligno, Ficino soon turned to Platonism. At the behest and with the support of Cosimo de' Medici he rapidly mastered Greek and began an ambitious program of translation: Homer, Hesiod, Proclus, the *Corpus Hermeticum,* Plotinus, and Plato. Begun in 1463, completed about 1470, and printed in 1484, Ficino's was the earliest complete translation of Plato into a Western tongue and was used for several centuries. The informal circle of friends who gathered about Ficino at the Medici villa in Careggi to discuss the teachings of the ancient philosophers has been called, somewhat misleadingly, the Platonic Academy.

The overriding concern in Ficino's literary labors among the classics of Greek thought was clearly religious. His spiritual bent had been demonstrated from an early age by such writings as the *Dio et anima* (1457) and the *De furore divino* (1457), and on Dec. 18, 1473, he was admitted to holy orders. In his most important original writing, the *Theologia Platonica* (1469-1474), Ficino stressed the perfect compatibility of philosophy and religion, the harmony between Platonic philosophy and Christian revelation. It is essentially a theological commentary on the doctrine of Plato and a demonstration of the existence and immortality of the soul. In Ficino's view, ancient philosophy was part of the process of divine revelation and had prepared for the coming of Christ. By his explication of Platonic doctrines he

hoped to persuade Jews, rationalists, and skeptics (among the last principally the Aristotelians, who rejected the immortality of the soul) to approach the true faith of Christianity. Ficino argued that in Platonic doctrine he found the rational philosophical arguments to buttress Christian theology.

Ficino's last years were troubled by the fall from power of his patrons, the Medici, and the narrow fanaticism of the followers of Savonarola. Ficino died at Careggi on Oct. 1, 1499. By disassociating antiquity from paganism he contributed to the reestablishment of harmony between Christian aspirations and the passion for the recovery of classical culture, which was one of the distinctive features of his age.

Further Reading

Selections from Ficino's *Epistolae* are translated as "Concerning the Mind" in Ernst Cassirer and others, eds., *The Renaissance Philosophy of Man* (1948). The most important study of Ficino is Paul Oskar Kristeller, *The Philosophy of Marsilio Ficino* (trans. 1943). Ficino's religious concerns are emphasized by Charles Edward Trinkaus, *In Our Image and Likeness: Humanity and Divinity in Italian Humanist Thought* (2 vols., 1970). □

Arthur Fiedler

Arthur Fiedler (1894–1979) delighted audiences of all ages as conductor of the Boston Pops for fifty

years, bringing a mixture of classical music and pop tunes to mass audiences around the world.

Arthur Fiedler garnered many distinctions during his fifty consecutive seasons as conductor of the Boston Pops. He helped bring classical music to mass audiences; conversely, he also gave lighter genres such as pop a respectability they would not have had if he had not performed and recorded their works with his orchestra. Fiedler's albums with the Pops have sold over fifty million copies, and his rendition of Danish composer Jacob Gade's "Jalousie" became the first record by a symphony orchestra to sell over a million copies. In addition to being the toast of the city of Boston while he led the Pops, Fiedler and his orchestra toured extensively throughout the United States and the rest of the world. For his musical efforts, the conductor received many tributes, including the United States' highest civilian award, the Medal of Freedom, and France's Legion of Honor. When Fiedler died in 1979, he was eulogized in *Newsweek* by Hubert Saal as "neither elitist nor specialist" and "renowned" for his "resoundingly middlebrow musical taste that embraced high and low with equal respect and zest."

Fiedler was born in Boston on December 17, 1894, to a musical family. His father played violin for the Boston Symphony, and his mother played the piano, though not professionally. So many of his father's ancestors had been violinists in Austria that over the years their surname became Fiedler, the German word for "fiddler." Not surpris-

ingly, Arthur Fiedler's father determined that his son should continue in the family tradition, and provided him with violin lessons in his childhood. Fiedler, however, told Stephen Rubin in the *New York Times* that he did not particularly enjoy either those or the piano lessons he also received. "It was just a chore, something I had to do, like brushing my teeth," he explained. When his family moved to Berlin, Germany in 1910, Fiedler briefly rebelled against his father's plans for him and became an apprentice at a publishing firm there. He quickly tired of the business, however, and returned to his musical efforts.

Supported Himself on the Violin

While his family was in Europe, Fiedler was fortunate enough to be accepted at Berlin's Royal Academy of Music. Though he concentrated on studying the violin, he also took classes in conducting, which, even then, he liked better. Fiedler used his violin to support himself, however, by playing in small orchestras and in cafes. He continued in this type of musical job when his family returned to the United States to avoid the dangers of World War I. By 1915 he had won a spot as a second violinist in the Boston Symphony Orchestra, hired by then-conductor Karl Muck.

After a brief period in the U.S. Army—from which he was discharged for having flat feet—Fiedler returned to the Boston Symphony in 1918. For some time he played the viola for the orchestra, and also served as a substitute on many other instruments, including the piano, organ, celesta, and, of course, the violin. He longed to conduct, however, and though he remained with the Boston Symphony, he began conducting smaller musical groups such as the MacDowell Club Orchestra and the Cecilia Society Chorus. With some of his fellow Boston Symphony musicians, Fiedler formed the Boston Sinfonietta, a small chamber orchestra that specialized in performing unusual and little-heard classical compositions. As Richard Freed reported in *Stereo Review,* the Sinfonietta was "perhaps the only permanently constituted chamber orchestra in the country in the 1930s." Freed went on to laud its achievements: "The Sinfonietta made the premiere recording of Hindemith's viola concerto *Der Schwanendreher,* with the composer as soloist. With organist E. Power Biggs there were works of Handel, Corelli, and Mozart. There were the big Mozart Divertimento in B-flat Major, K. 287, and the Wind Serenade in C Minor, K. 388, Telemann's *Don Quichotte* suite, and such rarities as the marvelous little *Christmas Symphony* of Gaetano Maria Schiassi and a suite by Esajas Reusner (the latter with the first U.S. recording of the Pachelbel Canon as filler)."

Initiated Free Outdoor Concert

Not content with his many musical activities, Fiedler in 1927 began an effort to gain support for free outdoor concerts. He later told *Newsweek:* "I believed people should have an opportunity to enjoy fine music without always having to dip into their pockets." By 1929 Fiedler had his way, and he conducted selected members of the Boston Symphony in the first of what became known as the Esplanade Concerts, on the banks of Boston's Charles River.

The following year, Fiedler became permanent conductor of the Boston Pops, an orchestra drawn from the Boston Symphony for the purpose of performing lighter classical music. At its helm, Fiedler led the group to heights of popularity that had hitherto escaped it. By the end of his first season as the Pops' conductor, he had achieved great personal fame in and around the Boston area. He began recording with the Pops in 1935, and their popularity began to spread to the rest of the United States—and to the rest of the world.

Embraced the Beatles and Beegees

Throughout his lengthy tenure with the Pops, Fiedler was not afraid of innovation. In addition to serving up renditions of lighter classics such as Strauss waltzes, he would often add to his programs versions of Broadway tunes or popular hits of the day. With the Pops, Fiedler made recordings of the songs of George and Ira Gershwin, and was one of the first "serious" musicians to recognize the worth of the Beatles' efforts, successfully featuring some of their songs—including "She Loves You"—in Pops concerts. Shortly before his death from cardiac arrest on July 10, 1979, Fiedler and the Pops made an album of songs from the disco-celebrating film *Saturday Night Fever,* aptly titled *Saturday Night Fiedler.* Saal quoted Fiedler about his approach to music selection: "I think the snobs are missing something. There's no boundary line in music, I agree with Rossini: 'All music is good except the boring kind.'" Similarly, a *Time* reporter recorded more of the conductor's words: "My aim has been to give audiences a good time. I'd have trained seals if people wanted them."

Though towards the end of his time as leader of the Boston Pops Fiedler's health was poor and he needed the help of assistant conductor Harry Ellis Dickson, he remained active with the group practically up to his death. As *Time* reported: "Toward the end, the proud old man would shuffle unsteadily to the podium. But then, invigorated by the music, he seemed to shed 20 years."

Further Reading

Dickson, Harry Ellis, *Arthur Fiedler and the Boston Pops: An Irreverent Memoir,* Houghton, 1981.
Moore, Robin, *Fiedler, the Colorful Mr. Pops: The Man and His Music,* DaCapo Press, 1980.
High Fidelity, February 1988.
Ladies' Home Journal, November 1977.
Newsweek, July 12, 1948; July 23, 1979.
New York Times, April 2, 1972.
Saturday Evening Post, September 1976.
Stereo Review, November 1979.
Time, July 23, 1979. □

Cyrus West Field

Cyrus West Field (1819-1892), American merchant and promoter, laid the first transatlantic telegraph cable.

Cyrus Field was born of Puritan stock in Stockbridge, Mass., on Nov. 30, 1819. He quit school at 15. After short periods of work in New York and Massachusetts, Field became a junior partner with a New York firm of paper dealers. When the company failed in 1841, he personally assumed its debts.

Field and his brother-in-law set up the mercantile firm of Cyrus W. Field and Company. By 1852 Field was free of debt and had built a personal fortune of $250,000. He retired from business to devote himself to his passion: to connect Europe and America by submarine telegraph cable.

From the British and American governments Field obtained charters and received promises of financial subsidies and naval ships to lay the cable. He enlisted financial backing from New York and London capitalists. Perhaps his most impressive feat was in acquiring the services of Britishers Charles Tilson Bright, the great engineer, and William Thomson (later Lord Kelvin), the distinguished physicist and authority on electricity. Thomson's invention of the reflecting galvanometer and the siphon recorder (which recorded telegraphic messages in ink that came from a siphon) assured the operation of the cable once it was laid.

After three attempts to drop the cable to the Atlantic floor failed, Field got more capital. In 1865 the fourth try also failed. Undaunted, Field organized a new company, the Anglo-American Telegraph Company, and rechartered the *Great Eastern* as the laying ship. In 1866 the 1,852 miles of cable were finally laid.

Field was honored the world over, and the venture made him wealthy. He maintained an elegant house in New York City, built a large country estate, and set up a son in a New York brokerage house, financially guaranteeing his operations.

Field became a stock-market operator and this, coupled with his princely way of life and financial obligations, was his undoing. He made money in western railroads and, in the late 1870s, acquired control of the New York Elevated Railroad Company, which also prospered. Then he went overboard. He invested heavily in the Manhattan Elevated Railroad, a holding company formed by financier Jay Gould that had a monopoly of New York's rapid transit, and speculated in wheat futures. But Gould outmaneuvered Field, and in 1887 the wheat market collapsed; these setbacks, compounded by his son's bankruptcy, drained Field's fortune. He died on July 12, 1892 in New York City.

Further Reading

Isabella Field Judson, ed., *Cyrus W. Field: His Life and Work* (1896), is a biography written from family documents by Field's daughter. A popular study is Samuel Carter, *Cyrus Field: Man of Two Worlds* (1968). Philip B. McDonald tells the Atlantic cable story in *A Saga of the Seas: The Story of Cyrus W. Field and the Laying of the First Atlantic Cable* (1937). The company history and the personalities involved are discussed in Henry M. Field, *The Story of the Atlantic Telegraph* (1892). An excellent review of the scientific and technological problems in Field's venture is Bern Dibner, *The Atlantic Cable* (1959; 2d ed. 1964). □

David Dudley Field

David Dudley Field (1805-1894), controversial American jurist, was a vigorous champion of legal reform.

David Dudley Field was born on Feb. 13, 1805, at Haddam, Conn. His brother Cyrus laid the first Atlantic cable, and another brother, Stephen, became an influential Supreme Court justice. He attended the Stockbridge Academy and Williams College but withdrew before graduating. Field studied law in Albany and New York City, was admitted to the bar in 1828, and became a partner in a New York firm. By 1840 his reported worth was $100,000, this affluence coming partly from his practice and partly from his marriage to a wealthy widow. Throughout his career he was known for his rigidity and single-mindedness, qualities that both helped and hindered him.

In 1839 Field had begun his long fight for legal reform through codification. New York's distinction between equity and common-law courts seemed chaotic to him. He believed that the laws ought to be systematized, contradictions eliminated, bad laws removed, and all placed in one book available to lawyer, magistrate, and client alike. But codification was considered a radical change in the legal system, and only one of his five codes, the penal, was adopted by New York (1881) due to opposition by the legal profession.

In other states Field's codes were better received. The civil procedure code was adopted in part by 24 American states and several foreign countries. The criminal procedure code had a similar reception outside New York. Partly through the efforts of Stephen Field, California adopted all five codes.

When his work on the domestic codes was completed in 1865, Field turned to international codification. He was largely responsible for the *Draft Outline of an International Code* (1872), which considered the peace-time relations of nations; a second edition (1876) had an added section on war.

Field split from the Democratic party over its territorial expansion and slavery policies. He became active in the Free Soil party, then in the new Republican party, and was an early supporter of Abraham Lincoln. He may have influenced Lincoln's appointment of his brother Stephen to the Supreme Court in 1863. In 1864, however, he was part of a move to oust Lincoln from the ticket. He finally returned to the Democratic party. He skillfully but unsuccessfully argued the case of Democrat Samuel Tilden in the disputed Hayes-Tilden presidential election of 1876. In the Reconstruction era he argued a number of important constitutional cases before the Supreme Court. In general his arguments helped protect civil liberties of white citizens but were detrimental to the civil rights of black freedmen.

Before the Civil War, Field had crusaded against lawyers' arguing cases in which they knew their client was wrong. But after the war his choice of clients, like robber barons Jay Gould and Jim Fisk, and some questionable tactics led to a report critical of his conduct by the Bar Association of New York City. He died on April 13, 1894, in New York City.

Further Reading

There is no modern biography of Field. The best source is *Speeches, Arguments and Miscellaneous Papers of David Dudley Field,* edited by A. P. Sprague (3 vols., 1884-1890). Background studies are Albert Wormser, *The Law: The Story of Lawmakers and the Law We Have Lived By from the Earliest Times to the Present Day* (1949), and William Seal Carpenter, *Foundations of Modern Jurisprudence* (1958).

Additional Sources

Field, Henry M. (Henry Martyn), *The life of David Dudley Field,* Littleton, Colo.: F.B. Rothman, 1995.

Van Ee, Daun, *David Dudley Field and the reconstruction of the law,* New York: Garland, 1986. □

Marshall Field

The American merchant Marshall Field (1834-1906) established one of America's first innovative wholesale and retail dry-goods businesses.

The son of a farmer, Marshall Field was born near Conway, Mass., and attended local schools until he was 17. He clerked in a dry-goods store in Pittsfield, Mass. In 1856 he went to Chicago, where he worked for Cooley, Wadsworth and Company, a wholesale dry-goods firm, in 1861 becoming the general manager and a partner. In 1864 Levi Z. Leiter, a large-scale real estate operator, joined the company as a silent partner. When Potter Palmer, an entrepreneur and real estate developer, joined his dry-goods business with Field's and Leiter's, the company became Field, Palmer and Leiter. When Palmer retired in 1867 and Leiter in 1881, the organization became Marshall Field and Company, owned almost entirely by Field and run directly by him. Field was in fact the source and inspiration of the ideas that revolutionized retail selling everywhere.

The Field enterprise was highly diversified. It sold wholesale dry goods through a sales force reaching small stores all over the Midwest; manufactured dry goods in factories in the British Isles, France, and elsewhere; had its own buying offices all over the world; and operated its retail department store, Marshall Field and Company, in Chicago. When Field died on Jan. 16, 1906, the store covered some 36 acres over 11 Chicago blocks, the largest establishment of its kind.

As a merchant, Field was responsible for many innovations. He introduced the one-price system, bought and sold for cash, and permitted exchange of goods. The reliability of his store was well known. Various customer services were

Marshall Field

also initiated or early adopted by Field: restaurants, personal shoppers, home delivery, an interior decoration department, and a bargain basement. His sales grew from $12 million annually in 1868 to $25 million in 1881 and $68 million in 1906.

Meanwhile, Field pushed the development of downtown Chicago, so that when he died, half of his fortune, estimated to be between $100 million and $150 million, was in Chicago properties. He wished to make Chicago a great educational and cultural center and gave large sums to various institutions. He helped found the Art Institute, donated the land on which the first buildings of the University of Chicago were erected, and contributed $1 million for the museum at the World's Columbian Exposition. This museum became Field's chief interest; in addition to gifts during his lifetime his $8-million bequest built the Field (later Chicago) Museum of Natural History.

Further Reading

John Tebbel, *The Marshall Fields: A Study in Wealth* (1947), is a family biography. An early company history is S. H. Ditchett, *Marshall Field and Company: The Life Story of a Great Concern* (1922). A popularized history is Lloyd Wendt and Herman Kogan, *Give the Lady What She Wants! . . . The Story of Marshall Field & Co.* (1952). □

Stephen Johnson Field

The American jurist Stephen Johnson Field (1816-1899) was an associate justice of the U.S. Supreme Court and a powerful partisan of unimpeded business expansion.

S tephen Field was born on Nov. 4, 1816, in Haddam, Conn., the son of a Congregationalist minister. He spent 2 years in Europe and the Middle East before entering Williams College, from which he graduated in 1837. He read law in the firm of his brother David in New York City, then moved to California in 1849.

The contradiction in Field's life between outrageous personal boldness and determination for law and order was a reflection of the frontier. At Yurbaville (later Marysville), Calif., as justice of the peace, Field was noted for his arbitrary but firm enforcement of the law. Despite an undignified controversy with another judge, he was elected in 1857 to the state's supreme court.

Field was a Unionist in the Civil War, and in 1863 President Abraham Lincoln appointed him to the U.S. Supreme Court. Notable among his early court writings were dissents in the *Slaughter-House Cases* (1873) and *Munn v. Illinois* (1873). In the latter Field presaged his philosophy of protecting business from the competition of governmentally created monopolies and from governmental regulation. This legal philosophy, referred to as "substantive due process," expressed the idea of putting limits on government in order to preserve liberty, along with the notion that government interference in the jungle of economic competition was unnatural.

Substantive due process came into full force in Field's circuit court opinion, later upheld by the Supreme Court, *San Mateo v. Southern Pacific R.R. Co.* (1882). Here, a corporation was defined as a "person" and was thus protected by the 14th Amendment from any deprivation of its rights by government intervention "without due process of law." This clause was a firm barrier against regulation, and with its protection, business enjoyed a legal immunity that lasted until the 1930s.

Field was a powerful voice in the Democratic party. He greatly resented being bypassed for the chief justiceship in 1888 by President Grover Cleveland. A gregarious man, he was not above sharing the hospitality of men whose corporations were engaged in litigation before the Supreme Court.

After serving on the Supreme Court longer than any other justice in its history, Field resigned in 1897. He died on April 9, 1899, in Washington, D.C.

Further Reading

Field's *Personal Reminiscences of Early Days in California* (1880; rev. ed. 1893) is illuminating. Carl Brent Swisher, *Stephen J. Field: Craftsman of the Law* (1930), is the standard biography. Also of value is the essay on Field in Robert G. McCloskey, *American Conservatism in the Age of Enterprise: A Study of*

William Graham Sumner, Stephen J. Field, and Andrew Carnegie (1951).

Additional Sources

The Fields and the law: essays, San Francisco: United States District Court for the Northern District of California Historical Society; New York: Federal Bar Council, 1986. □

Henry Fielding

The English author and magistrate Henry Fielding (1707-1754) was one of the great novelists of the 18th century. His fiction, plays, essays, and legal pamphlets show he was a humane and witty man, with a passion for reform and justice.

The English novel of today was largely created by Henry Fielding and Samuel Richardson. Richardson's works, written in the form of a series of letters, are experiments in psychological analysis. Fielding's novels, in which the author himself tells the story and controls the plot structure, are considered the first accurate portrayal of contemporary manners.

Henry Fielding was born on April 22, 1707, at Sharpham Park, Somersetshire, the estate of his maternal grandfather. In 1710 the Fieldings moved to East Stour,

Dorsetshire. When Henry was 11, his mother died. A suit for custody was brought by his grandmother against his charming but irresponsible father, Lt. Gen. Edmund Fielding. The settlement placed Henry in his grandmother's care, although he continued to visit his father in London. Henry was educated at Eton. At 17 he attempted to elope with a young heiress but was frustrated by her guardian.

Lady Mary Wortley Montagu, Fielding's cousin, described him about this time as a high-spirited youth, full of the joy of life, witty and humorous. He was handsome and more than 6 feet in height.

Career as a Playwright

Fielding's first play, *Love in Several Masques,* was presented in London in February 1728. The following month he entered the University of Leiden in the Netherlands, where he studied classical literature. He returned to London in 1730. For the next 7 years Fielding was active as a playwright and theater manager. He wrote masques, farces, comedies, and burlesques, including the famous burlesque *Tom Thumb* (1730). In 1734 he married Charlotte Cradock, who was the prototype of his heroines Sophia and Amelia. Two political satires, *Pasquin* (1736) and *The Historical Register for the Year 1736* (1737), so infuriated the Whig government of Robert Walpole that all London theaters, except two protected by royal patent, were ordered closed by the Licensing Act of 1737. Fielding's career as a playwright was at an end.

Fielding then turned to the study of the law and was admitted to the bar in less than 3 years. He continued to oppose the Walpole government by editing a political journal, *The Champion* (1739-1740), the first of four journals that he edited in his lifetime.

First Novels

In 1740 Richardson published a novel, *Pamela; or, Virtue Rewarded,* the story of a young servant girl who preserves her virtue against the repeated advances of her master, Squire B———, so impressing him at last that he marries her. The book was an immediate success, being read as a lesson in morality by all young ladies. Fielding could not resist spoofing this, to him, ridiculous tale in an unsigned pamphlet, *An Apology for the Life of Mrs. Shamela Andrews* (1741), in which the virtuous heroine is hilariously exposed as a conniving wench.

Continuing the attack on Richardson, Fielding wrote *The History of the Adventures of Joseph Andrews, and of His Friend Mr. Abraham Adams* (1742). His purpose in this book, however, was more than parody, for he intended, as he announced in the preface, a "kind of writing which I do not remember to have seen hitherto attempted in our language." In this new kind of writing, which Fielding called a "comic epic poem in prose," he creatively blended two classical traditions: that of the epic, which had been poetic, and that of the drama, but emphasizing the comic rather than the tragic. Another distinction of *Joseph Andrews* and of the novels to come was the use of everyday reality of character and action as opposed to the fables of the past.

Joseph Andrews is supposedly the brother of "the illustrious Pamela, whose virtue is at present so famous." He resists the advances of his employer, Lady Booby, in order to remain faithful to his true love, Fanny Goodwill. After escaping Lady Booby and surviving amusing adventures along the road with his companion, Parson Adams, Joseph is reunited with Fanny.

Fielding's law practice was not prospering, and the moderate income from *Joseph Andrews* was not sufficient to provide for his wife and children. Consequently he gathered for publication as *Miscellanies* (3 vols., 1743) some earlier works, including *The History of the Life of the Late Mr. Jonathan Wild, the Great,* a savagely ironic account of a notorious London thief whom he equated satirically with all "great men," Robert Walpole in particular.

Tom Jones

Fielding's eldest daughter died in 1742, his wife in 1744, and he himself was crippled with gout. The death of his beloved wife was such a shock to Fielding that his friends feared for his reason. Yet during these sad years Fielding was creating his comic masterpiece, *The History of Tom Jones, a Foundling,* which appeared in 1749.

The plot of *Tom Jones* is too ingeniously complicated for simple summary; its basis is Tom's alienation from his foster father, Squire Allworthy, and his sweetheart, Sophia Western, and his reconciliation with them after lively and dangerous adventures on the road and in London. The triumph of the book is its presentation of English life and character in the mid-18th century. Every social type is represented, and through them every shade of moral behavior. Fielding's varied style tempers the basic seriousness of the novel, and his authorial comment preceding each chapter adds a significant dimension to the conventionally straightforward narrative.

While he was writing *Tom Jones,* Fielding also edited two journals—*The True Patriot* (1745-1746) and *The Jacobite's Journal* (1747-1748)—which were undertaken to counteract popular enthusiasm for Prince Charles Edward Stuart, the Young Pretender. Fielding wrote a preface (1744) for *The Adventures of David Simple,* a novel by his sister Sarah, and another preface (1747) for its sequel. In 1747 he married Mary Daniel, his first wife's servant; their grief over her death had drawn them together. Together they had five children.

Career as a Magistrate

In 1748 Fielding was commissioned justice of the peace for Westminster and later for Middlesex as well. Most of his work was concerned with London's criminal population of thieves, informers, gamblers, and prostitutes. In a corrupt and callous society he became noted for his impartial judgments, incorruptibility, and compassion for those whom social inequities had forced into crime. The income from his office, which he called "the dirtiest money upon earth," dwindled because he refused to take money from the very poor. Fielding was assisted in his work by his blind half brother, Sir John Fielding (1722-1780), a justice of the peace, who was said to be able to recognize over 3,000 thieves by their voices. The brothers organized the Bow Street Runners, the first modern police force, and they lobbied continually in Parliament for enlightened criminal legislation.

Henry Fielding's experiences as a magistrate gave a more serious tone to his last novel, *Amelia* (1752). The sufferings of the heroine, Amelia Booth, and her husband, a soldier, are used to expose and condemn the civil and military establishments of the period. In his essays for his last periodical, the *Covent Garden Journal* (1752), Fielding criticized wittily and incisively politics, society, and literature.

Sick with jaundice, dropsy, and gout and worn out by overwork, Fielding resigned his post as magistrate and sailed to Lisbon, where he hoped to recuperate. Even this painful voyage was matter for his pen; he made it the subject of his last work, *The Journal of a Voyage to Lisbon,* which was published posthumously (1755). Fielding died in Lisbon on Oct. 8, 1754, and was buried in the English cemetery there.

Further Reading

There are two major critical biographies of Fielding: Wilbur L. Cross, *The History of Henry Fielding* (3 vols., 1918; repr. 1964), and Frederick H. Dudden, *Henry Fielding: His Life, Works, and Times* (2 vols., 1952; repr. 1966). A short biography is John E. Butt, *Fielding* (1954). The fullest treatment of the novels is in Aurélien Digeon, *The Novels of Fielding* (1925). The chapters on Fielding in the following books are useful: Ernest A. Baker, *The History of the English Novel,* vol. 4 (1932); Arnold Kettle, *An Introduction to the English Novel,* vol. 1 (1957); and Ian P. Watt, *The Rise of the Novel* (1957). Recommended for general historical background are Arthur S. Tuberville, *English Men and Manners in the Eighteenth Century* (2d ed. 1929); George M. Trevelyan, *English Social History* (2d ed. 1946); and Basil Williams, *The Whig Supremacy, 1714-1760* (2d ed., rev. by C. H. Stuart, 1962). ☐

W. C. Fields

The American comedian W. C. Fields (1879-1946) appeared in many of the classic early motion picture comedies.

The son of an immigrant Cockney vegetable peddler, W. C. Fields was born William Claude Dukenfield on April 9, 1879, in Philadelphia, Pa. At the age of 11 he became a vagrant on the city's streets. He survived by stealing, was frequently arrested, and so damaged his nose in alley fights that its swollen bulbosity later became part of his comic trademark, as did the hoarse voice that was partly produced by childhood colds.

Fields practiced juggling fanatically, becoming one of the most skillful performers in history. At 14 he got his first professional booking. Within 3 years he was an established entertainer and, driven by his obsessive fear of falling back into poverty, had begun his lifelong clamor for better pay and better billing.

By his early 20s (during which Fields entered a brief, though never legally dissolved, marriage) such comic inventions as his famous "pool table" act made him an international vaudeville star. Several years as a headliner in the Ziegfeld Follies and George White's Scandals (1915-1922) won him recognition as a "talking" comedian.

The starring role of Eustace McGargle in the 1923 hit play *Poppy* provided the rudiments of the comic character Fields would make his own. After completing his first four silent movies, which were unsuccessful, he returned to vaudeville, starring in Earl Carroll's *Vanities*. At 51 he headed for Hollywood—rich, famous, and determined to conquer the film industry.

It took Fields a year to get a job. His seven two-reelers for Mack Sennett led Paramount Pictures to give him a cameo part in a feature film; the comic sequence that Fields invented, with himself as the vengeful enemy of miscreant motorists, established his powerful screen personality. With *International House* (1932) he won a long-term contract for featured roles in 16 comedies, including *Tillie and Gus* and *Million Dollar Legs* (in which he met Carlotta Monti, his companion for the rest of his life).

In the mid-1930s Fields's rocklike constitution crumbled, partly because of his heavy drinking. During a convalescence he casually started a new career as a radio comedian, quitting 3 years later at the peak of nationwide popularity.

At 60 Field's health improved, and between 1938 and 1942 he enjoyed the (artistically) finest years of his life. He starred in *David Copperfield, You Can't Cheat an Honest Man, My Little Chickadee, Never Give a Sucker an Even Break,* and *The Bank Dick.*

After 1942 there were no more jobs. Fields spent his last days in a sanitarium. He died on Christmas morning, 1946. He left a character who entered American folklore: an engagingly pompous and malevolently cold-eyed humbug who spoke for all who ever secretly yearned to cheat at cards or retaliate against such institutions as the law, banks, and motherhood.

Further Reading

The best book about Fields is Robert L. Taylor's touchingly funny *W. C. Fields: His Follies and Fortunes* (1949). Carlotta Monti, *W. C. Fields and Me* (1971), is a memoir about Fields by his former mistress. Other useful works are Donald Deschner, *The Films of W. C. Fields* (1966), and William K. Everson, *The Art of W. C. Fields* (1967).

Additional Sources

Fields, Ronald J., *W.C. Fields: a life on film,* New York: St. Martin's Press, 1984.
Gehring, Wes D., *W.C. Fields, a bio-bibliography,* Westport, Conn.: Greenwood Press, 1984.
Taylor, Robert Lewis, *W.C. Fields: his follies and fortunes,* New York: St. Martin's Press, 1989. ☐

João Batista de Oliveira Figueiredo

João Batista de Oliveira Figueiredo (born 1918) was a Brazilian army general and president. In the latter role, he was noted for restoring political rights and allowing exiles to return to his country. He also brought to an end 21 years of military- dominated government and turned the presidency over to a civilian successor.

João Figueiredo served as president of Brazil (1979-1985) more from a sense of duty than because of pleasure or ambition. In 1981 he told a reporter that "I spend most of my leisure time trying to pretend that I am not President. . . . I wish they had chosen someone else for this job." Indeed, it was his predecessor, Ernesto Geisel (1908- 1996), who decided that he would be the last of the five army generals to rule Brazil as president following the overthrow of João Goulart in 1964. He expanded Geisel's policy of *distenção*—the relaxing of the military's political control— into a gradual *abertura,* the opening of the political system. He used the presidency's power to marginalize right-wing anti-democrats and to prevent the radicalization of the left as he moved Brazil through a six year transition to civilian government.

His commitment to constitutional democracy was rooted in family tradition. His father, Colonel Euclides de Oliveira Figueiredo, opposed the revolution of 1930. He was one of the principal commanders in the Constitutionalist Revolt of 1932 and was an opponent of the Getúlio Vargas dictatorship (1937-1945). João Batista was born in Rio de Janeiro on January 15, 1918. He received his secondary education in military schools in Porto Alegre and Rio de Janeiro before entering the Escola Militar do Realengo from which he graduated first in his class as an *Aspirante* in the cavalry in November 1937. An outstanding student, he won the Brazilian military's "triple crown": first in his Realengo class, first in the advanced officers' course, and first in the command and general staff course. After a three-year tour with the Brazilian military training mission in Paraguay, he went through the Escola Superior de Guerra and then joined the faculty at the general staff school in 1961, where he participated in the conspiracy that brought down João Goulart in 1964.

A Military/Political Career

Promoted to colonel in August 1964, he helped found the Serviço Nacional de Informações (SNI) as the federal government's principal intelligence agency. Before Geisel named him head of the SNI in 1974, he served as chief of the São Paulo state police (1966-1968) and as commander of the prestigious 1st Cavalry Regiment in Brasília (1968-1969). Promoted to brigadier general in 1969, he served as chief of staff of the Third Army headquartered in Porto Alegre and then in a like position at the SNI. When an

"electoral college" of generals named his superior, General Emílio Garrastazu Médici, to succeed ailing President (General) Artur da Costa e Silva (October 30, 1969), he made Figueiredo chief of the presidential military staff. This put him in the Planalto Palace during years of increased repression of political dissidents, as dramatic actions by regime opponents—such as the 1969 kidnapping of the U.S. ambassador—were met with wide-spread arrests, torture, and death-squad activity. As president, he would deny that he had been involved in such abuses and decree "mutual amnesty" for both accused political prisoners and state security agents. Perhaps the experience firmed his convictions regarding the military's proper role.

Figueiredo eventually earned the enmity of Médici by withholding information that would have made him choose someone other than Geisel as his successor. Once in office Geisel appointed General Figueiredo as chief of the SNI. In that position Figueiredo was promoted to general of division. From 1974 to 1977 he was the short, barrelchested general in dark glasses who avoided press contact. Even so, in early 1977 knowledgeable politicians began to see him as the likely candidate for the succession. His eight years of daily contact with the Planalto under two presidents and his extensive security background strengthened his chances.

Geisel maneuvered so as to diminish direct armed forces participation in the government's decision-making processes and to increase the power of the presidency by bending the military to his will. Neutralizing the military's political role gave him the space to select the man he believed would carry his policies to their logical conclusion.

The year of decision was 1977. In April Geisel briefly recessed the Congress to allow him to decree a package of measures that insured a safe electoral college to chose the next president in October 1978. In June Figueiredo's name was floated as a candidate. In October Geisel eliminated the opposition of Minister of Army General Sílvio Frota by firing him in a dramatic confrontation. And then, to avoid pushing through a promotion that would pass over senior generals, Geisel decided to ignore the custom that only four-star generals be considered as candidates. Minus the fourth star, he announced Figueiredo's candidacy.

With the attention of the nation suddenly focused, the press asked "Who is Figueiredo?" and scurried about for information. Figueiredo, seeking to project a more accessible image, began wearing clear lens, shortened his public name to João Figueiredo, and shook hands and kissed babies from one end of Brazil to the other. He allowed photographs while doing exercises and horseback riding. His open, honest, often blunt manner touched the hearts of Brazilians accustomed to his somber predecessors. Elected in October, he took office in March 1979 declaring his intention "to make this country a democracy."

Problems of the Presidency

Considering the problems, that objective was a gigantic task. He immediately faced strikes as workers reacted to the rapidly rising inflation that reached 110 percent by 1980, declining productivity, and an international debt of some

$50 billion that soared with the skyrocketing interest rates in the United States—each new percentage point cost the Brazilians another $100 million. To improve the political atmosphere, he signed into law a general amnesty. A total of 4,650 persons who had lost their political rights or been jailed, exiled, or dismissed from their jobs were affected. In November 1979 party reform eliminated the two recognized parties, which were replaced by an alphabet soup of multiple parties. Figueiredo's advisers argued that multiplication would split the opposition into competing factions.

The hard-line right-wing reacted to the regime's openness with a wave of terrorist bombings. Figueiredo challenged the terrorists to attack him instead of innocent people after a letter bomb killed a secretary at the lawyer's association. On April 30, 1981, a bomb exploded in a car outside a large convention center in Rio de Janeiro where 20,000 people were attending a concert sponsored by opposition groups. The army sergeant holding the device was killed and the captain driving the vehicle was severely injured. The incident confirmed direct military involvement in the bombings. Strong, but as yet unexplained, pressures prevented Figueiredo from punishing the guilty. The subsequent sloppy cover-up was headline material, and the tension on the president was so great that he suffered a heart attack in mid-September 1981. After hospitalization in Rio he was treated in Cleveland, Ohio. He paid a price in health for his position, suffering heart, eye, and back problems during the next several years.

The worsening international economic situation and the process of political liberalization jointly produced economic and social problems. Massive strikes in São Paulo's industrial zone in 1978 and 1980 led to the arrest of union leaders under the national security laws. Workers protested that their wage increases indexed to the inflation rate were far below a livable level. The government in turn was pressured by the International Monetary Fund to hold down wages as an anti-inflationary measure. Increasingly it became clear that debt repayment meant low incomes for Brazil's workers. In the north and northeast rural people began seizing unused lands, causing Figueiredo to create a new ministry to deal with land reform.

Tension with the Catholic Church, which was the major voice for societal change, reached a peak in the early 1980s with the expulsion of an Italian priest and the imprisonment of two French priests involved in political and land reform questions.

To confront the growing debt, the government invested massively in natural resources for export, opened Brazil to foreign petroleum exploration, and completed the huge Itaipú hydroelectric project. At the end of his term Figueiredo left growing inflation but also an extensive infrastructure to support Brazil's continued growth.

In foreign policy he continued the pragmatic position of his predecessors that Brazil should pursue any relations that contribute to its development. The days of automatic alignment with the United States of America were over. Pointedly, he kept a certain distance from Washington, while intensifying relations with Europe, Asia, Africa, and Spanish America. The North-South dialogue was the cornerstone of Brazilian foreign policy. He expressed his view in his 1982 speech to the United Nations when he declared that "the economic policies of the great powers are destroying resources without constructing anything in their place."

In 1984, there were nationwide demonstrations calling for the direct election of a new president. Figueiredo kept his word to allow them. In January 1985, Tancredo de Almeida Neves was chosen president by the electoral college. On the eve of his inauguration, he was rushed to the hospital and died five weeks later. On March 15, 1985, Vice President and civilian José Sarney donned the presidential sash, and the Revolution of 1964's last president eagerly began his retirement.

Further Reading

There are no biographies or other studies of Figueiredo in English. There is good summary of 20th-century Brazilian history in Thomas E. Skidmore and Peter H. Smith, *Modern Latin America* (1984); a helpful review of recent decades in Robert Wesson and David V. Fleischer, *Brazil in Transition* (1983); *Countries of the World* by James D. Rudolf (1991). ☐

José Figueres Ferrer

José Figueres Ferrer (1906 - 1990) served as President of Costa Rica for a total of 12 years. He served three different, non-consecutive terms.

José Figueres Ferrer was born in 1906. There is not much information regarding his early life.

A new epoch came into being in Costa Rica during 1940. It was then that Dr. Rafael Angel Calderen Guardin was elected the new president. He began to make sweeping changes, which appeared to be an attempt to move the country into a more stabilized one. Some of his policies included land reform, progressive taxation and guaranteed minimum wage. The country looked as if it was headed in the right direction.

The sanctuary, which Costa Rica had become, would take turn for the worse. Calderen's United Social Christian Party refused to leave office, or leave behind power. They had lost the 1948 election. A civil war ensued. The Calderen's were opposed by Jose (Don Pepe) Figueres Ferrer. Prior to the revolt, "Don Pepe" had been exiled to Mexico in 1942. He returned to fight a political battle, with the aid of both the Guatemalan and Cuban governments. He won the war, which lasted 40 days, and cost 2,000 lives.

Figueres Ferrer had been named the head of the Founding Junta of the Second Republic of Costa Rica. He made it his mission to reform Costa Rica. He included the positive aspects of Calderen's campaign and added some additional ones which were an attempt to make Costa Rica a more positive and progressive country. Figueres Ferrer gave women the right to vote, abolished all branches and divisions of the Costa Rican armed forces, nationalized banks,

etc. One of the more controversial rulings he made was the ban on all actions of the Communist party.

Figueres Ferrer led a national revolt in 1948. The revolt was an act of solidarity to ensure that the newly elected president Otilio Ulate could effectively take over the governmental control. Ulate placed Figueres Ferrer in the rank of provisional president. It was during this legislation period that Costa Rica developed some of it's most useful and socially conscious reforms. Figueres Ferrer was elected to the office presidency in fair and open elections in 1948. He served a total of 12 years. His terms were divided amongst 3 stints in office: 1948-1949, 1953-1958, and 1970-1974.

Figueres Ferrer died in 1990 knowing that to many Costa Ricans, he was a hero. He has been credited with bringing democracy to his country. His son, Jose Figueres Olsen currently serves as President of Costa Rica.

Further Reading

Information regarding José Figueres Ferrer can be obtained from *The Concise Columbia Encyclopedia*. Additional information on both José Figueres Ferrer and Costa Rica can be found at http://www.centralamerica.com and at http://www.pubweb.acns.nwu.edu □

Millard Fillmore

The major contribution of Millard Fillmore (1800-1874), thirteenth president of the United States, was his signing of the Compromise of 1850.

Millard Fillmore was born in Cayuga County, N.Y., the son of a poor farmer. Although he held several legal clerkships, he was largely self-taught in the law. He entered politics in association with Thurlow Weed and William H. Seward, helping to organize the Anti-Masonic party as a major third party in the North. As one of the party's leaders in the New York Assembly, Fillmore sponsored reforms, including abolishing debtor imprisonment and a bankruptcy bill. As a member of the U.S. House of Representatives in the 1830s and 1840s, he led his party into the newly formed Whig party. He was elected comptroller of New York State in 1846.

In 1848 Fillmore was elected vice president of the United States under Zachary Taylor. This proved an unpleasant experience, as he was excluded from all patronage and policy-making decisions. He was unable to prevent Taylor's opposition to Henry Clay's proposals for ending the sectional crisis over the extension of slavery into territories acquired by the Mexican War; but before Taylor could veto Clay's compromise bill, he died. Fillmore, now president, quickly accepted the five bills which made up the Compromise of 1850. This was the high point of his administration

and demonstrated his attempt to find a middle ground on the slavery question. However, he was attacked by antislavery groups, especially for his vigorous enforcement of the Fugitive Slave Law, which was part of the compromise. Fillmore believed that slavery was evil but, as long as it existed, had to be protected.

Fillmore's policies all aimed at turning the country away from the slavery question. His most important recommendation was that the U.S. government build a transcontinental railroad. His foreign policy, formulated with Secretary of State Daniel Webster, had similar goals. In marked contrast to the aggressive policy followed by the United States during the rest of the 1840s and 1850s (when Democratic administrations made every effort to acquire additional territory), Fillmore sought to encourage trade through peaceful relations. One of his major undertakings was to send Commodore Matthew Perry to open Japan to American commerce.

In 1852 Fillmore was repudiated by the Whigs. After he ran unsuccessfully for president in 1856 as the Know-Nothing party's candidate, he returned to Buffalo to devote himself to local civic projects. He died on March 8, 1874.

Further Reading

The definitive biography of Fillmore is Robert J. Rayback's objective *Millard Fillmore* (1959). For background on Fillmore's New York career see the books by Glyndon G. Van Deusen on the leaders of the Whig party in the Empire State: *Thurlow Weed: Wizard of the Lobby* (1947), *Horace Greeley: Nineteenth-Century Crusader* (1953), and *William Henry Seward* (1967). □

Sir Robert Filmer

The English political theorist Sir Robert Filmer (died 1653) was influential in the development of English conservative thought. His treatises formed the basis for a royalist or Tory theory of kingship and government.

The eldest son of Sir Edward Filmer, Robert Filmer was born in the last decade of Elizabeth I's reign. After being educated at Trinity College, Cambridge, he retreated to his country estates in Kent, where he devoted himself to scholarly pursuits and to winning the hand of Anne, daughter of the bishop of Ely. At the beginning of Charles I's reign Filmer was knighted, but he appears to have played no major role either in local government or in Parliament.

As the conflict between Crown and Parliament deepened, Filmer took a strong royalist stand. When civil war erupted in 1641, Filmer's response was to write his *Patriarcha or the Natural Powers of Kings*, which, though not published, was circulated in manuscript form. His writings earned him the active hostility of Charles's parliamentary opponents. His house was looted by a parliamentary force in 1643, and the next year he was temporarily imprisoned in Leeds Castle.

With the end of the first civil war, Filmer regained his freedom and apparently played no part in the second internecine struggle, which broke out soon after. He did, however, return to his writing, and before the execution of Charles I he authored his most thoughtful treatise, *The Anarchy of Limited or Mixed Monarchy,* in which he argued for the establishment of a "pure" monarchy such as existed in France. Like his earlier work, this was not published at the time.

After the establishment of the Commonwealth, Filmer retreated into deeper obscurity. He continued to write, but as his ideas were anathema to England's new rulers, publication was impossible. After an appeal to the landed classes to restore traditional government in *The Free-holders' Grand Inquest,* he undertook an analysis of Aristotle's *Politics* which dealt with the question of "mixt" as opposed to "pure" forms of government, and Filmer argued, as did the French writer Jean Bodin, for the superiority of the latter type.

In 1652 Filmer wrote *Observations Concerning the Original of Governments,* in which he enunciated a theory of absolutism that not only opposed the more liberal ideas of John Milton and Hugo Grotius, but that also differed with the more (to him) congenial ideas of his other contemporary Thomas Hobbes. Filmer rejected any sort of "social compact"—whether stemming from man's "natural goodness" as Milton would have had it or from his depravity as Hobbes averred—as the original basis for government. He also rejected extreme mechanism and thus alienated many contemporaries. Filmer was, however, a rationalist; before his death in 1653 he wrote two works which cast doubt on the validity of witchcraft, *An Advertisement to the Jurymen of England Touching Witches* and *The Difference between a Hebrew and an English Witch.*

After the Restoration a genuine wave of promonarchical sentiment existed, and Filmer's once unpopular ideas were gradually resurrected. In 1679 his treatises (except the *Patriarcha*) were published. The remaining work appeared in print the following year.

Further Reading

There is no modern study of Filmer, for the scarcity of information about him precludes a full-length treatment. Thomas I. Cook, ed., in his introduction to John Locke's *Two Treatises of Government* (1947) provides a thorough and sympathetic analysis of Filmer's importance. □

Rabbi Louis Finkelstein

As chancellor of the Jewish Theological Seminary, Rabbi Louis Finkelstein (1895-1992), a renowned scholar of classical Jewish history and literature, headed the American religious movement Conservative Judaism.

The son of Rabbi Simon and Hannah (Brager) Finkelstein, Louis Finkelstein was born in Cincinnati, Ohio, on June 14, 1895. In 1902 his family moved to the Brownsville section of Brooklyn. There, under the supervision of his father, Finkelstein continued his intensive religious education, rising early each day to pursue his religious studies prior to setting off for school. Finkelstein earned an A.B. from the City College of New York in 1915 and a doctorate from Columbia University in 1918. In 1919 he was ordained rabbi at the Jewish Theological Seminary in New York. In 1922 he married Carmel Bentwich; they had three children.

From 1919 to 1931 Finkelstein was rabbi to Congregation Kehillath Israel in the Bronx in New York City. At the same time he joined the seminary faculty, serving first as instructor in Talmud (1920-1924) and then as Solomon Schechter Lecturer in Theology (1924-1930). In 1931 Finkelstein left the congregational rabbinate to join the seminary full-time. He was promoted to full professor in 1931 and began to assume increasing administrative responsibilities, becoming assistant to president Cyrus Adler (1934-1937) and provost (1937-1940). Following Adler's death, he became president (1940-1951). In 1951 he was elevated to the newly created post of chancellor of the seminary (1951-1972), an institution, Finkelstein believed, that could synthesize modern American life with the traditional faith of Judaism.

Period of Expansion

When Finkelstein assumed the reins of leadership, Conservative Judaism was entering a period of extraordinary expansion. The number of synagogues affiliated with the movement more than doubled in the years between 1949 and 1963, and the funds raised for the seminary increased more than sevenfold between 1938 and 1944. This proportional growth enabled Finkelstein to expand the programming and educational activities of the seminary, bringing it to national prominence in Jewish and interfaith affairs. Under his leadership the seminary created the Jewish Museum in New York, sponsored the radio and television programs "The Eternal Light," founded the Institute for Religious and Social Studies to bring together clergy of different faiths, and inaugurated the Conference on Science, Religion and Philosophy to explore the moral issues of the new technological world. Finkelstein was determined to see Jewish civilization recognized as one of the great streams of thought in world civilization. He realized his goal as he saw many of the scholars trained at the seminary move out to teach in the more than 100 American universities sponsoring Jewish studies programs.

As the head of the largest denomination of Judaism in America, Finkelstein served as an adviser on Jewish affairs to President Franklin Roosevelt (1940-1945). He prayed at the inauguration of President Dwight Eisenhower and in 1963 was invited by President John Kennedy to join the American delegation sent to the Vatican for the installation of Pope Paul VI. He was also invited by President Richard Nixon to preach at the White House.

Literary Classicist

Finkelstein wrote and edited nearly 100 books on Judaism, religion, sociology, culture, and ethics. During the early years of his career he distinguished himself as an insightful scholar of the history and literature of classical Judaism. Among his most important works are *Jewish Self-Government in the Middle Ages* (1924); *Akiba: Scholar, Saint, Martyr* (1936), a biography of the second century rabbi and martyr to his faith at the hands of the Romans; and a work on the economic and social background of the second century B.C.E. Jewish religious sect *The Pharisees* (1938). He edited a major, three volume study, *The Jews: Their History, Culture and Religion* (1949), as well as *American Spiritual Autobiographies* (1948) and *Social Responsibility in an Age of Revolution* (1971). In 1985 he published the third and fourth volumes of a projected six volume critical edition of the Sifra, a fourth century commentary on the biblical book of Leviticus.

Finkelstein died November 29, 1991, at his home in New York City after a long bout with Parkinson's disease. He was 96 years old.

Further Reading

For additional information, see the article on Louis Finkelstein in the *Encyclopedia Judaica* (1972). For background on Conservative Judaism and on Finkelstein's role during its expansion period, see Herbert Rosenblum's *Conservative Judaism: A Contemporary History* (1983), available from the United Synagogue of America in New York City, and Marshall Sklare's *Conservative Judaism* (3rd ed., 1985). For Finkelstein's interpretation of Conservative Judaism, see his essay "Tradition in the Making," in *Tradition and Change* edited by Mordecai Waxman (1958). □

Further Reading

Carlos E. Finlay, *Carlos Finlay and Yellow Fever* (1940), is a valuable work by Finlay's son and includes most of the Cuban scientist's writings on yellow fever, as well as a section on his life. A collection of essays on Finlay published by the Cuban Ministry of Public Health is *Dr. Carlos J. Finlay and the "Hall of Fame"* (1959). See also Enrique Saladrigás y Zayas, *A Tribute to Finlay* (1952). □

Carlos Juan Finlay

The Cuban physician and epidemiologist Carlos Juan Finlay (1833-1915) discovered that certain mosquitoes transmit yellow fever.

Carlos Juan Finlay was born in Camagüey Province on Dec. 3, 1833, of a Scottish father and a French mother. He spent his early years on his father's coffee plantation but soon was sent to school in France and England. From there he traveled to the United States, where he received a degree in medicine at Jefferson Medical College, Philadelphia, in 1855. He returned to Cuba and began to practice medicine after revalidating his degree at the University of Havana. From Cuba he traveled to Peru, Trinidad, and France, working in various hospitals. In 1870 he settled in Cuba permanently, developing an interest in the island's sanitary and health problems.

When, in 1879, an American mission arrived in Cuba to study the causes of yellow fever, the Spanish government designated Finlay to work with the group. He developed the idea that the transmission of yellow fever required a vector. At the International Sanitary Conference, held in Washington in February 1881, he explained his theory. In August Finlay read before the Academy of Sciences of Havana his historic work showing a mosquito, *Culex fasciatus* or *Stegomyia fasciata* (later known as *Aedes aegypti*), to be the vector of the yellow fever organism. Although Finlay advanced numerous experiments and observations to support his conclusions, his theory was not accepted by the scientific world for almost 2 decades. In a report to the International Sanitary Conference held in Havana in 1901, Walter Reed confirmed Finlay's discovery.

When United States troops landed in Cuba in 1898 during the Spanish-American War, Finlay worked with the American army in Santiago de Cuba. He further tested his theories in practice and advocated a campaign against the mosquito. As a result of his urgings, W. C. Gorgas, United States health chief in Cuba, began a program, later extended to Panama, to exterminate the mosquito, thus putting an end to a sickness that had plagued the Caribbean for many years.

In addition to his work in the epidemiology of yellow fever, Finlay wrote extensively on ophthalmology, tuberculosis, tetanus, trichinosis, filariasis, leprosy, beriberi, cholera, and exophthalmic goiter. After the establishment of the Cuban Republic in 1902, he was appointed public health chief, and the Cuban government created in his honor the Finlay Institute for Investigations in Tropical Medicine. Finlay died in Havana on Aug. 20, 1915.

Charles Grandison Finney

Charles Grandison Finney (1792-1875), American theologian and educator, was a famous evangelist who brought frontier religion to the urbanized East.

Charles Finney was born on Aug. 29, 1792, in Warren, Conn.; his family moved to Oneida County, N.Y., about 1794. A self-assured young man, he decided after high school not to attend college. For several years he taught school in New Jersey, but his family finally persuaded him to return to western New York to study law.

Finney's interest in religion at this time was only perfunctory, because he found orthodox Calvinism unpalatable. Thus his route to a religious "awakening" was outside the institutional church. Observing that legal decisions often quoted Scripture, he began to read the Bible. He became concerned as to how man could achieve salvation, finally concluding that, instead of waiting upon God's regenerative spirit, any man could exert himself to give up sin and accept Jesus as a redeemer. In 1821 he had a mystical experience in which he believed he stood face to face with Jesus. From this time he devoted his energies to preaching revivals. He was licensed as a Presbyterian minister in 1824.

Finney was a masterful pulpit orator. He addressed the audience as sinners and prayed for them by name. He prolonged his meetings until early morning and even carried his ministry into the factories. Only his success at winning converts persuaded more orthodox clergymen to condone his techniques.

In 1828, after a fruitful campaign in western New York, Finney visited Philadelphia, Providence, and Boston. In 1832, at the invitation of several prominent businessmen, he moved to New York City. He was plagued with illness, and his sojourn was unhappy. Three years later he accepted the chair of theology at Oberlin College.

Finney devoted much of his time to teaching and writing. *Lectures on Revivals of Religion* (1835) was a manual on conducting revivals. His subsequent works, *Sermons on Important Subjects* (1836), *Views of Sanctification* (1840), and *Lectures on Systematic Theology* (1846), elaborated his belief in the perfectability of man. He supported the temperance movement and condemned the "sin of slavery." Drawing his following from the professional and business classes, he taught the value of charitable and philanthropic enterprises.

In 1851 Finney became president of Oberlin, a position he held until the end of the Civil War. Though hampered by illness, he conducted revivals until his death on Aug. 16, 1875, in Oberlin.

Further Reading

There is no modern biography of Finney. His *Memoirs of Rev. Charles G. Finney* (1876) is useful for factual data. By far the liveliest sketch of Finney's life is Bernard A. Weisberger, *They Gathered at the River: The Story of the Great Revivalists and Their Impact upon Religion in America* (1958). Equally important are Whitney R. Cross, *The Burned-over District: The Social and Intellectual History of Enthusiastic Religion in Western New York, 1800-1850* (1950), and Charles C. Cole, Jr., *The Social Ideas of the Northern Evangelists, 1826-1860* (1954).

Additional Sources

Drummond, Lewis A., *A fresh look at the life and ministry of Charles G. Finney,* Minneapolis, Minn.: Bethany House, 1985.

The autobiography of Charles G. Finney, Minneapolis: Bethany Fellowship, 1977.

The memoirs of Charles G. Finney: the complete restored text, Grand Rapids, Mich.: Academie Books, 1989.

Guldseth, Mark, *Streams: the flow of inspiration from Dwight Moody to Frank Buchman,* Homer?, Alaska: M.O. Guldseth, 1982.

Hambrick-Stowe, Charles E., *Charles G. Finney and the spirit of American Evangelicalism,* Grand Rapids, Mich.: W.B. Eerdmans Pub. Co., 1996.

Hardman, Keith, *Charles Grandison Finney, 1792-1875: revivalist and reformer,* Syracuse, N.Y.: Syracuse University Press, 1987. □

Firdausi

Firdausi (934-1020) was a Persian poet of the first rank in the long history of the Persian civilization. He wrote one of the greatest national epics in world literature.

Firdausi was born in the province of Tus, some 12 miles northeast of present-day Meshed. Firdausi was the pen name of the poet. His personal name and that of his father, according to al-Bundari, was Mansur ben Hasan. Firdausi's family was of old Iranian gentry stock and thus rich enough to be independent. He studied philosophy, astronomy, poetry, and astrology. He was happily married to an educated musician. They had a son, who died at the age of 37, and a daughter, who survived him.

Firdausi grew up in a world that had been controlled by the Islamic religion and the Arabs for about 300 years. This culture was foreign to the natural heritage of the Iranian peoples. It was thus with the writing of the *Shahnameh* (Book of Kings) by Firdausi that Persian literary influence began to grow in a nonpolitical way in the Arab world.

Firdausi began to write his masterpiece, the *Shahnameh,* at about the age of 40. His main motive in undertaking this great task was to revive the glory of ancient Iran. A youthful contemporary of Firdausi, the gifted but ill-fated Dakiki, originally conceived the idea of narrating the story of Iran's history in heroic verse, but he was assassinated. Thus Firdausi took up the task. His main sources were his own imagination and the *Khvatainamak* (Book of Sovereigns), a prose epic in the ancient language Pahlavi, compiled from earlier chronicles about A.D. 640 under the last Sassanian kings in Iran.

"Book of Kings"

The *Shahnameh* is an epic of nearly 60,000 couplets. It chronicles the story of Iran for a period reckoned traditionally as more than 4 millennia. The work is divided into several parts covering four dynasties, the Pishdadian, the Kayanian, the Ashkanian, and the Sassanian. The descriptions of the first two are drawn from mythology; the third is only partly historical; and the fourth is the most factual.

The narrative begins with a description of primitive rulers followed by the golden age of King Jamshid, presumably 3000 B.C. Then follows the thousand years of foreign rule under cruel tyrants such as Zahak, who typifies the sway of Semitic invaders. Gradually Iran frees itself, only to be subjected to new wars with the country of Turan.

The romantic episodes of the loves of Zal and Rudabah serve as a prelude to the birth of their son Rustam, the supreme hero of the epic, whose martial exploits and tragic fate—slaying his unknown son Sohrab in a battle between Iran and Turan—dominate the earlier portion.

With the end of the Kayanian dynasty come the epoch of the Achaemenian kings and then Alexander the Great. Finally, after scantily covering the 500 years of Parthian rule, Firdausi praises the rise of Sassanian rule from A.D. 226 to 650. Thus the poem, despite its length, keeps ever in view the unifying purpose to exalt the fallen glory of Iran.

Rejection and Travels

Firdausi was 40 when he began the poem and 71 when he finished it. His growing fame at this time led him to the court of Mahmud of Ghazni, in what is now Afghanistan. Firdausi traveled there to present his works. On reading the biographers one is led to believe that his main dissatisfaction was the inadequacy of his reward. But the underpinnings of disagreement went further.

In the first place, Firdausi was a Shiite and Mahmud a Sunnite—representing the opposite poles of Islam. Furthermore, Firdausi had praised a vizier hostile to Mahmud. Finally, Firdausi was offended by Mahmud's lack of interest in poetry. In fact, Mahmud was to pay Firdausi a gold dirhem for each couplet but reneged and gave him 60,000 silver dirhems instead, which Firdausi rejected. In rage, Firdausi broke with the ruler and had to flee for his life.

After 10 years of wandering in poverty he found refuge in Tabaristan southeast of the Caspian Sea. To his new princely benefactor he dedicated the long poem "Jusuf and Zulaikha," the love story of Potiphar's wife for Joseph, a masterpiece of romantic verse that he took from the Old Testament by way of the Koran. Firdausi spent his last years in Tus in relative quietude.

An Evaluation

In both the major extant works of Firdausi is seen a poet of extraordinary ability. He combined harmoniously what he drew from historical sources with his personal inspiration. As for his style, whether in the fantastic elements demanded by the epic or in the gracefulness of his descriptions of everyday life, he excels at describing and explaining facts or sentiments in a clear, concise manner. His style is firm but eloquent, never giving into baseless extremes.

His poetry very seldom contained Arabic words, except in his descriptions of Alexander the Great, which came largely from Arabic sources. Just as Dante did with Italian, Chaucer with English, or the Gutenberg Bible with the Latin Vulgate, he was in his day a popularizer of the vernacular. Arabic was the holy Islamic language of Allah in the Koran just as Latin was the lingua franca for the Catholic Church. It was the *Shahnameh* of Firdausi that recongealed the Persian language into a coherent force that soon was to be the court language for most of the Islamic world.

Further Reading

In English, the best translation of the *Shahnameh* is by George and Edmond Warner (9 vols., 1905-1925). Studies of Firdausi include a rare work, published by Columbia University, *Firdausi Celebration, 935-1935,* edited by David Eugene Smith (1936); Issa Sadiq, *Ferdousi* (1945); and P. B. Vachha,

Ferdousi and the Shahnama: A Study of the Great Persian Epic of the Homer of the East (1950). Excellent background works are Edward G. Browne, *A Literary History of the Persians* (1906), and Jan Rypka, ed., *History of Iranian Literature* (1956; trans. 1968).

Additional Sources

Ferdousi: a critical biography, Cambridge, Mass.: Harvard University, Center for Middle Eastern Studies; Costa Mesa, Calif., U.S.A.: Distributed exclusively by Mazda Publishers, 1991. □

Harvey Samuel Firestone

The American industrialist Harvey Samuel Firestone (1868-1938) organized the Firestone Tire and Rubber Company, a leading firm in the rubber industry.

Harvey Firestone was born at Columbiana, Ohio, on Dec. 20, 1868, the son of a prosperous farmer. During the 1890s he held various positions in the buggy industry. In 1896 Firestone established a tire company; it was sold 3 years later. In 1900 he founded the Firestone Tire and Rubber Company in Akron, Ohio, which was already a center of the tire industry catering to the bicycle.

Now Firestone shifted his attention to the automobile industry and the pneumatic tire, which replaced the solid tire. He obtained a substantial order from Henry Ford in 1906, and this became the foundation of a business and personal relationship. Firestone became one of the "big five" in rubber: the others were Goodyear, Goodrich, United States Rubber, and Fisk.

Firestone responded to the 1920-1921 business decline by reducing prices and refusing to participate in a price agreement with his competitors. Wages were cut in an effort to trim costs (like most mass production industries, the rubber industry was not yet unionized). In 1923 Firestone brought out the balloon tire, a product innovation which was widely copied.

The rubber tire industry was at this time completely dependent on imported raw material. The price of rubber, like that of most raw materials, fluctuated greatly: it rose during World War I and went down during the postwar depression. Under the sponsorship of Great Britain, which owned colonies producing much of the world's rubber supply, a short-lived cartel was started in 1922 to raise the price of rubber and restrict its output. Complaints from consumer nations arose, particularly from the United States, which, in the midst of an automobile revolution, was the largest consumer of rubber. In response, in 1924 Firestone and Henry Ford began to develop their own rubber supply in Liberia, Africa. The size of Firestone's Liberian rubber plantations made him an important factor in the economic life of that country. In 1930 a League of Nations inquiry into the slave traffic exonerated Firestone's labor policy there.

Firestone died on Feb. 7, 1938, in Miami Beach, Fla. His family-controlled company concentrated on a single line of products—rubber tires.

Further Reading

Firestone's *Men and Rubber,* in collaboration with Samuel Crowther (1926), presents his reminiscences. Alfred Lief wrote the popular biography *Harvey Firestone: Free Man of Enterprise* (1951) and *The Firestone Story: A History of the Firestone Tire and Rubber Company* (1951). The Liberian venture is examined in Wayne C. Taylor, *The Firestone Operations in Liberia* (1956). □

Ruth First

Ruth First (1925-1982) was a South African socialist, anti-apartheid activist, and scholar. She fled South Africa in 1963 after serving 117 days in solitary confinement in South African jails. She worked from exile in England until 1977 when she returned to hands-on political work in Mozambique. On August 17, 1982, she was killed by a parcel bomb in Maputo, Mozambique.

uth First was born in Johannesburg, South Africa, in 1925, the daughter of socialist immigrants Tilly and Julius First. Educated in Johannesburg, she completed a bachelor's degree in sociology at the University of the Witwatersrand in 1946. Her years as a university student were filled with political exploration and set her commitment to pursue the struggle for social justice for all South Africans. First was instrumental in the foundation of the non-racial Federation of Progressive Students and joined the South African Communist Party—the principal party open to whites forging inter-racial political activity.

Upon graduation First worked as researcher for the Johannesburg municipality and taught evening classes in black schools. As a Communist party member she collaborated in organization of the African Mine Workers Union. When the mine workers went out on strike in 1946, the government brutally suppressed the strike and arrested the Communist party's entire executive body. First resigned her research position to become acting party secretary and ultimately editor of the Johannesburg edition of the party newspaper, *The Guardian.*

Throughout the 1950s First engaged in intense investigative journalism, revealing the brutal reality of South African rule while also publicizing statements by the increasingly persecuted leadership of the African National Congress (ANC), the principal anti-apartheid party. She supported the ANC's 1952 Defiance of Unjust Laws Campaign and in 1954 helped found the Congress of Democrats branch of the Congress Alliance—a political coalition including the ANC, the South African Indian Congress, the South African Coloured People's Congress, and the South African Congress of Trade Unions. She helped draft the Congress Alliance's Freedom Charter, which called for "... a non-racial South Africa based on equal rights for all."

With the Suppression of Communism Act in 1951, *The Guardian* was banned. Despite a series of banning orders which cumulatively circumscribed First's ability to research, publish, and organize, she and her staff managed to publish a series of newspapers between 1952 and 1963. In 1956 First, her husband attorney Joe Slovo, and much of the Congress Alliance leadership was arrested and charged with high treason. After more than a year of litigation the case was dismissed, but this persecution set the tone for future events. When Hendrik Verwoerd, the principal architect of apartheid legislation, became prime minister in 1958, efforts to penetrate, undermine, and suppress the militant anti-apartheid movement redoubled. Within half a decade the Congress Alliance leadership was largely dismantled, murdered, imprisoned, or driven into exile.

First exploited the privileges of her race and sex to remain active in political activity after her colleagues were jailed. Although she was known to support the ANC and to be a respected strategist within the movement, First was not arrested in July 1963 when the government raided the underground headquarters of the Congress Alliance at a Rivonia farm house. Key ANC leaders were taken and charged in the so-called Rivonia trial (1963-1964). Nelson Mandela, Govan Mbeki, and Walter Sisulu, were sentenced to life imprisonment. When First was arrested in August

1963 under the 90 day detention act, she was told by a security officer: " . . . You could have been charged in the Rivonia case. But we didn't want a woman in that case." Shortly after her release in late 1963 First, her three daughters, and her mother joined the rest of the family in exile in England.

Banning and exile did not suffocate First's activism, but encouraged a qualitative change—from political journalism to activist scholar. Her first major monograph, a study of South Africa's continuing illegal domination of South West Africa, researched while under police surveillance in 1961, was widely acclaimed and remains a classic. Despite banning orders First edited ANC members' speeches and trial addresses and was instrumental in the publication of Mbeki's *South Africa: The Peasants Revolt* and Mandela's *No Easy Walk to Freedom.* In 1970, with the publication of *Power in Africa,* she won international recognition as a key African analyst. She became a lecturer at the University of Durham and during the 1970s combined scholarship, a sharp critical eye, and firm political commitment to author and co-author many important works on South African apartheid, African politics, and an outstanding biography of Olive Schreiner.

In 1977 First seized the opportunity to return to southern Africa as director of research at the Center for African Studies in Mozambique. Free from the constraints of banning orders and the frustration of exile, First flourished under the demanding task of training Mozambican cadres to develop appropriate, useful, and politically informed research techniques in an effort to stabilize the fledgling socialist state. She turned her talents as teacher, activist, strategist, and scholar to strengthen and sharpen the struggle for social justice.

First was never a politician, yet she was a towering force in political circles—the all important behind-the-scenes strategist, the gifted problem solver who never left a stone unturned, a question unasked, or a bold initiative untried. A prolific and influential writer, First left an important legacy of political analysis of modern Africa, and her work in Mozambique set the international pace for integrating social science research into the creation of socialism. She was at a highpoint in her life's work when she was cut down in 1982.

Further Reading

A selection of her writing and an important bibliography of her published works, including reviews of her works, news reports of her murder, and obituaries, collected by Gavin Williams, is contained in "A Tribute to Ruth First," *Review of African Political Economy,* Volume 25 (1984). The student's best introduction to Ruth First is *117 Days* (1965), her account of solitary confinement under the Verwoerd regime in South Africa. The book was re-issued after her death with a preface by her life-long friend Ronald Segal (1983). Her publications include: *South West Africa* (1963); *Power in Africa: Political Power in Africa and the Coup d'Etat* (1970); *Libya: The Elusive Revolution* (1973); *Black Gold: The Mozambican Miner, Proletarian and Peasant* (1983); and, with Ann Scott, *Olive Schreiner* (1980). □

Bobby Fischer

An eight-time U.S. chess champion, Bobby Fischer made his mark in the 1970s as one of the most skilled and controversial masters of the game. With his famous 1972 victory over Russian Boris Spassky and his youthful good looks and energy, he helped win over a new generation of chess enthusiasts.

The definitive child prodigy, the Mozart of chess, an eccentric, reclusive figure—Bobby Fischer has been labeled all of these and more throughout an acclaimed and controversial life behind a chessboard and before the eyes of an adoring public. In an era when the most highly publicized chess matches pit human against computer, Fischer represents the image of an earlier time that stressed the mental and emotional athletics of the game.

An eight-time United States chess champion, and the holder of several "world's youngest winner" titles, Fischer was a well-known name in chess circles long before his most famous match: the 1972 tournament that pitted him against Boris Spassky of Russia. That tournament, played out before millions via television coverage, became a less a contest between two gifted players and more a metaphor for Cold War politics. As Fred Waitzkin described it in his book *Searching for Bobby Fischer,* "Each man bore responsibility for his country's national honor. Spassky would be Russia's greatest hero if he won, and would fall into disgrace . . . if he didn't. Fischer wanted to annihilate the Russians, whom he had hated since he had decided as a teenager that they cheated in international tournaments. If he won he would instantly become a legend; if he lost he would be dismissed by many as a crackpot."

A New Kind of Idol

As history relates, Fischer won that tournament, and in doing so garnered much more than prize money. With his youthful good looks and unpredictable manner, Fischer helped turn a new generation of young people into chess enthusiasts. " Chess clubs proliferated during the early seventies, inspired by Bobby's success and charisma," reported Waitzkin. "Mothers pulled their sons out of Little League and ferried them to chess lessons. Talented young players with dreams of Fischer, television immortality and big chess money spurned college and conventional career choices to turn professional."

Bobby himself, however, was never comfortable with his fame. Born in Chicago in 1943 and raised in Brooklyn, New York, Fischer grew up in a single-parent family, his physicist father having left the family and the country after a 1945 divorce. The boy showed early promise in his chosen field when at age six he learned the rules of chess; by age eight Fischer was competing informally at the Brooklyn Chess Club. Eventually the youngster caught the eye of chess master John Collins, who became his key instructor, though as Collins noted in his book *My Seven Chess Prodigies,* no one person could claim credit for Fischer's talent:

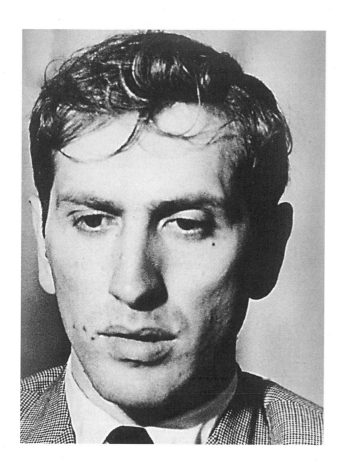

"Geniuses like Beethoven, Leonardo da Vinci, Shakespeare and Fischer come out of the head of [the mythic Greek god] Zeus, seem to be genetically programmed, know before instructed." As for formal educational instruction, that ended when Fischer was a teenager; he dropped out of school to concentrate on his game.

Fischer rose through the junior ranks quickly, and at age 13 won the United States Junior Championship, the youngest player to date to have taken the title. From there it was on to the United States Open Championship, where he competed against adults. Fischer took that title, too, at age 14. International play beckoned, and by age 17 Fischer became a challenger for the world title—and the youngest player ever to receive the title of international grand master.

But there was another side to Fischer's success. The young man, for all his brilliance, was considered something of a loose cannon, less than cooperative, and publicly scornful and egocentric. He would cancel out of matches unexpectedly, act demanding on tours, and maintain grudges that would last years. Fischer once accused Russian chess professionals of conspiring against him in international tournaments and at one point in the 1960s withdrew for five years from international competition.

The Big Match

By 1970 the master player returned to form, building up tournament credits in order to take on the reigning world champion, Fischer's longtime nemesis, Boris Spassky. In 1972 the arrangements were in place, and the chess world buzzed with the prospect of this historic challenge. Reykjavik, Iceland, was the chosen site, but as the event drew near, Fischer continued to demonstrate the eccentric behavior that "had the whole world wondering whether he would show up," as Waitzkin put it. "For several days, friends reserved space for him on flights to Reykjavik and pleaded with him to go. Plane after plane, loaded with passengers, waited on the runway while Fischer took walks and naps or ate sandwiches."

Even after he made a last-minute arrival in Iceland, Fischer maintained an aggressive presence. He "offended Icelanders by calling their country inadequate because of its lack of movie theatres and bowling alleys," wrote Waitzkin. "He wanted television coverage, but when a television deal was arranged . . . he refused to play in front of the cameras, claiming that they were too distracting. He forfeited a game and threatened to leave unless Spassky agreed to play in a small room with no audience and no cameras. He argued about the choice of chess table, about his hotel room about the noise in the auditorium, about the proximity of the audience to the players and about the lighting." And still, Fischer won the tournament with great style.

The chessman's life since that historic match was marked by a period of self-imposed obscurity that lasted nearly 20 years. He lost the world title after refusing to accept the challenge of Anatoly Karpov in 1975. Reports of a disheveled, reclusive Fischer living in the worst sections of Los Angeles brought out the detective in journalists. Those reporters who could get close to Fischer's friends heard tales of a man who wanted only to be left alone. In 1981 he was picked up by the police for resembling a fugitive bank robber; after spending a night incarcerated, Fischer (using the pseudonym Robert D. James) wrote a pamphlet titled *I Was Tortured in the Pasadena Jailhouse*. According to *Sports Illustrated* writer William Nack, the chapter headings included "Brutally Handcuffed, False Arrest, Insulted, Choked, Stark Naked, No Phone Call, Horror Cell, Isolation & Torture." As Waitzkin related, the pamphlet became a bestseller in chess clubs, although it doesn't once mention the game.

Controversial Views, Surprising News

In other areas of his life, Fischer demonstrated equally strong, if offbeat, convictions. For example, though his mother was Jewish, Fischer maintained decidedly anti-Semitic views, even extolling Nazism. Likewise, the chess champion believed that "everything was controlled by 'the hidden hand, the satanical secret world government,'" as Nack quoted a Fischer associate. He distrusted doctors, was sure the Russian government was out to kill him, and even, according to a *Maclean's* article, had his dental fillings replaced "because he feared that Soviet agents might be able to transmit damaging rays into his brain through the metal in his teeth."

In light of all the controversy surrounding Fischer, it was a surprising announcement in 1992 that had agreed to take on Spassky in another highly publicized challenge. At stake was $5 million in prize money. But perhaps more notable than the players themselves was the tournament site: the town of Sveti Stefan, in a region of the Yugoslav republic adjacent to the warring former republic of Bosnia-Herzegovina. At that time, U.S. President George Bush had imposed economic sanctions on Yugoslavia—sanctions that Fischer defied by taking on a commercial venture. At a press conference, Fischer spat on a letter from the U.S. Treasury Department, saying "this is my answer" to threats of fines and imprisonment if he played in Sveti Stefan.

The 30-game match ended in 15 draws, but Fischer had shown he still had some championship play in him. When the U.S. government handed down an indictment of Fischer in December of 1992, he chose to stay in eastern Europe. In the mid-1990s Fischer, the author of several chess books and inventor of a chess timing clock, was reportedly living in Budapest, Hungary, and had a girlfriend in the person of a 19-year-old Hungarian chess star, Zita Rajcsanyi.

In his *Searching for Bobby Fischer,* Waitzkin wonders about the prospect of his own chess-prodigy son growing up to be as unpredictable as Fischer and speculates on Fischer's youth, when his one and only interest was in his game: "In the early fifties, a child chess prodigy was perceived as odd rather than gifted. It would have been easier for [Fischer] if his genius had been for an admired endeavor like mathematics or playing the piano; in devoting his life to chess from the age of eight, he typecast himself as a weirdo and outcast. He must have felt tremendous pressure from his mother, from his teachers, who said he was wasting his life on a game, and from his schoolmates, who were learning about girls, Shakespeare and football. All this must have driven him further and deeper, and made him greater."

Further Reading

Collins, John, *My Seven Chess Prodigies,* 1974.
Maclean's, September 14, 1992, p. 42.
Sports Illustrated, July 29, 1985, pp. 72-84.
Waitzkin, Fred, "The World of Chess, Observed by the Father of a Child Prodigy," in *Searching for Bobby Fischer,* Random House, 1988. □

Emil Fischer

The German chemist Emil Fischer (1852-1919), perhaps the greatest of the organic chemists, is known for his work in the study of pure sugars and proteins.

Emil Fischer was born at Euskirchen, Prussia, on Oct. 9, 1852. After studying chemistry at the University of Bonn for a short time, he transferred to the University of Strassburg and received a doctoral degree in 1874. Fischer moved to Munich that year and spent 8 productive years there. He then went to Erlangen (1882) and to Würzburg (1885) and finished his career as professor of chemistry at the University of Berlin (1892).

Studies of Pure Sugars

Of the many natural products available for man's use, perhaps no group is so important as the carbohydrates. Until 1884, however, no exact scientific study of the carbohydrates had been undertaken, and little was known concerning their chemical constitution or the arrangement of their molecules. Between 1884 and 1900 Fischer successfully determined the inner structure of the sugar group and thus gave scientists the key to an understanding of other carbohydrates.

Fischer's first step in unraveling the mysteries of the sugar group was the discovery in 1875 of phenyl hydrazine, a compound which could be used as a general reagent for separating and isolating sugars. Through the use of phenyl hydrazine and its derivatives, he discovered the presence in sugars of the carbonyl group ($=CO$). By 1884 he was able to produce crystalline derivatives with various sugars; hitherto, these derivatives had been available only in impure mixtures which almost always were syrups. Fischer was also able to show that the best-known sugars contain six carbon atoms. Differences in the sugars could be detected through their effects, in solution, on polarized light, although not all of them were found to be optically active.

Fischer synthesized some of the known sugars such as fructose and glucose, and he identified 16 stereoisomeric forms of glucose. In addition, he synthesized a number of sugars that do not occur in nature and demonstrated their structural relationships. His work proved to be a vindication

of the asymmetry theory of J. H. van't Hoff and J. A. Le Bel; that is, mirror-image molecules do, in fact, exist.

Purine Group

At approximately the same time that Fischer was involved with the analysis and synthesis of sugars, he accomplished a great deal of research on another important group of compounds, the purine group, or purine derivatives. Among the purine derivatives are caffeine, xanthine, theobromine, and uric acid. The Swedish chemist Carl W. Scheele discovered uric acid in 1776, and Justus von Liebig and Friedrich Wohler studied its derivatives in the 1830s. Adolf von Baeyer was also interested in studies of this natural product of tissue waste and succeeded in presenting an orderly arrangement of the purine derivatives. However, the final determination of the structures of the purine group was done by Fischer during his years at the universities of Erlangen and Würzburg. Later, at Berlin, he synthesized xanthine, caffeine, theobromine, adenine, and the parent compound, purine. Before 1900 Fischer and his students had investigated no fewer than 130 purine derivatives. In 1902 he received the Nobel Prize for his work on sugars and purines.

Research in the Proteins

From his previous research, Fischer was led in 1899 to the study of an even more complex group of natural products, the proteins. The proteins themselves are made up of amino acids; therefore the first steps in his research had to be the investigation of the amino acids, and he proceeded with great skill to isolate and identify them.

The difficulties in these researches were such as to discourage any but the most persistent of investigators, for the proteins are noncrystalline, are sensitive to heat, alcohol, and acids, and cannot easily be produced in a pure state. Fischer's basic method was to prepare the esters of amino acids and then distill them fractionally. Once the amino acids were separated, they could be built up into more complex structures, which he called polypeptides. With this method, the number of possible variations was almost unlimited, and it became evident why such a large number of different proteins exist in nature. In this field of study his greatest achievement was perhaps his synthesis in 1907 of a simple, but real protein molecule.

Later Life and Character

Fischer continued to investigate new areas of organic chemistry. His vacations in the Black Forest of Bavaria led him to study the chemical substances in the lichens that were attached to the old evergreens, and he discovered a new group of compounds, the "depsides." He also studied the constitution and synthesis of tanning substances and initiated some research into the composition of fats.

During World War I Fischer held a position as scientific adviser to the German government, with the task of organizing industrial chemical production for the war effort. He increased the ammonia supply from coke ovens, stimulated the production of the synthetic nitric acid industry, and attempted to organize the production of "synthetic" food.

He also worked closely with the German dye industry but never accepted any of the lucrative industrial posts offered to him.

As a professor at Berlin, Fischer found himself called upon for many duties outside teaching and research. He was several times president and vice president of the German Chemical Society and was a member of the Prussian Academy of Sciences. Because of the pressure of these outside activities, he sought to establish private research facilities and to turn over his teaching duties to younger men. In this effort he helped to found the Kaiser Wilhelm Institute for Chemistry and the Kaiser Wilhelm Institute for Carbon Research.

Fischer was a scientist of great talent, imagination, and energy who spent his life in dedication to his field. He married Agnes Gerlach, the daughter of an anatomy professor at Erlangen, in 1885; they had three sons. Agnes Fischer died in 1892.

During the war Fischer suffered from ill health, first from chemical poisoning and then from cancer. He tried unsuccessfully to treat the disease with various chemicals and died on July 15, 1919. One of his colleagues, the Nobel Prize winner Richard Willstätter, said of Fischer's life and character, "He was the unmatched classicist, master of organic-chemical investigation with regard to analysis and synthesis, as a personality a princely man."

Further Reading

A sympathetic biographical essay on Fischer can be found in Burckhardt Helferich's contribution to Eduard Farber, ed., *Great Chemists* (1961). A brief account of Fischer's work is included in J. R. Partington, *A Short History of Chemistry* (1937; 3d ed. rev. 1957), and in Alexander Findlay, *A Hundred Years of Chemistry* (1937; 3d ed. 1965). □

Hans Fischer

The German organic chemist Hans Fischer (1881-1945) was awarded the Nobel Prize in Chemistry in 1930 for his researches into the constitution of hemin and chlorophyll and especially for his synthesis of hemin.

Hans Fischer, the son of Dr. Eugen Fischer, a manufacturer of chemicals, was born at Höchst am Main, on July 27, 1881. He entered the University of Lausanne in 1899, read chemistry and medicine, and subsequently transferred to the University of Marburg, where he graduated in chemistry in 1904. Two years later he qualified in medicine at Munich. In 1908 he graduated as a doctor of medicine at Munich. He was assistant to the chemist Emil Fischer at Berlin (1908-1910) and did some early work on bile pigments at Munich (1910-1912).

After a year as a teacher of internal medicine and three as lecturer in physiology at Munich, Fischer held the chair of medical chemistry at Innsbruck (1916-1918) and then at

Vienna (1918-1921). From 1921 until his death he was professor of organic chemistry at the Technische Hochschule in Munich.

From 1911 Fischer studied the pyrrole group of the heterocyclic compounds. In 1915 he showed that the urine and feces of a case of congenital porphyria, a disease then recently discovered, contained uroporphyrin and coproporphyrin.

Structure of Hemoglobin

Fischer then began to study hemoglobin, a very important member of the pyrrole group. Its molecule consists of the pigment heme combined with the protein globlin. Heme contains iron, and its chloride, which is easier to work with, is hemin. Hemoglobin possesses the unique property of forming a loose reversible combination with oxygen, so that oxygen taken up by it in the lungs can be given off in the tissues. In this loose combination the active part is heme, and heme combined with any other protein except globin does not possess the property of giving up combined oxygen. It was already known, partly through the work of Fischer himself, that hemin has the formula $C_{34}H_{32}O_4N_4FeCl$, and his problem now was to determine the steric arrangement of the 76 atoms in this molecule of hemin.

When Fischer started his work it was known that, when the iron atom is removed from hemin, porphyrins are formed. These substances occur widely in nature, and, though their exact chemical composition was unknown, it

was realized that they all contained the pyrrole ring, consisting of four carbon atoms with a nitrogen atom closing the ring. His first problem was therefore to clarify the structure of the porphyrins. At a later stage of this investigation he synthesized the substance "porphin," which is not known to occur naturally. Porphin consists of four pyrrole rings, arranged as at the four points of the compass. These four rings are linked together by four methene bridges ($=CH—$) so that the whole forms a closed square. Fischer then showed that all porphyrins contain this porphin nucleus, in which, in each of the four pyrrole rings, the two carbon atoms most distant from the nitrogen atom are each linked with an atom of hydrogen. He also showed that, in all naturally occurring porphyrins, these hydrogen atoms are replaced by substitution groups (methyl, ethyl, vinyl, and so on). The possible permutations are therefore considerable.

In 1926 Fischer discovered porphyrin syntheses, and he synthesized over 130 isomers. It was recognized that the iron atom in hemin was situated at the center of the porphin nucleus. He studied the substance ooporphyrin, a constituent of the spots on the eggs of certain birds. He found it identical with the protoporphyrin previously described by Kämmerer, and by introducing iron complexly into it Fischer produced hemin. By a short-term putrefaction of hemoglobin he produced protoporphyrin; and by putrefaction carried on for several months he produced deuterohemin, from which he obtained deuteroporphyrin by splitting off the iron.

By the mild reduction of hemin the substance called mesoporphyrin had previously been obtained. Fischer found that, by decarboxylating mesoporphyrin, etioporphyrin was formed, and he determined that etioporphyrin contained four methyl and four ethyl groups. He then found that, by introducing four methyl and four ethyl groups into the porphin nucleus, etioporphyrin was obtained. But, depending on the position assumed by these residues as side chains in the porphin nucleus, this introduction could be effected in four different ways. He synthesized these four etioporphyrins and related them to the ooporphyrins. He then turned to a study of the mesoporphyrins and found that there were 15 possible isomers. He synthesized 12 of the 15. He found also that mesoporphyrin IX was identical with the mesoporphyrin obtained from hemin. Further, mesoporphyrin IX was derived from etioporphyrin III, and the arrangement of the side chains in hemin was thus determined.

Fischer next determined the formula for deuteroporphyrin and synthesized that substance. By the introduction of iron, deuterohemin was obtained, and by a complex process two acetyl residues were introduced into the latter, producing diacetyl-deuterohemin. Partial reduction of diacetyl-deuterohemin yielded hematoporphyrin, and from it protoporphyrin was produced by the removal of two molecules of water. On the introduction of iron into protoporphyrin, a synthetic hemin was produced that was indistinguishable from natural hemin obtained from hemoglobin. Fischer completed this synthesis in 1929.

Structure of Chlorophyll

Meanwhile Fischer had also been working on chlorophyll. During his career he wrote nearly 130 papers on that subject. Richard Willstätter had shown about 1912 that plants contain two chlorophylls: chlorophyll a and chlorophyll b. From chlorophyll he obtained three different porphyrins, and from these etioporphyrin, which he considered identical with the etioporphyrin obtained from hemoglobin. Fischer started his researches here, and from the three porphyrins he obtained two distinct etioporphyrins. He synthesized very many isomers, and he converted pyroporphyrin into his mesoporphyrin IX. He then worked on the substance phylloerythrin, found in the gastrointestinal tract of ruminants. He showed that it is a porphyrin and that it exhibited an atypical linkage of two of the pyrrole nuclei. It was known that chlorophyll contains magnesium, and Fischer determined that the magnesium atom was situated at the center of the porphin nucleus.

Even with the lead that phylloerythrin gave Fischer, it required many years to enable him to put forward his formula for the structure of chlorophyll a, a formula which seems to be correct. This formula is notable not only for the atypical linkage of two of the pyrrole nuclei, but also for the presence of two surplus hydrogen atoms in 7-and 8-positions, and of a very complex phytyl group in the 7-position. He found that the formula for chlorophyll b is the same as that for chlorophyll a, except that in the former a formyl group replaces the methyl group in pyrrole ring II of the latter.

Bile Pigments

All Fischer's important work on this subject was done during the last few years of his life. Although the pigments biliverdin and bilirubin had been known for nearly a century, when Fischer began his investigations practically nothing was known of their chemical composition. He showed that, whereas the molecule of the porphyrins consists of four pyrrole rings linked by four carbon linkages to form a closed ring (the porphin nucleus), the molecule of a bile pigment is the same except that it lacks one of the carbon linkages. The pigment molecule can therefore be regarded either as an open ring or as a linear chain of four pyrrole nuclei linked by three carbon linkages. Fischer worked out the structural formulas for both biliverdin and bilirubin. In 1942 he synthesized biliverdin, and in 1944 he effected the even more difficult synthesis of bilirubin.

Later Life

Fischer was not only a superb research chemist but also a very fine administrator of a research institute, and he was extremely popular with his staff and students. He was a keen mountaineer, skier, and motorist, despite the fact that as a young man he had suffered from serious surgical tuberculosis. In addition to innumerable scientific papers Fischer was the author, with two colleagues, of a standard work on pyrrole chemistry, *Die Chemie des Pyrrols* (3 vols., 1934-1940).

The title of Privy Councilor (*Geheimrat*) was conferred on Fischer in 1925. He received the Liebig Memorial Medal in 1929 and the Davy Medal in 1937. In 1936 Harvard University conferred on him an honorary doctorate. He died in Munich on March 31, 1945.

Further Reading

There is a biography of Fischer in *Nobel Lectures, Chemistry, 1922-1941* (1966), which also contains his Nobel Lecture. For the chemical background to Fischer's work see P. Karrer, *Organic Chemistry* (trans. by A. J. Mee, 4th ed. 1950). See also C. W. Carter, R. V. Coxon, D. S. Parsons, and R. H. S. Thompson, *Biochemistry in Relation to Medicine* (3d ed. 1959), and A. White, P. Handler, and E. L. Smith, *Principles of Biochemistry* (3d ed. 1964, and later editions). ☐

Johann Bernhard Fischer von Erlach

Johann Bernhard Fischer von Erlach (1656-1723) was the greatest architect of baroque Austria. He blended Italian baroque ideas with French classicism and created an architecture magnificent enough to express imperial authority and grandeur.

On the upsurge of the arts that took place in central Europe after the lifting of the siege of Vienna (1683) and the subsequent expulsion of the Turks from Hungary and the Balkans, Austria, as the hereditary home of the Hapsburgs, and through them of the Holy Roman Empire, enjoyed what was probably its most important and splendid period of artistic development. Inspired by French and Italian examples, enough native artists appeared on the scene to compete with the Italians, who had dominated the arts north of the Alps since the Renaissance. Johann Bernhard Fischer von Erlach was one of the first figures in this group and certainly the most imposing.

Fischer was born in Graz on July 18, 1656. (When the artist was ennobled in 1696, von Erlach was added to his name.) The son of a Styrian sculptor, Johann was trained as a sculptor by his father. After a lengthy sojourn in Rome (about 12 years, it is believed), Fischer returned to Graz in 1687 and immediately found employment executing stucco decorations in the interior of the ducal mausoleum.

Fischer's study of architecture led to his appointment as instructor to the heir apparent of the crown, Archduke Joseph (later Joseph I), in civil architecture. While thus occupied Fischer also designed two triumphal arches for the entry of the Emperor into Vienna and, from 1690 to 1694, the Althan Palace at Frain (Vranov) in Moravia. This palace, his first important building, was particularly noteworthy for the large oval Great Hall, a form that became almost his trademark. The high dome of the room, pierced by oval windows, was decorated in fresco by Johann Michael Rottmayr.

Imperial and Princely Palaces

In 1696 Emperor Leopold I commissioned Fischer to design a new palace for Archduke Joseph at Schönbrunn on the outskirts of Vienna. The architect had submitted a plan, the famous "first project," some years earlier. It combined Italianate and French ideas with some suggestions from Fischer's studies of ancient site planning and was perhaps the most audacious design for a palace to come out of the baroque period. Obviously intended to overshadow Versailles, it placed the palace at the top of the hill at Schönbrunn, with huge ramps and stairways leading up from the entrance to the main building, which took as its inspiration Gian Lorenzo Bernini's design for the Louvre facade. The "first project" was too daring and grandiose even for the Emperor, and Fischer had to produce a more conservative design, with the palace at the foot of the hill, and only elaborate formal gardens leading up to a small summerhouse at the top. This plan was executed between 1696 and 1700, but much of it was changed some 40 years later for Maria Theresa.

Fischer was also employed by the prince bishop of Salzburg, for whom he produced some of his best church designs, including the Church of the Holy Trinity (1694-1702), the Ursuline Church (1699-1705), and the University Church (1696-1707). In Vienna he built a large number of palaces, such as the Winter Palace for Prince Eugene of Savoy (1695-1698), later altered by Johann Lucas von Hildebrandt, Fischer's greatest rival; the Batthyany Palace (1699-1706); the Trautson Palace (1710-1712); the Bohe-

mian Court Chancellery (1708-1714); and the Rofrano Palace (now Auersperg; 1721-1722).

As court architect, Fischer was in charge of all works under three emperors, and for the third, Charles VI, the last of the male Hapsburgs of the main line and the father of Maria Theresa, he produced his two most famous works, the Karlskirche (Church of St. Charles Borromeo) and the Hofbibliothek (Imperial Library). During this time Fischer was also working on a scholarly work dealing with the great buildings of the past as well as some of his own, called *Entwurf einer historischen Architektur* (*A Plan for a History of Architecture*), which he presented to Charles VI in manuscript form on his accession to the throne in 1712. It appeared in print, in an enlarged and fully illustrated version, in 1721, and it is as much a monument to Fischer's erudition as his buildings are to his talent. On the basis of descriptions and his own observations he reconstructed such buildings as the Forum of Trajan in Rome, the palace in Persepolis, the Porcelain Pagoda in Nanking, and Stonehenge in England.

The Karlskirche

In 1715 Fischer received the commission for the church, vowed by the Emperor in 1713 for the deliverance of Vienna from the plague. This is Fischer's masterpiece and one of the outstanding architectural creations in Western art. Using the oval form again, he designed a church that was to be seen on a height outside and above the city proper, as much a monument to imperial glory as to Faith triumphing over disease.

Drawing on his knowledge of the monuments of architecture past and present, Fischer placed before the church with its high drum and cupola a low facade incorporating French classicistic elements and references to the broad facade of St. Peter's in Rome. Probably inspired by the minarets of Moslem mosques (and those of the Hagia Sophia in Constantinople), he placed high Roman triumphal columns on either side of the entrance, with reliefs depicting scenes from the life of St. Charles, similar to those on the columns of Trajan and Antoninus Pius in Rome. The broad low front over which the huge dome hovers, flanked by the columns, achieves an interplay of vertical and horizontal movement and a projection and recession of forms that give an almost unparalleled grandeur to the whole.

The Hofbibliothek

Fischer did not live to see the Karlskirche completed; it was finished by his son, Joseph Emmanuel Fischer von Erlach (1693-1742). The same is true of Fischer's other great architectural achievement in Vienna, the Hofbibliothek, begun in 1722.

If the "first project" for Schönbrunn is one of the most daring plans of the whole period for a palace and its setting, and the Karlskirche one of the greatest churches, the Great Hall of the Hofbibliothek is certainly one of the period's greatest secular interiors. Here Fischer again used the oval cupola form but set transversely to the length of the hall. The exterior, following French ideas closely, for all its simplicity clearly reveals the interior arrangements, and it is dominated by the central dome (the projecting side wings enclosing the square in front of the main building are later additions). The interior blends the monumental with the practical in the high open bookshelves (inspired by Francesco Borromini's libraries in Rome) and the interrelation of the central space with the adjacent vaulted side halls. Like the first design for Schönbrunn and the Karlskirche, the significance of the building is not only the obvious one based on its function but is also a glorification of imperial power—in this case its patronage of the arts and sciences.

Fischer died on April 5, 1723. His son, Joseph Emmanuel, in spite of Hildebrandt's efforts to the contrary, took over his father's official position and commissions and completed the Hofbibliothek in 1735.

Further Reading

The best study of Fischer von Erlach in English, and one of the best books on Austrian baroque art, is Hans Aurenhammer, *Johann Bernhard Fischer von Erlach* (1972). Based on the author's catalog of the commemorative exhibition of 1956-1957 in Graz, Vienna, and Salzburg, it far exceeds, in scholarship and interpretation, the monograph in German by Hans Sedlmayr, *Johann Bernhard Fischer von Erlach* (1956). Fischer is discussed in surveys of central European art, such as John Bourke, *Baroque Churches of Central Europe* (1958; 2d ed. 1962); Nicolas Powell, *From Baroque to Rococo* (1959); and Eberhard Hempel, *Baroque Art and Architecture in Central Europe* (1965). □

Hamilton Fish

As secretary of state under President Ulysses S. Grant, Hamilton Fish (1808-1893) settled the Alabama Claims and avoided war with Spain over the Cuban insurrection.

Hamilton Fish was born on Aug. 3, 1808, in New York City. His father was a socially prominent lawyer and Federalist; his mother was from the old Stuyvesant family. Fish graduated with highest honors from Columbia College in 1827 and was admitted to the bar in 1830. He entered politics as a Whig; he was elected to Congress in 1842 and to the governorship in 1848. His administration expanded the New York canal system and established a statewide framework for public education. In 1851 he was elected to the U.S. Senate. Conservative in background and patrician in taste, he joined the upstart Republican party only after it was clear that the Whig party was dead beyond revival.

Fish was not known nationally when President U.S. Grant appointed him secretary of state in 1869. Fish accepted reluctantly but found the job to his liking and remained for the entire two terms. His influence helped rescue Grant's presidency from total failure.

Three major foreign policy problems confronted Fish during his tenure. The first was Grant's effort to annex Santo Domingo. Cool toward the project, Fish nevertheless set about loyally to carry out his superior's wishes. A treaty of annexation was concluded, but Charles Sumner, chairman of the Senate's Committee on Foreign Relations, blocked it. Fish was unsuccessful in mediating the quarrel between Sumner and Grant. Grant's lieutenants in the Senate deposed Sumner from his chairmanship. The annexation was defeated, but Fish emerged from the imbroglio with honor.

Fish's efforts to settle the Alabama Claims were more successful. These claims were damages demanded by the United States from Great Britain for the latter's negligence during the Civil War in allowing Confederate cruisers, especially the *Alabama,* to be built and supplied in England, in violation of British neutrality. The cruisers destroyed scores of American freighters during the war and all but drove the U.S. merchant marine from the seas. In addition, the North demanded reparations for other British actions during the war. Senator Sumner said at one point that the claims could be satisfied only by ceding Canada to the United States. Britain had no intention of acceding to any such extreme demands, and Fish intimated through diplomatic channels that a less extravagant settlement would be acceptable. A joint high commission met in Washington under Fish's watchful eye and negotiated the Treaty of Washington (1871), which provided for the arbitration of the Alabama Claims and of minor issues between the United States and Canada. The arbitration tribunal awarded the United States $15,500,000 in damages.

A Cuban insurrection was in process when Fish took office. He talked Grant out of issuing a recognition of rebel belligerency, which might have led to a conflict with Spain, and he tried unsuccessfully to work out a peace settlement

between Spain and the revolutionaries. In 1873 the *Virginius,* a rebel-owned steamer with illegal American registry engaged in carrying arms, was captured by the Spanish, and 53 crewmen and passengers, including several Americans, were executed as pirates. The incident could have led to war, but again Fish cool-headedly negotiated a settlement, which included indemnities for the families of dead Americans and a Spanish promise (never fulfilled) to punish the officer responsible for the executions.

Fish retired from public life in 1877 and busied himself in civic and social affairs. He died in New York on Sept. 6, 1893.

Further Reading

Amos E. Corning's *Hamilton Fish* (1918) has been largely superseded by Allan Nevins's rich and massive *Hamilton Fish: The Inner History of the Grant Administration* (1936; rev. ed. 1957), based on Fish's letters and diary. Also valuable is the essay on Fish by Joseph Fuller in volume 7 of Samuel Flagg Bemis, ed., *American Secretaries of State and Their Diplomacy* (1929).

Additional Sources

Fish, Hamilton, *Memoir of an American patriot,* Washington, D.C.: Regnery Gateway; Lanham, MD: Distributed by National Book Network, 1991. □

Andrew Fisher

Andrew Fisher (1862-1928) was an Australian labor leader. As the fourth prime minister of Australia, he pursued aims of greater social justice and initiated major projects in the new nation.

Andrew Fisher was born at Crosshouse, Ayrshire, Scotland, on Aug. 29, 1862. He was a miner before emigrating to Queensland in 1885. Working in the Burrum coal mines, he served as a union leader, meanwhile reading economics and social science. He became a pioneer member of the emerging Labor party, under whose banner he entered the Queensland Legislative Assembly in 1893.

In Australia's first federal elections (March 1901) Fisher won a seat in the House of Representatives. He won the deputy leadership of the party in 1904. He was minister for trade and customs in Labour's first federal ministry. When his leader, John Christian Watson, rebelled against caucus domination in 1908, Fisher was the party's almost unanimous choice to succeed him.

In November 1908 Fisher, a self-avowed Socialist, withdrew the support previously accorded Alfred Deakin and became prime minister and treasurer. Labour did not hold an outright majority, however, and the Fisher ministry lasted only 7 months before being ousted by a "fusion" of non-Labour forces.

The general election of April 1910 resulted in a Labour majority, opening the way for a spate of legislation. A federal land tax and compulsory military service were introduced, a government-owned bank (the Commonwealth Bank) was set up and private banks' notes withdrawn, maternity allowances were established as part of expanded social service benefits, and the transcontinental rail link was begun. After High Court rulings defined the limits of federal power in various fields important to Labour's objectives, Fisher in 1911 launched a referendum to amend the Constitution. It and a similar referendum in 1913 failed.

In the general election in mid-1913, Labour lost some seats and Fisher resigned, but a special poll in 1914 brought Fisher back to power. The third Fisher government fully supported Australia's participation in World War I and began immediate recruitment of an expeditionary force and deployment of the Royal Australian Navy. German possessions in the South Pacific area were taken over. Union pressure for social legislation was unabated, and as expectations for a quick end to the war faded, dissatisfaction grew. Amid signs of an impending party split Fisher resigned in October 1915 to become Australian high commissioner in London (1916-1920). He died in London on Oct. 22, 1928.

Further Reading

The background to Labour party developments and Fisher's emergence as leader is contained in Ian Turner, *Industrial Labor and Politics* (1965). The record of the Fisher governments is covered in H. Gyles Turner, *The First Decade of the Australian Commonwealth* (1911), and A. N. Smith, *Thirty Years: The Commonwealth of Australia, 1901-1931* (1933). The story of Australia's participation in World War I is given in Charles E. W. Bean and others, *The Official History of Australia in the War of 1914-1918* (12 vols., 1921-1942). □

Irving Fisher

The American economist Irving Fisher (1867-1947) made significant and original contributions in the fields of economics, mathematics, statistics, demography, public health and sanitation, and public affairs.

Irving Fisher was born in Saugerties, N. Y., on Feb. 27, 1867. He received his doctoral degree in mathematics at Yale in 1891. From 1892 until 1895 he taught mathematics at Yale; in 1895 he joined the faculty of political economy, where he remained until his retirement as professor emeritus in 1935.

It is virtually impossible to do justice to Fisher's many contributions to economics and statistics, but his writings on monetary theory and policy and index numbers have earned special acclaim. He brought to his writings the lucidity, analytical precision, and rigor of an accomplished mathematician. In *The Purchasing Power of Money* (1911) Fisher completely recast the theory of money into his classical quantity-theory-of-money equation $MV + M'V' = PQ$, which made the purchasing power of money (or its reciprocal, the general price level P) completely determined by the stock of money in circulation M, its velocity of circulation V, the volume of bank deposits M', their velocity of circulation V', and the total volume of transactions Q. Fisher translated his theory into a policy prescription of "100 percent money" (all bank deposits should be backed by 100 percent reserves rather than fractional reserves, used then and now by virtually all banking systems) on the grounds that such a policy would control large business cycles. He spent a large part of his private fortune promoting (unsuccessfully) the policy.

Fisher's *The Theory of Interest,* which draws heavily from John Rae and Eugen von Böhm-Bawerk, added clarity and rigor to one of the most complex concepts in economics. In his theory the rate of interest is based on the supply of savings and on the demand for capital as determined by the present and future outlook for investment opportunities. He also distinguished between the nominal and real rates of interest and developed the concepts of positive, negative, and neutral time preferences. Fisher's theory anticipated the later works of members of the Cambridge school.

Fisher made significant and original contributions in statistical theory, econometrics, and Index number theory. *The Making of Index Numbers* (1922) became a standard reference on the subject. After a methodical and quantitative analysis of various index number formulations, he developed his "ideal" index, the geometric mean of the Paasche and Laspeyre indexes. He considered this formulation "ideal" because it met his "time reversal" and "factor reversal" tests.

It has been said of Fisher's contributions to economics and statistics that he built grand columns and arches but he never quite completed the intellectual edifice that could be designated the Fisher theory or the Fisher economic system. It can also be said that he laid solid foundations on which others built their edifices.

Further Reading

The monumental variety and quantity of Fisher's writings defy description. His son, Irving Norton Fisher, compiled a 4,300-page bibliography of his known writings, *A Bibliography of the Writings of Irving Fisher* (1961); he also wrote a creditable biography, *My Father, Irving Fisher* (1956), that covers the essentials of his father's career. A valuable introduction to Fisher's many activities is William Fellner and others, *Ten Economic Studies in the Tradition of Irving Fisher* (1967).

Additional Sources

Allen, Robert Loring., *Irving Fisher: a biography,* Cambridge, Mass.: Blackwell Publishers, 1993. □

Sir Ronald Aylmer Fisher

The English statistician Sir Ronald Aylmer Fisher (1890-1962) introduced fresh ideas into the planning and interpretation of quantitative biological experiments. He was a pioneer in the mathematical theory of genetics.

Ronald Fisher was born in London on Feb. 17, 1890, and was educated at Cambridge University, where he specialized in mathematics and physics. In 1919 he was appointed to the new post of research statistician at the Rothamsted Experimental Station in Hertfordshire. His primary task there was the analysis and reinterpretation of a 66-year backlog of records on continuous agricultural experiments and associated meteorological data. In discharging this duty he revolutionized existing statistical techniques, and he expressed the new outlook in *Statistical Methods for Research Workers* (1925), which was to become, and to a large extent remains, the bible of applied statistics.

A central theme of Fisher's work in statistics was hypothesis testing. Many experiments, especially biological ones, are essentially devised to check whether or not some agent has a determinate effect on a test organism. This necessitates a direct and fair comparison between the organism tested with the agent (test organism) and the organism without it (control organism). Because of normal biological variation, it is unlikely that the two organisms will be the same even if the agent is wholly ineffective. Therefore the question arises whether an observed difference, in favor of the test organism, is entirely due to chance variation or is mainly due to the agent. Fisher termed the basic "no effect" situation the *null hypothesis,* which the experiment is de-

signed to check. Having satisfied himself that the null hypothesis is untenable, the experimentalist can go on to make quantitative estimates of the effect of the agent—especially if he has been wise enough to test it at different levels of application.

Another and cognate area that Fisher transformed was the planning of experiments in which considerable variation of results is to be expected and in which ancillary factors have to be taken into account. For example, in crop fertilization trials highly localized soil variations may exist, and Fisher developed schemes for the random allocation of subplots in ways that such nuisance factors are minimized without harm being done to the probabilistic model on which the hypothesis testing depends.

Darwinism versus Mendelism

Aside from his practical work on the methodology of experimentation, Fisher wrote perceptively on the rationale of statistical inference. He also established the exact distribution of several important statistical functions. At the same time he was probing a quite different matter: the quantitative side of the theory of natural selection. He became a leader in the reconciliation of Darwinism and Mendelism, and in 1930 he published his second great book, *The Genetical Theory of Natural Selection*. Ever since the rediscovery of Gregor Mendel's experimental evidence for particulate inheritance and the subsequent fashioning of the theory of genes, there had been an uneasy feeling that these ideas did not tie in with Charles Darwin's theory of natural selection. Fisher was one of the first to tackle the tough mathematical problems and conceptual difficulties in this area. He discovered just how the frequency of particular genes in a given population will fluctuate under the influence of natural selection. In the book he also put forward his views on eugenics; it is a classic of population genetics.

An important by-product of Fisher's work on genetics was his practical and theoretical interest in human blood grouping. In 1935 he set up a blood-grouping unit in London, and one of the outcomes was the unraveling of the mode of inheritance of Rhesus groups.

Fisher left Rothamsted in 1933 and moved on to professorships in London and, later, Cambridge University. He had been made a fellow of the Royal Society in 1929 and was knighted in 1952. After his retirement he emigrated to Australia, where he died on July 29, 1962.

Further Reading

A detailed biography of Fisher appeared in the Royal Society, London, *Biographical Memoirs of Fellows of the Royal Society*, vol. 9 (1963). Fisher's work in statistics is discussed in James R. Newman, ed., *The World of Mathematics* (4 vols., 1956), and Lancelot Hogben, *Statistical Theory: The Relationship of Probability, Credibility and Error* (1957).

Additional Sources

Box, Joan Fisher, *R. A. Fisher, the life of a scientist*, New York: Wiley, 1978. ☐

James Fisk

The American financial speculator James Fisk (1834-1872), a gaudy exemplar of the "gilded age," made money in wild forays in the stock market.

James Fisk was born on April 1, 1834, near Bennington, Vt. His father was a peddler, and young Fisk worked with him until he struck out for himself. He turned up in Boston in a mercantile firm. During the Civil War he made money buying Southern cotton for a Northern syndicate in areas occupied by the Northern armies. He then set up and failed as a dry-goods jobber in Boston.

In 1866 Fisk went to New York and attached himself to Daniel Drew, acting as Drew's agent in the sale of a steamboat company. Drew helped Fisk establish a brokerage house, installed Fisk on the board of directors of the Erie Railroad, and involved him in the "Erie war" against Cornelius Vanderbilt. Fisk, ever alert to the main chance, realized that Jay Gould was really calling the tune, and he became Gould's man. Following Gould's orders, Fisk played the market in Erie stock and flooded it with new securities. When Gould made peace with Vanderbilt, the Erie became Gould's private preserve and Fisk was retained on the board, while Drew was pushed out.

Fisk had made money; he made more in controlling and operating the Narragansett Steamship Company. He also ran the Fall River and Bristol steamboat lines. In 1869 Fisk became a partner in Gould's effort to corner the gold market, with Fisk buying gold while Gould sold. Gould had sensed that the U.S. Treasury would not tolerate a corner on the gold market and would release gold. When it did, Gould—but not Fisk—emerged relatively unscathed. In fact, Gould's brokerage firm denied responsibility for Fisk's operations. But the strange association continued, with Fisk acting as the front man when Gould became involved with the Wabash and the Union Pacific railroads. Fisk's banking house was taken into various syndicates for the sale of large blocks of stock of the New York Central and the Southern Pacific railroads.

Fisk used his ample funds to patronize the theater in New York; he bought Pike's Opera House and leased the Academy of Music. He was a big spender in New York's night life, where he was known as "Jubilee Jim." A rival shot him in a quarrel over a popular actress on Jan. 6, 1872, and Fisk died the next day.

Further Reading

Popular biographies of Fisk are Robert H. Fuller, *Jubilee Jim: The Life of Colonel James Fisk, Jr.* (1928), and W. A. Swanberg, *Jim Fisk: The Career of an Improbable Rascal* (1959). Charles F. Adams, Jr., and Henry Adams tell the story of the "Erie war" in *Chapters of Erie and Other Essays* (1871). An excellent account of the relations between Fisk and Gould is in Julius Grodinsky, *Jay Gould: His Business Career, 1867-1892* (1957).

came assistant librarian. At the same time he also began the career of public lecturer that he would continue until his death.

Outlines of Cosmic Philosophy (1874) revealed his basic philosophical premise: societies evolve like biological organisms, and the laws of their evolution, like the Darwinian laws of biological evolution, can be discovered. Though Fiske never succeeded in formulating any laws of history, he never doubted their existence.

At this point Fiske turned from philosophy to the study of history. In preparing a series of lectures on American history in 1879, he treated the United States as the climax of a historical evolution toward a free democratic republic. Thereafter he worked in the field of American colonial and Revolutionary history. His best-known work, *The Critical Period of American History* (1888), dealt with the period between the end of the Revolutionary War and the adoption of the Constitution. He published several books during the next decade.

By the 1890s Fiske had a considerable reputation as a lecturer, his previously unorthodox religious views having mellowed so that his middle-class public regarded him as a reconciler of science and Christianity. His scholarly reputation declined, however, as his popularity increased; professional historians noted the lack of original research in his books. While his mind was not deep, it was broad, and he had a genius for explaining other men's ideas clearly.

Additional Sources

McAlpine, R. W. (Robert W.), *The life and times of Col. James Fisk, Jr.,* New York: Arno Press, 1981.

Stafford, Marshall P., *The life of James Fisk, Jr.: a full and accurate narrative of all the enterprises in which he was engaged,* New York: Arno Press, 1981. □

John Fiske

John Fiske (1842-1901), American philosopher and historian, was responsible for applying the Darwinian theory of evolution to philosophical and historical studies in the United States.

Born Edmund Fisk Green (he later changed his name) on March 30, 1842, in Hartford, Conn., he was from an early age extremely bookish. His investigation of current scientific theories led him to doubt the validity of orthodox Christianity. He entered Harvard in 1860 but was disappointed to find the curriculum old-fashioned; he displeased college authorities with his unorthodox religious views.

After graduation Fiske entered Harvard Law School and passed his bar exam in 1864. He soon turned from practice of law to writing to solve his financial difficulties. In 1869 he obtained a teaching position at Harvard and in 1872 be-

For the last few years of his life Fiske suffered from bad health, complicated by obesity. He died on July 4, 1901, in Gloucester, Mass.

Further Reading

Unquestionably the best book on Fiske is Milton Berman, *John Fiske: The Evolution of a Popularizer* (1961). John Spencer Clark, *The Life and Letters of John Fiske* (2 vols., 1917), is not as critical or judicious but includes substantial selections from Fiske's correspondence. Jennings B. Sanders's essay on Fiske in William T. Hutchinson, ed., *The Marcus W. Jernegan Essays in American Historiography* (1937), places Fiske in the development of American historical writing. □

Minnie Maddern Fiske

The first important "realistic" actress in the United States, Minnie Maddern Fiske (1865-1932) became known primarily for her portrayals of the heroines of the Norwegian playwright Ibsen.

Minnie Maddern Fiske was born Mary Augusta Davey in New Orleans on December 19, 1865. Her father was the theatrical manager Thomas Davey, and her mother, Lizzie Maddern, was an actress whose surname the young "Minnie" adopted for her own stage name.

A true child of the theater, Minnie was brought upon the boards as an infant and continued to perform as soon as she could speak. As a child actress she drew attention as early as the age of four, when she made her first New York appearance. She ran the gamut of the so-called "infant prodigy" roles, which included that of Prince Arthur in *King John,* then gracefully graduated to those of the young ingenue by the age of 15. She starred in *Featherbrain, In Spite of All* (with Richard Mansfield), and *Fogg's Ferry*. She was happy to be pronounced a "new Lotta" by one critic for her work in the latter production, as Lotta Crabtree had been her idol.

In 1882 Fiske fell in love with and married Legrand White, a vaudeville musician. Their quarrels over the financing of *Caprice* initiated the break-up of their brief union. It was in this production that Fiske sang "In the Gloaming," popularizing the tune, and created another theatrical innovation by staying "in the setting"—that is, remaining seated by the hearth for the song rather than going to the edge of the stage, as was the custom.

At the age of 25 Fiske married Harrison Grey Fiske (1861-1942), four years her junior and the editor of the *New York Dramatic Mirror*. Harrison Fiske provided life-long support of all of his wife's theatrical ventures, serving in a variety of capacities: business manager, director, producer, dramaturg, critic. He remained her devoted "righthand man" until her death.

Upon her marriage, Fiske declared that she would give up the stage. However, she was drawn back to it four years later, after writing some of her own plays (several of which were produced) and studying a number of the socalled "new" dramas—in particular those of Ibsen, whose work was to have a profound effect upon her subsequent production and acting style. Fiske first played Nora in Ibsen's *A Doll's House* in 1894 and followed this success with the critically acclaimed *Tess of the D'Ubervilles* in 1897. The latter was performed at the only theater in New York City which was not controlled by the Syndicate, which acquired a virtual monopoly of the professional theatrical circuit both in New York and nation-wide. The Fiskes fought the Syndicate, even though it meant playing in opera and vaudeville houses and in the cruder accommodations that were afforded in burlesque halls and the basements of churches.

Finally, in 1901, the Fiskes were able to lease the Manhattan Theatre, and popular productions during their tenacy included Ibsen's *Hedda Gabler* (with Minnie in the title role), as well as his *Pillars of Society* and *Rosmersholm*. Later they produced Langdon Mitchell's *The New York Idea,* a sophisticated comedy about divorce; then Edward Sheldon's *Salvation Nell,* which included real-life slum residents in its cast and a famous ten-minute silent stare of Minnie, who portrayed the heroine.

By 1911 Fiske had sold his interest in the *Mirror* (which had been forbidden reading material for any actor who signed on with the Syndicate) and turned to producing fulltime. Fiske joined her husband in the role of producer, and they proved to be a compatible team. She also made a few adjustments of her artistic concerns and focussed the remainder of her career on classic and light contemporary comedy. Only occasionally would she return to serious roles, as she did in 1926 with a performance as Mrs. Alving in Ibsen's *Ghosts.* Stand-outs among her characterizations in her later years were as the title character in Harry James Smith's *Mrs. Bumstead-Leigh,* Mistress Page in *The Merry Wives of Windsor,* and another popular revival, Mrs. Malaprop in Sheridan's *The Rivals.*

Fiske's sensitivity was evident both on and off the stage. The intensity of her performances was such that she was easily distracted by any noise in the house and thus found it necessary to forbid the presence of babies and the eating of peanuts in her audiences. Outside of the theater she was well known for her support of the American Society for the Prevention of Cruelty to Animals, and she often cared for stray animals herself. She was devoted to a number of humane causes throughout her life, and she was a protester against the killing of animals solely for their fur, against bull-fighting, and against President Theodore Roosevelt's hunting expedition to Africa. She also helped to save the egret from extinction.

Fiske has been considered to be the first important realistic actress in the United States, as she was the first major performer in the roles of Ibsen's female protagonists and implemented naturalistic detail and innovation in her interpretations of the contemporary problem play. A pioneer in "psychological realism" years before the work of Stanislavski was evident in America, Fiske was known for a naturalness and simplicity in her acting and production style which countered the stage tricks and artificiality still prevalent on the early 20th-century stage. For each role she assumed she undertook an extremely detailed character study in order to appear unstudied and simple in performance. Her skillful employment of suggestion rather than overt display taught much to the new generation of actors who worked with her and watched her perform. Her subtleties were perhaps better suited for the emerging medium of film; however, that possibility was never explored as movies with sound did not appear until Minnie Fiske's dark beauty was beginning to fade.

She remained as contrary to the so-called "star system" as she had been to the powerful Syndicate, and she emphasized the importance of ensemble work in each production. Quietly and virtually single-handedly, she ushered in a new era of theater in America. Hers was a style different from that which was popular at the time, and much of the acknowledgment of her work by other actors and many critics did not come until the end of her career. A seemingly indefatigable performer, Fiske never really retired, working right up until several months before her death on Valentine's Day, 1932.

Further Reading

For additional information on Fiske see Archie Binns, *Mrs. Fiske and the American Theatre* (1955). □

John Fitch

John Fitch (1743-1798), an American mechanic and inventor, was the first to build and operate a steamboat successfully.

John Fitch was born on a farm in Hartford County, Conn. By the age of 10 he had left school and begun farming. To escape farming he spent the next 6 years at clerking and various other jobs. He was apprenticed to two different clockmakers, and when he reached his twenty-first birthday he set up his own brass shop in East Windsor, Conn. He always had trouble maintaining stable social relationships; in 1769 he deserted his wife and left the state.

Settling in Trenton, N.J., Fitch set up as a brass and silver smith. During the American Revolution he earned a modest living repairing guns and provisioning the Continental troops. In 1780 he went west for the first time, as a surveyor for a land speculation company. While running lines along the Ohio River he laid claim to 1,600 acres in Kentucky. On another trip west, in 1782, he was captured by Indians and turned over to their British allies. After his imprisonment in Canada, he was released and continued his speculations in western lands. Following his last trip in 1785, he drew and engraved a map of the Northwest Territory which brought him some fame and a small income.

After 1785 Fitch devoted himself to developing the steamboat. The idea was not new, but Fitch later claimed to have gotten it independently after seeing a picture of a steam engine in a book. He first thought to apply steam power to driving wagons, but he soon turned to the problem of making a boat go by the force of steam. By 1786 he was granted an exclusive privilege to employ steam on the waters of New Jersey, and in 1787 he received similar grants from Pennsylvania, New York, Delaware, and Virginia.

Fitch worked with the clockmaker and master mechanic Henry Voight of Philadelphia to perfect his idea. He lacked the funds to purchase an engine ready-made from England; furthermore, export of steam engines was banned by the British government. So he tried to make an engine himself—a task which detracted significantly from his chances for success. Nevertheless in August 1787, before a distinguished group of Federal and Pennsylvania state officials, he demonstrated his first boat on the Delaware River. One handicap was the method of propulsion—a row of steam-powered oars on each side of the boat. His future boats used the paddle wheel. During this period he expended much energy in a controversy with James Rumsey of Virginia, who disputed his claim to have originated the steamboat.

In July 1788 Fitch successfully launched a new and larger boat, which made many trips between Philadelphia and Burlington, N.J., carrying as many as 30 passengers at a time. In 1790 he put another boat into service that made regularly scheduled runs across the Delaware River. Despite this success, however, steamboat travel was not accepted by the public. This, combined with constant mechanical troubles and uncertain financial backing, resulted in the failure of Fitch's enterprise.

Fitch received a patent in August 1791 but was not able to capitalize upon it. He sought the patronage of the Federal government as well as of several states, and he even corresponded with the Spanish government over the possibility of operating boats on the Mississippi River. He traveled to France looking for backing but failed there too. He returned to the United States and in 1796 moved to Kentucky. Here he died, presumably by his own hand, 2 years later.

Something of the difficulty of Fitch's life may be understood from the bitter humor of a declaration (with misspellings) he once made: "I know of nothing so perplexing and Vexatious to a man of feelings, as a turbulant Wife and Steam Boat building. I experienced the former and quit in season, and had I been in my right sences I should undoubtedly [have] treated the latter in this same manner, but for one man to be teised with Both, he must be looked upon as the most unfortunate man in this World."

Fitch's attempt to establish the steamboat was followed by at least a dozen other experimenters before Robert Fulton's success in 1807.

Further Reading

Fitch told his own story in *The Original Steamboat Supported* (1788). The standard biography is still Thompson Westcott, *The Life of John Fitch, the Inventor of the Steam-boat* (1857), but it may be supplemented by Thomas A. Boyd, *Poor John Fitch, Inventor of the Steamboat* (1935). A balanced account of the rivalry between Fitch and others is James Thomas Flexner, *Steamboats Come True: American Inventors in Action* (1944).

Additional Sources

Fitch, John, *The autobiography of John Fitch,* Philadelphia: American Philosophical Society, 1976. □

Ella Fitzgerald

Ella Fitzgerald (1918-1996) was one of the most exciting jazz singers of her time and, because of the naturalness of her style, had a popular appeal that extended far beyond the borders of jazz.

Ella Fitzgerald was born on April 25, 1918, in Newport News, Virginia, but spent her formative years in Yonkers, New York, and received her musical education in its public schools. When only 16, she received her first big break at the Apollo Theater in Harlem, when she won an amateur night contest and impressed saxophonist-bandleader Benny Carter. He recommended her to drummer-bandleader Chick Webb, who hired her in 1935. She soon became a recording star with the band, and her own composition "A-tisket, A-tasket" (1938) was such a smash hit that the song became her trademark for many years thereafter. When Webb died in 1939, Fitzgerald assumed leadership of the band for the next year.

By 1940 Fitzgerald was recognized throughout the music world as a vocal marvel—a singer with clarity of tone, flexibility of range, fluency of rhythm, and, above all, a talent for improvisation that was equally effective on ballads and up-tempo tunes. Although for a long time her reputation with musicians and other singers outstripped that with the general public, she corrected the imbalance soon after joining Norman Granz's Jazz at the Philharmonic (JATP) in 1946. She made annual tours with the group and was invariably the concert favorite. Three of her unfailing showstoppers were "Oh, Lady Be Good," "Stomping at the Savoy," and "How High the Moon." Each would begin at a medium tempo and then turn into a rhythmic excursion as Fitzgerald moved up-tempo and "scatted" (that is, sang harmonic variations of the melody in nonsense syllables). The huge JATP crowds always responded tumultuously.

By the early 1950s Fitzgerald's domination of fans' and critics' polls was absolute. In fact, she won the *Down Beat* readers' poll every year from 1953 to 1970 and became known as "The First Lady of Song." In 1955 she terminated her 20-year recording affiliation with Decca in order to record for Norman Granz's Verve label and proceeded to produce a series of superlative "Songbook" albums, each devoted to the compositions of a great songwriter or songwriting team (Jerome Kern and Johnny Mercer; George and Ira Gershwin; Cole Porter; Richard Rodgers and Lorenz Hart; Irving Berlin; Duke Ellington). The lush orchestrations induced Fitzgerald to display the classy pop-singer side of herself; even in the two-volume Ellington set her jazzier side deferred to the melodist in her.

Under Granz's personal management Fitzgerald also began to play choice hotel jobs and made her first featured film appearance, in "Pete Kelly's Blues" (1955). In 1957 she worked at the Copacabana in New York City and gave concerts at the Hollywood Bowl. In 1958, in the company of the Duke Ellington Orchestra, she gave a concert at Carnegie Hall as part of an extended European and United States tour with the band. In the early 1960s she continued to work the big hotel circuit—the Flamingo in Las Vegas, the Fairmont Hotel in San Francisco, and the Americana in New York City—and to tour Europe, Latin America, and Japan with the Oscar Peterson trio, which was three-fourths of Granz's JATP house rhythm section. In 1965 and 1966 she was reunited with Ellington for another tour and record date.

Fitzgerald was always blessed with superb accompanists, from the full orchestral support of Chick Webb and Duke Ellington to the smaller JATP ensembles. In 1968 she teamed up with yet another, the magnificent pianist Tommy Flanagan, who headed a trio that served her into the mid-1970s. In 1971 Fitzgerald had serious eye surgery, but within a year she was performing again. Her singing, however, began to show evidence of decline: the voice that was once an instrument of natural luster and effortless grace became a trifle thin and strained. Nevertheless, so great was her artistry that she continued to excite concert audiences and to record effectively. She appeared after the mid-1960s with over 50 symphonic orchestras in the United States.

A large, pleasant-looking woman with a surprisingly girlish speaking voice, Ella Fitzgerald had a propensity for forgetting lyrics. This endeared her to audiences, who delighted in her ability to work her way out of these selfpainted corners. Unlike some other great jazz singers (Billie Holiday, Anita O'Day), Fitzgerald had a private life devoid of drug-related notoriety. She was twice married: the first marriage, to Bernie Kornegay in 1941, was annulled two years later; the second, to bassist Ray Brown in 1948, ended in divorce in 1952 (they had one son).

Was Ella Fitzgerald essentially a jazz singer or a pop singer? Jazz purists say that she lacked the emotional depth of Billie Holiday, the imagination of Sarah Vaughan or Anita O'Day, and the blues-based power of Dinah Washington and that she was often facile, glossy, and predictable. The criticisms sprang partly from her "crossover" popularity and ignored her obvious strengths and contributions: Fitzgerald was not only one of the pioneers of scatsinging, but, beyond that, she was an unpretentious singer whose harmonic variations were always unforced and a supreme melodist who never let her ego get in the way of any song she sang.

Fitzgerald died on June 15, 1996 at the age of 78. She left a legacy that won't soon be forgotten. In her lifetime she was honored with no less than 12 Grammys, the Kennedy Center Award, as well as an honorary doctorate in music from Yale University. In 1992 she was honored by President George Bush with the National Medal of Freedom. Fitzgerald's impressive financial estate was left in a trust, including the $2.5 million in proceeds from the sale of her Beverly Hills home.

Further Reading

There is no biography of Ella Fitzgerald, but there are excellent chapters on her in Leonard Feather's *From Satchmo to Miles* (1972) and Henry Pleasants' *The Great American Popular Singers* (1974). Also see *Jet* (December 28, 1992). □

Frances FitzGerald

Frances FitzGerald (born 1940) wrote one of the most influential books on the Vietnam War to appear while the conflict was still in progress.

Frances FitzGerald was not quite 32 years of age when her first book, *Fire in the Lake: The Vietnamese and the Americans in Vietnam* (1972), was published to immediate and extraordinary praise. *Fire in the Lake* was hailed for its "stunning clarity" by one reviewer and as "one of the best descriptions and analyses of Vietnam ever published in English" by another. *TIME* magazine was impressed that she had achieved "so fresh a blend of compassion and intelligence," and even the conservative *National Review*, which loathed it, predicted accurately that her book would "become gospel for the anti-war movement."

The young woman whose career had just taken such a remarkable turn was a journalist with a remarkable family and personal background. Her father, Desmond FitzGerald, was a deputy director of the Central Intelligence Agency (CIA) and an expert on Southeast Asia. Her mother, Mary Endicott Peabody FitzGerald Tree, was a former American ambassador to the United Nations. FitzGerald herself had graduated from Radcliffe College with a BA, *magna cum laude*, in 1962. Five years later she won the first of many honors, an Overseas Press Club award for best interpretation of foreign affairs.

FitzGerald prepared herself for the work to come by visiting Vietnam twice as a free-lance journalist, for a total of 16 months, and by studying Chinese and Vietnamese history and culture under Paul Mus, to whom, as also to the memory of her father, she would dedicate *Fire in the Lake*. Its publication resulted not only in superb reviews but in a whole series of honors including a Pulitzer Prize for contemporary affairs writing, a National Book Award, and the Bancroft Prize for historical writing—all in 1973. The Vietnam War was still strongly affecting America's political and cultural life at this time, and a good book on it was bound to win unusual attention. The Bancroft Prize, for example, is normally given to a professional scholar rather than a journalist.

But while the times partly explain her book's success, FitzGerald had earned it also, not by disclosing new information, but by viewing Vietnam from a different perspective. More than half of her book was devoted to explaining how the National Liberation Front (NLF or the Viet Cong, to most Americans) had adapted itself to Vietnam's unique culture and traditions. As she explained it, Marxism did not clash with local values. Rather, it was highly compatible with Confucianism, the basis of Vietnam's way of life, with the Communist party replacing the emperor as the source of wisdom and leadership. FitzGerald greatly admired the NLF. Although she acknowledged that it had committed atrocities and that land "reform" in North Vietnam entailed considerable brutality, she minimized the NLF's actions. Her book is not even-handed by any means, but for a work of advocacy is reliable.

Nevertheless, *Fire in the Lake* is a partisan book that aims to show the NLF in the best possible light. Despite admitted shortcomings, the Communists are portrayed as fundamentally decent, faithful, and true lovers of the peasantry and champions of the people. At one point FitzGerald says that in NLF controlled areas farm production actually rose. This might well have been true in selected cases, but North Vietnam, had crippled agriculture by ruthlessly imposing collective farming upon their unhappy peasants. That this would happen in South Vietnam too when the Communists won was a foregone conclusion.

Critics also resented her argument that because free elections have no place in Vietnamese culture, the absence of them means nothing. People who honor authoritarian regimes have always argued, as FitzGerald did, that voting is not a part of the national heritage in question, or that decisions are arrived at by consensus, making disputed elections unnecessary. FitzGerald pointed out that in South Vietnam the Communists were trying to attract support and respected local sentiments accordingly. What she didn't say, and perhaps did not believe, was that in North Vietnam, where the Communists were in power, they ignored public opinion. In 1973 the North's present was the South's future, a tragedy for both regions.

FitzGerald devoted the other half of her book to the evils of South Vietnam's various anti-Communist regimes and the folly of America's support for them. American intervention in South Vietnam was a ghastly mistake, not because the NLF was a band of political saints, but because, owing to the outrageous corruption and incompetence of the ruling elite in Saigon, there was no way to save the country.

FitzGerald's next book, *America Revised: History Textbooks in the Twentieth Century* (1979), is a trenchant critique of this debased educational medium, though to some readers it appeared that what FitzGerald objected to most was that textbooks did not give what she saw as the correct version of American history. The contrary objection was raised by her third book, *Cities on a Hill: A Journey Through Contemporary American Cultures* (1987), which described four different communities ranging from a retirement village in Florida to the followers of Bhagwan Shree Rajneesh in Oregon. Though her intent was to explore the effect of the 1960s on American culture, some critics held that while her book was delightfully descriptive, as analysis it did not seem to go anywhere.

Thus, in the years after *Fire in the Lake* appeared Fitz-Gerald continued to write, producing books that invariably strike reviewers as well-written and thoughtful.

Further Reading

For additional FitzGerald writing on Vietnam see "Life and Death of a Vietnamese Village," *New York Times Magazine* (September 4, 1966) and "The Tragedy of Saigon," *Atlantic Monthly* (December 1966). Probably the best full-length book on the Vietnamese conflict is Stanley Karnow's *Vietnam: A History* (1983). □

Francis Scott Key Fitzgerald

The American author Francis Scott Key Fitzgerald (1896-1940), a legendary figure of the 1920s, was a scrupulous artist, a graceful stylist, and an exceptional craftsman. His tragic life was an ironic analog to his romantic art.

On Sept. 24, 1896, F. Scott Fitzgerald was born in St. Paul, Minn. His family was Irish Catholic, his mother's side wealthy. The family lived for some years in Buffalo and Syracuse; but in 1908, when Scott's father lost his job, they returned to St. Paul. For the most part, Scott was privately educated; he attended Newman School in Hackensack, N.J., from 1911 to 1913.

Fitzgerald enrolled at Princeton University in 1913 and struck up enduring friendships with Edmund Wilson and John Peale Bishop. Because of ill health and low grades, he left college in 1915. He returned to Princeton in 1916 but left a year later without a degree and joined the Army with a second lieutenant's commission. Stationed in Alabama in 1918, he met Zelda Sayre, then 18 years old; he would marry her a few years later. After his Army discharge he took an advertising job briefly. Back home in St. Paul, he finished his first novel, *This Side of Paradise,* which was accepted by Scribner's in 1919, and that same year he had remarkable success placing nine short stories in leading commercial journals.

First Publications

Upon publication of *This Side of Paradise* (1920), Fitzgerald married Sayre in New York City. Of this period he later recalled riding up Fifth Avenue in a cab—young, rich, famous, and in love (he might easily have added handsome)—suddenly bursting into tears because he knew he would never be so happy again. He was right. Despite great earnings and fame, he and Zelda lived luxuriously, dissolutely, and tragically.

A daughter was born in 1921 after the couple had spent some time in Europe. When Fitzgerald's second novel, *The Beautiful and the Damned* (1922), and a collection of short stories, *Tales of the Jazz Age* (1922), sold very well, they rented a house on Long Island and ran into debt because of their extravagance. Fitzgerald attempted to recoup by writ-

ing a play, *The Vegetable* (1923), but it flopped quickly. The Fitzgeralds went to Europe for over 2 years. The high points of this sojourn were publication of *The Great Gatsby* (1925) and the beginning of Scott's friendship with Ernest Hemingway. In 1927 Scott went to Hollywood on his first movie assignment. Afterward the Fitzgeralds again went abroad several times.

Zelda's first major nervous breakdown, in 1930, and treatment in a Swiss clinic became the basis for Fitzgerald's next novel, *Tender Is the Night* (1934). Zelda spent the rest of her life in and out of sanitariums, and Fitzgerald's own life ran a parallel disastrous course.

Analysis of the Novels

This Side of Paradise (1920), an autobiographical novel, tells of the youth and early manhood of a Princeton undergraduate. In the climactic action his loyalties shift from football to literature, with a concomitant growth in his character. This patchy work struck a nerve in the reading public, chiefly for its new type of heroine—the "flapper," a young woman in revolt against the double standard, who smokes, drinks, dances, and is considered to be somewhat promiscuous.

The Beautiful and the Damned (1922) deals with a dissolute couple, Anthony Patch, grandson of a millionaire, and his debutante wife. They live indolently, extravagantly, and quarrelsomely on the expectations of Tony's inheritance, but the grandfather discovers Tony's alcoholism and profligacy and disinherits him; however, after the grandfa-

ther dies, the will is broken. Ironically, the inheritance reinforces Tony's spiritual disintegration. As with most of Fitzgerald's novels, the autobiographical elements are fairly obvious.

The Great Gatsby (1925) is an American classic, generally regarded as Fitzgerald's finest work. It extends and synthesizes the themes that pervade all of his fiction: the callous indifference of wealth, the hollowness of the American success myth, and the sleaziness of the contemporary scene. It is the story of Jay Gatz, a successful, vaguely disreputable man, who has a background of poverty and has pretentiously altered his name to "Gatsby." A naively vulgar parvenu, he nonetheless emerges as morally superior to the slightly covert snobs who free-load at his parties and the reckless rich whom he so hopelessly emulates. Gatsby dies quixotically attempting to reclaim his former love, Daisy.

With T. S. Eliot's poem *The Waste Land* and Ernest Hemingway's *The Sun Also Rises*, *The Great Gatsby* is a major contribution to the creative record of the barren spirituality of the 20th century. Ironically, in *Gatsby* an ash heap dominates the landscape between Long Island and Manhattan; Gatsby's memorabilia include rigorous self-improvement schedules and Benjamin Franklin homilies, but he rises to success as a bootlegger; Gatsby, whose notion of elegance is his pink suit, silk shirts, cream-colored car, and large house with swimming pool, has a similarly shallow knowledge of people and never sees Daisy's superficiality; finally, the green light on his dock, a multisymbol of lush vegetation (for the Pilgrims) or riches (for contemporary Americans), is ultimately a deceit—a forlorn, romantic image ending the novel.

Fitzgerald's characters are memorable despite his spare, ideographic method of delineation: Gatsby, whose pet term of address is "Old Sport," is seen only as "a pink suit"; Daisy's husband is identified by the wad of muscle beneath his suit jacket; Daisy has "a voice like money." Nowhere is Fitzgerald's contrast with contemporary author Thomas Wolfe better illustrated: Wolfe believed in "putting in," and Fitzgerald in "taking out," in extreme selectivity and economy in his art.

In its original form *Tender Is the Night* (1934; later restructured by Malcolm Cowley) is structurally imperfect. Set in Europe, chiefly on the Riviera, the first half is told by a 19-year-old starlet who has a crush on the hero, Dick Diver, a young American psychiatrist. The second half is seen through the eyes of Dick and of Nicole, the wealthy American schizophrenic whom he marries, cures, and is destroyed by. Dick ultimately returns to America and becomes a small-town practitioner and an alcoholic. The theme is parasitism—the health of one person gained at the expense of another—and the facts bear an unmistakable resemblance to Scott and Zelda's marriage.

The Last Tycoon (1941), published posthumously after Edmund Wilson put it together from Fitzgerald's unfinished manuscript, is the story of a movie producer. Though Wilson calls it Fitzgerald's most mature work, it has received minimal critical attention.

Short Stories

Some of Fitzgerald's best work is in the short-story form. The titles of his collections are extraordinarily representative of the spirit of the times. *Flappers and Philosophers* (1921) contains "The Off-Shore Pirate" and "The Ice Palace." *Tales of the Jazz Age* (1922) includes "May Day" and "The Diamond as Big as the Ritz," two exquisite stories. The best-known pieces in *All the Sad Young Men* (1926) are "Winter Dreams," a quintessential instance of Fitzgerald's romantic vision, and "The Rich Boy." Fitzgerald's final collection, *Taps at Reveille* (1935), includes "Babylon Revisited," perhaps his most widely anthologized story.

Last Years

Fitzgerald earned over $400,000 between 1919 and 1934, but he and Zelda lived so expensively that they barely managed to cover their bills. When *Tender Is the Night* failed to excite interest, financial problems became acute; by 1937 Fitzgerald owed $40,000 despite continued earnings from magazine stories. Zelda had been permanently returned to the sanitarium in 1934; and the years 1935-1937 saw Fitzgerald's own descent—increasing alcoholism and physical illness—which he described with poignant candor in articles appearing in *Esquire* in the mid-1930s.

In 1937 Fitzgerald signed a movie contract at a weekly salary of $1,000. His liaison with gossip columnist Sheilah Graham during the last 3 years of his life is described in her *Beloved Infidel* (1958). But the heartbreak and dissolution took their toll, and after two heart attacks Fitzgerald died on Dec. 21, 1940. Zelda Fitzgerald died in a fire in 1947 at Highland Sanitarium, Asheville, N.C., leaving a novel, *Save Me the Waltz* (1932, American edition).

Further Reading

Fitzgerald's *The Crack-up,* edited by Edmund Wilson (1945), is a revealing but fragmentary autobiographical collection of essays and letters. The standard work on Fitzgerald is Andrew Turnbull, *Scott Fitzgerald* (1962), a full and reliable biography, though not sufficiently critical. An exciting, sometimes inaccurate biography is Arthur Mizener, *The Far Side of Paradise* (1951). See also Alfred Kazin, ed., *F. Scott Fitzgerald: The Man and His Work* (1951); Sheilah Graham, *Beloved Infidel: The Education of a Woman* (1958); James E. Miller, Jr., *F. Scott Fitzgerald: His Art and His Technique* (1964); Robert F. Sklar, *F. Scott Fitzgerald: The Last Laocoön* (1967), a study of Fitzgerald as an intellectual; and Nancy Milford, *Zelda: A Biography* (1970), a brilliant study of Fitzgerald's wife and their marriage. For literary background see Alfred Kazin, *On Native Grounds: An Interpretation of Modern American Prose Literature* (1942). □

Garret Fitzgerald

The Irish taoiseach or prime minister Garret FitzGerald (born 1926) was deeply committed to religious and cultural tolerance and reconciliation in Northern Ireland and the Irish Republic and to constitutional and structural changes serving those ends.

arret FitzGerald was born on February 9, 1926, the son of Desmond and Mabel (McConnell) FitzGerald. Both parents had been involved in the Irish language restoration movement, the Gaelic League, the 1916 Easter Week uprising, and the insurrection of 1919-1921, although the mother was an Ulster Presbyterian. His father had been minister for external affairs, 1922-1927, and minister for defense, 1927-1932, of the Irish Free State.

FitzGerald received his primary education at St. Brigid's School in Bray, County Wicklow, and started his secondary education at an Irish-language boarding school, Coláiste na Rinne, in Dungarvan, County Waterford, but completed it at Belvedere College in Dublin. He studied economics at University College, Dublin, where he received a Ph.D. while also taking a law degree at King's Inn and being called to the bar. In 1947 he and Joan O'Farrell were married. They had three children, a daughter and two sons.

From 1947 to 1958 he was employed by Aer Lingus (Irish Air Lines). He also was Irish correspondent for the BBC, the *Economist,* and the *Financial Times* and economic correspondent for the *Irish Times*. He was a Rockefeller research assistant at Trinity College, Dublin, 1958-1959, and college lecturer in the Department of Economics, University College, Dublin, 1959-1973. He wrote two books in this period: *State-Sponsored Bodies* (1959) and *Planning in Ireland* (1968).

From 1965 to 1969 he was a member of Seanad Eireann, the upper house of the Irish legislature, which has essentially a delaying power in legislating. He was one of the talented younger figures in the opposition Fine Gael (Tribe of Gaels) Party. That party had evolved out of the Cumann na nGaedheal (League of Gaels) Party that had governed in the Free State era. Fine Gael was the opposition for all but two brief coalition ministries, 1948-1951 and 1954-1957. FitzGerald and associates sought to revitalize their party in the later 1960s by projecting a social justice theme in contrast to the conservative reputation the party had during the era of Fianna Fáil (Soldiers of Destiny) ascendancy, 1932-1973. Elected to Dáil Eireann (the Irish Parliament) in 1969, he served as opposition spokesman on education until 1972 and then as spokesman on finance.

The Problem of Northern Ireland

In February 1973 FitzGerald became minister of external affairs in a Fine Gael-Labour coalition government headed by Liam Cosgrave. He participated in the Sunningdale Conference, December 6-9, 1973, which set up a power-sharing executive for Northern Ireland that for the first time included minority (Catholic and Nationalist) political leaders. Alas, the experiment collapsed within a few months following a general strike by workers from the majority Protestant community.

FitzGerald made a favorable impression as a participant in, and later (January to June 1975) as president of, the Council of Ministers of the European Economic Community, which Ireland had formally entered in January 1973. Understandably, he became the almost automatic successor to Liam Cosgrave when the latter stepped down as Fine Gael leader following Fianna Fáil's return to power in the June 1977 election.

As opposition leader, FitzGerald modernized the party organization, and his efforts paid off when Fine Gael increased its seats in the Dáil in the June 1981 election by 22. That and the 15 Labour seats gave the coalition a two vote plurality over Fianna Fáil, but the ability to govern was dependent on the shaky tolerance of independent members more hostile to the Fianna Fáil leader, Charles Haughey, than sympathetic to the coalition.

The hunger strike in Northern Ireland by prisoners demanding political prisoner status was on at the time. It was only called off in October after 11 men had died. A month later FitzGerald and the British prime minister, Margaret Thatcher, met and institutionalized cooperation between their governments with the formation of an Anglo-Irish Intergovernmental Council.

The Irish government, however, fell in January 1982 when the independents joined with Fianna Fáil in opposing severe tax increments necessitated by an enormous deficit. The Fianna Fáil government that came to power after the February election also had only a plurality and was dependent on independent votes, which votes it lost the following November when it had to engage in fiscal conservatism.

Governing with a Majority

The election of November 24, 1982, the third in 18 months, gave the Fine Gael and Labour combination an absolute majority. FitzGerald's second government, with the new young Labour leader Dick Spring as tánaiste (deputy premier), sought to bring inflation and governmental indebtedness under control, to implement legal and constitutional reforms to make Ireland more congenial for religious pluralism, and to advance the Anglo-Irish process toward eventual accord in Northern Ireland.

In September 1983 a constitutional amendment protecting "the right to life of the unborn," which sought to add constitutional absoluteness to existing Irish statutes prohibiting abortion, was approved in a referendum by two-thirds of the voters. The Taoiseach had opposed the measure for being too legally imprecise, and leaders of the Irish Protestant community opposed it for being too reflective of a specifically Roman Catholic ethos. In 1985, despite the opposition of the Roman Catholic hierarchy, the government succeeded in legalizing the sale of contraceptives to adults. Later serious consideration was given to constitutional revision to allow under certain circumstances divorce or marital dissolution in Ireland. In June 1986 Ireland voted on the question of repealing the national ban on divorce. Despite the urging of Prime Minister FitzGerald, a strong majority voted to continue to prohibit divorce.

Inflation Woes

The government's fiscal policy, dictated by one of the world's largest per capita foreign indebtedness and national deficit, was painful, prompting a series of unfavorable results in public opinion polls, especially since unemployment and youthful emigration continued to grow. However, the inflation was brought under control.

In May 1983 the government convened a New Ireland Forum attended by representatives of all constitutional nationalist parties in the Republic and Northern Ireland. The forum's report, issued on May 2, 1984, made three suggestions for settling the Northern Irish imbroglio: a unitary Irish state, a federal arrangement between North and South, and/or Anglo-Irish joint sovereignty over Northern Ireland. However, the report also indicated an openness to any other suggestion that would allow tolerance and equity toward the two traditions in Northern Ireland.

After a meeting with FitzGerald in November 1984, Margaret Thatcher bluntly dismissed the three options of the forum. However, the Anglo-Irish consultations continued, culminating in a formal agreement signed on November 15, 1985, at Hillsborough in Northern Ireland by both premiers. The agreement gives the Irish Republic an unprecedented role as a participant in an on-going conference dealing with policy formulation in Northern Ireland on issues affecting the nationalist majority, but also specifically commits both governments to the guarantee that Northern Ireland will not be coerced into a united Ireland without the consent of the majority of its population. The extraordinary conference arrangement will disestablish itself to the degree that devolved institutions in Northern Ireland receiving the consensus of both communities come into being. The latter would be the beginning of that community reconciliation that FitzGerald, sensitive to Protestant anxieties because of his maternal relations as well as to Catholic grievances, always regarded as preliminary to the achievement of a "New" and/or "United" Ireland.

FitzGerald retired from Parliament in January 1993 but kept active in politics as a senior statesman. He wrote a weekly column in the *Irish Times* and was an active lecturer abroad, making appearances at many American colleges and universities. He was named Commander of France's Légion Honneur in 1995.

Further Reading

FitzGerald can best be understood by reading his book *Toward a New Ireland* (London, 1972) in which he set forth the views which generally governed his public career. For background on Irish politics up to the commencement of his second ministry see Bruce Arnold, *What Kind of Country* (London, 1984), and for more general background consult John A. Murphy, *Ireland in the Twentieth Century* (Dublin, 1975), and Ronan Fanning, *Independent Ireland* (Dublin, 1983).

Additional Sources

FitzGerald, Garret, *All In A Life: An Autobiography,* (1991). ☐

George Fitzhugh

George Fitzhugh (1806-1881), American polemicist and pioneer sociologist, was a prominent defender of slavery. By his methods of debate he broke new ground for social analyses.

George Fitzhugh was born on Nov. 4, 1806, in Prince William County, Va., of a well-regarded but only moderately well-off family. His title to aristocratic ancestry, of importance to him, was not firmly established. His father, a surgeon, soon moved the family to Alexandria, a gracious and aristocratic region that nourished young Fitzhugh's belief in the Southern way of life. Fitzhugh studied law, married, and moved to Port Royal, Caroline County, where he built a law practice.

Although the fact was not appreciated at the time, Fitzhugh was a pioneer analyst of society in such pamphlets as *Slavery Justified* and *What Shall Be Done with the Free Negroes?* (both 1850). He expanded his views in *Sociology for the South; or, The Failure of Free Society* (1854), in which the word "sociology" was employed for the first time in America. In his most notorious work, *Cannibals All! or, Slaves without Masters* (1857), he argued that capitalism, cruel and irresponsible, was justly condemned by idealists and socialists, who, however, failed to appreciate society's need for a proper master-slave relationship, such as the South provided.

Fitzhugh solicited correspondence with abolitionists, whose views he wanted to expose as contradictory. In 1855 he visited a New York relative, Gerrit Smith, one of the nation's wealthiest men and an outstanding abolitionist. Fitzhugh also talked with other abolitionists and lectured in Boston and New Haven, Conn., on the inadequacies of the free society.

Between 1855 and 1867 Fitzhugh wrote more than a hundred articles for *De Bow's Review,* an outstanding Southern journal. His subject matter included literary criticism, history, genealogy, and general topics, though all were directly or indirectly supportive of his major conviction of the validity of the slavery system. He also wrote editorials for Richmond newspapers, and contributed essays to Northern publications, including *Lippincott's Magazine* and the proslavery New York *Day Book.* Abraham Lincoln, developing his viewpoint in Illinois, used Fitzhugh's arguments as representative of Southern public opinion.

Fitzhugh served as a clerk in the U.S. Attorney General's Office (1857-1858). During the Civil War he held a minor post in the Confederacy's Treasury Department. Afterward he worked for the Federal Freedmen's Bureau, which he served conscientiously, though from a firmly paternalistic point of view. He continued to write, adapting his ideas to changed conditions, but with less effect. He died on July 29, 1881, in Huntsville, Tex.

Further Reading

The only full-length study of Fitzhugh is Harvey Wish, *George Fitzhugh: Propagandist of the Old South* (1943), which also contains a useful bibliography of proslavery writings and related works. A briefer study by Wish is *George Fitzhugh: Conservative of the Old South* (1938). For background information see Russel B. Nye, *Fettered Freedom: Civil Liberties and the Slavery Controversy, 1830-1860* (1949; rev. ed. 1964). ☐

Thomas Fitzpatrick

Thomas Fitzpatrick (1799-1854), American trapper, guide, and government agent for Native Americans, was one of the most prominent mountain men during the mid-19th century.

Thomas Fitzpatrick, one of eight children, was born in County Cavan, Ireland. Little is known about his early life, but by the time he was 17 he had arrived in the United States. In 1823 he accompanied William Ashley's fur trading expedition up the Missouri River, and he participated in the Arikara War that summer.

For the next 17 years Fitzpatrick and other trappers crisscrossed the Rocky Mountains and the central and northern plains searching for beaver. He worked for companies headed by Ashley and later by Jedediah Smith and others. In 1830 one company sold its business to Fitzpatrick, James Bridger, and three other trappers, who formed the Rocky Mountain Fur Company. Four years later the company was dissolved, although Fitzpatrick, Bridger, and Milton Sublette soon combined to continue trading. In 1836 the powerful American Fur Company forced them out of business, and Fitzpatrick became an employee of that organization.

That same year Fitzpatrick began his work as a guide; he led the Marcus Whitman and Samuel Parker missionary party west to the annual trappers' rendezvous in the mountains. In 1837 Fitzpatrick escorted Sir William Drummond Steward and artist Alfred Jacob Miller to the summer rendezvous. Four years later he led the Bidwell-Bartleson train to Ft. Hall and took a missionary party into country dominated by Flathead tribes. In 1843 Fitzpatrick led John C. Frémont's second expedition to California; he guided Col. Stephen W. Kearny's expedition to the Rocky Mountains in 1845. The next year, meeting Kearny's army marching to California, he guided it to Socorro in New Mexico, where he and Kearny met Kit Carson carrying dispatches to Washington, D.C. Kearny gave the messages to Fitzpatrick and sent him east. Then Kearny used Carson as guide to California.

In Washington, Fitzpatrick learned that he had been appointed agent for the tribes of the Upper Platte and Arkansas regions, so he returned west. The Native Americans knew and respected him, calling him Broken Hand or Bad Hand because of an injury he had received years earlier. For the next 8 years he worked with tribes such as the Arapahoe, Cheyenne, Shoshone, Sioux, Commanche, and Kiowa of the central plains. While serving as agent, Fitzpatrick married Margaret Poisal, and when he died in Washington, D.C., on Feb. 5, 1854, he left two small children, Andrew and Virginia.

Further Reading

The standard biography of Fitzpatrick is Le Roy R. Hafen and W. J. Ghent, *Broken Hand: The Life Story of Thomas Fitzpatrick* (1931). This was considered complete when written but is being revised to include new material. J. Cecil Alter, *James Bridger: Trapper, Frontiersman, Scout, and Guide: A Historical Narrative* (1925; new ed. entitled *Jim Bridger,* 1962), is an accurate account of a fellow mountain man and partner of Fitzpatrick. Dale L. Morgan, *Jedediah Smith and the Opening of the West* (1953), and John E. Sunder, *Bill Sublette: Mountain Man* (1959), also provide useful material.

Additional Sources

Hafen, Le Roy Reuben, *Broken Hand, the life of Thomas Fitzpatrick, mountain man, guide and Indian agent,* Lincoln: University of Nebraska Press, 1981; 1973. □

Hippolyte Armand Louis Fizeau

The French physicist Hippolyte Armand Louis Fizeau (1819-1896) is best remembered as the first to measure the speed of light without any recourse to astronomical observations.

Hippolyte Fizeau was born in Paris on Sept. 23, 1819, the son of a wealthy physician and professor at the Faculty of Medicine in Paris. Young Fizeau received his secondary education at the Collège Stanislas and first wanted to pursue a career in medicine, but because of poor health he had to discontinue regular attendance of classes. After a lengthy journey had restored him to health, he turned again to scientific studies. This time, however, he did not work for a degree, and instead of medicine he concentrated on physics.

It was mainly the experimental verification of theories that interested Fizeau, and he soon had a laboratory equipped for himself at home. His first achievement was an improvement on the daguerreotype process, a method discovered by Louis Daguerre in 1839 to produce photographic images. Fizeau substituted bromine for the iodine used by Daguerre. Through his work Fizeau developed a friendship with Léon Foucault, an enthusiast of the art of the daguerreotype. Together they collaborated to perfect the art for the use of celestial photography. The first authentic photograph of the disk of the sun came through their combined efforts.

It was in the field of optics that Fizeau earned a lasting reputation. The inspiration came from François Arago, who looked for a decisive test between the corpuscular and wave theories of light. If the wave theory was true, the velocity of light had to be greater in moving media, such as water flowing in a tube. The project implied the working out of a terrestrial method of measuring the speed of light, and Arago suggested that this could be done by using a rotating mirror. Fresnel and Foucault began to work together on the project, but the actual measurements were carried out individually. Meanwhile, Fizeau hit upon the cogwheel method of measuring the speed of light and by September 1849 obtained the value of 315,000 kilometers per second. His measurements with the rotating mirror were communicated to the academy in May 1850, almost simultaneously with those of Foucault. During the intervening months Fizeau had also succeeded in measuring the change of the velocity of light in a rapidly flowing column of water, which greatly strengthened belief in the wave theory of light.

In addition to the work on optics, Fizeau also established the velocity of electricity in wires, corresponding to one-third of the speed of light. He did valuable work in the development of induction coils, in the application of the Doppler effect in astronomy, and in the utilization of optical wavelengths for precision measurements.

Fizeau never held professorships but was elected to the Academy of Sciences in 1860. He died after a long illness in Venteuil near Jouarre on Sept. 18, 1896.

Further Reading

Two works which are useful for the study of Fizeau are William Wilson, *A Hundred Years of Physics* (1950), and George Gamow, *Biography of Physics* (1961). □

Robert Flaherty

Robert Flaherty (1884-1951) was an American documentary filmmaker who, beginning with *Nanook of the North*, created a vision of human good will, curiosity, and ingenuity in adapting to nature and civilization.

Robert J. Flaherty was born in Iron Mountain, Michigan, on February 16, 1884, the son of a mining engineer who took the boy along on prospecting expeditions and to gold mines that he managed in northern Canada. Flaherty had little formal education, starting late and finishing early. He was expelled from the Michigan College of Mines after seven months, during which he spent much of his time camping in the woods. But at the college he met Frances Hubbard, a Bryn Mawr College graduate and the daughter of a distinguished academic geologist. He later married her, and she became his lifelong collaborator.

Flaherty spent the years between 1900 and 1920 as an explorer and prospector, making several hazardous expeditions to northern Canada. From 1913 to 1915, on two expeditions, Flaherty shot 70,000 feet of motion picture film of Eskimo life. The negative of this film was destroyed in a darkroom fire when Flaherty dropped a cigarette; the one surviving positive print has been lost.

In 1920 Flaherty secured the backing of a fur-trading company, Revillon Freres, to return to the north and make a film about Eskimo life. The result, *Nanook of the North,* was released in June 1922 to modest reviews and box office receipts but has for many decades been regarded as a classic. The film shows Nanook, an Eskimo hunter, and his family as they travel by kayak and dogsled through a frozen wasteland, surviving by hunting, fishing, and trapping.

Hollywood, which had been disinterested in *Nanook,* now sought Flaherty out, and in 1923 Jesse Lasky commissioned Flaherty to produce a film for Paramount Pictures. Lasky told Flaherty to "make me another *Nanook.* Go where you will, do what you like." Flaherty chose American Samoa. In February 1926 the resulting film, *Moana,* opened in New York City. It was in a review of *Moana* that John Grierson, later the father of the British documentary film movement, first applied the term "documentary" to a motion picture. *Moana* is a film of great visual beauty in which Flaherty explored the possibilities of a newly developed panchromatic film stock and with it recorded the textures of sea and skin in a Polynesian paradise. Some reviewers objected that Flaherty inappropriately included a long sequence of body-tattooing to give his film an element of conflict and suffering.

Flaherty's next major film, *Man of Aran* (1934), described the hard life of fishing and farming on the Aran Islands off the west coast of Ireland. Flaherty had by this time become a world figure, generally recognized as the originator of documentary film, and *Man of Aran* was voted the best film of the year at the Venice Film Festival of 1934. His work, however, was becoming controversial within the documentary community and awkward for the film industry. The documentary movement that grew up in 1930s in Great Britain under the leadership of John Grierson was devoted to the capacity of film to describe and influence the social conditions of modern, industrial democracies. For these filmmakers, who were also articulate theorists and critics of documentary at the time, Flaherty's work seemed to have petrified into a romantic vision that evaded the real issues of the 20th century. And for the film industry, Flaherty was difficult in other ways. He preferred to work with a small crew and to shoot enormous amounts of film over an extended period of residence and reflection, which made him an awkward problem for the system of studio production.

Flaherty's last finished work was *Louisiana Story* (1945), which describes, from the point of view of a Cajun boy, the introduction of oil drilling in the bayous of Louisiana. The film, sponsored by the Standard Oil Company of New Jersey, was photographed by Richard Leacock, later a major figure in American documentary, and edited by Helen van Dongen.

Flaherty's films endure, largely because of their great visual beauty, the genuine respect he showed for his subjects, and their vision of the largeness of the human spirit. The people in his films know how to cooperate, how to laugh, and how to survive both permanent hardship and the mysteries of change.

Further Reading

Among the best works on Flaherty are Paul Rotha, *Robert J. Flaherty: A Biography* (1983); Arthur Calder-Marshall, *The Innocent Eye: The Life of Robert J. Flaherty* (1963); Frances Flaherty, *The Odyssey of a Film-Maker* (1960); and Richard Griffith, *The World of Robert Flaherty* (1953). For a guide to other sources, see William T. Murphy, *Robert Flaherty: A Guide to References and Resources* (1978). For a discussion of Flaherty's place in documentary film, see Erik Barnouw, *Documentary: A History of the Non-Fiction Film* (1974) and Richard M. Barsam, *Nonfiction Film: A Critical History* (1973).

Additional Sources

Rotha, Paul, *Robert J. Flaherty, a biography,* Philadelphia: University of Pennsylvania Press, 1983. □

Titus Quinctius Flamininus

Titus Quinctius Flamininus (ca. 228-174 B.C.) was a Roman general and diplomat whose victory over Philip V of Macedon at Cynoscephalae freed Greece from Macedonian domination but led to an increasing Roman involvement in Greek affairs.

Flamininus was a member of the Roman patrician nobility. About the age of 20, in 208 B.C., he was elected a military tribune and in 205 was put in charge of the southern Italian city of Tarentum, with the rank and powers of a propraetor. It was in this city, largely Greek in language and culture, that he probably formed the philhellenism which was to be of importance in his life and work.

After holding various minor offices, in (or before) 199 Flamininus became quaestor and in the same year was chosen consul for 198, although he had neither been aedile and praetor nor attained the required age of 30. His election was probably dictated by the combination of philhellenism and diplomatic skills which he had already displayed, for Rome was involved in the Second Macedonian War and needed the support of Greece.

Flamininus proceeded to Greece and after some preliminary victories entered into extensive diplomatic negotiations. His command in Greece as proconsul was extended from 197 to 194. In June 197 at Cynoscephalae in Thessaly, Flamininus defeated Philip V and in the peace treaty forced Philip's withdrawal from Greece proper. After settling various side issues of the war, Flamininus proclaimed the freedom of Greece at the Isthmian Games in 196. Danger from Antiochus III of Syria caused Roman troops to be retained in Greece, and in 195 Flamininus defeated the adventurer Nabis of Sparta. In 194 Flamininus departed from Greece, was honored by the Greeks as their liberator, and celebrated a magnificent triumph in Rome.

The following years were involved in defending Roman interests in, and the autonomy of, Greece, both through military action and diplomacy. In 189 Flamininus was made censor, but after this he played an increasingly less important and active role in politics, perhaps because of disagreement over Roman policy toward Greece, which grew ever more imperialistic. In 183 he led a Roman mission to Prusias, King of Bithynia, to demand the extradition of Hannibal, who had fled to him for protection, but Hannibal committed suicide.

Further Reading

The ancient sources for the life of Flamininus are Polybios, Livy, and Plutarch. A recent study of his career is E. Badian, *Titus Quinctius Flamininus: Philhellenism and Realpolitik* (1970). See also J. B. Bury and others, eds., *Cambridge Ancient History,* vol. 8 (1930); F. W. Walbank, *Philip V of Macedon* (1940); and H. H. Scullard, *Roman Politics, 220-150 B.C.* (1951). □

John Flamsteed

The English astronomer John Flamsteed (1646-1719), the first astronomer royal, was the author of an important set of star catalogs.

John Flamsteed was born at Denby near Derby on Aug. 19, 1646, the only son of Stephen Flamsteed. John attended the Free School in Derby until he was forced to leave because of illness. After a brief period of rest and treatment, he entered Jesus College, Cambridge, in 1670 to study astronomy.

Flamsteed's interest in astronomy was stirred by the solar eclipse of 1662, and besides reading all he could find on the subject he attempted to make his own measuring instruments. He came to astronomy more or less self-taught, and yet he became known through an article in 1670 in the foremost scientific journal of the day, *Philosophical Transactions of the Royal Society*. At Cambridge he observed the planets and the moon, and by these observations and research into written sources he deduced great quantities of data. After earning his degree in 1674 and taking Holy Orders, Flamsteed was invited to London by Sir Jonas Moore, Governor of the Tower, who offered him a private observatory in Chelsea. But events took a different course: it had been pointed out to King Charles II by his advisers, of whom Flamsteed was one, that if more accurate astronomical data were available to seamen, fewer ships and men would be lost. Sir Christopher Wren built an observatory at Greenwich, and Flamsteed was appointed in 1675 "our astronomical observator," the first astronomer royal.

Flamsteed's position was difficult: he had no instruments and no assistants. A clergyman without a living, he took private pupils in mathematics and astronomy to supplement his salary so that he could purchase the instruments he needed. For 13 years he worked single-handedly, with a sextant of 7-foot radius and other instruments that he had provided for himself, and made at least 20,000 observations. He improved the existing tables of known star positions and the tables of the moon's motion, and he attempted to amend existing lunar and planetary theories. Although Flamsteed repeatedly asked for a transit instrument, he was never provided with one; his observations could be made solely with his sextant, which gave only relative positions of the stars.

Isaac Newton badly needed the data from Flamsteed's observations to complete his lunar theory, but Flamsteed regarded them as his own property. The two quarreled, and eventually Flamsteed was obliged to turn his data over to the Royal Society, of which Newton was president. Shortly thereafter, in 1712, the data appeared without Flamsteed's consent, under the title *Historia coelestis Britannica*. Flamsteed died on Dec. 31, 1719, before the printing of his own edition was complete (1725).

Flamsteed was probably the first to make good use of a timepiece in addition to the usual angle-measuring instruments. He found the annual variation in the position of the polestar to be 40". His greatest achievement was perhaps his *British Catalogue of 2884 Stars,* which included critiques of many earlier catalogues.

Further Reading

Francis Baily, *Account of the Reverend John Flamsteed* (1935), is the main source of information. This originally made up the third volume of Flamsteed's *Historia coelestis Britannica* (1725), completed posthumously. Flamsteed is covered in Eugene Fairfield McPike, *Hevelius, Flamsteed and Halley* (1957), and Antonie Pannekoek, *A History of Astronomy* (1961). □

Hallie Flanagan

Hallie Flanagan (1890-1969) was a director, playwright, and educator who headed the Federal Theater Project, America's first national, federally-funded theater organization, from 1935 to 1939.

Born in South Dakota on August 27, 1890, and raised in Iowa, Hallie Flanagan attended Grinnell College where she subsequently taught drama. She first gained notice as a playwright when she won a regional contest sponsored by the Des Moines Little Theatre Society with her play *The Curtain.* Her successful productions at Grinnell College eventually led her in 1923 to a position as production assistant in Professor George Pierce Baker's creative Workshop 47 at Harvard University, where she also completed a Master's degree. Returning to Grinnell, she directed for its experimental theater. Her productions there continued to win her recognition as an innovative director and led to her appointment as professor of drama and director of the experimental theater at Vassar College in

1925. A year later she received a prestigious honor—a grant from the Guggenheim Foundation (the first to be awarded to a woman).

On the Guggenheim fellowship Flanagan travelled to Europe and the U.S.S.R. to observe the exciting new developments on the continental stage of the early 1920s and wrote of her experiences in *Shifting Scenes of the Modern European Theatre* (1928). Besides being stimulated by the modernist experiments in staging that she saw in Europe, Flanagan was also strongly influenced by European dramatic forms and themes steeped in folklore, mythology, and history—the classic theater of Greece, popular puppet shows, robust folk plays, expansive verse dramas. In particular, the theaters of the Russian directors Vsevolod Meyerhold and Alexander Tairov impressed Flanagan with their vitality and strength and solidified her own goals to create theater that truly responded to and challenged its audience.

Returning to Vassar in 1926, Flanagan began to put these varied ideas and influences into practice and to build Vassar Theatre's reputation as one of the nation's leading experimental stages. The repertoire at the theater was richly diverse, ranging from contemporary plays dealing with current topics to experiments in form to classic texts daringly reinterpreted for the present. One of Flanagan's most celebrated productions was *Can You Hear Their Voices?* (1931). Co-authored by Flanagan and Margaret Ellen Clifford, the play was a carefully documented dramatization of a recent Arkansas drought that was controversial in both form and content as it revealed a rural world of hunger and privation neglected by governmental bureaucracy. Flanagan remained at Vassar until 1942, at which time she left for a similar teaching and directing position at Smith College in Massachusetts. She retired from academia in 1955.

Undoubtedly, Flanagan's greatest contribution to American theater was as director of the Federal Theater Project from 1935 to 1939. As a program of the Works Progress Administration, the Federal Theater Project was the first nation-wide, federally-sponsored theater in the United States. It was created to provide employment to professional theater artists in socially useful jobs during a time of severe economic depression. Committed to theater that serves as a dynamic artistic and social force for people, Flanagan sought to make the Federal Theater Project a regionally-rooted, popular, educational art theater that reached the entire nation. In many respects, Flanagan succeeded.

At its peak the Federal Theater employed over 10,000 people; operated theaters in 40 states; published a nationally distributed theater magazine; conducted a play and research bureau that served not only its own theaters but 20,000 schools, churches, and community theaters throughout the country; charged admission for less than 35 percent of its performances; and played to audiences totalling many millions.

Flanagan organized an ambitious program of classic and modern plays, dance drama, musical comedy, children's plays, religious plays, marionette shows, and series of plays by established playwrights and by young, new drama-

tists. Critical reaction to the artistic quality of the project's work grew increasingly positive beginning in 1936.

One of the Federal Theater's major achievements was the Living Newspaper, a compact, cinematic production style that dramatized immediate social and economic issues such as agriculture, flood control, and housing. *Triple A Plowed Under, Power,* and *One-Third of a Nation* represent pioneer productions in this art form.

Other important programs of the project included the development of a Black theater which presented significant productions of *Macbeth, Haiti,* and *The Swing Mikado;* classical revivals of miracle and morality plays and numerous Elizabethan productions; an international cycle of plays from Euripides to Ibsen; simultaneous production in 21 cities of Sinclair Lewis' anti-Fascist *It Can't Happen Here;* nation-wide productions of plays by Elmer Rice, Eugene O'Neill, and George Bernard Shaw; and regional productions such as *The Sun Rises in the West* in Los Angeles and *The Lost Colony* in North Carolina which were specifically geared to speak to local concerns and history.

Following Flanagan's vision of theater as an arena for vital exchange between artists and audiences, the Federal Theater was clearly a people's theater addressing national and regional issues in powerful, dramatic terms. Indeed, its consistently candid questioning of economic policies, especially in the Living Newspapers, ultimately brought the project criticism from witnesses before the House Committee on Un-American Activities and before the subcommittee of the House Committee on Appropriations. Although all major film, stage, and radio organizations as well as many community and sponsoring agencies spoke in favor of the Federal Theater, the Congress heatedly debated the continuation of the project. The House voted to dissolve the theater; the Senate voted to maintain it. On June 30, 1939, the Federal Theater was ended by congressional action.

Throughout her career Hallie Flanagan was a prolific contributor on the subject of theater to many leading American journals. She died in 1969.

Further Reading

Besides *Shifting Scenes of the Modern European Theatre* (1928), Flanagan's own books on the theatre include *Dynamo* (1943), an account of her work with the Vassar Experimental Theater, and *Arena* (1940), a personal chronicle of the joys and struggles of the Federal Theater Project. Jane DeHart Mathews' *The Federal Theatre 1935-1939: Plays, Relief, and Politics* (1967) is an excellent study of the project's brief history as a national institution.

Additional Sources

Bentley, Joanne, *Hallie Flanagan: a life in the American theatre,* New York: Knopf: Distributed by Random House, 1988. □

John Bernard Flannagan

American sculptor John Bernard Flannagan (1895-1942) executed small-scale studies of animals that were bold and forthright in concept.

John B. Flannagan was born in Fargo, N.Dak. The father's death, when John was five, left his widow so destitute that she was forced to place her two children in an orphanage. John showed an aptitude for carving even as a boy. However, at the age of 19 he went to Minneapolis to study painting at the Institute of Arts. Three years later he joined the Merchant Marine. In 1922, following release from the service, he headed for New York City to continue his formal art education. Instead, he accepted the offer of painter Arthur B. Davies to work on his farm and receive art instruction from him. Encouraged by Davies, Flannagan decided to become a professional sculptor.

Flannagan went to New York City in 1923 and had his first exhibition. His earliest sculptures were executed in wood, but by 1926 he had begun to use stone, and 2 years later he was using nothing else. He lived in Woodstock and Rockland County. In 1927 he had his first one-man show at the Weyhe Gallery in New York, which awarded him a weekly stipend for sculpture in 1929—an arrangement that lasted until 1937. In 1930 he went to Ireland for a year and went again in 1932 on a Guggenheim fellowship.

Flannagan never embraced the prevailing neoclassical styles required for official, commemorative sculpture commissions. He worked in simple fieldstone because, as he said, "its very rudeness seems to me more in harmony with simple direct statement." Furthermore, he sought to endow his sculpture with a natural quality so that "it hardly feels carved, but rather to have always been that way." In *Figure of Dignity* (1932-1933) a mountain goat seems to emerge from the stone and appears to be ascending, having halted briefly to look backward. This simple and appealing piece suggests a meaning that goes beyond what is actually represented. Flannagan's art was so unaffected and direct that one cannot detect any outside influences in it, though, like many modern artists, he was influenced by Paul Klee. Flannagan was fascinated by the first stirring of life and the mystery of birth, when numb beings begin to adjust to a strange, and often hostile, world.

In 1937 and again in 1939 Flannagan was in automobile accidents. The latter required four operations, leaving him with a speech impediment and loss of balance. He had great difficulty working, although he made a few pieces cast in bronze. In 1942, on the eve of a retrospective exhibition of his work in New York, Flannagan committed suicide.

Further Reading

Essential to Flannagan scholarship is *Letters of John B. Flannagan* (1942), which contains an introduction by W. R. Valentiner. *The Sculpture of John B. Flannagan,* edited by Dorothy Miller and with a brief essay by Flannagan's closest friend, Carl Zigrosser, is the catalog of the Museum of Modern Art's 1942 exhibition. □

Gustave Flaubert

The French novelist Gustave Flaubert (1821-1880) was one of the most important forces in creating the modern novel as a conscious art form and in launching, much against his will, the realistic school in France.

Gustave Flaubert was born on Dec. 12, 1821, in Rouen. Rouen's medieval charm, the bustle of its business (which revolted him), and the comfortable bourgeois ease that flowed from his father's position as chief surgeon at the municipal hospital marked the sensitive child. Fearing his father, he found outlets for his overflowing affections in his mother and younger sister. His sister died in childbirth when Flaubert was 24, but his mother lived (usually with him) until his fiftieth year. He was tied to her by bonds of love and exasperation, which he never fully understood.

As an adolescent of 15, Flaubert fell platonically in love with an older married woman, Elisa Schlésinger, and remembered her ever after as a pure and unsullied love. A few years later he toyed briefly with the idea of marriage but never again seriously considered it. The young man was sent to Paris to study law, where his desultory efforts were largely unsuccessful. He had easy access to what he called "the bitter poetry of prostitution," and this led to venereal disease, from which he never recovered. His attitudes toward women were colored by these experiences, and the subject of love became an obsessive focal issue in his works. He early linked sexuality to religion, which he felt was a similar longing for certainty always frustrated by doubt. Both areas brought him notions of doom, death, and annihilation.

In 1845 Flaubert had his first attack of temporal-lobe epilepsy. He was helplessly crippled by his seizures, which became hideous terror for him and recurred at intervals throughout his life. In 1846 he had to face the deaths of his father and his beloved sister. He abandoned his legal studies, since any emotional excitement brought on an attack of his malady. He must, he felt, become an observer of life and not a participant in it; thereafter he gave himself fully only to his writing. He did have love affairs, but they were never central to his life; most important were his stormy affairs with the poet Louise Colet in 1846-1847 and again in 1851-1854 and his affectionate relationship with Juliet Herbert, the governess of his niece, which began in the mid-1850s and lasted to the end of his life.

In literature alone Flaubert found no unbearable conflict, for he had been slowly evolving away from his childhood romantic ideal of the writer caught up in wild emotion as he wrote. Even before his illness he was moving toward a concept of writing as "emotion recollected in tranquility," an esthetic of detachment easily concording with his physical state. It allowed quiet consideration of style, which he felt as essential to prose as it had long been considered to poetry. After several false starts he turned to writing *The*

Temptation of Saint Anthony, the story of the desert hermit of Egypt, which was a convenient focus for his concerns with religion and sexuality and for giving scope to his enjoyment of erudite research. He completed the first version in 1849, but unfortunately it proved unpublishable. This was a bitter blow, and during the next 25 years he intermittently revised the work.

After this failure Flaubert left immediately for a longplanned 20-month journey through the eastern Mediterranean, accompanied by his lifelong friend Maxime Du Camp. He had studied Egypt and the Holy Land for *Saint Anthony,* and their familiarity upon first sight confirmed his view that art could conjure up reality. He returned via Greece and Italy, the classical lands whose esthetic, with its insistence on simplicity, control, and serenity, formed a further focus in his work.

Madame Bovary

In 1851 Flaubert embarked upon *Madame Bovary,* on which he worked until 1856. It was published in 1857 and created a storm; Flaubert in fact was unsuccessfully tried on the charge of contributing to public depravity. In addition to satirizing the provincial bourgeoisie, this work tells of Emma Bovary, who as a girl attends a convent school where she acquires romantic notions of a lover who will live for her alone. She marries a good but simple doctor, Charles Bovary, who adores her but does not understand her romantic fantasies, and she then has two love affairs. When, at the end, she finds her dream world in shreds about her, she prefers death to accepting a world not consonant with her fantasies and commits suicide.

At a more profound level the book is the profession of faith of an author who had outgrown romanticism and knew its premises were false. The man of whom Emma dreamed could not exist; the only man who would tell her what she wished sought only an easy seduction. She was foredoomed from the moment she adopted romantic fantasies in the convent.

Madame Bovary can also be read as Flaubert's view of modern woman, who has been perverted by society to shallow or false ideals and thus cannot follow her own nature to its true fulfillment in real love, which would combine in one transcendent experience the fullest physical experiences with the richest spiritual ones. These concepts, coupled with Emma's death, embody Flaubert's principal themes: sexuality, religion, and annihilation. The book is a masterpiece because of these underlying concerns and Flaubert's analysis, and because of his success in giving them form in his novel.

Madame Bovary displayed a new technique for writing ironic novels which writers were to imitate for many generations. Flaubert's doctrines may be readily summarized. He believed writers must write of the observed, actual facts; his documentation became legendary. To this extent he partook of the scientism of his period. He wished the writer to be, like the scientist, objective, impartial, impersonal, and impassive. But while the scientist generalizes his truths into a law of nature, Flaubert asked the writer to generalize his observations into an ideal, a type, whose dynamic power becomes apparent through the artistry of its presentation. Finally, Flaubert was a convinced Platonist who accepted the Socratic dictum that the True, the Beautiful, and the Good are one. If the writer presented the True through the Beautiful, his work would also be morally good.

The publication of *Madame Bovary* made Flaubert a celebrity. A floundering school of French writers who called themselves realists (markedly inferior to their later American counterparts) imitated Flaubert's use of careful documentation and a rather commonplace subject and proclaimed him their master. In Paris he came to know most of the important people of his day: members of the imperial court, the Goncourt brothers, George Sand, to whom he became devoted, and later the younger men such as Émile Zola, Alphonse Daudet, and Ivan Turgenev. He withdrew, however, each spring to Croisset, a village near Rouen.

Flaubert's next work, *Salammbô* (1862), recounted the revolt of the mercenaries against Carthage in the 3d century B.C. In it he gave free rein to his penchant for archeological documentation and his delight in the ancient world. Unfortunately the novel is tedious and repetitious, and few readers have been moved by this mythological account of the fusion of sexuality with religion and their joint culmination in death and annihilation. Flaubert's scrupulously accurate reconstruction of antiquity, however, did influence later historical novels.

A Sentimental Education

In 1864 Flaubert started work on *A Sentimental Education,* which was published in 1869. His great Parisian novel, this work is the equal of *Madame Bovary* although less popular. It presents a satiric panorama of Flaubert's generation. The weak, cowardly hero, Frédéric Moreau, experiences early adoration for an older married woman, Marie Arnoux. This situation is drawn from Flaubert's own life, and Marie Arnoux is one of his greatest creations. Frédéric tries many careers and penetrates most of the important milieus of France at the mid-century. Each new episode is a new hope for him; each ends in disillusionment. "A symphony in gray," Flaubert's *Sentimental Education* suggests that unfulfilled dreams are always superior to reality, which annihilates them. Henry James, James Joyce, and the "new novel" in France since World War II all owe something to it.

The end of the 1860s and the start of the 1870s were a period of disasters for Flaubert. He was stunned by the deaths of many of his closest friends. The minor poet and dramatist Louis Bouilhet had been his constant counselor and confidant for 20 years, and his death in 1869 was an irreparable loss. Flaubert also mourned the deaths of the critic Charles Augustin Sainte-Beuve (1869) and the writer Théophile Gautier (1872). In 1872 he lost his mother, the culminating blow.

Flaubert's despair shows in his next work, a revision (the third) of his earlier *Temptation of Saint Anthony* (1874). It summarizes his lifelong preoccupation with religion and proposes the doctrines of his friend Ernest Renan that all religions are equally true and equally false, equally beautiful and equally a source of anguished nostalgia since they all must perish. Religion and annihilation thus inform the book; sexuality, too, leads to the same end.

Three Tales

Flaubert had brought up the orphaned niece of his beloved sister. His niece met financial disaster in 1875, and he sacrificed his fortune in a vain attempt to stave off her ruin. Impoverished, unable to help her further yet despairing over both their plights, he turned with a humility he had never known before to the preparation of his *Three Tales* (1877). The first two of these are among the best 19th-century French short stories.

"A Simple Heart" recounts the selfless devotion of a servant, Félicité, through a lifetime of service. The second, a retelling of the medieval "Legend of Saint Julian the Hospitaller," shows the saint killing his father and mother and making atonement during the rest of his life. Neither tale is ironic; each conveys a symbolic message. The third tale, "Hérodias," is less successful but states the message directly through John the Baptist, who gladly accepts his fate: for the Messiah to come, he, the predecessor, must willingly die. Félicité and St. Julian had also learned to put the welfare of others above their own and to seek happiness only in the fullness of love. It was the wisdom Flaubert had learned in his own sacrifices for his niece.

Flaubert began his uncompleted last work, *Bouvard and Pécuchet,* before the financial crisis of his niece; he continued it after he had finished the *Three Tales.* He thought of it as inaugurating a new genre, the philosophical novel; it has been the subject of much dispute. Two rather simple copy clerks come into an inheritance, retire to the country, and study one subject after another, each time with renewed excitement and hopefulness and each time ending in disaster. *A Sentimental Education* had reviewed all of contemporary society and found it hollow; all of religion had been examined in *Saint Anthony* and had been found wanting; so in *Bouvard and Pécuchet,* all knowledge is scrutinized and found futile. Much in *Bouvard and Pécuchet* is great satire; much is hilarious; much becomes deeply sad; but some of it has been deemed tedious. And in the absence of its second half, it is not absolutely clear what Flaubert intended to suggest. It was, however, a seminal work for James Joyce.

On May 8, 1880, Flaubert was struck down by a brain hemorrhage after having spent his last years in anguish.

Further Reading

The most comprehensive general study of Flaubert's life and works is Benjamin F. Bart, *Flaubert* (1967). A fine study of his early life through the publication of *Madame Bovary* is Enid Starkie, *Flaubert: The Making of the Master* (1967). The best study of Flaubert's writings is Victor H. Brombert, *The Novels of Flaubert: A Study of Themes and Techniques* (1966). Useful essays on the whole of Flaubert's works are in Raymond D. Giraud, *Flaubert: A Collection of Critical Essays,* edited by Benjamin F. Bart (1964). A representative sampling of critical opinion on Flaubert's first novel is included in Benjamin F. Bart, ed., *"Madame Bovary" and the Critics* (1966).

Additional Sources

Troyat, Henri, *Flaubert,* New York, N.Y., U.S.A.: Viking, 1992. Lottman, Herbert R., *Flaubert: a biography,* Boston: Little, Brown, 1989. □

Gisi Fleischmann

Czechoslovakian leader Gisi Fleischmann (1894-1944) worked tirelessly to rescue her fellow Jews during the Nazi Holocaust, organizing networks which allowed many to escape to safety.

G isi Fleischmann was born in 1894 into an Orthodox Jewish family in Bratislava, Slovakia. As a young woman she became a Zionist. She developed rapidly as a Zionist leader and soon became president of the Bratislava branch of WIZO, the Women's International Zionist Organization. In this post she showed ability as an organizer and public speaker, as well as diplomatic skill. About the time of her introduction to Zionism, she married the merchant Josef Fleischmann. The Fleischmanns had two daughters.

Soon after Hitler came to power in Germany in 1933 Jewish refugees began to arrive in the Bratislava area. Many of these refugees hoped to go on to the British-held Palestine

Mandate (now Israel), but hundreds were stranded in Slovakia. As a member of the Central Jewish Relief Committee of Bratislava, Fleischmann played a key role in providing for the needs of such people and helping them on their way. Many of them later remembered her with gratitude and affection.

In 1939 she was sent to London and Paris to try to persuade foreign governments to take in the Jews menaced by Nazism and to obtain more funds from Jewish relief organizations to deal with the refugee situation in Central Europe. But no government was interested in the rescue of Jews; and the organizations had no more money to give.

Meanwhile, Hitler had annexed Austria (1938) and much of Czechoslovakia (1939), but Slovakia proclaimed itself an independent state. The German leader decided to recognize Slovakian "independence," which was a matter of form only. Throughout World War II the country remained a staunch friend and ally of Nazi Germany. As the situation in Europe worsened, Fleischmann and her husband were able to send their daughters to safety in the Palestine Mandate. Like so many others, the family was never reunited. Josef Fleischmann died of natural causes in 1942.

Following the Nazi pattern elsewhere in Europe, the Slovakian government set up a nationwide "Jewish Council." Fleischmann and her friends joined the council. Although they understood that it was really designed to be used against Jews, they tried to use it instead as an instrument to save Jewish lives. Later they formed a secret resistance group within the setting of the council. This was known simply as the Working Group, and Fleischmann was its acknowledged leader.

In 1942 the Germans and Slovaks began deporting Slovakia's 80,000 Jews to Poland, where they faced death in work and concentration camps. Under Fleischmann's leadership the Working Group fought to end the deportations. Though they had little money, by bribery and promises to Slovak and German officials they managed to halt the transports to Poland while there were still 20,000 Slovakian Jews left. These 20,000 remained precariously safe for nearly two years.

Fleischmann's colleague Rabbi Michael Weissmandel then originated a plan to save all of Europe's remaining Jews by the payment of a large ransom. This, the Europa Plan, probably was the first effort by Jews to negotiate with the Nazis for the lives of their people. She originally opposed Weissmandel's plan. Later, though, when she became convinced that it was the only way to save large numbers of Jews, she became the plan's chief Jewish negotiator and its staunchest advocate with Jewish organizations.

Although some Nazi officers indicated an interest in the Europa Plan, it was never tried. The Working Group's rescue efforts never stopped, even while negotiations for the plan went on. Fleischmann and her friends organized a network to smuggle Jews, many of them children, out of Poland to safety. These rescues were known as "hikes."

In late summer 1944, as the result of a revolt in Slovakia, Germany took over direct control of the country and resumed deporting Slovakian Jews to Poland. Among the victims was Fleischmann. She was sent to the death camp at Auschwitz and was murdered there on or about October 18, 1944.

The noted Jewish lawyer Gideon Hausner wrote of her that her name "deserves to be immortalized in the annals of our people" as "a radiant example of heroism and of boundless devotion."

Further Reading

Gisi Fleischmann is mentioned extensively in Marie Syrkin's *Blessed Is The Match* (1947, 1976) and in Nora Levin's *The Holocaust* (1968). She is the subject of a pamphlet, *Gisi Fleischmann: The Story of a Heroic Woman* (1970), by her friend and colleague Y. O. Neumann.

Additional Sources

Campion, Joan, *Gisi Fleischmann and the Jewish fight for survival*, Miami, Fla.: Dvorion Books, 1983.
Campion, Joan, *In the lion's mouth: Gisi Fleischmann & the Jewish fight for survival*, Lanham, MD: University Press of America, 1987. □

Sir Alexander Fleming

The Scottish bacteriologist Sir Alexander Fleming (1881-1955) is best known for his discovery of penicillin, which has been hailed as "the greatest contribution medical science ever made to humanity."

Alexander Fleming was born on Aug. 6, 1881, at Lochfield, Ayrshire, one of the eight children of Hugh Fleming, a farmer. Nature, which he considered his first and best teacher, developed his power of observation and taught him to apply his powers of reasoning to what he observed and to act in accordance with his observations. Like many Scots who were forced to leave their native land for better career opportunities, Fleming, at the age of 13, left for London, where he lived with his brothers. He attended lectures at the Polytechnic School and worked for 4 years in a shipping office. In 1901 an uncle left Fleming a legacy that enabled him to study medicine, and he entered St. Mary's Hospital Medical School in Paddington, later a part of the University of London.

In 1906 Fleming received his licentiate from the Royal College of Physicians. He chose a career in bacteriology and immediately joined the Inoculation Department, now the Wright-Fleming Institute, where he spent his entire career. He assisted Sir Almroth Wright, the originator of vaccinotherapy (therapeutic inoculation for bacterial infection) and the first doctor to use antityphoid vaccines on human beings. Fleming's research at this time primarily involved the use of Paul Ehrlich's Salvarsan in the treatment of syphilis. In 1908 Fleming passed his final medical examinations, winning the Gold Medal of the University of London. He was awarded the Cheadle Medal for his thesis "Acute Bac-

terial Infections," which foreshadowed the line of work he followed throughout his life.

During World War I Fleming served in the Royal Army Medical Corps, specializing in the treatment of wounds by antiseptics. He noticed that phagocytosis (the ingestion and destruction of infectious microbes by the cells) was more active in war wound infections than in ordinary wound infections, and he advised surgeons to remove all necrotic tissue as soon as possible. He observed that antiseptics not only did nothing to prevent gangrene but actually promoted its development by destroying leukocytes. Although Fleming's later discoveries have overshadowed this work, some authorities believe that he never conceived anything more perfect or ingenious than these brilliant experiments by which he demonstrated the danger to human tissues of incorrectly administered antiseptics.

In 1915, while on leave, Fleming married Sarah Marion McElroy, an Irish nurse who operated a private nursing home in London. The couple had one son, Robert.

Lysozyme Research

In 1921, the year he became assistant director of the Inoculation Department at St. Mary's, Fleming discovered that nasal mucus, human tears, and, especially, egg whites contain a chemical substance with marked bactericidal properties. Inasmuch as it lysed (dissolved) microbes and had the properties of an enzyme, Fleming called it lysozyme. Élie Metchnikoff believed that bodily secretions removed microbes by mechanical rather than chemical

means, an opinion held in 1921 by most bacteriologists. Fleming now challenged this view, but his work met a cold reception. Between 1922 and 1927 he published five more articles on lysozyme: he proved that antiseptics then in use, even in much weaker solutions than necessary to fight septicemia, would destroy leukocytes, and that "whereas egg white . . . has no destructive effects on the leukocytes, it has considerable inhibitory or lethal effect on some of the bacteria."

Discovery of Penicillin

The leitmotiv of Fleming's career was his search for a chemical substance which would destroy infectious bacteria without destroying tissues or weakening the body's defenses. In 1928 an accidental observation, which was a direct result of his apparently disorderly habit of not discarding culture plates promptly, led to the fulfillment of his goal. Fleming noted that on a culture plate of staphylococci a mold (*Penicillium notatum*) which had been introduced by accidental contamination had dissolved the colonies of staphylococci—an example of antibiosis. He found that the broth containing the bactericidal substance (penicillin) produced by the mold was unstable and rapidly lost its activity. Furthermore, it could not be used for injections until freed from foreign protein. Clearly, a method of extraction and concentration of the crude substance was required. Fleming had no chemist or biochemist on his staff, and he encouraged others to attempt the task.

In 1935 Howard W. Florey, an Australian experimental pathologist, and Ernst B. Chain, a Jewish chemist who had fled from Nazi Germany, came to Oxford University, where in 1939 they took up Fleming's work on penicillin. By employing the relatively new technique of lyophilization, Florey and Chain isolated the drug in completely purified form, which was a million times more active than Fleming's crude substance of 1928, and in 1940 they published the results of their successful treatment of infected white mice. A completely successful test involving a human being was not accomplished until 1942 because of the limited supply of the drug. By 1943 factories in England and the United States were producing penicillin on a large scale, and it became available for military use. By 1944 the miracle drug became available for civilian use.

Fleming never collected royalties on penicillin. In 1945 he received the Nobel Prize in physiology or medicine and toured the United States, where he was hailed as a hero. American chemical firms collected $100,000 and presented it to him in gratitude for his contribution to medical science. He refused to accept the money personally but used it for research at St. Mary's.

In 1946 Fleming became director of the Institute, a position he held until 1955. In 1951 he was elected rector of Edinburgh University. His wife had died in 1949, and in 1953 he married Amalia Coutsouris-Voureka, a Greek medical worker who had come to London in 1946 to work with him. Fleming died on March 11, 1955, and was buried in the crypt of St. Paul's Cathedral in London. According to André Maurois, "No man, except Einstein in another field, and before him Pasteur, has had a more profound influence on the contemporary history of the human race."

Further Reading

Discussions of Fleming's life and work can be found in John D. Ratcliff, *Yellow Magic: The Story of Penicillin* (1945); Laurence J. Ludovici, *Fleming, Discoverer of Penicillin* (1952); Lloyd G. Stevenson, *Nobel Prize Winners in Medicine and Physiology, 1901-1950* (1953); John Rowland, *The Penicillin Man: The Story of Alexander Fleming* (1957); and, André Maurois, *The Life of Sir Alexander Fleming, Discoverer of Penicillin* (1959; trans. 1959). □

Sir Sandford Fleming

Sir Sandford Fleming (1827-1915) was a Scottish-born Canadian railway engineer who became a widely recognized publicist for various scientific, imperial, and public causes.

Sandford Fleming was born on Jan. 7, 1827, at Kirkcaldy, Scotland, where he studied engineering and surveying. He went to Canada West in 1845 and qualified as a civil engineer; he undertook surveys, road projects, and several early town plans between Hamilton and Peterborough.

In 1849 Fleming was prominent among a group of young scientists and engineers in founding the Canadian Institute at Toronto. Fleming also designed the first Canadian postage stamp, the threepenny beaver, in 1851. His marriage in 1855 to Ann Jean Hall of Peterborough (they had six children) marked the end of the period of his adjustment to Canada and the beginning of his distinguished career as a railway builder.

Railway Engineer and Builder

Fleming's reputation developed in the railway building boom of the 1850s, particularly when he was chief engineer of the Ontario, Simcoe, and Huron (later Northern) Railway, from 1857 to 1862. He also contributed to planning a major harbor development at Toronto.

In 1863 Fleming was unanimously chosen by the four colonial governments to survey the first link—from Rivière du Loup to Halifax—of a railway connecting Britain's scattered Canadian colonies. He also contributed to building a railway system in the Maritime Provinces. Appointed chief engineer of the Intercolonial Railway, he saw the project to completion in 1873 as one of the most efficiently constructed lines on the continent. He also began a lifelong attachment to the society and politics of the Maritimes, cooperating with journalists and politicians in the cause of the larger confederation. He never stood for public office, but his wide personal and professional contacts gave him prominence and considerable influence in Canadian public life.

In addition to his Intercolonial duties, Fleming was appointed in 1871 engineer in chief of the proposed Canadian Pacific Railway. The original scheme for private construction faltered with the famous "Pacific Scandal" of 1872 and the depression after 1873. Fleming's superintendence of the government's own exploratory and construction program then became even more important; it also became more delicate in view of the change from John A. Macdonald's Conservative administration to Alexander Mackenzie's Liberal regime. Fleming surveyed the Yellowhead Pass route, advocating a generally more northerly route in the prairies and mountains than was initially adopted. Many of his preferences were adopted in building the later transcontinental lines, Fleming having demonstrated the practicability of the Kicking Horse, Eagle, and Rogers passes. Politics at times persuaded Fleming's superiors to overrule his sound technical advice, but his opinions were always listened to with respect.

Fleming survived these political difficulties until 1880, when the Conservatives had returned to power and when new prospects of private Pacific railway construction conditioned his fall before the factionalism of Conservative politicians and financial interests. He had also, through his connection with Sir Charles Tupper, become embroiled in the struggles over the successor to the ailing Macdonald. In 1880 Fleming was forced to withdraw as Pacific engineer-in-chief and, spurning lesser posts, retired to a vigorous life, working for public causes during his last 35 years.

Later Years

Fleming's professional and scientific horizons were further broadened through his association with British imperial transportation and communications leaders, his experience as adviser on railway construction to Newfoundland's government, and his service on an international development board for Montreal harbor. From the early 1880s he devoted much travel and abundant correspondence to stirring interest in Britain, Australia, and New Zealand in a Pacific cable link with Britain through Canada. As a director of the Canadian Pacific Railway Company and the Hudson's Bay Company, he sought to match entrepreneurial interest with imperial loyalty and Canadian advancement. His imperial federation proposals faltered, but the Pacific cable project was completed in 1902.

Scientific matters also occupied Fleming, notably the question of universal or cosmic time. In 1884 he was rewarded when an International Prime Meridian Conference met in Washington and adopted the modern system of international standard time measurement.

Fleming was a charter member and early president (in 1888) of the Royal Society of Canada. He was also prominent in seeking improved professional standards of engineering education and organization. From 1880 until his death he was chancellor of Queen's University, Kingston, and lay leader of the Presbyterian Church in Canada. In the 1890s he lectured and wrote on questions of political representation. He represented Canada at colonial conferences in London in 1888 and Ottawa in 1894 and at the Imperial Cable Conference in London in 1896. He was knighted in 1897.

Fleming wrote many scientific papers and reports on railway surveys and construction. His books include *Railway Inventions* (1847); *A Railway to the Pacific through British Territory* (1858); *The Intercolonial* (1876); *England and Canada: A Summer Tour between Old and New Westminster* (1884); and *Canada and British Imperial Cables* (1900). Fleming died at Halifax on July 22, 1915.

Further Reading

There is a laudatory memoir prepared with Fleming's assistance and relying heavily on his writings: Lawrence J. Burpee, *Sandford Fleming, Empire Builder* (1915). Fleming's activities in surveying for the Canadian Pacific Railway are recounted in Don W. Thomson, *Men and Meridians: The History of Surveying and Mapping in Canada* (3 vols., 1966-1969). See also John Lorne McDougall, *Canadian Pacific: A Brief History* (1968).

Additional Sources

Green, Lorne Edmond, *Chief engineer: life of a nation builder—Sandford Fleming,* Toronto: Dundurn Press, 1993. □

Alice Cunningham Fletcher

The American anthropologist Alice Cunningham Fletcher (1838-1923) was a pioneer in the scholarly development and professional organization of the discipline of anthropology in the United States.

Born in Cuba of American parents on March 15, 1838, Alice Fletcher was privately educated and traveled widely in her youth before settling near Boston. Her interest in North American archeology and ethnology began prior to 1880, when she became informally associated with the Peabody Museum of Harvard University. In 1886 she was listed among the official personnel of the museum. She specialized in the ethnology of the Omaha Indians and other Plains Indian tribes, contributed to the early study of comparative ethnomusicology, and sought to justify aspects of Federal Indian policy of the late 19th century on the basis of anthropological theory.

Fletcher's first field work was undertaken in 1881, when on a camping trip with a missionary party she visited some Native American settlements in Nebraska and South Dakota. She then took up concentrated research of the Omaha tribe, who remained her primary interest, although she studied other Plains groups and published important works on them. Her best-known work, *The Omaha Tribe* (1911), was written with the assistance of Francis La Flesche, an educated member of the tribe.

Scholarly and Professional Activities

Fletcher's concern for the welfare of Native Americans preceded her serious study of ethnology. She believed that private property, agrarian economic pursuits, and assimilation into white society would quickly alleviate their socioeconomic distress. These convictions were bolstered by the cultural evolutionary theories current in her day and led her to justify "scientifically" and to promote vigorously the Omaha Allotment Act of 1882 and the General Allotment Act of 1887, which divided reservations into small, subsistence family farmsteads. Ironically, the measures in which Alice Fletcher placed so much faith further complicated the problems Native Americans faced, obstructing them in efforts to make rational adaptations of their land resources to opportunities offered by an increasingly industrialized society based on corporate rather than individual enterprise.

At a time when many professions were reluctant to accept women, prominent anthropologists were convinced that women were equally necessary to their discipline to obtain complete and accurate accounts of different societies. This cordiality extended to organizational activities as well. Alice Fletcher, for example, had charge of the Native American exhibit of the New Orleans Industrial Exposition of 1884-1885. In 1893, on the occasion of the World's Columbian Exposition in Chicago, she and several other women participated on equal terms with their male colleagues in the special Anthropological Congress. Matilda Stevenson had founded the Women's Anthropological Society in 1885, and Miss Fletcher served as president in 1893. This group disbanded in 1899, when the members were admitted to the heretofore all-male Anthropological Society of Washington, and by 1903 Alice Fletcher was president of the Washington society. Even earlier, in 1896, she had been vice president of the prestigious American Association for the Advancement of Science. In 1905 she served as president of the American Folklore Society. She died in Washington, D.C., on April 6, 1923.

Further Reading

Alice Fletcher's correspondence and other papers are deposited in the archives of the Bureau of American Ethnology, Smithsonian Institution, Washington, D.C. An extensive account of Fletcher is in the chapter by Nancy Oestreich Lurie, "Women in Early American Anthropology," in June Helm, ed., *Pioneers of American Anthroplogy* (1966), which compares her career with those of Erminnie Platt Smith, Matilda Stevenson, Zelia Nuttall, Frances Densmore, and Elsie Clews Parsons. J. O. Brew, *One Hundred Years of Anthropology* (1968), is recommended for general background.

Additional Sources

Mark, Joan T., *A stranger in her native land: Alice Fletcher and the American Indians,* Lincoln: University of Nebraska Press, 1988. □

John Fletcher

The works of the English playwright John Fletcher (1579-1625) are noted for their stylistic grace, ingenious plotting, and exciting theatricality.

John Fletcher was baptized on Dec. 20, 1579. His father was an Anglican minister who became chaplain to Queen Elizabeth and eventually bishop of London. John was educated at Cambridge and acquired a reputation as a literary man. It is not known when or why he turned to the stage, but by 1608 he had launched a long and fruitful career as a dramatist.

Although some 15 plays have been attributed to him as sole author, Fletcher did most of his work in collaboration with others. From about 1608 to about 1613, he and Francis Beaumont formed one of the most famous and successful partnerships in literary history. During this period he probably also assisted Shakespeare in one or two plays. After Shakespeare's death in 1616, Fletcher became the leading playwright of the King's Men, the most prestigious theatrical company of the period. From this time until his death in 1625, he generally served as senior partner in collaboration with Philip Massinger, Nathan Field, Samuel Rowley, and others.

Fletcher's plays were written for the elite, sophisticated audiences which frequented the "private" theaters of Jacobean London. Although his plays are still admired for their dramatic craftsmanship, they are commonly thought of as refined entertainments lacking the larger significance and universality of appeal which distinguish the work of his greater contemporaries.

Fletcher employed a variety of dramatic forms, including revenge tragedy (*Valentinian,* ca. 1614), satiric comedy (*The Humorous Lieutenant,* 1619), and farce (*Rule a Wife*

and Have a Wife, 1624). But his most characteristic kind of play is the "tragicomedy," which he described as a play which "wants [that is, avoids] deaths . . . yet brings some close to it [death]" (from his first play, *The Faithfull Shepherdess,* ca. 1608). But his description gives an inadequate idea of this new dramatic genre. A better illustration of Fletcherian tragicomedy is to be found in a play of narrowly averted incest, *A King and No King* (ca. 1611, probably written with Beaumont). Only in the last scene of this play, when King Arbaces is on the verge of yielding to his incestuous passion for Panthea, is it revealed that his beloved is not really his sister after all. Fletcher's principal concern is with the effects attending the sudden surprise which turns near-tragedy into comedy.

Fletcher died in 1625, reportedly a victim of the plague. He was buried at St. Saviour's Church in London.

Further Reading

Gerald Eades Bentley, *The Jacobean and Caroline Stage,* vol. 3 (1956), contains most of the essential information about Fletcher's life. For further information, some of it based on early gossip of questionable value, see the first volume of Alexander Dyce's edition of *The Works of Beaumont and Fletcher* (1843). Clifford Leech, *The John Fletcher Plays* (1962), discusses Fletcher's artistic merits. □

Joseph Francis Fletcher

Joseph Francis Fletcher (1905-1991) was a philosopher widely recognized for his work in moral theory and applied ethics. Best known for the method of consequentialist moral reasoning espoused in his book *Situation Ethics*, Fletcher was also acknowledged as the father of modern biomedical ethics.

Joseph Francis Fletcher was born in East Orange, New Jersey, on April 10, 1905. His parents separated when he was nine, after which his mother returned to her family home in Fairmont, West Virginia, to raise her two children. His experiences working for the Consolidation Coal Company and the Monongahela Coal Mine led to his lifelong sympathy for the working conditions of coal miners and set the stage for a life of social activism.

He entered West Virginia University at Morgantown when he was 17. Already a member of the education staff of the United Mine Worker's Association, Fletcher was jailed during his first college year for defying an injunction against speaking in public for the miner's union. A self-proclaimed democratic socialist, his interests in philosophy and history led him to study the utilitarians Bentham and Mill and the pragmatists Peirce, Dewey, and James.

Two significant things happened during his second year in college: he met his future wife, fellow student and poet Forrest Hatfield (of the famous feuding Hatfields), and he became an active Christian in the Episcopal Church. Fletcher embraced Christianity because of his social ideals. Through his work in the church he hoped to further the cause of social justice, especially economic democracy for workers.

An outstanding student, Fletcher was denied a degree by the university because he refused to participate in compulsory military training. Such training was required of male students in land-grant universities by federal law. However, an honorary doctorate was conferred on him by West Virginia University in 1984.

In 1922, after only three years of college, Fletcher entered Berkeley Divinity School. Working the summer of his first year in a program called "Seminarians in Industry," he was assigned to the Plymouth Cordage Company factory where he discovered and exposed a blacklist of union sympathizers that included Bart Vanzetti, the Italian anarchist. During his second summer he volunteered for the Sacco-Vanzetti Defense Committee in Boston. His last year at seminary was spent collaborating on a book with Spencer Miller, education adviser of the American Federation of Labor, titled *The Church and Industry* (1931).

After completing divinity school in 1928, Fletcher pursued graduate studies in economic history at Yale. There he won the John Henry Watson fellowship and in 1930 went to London to study under R. H. Tawney at the London School of Economics. During this period he formulated the tenets of his theology of social redemption. He was heavily influenced by theologians Walter Rauschenbusch, Washington Gladden, and William Temple.

On his return to America during the era of the Great Depression, Fletcher continued his union activism and teaching. In 1936 he became dean of St. Paul's Cathedral in Cincinnati, where he developed a school of social training for seminarians. He taught courses in labor history and New Testament at the University of Cincinnati and social ethics at Hebrew Union College. He also raised support for and taught volunteer courses in a labor education night school supported by local unions.

In 1944 Fletcher accepted the Robert Treat Paine Chair in Social Ethics at the Episcopal Theological School of Harvard University, where he taught Christian social ethics. For several years he also taught business ethics in the Musser Seminar at the Harvard School of Business Administration. He continued his social activist teachings for union organizations and was twice attacked and beaten unconscious by anti-union thugs while lecturing in the deep South. Along with two fellow Harvard professors, Fletcher was redbaited and subpoenaed by Senator Joseph McCarthy, who charged the professors with being Communists or at least Communist sympathizers.

The Lowell Lectures given by Fletcher at Harvard in 1949 were precursors of his treatise on ethical issues in medicine, *Morals and Medicine* (1954). This book gave a biological direction to his social ethic and was the first non-Catholic treatment of medical ethics. It is considered the pioneering work of a new discipline—biomedical ethics—and subsequently established Fletcher as the "father of modern biomedical ethics."

His basic bioethical premise is that humans should control and improve their natural condition by reasoned choice rather than by leaving things to chance. Natural biological processes (for example, methods of fertilization) are not inherently better than artificial (man-made) processes. The development and use of technology is a supremely human enterprise. However, the implications of new technologies should be considered prior to and during their development, not simply afterwards. An important influence on his thinking during this period was Garrett Hardin, the social biologist. Fletcher first coined the term "clinical ethics" in 1976 to reflect the specific nature of bioethics applied in clinical or patient-centered situations.

In 1966 Fletcher published the controversial best-seller *Situation Ethics*, which he described as his "fat pamphlet," setting forth his theory of moral action. Although written within the context of Christianity, the theory was and is independent of Christian presuppositions. Fletcher espoused a consequentialist ethic and methodology based on loving concern, or *agape*. He proclaimed that human beings are more important than moral rules and that appraisals of consequences rather than rules should guide moral decision making. Following rules without regard for the consequences is both immoral and an abdication of personal responsibility. His primary concern was with particular cases rather than general principles. "Situation Ethics" has been formally embraced as a category of consequentialist ethics.

In 1967 Fletcher gave up his faith in Christianity and subsequently eschewed any religious or secular dogma. Upon retiring from the Episcopal Theological School, he moved to Charlottesville, Virginia, where he was the first (and only) person to hold the title of professor of medical ethics in the Program in Human Biology and Society at the University of Virginia. He served as visiting scholar there until his death from cardiovascular disease on October 28, 1991.

A prominent speaker, Joseph Fletcher lectured at over 450 universities and medical schools throughout the United States, Europe, and Asia. He was a visiting scholar at St. Andrew's University in Scotland and Cambridge University in England, where he was a fellow of Clare College. He was also a visiting professor at the International Christian University in Tokyo. He was awarded honorary doctorates from West Virginia University, Berkeley Divinity School, and the Episcopal Theological School. In 1984 the Hastings Center awarded him the Beecher Award. He was an elected honorary member of Alpha Omega Alpha, the national medical honor society. In the early 1980s the Mohawk Nation made him a full-fledged brave in the Clan of the Turtle. He was also named "Humanist Laureate" by the Academy of Humanism in 1983.

Further Reading

A prolific author, Joseph Fletcher wrote over 250 articles, monographs, reviews, and books. Recommended readings include: *Situation Ethics: The New Morality* (1966), *Moral Responsibility: Situation Ethics at Work* (1967), *Morals and Medicine* (1954), *Humanhood: Essays in Biomedical Ethics* (1979), and *The Ethics of Genetic Control: Ending Reproductive Roulette* (1974). Also recommended is *The Situation Ethics Debate* (1968) edited by Harvey Cox. □

Abraham Flexner

Abraham Flexner (1866-1959) devoted his life to the improvement of teaching and research in America, initiating the modern American medical school and serving as first director of the Institute for Advanced Study at Princeton.

Abraham Flexner was born on Nov. 13, 1866, in Louisville, Ky. He attended the Louisville High School and returned to it as a teacher after his graduation from Johns Hopkins University in 1886. Four years later he opened a college preparatory school in Louisville and put to a successful test his belief that inspired teaching plus the enthusiasm and competitive spirit of youth made the usual administrative rules, records, reports, and classroom examinations unnecessary.

Flexner married in 1898. In 1905 he began graduate studies in education at Harvard University. His concern turned to the institutions and practices of graduate and professional training. He traveled in England, Germany, France, Canada, and the United States. In 1910 his report to the Rockefeller Foundation on medical education set into motion comprehensive reforms which led to the subsequent rise of American medical education to world leadership. Flexner followed this with an investigation of prostitution in Europe and with further research and writing on problems of teaching.

As a consultant with the Carnegie Foundation for the Advancement of Teaching and, from 1913 to 1917, as assistant secretary of the General Education Board of the Rockefeller Foundation, Flexner prepared a statement published as *A Modern School* (1916). In these pages Flexner emerges as one of America's chief spokespersons for what became known as educational progressivism. He believed in universal education for literacy and a rigorous and demanding academic curriculum for the gifted and interested. During most of the 1920s Flexner continued working for the improvement of medical education as the director of studies and medical education of the General Education Board.

Flexner next began examining higher education, visiting universities in England and Germany. In 1930 his *Universities: American, English, German* appeared. He saw universities not as popular institutions reflecting the desires and whims of society but as intellectual leaders. "Universities must at times give society, not what society wants, but what it needs," he wrote. In 1930 he was asked to establish the Institute for Advanced Study in Princeton, N.J., and to serve as its first director; now he could put his ideas concerning the place of research in society and the world of learning into practice. His answer to a new fellow who asked what his duties were was typical: "You have no

duties, only opportunities.'' He served as the institute's director until 1939 and as director emeritus thereafter. He died on Sept. 21, 1959, in Falls Church, Va.

Further Reading

Flexner's views on universities are discussed in Alexander D. C. Peterson, *A Hundred Years of Education* (1952). Further background on education is in Stuart G. Noble, *A History of American Education* (1938; 2d ed. 1954). □

Matthew Flinders

Matthew Flinders (1774-1814) was an English naval captain and hydrographer who prepared detailed charts of much of the Australian coastline.

Matthew Flinders was born on March 16, 1774, at Donnington, Lincolnshire, and educated in a local grammar school. Instead of becoming a surgeon like his father, he entered the Royal Navy at 15 and accompanied William Bligh on his second voyage to Tahiti in 1791. In 1794 Flinders saw action against the French in the English Channel and the following year went to New South Wales.

Accompanied in 1796 by George Bass, a naval surgeon, Flinders first explored Botany Bay and the coastline south of Sydney in an 8-foot open boat, the *Tom Thumb*. Between October 1798 and January 1799 Flinders and Bass, who had recently discovered the Bass Strait separating Tasmania from the mainland, sailed around Tasmania in the sloop *Norfolk*. In the summer of 1799 Flinders surveyed the coastline north of Sydney as far as Moreton Bay (Queensland).

After returning to England in 1800, Flinders published an account of his work, and the Admiralty decided that he should chart the whole Australian coastline. With the rank of commander, he was put in charge of H. M. S. *Investigator* and in July 1801, 3 months after his marriage, Flinders set out on a voyage which places him among the world's foremost navigators. From December 1801 Flinders made charts and collected botanical specimens along the unknown coast of the Great Australian Bight, and in April 1802 he met the French explorer Nicolas Baudin in Encounter Bay. After a refit, Flinders's expedition proceeded up the Queensland coast, passed through Torres Strait, and reached the Gulf of Carpentaria in November 1802. The *Investigator* became unseaworthy and, unable to complete the survey, Flinders sailed down the west coast and rounded the continent before returning to Sydney in June 1803.

In order to enlist support for a further expedition, Flinders embarked for England late in 1803. Forced to call at Mauritius, he was held captive for 6 years by the French governor because England and France were again at war. While Flinders worked on his journals, Baudin foreshadowed his discoveries by publishing maps of the ''Terre Napoleon.'' Flinders returned to England in 1810 in poor health and published *Voyage to Terra Australis* the day before his death on July 19, 1814.

Flinders ranks second only to James Cook among the explorers of the period. His life was dedicated to discovery, and his careful scientific observations have stood the test of time. Seafarers were indebted to him for observations on the action of tides and on compass error produced by iron in ships. Flinders wanted to name the new continent Australia, but the Admiralty preferred New Holland.

Further Reading

Several books have modified the picture of Flinders presented in Ernest Scott's pioneer biography, *The Life of Captain Matthew Flinders* (1914). A straightforward account of Flinders's career which deals at length with the 1801-1803 survey is K. A. Austin, *The Voyage of the Investigator* (1964). James D. Mack, *Matthew Flinders, 1774-1814* (1966), praises Flinders's scientific work. Sidney John Baker, *My Own Destroyer* (1962), explores a similar theme, attributing deficiencies in Flinders's character to the relationship between father and son. In Ernestine Hill, *My Love Must Wait* (1942), Flinders's career forms the basis of a charming novel.

Additional Sources

Ingleton, Geoffrey C. (Geoffrey Chapman), *Matthew Flinders: navigator and chartmaker*, Guildford, Surrey, England: Genesis Publications in association with Hedley Australia, 1986. □

Juan José Flores

Juan José Flores (1801-1864) was a South American general and the first president of Ecuador. He dominated Ecuadorian political life for 2 decades.

Juan José Flores was born in Puerto Cabello, Venezuela, on June 19, 1801, the illegitimate son of a rich Spanish merchant and Rita Flores. His father returned to Europe, and young Flores grew up in great poverty. He worked for a while in a Spanish military hospital and at the age of 14 enlisted in the army. When, as a sergeant, he was taken prisoner on Oct. 31, 1817, he joined the patriot army of Simón Bolívar. For his role in the victory of Carabobo (1821) Bolívar promoted Flores to lieutenant colonel. By 1824 he was a colonel and governor of the province of Pasto.

Soon after, Flores was appointed intendant of Quito. He retained this position until 1830, extending his authority over all of present-day Ecuador. As second in command under Gen. Antonio José de Sucre, he took part in the battle of Tarqui (Feb. 27, 1829), in which an invading Peruvian army was defeated. Flores was then promoted to general of division.

President of Ecuador

Left without rivals in Ecuador, where his position was strengthened by his marriage to a member of the aristocracy, Doña Mercedes Jijón, Flores convoked an assembly in Quito, which on May 13, 1830, declared the independence of Ecuador. A few months later, at the age of 29, he was elected its president for a 4-year term.

The first presidency of Flores was marked by his efforts to organize the republic. He was able to maintain himself with the backing of his Venezuelan troops and with the political support of the majority of the ruling class. However, a Liberal revolt broke out in Quito while Flores was on the coast facing an invasion by revolutionaries. The leader of the latter, Vicente Rocafuerte, fell into his hands. Showing his great political acumen and considering the important social connections of his prisoner in Guayaquil, Flores offered him the presidency. Rocafuerte accepted, and with the coastal region solidly under his control, Flores defeated the revolutionaries of Quito at Miñarica on Jan. 18, 1835.

During Rocafuerte's presidency Flores remained commander in chief of the army. He succeeded him for a second term in 1839, Rocafuerte moving to the politically very important post of governor of Guayaquil. Rocafuerte expected to continue alternating with Flores in the presidency, but the general decided to get himself reelected in 1843. A widespread revolt inspired by Rocafuerte forced a confrontation, and unable to reestablish his authority over the country, Flores signed an agreement with his opponents which guaranteed the safety of his family, his property, and his rank while in exile.

Exile and Return

Flores went to Europe, but when the new government rescinded the agreement, the general organized an expedition with the financial backing of the queen mother of Spain. The plan failed when the English government embargoed his ships. Flores then returned to his native country and spent several years in various Spanish American countries. An attempted invasion of Ecuador in 1852 was defeated by his erstwhile protégé Gen. José María Urbina.

In 1860 a Peruvian invasion of Ecuador led to civil war. The faction headed by Gabriel García Moreno—an admirer of Rocafuerte who began his political career as one of the most violent enemies of Flores—recalled the general to command its troops. Flores returned, took over the command, and ended the war on Sept. 24, 1860.

Flores then presided over the Constituent Convention of 1861, which legalized the García Moreno regime. The unwise foreign policy of the new president led to war with Colombia (New Granada), which ended with the defeat of Flores at Guaspud on Dec. 6, 1863. The following year he was back in Guayaquil, facing an invasion by former president Urbina. Seriously ill, Flores sallied forth against the revolutionaries and defeated them. He died on board the steamer that was carrying him back to Guayaquil on Oct. 1, 1864.

Further Reading

Discussions of Flores are in Lilo Linke, *Ecuador: Country of Contrasts* (3d ed. 1960), and George I. Blanksten, *Ecuador: Constitutions and Caudillos* (1964). See also Hubert Clinton Herring, *A History of Latin America from the Beginnings to the Present* (1955; 3d ed. 1968), and James Fred Rippy, *Latin America: A Modern History* (1958; rev. ed. 1968). □

Howard Walter Florey

The Australian experimental pathologist and teacher Howard Walter Florey, Baron Florey of Adelaide (1898-1968), helped isolate penicillin and develop it as a successful nontoxic antibacterial agent for use in medical treatment.

Howard W. Florey, the son of Joseph Florey, was born on Sept. 24, 1898, at Adelaide. After attending St. Peter's Collegiate School and Adelaide University (1916-1921), where he received a degree in medicine, he entered Magdalen College, Oxford, as a Rhodes scholar in 1921 and then Cambridge University in 1924. During 1925-1926 he was Rockefeller traveling fellow in the United States. In 1926 he was appointed Freedom research fellow at Cambridge. In the same year he married Mary Ethel Reed; they had two children.

Florey became successively Huddersfield lecturer in special pathology at Cambridge University in 1927, Joseph Hunter professor of pathology at the University of Sheffield in 1931, and professor and head of the Sir William Dunn

School of Pathology at Oxford University in 1935, a position which he held until 1962, when he resigned to become provost of Queen's College, Oxford. In 1935 he invited the chemist Ernst B. Chain to Oxford to direct the work of the biochemistry department. After numerous vicissitudes Florey and Chain succeeded (1940-1941) in isolating the drug penicillin in completely purified form, which turned out to be a million times more active than the crude substance first observed in 1928 by Alexander Fleming. Penicillin is usually measured in Oxford units, also called Florey units. In 1941 the Rockefeller Foundation brought Florey to the United States to persuade American authorities of the need to make major facilities available for the rapid development of penicillin production. His journey was eminently successful, and by the last stages of World War II large amounts of penicillin were in clinical use.

The research interests of Florey were wide-ranging, and he remained an active laboratory investigator all his life. Throughout his career he was preoccupied with the structure and function of the smaller blood vessels and their relation to the movement of lymph and cells in inflammation. His work on lysozyme led to his general study of antibiotics in collaboration with Chain. In temperament Florey was reserved but sure of himself. He was above all a skilled experimentalist with little liking for speculation.

Florey was the recipient of numerous prizes, honors, and honorary degrees, including the Nobel Prize in physiology or medicine in 1945; he was created a baron in 1965. In 1944 he became Nuffield visiting professor to Australia and New Zealand. He was largely responsible for the detailed planning and policy of the John Curtin School of Medical Research of the Australian National University. In 1965 he became chancellor of this university. He died on Feb. 21, 1968.

Further Reading

Lloyd G. Stevenson, *Nobel Prize Winners in Medicine and Physiology, 1901-1950* (1953), includes a sketch on Florey. Discussions of his life and work can also be found in John D. Ratcliff, *Yellow Magic: The Story of Penicillin* (1945); Laurence J. Ludovici, *Fleming, Discoverer of Penicillin* (1952); and André Maurois, *The Life of Sir Alexander Fleming, Discoverer of Penicillin* (1959; trans. 1959). □

Paul Flory

Paul Flory (1910-1985), founder of the science of polymers, was a researcher in macronuclear chemistry and was awarded the Nobel Prize in 1974.

Paul Flory is widely recognized as the founder of the science of polymers. The Nobel Prize in chemistry he received in 1974 was awarded not for any single specific discovery, but, more generally, "for his fundamental achievements, both theoretical and experimental, in the physical chemistry of macromolecules." That statement accurately reflects the wide-ranging character of Flory's career. He worked in both industrial and academic institutions and was interested equally in the theory of macromolecules and in the practical applications of that theory.

Paul John Flory was born in Sterling, Illinois, on June 19, 1910. His parents were Ezra Flory, a clergyman and educator, and Martha (Brumbaugh) Flory, a former school teacher. Ezra and Martha's ancestors were German, but they had resided in the United States for six generations. Both the Flory and the Brumbaugh families had always been farmers, and Paul's parents were the first in their line ever to have attended college.

After graduation from Elgin High School, Flory enrolled at his mother's alma mater, Manchester College, in North Manchester, Indiana. The college was small, with an enrollment of only 600. He earned his bachelor's degree in only three years, at least partly because the college "hadn't much more than three years to offer at the time," as he was quoted as having said by Richard J. Seltzer in *Chemical and Engineering News*. An important influence on Flory at Manchester was chemistry professor Carl W. Holl. Holl apparently convinced Flory to pursue a graduate program in chemistry. In June of 1931, therefore, Flory entered Ohio State University and, in spite of an inadequate background in mathematics and chemistry, earned his master's degree in organic chemistry in less than three months. He then began work immediately on a doctorate, but switched to the field of physical chemistry. He completed his research on the photochemistry of nitric oxide and was granted his Ph.D. in 1934.

Flory's doctoral advisor, Herrick L. Johnston, tried to convince him to stay on at Ohio State after graduation. Instead, however, he accepted a job at the chemical giant, Du Pont, as a research chemist. There he was assigned to a research team headed by Wallace H. Carothers, who was later to invent the process for making nylon and neoprene. Flory's opportunity to study polymers was ironic in that, prior to this job, he knew next to nothing about the subject. Having almost *any* job during the depths of the Great Depression was fortunate, and Flory was the envy of many classmates at Ohio State for having received the Du Pont offer.

Flory's work on the Carothers team placed him at the leading edge of chemical research. Chemists had only recently begun to unravel the structure of macromolecules, very large molecules with hundreds or thousands of atoms, and then to understand their relationship to polymers, molecules that have chemically combined to become a single, larger molecule. The study of polymers was even more difficult than that of macromolecules because, while the latter are very large in size, they have definite chemical compositions that are always the same for any one substance. Polymers, on the other hand, have variable size and composition. For example, polyethylene, a common polymer, can consist of anywhere from a few hundred to many thousands of the same basic unit (monomer), arranged always in a straight chain or with cross links between chains.

With his background in both organic and physical chemistry, Flory was the logical person to be assigned the responsibility of learning more about the physical structure of polymer molecules. That task was made more difficult by the variability of size and shape from one polymer molecule to another—even among those of the same substance. Flory's solution to this problem was to make use of statistical mechanics to average out the properties of different molecules. That technique had already been applied to polymers by the Swiss chemical physicist Werner Kuhn and two Austrian scientists, Herman Mark and Eugene Guth. But Flory really developed the method to its highest point in his research at Du Pont.

During his four years at Du Pont, Flory made a number of advances in the understanding of polymer structure and reactions. He made the rather surprising discovery, for example, that the rate at which polymers react chemically is not affected by the size of the molecules of which they are made. In 1937, he discovered that a growing polymeric chain is able to terminate its own growth and start a new chain by reacting with other molecules that are present in the reaction, such as those of the solvent. While working at Du Pont, Flory met and, on March 7, 1936, married Emily Catherine Tabor. The Florys had two daughters, Susan and Melinda, and a son, Paul John, Jr. Flory's work at Du Pont came to an unexpected halt when, during one of his periodic bouts of depression, Carothers committed suicide in 1937. Although deeply affected by the tragedy, Flory stayed on for another year before resigning to accept a job as research associate with the Basic Science Research Laboratory at the University of Cincinnati. His most important achievement there was the development of a theory that explains the process of gelation, which involves cross-linking in polymers to form a gel-like substance.

Flory's stay at the University of Cincinnati was relatively brief. Shortly after World War II began, he accepted an offer from the Esso (now Exxon) Laboratories of the Standard Oil Development Company to do research on rubber. It was apparent to many American chemists and government officials that the spread of war to the Pacific would imperil, if not totally cut off, the United States' supply of natural rubber. A massive crash program was initiated, therefore, to develop synthetic substitutes for natural rubber. Flory's approach was to learn enough information about the nature of rubber molecules to be able to predict in advance which synthetic products were likely to be good candidates as synthetic substitutes ("elastomers"). One result of this research was the discovery of a method by which the structure of polymers can be studied. Flory found that when polymers are immersed in a solvent, they tend to expand in such a way that, at some point, their molecular structure is relatively easy to observe.

In 1943, Flory was offered an opportunity to become the leader of a small team doing basic research on rubber at the Goodyear Tire and Rubber Company in Akron, Ohio. He accepted that offer and remained at Goodyear until 1948. One of his discoveries there was that irregularities in the molecular structure of rubber can significantly affect the tensile strength of the material.

In 1948, Flory was invited by Peter Debye, the chair of Cornell University's department of chemistry, to give the prestigious George Fisher Baker Lectures in Chemistry. Cornell and Flory were obviously well pleased with each other as a result of this experience, and when Debye offered him a regular appointment in the chemistry department beginning in the fall of 1948, Flory accepted—according to Maurice Morton in *Rubber Chemistry and Technology* —"without hesitation." The Baker Lectures he presented were compiled and published by Cornell University Press in 1953 as *Principles of Polymer Chemistry*. Flory continued his studies of polymers at Cornell and made two useful discoveries. One was that for each polymer solution there is some temperature at which the molecular structure of the polymer is most easily studied. Flory called that temperature the theta point, although it is now more widely known as the Flory temperature. Flory also refined a method developed earlier by the German chemist Hermann Staudinger to discover the configuration of polymer molecules using viscosity. Finally, in 1956, he published one of the first papers ever written on the subject of liquid crystals, a material ubiquitous in today's world, but one that was not to be developed in practice until more than a decade after Flory's paper was published.

In 1957, Flory became executive director of research at the Mellon Institute of Industrial Research in Pittsburgh. His charge at Mellon was to create and develop a program of basic research, a focus that had been absent from that institution, where applied research and development had always been of primary importance. The job was a demanding one involving the supervision of more than a hundred fellowships. Eventually, Flory realized that he disliked administrative work and was making little progress in refocusing Mellon on basic research. Thus, when offered the opportunity in 1961, he resigned from Mellon to accept a post at the department of chemistry at Stanford University. Five years later, he was appointed Stanford's first J. G. Jackson-C. J. Wood Professor of Chemistry. When he retired from Stanford in 1975, he was named J. G. Jackson-C. J. Wood Professor Emeritus. In 1974, a year before his official retirement, Flory won three of the highest awards given for chemistry—the National Medal of Science, the American Chemical Society's Priestley Medal, and the Nobel Prize in chemistry. These awards capped a career in which, as Seltzer pointed out, Flory had "won almost every major award in science and chemistry."

Flory's influence on the chemical profession extended far beyond his own research work. He was widely respected as an outstanding teacher who thoroughly enjoyed working with his graduate students. A number of his students later went on to take important positions in academic institutions and industrial organizations around the nation. His influence was also felt as a result of his two books, *Principles of Polymer Chemistry*, published in 1953, and *Statistical Mechanics of Chain Molecules*, published in 1969. Leo Mandelkern, a professor of chemistry at Florida State University, is quoted by Seltzer as referring to the former work as "the bible" in its field, while the latter has been translated into both Russian and Japanese.

Flory was also active in the political arena, especially after his retirement in 1975. He and his wife decided to use the prestige of the Nobel Prize to work in support of human rights, especially in the former Soviet Union and throughout Eastern Europe. He served on the Committee on Human Rights of the National Academy of Sciences from 1979 to 1984 and was a delegate to the 1980 Scientific Forum in Hamburg, at which the topic of human rights was discussed. As quoted by Seltzer, Morris Pripstein, chair of Scientists for Sakharov, Orlov, and Scharansky, described Flory as "very passionate on human rights. . . . You could always count on him." At one point, Flory offered himself to the Soviet government as a hostage if it would allow Soviet scientist Andrei Sakharov's wife, Yelena Bonner, to come to the West for medical treatment. The Soviets declined the offer, but eventually did allow Bonner to receive the necessary treatment in Italy and the United States.

Flory led an active life with a special interest in swimming and golf. In the words of Ken A. Dill, professor of chemistry at the University of California, San Francisco, as quoted by Seltzer, Flory was "a warm and compassionate human being. He had a sense of life, a sense of humor, and a playful spirit. He was interested in, and cared deeply about, those around him. He did everything with a passion; he didn't do anything half way." Flory died on September 8, 1985, while working at his weekend home in Big Sur, California. According to Seltzer, at Flory's memorial service in Stanford, James Economy, chair of the American Chemical Society's division of polymer chemistry, expressed the view that Flory was "fortunate to depart from us while still at his peak, not having to suffer the vicissitudes of old age, and leaving us with a sharply etched memory of one of the major scientific contributors of the twentieth century."

Further Reading

Morton, Maurice, "Paul John Flory, 1910–1985, part I: The Physical Chemistry of Polymer Synthesis," in *Rubber Chemistry and Technology*, May-June, 1987, pp. G47-G57.
Seltzer, Richard J., "Paul Flory: A Giant Who Excelled in Many Roles," in *Chemical and Engineering News*, December 23, 1985, pp. 27–30. □

Carlisle Floyd

Carlisle Floyd (born 1926) brought abilities as librettist and dramatist to the composition of opera. Writing mostly in the *verismo* tradition, Floyd achieved considerable success with his third opera, *Susannah*, although he continued to refine and develop his techniques in later works.

C arlisle Floyd was born in Latta, South Carolina, on June 11, 1926. He received his first piano lessons from his mother at the age of ten, but divided his attentions among literature, graphic arts, sports, and music throughout his high school years. At Spartanburg College, where he began studying in 1943 on a scholarship, Floyd's writing abilities earned him first prize in a contest for one-act plays. When in 1945 his piano teacher, Ernst Bacon, accepted a post at Syracuse University, Floyd followed him there in order to continue studying with him.

Floyd received his bachelor of music degree from Syracuse in 1946 and in the following year began teaching piano at Florida State University. In 1948 he organized a course—the first of its kind anywhere—dealing with the problems of relating music and text in the composition of opera. As professor of music he taught composition at Florida State University until 1976. In that year he accepted a post at the University of Houston where, in addition to the duties of professor, he became co-director of the Houston Opera Studio. He also served as chairman of the Opera Musical Theater of the National Endowment for the Arts.

19th Century Roots

Floyd was best known for his operas, most of which are in the *verismo* tradition. This movement has its roots in the realism of the 19th-century dramatists such as Zola, Flaubert, Ibsen, and Hauptmann, who replaced an idealistic and often fantastic subject matter with one grounded in believable events, often with a contemporary, moral message. Earlier operatic composers who allied themselves with this movement were Mascagni, Leoncavallo, and (to some extent) Puccini, and later Menotti and Moore.

Floyd's first major success and, indeed, perhaps his best-known work was his third opera, *Susannah,* (written 1953-1954) and first produced at Florida State University on February 24, 1955. It combined the features of *verismo* with

those of folk opera, and hence contained music reminiscent of hymns, folk songs, and square dances, though not actually using previously existing music. Floyd wrote his own libretto, as he did for all of his 11 operas. Here he borrowed the apocryphal story of Susannah and the Elders, but set it in the mountains of present-day Tennessee. The consequences of a conflict between narrow religious dogma and straightforward folk honesty were depicted through the seduction of the heroine by Reverend Blitch and the avenging of Susannah's dishonor by her brother, who kills Blitch. Both the libretto and the music are direct, uncomplicated, and emotional. The text was treated in a variety of ways. Many of the arias utilize modal scales characteristic of folk music. In addition to recitative, which is always sensitive to the natural inflections of speech, Floyd employed spoken sections and, briefly, *Sprechstimme* (halfway between speech and song). Conventional harmonic language serves the purposes of folk description.

In 1958 Floyd completed another major opera, *Wuthering Heights,* on a commission from the Santa Fe Opera. Floyd's libretto departed from his usual American setting in its basis on the Emily Brontë novel. He did, however, seek to have the characters speak in a manner that was essentially timeless in character rather than identifiably contemporary or Victorian. He also chose to use only the first half of the book, as he felt that both the shifting emphasis to Heathcliff and the introduction of a second generation in the second half would necessitate proportions unacceptable to opera.

Greater Acclaim to Come

Several of Floyd's later operas received higher critical acclaim than either *Susannah* or *Wuthering Heights,* chiefly for the greater sophistication of their melodies, but none became more popular. Among his later operas were: The *Passion of Jonathan Wade* (1962), commissioned by the New York City Opera on a grant from the Ford Foundation; *The Sojourner and Mollie Sinclair* (1963), a one-act opera commissioned by the Carolina Charter Tercentenary Commission and intended for television; *Markheim* (1966); *Of Mice and Men* (1969); *Bilby's Doll* (1976), commissioned by the Houston Opera with a grant from the National Endowment for the Arts and containing instances of atonal writing unusual for Floyd; and *Willie Stark* (1980), commissioned jointly by the Houston Opera and the John F. Kennedy Center for the Performing Arts. All revealed Floyd's gifts as a writer of lyrical melodies and his flair for the theater. Compositions outside the realm of opera include: *Pilgrimage* (1956), a cantata for voice and orchestra; a piano sonata (1957); *Introduction, Aria,* and *Dance* (1967) for orchestra; *Flower and the Hawk* (1972), a monodrama for soprano and orchestra; and *In Celebration* (1978), an overture for orchestra.

Not Just Opera

The non-operatic works of Floyd gained increasing attention in later years. In 1993, his orchestral song cycle *Citizen of Paradise,* based on the poems and letters of Emily Dickenson, premiered. *A Time to Dance* was commissioned by the American Choral Directors Association and in March 1994 performed by the Westminster Choir and the San Antonio Symphony at the association's biennial convention.

Awards and honors received by Floyd are numerous. Among the more notable are a Guggenheim Fellowship in 1956 and the National Opera Institute's Award for Service to American Opera, the highest honor the institute bestows, which he received in 1983. Additionally, Floyd in 1976 became the first chairman of the Opera/Musical Theater Panel when the program was created by the National Endowment for the Arts. He also was selected to be the keynote speaker at Opera America's annual conference in 1997.

In addition, Floyd continued teaching at the university level, sharing his gifts with others who someday might rival or surpass his stature in the operatic world. He was associated with the University of Houston School of Music for 20 years. When he retired from teaching in 1996, he left behind the school's distinguished M.D. Anderson Chair and the legacy of having helped build a highly respected music program. Upon his departure from academia, Floyd referred to his retirement as his "third act" and expressed the intention to pursue the creation of more operatic works.

Further Reading

David Ewen's *American Composers: A Biographical Dictionary* (1982) contains a complete but not always reliable biography. Floyd discussed his opera *Wuthering Heights* in a lengthy article in the *New York Times* (July 13, 1958). Howard Taubman reviewed the same opera in the *New York Times* (April 10, 1959), and *Susannah,* also in the *New York Times* (September 28, 1956). More recently in the same newspaper (October 15, 1983) Donal Henahan reviewed *Of Mice and Men.* □

Elizabeth Gurley Flynn

Elizabeth Gurley Flynn (1890-1964) devoted her life to the cause of the working class. She organized workers, defended the civil liberties of radicals, and was a leading figure in socialist and communist circles.

Elizabeth Gurley Flynn was born in Concord, New Hampshire, on August 7, 1890, to Thomas and Annie Gurley Flynn. From her parents she absorbed principles of socialism and feminism that would inform the rest of her life. After several moves, in 1900 the family settled in the Bronx in New York City, where Flynn attended public schools. At the age of 16 she gave her first public address to the Harlem Socialist Club, where she spoke on "What Socialism Will Do for Women." Her striking appearance and dynamic oratory made her an enormously popular speaker. Upon her arrest for blocking traffic during one of her soapbox speeches she was expelled from high school, and in 1907 she began full-time organizing for the Industrial Workers of the World (IWW).

In the IWW Flynn met Jack Archibold Jones, a miner and organizer, and they married in 1908. The marriage lasted little more than two years, during which their work separated them for much of the time. Their first child died shortly after its premature birth in 1909; the second, Fred, was born in 1910. Motherhood did not interrupt Flynn's career; she moved back to the Bronx, where her mother and sister cared for her son while she travelled on behalf of workers. Flynn did not remarry, but she carried on a long love affair with Italian anarchist Carlo Tresca, who lived with the Flynn family in New York.

Flynn's efforts for the IWW took her all over the United States, where she led organizing campaigns among garment workers in Minersville, Pennsylvania; silk weavers in Patterson, New Jersey; hotel and restaurant workers in New York City; miners in Minnesota's Mesabi Iron Range; and textile workers in the famous Lawrence, Massachusetts, strike of 1912. She spoke in meeting halls, at factory gates, and on street corners in cities and towns across the country from Spokane, Washington, to Tampa, Florida. As she participated in the IWW campaigns against laws restricting freedom of speech she was arrested ten times or more, but was never convicted.

Many of the workers whom Flynn sought to organize were women and children, and Flynn combined her class-based politics with recognition of the particular oppression

women experienced because of their sex. She criticized male chauvinism in the IWW and pressed the union to be more sensitive to the needs and interests of working class women. She was a strong supporter of birth control, and she reproached the IWW for not agitating more on that issue. While Flynn considered the women's suffrage movement largely irrelevant to working-class women and opposed mobilization of workers on its behalf as diversionary and divisive, she believed that women should have the right to vote and never opposed suffrage publicly as did some of her colleagues. Her feminist consciousness grew when she joined the Heterodoxy Club, a group of independent women who met regularly to discuss issues of concern to women.

By the later 1910s Flynn was devoting more and more of her time to defending workers' rights, which came under intensive attack during and after World War I. She was a founding member of the American Civil Liberties Union (ACLU) and chaired the Workers Defense Union and its successor, International Labor Defense. Besides making speeches, Flynn visited political prisoners, raised money, hired lawyers, arranged meetings, and wrote publicity on behalf of dozens of radicals, including Sacco and Vanzetti, whose defense went on for seven years.

In 1926 Flynn's health failed, and she spent the next ten years recovering in Portland, Oregon, where she lived with Dr. Marie Equi, an IWW activist and birth control agitator. In 1936 Flynn returned to New York and joined the Communist Party, on which she would focus her work for the rest of her life. Although she had announced her new affiliation to the ACLU and had been elected unanimously to a three-year term on its executive board, in the wake of the Nazi-Soviet pact of 1940 the ACLU expelled her for her party membership.

During World War II Flynn organized and wrote for the party with a special emphasis on women's affairs and ran on its ticket for congressman-at-large from New York. She joined other women leaders in advocating equal economic opportunity and pay for women and the establishment of day care centers and publicized women's contributions to the war effort. Fully supporting the war effort, she favored the draft of women and urged Americans to buy savings stamps and to re-elect Franklin D. Roosevelt in 1944. Flynn rose in party circles and was elected to its national board.

With other Communist leaders, Flynn fell victim to the anti-Communist hysteria that suffused the United States after the war. After a nine-month trial in 1952, she was convicted under the Smith Act of conspiring to teach and advocate the overthrow of the United States government. During her prison term from January 1955 to May 1957 at the women's federal penitentiary at Alderson, West Virginia, she wrote, took notes on prison life, and participated in the integration of a cottage composed of African-American women. Upon her release Flynn resumed party work and became national chairman in 1961. She made several trips to the Soviet Union. Falling ill on her last visit, she died there on September 5, 1964, and was given a state funeral in Red Square.

Further Reading

Flynn published two books about her life: *The Rebel Girl, An Autobiography: My First Life* (1906-1926; revised edition, 1973) and *The Alderson Story: My Life as a Political Prisoner* (1955). A summary of Flynn's IWW and labor defense activities can be found in Rosalyn Fraad Baxandall, "Elizabeth Gurley Flynn: The Early Years," in *Radical America* (January-February 1975). The following books provide discussions of Flynn in the context of women activists and labor radicals: Melvyn Dubofsky, *We Shall Be All: A History of the Industrial Workers of the World* (1969); Meredith Tax, *The Rising of the Women: Feminist Solidarity and Class Conflict, 1880-1917* (1980); and June Sochen, *Movers and Shakers: American Women Thinkers and Activists, 1900-1970* (1973).

Additional Sources

Camp, Helen C., *Iron in her soul: Elizabeth Gurley Flynn and the American Left,* Pullman, Wash.: WSU Press, 1995. □

John Flynn

The founder and superintendent of the Australian Inland Mission, John Flynn (1880-1951) established remote "bush" hospitals and communication through the unique pedal radio and his Flying Doctor Service.

K nown for over 50 years as "Flynn of the Inland," John Flynn was born on November 25, 1880, in the small country township of Moliagul in central Victoria, Australia. He commenced training as a school teacher, then in 1903 for the ministry of the Presbyterian Church. During this time he developed skills in photography and first aid. In 1910 he published a small book, *The Bushman's Companion,* containing practical advice for people living far from medical help.

In 1910 he volunteered for appointment to a remote pastorate extending from the Flinders Ranges of South Australia to the rail terminus at Oodnadatta 450 miles northwest. Here, 500 miles from a resident doctor, he established his first "bush" hospital. In 1912, with photographs to support his "Northern Australia Report," his presentation of the frightening hazards facing isolated pioneers resulted in the Presbyterian General Assembly appointing him as superintendent of a special ministry to the sparsely populated areas of Australia. Despite limited finances, but with great vision and growing support, he gradually added other "bush" hospitals, each staffed by two dedicated and highly trained nursing Sisters equipped to perform emergency operations. Flynn planned to have a patrol padre (itinerant pastor) associated with each hospital.

The first padre, based at Oodnadatta, used a string of five camels. Two riding camels were for himself and his "camel boy," and three pack animals were for food, water, cooking utensils, and bed-rolls. His longest patrol extended 750 miles northward along the overland telegraph line. One padre used a camel buggy and another used horses prior to the use of motor trucks. Flynn's commitment to staff support, work evaluation, and consultations with "bush" people kept him in the field for a great part of each year. In 1925 he purchased a specially designed Dodge buck-board in which he made some incredible journeys—the first lasted four months over inland desert tracks that were used in the 1980s only by four wheel drive vehicles.

Flynn recognized that his hospitals and padres could do little to alleviate the agony suffered by patients conveyed by camel, horse, or buggy over hundreds of trackless miles to his out-post hospitals. As early as 1919 he wrote in his *Inlander* magazine of the need for the wider mantle of safety that only radio and aircraft could supply. With the initial help of air force pilot Clifford Peel and later (Sir) Hudson Fysh, a founder of QANTAS, Flynn reached one of his goals when on May 17, 1928, a de Haviland 50, leased from QANTAS and named *Victory*, answered its first medical call.

In 1925, by chance, he met a young Adelaide radio enthusiast, Alfred Traeger, who expressed great interest in Flynn's vision. This meeting was destined to change the history of communication in remote areas of Australia. The following year Flynn invited Traeger to join his staff. Their first successful two-way transmission was from Alice Springs in November 1925. However, the heavy copper oxide batteries used were unsuitable for remote homesteads. Traeger persisted until he perfected a transceiver for which the current was provided by the operator using cycle pedals to drive a small generator. In June 1929 this unique pedal radio using a hand-operated Morse code transmitter went into service in remote homesteads and Flynn hospitals through the new Flying Doctor base at Cloncurry. The pedal radio provided the link between patient, hospital, and Flynn's Aerial Medical Service to complete his mantle of safety.

The final phase of Flynn's great service to the people of remote areas began with his merging of his Aerial Medical Service into an Australia-wide community service—now known as the Royal Flying Doctor Service of Australia (R.F.D.S.). Flynn had recognized that his Flying Doctor Service, supported by limited resources, could never achieve his vision of a service for two-thirds of Australia. With the support of the 1933 Australian State Premiers' Conference and his own church, he gave his Flying Doctor Service and all its transmitting equipment to the new organization and the pedal radios to the people of the outback. Flynn's work was publicly recognized in the award of the O.B.E. (Order of the British Empire) in 1933.

Flynn demonstrated an instinctive insight as a "community developer" and a recognition of the benefit the pedal radio would bring to the women and children of the outback in security, social communication, and education; for example, the Country Womens Association of the Air held meetings through a radio link-up and the Education School of the Air was carried by a radio network. He enjoyed a remarkable range of friendships, from the "battlers in the bush" to cabinet ministers. His fertile imagination developed projects that enriched people and places. He lived for a specific goal and refused to be sidetracked from a task that received his total commitment.

On May 7, 1932, at age 51, Flynn married Jean Baird. He died on May 5, 1951, and by his wish his ashes were interred at the foot of Mt. Gillen, Alice Springs.

The *Australian Dictionary of Biography* reports that

In 1939 Flynn was elected to the three-year term as Moderator-General of the Presbyterian Church of Australia. In 1940 and 1941 the degrees of D.D. were conferred on him by the University of Toronto and the Presbyterian College at McGill University, Montreal, Canada. When John Flynn said "A man is his friends" he expressed something akin to Martin Buber's philosophy that "All real living is in meeting." His meeting with other people often revealed a compulsive humanism which gave meaning to his own life as an ordained minister of his Church and to the faith by which he lived and served.

Further Reading

The *Australian Dictionary of Biography* article by Graeme Bucknall in Volume 8 provides a more detailed account of Flynn's life and work. W. W. McPheat, *John Flynn, Apostle to the Inland* (London, 1963) contains a definitive account of Flynn's life and work. M. F. Page, *The Flying Doctor Story, 1928-1978* (1977) was published for the Jubilee of the Royal Flying Doctor Service of Australia. The early chapters contain an accurate account of Flynn's role in establishing the service in 1928 at Cloncurry. Flynn's *Inlander* magazine published between 1913 and 1926, contains most of his published writings.

Additional Sources

Griffiths, Max., *The silent heart: Flynn of the inland,* Kenthurst, Australia: Kangaroo Press, 1993.
McKenzie, Maisie., *Flynn's last camp,* Brisbane, Qld.: Boolarong Publications, 1985. ☐

Ferdinand Foch

The French marshal Ferdinand Foch (1851-1929) was commander in chief of the Allied armies in World War I.

Ferdinand Foch was born on Oct. 2, 1851, at Tarbes. His early schooling revealed his "geometrical mind" and mathematical ability. He enlisted in the infantry during the Franco-Prussian War but did not see active service. Resuming his education, he graduated from the École Polytechnique in 1873 and was commissioned a lieutenant in the artillery.

By 1894 Foch had become lieutenant colonel and professor of strategy and tactics in the École Supérieure de Guerre (War School). His lectures were published in two volumes: *De la conduite de la guerre* (1897; *Precepts and Judgments*) and *Des principes de la guerre* (1899; *Principles of War*). Foch's doctrine of massive attack attracted much attention. He stressed both philosophical and material aspects of war and emphasized the importance of morale and the will to win. In 1900 Foch was transferred to regimental command and then to staff duty with the V Corps. In 1907 Premier Georges Clemenceau appointed him general and director of the War School, where he remained for 4 years.

At the beginning of World War I, Foch was in charge of the XX Army Corps and fought in Lorraine. Next he commanded the newly formed 9th Army and helped check the Germans in the first Battle of the Marne. Gen. Joffre then entrusted him with coordinating troops and operations in the north during the "race to the sea" from the Oise River to the Flemish coast. As commander of the Group of Armies of the North for 2 years, Foch presided over the Artois offensives of 1915 and the Battle of the Somme in 1916. The disappointing results of the Somme offensive led to replacement of both Foch and Joffre. After a brief interval Foch was appointed chief of the general staff by Gen. Pétain.

In the spring of 1918, when the Allies were threatened by the German grand offensive, Foch became chief commander of all Allied armies in France. He halted the Germans and launched a counteroffensive which drove them back and ended the war. On Nov. 11, 1918, Foch induced the German representatives to accept his armistice terms, including occupation of the left bank of the Rhine.

Acclaimed by the world after the war, Foch received many honors, including election to the French Academy and to the Academy of Sciences. He bitterly condemned the peace settlement for its failure to detach the left bank of the Rhine from Germany. Foch died in Paris on March 20, 1929, and was interred in the Invalides.

Further Reading

Valuable memoirs by Raymond Recouly, a friend of Foch, are *Foch: His Character and Leadership* (trans. 1920) and *Foch: My Conversations with the Marshal* (trans. 1929). Leading biographies of the marshal are George Grey Aston, *The Biography of the Late Marshal Foch* (1929) and Basil Henry Liddell Hart, *Foch, the Man of Orleans* (1932). Another useful work is Cyril Bentham Falls, *Marshal Foch* (1939). The postwar Rhineland question is explored in Jere C. King, *Foch versus Clemenceau: France and German Dismemberment, 1918-1919* (1960). □

Tom Foley

Former Speaker of the U.S. House of Representatives Democrat Tom Foley was swept out of office in 1994 in an election many Republicans referred to as a "Republican Revolution." Foley served from the 89th to 103rd Congress (1965-1995) and was speaker from 1989 to 1995 but fell out of favor with fellow House members following his handling of the House banking scandal of the early 1990s.

Tom Foley was born on March 16, 1929, in Spokane, Washington. His father, Ralph E. Foley, was a lawyer who was Spokane County prosecutor in the 1930s before becoming a superior-court judge for 35 years, the longest tenure in Washington state history. His mother was Helen Marie Higgins.

Although Foley grew up in a middle-class neighborhood populated mainly by Republicans, he gained much sympathy for the less fortunate from his parents and experienced blue-collar life in the summers of his high school years working in the Kaiser Aluminum plant in Spokane. Foley attended Gonzaga High School where he was an indifferent student, even flunking a course in algebra. He was little better at Gonzaga University where he matriculated in 1947. In fact, the dean of the school gave him an ultimatum: improve your grades or leave. Foley left, transferring to the University of Washington from which he earned a B.A. in 1951. He then entered Washington Law School with the goal of becoming a lawyer like his father. He managed to stay only one day, leaving after an assistant dean of the law school described the law as a business. Foley then enrolled in the University of Washington's Graduate School of Far Eastern and Russian Studies. After two years there Foley returned to the law school, graduating with an LL.B. in 1957.

His first legal position was as a partner in the law firm of Higgins and Foley in Spokane soon after graduation. Following in his father's footsteps, he became deputy prosecutor in Spokane County the following year. He held this post

for two years while, ironically, also instructing law students at Gonzaga University. In 1960 he became assistant attorney general for the state of Washington.

Foley's first taste of life in the nation's capital came when Senator Henry (Scoop) Jackson, a friend of his father's, hired him as special counsel to the Senate Interior and Insular Affairs Committee in 1961, a post he filled until 1964. At the urging of Jackson, he then ran for Congress from the Fifth District of Washington against a 27-year Republican veteran of the House, Walt Horan. The district was Republican and primarily rural, but it also included Spokane. The seat was considered so secure that no other Democrat had filed for the nomination when Foley made his last-minute decision to do so. Supported by the two Democratic senators from the state and organized labor, and helped by the Lyndon Johnson 1964 landslide, Foley won by a narrow margin in a campaign that was noticeably polite and positive.

Foley entered Congress as a Johnson liberal, supporting Great Society programs and only later opposing the Vietnam War. His positions remained generally liberal during his terms of office. He was pro-choice despite his Catholic background and supported the Equal Rights Amendment. He opposed capital punishment, a constitutional amendment allowing school prayer, aid to the contras, the MX missile, nuclear testing, term limits, and, a notable deviation, gun control. The last position was one in keeping with the traditions of the West and his own district. His popularity slipped in Nixon's re-election victory in 1972, and he

almost lost his seat in 1978 and in the Reagan victory in 1980.

In 1968 he married Heather Strachen and continued his steady and unspectacular rise in the House. In 1974 he became chair of the Democratic Study Group, which was energized by the large number of "Watergate" freshmen. Foley led the group's fight to end the seniority system and to open committee hearings. Despite this, he personally refused to help oust 75-year-old W. R. Poage of Texas, the chairman of the House Agricultural Committee on which Foley served. A grateful Poage, although defeated, nominated Foley for the chairmanship. Foley won and at age 45 became the youngest chair of a major congressional committee and the first westerner to chair the House Agricultural Committee. As chairman until 1981 and vice chair until 1986, he tried to re-orient the Agriculture Department toward nutrition and consumer interests instead of being primarily involved with livestock and grain producers.

Foley's next major post was as head of the Democratic Caucus, defeating Shirley Chisholm in 1976. He further solidified Democratic support for his mediating ways so that when John Brademus of Indiana lost his seat in the 1980 election, Foley assumed his position as House majority whip, the third highest ranking position in party leadership. Foley served in that capacity for three terms, through 1986. He moved up to House majority leader in 1987 as a consequence of Jim Wright vacating that position to assume the speakership. As majority leader in the trying years of 1987-1989 when the Iran-Contra affair was in the headlines, Foley proved to be a calming influence in his service on the Permanent Select Committee To Investigate Covert Arms Transactions with Iran. As a result, members of the House voted him its most respected member in 1988 and again in 1989.

In 1989 Jim Wright ran afoul of the House Ethics Committee, which charged him with financial improprieties, and he resigned as speaker. Foley then became the 49th Speaker of the House, the highest leadership post. In the early 1990s, Foley fell victim to controversy over House members' bounced checks at the House bank. Foley was sharply criticized by members of his own party for how he handled the House banking scandal, which received much media attention and raised the ire of the electorate. His greatest sin, according to critics, was not protecting his own flock in the House. At least one member called for Foley to resign his post at the end of 1992. "We're angry he knew about this mess and sat on his duff for three years," said one senior House member in 1992. "He was so concerned with the institution that he sacrificed his members."

Back home in Washington, members of an electorate said to be 60 percent in favor of term limits became incensed at Foley's pursuit of a 16th consecutive term in the House. Foley filed a lawsuit against a state initiative to limit terms, challenging such limits on federal officeholders as unconstitutional. In the state's September 1994 open primary, five Republican and Democratic candidates split the vote, allowing Foley to just squeak by with a meager 35 percent. It was the second-worst showing of his 16 congressional campaigns. Foley's Republican challenger, George

Nethercutt, capitalized on public sentiment and pledged to serve no more than three terms if elected. Further, he said, "I would never sue my constituents to save my job."

Foley's reelection campaign labored under at least two other burdens. Voters, who in the past had been accustomed to Foley's pork barrel-style politics, were growing doubtful such tactics were good for the country. "It's basically pork. Even though we live here, it just isn't right," said one voter. Foley also angered gun-toting voters in his state with efforts to pass a ban on assault-weapons. National Rifle Association (NRA) advertisements opposing the ban featured Foley as a target for defeat.

Foley lost to Nethercutt in the "Republican Revolution" of 1994. Representative Newt Gingrich, a Republican from Georgia, became speaker of the House and was considered by many to carry the banner of incoming Republicans, at least for the time being. Foley was critical of Republicans' description of their sweeping victory in the House. "They were wrong to use the term 'Republican Revolution.' This country isn't revolutionary. It's centrist." Foley later became chairman of President Bill Clinton's Foreign Intelligence Advisory Board.

Further Reading

Additional information on Tom Foley can be found in J. Newhouse "Profile," *New Yorker* (April 10, 1989); H. Gorey, "Waiting for Opportunity To Knock," *TIME* (June 5, 1989); *The New York Times* (August 18, 1982, and June 2, 7, and 8, 1989); A. Z. Posner, "Friendly Foley," *New Republic* (August 8-15, 1988); S. V. Roberts, "After Wright's Fall," *U.S. News and World Report* (June 5, 1989); and Fred Barnes, "Mission Accomplished," *New Republic* (July 3, 1989).

Additional Sources

Tumulty, Karen, "The Price of Pork," *Time,* November 7, 1994, v144, n19, p. 37.

Smolowe, Jill, "Speaker Foley's Folly," *Time,* October 10, 1994, v144, n15, p. 30.

Borger, Gloria, "Foley is Fighting Back, But Can He Save Himself?" *U.S. News & World Report,* April 13, 1992, p. 31.

Blow, Richard, "Foley Flexes," *Mother Jones,* January 1993. □

Jane Fonda

Jane Fonda (born 1937) was a member of a famous American theatrical family and recipient of the industry's highest awards. Her numerous radical activities during the period of the Vietnam War brought animosity from some and adoration from others. In the post-Vietnam era, her multi-faceted career included films, television, exercise videocassettes, and writing.

Jane Fonda, her father Henry, and her brother Peter comprise the "Fantastic Fondas" of the theater. Jane was born in New York City on December 21, 1937, to Henry and Frances Seymour Brokaw Fonda. Born into wealth, her maternal lineage can be traced to the American Revolution leader Samuel Adams. She herself became something of a revolutionary.

When Fonda was 13 her mother committed suicide after learning of her husband's interest in a much younger woman, Susan Blanchard. Told that her mother died from a sudden heart attack, Fonda learned the truth a year later from a magazine story. Both she and Peter had difficulty coping, although Fonda believes Blanchard, whom her father married, did much to provide a stable home life for them. Fonda attended schools in New York and Vassar College, where she admittedly "went wild." Thereafter, she engaged in a whirlwind of studies in Paris and New York. Her first stage appearance was in 1954, but she did not seriously decide on an acting career until four years later while visiting her father, who lived next door to Lee Strasberg, director of the Actors Studio in Malibu, California. Friends urged her to go into the profession; Strasberg accepted her as his student, and she paid for her acting lessons with a brief but successful modeling career.

Fonda probably inherited some theatrical genius; certainly hers was a meteoric rise to stardom. A number of persons influenced her career, including her godfather, Joshua Logan, first husband, Roger Vadim, and director Sidney Pollock. She received many of the industry's highest awards, including two Academy Awards for Best Actress

(*Klute,* 1971, and *Coming Home,* 1979). Both came before her famous father received one and after she was a controversial figure for her lifestyle, her rejection of many American traditional beliefs, and her outspoken anti-Vietnam War views.

Fonda became a heroine of the New Left for her activities in such causes as constitutional rights for American servicemen, Black Panthers, Native American rights, the Vietnam War, the anti-nuclear movement, and women's rights. Her life reflected the uncertainties, confusion, and rapidly changing values which began to rock America in the mid-1960s. To many she seemed mercurial, contradictory, and driven as the fighter for justice and peace. To others, she was naive, irritating, and an anti-American fool. Her causes were so numerous and undiscriminating that Saul Alinsky, fellow American radical, claimed that Fonda was "a hitchhiker on the highway of causes."

Fonda's first act of civil disobedience came in 1970 when she was arrested for illegally talking to soldiers against the military. Her radicalization was completed by what she saw and the people she met on a cross-country journey. Having left California as a left-wing liberal, she arrived in New York where she announced that she was a revolutionary woman, ready to support all struggles that were radical.

Fonda's support and fund-raising for the sometimes violent Black Panthers, including her relationship with Panther leader Huey Newton, led the FBI to place her under surveillance. Meanwhile, many differences with her father became public. As a life-long liberal, he sympathized with many of her views, but emphatically rejected her methods. Jane, in turn, rejected his idea that changes could be effected by electing the right officials into public office.

As her activities increased, government surveillance grew to at least six agencies at one time. Returning from Canada, she was infuriated when U.S. customs officials in Cleveland confiscated vials thought to be drugs. They proved to be vitamins and non-prescription food concentrates which she used to stabilize her weight.

Critics decried Fonda's exaggerations of American atrocities in Vietnam, which even supporters admitted were inflated. Many were astonished when she spoke as if she had visited Vietnam and witnessed the horrors she described. Ultimately, supporters arranged for her to go to Hanoi. When she publicly denounced American involvement there, she was labeled a "Communist" and "Hanoi Jane" by many back home. The State Department rebuked her, letters of protest filled newspapers, and at least one congressman demanded her arrest for treason. Yet Fonda seemed unperturbed by it all.

As the Vietnam War was ending, Fonda's radicalism diminished. Reconciliation with her father came in the early 1980s as they filmed *On Golden Pond,* a story which paralleled their own relationship in many ways. By the mid-1980s Fonda's popularity in films and television was such that to speak ill of her in Hollywood was to invite professional suicide. Her exercise salon, books, and videotapes became so popular that she may be remembered as much for them as for her films.

By 1985 she rarely spoke for radical causes. Rather, she seemed to have mellowed considerably. On a *CBS Morning News* television program she spoke of a new spiritual awareness during the filming of *Agnes of God,* and on CBS's *America* her comments and dress were quite subdued as she "plugged" her latest exercise videotape. She had moved from the radical to the respectable Jane Fonda.

Her personal life seemed stable as she and husband, former activist Tom Hayden, lived with her daughter Vanessa and their son Troy. Hayden sought a Senate seat from California in 1986, apparently both thinking that changes could be made by electing the "right" officials. Although her interests seemed to lie with her multi-faceted career and family, it seemed likely that Fonda could return to her former radical activism if she perceived that conditions demanded it.

In 1988 the "Hanoi Jane" issue raised its head again during filming of *Stanley and Iris,* which was being shot in a small Connecticut town. Old resentments among the townspeople about Fonda's role in Vietnam flared, leading her to issue her first public apology for her activities during the Vietnam War. She admitted that she'd been misinformed about aspects of the war, as well as some of her other causes at the time.

Fonda and Hayden were divorced in 1989. In 1991 she married media mogul Ted Turner, and settled into a much more domestic phase of her life. She announced that she was leaving her film career behind, and in 1996 confirmed that statement in a *Good Housekeeping* interview: "After a 35-year career as an actress, I am out of the business. That's a big change. Work, in many ways, defined me." Although she left behind her acting and producing career, Fonda was far from idle. In 1996 she published a cookbook, *Jane Fonda: Cooking for Healthy Living.* She also created a new series of workout tapes with the help of a physiologist called *The Personal Trainer Series.* Her goal with the new series was to design a program that anyone could stick with, stating in *Good Housekeeping,* "Anybody can do 25 minutes."

Further Reading

Although both are unauthorized biographies, *Jane Fonda: The Actress in Her Time* by Fred L. Guiles (1982) and *Jane: An Intimate Biography of Jane Fonda* (1973) by Thomas Kiernan provide interesting additional insights into the life of Jane Fonda and the sub-title of each accurately describes the contents. James Brough's *The Fabulous Fondas* (1973) gives considerable attention to Jane's life, but she shares space there with her father Henry and brother Peter. Also see Christopher Anderson's *Citizen Jane: The Turbulent Life of Jane Fonda* (1990) and *Good Housekeeping* (February 1996, page 24) □

Rubem Fonseca

Rubem Fonseca (born 1925) was Brazil's most highly regarded author of the late 20th century, with a string of critical and popular successes that com-

bined the conventional mystery/thriller format with a sophisticated, polished prose style and a focus on urban alienation.

Rubem Fonseca became one of Brazil's most widely read authors both because of his immense skill at creating believable characters and situations and because his themes addressed an urban population daily more distant from itself. Unlike many Latin American authors who fail to attract a following abroad, Fonseca was a thoroughly cosmopolitan writer who eschewed the exotic or picturesque—a fact that may explain his widespread popularity in Germany, France, and, increasingly, the English-speaking world.

In addressing the catholic human conditions of loneliness, alienation, and frustration, Fonseca was both a Brazilian writer and a universal writer. Using the outward trappings of the thriller and the detective story to frame his narrative, with *hommages* to the hard-boiled genre of Raymond Chandler and Dashiell Hammett, Fonseca was nevertheless deeply rooted in his own culture, accessible to both the casual reader and the professional critic.

Fonseca could easily be mistaken for a sensationalist seeking facile titillation in lurid violence. His themes and characters often dealt with the netherworld of pathology lying just beneath the surface of workaday lives, and his subject matter included such bizarre topics as "sexual coupling" contests, transvestites, death squads, professional hit men, and psychotic killers masquerading as humdrum businessmen whose lives of quiet desperation are punctuated by episodes of random, motiveless murder.

However unsavory, Fonseca's world was a metaphor for society, especially Brazilian society in the dying years of the 20th century. That he spoke to a large segment of the reading public can be seen in the runaway popularity of his three novels published between 1983 and 1988, all of which rose to the top of the best-seller list. He shared with Jorge Amado the rare position of one of the few Brazilian novelists whose eagerly awaited works were published in mass printings in a nation where a normal press run is 3,000 copies.

A Grande Arte (1983; translated as *High Art*, 1987) is a revenge story that demonstrates Fonseca's skill at revealing character through action. The protagonist is a lawyer who may be willing to skirt the limits of legality for a client but whose loyalty is unshakable. When his lover Berta is raped, he sets out after her assailant, vowing to use the same weapon, a knife, that had been employed in the crime. In the end he is thwarted by the one foe he cannot overcome—himself.

In *Bufo & Spallanzani* (1986; translated 1990) the narrator is a novelist whose twin obsessions—fornicating and eating—lead to complications when one of his lovers, the wife of a millionaire, is found dead in her car. (Among the novel's delights is Fonseca's playful and highly original mix of sexual and food images.) He becomes the target both of police investigation by a dogged inspector and of the woman's husband, furious upon discovering he has been cuckolded. This thoroughly post-modern work combines sex, violence, concepts of aesthetics, and metafiction in a witty black comedy.

Vastas Emoções e Pensamentos Imperfeitos (1988; *Vast Emotions and Imperfect Thoughts*) examines the despair of a film director whose lover, Ruth, has committed suicide. Seeking escape, he accepts a West German offer to film Isaac Babel's *Red Cavalry* in Europe, but not before he unwittingly becomes enmeshed in a mystery involving stolen gems and murder. In typical Fonseca fashion, the two themes come together in an emotionally satisfying manner at the end. Along the way, the reader learns a great deal about diamonds, Babel, and filmmaking.

For all his success as novelist, Fonseca first gained critical and popular recognition as a short story writer. His two best known collections, *Feliz Ano Novo* (Happy New Year, 1975) and *O Cobrador* (The Taker, 1979), display a mastery of technique and concision of style that in themselves would guarantee him a place in the front ranks of contemporary Brazilian authors. The title story in *Feliz Ano Novo,* which tells of a gang of bank robbers who invade a private party on New Year's Eve to rape and kill, was so graphically intense and thematically shocking that the book was suppressed by the military dictatorship; it was not until 1989 that Fonseca won a court case clearing him of offenses against "morality and good customs." The title story in *O Cobrador,* a journey into the mind of a psychopathic serial killer, is arguably even more stunning. "Ship Catrineta" is a black comedy about an urbane, sophisticated family in Rio de Janeiro who happen to be cannibals. Fonseca's only straightforward humorous tale is the hilarious "Lonelyhearts," in which a former police reporter goes to work as the advice columnist for a women's newspaper. In 1994 he published his sixth novel *O Selvegan da Opera* (The Savage of the Opera), which tells the story of opera composer Antonio Carlos Gomes (1836-1896).

The most reclusive of contemporary writers, Fonseca was often called the Greta Garbo of Brazil. Though he did not grant interviews, he could frequently be spotted soon after sunrise jogging along the beach in the Leblon section of Rio de Janeiro, where he lived with his wife Théa. Fonseca steadfastly refrained from commenting on the meaning of his writing, preferring to let his work speak for itself. He did, however, remark at one point, "Perhaps I am the Taker."

Despite his sometimes grisly themes and a relentlessly unsentimental treatment of his subject matter, Fonseca was to his intimates a warm, approachable individual with a delightful sense of humor and boundless joy for living.

Rubem Fonseca was born in 1925 in the state of Minas Gerais and lived in Rio de Janeiro from the age of seven. He and his wife, a former translator of English, had three children. He obtained a graduate degree in the United States and was a writer in residence in West Germany in 1988. In the late 1980s he became a computer enthusiast, composing his later works at the keyboard of his IBM-clone.

Further Reading

Fonseca's novels available in English include *High Art,* translated by Ellen Watson (1986); *Bufo & Spallanzani,* translated by Clifford Landers (1990); and *Vast Emotions and Imperfect Thoughts,* translated by Clifford Landers. His short stories have appeared in publications ranging from *Latin American Literary Review* ("The Ship Catrineta") and *Brazil/Brazil* ("Lonelyhearts") to *Ellery Queen Mystery Magazine* ("Night Drive"). A brief biography, which also details some of his stories, can be found in *World Authors 1985-1990* (1995). □

Theodor Fontane

The German author Theodor Fontane (1819-1898) was once famous for his ballads and lively travel accounts but is now best known for his realistic novels, which are usually set in Berlin.

Theodor Fontane born on Dec. 30, 1819, in Neu-Ruppin (Brandenburg). The son of an apothecary, he planned to follow in his father's footsteps but found the work uncongenial. Thereafter, he determined to pursue a literary career.

Two trips to England, one (1852) to study ballad origins and a longer sojourn (1855-1859) as an attaché of the Prussian embassy, were followed by an editorial appointment on a conservative Berlin newspaper, *Kreuzzeitung,* a post that Fontane held until 1870. The post made possible considerable travel, notably described in the *Wanderungen durch die Mark Brandenburg* (4 vols., 1862-1882). As a correspondent during the Franco-Prussian War, he was captured and narrowly escaped execution as a spy. In the postwar period he became, and remained for nearly 20 years, the theater critic of the *Vossische Zeitung* in Berlin.

Late in life Fontane discovered the literary form most congenial to his talents and produced the series of novels that reflect his long-continued, analytical, and objective scrutiny of late-19th-century society.

His novels *Vor dem Sturm* (1878) and *Schach von Wuthenow* (1883) are historically oriented; others concentrate on contemporary social problems. Three novels, *L'Adultera* (1880), *Cécile* (1886), and *Effi Briest* (1895), concern adultery. In the latter two works the situation is resolved tragically; in *L'Adultera* a divorce, followed by the marriage of the lovers, restores the necessary social equilibrium. "Marriage is order," Fontane believed, and without preaching he demonstrates the inevitably unhappy consequence when this "law" is flouted.

Irrungen, Wirrungen (1887) treats the "misalliance" between a member of the nobility and a simple, good-hearted girl of the people whose affair must end, for they make the hard decision that social dictates of "duty" and "order" must prevail. *Stine* (1890) recapitulates a similar theme with tragic overtones. *Frau Jenny Treibel* (1892) gently satirizes bourgeois pretensions, while the late novel *Der Stechlin* (1897) is a sharply observed study of the

Brandenburg nobility. Fontane died in Berlin on Sept. 28, 1898.

Fontane is no reformer but a mildly amused, somewhat reserved, and keen-eyed observer to whom "society" represents a manifestation of a principle of order. Though neither divinely nor naturally ordained, society still transcends the power of the individual to alter it; those who make an attempt do so at their peril. What has been called Fontane's "psychological naturalism" links the preceding tradition of poetic realism and the analytical approach so prominent in the 20th-century German novel.

Further Reading

Kenneth Hayens, Theodor Fontane: *A Critical Study* (1920), is still useful. A perceptive analysis is in Roy Pascal, *The German Novel: Studies* (1956). □

Dame Margot Fonteyn

Dame Margot Fonteyn (born Margaret Hookham; 1919-1991) was an outstanding and beloved classical ballerina with an extensive career, from 1934 to 1979. She danced for England's Royal Ballet, putting British ballet on the international map.

Margot Fonteyn was born in Reigate, England, on May 18, 1919 as Margaret Hookham. Her father was British and her mother, Hilda, was a daughter of an Irish mother and a Brazilian father. She had one brother, Felix. They grew up happily in the London suburb of Ealing. She began dance classes at age four at a local dance school. Her father accepted a position as chief engineer of a tobacco company in Shanghai when Fonteyn was eight years old. In Shanghai she took ballet lessons from the Russian George Goncharov. She loved to move and was always creating dances for herself. At age 14 her mother brought her to London to give her a chance to develop a dancing career. She started taking lessons with Serafina Astafieva, and a little later she went to the Sadler's Wells Ballet School with Vera Volkova. When she danced in England she got her stage name, Margot Fonteyn, which indirectly evolved from her mother's family name, Fontes.

Fonteyn devoted her entire career to the Royal Ballet. This company was founded by Ninette de Valois in 1928 as the Vic-Wells/Sadler's Wells Ballet. De Valois believed in Fonteyn's talent and pushed her through difficult moments. In her autobiography Fonteyn recalls her thoughts whenever faced with a new step: "What a beautiful step. I shall never be able to do it."

Her debut was as a snowflake in *The Nutcracker* in 1934. The next year a wealth of dance roles in the standard classics, such as *The Sleeping Beauty, Giselle,* and *Swan Lake,* became open to the young Margot due to the departure of the great ballerina Alicia Markova. Fonteyn loved to become the romantic heroines. Her first major role was in Frederick Ashton's new ballet *Le Baiser de la Fee* in 1935.

Her collaboration with choreographer Sir Frederick Ashton was exceptional. Fonteyn was his muse. In her autobiography she tells that although she had to work hard to master his creations, her happiest moments on stage were in Ashton ballets. He created leading roles for her in *Apparitions, Nocturne, Les Patineurs, A Wedding Bouquet, Horoscope, The Wise Virgins, Dante Sonata, The Quest, The Wanderer, Daphnis and Chloë,* and *Ondine.* De Valois also created roles for Fonteyn in *Orpheus and Euridyce* and *Don Quichotte.* She danced in revivals of *Firebird* and *Petrouchka* from the Diaghilev Ballets, staged by Leonide Massine. She was the first ballerina in George Balanchine's *Ballet Imperial.* During World War II the company had a full and hectic schedule. They were performing for all kinds of audiences, including the troops in Brussels. Her first performance in the United States in 1949 was triumphantly received.

Margot Fonteyn was at her best in a *pas de deux.* She loved working with a partner. She danced with Robert Helpmann and Michael Somes, each for many years. She appeared with Roland Petit for Les Ballets de Paris in *Les Demoiselles de la Nuit* in 1948. In her forties she started to think about retirement, but instead revived her career. She met Rudolf Nureyev, who had just left Russia at age 23. They became a dynamic team. The combination of his spirit and her technique, which was better than it had ever been before, made it joint artistry. They performed *Swan Lake, Giselle,* and *Romeo and Juliet.* Ashton created *Marguerite et Armand* and modern dance choreographer Martha Graham created *Lucifer* for them. For the next 15 years they performed all over the world. In 1965, an anecdote says, they once received a 40-minute ovation and had 43 curtain calls.

Fonteyn was the most versatile British ballerina after World War II. Her pale face, black hair, luminous eyes, and engaging smile were her trademarks. With her total musicality, her beautiful physique, her soft style of movement, her gentle loving manner, and her exquisite lines, she created a strong connection with audiences all over the world. She especially stood out in lyrical roles. She could dance the most difficult choreography with a disarming ease. Her presentation of Princess Aurora in *The Sleeping Beauty* is considered the ultimate interpretation of that role. She had an extraordinarily long career. At age 60 she had her farewell performance in London's Royal Opera House.

Her personal life started relatively late. Until age 35 her ballet career was all-consuming. In 1955, at age 36, she married in Paris a man she had met in her youth–Robert E. Arias, "Tito," the son of the former president of Panama. They met international celebrities and diplomats. He became the Panamanian ambassador in London and was actively involved in the politics of Panama. Attacked by a political opponent, he became paralyzed. The couple continued their separate careers, yet always remained connected, even when geography set them apart.

In 1951 Fonteyn was decorated a Commander of the Order of the British Empire, and in 1956 she became Dame of the Order of the British Empire, after which she was known as Dame Margot Fonteyn. In 1979 she received from the Royal Ballet in England the title "prima ballerina assoluta," a title only given to three ballerinas in the 20th century. She became president of the Royal Academy of Dancing in 1954 and annually organized and presented a gala matinee, persuading famous dancers from all the major companies to appear. She received several awards and honorary doctorates. She wrote her autobiography while still dancing in 1975. In 1979 she presented the television series and book "The Magic of Dance." A documentary was made on her Panamanian ranch to celebrate her 70th birthday. She died on February 21, 1991, at age 72, two years after her husband.

Further Reading

Probably the best source of information is Margot Fonteyn, *An Autobiography* (1969). K. Money wrote *The Art of Margot Fonteyn* (London, 1965) and *The Making of a Legend* (London, 1973). *Dance* magazine did a portfolio on Fonteyn in July 1973. A book about dance history mixed with personal experiences is *The Magic of Dance* (1979) by Margot Fonteyn. □

Michael Foot

Michael Foot (born 1913) was a left-wing journalist, a British Labour Party member of Parliament, and leader of the Labour Party from 1980 to 1983.

Michael Foot was born on July 23, 1913, in Plymouth, England. His father, Isaac Foot (1880-1960), was a major figure in the radical wing of the Liberal Party and represented Bodmin (Cornwall) in Parliament from 1922 to 1924 and again from 1929 to 1935. A passionate bibliophile, he built up a collection of more than 60,000 books—an enthusiasm which his son inherited.

Foot was a physically active child despite recurring bouts of eczema and asthma. He attended Leighton Park, a public school founded by Quakers and marked by an internationalist and pacifist ethos. In 1931 he entered Oxford and soon gravitated toward the debating society or Union, as it was called, becoming its president in 1933. He voted with the majority in the famous 1933 resolution that "this House will in no circumstances fight for its King and Country."

Liberal Turns Labour

Foot's first venture into national journalism was a 1934 article for the *News Chronicle* of London entitled "Why I Am a Liberal." He argued that Liberalism was a bulwark against war and fascism and called for a Rooseveltian New Deal for Britain. But he was not destined to remain a Liberal much longer. In 1934 he took a job in Liverpool, where he was appalled by the poverty and unemployment he saw around him. As a result he joined the Labour Party and met, for the first time, Aneurin Bevan, whose close friend, co-worker, and biographer he was later to become.

Foot fought his first parliamentary race in 1935, losing to a popular Conservative candidate at Monmouth. In 1937 he was adopted as the prospective Labour candidate for Plymouth Devenport. More immediately promising was the experience he was gaining in journalism. After short stints with the *New Statesman* and *Tribune,* Bevan was instrumental in finding him a job on the newspapers owned by Lord Beaverbrook. He worked for Beaverbrook from 1938 to 1944, rising to the acting editorship of the London *Evening Standard* in 1942. Under his guidance the paper moved sharply to the left.

The appearance of the book *Guilty Men* in 1940 made him notorious. Co-written by him under the pseudonym "Cato," *Guilty Men* was a slashing attack on the foreign and defense policies of the Conservative governments of the 1930s. A massive best-seller (by 1944 there were 43 printings), it became the leading anti-Tory critique of appeasement and stands as one of the great political tracts of 20th-century Britain and as a contributing factor to the Labour Party's victory in 1945.

Victory Over Tories

Foot won Plymouth Devenport in 1945, transforming a previous Tory majority of 11,000 into a Labour majority of 2,000. A back beach "loyal critic" of the government, he was the co-author of the 1947 pamphlet "Keep Left," which warned of the need for more rigorous socialist policies. In 1948 he became editor of *Tribune* and steered the editorial line toward support of Britain's entry into the North Atlantic

Treaty Organization (NATO) and support for the United States in the Korean War.

During the 1950s Foot was a leading spokesperson for the left wing of the Labour Party. He attacked the 1951 Labour government's budget, which raised defense spending and imposed fees on drug prescriptions and eyeglasses. He opposed German rearmament, the British invasion of Suez in 1956, and the Labour leadership's defense policy, which conditionally tolerated British first use of nuclear weapons. These controversial stands helped cause his defeat in the elections of 1955 and 1959.

Foot was flabbergasted when in 1957 his political hero Aneurin Bevan abruptly announced that Britain must maintain its nuclear deterrent so as not to "appear naked in the conference chamber" in negotiations with the Soviet Union. However, friendly relations between the two men were re-established by 1959. On Bevan's death in 1960 Foot was selected as his successor for the South Wales coalmining constituency of Ebbw Vale. He won election by over 16,000 votes and still held the seat in 1985.

Foot welcomed the emergence of Harold Wilson as leader of the Labour Party in 1963 and gave critical support to the 1964-1970 Labour government from the back benches. As he saw it, the greatest need was to keep the Tories out, even though he viewed the government's record as a "bloody catastrophe." In 1969 he ran unsuccessfully against James Callaghan for the post of Labour Party treasurer.

Becomes Employment Secretary

In 1970 Foot substantially modified his political stance. Previously a back bench critic of the Labour leadership, he now sought and won election to the shadow cabinet. In 1972 Wilson promoted him to shadow leader of the House of Commons, and after Labour's victory in the 1974 general election he accepted the cabinet post of employment secretary.

Foot was a powerful figure in the 1974-1979 Labour government. As employment secretary he was responsible for the repeal of the Conservative Industrial Relations Act of 1972. As leader of the House of Commons from 1976 to 1979 he used his encyclopedic knowledge of parliamentary procedure to guide legislation through a House of Commons in which the government did not command a majority. His goal throughout was to keep Labour in office for as long as possible, and he accordingly advised Callaghan, to whom he had become increasingly close, not to hold a general election in the fall of 1978.

But not even Foot's parliamentary skills could save the government from losing a vote of confidence in March 1979, and in the ensuing election Labour suffered a stunning defeat. Following Callaghan's resignation as party leader, Foot won a bitterly-fought contest against Denis Healy in November 1980. Foot's election, along with sweeping constitutional changes in the party's method of electing the leader and reselecting members of Parliament, led the far right of the party to split from Labour to form the Social Democratic Party (S.D.P.) early in 1981.

Defeat for Labour

Foot led a deeply divided and demoralized party into the general election of 1983. The result was an utter debacle for Labour, which only narrowly edged out the S.D.P. for second place with 27.6 percent of the votes. It was Labour's worst showing since the 1920s. On June 13, 1983, Foot resigned as party leader.

Ten years later, looking back over Foot's career on the occasion of his 80th birthday in July 1993, journalist Ian Aitken, writing in *New Statesman & Society,* lamented what he called a betrayal of Foot. "His leadership had been held—often by people who ought to know better—to be the cause of the disasters that engulfed the Labour Party in the early years of Thatcherism, culminating in the election loss of 1983. Yet this is nonsense, and cruel nonsense at that. What doomed Foot's leadership . . . was, quite simply, betrayal—and betrayal by the very people he could have expected to support him as the most left-wing, democratically minded leader they have ever had, or were ever likely to have."

Soviet Ties Alleged

Foot was attacked in an early 1995 *Sunday Times* article that claimed he had taken money from the Soviet secret police in the 1960s to subsidize a weekly newspaper he helped to found in 1937. The story also appeared in *The News of the World*. Both papers were owned by media mogul Rupert Murdoch. The stories caused a turmoil on London's Fleet Street, and Foot sued Murdoch and the papers for libel. *The News* printed an apology, but the *Times* edited Foot's response to the story. Not surprisingly, Foot had strong feelings about Murdoch, which he revealed during an interview with Bill Jones, writing for *New Statesman*. "It is impossible to overrate the injurious effect he's (Murdoch) had, and it's sad the other papers are inclined to follow his lead rather than restore any decent standards in British journalism, though I exclude some from this—the *Guardian* and *Observer* and some sincere journalists on other papers."

In the same interview, Foot blamed England's Tory government for corruption he sees as pervasive in English government. "Most people outside the House (of Commons) now see it as a corrupt place and they're right—it is corrupt from top to bottom. I exonerate Labour from these charges. Yet the way money is distributed in the Commons, and the (House of) Lords too, let's not forget, is an absolute outrage."

As reported by the journalism of the day, Foot was viewed as largely ineffectual in his later years. Reviewer Steven Fielding, writing in the January 1996 issue of *History Today* on a biography of Foot by Mervyn Jones, noted the "very low-ebb" of Foot's reputation. "Few, even in the party he led during the early 1980s, would now publicly endorse any of his core beliefs. Foot is as Old Labor as you could possibly get."

Further Reading

Simon Hoggart and David Leigh, *Michael Foot: A Portrait* (London, 1981), is accurate and on the whole sympathetic. A bruising account of his role in Labour's 1983 defeat is offered in David Butler and Dennis Kavanagh, *The British General Election of 1983* (London, 1984). The best approach, however, is through Foot's own writings. In addition to *Guilty Men* (London, 1940), the most important are *The Pen and the Sword* (London, 1957), *Aneurin Bevan, 1897-1945* (London, 1962), *Aneurin Bevan, 1945-1960* (London, 1973), and *Debts of Honour* (London, 1981). His side of the election of 1983 is presented in *Another Heart and Other Pulses: the Alternative to the Thatcher Society* (London, 1984).

Jones, Bill, "Interview: Michael Foot," *New Statesman,* January 10, 1997, v126, n4316, p. 30.

Aitken, Ian, "The Left's Betrayal of Michael Foot," *New Statesman & Society,* July 30, 1993, v6, n263, p. 9. □

John Forbes

The British general John Forbes (1710-1759) commanded the expedition that captured Ft. Duquesne during the French and Indian War.

Little is known of John Forbes's early life other than that he was the son of Col. John Forbes of Fifeshire, Scotland. Although trained as a physician, young John purchased a cornet's commission in the 2d Royal North British Dragoons. Serving in various staff positions during the 6 years he participated in the War of the Austrian Succession, he won rapid promotion. By 1745 he was a lieutenant colonel, and in 1750 he was appointed lieutenant colonel of his own regiment. In 1757 he became colonel of the 17th Foot. With the outbreak of the French and Indian War in the American colonies, he accompanied his regiment to Halifax, where, as adjutant general to the Earl of Loudon, he furthered his own cause by a number of valuable suggestions.

In December 1757 Forbes was made a brigadier general in America only, and William Pitt assigned him to command the expedition against the French stronghold Ft. Duquesne. His force was made up of Montgomery's Highlanders, a detachment of Royal Americans, and 5,000 provincials from Pennsylvania, Virginia, Maryland, and North Carolina. Young George Washington accompanied the expedition. Among the trials that beset Forbes were the reluctance of the Pennsylvania Assembly and the refusal of the Maryland Legislature to appropriate funds. Bickering between his officers and the provincials and the reluctance of the local inhabitants to furnish provisions contributed to delays. Forbes's Cherokee allies deserted early in the campaign, while the western Indians held back. The almost continuous rains made a morass of the road built by the army. Yet Forbes continued to press forward through the wilderness, building blockhouses along the way. His road across the Allegheny Mountains later became one of the most important routes of America's western expansion.

From the beginning of the campaign Forbes was troubled by illness, and his troops were spirited by his show of courage. Successful negotiations won over the western Indians to the British side. Although British skirmishing parties were twice defeated, the French evacuated Ft. Duquesne without firing a shot in its defense. On Nov. 25, 1758, five months after the campaign began, Forbes raised the British flag over the fort, now renamed Pittsburgh. He returned to Philadelphia "looking like an emaciated old woman of eighty" and died on March 11, 1759.

Further Reading

Forbes's letters are collected in Alfred Proctor James, ed., *Writings of General John Forbes Relating to His Service in North America* (1938). Alfred Proctor James and Charles Morse Stotz, *Drums in the Forest* (1958), has an excellent account of Forbes and his capture of Ft. Duquesne. The military situation is discussed in detail in William A. Hunter, *Forts on the Pennsylvania Frontier, 1753-1758* (1960). See also Leland D. Baldwin, *Pittsburgh* (1937). ☐

Malcolm Forbes

Millionaire Malcolm Forbes (1919-1990) was the publisher of *Forbes* magazine from 1957 to 1990.

T he entire world knew how old Malcolm Forbes was when he died in 1990; extensive press coverage of his lavish 70th (and last) birthday party thrown in Morocco in September of 1989 insured that everyone who had not been invited would know what they had missed. Characterized as a man who loved the spotlight, who shamelessly enjoyed the privileges his money afforded him, and who was always in pursuit of adventure, Forbes was a balloonist, a motorcyclist, and a sailor who took many trips on his huge yacht, the "Highlander." He collected anything precious and beautiful, most famously, Faberge eggs. His son Robert was quoted in the Chicago Tribune as emphasizing Forbes's playful nature in a eulogy: "He was so many things to so many of us. Boss, bon vivant, raconteur, balloonist, columnist, happiest millionaire, leader of the pack . . . source, mentor, friend, super this, mega that, father, grandfather, father-in-law, uncle, cousin and sparkling, naughty boy." Also ex-husband, as his wife of 39 years, Roberta Remsen Laidlaw, had divorced him in 1985. As Malcolm, Jr., explained in Forbes, his parents still loved each other but could no longer live together. Forbes was often seen in the company of movie star Elizabeth Taylor, and the two answered speculation about an impending marriage by saying that they were merely good friends.

Inherited Wealth

A savvy businessman by all accounts, Forbes inherited his wealth from his father, B.C. (Bertie) Forbes, who established him at the Fairfield Times newspaper as owner and publisher only days after his graduation from Princeton. As

he was fond of saying, he was loaded with "sheer ability, spelled i-n-h-e-r-i-t-a-n-c-e," as quoted in Forbes. He went on to publish the Lancaster Tribune in 1942, and four years later, after a stint in the Army on the European front of World War II, he joined the staff at Forbes magazine. He was first an associate publisher, then publisher, editor, editor-in-chief, vice-president, and, finally, president. As a politician, Forbes was less than successful; he said that he was "nosed out by a landslide" in a New Jersey race for governor in 1957.

Lavish Lifestyle

Forbes was loath to put a real figure to his income and holdings, though he published practically everybody else's value. Early in 1990, the *New York Post* estimated Forbes's holdings by toting up his collections, houses, and publications, but as *Time* magazine reported it, the estimates were generous; "Malcolm is a billionaire, but only if you swallow an estimate of $65 million for his flagship magazine's annual profits." *People* magazine lists eight houses, a palace in Tangier, Morocco, a chateau in Normandy and the island of Lauthala in Fiji as his dwellings. His famous birthday party was held in Tangier, and aroused the disgust of many outsiders who found the display gratuitously expensive. Forbes added some fuel to the flames by suggesting that the party be tax-deductible, as it was for business purposes. His company, Forbes Inc., actually did pay for the party, just as it would pay for any publicity campaign. Forbes's flamboyant consumerism served the firm well, and his enthusiastic spending habits earned him the nickname "the happiest millionaire." Although not as obviously a philanthropist, Forbes gave millions of dollars each year to charities, and had been at a charity bridge tournament the day he died. "Malcolm Forbes was a giant of American business," said then President George Bush, as quoted in *Forbes*. "His success in publishing reflected the tremendous vitality of our nation and served to inform and inspire a generation of successful business leaders. He was greatly admired and will be greatly missed." Former president Ronald Reagan offered a similar tribute: "Malcolm was truly a dear friend and we will miss him sorely. We hold our memories of him close to our hearts and are thankful to have known him." □

Robert Bennet Forbes

Robert Bennet Forbes (1804-1889), merchant and shipowner, was among the most prominent Americans engaged in the China trade in the 19th century.

Robert Forbes was born on Sept. 18, 1804, near Boston. His father, a merchant, was prosperous enough to educate him briefly in France and at the Milton Academy. When his father's business failed, young Forbes entered the employ of his uncles, James and Thomas H. Perkins, who were among the most successful New England merchants of the early 19th century.

In 1817 Forbes sailed in one of the Perkins' ships to China, for the first time seeing the country that would soon supply him with great personal wealth. He became a sea captain and trader with his uncles' firm. His chance for fortune came in 1830, when Perkins and Company joined another leading firm in the China trade, Russell and Company. Forbes settled in Canton, exporting Chinese silks, earthenware, and teas to America and importing sandalwood, textiles, furs, and opium. After a few lucrative years he returned to Boston as the agent for Russell and Company.

Hit hard by the economic panic of 1837, Forbes returned to China to regain his fortune. Remaining in Canton during the Opium War, he did a booming business until the British closed the harbor. He returned to Boston early in the 1840s and went back to China for several years at the end of that decade.

During the 1840s Forbes secured or constructed many trading vessels. He contributed a few minor inventions to the science of shipbuilding and made early use of metal hulls and screw propellers. During his last years he wrote pamphlets concerning his career in China, commerce, and improvements in shipbuilding and maritime safety, as well as his autobiography. He died in Boston in 1889.

Forbes and other merchants in the China trade enacted a colorful if somewhat inglorious chapter in American history. In the early decades of the American Republic they opened up commercial avenues that contributed to the young nation's economic growth. In their commerce with

China, however, they exploited the narcotics trade and were identified with other Western elements exploiting China. They may thus be said to have taken short-run profits at the cost of long-range political and moral considerations.

Further Reading

Forbes's autobiography, *Personal Reminiscences* (1876; 3d ed. 1892), is the most complete source on his life. For the story of the China trade and the participating American merchants, see Samuel Eliot Morison, *The Maritime History of Massachusetts: 1783-1860* (1921); Eldon Griffin, *Clippers and Consuls* (1938); Foster Rhea Dulles, *China and America: The Story of Relations since 1784* (1946); Earl Swisher, ed. and trans., *China's Management of the American Barbarians* (trans. 1951); and Te-kong Tong, *United States Diplomacy in China, 1844-60* (1964). □